D0295075

World History

World History

First published in this edition 1996 by Geddes & Grosset Ltd,
David Dale House, New Lanark, Scotland.

2 4 6 8 10 9 7 5 3 1

ISBN 1 85534 339 8

Printed and bound by Firmin-Didot (France),
Group Herissey. No d'impression : 35415.

Contents

1

Early Civilizations of Asia

Before History

Origins

Scientists estimate that the earth was formed some 4600 million years ago. Fossils of the simplest animals and plants have been found in rocks dating from 1000 million years later. The early development of life within those ancient seas was inconceivably slow. The first land plants and animals evolved in the Silurian age, over 400 million years ago. The great dinosaurs ruled the earth for the 160 million years of the Mesozoic Era, which ended some 65 million years BC. The extinction of these giants provided the opportunity for the family of mammals to begin their colonization of the planet.

Some two million years ago, several groups of primates living around the forest edge in Africa began to show characteristics that might be called 'human'. These creatures began to plan their hunting expeditions and their use of weapons. Other animals use tools—no other animal makes tools for something it plans to do tomorrow!

Still, the development of man into the species *homo sapiens* remained immensely slow. Some evolutionary pathways proved to be dead ends. But the spread of the family of man was relentless. For hundreds of thousands of years, small bands of these evolving people moved into new environments, hunting and gathering their food as they went. The animal, man, proved remarkably adaptable, surviving the cold of the ice ages and the heat of the tropics.

The First Agricultural Revolution

The last ice age rolled back some 12,000 years ago, leaving the world with much the same climate that it has retained until today. Comparatively shortly afterwards some people began to introduce major changes into the timeless pattern of life.

Wheat and barley live naturally in the area between eastern Turkey and the Caspian Sea. At some time people—probably the women—learnt that it was possible to plant the seeds and so reduce the work of gathering. Soon these new farmers began to select which seeds produced the best crop, and so improved the quality of the crops.

The introduction of cereal farming had radical effects on human life. Tribal groups lost their mobility as they had to settle in one place to tend the crops. When, in time, one group began to produce a surplus, it had to defend its goods against attack. Settlements then needed to be fortified and a military class grew up within the community. Once a community was producing a surplus of food, some people could undertake specialized roles within the community.

The domestication of animals was, no doubt, a long process. There was no sharp dividing line between the time when the people followed herds of wild animals as hunters, and the time when they drove the animals as herders. During the same years after the last ice age, people of southern Asia and Europe domesticated sheep, cattle and pigs. In the millennia that followed, tribesmen from the mountains of northern Iran and the steppes of Central Asia tamed the horse and camel.

Scholars differ about the pattern of development of settled agriculture. The traditional view was that all innovation happened in the Fertile Crescent of the Middle East, and skills spread outward, like ripples on a pond. Others hold that settled agriculture was discovered in many different places as conditions favoured it. Certainly the new methods appeared across Europe, as well as in India and Africa in the millennia that followed. Developments in the Far East and the Americas, at least, were independent of those in the Fertile Crescent. M'llet and rice were cultivated in China and South East Asia from about 6000 BC. Here chicken, water buffalo and, again, pigs were domesticated. Change came later in the Americas, where maize, potatoes and other important crops were added to the world's store.

The Growth of Cities

As the agricultural age continued, so people began to gather into yet larger communities. The earliest discovered is Jericho, which grew up before 8000 BC. Two thousand years later, Catal Hüyük, in Anatolia, covered 32 acres. These cities provided protection and allowed for greater specialization of role for the inhabitants.

New skills were, indeed, needed. Copper was smelted in Anatolia in about 7000 BC, introducing the age of metals. The earliest known pottery and evidence of the first woollen textiles have both been found in Catal Hüyük.

City life also provided a centre for religious worship. A temple lay at the heart of the community, and religion and government were always closely allied to each other. The change in lifestyle brought with it a change in religious practice. Cave paintings, such as those of southern France give a glimpse of the cults of the hunter gatherers, which focused on animals and sacred places. These have much in common with the practices of people, like some North American Indians, who lived similar lives within historical times.

Settled agriculture brought with it a new emphasis on birth and fertility, symbolized by the mother goddess figures found from widely dispersed areas of this early civilized world.

Sumerian Civilization

Irrigation

As would be expected, the earliest developments in city life happened in regions that had adequate natural rainfall. Some time after 5000 BC, however, groups from the north began to settle in the dry land of Mesopotamia. Here they drained the marshes and used the water from the twin rivers Tigris and Euphrates to irrigate the fertile land.

The Rise of the Sumerian Cities

It appears as though two of the most vital inventions in the history of humans—the wheel and the plough—were made in Mesopotamia in around 3500 BC. These enabled farmers to cultivate the irrigated land in a more concentrated manner, so increasing the surplus production, leading to a spectacular flourishing of cities.

The most famous city, Ur of the Chaldees, was only one; also prominent were Eridu, Uruk, Badtibira, Nippur and Kish. Each city had its own special deity, and it served as the centre for a surrounding region of villages and farm land.

The Invention of Writing

In about 3100 BC the people of these Sumerian cities learnt how to represent their spoken language by the use of writing. The earliest characters were pictographic, and remain largely undeciphered. The Sumerians later developed the more flexible cuneiform script. The invention of writing marks the beginning of history, but the earliest documents were unremarkable. Written on the tablets of clay are lists showing the ownership of jars of oil and bundles of reeds. They do show, however, that some of the inhabitants were gathering serious wealth, which could be measured in hundreds and thousands of units.

Life in Sumeria

The cities were walled, but it appears that, in the early centuries, this was not a world of warring cities. Disputes were controlled by the exchange of embassies and by dynastic marriages, rather than by conflict. The laws that governed behaviour were not particularly strict.

The area was short of both wood and stone, and the Sumerian people depended heavily on clay for building and many other functions. The skills of the artisans became ever more refined. Gold, silver, bronze and polished stones were made into fine objects for the decoration of people, homes and temples. Weavers, leather workers and potters followed their specialized crafts. The scribes of later centuries wrote down a fine oral tradition of myths, epics and hymns. The world in which small family groups of hunters lived in cooperation had now been left far behind. Everyday life was controlled by a highly developed bureaucracy, which - for good or ill - was to become a hallmark of civilization. Kings were now divine beings, who were buried, not only with treasure, but also with their whole retinue to see them safely into the next life.

Egypt

In about 3200 BC, King Menes united the whole of the land of the lower Nile. The deserts that stretched on both sides of the river largely protected the Egyptians against the invasions that plagued Mesopotamia. Egyptian rulers had to face the armies of Assyria and 'The People of the Sea' from the Mediterranean, but the remarkable endurance of Egyptian civilization owes much to its isolation. Despite this, the Egyptians owed much to the Sumerians. In particular, they borrowed the early Sumerian system of writing, and adapted this into their own pictorial script. *Hieroglyphics* means 'the writing of the priests' and the art remained a closely guarded secret within the priestly caste.

For more than two thousand years dynasties followed one another; the country experienced bad times as well as good, but a continuity was maintained, unparalleled in the history of the world. Even when the land later fell under foreign rulers, Egyptian culture retained its remarkable integrity.

The Nile Waters

Egypt depended on the Nile. This was a kindlier river than the Tigris and Euphrates because each year it flooded the land on either side, providing natural irrigation for the fertile soil. The whole of Egyptian life was attuned to the rise and fall of the great river. The ruler - or pharaoh, as he would later be called - was the owner of the land and the giver of its life, and the ceremonials of kingship centred on the fertility of the land. The Book of Exodus describes how the rulers of Egypt were able to organize the storage of surpluses from good years to guard against crop failures in bad years.

The Calendar

The Egyptians studied the movements of the sun and stars, and they were the first to work out the year, consisting of 364¼ days. For the Egyptian farmer, this year was divided into three parts, each of four months—one of flooding, one of planting and one of harvesting.

The Capital Cities

Menes set up his capital in Memphis. Later pharaohs moved it to Thebes, but neither were true cities, like those of Sumeria. Their role was more as a centre of religion than a focus for daily life.

The wide deserts provided more protection from enemies than any city walls. Because of this physical isolation, Egyptian life could remain focused on the villages, rather than on larger centres of population.

Monuments and Art

The massive monuments of ancient Egypt remain objects of wonder. Imhotep, builder of the Step Pyramid at Saqqara, has left his name as the first architect known to history. Many thousands were marshalled to build these tombs for the rulers, working without winches, pulleys, blocks or tackles.

A modern visitor will look with awe at the pyramids and other great stone monuments, but it is the more modest paintings that give insight into the daily lives of the people. They show scenes of busy rural life, where peasants gather crops and hunt wild fowl by the Nile. They are happily free from the scenes of carnage and inhumanity, which are all too common in much of the art of the period. It was a world in which women had a high status and beauty was admired.

No doubt the peasants had to work hard to keep not only themselves but the whole apparatus of royal and priestly rule, but the river was kind and the land was fertile, and there was usually enough for all.

Migration and Trade

Semites and Indo-Europeans

The Semites were herders of sheep who originated in the Arabian peninsula. They were a warrior people, reared in the stern disciplines of life at the desert edge. The most powerful group in those early years them were a people called the Amorites. They founded cities to the north of Sumeria—Babylon, Nineveh and Damascus. The Indo-Europeans were mainly cattle herders, who made their way into Mesopotamia from the north. Their gods emerge in the Pantheon of Greece and in the Vedic deities of India.

The Indo-Europeans had learned how to tame horses from their Asian neighbours.

Most importantly, they brought iron. Iron weapons and chariots gave them a technological advantage over the earlier inhabitants of Mesopotamia. Control of iron therefore became an essential precondition of political power. The slow spread of iron technology had other important effects. An iron plough could break in land that had hitherto been too hard for agriculture. This created a rise in production, and hence an increase in population.

The Growth of Trade

Newcomers from both north and south were drawn into Mesopotamia by the rich lifestyle of the cities. But it happened that the area had no significant iron deposits, and was generally poor in other metals. This urgent need for raw materials was to be the driving force for the development of trade in the ancient world.

Money

It is remarkable how much trade was carried on before the development of currency as a method of exchange. Merchants from the civilized Fertile Crescent were able to take a range of manufactured goods to exchange for metals and other raw materials. Goods were also moved around the world as tribute, taxes and offerings to temples. The first coins date from about 700 BC , but their use spread slowly. Egypt, for instance, did not introduce a currency until about 400 BC.

Land Transport

The wheel was of no value in a world without roads. Columns of pack animals began to spread out from the Near East into the highlands of Iran and, through the Balkans, into metal rich Europe, opening up trade routes that would be trampled for many centuries.

Sea Transport

Improvements in the design of ships followed. Oars and sails were developed and rigging improved; decks were made watertight. The Red Sea and Persian Gulf became navigable all the year round, and the Mediterranean at least in summer. The growth in sea transport would ultimately change the centre of gravity of early civilizations away from the inland rivers towards the coastal regions. Ideas and empires could now spread along sea as well as land routes.

Against this background, the empires of the ancient Near East rose and fell.

Babylon, Assyria and the Hittites

Babylon

In 1792 BC, a ruler called Hammurabi came to power in the Semite city of Babylon. He can be looked upon as the first great emperor ir the history of the world. Hammurabi's armies carried Babylonian power across most of the Fertile Crescent, from the Persian Gulf and the old Sumerian cities in the east, to the edge of mountains of Asia Mir.or and the borders of Syria in the west. Conquest was undertaken to secure essential supplies by the control of trade routes, and the exaction of tribute. Carvings show endless lines of conquered people bearing products to swell the stores of the great king, and the riches of Babylon became famous throughout the region.

Hammurabi was an absolute ruler, but he was anxious that his subject should know the laws under which they had to order their lives. He therefore set up pillars in the temples on which were engraved all the laws that governed his kingdom, so that his subjects would be able to come and refer to them. This Code of Hammurabi was the first statement of the principle of 'An eye for an eye'.

Astrology played a vital role in all decision taking, and this led to Babylonians to study the stars closely. By 1000 BC their astrologers had plotted the paths of the sun and the planets with great accuracy, and they were able to predict eclipses. They instituted the system under which the circle is divided into 360 degrees and the hour into 60 minutes.

The first great period of Babylonian power ended when the city was destroyed by the Hittites in 1600 BC After that, Babylon remained an important centre of trade and culture, but a thousand years would pass before the city would achieve a late flowering of political power, under the great king Nebuchadnezzar.

The Hittites

The Hittites, who destroyed the first Babylon, were an Indo-European people who had come into the area from the north, probably through the Balkans. After defeating Babylon, they dominated an even larger empire than that of Hammurabi, across the sweep of the fertile crescent, from their homeland in Anatolia, Asia Minor to the Persian Gulf and the borders of Egypt. The power of the Hittites was based on skill with iron. It was they who carried iron technology across the region.

Hittite power collapsed in its turn under pressure from the 'People of the Sea', who were also harassing Egypt at the same time. These People of the Sea, however, did not follow up their successes by founding an empire. Rather, they left a vacuum that was to be filled by the most terrible of the empires of the Ancient Near East.

Assyria

The centre of power now moved to the city of Nineveh on the middle reaches of the Tigris. Monuments of the great kings of Assyria, like Tiglath-Pileser I and Ashurbanipal show an empire based on brute military force and the use of terror to control conquered people. Whole populations, like the lost ten tribes of Israel, were moved from their homeland and resettled in other parts of the empire. In this way they lost the identity on which national resistance could be built.

Assyrian armies dominated the region from the twelfth to the seventh centuries BC. They marched north into the highlands of modern Turkey and Iran, looking for metals and other necessary supplies. They conquered Syria and Palestine, and, under Ashurbanipal in the mid-seventh century, they even drove the Pharaohs of Egypt out of the Nile delta.

The Hebrews

Among the Semite invaders into the Near East was a group known as the Hebrews. The Bible record tells how Abraham, the father of the people, left the city of Ur to return to a purer nomadic way of life. His descendants experienced a period of bondage in Egypt, from which they emerged in about 1300 BC.

The Hebrews made their home in Palestine, and they had set up a monarchy by about 1000 BC. Hebrew power reached its peak under King Solomon, who died in 935 BC. The kingdom then split; Israel, the northern kingdom, was destroyed by Assyria in 722 BC and Judah, the southern, by Babylon in 587 BC.

The Hebrews do not feature in world history by virtue of their political success but because of their religious faith. They proclaimed a single deity whom they called Yahweh. The sacred writings of the Hebrews have been one of the major influences on the subsequent history of the world. Some themes need, therefore, to be identified.

Monotheism

Initially Yahweh was seen as the God of the Hebrews, who was set over against the gods of other peoples of the area. In time, however, Yahweh began to develop a uniqueness that challenged the existence of other gods. A writer from the period of the Babylonian exile pronounced Yahweh to be the god of the non-Hebrew, as well as the Hebrew people.

Divine Law

The rulers of Babylon and Assyria were absolute monarchs, whose word was law and whose actions therefore could not be judged by any superior authority. The Hebrew prophetic tradition, in contrast, made it clear that a king, no less than any other person, operated under a divine law. Here, a ruler, who has unjustly taken a common man's vineyard, can be challenged by a prophet with the words 'Thou art the man!'

Man and Nature

The Hebrew creation myth, which was handed down verbally for many centuries before being written into the Book of Genesis, clearly sets man apart from the rest of creation. He is made in the image of God and given dominion over the beasts. The Bible has been the vehicle that has transmitted this perspective into Western culture.

Male-centred Religion

The Old Testament narrative describes the fierce rejection of female fertility gods of the Fertile Crescent, which the Hebrews described as The Abomination of Desolation. For the Hebrews divinity was uncompromisingly male, and woman is depicted as a secondary creation, born out of man's side. This rejection of the female strand of religion would later be modified in Catholic Christianity in the cult of the Virgin, but it has been influential in defining western attitudes on the relationship of the sexes.

Persia

In about the year 1000, Aryan people moved south into the land that is now Iran (the land of the Aryans). There were two dominant tribes; the Medes occupied the north of the country, while the Persians occupied the south.

In the early centuries the Medish tribes were subject to the Assyrians, but they rebelled against their masters, and in 612 BC Nineveh was sacked and the Assyrian Empire was destroyed by the army of the Medes. The success of the Medes, as of the Persians after them, was based on their successful harnessing of the horse as an instrument of war.

The power centre shifted south when the Persian King Cyrus united Medes and Persians to form what was to become the greatest empire of the Near East. At its height, it extended from Greece and North Africa in the west to the Indus valley and the edge of the Central Asian steppe in the east. Darius the Great had problems at either edge of the empire—with Greeks in the west and Scythians in the east—but the bulk of the empire held together well until 330 BC.

The official Persian religion was Zoroastrianism. This emphasized the struggle of good and evil, and was to give the Semites the concept of angels and hell fire. It did not, however, seek converts, and the people of the empire were left in peace with their own gods. Cyrus was greeted by the Jews as the instrument of Yahweh, and he even rebuilt King Solomon's temple.

Darius was not as successful a conqueror as Cyrus, but he was an administrator of genius. Once a region had been brought within the empire, the royal satrap worked to win the trust and loyalty of the conquered people. Regional traditions were respected and local people were given responsibility in managing their own affairs. The country was bound together by roads, which could be used for trade and even postal services, as well as for armies.

At its peak, the Persian Empire reached as far as the Indus valley. This was the home of another, distinct Asian civilization.

India

The Harappa Culture

Remains have been found in the Indus Valley of cities, dating from about 2550 BC. The pictogram writing of these early Harappa people has not been deciphered, but archaeologists have discovered houses, with bathrooms, built of burnt brick. There are remains of canals and docks, and Indian products from this period have been excavated in Mesopotamia. Rice was grown, which may indicate that the cities had contact with the Far East. Here is the first evidence of cultivated cotton.

The Harappan cities had houses, granaries and temples, but no palaces. This suggests that the civilization was centred around the priests, rather than around warrior kings. They were therefore probably ill equipped to meet the challenge of invaders.

The Aryans

In about 1750 BC Indo-European Aryans began to penetrate into the land from the north. They herded the cattle, which were to become sacred creatures. Their religion is enshrined in the oldest holy books of the world, known as the Vedas. From these it is possible to get an image of nomadic people, standing round their camp fire at night, chanting hymns to the sun and other forces of nature.

The Aryans overran the northern part of the continent, but they did not completely destroy the people who had been there before them. They slowly spread from the Indus, clearing the dense forest of the Ganges Valley and founding cities, such as Benares.

Hindu Castes

The racial structure of Aryan and non-Aryan people became enshrined in the caste system of India. There were three 'twice born' castes, which are assumed to originate from the Aryan invaders. The *Brahmins*, were the priests, the *Ksahiyas*, were warriors and the *Varsyas*, were farmers and merchants. Only members of these castes were permitted to take part in the Vedic rituals.

The *Sudras*, who came below the lowest member of the twice-born castes accommodated the conquered people. Below them were the unclean *outcasts*, who did not enjoy any caste status.

The Cults

As time passed, people looked for religious expressions that could engage the emotions more fully than the Vedic hymns. The cults surrounding the gods *Vishnu* and

Shiva, with their consorts, fulfilled their needs. It appears that Shiva, at least, was drawn from older pre-Aryan India. The cult of Shiva, who represented the great cycle of birth and death, life and destruction, was to express the Hindu world view most completely.

Buddhism

In the early part of the sixth century BC a prince of the warrior caste, called Siddartha Buddha, left his home to seek enlightenment. He first followed the strict Hindu practice of fasting, but he did not achieve his objective. In the end he found that true enlightenment could only be discovered by 'letting go' of his own self, and accepting that, in life, all things are changing. The Buddha rejected the caste system and his teachings took his followers out of Hinduism.

Although Hinduism and Buddhism separated, any contest for supremacy lay in the mind, for there were no wars of religion, like those that were to mark the West. The two religions share the same root. Both see man as an integral part of the natural world, not as a creature set apart from, and above it, as in the Hebrew tradition.

Buddhism received a great impetus with the conversion of the north Indian king Ashoka in 260 BC. He abandoned his career of conquest and administered his kingdom in the light of the teaching, providing the people with social works and good laws. In the end, Hinduism was to retain its hold on the subcontinent, apart from Ceylon (Sri Lanka) in the south and the mountains of Tibet in the north, while Buddhism made its impact further east.

Central Asia

Across the Himalayas from India lay the great land mass of central Asia. This can be divided into three bands. Furthest north was the great wall of the forests of Siberia. The centre consists of the Asian grasslands. In the south are the deserts and mountains. The last two are influential in world history from the earliest times until about 1500 AD.

In the grasslands of the steppe lived a selection of nomadic tribes. They survived in marginal land, much as, in later times, the Plains Indians would survive on the American prairie. The nomadic life could take peoples right across the grasslands, and they often fought each other for the control of land. Because the plain could only support a small population, drought, war or other impulses could set whole peoples on the move. This would produce a knock-on effect. Ripples could grow to waves. These would then break onto the boundaries of the lands that bordered on the steppes.

These were illiterate people, so their names and history are confused, but they appear in history as the Hsiungnu or Huns, the Avars, the Scythians, the Turks and the Mongols. They were terrible foes, who won their battles by great mobility and superb mastery of the horse.

Further south, in the desert region, lay the trade routes. From very early times Bactrian camels and horses carried goods along these trade routes, creating a link between Europe and the Near East to the west and China to the east. Most of the goods moved from east to west. At an early date, the Chinese learnt to make fine fabric from the web of the silk worm. Pepper and other spices also made light and high value loads. It was an immense and dangerous journey, but the profits were incentive enough to keep the caravans moving.

China

Isolation and Contact

The people of China have long known their nation as *Chung-hua,* the Central Nation. Educated people knew well of the existence of other cultures, but they were looked on as subordinate, and, indeed, tributaries of the great nation. Although the Chinese did maintain contact with the outside world, they were little influenced by it. Chinese culture was therefore able to establish a structure in the early centuries, which remained little altered throughout history.

The immediate concern of Chinese rulers, again from very early times, was to defend the northern borders against the steppe nomads. This border, which would be marked by the world's greatest building work, The Great Wall, lay along the line where the decline in rainfall made settled agriculture impracticable.

Culture and Language

The huge country centred on three rivers, the Hwang-Ho, the Yangtse and the Hsi. They were divided by great mountain ridges. A wide range of climates could be found within the nation. China has been politically divided for long periods, but she has maintained a unity of culture, beyond that achieved by any other people. An important reason for this is that, while the people of the west came to use to a phonic script, China retained the use of pictograms. The difference is fundamental. A phonic script is easily learned, but it needs to reflect the sounds of a language. People of different languages are therefore unable to communicate with each other without learning each other's language. This is inevitably culturally divisive. A pictogram script, in contrast, is hard to learn, but it is not linked to the sound of language. It can therefore be used to bind people who speak differently. China therefore developed a power to absorb and civilize the conquerors who, from time to time, spilled over her frontiers.

Literacy was the property of a cultured elite, whose whole education had, of necessity, been centred on diligence rather than creativity. This gave Chinese culture the twin characteristics of breadth and stability.

The State

Around 1700 BC, the first historical dynasty, the Shang, gained control of the northern Hwang-Ho river valley. Even at this early stage, the court had archivists and scribes. Like their successors of later dynasties, the kings saw themselves as the bringers of civilization to barbarian peoples.

About 1100 BC the Shang were overthrown by the Chou who carried royal power to the central Yangtse river valley. Then, around 700 BC, the Chou in their turn were overthrown by pastoralists from the north. This brought in the time graphically known as the Period of the Warring States.

Confucianism

During this period there lived K'ung-fu-tsu, who became known to the world as Confucius. He looked back from that period of unrest to an earlier time when the world was at peace and believed that the problems of his times arose from the fact that people had forgotten their proper duty. In an ordered world, everyone had a place in society. Some—rulers, parents, husbands—were 'higher'; others—subjects, children, wives—were 'lower'. Everyone, high and low, was bound together in ties of mutual duty and respect. The high had no more right to oppress the low than the low had to be disrespectful of the high. When these bonds were broken, the times became out of joint.

Confucianism therefore placed emphasis on 'conservative' institutions - the state, the civil service, scholarship, and, above all, the family. It was not a religion, in the sense of teaching about God, but it brought a religious dimension to the worship of ancestors.

Social Structure

K'ung-fu-tsu accepted the most fundamental division in Chinese society. The common peasants were not allowed to belong to a clan, and they therefore had no ancestors to worship. Their lives consisted of an endless round of toil.

For those who were, more fortunately, born into a clan, China would become a land of opportunity. Even boys from poor homes could study to pass the necessary examinations, which would open up the coveted civil service jobs. For those with more modest aspirations, growing cities offered opportunities in trade and the crafts.

The fortunate lived in an assurance that Chinese customs and the Chinese way offered the model of excellence, and all other people had to be judged according to the way in which they measured up to this standard.

2

Mediterranean Civilization

Early Seagoing People

Conquering the Oceans

The earliest civilizations centred on major river valleys. The rivers provided water and arteries of communication. Then the technology of sails and shipbuilding improved to a level that enabled men to venture onto the oceans. From early times, the Red Sea and the Persian Gulf provided important communication routes, which were orientated towards the east. The Mediterranean, particularly in winter, is subject to violent storms. Further advances in marine engineering, such as the construction of watertight holds and improvements in sails and rigging, were needed before sailors could master this environment.

By about 500 BC ships were able to move freely in the Mediterranean, at least in summer, so providing easier communication than was possible on land. There was then no distinction between a fertile north and an arid north shore. The whole region was fertile. Traders and rulers therefore saw the Mediterranean basin as a single unit, bound together by its ocean highway.

Minoa and Mycenae

In about 1900 BC a civilization grew up on Crete, which has been named after its King Minos. Its earliest writing has not been deciphered, but excavations reveal fine palaces and developed communities. Their cities stood beside the sea, and the builders were already confident enough in the control of their ships over the eastern Mediterranean to dispense with fortifications.

Objects found in Crete and Egypt show that there was a lively trade between the two cultures. The Minoan sailors probably traded in timber, wood, olive oil and grapes over the whole of the Mediterranean area.

Inhabitants of the Minoan cities were the first people to enjoy the benefits of piped drains and sewers, and wall paintings show them dancing and playing sports, including the Minoan speciality of bull leaping.

The Minoans set up colonies on the mainland, of which the most important seems to have been at Mycenae. This is the name that is given to Minoan civilization as it is found on the mainland. The culture spread across the Aegean to the coast of Asia Minor and to the city of Troy at the mouth of the Bosphorus.

The first Minoan civilization was destroyed by Indo-European people who poured into the region from the north. Some of these invaders settled in the Ionian peninsula to become Greeks. A later resurgence of Minoan civilization is thought to have been under Greek influence.

The stories written down centuries later by the poet Homer tell of the struggles between the Mycenaens of Troy and the less advanced Indo-European invaders.

The Phoenicians

Semite people, in general, liked to keep their feet on dry land. The exception were the people who lived in the area known as Phoenicia, which is now Lebanon and southern Syria. They developed remarkable skills as sailors and for centuries their ships dominated the trade routes. Phoenician sailors reached the Atlantic Ocean and traded with tin miners in distant Cornwall. The Greek historian Heroditus even reports that one expedition rounded the southern cape of Africa.

The Phoenicians planted colonies to protect their trade routes. Most important, in about 800 BC they founded the city of Carthage. The colony was strategically placed to protect the ships that brought metal from Western Europe.

Phoenicia was never a power on land and, when, in 868 BC the Assyrian king 'washed his weapons in the Mediterranean' Phoenicia lost its independence. But the rulers of the great empires needed these fine sailors, and the Phoenicians therefore exercised influence beyond their military power.

Phoenicia is best known for its sailors. It did, however, make another major contribution to western culture, by creating a phonic alphabet. The words alpha, beta and gamma are derived from the Phoenician words for an ox, a house and a camel.

The Greeks

In Mycenaean times, an iron-working Aryan people were moving south into the Greek peninsula. Myths of early battles with Mycenaean Troy are preserved in the works of the storyteller—or tellers—given the name of Homer.

The early culture was oral, but, in around 750 BC the Greeks adopted and modified the Phoenician alphabet and committed the ancient legends to writing. These were to provide the starting point for the world's first great literary culture.

The beginning of Greek civilization was dated from the first Olympian Games, held in 776 BC. This event, held once every four years, drew together people who shared the Greek language and culture. The participants did not, however, come under one unified government.

Government

The Greek political structure was dictated by the geography of the region in which they settled. This was a land of mountain ranges, with small coastal plains that faced outwards to the sea. Each of these plains was settled by a self-governing community, which initially contained only as many people as the land would support. This was the basis of the *polis*, or city state.

Homer's *Iliad* provides a picture of an early feudal society of kings, nobles and common fighting men. Each city then followed its own course in working out the structure of government. The first struggle lay between the kings (monarchy) and the nobles (aristocracy). Then pressure came from other influential citizens (oligarchy) and from the general mass of free male citizens (democracy). When a state plunged into chaos, a strong man (tyranny), who was often benevolent and public spirited, would emerge to bring order to the polis.

The Greek concept of democracy was specific to the confined structure of the city state. It did not operate through representative institutions, but through the direct participation of citizens in the decision taking process. The meeting place, or *agora*, not the temple or the royal palace, was now the centre of city life. The citizens who met here provided the city with its law courts and its political assembly. Debate and persuasion became vital skills. People could on occasion be swept away by the power of a demagogue, but within this forum they learned to listen and to analyse argument.

The fractured nature of Greek society did not provide peace and stability. The city states might join together in games, but they were as often at war with each other. For both good and ill, the people remained fiercely independent, more ready than any other people before, and perhaps even since, to question the structure of the society within which they lived.

Colonization

Since geography prevented expansion inland, the Greeks had an impetus to expand outwards, along the sea routes. Greek communities were established along the west and south coasts of Asia Minor, on the islands of the Aegean and as far east as Cyprus and westwards to Sicily and southern Italy, and even further into North Africa, France and Spain. These colonies were self-governing, but they often had links with powerful city states, such as Corinth or Athens. They served both as an overspill for excess population and also as trading bases across the Mediterranean Sea.

The Persian Wars

The conflict between Greece and Persia has been depicted as a struggle between an oppressive empire and a freedom loving people. Reality is more complex. Close links had long existed between the Greeks and the Persians and many Greeks served within the Persian army. The trouble started when Greek city states in Asia Minor rebelled against Persian rule and Darius moved to put down the insurrection. The Asians were supported by the European Greeks, and this brought the Persian Empire into conflict with an alliance of Greek cities, led by Athens and Sparta. The army of Darius was defeated at Marathon in 490 BC and the navy, led by his successor Xerxes, failed ten years later at Salamis. This war drew the boundary of the Persian Empire to the east of the area of Greek settlement.

Athens and Sparta

The alliance that had defeated Persia did not survive the victory. Athens was much the largest of the city states, with a larger population than its farm land could support. Prosperity was based on the control of silver mines, which were worked by thousands of slaves. The city's very survival therefore depended on a structure of trade and colonies. Whatever freedom may have been enjoyed by Athenian citizens within their city, their rule of others was often oppressive. The Athenians demanded heavy tribute from client states and put down rebellion as violently as any Persian army.

Other trading states, like Corinth, felt themselves continually threatened by Athenian power. They found allies in the conservative, agricultural state of Sparta. The Peloponnesian War lasted for 27 years, and ended with the defeat of Athens in 404 BC. This led to a reaction against an over-mighty Sparta, and the destructive sequence of wars continued into the fourth century. The Greeks may have provided the world with a vocabulary of politics and an ideal of democracy, but its outstanding achievement lies, not in politics, but in broader fields of culture.

Religion

Greek myth is drawn from the common Indo-European root, which created the Vedas (the sacred writings of Hinduism) in India. It has provided a fertile source of inspiration for western art and literature for more than 2000 years, but it is harder to look back through the twin filters of Semitic religion and rationalism, which have shaped modern attitudes, to understand what the world of gods meant to the Greeks themselves. On the one side, there was a piety of the common man, which condemned Socrates for blaspheming against the gods; on the other side there was a freethinking strain, expressed by Miletus a philosopher of the seventh century, who declared 'If an ox could paint a picture, its god would look like an ox'. The Greek religious tradition was real, but it was not an all-demanding way of life, like that of the Hebrews.

Philosophy and Science

The Greeks invented organized abstract thought and took it to a level that would dominate the philosophy of the Near East and Europe until very recent times. In the Greek perspective, there was no distinction between the arts, the sciences, and, indeed, religion. All were a part of the search for truth. In the sixth century, Pythagoras did not distinguish mathematics from philosophy and religion. The two greatest Greek thinkers defined the twin, often opposing, channels through which all philosophy, and later, all theology, would flow.

Plato, a pupil of Socrates, was 23 years old when his home city of Athens was defeated by Sparta. His attempt to achieve a mental order was therefore born of the political disorder of the post war years. Plato is the apostle of the *ideal*—the abstract of perfection, whether it be for the state, the individual, or in a mathematical equation. In his philosophy, all life is a striving towards an ideal of the good, containing truth, justice and beauty, which was the only reality in an imperfect world. Plato's Academy can lay claim to being the world's first university.

Aristotle came to Plato's Academy at the age of 17 and remained his master's devoted disciple. His interests, however, took him in the opposite direction, as he came to emphasize enquiry and experiment as the source of knowledge. While Plato stressed the *ideal*, Aristotle stressed the *real*; while Plato was drawn into the abstractions of mathematics, Aristotle found himself fascinated by the complexities of biology and literary criticism. For him, truth lay not in a distant abstract, but in a 'happy medium'. Aristotle is therefore seen as the father of the scientific method.

The Arts

Fifth-century Athens provided the most fertile environment for classical Greek culture. The architecture of the Parthenon, the sculptures of Praxiteles and Pheidias provide an illustration in stone of the Platonic ideal. They provided generations of architects and artists, particularly from Europe, with a standard of perfection. Literature also flourished. Aeschylus, Sophocles and Euripides used the ancient myths to explore depths of the human experience and create tragic drama, while the irreverent Aristophanes pioneered the tradition of comedy. The disasters of the Peloponnesian Wars also inspired Thucydides to become the world's first scientific and literary historian.

The contribution of Greece to the world's cultural store is a fundamental theme of history. By the middle of the fourth century, however, the advances were largely confined to the Greek speaking world. The diffusion of Greek culture into a wider world would be the work of a young and brilliant student of Aristotle.

The Hellenistic World

Alexander the Great

The state of Macedon lay to the north of Greece. It crossed the boundary that divided the civilized world from the barbarians. Philip II of Macedon developed his army into an efficient fighting machine and conquered the Greek city states. Philip died in 336 BC and was succeeded by Aristotle's pupil, his son, Alexander.

Alexander inherited his father's army and the Greek power base. The problem he faced was how he could pay the soldiers who had served Macedon so well. This search for money took Alexander the Great on spectacular campaigns. There was ample booty to be won across the Aegean in the Persian Empire. In 334 BC the Macedonian army defeated the Persians under their king, Darius III, at Issus. The army then marched south into Egypt, where Alexander founded the city that was to carry his name, Alexandria. He returned north, defeated the Persians once more and sacked the capital of Persepolis. Not content, he took his army eastward into Afghanistan and the Punjab. He would have gone further, but his soldiers insisted that the time had come to turn back.

The young man was one of the great soldiers of all time. The importance of his conquests, however, was that they were the catalyst that brought together the old civilizations of the Near East and the newer Greek culture. Alexander was Greek, but he was drawn to Eastern ways. He himself married the Persian emperor's daughter, and, in a great symbolic gesture, he married nine thousand of his soldiers to eastern women.

The Division of the Empire

Alexander died in Babylon in 323 BC at the age of thirty-two, leaving no heir to succeed to his enormous empire. The land was divided between his generals. The Ptolemies based their power in Egypt, the Seleucids in the region of Syria and the Attalids around Pergamum. Parthia later became independent of the Seleucids. These were centralized states under absolute monarchs. The age of debate and democracy was certainly past. Over most of the Hellenistic world, this was a time of economic growth, but the Greek cities themselves declined.

Hellenistic Culture

Greek was now the official and commercial language of the whole area. The learning of the scholars became widely known and great libraries were set up at Alexandria and Pergamum. Among the books preserved were many of the writings of Plato and Aristotle. Scholars in the Greek tradition worked in different parts of the Hellenistic world. Science flourished, as it would not do again for over fifteen hundred years. In Alexandria Euclid laid the foundation of geometry. Aristarchus correctly deduced the structure of the solar system eighteen hundred years before Copernicus and Eratosthenes measured the circumference of the earth. Archimedes of Syracuse had the widest ranging genius of all.

Philosophers, such as the Stoics, could no longer question the ways of government, so they turned their thoughts towards the inner life of man. They led a quest for virtue and true contentment. Classical Greek styles provided powerful models for painters and sculptors, but Hellenistic artists retreated from the Platonic search for an ideal and worked instead to project the humanity of their subjects.

Religion

Greek religion was too restricted a vehicle for this new, expansive world. Mystery cults began to spread, which demanded a more active devotion from their followers. Two of these became increasingly dominant. From Egypt came the myth of Isis and Osiris. This told of a dying and a rising god. From Zoroastrianism came the mystery of Mithras, with its powerful image of redemption through blood.

The End of the Hellenistic World

The Hellenistic empires in their turn fell to a new power from further west in the Mediterranean. The Roman victory at Actium in 31 BC marked the end of the era. No battle, however, could put an end to Greek culture. The Roman poet Horace summed it up by saying that, although Greece was defeated, it took its conquerors prisoner.

Republican Rome

The Etruscans

In the years before 509 BC, central Italy was dominated by a people called the Etruscans. They can be seen in lifelike tomb sculptures, but little is known about their culture. They appear to have been an Indo-European people, who achieved dominance over other people by bringing iron working to a high level of perfection. Etruscan kings, the Tarquins, ruled in Rome until they were expelled, according to tradition, in 509 BC. The expulsion of the kings remained a powerful myth within the Roman state. Men looked back to the days of the Tarquins as the time when the rights of the citizen were subjected to the will of a single individual.

The Structure of the State

The new Roman state was based on agriculture. Indeed, *pecunia*, the name for a flock or herd of animals, became the Latin word for money.

There were different groups within society. The old families who took pride in their status as *patricians*, assumed power in place of the deposed kings. The remaining free people were known as the *plebeians* or *plebs*. At first they were poor farmers, with little say in affairs of state. As Rome grew, however, many plebeians became more wealthy and they began to look for a share in the running of affairs.

Romans, be they patricians or plebs, took immense pride in their status as citizens. Roman citizenship became a unique badge of belonging to a pure and strong society, free from the softness and corruption of the Hellenistic world around them. Every man was liable to military service, which could be for as long as sixteen years in the infantry or ten years in the cavalry. Warlike virtues were admired by society and inculcated in boys through the home and education. At best, this could breed a self-sacrifice to the common good; at worst, it could bring a lust for battle and bloodshed.

The organization of the Roman Republic was not unlike that of a Greek polis. The Roman *forum* took the place of the Greek agora. The *senate*, which was an assembly of patricians, wielded the real power. Two consuls, elected from its ranks, commanded the army in war and were responsible for government in time of peace. The demand of the plebs to be represented was met by the appointment of two tribunes. It therefore became possible for an unusually talented man, from a low family, to rise in the state. This structure lasted for 450 years. It carried Rome from being a small city state to dominance in the Mediterranean basin.

Early Expansion

In the early centuries, Roman armies were occupied with winning control over the Italian peninsula. If there was a ruthless character to Roman expansion, there could also be generosity in the terms given on surrender. Conquered people were given Roman citizenship and allowed a large measure of self-government. Once within Roman rule, they too were expected to provide troops for the army.

The Punic Wars

As Rome expanded, she had only one serious rival. Carthage had expanded beyond North Africa. Her ships controlled the sea and Carthaginian colonies were established in Sicily, Southern Italy and Spain. The two powers were bound to clash for supremacy in the western Mediterranean. The Romans built up a navy, and in the First Punic War (264–241 BC) they defeated the Carthaginians at sea and won Sicily.

The Second Punic War (264–241 BC) marked the decisive struggle between the two powers. When Hannibal crossed the Alps and defeated Roman armies at Lake Trasimene and Cannae, it seemed as though Roman power would be broken. In 202 BC, however, Hannibal was in turn defeated at Zama and Carthaginian power was destroyed. In 149 BC Rome took an excuse to fight a third Punic War. This time Carthage was flattened and the ground on which the city had stood was ploughed over.

The Rise of the Generals

Victory over Carthage had been bought at a high cost, and that cost was paid by the poor. Many peasant farmers, who were citizens, sold their land to the rich and so lost their means of support. This led to a period of internal unrest.

Wars were now being fought far from home, in the Hellenistic east and to the north in the land they called Gaul. Roads were built across the empire, which enabled the army legions to move swiftly from one trouble spot to another. These distant armies could no longer be commanded by consuls, with a term of office of two years.

There therefore arose a new breed of professional generals. These men often became fabulously rich on the booty of war, and, with a loyal army at their back, they could pose a threat to the traditional institutions of the Republic. Marius made his name in Africa and Gaul, and then Sulla in the eastern Mediterranean. Julius Caesar was the most successful in this line of successful generals. In 49 BC he took an irrevocable step when he crossed the River Rubicon, which marked the boundary of Italy, and marched on Rome at the head of his army. By this action he started the chain of events that led to his murder and the founding of imperial Rome.

Christianity

Origins

The early years of the Roman Empire were to see the beginnings of another of the great religions of the world. The Jewish people had maintained a stubborn refusal to dilute their religion to meet the demands of Hellenistic rulers. At the time of Jesus of Nazareth, sects like the Essenes and the Zealots maintained a resistance to Roman rule.

Jesus was a Jew, but he appears to have rejected the path of political resistance and taught instead a message of the relationship of the individual to God and other men, closer to the teaching of some later rabbis. The content of Jesus' teaching was indeed to be influential, but his significance lay not in what he said but in what his disciples declared him to be.

The share of responsibility for his execution can not be determined from the documents preserved, so it is unclear whether he was executed as a danger to the Roman state or as a critic of Jewish practice. Whichever it was, his disciples declared that they had witnessed his resurrection, and proclaimed that he was the Son of God. They picked up the words of the writer from the Babylonian exile and announced him as the saviour of the world, and not just of a chosen people. The holy books of the new religion were written down in the Greek language of the Hellenistic world, rather than in the more restricted Aramaic language that Jesus himself spoke.

Christianity and the Mysteries

Paul of Tarsus carried the message in a series of missionary journeys through the Greek speaking world. There he spoke the language of the popular mysteries - of redemption through blood and of a dying and rising god. With Christianity, however, it was different, he declared. While the mysteries were based in mere images, Christianity was rooted in historical fact.

Paul and other missionaries always sought to found a Christian cell, which they called an *ecclesia*, the word used for the meeting of the Greek polis. Hellenistic culture provided a language for the new religion; Rome provided a structure that enabled it to spread. Missionaries could make use of the Roman roads, and they were not likely to be molested by bandits on the way.

There was no doubting the enthusiasm of the converts, but, for a long time, an outsider would not have readily recognized a fundamental difference between this religion and the mysteries. Heresies, like Gnosticism and Manichaeism were pulling Christianity away from its Semitic roots into the maelstrom of Hellenistic religion. The Roman army generally favoured Mithras. A long path of persecution lay ahead before Christianity would emerge as the dominant religion of the region.

Imperial Rome

The Emperor

At the battle of Actium in 31 BC, Julius Caesar's great-nephew, Octavian, brought Egypt into the empire and ended the years of civil war. Four years later he was given the title of Augustus and made consul for life. He was careful to preserve the honoured republican institutions, but the senate lapsed into impotence and all power now lay with him.

No rule of inheritance was ever established for the position of emperor. In the centuries that were to follow, incompetents would be matched by administrators and generals of ability, imbeciles by philosophers. Most emperors died violently. Succession first passed through the house of Caesar. During one century of good government, it became the practice for an emperor to adopt his successor. For long periods, however, power fell to the general who could command the largest army. But the mass of people would never see the emperor in person. For them, success or failure had to be judged on whether he was strong enough to prevent the huge empire from breaking into civil strife.

The practice of emperor worship was imported from the old Persian tradition. The act of reverence due to the god-ruler was the symbol that bound together the hugely diverse people who now lay under Roman rule. Pious Jews refused to perform this ritual, but this was recognized to be a part of their ancient tradition and it was generally overlooked. The refusal of Christians, who came from all parts and races, was looked upon as a serious threat to the unity of the empire.

Buildings

The great monuments of Rome date from the Imperial age. Augustus himself restored eighty-two temples and boasted, 'I found Rome of brick and left it of marble'. Aqueducts, arches and the huge Colosseum still stand as monuments to Imperial glory. The Romans were content to copy Greek styles to which they added impressive engineering skills.

The more prosperous Roman citizens built homes, such as have been preserved at Pompeii and excavated across the empire. Here they built for comfort, and artists, working in paint and mosaic, expressed a less pretentious view of life with humour and grace.

Natural frontiers

The Roman armies had now carried the empire across Europe, Asia and Africa, until it had ten thousand miles of land frontier. Beyond lay barbarians, ever willing to invade and plunder. The task of defence was made easier by natural boundaries - the African and Arabian deserts and the great rivers Rhine and Danube. This line of defence had two weak points, lying on either side of the Black Sea. In Asia the entrance to the steppes lay open across the land of the Parthians. In Europe generals were tempted to go beyond the Danube, across what is now Romania to the Carpathian Mountains. Roman armies suffered heavy defeats in both of these sectors. Claudius also carried the empire across the natural frontier of the North Sea to Britain. The expedition was designed to bring the glory of conquest and to win control of fabled metal mines of the wild island.

The City of Rome

By imperial times, Rome had grown to be a huge city. Since most of the work was done by slaves, much of the population was unemployed, and the citizens had become accustomed to a lifestyle supported by tribute from conquered peoples. No emperor could contemplate unrest in Rome, so the citizens had to be fed and kept amused on the famous diet of bread and circuses. Entertainments were on a massive scale. The Circus Maximus alone seated 190,000 people. Claudius built the huge harbour at Ostia, where grain, wild beasts and slaves were constantly being unloaded to feed the stomachs and the jaded palates of the people. The city gave nothing back to its empire.

East and West

Gradually a distinction began to emerge between the eastern and the western parts of the empire. The West, centred on Rome itself, covered western Europe and the old Carthaginian lands of North Africa. The east included the old Hellenistic world of Greece, Asia Minor, the Near East and Egypt.

The eastern side of the empire had a better balance to life. It contained ancient cities, but none dominated the region. It was self-sufficient in grain, wood, oil, wine and other essentials, with a surplus to buy in metal from the west and luxuries from the east.

The western part of the empire was not an area of ancient civilization. Since Carthage had been flattened, it had no cities to balance the metropolis of Rome, which constantly sucked in products, so upsetting the economic balance of the region.

In 285 the Emperor Diocletian appointed a co-emperor to rule the western sector. There was now an Empire of the East and an Empire of the West. In 324 Constantine accepted the dominance of the East by taking his capital to his new city of Constantinople.

The Triumph of Christianity

By this time, Christianity had established itself as a growing force. Diocletian tried to stem the tide, but Constantine accepted the new faith. Emperor worship may now have ceased, but even a Christian emperor could not shed the concept that he was the fountain of religion. He declared himself to be the thirteenth apostle and sat as chairman of the Council of Nicea, which established Christian doctrine. This set a precedent for the control of the church by the state.

At about the same time a group of hermits came together in Egypt to form the first monastery in the Christian tradition. This was destined to grow into an influential movement, capable of confronting the ambitions of Christian rulers.

The Barbarian Invasions

The century after Constantine saw increasing pressure on the European frontier of the Western Empire. Far away in the east, the Huns were on the move, and this created pressure on western tribes. The Huns themselves erupted into Europe under Attila in 440, to be defeated at Troyes in 451, but ahead of them, as if a prow wave, came Goths, Ostrogoths, Visigoths, Franks and Vandals.

The Romans found it difficult to defend the long land frontier and they recruited barbarians to strengthen the army. In 376 about 40,000 armed Visigoths were allowed across the frontier. Then in 410 the Goths sacked Rome. Vandals, who left their name for mindless destruction, crossed through Spain into North Africa and then returned for an even more destructive assault on the great city.

In northern Europe, Angles, Saxons and Jutes crossed the North Sea, first to ravage and then to settle in the British Isles. The Celtic inhabitants, no longer protected by Roman legions, were driven back to the highland area of the West, and into Ireland, where the Christian faith survived and flourished.

Byzantium

Her Frontiers

With the ancient capital in barbarian hands, the Roman Empire can be said to have fallen. Those who lived in the Empire of the East, however, recognized no such catastrophe. In 483 Justinian succeeded in Constantinople, and he set about the task of winning back the lost western lands. His armies recovered North Africa, Italy and Southern Spain. It appeared for a time as though the Roman Empire was still a reality.

His conquests, however, were ephemeral. From his time onwards, the Empire of the East was under continual pressure.

In the East, Persia was a power of consequence once again, and behind her the steppe nomads were ever menacing. In the south the empire faced growing Arab power. In the north, Slav people were pressing into the Balkans. The Emperor Heraclius led the Imperial armies in more successful campaigns, but the pressure was ever inwards towards what was to be the Byzantine heartland of Asia Minor, Greece, the Balkans and southern Italy.

Cultural Life

The people saw themselves as being direct inheritors of the old empire. Citizens of Constantinople still visited the bath houses; they still followed the chariot races with the passion of a modern football supporter. Justinian completed the work of centuries of Roman jurists by compiling the authoritative digest of Roman law.

Byzantium, however, soon developed a distinctive character that set it apart from the old empire. This drew both from the Greco-Roman and from Eastern traditions. Constantinople remained a home of classical scholarship. Plato was particularly popular, but his thinking became overlaid by layers of mysticism. Classical features were used in buildings, but the great dome that rose over Justinian's Church of the Holy Wisdom demonstrated new skills and a new aesthetic. Secular artists still worked within Hellenistic traditions, but religious artists, in paintings and mosaics, were beginning to express a particularly eastern Christian piety.

Religion

Early in the development of the eastern church there emerged a distinction between secular (living in the world) and religious (living out of the world) clergy. Secular clergy worked at the parish level and were allowed to marry. The ideal was set by the many hermits and monks who expressed their piety in extreme self-sacrifice. Religious icons became the focus of devotion for ordinary people.

The emperor maintained Constantine's position at the head of the church. Patriarchs, bishops and priests lay under his power. Emperors decided doctrine and mercilessly persecuted many of their subjects who held 'heretical' beliefs.

In the centuries after Justinian, the eastern and the western churches drew gradually further apart. In the west, the Bishop of Rome claimed primacy and began to build a centralized structure. The church finally divided into western and eastern parts in the Great Schism of 1054. This was partly about authority, partly about abstruse issues of theology, but it mainly stemmed from lack of understanding of each other's piety.

The Arabs

Mecca

The desert land of the Arabian peninsula was inhabited by fierce and independent minded Semitic tribes people, who were known as Arabs. They led a nomadic life of great hardship. One trade route between the Mediterranean and the Indian Ocean went across this land, passing through Mecca. The city was also a centre for pilgrimage to the sacred stone or *kaba*. The citizens of Mecca jealously guarded the revenues of both the trade and the pilgrimage.

Early in the seventh century a merchant, called Mohammed, had a vision and started preaching the message 'There is no god but Allah'. He came into conflict with the citizens of Mecca, and in 622 he left the city to live in Medina. This is the date from which the Arab world numbers its calendar.

Islam

The prophet Mohammed had met Christians and Jews and read many of their books, and the religion that he founded lies within the Semitic tradition. He preached one god, which for him ruled out the Christian concept of the Trinity. The word 'Islam' means 'submission', for the duty of the Moslem is to submit to the will of the one god. He gave his followers the five duties—daily prayers, alms, fasting, the keeping of Friday as a holy day, and the pilgrimage—but the message was one of great simplicity. Very quickly, the feuding tribes of the peninsula were given that sense of community, which has ever since been the distinguishing feature of Islam.

Mohammed taught his followers that Christians and Jews were 'people of the book'. They and their religion had, therefore to be treated with respect. Once they accepted Moslem rule, they might be taxed, but they should not be persecuted or converted by force.

The Arab Conquests

Once the Arabs were united, they started raiding towards the north in search of booty, into the lands controlled by Byzantium and Persia. Their invasions had startling and unexpected success, partly because the two empires had weakened one another by endless warfare. More important, however, was that taxation and religious persecution had made their governments deeply unpopular with the people. To 'heretical' Christians, the tolerant Moslem invaders seemed greatly preferable to either emperor.

The Persian Empire collapsed and Byzantium was pressed ever further backwards. Jerusalem fell in 638. It seemed as though Constantinople itself would fall, but in 717 the Arab armies were driven back from the city walls. By this time the Arabs not only controlled the Near East, but also North Africa and the whole of Spain. Their armies were even crossing the Pyrenees into the plains of Europe. Here, however, they found themselves in an alien environment of cold weather and barbarous people, so they turned back towards the south. The Arab armies carried Islam over this wide empire. Many conquered people converted; indeed Christianity disappeared completely from its old stronghold in North Africa.

The ultimate authority within the Islamic world lay with the caliphs. In 750 the ruling Umayyad house was overthrown and the new Abbasid rulers moved the capital to Baghdad.

Arab Culture

The Arabs possessed a powerful poetic tradition before the time of Mohammed and Islamic culture was founded in literature. The Koran, with its religious message and its classical language, provided a powerful unifying bond for one of history's more stable empires. Since the depiction of the human form was forbidden, art developed as elaborate geometric pattern. As the centre of empire moved out of the Arabian peninsula to Baghdad, so eastern influences became increasingly powerful. The Arabic language remained, however, the cement of the Islamic world. Although local dialects might vary, scholars from all parts continued to use the pure language of the Koran.

The Moslems did not come as the destroyers of civilization. The men from the desert quickly absorbed the cultures that they conquered. Their scholars read the Greek philosophers, and united them with the astronomy, mathematics and medicine of the east, so serving as the main channel for the ancient learning in a troubled world. Moslem civilization reached one of its peaks in Spain, where the university of Cordova was a major centre of learning.

The eastern Mediterranean remained the centre of thriving trade. War might bring temporary disruption, but trading links with the East were never long severed. From India came spices, pepper and sugar; from China came porcelain and silks. The wealthy of Byzantium had an insatiable taste for luxury goods and the Arabs soon came to share these sophisticated tastes. Byzantium controlled the overland routes to China, which ended at the Black Sea ports. The Arabs controlled the sea routes by the Persian Gulf and the Red Sea to India, with links beyond to China and the Spice Isles.

Threats to Arab Civilization

In time, Byzantium ceased to be a threat to the Islamic Empire; indeed it seemed only a matter of time before Constantinople must fall. From the eleventh century, for some 300 years, Arab civilization would be subjected to assaults by Christian crusaders from Europe (Chapter 3) and successive waves of nomadic invaders from the steppes of Asia (Chapter 4). The latter were by far the more threatening of the two, and it was they who finally brought the great days of Near Eastern civilization to an end.

3

The Formation of Europe

Church and State

The Papacy

In the year 590 a new Bishop of Rome was elected who would later be known as Gregory the Great. He was a Roman from a senatorial family, but, in the chaos of his day, he had made the choice to become a monk. For a devout Christian, the monastic life seemed to be the only safe course to heaven in a violent and turbulent world. But Gregory saw that it was pointless to live with regrets for past glories of Rome or hopes for help from Byzantium. The church now had a mission to the restless and threatening barbarian world. Gregory selected monks as missionaries and sent them to bring Christianity to the barbarian tribes. The best known of these was Augustine of Canterbury. At the same time, missionaries from Ireland were moving south from Scotland into England and northern Europe. The missionaries from Rome, however, succeeded in linking the growing church back to Rome.

For Gregory's successors the first priority was to establish the primacy of the bishopric of Rome, or papacy. Popes claimed that, since they stood in a direct line from St Peter, they had inherited his 'power to bind and loose'. A pope could therefore control men's eternal destiny by the weapon of excommunication. In an extreme situation, he could even place an interdict, which forbade the performance of any sacraments, on a whole country. In an age of faith this was a formidable sanction.

The Popes had first to bring the Christian clergy under their control. Ordinary parish priests were generally illiterate peasants; bishops were temporal lords who used the church as a means of expanding family lands. Most were married men, who expected to pass their lands and livings on to their children. Their prime allegiance was therefore to the king or chief, rather than to a distant pope.

Monasticism

Only the monks were free from these temporal ties. The Rule of St Benedict, which imposed poverty, chastity and obedience, was now widely accepted. The monks were also almost alone in being literate in an uncultured world. This meant that they could reach positions of influence in both church and state.

The popes used monks as their representatives, and, wherever possible, promoted them to high positions within the church. In time the popes worked to extend their control over the secular clergy by forbidding clerical marriage altogether.

A Time of Turbulence

In the early centuries after the fall of Rome, the pope and his monks were able to establish respect and authority because they provided the only apparent stability in a troubled society. Groups of barbarians roamed through Europe, bound to their leaders in simple tribal ties. When they settled down and adopted Christianity, much of the old way of life continued. Society still had no recognizable political structure, in the modern sense. Disputes were still settled by traditional 'rough justice', such as the ordeal and trial by battle.

Change continued slow in the dark forests of Germany. In time, however, the Franks and other groups in the western part of the European mainland adopted a form of Latin as their language, and paid some respect to the Roman legal system. The tribes who were more cut off in the British Isles, continued to speak their own German language, and developed law, based on past rulings, as preserved in the minds of the elders. So developed the divisions between the romance and Anglo-Saxon languages, and between Roman and common law which were to become important in later western civilization.

Political and social order was beginning to emerge by the end of the eighth century, but then Viking ships brought new danger to European coasts. It is never easy to say why a people go on the move, but it appears as though population growth and weather problems disturbed the balance of marginal Scandinavian farming. Certainly the feared Norsemen set off on 'land takings' and voyages of plunder. Their ships spread out across the North Atlantic to Iceland, Greenland and North America; they emerged into the Mediterranean; they sailed down the great rivers of central Asia, setting up the Russian state, and reaching Constantinople; they won control of northern Britain and Normandy. In 1066 a family of Norse descent won the crown of England.

The Norsemen were not the only raiders. Men from the steppes, this time the Magyars, were pillaging from the east and Moslem Saracen raiders came from the south. Hardly any part of Europe escaped. The unfortunate monks of Luxeil had their monastery burned by Norsemen, Hungarians and Saracens.

The Empire

For a brief period a new power arose in Europe. In 771 the ruthless and talented Charlemagne succeeded to the whole of the Frankish kingdom. For the next 40 years he led his armies to victories on all his borders, even mounting the first counterattack against Islam in Spain. Charlemagne was more than a conqueror. He was a devout Christian, and did much to spread the faith—by the sword if necessary—across Europe. He also respected learning, and he could read himself, although writing defeated him. He encouraged the clergy to respect books and learning, he founded schools and brought the best minds of the day to his court.

On Christmas Day, 800, he was crowned by Pope Leo III in the church of St Peter in Rome. The people cried, 'to Charles Augustus, crowned by God, great and peaceful Emperor of the Romans, Life and Victory. ' A new Roman Empire had been proclaimed.

The empire was based on one man's will, and, like Alexander's, it fell apart on Charlemagne's death. It was divided into three parts. The central kingdom did not survive, but the two other halves would ultimately become France and Germany. Charlemagne's eastern successor retained the title of Holy Roman Emperor, but his lands remained a loose confederacy. In 940 the Comte de Paris, Hughes Capet, won the French crown and established a monarchy that was to survive until the French Revolution. His family was the first European dynasty to establish the concept of a hereditary monarchy.

Powers Temporal and Spiritual

After Pope Leo III had placed the crown on Charlemagne's head, he stretched himself on the ground as a sign of honour to the emperor. Later popes would regret this gesture. The first objective of the popes was to win control within the church. This involved taking the right to appoint bishops away from the temporal rulers.

In the eleventh century, Pope Gregory VII and Emperor Henry IV came into conflict in the Investiture Controversy. Gregory was victorious, forcing Henry to stand barefoot in the winter snow as a sign of submission. Gregory then formulated the extreme claim that all power came from the pope, and he therefore had the right to appoint and depose kings and emperors. The Investiture Controversy was the first of a series of disputes between church and state. They involved, not only the Holy Roman Emperor, but also kings of France and England.

King, Lord and Parliament

The Feudal System

In those troubled times, people were prepared to sacrifice liberty in the interest of security. Kings and emperors were remote figures, so free men bound themselves to their local lord, who could give assistance when danger was near. When a man took an oath of loyalty he gave his lands to the lord, and then received them back as the lord's vassal. He had the obligation to follow the lord to war, but as a mounted knight, to set him apart from the common serfs. The lord, in his turn, bound himself to a higher lord, and the king stood at the apex of the pyramid. Only the serfs were nobody's vassal, because they had nothing to give in exchange for protection. These common people were not allowed to leave their villages, to go to school or to get married without their lord's permission.

By the end of the ninth century, this feudal system had spread to all but the most remote areas of Europe. Kings, like other lords, were concerned to extend their lands wherever they could by war and dynastic marriage. The two way nature of the feudal compact served as a check on royal power. In France, the Capetian kings stood at the apex of the pyramid, but for long periods their actual power did not extend beyond their own lands around Paris. So, when the King of England married a French heiress, he did homage to the French king for his lands in Aquitaine, but he did not permit any interference within his territory.

The Hundred Years' War between France and England was fought sporadically from 1337 to 1453. The English king may have laid claim to the crown of France, but it remained in essence a struggle between a dynastic monarch, determined to establish direct control over feudal lands on the one side, and an over-mighty subject, on the other. It was one of the catalysts that defined the meaning of the modern nation state. Writing some two hundred years later, Shakespeare would put words of nationalistic fervour into the mouths of John of Gaunt and Henry V. Such sentiments would have been incomprehensible in the time of Charlemagne or William the Conqueror, but they were beginning to have some meaning to their supposed speakers.

King and Parliament

William the Conqueror gave English kings more direct authority within their own realms. The feudal system was constructed to ensure that no lord could become 'over mighty'. Vassals, for their part were concerned that the king should not achieve unlimited power. In 1215 the lords forced King John to sign Magna Carta, which laid down two basic rights—that no free man could be imprisoned without a trial, and the king could not raise taxes without the consent of a Great Council. In 1295, King Edward I called what became known as the Model Parliament, because it set the pattern for future parliaments. Representation was by estates—the Lords temporal, the Lords Spiritual and the Third Estate, with the first two sitting together in an upper house. It was also established that parliament had the responsibility to act as the highest court in the land, to give advice to the king, to make laws and to vote taxes.

The Rise of the Towns

The inclusion of the third estate in Edward's Model Parliament was testament to the growing importance of trade in the European economy. Wealth was no longer the preserve of landowners and the church, so, to achieve maximum income, it was now necessary to consult with the representatives of the growing towns.

As towns grew in importance, kings gave them charters, which assured them freedom from interference by local landowners. Their walls were the symbol of their independence, and magnificent churches the evidence of their wealth. Trade provided a means by which low-born men could rise to positions of power within their own community, and even within the state. Different occupations were organized into guilds, which controlled terms of entry, quality standards and gave members a social structure.

The cities were often natural allies to kings who wanted to centralize power. Overmighty nobles might flourish in conditions of civil war, but merchants needed the peace that only a strong government could provide. Kings, for their part, recognized that the growing wealth that was the basis for national strength as well as royal revenue was generated not on noble estates but inside the town walls.

The Cloth Trade

The Lord Chancellor of England still sits in the House of Lords on a woolsack. This was a reminder to parliament that the nation's wealth rested on the woollen trade. England, however, stood in the lowly position of a primary producer; the business in finished cloth centred round Flanders. Flemish weavers jealously guarded the trade secrets that made their cloth the most sought after in Europe. From the thirteenth century, the economy of northern Europe became increasingly sensitive to fluctuations in the fortunes of the cloth trade.

The Crusades

The First Crusade

In 1095 the Byzantine emperor appealed to the pope for assistance against the Turks. The pope answered the call by preaching a Holy War. The motives of those, both noble and common folk, who took the cross, were very mixed. Many of the Norman lords who took the lead saw the opportunity of a new land taking, like those of their Viking ancestors. But there was also a real devotion. The two were not incompatible.

When the army arrived first in Byzantium and then in the Arab lands, they appeared like barbarians, with nothing to recommend them but their brute courage. Jerusalem fell to the crusaders, who waded through blood to give thanks for the victory.

Outremer

The crusaders established states in the conquered land. The Moslems resented these Christian enclaves in their territory, and they were therefore under constant pressure. In 1187 Saladin reconquered Jerusalem, and the crusaders were unable to win it back. In 1291 the last Christian outpost fell to the army of Islam. The crusades gave the West two centuries of contact with a higher culture. Knights returned home with a taste for oriental luxury goods. Some picked up an interest in learning and mathematics, and methods of castle construction and siege warfare were modernized on Arab models.

The Later Crusades

Eight campaigns between the eleventh and the thirteenth centuries are known as crusades, as well as tragic children's crusades. The movement turned inwards against European heretics. The simple crusaders were not always able to distinguish which enemy they should fight. The Venetians encouraged the fourth crusade to turn on Byzantium. In 1204 Constantinople was captured by the crusaders and the city remained in Christian hands until 1261. Although the rump of empire would survive into the fifteenth century, Byzantium never recovered from the disaster.

Spain

At the same time, Christian forces were counterattacking against the Moslem Moors in Spain. In 1212 the Moors were defeated and driven back to Grenada. The reconquest of the peninsula was completed in 1492. A great culture was replaced by a fanatical Christian state, in which the Inquisition was used as a tool of persecution against Moors, Jews and many Christians whose views did not please the authorities.

Learning, Art and Society

Scholarship and Authority

As long as there was no nation state, there were no sharply defined national boundaries. Latin provided a lingua franca and the church a broadly based structure within which the educated of their day could communicate.

Through the troubled times any learning remained behind monastic walls. The books of early Christian fathers were copied and became the intellectual authorities of the new world. Men had lost confidence in their own ability to reach conclusions, either through logic or through experiment, and all argument therefore referred back to authority. Even quite trivial issues of dispute would be decided by the weight of authority that could be mustered on the one side or the other.

The authors of antiquity were largely unknown until around the twelfth century. Then translations began to be made into Latin from copies preserved in Islamic Spain and Sicily. The ancient dichotomy between Plato and Aristotle began to be reflected in arguments between nominalist and realist theologians. Thomas Aquinas, in particular, baptised Aristotle. This did not, however, lead to an increase in experiment; classical authors joined the Christian fathers as valid sources of authority. In southern Europe, men still lived amidst the ruins of classical civilization. The classical and the

Christian came together until, as in Dante's *Inferno* and Michelangelo's Sistine Chapel, they became indistinguishable from each other.

By the twelfth century, learning was coming out from monastic walls into the more open atmosphere of universities. The first was at Salerno, where Islamic and Byzantine influence was strong. Then came Bologna, Paris, Oxford and many others. Crowds would follow teachers, like Peter Abelard, who spoke a new and more restless language. University students were in religious orders of some sort, but the educational impetus continued outwards into the wider population. By later medieval times, an increasing number of lay people, particularly in the towns, were acquiring literacy.

Architecture and Painting

In early medieval times most stone buildings were either castles or monasteries. Many were fine buildings, but they added little to the techniques of antiquity. By the twelfth century, architects were developing their own signature. The Romanesque style of Southern Italy was based closely on a study of classical models. In northern France and England there rose magnificent cathedrals in the Gothic style. Here the pointed arch and the flying buttress enabled them to give their structures both height and light.

Most painting, likewise, remained dedicated to the church. Altarpieces showed the Virgin and child, with patrons and saints; frescoes and stained glass windows reminded illiterate worshippers of Bible stories; monks, copying psalters and books of hours, under no pressure of deadlines, painted exquisite decoration. In Italy, the school of Sienna worked under direct influence from Byzantium. But painters, like architects and stone masons, were craftsmen who were happy to work for any patron, and, as the centuries passed, an increasing number of commissions were available for secular work.

Literature

Medieval literature, like that of any other period, was made up of different strands—folk tales and myths, national histories, historical chronicles, love poems and works of devotion. Early vernacular literature, like Norse sagas and the Anglo-Saxon *Beowolf*, helped to create national language areas. In the early centuries, however, Latin was the language of both secular and religious writing.

By the fourteenth century a new vernacular literature was emerging. The supreme example of in English is *The Canterbury Tales*, written by soldier and customs officer, Geoffrey Chaucer, for an audience of other lay people.

Times of Change

The Black Death

A sickness new to the human race was first reported in the Yangtze Valley in 1334 and, according to one estimate, some thirteen million Chinese died in the following years. Relentlessly it spread from east to west, leaving devastation in India and across Asia. In 1347 the plague spread across Northern Italy and in the following years it is estimated that between a quarter and a third of the population of Europe perished. This first outbreak was the worst, but the disease returned periodically until the second half of the seventeenth century. Although it was a worldwide phenomenon, its effects have been most closely studied in Europe.

Initially it brought economic collapse; prices of all goods fell sharply and much farm land returned to nature. As life recovered, employers were faced with an acute labour shortage. This created strains within the social structure of both town and country. Guild regulations were flouted and the feudal structure began to crumble. There were major peasant uprisings, in France in 1358, in Florence in 1378 and in England in 1381.

The Late Medieval Church

Pious Christians were unable to understand why God could have created such destruction. The plague accentuated a Christian piety that identified God as judge and destroyer and the saints, particularly the Virgin Mary, as protector.

The church, like all institutions, moves through cycles of corruption and reformation. In early medieval times, reformation came from within. The last of these reforming movements was the founding of the friars by Francis of Assisi in 1209. Now the impetus for reform had grown weak. In the fourteenth century popes taxed the faithful heavily to maintain a lavish lifestyle. After the Black Death these taxes fell all the more heavily on a smaller population. One fund raising technique was the offer of indulgences, by which punishment in the next world was remitted in exchange for payment in this world. During the fourteenth century the church lost its independence when it moved under the protection of the King of France in Avignon. The Great Schism, when rival popes competed from Rome and Avignon, further undermined spiritual authority. Some Franciscans denounced papal luxury and were burned as heretics but their message was heard by the people.

Before the end of the fourteenth century John Wycliffe in England and Jan Hus in Bohemia were preaching that man did not need the apparatus of the church to make contact with God. Hus founded what was to be the first protestant church, and Wycliffe translated the Bible into English.

The Reformation

In the early sixteenth century the pope set out to raise money for the building of St Peter's by selling indulgences. In 1517, the university lecturer Martin Luther challenged the papal representative to a debate by nailing 95 theses to the door of Wittenberg cathedral. The church authorities sought to have him condemned, like heretics of old, but he found protection from German princes. The protestant movement soon won followers, particularly in the trading towns and in Northern Europe.

Luther did not initially see himself as the leader of a movement that would split the western church, but, as he preached the supremacy of the Bible and faith over the sacraments and traditional authority, the division quickly became irreconcilable. He found himself leading a mass movement, based on individual piety. Luther was the catalyst for another round in the ancient struggle between lay and secular powers. He only survived to preach because he was adopted by German princes, who saw his movement as a useful weapon against the power of the church.

Eastern Europe

Russia

It appears as though the Norsemen who settled the rivers of Russia brought no women with them, so the process of assimilation was rapid. In 980 Vladimir established the kingdom of Kiev and he married a sister of the Byzantine emperor. It is said that Russian envoys visited Constantinople and the West to decide which form of Christianity should be adopted. They were overwhelmed by the splendour of Constantinople, and the eastern link was forged. Kiev was destroyed in 1169 and the centre of power was driven northwards to Moscow. Trading and cultural ties with Byzantium were largely lost, and Russia was increasingly isolated until it was overrun by the Mongols in the thirteenth century. Russian independence can then be dated to the victory over the Tartars in 1380. The Grand Princes of Moscow emerged as rulers and Ivan III (1462–1505) adopted the title of Tsar (Caesar) and the double headed eagle, to substantiate the claim that, with Constantinople in Ottoman hands, the Russian monarchy had now inherited the imperial tradition.

Poland

When Vladimir made his choice of the eastern church, the Poles on his western frontier had just turned in the other direction. The missionaries who brought western Christianity to Poland also acted as forerunners for waves of land-hungry German invaders, led by the fearsome Teutonic Knights. In late medieval times, a Polish state lay across the central European plain, with its prosperity based on grain exports to the west through the port of Danzig. It was, however, already showing signs of the damage that would be caused by its geographical location as a buffer between Western Europe, the Scandinavian north, Russia and the East and the disturbed cauldron of Slavs and Magyars in the Balkan south.

In both Russia and Poland the serfs lived in great poverty, under the control of a wealthy landed class. Rulers were faced with a perpetual challenge from over-mighty subjects without being able to look for the support of any considerable middle class.

4

The Wider World

Asia Before the Mongols

India

For centuries after Ashoka, the Indian subcontinent was divided into warring states. The south, behind its mountain barrier, remained the home of non-Aryan people. They maintained contact with the Mediterranean civilizations through the Red Sea and Persian Gulf trading routes. In the northwest, the frontier and Indus valley remained open to Asian invaders. Invading Hunas, probably Huns, devastated this region, as they did lands both to east and west.

In about 320 AD the Guptas united the whole of northern India. This marked the great age of Hindu culture. In the fifth century, the decimal system was invented, so opening new areas of mathematics. Sculpture and literature flourished, both achieving a broad unity of style, characterized by a warm sensuality. Buddhist culture declined as Hinduism spread across Asia and into the islands of the Pacific. The island of Bali remains today a marker of this great expansion.

The Hindu Empire was in time challenged by the rise of Islam. Moslem traders—always effective missionaries for the Prophet—would have visited the western ports in the seventh century. By the eighth century invaders were crossing the open north western frontier. By the twelfth century, they controlled the Punjab, and a century later they dominated the Ganges valley. The fateful religious divide was now established.

China

China was united more effectively by language and culture than it was by its political structure. The two most powerful dynasties were Han (*c.* 205 BC-AD 220) and T'ang (618–907). Their empires were comparable to that of Rome at its most powerful. During the T'ang Dynasty trade flourished, and China became a major sea power, with trade reaching from the Persian Gulf in the west to Indonesia in the east. The great Chinese dynasties had an expectation of life of about 300 years. They were founded by a great individual who combined military and administrative skills. In later years, as the succession passed to lesser men, the state would come under pressure from nomads to the north and rebellion at home. Imperial authority was upheld by officials, who preserved the traditions of K'ung-fu-tsu. Their main tasks were to take the census and keep the land register up to date. Beyond that, they maintained only a broad supervision over local lords, who raised taxes and performed the day to day tasks of administration themselves.

Great civil works were undertaken. The country was now bound together by canals, of which the most important was the Great Canal, which linked Peking with Hangchou. Huge irrigation projects were undertaken to provide food for the ever growing population. The casting of iron, printing, the magnetic compass, the use of paper money and explosives were all pioneered in China, but the conservative structure of society militated against the fullest exploitation of her inventions.

In the periods between the great dynasties, the country relapsed into warring states. There were times of disaster, when armies ravaged large areas, but in general, conditions changed little for the mass of peasants, whose life was always more closely governed by local lords than by distant emperors. But, while Europe remained divided into her warring states, China could always be drawn together once again by a dynamic new dynasty.

The Sung Dynasty (960–1279) was never as powerful as its great predecessors and in 1127 it lost the northern part of the country to Chin invaders. In the following century and a half the Southern Sung Dynasty lacked military power, but the period is viewed by many as the high point of Chinese culture. The Imperial capital of Hangchou was a centre of wealth, culture and leisured living, far beyond any other city in the world.

Sung art was influenced by the Zen school of Buddhism. Painters, such as Ma Yuan, worked with an economy of line and colour to make a visual statement about man's position within the world order. Potters made dishes that looked 'like ivory, but were as delicate as thin layers of ice'.

The Seljuk Turks

The name 'Turk' is given to widely dispersed people, originating on the Asian steppes, who spoke a common language. In the tenth century, a chief called Seljuk settled with his people near Samarkand and was converted to Islam. The tribe organized an army based on slaves, mainly recruited from southern Russia and the Caucasus, who were known as mameluks. Backed by these fearless warriors, Seljuk's grandsons built an empire, from Azerbaijan and Armenia, into the ancient lands of Middle East. They overran Persia, captured Baghdad, Jerusalem and Egypt and invaded Byzantine lands in Asia Minor.

Later Seljuk rulers found it difficult to hold this vast empire together. While their efforts were largely directed against European crusades, they faced trouble in other parts of the empire. In Egypt, for instance, mameluke soldiers established a virtually independent government. The Seljuk Empire therefore became vulnerable to another and greater threat from the Asian steppes.

The Mongols

Genghis Khan and his Successors

In 1206 a chief called Temujin, better known to the world as Genghis Khan, united the Mongol tribes who lived in the area today called Mongolia. These were wild, nomadic peoples in the tradition of the horsemen who had come from the steppes throughout recorded history. He then established dominance over the more numerous Turkish peoples from the land to the north of the Himalayas. Genghis Khan came to believe that he was destined to rule the world, and he embarked on the greatest programme of conquest in history. His followers were magnificent horsemen. As a nomad people, they could survive on dried milk and the blood of their horses. Released from the constraints of supply, they were therefore uniquely mobile. They were also utterly ruthless. Cities that accepted them were often treated with leniency; those that resisted were liable to be levelled to the ground, and the population massacred. As the reputation of the Mongol horde was carried ahead, rulers capitulated to avoid the dreadful destruction.

By the time that Genghis died in 1227, the Chin Empire of northern China had fallen, and Mongol armies had swept across the open grasslands of Asia as far as Russia and the Caucasus. Still the advance continued. In 1237–38 the Russian state was overwhelmed by horsemen who rode down the frozen rivers, achieving the winter conquest that would later elude both Napoleon and Hitler. When a Great Khan died the armies returned to their homeland to debate the issue of succession. Europe might have been overrun had Genghis Khan's successor not died in 1241. The armies did not again threaten Europe; to the Mongols, it seemed a poor land, hardly worth conquering. They did, however, return to the Middle East, capturing Baghdad and destroying the caliphate in 1258. The tide of conquest finally turned here too when, in 1260, the mamelukes of Egypt organized the armies of Islam to defeat a Mongol army at Ain Jalut, near the town of Nazareth.

Mongol China

The Mongol Empire was now divided into four, with the eastern section the portion of Genghis' grandson, Kublai. He led a Mongol assault on the Southern Sung Empire, which fell in 1279. Further expeditions were launched into South East Asia and even, unsuccessfully, against Japan. While his grandfather Genghis had devastated the north, Kublai respected the civilization that he conquered. Although he spoke little Chinese, he was a patron of literature and, like conquerors before him, he adopted Chinese ways. Mongol rule had now united the whole territory between Europe and China under a single authority and the ancient overland routes were opened once again. In 1275 members of the Polo family from far away Venice reached the court of Kublai Khan. When the young Marco Polo finally returned to Venice in 1299 he gave the west its first information about the civilization of the east. Readers in the more primitive Europe found it hard to believe that such a land of riches could exist far to the east, but some two centuries later a Genoan sailor called Christopher Columbus would own and make notes on a copy of the Venetian's narrative.

For the Chinese, however, the Mongols remained a dynasty of foreigners. Prosperity declined sharply and there was a wave of unrest, and the Mongols were overthrown in 1367 by a new Ming Dynasty. This survived its allotted three centuries until 1644 when it was in turn overthrown by new invaders from Manchuria, who established the Manchu Dynasty.

Later Mongol Conquests

In about 1370 Timur the Lame, a chief from the region of Samarkand, proclaimed that he was the man to revive the Mongol Empire. In the next thirty years, he ravaged the Middle East, Asia Minor, southern Russia and northern India with a brutality matched only by his distant kinsman Genghis Khan. The ancient lands of the Fertile Crescent, so long the focus of world civilization, never recovered from his invasion.

The Mongol Khanate of the Golden Horde in Russia was fatally weakened. He died in 1405, when on his way to carry his conquests into China.

In time the Mongol people of Central Asia and the Middle East came to accept the religion of Islam. The weakness in Mongol power lay in the fact that there was no established law of succession. Timur's successors, like other Mongols, were concerned with domestic issues as they contested succession. Fifth in line from Timur was the more attractive Babur, an accomplished soldier who was also interested in literature, music and architecture. The kingdoms of northern India were at that time in a state of permanent warfare. In 1526 Babur won a series of victories, and by his death in 1530 he had established Mongol—or Mogul—rule in northern India.

Mogul India

Akbar

In 1556 Babur's grandson, called Akbar, inherited a weak and divided empire as a boy of fourteen. He also inherited the ancestral belief that no empire can survive unless it is continually expanding, and throughout his reign he kept his armies constantly on the offensive. He continued old Mongol tactics. When a city, like Chittor, resisted it could be utterly destroyed and its people massacred; when people accepted his authority, they found him a generous ruler. By 1600 his Mogul empire controlled the whole of the subcontinent, except for Ceylon (Sri Lanka) and Vijayanagar in the south. Akbar built a huge capital at Fathpur-Siki, which was to be the model for Mogul public buildings of incomparable grandeur, culminating in Shah Jahan's Taj Mahal.

The country was divided into provinces, but all authority sprang directly from the emperor himself. Although a ruthless conqueror, Akbar was anxious to bind his people together effectively, and he was concerned at the religious division that existed between his Hindu and Moslem subjects. He was suspicious of all dogmatism, and devout Moslems accused him of backsliding when he abolished the poll tax payable by Hindus, and worked to find a compromise between the two religions.

The Decline of the Mogul Empire

Akbar was an outstanding ruler, but his empire suffered from weaknesses inherited from his Mongol tradition. In Europe, structures of government were coming into existence that transcended the personality of the ruler. In Mogul India, however, authority continued to be overdependent on the ability of one man. In his last years, even Akbar was plagued by rebellious sons. The instability of the empire can be illustrated by events at the end of the reign of Shah Jahan. In 1657 he fell ill, triggering a ferocious civil war between his sons. The victorious Aurangzeb was a devout and intolerant Moslem, and under his rule the united empire created by Akbar began to fall apart.

The Ottomans

The Foundation of Empire

Mongol successes in central Asia created more movement of nomad tribes out of the grasslands. In the late thirteenth century, one Ertughrul led a band of followers, who were equally devoted to Islam and to plundering, into the Seljuk lands of the Middle

East. Ertughrul's son, Othman overthrew the Seljuk sultans, and founded the great empire that was to bear his name.

Othman's successors defeated the Byzantine army. They captured Asia Minor, and, in 1361, crossed into Europe to establish Ottoman power in the Balkans. Constantinople was now an isolated fortress in Ottoman lands, and in 1453 it fell to the Sultan Mehmet II.

The Spread of Empire

Ottoman power reached its peak in the century after the fall of Constantinople. In the early sixteenth century Selim I marched southwards, defeating the Mamelukes of Egypt and capturing Mecca, where he was proclaimed Caliph of the Islamic world. His successor Suleiman I, the Magnificent, turned north. In 1526 he defeated the Hungarian army at the great battle of Mohacs. Three years later his armies laid siege to Vienna.

Africa

Trans-Saharan Trade

Historians of early sub-Saharan Africa are restricted by the lack of written records and the destructive capacity of termites, working on wood and mud brick. The continent, however, was far from isolated. A thriving trade existed across the Sahara trade routes between North Africa and the grassland region that lies across the continent from near the Atlantic to the Nile.

The staple product being carried southward was salt—an essential commodity for people living in a hot climate. The Moslem traders who crossed the desert carried various luxury goods, and also brought their religion and literacy in Arabic script. On the return journey they carried gold, slaves and leather goods. Before the time of Columbus, Europe was heavily dependent on African gold, and 'Morocco leather' has always originated south of the Sahara. A key focal point of this trade was Timbuktu, on the Niger, which became famous as the meeting point of the camel and the canoe. The town was already well enough known to be marked on a Spanish map in the late fourteenth century.

The gold and probably most of the slaves came from the forest region still further south, so trade reached out in both directions. Among the most active traders were the Hausa people, who were based on city states, such as Kano, and Zaria. They would be late recruits to Islam and they never organized into larger political units.

African Empires

Broadly based political structures did, however, come into existence in the Southern Sudan to control the two-way trade. The Empire of Ghana (eighth to the eleventh centuries) was succeeded by Mali (twelfth to fourteenth centuries) and Songhai (fourteenth to sixteenth centuries). Kings like Musa Mensa, who ruled Mali in the early fourteenth century, were well known for their wealth and learning across the Islamic world, and even beyond. The trade in gold appears also to have stimulated the growth of forest kingdoms, such as Benin and Oyo. These would grow in importance with the arrival of European ships on the coast in the fifteenth century. Far to the east, the kingdom of Ethiopia maintained its isolated Christian tradition, again with power based on trade with the north by way of the Nile.

There was also traffic in gold and slaves down the coast of East Africa. The unique stone ruins of Zimbabwe provide evidence to support the reports of inland states in this region.

America

America was the last continent to be settled by man and it remained the most isolated. Traditional hunter/gatherer lifestyles were successfully followed by people of widely differing culture across wide areas of North America and within the many forest regions of North America until they suffered under the impact of European invaders. The cultivation of maize and then of other crops, however, made possible the development of more complex civilizations.

Central America

The earliest civilization was that of the Olmecs, which flourished on the coast of the Gulf of Mexico in the seventh century BC. Many of the characteristics of later civilizations of the region can already be recognized in these people. In their capital of Teotihuacan they built huge pyramids, apparently dedicated to the same gods that would be worshipped by people of the region in later generations.

The most accomplished civilization of the region was the Maya, centred on the Yucatan peninsula, which reached its peak in the ninth century BC. The Mayans used a pictogram form of writing. Like the Babylonians, they laid emphasis on the calendar and the heavenly bodies and they developed great skill in mathematics and astronomy, working out the duration of the year and learning how to predict eclipses. They were the first people in the world's history to achieve a sense of the vast span of time. Mayan sites, like those of ancient Egypt, are not cities, but vast complexes of temples and other ceremonial buildings.

The Maya were succeeded by the Toltecs, and they were overthrown in their turn by the Aztecs, who dominated the region from the thirteenth century. They appear to have been the first to introduce mass human sacrifice. This practice came to dominate the whole of Aztec strategy for the region. As victims were best found in warfare, they had no motivation to create conditions of peace, but rather encouraged a general unrest among subject people.

The Aztecs had a tradition that the white-skinned and bearded god Quetzalcoatl would one day return from the east. When the invading Spaniards appeared to fulfil this prophesy, there were many subject people who were prepared to take their side against their feared Aztec masters.

The Andes

The long spine of the Andes is perhaps the most improbable setting for any of the world's civilizations. Between 600 and 1000 AD, a people called the Huari brought some political unity to this area. In the twelfth century, the Incas, based on Cuzco in modern Peru, were only one of many smaller groupings. They then conquered an empire that by the fifteenth century stretched 2000 miles from Quito in modern Ecuador to the deserts of Chile.

The Incas were a non-literate people. Instructions were carried to distant parts of the empire by messengers. Again, lacking the wheel, these messengers travelled on foot over a road network, built with great engineering skill. Inca power was centred on heavily fortified cities, where invading Spaniards were to find a wealth of beautiful objects made of gold and stone.

The Incas were not as oppressive to their subject people as the Aztecs, but there were still many who were prepared to support the small force of Spaniards who arrived in 1531 to conquer and loot the empire.

5

The Triumph of Europe

The Background to Conquest

New Perspectives

The Mappa Mundi, in Hereford Cathedral, illustrates the medieval perspective of the world. Jerusalem lies in the centre of the world, with the three known continents - Asia, Africa and Europe - arranged around the Mediterranean Sea. Phoenician and Viking ships may have sailed the wider oceans, but these lay at the edge of the known universe.

By the fifteenth century, changes were taking place. The reports of Marco Polo's travels in the East were becoming widely known. No profit orientated merchant could ignore his descriptions of markets loaded with silks, velvets and damasks. He had travelled beyond China to the islands of the Pacific and described how cheaply spices could be obtained. It was still impossible to keep meat animals alive through the European winter, so all except the breeding stock was slaughtered and salted down at Michaelmas. By spring it was barely edible without pepper, cinnamon and nutmeg to disguise the taste.

In 1400, a copy of the Hellenistic Ptolemy's *Geography* was brought from Constantinople and published in the west. It contained many errors, but did show that the world was round and not a flat dish. During the century, this became the accepted view of scholars.

The Ottoman conquests helped stimulate interest in alternative routes to East Asia. Through medieval times the majority of luxury goods had been brought by the Asian overland routes. These were now threatened by a hostile power. The Genoese, traditional allies of Byzantium, were particularly threatened by the new developments. Ottomans and Venetians alike combined to shut them out from the profitable business.

Logic demanded that traders should turn their attention to the oceans that lay beyond the enclosed Mediterranean world. Luxury goods were high value and low bulk cargo. Projected returns on investment on one cargo reaching Europe were astronomical.

Technical advance

During the fifteenth century major technical advances were also made in Europe, which brought such a project within the bounds of the possible. Before that time European ships had been square rigged on a single main mast. Such a ship could be manned by a small crew, but could not sail efficiently into the wind. Arab ships used a lateen sail. This could sail into the wind, but such a large crew was needed that it could never go far from land where food could be obtained. Shipbuilders now constructed multi-masted vessels, with both square and lateen sails, which could both be handled by a small crew and sail into the wind.

If ships were to sail far out from land, then navigational techniques needed to improve. By 1500 European sailors were skilled in the use of the magnetic compass, either re-invented or brought from China, and in measuring latitude. Almost 200 years more years would pass before similar advances were made in calculating longitude. Great advances were also made in cartographical techniques, with the Dutch leading the way.

European craftsmen also developed gunnery to new levels. King John II of Portugal took particular interest in the problems of mounting modern guns on board ship. Success in these experiments meant that European ships could command the seas. In previous centuries, ships came together with grappling hooks to allow soldiers to fight a conventional battle. Now the European ship could sink an enemy ship without allowing it to come close enough to bring the soldiers into action.

Population and Prices

The intellectual climate was favourable, commercial incentives were strong, and the required technology was available. As with Norsemen and Mongols, however, a further 'push factor' was needed to trigger off a major movement of European people. Demographers have shown that Western Europe had recovered from the Black Death and a cyclical population increase was in progress. Pauperism was on the increase, and also, in populations organized on the basis of primogeniture, landless younger sons of gentry families were looking for any way of making a fortune.

Historians now link the population rise with an inflationary trend that persisted through the sixteenth century. On average, prices quadrupled between 1500 and 1600. Since wages and savings did not always keep up with the rising prices, this created conditions of hardship that could make emigration attractive.

Religion

Christians of the period generally held that unbelievers possessed no rights. The Pope declared that Christian kings had a right to conquer heathen lands. Some Catholic friars and, later, Jesuits did identify with the cause of the native people, but even their mission stations were instruments of colonial control. The Protestant record was, if anything, worse. 300 years would pass before protestant Christians made any serious attempt to protect the rights of and to share their faith with non-European people.

Asia

The Portuguese

By 1400 Portugal was free from Moslem rule and had established itself as a separate country from Spain. Its geographical position made it a natural Atlantic pioneer. In the first half of the fifteenth century, the king's brother, Henry 'The Navigator' established a school for sailors at Sagres, by Cape St Vincent, and sent out expeditions to explore ever further south into the Atlantic. Slowly they pushed the boundaries of exploration beyond the Azores and to Senegal.

In 1487, twenty-seven years after Henry's death, Bartholomew Diaz rounded the

Cape of Good Hope and established that the way to India lay clear. In 1498 Vasco da Gama took his ship to Calicut in south India. Indian merchants were happy to sell to the newcomers as they offered higher prices than the Arabs. He returned with a cargo of pepper, cinnamon, ginger, cloves and tin. It was reported that the King of Portugal and Vasco da Gama's other backers made a 6000 per cent return on their investment. A century of human and financial investment had finally paid a dividend. In 1503 the Portuguese established a permanent base in India, at Cochin, followed in 1510 by Goa, and later by Seurat.

In 1509 the Arabs sent a fleet, manned by 15,000 men, to drive the Portuguese from their seas, but the European superiority in ships and gunnery proved decisive in a battle off Diu. From that time European fleets exercised control over the world's oceans. Arab and oriental sailors could no longer confront them in battle, but only operate as pirates.

In 1517 the first Portuguese ship arrived off the coast of China and, according to European custom, fired their guns in salute. The Chinese found these barbaric Europeans 'crafty and cruel', but had to respect their guns, which 'shook the earth'. In 1521 Portuguese ships had reached the Spice Islands. In 1557 they established their trading base at Macao, off the Chinese mainland.

The Dutch

The Portuguese successfully protected their Africa route against encroachment by other European nations until the last years of the sixteenth century. Then in 1594 a group of Dutch businessmen fitted out four ships to sail to the Far East. They carried the products of Europe—woollen and linen fabrics, glassware, ornaments and different kinds of ironware, including armour. The ships reached East Asia and found that the people welcomed their quality goods. In 1602, the Dutch parliament, the Estates, set up the Dutch East India Company to follow up this initiative. The Malacca Strait, in modern Indonesia, became the focus of the empire, with headquarters on the island of Java. The Dutch then set about driving the Portuguese out of their Asian empire. Only a few Portuguese outposts, such a Goa and Macao survived the assault.

Once in control, the Dutch traders ruthlessly set about eliminating all competition. In 1623 ten English merchants were tortured and killed at Amboyna. But they were not content to exclude other European competition from their market. Chinese junks were shut out of their traditional markets as even local trade was channelled into Dutch ships. By now Europe was becoming glutted with spices, so the Dutch governor, Jan Coen set about controlling production to keep prices high. On one occasion he destroyed all the nutmeg trees on the Banda Islands and either killed or sold into slavery the entire population of 15,000 people. He burnt villages along the coast of China in an attempt to control the whole region, but complained that China, like India, was 'too extensive for discipline'.

The English

The English East India Company was founded two years earlier than the Dutch, but it lost the race to control the Spice Islands. After Amboyna, the Dutch and the English were bitter commercial rivals. The English had to accept that the prize of the Pacific trade was closed to them and had to make do as a second best with establishing themselves in India. The trade in coffee, tea and cotton goods was of lower value than that from further east, but as the English trading stations at Madras, Bombay and Calcutta grew in importance tea gained status as a fashionable drink. When Dutch power waned in the later years of the seventeenth century, English ships were able to use their Indian bases for trading with China and the Pacific Islands.

The French

The French East India Company had now replaced the Dutch as the main competition. French merchants, however, operated under difficulties. They came from a nation whose power was centred on its land army. While naval and commercial interests were influential in London, they carried little weight in Paris. In times of war, French ships were exposed to the powerful English navy and French overseas outposts were at all times starved of resources.

It long seemed impossible that any European nation would establish political control in the sub continent. Then the death of Aurangzeb in 1707 marked the end of the Mogul Empire as an effective force, and the subcontinent split into warring states. From that time, the trading companies became increasingly involved in politics.

America

The Spanish

On 2 January 1492 the troops of the 'Catholic Monarchs', Isabella of Castile and her husband, Ferdinand of Aragon, finally drove the Moors out of Grenada. In the cheering crowd was a Genoese sailor, Christopher Columbus. Like another Genoese, John Cabot, he had decided that the Indes could best be reached by sailing westwards. Both turned to western European monarchs, with a natural interest in Atlantic trade. Columbus won the support of Isabella, and in August his three ships sailed from Palos, to reach San Salvador on 12 October.

Columbus was bitterly disappointed that he did not find the eastern markets described by Marco Polo. In later voyages he explored the Caribbean Islands and reached the mainland. He died in 1506, still convinced that he had reached the Indes. Before then, however, another Italian, Amerigo Vespucci, this time in Portuguese pay, had established that this was indeed the continent that subsequently carried his name. In the year that Columbus sailed, the Spanish Pope, Alexander VI issued a bull, awarding to Spain and Portugal all lands already discovered or to be discovered in the West, towards the Indes or the ocean seas, with the dividing line between the two on the line of longitude 45 degrees west. This ruling gave Brazil to Portugal and the rest of the continent to Spain. The Spanish, however, never established effective control to the north of a line from modern Georgia in the east to California in the west.

In 1519 Magellan led an expedition to explore this new world. When the remains of his expedition returned in 1522, having circumnavigated the globe, the basic facts of world geography were finally established.

Meanwhile the Spaniards were establishing their power in the New World. In 1513 Balboa crossed the Isthmus of Panama and reached the Pacific Ocean. In the east, Portuguese guns could win naval battles, but they could never bring down great empires. In the west, however, the Spaniards found that civilizations crumbled before them. There was too large a gap between the technology of the 'New World' on one side and the firearms, horses and armour of the 'Old World' on the other. Perhaps most important, the American 'Indian' people were psychologically ill equipped to confront the brutal European soldiers. Many were killed by the newcomers; many lost the will to live when forced to work in unfamiliar ways; even more died of the plague and other diseases for which they lacked immunity. According to one estimate, twenty-five million people lived in what was to become New Spain when Columbus landed, but only a million and a half survived a century later.

The Spaniards may not have found silks and spices, but they found gold. What to the native Americans was a decorative metal was, to the Spaniards, the basic unit of exchange and measurement of wealth. For gold Cortes and Pizarro destroyed the Aztec and Inca civilizations. Unsuccessful searches for gold established Spanish rule in what is now the south of the United States, from Florida to the Great Plains, and the Californian coast. All kinds of gold objects were melted down and shipped back to Spain, where the new riches funded the emergence of Spain as a major power.

The gold was soon plundered, and no significant mines were discovered. A sustainable flow of wealth was, however, established by the opening of silver mines in Peru. Spain now controlled both sides of the Isthmus of Panama and a merchant fleet was built on the westward, Pacific side. A trading base was established at Manila in the Philippines, and galleons carried trading goods across the wide Pacific. These luxury goods from the Orient, along with silver from Peru, were then carried across the Isthmus of Panama and loaded onto the Atlantic treasure fleet for Spain.

In the early years of colonization few women left Spain for the New World, and settlers took Indian wives. The culture, and even the religion of New Spain therefore developed a syncretism between Spanish and Indian traditions. In time the importation of black slaves from Africa further complicated the ethnic mix. It has, however, remained generally true, even into modern times, that the social position and wealth of any individual could be gauged by skin colour.

The English

John Cabot was convinced that Columbus had got his sums wrong. He believed correctly that China was far out of range of any ship following a southerly route. By his calculation, the journey could be made at a more northerly latitude. Sailors from Bristol, England, were already fishing the Newfoundland banks and knew the North Atlantic well. Cabot therefore won support from King Henry VII of England and in 1496 reached the coast of North America. It was not obvious that the north of the continent was embedded in the Arctic ice and Cabot's son, Sebastian led a long line of English sailors in search of the North West Passage. The English sea dogs, Drake and Hawkins preferred the warm waters of New Spain to the cold northern seas. They first operated as traders, and then, after being attacked by Spaniards, as privateers.

The gold of New Spain and the luxury trade of the Orient offered instant riches. Returns on investment in North America were likely to be less spectacular. By the 1580s, however, Sir Walter Raleigh and others were advocating colonization of the land of Virginia, which was now claimed by England. Attempts were made to establish colonies in 1585 and 1589, but both failed. The first successful colony was established at Jamestown in 1607. In 1620 a group of 'Pilgrim' refugees set up a colony at New Plymouth, Massachusetts, and later moved to the better site of Boston.

The English settlements were based on a farming economy. Disease, spreading from New Spain had recently ravaged the native American tribes, leaving much of the land vacant. The surviving people practised a mixed hunting and farming economy, based on shifting cultivation, so to newcomers much of the land appeared to be empty. As land-hungry settlers kept on arriving and pushing inland towards the Appalachian Mountains conflict with the Indian people was inevitable.

The Dutch

In 1614 the United New Netherlands Company established a colony at the mouth of the Hudson River. The Dutch recognized the potential of the trade in beaver fur and used the Hudson to make contact with Indian people of the interior. This settlement divided the English colonies of Virginia and New England, and hostility between the two Protestant countries, aroused in the far Spice Islands, spilled over into the New World. In 1664 the English drove the Dutch from North America.

At the height of their powers, the Dutch carried their assault on the Portuguese Empire into the New World by annexing Brazil in 1637. The Portuguese settlers rebelled against them and they were driven out in 1654, leaving Brazil as the western outpost of a once great Portuguese Empire.

The French

In 1603 the French explorer de Champlain sailed into the St Lawrence River. He too was still searching for the elusive route to the east. He established settlements that were to become Montreal and Quebec and pressed on to explore the inland waterways of the interior. The French settlers were comparatively few in number and they received little support from their home government. Champlain and those who came after him exploited Indian rivalries to establish a flourishing trading empire, based on the fashion trade in beaver fur. As the animals were hunted to near extinction in the east, the 'beaver frontier' moved west, taking the hardy French after them.

French explorers followed the Great Lakes waterway into the interior and then the Mississippi to the Gulf of Mexico. Here they established the French outpost of New Orleans. The North American empire, named Louisiana, after Louis XIV, now followed the waterways in a huge, but lightly populated arc. At first the French and English colonists only came into contact with each other in the Hudson Valley. The risk of conflict grew, however, when the French tightened the noose around the English colonies by taking control of the Ohio River. At the time, however, colonial wars, which decided the fate of India and North America, were seen as little more than a sideshow beside the main European conflicts.

The Old Colonial System

The Dutch can be credited with the development of mercantilism, which became known as the old colonial system. This was not developed specifically for North America, but, when applied by the English in their American possessions, it became a root cause of later conflict between the colonists and the mother country. It was assumed that overseas colonies existed to promote the interests of the mother country, by extending its economic base. Colonists were expected to produce cash crops. Some, like rice from the Carolinas or tobacco from Virginia, could not be produced in northern Europe. Softwood timber from New England was also of vital strategic importance for shipbuilding at a time when European forests were finally disappearing. Buying these goods from a national source saved the mother country the foreign exchange, which would be required to purchase them from abroad. By selling these crops, the colonists earned money that would be spent on the manufactured goods. This in turn assisted the manufacturing industries and strengthened the merchant marine of the mother country. Any business between the colony and a third country had to be transacted through the mother country. This had the further benefit of boosting customs revenue.

The trade-off was that the mother country was responsible for providing the colonists with protection, be it from local populations or from hostile Europeans. This involved the Westminster government in the expense of funding wars against the French and their Indian allies. The system came under pressure when the colonies began to develop out of their original role as providers of raw materials to develop their own manufactures.

Africa

The Atlantic Slave Trade

The Portuguese were the first to discover that West Africa had human resources, which were to be exploited in a slave trade, which continued for some 350 years. A base was established on the coast as early as 1448, from which comparatively small numbers of slaves were shipped back to Portugal.

An acute labour problem then began to develop in the new American plantations. The obvious solution was to recruit American Indians. Heavy field work, however, proved alien to them. Many died, often by suicide, when forced to work on European plantations. European labour was also brought in, both by the forcible transportation of convicts, and by indentured labour schemes, under which immigrants were bound to their masters for a given number of years. Again, however, expectation of life was short, and the labour problem remained unresolved.

Portuguese ships then began to take slaves directly to their colony of Brazil. In 1562 John Hawkins began the English slave trade between West Africa and the Caribbean. Dutch, French, Danes and later sailors from both North and South America joined in the business. European nations established forts on the West African coast to protect the interests of their slave traders.

It is estimated that some eight to ten million slaves were carried across the Middle Passage to America. The economies of European cities, such as Nantes, Bristol and later Liverpool, were based on slaving, and the business was accepted as a part of the national commercial interest.

The individual suffering of slaves would ultimately receive wide publicity; the impact the trade had on African society is harder to quantify. European sailors rarely penetrated inland to find their own captives. Domestic slavery already existed on the continent, and Africans initially sold their own slaves to purchase European goods. In time, however, demand outstripped this source of supply. Military confederacies, such as Dahomey and Ashanti, grew up to fulfil the double function of protecting their own members, and feeding slaves to the European forts. When Europeans later penetrated the continent, they discovered that these states often acted with a savagery untypical of African society further inland. The demand for slaves created an endemic state of war that penetrated inland, far beyond any direct European contact. The resulting depopulation appears, however, to have been largely balanced by improvements in the African diet as a result of the importation of American crops, such as the yam and cassava.

Colonization

The first African colonies had the prime function of protecting and providing staging posts for national ships on the eastern trade routes. The Portuguese previously established the outposts in Mozambique and Angola that would achieve the distinction of being the longest lasting European overseas colonies. In 1652 Jan van Riesbeck set up the Dutch colony at the Cape of Good Hope, to serve the eastern convoys as a 'tavern of the seas'. In the eighteenth century, the French established an interest in the Indian Ocean island of Madagascar, along with Mauritius, and Reunion. The slave coast of West Africa remained unattractive for colonization. European slavers and soldiers themselves suffered a high mortality rate from tropical diseases, particularly yellow fever and malaria.

East Africa

At this time, East Africa lay off the main trading routes, and the region offered little to attract European merchants. Arab dhows still sailed undisturbed to Zanzibar and their caravans penetrated deep inland. Here again, slaves featured prominently as a trading commodity alongside gold and ivory. The area remained an Arab area of influence until European missionaries and traders penetrated the area in the nineteenth century.

6

The Nations of Europe

Italy and the European Powers

The City States and the Papacy

In the fifteenth century, the northern half of Italy was the most advanced part of Europe. The great trading cities of Genoa and Venice brought in wealth and broad contact was maintained, both through trade and cultural exchange with Arab and Byzantine civilizations. The country probably benefited from the fact that it was never brought under unitary political control.

The broken terrain of Tuscany and Umbria suited the development of independent city states, not unlike those of ancient Greece. Florence and Sienna, like Athens and Sparta of old, built up confederacies to counterbalance the power of the other. In the late fourteenth century, the banking family of Medici took power in Florence. Times were not always easy, but they led the city to its unique flowering of culture.

In the north, another ring of states, with Milan as the most powerful, controlled the trading routes across the Alps. In the centre, the pope ruled the Papal States as any other temporal monarch, and involved himself in the politics of the peninsula, attempting always to extend the patrimony of St Peter. During this period the lifestyle of the popes was little different from that of any other monarch. They led troops into battle, promoted family interests, including those of their children, and built themselves enormous monuments. Julius II's decision to build himself a tomb set off the chain of events that triggered the Reformation in distant Germany; the tomb would be too large for St Peter's, so the church had to be rebuilt; this involved raising money by the granting of indulgences.

The Theory of Kingship

Within this turbulent world of Italian politics, only the fittest survived. Niccolo Machiavelli worked for the Florentine state, travelling widely as a diplomat. He wrote a book, called *The Prince*, which was based on these experiences, which contained advice for the Medici family on the theory and practice of government. Political decisions, he argued, could only be taken on a cool, indeed callous, assessment of the security needs of the state and of its ruler. Medieval concepts of the mutual duties of ruler and subjects were cut away in this first exposition of what would later come to be called 'real politik'.

Medieval monarchy was based on a feudal alliance between king and his tenants in chief. In the sixteenth century, power was being drawn to the centre at the expense of both the magnates and of representational institutions. For Machiavelli's prince, power was its own justification. The theory of centralization was later taken further with the formulation of the concept of the divine right of kings. Rulers, it was said, held power directly from God. Rebellion was a sin and criticism of the royal will was tantamount to treason.

Foreign Invasion

In 1494 Charles VIII of France crossed the Alps at the head of an army of 30,000 men. He laid claim to the Kingdom of Naples and on his way south, through Rome itself, his army left a trail of destruction. Other foreign armies followed. Artists still worked on, producing some of the greatest works known to man, but the days of the city state were over and Italy would henceforth be a pawn in the real politik of the great powers. In 1527 the ragged, unpaid and hungry army of the great emperor, Charles V, ran wild in the streets of Rome, and the city was sacked for the first time since the barbarian invasions.

The Empire of Charles V

Throughout medieval times, kingship was fundamentally a matter of family inheritance. Charles was the ultimate beneficiary of this dynastic system. From his mother, the mad Joanna, he inherited his grandparents' crowns of Castile and Aragon. On the paternal side, he inherited from his grandfather the title of Holy Roman Emperor, and from his grandmother the lands of the Duchy of Burgundy. As king of Castile he controlled Spanish land in the New World; as Emperor he ruled Austria, Hungary, Bohemia and much of Germany; as Duke of Burgundy he possessed the Netherlands, which was the richest part of all Europe. His empire was larger than that of Charlemagne.

France was now shut in on all sides, and its king was determined not to let Italy fall to Charles' empire. The crusading spirit was finally laid to rest as Pope and King of France allied with the Ottoman Turks against Charles.

This great empire, like that of Charlemagne, carried the seeds of its own destruction. Charles was unable to function adequately as ruler of such dispersed lands, and resentment grew, particularly in the Netherlands, at the taxes raised to support Italian wars. Charles was also depressed at his inability to control the spread of Protestantism within his own lands. He abdicated in 1556 and the empire was divided. The title of Emperor passed to his brother Ferdinand I, while the more valuable western share, consisting of Spain and the old Burgundian lands, went to his son, Philip II. There were now two Hapsburg dynasties in Europe.

Protestantism and the Counter Reformation

The Spread of Protestantism

Luther's new beliefs found most followers in northern Europe, particularly in Germany itself and in Scandinavia. The impetus behind the further spread of Protestantism came, not from Germany but from Geneva. John Calvin was French, but he achieved prominence in the Swiss canton. He preached a harsh form of Protestantism; since God was all-powerful, he had predestined a minority of people—the elect—to salvation and the rest to damnation. The elect had to show their status by a strict adherence to a way of life. Within Geneva, moral sins like adultery and even disobedience by a child to parents, were severely punished. Calvinism proved to be a more militant faith than Lutheranism. It appealed in the Netherlands, in England and on the west coast of France, in Scotland and later in the Lutheran heartland of Germ ny.

All Protestantism stressed the direct communion of the individual with God, and it is not therefore surprising that it quickly showed a capacity to fragment. In 1532 an extreme group, the Anabaptists, took control of the German city of Münster, preaching not only rejection of infant baptism, but polygamy and a radical social gospel. In the extreme Protestant sects, authority lay not in any higher political or ecclesiastical power, but in the local 'gathered church'. These separatist churches were persecuted in Protestant and Catholic countries alike, but it was this tradition that would ultimately implant itself in the New England colonies of North America, and profoundly influence the development of American society.

Tolerance was not a cherished ideal in sixteenth century Europe, but by 1530 it had become clear that Protestantism was too powerful a movement to be readily suppressed. In that year the Peace of Augsburg laid down the principle of 'cuius regio, eius religio'—the country would follow the religion of the ruler. This left rulers free to persecute within their own dominions.

Sweden and England Break with Rome

Two European monarchs took their nations out of communion with the Roman church. Both were motivated by national and financial, rather than by religious reasons. In 1523 the young Swedish nobleman, Gustavus Vasa, succeeded in his struggle to make Sweden independent from Denmark, and was proclaimed king. Lutheranism had already made progress among his people. In 1527 he broke with Rome as a symbol of the new national independence, and he enriched his hard pressed government with church lands.

Henry VIII of England had showed no personal inclination towards the reformed religion; indeed he had written a pamphlet attacking Luther, and had persecuted Protestants. In 1530, however, he became involved in a dispute with the pope over his divorce to Catherine of Aragon. Using selective intimidation, he won the support of parliament for a breach with Rome, and then for the plundering of the monastic lands. The Church of England, reformed in doctrine, but conservative in practice, was the creation of Henry's Archbishop of Canterbury, Thomas Cranmer. After a short return to Catholicism under Mary I, Henry's daughter, Elizabeth, declared that the English church should be a home for all men of goodwill. Separatist Protestants and politically active Catholics were still persecuted, but England did escape the worst violence of these years.

The Counter Reformation

The Roman church had been on the defensive against an aggressive Protestantism for twenty-five years when Pope Paul III called his bishops together for the Council of Trent. Paul represented a new generation of Popes, anxious to clear away the scandals of the past, and re-establish the western church on a firm footing. The discussions were dominated by bishops from Spain and Italy, where Protestantism had found no foothold. The Council brought in reforms—indulgences, for instance, were abolished - but it made no concessions to Protestant faith. By the time that the Council had finished its debates in 1563, the lines of division were clearly drawn.

Catholicism was now on the counter offensive. As in the past, monasticism provided the papacy with its front line troops. In 1540, Ignatius Loyola, who had been a fellow student in Paris with John Calvin, established the Society of Jesus, or Jesuits. Members were bound to total loyalty to the Pope, and this provided the reforming papacy with a means of circumventing special interests within the church. Jesuits became particularly prominent in education and in missionary work.

Spain and the Netherlands

The Expulsions

Even without Charles' eastern lands, Philip II's Spain remained the dominant power in Europe. He controlled southern Italy and Sicily and succeeded in conquering Portugal. Spain's European power was now underpinned by the revenues of a two huge overseas empires.

The nation's weakness was not clearly evident at the time. When the Moors were finally defeated, Moslems and Jews had been promised security within the Christian state. The presence of infidels, however, proved too much for Catholic rulers, still driven by the intolerance of the Inquisition. Moors, Jews, and converted Moors, the Moriscos, were all driven out of the country. These, however, were the very tradespeople and skilled craftsmen on whom the economy of the nation rested. As a result, Spain became heavily dependent on imported goods, particularly from the prosperous northern Netherlands. On occasions the Panama fleet had to be diverted and sailed direct to unload its treasure in the Netherlands.

The Spanish Netherlands

The old Burgundian lands covered both of the modern states of Belgium and Holland. The greatest centres of prosperity, with Antwerp outstanding, lay in the south. The northern part, mostly consisting of land drained from the Rhine delta, contained the finest farmland in Europe, but, even with intensive agriculture, it could not feed the growing towns. Calvinist Protestantism had won adherents both in the north and in the south.

Charles V was born in the Netherlands, and during his reign the two religions coexisted with reasonable tolerance. The accession of Spanish born Philip II, however, brought change. As king, he was determined to bring the old Burgundian noble families under his control, and, as a faithful son of the church, he meant to stamp out heresy in his land. The Spanish Duke of Alva was sent with an army to bring the area under control.

Dutch Independence

In 1572, William Prince of Orange led the People of the Netherlands in revolt. As Spanish armies established control of the south, many Protestants moved north behind the protection of the dykes, and the religious division between the Catholic south and the Protestant north was established. In 1581 the followers of William of Orange declared their independence from Spain. No matter how bitter the fighting, the trade between Spain and her rebellious provinces never ceased. Philip was in no position to cut off this channel of supplies for his people and the Dutch were happy to drain the enemy of wealth. William was murdered on Philip's orders in 1584, but the struggle continued until Spain made a truce in 1609. Almost forty years would pass before Spain finally recognized the independence of the Dutch people, but in practice Holland had established its independence from its traditional ruling house.

The Dutch Republic

The new nation was unique in that power was based on trade, rather than on inherited land. A successful Dutchman did not plan for the day when he would put aside the cares of trade and live as a gentleman—his objective was to hand a thriving business to his heirs. The people lived by a strict work ethic, and made the most of the limited resources of their small land.

National wealth was founded on north-south trade, carrying products such as grain, timber and iron from the Baltic to the overpopulated Mediterranean lands. Dutch flyboats, little more than floating holds, plied the oceans. 'Norway was their forest, the banks of the Rhine and the Dordogne their vineyard; Spain and Ireland grazed their sheep; India and Arabia were their gardens and the sea their highway. ' Scholars also provided vital information for the sailors and, in doing so, laid the foundation of modern geography.

The Decline of Spain

The loss of the Netherlands was the clearest marker of Spain's fall from the position of being Europe's dominant power. In 1588 a Spanish naval armada was also defeated by the English fleet. In 1640 Portugal re-established her independence under the house of Breganza. The nation could have overcome military reverse; the basic problem was that Philip II and his successors concentrated on military and colonial affairs at the expense of the economy, which had been shattered by the mass expulsions.

The French Wars of Religion

The French Monarchy

In the middle of the sixteenth century, French royal power stood at a low ebb. Financial stringency led to offices being sold to the highest bidder, and, partly as a result, the size and independence of the aristocracy was ever increasing. Calvinism was strong in Brittany and Normandy, and growing in power further south on the Atlantic coast and in Languedoc. Its strength was based on craftsmen and some poorer nobles, followed by a growing number of peasants. By 1562 there were over fifteen hundred 'Huguenot' congregations, many led by Geneva-trained pastors. The Catholics themselves were divided into two parties—the moderates, led by the Regent, Catherine de' Medici, who at first planned to keep the peace by giving a measure of toleration to the Protestants, and an extreme Catholic party, who wanted to see heresy stamped out.

The Wars

Fighting broke out after extremist Catholics massacred a Huguenot congregation at Vassy in 1562. The ensuing wars were fought with great ferocity on both sides. In 1572 three thousand Huguenots were massacred in Paris on St Bartholomew's Day, and in 1588 the king, Henry III, was ejected from his own capital by extreme Catholics. In 1584 the Huguenot Henry of Navarre had become heir to the throne. He succeeded in bringing the war to an end by turning Catholic and reaching an agreement with his former Protestant followers in the Edict of Nantes. This left the Huguenots with freedom of worship in large areas of the country, as well as certain fortified cities. These now effectively lay outside royal control.

Germany

The Empire after Charles V

Emperor Charles V's brother Ferdinand saw himself as a faithful Catholic and soldier of the Counter Reformation. His own lands and the south of Germany remained Catholic. The Protestant forces set against him were divided. In the north were the Lutheran powers of Denmark, Saxony and Brandenburg. The Calvinist stronghold lay to the west around the Rhine. Ferdinand dreamed of winning back the whole of Germany to Catholicism, while at the same time bringing it once again under imperial rule.

Ferdinand was unable to achieve his ambition because his empire was exposed on its eastern flank. In the south, the Ottoman Empire reached the peak of its power under Suleiman 1, and even threatened Vienna itself. In the north, Sweden was establishing control of the Baltic Sea while Poland and Russia both pressed on German land.

The Thirty Years' War

In the early seventeenth century, the religious divisions became more sharply fixed. In 1608–1609 the Catholic League and the Calvinist Union were set up as rival military blocks. The first of a series of wars broke out in 1618, when the Calvinist Elector Palatine was elected King of Bohemia. The Catholic armies, led by virtually independent war lords, won early successes, but this rallied the Lutheran armies to the Protestant cause. The Protestant champion turned out to be Gustavus Adolphus, King of Sweden, who won a series of battles before he was killed at Lützen in 1632.

By this time the religious battle lines were becoming blurred. Catholic France, under Cardinal Richelieu, was prepared to fund Protestant armies and even to intervene directly to prolong the war and so prevent a re-emergence of imperial power in Germany. This brought in Catholic and Hapsburg Spain on the imperial side.

The war was a disaster for the people of Germany. Roaming armies stripped the countryside of food; the devastation caused by the imperial sack of Magdeburg in 1629 rivalled that of a Mongol army. When the war limped to a close in 1648, the countryside was impoverished and depopulated. Ferdinand's ideal of a Catholic Germany, united under the empire, was destroyed. Protestantism was unassailable in the north, and the effective power of the emperor in the German-speaking lands was henceforth limited to his Austrian heartland. In the Treaties of Westphalia the Emperor had to accept the independence of Switzerland—a reality since the end of the fifteenth century—and the King of Spain that of the Netherlands. France and Spain both made achieved territorial gains in German lands. Most significant for the future, the new power of Brandenburg had emerged in the north.

Brandenburg-Prussia

In 1640, 'The Great Elector' Frederick William of the House of Hohenzollern, inherited Brandenburg and the eastern territory of Prussia. A man of great energy, he set about creating a well-run, modern state. His twin tools were an efficient civil service and a highly disciplined army, which served as a model for later German armies. The Great Elector's work was consolidated a century later by Frederick II 'the Great'. He had no vision of a united Germany, but he ruthlessly expanded his family lands at the expense of the Empire.

The Hegemony of France

Richelieu

Henry IV was assassinated in 1610 by a Catholic fanatic, leaving a country at peace, but with many problems. The Huguenots were a state within a state; the nobles were over powerful and contributed little to the national life; the peasants were desperately poor and over-taxed.

In 1624 Henry's son and successor, Louis XIII, appointed Cardinal Richelieu as head of the royal council. For eighteen years, Richelieu worked single-mindedly to establish royal power within the nation. He had no wish to persecute the Protestants, but he destroyed the independent Huguenot fortresses, including La Rochelle and Montauban. He made examples at a high level to bring the nobles under his control. Regional government was delegated to directly appointed intendants, who exercised the complete range of royal power.

Richelieu's foreign policy was directed at limiting the power of Spain and improving national security by achieving 'natural frontiers' at the Rhine and the Alps. For this, he was prepared to ally with Protestants and to prolong the misery of the Thirty Years' War.

Richelieu represented the apotheosis of the Machiavellian ideal; his policy was driven by a cold analysis of *raison d'etat*. He did not, however, recognize that some improvement in the lot of the poor was essential if the state was to be securely based. Shortly after Richelieu and his royal master died in 1642–43, there was a series of popular uprisings across the country, which were known as the Frondes.

Louis XIV

The young king who succeeded was to rule the country until 1715. His domestic and foreign policy was a continuation of that laid down by Richelieu. All real power lay in the hands of non-noble ministers and the intendants, while the nobles were emasculated by being drawn into the glittering court of Versailles.

Unlike Richelieu, however, Louis determined that he would not rule over heretics. He revoked the Edict of Nantes, facing Protestants with the choice of conversion or expulsion. Like Isabella of Castile, he was hereby driving a productive group out of the nation. Economic conditions did improve, but the poor continued to suffer harshly enforced penal taxation.

Much tax revenue was spent on foreign wars. As France had organized leagues to limit the power of Spain, so now others united to contain France. The driving force in the anti-French Grand Alliance was William of Orange, Stadholder of the Netherlands. His power strengthened when, in 1688 he also became king of England as William III. The War of the Grand Alliance (1689–97) was followed by the War of the Spanish Succession (1701–14), which sought to prevent Louis from unifying the crowns of Fence and Spain by dynastic succession.

Eighteenth-century France

In 1715 France was clearly the leading power in Europe. Major losses of overseas territory to England in India and North America during the Seven Years' War (1756–73) did not appear as significant at the time as they were later to become. Financial weakness, however, underlay the pageantry of the France monarchy. The huge noble class—estimated at up to a quarter of a million strong—had lost political power but not financial and legal privilege. The state sank ever more deeply into debt, but had no means of tapping the huge reserves of noble wealth. Here lay the seeds of revolution.

England

Sea Power

When Roman soldiers were posted to Britain, they considered that they were being consigned to the edge of the civilized world. Through medieval times, the British Isles remained on the periphery of the known world. The discovery of America moved the centre of gravity away from the Mediterranean towards the Atlantic Ocean. Geography therefore now favoured England.

As an island nation, the English were perforce a seafaring people. By 1500, however, this seafaring tradition had not been converted into naval power. The defeat of the Spanish Armada in 1588 proved to be a turning point. The battle was won by strategy rather than by fighting force, but the Elizabethan sea dogs created a national myth that would survive into modern times. Governments, reluctant to involve troops in European land battles, laid the greatest stress on building up naval power and securing naval supplies. The navy provided protection for the island, maintained links with overseas colonies, and secured trade routes against competition.

Monarchy and Parliament

The Tudor monarchs, Henry VIII and his daughter Elizabeth, dominated sixteenth-century English politics. The English nobility were few in number, and were generally content to concentrate their efforts on field sports and the efficient management of their estates. While parliamentary government was withering on the continent, in England the old institutions remained robust. Henry found it convenient to use the House of Commons as his ally against the Church, and Elizabeth was able to manage parliament, even if sometimes with difficulty, both as a source of revenue and as a channel of government.

When Elizabeth died in 1603, the succession passed to the Scots House of Stuart, which, through family and cultural ties, was more influenced by the French model. Very early, James VI of Scotland and I of England became involved in disputes with both the legal and parliamentary establishment. James proclaimed the divine right of kings, which, he claimed, gave the king the power to appoint and dismiss judges and to raise taxes. Jurists recovered documents such as Magna Carta from obscurity to defend ancient privileges against the new royal pretensions. Implicit in their arguments lay the notion that royal power was derived from the consent of the people—however the people might be defined. The conflict was made more acute by the fact that personality did not match pretension. The Tudors had maintained authority through the force of their personalities, rather than through modern concepts of kingship. James was intelligent but personally unimpressive; his son Charles I was an inadequate recluse.

The Civil War

Charles I soon found himself in direct confrontation with parliament. In 1628 parliament presented a Petition of Right against the use of arbitrary royal power; in 1629 Charles dissolved parliament and began eleven years of direct rule. Many aspects of royal government were unpopular to influential subjects. An attempt was made to impose 'high church' worship, not only on England but also on Calvinist Scotland. An increasing number of cases were heard in royal prerogative courts, rather than in the courts of common law. Direct taxes, such as ship money, were levied without parliamentary approval. It seemed to many as though Charles would soon follow Richelieu's example and centralize all government.

The outbreak of war in Scotland brought financial disaster and Charles was forced to recall parliament in 1640. A struggle for power led to the outbreak of war in 1642. Historians have long argued the economic, religious and social issues that lay behind the conflict; certainly it was very different in nature from the violent upheavals that would later shake France and Russia. Parliamentary power was based in the rich south east, while the king's was centred in the poorer north and west. The parliamentary victory was due both to this difference in resources, and to the leadership of Oliver Cromwell, who emerged as the outstanding general in the conflict. He kept his New Model Army under such firm control that it could march across countryside and leave fields and property as they had been before the army passed.

The Commonwealth

The parliamentary broke into factions after the defeat of the king. In 1648 one faction seized power, with army support and staged the trial of Charles I. The execution of the king in 1649 provoked a shocked response across Europe. No action could have expressed the rejection of divine kingship more vividly. In 1653, Cromwell staged a military coup and assumed power as Lord Protector. Cromwell died in 1658, and a brief attempt was made to continue the protectorate under his son. This failed, however, and in 1660 the army again was responsible for bringing Charles II back to London.

The Glorious Revolution

The saga of the conflict between the Stuarts and their parliaments was not, however, over. Charles was mistrusted, both for his French sympathies and for his leaning towards Catholicism, but he still depended on parliament for revenue. In 1685 he was succeeded by his Catholic brother, James II. Three years later James was forced to leave the country, to be replaced by his Protestant daughter, Mary and her husband, the Dutch William of Orange, who exercised the practical power. William was more interested in securing the English alliance against France, than he was in pursuing power struggles with the English parliament. He therefore accepted laws that established that the king would henceforth require parliamentary consent to raise money and keep a standing army in peace time. It was also agreed that he could not alter or suspend any act of parliament.

In 1714 the English throne passed to the German house of Hanover. Since the new king could not speak English, day to day government passed to a prime minister and a cabinet, drawn from the majority party in the House of Commons. Political power had now finally passed from the monarchy to the property owning classes, who were represented in parliament. In the century that followed, parliament largely used its power to improve the position of the landowning class, often at the expense of the poor. English politics had, however, run against the European tide, which favoured greater centralization in the hands of the monarch.

The Act of Union

Throughout history, there had been strife between England and her smaller, poorer northern neighbour, Scotland. The union of the crowns in 1603 did not put an end to this. In 1707, however, the two countries became formally united in the Act of Union. Two clan uprisings followed in 1715 and 1745, in favour of the exiled Stuarts, but these were suppressed. Scots engineers, doctors and scholars were shortly after to make a major contribution to the great surge in national prosperity of the united Great Britain.

Russia

Boyars and Serfs

Across the continent the Russian state was following a very different pattern of development. The noble boyars held their land from the Tsar in return for defined services. Since Russia had no law of primogeniture, this class was getting ever larger, and most of its members poorer, as estates were split one generation after another. The mass of the people remained in the medieval condition of serfdom. Families were owned by their masters, had no right to move of their own free will and had no redress except in their masters' court.

The relationship of Tsar and boyars was often marked by bloody conflict. Ivan IV 'The Terrible' allied himself with the merchant class and the common people in an attempt to break noble power. He achieved many real reforms before mental disorder led him, in the latter years of his reign, to behaviour that anticipated that of Joseph Stalin in the twentieth century.

National Objectives

Russian development was hindered by the lack of a warm weather outlet to the ocean. The port of Archangel was ice-bound in winter, and all year the journey round northern Scandinavia was long and dangerous. The port of Rostov in the south was of little use as long as the Ottomans controlled the mouth of the Sea of Azov and the Dardanelles. National policy therefore became directed at winning a port on the Baltic Sea. This brought Russia into conflict with the advanced military state of Sweden, which regarded the Baltic as a Swedish lake.

The Russian tsar could mobilize huge armies, by raising levies, but there was no adequate support structure. Forces were sent to war with the vague hope that they would be able to live off the land. Often countless thousands of soldiers starved, and those who did manage to survive were in no condition to fight the world's most efficient army.

Peter the Great

Peter succeeded to the throne in 1682 at the age of ten, and suffered huge indignities from guards and boyars while still a child. Once a man, he announced his intention to bring his nation up to date and orientate it towards the West. A man of little education but enormous energy, he immersed himself in every detail of western science and technology. In a famous visit to the west he was equally at home working in disguise as a dock worker in Holland and meeting with scientists in England. His methods of enforcement were effective, if sometimes eccentric.

The vindication of Peter's work came in 1709 when his army won a decisive victory over the Swedish army under Charles XII at Poltava. Russia had won its outlet to the Baltic Sea, and here Peter decided to build his capital of St Petersburg.

Peter's great failure was that, like Louis XIV in France, he failed to do anything to improve the lot of the Russian poor. Someone had to pay for wars against Turkey and Sweden, for the modern weapons, for new ships and for the fine capital city. The poor were taxed and taxed again until they were left with the barest minimum necessary to keep themselves and their families alive. It is a measure of the depth of the misery and the capacity of the Russian people to absorb suffering that revolution did not erupt in violence for another 200 years.

7

The Western Mind

The Renaissance

Italy

The word *renaissance* was coined in the nineteenth century to describe the rebirth in Italy of the classical ideal in art, architecture and letters. The 'Middle Ages' was looked upon as a dark period before the great transformation of the fifteenth and early sixteenth centuries. Recent study has shown that the picture was more complicated; classicism remained strong throughout the Middle Ages, and there was more cross fertilization between Europe north and south of the Alps than had been assumed.

Any gallery visitor can, however, see the astonishing change that happened in visual perception within a comparatively few years. Across northern Italy artists experimented with new forms. In the words of the art historian, Giorgio Vasari, Giotto 'restored the art of design'. In Umbria, Piero della Francesca used mathematics to work out laws of perspective, well beyond any classical achievement. In Florence, Michelangelo combined an analytical eye with his huge talent to create a new vision of the human—or at least male—form. Even when painters and sculptors continued to work on church commissions, they now used live models to give a new sense of naturalism.

There was a keen awareness among the artistic community that they were living in an exciting new age. The Medici and other patrons commissioned works with secular themes, often drawn from Greek mythology. Artists were no longer faceless craftsmen who had produced so many medieval treasures. Art had found a new self-consciousness.

The same, secular driven, innovation was reflected in music and literature. There was a passionate interest in all aspects of antiquity. Some sculptors even buried their own work and dug it up again, claiming it as a classical discovery. Old manuscripts were found in monastic libraries or brought from the east and studied with a new intensity. Enthusiasm for antiquity did not preclude Christian belief; rather the classical tradition was seen as one element in divine revelation, so producing a syncretism that alarmed conservative churchmen.

By the mid-sixteenth century the Italian renaissance was losing its impetus. The first unique burst of innovation could not be maintained. The Counter Reformation church now demanded a more orthodox treatment of subject matter, both in literature and in painting. Much great work continued to be done, particularly in the Veneto. Paladio used Roman models in creating the architectural style that would bear his name, while Titian and his contemporaries were laying the foundations of what would become the baroque style. Generations of artists and patrons continued to travel to Italy to absorb the culture both of its classical past and of the present.

The Northern Renaissance

Some of the great painters of the Flemish school crossed the Alps and were much admired by Renaissance artists. Perhaps because they were not surrounded by antiquities in their home environment, however, they never made the sharp break with the gothic. Italian styles took many years to become established north of the Alps.

Northern Europe's unique contribution came in the field of scholarship and literature. Here writers were free from the restrictions of the Counter Reformation and fear of the Inquisition. Protestants wanted to make the Bible available to all. The translations of the scriptures by Martin Luther and William Tyndale were immensely influential in formalizing the written forms of German and English respectively. Traditional interpretations of the Bible were challenged when Erasmus of Rotterdam produced a version of the New Testament in the original Greek. Latin was now ceasing to be the universal language of scholarship. While a return to the vernacular liberated learning from the cloisters of the church, it also fractured the international culture, which had reached its peak in the twelfth century.

A strong secular tradition now flourished in England. Chaucer had already written for the newly educated merchant class. In 1510 John Colet, Dean of St Paul's Cathedral and close friend of Erasmus, made a gesture to the secularization of learning when he closed his cathedral school and refounded it under the control of a trading guild. The combination of Tyndale's language and renaissance scholarship had created a uniquely favourable environment when in 1585 an actor called William Shakespeare left his native Stratford to chance his fortune in London.

The great flowering of French literature came in the seventeenth century. Corneille and Racine were still in essence renaissance writers, handling classical themes with a paladian sense of form and style.

Printing

Most importantly, the re-invention of printing by movable type provided the means of dissemination of both religious and secular literature. Whether the innovation be credited to Johannes Guttenberg of Mainz or Lourens Coster of Haarlem, the technique provided the means of dissemination of the works of any author. Books became cheaper as print runs grew longer. In the following centuries print was used to promote colonies, to circulate scurrilous pamphlets to produce works on magic—as well as to disseminate works of scholarship, religion and literature. In 1702 *The Courant*, the world's first daily newspaper, was published in London. Soon afterwards works of popular fiction began to come off the presses. Print had become an integral part of Western life.

The Advancement of Science

The Copernican Revolution

In Hellenistic times the idea had been posited that the earth rotated round the sun, but this had not won general acceptance and in the sixteenth century it was still generally accepted that the heavenly bodies rotated around a stationary earth. In 1543, however, the Polish scholar Copernicus published a book arguing the theory of heliocentric astronomy.

Copernicus' theory received little attention. During this time, however, Dutch craftsmen were experimenting with glass lenses. They made spectacles and also telescopes for use at sea. One of these telescopes fell into the hands of the Italian teacher, Galileo Galilei, and he turned the instrument towards the skies. By studying sun spots, the phases of Venus and the rings of Jupiter, he provided clear proof that Copernicus had been correct.

Galileo delayed publishing his findings because he recognized that they must arouse a storm of controversy. Authority, both of the Bible and of ancient authors clearly supported a geocentric universe, and the church still held to authority as the arbiter of truth. He published his findings in 1632, but, faced with the terror of the Inquisition, he recanted in 1633.

Descartes—the Turning Point

Tradition states that, after formally accepting that the earth remained stationary, Galileo muttered 'it goes on moving'. Certainly the scientific impetus continued. In 1637 the French philosopher Descartes published *Discours de la Méthode*, which laid down what has become known as the Cartesian method. He argued that the experimental scientific process was the arbiter of truth. The pursuit of truth now involved breaking down knowledge into ever smaller areas of study. Medicine, for instance, became concerned with analysing the symptoms of disease in minute detail—arguably at the expense of a more integrated approach to the healing process.

In his dictum, *cogito ergo sum*, Descartes proclaimed the individualism that was to be the hallmark of modern European society. Western man had at last emerged from the shadow of past authorities, be they religious or classical. Personally a devout Catholic, Descartes rejected authority as an arbiter of faith and proclaimed that it had to be discovered through the human intellect. This was recognized as a fundamental challenge to the church, and Louis XIV personally ensured that Descartes was denied Christian burial.

Northern Europe

The condemnation of both Galileo and Descartes, and continued activities of the Inquisition placed scientists who lived in Catholic countries in an invidious position. In Protestant countries, scientists might meet hostility from those who defended religious authority, but they did not face persecution. The impetus for scientific innovation therefore passed to Northern Europe.

The first protestant scientist was the German, Kepler, who provided information on the movements of planets. Dutch scientists, continuing their work with lenses, developed the microscope. This opened up whole new areas of study in such areas as the biological sciences. In England the cause of experimental science was argued by the Lord Chancellor, Francis Bacon, who had early visions of its potential. In 1619, William Harvey demonstrated the mechanism of the circulation of the blood.

The advances in navigation, first in Holland, and then in France and, above all, in England, drove forward skills in cartography and geographical study. Progress in astronomy and in the construction of clocks were spin-offs from this navigational programme. Landsmen could now own clocks and watches that told the time with great accuracy. People began to organize their lives around them, and to treat the hours and minutes of the day with a new respect.

The revolution started by Copernicus was completed by Isaac Newton, who published his *Principia Mathematica* in 1687. While Galileo argued the structure of the universe, Newton demonstrated the gravitational mechanism by which it worked. In the words of the poet Alexander Pope;

Nature and nature's laws lay hid in night:
God said, 'Let Newton be!' and all was light.

Until Newton's time, humans were uncomprehending playthings of fate or divine providence. Now they began to understand that the everyday events of life were driven by a structure of causation. Later generations of scientists have maintained the process. Mendel worked out the structure of genetic inheritance, Darwin illustrated the mechanism evolution, Pasteur demonstrated the causes of disease, Crick and Watson unravelled the DNA code. These and many other insights make up the intellectual baggage of Western man.

Enlightenment to Romanticism

The Philosophes

The new enlightenment was to find its home in France, but the pattern of thinking owed much to seventeenth-century British writers, notably John Locke, who published his *Essay Concerning Human Understanding* in 1690. Locke said that many religious issues were beyond human knowledge, and he argued for tolerance and reliance on reason and reasonableness. His work reflected a wide change of mood, signalling the end of two centuries of religious strife; never again would the battle lines of Europe's terrible wars be drawn along religious lines.

The scientific advances of the seventeenth century encouraged philosophers of the following century to see the world as an ordered machine, much like one of the new clocks. There was an optimistic view that the universe was driven by a well-oiled logic, and, if people could only behave in a reasonable manner, the world's problems could be readily overcome. Past religious passions now appeared irrelevant. Many thinkers no longer saw God as an imminent cause of good or evil, but as a great watchmaker, an ultimate mover, who no longer had immediate relevance to life. The poet Pope, himself a Catholic, again provided the aphorism of the age with the couplet;

Know then thyself; presume not God to scan;
The proper study of mankind is man.

The dominant personality among the *philosophes* was the Frenchman, Voltaire. He was a satirist, rather than an original thinker, and he turned his barbed pen on anything that he saw as repressive or pretentious. Voltaire had problems with the French authorities, but he and his circle sewed seeds of scepticism about the old order, which would have immense repercussions in the later years of the century.

Evangelicalism

The first reaction against the intellectual emphasis of the age came with a religious revival that developed in parallel in England and her North American colonies, both within and outside the Church of England. John Wesley set the emotional tone of the movement, sharply in contrast with the language of the *philosophes*, when he described how he 'felt his heart strangely warmed'. This new Protestantism appealed primarily not to authority, but to the conversion experience. Until then, the Protestant churches had left missionary work almost entirely to the Catholic orders, but, by the end of the century, the worldwide tide of Protestant missions was beginning to flow, with incalculable, if often ambiguous, effects on non-European cultures.

Romanticism

If John Wesley represented the religious, Swiss-born philosopher, Jean Jacques Rousseau, led the secular reaction against Cartesian intellectualism. He proclaimed that man was pure when in the simple state, be that the uncorrupted form of a noble savage, or a new born child. The quest for goodness therefore involved a return to nature. Rousseau, more than any other person, taught people to look on their environment as a place of beauty. Since the time of Hannibal, travellers had crossed the Alps, without pausing to recognize them as anything other than a barrier on the road to Italy. Now, as if overnight, Rousseau's Swiss mountains were discovered as majestic things of beauty.

As romanticism emphasized the emotions above the intellect, so it elevated the creative artist, as the person most able to express those emotions. The great milestones of the movement, such as Wordsworth and Coleridge's *Lyrical Ballads*, Beethoven's *Eroica Symphony*, the late paintings of Turner, explored new forms and emotions. This could lead to excess, but it also opened the way to the achievements, such as those of French impressionist painters and the great romantic composers.

Social Reform

At about the same time, first clearly surfacing in the 1770s, a transformation began to occur in attitudes to social issues. For centuries, Europeans had been shipping Africans to slavery with no apparent compunction. Now powerful antislavery movements made themselves heard in France, Denmark, England and other countries. Movements for the reform of vicious penal systems, the abolition of the 'hanging codes' and for the humane treatment of the insane can be dated to the same time. Educational reform also became a cause for the future.

Credit for this new mood of social reform has been given to the pen of Voltaire, the preaching of Wesley and the ideals of Rousseau. All played their part. In education, for instance, evangelical passion to bring truth to the poor led directly to the opening of ragged schools, while Rousseau was laying the foundations for the quite separate development of child-centred learning, which was carried forward by the Swiss educator, Pestalozzi. The cause of reform was uniquely in the air, and the traditional political structures were ill equipped to contain it. Europe was ready for the cataclysm of the French Revolution.

8

Revolution

The French Revolution

The Estates General

In 1776 the British government was faced with a major revolution in its American colonies (Chapter 11). King Louis XVI of France, recognizing this as an opportunity of regaining some of the ground lost in the Seven Years War, involved France in the conflict. In military terms the intervention was successful; in financial terms it was a disaster. The French government, always in financial straits, was now unable to function. The shortfall could no longer be met by the time honoured device of increasing taxes on the poor, but those able to pay could only be taxed with their own consent. Members of the aristocracy recognized an opportunity of winning concessions from the monarchy in return for money, and they insisted that Louis should recall the French parliament, the *Estates General*, which had not met for 150 years.

The body met in three separate houses - aristocracy, clergy and the third estate. This last house represented the property owning middle classes and was largely made up of professional men. They had no vision of themselves as revolutionaries, but they were influenced by the ideas of the *philosophes* and of the American Declaration of Independence. Louis anticipated doing his business with the other two houses before disbanding the body, but the Third Estate had equal representation with the other two, and could count on considerable support in the House of Clergy. In the summer of 1789 the Third Estate declared that it constituted a National Assembly. Louis gave way before its demands and the body set about a huge programme of constitutional, administrative and social reform.

Popular Unrest

Since the time of the Frondes, French kings had been acutely aware of the dangers of uprisings among the poor, who remained unrepresented in the National Assembly. There was unrest in many parts of the countryside, where chateaux were attacked and hated rent books burned. The most immediate danger, however, came from the poor of Paris, who found themselves caught in a spiral of inflation, most crucially in the price of bread. By 14 July, it was estimated that only three days' supply remained in the storehouses of the capital.

The mob possessed armaments, but little ammunition. This lay under close guard in the royal castle of the Bastille. On 14 July the mob stormed the Bastille, leaving Louis quite helpless. He could not use his army because the loyalty of rank and file soldiers was in doubt. Many of the aristocracy were now fleeing France and in June

1791 Louis and his family made their bid to escape. They were captured and brought back as prisoners to the capital. The Assembly maintained the King as a figurehead until he signed the new Constitution in September. The body disbanded itself to make way for the new Legislative Assembly.

War and the Terror

Since the National Assembly had barred any of their number from seeking re-election, the new body was made up of inexperienced men. The dominant figures were Danton, who surrounded himself with members from the Gironde, in southern France, and the little lawyer Robespierre, whose power was based on the Jacobin Club. Protagonists of the new order now felt under siege. The King could still serve as a focal point for a royalist counter-revolution, and both Austria and Prussia were issuing threats. Robespierre argued that peace should be preserved, but Danton believed that the nation could only be united by war. He urged his fellow countrymen to 'dare and dare and dare again', and Frenchmen responded to his cry that the *patrie* was in danger. In April 1792, France declared war on Austria, and Prussia came in on the side of Austria. Early news from the war was disastrous, and the capital was gripped in a fever. On 30 July a contingent marched into the capital, singing the song that would become the national anthem. They demanded that Louis should be dethroned and a republic proclaimed. The men of Marseilles were soon joined by a huge citizen army that, chanting the *Marseillaise*, threw itself on and routed mercenary enemy soldiers at Valmy on 20 September. Two days later, France was declared a republic. Louis was placed on trial in December and executed on 21 January 1793.

The citizens' army swept across the Netherlands and at last achieved the 'natural frontiers' that had been beyond the reach of the armies of Louis XIV. The victors proclaimed liberty and equality for the poor of all lands, but in practice all too often they laid new tax burdens on those same poor to pay the cost of war.

In February 1793 France faced a coalition of Britain, Austria, Prussia, Holland, Spain, Sardinia and Italian states. Action taken against the Catholic church also provoked civil war in the conservative regions of the Vendée and Brittany. Effective power now passed from the Assembly to a Committee of Public Safety. In June, Danton's Gironde fell to Robespierre's Jacobins, and the period known as the Reign of Terror began. Among the victims were successive waves of politicians, including both Danton and his Girondins, and Robespierre and the Jacobins. As a result, power passed to a new generation of second rate men, who could not command the respect of the nation.

Meanwhile, the French citizen army, now reinforced by the first use of conscription in modern times, was more than holding its own in the war. Britain, while formidable at sea, was poorly equipped for a land war and the old enemies, Prussia and Austria, failed to coordinate their effort. The French armies, now led by a new generation of generals, remained firmly entrenched on the Rhine.

The Empire

The rise of Napoleon

In May 1798 a French army, led by the Corsican Napoleon Bonaparte, was sent to invade Egypt in an attempt to cut British trade routes. Land victories were made worthless when the British fleet, commanded by Admiral Nelson, destroyed the French supply fleet, and so cut the army off from Europe. In August 1899 Napoleon abandoned his army and returned to France to challenge the discredited leaders of the nation. His gambler's throw succeeded and on 9 November he staged a coup d'etat and assumed the title of First Consul. He set about centralizing power in his own hands; in 1802 he became consul for life, and in 1804, he followed the example of Charlemagne by crowning himself as Emperor Napoleon I. Any dismay at this negation of the ideals of the revolution was overwhelmed by the relief of ordinary Frenchmen at the return of ordered and firm government.

Imperial Government

Napoleon had a genius for administration. After an initial purge of remaining Jacobins, he set about healing old divisions and reuniting the country. He recognized that the continuing civil war in the Vendée could not be brought to an end unless the state came to terms with the Catholic church, so the old religion was restored to its position as the national faith. He set about recruiting the ablest men into government, regardless of whether they held republican or royalist sympathies. Most enduringly, he personally supervised a detailed revision of the whole of the French legal system into the *Code Napoleon.* Had Napoleon been content to hold the Rhine frontier and bring sound administration to France, his rule could have been outstandingly successful. But he was by instinct a general and the symbolic identification with Charlemagne at his coronation illustrated his determination to build the greatest empire that the world had seen. 'I am destined to change the face of the world. ' he declared. But Napoleon, like Louis XVI, discovered that wars could only be fought at a financial cost, which had to be passed on in taxes to the ordinary people of France and the conquered countries.

The Napoleonic Wars

The great struggles of previous centuries had achieved little more than change the line of a frontier here and there. In the three years from 1805, Napoleon completely redrew the map of Europe. He owed his success to the army that he had inherited from the revolution. Opposing generals recognized that the citizens' armies of France were carried forward on a tide of national energy, which had been released by the revolution. Napoleon added to this a military professionalism, identified with the magnificent Imperial Guard. The surge of victories carried the army across Europe as far as Bohemia, north into Scandinavia and south into Italy and Spain. Ancient rulers were replaced by members of the Bonaparte family or generals from the army. Even then, however, Britain, Spain and Russia remained as weak points remained in the French Continental System.

Giving priority to the invasion of Britain, Napoleon gathered barges at the channel ports. Any hope of carrying out this operation, however, ended in 1805 when the French fleet was destroyed at the Battle of Trafalgar. Britain therefore remained an implacable foe across the Channel.

The victorious French army in Spain found itself unable to overcome a fierce guerilla resistance that made full use of the broken terrain. The British despatched a force under the general who would later become the Duke of Wellington. In August 1812, after a relentless campaign, Wellington led his army into Madrid.

As Madrid fell, Napoleon was on the other side of Europe, leading 450,000 men on his disastrous campaign against Russia. He had already heavily defeated the Russian army and he believed that serfs would flock to join him once they heard that he had proclaimed their emancipation. He defeated the Russian army again at Borodino and marched on across the scorched countryside to occupy Moscow. But, when the Russians burned their own capital city around his army, and winter began to set in, he was forced to order the terrible retreat. In the end, only a tenth of his great army survived the ordeal. The Imperial Guard was reduced to some 400 men; 80,000 horses had died, leaving the emperor with no effective cavalry to put in the field.

Defeats in Spain and Russia shattered the myth of invincibility and by 1814 Napoleon had lost everything. Paris fell on 30 March, and he abdicated his imperial crown on 11 April. In France, however, loyalty to the deposed emperor remained strong, and, when he escaped from exile in 1815, men flocked to join his army. The hundred days' adventure ended when he was defeated by the combined British and Prussian armies Waterloo on 18 June.

Napoleon passed the remainder of his life in well-guarded exile, but the Napoleonic legend lived on. As French power declined, people remembered that it was the Little Corporal who had led them to glory.

Reaction and Revolution

The Return of the Old Order

After the defeat of Napoleon, members of the old ruling houses moved back into their palaces. The statesmen met in Vienna to reorganize the continent. The treaty took little account of nationalist aspirations. Poland was awarded to Russia; Venice and Lombardy to Austria; the Rhineland was taken from France and given to Prussia; the southern Netherlands were incorporated into Holland; Norway was made a part of Sweden.

The Austrian Prince Metternich was the main architect of this restoration of the old order. He fully recognized the huge changes in political consciousness brought about by the French Revolution, but he believed that these had to be suppressed, and that structures should return to return to their dynastic roots. He opposed all representative institutions, and established the Holy League as a coalition of powers dedicated to suppress ideas of liberty and nationalism, wherever they might show themselves. Of the major powers, only Britain—itself, however imperfectly, a representative government—stood apart to uphold a more liberal tradition.

The policy of intervention was successfully invoked when the Spanish people rose in rebellion in 1820. Austria also put down rebellion in her Italian possessions. Metternich was wise enough to see himself as the defender of a dying way of life. In 1821 the people of Greece rose against their Turkish masters. True to his principles, Metternich gave Austrian support to the Ottoman Turks, but the rebels won backing from Russia and Britain and achieved their independence in 1830.

Also in 1830 the people of Paris rose again and replaced the conservative king with his more liberal cousin, Louis Philippe and revolutions broke out in Poland and across Germany. In the same year, the Catholic Belgians rebelled against their Dutch masters. The conservative powers threatened to intervene, but Britain, in a gesture that would be called in eighty-four years later, guaranteed Belgian independence.

The Year of Revolutions

The unrest of 1830 was a prelude to much greater upheavals of 1848. In January, rebellion broke out in Sicily. In February the people of Paris drove Louis Philippe, now a figure of fun, into exile. In March, Venice, Parma, Milan and Sardinia all rose against Austria. As the year progressed, there was revolution in Poland and Hungary. Smaller German princes fell, most never to return. Uprisings in Berlin and Vienna even brought the powerful Prussian and Austrian states to the point of collapse, and the elderly Metternich had to follow Louis Philippe into exile.

The Hughes Capet French monarchy was finished for ever, and, after a period of civil war the French people turned again to the magic name of Napoleon, in the person of his nephew, Louis Napoleon. He followed family tradition by staging a coup d'état and assuming the title of Emperor Napoleon III. Across the rest of Europe, the ruling houses re-established control over their dominions.

New Nations

The Unification of Italy

A decade later, Camillo Cavour, a statesman in the Italian kingdom of Savoy, set about achieving by, political means, what had been beyond the powers of the revolutionaries. In 1858 he met with Napoleon III to discuss how Austrian rule might be ended and Italy unified under his King, Victor Emmanuel of Savoy. In 1859 French armies inflicted heavy defeats on the Austrians at Magenta and Solferino. In 1860, the popular soldier Garibaldi led 'the thousand' against the rulers of Sicily and Naples. He handed these territories over to Victor Emmanuel. For a time, Austria held on to Venice but the city fell in 1866. Finally the Papal States were brought into a united Italy in 1870. The political task was complete, but the new country faced formidable problems of poverty, and large numbers, particularly from the south, emigrated to find a better life.

The Unification of Germany

In 1862 Otto von Bismark, a nobleman of Junker descent, became Prime Minister of Prussia. His first speech was ominous for the future of European peace. 'The great issues of our day cannot be solved by speeches and majority votes—but by blood and iron.' The German-speaking people were already showing a formidable potential, but to achieve it all they had to be united into a nation state. Only Austria or Prussia could be the focus of such a state. Bismark determined that it should be Prussia.

In 1864 the two powers collaborated to annex the German-speaking lands of Schleswig and Holstein from Denmark. Then, two years later, Prussia went to war with Austria. On 3 July 1866 the Hapsburg army was devastatingly defeated at Sadowa. The Hapsburg monarchy retained Austria, but Germany was now effectively united. In 1870 Germany went to war with France, and the Napoleonic legend was laid forever on the field of Sedan.

As Bismark's army occupied Paris, there could no longer be any doubt that Germany was the dominant power in continental Europe. The violent methods by which this had been achieved were no innovation in European politics. The new state was based on admirable organization. German cities were models of organization and sanitary efficiency. A state school place was provided for every child, and illiteracy

rates became the lowest in the world. The poor, who until that time had emigrated in large numbers, now showed their confidence in the government of their country by staying at home, and by playing their part in constructing the impressive industrial base of the new nation.

9

A Changing World

The Infrastructure of Change

Population

The population of Europe had been growing relentlessly since the time of the Black Death. Demographers have argued why, for instance, the increase was particularly pronounced in the sixteenth century. It appears as though women started marrying younger, and therefore having a longer child bearing life. But this leaves unanswered the question why such a social change should have occurred. The eighteenth century again saw a steady increase across western Europe, which predated major medical advances of the following century. A modest alleviation of the harsh conditions of rural life, the improvement of the housing stock, and some advances in public health may all have contributed to a reduction in the death rate.

Rulers generally welcomed a rising population; it provided an larger manpower pool for the military, and increased the tax base of the nation. In 1798, however, an English clergyman, called Thomas Malthus, published his *Essay on Population*. The world, he argued, possesses limited resources. As population grows, so the most vulnerable—the poor—must inevitably experience disaster and hunger. Malthus' work was influential, but his warnings were not, in the short term, authenticated by events. The reason for this was that, at the same time that the population was increasing, Europe was experiencing a green revolution, which greatly increased the amount of food available to meet the growing demand.

The Second Agricultural Revolution

The first great change in farming practice came with the introduction of settled agriculture at the beginning of historical times (Chapter 1). Even in Babylonian cities, farming families had to produce a surplus to feed craftsmen, priests and warriors. By the beginning of the eighteenth century, little had changed. It is estimated that in England eight out of ten people still lived in the countryside and that, on average, one farming family had to keep one other family from the produce of its land. People still ate bread baked from their own wheat and drank beer brewed from their own barley. Animals, except for breeding stock were still slaughtered and salted down for the winter.

Once again, change originated in small, highly urbanized, seventeenth century Holland. Dutch farms had to be more efficient than those of their larger neighbours, and major improvements were pioneered, particularly in the development of root vegetables, largely for animal winter feed, and in high yield artificial grasses, such as alfalfa and lucerne.

In the eighteenth century, the English gentry, unlike their neighbours in France, lived on their estates and it became fashionable to take an interest in farming. George III set the tone by contributing articles to a farming journal. Some began to introduce the Dutch innovations on their estates. New crops and methods of rotation were introduced and selective breeding produced remarkable improvements in the quality of livestock.

These improvements could not be introduced without radical changes in the organization of the countryside. Improved agriculture could not be successfully introduced in the old communal fields, so enclosures, which had been taking place for two centuries, were given a new impetus. In the change from peasant holdings to larger farms, worked by landless labourers, many lost land and ancient rights. The production of food, however, became a much more efficient process. By the late eighteenth century, British farmers were in a position to support a huge increase in the nation's urban population.

Financial and Human Resources

Any major economic expansion needs to be built on a sound financial base. Britain's growing international trade brought prosperity, and her island position meant that wealth did not have to be dissipated on the maintenance of a large standing army. By the standards of the time, she also had a sophisticated and well-capitalized banking industry.

It is harder to establish a link between the skills required for technological advance and the social and educational structure of the day. Few of the innovators of the new age came from the conventional academic background, which had produced Isaac Newton; they were more typically self-taught, or the products of Scottish or dissenting education.

Economic Theory

In 1776 Adam Smith published *The Wealth of Nations*, which laid the basis of modern economics. He argued the benefits of competition in a free economy, against both state control and the abuses of monopoly powers. His arguments were influential both in government and business circles, initially in Britain and later in the United States and elsewhere.

The First Industrial Revolution

Iron and Coal

Since the time of the Hittites, iron working had been centred on the great forests. The charcoal used in the smelting process consumed large quantities of timber, which was also vital for building and naval supplies. Over the centuries, the forests receded to the more remote areas. By the end of the seventeenth century, Britain faced something of a crisis. In the fourteenth century, German craftsmen of the Rhineland had learnt how to make cast iron, so that the metal could now be used to make a wider range of products, but there was an acute shortage of the wood needed to drive the blast furnaces.

Early in the eighteenth century, the Darby family of Shropshire finally solved the problem of how iron could be smelted from coal. As this technique became widely known, industry moved from the forests to the great coal fields that lie across Europe in a band from mid-Russia to Wales. Surface coal was soon exhausted and deep mines were sunk to exploit the seams. Iron goods could now be produced in bulk.

Steam Power

As early as Hellenistic times, it had been recognized in theory that steam could be used to drive an engine, but the technological basis was lacking. The need for pumps to drain the new deep mines made progress all the more essential. The Scottish engineer, James Watt made the essential breakthrough when he separated the cylinder from the condenser. As a result, industry could now be liberated, not only from the forests, but also from the banks of fast flowing rivers.

Water Transport

Before the eighteenth century, land transport was rudimentary over most of Europe. Once again, the Dutch had pioneered the use of the canals, which drained their country for transporting loads. The French government also constructed the magnificent Canal du Midi, designed to prevent goods having to be carried around the coast of Spain. France also had a high quality road network, built by forced labour, but these, like those of the Romans, were built for military use.

In 1861 the Duke of Bridgwater opened a canal that linked his coal mine at Worsley with the growing town of Manchester. The potential for improved communications to lubricate economic growth was illustrated when the price of coal in Manchester fell immediately by a half. The great revolution occurred, however, when steam power was applied to locomotion. Here the initiative was taken in the United States, where inland waterways provided the essential communication links for the new nation. In 1807, Robert Fulton sailed *The Steamboat* from New York to Albany in 32 hours—a journey that had previously taken four days. Two years later, steam power was applied to ocean navigation.

Railways

The world's first commercial railway was opened in Britain in 1825, between Stockton and Darlington. Huge sums of money were invested in railway building in many nations, but, despite massive construction programmes, especially in the United States and Germany, Britain retained her initial advantage. The age of cheap and rapid communication brought important social, as well as economic, change as the structure of society began to reflect the new mobility.

Cotton and the Factory System

There had long been a market for fine fabrics in western Europe. By the early eighteenth century a substantial silk industry had grown up in France, which reduced dependence on imports. At this time, cotton was still a luxury fabric, and ready woven cloth was imported from India. Entrepreneurs then began to import raw cotton, which was put out for manufacture to domestic workers. Whole families worked immensely long hours at carding, spinning and weaving to earn a modest subsistence. The early machines were invented by enterprising craftsmen to help boost domestic output.

The first large spinning factory was built by Richard Arkwright at Cromford, near Derby in 1771. By the early nineteenth century all the stages of cotton cloth production had been brought within the factory system. Britain, backed by her huge merchant marine, had established a dominant position in the world supply of textiles. One machine, tended by a woman or a girl, could now do the work of many domestic workers, and traditional producers, from Britain itself to India, lost their livelihood.

Despite being a closely guarded secret, the new technology was bound to become known. The United States was already showing itself a fertile ground for industrial development and a substantial industry grew up in New England.

Urban Growth

The population of Europe continued to grow rapidly throughout the nineteenth century, but the increase was now concentrated in the urban centres. In the nineteenth century, the population of London increased from about 900,000 to some 4.7 million, that of Paris from 600,000 to 3.6 million; small country towns turned into conurbations. This growth in Europe was matched by comparable expansion of New York and the Midwestern cities of the United States.

The urban centres grew faster than their service infrastructure, and so the industrial revolution became identified with slum housing, malnutrition and cholera, on a scale that remains common in the burgeoning cities of modern developing countries. For most of the workers, however, the change from rural to urban poverty was not the disaster that has often been painted. The poor had always lived on the edge of subsistence; there were indeed reverses, as during the 'hungry forties', but the overall tendency was towards an improvement in living standards. Pasteur's discovery of the germ causation of disease stimulated major sewage and other sanitation projects in the second half of the century.

The Second Industrial Revolution

The Decline of Britain

Visitors to the Great Exhibition, which was held in London in 1851, would not have readily recognized that the age of British industrial supremacy was already nearing its end. Britain possessed half of the world's mileage of railway lines, and half of its merchant marine. Five years later, the British inventor, Henry Bessemer would present his Convertor, which made possible the mass production of steel. The nation's lead still appeared unassailable.

In hindsight it is, however, possible to recognize the signs of decay. Too much investment lay in the industries of the first industrial revolution, which were vulnerable to competition from low cost countries; the educational system, both for the rich and poor was ill equipped to train in the more technical skills needed to meet the ever growing complexities of industry; British industry was already at times failing to capitalize on the skills of the inventors.

Germany and the United States

In the second half of the century two powers demonstrated great economic potential. German military expenditure funded the expansion of the mighty firm of Alfred Krupp, which was soon competing with British companies for the supply of railway and shipyard equipment. The electric dynamo was invented simultaneously in Britain and Germany, but the German firm of Siemens reaped the benefits. In 1885 Carl Benz produced the first working automobile using the internal combustion engine, so initiating the greatest transport revolution in the world's history.

The United States was also showing both creativity and economic power. Inventive geniuses, like Bell and Edison, found that the young nation, with its growing market base, provided an ideal environment for the exploitation of new technology. The telegraph, the telephone, the domestic sewing machine, mechanized agricultural machines, the safety lift, air conditioning, the electric light, the phonograph, the cine camera and the aeroplane were all American contributions to the more sophisticated second phase of industrialization. Andrew Carnegie and Henry Ford also showed the American capacity to build great operations on the inventions of others.

Capital and Labour

Trades Unions

Throughout history, there had always been a sharp divide between the rich and the poor, but the working people within the new factory system became acutely aware of the polarization between those who owned the means of production and their employees. By gathering workers together in large units of production, the owners made it practicable for them to organize in defence of their living conditions.

Robert Owen, a working man turned successful cotton master, attempted to establish a model industrial society at New Lanark, Scotland; he introduced schools and all kinds of leisure activities for the working people, and still was able to show a profit for the mill. He became dissatisfied with this paternalistic approach and set up a cooperative venture in New Harmony in America. This proved less successful, and he returned to Britain, where he founded the ambitious Grand National Consolidated Trades Union. This was a bid to harness the power of the working people, so that they could control the industries in which they worked. Owen's union failed, as did most of the early attempts to organize labour. Unskilled workers, faced by organized management, lacked credible bargaining power. Over much of Europe, they were further weakened by being divided between opposing Christian and socialist unions.

The battle between capital and labour could be seen in its rawest state in the United States. The owners mobilized city and state authorities and hired private armies to break strikes. Also there were as yet no antitrust laws to prevent employers from combining to achieve their objectives. The workers responded by organizing themselves into violent secret societies, like the Molly Macguires of the Pennsylvania coal mines. At Andrew Carnegie's Homestead works at Pittsburgh in 1892, the two sides confronted each other in pitched battle.

At Homestead, as elsewhere, management emerged victorious because there was always unskilled 'blackleg' labour on hand to fill the jobs of those who went on strike. At the end of the century, however, there emerged a new generation of union leaders who recognized that progress could best be made by organizing the skilled labour that was now vital for the more sophisticated industries. In The United States, in 1886, Samuel Gompers organized these skilled trades into the more successful American Federation of Labour. In the years that followed, the rights of organized labour were increasingly recognized by the legal systems of the industrialized nations.

Socialism

During the time that Robert Owen was experimenting with new structures, continental thinkers were beginning to challenge the laissez-faire theories of Adam Smith. Most influential was the French nobleman, Claude de Saint-Simon, often looked on as the founder of socialism, who published his critique of the new industrial age in the 1820s. He argued for the replacement of the existing ruling elite by a 'meritocracy', which would manage the economy for the general good of the population, rather than for individual gain.

Saint-Simon's ideas gained ground in France. In 1848 Paris experienced two distinct revolutions. The first unseated the king; the second was a bloody confrontation between workers, proclaiming the new socialists ideas, and the bourgeoisie, who defended traditional property rights.

Communism

Karl Marx watched the destruction of the Paris workers in 1848 with distress but without surprise. He had been associated with the revolutionary movement in his native Germany before being forced into exile. He believed that history showed two struggles. The first, as in all earlier revolutions, had been between the feudal authorities and the bourgeoisie. The second, in his own day, lay between the bourgeoisie and the proletariat.

Marx held that the value of goods lay in the labour that had been expended in its production, and the interests of the proletariat lay in winning a fair return for that labour. That was in conflict with the interests of the owners, or bourgeoisie, who were dedicated to achieving a profit on the product. Within a capitalist society the proletariat was therefore alienated from the production process, and both sides were inevitably locked in class war. The objective for the proletariat was to win control of the machinery of government by revolution, and then to use the new communist state to control the 'commanding heights of the economy'—land, transport, factories and banks.

Marx and his friends tried to gather the revolutionary movement into the unity without which he believed it could never be effective. In 1864 the First International meeting of the Communist party was held in London, with delegations from France, Germany, Italy, Switzerland and Poland, as well as Britain. The party, however, quickly showed its capacity for splitting into factions. When, by the beginning of the next century, none of the great industrial nations had fallen, many thought that the communist challenge had passed away. It was not anticipated that the revolution would come in Russia, which, under Marx's definition, still lay within the feudal stage of development.

Change and Society

Education

The movement for educational reform can be traced to the late eighteenth century, but another century had to pass before change affected the lives of working people. In Germany and the United States, and later in Japan, politicians recognized that, if a nation were to remain competitive in the new world, it needed an educated labour force. All across the industrial world there was a huge increase, not only in basic education but in the provision of higher education. Literacy and numeracy were at last seen as functional skills, rather than as the prerogative of a privileged élite.

The Women's Movement

Before the middle of the nineteenth century individual voices had been raised to protest against the subjugation of women in western society, but the origin of a formal movement can be placed in 1848, the year of revolutions. In that year a group of women, with men supporters, met at Seneca Falls in New York State and laid out a programme that was to be the blueprint for the women's movement. The resolutions demanded voting rights, equality before the law, the right to hold property, justice in marriage, equal opportunity in education, free access to jobs and an end to the pervasive double standard in morality. The political struggle became identified with the names of Susan Anthony in the USA and later with the Pankhurst family in Britain. Many advances were made, particularly in educational provision, but the radical change came with the First World War. Women who undertook a wide range of men's work could no longer be denied basic rights.

Leisure

Towards the end of the century working hours began to be reduced and, perhaps for the first time in history, the less privileged found themselves with time for leisure activities. Virtually all the major sports that are popular across the world today were codified during these decades, and this happened mainly in Britain, where the industrial achievements brought the earliest benefits. By the beginning of the twentieth century, the bicycle and the railway excursion were giving urban dwellers a new sense of freedom. Many problems remained, but those who lived in the industrial societies experienced a genuine improvement in the quality of life. This improvement made the programmes of the revolutionaries less attractive than Karl Marx and his followers had anticipated.

10

America

The Birth of the United States

The Causes of Conflict

When the Seven Years' War ended in 1763 it appeared that Britain had achieved her aims in the New World. The French colonies in Canada had fallen under British rule and the stranglehold on the Thirteen Colonies by French forts on the Ohio River had been broken. Very shortly, however, it became clear that strains were building up in the relationships between the American colonists and the mother country.

Under the mercantilist system, it was taken for granted that the colonies existed for the benefit of the other country. As American economies strengthened, however, they began to generate their own momentum. Slaving ships from New England, for instance, now competed directly with those from Bristol on the Guinea Coast.

The American colonists had already developed the westward momentum, which remains a feature of the nation today. Pioneers were penetrating into the rich lands to the west of the Appalachians. Britain, as the colonizing power, was responsible for security, and the London government therefore had to decide whether to expand budgets to provide protection to these pioneers. To the annoyance of many colonists, a decision was taken that a limit should be drawn along the ridge of the Appalachians. The government further decided that the American colonies should be taxed to help pay security costs. When the traditional colonial assemblies refused to vote the funds, the British government decided to establish the principle of its right to impose direct taxation. The Stamp Act, the Sugar Act and the duty on tea were all stages in the deteriorating relationships. None were in themselves onerous, but they created genuine anxiety. Sugar molasses, for instance, was turned into rum, which was the staple of the slave trade. Any tax could be used to make American ships uncompetitive with their British rivals.

Independence

Tension centred on the largest city and trading port of Boston, where fighting started in 1775. In the following year representatives from the Thirteen colonies, now to become states, met in Philadelphia to declare themselves independent. The famous and highly influential Declaration of Independence, drafted by Thomas Jefferson, justified the act of rebellion in terms that drew from Locke and the *philosophes*. It declared that government derives from the consent of the governed and the misgovernment, listed in detail, broke that tie of consent.

The colonists faced serious problems in organizing themselves to fight a major European power; there was little natural unity, and money to fund the conflict proved as hard to raise as it had been under British rule. American success was largely the result of the outstanding leadership qualities of George Washington and the ability of the colonists to adapt to a guerilla style of warfare, well suited to the heavily forested terrain. In 1781, the British army surrendered at Yorktown and two years later, Britain accepted defeat.

The Constitution

It was not immediately clear, however, whether one or thirteen new nations had emerged from the conflict. Many of Washington's army remained unpaid and no mechanism existed for a central government to raise money from the states. The Constitutional Convention of 1787 was faced with serious division between the interests of large and of small states, and between those who wanted to see a strong central government and those who preferred to see real power continue to lie with the individual states. The final document, which was ratified in 1788, steered a compromise course between the interests. The Executive, Legislature and Judiciary all had their own spheres of responsibility, and acted as a control on one another by a complex structure of checks and balances.

Canada

The successful rebellion by the American colonies left the British government reluctant to expend further effort and resources on colonization. Many loyalists from the south had moved north, and the division between the French and English population remained deep. The colonies covered much sparsely populated territory and communications remained poor. The people were united only in a common hostility to any threat of annexation by the more powerful neighbour to the south.

In the first half of the nineteenth century, progress was made towards the establishment of a confederacy. In 1867, The British North America Act brought together four provinces into a federal Dominion of Canada. To protect minority French interests, language and education remained provincial concerns and other provinces joined the federation in subsequent years. In 1885, the last rivet was driven into the Canadian Pacific Line, bringing together east and west and opening up the prairies for agricultural development.

Latin America

To the south, the countries of Latin America remained under the colonial control of Spain and Portugal. The successful rebellion of the British colonies was shortly followed by the collapse of the old monarchies in the face of Napoleon's army. Links with the old countries were cut during the European wars, and this generated an outburst of nationalist fervour.

Spain fought a series of devastating wars to recover control of her American empire. In 1810, the Mexican priest Manuel Hidalgo y Costilla led the poor in a rising, but independence was not finally won until 1821. Power then passed, not to the poor, but to the wealthy classes of Spanish descent. Rulers like Santa Anna treated the country as a personal *hacienda*, and the situation of the poor became, if anything, worse than it had been in colonial days.

In 1811 Venezuela declared its independence under the 'Great Liberator', Simon

Bolivar. He had travelled in Europe and was particularly influenced by the writings of Voltaire, and he now saw himself as the George Washington who would bring unity to the Spanish-speaking countries of South America. He won a series of victories against Spain, and independence seemed assured, provided the conservative European powers did not follow Metternich's plan and intervene to uphold the old order. This was prevented by American President Monroe, who warned off any intervention by proclaiming his doctrine of 'hands off America'.

Bolivar seemed on the verge of creating a United Republic of Columbia, which could be a comparable power to the USA. He was, however, unable to hold the new country together, and one part of the country after another broke off to form new nations. As in Mexico, the privileged classes preserved power for themselves. The European nations competed to invest, particularly in Argentina, and there was a steady stream of immigration from the Old World, but the old inequalities remained, and the economies of many of the new Latin American countries became dangerously dependent on single primary products.

The path to independence was smoother in Brazil. The Portuguese royal family decided not to defend its rights, and in 1822 the country was declared an independent empire by consent. Here, too, old social inequalities remained and, as late as 1888, Brazil was the last American country to abolish the Atlantic slave trade.

Slavery and the Civil War

King Cotton

Dr Samuel Johnson spoke for many when he poured scorn on American ideals of liberty, which were denied to the black slave population. The continuance of the institution was one of the issues discussed in the Constitutional Convention. There were three broad points of view. Opponents of slavery wished to see the institution outlawed in the new nation; representatives of the southern states would not contemplate joining a union that deprived them of their property; moderates, like Washington himself, opposed slavery, but they believed that they could let history take its course. Slavery, they argued, was outdated and it would wither away of its own accord. Events proved them wrong.

The new English cotton mills created an insatiable demand for raw cotton. The native short staple cotton was an uneconomic crop until in 1793 Eli Whitney invented a gin, which enabled it to be cleaned in large quantities. In the decades that followed huge areas of the south was given over to cotton cultivation. This created a demand for slaves. The Atlantic slave trade was declared illegal, but many were smuggled into the country; others were 'sold down the river' by plantation owners from the more northerly slave states.

This resurgence of slavery led to widespread unrest. Slave risings broke out and an increasing number of slaves used the freedom road to escape north. White and black activists combined in a highly organized antislavery movement. Anger rose when in 1850 Congress passed the Fugitive Slave Law, which gave southern owners the right to pursue their property into the free northern states.

Slave and Free States

The House of Representatives, elected by population, was dominated by the free states. The Senate was more finely balanced. As new states were added to the Union, the balance was maintained. California and Oregon tilted the balance towards the free states. 'Bleeding' Kansas, a fierce bone of contention, fell to the slave party. When, in 1860, a republican from Illinois called Abraham Lincoln was elected president, the slave states felt that the political balance had swung irretrievably against them. In March 1861 eleven southern states declared their secession from the Union and the following month they attacked the federal Fort Sumter.

The Civil War

Over six hundred thousand men died in the four years of war that followed. The southern armies were highly motivated and generally well commanded, but they were bound to lose a long war of attrition. The industrial north had a larger population, more industrial production and more miles of railway. This was the first major war in history fought with armaments that were the products of the industrial revolution, and great battles, like Antietam and Gettysburg presaged the terrible loss of life at Verdun and on the Somme half a century later. When the war ended in April 1865, the south lay devastated. Lincoln was assassinated five days later.

Civil Rights

The war had been fought over the right of the south to secede from the Union. Slavery was abolished in the process. Lincoln's emancipation decree was given the force of law by the Thirteenth Amendment of 1865, and further amendments wrote civil rights into the constitution. In the years of reconstruction, black legislators took their seats, and it appeared as though political and social equality might be close. Gradually, however, by a process of manipulation and terrorization, the white supremacists regained control of the southern states. The liberal fervour of the antislavery years was now spent, and the Supreme Court proved unwilling to uphold even the most clearly defined constitutional rights. Disillusioned, many blacks migrated to the booming industrial cities of the north, where they encountered new forms of discrimination.

The situation only began to improve with the great Civil Rights movement of the 1960s, when Dr Martin Luther King provided a rallying point for his people's aspirations and liberal white sympathizers were again mobilized, as they had been a century before in the antislavery campaign.

The Westward Movement

Thomas Jefferson

Of all the founding fathers, Jefferson had the clearest vision that the new nation could become a great power and that this had to be based on an exploitation of the great potential of the continent. He was the architect of the system whereby new states could be added to the Union. By 1803 Napoleon had decided that the Mississippi lands of Louisiana, which remained French, were of no value, and Jefferson, now president, negotiated to buy them for $15,000,000—and so doubled the land area of the United States. In 1804 he sent out an expedition led by Lewis and Clark to cross the continent and report back on its potential.

Jefferson's vision of the west as the land of opportunity gradually captured the American imagination. It was argued that the American people—by which was meant the white American people—had a 'manifest destiny' to possess the continent from the Atlantic to the Pacific Oceans.

The Dispossession of the Indian People

During the early years of the nineteenth century, Americans of European origin were pushing into traditional Indian territory beyond the Appalachians. Every expedient was used, from purchase to forced expulsion, to drive the Indian people back into the western grasslands, which remained unattractive to white settlement.

The nomadic buffalo culture of the plains Indians was based on horses originally acquired form the southern Spanish settlements, and it was therefore a comparatively recent development. In the middle of the century, migrants were attracted, not to the featureless plains with their extremes of climate, but to the far west. For a brief period, wagon trains and nomadic Indians were able to coexist. By the 1870s, however, the white men began to move into these last hunting grounds. The buffalo were hunted to deprive the Indian people of their livelihood and provide food for railway construction workers; then the railway link with the eastern markets made the grasslands attractive for cattle farming. Finally new agricultural machinery and irrigation techniques made large scale wheat farming economic. With the buffalo herds destroyed, and their whole way of life undermined, the surviving Indian people were driven back into ever more arid and infertile reservations.

Oregon Country

Lewis and Clark reported on fertile land on the Pacific coast around the mouth of the Columbia River. Many Americans were prepared to go to war with Britain over British Columbia, but agreement was reached on the 49th parallel boundary. This left ample scope for colonization in the north west. The wagon trains that followed the Oregon trail brought farming families into this attractive region.

The Southwest

The new Mexican state claimed the whole of the southwest of the country, from Texas to California and as far north as Utah and southern Wyoming. Spanish settlement had been based on missions, which were often widely dispersed, and the non-Indian population of the region remained low. Between 1836 and 1847 the United States and Mexico were in an intermittent state of war, which ended with the capture of Mexico City and defeat for Mexico. Under the treaty, the United States won the whole of the southwest. Existing property rights of the Spanish speaking people were, in theory, protected, but, in practice, they had no means of protecting them against the newly arrived 'Anglos', who controlled the courts.

Shortly before the treaty was signed, gold was discovered at Sutter's Mill in Northern California. This set off the Gold Rush, which brought fortune hunters flocking to California from the east, and, indeed, from many parts of the world. The influx of population in turn created a farming boom and California was rapidly converted from a thinly populated region, largely consisting of mountains and desert, to the world's most rapidly expanding economy.

Immigration

From Europe

Any measurement of the population rise of Europe from the middle of the eighteenth to the end of the nineteenth centuries should properly include, not only statistics on those countries themselves, but also of the millions who emigrated to destinations in many parts of the world—as well as their descendants. Figures cannot be collated, but people of European stock took over great areas of the world, often at the expense of the indigenous population.

In order to overcome human reluctance to disrupt living patterns, there needs to be a 'push factor' propelling people from their homes, and a 'pull factor' drawing them to a new environment. As in the early years of colonization, the growing wealth of the United States drew economic, political and religious refugees from Europe. The British still came. Many of the Mormons who pulled their handcarts across the plains to Utah originated from among the cotton mills of Lancashire. The depopulation of the Scottish glens provided a new stream, although most preferred to go to Canada. The Catholic Irish, angered by English protestant rule and by unjust land laws had long been ready recruits; the disastrous potato famine of 1845–46, which is estimated to have claimed the lives of a million people, turned the stream into a flood.

People now came from new countries of origin. Norwegian families, long accustomed to extremes of climate, left their marginal fiord farms to farm in the harsh environment of Wisconsin and the Dakotas. Germans fled from the political and social upheavals of their country. Peasants from southern Italy, condemned to live on the brink of subsistence under rapacious landlords, took the boat to America. Towards the end of the century, people were coming from further east. Russian Jews fled the pogroms; Poles fled Russian oppression. All funnelled through Ellis Island to emerge, often penniless, and speaking no English, onto the streets of New York. They worked as they could, in clothing sweatshops, on construction, in domestic service. Each new national group faced discrimination as those who were settled in jobs and homes tried to protect their position from the work-hungry newcomers.

The New Immigration. The capture of the south west brought a significant Spanish speaking population within the United States. Civil war in Mexico and an increasing divergency of the standards of living brought an increasing number of immigrants across the border. Most came as migrant workers, following the crops into California and far beyond. In good times, they were welcomed as cheap labour, but in times of depression they proved easy targets for discrimination. In the twentieth century immigrants from Puerto Rico and other Caribbean islands have also increased the Hispanic population of the eastern side of the country.

Asian immigration began when Chinese labourers were recruited to work in the 1849 Gold Rush. Distinctive in those early days in their 'queues' and national clothing, they found themselves at the bottom of the immigrant 'heap', increasingly shut out from desirable employment and property ownership by Chinese Exclusion Acts. They, like subsequent Asian immigrants, preserved a respect for education, which enabled them to improve their status rapidly when the legal discrimination was brought to an end.

The United States Abroad

The Continent

The Monroe Doctrine was originally proclaimed to protect emerging Latin nations seeking to establish independence from European colonial powers. In the later years of the century it was used to promote the continent as a sphere of US interest.

One major thrust lay through the Caribbean towards South America. In 1903 effective control over the Isthmus of Panama was wrested from Columbia and the Panama Canal linking the two oceans was opened in 1914. War with Spain in 1898 also ended with the acquisition of Puerto Rico and Cuba.

American interests also led expansion across the Pacific. Alaska was purchased from Russia in 1867, providing the westward bridge of the Aleutian Islands. Midway Island was won in the same year, followed by Samoa and the Hawaiian group. The war with Spain finally brought Guam and the Philippines within the American empire.

Although the United States was no longer a new country, the need to absorb waves of immigrants fostered an introversion and at times an aggressive nationalism. Many American statesmen, wishing to distance their country from what they saw as the destructive quarrels of the old world, proclaimed a policy of isolationism. The history of the twentieth century was to show that the world's greatest power could not successfully stand back from international events.

11

The Age of Imperialism

India

The East India Company

The battles in the eighteenth century between rival trading companies were fought, not to win territory, but to establish trading advantage. In 1757, however, the British East India Company's army in Bengal first captured the French trading station and then defeated the Nawab's army at Plassey. The company then found itself, by default, the inheritor of Mogul power. Now irretrievably involved in politics, it gradually extended its control over large areas of the subcontinent.

Company officials never lost sight of the fact that their objective was to turn in a profit. As the company extended its control over all internal as well as external trade, the standard of living of many Indians declined. Company officials took the opportunity of amassing private fortunes, often by corrupt means. In the days before steam ships and the opening of the Suez Canal, India was far distant from home. Men travelled out as bachelors and many took local women and lived much as Indian princes.

After the American revolution, the British government was reluctant to become involved in further colonial expansion. To bring the Company under control, however, it assumed dual control of the Indian possessions in 1784. The writings of Adam Smith had discredited the old mercantilist ideas, which had been the justification for early colonization. In line with prevailing doctrines of free trade, the company therefore lost its monopoly trading rights and was reduced to an administrative organization.

Modernization

The evangelical fervour of the age brought Protestant missionaries of many denominations to the subcontinent. Most had a simple desire to replace the traditional religions of Hinduism and Islam. They started schools that offered western education and encouraged converts to adopt western dress and habits. These missionaries looked to the Christian rulers for protection and active encouragement.

The new generation of administrators was less directly motivated by the profit motive and more by a desire to bring the benefits of modern life to the people of India. Many had a genuine, albeit paternalistic, respect for Indian culture, and they resisted the missionaries' attempt to overturn traditional ways. These administrators did, however, believe in reform. Laws, based on western practice, were introduced to stamp out traditional practices, such as the burning of widows and the killing of infant girls. The products of the industrial revolution, such as the electric telegraph and railways were also enthusiastically introduced.

The Mutiny

The modernization programme inevitably created tension. Railways, for instance, were looked upon as a threat to the caste system. There was also powerful resentment against British acquisition of new land, particularly in the northern province of Oudh. The introduction of a new form of greased cartridge was the immediate cause of the Indian Mutiny of 1857. This was as much a traditionalist reaction against modernization as it was a rebellion against the ever expanding foreign rule. Many educated Indians, like the operators of the Delhi telegraph, died at the hands of the mutineers. The mutiny was put down with as much ferocity as it had been waged. The British parliament at last accepted direct responsibility for government. In 1877 Queen Victoria was proclaimed Empress of India and her rule over the subcontinent became the symbol of British power. The true age of imperialism had begun.

The Raj

The new rulers determined that mistakes that had led to the mutiny should not be repeated. They therefore took care to respect the rights of the traditional ruling class. When early representative institutions were introduced, this ruling class was called upon to represent the Indian people. The aspirations of the rising intelligentsia were therefore overlooked. Indeed, the contempt for the educated 'westernized native', which was to be characteristic of British imperialism, was first shown in India. The first meeting of the Indian National Congress was held in Bombay in 1885, but a further twenty years would pass before independence appeared on the Congress agenda.

Throughout history, India, like China, had shown a capacity to absorb its conquerors; the British alone resisted assimilation. The new rulers of the Indian Civil Service were drawn from the elite and many acquired a knowledge of Indian language and customs, but, in the wake of the Mutiny, a barrier existed between the two races that could not be crossed. Fast and comfortable steam ships now linked Europe and India, and the journey time was much reduced when the Suez Canal opened in 1869. Administrators and traders increasingly kept their roots in Britain, while serving tours of duty overseas. Also men were now joined in India by their womenfolk. Few of these *memsahibs* had work that brought them into contact with Indian people, so their cultural values were never seriously challenged.

In the second half of the century new concepts of racial superiority were fashionable, particularly in northern Europe. Europeans had long treated other races as inferior, but they had not theorized about it. Now concepts of racial superiority were becoming fashionable, partly based on popular Darwinianism. The European rulers of India, as of other colonized people, were therefore ill equipped to understand the nationalist aspirations when they did come to the surface.

China

The Manchu Empire

In the middle of the seventeenth century, invaders from Manchuria overthrew the Ming emperor and established the foreign Manchu (Ch'ing) Dynasty. Following the ancient pattern, the early rulers were able men, who established a working relationship with the mandarin administrators, and for more than a century the land experienced one of its more prosperous periods.

By the end of the eighteenth century, however, problems were growing. It is estimated that the population trebled, from 100 to 300 million between 1650 and 1800, and it would reach 420 million by 1850. In China, Malthus' forecasts on the effects of population growth proved accurate. All available land was already under cultivation, so production could not match increased demand. The situation became disastrous in the terrible northern famine of 1887–89, when some ten million people starved to death. As social problems became worse, so the quality of imperial government deteriorated into corruption and mismanagement. Resentment boiled and people remembered that the Manchu were a foreign race.

In 1786 rebellion broke out in Shantung, and this was followed in 1795 by the White Lotus Uprising on the borders of Szechwan and Shensi. These were the preludes of a century of peasant unrest on a scale far beyond anything experienced in human history before that time. It is estimated, for instance, that more people died in the T'ai-p'ing Rebellion of 1850–64 than in the whole of the First World War, while huge Islamic risings of the north and southwest left wide areas of the country devastated. The Manchu Dynasty, however, managed to cling to power through all these upheavals.

China and the West

Since the earliest times, China had always had a favourable balance of trade with Europe. There was a demand in the West of porcelain and silks, but, apart from a few clocks and toys, Europe had little to offer in return. Towards the end of the eighteenth century the balance took a turn for the worse. There was a fashion in Europe for Chinoiserie, reflected in some of the art of the period. More important, tea became the staple drink of many Europeans. This could only be bought by a steady drain of bullion.

Western merchants were convinced a huge Chinese market, was waiting to be opened up, but contact was strictly controlled through a few merchants in Canton. Attempts to open the market ended in frustration. In 1793 George III of Britain sent an emissary to the Manchu court with gifts. The Emperor thanked King George for his 'submissive loyalty in sending this tribute mission' from 'the lonely remoteness of your island, cut off from the world by intervening wastes of sea', but the mission achieved nothing of substance.

The Opium Wars

In the early years of the nineteenth century British traders found that the drug opium could right the adverse balance of trade. A great deal of Indian farmland was placed under the crop and the flow of bullion into China was quickly reversed. Apart from the direct damage done by the opium, the Chinese government found that the drain of wealth quickly created financial crisis. The opium trade was a breach of Chinese law, and in 1839 a large quantity was destroyed. In the following First Opium War the Chinese forces proved ill equipped to fight a modern war, and they were defeated. In 1842, China was forcedly opened up to foreign trade and missions, and Britain won control of the trading outpost of Hong Kong.

Thirteen years later, the British Prime Minister, Lord Palmerston, decided to assert British authority once again. His declared policy that half civilized governments such as those of China 'all need a dressing every eight or ten years to keep them in order' made him popular at home. He was prepared to defend British citizens against the valid operation of foreign law and in 1856 he defied parliament to take Britain, with French help, to war with China again. The imperial army was weakened by the T'ai-p'ing Rebellion and in 1860 the allied army marched into Peking and burned the Imperial palace.

European Influence and Reaction

Although China herself remained nominally independent, her influence in Asia was much reduced. Russia used the British and French invasion as a cover for occupying the northern Amur river, so winning the Pacific outlet of Valdivostok; Britain won Burma, against fierce local opposition; France defeated Chinese armies to win Indo-China; Korea won its independence, later to fall to Japan; Japan conquered Taiwan; even the United States closed in by conquering the Philippines, again in the face of fierce nationalist resistance. Within China itself, the European powers jockeyed for privileges. Even more threateningly, the country was now open to western missionaries who, along with the Christian gospel, brought cultural assumptions profoundly at odds with traditional Confucian values.

The End of the Manchu Empire

By the last years of the century the ancient civilization was beginning to collapse. In 1898 the young emperor and his advisers decided that China must follow the Japanese example and adopt western ways. The experiment was short lived as the dowager Empress led the faction of reaction. She imprisoned the emperor and gave support to the xenophobic Boxers, who were attacking mission stations and other western interests across the country, and the embassy area of Peking was besieged. The western powers replied by sending a combined army to relieve the city. Still the Manchu rulers clung to power, but they were threatened from two directions. The army war lords were now unreliable, and outside the country, young foreign educated men plotted to overthrow the dynasty. In 1911–12 the two combined to bring down the Manchu Dynasty. The foreign educated Sun Yat-sen became president, but one year later he gave way to one of the military commanders.

Japan

The Shogunate

In 1603, at a time when the imperial family had lost effective power, the military leader, or Shogun, Tokugawa Ieyasu established power over the whole of Japan. In the centuries that followed, the Tokugawa shogunate closed Japan off from the outside world. The Japanese were prohibited from travelling abroad; Jesuit missionaries were expelled and their converts persecuted; only a few Dutch traders were allowed to operate from the city of Nagasaki. For Japanese urban entrepreneurs, however, the cost was a small price to pay for the peace and prosperity brought by the powerful shoguns. Educational reforms created a high level of literacy and a vigorous free enterprise economy was permitted to flourish in the growing towns. The growing prosperity of the towns was not matched in the countryside, where both the traditional lords, and the peasants tended to become poorer.

The Opening of Japan

In 1854 the navy officer Matthew Perry was commissioned by the President of the

USA to open up the Japanese market. His Treaty of Kanagawa brought the years of isolation to an end. The shogunate did not long survive it, and the Emperor resumed direct power in 1868. There was now a fierce debate within Japan as to whether the country should adopt western ways wholeheartedly, or follow the example of China and remain separate. The reformers were able to point to the disastrous results of conservative policies, as applied in China. The largest feudal families voluntarily surrendered their rights and the government systematically set about the modernization of their country. The changes were based on the solid structure, bequeathed by the Tokugawa shogunate, but there remains no example in history of a comparable change in social life within a single generation. By 1900 an advanced system of state education had been constructed, western experts were imported to train the people in engineering, and young Japanese students were sent to study overseas. At first the new industries, like textiles and shipbuilding, were faithful copies of western prototypes, but they gained an increasing share in world markets. By the 1920s Japan was a formidable industrial competitor to the European nations.

Japanese Expansionism

The era of peace had left the samurai caste deprived of employment. They bequeathed an aggressive nationalism to the new state. The Japanese also recognized that European world domination had been based on the use of force. The now popular motto 'Asia for the Asians' was intended as a Monroe Doctrine for a Japanese sphere of influence.

Russian power was particularly menacing. The transcontinental railway had now reached Vladivostok, and the Russians were showing interest in the newly independent Korea. In 1902 Japan concluded a treaty with Britain, which provided security against intervention and two years later she attacked Russian shipping in the Manchurian Port Arthur. The city fell in January of the next year and the Russian Baltic fleet was destroyed in the Tsushima Straits in May.

This victory of an Asian over an essentially European power in the Russo-Japanese War marked the end of the European military domination of the world, which had survived since the fifteenth century. In the years that followed, Japan continued to build an empire, first by the annexation of Korea and then by the acquisition of wide Chinese lands. These conquests were accepted as a fait accompli by the European powers at the Treaty of Versailles in 1919.

The Pacific

The Aborigines of Australia

Over 50,000 years ago, great ice caps in the polar regions made the world's seas lower than they are today. The Indonesian islands formed a great peninsula, and Australia was joined to Tasmania and New Guinea in a single land mass. At this time the ancestors of the Australian aborigines arrived in their isolated home. Despite the lower waters, they had still crossed a wide stretch of ocean, making them possibly the world's first seafaring people. These early settlers brought their dogs, but the other animals would have provided a strange sight to people accustomed to the fauna of Asia. In their new home, they adopted a hunter-gatherer lifestyle, delicately in balance with the unique environment.

The Polynesians

Much later, some 3–4,000 years ago, a different race of people began to spread out across the islands of the Pacific Ocean. The methods by which they navigated their great canoes are little understood; they probably followed the paths of migrating birds, and it is suggested that they could feel the current off distant land masses on the surface of the water with their hands. Certainly they made successful voyages of up to 2000 miles to colonize unknown islands. It appears that they went via Fiji and Samoa to the remote Marquesas Islands, from where they fanned out, north to Hawaii, south east to Easter Island and southwest to New Zealand, which they called Ao-te-roa, or Long White Cloud. The earliest settlers were probably fleeing from war, but in time warfare followed them to their new homes.

The Arrival of the Europeans

Australian aborigines and Polynesian islanders alike were for long protected from European ships by unfavourable trade winds. In the seventeenth century several Dutch sailors, operating from the East Indes, made voyages in the area, but they were not attracted by what they saw as the region offered no prospect of profitable trade. In 1770 the English Captain James Cook sailed along the east coast of Australia and landed at Botany Bay. He later commanded two more voyages through the Pacific Islands. The sailors found the Pacific island societies to be living examples of the 'noble savage' existence, extolled by writers such as Rousseau—and bequeathed the devastations of syphilis to the islanders.

Australia

The Penal Colony

The war with the American colonies shut Britain off from the penal colonies of Georgia and the Carolinas, and so posed the British government with a problem of how to dispose of its surplus criminal population. As long as the war was in progress, convicts were kept in hulks moored in river estuaries.

One of those who had landed off Captain Cook's ship in Botany Bay was a geographer and scientist called Joseph Banks. In the years that followed he had become the driving force behind an exploration movement, intended to open new areas of the world to British trade. Banks argued the case for establishing a penal colony in Botany Bay. The land was good, he argued, the climate mild and the natives few in number.

The first convoy sailed in 1787, under the command of Captain Arthur Phillip, carrying 571 male and 159 female convicts, supervised by over 200 marines. Most of those transported were hard-core criminals, but there were also a significant number of political prisoners, particularly from rebellious Ireland. Large numbers of enforced immigrants suffered dreadfully on the long journey and in the penal settlements, and many continued to nurse resentment against the 'old country' and the forces of law and order.

Exploration

By the end of the century it was established that New South Wales in the east was linked to New Holland in the West in a single continent. In 1813 pioneers crossed the Great Dividing Range, which hemmed in the eastern coastal plain to discover the broad grasslands of the interior. By 1859 the landmass of the continent had been divided into six colonies.

It is said that, when these first white men appeared on the central plain, an aborigine scrambled into a tree and let out a long, high-pitched shriek. The establishment of European civilization in Australia was an immense achievement, but, yet again, the heaviest price would be paid by indigenous people in the age-old clash of interests between nomadic hunter-gatherers and settled agriculturalists.

Economic growth

The earliest settlers did not readily find cash crops to make the colony self-sufficient. Lieutenant John Macarthur is credited with recognizing the immense potential of the interior for sheep farming. He developed new breeds that would flourish in the New South Wales grasslands and was able to live in the style of an English country gentleman. His example was followed by emancipated convicts and a new generation of free settlers. The influx of cheap Australian wool to the home country stimulated the Yorkshire woollen industry at a time when woollen fabrics were gaining popularity in world markets. Towards the end of the nineteenth century the development of refrigerated ships boosted the meat trade. Then, in the early years of the twentieth century, strains of wheat were developed to suit the dry climate.

Early on, it was also established that the continent possessed great mineral wealth. Gold and copper mines were in operation by the middle of the nineteenth century, and the great Broken Hills complex was opened up in 1883. Despite such development in the interior, the cities proved to be the main beneficiaries. By 1901, 65 per cent of the population lived in the six capital cities.

Political Development

Progress with self-government in Canada encouraged the British government to devolve increasing political responsibility in its colonies of European settlement. In 1901 the six colonies became states to form the Commonwealth of Australia. Old links proved decisive when Australian soldiers fought with the British army in the wars of the twentieth century.

During World War Two, however, the nation's leaders, recognizing that Britain could contribute little against an expansionist Japan, turned to the United States for support. Since the war, extensive non-British immigration into Australia, and the increasing orientation of Britain towards Europe has further weakened traditional ties.

New Zealand

European Settlement

In 1814 a group of missionaries arrived in the land that had been described by Captain Cook. It is estimated that at that time there was a population of about a quarter of a million Maori people, who had lived in complete isolation for many centuries. In 1839 Edward Gibbon Wakefield established the New Zealand Association, with a view to buying land from the tribes and organizing settlements. The British government, hoping to control the movement, formally annexed the country in the following year.

The British proclaimed equality between Maori and European people, but practice never matched theory, and the colonists' land hunger provoked the Land War of

1845–48. After further settlers arrived, many from Scotland, war broke out again in the 1860s. By 1870 the Maori people had effectively lost control of their land.

Constitution and Economy

The country was granted a constitution in 1852 and in 1907 it became a self-governing dominion within the British Empire. Its dependence on agriculture, however, left it heavily dependent on the British economy. Early prosperity was based on wool and gold, but the introduction of refrigerated shipping in the last years of the nineteenth century favoured low cost New Zealand farmers, at the expense of their British competitors. This brought a period of prosperity, and ties with Britain were reinforced by disproportionate contribution made in two world wars. As with Australia, these have weakened in the second half of the twentieth century, during which time the country has suffered from its heavy dependence on primary products.

Japan and The United States

By 1914 Britain was withdrawing from direct involvement in the Pacific region but neither the emerging Australia or New Zealand were showing potential as a regional power. The Dutch still controlled the East Indies, modern Indonesia, but only at the cost of a series of major struggles against an emerging nationalism on Bali, Sumatra, and Java. Two powers now faced each other: the United States, with forward bases in Samoa, Guam and the Philippines and the emerging power of Japan. The foundations of a major regional conflict were already laid.

North Africa

Egypt

In classical times, North Africa had been an integral part of Mediterranean civilization. After the early flowering of Islamic civilization, however, it became increasingly cut off from the countries on the northern, Christian shore of the inland sea. Egypt was for centuries isolated under Mameluke rule. When Napoleon led an army into Egypt in 1798, he took with him not only fighting men, but also scholars, who would be able to interpret the remains of the country's fabled ancient civilization.

French interest in the area survived the fall of Napoleon, and, when Mehemet Ali broke the power of the mamelukes and established effective independence from Ottoman rule, French influence remained powerful. Under Mehemet Ali and his grandson Ishmael, Egyptian power was taken south into the Sudan and along the Red Sea. Ishmael contracted with France for the construction of the Suez Canal, which was opened in 1869. He staved off financial collapse, however, by selling a controlling interest in the canal to Britain, who now controlled this lifeline to India. In 1881 the Egyptian government was threatened by a nationalist rising in Egypt and by the Mahdi in the Sudan, and Britain responded by sending a force to protect the canal. It was not intended as an army of occupation, but Britain became involved in a protracted war in the Sudan and in administering a protectorate over Egypt.

Algeria

The coast of Algeria to the west had long been the home of Barbary pirates. In the 1830s, France began a major advance into the area. The pirates were driven from their harbours, and the French moved south to the Atlas mountains. Here they met fierce resistance, led by Abd el Kadir, but they won control of the mountain passes. Military success was followed by an influx of French settlers into the coastal region.

Sub-Saharan Africa

An Unknown Continent

For centuries the interior of Africa had been viewed by the outside world as little more than a source of human merchandise. European merchants had shipped slaves by the million out of the west coast. Bedu and Tuareg tribesmen had driven them across the Sahara to the markets of North Africa; they had been carried across the Red Sea in dhows by Arab traders; they had been beaten into submission by Dutch settlers in the south. The slave trade had had a profoundly brutalizing effect on African life, far beyond the boundaries of foreign exploration.

Yet in the early nineteenth century, Africa had its own political movements. In the grasslands of West Africa, an aggressive Islam was expanding in Hausaland under the Fulani Uthman dan Fodio and in Futa Jallon, under Al-hajj Umar. Far away, in the southwest, the Bantu people were experiencing a period of unrest. Shaka founded the Zulu kingdom in 1818, setting neighbouring people on the move.

European Explorers and Missionaries

In the early days of the industrial revolution, there was a general view, vigorously fostered by Joseph Banks, that Africa was a land of unbounded wealth, which offered untapped opportunities for trade. Since Britain had most to sell, British interests funded the earliest explorers. Early explorers, such as Mungo Park, acted as commercial travellers, carrying samples of Lancashire textiles and other manufactures. Results were disappointing but some solid business was established on the coast in products such as palm oil.

By the middle of the century European interest was increasingly focused on 'the dark continent', and explorers, such as David Livingstone and H. M. Stanley became major celebrities. Livingstone maintained an interest in 'legitimate trade', which he hoped would displace the continuing traffic in slaves in Central Africa, but he travelled as a missionary. European civilization had now achieved an unassailable self-confidence. Romantic concepts of the noble savage were forgotten and it was readily assumed that Africa was in need of Christianity, Western customs, and the post-industrial working practices that alone could provide the basis for economic advance.

Explorers, mainly following the routes of the great rivers, penetrated deep into the continent. They were followed by missionaries from a wide range of denominations from Europe and America, who were at times almost as much at competition with each other as they were with traditional practice. Expectation of life for explorers, traders and missionaries in malarial West Africa could be measured in months until quinine was introduced as a prophylactic in the 1840s and even afterwards the coast was still considered unfit for European settlement.

The Scramble for Africa

In 1880 active European political interest in Africa was limited to the French colony in Algeria in the north and the British Cape Colony in the south. The old Portuguese colonies, various ex-slaving trading outposts and settlements of freed slaves retained only tenuous links with Europe. By 1914 in the whole continent, only Ethiopia was a truly independent nation. In the intervening decades the continent was divided up between colonizing powers. Lines were drawn on maps in European capitals; boundaries sometimes followed rivers, often placing a village in one country and its farm land in another. The colonizing movement was in places the focus of national policy; elsewhere it was the product of adventurers or commercial companies working on their own initiative.

The British assumption of control in Egypt provoked the jealousy of other European countries. In particular, the French army was suffering from the bitter humiliation of the defeat at Sedan in 1870. Africa offered a forum for the recovery of a lost military prestige.

France and Britain were the main protagonists in the northern half of the continent. French colonization followed two thrusts. The first came south across the Sahara from Algeria into the grasslands of West Africa. The second went east from Senegal along the upper Niger to Lake Chad towards the Nile. The British also had a dual thrust, south from Egypt and north from South Africa. The imperialist Cecil Rhodes dreamed of establishing an unbroken chain of British possessions from the Cape to Cairo. French and British forces met where the thrusts intersected at Fashoda in the southern Sudan in 1898, when for a time it seemed likely that the two countries would be involved in a colonial war.

Meanwhile the British had also established West African colonies, based on their old slaving stations. The Germans were active in West, South West and in East Africa. King Leopold of the Belgians gained control of the Congo as a private venture. This was taken over by the Belgian state in 1908. Spain won control of much of the northwestern Sahara and shared influence in Morocco with France. Italy belatedly joined the scramble by invading Libya in 1911.

In the early years colonization was largely bloodless, but the process became increasingly violent. Britain faced African revolts as far apart as the Gold Coast and Rhodesia and France the Niger and Madagascar. The brutality of King Leopold's exploitation of the Congo was exposed in 1904. In the same year a major rebellion broke out against the Germans in South West Africa, which ended when they drove the Herero people to virtual extinction in the desert. The Italian invasion of Libya was also conducted with widespread brutality. By the beginning of 1914 the redrawn map of Africa could be seen as a symbol of a dangerously aggressive and expansionist mood within Europe.

South Africa

The Great Trek

During the Napoleonic Wars Britain occupied the Cape of Good Hope, and the territory was retained, as the Cape Colony, in 1814 for its strategic value in controlling the sea routes to the east. At that time, however, there were no British settlers, the land being shared between nomadic Bushmen and Hottentots and Afrikaans-speaking Boers of Dutch and French Huguenot origin. Soon the new government began to bring in thousands of British settlers. The Boers were angered when their black slaves were freed and laws were introduced that they considered to be unduly favourable to the previously subject black people. In 1835 some 10,000 Boers left their homes at the Cape and settled on land of the Vaal and Orange Rivers. More Boers followed when the British annexed their republic of Natal. The settlers set up the new republics of Transvaal and the Orange Free State where they could live free from British interference.

The movement of the Boers from the south coincided with migrations of Bantu people, displaced by the Zulu kingdom. The two people clashed, but the main losers were the native nomadic people, who were driven to a precarious existence in the desert.

The Boer War

Resentment between Boers and the British continued to grow. The British briefly annexed the Transvaal, and, although they withdrew, this left the Boers feeling that they would never be left in peace. Then, in 1886, gold was discovered in the Transvaal, and, within a few years, a new city of Johannesburg had grown to a population of 100,000. Most of the newcomers were British, but they were excluded from the running of the republic. Angry that the world's great empire, the modern Rome, could be frustrated by a small number of intransigent Boer farmers, Cecil Rhodes provoked a confrontation. President Kruger of the Transvaal, an implacable opponent of British rule, responded with an ultimatum, and war broke out in 1899.

Liberal opinion in Britain and Europe saw the Boers as an oppressed minority, and, when they were finally defeated in 1902, there was pressure for a generous settlement. A few voices were raised in the British parliament to defend the rights of the black peoples, but these found no support. In 1909 the four territories were brought together into the self-governing Union of South Africa, which lost little time in passing laws that discriminated against the non-white peoples. In 1948 the Afrikaans-speaking people won power within the country and put in place the formal structure of apartheid.

12

The Nation State in Crisis

The Eastern Question

The Decline of Ottoman Power

In 1683 armies of the Ottoman empire laid siege to the city of Vienna for the second time and Europe was threatened once more from the East. The armies withdrew, but the Emperor at Istanbul still controlled almost three quarters of the Mediterranean coastline—North Africa, the Arab lands of the Middle East, the homeland of Turkey, Greece and the Balkans.

By the eighteenth century, statesmen could recognize that the Ottoman Empire, like other empires before it, was in decline. Administration was clumsy, and the sultan had to rely on local rulers, whose loyalty was often in doubt. Also, the social military structure of the empire was becoming increasingly out of date.

Russian Objectives

Russian statesmen took the closest interest in the Ottoman decline. Peter the Great had won a warm water port, but, for both trade and strategic reasons, the country still badly needed an outlet into the Mediterranean Sea. In 1768–74 Catherine the Great fought a successful war against the Turks and won the Crimea and other territory on the north bank of the Black Sea along with rights of navigation into the Mediterranean. She also established that Russia had the right to act as protector of eastern Christians within the Turkish dominions.

Russia continued to make advances after the defeat of Napoleon. She won control of the ancestral Ottoman homeland in the grasslands east of the Caspian Sea, taking her empire as far as the mountain passes of the Himalayas. Still further east, she won the Pacific port of Vladivostok from the Chinese. Russian territorial ambitions were backed by huge military forces, and other European powers perceived her as an aggressive imperial power.

Concern focused on the fate of the Turkish European territories. In a private conversation with the British ambassador, Tsar Nicholas I described Turkey as 'the sick man of Europe'. He implied that it would be better for the powers to consider how to share the sick man's possessions, rather than to wait and fight over them when he died. Other powers, however, preferred to support Turkey so that it could continue to act as a check on Russian ambitions in Eastern Europe.

In 1841 the European powers came together in the Convention of the Straits to guarantee Turkish independence. It was agreed then that the Bosphorus should be closed to all ships of war. This shut Russia out of the Mediterranean, and meant that she could not protect her merchant ships, now carrying increasing grain exports by the Black Sea.

The Crimean War

In 1851 Russia invaded Turkey's Danube lands, and in 1853 her navy sank the Turkish fleet, so winning back her outlet to the Mediterranean. Excitement ran high in Paris and London. Napoleon III was looking for a way of rebuilding the family's military prestige. Britain was concerned for her links with India, for, although the Suez Canal was not yet built, traffic was already following the Mediterranean route. In March 1954 the two powers declared war on Russia in support of Turkey. Combined forces were despatched to capture the Russian naval base at Sebastopol in the Crimea. The huge Russian army was unable to dislodge the invading force and in 1856 she was forced to accept peace on the terms that she would keep no fleet in the Black Sea and build no bases on its shores.

The battles of the Crimean War were made famous because the armies were followed by a journalist, who published detailed reports in the London *Times*. For the first time in history, the public was able to read first hand reports of the sufferings of the soldiers. The modern profession of nursing dates itself from the work done by Florence Nightingale and her staff in this campaign.

Disintegration

Victory over Russia in the Crimean War could not long delay the final disintegration of the Ottoman Empire. France and Britain, who had fought as allies of the Turks, were happy to help themselves to territory in North Africa. Britain also occupied Cyprus and extended her influence in the Middle East. Russia continued her forward movement in the less sensitive territory to the east of the Caspian Sea. In Eastern Europe, Greece was already independent and in the half century after the end of the Crimean War, Serbia, Romania and Bulgaria would also break free. Russia, always ready to stand as protector of the oppressed Slav peoples, went to war with Turkey again in 1877. For a time Europe stood on the brink of another war as the powers prepared to shore up the tottering empire once again. However, in 1878, Russia, faced by the combination of Prussia, Austria and Britain, was forced to accept terms at the Congress of Berlin.

In 1907 rebellion broke out in Turkey itself. A group, who called themselves the Young Turks, demanded constitutional reforms, along European lines. In 1909 the long reigning Abdul-Hamid was deposed. The new rulers dressed their government as a constitutional monarchy, but it was effectively a dictatorship, dedicated to reviving Turkish power, at home and in the remaining Ottoman lands of the Middle East.

Nationalism

Western Europe

The Napoleonic conquests and the reactions against them had aroused fierce emotions of nationalism, which were to influence European politics. Germany and Italy began their discovery of a national identity (Chapter 8), but the mood also affected smaller peoples, such as Belgians and Norwegians. Britain had her own problems in Ireland. The situation was complicated by the fact that Westminster politicians had to reconcile two vocal nationalist groups. The majority Catholics considered themselves to be under a foreign power, discriminated against in their religion and insecure in their land holding. The minority Protestants of the north, mostly of Scots descent, used their political connections with English conservatives to defend accustomed privileges. After 1848, however, concern on issues of nationality centred on eastern Europe.

Poland

Russia might stand as the liberator of oppressed Slav peoples in the Balkans, but, on her own western frontier, she was the oppressor. The decline of Poland began with long wars against Sweden, which ended in 1709. Depopulated and weakened, with no natural frontiers, she stood between aggressive powers to east and west. In the last decades of the eighteenth century, she was partitioned between Russia, Austria and Prussia. A supposedly free Poland, created in 1815, was effectively a Russian colony. A series of nationalist rebellions were a failure and Russian administrators tried to eliminate all traces of Polish nationalism, insisting that even primary school children should be taught in the Russian language.

The Austro-Hungarian Empire

Metternich recognized very clearly that the new nationalism could undermine the whole structure of the Austrian empire. The house of Hapsburg ruled over different nationalities, speaking a wide range of languages. Defeat by Prussia and then the loss of Italy had pushed the western boundaries of the once great empire back to the Austrian heartland. Alone of all the major European powers, landlocked Austria was not in a position to participate in the scramble for colonial possessions. Any expansion had to be towards the east, and foreign policy now focused on the Danube and the Balkans.

The new nationalists of the region, however, saw Austria, as much as Turkey as a threat to their aspirations. The Hungarians exploited the weakness of the Empire after the Prussian victory at Sadowa to negotiate a new Covenant with Vienna. The Hapsburgs now ruled a dual Austro-Hungarian empire, in which military and foreign policy was coordinated, but in other ways the eastern part had virtual self-government. The new Hungarian section of the Empire contained a number of national minorities, and trouble was never far from the surface.

In 1878, after the war between Russia and Turkey, Bosnia and Herzegovina were placed under Austrian administration, and in 1908 they were annexed by Austria. The independent Serbia, with Russian support, now stood as the focus of pan-Slavic aspirations, and so as protector of the nationalist movements in the two territories. The Austrian government, angry at this subversion, looked for an opportunity of crushing Serbia.

Russia

Despotism

In the decades before the Crimean War, Russia was ruled by the autocratic Tsar Nicholas I. He tried to keep all western ideas of liberalism and socialism at bay by a suffocating censorship. At the same time the administration became ever more corrupt and inefficient. The repression of this period was primarily directed against the intelligentsia, who were traditionally close to developments in the west. Nicholas did recognize, however, that the position of the serfs had become such an anomaly that it endangered the Russian state. As in France before the Revolution, these poorest people had to carry by far the bulk of the load of taxation. Nicholas declared a desire to make changes and he did make progress in codifying peasants' rights and bringing them within the legal system. He was unable, however, to tackle the medieval structure of serfdom, which tied the mass of the people to their villages, and left them as the virtual possessions of their masters.

Emancipation and Reform

Nicholas was succeeded by his son, Alexander II, during the Crimean War. The failure of the superior Russian armies and the humiliating nature of the peace, left no doubt that the state needed radical overhaul. Although conservative by nature, the new Tsar supervised a major overhaul of the army, the law and the administrative system.

Most difficult, he put in train the process of emancipation for the serfs. 'Better,' he said, 'to abolish serfdom from above, than to wait till it begins to abolish itself from below.' Emancipation was pronounced in 1861, but problems still remained to be solved. Landlords needed to be compensated and a system had established whereby the peasants could buy their own land. This took the form of a tax, which left many, in practice, worse off than they had been before emancipation.

The Prelude to Revolution

The first shot was fired at Alexander only five years after his emancipation decree; he was assassinated in 1881. The reforms of his reign were matched with a continued autocracy, which aroused profound frustration, particularly amongst the intelligentsia. The education system, in particular, was subject to the tightest control by a reactionary bureaucracy. Also during these years, individuals within government gave support to pogroms against the Jews. After the murder of Alexander II in 1881, government fell increasingly into the hands of the opponents of reform.

Opposition was divided between liberals, socialists and groups of nihilists, all of whose leaders were drawn from the intelligentsia. They appealed first to the suffering peasants, demanding a programme of land reform. Towards the end of the century, however, large numbers of peasants were leaving the land to make up the industrial proletariat of the long delayed industrial revolution. Revolutionary activists now found it productive to work in the growing slums of the cities, building up revolutionary cells of workers.

Success is the ultimate justification of autocratic government, and defeat by Japan in 1905 brought the imperial government to the brink of collapse. The battleship *Potemkin* mutinied and terrorized the Black Sea. Massive strikes, particularly by railway workers, crippled the economy. In October 1905 the Socialist groups organized themselves into the First Soviet, based on the principle of the cells that had been established in the factories. Nicholas II, like Louis XVI before him, was forced to attempt to rally national unity by calling a national parliament, or *duma*. Experiments in representative democracy were, however, halfhearted and failed. In the years that followed, the weak Tsar shut himself increasingly within his family circle, now increasingly dominated by the eccentric Rasputin. When the European war broke out in 1914, Russia was ill prepared for such a disaster.

The Armed Peace

The Alliances

In the years after 1871, there were two fixed points in European diplomacy. Austria and Russia faced each other over the control of the liberated Turkish lands in the Balkans. Fighting could break out at any time within the region, leading to the risk of 'superpower involvement'. France also, smarting from defeat at Sadowa and the occupation of Paris, was chronically hostile to Germany. She was, however, militarily weak and the autocratic powers of Austria and Russia looked on her as a threat, and so she remained isolated and impotent.

In previous centuries, alliances had been formed under the immediate threat of war, and they had disintegrated immediately after the threat was over. During these decades, however, the European powers began to form themselves into permanent alliances, committed to help each other in the event of war. By the beginning of the twentieth century, a new alignment of powers had become established. Germany allied with Austria, and they were later to be joined by Italy to form the Triple Alliance. To meet this threat, France and Russia joined to form the Dual Alliance. Britain was not a significant continental power, and as late as 1898 the two countries narrowly avoided a colonial war. In 1904, however, policy changed dramatically as Britain concluded a nonbinding *entente cordiale* with France, which was followed by a similar agreement with Russia. Hostility towards Germany increased as the German government set about a major naval construction programme, which was interpreted as a direct threat to Britain. The British government responded with its own programme, and a major arms race was under way.

Military Strategy

With Europe organized into armed camps, the generals considered strategy in the event of conflict. Failing to take account of the bloody attrition of the American Civil War, they assumed that events would be settled, as in Bismark's wars, by one swift, decisive campaign. Germany was faced with the prospect of fighting on two fronts. Strategists decided that, while the Russian war machine was massive, the bureaucratic inefficiency would prevent rapid deployment of forces. They therefore developed a plan that, in the event of impending war, the German army would make a first strike to knock out France, so that it could then give its full attention to the eastern front.

In the early years of the century, there was a mood of militarism throughout Europe, fed by accounts of colonial wars and victories against non European people. It was most evident in Germany, where theorists declared that war was the natural state of man, but it spread much wider. In Britain, for instance, metaphors of war and sport were subtly mingled in the public school education of the nation's elite.

The Outbreak of War

Austria and Serbia

By the summer of 1914 Serbian support for rebels in Bosnia and Herzegovina had brought relationships with Austria to a low state. On 28 June 1914 the heir to the throne, the Archduke Franz Ferdinand, and his wife were murdered in the Bosnian capital of Sarajevo. Encouraged by her ally Germany, Austria used this as a pretext for invading Serbia on 28 July. On 30 July Tsar Nicholas II ordered mobilization, not only in the Balkans, but along the whole border.

First Strike

It appears that, at the last moment, Kaiser Wilhelm II of Germany may have had doubts about plunging Europe into war. The British foreign minister tried to gather support for a conference to localize the conflict, but the German war machine was now moving under its own impetus. On 3 August Germany attacked France through undefended neutral Belgium. Italy declared that the conflict was none of her concern, so the central powers of Germany and Austria faced France and Russia. Britain had no treaty obligation to enter the war on behalf of France, but did consider herself bound by the guarantee made to Belgium after the 1830 uprising. Her formal position for taking up arms was therefore as defender of the rights of small nations. Italy later entered the war on the side of the Allies, as they were now called, while Turkey and Bulgaria aligned themselves with the Central Powers. Military enthusiasts forecast a short war, to be decided by Christmas, but the British Foreign Secretary, Sir Edward Grey warned, 'The lamps are going out all over Europe. We shall not see them lit again in our lifetime.'

War and Revolution

Stalemate

The German first strike strategy involved high risk. Russia mobilized more rapidly than anticipated and the German army was defeated at Grumbinnen on 20 August. In early September the western offensive became bogged down on the Marne. Germany was fighting the war on two fronts, which her generals had feared. On the western front, the opposing armies dug in for their long years of attrition. The new German navy remained in port as the British fleet set about sapping German resistance by blockade. Allied attempts to break the stalemate by offensives in the Dardanelles and Salonika, were unsuccessful.

The Russian Revolution

The huge open spaces of the eastern front kept war more mobile. Early Russian success was undermined by the failure of the political structure. In March 1917 a wave of unrest swept the Tsar from power. The opposition was divided between liberal politicians, who now set up a provisional government and the socialist Soviet—itself divided between the moderates and a radical Bolshevik wing. The moderate provisional government pledged itself to continue the war, but in April the Bolshevik, Vladimir Ilyich Lenin, returned from exile and announced the arrival of world revolution. Russian workers, he claimed, should not be dying in a bosses' war. The provisional government staked everything on a last great offensive, but this failed, and on 7 November, Lenin staged a Bolshevik coup d'état. In March 1918 he concluded peace between his newly born Soviet Union and the Central Powers at Brest Litovsk. In July of 1918 the Tsar and his family were shot at Yekaterinburg.

American Intervention

Germany now had to fight on only one front, but, during this period, another, even more formidable enemy had been drawn into the war. Desperate at the success of the British naval blockade, the German navy mounted its own submarine blockade of

Britain. To be successful it had to attack American ships that were carrying supplies to Britain. This brought the United States into the conflict in April 1917. The German High Command recognized that the intervention of American troops would tilt the battle against the Central Powers, but it staked everything on defeating Britain and France before the Americans arrived. 1917 and 1918 saw huge and costly offensives from both sides on the western front. In the Autumn of 1918 Germany's allies, Austria and Bulgaria began to crumble, the German fleet mutinied and there was increasing unrest in the German cities. Finally the Kaiser abdicated and the generals sued for peace.

The World of Versailles

The Cost of War

All the major continental nations emerged weakened from the First World War. Russia, involved in civil war, was no longer a factor in international politics. France, although victorious, had suffered grievously. Austria was now not a power of significance. Germany, although defeated, was no longer surrounded by serious rivals. Loss of life had been severe in all the combatant nations, but wealth had also drained away. The United States was the main beneficiary of the war at a cost of fewer casualties than had been suffered by the Dominion of Australia. In the past she had been a major debtor nation, but now she moved into a period of being the world's main creditor nation.

A New World

The war was also an emotional and intellectual landmark. It was as if the great optimism, which had buoyed up a successful and expansionist Europe was suddenly pierced. The belief in an inevitable tide of progress, prevalent since the time of Descartes, no longer seemed tenable in the face of sustained barbarity on European soil. Liberal thinkers, in disciplines such as theology as well as in politics, found themselves on the defensive. New absolutisms, of both left and right, emerged in confrontation, both threatening to overwhelm traditions of representative government.

The conflict had also brought permanent changes in the structure of society. Women, who had been mobilized to fill men's jobs, could no longer be denied political and a growing economic emancipation. The war brought technological advances in areas such as aeronautics and the development of motor vehicles. Output had increased to meet the demands of a technological war, and, in the process, labour unions had established a stronger position for themselves. Many felt threatened by the rapid social change, evident in almost every field of life.

In the years before the war, artists had already been working in strange and disturbing new forms. Stravinsky's *Rite of Spring* and Picasso's *Demoiselles d'Avignon* created scandal in their fields. In 1922, Joyce's *Ulysses* dispensed with the convention of the English novel. It seemed as though all recognizable values were now fractured as creative artists abandoned both classical and romantic forms to explore abstraction and an inner life, now provided with a whole new vocabulary by the works of Sigmund Freud. The arrival of jazz from America, exploiting the interaction between African and European popular music, only served to heighten the alarm of traditionalists.

The Treaties

The Treaty of Versailles, ratified by Germany in July 1919, was the first of a series of treaties imposed on the defeated Central Powers. The leading architects of the new order were President Woodrow Wilson of the United States, Georges Clemenceau, premier of France and David Lloyd George, prime minister of Britain. Clemenceau, recognizing the continuing potential of Germany, pressed for financial reparations, intended to retard industrial recovery, the return of Alsace-Lorraine to France, and the demilitarization of the Rhineland. The map of eastern Europe was redrawn, with Poland, Hungary, Czechoslovakia and Yugoslavia created as new nations. In the north, Finland, which had won independence from Russia in 1917, was joined by the three newly independent Baltic States, Estonia, Latvia and Lithuania. The pattern of nationalities was, however, more complex than could be accommodated within national boundaries, and all these nations had substantial minorities. Of greatest significance for the future, substantial numbers of German-speaking people found themselves within Czechoslovakia and Poland. The treaties attempted to protect minority rights, but there was considerable movement of peoples across national boundaries. The largest movement came at the end of the war between Greece and Turkey from 1920 to 1922. In particular, Greek people left the coast of Asia Minor, where they had lived since ancient times. The two communities continued in uneasy coexistence in Cyprus.

The treaties also changed the wider world. Germany's East and West African possessions were divided between Britain and France, while Southwest Africa, the future Namibia, was placed under the trusteeship of South Africa. The concept of trusteeship was also used to extend western influence over the old Ottoman territories of the Middle East.

The League of Nations

President Wilson hoped that his country, with its democratic tradition, could take the lead in creating a new atmosphere of goodwill. He therefore proposed a League of Nations, which would serve as guardian of world peace. Wilson was to be bitterly disappointed when his own Congress refused to let the United States join the new body. Unhappy about the way in which their country had been plunged into European affairs, the majority of Americans were anxious to return to a traditional isolationism. It became evident that the new body lacked credibility as early as 1920, when Poland successfully seized Vilna from Lithuania. Later incidents reinforced the fact that successful international collaboration to repel aggression could not be organized through the League. The Italian government took full advantage when, in Europe's final African venture, it launched an attack on Ethiopia in 1935.

Ireland

Attempts by prewar Liberal administrations to give home rule to Ireland had been frustrated by the collaboration of Ulster Protestants and conservative politicians. Prime Minister Lloyd George now faced destructive guerilla warfare from nationalists. In 1921 the moderate nationalists accepted partition of the island, which left a significant Catholic minority within the Protestant-dominated northern provinces. This led to civil war within the new Irish Free State, and laid the foundations of continuing strife in the north.

The World Economy

The Postwar Boom

During the 1920s world trade appeared to be returning to its prewar vigour, but, even during these boom years, there were signs of problems ahead. The war had created an increased potential for production, but demand was stagnant. The Soviet Union was in no position to import goods from abroad, and new nations raised tariff barriers to protect fledgling industries. The United States now produced over half of all the world's manufactures, but American consumers, like the Japanese 70 years later, showed little desire to buy goods from abroad and domestic industry was protected by import duties.

As industry boomed, so the price of raw materials, including agricultural products, decreased, creating problems for primary producers. At the same time, the fact that workers did not share the profits of their industries, brought outbursts of industrial unrest, such as the British General Strike of 1926.

The Great Depression

By 1928 world trade had become heavily dependent on American finance. In that year Wall Street experienced The Great Bull Market as the price of shares rose to unrealistic heights. Then, on 28 October 1929, the stock market crashed. American capital for investment dried up, leading to a rapid world wide collapse of industrial confidence. Governments took what action they could to protect their own industries against imports, so further inhibiting world trade. It is estimated that at the depth of the recession in 1932 industrial production in the United States and Germany was only half of what it had been three years earlier. Unemployment reached record levels in all the industrial countries, bringing times of great hardship.

The New Deal

In America, the parties divided over the political response to the problems. The Republicans, favouring a traditional *laissez-faire* approach, were defeated in the 1932 elections by a Democratic party, led by Franklin Roosevelt. He instituted a New Deal, based on substantial public investment. The showpiece was the publicly owned Tennessee Valley Authority. Designed to provide an industrial infrastructure for one of the country's poorest regions. Roosevelt won great popularity, going on to win an unprecedented four presidential elections, but the improvement brought by the New Deal was as much psychological as practical, and real recovery had to await the stimulus of a second world war.

The Rise of the Dictators

Italy

In the elections of 1921, a new party won just 36 seats in the Italian parliament. Its leader, Benito Mussolini had a background as a socialist, but he now proclaimed that he would save Italy from the menace of communism. The party appealed to ancient Rome in its extended arm salute and the symbol of the *fasces*, which gave the movement its name. The black-shirted fascists used intimidation, first to come to power and then to eliminate all political opposition. Mussolini's rule achieved some legitimacy when, in 1929, he negotiated a treaty with the highly conservative papacy.

Germany

The Austrian-born Adolf Hitler became leader of the German National Socialist, or Nazi, party in 1921. Having failed in an early attempt to take control of the Bavarian government, he set about reorganizing his party as a military movement, not hesitating to purge his own followers. He directed his appeal to a German people, who were frustrated by military defeat, humiliated by the loss of empire and European territory, and, in many cases, impoverished by hyper-inflation. Hitler's philosophy was laid out in his early book *Mein Kampf*. This described both his military ambitions for Germany, and his obsessive hatred of the Jewish people.

The struggle appeared to lie between Hitler's new right, and the parties of the left. But the left was divided. The communists, taking their orders from Moscow, attempted, and sometimes succeeded, in fomenting revolution. The social democrats were therefore forced into alliance with conservative military leaders. Capitalizing on these divisions and on the economic problems brought by the Depression, Hitler took his Nazi party to power in 1933. He then quickly set up a reign of terror. While the Jews were the prime target, political opponents, gypsies, the handicapped, and anybody not considered to be of true Aryan descent also suffered. Despite this, his popularity remained high among most Germans. His armaments and other public works programmes appeared to be bringing a return of prosperity, while military success retrieved national pride.

The Soviet Union

The Bolshevik revolution of 1917 was followed by three years of civil war, during which White Russian armies, supported by foreign troops, tried to overthrow the new communist state. Lenin and his followers emerged successful, but at huge cost. It is estimated that some 13 million died in the war and through the famine it caused; economic life was at a standstill. In 1921, as an emergency measure, Lenin largely freed the economy and recovery followed rapidly.

Lenin died in January 1924, leaving two men contending the succession. Trotsky proclaimed that the new society could only flourish within a communist world, and the prime task was therefore to export the revolution. His opponent, Stalin, argued that the priority was to rebuild the Soviet Union, by creating 'communism within one state'. When Stalin emerged victorious, it appeared as though the forces of moderation had prevailed.

Stalin assumed autocratic power and created a personality cult, not dissimilar to those constructed around the fascist dictators. He set himself the objective of changing the Soviet Union from a largely medieval economy, to a major modern state within a few decades. This involved the conversion of agriculture from its peasant structure by wholesale collectivization, and the rapid development of heavy industry. The programme was forced through at huge human cost. Industrially the results were dramatic. Production of coal, iron and steel and other basics increased many times over. The expansion of heavy industry was, however, bought at the expense of consumer goods, and the people, were constantly disappointed in the promised general improvement in living standards. Peasants on the collective farms, also resentful at being expected to produce low cost food for the growing cities for little return, remained obstinately unproductive.

Stalin's increasingly paranoiac behaviour was now demonstrated in a series of show trials and purges. Virtually all the old political leaders and a high proportion of military officers were executed to ensure that nobody would be able to challenge for power. Millions more suffered and died in labour camps. The new administrators of the country were tied to Stalin by a common guilt, and by an increasing web of petty corruption.

Spain

By the 1930s the days in which Spain had been a great European power were long past, and she had therefore avoided involvement in the First World War. In 1933 a right wing government came to power, which provoked rebellion by national minorities. In early 1936 a left wing government was elected with a large majority. General Franco, modelling himself on the fascist dictators, led a mutiny of the army in Morocco and invaded the mainland. The army, the political right and the Roman Catholic church aligned with Franco, while left wing groups and the national minorities aligned with the elected government. Franco received assistance from the fascist states, while the government was supported by the Soviet Union and a variety of international volunteers. The bitter war lasted until 1939, when Franco achieved the position of dictator, which he held until his death in 1975.

The Second World War in the West

German Expansion

From the beginning, Hitler followed a programme for the creation of a German empire in central Europe. His first objective was to win back land lost at Versailles; he then planned to conquer the whole of mainland Europe, including European Russia, and create an empire in which 'lower' races, such as the Slavs, would be reduced to a servile status. He exploited the weakness of the League of Nations, American isolationism, and lack of unity among other European powers in a series of successes—the recovery of the Saarland by plebiscite, the remilitarization of the Rhineland, unification with Austria, and finally the dismemberment of Czechoslovakia. When Britain and France acquiesced to the last of these at Munich, it appeared as though no other power had the will to frustrate his ambitions.

In 1939 Hitler and Stalin concluded the Nazi-Soviet Pact to preserve Russian neutrality. The Soviet Union was awarded eastern Poland and took the opportunity to advance further into the Baltic States and Finland, where Russian armies were halted by fierce national resistance. Unlike Czechoslovakia, Poland was protected by treaty links with Britain and France, and the German invasion provoked a joint ultimatum and war. Mussolini took the opportunity of entering the war in support of Germany and invading Greece.

German Successes

After defeating Poland, in 1940, the German army repeated the 1914 tactic of invading France across Belgium. This time Paris fell and a puppet government was installed in southern France. Successful campaigns to the north and south reduced Denmark, Norway, Yugoslavia and Greece. In early 1941 the Afrika Corps landed in Libya and within two months was threatening Cairo and the Suez Canal. Britain, now rallied by the charismatic leader, Winston Churchill, held off an air offensive, intended to prepare the way for invasion, in the Battle of Britain.

On 22 June 1941 Hitler launched Operation Barbarossa against an unprepared Soviet Union. The invasion followed the logic of Hitler's master plan, but it dangerously overstretched German resources. The imbalance was made greater when the Japanese attack on Pearl Harbour brought the United States into the war in December of the same year. Stalin demonstrated his character as a national leader in rallying his people for a massively costly defence. The war turned in November 1942, when the Russians broke the German front at Stalingrad and a British army defeated the Afrika Corps at El Alamein. Once the Allies had re-established a western front with the Normandy landings of June 1944, the final defeat in 1945 was inevitable.

The years from 1939–45 gave a new and terrible meaning to warfare. The Germans mobilized conquered people for slave labour, and perpetrated mass genocide on European Jewry; the Russians deported whole national populations for alleged collaboration; residential areas of cities were targeted in indiscriminate bombing by both sides. Among some 50 million dead were an estimated 27 million Russians, 6 million Jews and $4^1/_2$ million Poles.

Europe Divided

The Yalta Settlement

The future political shape of Europe was negotiated in February 1945 at a conference at Yalta in the Crimea, attended by Stalin, Roosevelt and Churchill. Germany was to be partitioned and the countries of Eastern Europe were to form a zone of Russian influence. In the event, Austria and Greece—the latter after civil war—remained within the western sphere.

The Recovery of Western Europe

At the end of the war, western Europe was in a state of serious economic collapse. Once again, there were large movements of displaced people, and food shortages continued for years after the war. In June 1947, the US Secretary of State, George Marshall, announced a major aid programme, directed, 'not against any country or doctrine, but against hunger, poverty, desperation and chaos'. The Soviet Union was offered the chance of participating but turned it down. The Marshall Plan provided much needed capital for reconstruction.

The United Nations

During the last years of the war, thought was given to the reasons why the League of Nations had failed to preserve world peace. In 1945 representatives of the nations met in San Francisco to set up the new United Nations. In its constitution, great influence was given to the Security Council, which had five 'great powers' as permanent members and representatives of other nations. The right of veto given to the great powers, but at least all the major powers were now involved in the organization and debates were subject to the scrutiny of the world media.

The European Community

Some European leaders now argued that the nation state was no longer capable of providing a secure structure for world peace. In particular, the long standing enmity between France and Germany was no longer tolerable. In 1952, the Federal Republic of Germany, France, Italy, Holland, Belgium and Luxembourg, formed the European Economic Community. This was designed to be both a trading group, capable of competing with the new superpowers, and also a stabilizing influence on the volatile European political scene.

The Cold War in Europe

It soon became clear that European nationalism had run its destructive course, and the danger to world peace now lay in the confrontation of the United States and the Soviet Union. In the words of Winston Churchill, an 'iron curtain' had descended across Europe.

The Soviet Union emerged from the Second World War in control of a vast empire. It had inherited imperial conquests, and had further added the Baltic Republics. It also now controlled puppet regimes in Eastern Europe, bound together in the Warsaw Pact, which maintained huge land forces on its western front. Stalin's policy was still primarily directed at preserving national security, which had been so devastatingly violated by Hitler's army. He and later Soviet leaders therefore felt threatened by American superiority in nuclear weapons. A crash nuclear programme was put in hand and advances in rocketry were clearly illustrated when, in April 1961, Yuri Gagarin became the first man to be launched into space.

America and her allies in the North Atlantic Treaty Organization (NATO) relied heavily on nuclear superiority. The Americans responded to the Russian space programme and, in July 1969, with a wondering world watching on television, men were placed on the moon.

Berlin, divided between the four occupying powers, lay exposed within the Russian area of influence and in 1948–49 conflict loomed as the Russians shut off western communications with the city. A later crisis ended with the building of the Berlin Wall in 1961. This stood for the next 28 years as a potent symbol of the Cold War and the division of Europe into two hostile camps.

13

After Empire

The Expansion of Japan.

The Beginnings of Aggression

The 1914–18 war brought prosperity to the rising Japanese economy. European competition in Asian markets was reduced and Japanese factories were able to export to the combatants. During this period, heavy industries, such as shipbuilding, were able to build up a firm base. Competition returned in the postwar boom years, but Japan continued to export successfully. During the boom years, companies reinvested profits in preparation for more difficult times. Japanese industry, none the less, suffered badly in the Depression. With foreign markets closed and the home market as yet undeveloped, industry worked at only a fraction of capacity. The weakness was exacerbated by the country's lack of raw materials. Foreign policy therefore became directed at the winning control of the export markets and natural resources of East Asia. China was the first target for expansion.

China's Weakness

After the fall of the Manchu Empire in 1912, China plunged back into chaos. Sun Yat-sen's Nationalist (Kuomintang) party struggled for power with independent war lords. During this time communist cells were coming into existence. Following Marxist orthodoxy, they initially concentrated on the cities, but later, under the influence of the rising Mao Tse-tung, they worked increasingly among the mass of the peasants, who had suffered greatly during the upheavals. Under his influence, the communists built up communes in scattered and remote areas. Sun Yat-sen died in 1925, to be succeeded as Kuomintang leader by the more conservative Chiang Kai-shek. After a period of collaboration, Chiang attempted to exterminate the communist opposition. Driven from their southern bases, the communists only survived by coming together in the Long March of 1934–35 and establishing a new northern headquarters, based on Yenan.

The War in the East

The Attack on China

Japan exploited the weakness and growing corruption of the Kuomintang government by strengthening its control over Manchuria and areas of the north in the early 1930s. In 1936 the Kuomintang and the communists made common cause against the foreigners, but in the following year, Japan launched a major assault on China. In December 1937 the Japanese army captured the capital at Nanking and the Chinese government had to retreat to remote Szechwan, leaving the Japanese in control of the north, and most of the Pacific coast, including the major industrial cities.

Victory brought Japan into conflict with the Pacific colonial powers, and their concessionary ports were blockaded. The Americans and British responded by supplying Chiang Kai-shek along the Burma Road, and the United States renounced its commercial agreement with Japan.

Control of the Pacific

Japanese foreign policy was now set on winning control over the whole of the Pacific rim. With the outbreak of war in Europe, she allied herself with Germany. Then in 1941, as German troops were sweeping into Russia, she launched her first attack on French Indo-China. On 7 December 1941 her air force attacked the American navy in Pearl Harbour, Hawaii, and, at the same time, she launched assaults on the Dutch in Indonesia and the British in Malaysia and Burma. The campaigns were brilliantly successful and by mid-1942 both India and Australia were under threat.

Defeat and the Atom Bomb

The attack on Pearl Harbour put and end to isolationism and united Americans behind President Roosevelt. As the world's greatest industrial power became geared for war, the tide turned against Japan. In June 1942 the Japanese fleet suffered a reverse at the battle of Midway Island, and thereafter a relentless American offensive drove them from their Pacific conquests, while the British also fought back through Burma. From November 1944 the Japanese cities came under direct air attack. The war ended with the use of the new atomic weapon on the cities of Hiroshima and Nagasaki in August 1945.

Decolonialization

The Japanese victories, and, in particular, the fall of Singapore on 15 February 1942, involved a profound loss of face for the colonizing powers. The invading armies were seen by many Asians as liberators from western regimes. Many of those who had assumed control, under Japanese direction, now became prominent in independence movements. The United States handed over political control of the Philippines in 1946 after negotiating a continued military presence. The Dutch, themselves newly liberated, at first fought to preserve their possessions but in 1948 they accepted the independence of the Republic of Indonesia. The British fought a communist rebellion in Malaya before handing over to a more acceptable national government in 1957. The French became involved in a long war for Indo-China before being defeated in 1954.

China and her Neighbours

Communist China

The fall of Japan left the two forces of the Kuomintang and the communists vying for the control of China. China's miseries continued when civil war broke out in 1947. In one battle, half a million men were engaged on each side. By 1949 the communists were gaining the upper hand and in May 1950 Chiang Kai-shek retreated to Taiwan with his government.

The new communist government was faced by a huge task of reconstruction. According to Mao's estimate, some 800,000 'enemies of the people' were executed, largely from the old village landlord class. The communists had long experience with the collectivization of agriculture within their own territories, and they did not follow Stalin's example of imposing it from above. Peasants were organized to control their own operations and, despite setbacks, the conditions of life for the mass of people improved.

Mao Tse-tung capitalized on the age-old Chinese respect for authority to provide a strong central government, which had for so long been lacking. He adapted western Marxist ideology to traditional thought patterns, and showed a strong hostility to western culture, which was given full rein in the Cultural Revolution, which he launched in 1966.

To western eyes, China appeared now to be a part of a united Communist bloc, intent on achieving world dominance. In practice, however, Mao had largely rejected the Russian brand of communism. By the 1960s, acute strains were appearing in the relationship between the two countries. When China developed its own nuclear capability in 1964, it was primarily as a deterrent against potential Russian aggression. The Chinese reconquest of the old province of Tibet also led to a successful war with India in 1962.

The Korean War

In 1945 the Japanese colony of Korea was occupied by Russian troops from the north and Americans from the south. This led to partition, with both governments claiming the whole country. In 1950 the northern armies invaded the south. The United States and other western nations, with the backing of a United Nations resolution, responded by sending forces to support the south.

For a time it appeared as though the north would be defeated, but China, concerned at her own security, sent an army across the border. The American President Truman refused to become involved in a war on Chinese soil, and the war was concluded in 1953 by an armistice that perpetuated partition.

Conflict of Ideologies

American analysts saw the communist strategy in South East Asia and being a process of 'slicing the salami'. Territories were to fall to communism, not in one major conflict, but one by one. The communist uprisings, which faced almost every nation of South East Asia in the coming decades, were in fact little coordinated and variously owned allegiance to Moscow, Peking or neither. That in the new nation of Indonesia was put down with great violence.

American policy became dedicated to holding the line against communism in the region. This involved providing support to noncommunist regimes, including Chinese nationalist government in Taiwan. The United States was therefore deeply involved in the politics of the region.

The French defeat in Indo-China left the new country of Vietnam divided, with a communist regime under the old nationalist Ho Chi Minh established in the north. The United States became increasingly involved in the struggle, supporting unstable noncommunist administrations, based in the southern capital of Saigon. In 1965, faced with the possibility of the defeat of the client regime by the northern-backed Vietcong guerillas, President Johnson authorized massive involvement in the conflict. The weight of American fire-power proved ineffective against a highly motivated enemy. In 1973 the American government, confronted by a mounting antiwar campaign at home, withdrew from the conflict. In the next two years the three countries of Indo-China fell to the communists. The people of Cambodia, having experienced American bombing, now suffered from the worst aberrations of Marxism, as interpreted by the Pol Pot regime.

The Pacific Rim

Japanese Reconstruction

United States troops occupied Japan, in an enlightened manner, from 1945 until 1952. The first objective was to ensure that the expansionist phase was over. A new democratic constitution was established, the Emperor renounced his divinity, and expenditure on defence and armaments was radically curtailed. As with Germany, industrial reconstruction followed fast. After the humiliation of defeat, both nations needed to experience success. Also, the imposed limitation of defence expenditure proved a powerful boost to the civilian economy.

The Technological Revolution

Soon Japan was no longer a low cost economy and her heavy industries began to suffer some of the problems experienced in the West. By this time, however, the nation had developed skills that enabled it to take the lead in the third, technological phase of world industrialization. Automobile production boomed, winning markets in Europe and North America, and Japanese labour and management skills proved highly suitable to the detailed work involved in the production of hi-tech goods. Supported by a huge balance of payments surplus, she has established a position of dominance in world markets in a wide range of product areas.

An Area of Growth

In the last decade of the twentieth century it became clear that the region of the Pacific rim is established as a formidable competitor to the established industrialized regions of western Europe and North America. It remained, however, a region of wide diversity. South Korea, Taiwan, Singapore and—at least until reunification with China in 1997—Hong Kong participated in the economic prosperity pioneered by Japan. At the other extreme, peoples of many of the nations of Southeast Asia continue to survive on low per capita incomes. China herself emerged from the isolation of the Cultural Revolution to rebuild international links, but, unlike communist regimes to the west, it has successfully repressed those who wished to liberalize the political structure of the nation.

The Indian Subcontinent

The Independence Movement

Indian troops made a significant contribution to the allied victory in the First World War, and in 1918, nationalist politicians looked to see their country start its progress towards the self-government that had already been given to the white dominions. In 1919, however, a British general ordered troops to fire on a demonstration in Amritsar, killing some four hundred people and injuring many more. Although the government disavowed the act, many British residents were loud in support, fuelling bitterness between the two communities. One of those radicalized by the Amritsar massacre was Mohandas Gandhi, known as Mahatma (Great Soul). During the next decades, he led a civil disobedience movement, based, if not always successfully, on nonviolent principles.

In the face of opposition at home, as well as from residents in India, the British government slowly moved towards accepting the principle of granting dominion status to India, and the Government of India Act of 1935 gave substantial power to elected representatives. The movement for complete independence, however, continued to grow. With the outbreak of the World War Two, some Indians sided with Japan in the hope of bringing down the colonial power.

Partition

The independence movement still faced the problem of reconciling the two major religious groupings of the subcontinent. Mohammed Ali Jinnah emerged as leader of the Muslim League, which now demanded that an independent state of Pakistan should be established at independence for the Islamic community. In 1945 a Labour government was returned in Britain and in March 1946 it made an offer of full independence. As disputes continued, it announced that Britain would withdraw not later than June 1948. Faced with this ultimatum, the Hindu leaders accepted partition - for which decision Gandhi was assassinated by an extremist Hindu.

The new state of Pakistan was established in two blocks in the north west and north east. The rulers of princely states on the boarder of the two nations were permitted to decide their allegiance, leaving Kashmir as disputed territory. Independence was marked by communal rioting, which left some half a million dead, and the mass movement of peoples in both directions across the frontier.

Independence

Jinnah died in 1948, and a decade later the army took control of Pakistan. Leadership of India fell to Jawaharlal Nehru and later passed to his daughter, Indira and grandson Rajiv Gandhi. The new country faced formidable problems. Independence was quickly followed by famine in 1951, and, with rising population it appeared as though Malthusian disaster was imminent. A combination of a reduction in the rate of population growth and an agricultural 'green' revolution has, however, improved the supply of food. The fragile ecology of eastern Pakistan, however, continued to bring disasters, and a cyclone in 1970 led to rebellion that, with Indian help, brought into being the separate Islamic state of Bangladesh.

Partition did not bring the end of India's communal problems. Indira Gandhi was assassinated by discontented Sikh nationalists, and her son Rajiv by Tamils of the south. Mahatma Gandhi allied himself with outcasts and hoped to see the end of the caste system, but this has been frustrated by a resurgence of Hindu fundamentalism. For all its problems, however, India remains the world's largest democracy.

Sub-Saharan Africa

Decolonialization

British governments of both parties continued the policy of giving independence to colonies, which had begun with India. The sheer size of the British Empire had meant that expatriate manpower was spread thinly. The second layer of administration was already staffed by African personnel and a machinery of local government was in place. Riots in the Gold Coast in 1948 gave notice of a growing nationalist movement. In 1957 the Gold Coast became the first independent country, within the British commonwealth, under its new name, Ghana. Three years later the much larger Nigeria became a sovereign state.

Across the continent, in Kenya and Rhodesia the problem was complicated by the presence of a white settler population, bitterly opposed to any move towards majority rule. The most serious challenge was posed by the Mau Mau disturbances in Kenya of 1952–56. Many of the white minority left the country when it received its independence in 1963. Two years later the white minority government of Southern Rhodesia declared unilateral independence and seceded from the British commonwealth. The British government failed to take effective action against this colonial rebellion and war continued between the white government and black nationalist groups, until the latter won to set up the state of Zimbabwe in 1976.

French governments, disillusioned by prolonged war in Indo-China and Algeria, gave independence at an even faster pace. In 1960 the Sub-Saharan colonies were offered either complete separation, in which case, they would receive no continued assistance, or association with France, within a French Community.

The two largest African empires were therefore dismantled within a few years with comparatively little strife. Independence for the remaining colonies proved a more painful process. In 1960, the Belgians withdrew from the Congo, which became the state of Zaire. Until that time, Africans held no positions of responsibility, and there was little preparation for the event. When the mineral-rich area of Katanga attempted to secede, the Cold War superpowers became involved in the ensuing civil war.

The last African empire was also the oldest. The Portuguese colonies of Guinea-Bissau, Mozambique and Angola achieved independence only after prolonged struggle.

After Independence

The emergent nations faced formidable problems. Some new nations spent unwisely on and military prestige projects, but, even where this was avoided, as, for instance, in Tanzania, falling world commodity prices led to a serious reduction in government revenue. Industrialization has proved unattainable, both through lack of capital, but also because it has proved hard for products from new nations to break into the controlled markets of the developed world.

Independent African nations found themselves caught in the Malthusian nutcracker of increasing population and falling revenue. This led to a decline in already low living standards and a failure by governments to deliver the public health and education programmes expected within a newly liberated nation. This exacerbated traditional communal rivalries, which in turn frequently erupted into civil war, like the Nigerian Biafran War of 1967–70 and later struggles in the Sudan, Ethiopia and the Horn of Africa. Political instability led to the emergence of authoritarian, often military, regimes. An already difficult situation has been made worse for nations immediately south of the Sahara by climatic change and desertification, which have destroyed large areas of productive land.

South Africa

The violently imposed apartheid system led to South Africa being increasingly ostracized from the world community. She withdrew from the British Commonwealth in 1961 and was later expelled from the United Nations. Economic sanctions imposed by the USA and a world sporting boycott had an effect, and in the early 1990s the legal apparatus of apartheid was dismantled. Following the country's first all-race elections, held in 1994 and won by the African National Congress (ANC), led by Nelson Mandela, South Africa re-entered the world fold.

Latin America

Capital and Industrialization

In the years before the First World War there was heavy European involvement in the economy of Latin America. The war then led to a drying up of European capital and the United States became the main investor in the region.

The world depression of the 1930s hit the region hard. The price of primary products, which were the mainstay of the economies, collapsed. After the war many of the larger nations instituted industrialization programmes, at times with a measure of success, but this was achieved only by borrowing the required capital, which left the nation with a heavy burden of debt and vulnerable to currency and interest rate fluctuations on the international market.

Economic problems created political instability. The rural poor had always lived in conditions of poverty, but they did not pose the same immediate problem to political stability as the growing and highly volatile urban populations.

Political Structures

The economic problems of the region meant that reforming governments did not have the revenue to deliver the social programmes needed to combat deprivation. When reforms were attempted they created inflation that weakened the economic base of society. Reforming democracies have therefore been under constant pressure from more authoritarian systems of government. These took three broad forms—popularist leaders, military regimes and revolutionary governments.

The archetype popularist leader was Getulio Vargas, who came to power in Brazil in 1930, and the best-known Juan Peron, who ruled the Argentine from 1943–55 and then returned briefly in 1973. Both drew comparison with European dictators, but they had wide support among the urban poor, who believed that they alone could take on powerful vested interests on behalf of the people. They depended, however, on army support, and both were vulnerable when this was withdrawn.

Cuba and Revolution

The revolutionary movement had early roots in Mexico, but it became focused on Cuba with the success of Fidel Castro's revolution in 1959. An attempt by the United States to undermine the revolution came to disaster at the Bay of Pigs in April 1961 when they were overwhelmed by Cuban troops. In the following years Cuba, now aligned with Russia, exported revolution into Latin America. Che Guevara, a symbol to the new left across the world, was killed fighting with Bolivian guerillas in 1967. The United States became involved, supporting anti-communist regimes within the region, even when these had a poor human rights record. The democratic left wing government of Salvadore Allende in Chile, for instance, was overthrown by the military in 1973 with American support. Contra rebels against the Cuban-inspired government of

Nicaragua were funded from Washington, and the government of the island of Grenada was overthrown by American invasion in 1983.

The Missile Crisis

In 1962 Cuba was the focus of the most dangerous crisis of the Cold War. In October, intelligence reports showed that sites were being built on Cuba from which missiles would be able to reach any city in the United States. President Kennedy demanded that all missiles in Cuba should be withdrawn and announced that ships bringing more would be intercepted. The superpowers stood poised for nuclear confrontation, but the Russian President Khrushchev broke the crisis by agreeing to withdraw the missiles. President Kennedy had successfully reasserted the Monroe Doctrine that the American continent would remain an area of United States influence, and the powers would not again come so close to open war.

The Middle East and North Africa

The New Turkey

In 1918, a proposal was put forward that Turkey itself should be divided into French, British and Italian spheres of influence. The successful general, Mustafa Kemal, led resistance against Greek and French forces, and established independence for the new, smaller nation. He set about a process of modernization of the nation, which went as far as westernizing its script and converting the country into a secular state. His people gave him the name of Ataturk—'father of the Turks'.

The Mandates

The old Ottoman lands of the Islamic Middle East, now finally separated from the Ottoman Empire, had acquired new strategic importance with the early development of oil reserves—although the scale and future importance of these were not as yet recognized. National boundaries were drawn up and the region was divided between France and Britain under the mandate of the League of Nations. This implied that the newly defined countries were destined to move towards self-governing status. France was awarded Lebanon and Syria, although she had to take possession of the latter by force, and continued to rule it with considerable oppression. Britain received Palestine, Iraq, and Trans-Jordan, and she also controlled the emirates of the Persian Gulf. In 1932, Britain largely withdrew from Iraq, but the Palestinian mandate turned out to be something of a poisoned chalice.

The Founding of Israel

The objective of founding a Jewish national home in Palestine was first put forward in a Zionism Congress as early as 1897. It was to be a refuge for Jewish people who were persecuted in the pogroms of eastern Europe, and it also attracted many from minority Jewish communities within the Arab world. In 1917, the British government gave support to the project, with the contradictory provision that it should not interfere with the rights of the indigenous people. The movement was given further impetus by German persecution of the Jews under Hitler. In the post war years, large numbers of European Jews sought entry, and the British authorities had the impossible task of reconciling the opposing interests. In 1947 the United Nations voted for the partition of Palestine in the face of opposition from the Arab states and in 1948 the British withdrew. In the ensuing war, large numbers of Arabs left their homes for refugee camps in the neighbouring countries. The Arab states refused to accept the existence of a Jewish state in the Islamic heartland. The refugees remained, unsettled, waiting to return to their homeland as Israel and her neighbours continued in a state of war.

North African Independence

After the Second World War the British presence in Egypt was restricted to a defensive force in the canal zone and, by 1956, Libya, Tunisia and Morocco had shaken off foreign ties. Armed conflict centred on Algeria, where over one million French settlers resisted any move towards independence. The country was declared an integral part of metropolitan France and a bitterly fought dispute continued from 1954–62. When General de Gaulle finally decided to give independence, colonists allied with army generals and France itself was taken to the brink of civil war.

Nasser and Pan-Arabism

In 1952 a group of Egyptian army officers overthrew the monarchy. Two years later, Gamal Abdel Nasser became president of the country. His objective was to establish Egypt as the unquestioned leader of a new and more coherent Arab people. Lacking oil resources, however, Egypt remained a poor country and Nasser planned a development programme based on the construction of the Aswan High Dam on the Nile. When the Americans and British withdrew offers of funding, Nasser turned to the communist bloc for support, so introducing cold war politics into the Middle East.

In 1956 he nationalized the company that administered the Suez Canal. In October the Israelis invaded Egyptian territory, ostensibly to destroy guerilla bases and this was followed by a joint attack by the British and French on the Suez Canal zone. World opinion was outraged, and the American government applied pressure that forced the invaders to withdraw.

The Suez fiasco left Nasser as the leading figure within the Arab world, but his attempts to take this towards political union were unsuccessful. In 1967 he closed the Straits of Tiran to Israeli shipping and the Israeli army launched a 'first strike' in what has become known as the Six Day War. After a successful campaign, Israel controlled new territory, including, from Jordan, the whole West Bank of the River Jordan, and, from Syria, the tactically important Golan Heights. Jerusalem, a city of great symbolic importance to all three Semitic religions, now passed under full Israeli control. Successive Israeli governments, in time reinforced by the possession of nuclear weapons, have failed to comply with United Nations resolutions demanding withdrawal from the occupied territories. Indeed, increasing numbers of Jewish immigrants have been established in West Bank settlements. As Israel's neighbour, the Lebanon, collapsed into civil war, many Arabs resorted to international terrorism.

The Oil Crisis

In 1961 Britain withdrew from her interests 'east of Suez'. Much of the, now increasingly vital, oil production of the region, however, remained under the control of western companies. A further outbreak of hostilities between Israel and her neighbours in 1973 led the Arab countries to 'play the oil card' by taking more direct control over their own reserves and withholding supplies from Israel's allies in the developed world. This led to an increase in price, which had a sharp effect on the world economy. The Arab nations, and other oil-producing nations, led by Saudi Arabia now organized themselves into OPEC (Organization of Petroleum-Exporting Countries) with a view to controlling world prices. This was less successful than had been anticipated because the depression caused by the price rise restricted world demand, and Britain and Norway, opening new North Sea reserves, stood outside the cartel.

In 1978 Nasser's successor, President Sadat, made peace with Israel under American sponsorship at Camp David. This did not end the conflict within the region, but rather took Egypt out of the mainstream of Arab politics.

Iran and Islamic Fundamentalism

With Egypt returned to the American sphere of influence after Camp David, the Soviet Union turned increasingly to the radical, though mutually hostile, governments of Syria and Iraq. The United States, looking for a buffer between the Soviet Union and the oil-rich Middle East, put heavy backing behind the conservative and corrupt administration of the Shah of Iran. In 1979 discontent erupted into revolution, and the Shah was replaced by a fundamentalist regime, dominated by the Ayatollah Khomeni. This sparked a wave of Islamic fundamentalism that gave expression to pent-up Arab anger at the imposition of alien values by aggressive western societies. Equally hostile to capitalist and to communist ideologies, Islamic fundamentalism has threatened governments of different complexions, from Afghanistan to Algeria. Indeed, the failure of the 1979 Soviet invasion of Afghanistan in support of a crumbling Marxist regime demonstrated militant Islam to be a highly effective barrier against further Russian expansion in the region.

Iraq

In 1979 Iraq came under the full control of a determined and ruthless leader, Sadaam Hussein. He had ambitions to revive Nasser's pan-Arab vision, this time based on Iraqi military power. He received wide western and Arab backing when he took his country to war with Iran, but he failed to achieve any of his war objectives. In 1990, he attacked and occupied Kuwait, provoking an international response in 1991, which left his country damaged, but his own power intact.

The Collapse of the Russian Empire

Cracks in the Structure

As early as 1953, the year that Stalin died, there were signs of unrest among subject people of the Russian Empire. Yugoslavia, while remaining communist, had already loosened her ties with the Soviet bloc. Anti-Soviet riots in East Germany in 1953 and in Poland in 1955 were followed by rebellion in Hungary in 1956. The last was suppressed by military force, launched under the cover of the Anglo-French attack on Suez. The profound unpopularity of Russian domination and of the repressive puppet regimes continued to be demonstrated by a haemorrhage of refugees crossing from East to West Germany. In 1961 the East German authorities responded by building that ultimate symbol of the Cold War—the Berlin Wall. In 1968 a reforming communist government in Czechoslovakia was again overthrown by Soviet tanks. By this time large Russian forces were also tied down on the eastern frontier to check an increasingly hostile China.

Collapse

Meanwhile the government was coming increasingly under strain within the Soviet

Union. Khrushchev's denunciation of Stalin at the Twentieth Congress of the Soviet Communist Party and the termination of the worst excesses of the secret police enabled citizens to express dissatisfaction. Industrialization had been bought at the expense of the production of consumer goods, The corrupt and petty bureaucracy was increasingly exposed, and agriculture remained in the disastrous condition bequeathed by Stalin's collectivization.

In 1985 President Gorbachev inherited a collapsing empire. Constricted by domestic pressures, he chose not to intervene when, in a few dramatic months of late 1989 and early 1990, communist governments of Eastern Europe collapsed under popular pressure and new regimes declared themselves independent of Soviet control. The tearing down of the Berlin Wall, and subsequent reunification of Germany (3 October 1990) was the most powerful symbol of change. The situation was little better in the republics that constituted the Soviet Union. The people were increasingly disillusioned by falling living standards and inefficient government. Powerful nationalist forces, from the southern republics of Armenia to Azerbaijan to the old Baltic States in the north now threatened to break up the Soviet Union from within. In August 1991 an attempt by communist 'hard-liners' to restore the old system in a coup d'état failed, leaving the central Soviet government stripped of any real power. As one republic after another announced secession it was quickly clear that the world possessed another 'sick man'—with all the attendant dangers.

The collapse of the Russian Empire at least signalled the end of superpower confrontation. Faced with mounting problems at home, Gorbachev looked for support from America and other wester. nations, and the Strategic Arms Limitation Treaty of July 1991 began the long process of disarmament. The benefits for world peace were illustrated when the Soviet Union refrained from backing Iraq in the Gulf War, so preventing a regional conflict being inflated into a confrontation of superpowers. At the time of writing, the formidable problems of the Soviet Union itself, and of the emerging democratic states of Eastern Europe, remain unresolved, but the fear of the human race being destroyed by its own weapons has—rightly or wrongly—been overtaken by new environmental concerns, which centre on the rate at which the post-industrial world is consuming the natural resources of the planet.

A–Z of People, Facts and Events

A

A1 first British car registration, issued to the 2nd Earl Russell 1903.

Aachen *or* **Aix-la-Chapelle** a university city and spa town in western Germany on the Belgian border, founded 125; Charlemagne's capital, free city of the Holy Roman Empire, burnt 1656; captured by American troops 1944.

Aalto, [Hugo] Alvar [Henrik] (1898–1976) Finnish architect and designer of Artek furniture. He moved away from the geometric shapes of Constructivism towards softer curves and more irregular forms. Notable works include the Finlandia Concert Hall, Helsinki.

Abbado, Claudio (1933–) Italian conductor. He became musical director of La Scala (1971), principal conductor of the London Symphony Orchestra (1979) and of the Berlin Philharmonic Orchestra (1989).

Abbas, Ferhat (1899–1985) Algerian nationalist leader.

Abbas I (1813–54) Egyptian pasha. He was assassinated.

Abbas the Great (*c.*1557–1628) shah of Persia.

Abbasid dynasty of caliphs who ruled Baghdad, founded by Abdul Abbas 750, ended 1258.

Abbeville, Treaty of (Treaty of Paris), relinquishing English claims to several French territories, signed 20 May 1259.

Abbey, Edwin Austin (1852–1911) American-born painter who worked in the US and England. He was the official painter at the coronation of Edward VII (1902).

Abbey Theatre, Dublin, founded in 1904 by W. B. Yeats and Lady Gregory, burned down 1952, rebuilt 1966.

Abbot, Bud (1895–1974) American film comedian.

Abbot, George (1562–1633) archbishop of Canterbury (1611–33).

ABC (American Broadcasting Company) formed 1943.

Abd-el-Kader (1808–83) Algerian revolutionary leader.

Abd-el-Krim (1882–1963) Rif revolutionary leader.

Abdication the formal renunciation of a throne. In Britain, James II abdicated in 1688, Edward VIII on 10 December 1936.

Abdominal operation first successfully performed by American surgeon Ephraim McDowell (1771–1830).

Abdul Latif (1162–1231) Arabian writer.

Abdur Rahman Khan (*c.*1844–1901) emir of Afghanistan.

Abe, Kobo (1924–) Japanese writer.

à Becket, Thomas *see* BECKET, THOMAS À.

à Beckett, Gilbert Abbott (1811–56) English humorous writer who studied for the bar but became one of the original staff of *Punch* and a leader writer for the *Times.*

Abel, Sir Frederick Augustus (1827–1902) scientist, inventor (1879) of apparatus for determining flashpoint of petroleum.

Abelard, Peter (1079–1142) French theologian and philosopher who advocated nominalism and was condemned for hersey twice (1121, 1142). His love affair with his pupil Héloïse (1101–64), whose uncle had him castrated, with its combination of intellectual and physical passion described in their letters to each other, was to haunt the imagination of many poets, notably Alexander Pope.

Abercrombie, Lascelles (1881–1938) English poet.

Abercromby, Sir Ralph (1734–1801) British general who served in the French Revolutionary and Napoleonic Wars. As commander in chief in the West Indies, he captured the islands of Grenada, St Lucia, St Vincent and Trinidad, and as commander in chief in Egypt he landed after severe fighting at Aboukir and secured a victory over the French at Alexandria but was mortally wounded.

Abercromby, Sir Robert (1740–1827) commander of the Indian forces.

Aberdeen a city and fishing port in northeast Scotland, incorporated by David I, granted charter by William the Lion 1179, burnt by Edward III 1336.

Aberdeen, George Gordon, Earl of (1784–1860) British statesman who was prime minister 1852–55 but was forced to retire during the Crimean War.

Aberdeen University founded 1494 by Bishop Elphinstone, united with Marischal College 1860.

Aberfan disaster two million tons of coal waste slid onto a Welsh village, killing 192 people including 113 children, 21 October 1966.

Aberration of light discovered 1729 by the English astronomer James Bradley (1693–1762).

Abershaw, Jerry(*c.*1773–1795) English highwayman. He was hanged.

Aberystwyth a resort and university town on Cardigan Bay in Mid-Wales, founded 1109, granted first charter 1277, college erected there 1872.

Abhorrers a political group (connected with the Tories) that first came into prominence 1680. Its members expressed abhorrence at those who petitioned Charles II to summon Parliament.

Abington, Mrs Frances (1737–1815) English actress.

Abjuration, Oath of an oath that had to be taken by all holders of public offices, clergymen, teachers, members of the universities and lawyers, rejecting the Stewarts, first required 1701. It was superseded in 1858 by a more comprehensive oath declaring allegiance to the royal family.

ABM (Anti-Ballistic Missile) Treaty between the USA and USSR signed 26 May 1972.

Abolition of slavery in British possessions 1834; in French possessions 1848; throughout the USA 1862.

Aboukir a small village on the Egyptian coast, east of Alexandria. Aboukir Bay was the scene of a naval battle in which Nelson annihilated a French fleet under Brueys on the night of 1 and 2 August 1798, thus totally destroying the naval power of France in the Mediterranean. Near Aboukir, on 25 July 1799, Napoleon defeated the Turks under Mustapha, and on 8 March 1801, Sir Ralph Abercromby effected the landing of a British army against the French.

About, Edmond [Edmond François Valentin] (1828–85) French writer who wrote many popular novels and other miscellaneous works. He was elected a memger of the Academy in 1884. His novels invlude *Le roi des montagnes* (1856).

Abraham *or* **Abram** the greatest of the Hebrew patriarchs, who was born at Ur and migrated to Palestine *c.*2000–1500 BC.

Abraham, Battle of the Heights of a battle of the Seven Years' War fought near Quebec between the British under Wolfe and the French under Montcalm 13 September 1759. It was a British victory but both Wolfe and Montcalm were killed.

Abraham, Robert (1773–1850) English architect.

Abram *see* ABRAHAM.

Abruzzi earthquake an earthquake in southern central Italy that killed 15,000, 3 November 1706.

Absolute zero (–273°C; –459°F) idea introduced by Lord Kelvin (1824–1907).

Abu Nidal (1937–) Palestinian terrorist.

Abu Nuwas (*c.*756–810) Arabian poet.

Abyssinia *see* ETHIOPIA.

Abyssinian Expedition carried out by British troops from India 1867–68.

Abzug, Bella (1920–) American political activist.

Académie des Jeux Floreux in Paris, constituted an academy by Louis XIV 1694.

Académie Française a literary academy founded in Paris 10 February 1635 by Cardinal Richelieu to supervise and protect the purity of the French language. It has 40 members ('the immortals').

Academy Awards given annually since 1927 to films, actors and technicians by the American Academy of Motion Picture Arts and Sciences for merit in the form of statuettes called Oscars.

Accademia della Crusca in Italy, a leading Italian academy, founded 1582.

Accoramboni, Vittoria (1557–85) Webster's 'White Devil', he was assassinated.

Accordion a musical instrument invented by the German Friedrich Buschmann 1822.

Accountants of Scotland, The Institute of Chartered chartered 1854.

Accountants, Institute of Chartered, in England and Wales, founded (as the Institute of Accountants) 1870; chartered 1880.

Acetylene a colourless soluble gas discovered 1836 by the British scientist Edmund Davy (1785–1857).

Achaean League a confederation of Peloponnesian cities in Greece for political and military purposes, particularly in resisting Macedonia; formed *c.*280; Aratus became leader 245 BC; Philopoemen became leader 208 BC; dissolved 146 BC. It was involved in several battles: Megalopolis 226 BC against the Spartans; Larissus 209 BC against the Aetolians and Eleians; Mantinea 208 BC and Barbosthenian Mountains 192 BC against the Spartans; Leucopetra 146 BC and Scarpheia 146 BC against the Romans, when the League was defeated.

Achaemenid dynasty a dynasty that ruled Persia from *c.*550 to 300 BC.

Achebe, Chinua (1930–) Nigerian novelist and poet whose work focuses on Ibo society and the legacy of colonialism. He was awarded the Nobel Prize for literature in 1989.

Acheson, Dean [Gooderham] (1893–1971) US lawyer and statesman who was responsible for formulating and developing several important strands of American foreign policy, notably the Marshall Plan and the establishment of NATO.

Achille Lauro Italian cruise liner hijacked by Palestinian terrorists, 7–9 October 1985.

Achromatic telescope invented *c.*1757 by the English optician John Dollond (1706–61); and independently in 1733 by the English amateur Chester Moor Hall (1703–71).

Ackermann, Rudolph (1764–1834) German-born publisher of illustrated books.

Aconcagua the highest mountain in the Andes (6960

metres/22,834 feet), first climbed by the Fitzgerald Expedition 1897.

Acre a city now in Israel; a trading port since the days of the Phoenicians, it was taken by the Crusaders 1110, captured by Saladin 1187, recaptured by Richard Coeur de Lion 1191, finally lost to Christendom 1291; defended by the Turks against Napoleon 1799; taken by Ibrahim Pasha and bombarded by a British, Austrian and Turkish fleet and restored to Turkey 1840; occupied by British troops 1918.

Acridine a chemical compound isolated by the German scientists Carl Graebe and H. Caro 1890.

Actinium a radioactive element discovered 1900 by the French scientist André Debierne (1874).

Actinometer a machine for measuring intensity of radiation invented 1825 by Sir John Herschel (1792–1871).

Actium, Battle of a naval battle of the War of the Second Triumvirate between Octavian and Mark Antony, 2 September 31 BC. Mark Antony was defeated.

Act of Settlement an Act of Parliament securing Hanoverian succession to the English throne, passed 1701.

Act of Toleration an Act of Parliament by which Protestant dissenters from the Church of England were relieved from the restrictions under which they had formerly lain, passed 1689.

Act of Uniformity an Act of Parliament enjoining all ministers in England to use the Book of Common Prayer, passed 1662.

Acton, John Emerich Edward Dalberg [1st Baron Acton] (1834–1902) English historian who was professor of modern history at Cambridge and undertook the editorship of *The Cambridge Modern History*.

Acton, Sir Harold [Marino Mitchell] (1904–94) English poet, historian and writer. The scion of an aristocratic Anglo-Italian Roman Catholic family, he was the inspiration for several characters in the novels of his friend, Evelyn Waugh.

Adad Nirari III king of Assyria. Too young to rule after the death of his father, Shamshi-Adad in 811 BC, his mother, Sammuramat, took power until 806 BC.

Adalbert (*c.*1000–1072) German archbishop.

Adalbert, Saint (*c.*957–997) German-born priest who was appointed bishop of Prague in 983 and attempted to convert the pagan Bohemians but was martyred.

Adam, James (1730–94) Scottish architect. The brother of Robert Adam, he worked with him as a draughtsman and also designed buildings of his own.

Adam, Robert (1728–92) Scottish architect famous for his individualistic interpreations of Palladian and Renaissance styles in domestic architecture. His designs usually included interior decor and furnishings down to the smallest details, and his style has been widely imitated. Notable works include Culzean Castle in Ayrshire and Keddleston House in Derbyshire.

Adams, Ansel [Easton] (1902–84) American photographer noted for his detailed, deep-focus studies of American landscape.

Adams, Francis William Lauderdale (1862–93) Australian writer. He committed suicide.

Adams, Henry Brooks (1838–1918) American historian whose nine-volume *History of the United States* (1889–91) is a landmark in American historical writing. He was the great-grandson of John Adams and grandson of John Quincy Adams.

Adams, John (1735–1826) American statesman and 2nd president of the USA (1797–1801) who helped draft the Declaration of Independence in 1776. After taking part in the peace negotiations following the American War of Independence he was the first American ambassador in England (1785–88), and was vice-president under Washington. His son was John Quincy Adams.

Adams, John Bertram(1920–84) English nuclear physicist, founder member of CERN.

Adams, John Couch (1819–92) English astronomer who predicted the position of the planet Neptune (1845). He was professor of mathematics at Aberdeen University, and in 1859 was appointed professor of astronomy and geometry at Cambridge.

Adams, John Quincy (1767–1848) American statesman and 6th president of the USA (1825–29) who was the son of John Adams.

Adams, Richard [George] English novelist. His best-known work is *Watership Down* (1972), a fantasy about a colony of rabbits, which has become a modern classic of children's literature.

Adams, Samuel (1722–1803) American statesman.

Adams, Sarah Flower (1805–48) English hymnwriter (*Nearer to Thee*).

Adams, William Bridges (1797–1872) English inventor.

Addams, Charles Samuel (1912–88) American cartoonist. He worked for *New Yorker* magazine from 1935 and was famous for his humorously macabre style, which inspired 'The Addams Family' TV series.

Addams, Jane (1860–1935) American social reformer. She founded Hull House in Chicago and was awarded the Nobel Peace Prize in 1931.

Adding machine first model built 1642 by the French scientist Blaise Pascal (1623–62).

Addington, Henry [1st Viscount Sidmouth] (1757–

1844) English statesman, Tory prime minister (1801–04).

Addinsell, Richard(1904–77) English composer of incidental music (*Warsaw Concerto*.

Addis Ababa the capital of Ethiopia, founded by Menelek II 1892.

Addison, Joseph (1672–1719) English essayist and poet. With his friend Richard Steele he founded the influential magazine *The Spectator* in 1711.

Addison, Thomas (1793–1860) English discoverer (1855) of Addison's disease.

Addled Parliament of James I's reign sat 5 April to 7 June 1614.

Adelaide (1792–1849) queen, wife of William IV.

Adelaide the state capital of South Australia, founded 1836 and named after Queen Adelaide.

Aden a major port in southern Yemen, formerly the capital of South Yemen; annexed to British India 16 January 1839; Crown Colony 1 April 1937; it became part of the People's Republic of Southern Yemen 1967.

Adenauer, Konrad (1876–1967) German statesman who was imprisoned twice by the Nazi regime (1934, 1944). As chancellor of West Germany (1949–63) he had a major role in world politics.

Adler, Alfred (1870–1937) Austrian psychiatrist. He was an associate of Freud, whose emphasis on sexuality he rejected, founding a school of psychoanalysis based on the individual's quest to overcome feelings of inadequacy (the 'inferiority complex').

Adler, Larry (1914–) American harmonica player.

Adler, Nathan Marcus (1803–90) Chief Rabbi and founder 1855 of Jews' College, London.

Admiralty, London, founded 1512.

Admiralty Islands an island group in the southwest Pacific, part of Papua New Guinea in the Bismarck Archipelago, first colonized by the Dutch 1616.

Adoption in England and Wales governed by the Adoption Act 1976, as amended by the Children Act 1976.

Adrenaline a hormone isolated 1901 by the Japanese scientist Jokichi Takamine (1854–1922).

Adrian I pope (772–795).

Adrian II pope (867–872).

Adrian III, Saint pope (884–885).

Adrian IV [Nicolas Breakspear] (*c.*1100–59) pope, first and only English pope (1154–59).

Adrian V pope (1276).

Adrian VI [Adrian Florensz] (1459–1523) pope (1522–23).

Adrian, Edgar Douglas, Baron (1889–1977) English physiologist who worked on neurons. He shared the Nobel prize for physiology and medicine in 1932.

Adrian, Saint martyred 4 March 303.

Adrianople, Battle of 378; taken by the Ottomans 1360, and their capital 1366–1453.

Advent Christian festival comprising the period encompassed by the four Sundays before Christmas.

Advertisement Duty, Newspaper introduced in England under Cromwell, abolished 1853.

Ady, Endre (1877–1919) Hungarian poet.

'AE' [George William Russell] (1867–1935) Irish poet.

Aed (d.879) king of Scots (879) *see* Appendix.

Aed Find (d.*c.*778) king of Scots (768–778) *see* Appendix.

Aegates Islands, Battle of a battle of the First Punic War, 241 BC, which was a Roman naval victory and led to the end of the war, with cession of Sicily to Rome.

Aelfric (*c.*955–*c.*1020) English monk, scholar and writer. He wrote works in old English on the lives of the saints and translations from Latin and the Bible. He has been highly regarded as a prose stylist.

Aegina a city state of ancient Greece. It was conquered by Athens in 456 BC.

Aegospotami, Battle of 405 BC a naval victory in the Peloponnesian War by Sparta under Lysander over Athens.

Aelfwald (d.749) king of East Anglia (713–749) *see* Appendix.

Aelle (1) (d.*c.*514) king of Sussex *see* Appendix.

Aelle (2) (d.588) king of Deira (*c.*560–588) *see* Appendix.

Aelle (3) (d.867) king of Northumbria (866–867) *see* Appendix.

Aemilian Way Roman road, constructed 187 BC.

Aerodynamics study founded by Sir George Cayley 1809.

Aeroplane steam model patented 1842 by W. S. Henson; successful model flown 1903 by Wright brothers; flights of Blériot, Brabazon and Cody 1909.

Aesc (d.512) king of Kent (488–512) *see* Appendix.

Aescwine (1) king of Essex (*c.*527–*c.*587) *see* Appendix.

Aescwine (2) king of Wessex (674–676) *see* Appendix.

Aeschines (389–314 BC) Greek orator.

Aeschylus (524–456 BC) Greek dramatist regarded as the founder of Greek tragedy. Seven of his plays survive, including *Prometheus Bound* and the *Oresteia* trilogy, and *Seven against Thebes* (467 BC).

Aesop (*c.*620–*c.*560 BC) Greek writer of fables in which human characteristics are satirized in the form of dialogues between animals.

Aetius, Flavius (*c.*390–454) Roman leader who defeated Attila (451). He was murdered.

Afghanistan a landlocked country in sothern Asia; independent republic since 1919; invaded by Soviet troops 1979, withdrawn 1988–89.

Afghan Wars between British and Afghans 1839–42, 1879–80, 1919.

African National Congress (ANC) African nationalist movement opposed to apartheid in South Africa; founded 1912, banned 1960, leader Nelson Mandela imprisoned 1962, released 1989; negotiated new constitution with President de Klerk 1990–93; ruling party in first free election 1995.

Agadir a port and resort in Morocco; incident of 1911; earthquake 1960.

Aga Khan heriditary title of the spiritual leader of the Ismaili sect of Islam.

Aga Khan IV (1936–) spiritual leader of the Ismaili sect of Islam.

Agapemonites religious sect founded 1846 by the Rev. Henry James Prince (1811–99).

Agapitus II pope (946–955).

Agapitus, Saint pope (535–536).

Agassiz, Jean Louis Rodolphe (1807–73) Swiss naturalist.

Agatha, Saint martyred 5 February 251.

Agatho, Saint pope (678–681).

Agee, James (1909–55) American author (*Let Us Now Praise Famous Men* 1941).

Agent Orange chemical defoliant used by US Air Force in Vietnam 1962–70.

Agesilaus (d.361 BC) king of Sparta (398–361 BC). At the battle of Coronea in the Corinthian War, 394 BC, he led the Spartans to a victory over the confederacy against them.

Aghrim, Battle of fought in Ireland against James II 12 July 1691.

Agincourt, Battle of fought between Henry V and the French 25 October 1415.

Agis I king of Sparta (*c*.1032 BC).

Agis II king of Sparta (427–398 BC).

Agis III king of Sparta (338–331 BC). During the Macedonian Wars Spartan troops under Agis were defeated at the battle of Megalopolis in 331 BC by the Macedonian regent Antipater 331 BC. Agis died in the battle.

Agis IV king of Sparta (244–240 BC). He attempted to reform Sparta and introduce land reform but was killed by the ephors, or rulers.

Agnes' Eve, St 20–21 January.

Agnew, Spiro [Theodore] (1918–) American Republican politican, vice-president (1969–73) in Nixon's administration. He resigned from office following revelations of political corruption and was sentenced to three years' probation.

Agnostic term first introduced 1869 by the English scientist Thomas Henry Huxley (1825–95).

Agrarian Law the first Agrarian Law for land reform in Rome passed by Spurius Cassius 486 BC.

Agricola [Georg Bauer] (1490–1555) German 'father of mineralogy'.

Agricola, Gnaeus Julius (37–93) Roman general. He conquered Britain in AD 78.

Agriculture administered by Ministry of Agriculture, Fisheries and Food (formerly Board of Agriculture), formed 1889.

Agriculture, Department of, USA, created 15 May 1862.

Agrigentum (Agrigento) a town on the south coast of Sicily. Founded *c*.582 BC, it was one of the great cities of classical antiquity.

Agrigentum, Battle of a battle of the First Punic War. It was a Roman victory over Carthage 262 BC.

Agrippa, Marcus Vipsanius (63–12 BC) Roman general.

Aguilar, Grace (1816–47) English writer (*The Vale of Cedars* 1850).

Ahab king of Israel (869–850 BC). An able warrior king, he took part in the battle of Karkar 854 BC, when a coalition of kings of Syria and Palestine withstood the growing threat of Assyria. He married Jezebel, a Phoenician princess, who brought to Israel the worship of Baal. Elijah protested at this and by challenging Ahab was able to stop the pagan cult.

Ahaz king of Judah (*c*.734–715 BC) who was warned by Isaiah to avoid joining Syria and Israel in a siege of Jerusalem. He appealed to Tiglath-Pileser III of Assyria for help, and when the Assyrians destroyed Syria and Israel, Judah became a vassal state.

Ahmed I (1589–1617) Turkish sultan (1603–17).

Ahmed II (1643–95) Turkish sultan (1691–95).

Ahmed III (1637–1736) Turkish sultan (1703–30).

Ahmedabad a city in western India founded by Ahmed Shah 1411.

Ahmediya Movement Muslim sect founded 1889 by Mirza Ghulam Ahmed (1839–1908).

Ahmednagar Indian city founded by Ahmed Nizam Shah 1494.

Aidan, Saint (d.651) Irish missionary in Northumbria. He founded a monastery at Lindisfarne (635) and was first bishop of Lindisfarne. His feast day is 31 August.

Aiden (d.606) king of Scots (*c*.575–606) *see* Appendix.

Aids (acquired immune-deficiency syndrome) first recognized in USA 1981; retrovirus first isolated in France 1983.

Ainsworth, William Harrison (1805–82) English historical novelist (*The Tower of London* 1840).

Air composition first analysed 1771 by the French chemist Antoine Laurent Lavoisier (1743–94).

Air conditioning first primitive system designed by

Stuart W. Cramer 1906; first associated with Legionnaire's Disease 1970s.

Airdrie, Lanarkshire, founded 1695.

Air gun invented 1656 by Guter of Nuremberg.

Airmail post first organized in Britain by the *Empire Illustrated* 10 August 1910.

Airmail Service first regular inaugurated by the US government 1918.

Air pump invented by the German scientist Otto von Guericke (1602–86).

Airship models constructed by Giffard in 1852 and by Renard and Krebos in 1884; rigid model constructed by Zeppelin in 1900.

Airy, Sir George Biddell (1801–92) British astronomer who estimated the density of the earth by measuring gravity in mines. he was astronomer royal (1835–81).

Aisne, Battle of the First World War battle 13–28 September 1914.

Aix, Battle of battle of the Cimbric War when Barbarian Teutones moving to invade Italy were defeated by Marius 102 BC.

Aix-la-Chapelle (Aachen) founded 125. Congresses 1668, 1748 and 30 September–21 November 1818.

Ajaccio capital and main port of Corsica, founded 1492 by the Genoese. It was the birthplace of Napoleon.

Ajanta Cave Paintings, India, dated approximately 600.

Akbar, Jalaluddin Mohammed (1542–1605) Mogul emperor of India (1556–1605).

Akerman, John Yonge (1806–73) English founder of the *Numismatic Journal.*

Akhmatova, Anna (1889–1966) Russian poet. Her masterpiece, Requiem (1963), describes the suffering of the Russian people under Stalin.

Akhnaton (*fl* fourteenth century BC) heretic pharaoh of Egypt (Amenhotep IV).

Akihito (1933–) emperor of Japan (1989–).

Akkadian Empire in Mesopotamia founded by Sargon 2650 BC. His son, Naram-Sin, succeeded 2600 BC.

Akron a city in northeast Ohio, USA, founded 1825, chartered 1865.

Aksakov, Sergei Timofeievich (1791–1859) Russian writer (*Family Chronicle* 1846–56).

Alabama, The Confederate warship built at Birkenhead 1862, attacked US shipping 1862–64, sunk off Cherbourg by *Kearsage* 1864.

Alabama a state of the USA, created Territory 1817, admitted as state to the Union 1819.

Alamein, Battle of Second World War battle 23 October–4 November 1942.

Alamo, The a Spanish mission near San Antonio, Texas, where Davy Crockett and 186 other Texans died defending their fort against a Mexican army, 1836.

Alanbrooke, Alan Brooke, Viscount (1887–1963) British soldier. He was chief of the Imperial General Staff in the Second World War (1941–46).

Alaric (d.410) Visigoth king.

Alaska the largest and most northerly state of the USA, discovered by Vitus Bering 1741; purchased from the Russians by USA 1867; incorporated as Territory 1912; became 49th US state 1959.

Alaska Highway runs 1,523 miles (2,452 km) from Dawson Creek, British Columbia, to Fairbanks, Alaska, built 1942 by the US Army and originally called the Alcan Highway.

Alba *or* Alva, Ferdinand Alvarez de Toledo, Duke of (1507–82) Spanish soldier. He suppressed a Protestant revolt in the Spanish Netherlands (1567–72) and conquered Portugal (1580).

Albania a small mountainous country in the eastern Mediterranean; under Turkish rule 1467–1912; principality 1912–24; republic 1925–28; monarchy 1928–46; republic from 1946.

Albany, Louisa, Countess of (1753–1824) wife of Prince Charles Edward.

Albee, Edward [Franklin] (1928–) American dramatist. His plays include *Who's Afraid of Virginia Woolf* (1962) and *Three Tall Women* (1994).

Albeniz, Isaac (1860–1909) Spanish pianist and composer. He was a child prodigy and went on to write operas, orchestral pieces and songs. He is best known for his piano suite *Iberia* (1906) comprising twelve technically demanding pieces redolent of the rhythms of Spanish folk music.

Albert anti-pope (1102).

Albert, Prince [Albert Francis Augustus Charles Emmanuel, Prince of Saxe-Coburg-Gotha] (1819–61) German-born consort of Queen Victoria who was naturalized as a British citizen on his marriage in 1840. He was a cultured and knowledgeable man and became a dominant influence on Victoria, and after his death she withdrew from public life.

Albert I (1875–1934) king of the Belgians (1909–34).

Alberta a province of western Canada, organized as district 1875; created province 1905.

Albert Hall, Kensington, built in memory of Prince Albert (1867–71).

Alberti, Domenico (*c.*1710–40) Italian singer, composer and harpsichordist. He wrote many works, e.g.*Endimione,* but is largely remember for his use of 'broken' chords in his pieces for harpsichord.

Alberti, Leone Battista (1404–72) Italian architect, painter, sculptor and writer. Born in Genoa, he worked mainly in Rome and Florence (facade of Santa Maria Novella). His writings include *On*

Painting (1435), but little of his painting or sculpture has survived.

Albert Memorial, Hyde Park, begun 1864, completed 1876.

Albert Nyanza a lake in East Africa, discovered 1864 by Sir Samuel White Baker (1821–93).

Albertus Magnus, Saint [Albert, Count von Böllstadt] (*c.*1200–80) German philosopher and teacher of Thomas Aquinas. His feast day is 15 November.

Albigenses French heretics active *c.*1200, destroyed 1209–29.

Albinoni, Tomaso (1671–1750) Italian composer. He was among the earliest to write concertos for solo violin. He wrote more than forty operas. Bach composed fugues on themes by Albinoni.

Albion a name given to Britain by the Romans. The word may be Celtic, but the Romans were struck by the whitness of the cliffs near Dover and associated it with their word *albus*, 'white'.

Albuera, Battle of a battle of the Peninsular War, fought between the British and French 16 May 1811, which was a British victory.

Albuquerque a university city of New Mexico, USA, founded 1706.

Alchred *or* **Elhred** king of Northumbria (765–774) *see* Appendix.

Alcibiades (*c.*451–404 BC) Greek general and statesman. He took part in the Peloponnesian War on the side of Athens.

Alcock, Sir John William (1892–1919) pioneer aviator. He made the first nonstop flight across the Atlantic with A. W. Brown (1919).

Alcoholics Anonymous (AA) self-help group founded 1935.

Alcott, Louisa May (1832–88) American writer. She was an active social reformer and prolific author, but is ow remembered chiefly for her hugely successful children's novel, *Little Women* 1868–69), and its sequels, *Jo's Boys* (1886) and *Little Men* (1871).

Alcuin (*c.*735–804) English scholar and theologian. He was an adviser to Charlemagne.

Aldeburgh Festival an annual music festival held in Aldeburgh, Suffolk, in June, founded by Benjamin Britten and Peter Pears in 1948. It maintains its strong association with Britten, many of whose works were first performed there.

Aldhelm (*c.*640–709) bishop of Sherborne.

Aldington, Richard (1892–1962) English poet and dramatist. His novel *Death of a Hero* (1929) is a thinly disguised semi-autobiographical account of his war experiences.

Aldol chemical compound discovered by the French chemist Charles Adolphe Wurtz (1817–84).

Aldrich, Robert (1918–83) American film director whose films include *Whatever Happened to Baby Jane?* (1962).

Aldrich, Thomas Bailey (1836–1907) American poet, novelist and editor of the *Atlantic Monthly* (1881–90).

Aldrin, Edwin ('Buzz') (1930–) American astronaut. He accompanied Neil Armstrong and Michael Collins on the Apollo 11 moon landing mission as the pilot of the lunar module and was the second man to walk on the moon.

Aldwulf (1) king of East Anglia (663–713) *see* Appendix.

Aldwulf (2) king of Sussex (*c.*765) *see* Appendix.

Aldwych London theatre, opened 18 October 1905.

Aleichem, Sholem [Shalom Rabinovich] (1859–1916) Yiddish writer.

Aleman, Mateo(1547–*c.*1616) Spanish writer (*Guzmán de Alfarache* 1599–1604).

Alembert, Jean le Rond d' (1717–83) French scientist and philosopher. He collaborated with Diderot on the *Encyclopédie*.

Alesia, Battle of battle of the Gallic Wars 52 BC. Vercingetorix, leader of the Gauls, defeated and captured by Cæsar.

Aleutian Islands a chain of islands, southwest of the Alaska Peninsula between the North Pacific Ocean and the Bering Sea, discovered by Vitus Bering 1725; bought from Russia by USA 1867.

Alexander (1888–1934) king of Yugoslavia (1921–34). He was assassinated at Marseilles 9 October 1934.

Alexander, Mrs Cecil Frances (1818–95) hymnwriter ('There is a green hill far away').

Alexander, Sir George (1858–1918) English actor-manager.

Alexander, Harold, Viscount (1891–1969) British soldier.

Alexander I, Saint pope (105–119).

Alexander II [Anselmo Baggio] (d.1073) pope (1061–73).

Alexander III [Rolando Bandinelli] (d.1181) pope (1159–81) who actged with great vigour against Henry II when the latter was accused of the assassination of Thomas à Becket. He also excommunicated Barbarossa.

Alexander IV [Rinaldo di Segni] (d.1261) pope (1254–61).

Alexander V [Peter Philargès] anti-pope (1409–10).

Alexander VI [Rodrigo Borgia] (1431–1503) pope (1492–1503) who was made a cardinal at the age of twenty-five by his uncle, Pope Calixtus III. He bribed his way to the papal throne in succession to Innocent VIII and once there used it to reduce the power of the Italian princes and seize their possessions for the benefit of his own family. He extracted money from all Christian countries under various pretexts and sold indulgences, his excesses bringing on him the condemnation of Savonarola. Despite this, he interested himself in the welfare of the people and was a patron of the arts. He had two illegitimate children, Cesare and Lucrezia Borgia.

Alexander VII [Fabio Chigi] (1599–1667) pope (1655–67).

Alexander VIII [Pietro Ottoboni] (1610–91) pope (1689–91).

Alexander I (1777–1825) Russian emperor (1801–25) who concluded peace with Britain, against which his predecessor had declared war, helped to defeat Napoleon and formed the Holy Alliance.

Alexander II (1818–81) Russian emperor (1855–81) who succeeded his father, Nicholas I, before the end of the Crimean War. He abolished serfdom in Russia in 1861. He was assassinated by Nihilists and succeeded by his son, Alexander III.

Alexander III (1845–94) Russian emperor (1881–94) who abandoned the reforms begun by his father, Alexander II, and ruled in the old autocratic fashion, restricting the liberties of Finland and the Baltic provinces and encouraging persecution of the Jews. He was succeeded by his son, Nicholas II.

Alexander I (*c.*1078–1124) king of Scotland (1107–24) *see* Appendix.

Alexander II (1198–1249) king of Scotland (1214–49) *see* Appendix.

Alexander III (1241–85) king of Scotland (1249–85) *see* Appendix.

Alexander Balas (d.146 BC) usurper of the Syrian throne (150–146 BC). He claimed to be the son of Antiochus Epiphanes and was supported by the Roman senate. He invaded Syria 152 BC but was defeated by Demetrius I. In 150 he again invaded and this time defeated Demetrius, who died in the battle. He antagonized his father-in-law, Ptolemy VI, by plotting against his life and met him in battle at Oenoparas. Although Ptolomy died, Alexander was completely defeated and afterwards murdered.

Alexander Severus (d.235) Roman emperor (222–235) who succeeded after the murder of his cousin Heliogabalus by the praetorian guard. He was at war with Persia 231 and defeated Artaxerxes. His failure to control his armies led to him and his mother being murdered in Gaul by mutinous troops during a war against the invading Germans. He was succeeded by Maximian.

Alexander the Great (356–323 BC) Macedonian king (336–323 BC). The pupil of Aristotle, he inherited the kingdom of Macedon from his father Philip II (382–336 BC). He conquered Greece in 336, Egypt in 331, and the Persian empire by 328. He extended his conquests to the east and defeated an Indian army in 326. He died in Babylon and was buried in the city he founded, Alexandria.

Alexander Zebina (d.122 BC) the son of a merchant who was set up by Ptolemy VII as a pretender to the Syrian throne shortly after the death of Antiochus VII and the return of Demetrius II. He never succeeded in obtaining power over the whole of Syria. In 125 BC he defeated Demetrius, who fled to Tyre and was there killed, but in the middle of the same year Alexander's patron, Ptolemy, set up against him Antiochus VIII by whom he was defeated in battle. Alexander fled and was captured by robbers who delivered him up to Antiochus, who put him to death.

Alexandra (1844–1925) British queen, wife of Edward VII, whom she married 10 Mardh 1863.

Alexandria the main port of Egypt on the Nile delta, founded 331 BC by Alexander the Great; Ptolemy I made it the intellectual centre of the Hellenic world; the library was founded during 3rd century BC and damaged 47 BC destroyed AD 272.

Alexandria, Battle of a battle of the Napoleonic Wars, when the British under Sir Ralph Abercromby defeated the French but Abercromby was mortally wound, 21 March 1801.

Alexandrian Era began 5503 BC.

Alexios Comnenos (1048–1118) Byzantine emperor (1081–1118).

Alfarabi, Abu Nasr (*c.*900–950) Arabian philosopher who wrote commentaries on Artistotle and wrote The Perfect City, his own political philosophy of a Utopian society.

Alfieri, Count Vittorio (1749–1803) Italian poet and tragedian. His many works, including 21 tragedies (*Saul* 1782), six comedies and an autobiography, display a strong enthusiasm for Italian nationalism and reform.

Alfonso *see* ALPHONSO.

'Alfred Jewel', The Ashmolean Museum, Oxford, found at Athelney 1693.

Alfred the Great (849–899) king of England (871–899) *see* Appendix.

Algardi, Alessandro (*c.*1595–1654) Italian Baroque sculptor and architect who worked in Rome from 1625. His patron was Pope Innocent X, and his major works include the tomb of Leo XI (*c.*1645) and the Villa Doria-Pamphili in Rome.

Algeciras, Conference of concerning Morocco, held 1906.

Algeria a North African country that fringes the Mediterranean Sea in the north, annexed to France 1842; conquered by Allies from Axis 1942; nationalist revolt began 1954; achieved independence 1962.

Algren, Nelson [Nelson Algren Abraham] (1909–81) American novelist. He wrote four novels, two of which, *The Man with the Golden Arm* (1949) and *A Walk on the Wild Side* (1956), are classic portrayals of urban American underclass life.

Alhambra, The Moorish palace near Granada, built between 1248 and 1354.

Ali (*c*.600–660) Muslim leader. He was killed

Ali, Muhammad [Cassius Clay] (1942–) American boxer and three times world heavyweight champion (1964–67, 1974–78, 1978). His licence to box was withdrawn in 1967, after his refusal to be conscripted into the armed forces to serve in Vietnam.

Aliwal, Battle of First Sikh War battle fought between the British and the Sikhs 28 January 1846.

Alizarin red dye synthetized 1868 by the German scientist Karl Liebermann (1842–1914).

Alken, Henry (d.1831) English etcher.

Allan, David (1744–96) Scottish painter.

Allen, Grant (1848–99) Canadian-born writer (*The Woman Who Did* 1895).

Allen, Woody [Allen Stewart Konigsberg] (1935–) American film director, actor and writer noted for his satirical films about the neuroses of New York intellectuals. His films include *Manhattan* (1979).

Allenby, Edmund, Viscount (1861–1936) British soldier.

Allende [Gossens], Salvador (1908–73) Chilean politician. He was elected president of his country in 1970, thus becoming the first freely elected Marxist president in Latin America. He was overthrown and killed in a coup that brought Pinochet to power.

Allende, Isabel (1942–) Chilean-born novelist (*The House of the Spirits* 1985).

Alleyn, Edward (1566–1626) English actor-manager, founder of Dulwich College 1619.

All Fools' Day *see* April Fool's Day.

All Hallows' Eve 31 October.

All Saints festival, instituted 625; celebrated at Rome 13 May.

All Saints' Day celebrated 1 November.

All Souls' College, Oxford University, founded 1437 by Henry Chichele (1362–1443).

All Souls' Day celebrated 2 November (except when Sunday of festival is of the first class when it is celebrated 3 November).

'All the Talents', Administration of cabinet formed under Grenville 1806, resigned 1807.

Alma, Battle of the a battle of the Crimean War in which the Allies fought the Russians 20 September 1854.

Alma-Tadema, Sir Lawrence (1836–1912) Dutch-born painter who moved to England in 1870, where he enjoyed a successful career as a painter of historical scenes, in particular of classical Greece and Rome. His paintings often included beautiful women.

Almack's London club founded 1763 by William Almack (d.1781); established as Brooks's 1778.

Almanza, Battle of a battle of the War of the Spanish Succession, 25 April 1707, when the French fought the British and Portuguese, who were victorious.

Almeida, Portugal, captured by the Spaniards 25 August 1762; by the French 1810; and recaptured by the Allies under Wellington 1811.

Almond, Dr Hely Hutchinson (1832–1903) Scottish educational reformer.

Almoravides (*Murabitim*) Berber Muslim sect, who ruled North Africa and Spain during the 11th and 12th centuries.

Almqvist, Karl (1793–1866) Swedish writer.

Alpaca fabrics first manufactured (1852) in England by Sir Titus Salt (1803–76).

Alpha rays discovered 1896 by Lord Rutherford (1871–1937).

Alphage, Saint (954–1012) archbishop of Canterbury.

Alphonso I (1094–1185) king of Portugal (1112–85).

Alphonso II (Alphonso the Fat) (1185–1223) king of Portugal (1211–23).

Alphonso III (1210–79) king of Portugal (1248–79).

Alphonso IV (1290–1357) king of Portugal (1325–57).

Alphonso V (Alphonso Africano) (1432–81) king of Portugal (1438–81).

Alphonso VI (1643–75) king of Portugal (1656–68).

Alphonso I king of Spain (739–757).

Alphonso II (Alphonso the Chaste) king of Spain (789–842).

Alphonso III (Alphonso the Great) king of Spain (866–914).

Alphonso IV king of Spain (924–931).

Alphonso V king of Spain (999–1028).

Alphonso VI (d.1109) king of Spain (1065–1109).

Alphonso the Emperor king of Spain (1126–57).

Alphonso the Wise king of Spain (1252–84).

Alphonso XI king of Spain (1312–50).

Alphonso XII (1857–85) king of Spain (1870–85).

Alphonso XIII (1886–1941) king of Spain (1902–31). He abdicated 14 April 1931 when the republic was established.

Alphonso VIII (Alphonso the Noble) king of Castile (1158–1214).

Alphonso IX king of Leon (1188–1230).

Alphonso X (Alphonso the Wise, Alphonso the Astronomer) (1221–84) king of Leon and Castile (1252–84).

Alpin (d.*c*.840) king of Scots (*c*.837–*c*.840) *see* Appendix.

Alric king of Kent (747–762) *see* Appendix.

Alsace-Lorraine a region in northeast France; ruled by

Germany 1871–1918, by France 1918–40, by Germany 1940–44, by France since 1944.

Altamira cave paintings prehistoric rock paintings, dating from about 13000 BC, discovered in 1879 near Santander in northern Spain, by the daughter of Marcelino de Sautuola.

Altdorfer, Albrecht (*c.*1480–1538) German painter and printmaker. He was a major figure of the Danube School, his work is characterized by inventiveness, distortion of figures and brilliant effects of colour and light.

Altman, Robert (1922–) American film director (*M.A.S.H.* 1970).

Altmark, Battle of the Second World War battle 16 February 1940.

Aluminium a very light white metallic element first isolated 1854 by the French scientist Henri Ste.-Claire Deville (1818–81).

Alva *see* ALBA.

Alyattes (d.560 BC) king of Lydia. A five-year war with Media was ended when during a battle in 610 BC an eclipse of the sun terrified both sides.

Amado, Jorge(1912–) Brazilian novelist (*Gabriella, Clove and Cinnamon* 1958).

Amasis I king of Egypt. He drove the Hyksos from Egypt and founded the New Empire 1600 BC, conquering Palestine and Phoenicia.

Amasis king of Egypt (569–525 BC). He established links with Greece and conquered Cyprus, extending trade.

Amateur Athletic Association in the United Kingdom founded 1880.

Amati, Niccolo (1596–1684) Italian violin-maker, the most famous member of a family of violin-makers who worked in Cremona, Italy, in the 16th and 17th centuries. He taught Antonio Stradivari and Andrea Guarneri.

Amazon River a South American river rising in the Andes and flowing east to the Atlantic, discovered 1500 by the Spanish navigator Vicente Yañez Pinzón (*c.*1460–*c.*1524).

Ambassadors first legally protected in England 1708.

Ambon (formerly Amboyna) an island and capital of the Spice Islands in the Maluku group in eastern central Indonesia; discovered by the Portuguese 1511; seized by the Dutch 1605; Massacre of 1623.

Ambrose, Saint (*c.*340–397) bishop of Milan. He greatly influenc ed church singing and may have introduced the antiphonal singing of the Syrian church. Despite bearing his name, the earliest surviving Ambrosian chants were composed long after his death.

Ambulances introduced 1792 by Baron Dominique Jean Larrey (1766–1842).

Amelia (1783–1810) princess, daughter of George III.

Amenophis III king of Egypt (1450 BC). He was a noted temple-builder.

Amenophis IV king of Egypt (1415 BC). He replaced the old religion by sun worship.

America the continent lying between the Atlantic and Pacific Oceans; discovered by Christopher Columbus 1492. Vikings believed to have reached America *c.*1000.

American Academy of Arts and Sciences founded in Boston 1780.

American Academy in Rome, founded 1905.

American Antiquarian Society founded 1812.

American Bar Association organized 1878.

American Bible Society founded 1816.

American Civil Liberties Union founded 1920.

American Civil War Veteran last surviving, Walter Williams (1843–1959).

American Civil War fought 1861 to 1865.

American Constitution came into force 21 June 1788.

American Declaration of Independence made 4 July 1776.

American Dialect of English first mentioned 1740.

American Duties Act passed 1764; on tea 1767.

American Ephemerus and Nautical Almanac founded 1849 by Charles Henry Davis (1807–77).

American Federation of Labor founded 1886.

American Football adopted present form 1880.

American Legion founded 1919.

American Philosophical Society founded by Benjamin Franklin at Philadelphia 1734.

American Society for the Prevention of Cruelty to Animals founded 1866.

American States, Organization of formed 1948.

American War of Independence fought 1775 to 1783.

America's Cup an international prize of a silver cup offered to yacht owners of any nation competing in a race for large yachts. It is called the America's Cup after the yacht of that name, which won the trophy in 1851. Yachts from Britain, Canada and Australia compete for it unsuccessfully 24 times before it was won by an Australian yacht, *Australia II*, in 1983. The catamaran *Stars and Stripes* regained it for the USA in 1987.

Ames, Joseph (1689–1759) English bibliographer (*Typographical Antiquities* 1749).

Amherst College, Hampshire Co., Mass., USA, opened 1821, chartered 1825.

Amiel, Henri Frédéric (1821–81) Swiss philosopher.

Amiens, Treaty of between Great Britain, France, Spain and the Netherlands, signed 25 March 1802.

Amiens Cathedral constructed 1220–88.

Amin [Dada], Idi (*c.*1925–) Ugandan soldier and politician, military dictator (1971–79). He appointed himself president for life in 1976, but was overthrown by the Tanzanian army's invasion in 1979.

Amines derivatives of ammonia, discovered 1849 by the French chemist Charles Adolphe Wurtz (1817–84).

Amis, Sir Kingsley (1922–95) English novelist and poet whose first novel *Lucky Jim* (1954), a satire on academic life, is a comic masterpiece. His later novels are darker in tone. He was the father of Martin Amis.

Amis, Martin (1949–) English novelist, the son of Kingsley Amis. His novels, including *London Fields* (1989), are cleverly plotted and written but display an underlying violence.

Amman, Jost (1539–91) Swiss artist.

Ammonia gas discovered 1774 by Joseph Priestley (1733–1804).

Amnesty International founded 1961; Nobel peace prize 1972.

Amoy (Xiamen) a port on an island off the southeast coast of China, one of the first treaty ports opened to European trade (1842).

Ampère, André Marie (1775–1836) French physicist.

Amphipolis, Battle of a battle of the Peloponnesian War 422 BC. Athenians were defeat by Sparta.

Amritsar a city in northern India, founded 1577 by Ram Das as the holy city of the Sikhs. Riots 10 to 15 April 1919; Golden Temple attacked by Indian troops 1981.

Amundsen, Roald (1872–1928) Norwegian explorer and navigator, leader of the first expedition to reach the South Pole in 14 December 1911.

Amyot, Jacques (1513–93) French translator of Plutarch.

Anabaptists a religious movement that rejects infant baptism and administer rites only to adults and that began in Münster, Germany, in 1521 and first reached England in 1549.

Anacletus *or* **Anencletus, Saint** pope (76–78).

Anacletus II anti-pope (1130–38).

Anacreon (*c*.550–*c*.465 BC) Greek lyric poet. His poems (mostly on love and wine, and many of doubtful attribution) were translated into French and English in the mid-16th century and were much imitated.

Anaesthesia, General nitrous oxide used 1799 by Humphry Davy, 1844 by Horace Wells (USA); ethyl chloride used 1848 by Heyfelder; ether used 1846 by William Morton (USA); chloroform demonstrated 1847 by James Young Simpson, administered to Queen Victoria 1853 by John Snow. Local freezing used 1812 by Baron Larrey (in Napoleon's army); cocaine used 1884 by Carl Koller; procaine used 1905 by Einhorn.

Anarawd king of Gwynedd (878–916) *see* Appendix.

Anastasia (1901–1918?) grand duchess of Russia.

Anastasius anti-pope (855–858).

Anastasius I, Saint pope (399–401).

Anastasius II, Saint pope (496–498).

Anastasius III pope (911–913).

Anastasius IV pope (1153–54).

Anastasius I (*c*.430–518) Roman emperor (491–518).

Anastasius II Roman emperor (from 713), executed 721.

Anaxagoras (*c*.500–*c*.428 BC) Greek philosopher.

Anaximander (611–546 BC) first world map designer.

Anaximenes (*fl* 6th century BC) Greek philosopher.

ANC *see* AFRICAN NATIONAL CONGRESS.

Anchor escapement in clockmaking invented by the English clockmaker Robert Hooke (1635–1703).

Ancon, Treaty of almost ending the War of the Pacific (1879–84) signed 20 October 1883.

Andaman Islands island group in the Bay of Bengal, used as penal settlement at intervals from 1858 until 1942; occupied by Japanese 1942–45; administered together with the Nicobar Islands by the government of India.

Andersen, Hans Christian (1805–75) Danish writer, best known now for his fairy tales, e.g. 'The Emperor's New Clothes'.

Anderson, Carl David *see* HESS, VICTOR FRANCIS.

Anderson, Elizabeth Garrett (1836–1917) first British woman doctor, qualified 1856.

Anderson, Lindsay [Gordon] (1923–95) British film director and critic (*This Sporting Life* 1963).

Andhra Pradesh a state in southeast India, constituted separate state 1953; on enlarging boundaries assumed present name 1956.

Andorra a tiny state in the eastern Pyrenees, between France and Spain; traditionally granted independence by Charlemagne *c*.778; created a coprincipality 1278.

Andrássy, Julius, Count (1823–90) Hungarian statesman.

Andre, Carl (1935–) American minimalist sculptor. His systematic arrangements of single objects in horizontal pattern are intended to focus attention on the relationship between objects and their surrounds. Famous among his works is *Equivalent VIII* (1976), the 'Tate bricks' that outraged the British public.

André, Major John (1751–80) British spy in America. He was hanged.

Andrea del Sarto (1487–1531) Italian painter in Florence who worked in an elegant classical style and was a major figure of the high Renaissance. His works include his Uffizi altarpiece, *The Madonna of the Harpies*.

Andrée, Salomon August (1854–97) Swedish polar explorer.

Andrew, Saint martyred 30 November 69.

Andrew I king of Hungary (1047–61).

Andrew II (1175–1235) king of Hungary (1205–35).

Andrew III king of Hungary (1290–1301).

Andrewes, Lancelot (1555–1626) theologian and bishop of Winchester. He was one of the translators of the Authorized Version of the Bible.

Andrews, Julie (1934–) British-born film star (*The Sound of Music* 1965).

Andreyev, Leonid Nikolaievich (1871–1919) Russian playwright (*He Who Gets Slapped* 1916).

Androco (*fl* 1st century AD) high king of the British tribes *see* Appendix.

Andronicus I, Comnenus (d.1185) Byzantine emperor (from 1183–85). He was murdered.

Andronicus II, Palaeologus (1260–1332) Byzantine emperor (1282–1328). He was forced to abdicate by his grandson, Andronicus III.

Andronicus III, Palaeologus (*c.*1296–1341) Byzantine emperor (1328–41) .

Andronicus IV, Palaeologus (d.1385) Byzantine emperor (1376–79).

Andropov, Yuri [Vladimirovich] (1914–84) Soviet statesman. Former head of the KGB and president of the USSR (1983–84).

Angas, George Fife (1789–1879) South Australian pioneer.

Angel gold coin first used in France 1340, in England 1465.

Angelico, Fra [Guido di Pietri] (1387–1455) Dominican monk and Italian painter in Florence. All his work is religious in character but also progressive in its understanding of perspective. His paintings include *Descent from the Cross* (1440).

Angell, Sir Norman [Ralph Norman Angell Lane] (1874–1967) British economist (*The Great Illusion* 1910).

Angelo, Domenico (1716–1802) fencing master (*L'Ecole d'armes* 1763).

Angelo, Henry (1760–*c.*1839) fencing master (son of Domenico).

Angelou, Maya [Marguerite Ann Johnson] (1928–) American dramatist, poet, short-story writer and singer, one of the leading black writers of the 20th century (*I Know Why the Caged Bird Sings* 1970).

Angerstein, John Julius (1735–1823) important figure in the development of Lloyds.

Angiosperms plants whose seeds ripen in a container first defined by Paul Hermann 1690.

Angkor Vat the ruined ancient capital of the Khmer empire in Cambodia, constructed *c.*1112–52.

Angles a Germanic tribe who in the earliest historical period lived in the district about Angeln in Schleswig-Holstein and who in the 5th century and subsequently crossed over to Britain along with bands of Saxons and Jutes (and probably also Frisians) and colonized a great part of what from them has acquired the name of England, as well as a part of the Lowlands of Scotland. The Angles formed the largest body among the Germanic settlers in Britain, and founded the three kingdoms of East Anglia, mercia and Northumbria. *See also* Appendix.

Anglesey an island off the northwestern tip of Wales, conquered by the Romans 61; by the English 1295.

Anglican Church (Church of England) established by Augustine 597, separated from Catholic Church 1534.

Anglo-Afghan Treaty concluded by the Dobbs Mission in Kabul 22 November 1921.

Anglo-Irish Treaty, setting up the Irish Free State, signed 6 December 1921.

Anglo-Persian Oil Company, now British Petroleum Company, formed April 1909.

Anglo-Saxons the name commonly given to the people formed by the amalgamation of the Angles, Saxons and Jutes who came from northern Germany and are said to have first landed in Britain *c.*449 and to have been led by Hengist and Horsa. From the preponderance of the Angles, the whole country came to be called *Engla-land*, i.e. the land of the Angles or English. *See also* Appendix.

Angola (formerly Portuguese West Africa) a country on the Atlantic coast of west-central Africa, discovered by the Portuguese navigator Diogo Cão 1482–85; Portuguese possession from 1575 until independence in 1975.

Angstrom unit (one millionth of 1 mm) named after the Swedish physicist Anders Jöns Angström (1814–74).

Anhydrite discovered 1794; named 1804 by Abraham Gottleb Werner (1750–1817).

Anicetus, Saint pope (155–166).

Aniline discovered by O. Unverdorben 1826, present name given by C. J. Fritzsche 1841.

Aniline dyes discovered 1856 by Sir William Henry Perkin (1838–1907).

Animism philosophical doctrine propounded in the 18th century by Georg Ernst Stahl (1660–1734).

Ankara a city in east-central Turkey, capital of Turkey since 1920.

Anna (d.654) king of East Anglia (*c.*633–654) see Appendix.

Ann Arbor, Michigan, first settled 1824; incorporated 1851.

Anna Comnena (1083–1148) Byzantine princess.

Annam former kingdom (3rd century–1428), empire (1428–1884) and French protectorate (1884–1945) in eastern Indochina, now in Vietnam.

Annapolis the capital of the state of Maryland, first settled (under the name Providence) 1649; assumed present name 1694; incorporated 1708.

Anne (1) (1456–85) queen of Richard III.

Anne (2) (1665–1714) queen of England (1702–14) *see* Appendix.

Anne (3) (1693–1740) Russian empress (1730–40).

Anne Boleyn (*c.*1507–36) granddaughter of the Duke of Norfolk who became lady in waiting to Catherine of Aragon. Henry VIII feel in love with her and, without waiting for the official completion of his divorce from Catherine, married her in January 1533. When her pregnancy revealed the secret, Cranmer declared the first marriage void and the second valid and she was crowned at Westminster. She was soon supplanted by her own lady in waiting, Jane Seymour. Suspicions of infidelity were alleged against her, and in 1536 she was tried for treason and adultery and beheaded.

Anne of Austria (1602–66) daughter of Philip III of Spain who married Louis XIII of France and was regent for her son, Louis XIV, after her husband's death in 1643. In 1661 she transmitted the royal authority to her son.

Anne of Bohemia (1366–94) first queen of Richard II.

Anne of Brittany (1477–1514) wife successively of Maximilian of Austria and of Louis XII.

Anne of Cleves (1515–57) fourth wife of Henry VIII, who married and divorced her in 1540. The marriage had been arranged by Thomas Cromwell, who suffered the ultimate fate for the king's dislike of his queen.

Anne of Denmark (1574–1619) queen of James I.

Anning, Mary English discoverer 1811 onwards of saurian remains (1799–1847).

Annual Register first issued 1759.

Annunciation, Feast of the celebrated in the Christian Church 25 March each year.

Annunzio, Gabriele d' (1863–1938) Italian writer (*Francesca da Rimini* 1901).

Anouilh, Jean (1910–87) French dramatist. His first play was an updating of Sophocles's *Antigone*, in which the eponymous heroine becomes a thinly disguised representation of the spirit of France under German occupation. Other plays include *Waltz of the Toreadors* (1952) and *Beckett* (1959).

Anselm, Saint (*c.*1033–1109) an Italian-born priest who succeeded Lanfranc as archbishop of Canterbury.

Ansermet, Ernest (1883–1969) Swiss conductor.

Anson, George, Baron Anson (1697–1762) explorer, sailed round the world 1740–44.

Anstey, Christopher (1724–1806) English writer (*The New Bath Guide* 1766).

Anstey, F. [Thomas Anstey Guthrie] (1856–1934) writer (*Vice-versa* 1882).

Antakya *see* **Antioch.**

Antalcidas, Peace of a peace in 387 BC ending the Wars of the Greek City States between Sparta and Persia.

Anterus, Saint pope (235–236).

Antheil, George (1900–1959) American composer and pianist of Polish descent. He incorporated the sounds of motor horns, doorbells and aeroplane engines in some of his compositions, e.g. *Ballet mécanique* (1926). He also compose operas as well as piano sonatas, symphonies and film scores.

Anthesteria Athenian festival in honour of Dionysus, 11–13 month of Anthesterion (February-March).

Anthony, Saint (*c.*250–356) the Great, first Christian monk.

Anthony of Padua, Saint (1197–1231).

Anthrax bacteria first discovered independently by Pollender and Brauell 1849.

Anthropometry the exact measurement of the human body to discover, size, proportion, etc, first so named 1872 by Cesare Lombroso (1836–1909).

Anthroposophy form of theosophy founded by Rudolf Steiner (1861–1925).

Anti-aircraft defence first used in siege of Paris 1870.

Anti-Corn-Law League founded 1838 by Richard Cobden (1804–65).

Antibiotics first, penicillin, discovered by Sir Alexander Fleming (1881–1955).

Anticosti Canadian island first sighted 1534 by the French explorer Jacques Cartier (1491–1557).

Antietam, Battle of a battle of the American Civil War fought 16–17 September 1862.

Antigua an island on the eastern side of the Leeward Islands, discovered by Christopher Columbus 1493; British colony until 1967; became independent as part of the state of Antigua and Barbuda in 1981.

Antimony a bluish white, very brittle metallic element discovered (according to tradition) by 'Basilius Valentinus' (possibly a 16th-century monk).

Antinomian Controversy between Agricola and the Lutherans 1527–40.

Antioch (modern Antakya) a city in southern Turkey. It was founded by Seleucus 300 BC as capital of his Syrian kingdom. Here the disciples were first called Christians AD 42. It was taken by the Persians 540; by the Saracens *c.*638; recovered for the Eastern emperor 966; lost again 1086; retaken by the Crusaders 1098, who held it until 1268 when it was captured by the Sultan of Egypt. It was taken from the Turks in the Syrian War, 1 August 1832, by Ibrahim Pasha but restored at the peace.

Antioch, Era of used by the early Christian writers of

Antioch and Alexandria. It placed the Creation at 5492 BC.

Antiochus I [Soter] (*c*.324–261 BC) king of Syria (280–261 BC) who succeeded his father, Seleucus I. Much of his reign was taken up by wars with the Gauls who had invaded Asia Minor, and he was killed in battle against them. He was succeeded by his son, Antiochus II.

Antiochus II [Theos] (d.246 BC) king of Syria (261–246 BC) who succeeded his father, Antiochus I. Soon after his accession he became involved in war with Ptolemy II of Egypt, which led to the loss or rebellion of several of his provinces. In return for peace, which was granted 250 BC, he agreed to marry Ptolemy's sister Berenice in place of his wife Laodice. On Ptolemy's death he recalled Laodice, but she had him, Berenice and their son murdered. He was succeeded by Seleucus II, his son by Laodice.

Antiochus III [Antiochus the Great] (242–187 BC) Seleucid king of Syria (223–187 BC). A son of Seleucus II, he succeeded his brother, Seleucus III. He recovered the provinces in Asia Minor that had been taken by Attalus I of Pergamus and attempted to extend his empire through wars with Egypt and Macedonia but was defeated by the Romans at the battle of Magnesia in 190 BC and forced to give up most of Asia Minor. He was killed by a mob when he plundered a wealthy temple to obtain money to pay tribute to Rome. He was succeeded by his son Seleucus IV.

Antiochus IV [Epiphanes] (d.164 BC) king of Syria (175–164 BC) who succeeded his brother, Seleucus IV. He conducted four campaigns against Egypt (171–168) and took Jerusalem (170 and 168 BC). His attempt to eradicate the Jewish religion and introduce the worship of the Greek gods led to the revolt of the Jews under Judas Maccabaeus. He was succeeded by his son, Antiochus V.

Antiochus V [Eupator] (*c*.173–162 BC) king of Syria (164–162 BC) who succeeded his father, Antiochus IV, at the age of nine. He was killed and succeeded by his uncle, Demetrius I, who laid claim to the throne.

Antiochus VI [Theos] king of Syria (144–142 BC) and son of Alexander Balas, usurper of the Syrian throne. Two years after his father's death, while he was still a youth, he was brought forward as a claimant to the crown against Demetrius II by Tryphon, who had been one of his father's chief ministers. Tryphon obtained the support of the Jews and Antiochus was acknowledged as king by the greater part of Syria. But Tryphon had the young prince put to death and ascended the throne himself.

Antiochus VII [Sidetes] king of Syria (137–128 BC) the younger son of Demetrius I and brother of Demetrius II, who obtained possession of the throne after conquering the usurper Tryphon. He carried on the war against the Jews and took Jerusalem 133 BC after almost a year's siege. He granted the Jews a favourable peace, and died in battle against the Parthians.

Antiochus VIII [Grypus] king of Syria (125–95 BC) a son of Demetrius II and Cleopatra (4) who succeeded his brother, Seleucus V, after his mother had had him assassinated. At first he let his mother wield the power, but with the assistance of Ptolemy VII of Egypt he conquered the usurper Alexander Zebina and became master of the whole of Syria. his mother became jealous of him and plotted against his life, but her son compelled her to drink the poison she had prepared for him. He reigned in peace for some time but in 112 BC a civil war began when his half-brother, Antiochus IX, became master of almost the whole of Syria. In 111 BC Antiochus VIII regained a considerable part of his dominions, and it was agreed that the kingdom should be shared between them. He had five sons who continued the civil wars in Syria.

Antiochus IX [Cyzicenus] king of Syria (111–95 BC) the son of Antiochus VII and Cleopatra (4), who shared the kingdom with his half-brother, Antiochus VIII. On the death of his brother, he attempted to obtain possession of the whole of Syria, but his claims were resisted by Seleucus VI, the eldest son of Antiochus VIII, by whom he was killed in battle. His son was Antiochus X.

Antiochus X [Eusebes] (d.*c*.83 BC) king of Syria (95–83 BC) the son of Antiochus IX, he defeated Seleucus VI, who had conquered his father, and compelled him to flee Syria, but he then had to contend with the brothers of Seleucus, Antiochus XI, Philippus and Demetrius III. He defeated Philippus and Antiochus XI in battle near the Orontes river, when the latter was drowned. The crown was assumed by Philippus who continued to prosecute the war assisted by Demetrius. The Syrians, worn out by the civil wars, offered the kingdom to Tirgranes, king of Armenia, who accordingly took possession of Syria in 83 BC and ruled over it until he was defeated by Lucullus in 69 BC.

Antiochus XI [Epiphanes] king of Syria (95–83 BC). Son of Antiochus VIII and brother of Seleucus VI, he continued the civil war against Antiochus X but was defeated in battle at the Orontes river and was drowned.

Antiochus XII [Dionysus] king of Syria (95–83 BC, 83–69 BC). The youngest son of Antiochus VIII, he assumed the title of king after his brother Demetrius

III was taken prisoner by the Parthians. He died in battle against the Arabians.

Antiochus XIII [Asiaticus] last Seleucid king of Syria (69–65 BC). Son of Antiochus X, he remained in Rome during the time that Tigranes ruled in Syria. On the defeat of Tigranes in 69 BC, Lucullus allowed him to take possession of the kingdom, but he was deprived of it in 65 BC by Pompey, who made Syria a Roman province.

Antipater (*c.*397–319 BC) Macedonian general and regent of Macedonia (334324, 323–319 BC). As regent during Alexander the Great's campaigns abroad, he defeated the Spartans at Megalopolis 331 BC. In 324 BC he took fresh troops to Alexander in Asia. After Alexander's death he was again regent and became involved in the Lamian War against a strong confederacy of Greek states with Athens at the head. He defeated the Greeks at Crannon in 322 BC.

Antipopes rival popes elected at various times, especially by the French and Italian factions 1305–1439.

Antislavery Society in the USA, founded *c.*1833 by William Lloyd Garrison (1805–79).

Antisthenes Greek philosopher (*c.*444–*c.*365 BC.

Antitoxins study initiated by the French scientist Pierre Paul Emile Roux (1853–1933).

Antofagasta a port in nothern Chile and capital of the region of the same name, founded 1870.

Antonello da Messina (*c.*1430–1479) Italian painter working in Sicily. His work, which helped to popularize oil painting in Italy, displays a strong Flemish influence in its light, atmosphere and attention to detail.

Antonine Wall Lollius Urbicus defensive wall between the Forth and Clyde Rivers in Scotland built by Lollius Urbicus 140–142.

Antoninus, Saint (1389–1459).

Antoninus Pius (86–161) Roman emperor (138–161).

Antonioni, Michelangelo (1912–) Italian film director. His films include *L'Avventura* (1959) and *Blow-Up* (1967), the latter regarded as a landmark of the 'Swining Sixties' English cultural landscape. Other films include *The Passenger* (1974).

Antony, Mark [Marcus Antonius] (*c.*83–30 BC) Roman soldier who fought with Julius Caesar in the Gallic Wars. He became a member of the Second Triumvirate with Octavian and Ledpidus 43 BC, and after Caesar's assassination defeated Brutus and Cassius at the battle of Philipi, 42 BC. He deserted his wife for the Egyptian queen, Cleopatra, their forces being defeated by his brother-in-law, Octavian, at the naval battle of Actium 31 BC. He and Cleopatra committed suicide.

Antraigues, Comte Emanuel d' (1755–1812) French diplomat. He was murdered 1812.

Anzac Day first celebrated in London 25 April 1916.

Anzio Landings World War II landings 22–25 January 1944.

Apartheid South African policy of separate political and cultural development for white and black races, first so named by the Rev. J. C. du Plessis at Kroonstad 1929; official policy of the government of South Africa 1948–90.

Apelles (*fl* 4th century BC) Greek painter who became court painter to Philip II of Macedonia and Alexander the Great. None of his work has survived, and his fame is due to the enthusiasm of classical authors whose detailed descriptions of his work later inspired Renaissance artists such as Botticelli and Titian.

Apollinaire, Guillaume [Wilhelm Apollinaris Kostrowitzky] (1880–1918) French art critic and writer who had great influence among avantgarde artists and poets at the beginning of the 20th century. A friend of Picasso and champion of Cubism, he also supported Orphism and Futurism and originated the term Surrealism.

Apollinaris, the Younger (d.*c.*390) bishop of Laodicea.

Apollo project American space programme initiated 1962 by President J. F. Kennedy; first lunar landing Apollo 10, 24 July 1969; discontinued 1975.

Apothecaries Company, London, incorporated 1606 and 1617.

Apperley, Charles James, 'Nimrod' (1779–1843) sporting writer.

Appian Way a Roman road connecting Rome with southern Italy was constructed 312–308 BC.

'Appleseed, Johnny' [John Chapman] (*c.*1775–1847) American pioneer.

Apponyi, Albert, Count (1846–1933) Hungarian statesman.

Apraksin, Feodor Matveievich (1671–1728) founder of the Russian Navy.

Apricots first planted in England *c.*1540.

Apries (Hophra) king of Egypt (596–569 BC). He conquered Palestine and Phoenicia and for a short time re-established Egyptian influence in Syria, which had been overthrown by Nebuchadnezzar, but the failure of an expedition he sent against Cyrene led to a revolt by the army, who elected Amasis in his place. He was defeated in battle and executed.

April Fools' Day (All Fools' Day) 1 April, supposed to be connectd with the fruitlss first errand of the dove from the ark or the sending of Christ to Herod by Pilate. There is a similar Indian custom, the Feast of Huli, 31 March.

Apsley, Sir Allen (1616–83) royalist leader.

Apuleius, Lucius (*fl* 2nd century AD) North African

Latin writer of a romance called *The Golden Ass* (*c.*125), a satirical novel narrated by a man turned into an ass.

Aquatint a method of etching on copper invented in France 1768.

Aquinas, Thomas *see* THOMAS AQUINAS.

Aquino, [Maria] Corazon (1933–) Filipino politician. She was president of the Philippines (1986–92) following the assassination of her husband, Benigno Aquino, the most prominent opponent of Marcos.

Arab League founded at Cairo 1945.

Arab-Israeli Wars: Six Day War 5 –10 June 1967; Yom Kippur War 6 –24 October 1973.

Arabella Stewart *see* STEWART, ARABELLA.

Arachnidae family to which spiders belong first distinguished 1815 by the French naturalist Jean Lamarck (1744–1829).

Arafat, Yasser (1929–) Palestinian leader who helped found the anti-Israeli guerrilla force *Al Fatah* and became chairman of the Palestine Liberation Organization in 1968.

Arago, Dominique François Jean (1786–1853) French scientist.

Aragon, Louis (1897–1982) French poet, essayist and novelist, one of the founders of both Dadaism and Surrealism. His works include the Surrealist novel *Nightwalker* (1926) and several collections of verse.

Aram, Eugene (1704–59)murderer. He was hanged.

Ararat, Mount [Büjük Agri Dagi] a mountain peak in eastern Turkey, reputed resting place of Noah's Ark after the Great Flood, first climbed 1829 by the German Dr Johann Jacob Parrot (1792–1840).

Aratus (271–213 BC) Greek statesman. He became leader of the Achaean League 245 BC. His great aim was to unite all the Greek states into one nation but in the face of the domination of Macedon and its Greek allies he was unsuccessful.

Arbela (Gaugamela), Battle of 331 BC a battle of Alexander the Great's Campaigns, when he defeated the Persians under Darius.

Arber, Edward (1836–1912) English bibliographer and scholar.

Arber, Werner (1929–) Swiss microbiologist, shared Nobel prize 1978 for work on DNA and monoclonal antibodies.

Arblay, Madame d' [Frances Burney] (1752–1840) English novelist (*Evelina* 1778).

Arbroath Abbey in eastern Scotland, scene of the barons of Scotland's Declaration of Independence to Pope John XXII, 1320.

Arbuckle (Roscoe), 'Fatty' (1887–1933) American comedy actor.

Arbuthnot, Alexander (d.1585) printer of the first Bible issued 1575 in Scotland.

Arbuthnot, John (1667–1735) Scottish writer (*Martin Scriblerus*).

Arc de Triomphe, Paris, constructed in honour of the Grande Armée 1806–36.

Arcadius (378–408) Roman emperor (395–408).

Arcesilaus (1) *see* BATTUS.

Arcesilaus (2) (*c.*316–*c.*241 BC) Greek philosopher.

Archangel port on the Dvina delta on the White Sea in Russia, founded 1584.

Archangel Passage discovered 1553 by the English navigator Richard Chancellor (d.1556).

Archer, Frederick (1857–86) outstanding English jockey. He committed suicide.

Archer, William (1856–1924) drama critic.

Archibald, Sir Adams George (1814–92) Canadian statesman.

Archimedes (*c.*287–212 BC) Greek mathematician born in Syracuse. He was noted for his work in geometry, hydrostatics and mechanics. When Syracuse was taken by the Romans, he was killed by soldiers ignorant of who he was.

Archipenko, Aleksandr (1887–1964) Ukrainian-born American sculptor. He explored extreme simplification of form and became a major influence on contemporary artists through his teaching.

Ardashir I ruler of Persia (229–) who established the Sassanid Empire by overthrowing the Parthians. He re-established the Zoroastrian religion.

Arden, Edward (*c.*1542–83) English High Sheriff. He was hanged.

Arden, John (1930–) English dramatist, whose early plays were innovative assaults on social corruption and violence, effectively using song, declamation and harshly poetic dialogue.

Arderne, John (*fl* 14th century) English pioneer surgeon.

Arditi, Luigi (1822–1903) Italian composer (*Il Bacio*).

Arendt, Hannah (1906–75) German-born American philosopher. Her best-known work is *The Origins of Totalitarianism* (1951), which argued that the similarities between Hitler's Germany and Stalin's Russia could be traced back to a common 19th-century ancestry.

Arensky, Anton Stepanovich (1861–1906) Russian composer. He studied with Rimsky-Korsakov and wrote three operas as well as symphonies, a violin concerto, and church and chamber music. His works include *Raphael* (1894).

Areopagus Greek tribunal founded *c.*1507 BC. Its powers were limited by Ephialtes 463 BC in democratic reform in Athens.

Arequipa city in Peru, founded 1539 by the Spanish conquistador Francisco Pizarro.

Aretino, Pietro (1492–1556) Italian poet and playwright whose name became a bywod in Elizabethan times for witty licentiousness.

Argenson, Marc, Comte d' (1696–1764) French army reformer.

Argentina country on the eastern coast of South America, discovered by the Spanish explorer Don Juan Diaz de Solis 1516; ruled by Spain until 1816; independent series of governments from 1816; constitutional republic since 1852.

Arginusae, Battle of 406 BC naval battle of the Peloponnesian War, which was an Athenian victory.

Argon an inert gas discovered 1894 by the British scientists Lord Lister (1827–1912) and Sir William Ramsay (1852–1916).

Arian movement heretical Christian movement founded *c.*314 by the Libyan theologian Arius (d.336).

Ariosto, Lodovico (1474–1533) Italian poet. His *Orlando Furioso* (1516), an epic romance in verse set in Charlemagne's time, enjoyed European-wide popularity.

Ariovistus (*fl* 1st century BC) German chieftain. He commanded the Helvetii at Bibracte in 58 BC but was defeated by Caesar, beginning the conquest of Gaul.

Aristarchus of Samos (*c.*310–*c.*250 BC) Greek astronomer at Alexandria.

Aristarchus of Samothrace (*c.*214–143 BC) Greek writer.

Aristides (d. *c.*468 BC) Athenian general.

Aristippus (*fl* 5th-4th centuries BC) Greek philosopher.

Aristophanes (*c.*448–387 BC) Greek comic dramatist, eleven of whose comedies survive. The objects of his satire ranged from politicians to his fellow dramatists (Euripides being one) and his plays are a valuable record of the intellectual debates of the day. The most popular of his plays now is *Lysistrata.*

Aristotle (384–322 BC) Greek philosopher. He taught at Plato's Academy for 20 years and became tutor to Alexander the Great and formed his own school (the Lyceum) in Athens in 335. His works, including *Nicomachean Ethics, Poetics* and *Politics*, were reintroduced to the Western world in the Middle Ages via Arabian scholarship and had a profound influence on almost every field of intellectual inquiry until the Renaissance.

Arithmetic of cardinal numbers axiomatized by the Italian mathematician Giuseppe Peano 1899.

Arius (d.336) Libyan theologian and leader of the Arian Movement.

Arizona a state in the southwest of the USA, settled 1732; created a Territory 1863; admitted to the Union 1912.

Arkansas a state in the south of the USA, settled 1686; created a Territory 1819; admitted to the Union 1836.

Arkhangelsky, Aleksandr (1846–1924) Russian composer (*Mass for the Dead*).

Arkwright, Sir Richard (1732–92) English inventor 1768 of the spinning frame who later established a water-powered spinning factory in Derbyshire.

'Arlen, Michael' [Dikran Kouyoumdjian] (1895–1956) Armenian-born novelist whose best-known work is *The Green Hat* (1924).

Arles, Synod of convened by the Emperor Constantine 314.

Arletty [Leonie Bathiat] (1898–1992) French stage and screen actress whose best-known film is *Les Enfants du Paradis* (1944).

Armada, Spanish a fleet of 130 Spanish ships, which was assembled in 1587 and in 1588 attacked an English fleet of 80 ships. The Armada was defeated because of excellent manoeuvring of the English ships, the use of fire-ships and a gale. Elizabeth I had a medal struck bearing in Latin the inscription, 'God blew, and they were scattered.'

Armaments, Limitation of Conference held Washington DC 1921–22.

Armani, Giorgio (1935–) Italian fashion designer who founded his own label in 1975.

Armenia a former kingdom created a Soviet Socialist Republic 1920; proclaimed a constituent Republic of the USSR 1936; became independent state on dissolution of USSR 1991.

Armenian Church separate since 451.

Arminianism religious movement founded by the Dutch theologian Jacobus Arminius (Hermandzoon) (1560–1609).

Arminius German leader (17 BC–AD 21), routed Roman army under Varus AD 9.

Armistice Day (Day of Remembrance) First World War, 11 November 1918.

Armory Show international exhibition of modern art held 1913 at the 69th Regimental Armory, New York, comprising 1,600 works. It toured the US, arousing controversy and excitement, and restoring vitality to contemporary art.

Armour plate first proposed for ships of war 1805 by the English scientist and politician Sir William Congreve (1772–1828).

Armstrong, Henry Edward (1848–1937) English chemist and educationist.

Armstrong, [Daniel] Louis 'Satchmo' (1900–71) American jazz trumpeter, singer and leader of many popular jazz bands. He had a genius for improvisation and became one of the best-loved entertainers of the 20th century. The name Satchmo means 'satchel mouth'.

Armstrong, Neil [Alden] (1930–) American astronaut. He commanded the Apollo 11 moon landing mission, in which he became the first man to walk on the moon, 20 July 1969.

Armstrong, William George, Baron (1810–1900) English engineer and inventor.

Arne, Thomas Augustine (1710–78) English composer of operas, oratorios and instrumenta pieces. His best-known work is his masque *Alfred*, which contains the song 'Rule, Britannia!' (1740).

Arnhem, Battle of Second World War battle, 19–28 September 1944.

Arnold, Benedict (1741–1801) American soldier.

Arnold, Bion Joseph (1861–1942) American electrical engineer and inventor 1900 of the magnetic clutch.

Arnold, Sir Edwin (1832–1904) English writer (*The Light of Asia* 1879).

Arnold, Malcolm (1921–) English composer, trumpeter and conductor. His works include symphonies, ballet music, and concertos for various instruments, as well as chamber, choral and orchestral pieces. He has also written film scores, e.g. *The Bridge on the River Kwai* (1957).

Arnold, Matthew (1822–88) English educationist and poet, the son of Thomas Arnold. He became one of the most important commentators on Victorian society. His poems include *Sohrab and Rustum* (1853).

Arnold, Thomas (1795–1842) English educational reformer and headmaster of Rugby (1828–42).

Arnolfo di Cambio (*c.*1232–*c.*1310) Italian sculptor and architect from Pisa who worked in Rome, principally on papal tombs, and became one of the most important Italian architects in the Gothic style. He was one of the architects of Florence Cathedral.

Arnulf (1040–1124) bishop of Rochester.

Aroostook 'War' American boundary dispute between Maine and New Brunswick 1839.

Arp, Jean *or* Hans (1887–1966) German-born French sculptor and painter. A founder of Dadaism, his work was abstract in form.

Arpád (d.907) Magyar leader. His dynasty ruled Hungary until 1301.

Arras, Treaty of between Charles VII and Philip the Good signed 1435.

Arrau, Claudio (1903–91) Chilean pianist. He taught in Berlin 1925–40 and opened his own piano school in Santiago, Chile. He was one of the greatest interpreters of works by Beethoven and was also admired for his playing of Chopin, Liszt, Brahms and Schumann.

Arrhenius, Svante August (1859–1927) Swedish chemist.

Arrowsmith, Aaron (1750–1823) English geographer and map publisher.

Arsacid dynasty ruled Persia 227 BC to AD 224.

Arses king of Persia (338–336 BC). The youngest son of Artaxerxes III, he was placed on the throne by the eunuch Bagoas who had poisoned his father. Arses rebelled against Bagoa who had him and his children put to death, ending the royal house.

Artagnan, Charles de Baatz d' (1611–73) French captain of the Musketeers.

Artaud, Antonin (1896–1948) French playwright, poet, actor and theorist, His essays on the theatre, *The Theatre and its Double* (1938), have had a lasting effect on Western drama.

Artaxerxes I king of Persia (465–425 BC). He succeeded his father, Xerxes, who had been murdered, and his reign was marked by several insurrections by his satraps (provincial governors).

Artaxerxes II king of Persia (404–358 BC). He succeeded his father, Darius II as king while his brother Cyrus became satrap of western Asia. Cyrus with a force of Greek mercenaries (among them Xenophon) rebelled against Artaxerxes and defeated his brother at Cunaxa in 401 BC, but was killed in the battle.

Artaxerxes III king of Persia (358–338 BC). He succeeded his father, Artaxerxes II, and kept his throne by treason and murder. He was poisoned by the eunuch Bagoas and was succeeded by his youngest son, Arses.

Artevelde, Jacob van governor of Flanders, killed 1345.

Artgal (d.871) king of Strathclyde *see* Appendix.

Arthur (*fl.* 5th or 6th century AD) British tribal king *see* Appendix.

Arthur (1187–1203) duke of Brittany. He was murdered.

Arthur, Chester Alan (1830–86) 21st US president (1881–85).

Arthur, Sir George (1784–1854) governor of Bombay (1842–46).

Artichokes first grown in England in the 16th century.

Articles of Religion six published by King Henry VIII 1536; 42 published without Parliamentary consent 1552; reduced to 39 1563 and received Parliamentary authority 1571.

Artificial radioactivity discovered 1934 by the French physicist Jean Frédéric Joliot-Curie (1900–1958).

Artificial silk made 1883 by the English electro-chemist Sir Joseph Wilson Swan (1828–1914). Industry founded *c.*1885 by the French scientist Hilaire, Comte de Chardonnet (1839–1924).

Artigas, José Gervasio (1774–1850) Uruguayan revolutionary leader.

Arts and Crafts Movement English movement in the decorative arts at the end of the 19th century. It took is name from the Arts and Crafts Exhibition Society, formed in 1888, and its aim was to re-establish the value of handcrafted objects at a time of increasing mass production. Its most active and important leader was William Morris.

rts Council of Great Britain founded in London as the Council for the Encouragement of Music and the Arts (CEMA) in 1940; incorporated under present name in 1946.

rtsybashev, Mikhail Petrovich (1878–1927) Russian-born writer (*Sanine* 1907).

rundel, Thomas (1353–1414) archbishop of Canterbury (1396–1414).

rundel, Thomas Howard, 2nd Earl of (1586–1646) English patron of the arts, collector and antiquarian, and also a prominent figure at the court of Charles I. His art collection was broken up after his death, but the bulk of the Arundel Marbles, his classical sculpture, is in the Ashmolean Museum, Oxford.

saph, Saint (d.*c*.596).

sbury, Francis (1745–1816) English-born Methodist leader in America.

scalon, Battle of fought between the Crusaders and the Moslems 15 August 1099.

scension Day celebrated on a Thursday each year 40 days after Easter Sunday.

scension Island a tiny volanic island in the South Atlantic Ocean, discovered by the Portuguese navigator João da Nova on Ascension Day 1501.

sch, Sholem (1880–1957) Yiddish writer (*Dos Shtelt* 1904).

scham, Roger (*c*.1515–1568) English educationalist and classics tutor to Elizabeth I. His book, *The Scholemaster* (1570), which criticizes corporal punishment, is a notable landmark in humanist educational theory.

sclepiades (*fl.* 2nd century BC) Greek physician.

scot Gold Cup instituted 1807.

scot Race Meeting first held 11 August 1711.

sculum, Battle of 279 BC Romans defeated by Pyrrhus, king of Epirus, when he invaded Italy.

sen dynasty ruled Bulgaria 1185–1258.

shanti former West African kingdom formally annexed by Britain 1901 and incorporated within the colony of the Gold Coast (now Ghana).

shanti Wars four wars between the British and the Ashanti people of West Africa: 1824–26, 1863–64, 1873–74 and 1895–1900.

shcan School a group of American painters of urban realism between 1908 and 1918.

shcroft, Dame Peggy [Edith Margaret Emily Ashcroft] (1907–91) English actress. One of the most popular stage and film actresses of her generation, she won an Oscar for her role in *A Passage to India* (1984).

shdown, Paddy [Jeremy John Dunham Ashdown] (1941–) English Liberal politician who was elected leader of the Liberal and Social Democratic Party in 1988.

Ashdown, Battle of between the Saxons and the Danes 6 January 871.

Ashe, Arthur (1943–93) American tennis player. The first black tennis player to win the US open (1968), the Australian open (1970) and the Wimbledon men's competition (1975), he contracted the HIV virus from a blood transfusion following heart bypass surgery in 1983 and developed full-blown Aids in 1988.

Ashendene Press private press founded and operated by C. H. St John Hornby (1895–1923).

'Ashes, The' instituted 1882.

Ashford, Daisy (1881–1972) English writer (*The Young Visiters* 1919).

Ashkenazy, Vladimir (1937–) Russian-born Icelandic pianist and conductor, known for his recordings of works by Mozart and Russian composers such as Scriabin and Rachmaninov.

Ashley, Laura (1926–85) Welsh-born designer and retailer of clothes and furnishings.

Ashmolean Museum in Oxford, founded *c*.1677 by the English antiquary Elias Ashmole (1617–92); opened 1682.

Ashmun, Jehudi (1794–1828) American reformer in Liberia.

Ashton, Sir Frederick [William Mallandaine] (1906–88) Ecuadorian-born British choreographer. He was cofounder of the Royal Ballet of which he was director (1963–70). His ballets include *A Month in the Country* (1976).

Ash Wednesday the first day of Lent.

Asimov, Isaac (1920–92) Russian-born American science fiction author whose many novels and short stories, e.g. *I Robot* (1950), have been influential in the science fiction genre.

Aske, Robert (d.1537) English leader 1536 of the Pilgrimage of Grace, he was executed.

Aslib, London, founded as the Association of Special Libraries and Information Bureaux 1924.

Asoka (273–232 BC) Indian emperor.

Aspdin, Joseph (1779–1855) English stonemason and inventor (1824) of Portland cement.

Aspirin developed 1899 by German physician Felix Hoffman.

Asquith, Herbert Henry [1st Earl of Oxford and Asquith] (1852–1928) British statesman. He was leader of the Liberal Party (1908–26) and prime minister (1908–16). He refused to serve under his successor, Lloyd-George, who had engineered his downfall.

Assam a state of northeast India, conquered by the

British 1842, incorporated into Bengal by 1914, became separate province 1924.

Asser (d.*c.*909) English historian and Bishop of Sherborne.

Assignats French Revolutionary paper money used 1789–97.

Assumption of the Blessed Virgin Mary, Feast of the celebrated each year 15 August; Catholic dogma defined 195.

Assur the oldest city of ancient Assyria, on the River Tigris, founded not later than 2300 BC.

Assurbanipal (d.626 BC) king of Assyria (*c.*669–626 BC). He subdued Babylon and overthrew Elam 668 BC.

Assyria an ancient kingdom of Mesopotamia. At its height, it extended from Egypt to the Persian Gulf. Its major cities were Assur and Nineveh. It became independent of Babylonia *c.*1700 BC; conflict with Babylonia began 1410 BC; conquered Babylonia 1290 BC; under Shalmaneser II Babylon and Syria were subdued 860 BC and under Tiglath-Pileser 721 BC; attack on Jerusalem 701 BC by Sennacherib failed; Taharka, Ethiopian king of Egypt, defeated by Esarhaddon 680 BC and Memphis captured 670 BC; Babylon again subdued and Elam overthrown 668 BC; Nineveh captured and destroyed by Nabopolassar of Babylon and Cyaxares of Media 612 BC; end of the Assyrian Empire.

Astaire, Fred [Frederick Austerlitz] (1899–1987) American dancer, singer and actor. His partnership with Ginger Rogers [Virginia McMath] (1911–95) resulted in a series of classic song-and-dance films, e.g. *Top Hat* (1935).

Asteroids minor planets that move around the sun between the orbits of Mars and Jupiter. The first to be discovered was Ceres, 1801, by the Italian astronomer Giuseppe Piazzi (1746–1826).

Astley's Circus founded 1770 by the English equestrian Philip Astley (1742–1814).

Aston, Francis William (1877–1945) English inventor of the mass spectograph.

Astor, John Jacob (1763–1848) American millionaire.

Astor, Nancy Witcher [Langhorne] [Viscountess Astor] (1879–1964) American-born British politician. She was elected to parliament as a Conservative MP, becoming the first woman to take her seat in House of Commons (1919).

Astrolabe, Mariner's adapted from the astronomer's astrolabe *c.*1480 by the German Martin Behaim (*c.*1459–1507).

Astrophysics the branch of astronomy that deals with the physical and chemial constitution of the stars, founded 1855 by the English scientist Sir William Huggins (1824–1910).

Astyages king of Media (595–560 BC) son and successor of Cyaxares, he was the last king of the Medes.

Asurnasirpal III king of Assyria 884 BC.

Aswan Dam, southern Egypt, completed 1902.

Aswan High Dam, southern Egypt, completed 1971.

Atahualpa last Inca of Peru (1532–33). He was executed.

Atatürk, Kemal [Mustafa Kemal Atatürk] (1881–1938) Turkish general and statesman, regarded as the creator of the modern Turkish state, he was prime minister 1923–38.

Athanasius, Saint (*c.*298–373) patriarch of Alexandria. The Athanasian Creed took its name from him as he was supposed to be its author.

Athelstan *see* ETHELSTAN and Appendix.

Athenaeum British periodical, began publication 1828; absorbed into *The Nation* 1921.

Athenaeum Club, London, founded 1824.

Athens ancient Greek city state and historic capital and principal city of Greece: end of monarchy 683 BC; legislation of Draco 621 BC; legislation of Solon 594 BC; Salamis conquered by Athens 570 BC; Pisistratus, Tyrant of Athens, 560–555 BC, 550–549 BC, 540–528 BC; Hippias and Hipparchus in power 528 BC; Pisistratid Tyranny at Athens ends and Hippias expelled 510 BC; Athens joins Peloponnesian League 510 BC Reforms of Cleisthenes 507 BC Athenians assist in the burning of Sardis 497 BC; Athenians under Themistocles defeat Persians at Salamis 480 BC; Confederacy of Delos founded by Athens for defence against Persia 477 BC; democratic reform in Athens, powers of the Areopagus limited by Ephialtes 463 BC; influence of Pericles begins 462 BC; Long Walls to Piraeus built 458 BC; Aegina conquered by Athens 456 BC; failure of an Athenian expedition to Egypt after initial success 454 BC; treasury of Confederacy of Delos removed to Athens 453 BC; Athenian empire at its height. Building of Parthenon began 447 BC; loss of Boeotia 447 BC; beginning of the Peloponnesian War between Athens and allies against Sparta and allies 431 BC, Thucydides its historian; Peace of Nicias 421 BC; end of Peloponnesian War 404 BC; Spartans entered Athens and set up the Thirty Tyrants; Thirty Tyrants overthrown 403 BC; Cnidus, Battle of Wars of Greek City States 394 BC: Spartan fleet destroyed by a combined Persian and Athenian fleet. Chaeronea, Battle of Amphictyonic War 338 BC: Athens and Thebes defeated by Philip of Macedon, who becomes supreme in Greece. Aristotle begins teaching at Athens 335 BC; schools closed 529; ruled by Turks 1456–1832.

Atkinson, Sir Harry (1831–92) New Zealand prime minister (1876–77, 1883–84, 1887–91).

Atlantic Charter signed 1941.

Atlantic Flight, First solo Trans- New York to Paris, made 1927 by the American aviator Charles Augustus Lindbergh (1902–74).

Atlantic Telegraph Cable a cable laid on the floor of the Atlantic Ocean was first suggested by Samuel Morse in 1843. An unsuccessful cable was laid in 1858. The first successful cable was laid by the SS *Great Eastern* 1866.

Atlantic Telephone Cable first opened for traffic 1956.

Atlantic Treaty, North signed in Washington DC 1949.

Atmosphere the layer of gases that encloses the earth, the composition of which was determined by the British scientist Henry Cavendish (1731–1810).

Atom the smallest part of a chemical element, which was thought to be indivisible until it was split in 1919 by the New Zealand-born scientist Lord Rutherford (1871–1937).

Atom bomb first used in warfare on Hiroshima and Nagasaki August 1945.

Atomic bomb explosion first carried out by the USA in New Mexico 1945.

Atomic Energy Agency, United Nations agency based in Vienna, established 1957.

Atomic nucleus first split (and the atom's energy released) by Sir John Cockcroft and Dr Walton 1932.

Atomic numbers of elements determined by the British scientist Henry Gwyn Jeffreys Moseley (1887, killed in battle 1915).

Atomic pile first started operating in Chicago 2 December 1942

Atomic-powered ship world's first, the Russian ice-breaker *Lenin,* launched 1957, put to sea 1958.

Atomic shell first fired in Nevada, USA, 1953.

Atomic theory classical version postulated by Leucippus of Miletus *c.*475 BC; modern version developed by the English chemist John Dalton (1766–1844).

Atomic weights pioneer work done by the Swedish chemist Baron Berzelius (1779–1848).

Atrebates ancient inhabitants of that part of Gaul that is now Belgium, afterwards called Artois. A colony of them settled in Britain, in a part of Berkshire and Sussex. *See also* Appendix.

Atropine drug extracted from belladonna discovered by the German scientist Philipp Lorenz Geiger 1833.

Attalus I (*c.*269–197 BC) king of Pergamus (241–197 BC) who defeated the Gauls and by 226 BC had made himself master of much of Asia Minor, but Seleucus III attacked him and by 221 BC his kingdom was limited to Pergamus itself.

Attalus III (d.133 BC) king of Pergamom (138–133 BC). He bequeathed his dominions to Rome, which formed the province of Asia 133 BC.

Attenborough, Sir David [Frederick] (1926–) English naturalist and broadcaster. He is Richard Attenborough's brother.

Attenborough, Sir Richard [Samuel] (1923–) English film director, producer and actor. He was created a life peer in 1993. His films as an actor include *Brighton Rock* (1947) and as a director *Gandhi.*

Atticus, Titus Pomponius (109–32 BC) Roman scholar.

Attila ('Scourge of God') (*c.*406–453) king of the Huns who invaded the Roman empire with an army that included Franks, Vandals and Ostrogoths. He was practically unbeaten in Europe until the battle of Chalons in 451, when his forces were annihilated by the son of Theodoric after his father had fallen on the battlefield.

Attlee, Clement [Richard] [1st Earl Attlee] (1883–1967) British statesman. Leader of the Labour Party (1939–55) and prime minister (1945–51), his 1945 administration introduced widespread nationalization and a programme of social security reforms.

Attorney General first English, William Bonneville 1277.

Attwood, Thomas (1765–1838) English composer and organist. A pupil of Mozart in Vienna, he became organist at St Paul's Cathedral, London. He was a friend of Mendelssohn and wrote anthems for the coronations of George IV and William IV.

Atwood, Margaret Eleanor (1939–) Canadian novelist and poet. Her works explore the common Canadian concern for cultural identity in relation to the US and also the question of female identity in a male-dominated world, e.g.*The Handmaid's Tale* (1986).

Auber, Daniel François Esprit (1782–1871) French composer. He wrote over forty operas, including *Fra Diavolo* (1830). In 1842 he followed Cherubini as director of the Paris Conservatoire.

Aubrey, John (1626–97) English antiquary and biographer. His *Lives of Eminent Men*, brief biographies of (mostly) his contemporaries, was first published in 1813 and is an invaluable and highly entertaining collection of biographical anecdotes, e.g. on Shakespeare and Jonson.

Auchinleck, Sir Claude (1884–1981) British soldier.

Auden, W[ystan] H[ugh] (1907–73) English-born American poet. The leading left-wing poet of his generation, he later drifted away from Marxism towards a Christian and socially conservative position. His works include *The Orators* (1932).

Audenarde (Oudenarde), Battle of fought between the English and the French 30 June–11 July 1708.

Audubon, John James (1785–1851) West Indian-born

American naturalist and artist. He studied drawing with David in Paris before moving to the US, where his interest in ornithology resulted in his *Birds of North America* (1827–38), one of the most beautiful of illustrated books.

Auer von Welsbach, Karl (1858–1929) inventor 1885 of gas mantle.

Augsburg, The Confession of Lutheran creed prepared 1530.

Augustine, Saint [Augustine of Hippo] (354–430) Latin Church Father. Born in what is now Tunisia, his father was a pagan and he was brought up a Christian by his mother. Reacting against the licentious life he led in Carthage, he converted to Manichaeanism for a while before returning to the Church. He was Bishop of Hippo (396–430) and wrote a spiritual autobiography, *Confessions*, and *City of God*, a major work of Christian apologetics.

Augustine, Saint (d. 604) Italian monk. He was dispatched to Britain in 597 by Pope Gregory I to convert the Anglo-Saxons to Christianity and impose the authority of Rome on the Celtic Church. He became the first Archbishop of Canterbury in 601.

Augustus *see* OCTAVIAN.

Augustus II (1670–1733) king of Poland (1697–1733).

Augustus III (1696–1763) king of Poland (1736–63).

Aulus Platonius Nepos (*fl* 1st century AD) Roman general who was sent by the emperor Claudius to subdue Britain 43–47 AD.

Aulus Platorius Nepos (*fl* 2nd century AD) Roman governor of Britain. The building of Hadrian's Wall across northern England from the Solway to the Tyne, which had begun in 122, was completed under his governorship.

Aurangzeb (1618–1707) Mogul emperor of India (1659–1707).

Aurelian [Lucius Domitius Aurelianus] (*c.*212–275) Roman emperor (270–275). He was assassinated.

Aurelius, Marcus *see* MARCUS AURELIUS.

Auric, Georges (1899–1983) French composer, the youngest member of Les Six. He wrote operas and ballets, e.g. *Les Matelots* (1925), piano and chamber pieces as well as music for films, particularly those of René Clair and Jean Cocteau.

Auschwitz (Oswiecim) a small town in Poland, site of the largest of the Nazi concentration camps, 1940–45.

Auscultation by stethoscope medical examination introduced by the French physician René Théophile Hyacinthe Laënnec (1781–1826).

Austen, Jane (1775–1817) English novelist. Her six great novels, *Sense and Sensibility* (1811), *Pride and Prejudice* (1813), *Mansfield Park* (1814), *Emma* (1816) and *Northanger Abbey* and *Persuasion* (1818) are set within the confines of the society in which she lived, the well-bred essentially rural middle class of Regency England. She is renowned for her masterly dialogue, finely tuned satire and moral sense.

Austerlitz, Battle of a battle of the Napoleonic Wars between the French, and the Austrians and Russians 2 December 1805. It was Napoleon's greatest victory.

Austin, Alfred (1835–1913) English poet, who, despite his jingoistic verse, was appointed poet laureate (1896–1913).

Austin, John Langshaw (1911–60) English philsopher. He stressed the need for simplicity and use of ordinary language in philosophical specualation, as seen in his posthumously published lectures, Sense and Sensibilia and How to do Things with Words (both 1962).

Australia the world's smallest continental landmass, an island state in the southern hemisphere; circumnavigated 1642–43 by the Dutch navigator Abel Janszoon Tasman (*c.*1603–59). Reached by air from England by Ross and Keith Smith 1919.

Australia, The Commonwealth of created 1 January 1901.

Austria a landlocked country in Central Europe; ruled by Hapsburgs 1278–1918; republic 1918–38; annexed by Germany 1938; occupied 1943–55; regained independence 1955.

Austrian Succession, War of the 1740–48.

Authorized Version of the Bible a translation of the Bible made at the order of James I and first published 1611. It is based for the most part on William Tyndale's translation of 1525.

Autogyro invented by La Cierra 1920.

Avars entered Europe *c.*555; defeated by Franks in 8th and 9th centuries.

Averroës (1126–98) [Ibn Rushd] Arab philosopher. Born in Spain, he became a judge, scholar and court physician in Morocco. His works, notably his Commentaries on Aristotle, which attempted a synthesis of Aristotelian and Islamic philosophy, were profoundly influential on European scholarship.

Avery, 'Tex' [Frederick Bean] (1907–80) American animator, created Daffy Duck, Bugs Bunny.

Avicenna (*c.*980–1037) (Ibn Sina) Persian philosopher.

Avignon a city on the River Rhone in southern France; ceded to the papacy 1274; seat of papacy 1309–1418; annexed to France 1791.

Avoirdupois a system of weights that generally superseded the merchants' pound in England 1303.

Avus, Battle of 198 BC a battle of the Second Macedonian War, when the Macedonians under Philip were defeated by the Romans.

Axminster carpet introduced into Britain from the USA *c.*1878.

Ayckbourn, Alan (1939–) English playwright and theatre director noted for his often rather dark comedies of middle-class life in suburban England, e.g. *The Norman Conquests* (1974) trilogy, which depicts identical events through the eyes of different characters.

Ayer, Sir A[lfred] J[ules] (1910–89) English philosopher, whose work is based on 'logical positivism' and the rejection of metaphysics and has been highly influential on British 'common-sense' philosophy. His works include *Language, Truth and Logic* (1936).

Ayub Khan, Mohammed (1907–74) Pakistani field marshal and statesman, president of Pakistan (1958–69). He was the first commander-in-chief of his country's army (1951–58) and introduced some reforms during his presidency. His suspension of civil liberties and increasingly dictatorial style of leadership eroded his power base and led to his fall in 1969.

Azañay Diaz, Manuel de (1880–1940) Spanish statesman (last republican president).

Azerbaijan a country on the southwest coast of the Caspian Sea; a republic of the former Soviet Union, it declared itself independent in 1991.

Azikiwe, [Benjamin] Nnamdi (1904–) Nigerian statesman, first president of Nigeria (1963–66). During the Nigerian civil war he joined the Biafran secessionist government, but accepted the reunification process once the war was over, when he (unsuccessfully) stood once more for president. He has been described as the 'father of modern Nigeria'.

Aztecs one of the former tribes of Mexico that had established an empire in the 14th century and were at the height of their power when they were discovered by the Spaniards, who had destroyed the empire by the early 16th century.

B

Baader, Franz Xaver von (1765–1841) German theologian.

Baader-Meinhof Group (Red Army Faction) West German urban guerrilla group (1968–72) led by Andreas Baader (1943–77) and Ulrike Meinhof (1934–76); both committed suicide in prison.

Baal-Shem-Tov [Israel ben Eliezer] (1700–60) Russian founder of the modern Hasidim (Jewish sect).

Baalbek Syrian city, destroyed by earthquake 1759.

Babar *see* **Baber.**

Babbage, Charles (1792–1871) English mathematician and founder of the Royal Astronomical Society. He designed an 'analytical engine' (1827–47), the prototype for modern computers.

Babbitt Metal anti-friction alloy invented 1839 by the American Isaac Babbitt (1799–1861).

Babel, Isaac Emmanuilovich (1894–1941) Russian writer (*Red Cavalry* 1926).

Baber, Babar *or* **Babur** (*c.*1483–1530) founder of the Mogul dynasty and conqueror of North India (ruled 1526–30).

Babeuf, François Noël (1760–97) French revolutionary leader who prepared the Babouvist conspiracy in 1796. He was guillotined.

Babi Persian religious sect founded 1844 by Mirza Ali Mohammed (1821–50). He was killed.

Babington Plot to murder Queen Elizabeth I in 1585, devised by Anthony Babington (1561–86). Babington was executed.

Babur *see* BABER.

Babylon first dynasty established 2100 BC by Sumu-Abu after the fall of Isin; Sumerians finally give way to the Semites; agricultural improvements and law reform under Hammurabi, greatest king of the first dynasty; ruled by Kassite invaders 1800-1200 BC; Assyria independent of Babylon *c.*1700 BC; conflict between Assyria and Babylonia 1410 BC; conquered by Tukultininib, king of Assyria, 1290 BC; subdued by Shalmaneser II, king of Assyria, 860 BC; subuded by Tiglath-Pileser III 729 BC; Assyrian power in Babylon ended by Merodachbaladan 721 BC; Babylon again subdued by Asurbanipal, king of Assyria 668 BC; capture and destruction of Nineveh by Nabopolassar of Babylon and Cyaxares of Media, end of Assyrian Empire 612 BC; Egyptian power in Syria overthrown by Babylon 605 BC at Battle of Carchemish; Jerusalem taken by Nebuchadnezzar 597 BC, Jehoiachin, the king, Esekiel, the prophet and others taken to Babylon; Zedekiah made king of Judah; Zedekiah's revolt against Babylonian rule; Jerusalem taken and destroyed by Nebuchadnezzar 586 BC; Babylon conquered by Cyrus 538 BC, declined in importance after this; Persian conquest 520 BC; submission of Babylon to Alexander 331 BC; death of Alexander at Babylon 323 BC; Seleucid Dynasty in Asia founded by Seleucus I (Nicator) 312 BC, capital at first Babylon.

Babylonian Captivity of the Jews 586–516 BC; dedication of the New Temple at Jerusalem after the return from the Babylonian Captivity 515 BC; return of Ezra with many Jews from Babylon to Jerusalem 458 BC.

'Babylonish Captivity' of the popes 1309–77.

Bacall, Lauren [Betty Joan Perske] (1924–) American film and stage actress (*The Big Sleep* 1946). She married Humphrey Bogart in 1944.

Baccarat Case in which future Edward VII gave evidence concerning gambling at Tranby Croft, tried June 1891.

Bacchelli, Riccardo (1891–1985) Italian novelist (*Il Diavolo al Pontelungo* 1927).

Bach, Johann Christoph Friedrich (1732–95) German composer, mainly of church music. He was the ninth son of of Johann Sebastian Bach.

Bach, Johann Sebastian (1685–1750) German composer. His works include some of the greatest music in several forms, e.g. his six cello suites, choral masterpieces such as the *St Matthew Passion*, and works for harpsichord, clavichord and the organ, such as *The Well-Tempered Clavier* and *The Art of Fugue*. Four of his sons were also composers.

Bach, Johann [John] Christian (1735–82) German composer and eleventh son of Johann Sebastian Bach, he became a court musician in London, where he was known as 'the English Bach' and influenced Mozart.

Bach, Karl Philipp Emmanuel (1714–88) German composer and son of Johann Sebastian Bach.

Bach, Wilhelm Friedemann (1710–84) German composer and organ player, the eldest son of Johann Sebastian Bach.

Bache, Alexander Dallas (1806–67) American founder 1863 of the National Academy of Sciences.

Bacon, Francis [Baron Verulam] (1561–1626) English philosopher and statesman. He served both Elizabeth I and her successor James VI and I in various offices until his conviction and disgrace for bribery in 1621. His writings on philosophy and the need for rational scientific method are landmarks in the history of human thought.

Bacon, Francis (1909–92) Irish-born British painter. His works feature twisted and contorted human shapes, often in weird landscapes or spaces, e.g. *Three Studies for a Crucifixion* (1962).

Bacon, Nathaniel (*c.*1647-1676) American colonial leader. He made several raids against the native American population. He was declared a rebel by the English governor, Sir William Berkeley, in 1676 and subsequently captured and burned at Jamestown, Virginia.

Bacon, Roger (*c.*1214–*c.*1294) English philosopher and scientist. Although he believed in astrology, he made some great discoverfies in physics and other branches of science. The extent of his knowledge caused him to be considered as a magician and he was imprisoned in Paris for magic.

Bacon's Rebellion American revolt 1676 in Virginia, led by Nathaniel Bacon (1647–76).

Bacteria discovered 1680 by the Dutch scientist A. van Leeuwenhoek (1632–1723); classified by F. J. Cohn 1872.

Badajoz, Battle of Peninsular War battle between Wellington and the French 1812.

Baden-Powell, Robert, Lord (1857–1941) founder 1908 of the Boy Scouts.

Badminton game played with shuttlecock, first played in England *c.*1873.

Badoglio, Pietro (1871–1956) Italian field marshal.

Badon, Mount legendary battle between British and Saxons *c.*500.

Baedeker, Karl (1801–59) German publisher in Cologne who made his name famous in connection with a series of guidebooks to various countries.

Baer, Karl Ernst von (1792–1876) Estonian scientist and discoverer 1827 of the mammalian ovum.

Baer, Max (1910–59) world heavy-weight boxing champion 1934.

Baeyer, Johann Friedrich Wilhelm Adolf von (1835–1917) German scientist and Nobel Prize winner 1905.

Baez, Joan (1941–) American folksinger, renowned for her 'protest songs' on civil rights and the Vietnam war in the 1960s.

Baffin, William (*c.*1584–1622) English sailor and explorer. He visited Greenland and Spitzbergen and surveyed the Hudson Strait and the large island now called after him.

Baffin Bay a part of the Northwest Passage, lying between Baffin Island and Greenland, discovered 1616 by William Baffin.

Baffin Island a large island lying between Greenland and Hudson Bay, the largest island of the Canadian Arctic, discovered and surveyed 1616 by William Baffin.

Bagehot, Walter(1826–77) English sociologist and editor of the *Economist.* His most important works are *The English Constitution, Physics and Politics* and *Lombard Street.*

Baghdad Railway started 1888, completed 1940.

Bagration, Piotr Ivanovich (1765–1812) Russian general who fought (1812) Napoleon at Borodino.

Baha'i religious sect developed from Babi by Mirza Hozain Ali (1817–92) and his son Abbas Effendi (1844–1921).

Bahamas West Indian islands discovered 1492 by Christopher Columbus; British colony 1783–1964; independent within the Commonwealth since 1973.

Bahrain Persian Gulf, British Protectorate from 1861 to independence in 1971.

Baïf, Jean Antoine de (1532–1589) French poet.

Baikie, William Balfour (1825–64) Scottish explorer of West Africa.

Bailey bridge invented 1941 by Sir Donald Bailey (1901–85).

Baillie, Joanna (1762–1851) Scottish dramatist and poet.

Bain, Alexander Scottish philosopher (1818–1903).

Baird, John Logie (1888–1946) Scottish engineer who invented a mechanically scanned system of television in the mid–1920s.

Bairnsfather, Bruce (1888–1959) English cartoonist and creator of the character 'Old Bill'.

Bajazet I (1347–1403) Turkish sultan.

Bajazet II (1446–1513) Turkish sultan.

Bakelite invented 1907 by the American Leo Hendrik Baekeland (1863–1944).

Baker, Sir Benjamin (1840–1907) English designer of the Forth Rail Bridge.

Baker, Chet [Chesney] (1929–88) American jazz trumpeter and vocalist.

Baker, Dame Janet [Abbott] (1933–) English mezzo-soprano who became one of Britain's most popular opera singers in the 1960s and had parts created for her by composers such as Britten. She was appointed a DBE in 1976.

Baker, Josephine (1906–75) American-born dancer, singer and civil rights activist.

Baker, Sir Samuel White (1821–93) English explorer of Africa, discoverer (1864) of Albert Nyanza. He wrote many travel books.

Bakerloo Line London Underground, opened 1906.

Bakewell, Robert (1725–95) English agricultural pioneer.

Bakst, Leon (1866–1924) Russian-born stage designer.

Bakunin, Mikhail (1814–76) Russian anarchist leader.

Balakirev, Mili Alexeivich (1836–1910) Russian composer.

Balaklava a port on the Black Sea, a few miles from Sebastopol, which has a landlocked harbour with a very safe anchorage. It was the British headquarters during the Crimean War and the scene of the battle of Balaklava.

Balaklava, Battle of a battle of the Crimean War, 25 October 1854, the outcome of which was indecisive but part of which was the famous Charge of the Light Brigade, when 600 British cavalry troops charged and took a Russian battery. Although a brilliant feat of arms, it was made under an erroneous interpretation of orders.

Balanchine, George (1904–83) Russian-born ballet dancer.

Balas, Alexander *see* ALEXANDER BALAS.

Balbinus, Decimus Caelius (d.238) Roman statesman and joint emperor with Maximus (238) They were proclaimed joint emperors by the Senate after the death of the Gordians and in the face of the threat from Maximin. Maximin was murdered by his own troops; Maximus and Balbinus were murdered by the Praetorian guard, leaving the third Gordian sole emperor.

Balboa, Vasco Núñez de (1475–1517) Spanish discoverer (1513) of the Pacific Ocean. He was beheaded.

Balbus, Lucius Cornelius (*fl.* 56–40 BC) Roman consul defended by Cicero.

Balchin, Nigel (1908–) English writer (*The Small Back Room* 1943).

Baldovinetti, Alessio (*c.*1425–1499) Italian painter.

Baldwin, James [Arthur] (1924–87) American novelist, dramatist and essayist. His main concern was with the role of blacks in American society, and, to a lesser extent, that of homosexuals. His novels include *Go Tell it on the Mountain* (1953).

Baldwin, Robert Canadian statesman (1804–58).

Baldwin, Stanley [1st Earl Baldwin of Bewdley] (1867–1947) British statesman and Conservative prime minister (1923–24, 1924–29, 1935–37) Notable aspects of his premierships include the passing of a state of emergency during the 1926 General Strike, his refusal to accept Wallis Simpson as Edward VIII's wife (*see* WINDSOR) and his failure to deal with the rise of European totalitarianism.

Baldwin I (1171–1205) emperor at Constantinople. He was killed.

Baldwin II (1217–1273) emperor at Constantinople.

Baldwin I (1058–1118) first king of Jerusalem.

Baldwin II (d.1131) king of Jerusalem (1118–1131) and brother of Godrey de Bouillon.

Baldwin III (1130–1162) king of Jerusalem.

Baldwin IV (*c.*1161–1185) king of Jerusalem.

Baldwin V (1178–1186) king of Jerusalem.

Bale, John (1495–1563) English dramatist.

Balearic Islands a group of islands in the Mediterranean, off the east coast of Spain, including Majora and Menorca; annexed by Rome 123 bc; taken by the Vandals under Genseric and by the Moors in the 8th century; taken by James I, king of Aragon, and constituted a kindom; united to Spain 1343; taken by Britain in the Napoleonic Wars; finally ceded to Spain 1803.

Balfe, Michael William(1808–70) British singer and composer who was born in Dublin and made his debut at the age of nine. He had a good baritone voice and composed some popular operas, e.g. *The Bohemian Girl* (1843).

Balfour Declaration favouring the creation of a Jewish national home in Palestine made by the British Government 2 November 1917.

Balfour, Arthur James, Earl Balfour (1848–1930) British statesman (prime minister 1902–1905).

Bali Indonesian island, first reached by the Dutch 1597.

Baliol *see* BALLIOL.

Balkan Wars fought by the Balkan powers over the division of the Turkish empire in Europe 1912–13.

Ball, John (d.1381) English priest and peasants' leader. He was executed.

Ball, Lucy [Lucille Desirée] (1911–89) American comedy actress, star of TV series 'I Love Lucy' (1951–55).

Ballantyne, R[obert] M[ichael] (1825–94) Scottish writer of boys' stories. He lived in the Hudson Bay Company's fur-trapping lands from 1841 to 1847, where he accumulated material for many of his stories.

Ballard, J[ames] G[raham] (1930–) English novelist (*Empire of the Sun* 1984).

Balliol *or* **Baliol, Edward** (1287–1364) king of Scots (1332–41) *see* Appendix.

Balliol *or* **Baliol, John de** (1249–1313) king of Scots (1292–96) *see* Appendix.

Balliol College Oxford University founded *c.*1263 by John de Baliol (d.1269), the third son of John de Balliol.

Ballistite smokeless powder invented 1888 by the Swedish chemist Alfred Nobel (1833–96).

Balloons invented by the brothers Joseph and Etienne Montgolfier 1783, first ascent by Montgolfier and Pilâtre de Roziers 21 November 1783; first ascent in hydrogen balloon made by the physicist J. A. C. Charles 1 December 1783; first ascents in Britain made 1784.

Ballot voting by ballot made compulsory in Britain 1872.

Balmoral Castle a British royal residence in Aberdeenshire, completed 1855.

Balsamo, Giuseppe ('Count Alessandro di Cagliostro') (1743–95) Italian charlatan and alchemist born at Palermo. In England he established an order of what he called Egyptian masonry, in which, as *grand kophta*, he pretended to reveal the secrets of the future and duped many people. In Paris he was implicated in the affair of the diamond necklace, which caused a scandal in the reign of Louis XVI, and was imprisoned in the Bastille but managed to escape. In 1789 he went to Rome where he was imprisoned. He died in prison.

Baltic, Battle of the *see* COPENHAGEN, BATTLE OF.

Baltic Exchange (The Baltic Mercantile and Shipping Exchange), London, developed from informal 17th-century coffee-house transactions to the formal establishment of the Baltic Club 1823.

Baltimore, Maryland, formally founded 1729; settled about fifty years earlier.

Baluchistan merged in West Pakistan 14 October 1955.

Balzac, Honoré de (1799–1850) French novelist. His great collection of novels and short stories describe the lives of French men and women of every class. His works include *La Comédie humaine* ('the Human Comedy' 1829–50).

Bampton Lectures a series of lecture delivered annually at Oxford University since 1780, founded by John Bampton (*c.*1690–1751).

Bancroft, Anne *see* BROOKS, MEL.

Bancroft, George (1800–91) American historian.

Bancroft, Sir Squire (1841–1926) English actor-manager.

Banda, Hastings [Kamuzu] (1905–) Malawi statesman, first president of Nyasaland from 1963 and president of Malawi (formerly Nyasaland) from 1966. One of the longest-ruling leaders in the world, he was appointed president for life in 1971.

Bandung Conference of Asian-African countries held 18–27 April 1955.

Bangalore Mysore capital founded 1537.

Bangkok made capital of Thailand by Paya Tak 1782.

Bangladesh formerly East Pakistan; became independent republic after civil war 1971.

Bank for International Settlements founded 13 November 1929.

Bank for Reconstruction and Development, International proposed at Bretton Woods Conference 1944, constituted December 1945, started operations 27 June 1946.

Bank of England founded 1694 by William Paterson (1658–1719); nationalized 1946.

Bank of France founded by Napoleon I 1800.

Bank of Scotland founded by the Scottish Parliament 1695.

Bank of the United States: first founded by the Federalists 1791, ended 1811; second founded 1816, ended 1836.

Bankhead, Tallulah (1903–68) American stage and film actress (*Lifeboat* 1944).

Bankruptcy Act abolished imprisonment for debt 1870.

Banks, Sir Joseph (1743–1820) English botanist and explorer. He sailed with Cook on his 1768–71 voyage round the world as a representative of the Royal Society and discovered many species of animals and plants. He was

Bannister, Sir Roger [Gilbert] (1929–) British amateur athlete and doctor who became the first man to run a mile in four minutes on 6 May 1954.

Bannockburn, Battle of fought between Scots and English 24 June 1314.

Banting, Sir Frederick [Grant] (1891–1941) Canadian physician whose research into diabetes with the American physiologist Charles Herbert Best (1899–1978) resulted in the isolation of the hormone insulin in a form suitable for treating diabetes. He was killed in an air crash.

Banting, William (1797–1878) English undertaker and pioneer in slimming by diet.

Bantock, Sir Granville (1868–1946) English composer (*The Great God Pan* 1903).

Bantry Bay, Battle of when French attempted the invasion of Ireland 1689; and again in 1796.

Baptist Church a Christian church that opposes infant baptism, first English church formed 1609 at Amsterdam and 1611 in London. The Baptist Union of Great Britain and Ireland formed 1891. In USA first Baptist church formed at the Providence settlement of Narragansett Bay in 1639.

Barbados visited by the English 1605; formally occupied by the English 1625; became part of the British Caribbean Federation 1956.

Barbarossa the nickname of Frederick I, Holy Roman emperor (*c.*1123–1190).

Barbarossa Brothers Turkish pirates who terrorized Christian shipping in the Mediterranean in the early 16th century.

Barbed Wire invented 1873 by the American Joseph Farwell Glidden (1813–1906).

'Barbellion, W. N. P.' [Bruce Frederick Cummings] (1889–1919) English writer, whose works include

The Journal of a Disappointed Man (1919).

Barber, Samuel (1910–81) American composer who worked with recognizably 19th-century harmonies and forms. His works include the popular *Adagio for Strings* (1936), *Essay for Orchestra* (1938).

Barbey d'Aurevilly, Jules (1808–89) French writer.

Barbirolli, Sir John (1899–1970) conductor of the Hallé Orchestra from 1943.

Barbizon School French art movement 1830–70.

Barbon, Nicolas (1640–98) English pioneer of fire insurance. He was the son of Praise-God Barebone.

Barbusse, Henri (1873–1935) French writer (*Le Feu* 1916).

Barcelona Cathedral erected 1298–1448.

Barcelona University founded 1430.

Barcochba Jewish leader of a revolt 131.

Bard College, Annandale-on-Hudson, NY, founded 1860, chartered in its present form and name 1935.

Bardeen, John (1908–91) American physicist and electrical engineer. He won two Nobel prizes, the first in 1956 for research that led to the invention of the transistor, the second in 1972 for research into the theory of superconductivity.

Bardot, Brigitte (1934–) French actress. The leading 'sex symbol' of the 1950s, her films included *And God Created Woman* (1956). Since the 1970s she has devoted herself to animal rights and welfare.

Barebone's Parliament an assembly of Roundheads called by Cromwell during the Commonwealth, sat 4 July to 12 December 1653. It was named after one of its members, the clergyman Praise-God Barebone (*c.*1596–1679).

Barenboim, Daniel (1942–) Argentinian-born Israeli concert pianist and conductor. He married the cellist Jacqueline du Pré in 1967 and was awarded the Legion of Honour in 1987.

Barents Sea named after William Barents (d.1597), the Dutch explorer, who made great efforts to discover the Northeast Passage to Asia.

Barham, Richard Harris (1788–1845) English writer (*The Ingoldsby Legends* 1837–40).

Barhebraeus (Abulfaraj) (1226–86) Armenian writer and bishop of Aleppo.

Baring, Maurice (1874–1945) English writer (*In My End is My Beginning* 1931).

Baring Brothers English merchant bankers, founded by John Baring (1730–1816) and Francis Baring (1740–1810). It was forced into collapse in 1995 by the activities of one of its employees in Singapore, Nick Leeson, who was imprisoned.

Baring-Gould, Sabine (1834–1924) English writer and hymn-writer ('Onward, Christian soldiers' 1865).

Barium first investigated by V. Casciorolus of Bologna 1602, discovered 1808 by Sir Humphry Davy (1778–1829).

Barker, Granville (1913–) English poet and novelist (*Alanna Autumnal* 1933).

Bar-Kochba, Simon (d.135) Jewish leader in revolt against Romans (131–135). He was killed fighting.

Barlach, Ernst (1870–1937) German artist.

Barnabites Catholic religious order founded 1537 by St Antony Mary Zaccaria (d.1539).

Barnard, Christian [Neethling] (1923–) South African surgeon, who performed the first heart transplant operation on 2 December 1967.

Barnardo's Homes, Dr homes for destitute children, founded 1867 by Dr Thomas Barnardo (1845–1905).

Barnato, Barnett (1852–97) English-born South African financier. He committed suicide.

Barnes, Barnabe (*c.*1569–1609) English poet.

Barnes, Thomas (1785–1841) English journalist and editor of *The Times* (1817–41).

Barnes, William (1800–86) English dialect poet.

Barnet, Battle of a battle of the Wars of the Roses, 14 April 1471, which was a Yorkist victory.

Barnet Fair, Hertfordshire, held during first week in September.

Barnfield, Richard (1574–1627) English pastoral poet.

Barnum's Show founded 1871 by the American Phineas Taylor Barnum (1810–91).

Baroja, Pio Spanish novelist (1872–1956).

Barometers invented 1644 by Evangelista Torricelli (1608–47).

Baronet title created by King James I of England 1611 to provide funds for the colonization of Ulster. The first baronet was Sir Nicholas Bacon, and fee was fixed about about £1000, a stipulation being made that there should never be more than 200 baronets.

Barr, Robert (1850–1912) Scottish writer (*In the Midst of Alarms* 1894).

Barren Grounds a large tract in the Northwest Territories of Canada, first crossed 1770–72 by the English explorer Samuel Hearne (1745–92).

Barrès, Maurice (1862–1923) French politician and writer (*Le jardin de Bérénice* 1891).

Barrie, Sir J[ames] M[atthew] (1860–1937) Scottish dramatist and novelist, remembered principally for *Peter Pan* (1904).

Barrington, George (1755–1804) Irish pickpocket who became an Australian chief constable.

Barrister first English woman barrister qualified 25 May 1921.

Barrow, Sir John (1764–1848) English explorer and founder (1830) of the Royal Geographical Society.

Barry, Sir Charles (1795–1860) English architect of the House of Commons.

Barrymore family of American stage and film performers: **Lionel Barrymore** (1878–1954), **Ethel Barrymore** (1879–1959) and **John Barrymore** (1882–1942). They appeared together only once, in *Rasputin and the Empress* (1932).

Bart, Jean (1650–1702) French admiral.

Barth, Hans (1897–1956) German composer.

Barth, Heinrich (1821–65) German traveller and scientist.

Barth, Karl (1847–1922) German pianist.

Barth, Karl (1886–1968) Swiss Protestant theologian whose theology was based on an orthodox 'theocentric' conception of divine grace and is seen as a reaction against the simplifications of 19th-century liberal theology. He was a committed and courageous opponent of Nazism.

Barthes, Roland (1915–80) French literary and cultural critic and philosopher, whose semiological studies were regarded as necessary reading in the 1960s and 1970s. His works include *Elements of Sociology* and *Mythologies* (1957).

Bartholdi, Frédéric Auguste (1834–1904) French sculptor (*Statue of Liberty*).

Bartholomew, John George (1860–1920) Scottish cartographer.

Bartholomew, Massacre of St *see* St Bartholomew Days' Massacre.

Bartholomew Fair held at West Smithfield, London, on St Bartholomew's Day (24 August OS) from 1133 to 1855.

Bartholomew's Hospital, St *see* St Bartholomew's Hospital.

Barthou, Jean (1862–1934) French statesman who was a member of several cabinets and was appointed prime minister in March 1913 but resigned in December of the same year. As foreign minister in 1934 he sought to strengthen alliances with Russia, Italy and Yugoslavia, but he was assassinated in Marseilles with King Alexander I of Yugoslavia by a Croat terrorist.

Bartlett, John (1820–1905) American bookseller and editor who compiled *Familiar Quotations* (1855), which has become a standard reference work in its field.

Bartók, Béla (1881–1945) Hungarian composer and pianist. He was a noted collector of folk songs, upon which many of his works are based. His works include the ballet *The Miraculous Mandarin*, string quartets, *Concerto for Orchestra* and *The Castle of Duke Bluebeard* (1918).

Bartolommeo, Fra [Baccio Della Porta] (*c.*1470–1517) Italian painter who studied in Florence. He was a follower of Savonarola, on whose death he joined the Dominican order and took the name of Fra Bartolommeo. His colouring, in vigour and brilliance, comes near to that of Titian ad Giorgione. His *Holy Family* is in the National Gallery, London.

Bartolozzi, Francesco (1727–1815) Italian engraver from Florence who worked all over Italy before living in London for forty years. He became director of the National Academy at Lisbon, Portugal.

Bartram, John (1739–1823) first American botanist.

Baruch, Bernard Mannes (1870–1965) American financier.

Barye, Antoine Louis (1795–1875) French sculptor.

Baseball the national game of the USA, the invention of which is attributed to Abner Doubleday (1819–83) of Cooperstown, New York.

Basevi, George (1794–1845) English architect of the Fitzwilliam Museum, Cambridge (1837).

Bashkirtsev, Marie (1860–84) Russian painter and writer (*Journal* 1887).

Basic English produced 1930 by C. K. Ogden.

Basie, 'Count' [William] (1904–84) American jazz pianist, composer and bandleader. He was a jazz pianist of great ability, and his big band featured singers such as Ella Fitzgerald and Frank Sinatra.

Basil, Saint (Basil the Great) (*c.*330–379) Greek priest who became bishop of Caesarea. He worked towards the regulation of clerical discipline and advocated monasticism. The vows of obedience, chastity and poverty frame by him are essentially the rules of all the Christian orders, although he is particularly the father of the Eastern orders as St Benedict is the patriarch of the Western orders.

Basil I (*c.*813–886) Byzantine emperor (867–886) who came from Macedonia and succeeded in gaining the favour of Michael III and became his colleague in the empire 866. After the assassination of Michael in 867, he became emperor. Although he had worked his way to the throne by a series of crimes, he proved an able and equitable sovereign.

Basil II (*c.*958–1025) Byzantine emperor (963–1025). On the death of his father, Romanus II, in 963 he was kept out of the succession for twelve years by two usurpers. He began to reign in conjunction with his brother Constantine, 976. His reign was spent in almost perpetual warfare, his most important struggle being that which resulted in the conquest of Bulgaria, 1018.

Baskerville, John (1706–75) British printer and typefounder.

Basketball invented by James Naismith at Springfield, Mass., 1891.

Basle University founded by Pope Pius II 1460.

Bass & Co. British brewers founded 1777 by William Bass (b.1720).

Bassano, Jacopo da [Giacomo da Ponte] (1510–92)

Italian painter who worked in Venice. He painted historical pieces, landscapes, flowers, etc, and also portraits. He had four sons who all became painters, Francesco being the most distinguished.

Bassompierre, François de (1579–1646) French soldier who was made Marshal of France by Louis XIII in 1622 and took part in the siege of La Rochelle (1628–29). He was imprisoned by Richelieu in 1631 and not released until 1643 after the cardinal's death. During his imprisonment he wrote his memoirs.

Bass Strait the channel between Australia and Tasmania, discovered 1798 by George Bass, English naval surgeon (d.1812).

Bastien-Lepage, Jules (1848–84) French realist painter who painted subjects connected with the country and everyday life, e.,g. *The Potato Harvest.*

Bastille, The the state prison and citadel of Paris, built 1369 by Hugues Aubriot (d.1383); destroyed 14 July 1789.

Bataille, Henri (1872–1922) French writer.

Batavia, Java, founded by the Dutch governor-general Pieter Roth 1619.

Bates, H[erbert] E[rnest] (1905–74) English novelist and short-story writer. His works include *My Uncle Silas* (1939) and the comic novel *The Darling Buds of May* (1958) featuring the Larkins, an unruly farming family.

Bath, Order of the (custom in existence by 1127), founded by George I in 1725.

Batoni, Pompeo Girolamo (1708–87) Italian painter.

Battenberg the title conferred on Julia von Hanke in 1851 on the occasion of her morganatic marriage with Prince Alexander of Hesse; son Louis changed the name to Mountbatten in 1917.

Battle, Ordeal by valid in English law until 1818.

'Battle Hymn of the Republic, The' written 1862 by the American poet Mrs Julia Ward Howe (1819–1910).

Battle of Britain the night bombing of Germany by Britain in the Second World War, fought 8 August to 5 0ctober 1940.

Battle of the Atlantic in the Second World War the struggle for the control of the sea routes around the UK, especially 1940–43.

Battle of the Bulge a Second World War battle fought in France December 1944 to January 1945.

Battle of the Spurs *or* **Battle of Guinegate** a battle fought between Henry VIII and the French 16 August 1513. It was an English victory.

Battus legendary founder of the Greek colony of Cyrene in Libya *c.*650 BC. There were eight rulers of the family founded by him, bearing alternately the names Battus and Arcesilaus.

Batu Khan Mongol ruler (1224–55) of the Western conquests of his grandfather, Genghis Khan. He overran Russia, Poland, Hungar and Dalmatia, holding Russia for ten years.

Baudelaire, Charles (1821–67) French poet noted for his fascination with the macabre and alleged Satanism. He became a leading Symbolist poet and his works include *Les Fleurs du mal.* (1857).

Bauhaus architectural and design movement founded 1919 by Walter Gropius (1883–1969).

Bauxite discovered by the Belgian P. Berthier 1821.

Bavaria formerly a kindom in the south of Germany, ruled by Wittelsbachs 1180–1918.

Bavarian Succession, War of the fought 1778–79.

Bax, Sir Arnold (1883–1953) composer (*The Poisoned Fountain* 1920).

Baxter, George (1804–67) English engraver and colour printer.

Baxter, Richard (1615–91) English clergyman and writer who became chaplain to Charles II on the Restoration. Following the passage of the Act of Uniformity he threw in his lot interely with the nonconformists. He was imprisoned 1685–91. He left many treatises, of which *The Saints' Everlasting Rest* (1650) was one of the most popular.

Bayard, Pierre du Terrail, Seigneur de (*c.*1474–1524) French general who served Charles VIII and Louis XII in Italy and became known as *Le chevalier sans peur et sans reproche* ('the fearless and blameless knight' He was killed in battle during the invasion of Lombardy.

Bay Bridge, San Francisco, built 1936.

Bayeux Tapestry a piece of needlework on a linen strip, 18 inches wide and 204 feet long, on which are worked in coloured threads 72 scenes connected with the invasion of England by William I. It is supposed to be the work of Matilda, William's queen, and was probably embroidered in the 12th century; first recorded mention 1476.

Bayle, Pierre (1647–1706) French critic and writer who became professor of philosophy at Sedan and Rotterdam. He was removed from his post in 1693 as the result of the activities of a rival and devoted himself to his *Dictionnaire Historique et Critique* (1691).

Baylis, Lilian Mary (1874–1937) British theatre manager. She founded the Old Vic theatre in London in 1912 and Sadler's Wells Company for opera and ballet in 1931.

Bay of Pigs, Invasion of the abortive attempt to invade Cuba by anti-Castro exiles funded and equipped by the US government, April 1961.

Bayreuth a town in Bavaria in southern Germany, founded 1194. It was the home and is the burial place of Richard Wagner, who built the Bayreuth Theatre.

ayreuth Theatre a theatre in Bayreuth, Germany, designed by Richard Wagner for the performance of his operas, built 1872, opened 1876. There are annual festivals of his music.

ay Psalm Book the earliest American printed book, published at Cambridge, Mass., 1640.

azin, René (1853–1932) French novelist who was professof law at Angers before turning to writing. His works include *Les Oberté* (1901).

eadle, George Wells (1903–89) American geneticist who worked with Edward Tatum on experiments to show that biochemical reactions in cells are controlled by particular genes. He shared the 1958 Nobel prize for physiology or medicine with Tatum and Lederberg.

ealdred king of Kent (807–825) *see* Appendix.

eale, Dorothea (1831–1906) principal of Cheltenham Ladies' College.

ear-baiting the sport of baiting bears with dogs, prohibited in Britain by Act of Parliament 1835. The places where bears were publicly baited were called bear gardens.

eardsley, Aubrey Vincent (1872–98) English artist who worked in black and white and who showed great technical skill, originality and disregard of conventionality, with sometimes a tendency towards the morbid. He illustrated *The Yellow Book* (1894–95).

eatles, The ('Fab Four') English pop group founded 1963, disbanded 1970: John Lennon (1940–80), Paul McCartney (1942–), George Harrison (1943–), Ringo Starr (1940–).

eattie, James (1735–1803) Scottish poet and philosophical writer. His Essay on the Nature and Immutability of Truth (1770) atttacked Hume and advocated what was afterwards called the doctrine of Common Sense, but he is best remembered by his poem, *The Minstrel* (1771–74).

eatty, David, 1st Earl Beatty (1871–1936) British admiral who distinguished himself in the battle of Jutland 1916 and was in command of the Grand Fleet in the First World War until he became First Sea Lord in 1919.

eaufort, Margaret, Countess of Richmond and Derby (1443–1509) philanthropist.

eauharnais, Eugène de (1781–1824) Prince of Venice. The son of Josephine by her first husband, he accompanied his stepfather, Napoleon, to Egypt in 1798, rose rapidly in the army and was appointed viceroy of Italy in 1805.

eaumarchais, Pierre Augustine Caron de (1732–99) French playwright noted for his comedies, e.g.*The Barber of Seville* (1775) and *The Marriage of Figaro* (1784), which have given him a permanent reputation.

Beaumont, Sir Francis (1584–1616) English dramatist who collaborated with John Fletcher from 1606 to 1613. Their best-known work are tragicomedies, a genre they had a significant influence on, e.g. *The Maid's Tragedy* (1610–11). The only play that Beaumont wrote alone was *The Masque*.

Beauvoir, Simone de (1908–86) French novelist and essayist whose works explore the female predicament from the standpoint of existential feminism, e.g. *The Second Sex* (1949).

Beaverbrook, Max [William Maxwell Aitken, 1st Baron Beaverbrook] (1879–1964) Canadian-born British newspaper proprietor and Conservative politician. In the First World War he served as minister of information (1918) and in the Second World War as minister of aircraft production (1940–41).

Bebop dance movement and jazz style dating from about 1941.

Bechet, Sidney (1897–1959) American jazz saxophonist and clarinettist. He never learned to read music but became one of the greatest soprano saxophone virtuosos of the 20th century.

Bechuanaland *see* BOTSWANA.

Becker, Boris (1967–) German tennis player, youngest competitor to win Wimbledon men's singles title 1985.

Becket, Thomas à (1118–70) English saint. Of Norman descent, he became Chancellor of England in 1155 and Archbishop of Canterbury in 1162. Relations between Becket and Henry II deteriorated because of the former's strong allegiance to Church rather than king, and Becket was murdered by four of the king's knights. Becket was canonized in 1173.

Beckett, Gilbert Abbott à *see* À BECKETT, GILBERT ABBOTT.

Beckett, Samuel (1906–89) Irish dramatist and novelist. His works, generally bleak and existentialist in philosophy, include the play *Waiting for Godot* (1952) and the short novel *Malone Dies* (1951).

Beckford, William (1759–1844) English writer who was famous in his time for his immense wealth and his eccentricities. He travelled much and spent an enormous sum on building and rebuilding Fonthill Abbey in Wiltshire. He is known for his *History of the Caliph Vathek* (1787), which he wrote in French and which was highly commended by Byron.

Becquer, Gustavo Adolfo (1836–70) Spanish writer.

Becquerel, Antoine Henri (1852–1908) French scientist and discoverer (1896) of radioactivity in uranium. He worked with Pierre and Marie Curie. He was awarded the Nobel prize for physics in 1903.

Beddoes, Thomas Lovell (1803–49) English writer who published *The Bride's Tragedy* (1822) while he was still a student. His most important work is

Death's Jest-book, or The Fool's Tragedy, which appeared in 1850, after his death by suicide.

Bede, the Venerable, Saint (*c*.673–735) Anglo-Saxon monk and historian. Prodigiously learned, he settled for life in the monastery at Jarrow in 682. He translated St John's Gospel into Anglo-Saxon. His most valuable book is his ecclesiastical history, *Historia Ecclesiastica Gentis Anglorum*.

Bedlam (Bethlehem Hospital) a religious house in London, founded by Simon Fitzmary 1247 and converted by Henry VIII into a hospital for lunatics. The lunatics were at one time treated as little better than wild beasts, hence Bedlam came to be typical of any scene of wild confusion.

Beecham, Sir Thomas (1879–1961) English conductor and composer, noted for his interpretations of the works of Delius, Strauss and Sibelius, and for his sharply witty ripostes.

Beecher, Henry Ward (1813–87) American writer, preacher and social reformer.

Beefeater *see* YEOMEN OF THE GUARD.

Beerbohm, Sir [Henry] Max[imilian] (1872–1956) English parodist, caricaturist and essayist. The parodies of authors such as Henry James and Kipling established him as one of the greatest of all parodists. His only novel is *Zuleika Dobson* (1911).

Beet sugar discovered 1747 by the German chemist Andreas Sigismund Maggraf (1709–82).

Beethoven, Ludwig van (1770–1827) German composer. Regarded as the greatest Romantic composer, he became famous throughout Europe in the 1790s as a brilliant pianist with a special gift for improvisation. His works include a violin concerto, nine symphonies, piano sonatas, string quartets, masses, and one of the greatest operas, *Fidelio* (1805).

Beeton, Mrs [Isabella Mary Beeton] (1836–65) pioneer arbiter of British housekeeping.

Beggars of the Sea a force of Dutch privateers licensed by William of Orange to help him invade the Spanish Netherlands first appeared 1569. Originally based in Dover, they were forbidden to used English ports 1571. They captured Brill, Flushing and other ports.

Begin, Menachem (1913–92) Polish-born Israeli statesman. He was commander of the Irgun militant Zionist group (1943–48) and prime minister of Israel (1977–83). He and Sadat were awarded the Nobel Peace Prize in 1978, after Egypt and Israel signed a peace treaty.

Beguines lay sisterhood founded *c*.1180 at Liège by Lambert le Bègue (b. *c*.1187).

Behan, Brendan (1923–64) Irish dramatist and poet. He was an Irish Republican Army supporter from an early age, and two of his works were directly based on his imprisonment for IRA activity, *The Quare Fellow* (1954) and *Borstal Boy* (1958). He also wrote *The Hostage* (1950).

Behn, Mrs Aphra (1640–89) English writer (*Oronooko* 1688).

Behring, Vitus *see* BERING, VITUS.

Beiderbecke, [Leon] Bix (1903–31) American jazz cornetist, pianist and composer, who is regarded as one of the few white jazz musicians to have had any significant influence on the development of jazz.

Beit, Alfred (1853–1906) German-born British South African financier and philanthropist.

Belasco, David (1853–1931) American actor-manager.

Belgian Congo *see* ZAIRE.

Belgium part of Burgundian and Spanish Netherlands until 1572; Spanish rule until 1700; Austrian rule 1713–94; part of Netherlands 1815–30; became independent kingdom 1830.

Beli (d.722) king of Strathclyde *see* Appendix.

Belisarius (505–565) Byzantine general and defeater of Persians, Vandals and Ostrogoths.

Belize, formerly British Honduras, first settled by the English 1638; declared a British colony 1862; renamed Belize 1973; became independent 21 September 1981.

Bell, Alexander Graham (1847–1922) Scottish-born American inventor and scientist. He succeeded in producing a device for transmitting the voice in 1875 and patented the telephone the following year (1876). He founded the Bell Telephone Company in 1877, and patented the gramophone in 1887.

Bell, Gertrude (1868–1926) English explorer in Arabia.

Bell, John (1745–1831) English bookseller and introducer *c*.1788 of 'modern face' type.

Bellarmine, Robert (1542–1621) Italian Jesuit writer (*Disputations* 1581).

Belleau Wood, Battle of First World War battle fought between US Marines and Germans 6–10 June 1918.

Belle Sauvage, London, one of England's oldest coaching inns, first mentioned 1453.

Bellini, Giovanni (*c*.1430–1516) Italian painter (*Agony in the Garden*). The most prominent of a family of noted artists, including his father **Jacopo Bellini** (*c*.1400–*c*.1470) and his brother **Gentile Bellini** (*c*.1429–*c*.1507).

Belloc, Hilaire (1870–1953) French-born English poet, essayist, historian and Liberal MP noted for his prolific output of all kinds of books, and for his robust Roman Catholicism, anti-imperialism and nationalism. His works include *The Path to Rome* (1902).

Bellow, Saul (1915–) Canadian-born American novelist, widely regarded as one of the greatest living writers. His novels include *Dangling Man* (1944),

Herzog 1964) and *More Die of Heartbreak* (1987). He was awarded the Nobel prize for literature in 1976.

Bell Rock Lighthouse, North Sea, completed 1812.

Belmondo, Jean-Paul (1933–) French film actor (*A Bout de Souffle* 1960).

Belo Horizonte capital of Minas Gerais, Brazil, founded 1895.

Belvoir Hunt, Leicestershire and Lincolnshire, dates from 1750; became a fox pack 1762.

Belzoni, Giovanni Battista (1778–1823) Italian archaeologist in Middle East.

Bembo, Cardinal Pietro (1470–1547) Italian poet.

Benavente, Jacinto (1866–1954) Spanish playwright.

Ben Bella, [Mohammed] Ahmed (1916–) Algerian statesman. A leading figure of his country's independence movement in the late 1940s and 1950s, he became prime minister in 1962 shortly after independence. He was deposed in 1965 following a military coup and was imprisoned until 1980.

Benbow, John (1653–1702) English admiral.

Benchley, Robert (1889–1945) American humorous writer.

Benedict of Nursia, Saint (*c.*480–*c.*544).

Benedict I pope (575–579).

Benedict II pope (684–685).

Benedict III pope (855–858).

Benedict IV pope (900–903).

Benedict V pope (964–965).

Benedict VI pope (973–974). He was murdered.

Benedict VII pope (974–983).

Benedict VIII [Theophylactus] pope (1012–24).

Benedict IX [Theophylactus] (*c.*1021–1056) pope (1032–48).

Benedict X [Johannes Mincius] anti-pope (1058–59).

Benedict XI [Niccolo Boccasini] (1240–1304) pope (1303–1304).

Benedict XII [Jacques Fournier] pope (1334–1342).

Benedict XIII [Pedro de Luna] (*c.*1328–*c.*1423) anti-pope (1394–1417.

Benedict XIII [Piero Francesco Orsini] (1649–1730) pope (1724–30).

Benedict XIV [Prospero Lorenzo Lambertini] (1675–1758) pope (1740–58.

Benedict XV [Giacomo della Chiesa] (1854–1922) pope (1914–22).

Benedict Biscop (*c.*628–690) English churchman and founder of monastery at Wearmouth.

Benedictine Order founded 529 by St Benedict of Nursia (*c.*480–*c.*544).

Benes, Eduard (1884–1948) Czech statesman.

Benét, Stephen Vincent (1898–1943) American writer (*John Brown's Body* 1928).

Beneventum, Battle of 275 BC during Pyrrhus' invasion of Italy; Pyrrhus defeated by Romans and driven from Italy.

Bengal became English settlement *c.*1652; made Chief Presidency 1773; divided between India and Pakistan 1947; East Bengal fought war of independence and became Bangladesh in 1971.

Benghazi Second World War, captured by British 7 February 1941; by Rommel 3 April 1941; recaptured by British 24 December 1941, and again 20 November 1942.

Ben-Gurion, David [David Gruen] (1886–1973) Polish-born Israeli statesman, 'Father of Israel'. He settled in Palestine in 1906, where he was active in the socialist wing of the Zionist movement. He was the first prime minister of Israel (1948–53) and was prime minister again (1955–63).

Benin, West Africa, incorporated into French West Africa by 1904; independent as Dahomey 1960; named changed to Benin in 1975; held first free presidential elections in 30 years in 1991.

Benn, Tony [Anthony Neil Wedgwood Benn, formerly Viscount Stansgate] (1925–) British Labour politician. Since the late 1970s he has been regarded as one of the leading figures of the radical left in the Labour Party.

Bennet, Alan (1934–) English actor and playwright (*Kafka's Dick* 1986).

Bennett, [Enoch] Arnold (1867–1931) English novelist, dramatist and essayist. His most popular novels centred on industrial life in the Black Country Potteries and include *The Old Wives' Tale* (1908) and the Clayhanger trilogy, *Clayhanger*, *Hilda Lessways* and *These Twain*.

Benno, Saint (1010–1106) bishop of Meissen. He was canonized in 1523.

Bentham, Jeremy (1748–1832) English philosopherand social reformer. He is famous for his proposition that the prime aim of political and philosophical inquiry should be the 'greatest happiness of the greatest number', expounded in his *Introduction to the Principles of Morals and Legislation* (1789).

Bentine, Michael *see* MILLIGAN, SPIKE.

Bentley, Edmund Clerihew (1875–1956) English journalist, noted for his classic detective novel, *Trent's Last Case* (1913), and his invention of the clerihew.

Bentley, Richard (1662–1742) English literary critic (*Dissertation on the Epistles of Phalaris* 1699).

Beonna king of East Anglia (*c.*760) *see* Appendix.

Beonred king of Mercia (757) *see* Appendix.

Beorhtwulf (d.853) king of Mercia (840–853) *see* Appendix.

Beornwulf (d.827) king of Mercia (823–827) *see* Appendix.

Beortric (d.802) king of Wessex (757–802) *see* Appendix.

'Beowulf' Anglo-Saxon epic poem written *c.*1000.

Béranger, Pierre Jean de (1780–1857) French songwriter (*Chansons Nouvelles* 1830).

Bérard, Christian (1902–49) French painter (*Seated Acrobat*).

Berchtold's Day Swiss annual festival held 2 January.

Berdyaev, Nicholas Russian-born philosopher (1874–1948).

Berenice (d.55 BC) queen of Egypt (58–55 BC). The daughter of Ptolemy XI and eldest sister of Cleopatra (6), she was placed on the throne by the Alexandrians when they drove out her father, but he was reinstated by the Romans, and her father put her to death.

Berenson, Bernard (1865–1959) Lithuanian-born American art critic. Highly influential in the early development of art history.

Berg, Alban (1885–1935) Austrian composer. He studied under Schoenberg and adopted his atonal twelve-tone technique. His works include songs, chamber works and the operas *Wozzeck* (1922) and *Lulu*.

Bergerac, Cyrano de (1619–55) French writer and soldier.

Bergh, Henry (1811–88) founder (1866) of the American Society for the Prevention of Cruelty to Animals.

Bergman, Ingmar (1918–) Swedish film and stage director. His films, which include *The Seventh Seal* (1957), *Wild Strawberries* (1957) and *Cries and Whispers* (1972), are claustrophobic psychological studies which have been very influential.

Bergman, Ingrid (1915–82) Swedish actress regarded as one of the most talented and beautiful actresses of her generation. Her films include *Casablanca* (1943).

Bergson, Henri Louis (1859–1941) French philosopher whose writings expound his theory of a 'vital spirit' moving in the world, bridging the apparent chasm between metaphysics and science. He was awarded the Nobel prize for literature in 1927.

Berhtun (d.686) king of Wessex (686) *see* Appendix.

Beria, Lavrenti Pavlovich (1899–1953) Georgian-born Soviet politician. He rose to power in the 1930s under Stalin, and became head of the secret police (1938–53). After Stalin's death, he was tried for treason and executed.

Bering *or* **Behring, Vitus** (1681–1741) Danish-born Russian explorer.

Bering Strait discovered 1725 by Vitus Bering.

Berio, Luciano (1925–) Italian composer whose works are based on a system of serialism and often feature electronic components.

Berkeley, Busby [William Busby Enos] (1895–1976) American film director, noted especially for his elaborate, often surreal, dance choreography.

Berkeley, George (1685–1753) Irish philosopher.

Berlin captured by the French 1806. Decree of Berlin, 21 November 1806. Congress of Berlin 1878; Treaty of Berlin signed 13 July 1878. Berlin Blockade began 28 June 1948; lifted 12 May 1949; Berlin Wall built to prevent exodus of East German citizens, August 1961; Wall begins to be dismantled November 1989 as democracy sweeps Eastern Europe following the collapse of the USSR.

Berlin, Irving [Israel Baline] (1888–1989) Russian-born American songwriter. He began his career as a street singer, and eventually wrote around a thousand songs, many of which featured in highly successful shows and in several film musicals (*Alexander's Ragtime Band* 1911).

Berlin, Sir Isaiah (1909–) Latvian-born British philosopher and historian. His works focus on the history of ideas, with particular reference to historical determinism.

Berlioz, Hector (1803–69) French composer. Regarded as a founder of modern orchestral techniques, his works include *Symphonie Fantastique* and the opera *The Trojans*.

Bermuda discovered by the Spaniard Juan Bermúdez 1503; settled by the English 1609 and formally taken over 1684.

Bernadette (Soubirous), Saint (1844–79) of Lourdes (visions 1858).

Bernadotte, Count Folke (1895–1948) Swedish humanitarian. He was assassinated..

Bernadotte, Jean Baptiste (1763–1844) French general who became king of Sweden (1818–44).

Bernanos, Georges (1888–1948) French writer (*Diary of a Country Parson* 1936).

Bernard, Saint (1091–1153) abbot of Clairvaux.

Bernardin de St Pierre, Jacques-Henri (1737–1814) French writer (*Paul et Virginie* 1787).

Bernhardt, Sarah (1844–1923) French actress.

Bernicia an ancient Anglian kingdom stretching from the Firth of Forth to the Tees. It was united with Deira and became part of the kingdom of Northumbria.

Bernini, Giovanni Lorenzo (1598–1680) Italian sculptor and architect.

Bernoulli's Numbers mathematics discovered by Jacques Bernoulli (1654–1705).

Bernoulli's Principle of the flow of liquids formulated by Daniel Bernoulli (1700–82).

Bernstein, Leonard (1918–90) American composer, pianist and conductor. He was musical director of the New York Philharmonic (1958–70), and a tireless popularizer of classical music. His works include chamber and choral music and several very popular musicals, e.g. *West Side Story* (1957).

Berruguete, Alonso (*c.*1480–1561) Spanish artist.

Berry, Chuck [Charles Edward] (1926–) American rock and roll singer-songwriter ('Johnny B Goode' 1958).

Berthelot, Marcelin (1827–1907) French organic chemist.

Bertillon System criminal investigation by anthropometry devised 1880 by the Frenchman Alphonse Bertillon (1853–1914).

Bertolucci, Bernardo (1940–) Italian-born film director. His films are among the most influential in modern cinema and include *Last Tango in Paris* (1972).

Berwick, Peace of signed (between England and Scotland) 1639.

Beryllium isolated 1828 by the German scientist Friedrich Wöhler (1800–82).

Berzelius, Baron Jöns Jakob (1779–1848) Swedish chemist.

Besant, Mrs Annie (1847–1933) British theosophist and reformer.

Bessel Functions invented 1817, fully developed 1824, by the German astronomer Wilhelm Bessel (1784–1846).

Bessemer Converter invented 1856 by the English engineer Sir Henry Bessemer (1813–98).

Bessemer Steel Process first used in USA at Phillipsburg 1856.

Best, Charles Herbert *see* BANTING SIR FREDERICK.

Best, George (1946–) Northern Irish soccer player. One of the world's finest and most entertaining wingers, his career slowly folded in a haze of alcohol abuse and general dissipation.

Beta Rays discovered 1896 by Lord Rutherford (1871–1937).

Bethlen, Gábor (1580–1629) Hungarian leader.

Bethmann-Hollweg, Theobald von (1856–1921) German chancellor.

Betjeman, Sir John (1906–84) English poet, essayist and broadcaster whose work was popular with critics and public alike. His works include *New Bats in Old Belfries* (1945). He was appointed poet laureate in 1972 and also wrote widely on architecture.

Betterton, Thomas (1635–1710) English actor-manager.

Bevan, Aneurin (1897–1960) Welsh statesman. He was Labour MP for Ebbw Vale for 30 years (1929–60) and one of the main spokespeople for the radical socialist opposition during the Second World War. As minister of health (1945–51), he oversaw the formation of the welfare state (*see* BEVERIDGE).

Beveridge, William Henry [1st Baron Beveridge] (1879–1963) Indian-born English economist. His 'Beveridge Report', the *Report on Social Insurance and Allied Services* (1942), became the basis for the welfare state introduced by Attlee's administration.

Beveridge Plan national insurance scheme for Britain conceived by Lord Beveridge; published 20 November 1942.

Bevin, Ernest (1881–1951) English trade unionist and Labour statesman. He helped found the Transport and General Workers Union (1922) and was minister of labour (1940–45) in the coalition war government and Labour's foreign secretary (1945–51).

Bewick, Thomas (1753–1828) English wood engraver.

Béza, Theodore (1519–1605) French religious reformer.

Bhave, Vinobha (1895–1982) Indian social reformer and spiritual leader.

Bhopal, India, founded 1728; capital city of the State of Madhya Pradesh 1956; scene of worst industrial (chemical) accident in history 1984: 2,000 killed and 50,000 injured by toxic gas leak.

Bhutan, Himalayan State, concluded treaty with East India Company 1774; subsidized by British from 1865, by Indian government from 1942; new treaty with government of India, 1949; restoration of National Assembly 1953; became democratic monarchy 1969.

Bhutto, Benazir (1953–) Pakistani politician, daughter of the former prime minister Zulfikar Ali Bhutto. After her father's death she lived in exile in Britain. She returned to Pakistan in 1986 and was prime minister of Pakistan (1988–90) and was re-elected in 1993. She bore a child while in office in 1990, the first modern head of government to do so.

Bhutto, Zulfikar Ali (1928–79) Pakistani statesman. He was the first civilian president of Pakistan (1971–73), then prime minister (1973–77). He was deposed in a coup and executed. His daughter is Benazir Bhutto.

Bibliographical Society, London, founded 1892.

Bibliothèque Nationale, Paris, founded 1721.

Bibracte, Battle of 58 BC battle of the Gallic Wars; defeat of Helvetii under Ariovistus, the German leader.

Bicycles: pedal-operated model invented by the British inventor Kirkpatrick Macmillan 1838; 'penny-farthings' popular 1870s; Rover 'safety' bicycle 1885; inflated tyres invented 1888.

Bifocal Lens invented 1780 by Benjamin Franklin (1706–90).

Big Ben, London, hour bell cast 10 April 1858. Clock went into service 31 May 1859. Chimes first broadcast 31 December 1923.

Big Bertha German long-range gun that shelled Paris March 1918.

Big Brother Movement scheme for emigration of boys from Britain to Australia founded by New Zealand-born Sir Richard Linton (1879–1959).

Bihar, Indian State, treaty made with East India Company 1765; separated from Bengal Province 1912 and united with Orissa. Made separate province 1936.

Bikaner, capital of Bikaner State, India, founded 1488.

Bikini Atoll, Marshall Islands, scene of atom-bomb tests started by US Navy 1946.

Biko, Steve [Bantu Stephen Biko] (1947–77) South African black radical leader who helped found the Black People's Convention in order to build confidence in South African blacks that they could defeat apartheid. His death in police custody while awaiting trial was universally regarded as murder.

Billiards believed to have been invented by Henrique Devigne, French artist, *c.*1571.

Bill of Rights, English based on Declaration of Rights (February) and passed by Parliament October 1689.

Bimetallism use of gold and silver for currency first so termed 1869 by Henri Cernuschi, Italian economist (1821–96).

Binomial Theorem invented before 1676 by Sir Isaac Newton (1642–1727).

Binyon, Laurence (1869–1943) English poet (*For the Fallen*).

Bioko island off West Africa discovered by the Portuguese navigator Fernão de Po *c.*1470.

Birkbeck College, London University, founded (as the London Mechanics' Institution) 1823 by Dr George Birkbeck (1776–1841).

Birkenhead, Frederick Edwin Smith, 1st Earl of (1872–1930) British statesman.

Birmingham University founded 1875 as Mason College by Sir Josiah Mason (1795–1881). Charter granted 1900.

Birrell, Augustine (1850–1933) English writer and statesman.

Birth Control Clinics world's first at Amsterdam 1881; first English in London 1921; first American in New York 1923 (previously opened 1916 and closed by police).

Birtwistle, Sir Harrison (1934–) English composer regarded with Maxwell Davies and others as a leading postwar composer. His works include *Gawain and the Green Knight* (1991)).

Bischof, Werner (1916–54) Swiss photographer. He was killed in a car accident.

Bisley National Rifle Association first met at Bisley 1890. First woman (Miss M. E. Foster) to win King's Prize 19 July 1930.

Bismarck, Prince Otto Eduard Leopold, Prinz von (1815–98) German statesman who was prime minister of Prussia (1862–90) and defeated first Austria during the 'Seven Weeks' War' (1866) and then France (1870–71). He became the first chancellor of united Germany and was dubbed the 'Iron Chancellor'.

Bismarck, Battle of the a Second World War naval battle 24–27 March 1941, when the German battleship *Bismarck* was sunk.

Bismarck Sea, Battle of the a battle of the Second World War, 2–4 March 1943, when a Japanese convoy carrying troops to new Guinea was destroyed by the American and Australian air forces.

Bismuth chemical element identified 1530 by the German scientist Georg Agricola (1490–1555).

Bizet, Georges (1838–75) French composer who is best known for his operas, e.g. *The Pearl Fishers*, *Carmen* (1875), but who also wrote a symphony, several songs and the *L'Arlésienne* suits.

Björnson, Björnstjerne (1832–1910) Norwegian writer (*Synnöve Solbakken* 1857).

Black, Joseph (1728–99) British scientist who developed (about 1765) the theory of latent heat.

'Black and Tans' auxiliary police used against Irish republicans 1920–21.

Black Death, The plague pandemic affecting Asia and North Africa, Italy 1340, England 1348–49.

Blackfriars Dominican convent established in London 1276.

Blackfriars Bridge, London, erected 1865–69.

Black Friday American financial disaster, 24 September 1869.

Black Hawk (1767–1838) North American Indian chief.

Black Hole of Calcutta scene of imprisonment of English by rebels 20–21 June 1756.

Black Letter for English newspaper titles first used 1679.

Black phosphorus first prepared by the American physicist Percy Williams Bridgman (1882–1961).

Black Prince, The *see* EDWARD (1).

Black Rod, House of Lords, first appointed 1350.

Blackmore, Richard Doddridge (1825–1900) English novelist (*Lorna Doone* 1869).

Blackstone's Commentaries (1765–69), legal guide, written by Sir William Blackstone, English jurist (1723–80).

Black Watch Highland regiment formed 1725, became Royal Highland Black Watch 1739.

Blackwell, Dr Elizabeth (1821–1910) first (1859) British registered woman doctor.

Blackwood's Magazine founded 1817 by William Blackwood (1776–1834) of Edinburgh.

Blades, William (1824–90) London printer.

Blaeu, Willem Janszoon (1571–1638) founder of Dutch firm of mapmakers.

Blair, Robert (1699–1746) Scottish poet (*The Grave* 1743).

Blake, Robert (1599–1657) English admiral.

Blake, William (1757–1827) English poet and artist.

His main poetic and artistic theme was innocence crippled by cynical experience. He is one of the greatest of English Romantic poets. His works include *The Marriage of Heaven and Hell* (1790).

Blanc, Mont the highest mountain in western Europe (4808 metres/15,774 feet), first climbed june 1786 by the French mountaineer Jacques Balmat (1762–1834) and Michel Paccard 1786.

Blanche of Castile (1188–1252) wife of Louis VIII.

Blanqui, Louis (1805–81) French revolutionary leader.

Blatchford, Robert (1851–1943) British socialist writer.

Blavatsky, Madame Helena (1831–91) Russian-born founder of the Theosophical Society.

Bleaching Powder discovered 1798 by the English scientist Smithson Tennant (1761–1815).

Blenheim Palace, Oxfordshire, built 1705–22.

Blenheim, Battle of between the English and the French 13 August 1704.

Blériot, Louis (1872–1936) French aviator and aeronautical engineer. A pioneer in aircraft design, he invented the monoplane and made the first flight across the English Channel in one, 27 July 1909.

Blessed Virgin Mary, The Assumption of The celebrated 15 August.

Bligh, Admiral William (1754–1817) captain of *The Bounty*. Mutiny of the Bounty 28 April 1789.

Blind books letters first printed in relief 1771 by the French philanthropist Valentin Haüy.

Bliss, Sir Arthur [Edward Drummond] (1891–1975) English composer whose work includes a choral symphony, ballets and film music. He was Master of the Queen's Music (1953–75).

Blitz (from German *Blitzkrieg*, 'lightning war') military technique of surprise attack, 1939–41; applied in England to heavy bombing 1940–41

Bloch, Ernst (1880–1959) Swiss-born composer (*America* 1926).

Bloch, Jean Richard (1884–1947) French novelist (*Et Compagnie* 1918).

Blok, Alexander Alexandrovich (1880–1921) Russian poet.

Blom, Eric (1888–1959) English music critic and historian.

Blomfield, Sir Arthur William (1829–99) English architect of the London Law Courts in Fleet Street.

Blondin, Charles French acrobat (1824–97). He crossed Niagara Falls on a tightrope 1859.

Blood, Colonel Thomas (*c.*1618–1680) Irish malcontent, attempted to steal the Crown Jewels 9 May 1671.

Blood circulation discovered 1615 by William Harvey (1578–1657).

Blood groups defined 1901 by Karl Landsteiner (1868–1943).

Bloody Assizes held 1685 by Judge Jeffreys (*c.*1644–1689).

Bloody Sunday massacre of St Petersburg workers 22 January 1905; also killing of 13 Roman Catholic protesters by British troops in Londonderry, Northern Ireland, 30 January 1972.

Bloomer, Amelia Jenks (1818–94) American women's rights campaigner and dress reformer.

Bloomfield, Robert (1766–1823) English poet (*The Farmer's Boy* 1800).

Blow, John (*c.*1648–1708) English composer.

Blücher, Gebhard Leberecht von (1742–1819) German field marshal.

Blueprint process for copying plans, etc, first used 1842 by the English astronomer Sir John Herschel (1792–1871).

Blum, Léon (1872–1950) French statesman, the first socialist and Jewish prime minister of France (1936–37, 1938, 1946–47).

Blunden, Edmund [Charles] (1896–1974) English poet and writer (*Undertones of War* 1928).

Blunt, Anthony [Frederick] (1907–83) English art historian, who was knighted in 1956, and was appointed Surveyor of the Queen's Pictures in 1945, a post he held until 1972. He was stripped of his knighthood in 1979, following the public revelation that he had been a Soviet spy.

Blunt, Wilfrid Scawen (1840–1922) English writer.

Blyton, Enid [Mary] (1897–1968) English children's writer whose most well-known books have featured such characters as Noddy and Big Ears and, for older children, *The Famous Five*.

Boadicea *see* BOUDICCA and Appendix.

Board of Trade, London, founded 1661; now Department of Trade and Industry, and incorporating (since 1992) the Department of Energy.

Boas, Franz (1858–1942) German-born American anthropologist whose emphasis on linguistic structure and scientific methodology has been very influential on anthropology.

Boccaccio, Giovanni (1313–75) Italian writer (*The Decameron* 1348–58).

Boccherini, Luigi (1743–1805) Italian composer.

Boccioni, Umberto (1882–1916) Italian painter and sculptor who became the leading Futurist artist of the early 20th century and one of the movement's principal theorists.

Bodichon, Barbara (1827–90) English founder 1869 of Girton College, Cambridge University.

Bodin, Jean (*c.*1530–1596) French political thinker (*Six Livres de la République* 1576).

Bodleian Library, Oxford, founded 1598, opened

1602, by Sir Thomas Bodley (1545–1613); new library opened 1946.

Bodoni, Giambattista (1740–1813) Italian printer and typographer.

Boece, Hector (*c.*1465-1536) Scottish historian who was educated at Paris University where he met Erasmus. His *History of Scotland* was published in 1527.

Boecklin, Arnold (1827–1901) Swiss painter.

Boer War, South Africa, began 11 October 1899, ended 31 May 1902.

Boeotia a region of ancient Greece made up of ten city states, forming the Boeotian League. Athens lost Boeotia at the Battle of Coronea 447 BC.

Boethius (*c.*473–524) Roman statesman and philosopher (*De Consolatione Philosophiae*). He was executed.

Bogarde, Sir Dirk [Derek Jules Gaspard Ulric Niven van den Bogaerde] (1920–) English actor and author whose films include *Death in Venice* (1970). He has written a highly acclaimed autobiography and several novels.

Bogart, Humphrey (De Forest) American film actor (*The Maltese Falcon* 1941) (1899–1957).

Bogart, Humphrey [De Forest] (1899–1957) American actor. He formed one of the best-known screen partnerships with his (fourth) wife, Lauren Bacall.

Bogotá Colombian capital founded by Gonzalo Jiménez de Quesada 1538.

Bohemia ruled by Hapsburgs 1526–1918; part of Czechoslovakia 1918–93.

Bohemian Brethren Christian sect founded among followers of Hus by Peter Chelcicky in early 15th century.

Bohr, Aage Niels (1922–) Danish nuclear physicist.

Bohr, Niels [Henrik David] (1885–1962) Danish physicist. He was the first to apply quantum theory to explain the stability of the nuclear model of the atom. He was awarded the 1922 Nobel prize for physics.

Boileau, Nicolas (1636–1711) French writer and critic.

Boito, Arrigo (1842–1918) Italian composer (*Mefistofele* 1868).

Bojer, Johan (1872–1959) Norwegian novelist (*Troens Magt* 1903).

'Boldrewood, Rolf' [Thomas Alexander Browne] (1826–1915) English-born Australian writer (*Robbery under Arms* 1888).

Boleslaus I (d.1025) Polish king (992–1025).

Boleslaus II (1039–*c.*1081) Polish king (1058–79).

Boleslaus III (1086–1139) Polish king (1102–39).

Boleyn, Anne (*c.*1507–1536) English queen. She married Henry VIII in 1533 and was beheaded.

Bolingbroke, Henry St John [Viscount Bolingbroke] (1678–1751) English statesman and writer (*The Idea of a Patriot King*).

Bolivar, Simon (1783–1830) Venezeulan-born revolutionary. He overthrew Spanish rule in Venezuela, Ecuador, Colombia and Peru (1810–24). Upper Peru was renamed Bolivia in his honour.

Bolivia an inland country of South America, conquered by the Incas 13th century; colonized by Spain from 1538; proclaimed a republic 1825; boundary with Chile fixed after war 1879–82; with Paraguay after war 1932–35; with Peru after war 1935–38.

Bologna, Giovanni da (1524–1608) Flemish sculptor.

Bolsheviks majority faction of Russian Social Democrat Party at Congress in Brussels and London, 1903; became Communist Party 1918.

Boltzmann, Ludwig (1844–1906) Austrian physicist. He committed suicide.

Bombay University founded 1857.

Bonaparte (Buonaparte until 1796), Napoleon (1769–1821) emperor of France (1804–13); Jerome (1784–1860) king of Westphalia (1807–13); Joseph (1768–1844) king of Naples (1806–1807) and Spain (1808–13); Louis (1778–1846) king of Holland (1806–10); Louis Napoleon (1808–73) emperor of France (1851–70).

Bonar Law, Andrew (1858–1923) British statesman (prime minister 1922–23).

Bonaventura, Saint (1221–1274).

Bond, Edward (1934–) English dramatist and screenwriter. His work was often controversial and public debate over one of his plays, *Saved* (1965), led to the abolition of stage censorship in Britain.

Bondfield, Margaret (1873–1953) first (1929) woman privy councillor.

Bone, Henry (1755–1834) English enamel-painter.

Bone, Muirhead (1876–1953) Scottish artist.

Bonesetting (osteopathy) practice founded 1874 by the American surgeon Andrew Taylor Still (1828–1917).

Bonheur, Rosa (1822–99) French painter.

Bonhoeffer, Dietrich (1906–45) German Lutheran pastor and theologian who was active in the anti-Nazi Resistance during World War II and hanged by the Gestapo in 1945. His writings are among the key spiritual works of the 20th century.

Boniface, Saint (*c.*680 murdered 754).

Boniface I, St pope (418–22).

Boniface II pope (530–32).

Boniface III pope (607).

Boniface IV pope (608-615).

Boniface V pope (619–625).

Boniface VI pope (896).

Boniface VII anti-pope (974).

Boniface VIII [Benedetto Gaetano] (1235–1303) pope (1294–1303).

Boniface IX [Piero Tomacelli] (*c.*1345–1404) pope (1389–1404).

Bonington, Chris [Christian John Storey] (1934–) English mountaineer, reached summit of Everest 1985.

Bonington, Richard Parkes (1802–28) English painter (*Grand Canal Venice*).

Bonn capital of German Federal Republic 1949–90.

Bonnard, Pierre (1867–1947) French painter and lithographer. His work is notable for being intensely colourful, especially in his interior work.

Book auction first, the sale of George Dousa's library, held in Leyden 1604.

Book jackets *or* **dust-wrappers** first used in England 1832; came into general use *c.*1890.

Book of Common Prayer, Church of England, *First* published 1549, *Second* 1552, *Elizabethan* 1559, *revised* 1662, controversial *modernized* 1980.

Bookplates to mark ownership first introduced in Germany *c.*1450.

Booksellers Association of Great Britain and Ireland founded as the Associated Booksellers 1895; assumed present name 1948.

Boole, George (1815–64) English mathematician and originator of Boolean algebra.

Boone, Daniel (1734–1820) American explorer.

Booth, Edwin Thomas (1833–93) American actor.

Booth, John Wilkes (1838–1865) murderer (1865) of Abraham Lincoln. He was shot.

Booth, William (1829–1912) English religious leader who established a Christian mission in London's East End in the 1860s and founded the Salvation Army in 1878.

Booth, William Bramwell (1856–1929) English religious leader who succeeded (1912) his father, William Booth, as General of the Salvation Army.

Bordeaux, Henri (1870–1963) French novelist (*Le Feu*).

Borg, Bjorn (1956–) Swedish tennis player who won five consecutive Wimbledon championship titles (1976–80).

Borges, Jorge Luis (1899–1986) Argentinian short-story writer, poet and critic who had a remarkable gift for creating short fictions with a beguiling metaphysical content.

Borgia, Cesare (1476–1507) Italian soldier and politician. The son of Rodrigo Borgia, he became a cardinal in 1493 after his father became pope as Alexander VI in 1492. He attempted to bring Italian affairs under his control in an atmosphere of intrigue, war and assassination, and was the model for Machiavelli's *Prince*. His sister was Lucrezia Borgia. He was killed in battle.

Borgia, Lucrezia, Duchess of Ferrara (1480–1519) illegitimate daughter of Pope Alexander VI (Rodrigo Borgia) and sister of Cesare Borgia, she was a patron of the arts and also acquired a reputation for conspiracy.

Borgia, Rodrigo *see* ALEXANDER VI.

Boric acid first prepared 1702 by the Dutch chemist Willem Homberg (1652–1715).

Boring machine first practical invented 1769 by the English engineer John Smeaton (1724–92).

Boris Godunov (*c.*1551–1605) Russian tsar.

Boris II (1894–1943) Bulgarian tsar.

Borneo discovered by the Portuguese 1521. North Borneo made British Protectorate 1881.

Borodin, Alexander (1833–87) Russian composer (*Prince Igor* 1869–91).

Borodino, Battle of fought between Napoleon and the Russians 7 September 1812.

Boron chemical element isolated 1808 by Sir Humphry Davy (1778–1829).

Borromeo, Saint Charles (1538–1584).

Borromini, Francesco (1599–1667) Italian architect.

Borrow, George Henry (1803–81) English writer (*Lavengro* 1851).

Boru, Brian *see* BRIAN BORU and Appendix.

Bosanquet, Bernard (1848–1923) English philosopher.

Bosch, Hieronymous [Jerome van Aeken *or* Aken] (*c.*1450–1516) Dutch painter, known for his fantastic and often grotesque allegorical paintings which use imagery drawn from folk tales and religious symbolism (*The Temptation of St Anthony*).

Boscobel, Shropshire, scene of the hiding-place (in an oak) of Charles II in 1651.

Bose, Sir Jagadis Chandra (1858–1937) Indian physicist and plant physiologist. He invented the crescograph, a device that automatically records plant movements.

Bose, Subhas Chandra (1897–1945) Indian nationalist leader. He was president of the Indian National Congress (1938–39) and, in collaboration with the Japanese during World War II, organized the Indian National Army to combat British rule in India.

Bosnia-Hercegovina ruled by Austria 1878–1918; part of Yugoslavia since 1918.

Bossuet, Jacques Bénigne (1627–1704) French theologian.

Boston, Massachusetts, settled by John Winthrop 1630.

Boston Massacre occurred 1770.

Boston Symphony Orchestra founded 1881 by the American philanthropist Henry Lee Higginson (1834–1919).

Boston Tea Party American revolutionary incident 16 December 1773.

Boswell, James (1740–95) Scottish biographer and

diarist best known for his *Life* of Dr Samuel Johnson. He also wrote *The Journal of a Tour to the Hebrides with Samuel Johnson LLD* (1785).

Bosworth Field, Battle of a battle of the Wars of the Roses, fought between Henry VII and Richard III, 22 August 1485. Richard was defeated and killed, and Henry vecame king of England, the first of the Tudor dynasty.

Botany Bay, New South Wales, discovered 28 April 1770 by Captain James Cook (1728–79); became British penal settlement 1786; transportation ceased 1840.

Botha, Louis (1862–1919) South African general and statesman. As general of the Transvaal army, he led the Boer forces against the British during the Boer War. He supported the Allies during World War I, and became first prime minister of South Africa (1910–19).

Botha, P[ieter] W[illem] (1916–) South African politician. As prime minister (1978–84) and then president (1984–89), he introduced limited reforms of apartheid.

Botham, Ian (1955–) English cricketer. A talented all-rounder, he captained England (1980–81) and scored 5,057 runs in Test matches (including 14 centuries).

Bothwell Bridge, Battle of fought between the English and the Scottish Covenanters 1679.

Bothwell, James Hepburn, Earl of (*c.*1537–1578) husband of Mary, Queen of Scots.

Botswana former British protectorate of Bechuanaland from 1885; became independent state within the Commonwealth 1981.

Botticelli, Sandro (1444–1510) Florentine painter, best known for his graceful and serene religious works. He also painted *The Birth of Venus*.

Bottomley, Horatio (1860–1933) English politician, financier and founder (1906) of *John Bull*; in prison for fraud 1920–27.

Boucher, François (1703–70) French painter (*The Toilet of Venus*).

Boucicault, Dion (1822–90) Irish-born playwright (*The Colleen Bawn* 1860).

Boudicca *or* **Boadicea** (d.62) British queen of the Iceni *see* Appendix.

Bougainville, Louis Antoine de (1729–1811) French explorer.

Boughton, Rutland (1878–1960) English composer (*The Immortal Hour* 1913).

Boulanger, George Ernest Jean Marie (1837–91) French general and politician. He committed suicide.

Boulder Dam harnessing the Colorado River, began 1928.

Boulez, Pierre (1925–) French composer and conductor who developed a composition style based on total serialism and electronic instruments. His works include *Memoriales* (1975).

Boulsover, Thomas English inventor (1743) of Sheffield plate.

Boulton, Matthew (1728–1809) English engineer and inventor.

Bounty, Mutiny of the 28 April 1789.

Bourbon Dynasty ruled France 1589–1792, 1814–48; Spain 1700–1808, 1814–68, 1874–1930; Naples 1759–99, 1799–1806, 1815–60; Parma 1748–1815, 1847–60.

Bourges Cathedral constructed between 1220 and 1260.

Bourne, Francis (1861–1935) English cardinal.

Bourse, The Paris French Stock Exchange founded 1724.

Bouts, Dirk (*c.*1410–1475) Dutch painter.

Bouvet Island South Atlantic, discovered 1739 by the French navigator Jean Baptiste Lozier Bouvet; annexed by Norway 1927–30.

Bow porcelain manufactured 1745–76.

Bow Street Runners, London, superseded by the Police 1829.

Bowdler, Thomas (1754–1825) English self-appointed censor of the classics.

Bowdoin College, Maine, founded 1794.

Bowen, Elizabeth (1889–1973) Anglo-Irish writer (*The Death of the Heart* 1938).

Bowen, York (Edwin) (1884–1961) English composer (*The Lament of Tasso* 1903).

Bowles, Jane (1917–73) American writer (*Plain Pleasures* 1966).

Bowles, Paul (1910–) American novelist and composer (*The Sheltering Sky* 1949).

Boxer Rising, Peking, in which the Chinese rose against foreigners in China, June and July 1900.

Boxing legalized in England 1901.

Boyce, William (1710–79) English organist and composer.

Boycott, Captain Charles Cunningham (1832–97) Lord Erne's English land agent in Co. Mayo, who was 'boycotted' from 24 September 1880.

Boycott, Geoffrey (1940–) English cricketer. He is regarded as one of England's greatest modern batsmen. He captained Yorkshire (1970–78) and played for England (1964–74, 1977–81).

Boyd-Orr, John, Baron (1880–1971) Scottish nutritionist.

Boyle, Richard, Earl of Cork (1566–1643) British Lord High Treasurer.

Boyle, Robert (1627–91) Irish-born scientist and discoverer (1667) of Boyle's Law.

Boyle's Law a scientific law, discovered 1667 by Robert Boyle, that states that at a constant temperature, the volume of a gas varies inversely with the pressure.

Boyne, Battle of the fought between William III and James II, 1 July 1690.

Boys' Brigade, The founded 1883 by Sir William Alexander Smith (1854–1914).

Boy Scout Movement began with camp for 20 boys in 1908 held by Lord Baden-Powell on Brownsea Island. First Rally and Conference, Crystal Palace, London, 4 September 1909. Incorporated in USA 1910. The movement was so successful that Baden-Powell left the army in 1911 to devote his time to it. It was given a royal charter in 1912.

Brabançonne, La Belgian national anthem composed by François van Campenhout (1779–1849).

Bracegirdle, Anne (*c.*1664–1748) English actress.

Bradlaugh, Charles (1833–91) English politician and social reformer.

Bradley, Andrew Cecil (1851–1935) English critic.

Bradley, Francis Herbert (1846–1924) English philosopher.

Bradley, Henry (1845–1923) one of the editors of the *New (Oxford) English Dictionary*.

Bradman, [Sir] Don[ald George] (1908–) Australian cricketer. A brilliant batsman, he scored 117 centuries during the 1930s and 1940s. He was Australian captain (1936–48).

Bradshaw's Railway Guide, Great Britain, first published 1839 by George Bradshaw (1801–53; discontinued 1961. Continental Bradshaw established 1848.

Bradshaw, John (1602–59) English regicide, president of court that condemned Charles I (1649).

Brady, Matthew B. 'Lincoln's cameraman', (*c.*1823–96) American pioneer photographer.

Bragg, Melvyn (1939–) English novelist and broadcaster. He is best known as a television presenter of arts programmes.

Bragg, Sir William Henry (1862–1942) English scientist.

Brahe, Tycho (1546–1601) Danish astronomer.

Brahms, Johannes (1833–97) German composer. He regarded himself as firmly in the Classical (as opposed to Romantic) tradition. His works include the great choral *German Requiem* (1869), four symphonies and chamber music.

Braid, James (*c.*1796–1860) Scottish pioneer in study of hypnotism.

Braille Alphabet for the Blind invented 1834 by the blind Frenchman Louis Braille (1809–52).

Braine, John (1922–86) English novelist (*Room at the Top* 1957).

Bramalea, near Toronto, Canada's first satellite city, founded 1959.

Bramante, Donato (1444–1514) Italian architect.

Branagh, Kenneth (1961–) Irish-born British actor and director. He founded the Renaissance Theatre Company in 1986 and has appeared regularly in films with his wife, the actress **Emma Thompson** (1959–). They separated in 1995.

Brancusi, Constantin (1876–1957) Romanian-born sculptor.

Brandeis, Louis Dembitz (1856–1941) American chief justice.

Brando, Marlon (1924–) American actor. Brando's many celebrated screen performances display the highly influential method acting style. His films include *A Streetcar Named Desire* (1947), *The Godfather* (1972) and *Last Tango in Paris* (1972).

Brandt, Willy [Karl Herbert Frahm] (1913–92) German statesman. He was active in the German Resistance during the Second World War and became mayor of Berlin (1957–66) and chancellor of West Germany (1969–74). He was awarded the Nobel Peace Prize in 1971 and produced the Brandt Report (1980) urging increased economic aid for the Third World.

Brandywine, Battle of, Delaware, fought between the British and the Americans 11 September 1777.

Brangwyn, Frank (1867–1935) British artist.

Brant, Sebastian (1457–1521) German writer (*Das Narrenschiff* 1494).

Braque, Georges (1882–1963) French painter. The term Cubism was coined in 1909 to describe his works. He also pioneered the use of collage in modern painting.

Brassey's Naval Annual founded 1886 by Lord Brassey (1836–1918).

Bratby, John (1928–) English painter.

Brattain, Walter *see* SHOCKLEY, WILLIAM BRADFORD.

Braudel, Fernand (1902–85) French historian. His influential works focused on socio-economic trends and the changing relationship between man and the environment rather than on politics or military events.

Braun, Wernher von (1912–77) German-born scientist and developer of ballistic missiles and satellites.

Bray, The Rev. Thomas (1656–1730) English pioneer in the provision of libraries.

Brazil discovered 500 by Vicente Yáñez Pinzón (*c.*1460–*c.*1524; independent empire 1822–89, republic since 1889.

Breakspear, Nicolas (Adrian IV) (1154–1159) only English Pope.

Breasted, James Henry (1865–1935) American Egyptologist.

Brecht, Bertolt (1898–1956) German dramatist who devised the theatre of alienation, which he used in

The Threepenny Opera (1928), for which Weill wrote the music, and developed in plays such as *Galileo* (1938) and *Mother Courage* (1941). He settled in the US during Nazi rule in Germany, returning to East Berlin in 1949 where he founded the Berliner Ensemble theatre.

Bred (d.842) king of Picts (842) *see* Appendix.

Breda, Peace of between England and the United Netherlands 1667.

'Breeches' Bible published by the Calvinists at Geneva 1558.

Breechloading cartridge case first adopted in principle by the Prussians *c.*1841.

Bremen belonged to Hanseatic League 1260–85, 1358–1422, 1433–1646; became free city 1648; became German 1867.

Brendan, Saint (484–577).

Brenner Pass, Swiss Alps; road built 1772, railway 1864–67.

Brennus leader of the Gauls, who in 390 BC crossed the Apennines, took Rome and overran the centre and south of Italy. He was bought off by the Romans and returned to Gaul.

Breslau capital of Silesia, founded *c.*1000; since 1945 included in Poland and called Wroclaw

Brest-Litovsk, Treaty of World War I confirming Russian Armistice with the Central Powers, signed 3 March 1918.

Breton, Nicholas (*c.*1545–*c.*1626) English writer.

Bretton Woods Conference on international monetary policy held July 1944.

Breughel *see* BRUEGHEL.

Breuil, Henri (1877–1961) French priest and archaeologist and expert in cave paintings.

Brezhnev, Leonid Ilyich (1906–82) Soviet statesman. He helped organize Khrushchev's downfall in 1964, and became general secretary of the Communist Party (1977–82) and Soviet president (1977–82). The period of his rule is now described as the 'period of stagnation' in the USSR.

Brian Boru (*c.*941–1014) king of Munster (976–1014) and high king of Ireland (1002–14) *see* Appendix.

Brian, [William] Havergal (1876–1972) English composer, frequently described as 'post-Romantic'. His more than 30 works include the huge *Gothic Symphony* (1919–27) and five operas.

Briand, Aristide (1862–1932) French statesman.

Bricks size standardized in England *c.*1625; taxed in England 1784 to 1850.

Bride, Saint (453–523).

Bridei I (d.586) king of Picts (556–586) *see* Appendix.

Bridei II (d.641) king of Picts (635–641) *see* Appendix.

Bridei III (d.692) king of Picts (671–692) *see* Appendix.

Bridei IV (d.706) king of Picts (696–706) *see* Appendix.

Bridei V (d.763) king of Picts (761–763) *see* Appendix.

Bridge card game, first recorded mention in England 1886.

Bridge first iron bridge built 1779 by Wilkinson and Darby at Ironbridge, Shropshire.

Bridge of Sighs, Venice, built 1597.

Bridges, Robert (1844–1930) English poet (*The Testament of Beauty* 1929).

Bridget, Saint (*c.*1303–1373) Swedish visionary.

Bridgewater Canal, Worsley to Manchester, constructed 1756–61 by the Duke of Bridgewater (1736–1806; engineer James Brindley (1716–72).

Bridie, James [Osborne Henry Mavor] (1888–1951) Scottish playwright.

Brieux, Eugène (1858–1932) French playwright (*Les Avariés* 1901).

Briggs, Henry (1561–1631) English mathematician and pioneer in the study of logarithms.

Bright, John (1811–89) English statesman.

Brighton bombing IRA attack on a Brighton hotel used by Conservative politicians (including prime minister Margaret Thatcher) during the Party Conference 12 October 1984.

Bright's Disease identified 1827 by Dr Richard Bright (1789–1858).

Brillat-Savarin, Anthelme (1755–1826) French gastronome.

Brindley, James (1716–72) English engineer whose works included the Bridgewater Canal.

Brisbane, Queensland capital, founded by the English explorer John Oxley 1824; named after General Sir Thomas Brisbane (1773–1860), governor of New South Wales (1821–25).

Bristol porcelain manufactured 1750–80.

Bristol University, England, founded as University College 1876; granted Royal Charter 24 May 1909.

Britain the island in northern Europe shared by England, Scotland and Wales; Agricola began his conquest in Britain 78; first invaded by Julius Caesar 55 BC, again invaded by Caesar 54 BC.

Britannia the Roman name for the southern part of the island of Britain.

Britannia Royal Naval College, Dartmouth, founded 1857 at Portland; transferred to Dartmouth 1863.

British Academy, London, granted charter 8 August 1902.

British Association for the Advancement of Science founded 1831.

British Broadcasting Corporation (preceded by British Broadcasting Company, formed 1922), constituted under Royal Charter 1 January 1927.

British Cameroons *see* CAMEROON.

British Columbia, Canada, constituted British Crown Colony 2 August 1858. Became a Province of the Dominion of Canada 1871.

British Council, London, established 1935; chartered 1940.

British Empire Exhibition, Wembley, London, opened 23 April, closed 1 November 1924.

British Empire, Order of founded by George V in 1917.

British Film Institute, London, founded 1933.

British Guiana issued the most valuable postage stamp (only one copy known) February 1856.

British Guiana *see* GUYANA.

British Honduras *see* BELIZE.

British Interplanetary Society founded at Liverpool 1933.

British Legion founded in London by Earl Haig 24 May 1921; became Royal British Legion in 1971.

British Museum, London, founded 1753; opened 16 January 1759.

British North American Act, by which the Dominion of Canada was created, proclaimed 1 July 1867.

British Pharmacopoeia first published 1864.

British Railways amalgamating existing regional railway companies under national ownership, inaugurated 1 January 1948.

British Red Cross Society founded 1905; received Royal Charter 1908.

British Somaliland former British protectorate (1884–1960), together with Italian Somaliland became the Somali Republic in 1960.

British Standards Institution founded 1901 as the Engineering Standards Committee; incorporated by Royal Charter 1929.

British Telecom (BT) created 1980 when the telephone service split from the Post Office; BT privatized as a public limited company 1984.

Britons the early Celtic inhaitants of southern Britain. After the invasions of the Angles, Saxons and Jutes they were gradually dispossessed and moved west and north, into Wales and Scotland. *See also* Appendix.

Britten, [Edward] Benjamin [1st Baron Britten] (1913–76) English composer and pianist. His works include the operas *Peter Grimes* (1945), *Billy Budd* (1951) and *A Midsummer Night's Dream* (1960), chamber music, orchestral works and song cycles. His works are noted for their romantic lyricism. He was created a peer in 1976.

Britton, John (1771–1857) English topographical writer (*The Beauties of England and Wales* 1803–14).

Broadcasting American daily, began from KDKA 2 November 1920; British daily, began from 2LO 14 November 1922.

Broadmoor, England, criminal lunatic asylum, opened 1863.

Brockhaus Conversations-Lexikon German national encyclopedia first published 1810–11 by Friedrich Arnold Brockhaus (1772–1823).

Brod, Max (1884–1968) Czech writer (*Tycho Brahe* 1914) and literary executor of Kafka.

Broglie, Prince Louis Victor de (1892–1987) French physicist.

Broken Hill, New South Wales, silver lode discovered 1883.

Bromine discovered 1826 by Antoine Jérôme Balard (1802–76).

Brontë sisters English novelists: Anne (*Agnes Grey* 1850) (1820–49; Charlotte (*Jane Eyre* 1847) (1816–55; Emily (*Wuthering Heights* 1847) (1818–48).

Brontë, Anne (1820–49), **Charlotte** (1816–55) and **Emily** (1818–48) English novelists and poets. Charlotte's *Jane Eyre*, based on her experiences as a teacher and governess, was published in 1847, and Anne's *Agnes Grey* and Emily's *Wuthering Heights* followed in 1848. Anne's *Tenant of Wildfell Hall* was published in 1848, in which year Emily died of consumption. Charlotte wrote two more novels: *Shirley* (1849) and *Villette* (1853).

Bronze Age the period of history characterized by the spread of bronze tools and weapons, which began in the Middle East *c.*4500 BC. It followed the Stone Age and preceded the Iron Age.

Brook, Peter [Stephen Paul] (1925–) English stage and film director based in Paris. He is regarded as one of the finest experimental directors of the modern era.

Brooke, Henry (1708–83) Irish writer (*The Fool of Quality* 1766).

Brooke, Sir James (1803–68) Indian-born rajah of Sarawak.

Brooke, Rupert [Chawner] (1887–1915) English poet. His war poems were very popular with the public for their idealized vision of the nobility of war.

Brookings Institution, Washington, founded 1922 for research in administration and economics by Robert Somers Brookings, American philanthropist (1850–1932).

Brooklands motor racecourse opened 6 July 1907.

Brooklyn Bridge, New York, built 1870–83 by the German-born engineer John Augustus Roebling (1806–69).

Brooks, Mel [Melvin Kaminsky] (1926–) American comedian, film writer and director, best known for his fast-moving, irreverent comedy films. His wife is the actress **Anne Bancroft** [Anna Maria Italiano]

(1931–) who is noted for her serious acting.

Brooks's Club, London, established 1778. Formerly known as Almack's, founded 1763.

Brougham, Henry, Lord Brougham and Vaux (1778–1868) British statesman.

Brouwer, Adriaen (*c.*1605–1638) Dutch painter.

Brown, Christy (1932–81) disabled Irish writer and painter (*My Left Foot* 1954).

Brown, Ford Maddox (1821–93) French-born painter (*Romeo and Juliet*).

Brown, George Douglas ('George Douglas') Scottish writer (*The House with the Green Shutters* 1901) (1869–1902).

Brown, George MacKay *see* DAVIES, SIR PETER MAXWELL.

Brown, John (1) (1736–88) Scottish medical pioneer.

Brown, John (2) (1800–1859) American abolitionist. He was hanged.

Brown, Louise (1978–) first 'test-tube' baby.

Browne, Hablot Knight ('Phiz') (1815–82) English artist and illustrator.

Browne, Robert (*c.*1550–1633) English religious leader (founded Brownist sect – later Congregationalists – 1582).

Browne, Sir Thomas (1605–82) English writer (*Hydriotaphia* 1658).

Browning machine gun invented by the American John Moses Browning (1855–1926).

Brownian Motion physics discovered 1828 by the Scottish botanist Robert Brown (1773–1858).

Browning, Elizabeth Barrett (1806–61) English poet and wife of Robert Browning (*Aurora Leigh* 1856).

Browning, Robert (1812–89) English poet renowned for his innovative experiments in form and narrative skill. His wife, Elizabeth Barrett Browning, whom he married in 1846, was also a major poet. His works include *Andrea del Sarto* (1855).

Brown University, Providence, Rhode Island, founded 1764 as Rhode Island College.

Brubeck, Dave (1920–) American jazz composer and pianist. He studied musical composition with Schoenberg and Milhaud, forming his 'Dave Brubeck Quartet' in 1951.

Bruce, Sir David (1855–1932) British pioneer in tropical medicine.

Bruce, Edward (1276–1318) high king of Ireland (1315–18) *see* Appendix.

Bruce, James (1730–94) Scottish explorer of Abyssinia.

Bruce, Lenny [Leonard Alfred Schneider] (1925–66) American stand-up comedian who developed an influential style of satirical and often scabrous comedy which frequently resulted in being prosecuted for obscenity (1925–66).

Bruce, Robert (1274–1329) Scottish king. *See* Appendix.

Bruce, William Speirs (1867–1921) Scottish polar explorer.

Bruch, Max (1838–1920) German composer (*Violin concerto* 1865–67).

Bruckner, Anton (1824–96) Austrian composer (*Missa Solemnis* 1854).

Brude (d.845) king of Picts (843–845) *see* Appendix.

Bruegel *or* **Brueghel, Pieter (the Elder)** (*c.*1525–1569) Flemish painter who painted peasant scenes and allegories. He is best known for his magnificent landscape painting *The Hunters in the Snow* (1565). His sons **Jan Brueghel** (1568–1625) and **Pieter Brueghel (the Younger)** (*c.*1564–1637) were also painters.

Brulé, Etienne (*c.*1592–1632) French explorer of North America. He was murdered.

Brumaire 2nd month (mid-October to mid-November) in the French Revolutionary calendar established 1793.

Brummell, 'Beau' [George Bryan Brummell] (1778–1840) English dandy.

Brunei northwest Borneo state, sultanate placed under British protection 1888; achieved independence in 1983.

Brunel, Isambard Kingdom (1806–59) English civil engineer. He designed steamships, e.g. *Great Eastern* (1858), and in the late 1820s planned and designed the Clifton Suspension Bridge. His father was Sir Marc Isambard Brunel.

Brunel, Sir Marc Isambard (1769–1849) French-born engineer who designed a tunnel under the Thames in London. He was the father of Isambard Kingdom Brunel.

Brunelleschi, Filippo (1377–1446) Italian architect.

Brunet, Jacques Charles (1780–1867) French bibliographer (*Manuel du libraire* 1810).

Brüning, Heinrich (1885–1970) German statesman who was chancellor 1930–32.

Brunner, Heinrich (1840–1915) German historian.

Brunner, Thomas (1821–74) English explorer in New Zealand.

Bruno, Giordano (1548–1600) Italian philosopher. He was burnt at the stake.

Bruno, Saint (*c.*1030–1101) German-born founder (1084) of the Carthusian Order.

Brussels Belgian capital founded by St Gery of Cambrai in the 7th century.

Brussels Treaty concerning Western Union signed 17 March 1948; came into force 25 July 1948.

Brutus, Marcus Junius (85–42 BC) Roman patriot. One of the leaders, with Cassius, of the revolt against Caesar and his subsequent assassination. Following their defeat at the Battle of Philippi 42 BC, they committed suicide.

Bryan, William Jennings (1860–1925) American statesman.

Bryce, James, Viscount Bryce (1838–1922) British statesman.

Bryn Mawr College, Philadelphia, American women's college founded 1880.

Brynner, Yul (1915–85) American film actor of Swiss-Mongolian descent (*The King and I* 1956).

Buber, Martin (1878–1965) Austrian-born Jewish theologian and existentialist philosopher. His philosophy, which centres on the relationship between man and God, has had a large impact on both Jewish and Christian theology.

Bubonic plague bacillus discovered 1894 by the French scientist Alexandre Emile John Yersin (1863–1943).

Buccaneers French and English pirates active in Caribbean between 1625 and 1700.

Bucer, Martin (1491–1551) German religious reformer.

Buchan, John [1st Baron Tweedsmuir] (1875–1940) Scottish novelist, statesman and historian. He wrote several best-selling adventure novels, e.g. *Greenmantle* (1916), was created a peer in 1935, and was appointed governor-general of Canada (1935–40).

Buchanan, George (1506–82) Scottish scholar.

Buchanan, James (1791–1868) 15th US president (1857–61).

Buchanites Scottish religious sect founded by Elspeth Buchan (1738–91).

Buchan's days weather predictions defined 1869 by Alexander Buchan (1829–1907).

Buchman, Frank [Nathan Daniel] (1878–1961) American evangelist who founded the Oxford Group and the longer-lived Moral Rearmament (1921), which were intended to provide ideological alternatives to both capitalism and communism.

Büchner, Georg (1813–37) German playwright (*Dantons Tod* 1835).

Buckingham Palace built by the Duke of Buckingham 1703; rebuilt 1825–37.

Buckingham, George Villiers, Duke of (1592–1628) favourite of James I. He was assassinated.

Buckingham, George Villiers, 2nd Duke of (1627–87) favourite of Charles II.

Buckle, Henry Thomas (1821–62) English historian.

Buddha, Gautama Siddharta (*c.*563–*c.*480 BC) the Indian founder of Buddhism.

Budé, Guillaume (1467–1540) French classicist.

Budge, Sir Ernest Alfred Wallis (1857–1934) English Egyptologist.

Buell, Abel (1742–1822) American map engraver, silversmith and inventor.

Buenos Aires founded 1536 by Don Pedro de Mendoza (*c.*1487–1537).

Buenos Aires Standard first English-language South American daily newspaper, founded 1861 by the Irish-born economist Michael George Mulhall (1836–1900).

'Buffalo Bill' [William Frederick Cody] (1846–1917) American frontiersman and showman.

Buffon, Georges Louis Leclere, Comte de (1707–88) French naturalist.

Buhl Cabinets style introduced by the French furniture maker André Charles Boulle (1642–1732).

Büjük Agri Dagi *see* ARARAT, MOUNT.

Bukharin, Nikolai Ivanovich (1888–1938) Russian Communist leader. He was tried and shot.

Bulawayo mining city in Zimbabwe founded 1893.

Bulganin, Nikolai Aleksandrovich (1895–1975) Soviet leader.

Bulgaria established in 7th century, conquered by Byzantines in 10th century, revived in 12th century, conquered by Turks in 14th century; Principality under Turkish suzerainty 1878; independent kingdom 1908; Communist republic 1946; democratic constitution adopted 1991.

Bull Run, Battles of American Civil War battles, first on 21 July 1861; second on 30 August 1862.

Bull-baiting prohibited in England by Act of Parliament 1835.

Buller, Sir Redvers Henry (1839–1908) British soldier.

Bullinger, Heinrich (1504–75) Swiss Reformation leader.

Bülow, Prince Bernhard von (1849–1929) German chancellor (1900–1909).

Bunche, Ralph Johnson (1904–71) American diplomat and UN official. The grandson of a slave, he became the first Black to be awarded the Nobel Peace Prize, in 1950, for his attempt at reconciling Israel and the Arab states (1948–49).

Bunin, Ivan Alexeyevich (1870–1954) Russian writer in exile.

Bunker Hill, Battle of American Revolution fought between Americans and English 17 June 1775.

Bunsen burner invented for use in laboratories by the German scientist Robert Wilhelm Bunsen (1811–99).

Bunsen, Christian Karl Josias, Baron (1791–1860) German diplomat.

Buñuel, Luis (1900–83) Spanish-born film director. His early films were made in collaboration with Salvador Dali, and he is regarded as a master of Surrealist cinema.

Bunyan, John (1628–88) English religious leader and author. Writer of several devotional works, the most famous being the remarkable allegory *Pilgrim's Progress* (1678–84).

Buonarroti, Philippe (1761–1837) French revolutionary leader.

Buononcini, Giovanni Battista (1672–*c.*1750) Italian composer (*Muzio Scevola* 1710).

Burbage, Richard (*c.*1567–1619) English actor.

Burbank, Luther (1849–1926) American horticulturalist.

Burchell, William John (*c.*1782–1863) English explorer.

Burckhardt, Jacob (1818–97) Swiss historian.

Burdett, Francis English politician (1770–1844).

Burgess, Anthony [John Anthony Burgess Wilson] (1917–93) English novelist, critic and composer. His novels include the controversial futuristic fantasy of juvenile crime *A Clockwork Orange* (1962, filmed by Kubrick in 1971).

Burgess, Guy [Francis de Moncy] (1910–63) English diplomat and spy. Recruited by Soviet Intelligence in the 1930s, he worked for MI5 during World War II and served with Philby at the British Embassy in Washington DC after the war. With his fellow agent, **Donald Maclean** (1913–83), he defected to the Soviet Union 26 May 1951.

Burghley, William Cecil, Lord (1520–1598) English statesman.

Burgkmair, Hans (1473–1531) German artist.

Burgoyne, John (1723–92) English general in American Revolution.

Burgred king of Mercia (853–874) *see* Appendix.

Burke, Edmund (1729–97) Irish-born statesman, writer and philosopher. He entered parliament for the Whigs in 1765 and was soon established as the dominant political thinker of the day. His works include the cornerstone of conservative political thought, *Reflections on the Revolution in France* (1790).

Burke, Robert O'Hara (1820–61) Australian pioneer who was the first person to cross Australia from south to north (1860–61).

Burke, William (1792–1829) Irish criminal and body-snatcher (with William Hare). He was hanged.

Burke's Peerage founded 1826 by Sir John Bernard Burke (1814–92).

Burlington Arcade, Piccadilly, London, opened 20 March 1819.

Burlington House, Piccadilly, London, built *c.*1664 by Sir John Denham (1615–69; rebuilt 1731.

Burma gained independence as a republic 4 January 1948.

Burne-Jones, Sir Edward (1833–98) English painter (*Cophetua and the Beggarmaid*).

Burnet, Sir Frank Macfarlane *see* MEDAWAR, SIR PETER BRIAN.

Burnet, Gilbert (1643–1715) British writer and divine.

Burnett, Mrs Frances Hodgson (1849–1924) English-born writer (*Little Lord Fauntleroy* 1886).

Burney, Charles (1726–1814) English musicologist.

Burney, Fanny [Madame d'Arblay] (1752–1840) English writer (*Evelina* 1778).

Burning to death British punishment for women last inflicted 1729; legally abolished 1790.

Burns, John (1858–1943) British socialist leader.

Burns, Robert (1759–96) Scottish poet, renowned as both a lyric poet and a satirist. The son of a farmer, his identification with folk tradition and his rebellious lifestyle also contribute to the unwavering popularity of his work in Scotland.

Burr, Aaron (1756–1836) American statesman.

Burroughs, William S[eward] (1914–) American novelist. A friend of Ginsberg and Kerouac, Burroughs became a heroin addict in the 1940s. His luridly obscene fiction features the squalid, nightmarish underworld of drug addiction.

Burton, Decimus (1800–1881) English architect.

Burton, Richard [Richard Jenkins] (1925–84) Welsh actor, regarded by his peers and critics as one of the most talented actors of his generation. He formed a screen partnership with Elizabeth Taylor, to whom he was married twice (1964–70, 1975–76). His films include (*The Spy Who Came in from the Cold* 1965).

Burton, Sir Richard Francis(1821–90) English explorer and translator of *The Arabian Nights*.

Burton, Robert (1577–1640) English writer (*The Anatomy of Melancholy* 1621).

Bus first in London ran from Marylebone Road to the Bank 4 July 1829.

Busby, Sir Matt[hew] (1909–94) Scottish footballer and manager of Manchester United (1946–69). Many members of his highly regarded team of 1958 died in a plane crash at Munich. His rebuilt team of 'Busby Babes' became the first English team to win the European Cup (1968).

Busch, Wilhelm (1832–1908) German humorous artist.

Bush, George [Herbert Walker] (1924–) American Republican politician and 41st president of the US (1989–93). The son of a wealthy senator, he served in the US Navy (1942–45), became US ambassador to the UN (1971–73), special envoy to China (1974–75) and CIA director (1976). He served under Reagan as vice-president (1980–88) before being elected president in 1988.

Bushell, Edward (*fl* 1670–71) English champion of juries.

Busoni, Ferruccio (1866–1924) Italian composer (*Die Brautwahl* 1912).

Buss, Frances Mary(1827–94) English pioneer of high schools for girls.

Butcher, Samuel Henry (1850–1910) Irish classicist.

Bute, John Stuart, Earl of (1713–92) British statesman.

Buthelezi, Chief Gatsha (1928–) South African Zulu chief and politician. He helped found the paramilitary organization Inkatha.

Butler, Joseph (1692–1752) bishop of Durham.

Butler, Josephine (1828–1906) social reformer.

Butler, R[ichard] A[usten], [Baron] (1902–82) English Conservative politician. As minister of education (1941–45), he introduced the Education Act of 1944. He was also chancellor of the exchequer (1951–55), home secretary (1957–62) and foreign secretary (1963–64). He was created a life peer in 1965.

Butler, Samuel (1612–80) English poet (*Hudibras* 1663–78).

Butler, Samuel (1835–1902) English writer (*Erewhon* 1872).

Butlin, William Edmund ('Billy') (1900–80) South African-born pioneer of holiday camps.

Butt, Dame Clara (1873–1936) English contralto.

Butt, Isaac (1813–79) Irish nationalist politician.

Buxtehude, Dietrich (1637–1707) Danish-born organist and composer.

Byng, George, Viscount Torrington (1663–1733) English admiral.

Byng, John (1704 shot 1757) English admiral. He was shot.

Byrd, Richard Evelyn (1888–1957) American polar aviator.

Byrd, William (*c.*1542–1623) English composer.

Byrom, John (1692–1763) English shorthand pioneer.

Byron, Lord George Gordon Noel [6th Baron Byron of Rochdale] (1788–1824) English poet. His works include many superb lyrics and the long satirical poem *Don Juan* (1819–21).

Byzantine empire existed 330–1453.

Byzantium founded 658 BC; rebuilt as Constantinople AD 330; conquered by the Turks 1453 and renamed Istanbul.

C

Cabal ministry formed 1668 by King Charles II of England, ended 1673 (from names of members: Clifford Ashley, Buckingham, Arlington, Lauderdale).

Cabell, James Branch (1879–1958) American novelist (*Jurgen* 1919).

Cabinet Noir French postal censorship instituted in reign of Louis XI, formally constituted in reign of Louis XV, abolished 1868.

Cabinet form of British government introduced by Charles II, formally instituted by William III 1693, principles developed by Sir Robert Walpole (1676–1745).

Cable first Atlantic completed 5 August 1858 by Sir Charles Tilston Bright (1832–88); first successful cable laid completed 7 September 1866.

Cabochiens Parisian rioters led by Simon 'Caboche' (real name Lecoustellier) active 1413–14.

Cabot, John (1451–98) Italian-born explorer (discovered Newfoundland 1497).

Cabral, Pedro (*c.*1467–*c.*1520) Portuguese explorer.

Cabria, Battle of 72 BC a battle of the Third Mithridatic War, when a Roman army under Lucullus defeated Mithridates..

Cabrillo, Juan Rodriguez (d.1543) Spanish explorer.

Cadbury, George (1839–1922) English businessman, social reformer and philanthropist. With his brother **Michael Cadbury** (1835–99) he established the model village of Bournville, near Birmingham, for the Cadbury work force.

Cade, Jack (d.1450) English revolutionary leader. He was killed.

Cadets Russian political party formed 1905 by Paul Milyukov.

Cadillac, Antoine de la Mothe, Sieur (*c.*1656–1730) governor of Louisiana (1713–16).

Cadiz, Naval Battle of fought between Sir Francis Drake and the Spaniards 1587.

Cadmium chemical element first isolated by the German scientist F. Stromeyer 1817.

Cadogan, William, 1st Earl Cadogan (1675–1726) Irish general.

Cadwalader (*c.*658–689) king of Wessex (685–688) *see* Appendix.

Cadwalladr (d.1172) Welsh prince.

Cadwallon (d.633) king of Gwynedd (*c.*625–633) *see* Appendix.

Caedmon (d. *c.*680) English poet.

Caesar, [Gaius] Julius (100–44 BC) Roman soldier and historian. He negotiated and formed the 'First Triumvirate' with Crassus and Pompey in 60, after which he fought in Gaul for nine years and invaded Britain in 55 and 54. He crossed the Rubicon and invaded Italy 49. Appointed dictator by the Senate in 49, he defeated Pompey at Pharsalia in 48. He was under the influence of Cleopatra, Queen of Egypt 48-47 BC. He defeated Pharnaces, king of Pontus at the Battle of Zela 47 BC and the republicans at the Battle of Thapsus in Africa in 46 BC and Pompey's sons at the Battle of Munda in Spain 45 BC. He reformed the calendar in 46 BC and was appointed perpetual dictator in 44 BC. He was assassinated by a largely aristocratic group of conspirators, led by Brutus and Cassius.

Caesarian Section performed on living woman as early as 1500.

Caesium chemical element first isolated 1860 by the German scientist Robert Wilhelm Bunsen (1811–99).

Cafe Royal, London, founded 1864, bombed 1940.

Cage, John (1912–92) American composer. His experimental music, e.g. *4 minutes 33 seconds* (1952), in which the performers remain silent, has been derided and admired in equal proportions.

'Cagliostro, Alessandro' *see* Balsamo, Giuseppe.

Cagney, James (1899–1986) American film actor of Irish descent, originally a dancer (*Yankee Doodle Dandy* 1942) but best remembered for his many portrayals of gangsters, e.g. in *The Public Enemy* (1931), *Angels with Dirty Faces* (1938).

Cahiers statements of local grievances submitted to the French States-General 1789.

Caicos Islands, West Indies, part of British colony of Turks and Caicos Islancds, discovered *c.*1512.

Caine, Michael [Maurice Joseph Micklewhite] (1933-) British film actor whose films include *Alfie* (1966) and *Hannah and Her Sisters* (1986) for which he won an Oscar as best supporting actor.

Caine, Sir Hall (1853–1931) British novelist (*The Deemster* 1887).

Ça Ira French revolutionary song written by Ladré 1789.

Caius College, Gonville and, Cambridge University, founded as Gonville Hall by Edmund Gonville (d.1351) in 1348; assumed present name under Royal Charter 1557.

Caius, John (1510–93) English physician to the Royal family.

Caius, Saint pope (283–296).

Cajetan, Cardinal Thomas (1469–1534) Italian theologian.

'Calamity Jane' [Martha Jane Burke] (*c.*1852–1903) American pioneer.

Calamy, Edmund (1671–1732) English historian of nonconformity (*Account of the Ejected Ministers* 1702).

Calas, Jean (1698–1752) French Calvinist. He was tortured to death.

Calcium discovered 1808 by Sir Humphry Davy (1778–1829).

Calculating machine first model built 1694 by the German scientist Gottfried Wilhelm Leibniz (1646–1716).

Calculus *Infinitesimal* invented 1675 by the German scientist Gottfried Wilhelm Leibniz (1646–1716; *Integral and Differential* invented independently by Leibniz and Isaac Newton (1642–1727).

Calcutta founded 1686–90 by the English official Job Charnock–1693; Black Hole of, episode occurred 20 June 1756.

Calderón de la Barca, Pedro (1600–1681) Spanish playwright (*La Vida es Sueño*).

Caledonia the name by which the northern portion of Scotland first became known to the Romans, when in the year ad 80 Agricola occupied the country up to the line of the firths of Clyde and Forth. He defeated the Caledonians in 83, and again at Mons Graupius in 84, a battle of which a detailed description is given by Tacitus. In the early part of the third century the people of Caledonia bravely resisted Severus, but the name then lost is historic importance.

Caledonian Canal, Scotland, constructed 1804–22 by the Scottish engineer Thomas Telford (1757–1834).

Calendar, French Revolutionary instituted 1793, abolished 1806.

Calendar, Gregorian reformed version of Julian Calendar, introduced by Pope Gregory XIII 1582; adopted in Britain September 1752.

Calendar, Hebrew calculated from 3761 BC; system adopted AD 358.

Calendar, Julian reformed version of Roman Calendar, introduced by Julius Caesar 46 BC.

Calendar, Mohammedan calculated from the Hegira 622.

Calendar, Roman calculated from the supposed date of the foundation of Rome, 754 BC.

Calhoun, John Caldwell (1782–1850) American statesman.

California a state of the USA on the Pacific coast, first settled 1769; ceded by Mexico to the USA 1848; admitted to the Union 1850.

California, University of founded at Berkeley 1868.

Californian gold fields discovered December 1847.

Caligula [Gaius Caesar Augustus Germanicus] (12–41) Roman emperor (37–41) who became tyrannical and was assassinated by a conspiracy and succeeded by his uncle, Claudius.

Caliphate of the Islamic Empire Umayyad 661–750; Abbasid established 750, extinguished by the Mongols 1258.

Caliphate, Egyptian extinguished by Ottoman conquest 1517.

Caliphate, Ottoman extinguished by the Kemalist Revolution 1923.

Callaghan, [Leonard] James [Baron Callaghan of Cardiff] (1912–) British Labour statesman prime minister (1976–79). After a vote of no confidence in his premiership in the House of Commons, he called a general election, which Labour lost.

Callas, Maria (1923–77) American-born Greek operatic soprano, renowned both for her voice and acting skills, which made her one of the most revered opera singers of the 20th century.

Callimachus Greek poet who lived in the 3rd century BC.

Callisthenes (*c.*360–328 BC) Greek historian. He was executed.

Callistus I, Saint pope (217–222).

Callistus II (Guido) pope (1119–24).

Callistus III [Alfonso de Borja] pope (1455–58).

Callistus III anti-pope (1168–79).

Callot, Jacques (1592–1635) French engraver.

Calloway, Cab(ell) (1907–) American band leader, singer and composer.

Calorimeters invented 1865 by the French scientist Pierre Eugène Marcelin Berthelot (1827–1907).

Calpurnia (*fl.* 50–40 BC) wife of Julius Caesar.

Calvin, John [Jean Cauvin] (1509–64) French religious reformer who had to flee from France to Switzerland, where, in 1536, he published his *Institutes of the Christian Religion* (1535), a summation of his Protestant faith and the founding text of Calvinism. He settled in Geneva, where he established the first Presbyterian government.

Calvino, Italo (1923–85) Cuban-Italian novelist, essayist and critic. His early novels belonged in the Italian realist tradition, while his later, highly complex explorations of fantasy and myth have been compared to Latin American 'magic realism'. His works include *Invisible Cities* (1972).

Camargo, Marie Anne French dancer (1710–70).

Cambodia, IndoChina, made French Protectorate

1863; granted independence 1955; 1970 Prince Norodom Sihanouk overthrown by Lon Nol and monarchy abolished; Khmer Rouge captured Phonm Penh 1975, renamed Kampuchea; murderous regime of Pol Pot 1975–79; invasion by Vietnam 1979–89.

Cambrai, Treaty of (The Ladies' Peace) renewing Treaty of Madrid signed 1529.

Cambrian Period Earth history 520 million years ago.

Cambridge University Observatory opened 1820.

Cambridge University Press founded 1583 by Thomas Thomas (1553–1588).

Cambridge University founded in 13th century, granted Royal Charter 1231.

Cambyses (d.*c*.522 BC) son of Cyrus the Great and king of the Medes and Persians (529–522). He conquered Egypt in 525 BC. A tyrannical ruler, he died of a accidental wound in the thigh while pursuing a pretender to his throne.

Camden, Charles Pratt, Earl (1713–94) English reforming judge.

Camden, William (1551–1623) English antiquary (*Britannia* 1586).

Camden, Battle of a battle of the American War of Independence, 16 August 1780, when the British defeated the Americans.

Camera lucida invented by English scientist William Hyde Wollaston (1766–1828).

Camera obscura described 1569.

Camera first roll-film marketed 1888 by the American inventor George Eastman (1854–1932).

Cameron, Sir David Young (1865–1945) Scottish artist.

Cameron, James (1911–85) Scottish newspaper and TV journalist.

Cameroon, West Africa, German colony 1884–1916; divided 1919 into British Cameroons and French Cameroun; South Cameroons and Cameroun united as a republic in 1961.

Camisards French Protestant rebels in the Cevennes active from 1685 to 1705.

Camões, Luis de (*c*.1524–1579) Portuguese poet (*Os Lusiadas* 1572).

Camorra, The Neapolitan secret society formed in the 16th century, suppressed in the late 19th century.

Camouflage, Thayer's Law of defined 1910 by the American painter Abbott Henderson Thayer (1849–1921).

Camp David official US presidential retreat near Washington DC, named by President Eisenhower after his grandson, 1953.

Campagnola, Domenico (*c*.1490–*c*.1565) Italian painter (*The Holy Family*).

Campaign for Nuclear Disarmament (CND) founded in Britain 1958 by Bertrand Russell and Canon John L. Collins.

Campanella, Tommaso (1568–1639) Italian philosopher (*Città del Sole*).

Campbell, Sir Colin (1792–1863) British field marshal.

Campbell, Donald [Malcolm] (1921–67) English car and speedboat racer, the son of Sir Malcolm Campbell. He set world speed records in 1964 on water (276.3 mph) and land (403.1 mph) but was killed in his boat *Bluebird* in a crash on Lake Coniston 1967. while trying to break his water speed record

.**Campbell, Kim [Avril]** (1947–) first woman prime minister of Canada (1993–95).

Campbell, Mrs Patrick [Beatrice Stella Tanner] (1865–1940) English actress. She was regarded as one of the finest (and wittiest) actresses of her generation.

Campbell, Sir Malcolm (1885–1948) English sportsman and racing driver, holder of world speed records on land and water from 1927. He was awarded a knighthood in 1931, the year he set a land speed record of 246 mph, for his achievements in setting land and water speed records. His son was Donald Campbell, (1921–67)

Campbell, Thomas (1777–1844) Scottish poet (*Ye Mariners of England*).

Campbell-Bannerman, Sir Henry (1836–1908) British statesman. He was Liberal prime minister (1905–1908) and played a major part in healing rifts in the Liberal party after the Boer War.

Campeggio, Cardinal Lorenzo (1472–1539) Italian divine.

Camperdown, Battle of naval engagement fought between the British and the Dutch fleets, 11 October 1797.

Campion, Edmund (1540–81) Jesuit missionary to England. He was hanged. He was beatified in 1886.

Campo Formio, Treaty of between Napoleon I and Austria signed 1797.

Camus, Albert (1913–60) French novelist, essayist and dramatist, and a leading Existentialist writer. He joined the French Resistance during the war, and was awarded the Nobel prize for literature in 1957. His major works include the novel *The Outsider* and *The Rebel*, a study of 20th-century totalitarianism. He was killed in a car accident.

Canada granted constitution as a Dominion 1867; associated as a member of the British Commonwealth of Nations 1926.

Canadian-Pacific Railway completed 1886.

Canadian-USA frontiers defined 9 August 1842.

Canal chief period of construction in England 1755–1827.

Canaletto, Giovanni Antonio Canal (1697–1768)

Venetian painter. An unrivalled architectural painter with an excellent sense of composition, his work includes many views of Venice (*S. Maria della Salute*).

Canary Islands Spanish territory in the Atlantic, occupation completed by Spain 1496.

Canberra the Australian federal capital, founded 1923 in a Federal Territory of its own in the southwest corner of New South Wales; Parliament House opened 1927.

Cancer Research Institute, London, founded 1902.

Candlemas Festival of the Purification of the Virgin 2 February.

Cannae, Battle of 216 BC Second Punic War battle in Italy between Romans and Carthaginians; Hannibal was victorious.

Cannes Film Festival first held 1946.

Canning, George (1770–1827) British statesman (prime minister 1827).

Canning to preserve food pioneered by François Appert 1809; patented in England by Durand 1810.

Canon law study developed by the 12th-century Italian monk Gratian in his *Decretum* published *c.*1140.

Canossa, Italy, scene of penance of the emperor Henry IV 1077.

Canova, Antonio (1757–1822) Italian sculptor (*Perseus*).

Canterbury ecclesiastical centre of England since 597.

Canterbury Cathedral, England, built 1070–1495.

Cantor, Georg (1845–1918) German mathematician.

Canute (*c.*994–1035) Danish king of England (1016–35) *see* Appendix.

Capa, Robert [André Friedmann] (1913–54) Hungarian-born American photographer, co-founder of Magnum Agency (1946). He became one of the best-known war photographers of the century and was killed by a mine in Indochina.

Capablanca, José Raúl (1888–1942) Cuban chess player, world champion (1921–27).

Cape Horn, South America, discovered by the Dutch navigator Willem Cornelis Schouten 1616.

Capek, Karel (1890–1938) Czech dramatist, novelist and essayist. His works include (*R.U.R.* 1920). With his brother **Josef Capek** (1887–1945), he wrote *The Insect Play* (1921), a prophetic satire on totalitarianism.

Cape of Good Hope, South Africa, first doubled 1488 by the Portuguese navigator Bartolomeu Diaz–1500.

Cape of Good Hope Triangular Postage Stamps first issued 1 September 1853,

Cape Province settled by Dutch 1652, bought by Britain 1814.

Cape St Vincent, Naval Battle of fought between British and Spanish fleets 14 February 1797.

Capet Dynasty ruled France 987–1328, Naples 1265–1435, Hungary 1308–82.

Cape Verde Islands independent republic in the Atlantic, Portuguese overseas province until 1975, discovered by the Portuguese navigator Diogo Gomes 1460.

Capgrave, John (1393–1464) English theologian.

Capone, Al[phonse] (1899–1947) Italian-born American gangster. Nicknamed 'Scarface', he established his powerful criminal empire, specializing in bootleg liquor, prostitution and extortion, in Chicago during the prohibition era. He was eventually jailed for tax evasion and died of syphilis.

Caporetto, Battle of First World War battle fought between Austrians and Italians 24 October 1917.

Capote, Truman (1924–84) American novelist and socialite. His varied works include light romances, e.g. *Breakfast at Tiffany's* (1958), as well as realist explorations of murder (*In Cold Blood* 1966).

Capra, Frank (1897–1991) Italian-born American film director. His comedies, usually portraying an ultimately successful struggle by a decent, everyday American against the flawed political system, were enormously popular in the 1930s (*Mr Smith Goes to Washington* 1939) (1897–1991).

Capuchin Order founded 1528 by Matteo di Bassi.

Caracalla (188–217) Roman emperor (211–217). He was assassinated.

Caradoc *or* **Caratacus** (d. *c.*54) king of the Catuvellauni tribe *see* Appendix.

Caramanlis, Constantine (1907–) Greek statesman (premier 1955–63, 1974–80; president 1980–85).

'Caran d'Ache' [Emmanuel Poiré] (1858–1909) Russian-born humorous artist.

Carausius, Marcus Aurelius Mausaeus British leader in 3rd century.

Caravaggio, Michelangelo Merisi da (1573–1610) Italian painter. Noted for his bold, expressive use of chiaroscuro, his religious paintings caused controversy by using everyday people as the models for his Biblical characters (*The Supper at Emmaus*).

Caravaggio, Polidoro Caldara da (*c.*1492–1543) Italian painter. He assisted Raphael and his other works include *Christ bearing the Cross.* He was murdered by his servant.

Carbolic first used 1863 as a disinfectant by Lord Lister (1827–1912.

Carbonari Italian secret revolutionary society formed *c.*1810.

Carboniferous Period Earth history 275 million years ago.

Carchemish, Battle of a battle at the ancient city of Carchemish on the Euphrates, 605 BC, the result of which was the defeat of the Egyptian army by

Nebuchadnezzar of Babylon who thus gained power over the whole of the Middle East.

Cardin, Pierre (1922–) French fashion designer.

Carducci, Giosuè (1835–1907) Italian poet.

Carew, Thomas (*c.*1598–1639) English poet.

Carey, George Leonard (1935–) archbishop of Canterbury (1990–).

Carey, Henry (*c.*1690–1743) English poet (*Sally in our Alley*).

Cargill, Donald (*c.*1616-1681) Scottish Covenanter and clergyman. He was ejected from the post of minister of the Barony parish in Glasgow for denouncing the Restoration. He fought at the Battle of Bothwell Brig (1679), and took part in the Sanquar declaration (1680). He was executed in Edinburgh.

Carl Rosa Opera Company founded by Carl Rosa (1843–89).

Carleton, William (1794–1869) Irish writer (*Traits and Stories of the Irish Peasantry* 1830).

Carlile, Richard (1799–1843) English radical.

Carlile, The Rev. Wilson (1847–1942) English founder of the Church Army (1882).

Carlisle, Cumbria, English city, granted charter 1158 by King Henry II.

Carlists supporters of the claims of Don Carlos (1788–1855) and his heirs to the Spanish throne; formed early in 19th century, suppressed 1878.

Carlos, Don (1545–68) heir of Philip II of Spain.

Carlotta (1840–1927) empress of Mexico (1863–67).

Carlowitz, Treaty of between the Turks and the Allies, signed 1699.

Carlsbad Decrees repressing growth of German democratic movements signed by the German states 1819.

Carlyle, Jane Welsh (1801–66) wife of Thomas Carlyle.

Carlyle, Thomas (1795–1881) Scottish historian and essayist. Hailed by many of his contemporaries as a great social critic and philosopher, he frequently attacked the materialism of the Industrial Age. His works include *The French Revolution* (1837).

'Carmagnole, La' French revolutionary song (possibly of Italian origin) composed 1792, suppressed 1799.

Carmelite Order founded *c.*1150 by the Crusader Berthold; monastic order recognized 1224.

'Carmen Sylva' [Elizabeth] (1843–1916) queen of Romania.

Carmichael, Hoagy [Hoagland] (1899–1981) American jazz composer and actor.

Carnap, Rudolf (1891–1970) German-born American philosopher. Regarded as a leading logical positivist, he attempted to develop a formal language that would remove ambiguity from scientific language.

Carnarvon, Henry Howard Molyneux Herbert, Earl of (1831–90) British statesman.

Carné, Marcel (1909–) French film director. His films include the highly acclaimed theatrical epic *Les Enfants du paradis* (1944), filmed during the German occupation of France.

Carnegie Endowment for International Peace, Washington, founded 1910.

Carnegie, Andrew (1835–1919) Scottish-born American industrialist and philanthropist who believed that personal wealth should be used for the benefit of all members of society.

Carnegie, Dale (1888–1955) American salesman, lecturer and author (*How to Win Friends and Influence People* 1936).

Carnot, Lazare Nicolas Marguerite (1753–1823) French revolutionary leader.

Carol I (1839–1914) Romanian king (1866–1914).

Carol II (1893–1953) Romanian king (1930–40).

Caroline, Queen (1768–1821) wife of George IV.

Caroline of Anspach (1683–1737) queen of England, wife of George II.

Carolingian Dynasty ruled the Franks 751–887.

Carpaccio, Vittore (*c.*1455–1522) Italian painter (*The Presentation in the Temple*).

Carpenter, Edward (1844–1929) English writer and social reformer (*Towards Democracy* 1905).

Carpet-sweeper invented 1876 by the American businessman Melville R. Bissell.

Carpetbaggers Northern businessmen who 'invaded' the Southern States of the USA after the American Civil War 1865.

Carracci, Ludovico (1555–1619) Italian painter (*Transfiguration*).

Carreras, José [Maria] (1946–) Spanish lyric tenor, one of the finest tenors (with Domingo, Pavarotti) of the late 20th century.

Carrhae, Battle of 53 BC a battle of the Parthian War between Rome and the Parthians; Crassus was defeated and killed.

Carroll, Lewis [Charles Lutwidge Dodgson] (1832–98) English author, clergyman and mathematician. His most famous works are the two remarkable 'Alice' books, *Alice's Adventures in Wonderland* (1865) and *Through the Looking Glass*.

Carson, Edward, Baron (1854–1935) British politician.

Carson, Kit (1809–78) American pioneer.

Cartagena, Colombia, founded 1533 by Pedro de Heredia, captured by Sir Francis Drake 1585.

Carter, Jimmy [James Earl Carter] (1924–) American Democratic statesman and 39th president of the US (1977–81). A successful peanut farmer, he became governor of Georgia (1974–77) and defeated Gerald

Ford in the 1976 presidential campaign. His administration made significant attempts at linking overseas trade with human rights issues.

Carteret, Sir George (*c.*1610–1680) Jersey-born English administrator.

Carteret, John, Baron (1690–1763) British politician.

Cartesian coordinates theory first propounded 1637 by the French philosopher René Descartes (1596–1650).

Carthage Phoenician city on north African coast, traditionally founded 850 BC; treaty between Rome and Carthage 508 BC; Carthaginian attack on Sicily at the Battle of Himera 480 BC repelled by Sicilian Greeks; First Punic War between Rome and Carthage (264–241 BC) ends with cession of Sicily to Rome; conquest of Spain 237 BC; Hannibal captures Saguntum 219 BC; Second Punic War (218–202 BC); Scipio carries the war into Africa 204 BC; Hannibal completely defeated at Battle of Zama near Carthage by the younger Scipio; Third Punic War (149–146 BC); Carthage destroyed and made Roman province of Africa; finally destroyed by the Arabs AD 648.

Carthusian Order founded 1084 by St Bruno (*c.*1030–1101).

Cartier, Jacques (1491–1557) French discoverer 1534 of the St Lawrence River.

Cartier-Bresson, Henri (1908–) French photographer and film director. His documentary black-and-white photographs were taken without prior composition and an uncropped frame.

Cartimandua (*fl* 1st century) queen of the Brigantes *see* Appendix.

Cartland, Barbara Hamilton (1901–) English romantic novelist, for some years the world's best-selling author.

Cartwright, Edmund (1743–1823) English inventor 1785 of the power loom.

Cartwright, Thomas (1535–1600) English religious leader.

Caruso, Enrico (1873–1921) Italian opera tenor. Born in Naples, he sang most of the great tenor roles in Italian and French opera and is regarded as perhaps the most outstanding operatic tenor of all time. He was one of the first great singers to make recordings.

Carver, John (*c.*1576–1621) English leader of the Pilgrim Fathers.

Carver, Raymond (1938–88) American short-story writer (*What We Talk About When We Talk About Love* 1981).

Cary, Joyce (1888–1957) Anglo-Irish writer (*The Horse's Mouth* 1945).

Casablanca, Moroccan port, founded 1468.

Casablanca Conference Second World War meeting between Franklin D. Roosevelt and Winston Churchill at which 'unconditional surrender' formula was agreed, held 14–20 January 1943

Casals, Pablo (1876–1973) Catalan Spanish cellist, pianist and composer. His recordings of Bach's cello suites and of the Dvorak cello concerto are particularly highly regarded.

Casanova, Giovanni Giacomo (1725–98) Italian adventurer and writer (*Memoirs*).

Casaubon, Isaac (1559–1614) Swiss-born classical scholar.

Casca, Publius Servilius (d. *c.*42 BC) Roman conspirator and assassin of Julius Caesar.

Casement, Sir Roger [David] (1864–1916) British consular official and Irish nationalist. While working for the British colonial service, he exposed the repression of the people of the Congo by its Belgian rulers in 1904. Knighted in 1911, he adopted Irish nationalism shortly afterwards and was hanged for treason.

Cash register invented by the American John Ritty of Ohio 1879.

Casimir I (1015–58) Polish king (1040–58).

Casimir II Polish king (1177–94).

Casimir III (1310–70) Polish king (1333–70).

Casimir IV (1427–92) Polish king (1447–92).

Casimir V [John II Casimir] (1609–72) Polish king (1648–68).

Caslon, William (1692–1766) English typefounder.

Cassander (*c.*354–297 BC) ruler of Macedonia (318–297) and king (305–297 BC). The son of Antipater, he blockaded Olympias in the city of Pydna 317–316 BC and when she was compelled to surrender had her put to death.

Cassatt, Mary (*c.*1845–1926) American painter.

Cassel, Gustav (1866–1945) Swedish economist.

Cassell, John (1817–65) English publisher.

Cassianus, Joannes (365–435) French-born pioneer founder of monasteries.

Cassini, Giovanni Domenico (1625–1712) Italian astronomer.

Cassino, Monte monastery founded by St Benedict 529, destroyed by Allies May 1944.

Cassiodorus (*c.*478–570) Roman statesman and scholar.

Cassius (d.42 BC) Roman patriot. One of the leaders, with Cassius, of the revolt against Caesar and his subsequent assassination. Following their defeat at the Battle of Philippi 42 BC, they committed suicide.

Castagno, Andrea del (1390–1457) Italian painter.

Castelnau, Michel de (*c.*1520–1592) French soldier and ambassador to the English court.

Castillon, Battle of a battle of the Hundred Years' War between the French and the English, 17 July 1453. It was a French victory ended the war.

Castle, Barbara [Anne] (née Betts) (1911–) British Labour politician. She was Ministrer of Transport (1965–68), Secretary of State for Employment (12968–70) and Minister of Health and Social Security (1974–78). Member of European Parliament since 1979.

Castlereagh, Robert Stewart, Viscount (1769–1822) Ulster-born statesman. He committed suicide.

Castro [Ruz], Fidel (1927–) Cuban statesman, prime minister (1959–76) and president (1976–). He led a coup in 1959, and shortly afterwards announced his conversion to communism. He survived several attempts at overthrow by exiled opponents and the CIA, e.g. the Bay of Pigs invasion in 1961, but survived with Soviet subsidies which began to decrease in the late 1980s.

Caswallon (d.*c*.60) high king of the British tribes *see* Appendix.

Catalysis chemical action discovered 1836 by the Swedish scientist Baron Berzelius (1779–1848).

Catesby, Robert (1573–1605) English conspirator. He was killed.

Cathal O'Connor (d.1224) king of Connaught (1202–24) *see* Appendix.

Catherine I (1684–1727) Russian empress (1725–27).

Catherine II (Catherine the Great) (1729–96) Russian empress (1762–96). She became empress on the death of her husband, Peter III (1728–62), who was murdered by one of her lovers. She consolidated and expanded the Russian Empire by conquest, and scandalized European opinion by having a supposedly legion number of paramours and heading an intrigue-raddled court, while patronizing Enlightenment philosophers such as Voltaire and Diderot.

Catherine de' Medici *see* MEDICI, CATHERINE DE'.

Catherine Howard (*c*.1521–1542) fifth wife of Henry VIII (*see* Appendix). She was beheaded.

Catherine of Aragon (1485–1536) first wife of Henry VIII (*see* Appendix).

Catherine of Siena, Saint (1347–80). Her feast day is 30 April.

Catherine Parr (1512–1548) sixth wife of Henry VIII (*see* Appendix).

Cathode rays discovered by the English scientist Sir William Crookes (1832–1919).

Catholic emancipation in Britain April 1829.

Catholic reform commenced *c*.1522, completed 1590.

Catiline conspiracy a conspiracy against Cicero organized by the Roman politician Lucius Sergius Catilina (*c*.108–62 BC), exposed and foiled by Cicero 63 BC. Catiline fled and was killed in battle in Etruria.

Catlin, George (1796–1872) American artist who depicted North American Indians and their life.

Cato Street Conspiracy unsuccessful plot to assassinate members of the British Cabinet 1820, planned by Arthur Thistlewood (1770–1820). He was executed.

Cato the Elder [Marcus Portius Cato] (234–149 BC) Roman statesman.

Cato the Younger [Marcus Portius Uticensis] (95–46 BC) Roman statesman. He committed suicide after Caesar's defeat of the republicans at the Battle of Thapsus during the civil war between Caesar and Pompey rather than survive the republic 46 BC.

Catt, Carrie Chapman (1859–1947) American suffragette and peace campaigner.

Cattermole, George (1800–1868) English painter.

Catullus, Valerius (*c*.84–*c*.54 BC) Roman poet.

Caudine Forks, Battle of the 321 BC the capture of a Roman army by the Samnites at the Caudine Forks.

Caughley porcelain manufactured 1772–99.

Caulaincourt, Armand, Marquis de (1772–1827) French statesman.

Cavalcanti, Guido (*c*.1230–1300) Italian poet.

Cavell, Edith [Louisa] (1865–1915) English nurse and patriot. She treated both German and Allied casualties in Brussels during the German occupation, and was executed (12 October 1915) by the German authorities, who accused her of helping British soldiers to escape to Holland.

Cavendish, Henry (1731–1810) English scientist and eccentric.

Cavour, Count Camillo (1810–61) Italian statesman.

Cawnpore (Kanpur), **Mutiny of** in which rioters murdered the English garrison and their families, 6 June 1857.

Caxton, William (*c*.1422–91) English printer and translator. His *Recuyell of the Historyes of Troy* (printed at Bruges 1475) is the first book to be printed in English.

Cayenne capital of French Guiana, founded 1664.

CBS (Columbia Broadcasting System) major American TV network founded 1927.

Ceausescu, Nicolae (1918–89) Romanian dictator. Secretary general of the Romanian Communist Party from 1969 and president of Romania from 1974, his regime was overthrown by dissident Communists in 1989, and he and his wife were executed.

Ceawlin (d.*c*.593) king of Wessex (577–591) *see* Appendix.

Cecil, Robert, [1st Earl of Salisbury] (*c*.1563–1612) English statesman.

Cecil, William [1st Baron Burghley] (1520–98) English statesman who served with skill and dexterity both Henry VIII and Mary I (converting to Roman Catholicism under Mary) and was one of the prime architects of Elizabeth I's succession.

Cecilia, Saint martyred 230. Her feast day is 22 November.

Cedar Creek, Battle of American Civil War battle, 17 October 1864.

Celebes *see* SULAWESI.

Celestine I, St pope (422–432).

Celestine II anti-pope (1124–30).

Celestine II pope (1143–44).

Celestine III [Giacinto Bobo] pope (1191–98).

Celestine IV [Godfrey Castiglione] pope (1241–43).

Celestine V [St Peter Celestine] (1215–1296) pope (1294).

Cell theory botany developed *c.*1850 by the German botanist Hugo von Mohl (1805–72).

Cellini, Benvenuto (1500–1571) Italian artist and writer (*Autobiography*).

Cellophane invented *c.*1900 by the Swiss scientist J. E. Brandenberger.

Cellular composition of plant tissue proved 1838 by the German botanist Matthias Jakob.

Celluloid patented 1855 by the English chemist Alexander Parkes; successfully invented 1870 by the American chemist John Wesley Hyatt (1837–1920).

Cellulose nitrate first synthetic plastic material invented 1855 by the British chemist Alexander Parkes (1813–90).

Celsius, Anders (1701–44) Swedish astronomer and inventor (1742) of the centigrade thermometer.

Celsus, Aulus Cornelius (*fl* 1st century) Roman medical writer (*De Medecina*).

Celts a people who inhabited Britain, Gaul, Spain and other parts of western and central Europe in pre-Roman times. *See also* Appendix.

Cenci, Beatrice (1577–99) Italian heroine and possibly murderess. She was executed.

Cenfus king of Wessex (674) *see* Appendix.

Cenotaph, Whitehall, London, memorial to the dead of both World Wars, unveiled 11 November 1920.

Cenozoic Era Earth history between 1 and 70 million years ago.

Cenred king of Mercia (716–718) *see* Appendix.

Censorship of printed books begun in Mainz in 1486.

Census first in Britain made 1801.

Centigrade thermometer invented 1742 by the Swedish scientist Anders Celsius (1701–44).

Centlivre, Susannah (*c.*1667–1723) English dramatist and actress.

Central African Republic former French colony of Ubanghi Shari took name, elected to stay in French Community 1958; became independent in 1960; parliamentary monarchy 1976; republic 1979.

Central Intelligence Agency (CIA) US organization to coordinate and analyze foreign intelligence founded 1947.

Central London electric railway opened 27 June 1900.

Central Treaty Organization (CENTO) set up as the Baghdad Pact Organization 1956 (Treaty signed 1955). Adopted present title 1958.

Centwine king of Wessex (676–685) *see* Appendix.

Cenwahl king of Wessex (643–672) *see* Appendix.

Ceres first planetoid sighted discovered 1801 by the Italian astronomer Giuseppe Piazzi (1746–1826).

Cerium chemical element isolated 1803 by the Swedish chemist Baron Berzelius (1779–1848).

CERN (Centre Européen pour la Recherche Nucléare) European research facility for particle physics, established 1954.

Ceol king of Wessex (591–597) *see* Appendix.

Ceolred king of Mercia (709–716) *see* Appendix.

Ceolwulf (1) king of Wessex (597–611) *see* Appendix.

Ceolwulf (2) king of Northumbria (729–737) *see* Appendix.

Ceolwulf I king of Mercia (821–823) *see* Appendix.

Ceolwulf II king of Mercia (874–*c.*880) *see* Appendix.

Ceorl king of Mercia (*c.*606–626) *see* Appendix.

Cerdic king of Wessex (519–534) *see* Appendix.

Cervantes [Saavedra], Miguel de (1547–1616) Spanish novelist, dramatist and poet. His most famous work was the satirical masterpiece *Don Quixote de la Mancha.*(1605–15).

Cesarewitch Stakes, Newmarket, first run in 1839.

Cetewayo (*c.*1836–1884) Zulu king (1874–84) who annihilated a column of the British army at Isandhlwana in 1879 but was defeated at Ulundi and later captured.

Ceylon *see* **Sri Lanka**.

Cézanne, Paul (1839–1906) French painter whose works include landscapes and still lifes. He was very influential on succeeding generations of painters, notably the Cubists.

Ch'ing dynasty, China, 1644–1912.

Chabrier, Emmanuel (1841–94) French composer (*España*).

Chad, Equatorial Africa, became autonomous republic within the French Community 1958; became indepedent 1960.

Chadwick, Sir Edwin (1800–1890) English pioneer in public health.

Chadwick, Sir James (1891–1974) English physicist. He discovered the neutron in 1932 and was awarded the Nobel prize for physics in 1935.

Chaeronea, Battle of (1) 338 BC a battle of the Amphictyonic War, when Athens and Thebes were defeated by Philip of Macedon, who became supreme in Greece. (2) 86 BC a battle of the First Mithridatic War, when the Roman army under Sulla won a victory over Mithridates' army.

Chagall, Marc (1887–1985) Russian-born French painter. His vividly coloured work features unusual compositions drawing on symbolism from Russian and Jewish folk art.

Chain, Sir Ernst Boris (1906–79) German-born British biochemist. He prepared penicillin for clinical use, and with Florey and Alexander Fleming shared the 1945 Nobel prize for physiology or medicine.

Chalcedon, Battle of 74 BC naval battle of the Third Mithridatic War, when a Pontic fleet destroyed the Roman fleet.

Chalcedon, Council of Fourth Ecumenical Council held 451.

Chalgrove Field, Battle of (Oxfordshire) English Civil War battle fought between the Royalists and the Parliamentarians 1643.

Chaliapin, Fyodor Ivanovich (1873–1938) Russian operatic singer.

Challenger disaster explosion of US space shuttle on lift-off killing all seven astronauts on board, 28 January 1986.

Châlons, Battle of fought between the Romans and the Goths and Huns 451.

Chamber of Commerce first in Britain founded in Glasgow in 1783.

Chamberlain porcelain manufactured 1786–1840.

Chamberlain, Austen (1863–1937) British statesman.

Chamberlain, Houston Stewart English-born racialist (1855–1926).

Chamberlain, Joseph (1836–1914) British statesman.

Chamberlain, [Arthur] Neville (1869–1940) British statesman and Conservative prime minister (1937–40). He pursued a policy of appeasement towards the totalitarian powers of Germany, Italy and Japan in the 1930s. He died shortly after illness forced his resignation from Churchill's war cabinet.

Chambers's Encyclopaedia founded 1859–68 by the Scottish publisher William Chambers (1800–1883).

Chambre Ardente French special court for trial of heretics, etc, instituted 1535, abolished 1682.

Chamisso, Adalbert von (1781–1838) German poet.

Champaigne, Philippe de (1602–1674) Flemish painter.

Champion Hurdle, Cheltenham, first run 1927.

Champlain, Battle of fought between the Americans and the British 1814.

Champlain, Samuel de (1567–1635) Lieutenant of Canada (1612–29).

Champollion, Jean François (1790–1832) French Egyptologist and decipherer of the Rosetta Stone.

Chancellor, Richard (d.1556) English navigator and instigator of the Muscovy Company. He died in a shipwreck.

Chandernagor [Chandannagar] a port in southwest Bengal, former French settlement 1686–1950.

Chandler, Raymond [Thornton] (1888–1959) American novelist and screenwriter. His detective novels (*Farewell, My Lovely* 1940) and screenplays (*The Big Sleep* 1939), are classics of the genre.

Chanel, Coco [Gabrielle Bonheur Chanel] (1883–1971) French couturière and perfumer who originated the thin, low-waist style for women's dresses.

Channel Islands under German occupation June 1940–May 1945.

Channel, English: submarine cable first laid 1850; first crossed by balloon 1785 by Blanchard and Jeffries; first swum 1875 by Matthew Webb; first flown by aeroplane 1909 by Louis Blériot; first woman flier Harriet Quimby 1912; tunnel scheme abandoned by British government 1924, revived as private venture 1980s, opened 1994.

Channing, William Ellery (1780–1842) American Unitarian leader.

Chantrey Bequest to Royal Academy (and now at Tate Gallery, London) made by Sir Francis Legatt Chantrey (1781–1841).

Chaplin, Sir Charlie [Spencer] (1889–1977) English comedian and film actor and director. His gentleman-tramp character with a beguiling shuffle, bowler hat and cane became perhaps the most famous comic creation of the 20th century.

Chapman, George (*c.*1559–1634) English poet and dramatist (*Bussy d'Ambois* 1607).

Chappaquiddick Incident death of Senator Edward Kennedy's secretary in a car crash after leaving a party, 18 July 1969; Kennedy was driving and left the scene before help arrived.

Chapter of Mitton battle fought between Scots and English 1319.

Chardin, Jean Baptiste Siméon (1699–1779) French painter (*La Bénédicité*).

Charge of the Light Brigade *see* BALAKLAVA, BATTLE OF.

Charlemagne (*c.*742–814) king of the Franks (768–814), king of Lombards (774–814), Holy Roman emperor (800–814). In 771 he became sole ruler of the Frankish kingdom and spent the early part of his reign conquering (and converting to Christianity) neighbouring kingdoms. He led an army into Spain to fight the Moors in 778. In 800 he was crowned emperor after crushing a Roman revolt against the Pope.

Charles, Prince [Charles Philip Arthur George, Prince of Wales] (1948–) born 14 November, heir apparent to Elizabeth II of the United Kingdom. He married Lady Diana Spencer (1961–) in 1981, and they had two children. They separated in 1992 and divorced in 1996. *See also* Appendix: Elizabeth II.

Charles, Ray [Ray Charles Robinson] (1930–) American singer, pianist and songwriter. Originally a blues/jazz singer, he became one of the most popular singers in the world.

Charles I (1887–1922) emperor of Austria (1916–18).

Charles II (Charles the Bald) (823–881) king of France and Holy Roman emperor (875–881).

Charles III (Charles the Simple) (879–929) king of France.

Charles IV (Charles the Fair) (1294–1328) king of France (1322–28).

Charles V (Charles the Wise) (1337–80) king of France (1364–80).

Charles VI (Charles the Foolish) (1368–1422) king of France (1380–1422).

Charles VII (1403–61) king of France (1422–61).

Charles VIII (1470–98) king of France (1483–98).

Charles IX (1550–74) king of France (1560–74).

Charles X (1757–1836) king of France (1822–30).

Charles I (1600–1649) king of Great Britain and Ireland (1625–49) *see* Appendix.

Charles II (1630–85) king of Great Britain and Ireland (1660–85) *see* Appendix.

Charles I title as Holy Roman emperor of Charlemagne.

Charles II title as Holy Roman emperor of Charles II of France.

Charles III (Charles the Fat) (839–891) Holy Roman emperor (881–891).

Charles IV (1316–78) Holy Roman emperor (1347–78).

Charles VI (1697–1745) Holy Roman emperor (1711–42).

Charles VII (1697–1745) Holy Roman emperor (1742–45).

Charles II (1661–1700) king of Spain (1665–1700).

Charles III (1716–88) king of Spain (1759–88).

Charles IV (1748–1819) king of Spain (1788–1808).

Charles V (1500–1558) king of Spain and Holy Roman emperor (1519–55) who presided over the Diet of Worms.

Charles I to **Charles VI** legendary kings of Sweden.

Charles VII (d.1167) king of Sweden (1160–67).

Charles VIII (d.1470) king of Sweden (1436–41, 1448–70).

Charles IX (1550–1611) king of Sweden (1600–1611).

Charles X (1622–60) king of Sweden (1654–60).

Charles XI (1655–97) king of Sweden (1660–97) .

Charles XII (1682–1718) king of Sweden (1697–1718). He was killed.

Charles XIII (1748–1818) king of Sweden (1809–18).

Charles XIV (1763–1844) king of Sweden (1818–44).

Charles XV (1826–72) king of Sweden (1859–72).

Charles Borromeo, Saint (1538–1584).

Charles Edward (1720–88) the Young Pretender to the English throne.

Charles Martel (*c.*689–741) ruler of the Franks.

Charles the Bold (1433–77) duke of Burgundy (1467–77). He was killed.

Charleston, South Carolina, founded 1670, by the Englishman William Sayle–1671.

Charlotte Sophia (1744–1818) wife of George III.

Charlton, Bobby [Robert Charlton] (1937–) English footballer, capped over 100 times for England. His brother Jack Charlton [John Charlton] (1935–), also an England player, became the manager of the Irish international team and led them to the World Cup finals in 1990 and 1994..

Charter, Great (Magna Carta) 1215; People's (Chartist) 1836.

Chartist Movement English social reform begun 1836, ended *c.*1858; petitions rejected by Parliament 1839, 1842 and 1848.

Chartres Cathedral constructed 1194 to 1260.

Chartreuse liqueur manufactured at La Grande Chartreuse Monastery near Grenoble 1607–1901, when the monks left France for Tarragona in Spain.

Chastelard, Pierre de (1540–64) French poet. He was hanged.

Chateaubriand, François René, Vicomte de (1768–1848) French statesman.

Chatham, William Pitt, 1st Earl of *see* Pitt, William.

Chatham, William Pitt, Earl of (1708–78) British statesman (prime minister 1766–67).

Chattanooga, Battle of American Civil War battle, 23–25 November 1863.

Chatterton, Thomas (1752–70) English forger and poet (*The Rowley Poems*). He committed suicide.

Chaucer, Geoffrey (*c.*1340–1400) English poet. His great narrative skill is displayed at its finest in *The Canterbury Tales* (*c.*1387–1400), a masterpiece of wit and humour in which various pilgrims tell each other stories..

Chausson, Ernest (1855–99) French composer.

Cheka Soviet secret police, established 1917, became GPU in 1922, later OGPU which was superseded by NKVD in 1934.

Chekhov, Anton Pavlovich (1860–1904) Russian dramatist and short-story writer. A physician, he became one of the greatest writers of his age, his works, notable for their wit and dramatic power, including the plays *Uncle Vanya*, *Three Sisters* and *The Cherry Orchard* (1903) and the short story 'The Lady with the Little Dog'.

Chelcicky, Petz Bohemian religious leader in 15th century.

Chelsea-Derby porcelain manufactured 1770–84.

Cheltenham Gold Cup first run 1924.

Chemical wood pulp for paper manufacture invented 1857.

Cheng-hua period China 1465–87.

Cheng-têh period China 1506–21.

Chénier, André (1762–94) French poet. He was guillotined.

Cheops (*fl. c.*2900 BC) Egyptian king.

Cheques first printed by the English banker Lawrence Childs *c.*1762.

Cherenkov, Pavel Alekseievich (1904–) Soviet physicist. In the mid–1930s, he discovered the form of radiation known as Cherenkhov radiation, and was awarded the 1958 Nobel prize for physics.

Chernobyl disaster explosion and fire at a Soviet light-water nuclear reactor in the Ukraine April 1986.

Cherokee North American Indian people, disbanded 1906.

Cherubini, Luigi (1760–1842) Italian composer who settled in Paris. He wrote operas, e.g. *Médée*, and other works and was much admired by Beethoven, whose opera, *Fidelio*, followed the story of *Médée* closely in its study of feminine psychology and stress on democratic values.

Cherypnin, Nikolai (1873–1945) Russian-born composer (*Le Pavillon d'Armide* 1903).

Chesapeake Bay battle between French and British fleets, 5 September 1781.

Chess played in India by 7th century AD, brought to Spain between 8th and 10th centuries, to England in late 13th century.

Chester Cathedral, England, founded 1093; created cathedral by Henry VIII 1541.

Chesterfield, Philip Dormer Stanhope, Earl of (1694–1773) British statesman and writer of the *Letters*.

Chesterton, G[ilbert] K[eith] (1874–1936) English essayist, novelist, critic and poet. With his friend Belloc, he became known as a gifted disputant for what they saw as the glory of old, rural Roman Catholic England. He is best known for his Father Brown detective stories.

Chetham's Library, Manchester, founded 1653 by the English manufacturer Humfrey Chetham (1580–1653).

Chevalier, Albert (1861–1923) English music-hall artist.

Chevalier, Maurice (1888–1972) French actor.

'Chevalier sans peur et sans reproche' [Pierre du Terrail, Chevalier de Bayard] (1474–1524) French soldier. He died in battle.

Chevy Chase, Battle of fought between Scots and English 1388.

Chia Ching period China 1522–66.

Chiang Ch'ing *or* **Jiang Qing** (1914–91) Chinese Communist politician and actress. She married Mao as his third wife in 1939 and was the main force behind the savage purges of the Cultural Revolution in the late 1960s. After Mao's death, her power waned, and she was arrested in 1976 with three confederates (the 'Gang of Four') and charged with murder and subversion. She was sentenced to death in 1981, the sentence later being suspended. She committed suicide.

Chiang Kai-shek *or* **Jiang Jie Shi** (1887–1975) Chinese general and statesman. He was president of China (1928–31, 1943–49), then, after losing the civil war to Mao Tse-tung and his forces, fled the mainland to establish the nationalist republic of China in Formosa, of which he was president (1950–75).

Chicago, Illinois, settled at the beginning of the 19th century; partly destroyed by fire 1871.

Chicago University founded 1890.

Chichester, Sir Francis (1901–72) English sailor and adventurer, made the first non-stop solo voyage around the world 1966.

Chickamauga, Battle of American Civil War battle fought 19–20 September 1863.

Childermas Holy Innocents' Day, 28 December.

Childers, [Robert] Erskine (1870–1922) Irish Republican and writer (*The Riddle of the Sands* 1903). He was executed 1922).

Children's Crusade set out from France and Germany to the Holy Land 1212.

Chile, South America, settled by the Spaniards 1540-1565; national government set up 1810; independence from Spain achieved 1818; military junta seized power from Salvador Allende September 1972; General Pinochet ousted by democratic elections December 1989.

Chiltern Hundreds first granted to an MP as grounds for resignation 1750.

Chimborazo volcanic mountain in Ecuador, first climbed 1880 by English mountaineer Edward Whymper (1840–1911).

China empire from at least the 23rd century BC until 1912; republic since 1912; the Communist People's Republic of China, governing the whole of China except Taiwan, proclaimed 1 October 1949.

China, Great Wall of constructed as a defence against the Mongols 214 BC, rebuilt 15th century.

Chinese Law first codified *c.*950 BC.

Chippendale, Thomas (1718–79) English furniture maker.

Chirac, Jacques (1932–) French politician (prime minister 1974–76, 1986–88, president 1995–).

Chirico, Giorgio de (1888–1978) Greek-born Italian

painter whose dreamlike pictures of open, deserted squares were hailed by the Surrealists as precursors of their own works in the early 1920s.

Chiswick Press, London, founded 1810 by the English printer Charles Whittingham (1767–1840).

Chladni figures acoustic phenomenon discovered 1787 by the German physicist Ernst Chladni (1756–1827).

Chlorine first isolated 1774 by the Swedish chemist Karl Wilhelm Scheele (1742–86).

Chloroform discovered 1831 by the German scientist Justus Liebig (1803–73. First used as an anaesthetic 1847.

Chocolate (Cocoa) brought to Europe during 16th century.

Choiseul, Etienne François, Duc de (1719–85) French statesman.

Cholera bacillus discovered 1883 by the German scientist Robert Koch (1843–1910); last major epidemic in England 1866.

Chomsky, Noam [Avram] (1928–) American linguist, philosopher and political activist. His innovative work in linguistics is based on the principles that humans are born with an innate capacity for learning grammatical structures. He was a notable opponent of the Vietnam war. His works include *American power and the New Mandarins* (1969).

Chopin, Frédéric [François] (1810–49) Polish-born pianist and composer. His emotional, melancholy works, often regarded as quintessentially Polish in mood, include over 50 mazurkas, two piano concertos and 25 preludes.

Chosroes I (d.579) Persian ruler (531–579).

Chosroes II (d.628) Persian ruler (591–628). He was murdered.

Chouans Breton royalists formed 1792, suppressed 1800.

Chou dynasty China 1122 to 255 BC.

Chou En-Lai *or* **Zhou En Lai** (1898–1976) Chinese Communist statesman. He was foreign minister (1949–58) and prime minister (1949–76) of the People's Republic of China and was regarded as a moderate during the chaos of China's Cultural Revolution in the late 1960s.

Chrétien de Troyes (*fl* 12th century) French poet (*Conte del Graal*).

Christ title of Jesus of Nazareth, founder of Christianity, born between 5 BC and AD 2, crucified between 30 and 33.

Christadelphians religious movement founded by John Thomas (1805–71).

Christ Church, Oxford University, founded 1525.

Christian, Fletcher leader of the 1789 mutiny on the *Bounty*; may have lived until after 1810.

Christian I (1426–81) Danish king (1448–81).

Christian II (1481–1559) Danish king (1513–23). He died in prison.

Christian III (1503–59) Danish king (1535–59).

Christian IV (1577–1648) Danish king (1588–1648).

Christian V (1646–99) Danish king (1670–99).

Christian VI (d.1746) Danish king (1730–46).

Christian VII (1749–1808) Danish king (1766–1808).

Christian VIII (1786–1848) Danish king (1839–48).

Christian IX (1818–1906) Danish king (1863–1906).

Christian X (1870–1947) Danish king (1912–47).

Christian Era calculated from ostensible date of Incarnation, adopted in Italy in 6th century.

Christianity religious movement founded by Jesus of Nazareth in 1st century.

Christian Science religious movement founded 1879 by the American Mrs Mary Baker Eddy (1821–1910).

Christian Socialism founded 1850 by John Ludlau (1821–1911).

Christian Tract Society London, founded 1809 by the Unitarian minister Robert Aspland (1782–1845).

Christie, [Dame] Agatha [Clarissa Mary] (1890–1976) English detective story writer whose ingeniously plotted novels, e.g. *The Murder of Roger Ackroyd*, established her as one of the great writers in the genre.

Christie, John Reginald Halliday (1898–1953) English murderer. He was hanged.

Christie's London auctioneers founded 1766 by James Christie (1730–1803).

Christina (1626–1689) Swedish queen (1632–54).

Christmas cards first examples designed in Britain 1843.

Christmas Day 25 December (Spain: 6 January; Russia and Greece: 7 January).

Christmas Island, Western Pacific, discovered 1777 by Captain James Cook; annexed 1888 by Britain; administered by Singapore 1900–1958, and now by Australia; called Kiritimati from 1981.

Christophe, Henry (1767–1820) king of Haiti . He committed suicide.

Christ's College, Cambridge University, founded as God's-House 1448 by King Henry VI; refounded and enlarged by the Lady Margaret Beaufort, Countess of Richmond and Derby, 1505.

Chromium first isolated 1797 by the French chemist Louis Nicolas Vauquelin (1763–1829).

Chromosphere layer of the sun's atmosphere so named by the English astronomer Sir Joseph Norman Lockyer (1836–1920).

Chronometers invented 1726 by the English inventor John Harrison (1693–1776).

Church Army founded in London 1882 by the English Rev. Wilson Carlile (1847–1942).

Churchill College, Cambridge University, opened 1960.

Churchill, Charles (1731–64) English satirical writer (*The Rosciad* 1761).

Churchill, Lord Randolph (1849–94) British statesman.

Churchill, Sarah (1660–1744) Duchess of Marlborough.

Churchill, Sir Winston [Leonard Spencer] (1874–1965) British Conservative statesman and writer. After an adventurous early life which included escape from imprisonment by Louis Botha during the Boer War, he held several posts under both Liberal and Conservative governments. He opposed Chamberlain's policy of appeasement in the 1930s and served as prime minister (1940–45) during the Second World War and 1951–55. His works include *History of the English-Speaking Peoples*. He was awarded the Nobel prize for literature (1953).

Church of England established by St Augustine 597, separated from the Catholic Church by the Act of Supremacy 1534.

Church of Ireland (Anglican) disestablished 1869.

Church of Scotland, The Reformed established 1560.

Church of Wales (Anglican) disestablished 1919.

Churriguera, José de (*c.*1650–1725) Spanish architect.

CIA *see* CENTRAL INTELLIGENCE AGENCY.

Ciano, Galeazzo (1903–44) Italian politician. He was shot.

Cibber, Colley (1671–1757) English poet laureate (1730–57).

Cicero, Marcus Tullius (106–43 BC) Roman statesman and writer. A friend of Pompey, he became consul 63 BC, in the same year exposing the Catiline conspiracy. He was killed by agents of the triumvirate of Mark Antony, Lepidus and Octavian following his denunciation of Mark Antony in his *Philippics*.

Cid, El [Rodrigo Diaz] (*c.*1026–1099) Spanish hero.

Cigarettes introduced into Britain 1854; link with lung cancer established 1950.

Cigars introduced into Britain from Cuba 1762.

Cimabué, Giovanni [Cenni di Pepi] (*c.*1240–1302) Italian painter (*St Francis*).

Cimarosa, Domenico (1749–1801) Italian composer (*Il Matrimonio Segreto* 1792).

Cimbri a Germanic people from Jutland who moved towards Rome and were defeated by Marius at the battle of Vercellae in 101 BC.

Cimon (d.449 BC) Athenian naval and military leader. The Persians were defeated by him at the Battle of Eurymedon 465 BC.

Cinchona introduced 1860 to India from South America by the explorer Sir Clements Robert Markham (1830–1916).

Cinchonine an alkaloid discovered by the French scientist Pierre Joseph Pelletier (1788–1842).

Cincinnatus, Lucius Quinctius (519–438 BC) Roman patriot.

Cinema projector first model constructed by the French inventor Etienne J. Marey 1893.

Cinematograph first model constructed by the French brothers Auguste and Louis Lumière 1895.

Cinioch (d.631) king of the Picts *see* Appendix.

Ciniod king of Picts (763–775) *see* Appendix.

Cinna, Lucius Cornelius (d.84 BC) Roman patrician and consul. An opponent of Sulla, he allied himself with Marius in attempting to seize power, causing massacres in Rome 87 BC. He was killed when his troops mutinied before he could meet Sulla in battle.

Cintra, Treaty of concerning the French evacuation of Portugal, signed August 1808.

Circulation of the blood discovered 1615 by the English physician William Harvey (1578–1657).

Circumcision, Christian Feast of the celebrated 1 January.

Cisalpine Republic existed in North Italy 1797–1802.

Cissa king of Sussex (*c.*514) *see* Appendix.

Cistercian Order founded 1098 by St Stephen Harding (d.1134).

Cîteaux French monastery founded by St Robert of Molesme 1098.

City and South London Railway first electric underground line, opened 18 December 1890 between King William St. and Stockwell.

Civil Engineers, Institution of, London, founded 1818; granted Royal Charter 1828.

Civil List the money voted annually by Parliament for the support of the royal family. Originally, the revenues from the the lands that belonged to the Crown ('His Majesty's Woods and Forests') were used to pay the expenses of government and provide an income for the sovereign. In 1810 George III surrendered the Crown lands in return for a fixed annual payment, the Civil List, and since then commissioners have collected the revenues on behalf of the public and paid them into the Exchequer.

Civil War, American 1861–65.

Civil War, English first 1642–46, second 1648.

Civil War, Spanish 1936–39.

Clair, René (1898–1981) French film producer.

Clairvaux French abbey founded 1115 by St Bernard (1091–1153).

Clapton, Eric (1945–) English rock guitarist and vocalist. Recognized as one of the most influential rock guitarists, he played with the Yardbirds (1963 –65) and Cream (1966–68).

Claque existed in the Théâtre Français until 1878.

Clare, John (1793–1864) English poet who acquired a

wide following in the 1820s and 1830s with such volumes as *The Shepherd 's Calendar* (1827). As with Burns, his popularity derived from his poems on rural life. From 1837, he spent most of his life in insane asylums, where he wrote many of the original and beautiful poems on which his reputation rests.

Clare College, Cambridge University, founded 1326 as Union Hall by Richard Badew, Chancellor of Cambridge; refounded 1336 by Lady Elizabeth de Clare (*c.*1291–1360).

Clarendon, Constitutions of royal proclamation issued 1164.

Clarendon, Edward Hyde, Earl of (1608–74) British statesman (chief minister 1660–67).

Clark, Jim [James Clark] (1936–68) Scottish racing driver who was World Champion in 1963 and 1965 and winner of 25 Grand Prix events. He was killed in a crash in West Germany.

Clark, William George (1821–78) Shakespearean editor.

Clarke, Arthur C(harles) (1917–) British sci-fi author (*2001, A Space Odyssey* 1968).

Clarke, John (1609–76) pioneer settler 1638 in Rhode Island.

Clarkson, Thomas (1760–1846) English opponent of slavery.

Claudel, Paul (1868–1955) French writer and diplomat.

Claudius I [Tiberias Claudius Drusus Nero Germanicus] (10 BC–54 AD) Roman emperor (41–54) who extended the Empire, initiated the conquest of Britain in 43 and extended Roman citizenship. He may have been poisoned by his fourth wife (and niece), Agrippina, who was the mother of his successor Nero.

Claudius II (d.270) Roman emperor (268–270).

Clausewitz, Karl von (1780–1831) Prussian strategist (*On War*).

Claverhouse, John Graham of (*c.*1649–1689) Scottish soldier. He died in battle.

Clay, Henry (1777–1852) American statesman.

Cleese, John [Marwood] (1939–) English comedy actor and writer. He was one of the main talents involved in the highly influential TV comedy series, *Monty Python's Flying Circus* (1969–74).

Cleisthenes (*fl* 6th century BC) Athenian statesmen. He introduced reforms of Cleisthenes in Athens 507 BC.

Clemenceau, Georges [Eugène Benjamin] (1841–1929) French statesman. A leading left-winger, he was an outspoken critic of the French government's war policy in the early days of World War I. He was prime minister (1906–1909, 1917–20) and his forceful negotiation of the Versailles Treaty is believed to have led directly to World War II.

Clement I, St pope (88–97).

Clement II [Suidger] pope (1046–47).

Clement III [Paolo Scolari] pope (1187–91).

Clement IV [Gui Foulques] pope (1268–71).

Clement V [Bertrand de Gouth] (*c.*1264–1314) pope (1305–14). He abolished the order of the Knights Templar in 1312.

Clement VI [Pierre Roger] (1291–1352) pope (1342–52).

Clement VII [Giulio dei Medici] (d.1534) pope (1523–34).

Clement VII [Robert of Geneva] (d.1394) anti-pope (1378–94).

Clement VIII [Aegidius Muñoz] (d.1446) anti-pope (1425–29).

Clement VIII [Ippolito Aldobrandini] (1535–1605) pope (1592–1605). During his reign the Vulgate was adopted by the Church.

Clement IX [Giulio Respigliosi] (1600–1669) pope (1667–69).

Clement X (1590–1676) [Emilio Altieri] pope (1670–76).

Clement XI [Gian Francesco Albani] (1649–1721) pope (1700–1721).

Clement XII [Lorenzo Corsini] (*c.*1652–1740) pope (1730–40).

Clement XIII [Carlo della Torre Rezzonico] (1693–1769) pope (1758–69).

Clement XIV [Lorenzo Ganganelli] (1705–74) pope (1769–74).

Clementi, Muzio (1752–1832) Italian composer (*Gradus ad Parnassum* 1817).

Clement of Alexandria Greek theologian in 2nd century.

Cleomenes III (d.*c.*220 BC) the last king of Sparta (236–222 BC). He was defeated by the Achean League at Sellasia 222 BC and thereafter fled to Egypt where he committed suicide.

Cleopatra (1) (d.336 BC) the second wife of Philip of Macedonia, who married her when he divorced Olympias in 337 BC. After his murder she was put to death by Olympias together with her infant child.

Cleopatra (2) daughter of Antiochus the Great of Syria who married Ptolemy V of Egypt 193 BC.

Cleopatra (3) daughter of Cleopatra (2) and Ptolemy V of Egypt who married her brother Ptolemy VI. She had a son by him, who was put to death in 146 BC by another brother, Ptolemy VII, who married her but soon divorced her to make way for her own daughter by her former marriage.

Cleopatra (4) (d.120 BC) Syrian queen, daughter of Ptolemy VI and Cleopatra (2), who married first, in 150 BC, Alexander Balas, the Syrian usurper, and on his death Demetrius II. During the latter's captivity in Parthia she married Antiochus VII, his brother. She murdered her son Seleucus V, who on the death of his father, Demetrius II, had assumed the government without her consent. Her other son by Demetrius, Antiochus VIII, succeeded to the throne 125 BC through her influence, but when she found him unwilling to give her sufficient power, she attempted to poison him. He had learnt her intention and forced her to take the poison instead. Antiochus IX was her son by Antiochus VII.

Cleopatra (5) (d.90 BC) queen of Egypt (117–90 BC). Another daughter of Ptolemy VI and Cleopatra (3), she married her uncle, Ptolemy VII. and after his death, was left heir to the kindom in conjunction with whichever of her sons she chose. She was compelled by her people to choose the elder, Ptolemy VIII, but she soon prevailed on them to expel him and make room for her younger son, Ptolemy IX. She sent an army against Ptolemy VIII in Cyprus and put to death the general who commanded it for allowing him to escape alive. Terrified at her cruelty, Ptolemy IX also retired but was recalled by his mother, who attempted to assassinate him but was herself put to death by him before she could achieve her object.

Cleopatra (6) [Cleopatra Berenice] queen of Egypt (81 BC). The daughter of Ptolemy IX, she succeeded her father and married her first cousin, Ptolemy X, who murdered her nineteen days after their marriage.

Cleopatra (7) (69–30 BC) Egyptian queen. She was the mistress of Caesar during his time in Egypt (48–47 BC) and committed suicide with her lover, Mark Antony, following the Battle of Actium (31 BC). Egypt became a Roman province 30 BC.

Cleopatra's Needle transferred from Egypt to London 1877 by the English surgeon Sir Erasmus Wilson (1809–84).

Clerk-Maxwell, James (1831–79) Scottish physicist.

Clermont the first steamship, built 1807 by the American engineer Robert Fulton (1765–1815).

Cleve, Joos van (*c.*1518–1556) Flemish artist.

Cleveland, Stephen Grover (1837–1908) 22nd and 24th US president (1885–89, 1893–97).

Clift, Montgomery (1920–66) American screen and stage star (*From Here to Eternity* 1953).

Clifton Suspension Bridge opened 1864.

Clinton, Bill [William Jefferson Davis Clinton] (1946–) American politician and 42nd President of the United States (1993–). A lawyer, he became Arkansas attorney general (1974–79), then state governor (1979–81, 1983–92). He defeated George Bush in the 1992 presidential election. *See also* GORE.

Clive, Kitty *see* Garrick, David.

Clive, Sir Robert [1st Baron Clive of Plassey] (1725–74) English general and administrator in India. He worked for the East India Company (1743–46) before joining the Indian army. He was an MP in England (1760–62) and governor of Bengal (1764–67). He committed suicide.

Clontarf, Battle of between the Irish and the Danes 1014.

Clotaire I king of the Franks (558–561).

Clotaire II king of the Franks (584–628).

Cloth of Gold, Field of the, near Calais, conference between Henry VIII and Francis I, 6 June 1520.

Clothworkers Livery Coı pany, London, founded before 1480; incorporated 1523.

Cloud chamber expansion chamber invented by the Scottish scientist Charles Thomson Rees Wilson (1869–1959).

Cloud, Saint (*c.*520–560).

Clouet, Jean (*c.*1485–*c.*1541) French miniaturist.

Clovis (465–511) first Merovingian king of the Franks.

Cluny Abbey founded 910.

Clynes, Joseph Robert (1869–1949) British politician.

Cnidus, Battle of 394 BC battle of the Wars of Greek City States, when a Spartan fleet was destroyed by a combined Persian and Athenian fleet.

'Colette' (Sidonie Gabrielle Colette) French novelist (1873–1954).

Coal gas invented 1792–96 by the Scottish engineer William Murdock (1754–1839). First used for lighting in Soho 1803.

Coal industry in Britain taken over by State 1938, nationalized 1947. Privatized 1993

Coalitions in Britain 1757, 1782, 1852, 1915, 1931, 1940.

Coalport porcelain manufactured from 1790.

Cobalt first isolated by the German scientist Georg Brandt 1735.

Cobbett, William (1763–1835) English politician, writer (*Rural Rides* 1830).

Cobden, Richard (1804–65) English political reformer.

Cockcroft, Sir John Douglas (1897–1967) English nuclear physicist. With the Irish physicist **Sir Ernest [Thomas Sinton] Walton** (1903–), he produced the first laboratory splitting of an atomic nucleus, for which they shared the 1951 Nobel prize for physics.

Cockerell, Sir Christopher Sydney (1910–) English engineer. He invented the hovercraft, the prototype of which first crossed the English Channel in 1959.

Cockfighting made illegal in England 1849.

Coco-Cola® American soft drink, the most widely consumed beverage in the world, invented 1866.

Cocos Islands a cluster of 28 small coral islands in the eastern Indian Ocean, discovered by Captain William Keeling of the East India Company 1609;

settled 1826; annexed by Britain 1857; a Territory of Australia since 1955.

Cocteau, Jean (1889–1963) French film director, novelist, dramatist, poet and critic. His experimental, surreal films were highly influential on modern filmmakers. The best known of his hovels is *Les Enfants Terribles*.

Code Napoléon promulgated as the French civil law code 1804; assumed its present name 1807.

Codex Sinaiticus purchased from the Soviet Government by Britain 1933.

Cody, Colonel Samuel Franklin (1862–1913) American aviation pioneer. He was killed in a flying accident.

Cody, William Frederick ('Buffalo Bill') (1846–1917) American frontiersman and showman.

Coel (*fl* 5th century) *see* Appendix.

Coello, Alonzo Sánchez (1515–90) Spanish painter.

Coello, Claudio (*c.*1621–1693) Spanish painter.

Coenred king of Mercia (704–709) *see* Appendix.

Coenwulf king of Mercia (796–821) *see* Appendix.

Coffee brought to England *c.*1650.

Cogidummus (*fl* 1st century) king of the Regni tribe *see* Appendix.

Coimbra, University of founded 1288 in Lisbon and transferred to Coimbra 1537.

Coke, Sir Edward (1552–1634) English statesman and jurist.

Coke manufacture of patented 1621 by Dud Dudley, the ironmaster (1599–1684).

Coke Ovens invented by Friedrich Hoffmann 1893.

Colbert, Jean Baptiste (1619–83) French statesman.

Colburn, Zerah (1804–40) American calculating prodigy.

Coldstream Guards raised 1659.

Cole, Douglas (1889–1959) English political writer.

Cole, Nat 'King' [Nathaniel Adams Coles] (1919–65) American jazz and popular music vocalist and pianist.

Colenso, William (1811–99) English missionary and explorer in New Zealand.

Coleridge, Samuel Taylor (1772–1834) English poet and critic. With Wordsworth he published *Lyrical Ballads* in 1798, a landmark in English poetry in its rejection of a special 'poetic' language and advocacy of clear everyday language. His works include *The Ancient Mariner* (1798).

Coleridge-Taylor, Samuel (1875–1912) English composer (*The Song cf Hiawatha* 1898–1900).

Colet, John (*c.*1467–1519) English divine and scholar.

Colette, [Sidonie Gabrielle] (1873–1954) French novelist. Her novels, e.g. *Chéri* and *Gigi*, are often erotic and display a strong sympathy for animals and the natural world.

Coligny, Gaspard de (1519–72) French statesman. He was murdered during the St Bartholomew's Day Massacre..

College postal stamps first used by Keble College, Oxford University, 1871; suppressed by the Postmaster-General December 1885.

Collingwood, Cuthbert Lord (1750–1810) English admiral.

Collingwood, Robin George (1889–1943) English historian and philosopher.

Collins, Michael (1890–1922) Irish Republican politician. A Sinn Fein leader, he negotiated the 1922 peace treaty with Britain that resulted in the establishment of the Irish Free State. He was killed in an ambush during the civil war that followed.

Collins, Wilkie (1824–89) English novelist (*The Moonstone* 1868).

Collins, William (1721–59) English poet (*How Sleep the Brave* 1746).

Collodion process invented 1850 by the English photographer Frederick Scott Archer (1813–57).

Colloidal chemistry study initiated 1861 by the Scottish chemist Thomas Graham (1805–69).

Collotype illustrations printing process invented by the French inventors Tessie du Motay and C. R. Maréchal 1865.

Colman, George the elder (1732–94) English dramatist (*The Jealous Wife* 1761).

Colman, George the younger (1762–1836) English dramatist (*The Heir at Law* 1797).

Cologne University founded 1388.

Colombia achieved freedom from Spanish rule 1819; formed part of the State of Greater Colombia 1819–30; became the Republic of New Granada 1830; transformed into the Confederación Granadina 1858; adopted the name of the United States of Colombia 1863; became the Republic of Colombia 1886.

Colon, Cristobal *see* COLUMBUS, CHRISTOPHER.

Colorado, USA, first settled 1858; made a Territory 1861; admitted to the Union 1876.

Colorado beetle reached Europe 1922.

Colosseum Roman amphitheatre built 75–80.

Colossus of Rhodes statue built *c.*285 BC; destroyed by an earthquake 224 BC.

Colour photography invented 1907 by the French pioneer in cinematography Auguste Lumière (1862–1954).

Colour television first experimental transmission to include 'live' pictures made from Alexandra Palace, London, 1956.

Colt revolver invented 1835 by the American manufacturer Samuel Colt (1814–62).

Coltrane, John [William] (1926–67) American jazz saxophonist. A virtuoso on the tenor and soprano saxophones, he became an influential and popular jazz musician.

Colum, Pádraic (1881–1972) Irish poet.

Columba, St (521–597) Irish missionary. Accused of being involved in one of Ulster's many bloody civil conflicts, as penance he fled to the Western Isles of Scotland to proselytise for Christianity. He established a monastic settlement on the island of Iona.

Columban, Saint (*c.*540–615).

Columbia Broadcasting System *see* CBS.

Columbia River discovered 1792 by the American explorer Robert Gray (1755–1806).

Columbia University, New York, founded 1754 as King's College; reopened with present name 1784.

Columbium (niobium) isolated 1801 by the English chemist Charles Hatchett (*c.*1765–1847).

Columbus Day commemorating the discovery of America: 12 October.

Columbus, Christopher (1451–1506) Italian-born navigator and explorer. Under the patronage of Spain, he led an expedition to seek a western route to the Far East. He discovered the New World in 1492, making landfall in the West Indies and made two subsequent voyages in 1493 and 1498, reaching South America on the third.

Combe, William (1741–1823) English writer (*Dr Syntax* 1812–21).

Combine harvester-thresher invented in California 1875.

Comédie-Française, Paris, instituted 1658; assumed present name 1680.

Comenius [John Amos Komensky] (1592–1671) Moravian scholar.

Comets studied 1698–1705 by Edmund Halley (1656–1742).

Comic strips originated by the German artist Wilhelm Busch (1832–1908).

Cominform international Communist body founded 1947, abolished 1956.

Comintern international Communist body founded 1919, dissolved 1943.

Comitia Tributa popular assembly established 471 BC in Rome under the *Lex Publilia* laws to choose the tribunes; after the second secession of the Plebeians 448 BC its powers were greatly increased; in 339 BC its decrees were altered to make one censor a Plebeian; *Lex Hortensia* 286 BC made it the supreme legislative power.

Commedia dell'Arte came into being in Italy 1567.

Commius (*fl* 1st century) king of the Atrebates *see* Appendix.

Commodus (161–192) Roman emperor (180–192). He was murdered.

Commonwealth republican regime in England 1649–53.

Commonwealth Day, British founded as Empire Day, 24 May 1902.

Commonwealth of Nations, British title first used during First World War 1914–18.

Commonwealth Relations Office founded 1925 as the Dominions Office; assumed present name 1947; combined with Foreign Office.

Commune of Paris revolutionary regime March–May 1871.

Communism origins in the Parisian secret societies of the 1830s. Karl Marx's *Communist Manifesto* issued by Communist League 1848.

Commynes, Philippe de (1445–1509) French historian.

Comoro a Protectorate of France until 1912; proclaimed a French colony 1912; attached to the Government-General of Madagascar 1914; a French Territory from 1947; became independent (except Mayotte) 1976.

Compass, magnetic described 1269 by Peter Peregrinus of Picardy.

Compensated pendulum invented 1722 by the English mechanician George Graham (1675–1751).

Complutensian Bible first polyglot Bible, prepared 1514–22.

Compressibility of water first demonstrated 1762 by the English scientist John Canton (1718–72).

Comptometer invented 1884 by the American inventor Dorr Eugene Felt (1862–1930).

Compton, Arthur Holly (1892–1962) American physicist. He was a prominent researcher into X-rays, gamma rays and nuclear energy, and discovered the Compton effect. He was awarded the 1927 Nobel prize for physics.

Compton, Denis [Charles Scott] (1918–) English cricketer, who played for Middlesex and England (1937–57) and who was regarded as one of the best all-rounders ever in cricket.

Compton-Burnett, Dame Ivy (1892–1969) English novelist. Her novels were mostly in dialogue and featured the traumas of upper-middle-class Edwardian family life.

Computer first mechanical model discussed in Italy 1840–41 by the British mathematician Dr Charles Babbage (1792–1871); first complete (the Harvard Mark I), built by the American Howard Aiken and IBM 1939–44; first digital (ENIAC) developed 1946; first transisterized developed by IBM 1959; first personal computer Apple II, 1977.

Comstock, Anthony (1844–1915) American pioneer in censorship.

Comstock silver lode, Nevada, discovered *c.*1856 by the American trapper Henry Tompkins Paige Comstock (1820–70).

Comte, Auguste [Isidore Xavier] (1798–1857) French positivist philosopher.

Conall king of the Picts (787–789) *see* Appendix.

Concentration camps first used as prison camps for Afrikaner women and children by the British during the Boer War 1899–1901; used in Nazi Germany (1933–45) as part of the 'Final Solution' to exterminate Jews, Gypsies, homosexuals and other political opponents. First: Dachau 1933; most notorious: Auschwitz, opened 1941; first to be liberated (by Red Army): Maidenek July 1944.

Concepción Chilean city founded 1541 by the Spanish conquistador Pedro de Valdivia (*c.*1510–1554.

Concert hall London's first public, Hickford's Room, The Haymarket, opened 1697.

Concertina invented 1829 by Charles Wheatstone.

Conclave of cardinals to elect a pope (Gregory X) first held at Viterbo 1268–71).

Condé, Louis II de Bourbon, Prince de (1621–86) French general.

Condell, Henry (d.1627) first Shakespearean editor.

Condensed milk process invented 18S6 by the American inventor Gail Borden (1801–74).

Conder, Charles (1868–1909) English painter.

Condillac, Etienne Bonnot de (1715–80) French philosopher.

Condorcet, Marie Jean Antoine Nicolas Caritat, Marquis de (1743–94) French philosopher. He committed suicide.

Confederate States of America formed 4 February 1861; defeated by Union 1865.

Confederation of British Industries founded 1965.

Confederation of the Rhine Napoleonic organization of German states formed 1806; ended 1813.

Confession of Augsburg Lutheran creed prepared 1530.

Confucianism religious movement founded *c.*531 BC by the Chinese sage Confucius (551–478 BC).

Congo River discovered by the Portuguese navigator Diogo Cão 1482.

Congregational Movement founded *c.*1580 by the English leader Robert Browne (*c.*1550–*c.*1633).

Congress of Industrial Organizations, USA, founded 1936.

Congress of the United States of America instituted 1787.

Congreve, William (1670–1729) English playwright (*The Way of the World* 1700).

Connecticut, USA, first settled 1635; organized commonwealth since 1637; one of the original states of the Union.

Connelly, Marc (1890–1980) American playwright (*Green Pastures* 1930).

Connery, Sean [Thomas] (1930–) Scottish film actor. One of the finest film actors of his time, he initially achieved worldwide fame as Ian Fleming's character James Bond.

Conrad I (d.918)) German king (911–918).

Conrad II (*c.*990–1039) German king (1024–39).

Conrad III (*c.*1093–1152) German king (1138–52).

Conrad IV (1228–1254) German king (1250–54).

Conrad, Joseph [Teodor Josef Konrad Korzeniowski] (1857–1924) Polish-born English writer. He qualified as a master mariner in 1886 and his many works often featured isolated characters in exotic locations. His novels include *Heart of Darkness* and *Lord Jim* (1900).

Conscription in England 1916–18, 1939–60; (women) 1941–47.

Conservation of energy principles defined 1847 by the German physicist Hermann von Helmholtz (1821–94).

Conservation of matter principle defined 1789 by Lavoisier.

Conservative Party, British origins *c.*1680 in the Tories; present name began to be adopted 1824–32.

Consols British consolidated annuitites first consolidated between 1750 and 1757.

Constable, John (1776–1837) English painter. Drawing inspiration from nature, he produced works such as *View on the Stour* and *The Hay Wain*, which were initially more influential in France than England. He and Turner are considered to be the most important English landscape painters.

Constans I (*c.*320–350) Roman emperor (337–350). He was assassinated.

Constans II (630–668) Byzantine emperor (641–668). He was murdered.

Constant, Benjamin (1845–1902) French painter (*Samson et Délilah*).

Constantine pope (708–715).

Constantine anti-pope (767).

Constantine (d.820) king of Picts (789–820) *see* Appendix.

Constantine I (*c.*288–337) Byzantine emperor (309–337).

Constantine II (316–340) Byzantine emperor (337–340). He was killed in battle.

Constantine III (d.641) Byzantine emperor (641).

Constantine IV (d.685) Byzantine emperor (668–685).

Constantine V (718–775) Byzantine emperor (740–775).

Constantine VI (b.*c.*770) Byzantine emperor (780–797).

Constantine VII (905–959) Byzantine emperor (913–919, 944–959).

Constantine VIII Byzantine emperor (1025–28).

Constantine IX Byzantine emperor (1042–55).

Constantine X (d.1067) Byzantine emperor (1059–67).

Constantine XI (d.1453) last Byzantine emperor (1448–53). He was killed.

Constantine I (*c.*274–337) Roman emperor. He became the first Christian emperor in 312, when, before a battle, he reportedly saw a cross in the sky inscribed 'In this sign conquer'. He moved the capital to Byzantium (which he renamed Constantinople) in 330. Christianity became the Empire's official religion in 324.

Constantine I (1868–1923) king of the Hellenes (1913–17, 1920–22).

Constantine I (d.878) king of Scots (862–877) *see* Appendix.

Constantine II (d.952) king of Scots (900–942) *see* Appendix.

Constantine III (d.997) king of Scots (995–997) *see* Appendix.

Constantinople founded as Byzantium 658 BC; rebuilt as Constantinople AD 330; captured by the Turks 1453 and renamed Istanbul.

Constantius I (*c.*250–306) Roman emperor (305–306).

Constantius II Roman emperor (317–361) (337–361).

Constantius III (d.421) Roman emperor (421).

Consulate, The French Napoleonic government established 1799, abolished 1804.

Contact lenses first suggested 1827 by the English astronomer Sir John Herschel (1792–1871; first made by the German lens maker F. E. Müller 1887.

Continental Congress American Federal legislative body established 1774, ended 1789.

Continental Drift theory developed 1910 by the German geologist Alfred Wegener (1880–1930).

Continental System blockade carried out by Napoleon 1804–12.

Conventicle Acts to suppress nonconformist worship in Britain, enacted 1593 and 1664; repealed 1689.

Convulsionaries Jansenist group in Paris who venerated François de Paris–1727.

Cook Strait, New Zealand, discovered by Captain James Cook 1770.

Cook, (Captain) James (1728–79) English explorer and mariner who in his first and second voyages (1768–71, 1772–75) charted and claimed the east coast of Australia for Britain and discovered New Caledonia. On his third and last voyage to the Pacific (1776–79), he was killed by islanders in Hawaii.

Cook, Thomas (1808–92) English pioneer travel agent.

Cooke, Alistair (1908–) Anglo-American journalist, author and broadcaster ('Letters from America').

Cooke, Jay (1821–1905) American financier.

Coolidge, Calvin (1872–1933) 30th US president (1923–29).

Coolidge, Susan (1845–1905) American writer (*What Katy Did*).

Cooper, Gary [Frank James Cooper] (1901–61) American film actor who specialized as the quiet, courageous hero in many westerns and adventure films, e.g. *High Noon* (1952).

Cooper, James Fenimore (1789–1851) American novelist. His adventure novels, such as *The Last of the Mohicans* (1826), established the enduring 'frontier myth' of America.

Cooper, Samuel (1609–1672) English miniaturist.

Co-operative Congress first held London 1869.

Co-operative Party, Great Britain, formed 1917; first MP elected 1919.

Co-operative Societies origins in England in the Rochdale Society founded 1844.

Copeland, William Taylor (1797–1868) English potter.

Copenhagen, Battle of *or* **Battle of the Baltic** a battle between the British and Danish fleets, 2 April 1801, when the British destroyed the Danish fleet. It was at this battle that Nelson, as second in command, made use of his blind eye not to see the signal sent to him to cease fighting.

Copenhagen University founded 1479.

Copernicus, Nicolaus [Mikdaj Kopernik] (1473–1543) Polish astronomer. His great work *De Revolutionibus* (1543) sets out his theory that the earth and planets revolve around the sun.

Copland, Aaron (1900–1990) American composer, pianist and conductor. He was influential in American music in incorporating elements from traditional American folk songs in his compositions. His works include the ballet score *Rodeo* and *Billy the Kid* (1938) (1900–1990).

Copley, John Singleton (1737–1815) American painter (*The Death of Chatham*).

Coppard, Alfred Edgar (1878–1957) English writer (*Adam and Eve and Pinch Me* 1921).

Coppée, François (1842–1908) French writer (*Le Réliquaire* 1866).

Coppola, Francis Ford (1939–) American film director and screenwriter. His most successful films include the modern classics, *The Godfather* (1972) and *Apocalypse Now* (1979).

Coptic Church separated from Orthodox Church 451.

Coptic Era began 29 August 284.

Copyright first Act passed in England 1709; law consolidated by Act of 1911.

Coquelin, Benoît Constant (1841–1909) French actor.

Coral Sea, Battle of the a naval battle of the Second

World War, 7–9 May 1942. The Japanese were forced to withdraw from the Coral Sea.

Coram, Thomas (1668–1751) English philanthropist.

Corday, Charlotte (1768–93) French murderer of Jean Paul Marat. She was guillotined.

Cordite invented by Sir Frank Augustus Abel (1827–1902) and Sir James Dewar (1842–1923) and adopted by the British Government 1891.

Corelli, Arcangelo (1653–1713) Italian composer (*La Follia*).

Corelli, Marie (1854–1924) English popular novelist (*Sorrows of Satan* 1895).

Corinth, Lovis (1858–1925) German painter.

Corinth a city state of ancient Greece near the modern city of the same name.

Corinth, Battle of (1) 429 BC a naval battle of the Peloponnesian War, when an Athenian fleet defeated a Peloponnesian fleet. (2) 394 BC a battle of the Corinthian War, when the Spartans defeated the Athenians and allies but failed to gain the isthmus. (3) 147 BC a battle of the fourth Macedonian War, when a Roman victory under Mummius led to Macedonia becoming a Roman province.

Corinthian War 394–387 between Sparta, led by Agesilaus, and various confederacies. Sparta was supreme.

Cormac mac-Art (d.*c*.360) high king of Ireland *see* Appendix.

Corman, Roger (1926–) American film director and producer. Known primarily in the 1950s and 1960s as a creator of cheap B movies he also fostered the careers of many prominent American directors and actors, including Coppola, De Niro and Scorsese. His films include *Little Shop of Horrors* (1960).

'Corn Law Rhymer, The' [Ebenezer Elliott] (1781–1849) English poet (*Battle Song*).

Corn Laws enacted in Britain 1815, 1828, 1842; repealed 1844, 1869.

Corneille, Pierre (1606–84) French playwright (*Le Cid* 1636).

Cornelius, St pope (251–253).

Cornell University, Ithaca, NY, founded 1865 by the American financier Ezra Cornell (1807–74).

Cornet cavalry rank abolished 1871.

Cornish language spoken until 18th century.

Cornwallis, Charles, Marquis (1738–1805) governor-general of India.

Coronado, Francisco Vásquez de (*c*.1510–1554) Spanish explorer of southwest USA.

Coronation Cup, Epsom, first run 1902.

Coronation Stone (Stone of Scone) placed in Westminster Abbey 1296 by King Edward I. Stolen by the Scottish Nationalists 1950; returned to Westminster 1952.

Coronea, Battle of (1) 447 BC Athens lost Boeotia. (2) 394 BC a battle of the Corinthian War; Spartans under Agesilaus defeated a confederacy against them.

Corot, Jean Baptiste Camille (1796–1875) French painter.

Corps of Commissionaires founded 1859 by the English soldier Sir Edward Walter (1823–1904).

Corpus Christi feast day founded 1264 by Pope Urban IV, celebrated on the Thursday after Trinity Sunday.

Corpus Christi College, Cambridge University, founded by the united Guilds of Corpus Christi and of the Blessed Virgin Mary 1352.

Corpus Christi College, Oxford University, founded 1516 by the statesman Richard Foxe (1448–1528).

Corpus Juris Civilis Roman legal code compiled at the Emperor Justinian I's orders 528–533.

Corpuscles, red first discovered by the Dutch naturalist Jan Swammerdam (1637–1680).

Correggio, Antonio Allegri da (1494–1534) Italian painter (*The Assumption of the Virgin*).

Corsica settled by the Greeks *c.* 560 BC; sold by Genoa to France 1768.

Cortés, Hernando (1485–1547) Spanish *conquistador* of Mexico (1519–21).

Cortisone discovered 1936 by the American biochemist Edward Calvin Kendall (1886–1972).

Cortona, Pietro da (1596–1669) Italian artist.

Cortot, Alfred (1877–1962) Swiss pianist.

'Corvo, Baron' [Frederick Rolfe] (1860–1913) English novelist (*Hadrian the Seventh* 1904).

Coryate, Thomas (*c*.1577–1617) English traveller and writer (*Crudities* 1611).

Cosgrave, Liam (1920–) Irish politician. The son of W. T. Cosgrave, he became Fine Gael prime minister of the Republic of Ireland (1973–77).

Cosgrave, W[illiam] T[homas] (1880–1965) Irish nationalist politician. He became first president of the Irish Free State (1922–32). His son is Liam Cosgrave.

Cosmic rays discovered 1925 by the American scientist Robert Andrews Millikan (1868–1953).

Costa Rica, Central America, discovered 1502 by Christopher Columbus; achieved independence from Spanish rule 1821.

Costa, Lorenzo (1460–1535) Italian painter (*Madonna and Child Enthroned*).

Costello, Lou [Louis Cristillo] (1906–59) American comedian, partner of Bud Abbot.

Cosway, Richard (*c*.1742–1821) English miniaturist.

Côte d'Ivoire, West Africa, autonomous republic within the French Community since 1960.

Cotman, John Sell (1782–1842) English painter.

Cotton, Charles (1630–87) English poet (*New Year Poem*).

Cotton, Sir Robert Bruce (1571–1631) English collector of the Cottonian Collection (now in the British Museum).

Coué, Emile (1857–1926) French founder of auto-suggestion.

Coulomb, Charles Augustin de (1736–1806) French physicist.

Council of Chalcedon fourth Ecumenical Council, 451.

Council of Constance Catholic general council, 1414–18.

Councils of Constantinople second Ecumenical Council 381; fifth Ecumenical Council 533; sixth Ecumenical Council 680.

Council of Elders French revolutionary government, 1795–99.

Council of Ephesus third Ecumenical Council, convened 431.

Council of Europe statute signed at 10-power London conference, came into effect 1949.

Council of Five Hundred French Revolutionary government 1795–99.

Council of Nicaea 1st Ecumenical Council, 325; 7th Ecumenical Council, 787.

Council of Ten Venetian cabal set up 1310; abolished *c.*1797.

Council of Trent Catholic General Council, began 1545; ended 1563.

Council, Vatican Catholic General Council 1869–70.

Counter-Reformation within the Catholic Church began 1513; completed 1563.

Countess of Huntingdon's Connection Calvinist Methodist sect founded in the 1740s.

Couperin, François (1668–1733) French composer (*Les Nations* 1726).

Couperus, Louis (1863–1923) Dutch writer.

Coupon election held 1918.

Courbet, Gustave (1819–77) French painter. Considered to be the founder of Realism, his work was frequently condemned as 'socialistic' because he scorned the established classical outlook.

Courtauld, Samuel British silk manufacturer (1793–1881).

Courtauld Institute of Art, London, established 1930, relocated to Somerset House 1990.

Courtrai, Battle of (The Battle of the Golden Spurs) between the Flemish and the French 1302.

Cousin, Jean (*c.*1500–*c.*1590) French painter (*The Last Judgment*).

Cousins, Samuel (1801–87) English engraver.

Cousteau, Jacques [Yves] (1910–) French oceanographer. He invented the aqualung (1943) and developed techniques of underwater cinematography that were influential in raising awareness of the world's oceans.

Coutts & Co. British bankers founded by the Scottish banker Thomas Coutts (1735–1822).

Covenanters Scottish signatories of the National Covenant of 1638, and the Solemn League and Covenant of 1643, who pledged to establish and defend Presbyterianism. They suffered persecution until 1690 when Presbyterianism was restored.

Covent Garden Theatre, London, opera house built 1858.

Coventry Cathedral built in the 15th century; destroyed in World War II 1940; rebuilt 1954–62.

Coverdale's Bible translated into English by the English divine Miles Coverdale (1488–1568); published 1535).

Coward, Sir Noel [Pierce] (1899–1973) English dramatist, actor and composer. His witty, sophisticated comedies and amusing songs were regarded as mildly shocking in their day and include *Private Lives*, *Blithe Spirit*. and *Bitter Sweet* (1929).

Cowley, Abraham (1618–1667) English writer (*The Mistress* 1647).

Cowper, William (1731–1800) English poet. Best known in his own day as an engaging satirist and nature poet, his darker religious poems are now seen as of more lasting importance. His works include *The Task* (1785).

Cox, David (1783 d.1859) English painter.

Coxwell, Henry Tracey (1819–1900) English balloonist.

Cozens, John Robert (1752–99) English watercolour artist.

Crabbe, George (1754–1832) English poet (*The Borough* 1810).

Craig, Edward Gordon (1872–1966) English theatre director and designer.

Craigavon, James Craig, Viscount (1871–1940) first prime minister of Northern Ireland.

Craik, Mrs [Dinah Maria Mulock] (1826–87) English writer (*John Halifax, Gentleman* 1857).

Cramer, Johann Baptist (1771–1858) German-born pianist and music teacher.

Cranach, Lucas (1472–1553) German painter (*The Judgment of Paris*).

Crane, Hart (1899–1932) American poet.

Crane, Stephen (1871–1900) American writer (*The Red Badge of Courage* 1896).

Crane, Walter (1845–1915) English artist.

Crane hydraulic invented *c.*1845 by William George Armstrong (1810–1900), later Baron Armstrong,

Cranmer, Thomas (1489–1556) English prelate. Appointed Archbishop of Canterbury in 1533 (while secretly married), he pronounced the annulment of the marriage of Henry VIII to Catherine of Aragon in 1533. A moderate Protestant reformer, he was executed at the stake by Mary I.

Crannon, Battle of 322 BC a battle of the Lamian War, when Antipater, regent of Macedonia, defeated insurgent Greeks.

Crashaw, Richard (*c.*1613–1649) English poet (*Steps to the Temple* 1646).

Crassus, Marcus Licinius (*c.*114–53 BC) one of the First Triumvirate with Caesar and Pompey 60 BC. He was defeated and killed by the Parthians at Carrhae.

Crawford, Joan [Lucille le Sueur] (1908–77) American film actress. One of the first leading women in Hollywood although many of her films were formulatic melodramas.

Cream separator first centrifugal model invented 1877 by the Swedish engineer Carl Gustaf de Laval (1845–1913).

Crébillon, Claude Prosper Jolyot de (1707–77) French writer (*Le Sofa* 1742).

Crébillon, Prosper Jolyot de (1674–1762) French playwright (*Catilina* 1748).

Crécy, Battle of between the English and the French, 26 August 1346.

Creevey, Thomas (1768–1838) English diarist.

Cremona Cathedral, Italy, built 1107–1606.

Creoda (d.593) king of Mercia (*c.*585–593) *see* Appendix.

Creosote discovered 1833 by the German manufacturer Baron von Reichenbach (1788–1869).

Crespi, Giuseppe Maria ('Lo Spagnuolo') (1665–1747) Italian painter.

Crete the largest and most southerly of the islands of Greece; Early Minoan Age began 2500 BC; Middle Minoan Age 2000–1850 BC; Late Minoan Age 1800–1600 BC; ruled by Venetians 1204–1645, by Turks 1645–1898; part of Greece since 1913.

Crewe, Robert Offley Ashburton Crewe Milnes, Marquess of (1858–1945) British statesman.

Crichton, The Admirable' [James Crichton] (1560–82) Scottish scholar. He was killed.

Crick, Francis [Harry Compton] (1916–) English molecular biologist. With James Dewey Watson, he discovered the double helix model of the structure of DNA, and was awarded the 1962 Nobel prize for physiology or medicine.

Cricket played in England since 13th century; MCC founded 1787.

Crimean War between the Allies (Britain, Turkey, France) and Russia, 1854–56.

Criminology study founded by the Italian Cesare Lombroso (1836–1909).

Crippen, Hawley Harvey (1862–1910) American doctor who poisoned his wife in London in 1910. His dramatic capture on board ship involved the first use of radio for police purposes. He was hanged.

Cripps, Sir [Richard] Stafford (1889–1952) British Labour statesman. A leading left-winger, he became chancellor of the exchequer (1947-50), and introduced a programme of high taxation and wage restraint to deal with Britain's economic problems.

Crivelli, Carlo (*c.*1434–1493) Italian painter.

Croatia independent 925–1102; part of Hungary 1102–1918, of Yugoslavia 1918–91; became independent from the former Yugoslavia 1991.

Croce, Benedetto (1866–1952) Italian philosopher.

Crockett, David (1786–1836) American pioneer. He was killed in battle.

Crockett, Samuel Rutherford (1860–1914) Scottish novelist (*The Stickit Minister* 1893).

Croesus the last king of Lydia (560–546 BC), noted for his wealth. He subdued the Greek cities in Asia Minor 560 BC but waged war with Persia, being defeated by Cyrus and executed.

Croker, John Wilson (1780–1857) Irish politician.

Crome, John (1768–1821) English painter.

Cromer, Evelyn Baring, Earl of (1841–1917) British agent and Consul-General in Egypt (1883–1907).

Crompton, Richmal [Richmal Crompton Lamburn] (1890–1969) English writer (*Just William* 1922).

Crompton's mule spinning machine invented 1779 by the English weaver Samuel Crompton (1753–1827).

Cromwell, Oliver (1599–1658) English soldier and statesman. A Puritan country squire and MP, he was a noted critic of Charles I during the 1628–29 Parliament. He displayed a strong grasp of military skill during the opening year of the Civil War (1642), forming his 'Ironsides' regiment the following year. He led Parliament's New Model Army to victory at Naseby (1645) and crushed Welsh and Scottish rebellions before signing Charles I's death warrant in 1649. After a murderous conquest of Ireland in 1649, his victory over a second Scottish rebellion in 1651 ended the Civil War. He was nominated 'Lord Protector' of the Commonwealth (1653–58) and established an authoritarian rule, dissolving parliament when it displeased him. He was succeeded as Protector (1658–59) by his son, Richard Cromwell.

Cromwell, Richard (1626–1712) Lord Protector of England (1658–59). He was the son of Oliver Cromwell.

Cromwell, Thomas [Earl of Essex] (*c.*1485–1540) English statesman. Of humble origin, he rose to power through the patronage of Cardinal Wolsey, and became Henry VIII's chief minister (1533–40). He fostered the passing of Reformation legislation, established the king's legal status as head of the Church in England, and oversaw the dissolution of the monasteries. He was beheaded.

Cronin, Archibald Joseph (1896–1981) Scottish novelist (*Hatter's Castle* 1931).

Cronkite, Walter (1916–) American radio and TV broadcaster.

Crookes tube high vacuum tube invented by the English scientist Sir William Crookes (1832–1919).

Crosby, Bing [Harry Lillis Crosby] (1904–77) American singer and actor. His relaxed, jazz-influenced style of 'crooning' made him one of the most popular and imitated singers of the century.

Crossbow first used in Europe *c.*1090.

Crossword puzzles first introduced in England at the beginning of 19th century.

Cruden's Concordance published 1737, compiled by Alexander Cruden (1701–70).

Cruikshank, George (1792–1878) English artist.

Crusades in Eastern Mediterranean 1095–1291.

Crusoe, Robinson story founded on the experiences of Scottish sailor Alexander Selkirk (1676–1721).

Crystal Palace designed by Sir Joseph Paxton (1801–65); erected in Hyde Park 1851, moved to Penge 1854, destroyed by fire 1936.

Cuba discovered 1492 by Christopher Columbus; achieved independence from Spanish rule 1898; declared a People's Republic under Castro in 1960.

Cube sugar manufacturing process invented by Sir Henry Tate (1819–99).

Cubism art movement founded in France *c.*1909.

Cui, César (1835–1918) Russian-born composer (*The Saracen* 1899).

Cuilean (d.971) king of Scots (966–971) *see* Appendix.

Cullen, Countée (1903–46) black American poet.

Cullinan diamond found at Pretoria 1905, presented to Edward VII on behalf of the people of Transvaal, 9 November 1907.

Culloden, Battle of fought between the Duke of Cumberland and the Young Pretender 16 April 1746 (last battle fought in Britain).

Culpeper's Herbal published 1653, compiled by Nicholas Culpeper (1616–54).

Cumberland, Richard (1631–1718) bishop of Peterborough and philanthropist.

Cumberland, William Augustus, Duke of (1721–65) British military commander.

Cumbria an ancient British principality, comprising, besides part of modern Cumbria, the Scottish districts of Galloway, Kyle, Carrick, Cunningham and Strathclyde, its capital being Dumbarton. It was possibly at one time the chief seat of the power of Arthur, and in the 6th century was an important and powerful kingdom. It speedily, however, fell under Saxon domination, and early in the 11th century was given by Edmund of Wessex to Malcolm of Scotland to be held as a fief of the crown of England.

cummings, e[dward] e[stlin] (1894–1962) American poet, novelist and artist. His experimental free verse and distinctive use of typography influenced many other poets. His works include (*The Enormous Room* (1922).

Cunard, Sir Samuel Nova Scotia manufacturer, founder of the first regular Atlantic steamship service (1787–1865).

Cunard Company founded by Samuel Cunard, George Burns and David MacIver, 4 May 1839; merger of Cunard and White Star Lines 1934.

Cunaxa, Battle of 401 BC a battle during the rebelleion of Cyrus against his brother, Artaxerxes II, when a force of Greeks, among them Xenophon, helped Cyrus. Cyrus was defeated and killed but his Greek allies were allowed to leave.

Cunedda (*fl* 4th century) Welsh tribal king *see* Appendix.

Cuneiform writing first deciphered 1835 by Sir Henry Rawlinson.

Cunninghame Graham, Robert Bontine (1852–1936) Scottish writer.

Cunobelinus *or* **Cymbeline** (d.*c.*43) high king of the British tribes and king of the Catuvellauni *see* Appendix.

Curaçao island in Netherlands Antilles, discovered, became Dutch colony 1634.

Curare discovered *c.*1740 by the Frenchman Charles Marie de Lacondamine (1701–74).

Curé d'Ars', The [Jean-Marie Vianney] (1787–1859) patron saint of parish priests.

Curfew introduced at Oxford by King Alfred to reduce fire risks 872.

Curie, Marie [Marie Sklodowska] (1867–1934) Polish-born French chemist. With her husband **Pierre Curie** (1859–1906), also a chemist, and the physicist Antoine Henri Becquerel, she was awarded the 1903 Nobel prize for physics for work on radioactivity, the first woman to win a Nobel prize. She subsequently became the first person to win two Nobel prizes when her discovery of radium and polonium led to her being awarded the 1911 prize for chemistry.

Curie, Pierre *see* CURIE, MARIE.

Curie, Professor Frédéric Joliot- (1900–1958) French physicist.

Curll, Edmund (1675–1747) English bookseller.

Curragh, Meeting of the, Ireland, March 1914.

Curran, John Philpot (1750–1817) Irish judge and patriot.

Curtiss, Glenn Hammond (1878–1930) American aviation pioneer.

Curzon, George Nathaniel, Marquess (1859–1925) British statesman and viceroy of India (1899–1905).

Curzon Line dividing Poland on linguistic lines 1919.

Cust, Sir Lionel Henry (1859–1929) English art historian and critic.

'Custer's Last Stand' made 25 June 1876 at Little Big Horn, Montana, by George Armstrong Custer (1839–76).

Cuthbert, Saint (*c*.635–687).

Cuthred (d.756) king of Wessex (740–756) *see* Appendix.

Cuyp, Albert (1620–91) Dutch painter (*Piper with Cows*).

Cyanide invented 1905 by the German chemist Heinrich Caro (1834–1910).

Cyanogen first isolated 1815 by the French scientist Joseph Louis Gay-Lussac (1778–1850).

Cyaxares (d.607) king of Media (624–607 BC). He waged war (615–610) against Alyattes of Lydia, but following a battle in 610 when an eclipse of the sun terrified both sides peace was made between them. For much of his reign he was subject to Assyria, but he allied himself with Nabopolassar of Babylon and in 612 BC they captured and destroyed Nineveh and ended the Assyrian Empire.

Cyclotron invented 1929 by the American physicist Ernest Lawrence (1901–58).

Cymbeline *see* CUNOBELINUS and Appendix.

Cynewulf (1) (d.786) king of Wessex (757–786) *see* Appendix.

Cynewulf (2) (*fl* 8th century) Anglo-Saxon poet (*The Dream of the Cross*).

Cynoscephaloe, Battle of 197 BC a battle of the second Macedonian War, when a Roman victory ended the war.

Cynossema, Battle of 411 BC a naval battle of the Peloponnesian War which was an Athenisan victory.

Cynric king of Wessex (534–560) *see* Appendix.

Cyprian, Saint (*c*.200–258) he was martyred 14 September.

Cyprus taken from the Venetians by the Turks 1571; ceded to Britain 1878; made British Crown Colony 1925; became republic 1960; partitioned in 1974 after Greek military coup and invasion by Turkey.

Cyrano de Bergerac, Savinien (1619–55) French soldier, poet and dramatist. Most famous in the popular imagination for having an enormous nose and for having (reputedly) fought around a thousand duels. His works include several satires, and his life was dramatized by Edmond Rostand in a verse drama.

Cyril, Saint of Alexandria (d.444).

Cyril, Saint of Jerusalem (*c*.315–386).

Cyrillic alphabet invention attributed to Saint Cyril (827–869).

Cyrus the Great (d.529 BC) king of Persia (563–529 BC). He conquered Media 550 BC and founded the Persian empire, going on to conquer Lydia 546 BC and Babylon 538 BC.

Cyrus the Younger (424–401 BC) Persian satrap, the brother of Artaxerxes II. He rebelled against his brother and was killed at Cunaxa.

Cyzicus, Battle of (1) 410 BC a naval battle of the Peloponnesian War when an Athenian fleet under Alcibiades defeated the Spartans under Mindarus in Asia Minor. (2) 88 BC a battle of the First Mithridatic War, when the Romans defeated Mithridates.

Czechoslovakia Republic founded 28 October 1918; annexed by Germany 1939; liberated 1944–45; Communist regime 1948–89; free elections held 1990; split into two separate states, Czech Republic and Slovak Republic 1994.

Czerny, Karl (1791–1857) Austrian pianist and composer (*Daily Studies*).

D

Dabrowski, Jan Henryk (1755–1818) Polish military leader and national hero.

Dadaism art movement founded *c.*1915 in Zurich; ended *c.*1922.

Dafydd ap Llywelyn (d.1246) king of Gwynedd (1240–46) *see* Appendix.

Dafydd ap Opwain (d.1194) king of Gwynedd (1170–94) *see* Appendix.

Dagobert I (d.639) king of the Franks (629–639).

Daguerrotype process invented between 1826 and 1839 by the French artist Louis Jacques Mandé Daguerre (1789–1851).

Dahl, Michael (1656–1743) Swedish painter (*Queen Christina*).

Dahl, Roald (1916–90) English author (of Norwegian parentage) known for his children's stories, e.g. *Charlie and the Chocolate Factory*, and humorous poems. Stories for adults include the collection *Kiss, Kiss.*

Dahlgren, John Adolf (1809–70) American ordnance specialist and inventor.

Dahomey *see* Benin.

Dail Eireann Irish Free State Chamber of Deputies formed in Dublin January 1919.

Daily Courant, The first English daily newspaper, founded 1702, ran until 1735.

Daily Express, The British newspaper founded 1900 by C. Arthur Pearson.

Daily Graphic, The British newspaper founded 1890 by W. L. Thomas; absorbed by *Daily Sketch* 1925.

Daily Herald, The British newspaper, began publication 16 April 1912; placed under joint control of Odhams and the TUC in 1929.

Daily Mail, The British newspaper founded 1896 by Lord Northcliffe (1865–1922).

Daily Mirror, The British newspaper founded 1903 by Lord Northcliffe (1865–1922).

Daily News, The British newspaper founded 1846, merged in *News Chronicle* 1930.

Daily Sketch, The British newspaper founded 1909 by Edward Hulton.

Daily Telegraph, The British newspaper re-founded 1855 by Joseph Moses Levy–1888.

Daimler, Gottlieb German automobile manufacturer (1834–1900).

Daladier, Edouard (1884–1970) French socialist statesman. He was prime minister (1933, 1934, 1938–40) and signed the Munich Pact of 1938. He denounced the Vichy government in 1943, and was then imprisoned for the duration of the war.

Dalai Lama highest ecclesiastical and secular official of Tibet since 15th century.

Dalai Lama [Tenzin Gyatso] (1935–) Tibetan spiritual and temporal leader. He became the 14th Dalai Lama in 1940, assumed full power in 1950, and escaped to India in 1959 following the Chinese invasion of his country. He was awarded the 1989 Nobel Peace Prize in recognition of his commitment to the non-violent liberation of his homeland.

Dalcroze eurhythmics music educational system invented by the Swiss composer Emile Jaques-Dalcroze (1865–1950).

Dale, David (1739–1806) Scottish industrialist and philanthropist.

Dale, Sir Henry Hallett (1875–1968) English physiologist. He and **Otto Lowei** (1873–1961) were awarded the 1936 Nobel prize for physiology or medicine for their work on the chemical basis of nerve impulse transmission.

Dalhousie, James Andrew Brown Ramsay, Marquis of (1812–60) governor-general of India (1848–56).

Dali, Salvador (1904–89) Spanish surrealist painter. His finely executed paintings, or 'dream photographs', did much to popularise the surrealist movement. They include *The Persistence of Memory* (1931). He also collaborated on surreal films with Luis Buñuel.

Dallas, Texas, first settled 1841, assumed present name 1845, in honour of the American statesman George Mifflin Dallas (1792–1864).

Dalmatia ruled by Venice 1718–97, by Austria 1797–1918; part of Croatia in former Yugoslavia 1918–91.

Dalriada an ancient kingdom in Argyll founded in the 6th century by Scots from Ireland. After being almost extinguished, the Dalriadic line revived in the 9th century with Kenneth mac-Alpin.

Dalton Plan educational system introduced at Dalton, Mass., by Helen Parkhurst *c.*1920.

Dalton's Law, defined 1803 by the English scientist John Dalton (1766–1844).

Daman and Diu discovered by Vasco de Gama 1498; district of Portuguese India 1559–1961; part of Union Territory of Goa Daman and Diu 1961–87.

Damasus I, Saint pope (366–384).

Damasus II pope (July-August 1048).

Damian, St martyred 303.

Damiani, Pietro (*c.*1007–1072) Italian papal legate and reformer.

Damien, Father Joseph [Joseph de Veuster] (1840–89) French leper missionary in Hawaii.

Dampier, William (1652–1715) English navigator.

Damrosch, Leopold (1832–85) German composer and conductor.

Dana, Charles Anderson (1819–97) American writer and editor.

Dana, Richard Henry (1815–82) American writer (*Two Years Before the Mast* 1840).

Dance, George (1) (1700–1768) English architect of the Mansion House, London.

Dance, George (2) (1741–1825) English architect, the son of George Dance (1) (College of Surgeons).

Danegeld tax first levied in England 991; finally abolished 1163.

Danelaw name applied in 11th century to area of eastern England settled by Danes in 9th and 10th centuries.

Daniel, Samuel (1562–1619) English writer *(Defence of Rhyme* 1602).

Daniell cell invented by the English scientist John Frederick Daniell (1790–1845).

Danish invasion of England began *c.*835.

D'Annunzio, Gabriele (1863–1938) Italian poet, novelist, dramatist and political adventurer. As a writer, the sensuous imagery of much of his work has been widely admired and his oratory was credited with Italy's joining the allies in the First World War. He seized the city of Fiume in 1919, which he ruled until 1920 and became a supporter of Mussolini.

Dante [Alighieri] (1265-1321) Italian poet. Expelled from Florence in 1309 for political reasons, he spent 20 years in wandering exile, during which he wrote his masterpiece, the *Divine Comedy*. His literary influence was enormous, and resulted in Tuscan becoming the language of literary Italy.

Danton, Georges Jacques (1759-94) French revolutionary leader. After the fall of the monarchy in 1792, he became minister of justice and voted for the death of Louis XVI. His efforts to moderate the Revolutionary Terror failed, despite his eloquence. He was outmanoeuvred by Robespierre and guillotined.

Danube Navigation European Commission appointed under the Treaty of Paris 1856; Statute 2 December 1861; International Commission appointed 1904.

Danzig (Gdansk), Poland, made capital of the dukes of Pomerania 1230; Free City 1466–1793, 1807–14, 1919–39; annexed by Germany 1939; returned to Poland 1945.

Dardanelles Expedition First World War expedition, February–March 1915.

Darien, Central America, discovered 1501 by the Spanish explorer Rodrigo de Bastidas.

Darien Scheme Scottish overseas trading venture conceived 1684 by the Scottish merchant William Paterson (1658–1719). Darien expedition set out for Panama 1698.

Darius I (Darius the Great) (548–486 BC) king of Persia (521–486 BC) who gained the throne from a usurper in a conspiracy with six others. He extended and consolidated the Persian empire, taking Babylon *c.*516 and invading Greece twice. He was defeated at Marathon 490.

Darius II (d.404 BC) king of Persia (424–404 BC) whose reign was marked by insurrections and plots against him. He was succeeded by his eldest son, Artaxerxes II.

Darius III (d.330 BC) Persian king (336–330 BC) who was unable to oppose the power of Alexander the Great who defeated him at Issus 333 and Arbela (Gaugamela) 331. The Persian empire ended with his death.

Darling River, Australia, discovered 1828 by the English explorer Charles Sturt (1795–1869).

Darling, Grace (1815–42) English heroine of the rescue of the *Forfarshire*'s survivors on 7 September 1838.

Darnley, Henry (1545–67) husband of Mary Queen of Scots. He was murdered, probably James Hepburn, Earth of Bothwell, who later married Mary.

Dartmouth College (Britannia Royal Naval College) opened 1905.

Dartmouth College, New Hampshire, founded 1769.

Darwin, Charles [Robert] (1809-82) English naturalist. The grandson of the physician and poet Erasmus Darwin, he sailed as a naturalist to South America and the Pacific (1831-36) where his studies among the rich animal and plant life of the area formed the basis for his revolutionary theory of evolution by natural selection. Darwin's theory rapidly found acceptance not only amongst scientists but among society at large. His famous work, *The Origin of Species*, was published in 1859.

Darwin, Erasmus (1731–1802) English physician and writer (*The Botanic Garden* 1789–92).

Dasent, Sir George Webbe (1817–96) British Nordic scholar (*Burnt Njal* 1861).

Daubigné, Théodore Agrippa (1552–1630) French historian.

Daudet, Alphonse (1840–97) French writer (*Tartarin de Tarascon* 1872).

Daughters of the American Revolution, Washington, DC, founded as a national society 1890.

Daumier, Honoré (1808-79) French cartoonist, painter and sculptor. One of the most proficient satirists of all time, his caricatures of the king resulted in a term in jail. He was also an innovative lithographer, painter and sculptor. His works include *The Good Samaritan*).

D'Avenant, Sir William (1606–68) English writer (*The Wits* 1633).

Davenant porcelain manufactured 1793–1882.

David king of the Hebrews (1000–962 BC) who formed Israel as a kingdom and made Jerusalem its capital.

David, St (Dewi) lived in Wales in 6th century.

David, Gerhard (*c.*1450–1523) Flemish painter (*Pieta*).

David, Jacques-Louis (1748-1825) French painter. The leading artist of the French Revolution, he was imprisoned after the death of Robespierre but survived to become painter to Napoleon. His works include *Madame Recamier*.

'David, Pierre' [David d'Angers] (1789–1856) French sculptor (*Lafayette*).

David I (*c.*1081–1153) Scottish king (1124–53) *see* Appendix.

David II (1324–71) Scottish king (1329–71) *see* Appendix.

Davidson, Randall (1848–1930) archbishop of Canterbury (1903–28).

Davies, Emily (1830–1921) English founder 1866–69 of Girton College, Cambridge.

Davies, Sir John (1569–1626) English poet (*Nosce teipsum* 1599).

Davies, Sir Peter Maxwell (1934–) English composer and conductor. With Birtwistle, he founded the Pierrot Players (later called the Fires of London). Since 1970 he has been based in Orkney and frequently collaborated with the Orcadian poet, novelist and short-story writer **George Mackay Brown** (1921–96).

Davies, Sir Walford (1869–1941) English composer (*Everyman* 1904).

Davies, William Henry (1871–1940) English poet (*The Autobiography of a Super Tramp* 1906).

Davis Strait, Greenland, discovered 1587 by the English navigator John Davis.

Davis, Bette [Ruth Elizabeth Davis] (1908–89) American actress, whose electrifying and commanding screen presence made her a highly rated film actresses. Her films include *Dark Victory* (1941) and *All About Eve* (1950).

Davis, Sir Colin [Rex] (1927–) English conductor. Noted particularly for his interpretations of Berlioz, he was conductor of the BBC Symphony Orchestra (1967–71).

Davis, Jefferson (1808–89) president (1861–65) of the Southern Confederacy.

Davis, John (*c.*1550–1605) English explorer and discoverer (1587) of Davis Strait. He was killed.

Davis, Miles [Dewey] (1926–91) American jazz trumpeter, composer and bandleader, he was the leading exponent of the influential 'cool jazz' school.

Davis, Richard Harding (1864–1916) American writer (*Soldiers of Fortune* 1897).

Davis, Sammy, Jnr (1925–90) American singer, actor and dancer.

Davisson, Clinton Joseph *see* THOMSON, SIR GEORGE PAGET.

Davitt, Michael (1846–1906) Irish patriot.

Davy, Sir Humphry (1778-1829) English chemist. An ingenious experimenter, he discovered many new metals, e.g. sodium and potassium, and developed ground-breaking studies in electrochemistry. He was knighted in 1812, and invented the 'Davy lamp' for miners in 1815.

Dawes Plan concerning reparations for World War I devised by the American statesman Charles Gates Dawes (1865–1951).

Dawes, Charles G[ates] (1865–1951) American banker. He devised the Dawes Plan of 1924 for German reparation payments after World War I. He was US vice-president (1925–29) and was awarded the 1925 Nobel Peace Prize.

Dawkins, Richard (1941–) British ethologist (*The Selfish Gene* 1976).

Dawson, Henry (1811–78) English painter (*The Wooden Walls of Old England*).

Day, Doris [Doris Kappelhoff] (1924–) American film actress, famous for her light-hearted, girl-next-door image.

Day, John (1522–84) English printer.

Day mean terrestrial, 23 hr, 56 min, 4.1 sec; mean solar, 24 hr, 3 min, 56.6 sec; mean sidereal, 23 hr, 56 min, 4.091 sec.

Day, Thomas (1748–89) English writer (*Sandford and Merton* 1783–89).

Dayan, Moshe (1915–81) Israeli general and statesman. He commanded the Israeli forces during the Sinai invasion (1956) and was minister of defence during the Six Day War of 1967. He played an important part in the talks leading to the Israel-Egypt peace treaty of 1979.

Daye, Stephen (*c.*1600–1668) English-born first New England printer.

Day Lewis, Cecil (1904–72) Irish-born English poet. In the 1930s he was regarded as part of the 'Auden generation' of left-wing poets. He was poet laureate (1968–72).

Daylight saving, pioneered in Britain by William Willett (1856–1915) and was officially adopted 1916.

Day of Atonement (*Yom Kippur*) Jewish holy day, falls

during last fortnight of September and first fortnight of October (10th day of Tishri).

D-Day Second World War invasion by Allies, landed in Normandy, 6 June 1944.

DDT (dichloro-diphenyl-trichloroethane) insecticide invented by the German scientist Zeidler 1874. First used as insecticide 1939.

'Deadwood Dick' [Richard W. Clarke] (1845–1930) American pioneer.

Deaf and dumb school first British school set up 1760 at Edinburgh by the Scottish teacher Thomas Braidwood (1715–98).

Dean, Christopher *see* TORVILL, JAYNE.

Dean, James [Byron] (1931–55) American film actor. He became a cult figure in the 1950s for his portrayal of troubled, disaffected adolescence, e.g. in *East of Eden* and *Rebel Without a Cause* (both 1955). He was killed in a car crash.

Death penalty for murder abolished in Britain 1965.

de Beauvoir, Simone (1908–86) French philosopher, novelist and essayist (*The Second Sex* 1953).

Debrett's Peerage first published 1802 by the English publisher John Debrett (d.1822).

Debs, Eugene (1855–1926) American socialist leader.

Debussy, [Achille] Claude (1862–1918) French composer. Regarded as the founder of impressionism in music and one of the strongest influences on modern music, his works include orchestral pieces, e.g. *L'Après-midi d'un Faune* (1892–94) and *La Mer*, and the opera *Pelléas et Mélisande*.

December Rising Russian revolt concerning the succession of Tsar Nicolas I, 1825.

Decemvirs ten magistrates in ancient Rome who were appointed 452 BC to draw up a code of laws, the Twelve Tables (450), and to whom for a time the whole government of the state was committed. At first they ruled well but became more tyrannical and were forced to resign following an insurrection.

Decimal classification for books invented 1876 by the American Melvil Dewey (1851–1931).

Decimal curency introduced in Britain 15 February 1971.

Decimal numbers first used extensively by Simon Stevin (1548–1620).

Decius (201–251) Roman emperor (249–251). He was killed in battle.

Decker, Sir Matthew (1679–1749) Dutch-born economist.

Declaration of Independence, American Revolution, adopted 4 July 1776.

Declaration of Right, England, February 1689.

Decree of Union (Laetentur caeli), uniting the Latin and Greek Churches, issued 6 July 1439.

Dee, John (1527–1608) English alchemist.

Defender of the Faith English royal title first bestowed by Pope Leo X on Henry VIII in 1521; continued by English Parliament 1544.

Defoe, Daniel (1660-1731) English novelist and pamphleteer. His works include two remarkable novels, *Robinson Crusoe* (1719) and *Moll Flanders* (1722), although he was better known in his lifetime as a skilled and prolific propagandist.

Degas, [Hilaire Germain] Edgar (1834-1917) French painter and sculptor. He met Monet in the 1860s, after which he began exhibiting with the Impressionists. He is especially noted for his paintings and pastel drawings of racehorses and ballet dancers, e.g. *The Rehearsal*.

de Gaulle, Charles [André Joseph Marie] (1890–1970) French general, statesman and first president (1958–69) of the Fifth Republic. An opponent of the Vichy regime, he fled to Britain in 1940, where he led the Free French forces. Elected president of the provisional government in 1945, he resigned in 1946 after disagreement over his executive powers. He was asked to form a government in 1958, during the Algerian crisis. He granted independence to France's colonies in Africa (1959–60), oversaw increased economic prosperity, fostered an independent nuclear deterrent policy and strongly opposed the UK's entry into the Common Market. He resigned after being defeated on constitutional reform.

De Grey, Walter (d.1255) archbishop of York (1215–55) and chancellor of England (1205–14).

Dehydration of food first extensively employed during the American Civil War, 1861–65.

Deira an ancient Anglian kingdom, stretching from the Tees to the Humber. With Bernicia it formed the kingdom of Northumbria.

Deioces founder of the Medean monarchy 700 BC.

Dekker, Thomas (*c.*1570–*c.*1640) English playwright (*The Shoemaker's Holiday* 1599).

De Klerk, Frederick Willem South African politician (president since 1989) (1936–).

de Klerk, F[rederik] W[illem] (1936–) South African statesman who succeeded P. W. Botha as leader of the ruling National party and president (1989–94) and continued the policy of dismantling apartheid, in 1990 legalizing the African National Congress and organizing Mandela's release from prison. He presided over South Africa's first free elections in 1994 but was defeated by Mandela.

de Kooning, Willem (1904–88) Dutch-born American painter.

Delacroix, Eugène (1798-1863) French painter. His early work, while Romantic in subject matter, owes much to classical composition. He studied Constable's work and in turn influenced other artists, particularly those of the Barbizon School. His works include *The Triumph of Apollo*.

De la Mare, Walter [John] (1873–1956) English poet and novelist. Much of his work was written for children and the loss of childhood innocence is a major theme in his work. His works include the poetry collection *The Listeners* and *Peacock Pie* (1913).

Delaroche, 'Paul' [Hippolyte Delaroche] (1797–1856) French painter (*The Finding of Moses*).

De La Rue, Thomas (1793–1866) British printer and founder of the playing-card publishing firm.

Delaunay, Robert (1885–1941) French painter who founded the movement called 'Orphism', the name given by Apollinaire to Delaunay's introduction of colour abstraction into his Cubist-style paintings. He influenced many other artists, notably Klee.

Delaware state of the USA, first settled 1638; entered the Union 1787.

Deledda, Grazia (1875–1936) Italian novelist (*Cenere*).

Delibes, Léo (1836–91) French composer (*Lakmé* 1883).

Delium, Battle of 424 BC a battle of the Peloponnesian War which was an Athenian defeat.

Delos the smallest of the Cyclades island group in Greece, said to be the birthplace of the god Apollo. It was the headquarters of the Confederacy of Delos 477–453 BC.

Delos, Confederacy of a confederacy founded by Athens for defence against Persia 477 BC. Its treasury was removed to Athens 453 BC, when the Athenian empire was at its height.

Delius, Frederick (1862–1934) English composer. Unconnected to any traditional school, he is noted for his six operas, including *A Village Romeo and Juliet*, and large orchestral pieces. Other works include *Brigg Fair* (1907).

Della Robbia, Luca (*c.*1400–1482) Italian sculptor.

Delorme, Philibert (*c.*1512–1570) French architect.

Delphin classics published by the French printer François Ambroise Didot (1730–1804).

Demarcation, Bull of issued by Pope Alexander VI, dividing discoveries in the known world between Spain and Portugal, 1493.

Demetrius I (337–283 BC) king of Macedonia (294–283 BC) and soldier who, before his accession, lost Syria to Ptolemy I 312 BC but gained Cyprus 306 BC. He unsuccessfuly besieged Rhodes 305 BC. In 307 and 303 he liberated several Greek cities from Ptolemy's rule.

Demetrius II (d.229 BC) king of Macedonia (239–229 BC) who opposed the Achaean league and cultivated friendly relations with the tyrants of the different cities in the Peloponnese.

Demetrius I [Soter] (*c.*187–150 BC) king of Syria (162–150 BC) and grandson of Antiochus the Great who succeeded Antiochus V, his nephew, whom he had put to death. His measures against the Jews drove them to take up arms again under Judas Maccabaeus, who defeated Nicanor, Demetrius's general, and concluded an alliance with the Romans by which they declared the independence of Judaea and forbade Demtrius to oppress them. He was killed in battle against Alexander Balas, the usurper of his throne, who was supported by Rome and Jonathan Maccabaeus.

Demetrius II [Nicator] (d.125 BC) king of Syria (146–137, 128–125), the son of Demetrius I. Unable to take the throne on his father's death because of the usurper Alexander Balas, he invaded Syria with a mercenary army and secured the support of Ptolemy VI. They met Alexander in battle at the River Oenoparas, when Ptolemy was killed and Alexander defeated. Alexander Balas was murdered by his followers and Demetrius gained the throne. Two years later, Tryphon claimed the throne for Alexander's infant son, Antiochus VI, and gained the powerful support of Jonathan Maccabaeus in establishing power in a great part of Syria and in Antioch. Demetrius retired to Babylon and then led an expedition against the Parthians, in which he was initially successful but was finally defeated and captured 137 BC. While he was in prison, his brother Antiochus VII ruled in Syria and engaged in war with the Parthians. Demetrius was released 128 and sent to Syria to operate a diversion against his brother. Antiochus was killed in battle and Demetrius regained his throne, but Ptolemy VII of Egypt set up Alexander Zebina against him and he was compelled to flee to Tyre where he was assassinated while trying to escape by sea.

Demetrius III [Eucaerus] (d.88 BC) king of Syria (95–83), fourth son of Antiochus VIII and grandson of Demetrius II. During the civil wars that folloed the death of Antiochus VIII, he was set up as king of Damascus, and after the death of Antioch X he and his brother Philippus for a time held the whole of Syria. At first they ruled jointly, but war broke out between them and he was blockaded in his camp and forced to surrender.

de Mille, Cecil B[lount] (1881–1959) American film producer and director. With Goldwyn, he is credited with creating the mass movie industry of Hollywood. His films were extravagantly produced epics that achieved enormous success throughout the world, e.g. *The Ten Commandments* (1923) and *The Greatest Show on Earth* (1952).

Democritus (d.370 BC) Greek philosopher.

De Morgan, Augustus (1806–71) English logician (*Budget of Paradoxes* 1872).

De Morgan, William Frend (1839–1917) English writer (*Joseph Vance* 1906)..

Demosthenes (*c.*384–322 BC) Greek orator. He committed suicide.

Dempsey, Jack [William Harrison Dempsey] (1895–1983) American boxer. An ex-miner who became one of the most popular boxers of his day, he was world heavyweight champion (1919–26).

Deneuve, Catherine [Catherine Dorleac] (1943–) French film actress (*Belle de Jour* 1967).

Dengue disease first described 1780 by the American physician Benjamin Rush (1745–1813).

Deng Xiaoping *or* **Teng Hsiao-p'ing** (1904–) Chinese Communist statesman. Denounced in the Cultural Revolution of the late 1960s as a 'capitalist roader', he re-emerged as a powerful figure in the late 1970s. He introduced economic reforms and developed friendly relations with the West but also sanctioned the Tienanmen Square massacre of dissident students in June 1989.

De Niro, Robert (1943–) American actor, who is regarded as one of the finest modern screen actors, with a remarkable facility for submerging himself in a wide variety of roles. His films include *Taxi Driver* (1976), *Midnight Run* and *The Godfather II* (1974), for which he won an Oscar, and *Raging Bull* 1979).

Denmark kingdom since the 10th century; new constitution granted 1953.

Dennis, John (1657–1734) English playwright (*Appius and Virginia* 1709).

Denny, Sir Archibald (1860–1936) Scottish shipbuilder.

Dental forceps invented by the English dental surgeon Sir John Tomes (1815–95).

Depardieu, Gerard (1948–) French actor. Established in the 1970s as a leading man in French films, his strong performances and independent character have made him popular worldwide, notably in *Danton*, *Cyrano de Bergerac* and *Jean de Florette* (1985).

De Paul University, Chicago, founded 1898.

De Pauw University, Indiana, founded 1837 as the Indiana Asbury College; assumed present name 1884.

Deposition, Bull of first issued by Pope Paul III excommunicating King Henry VIII, 1535; second issued by Pope Pius V excommunicating Queen Elizabeth I, 1570.

Depression, The began in USA in October 1929.

DeQuincey, Thomas (1785–1859) English writer (*Confessions of an English Opium Eater* 1821).

Derain, André (1880–1954) French painter. He was influenced by Picasso and Braque, and became one of the leading Fauvist painters.

'Derby, The', Epsom Downs, first run 4 May 1780.

Derby porcelain manufactured 1750 to present day.

Derby-Chelsea Porcelain manufactured 1770–84.

Dermot Mac Murragh (d.1170) the last Irish king of Leinster (1140–70) who enlisted the aid of the English soldier Strongbow in recovering his lands from Rory O'Connor. He was succeeded by Strongbow, who had married his daughter.

Derrida, Jacques (1930–) French deconstructionist literary critic and philosopher.

Desai, Anita (1937–) Indian novelist (*Fire on the Mountain* 1977).

Desai, Morarji [Ranchhodji] (1896–) Indian statesman. He held several posts under Nehru, founded the Janata party in opposition to Indira Gandhi's Congress Party, which he defeated in the 1977 general election, and was prime minister (1977–79).

Descartes, René (1596-1650) French philosopher and mathematician. He proposed a dualistic philosophy based on the separation of soul and body, mind and matter, and sought to establish his system on mathematics and pure reason, his most famous dictum being '*Cogito ergo sum*', 'I think, therefore I am'.

De Sica, Vittorio (1902–74) Italian film director and actor. His early films, e.g. *Bicycle Thieves* (1948), are regarded as among the finest Italian neo-realist films for their compassionate insight into the lives of the poor.

Desmoulins, Camille (1760–94) French Revolutionary leader. He was guillotined.

DeSoto, Hernando (*c.*1498–1542) Spanish explorer of North America.

Despard's Plot against the British Government devised by the English officer Edward Marcus Despard (1751–1803), who was executed.

Determinants mathematical theory developed 1851 by the English scientist William Spottiswoode (1825–83).

Detroit University, Michigan, founded 1877.

Deusdedit I, St pope (615–619).

Deusdedit II, pope (672–676).

De Valera, Eamon (1882–1975) American-born Irish statesman. He was sentenced to death by the British government for his part in the 1916 Easter Rising, but was reprieved after US intervention. He became president of Sinn Féin (1917–26). He opposed the Anglo-Irish Treaty (1921), gave largely symbolic leadership to the anti-Treaty forces during the civil war (1922–23), and was imprisoned (1923–24). He became prime minister (1937–48, 1951–54, 1957–59) and president (1959–73).

De Vere, Aubrey (1814–1902) British poet.

Devil's Island (Cayenne), French Guiana, used as a penal settlement 1854–1938.

Devine, George [Alexander Cassady] (1910–65) English stage director and administrator. He became one of the most prominent influences on the British stage as artistic director of the English Stage Company at the Royal Court.

Devolution, War of enforcing the queen of France's claim to parts of the Spanish Netherlands 1667–68.

De Vries, Hugo [Marie] (1848–1935) Dutch botanist and geneticist. He rediscovered the genetic principles first put forward by Mendel, and developed the theory of evolution through the mutation of genes.

Dew nature discovered by the American-born physician William Charles Wells (1757–1817).

De Wet, Christian Rudolf (1854–1922) Boer patriot.

Dewey, John (1859–1952) American philosopher.

Dewey, Melvil (1851–1931) American inventor (1876) of the Decimal Classification for printed material.

De Wint, Peter (1784–1849) English painter (*A Cornfield*).

De Witt, Johan (1625-72) Dutch statesman who opposed the House of Orange and wanted to abolish the position of stadholder altogether. Bargained with Cromwell in a treaty that the House of Orange would be deprived of all power of state. He resigned in 1672, and two weeks later, when visiting his brother, Cornelius (who had been jailed for conspiracy), was attacked by an angry mob of Orange partisans who lynched them both.

Diabelli, Anton (1781–1858) Austrian music publisher and composer.

Diaghilev, Sergei [Pavlovich] (1872–1929) Russian impresario and ballet master. Founder of the Ballet Russe de Diaghilev in 1911, he became a very influential ballet impresario, drawing on the talents of composers such as Stravinsky and artists such as Picasso.

Diagnosis, medical established as an exact science by the English physician Thomas Sydenham (1624–89).

Diamond necklace affair, involving Queen Marie Antoinette, took place 1784–85; tried 1786.

Diamonds carbon composition demonstrated 1796 by the English scientist Smithson Tennant (1761–1815).

Diamonds, first discovered in South Africa 1867.

Diaz, Bartolomeu (d.1500) Portuguese explorer.

Dick Tracy world's most popular comic strip first syndicated 12 October 1931.

Dickens, Charles [John Huffam] (1812-70) English novelist. His prolific output included plays, pamphlets and lectures, as well as novels and short stories. Immensely popular with both the American and British reading public, he continues to be one of the most widely read writers in the English language. His novels include *Pickwick Papers* (1836–38), *Bleak House* and *Great Expectations*.

Dickinson, Emily (1830-86) American poet. Although only seven of her *c.*2000 poems were printed in her lifetime she became recognized as a uniquely gifted poet following the wider publication of her work in the 1890s.

Dictaphone invented by the American electrician Charles Sumner Tainter (1854–1940).

Dictionary of American Biography first published 1872; compiled by Francis Samuel Drake (1828–85).

***Dictionary of National Biography*, British** founded 1882 by George Smith (1824–1901); first published 1885–1901; supplemented each decade.

Diderot, Denis (1713-84) French philosopher and writer. With others, he edited the great *Encyclopédie*, 17 volumes of which appeared under Diderot's overall direction between 1751 and 1772.

Didius Julianus (d.193) Roman emperor (193). He was murdered.

Diemen, Antony van (1593–1645) governor-general of Batavia.

Diesel engine invented 1893 by the German engineer Rudolf Diesel (1858–1913).

Diet of Worms concerning Martin Luther's actions and writings, held 1521.

Dietrich, Marlene [Maria Magdelene von Losch] (1902–92) German-born American singer and film actress, notable for her strong sexual presence and husky, alluring voice. Her films include *The Blue Angel* (1930).

Differential motor gear invented 1885 by the German engineer Karl Benz (1844–1929).

Digby, Sir Kenelm (1603–65) English writer (*Private Memoirs*).

Diggers group of English communists led by Gerrard Winstanley, active 1648–52.

Dilke, Sir Charles (1843–1911) British statesman.

Dimitrov, Georgi (1882–1949) Bulgarian communist leader (prime minister 1945–49).

Dingaan's Day South African anniversary commemorating the rout of the Zulu chief, Dingaan, 16 December 1838.

Diocletian (245–313) Roman emperor (284–305).

Diode valve invented 1904 by the English electrical engineer Sir John Ambrose Fleming (1849–1945).

Diodorus Siculus (*fl.* 1st century BC) Greek historian.

Diogenes (*c.*412–323 BC) Greek cynic philosopher.

Dionysius, St pope (259–269).

Dionysius of Syracuse *c.*431–367 BC) tyrant of Syracuse (405–367) who conducted several campaigns against Carthage.

Diophantine equations invented by the Greek mathematician Diophantus of Alexandria (*fl.* 3rd century).

Dior, Christian (1905–57) French couturier who created the 'New Look' of the late 1940s, with a narrow waist and full pleated skirt, which was very popular in the austerity of postwar Europe.

Dioscorus anti-pope (530).

Dirac, Paul Adrien Maurice (1902–84) English physicist. He devised a complete mathematical formulation of Einstein's theory of relativity and predicted the existence of antimatter. He shared the 1933 Nobel prize for physics with Schrödinger.

Discontent, Winter of, 1978-79, time of pay freezes and strikes under the Labour government of James Callaghan, led to Labour losing the 1979 general election.

Disney, Walt[er Elias] (1901–66) American cartoonist and film producer. His cartoon films of the 1930s and 1940s achieved high critical and popular acclaim, Mickey Mouse and Donald Duck being two of his famous creations. Other films include *Fantasia* (1941). He built Disneyland amusement park in California (1955) and planned Disney World in Florida (1971).

Disneyland, Anaheim, California, the first of the Disney amusement parks, opened 1955.

Dispensing in the USA first dispensary was opened in 1785 in Philadelphia by the American physician Benjamin Rush (1745–1813).

Disraeli, Benjamin [1st Earl of Beaconsfield] (1804–81) British statesman and novelist. He became a Tory member of parliament in 1837 and prime minister (1868, 1874-80). He promoted protectionism and a romantic imperialism which appealed to Queen Victoria and most of the British public, much to the ire of his great rival, Gladstone. His novels include *Coningsby* (1844).

d'Israeli, Isaac (1766–1848) English writer (*Curiosities of Literature* 1791–93, 1823).

Dissolution of the monasteries in England, 1536–40.

District nursing movement introduced in Britain 1859 by the English philanthropist William Rathbone (1819–1902).

Dittersdorf, Karl Ditters von (1739–99) Austrian violinist and composer.

Divorce for grounds other than adultery made legal in England 1937.

Djibouti northeast coast of Africa, former overseas territory of the French Republic (called French Somaliland then Territory of the Afars and Issas) acquired between 1856 and 1883; became independent 27 June 1977.

DNA (deoxyribonucleic acid) complex molecule that constitutes genetic material of living organisms, its double helix structure was first identified by James Watson and Francis Crick in 1953.

Dobson, Austin (1840–1921) English poet (*At the Sign of the Lyre* 1885).

Dobzhansky, Theodosius (1900–1975) Russian-born American geneticist. His seminal studies of genetic variation linked Darwin's evolutionary theory with Mendel's heredity laws.

Docking of horses' tails prohibited by law in Britain since 1950.

Doctor Wall (Worcester) porcelain manufactured 1751–83.

Doctor Who British children's BBC TV series began 1963.

Documentary film term dates from1929; first significant example was *Nanook of the North* (1920) by Robert Flaherty (1884–1951).

Dodo became extinct *c.*1680.

Dod's Parliamentary Companion founded 1832 by the English journalist Charles Roger Phipps Dod (1793–1855).

Dodsley, Robert (1703–64) English publisher.

Doenitz, Karl *see* DÖNITZ, KARL.

Doggett's Coat and Badge Prize Thames rowing competition founded 1715 by the English actor Thomas Doggett (d.1721).

Dog licence required in Britain by Act of Parliament 1878.

Dohnanyi, Ernst von (1877–1960) Hungarian composer *(Ruralia Hungarica* 1924).

Dolabella (*c.*70–43 BC) Roman general.

Dolci, Danilo (1924–) Italian social reformer. Described as the 'Gandhi of Italy', he built schools and community centres in poverty-stricken Sicily in the face of fierce opposition from an unholy alliance of church, state and Mafia.

Dole British unemployment payments, first so named by the *Daily Mail* 1919.

Dollar first issued in USA 1794, in England 1804.

Dollfus, Engelbert (1892–1934) Austrian statesman. A devout Roman Catholic, he became leader of the Christian Socialist Party and was elected chancellor (1932–34). He opposed the German Anschluss and was assassinated by Austrian Nazis.

Döllinger, Johann (1799–1890) German theologian.

Dolomite rock nature first studied 1791 by the French geologist Déodat de Gratet de Dolomieu (1750–1801).

Domagk, Gerhard (1895–1964) German pathologist. He was awarded Nobel prize 1938.

Domesday Book William the Conqueror's survey of England prepared 1085–86.

Domingo, Placido (1941–) Spanish tenor who studied in Mexico City. He is regarded as one of the finest modern operatic tenors for his sophisticated vocal technique and considerable acting ability.

Dominic, Saint (*c.*1170-1221) Spanish monk. Noted for his asceticism, he founded the Dominican Order of monks and helped the forces of the Inquisition in their barbarous treatment of the Albigensians in Southern France. He was canonized in 1234.

Dominican Order founded by St Dominic 1216.

Dominican Republic discovered 1492 by Christopher Columbus; achieved independence from Spanish rule 1821; the Republic founded 1844; new constitution granted 1924.

Dominion Day, Canada, celebrated 1 July.

Domitian (51–96) Roman emperor (81–96). He was assassinated.

Donald I (d.862) king of Scots (858–862) *see* Appendix.

Donald II (d.900) king of Scots (889–900) *see* Appendix.

Donald III Bane (1031–1100) king of Scots (1093–1097) *see* Appendix.

Donald Breac (d.642) king of Scots (*c*.635–642) *see* Appendix.

Donatello [Donato di Niccolò di Betto Bardi] (*c*.1386-1466) Florentine sculptor. One of the leading sculptors of the early Renaissance, his most famous work is the huge bronze statue of *David* (1430s).

Dongan, Thomas [Earl of Limerick] (1634–1715) Irish-born governor of New York (1682–88).

Dönitz *or* **Doenitz, Karl** (1891–1980) German admiral. He was commander of the German navy (1943–45). As head of the Nazi state following Hitler's suicide (May 1945), he surrendered unconditionally to the Allies and was sentenced at Nuremberg to ten years imprisonment for war crimes.

Donizetti, Gaetano (1797–1848) Italian composer (*Lucia di Lammermoor* 1835).

Donleavy, J[ames] P[atrick] (1926–) American-born Irish novelist. His most popular works are comic adventures set in Dublin's undergraduate community, e.g. *The Ginger Man*.

Donne, John (1573-1631) English poet and divine. After occasional hazardous adventures, such as accompanying Sir Francis Drake on his raid on Cadiz, he became Dean of St Paul's in 1621 and was regarded as one of the greatest preachers of his day. His poetry is among the finest metaphysical verse.

Donnybrook Fair, Ireland, licensed by King John 1204; suppressed 1855.

Donus pope (676–678).

Doolittle, Hilda ('HD') (1886–1961) American poet (*Hymen* 1921).

Doppler effect in physics predicted 1842 by the Austrian scientist Christian Doppler (1803–53).

Doré, Gustave (1832-83) French sculptor, painter and illustrator. Trained as a caricaturist, he became well known for his book illustrations and realistic drawings of London slums. He also illustrated Dante's *Inferno*.

Dorr's Rebellion to extend the suffrage to Rhode Island led (1841) by the American politician Thomas Wilson Dorr (1805–54).

Dort, Synod of held to discuss the Arminian heresy, 1618–19.

Dortmund-Ems Canal, Germany, constructed 1892–99.

DosPassos, John (1896–1970) American novelist (*U.S.A.*).

Dostoyevsky, Fyodor Mikhailovich (1821-81) Russian novelist. His novels, e.g. *Crime and Punishment*, *The Brothers Karamazov* (1880), are profound explorations of sin and redemption through suffering. With Tolstoy he was profoundly influential on modern literature.

Douai Bible first English Catholic translation published 1609–10.

Double Eagle II, flight of the the first transatlantic crossing by balloon (Maine to France, 137 hours 18 minutes), 17 August 1978.

Double refraction theory developed by the French physicist Etienne Louis Malus (1775–1812).

Double valency study (contributing to the study of Isomerism) developed 1893 by the Swiss chemist Alfred Werner (1866–1919).

Doughty, Charles Montagu (1843–1926) English explorer and writer (*Arabia Deserta* 1888).

Douglas, Norman (1868–1952) Scottish-born writer (*South Wind* 1917).

Douglas of Douglas, Sir James (*c*.1286–1330) Scottish patriot. He was killed in battle.

Douglas-Home, Sir Alec [Baron Home of the Hirsel] (1903–95) Scottish Conservative politician. He became the 14th Earl of Home in 1951, renouncing his title in 1963 to contest (and win) the seat of Kinross after succeeding Harold Macmillan as prime minister (1963–64). The furore over his unexpected emergence as party leader resulted in reform of the Tory leadership election process.

Dounreay site in Caithness of Britain's first fast-breeder reactor; first experimental started 1955; first large-scale prototype1974.

Dover, Treaty of to re-establish Catholicism in England signed between Charles II and Louis XIV, 1670.

Dowland, John (1563–1626) English poet and composer.

Downing College, Cambridge University, founded by Sir George Downing (1684–1749); built 1807.

Doyle, Sir Arthur Conan (1859–1930) Scottish novelist, short-story writer and physician. His most famous creation is the amateur detective Sherlock Holmes.

Doyle, Richard (1824–83) English caricaturist.

D'Oyly Carte, Richard (1844–1901) English impresario (the Gilbert and Sullivan operas).

Draco (*fl* 7th century BC) Athenian statesman and lawmaker whose swingeing legislation of 621 BC prescribed death for most offences.

Dragonades expeditions by French soldiers to persecute the Huguenots in the provinces, 1685.

Drake, Sir Francis (*c.*1540-1596) English navigator and pirate. He became a highly popular hero to the English following his successful depradations upon Spanish ships and settlements in the Caribbean in the early 1570s. He circumnavigated the world (1577-80) and was one of the leading lights in the victory over the Spanish Armada (1588).

Draper, Ruth (1889–1959) American actress and diseuse.

Drayton, Michael (1563–1631) English poet.

Dreadnoughts heavily armed warships introduced into Britain by Lord Fisher, 1905.

Dresden china originated by the German Johann Friedrich Böttger (1628–1719).

Drest I king of Picts (663–671) *see* Appendix.

Drest II (d.729) king of Picts (724–729) *see* Appendix.

Drest III (d.780) king of Picts (780) *see* Appendix.

Drest IV (d.837) king of Picts (834–837) *see* Appendix.

Dreyfus, Alfred (1859-1935) French army artillery officer who was tried in 1984 on a false charge of espionage and imprisoned on Devil's Island. The 'Dreyfus affair' scandalized much of Europe for the anti-semitism of the prosecution case. Zola's magnificent pamphlet, *J'accuse* (1898), was written in his defence, and Dreyfus was released and rehabilitated in 1906.

Drinkwater, John (1882–1937) English writer (*Abraham Lincoln* 1918).

Drive-in bank first British (Westminster) opened at Liverpool January 1959.

Drogheda, Ireland, sacked by Cromwell, 10 September 1649.

Drummond, Thomas (1797–1840) Scottish engineer and inventor.

Drummond, William, of Hawthornden (1585–1649) Scottish writer (*The Cypresse Grove* 1623).

Drury Lane theatres in London opened 1663, 1674, 1794, 1812.

Druses heretical Muslim sect, followers of Egyptian Caliph al Hakim (996–1020).

Drust (d.848) king of Picts (845–848) *see* Appendix.

Dryden, John (1631-1700) English poet, dramatist and critic. One of the most important literary figures of his time, he was also a highly significant contributor to the religious and political controversies of the day. He was also the first great English critic and an outstanding poet. His works include the social comedy *Marriage à la Mode* and the verse tragedy *All for Love* (1678). He became poet laureate in 1668 but lost the post in 1688 in the political upheaval surrounding the replacement of King James II by William III and Mary.

Du Barry, Madame (1741–93) mistress of King Louis XV of France. She was guillotined.

Du Bartas, Guillaume de Sallust (1544–90) Huguenot poet .

Dubcek, Alexander (1921–92) Czech statesman. As first secretary of the Communist Party (1968–69), he introduced political reforms which ended with the Russian invasion of 1968. Following Czechoslovakian independence, he was appointed chairman of the federal assembly (1989).

Du Bellay, Joachim (1522–60) French poet.

Dubh (d.966) king of Scots (962–966) *see* Appendix.*

Dubuffet, Jean (1901–85) French painter. He devised the concept of 'Art Brut' in reaction against 'museum art', and made paintings assembled from bits of rubbish, broken glass, etc.

Duchamp, Marcel (1887–1968) French-born American painter, sculptor and art theorist. One of the early pioneers of Dadaism, he introduced the concept of the 'found object'. His works include *Nude Descending a Staircase* (1912).

Duel last fought in England at Priest Hill, Egham, Surrey, 1852.

Dufy, Raoul (1877–1953) French painter.

Dugdale, Sir William (1605–86) English antiquarian writer (*Monasticon Anglicanum* 1655–73).

Duhamel, Georges (1884–1966) French writer (*Civilization*).

Dukas, Paul (1865–1935) French composer (*L'Apprenti-Sorcier* 1897).

Duke University, North Carolina, founded 1838; assumed present name 1930.

Dulles, John Foster (1888–1959) American Republican statesman and lawyer. He was secretary of state (1953–59) under Eisenhower, and developed the confrontational foreign policy of 'brinkmanship' in the Cold War against the USSR.

Dumas, Alexandre [*Dumas père*] (1802-70) French novelist and dramatist, whose entertaining Romantic novels, e.g. *The Three Musketeers* (1844), achieved instant and lasting popularity. His illegitimate son was Alexandre Dumas *fils*].

Dumas, Alexandre [*Dumas fils*] (1824–95) French writer. Illegitimate son of Alexandre Dumas *père*, he also wrote novels and plays, e.g. *Camille*, *La Dame aux Camélias* (1848).

Du Maurier, Dame Daphne (1907–89) English novelist and short-story writer. Several of her works have been made into successful films, e.g. the novels *Rebecca* and *Jamaica Inn*, and the stort story 'Don't Look Now'.

Du Maurier, George [Louis Palmella Busson]

(1834–96) French-born novelist (*Trilby* 1894). He was the grandfather of Daphne Du Maurier.

Dumbarton Oaks Conference at which the foundations of the United Nations were laid held Washington DC, 1944.

Dumdum bullets use banned by the Hague Conference 1907.

Dunant, Henri (1828–1910) Swiss founder (1864) of the International Red Cross.

Dunbar, Battle of between the English and the Scots, 3 September 1650.

Dunbar, William (*c.*1460–*c.*1520) Scottish poet (*Lament for the Makaris*).

Duncan, Isadora (1878–1927) American dancer and choreographer. She developed a free, interpretative style of dancing that was very influential on the development of modern dance (e.g. on Diaghilev). Her ardent feminism and unconventional lifestyle alienated many of her contemporaries. She died when the long scarf she was wearing caught in the wheel of her car.

Duncan I (1010–40) king of Scots (1034–40) *see* Appendix.

Duncan II (1060–94) king of Scots (1094) *see* Appendix.

Dunes, Battle of a battle at Dunkirk between the French and Spanish, 4 June 1658. It was a French victory.

Dungi king of Ur (2382–2328 BC) who succeeded his father, Ur-Engur, and extended his empire over the whole of Babylonia and also conquered Elam.

Dunkirk sold to France by King Charles II 1662

Dunkirk, Battle of Second World War battle, 22 May to 4 June 1940.

Duns Scotus (*c.*1266–1308) Scottish philosopher.

Dunstan, Saint (*c.*910–988) archbishop of Canterbury (959–988).

Dupes, Day of dissembling the triumph of the Spanish policy in France, 12 November 1630.

Dupleix, Joseph(1697–1763) governor-general of India under the French.

du Pré, Jacqueline (1945–87) English cellist. She became recognized as one of the world's finest cellists in the 1960s and married Daniel Barenboim in 1967, with whom she frequently performed. Her performing career came to an end in 1973, after she developed multiple sclerosis. Although confined to a wheelchair, she pursued an active teaching career until her death.

Durand Line defining the frontier between India and Afghanistan determined 1893.

Dürer, Albrecht (1471-1528) German engraver and painter. A leading figure of the Northern Renaissance, his work is outstanding in its attention to detail and its emotional content. A superb draughtsman, his albums of engravings were highly influential on other artists. His works include (*St Jerome*).

Durham University founded by William Van Mildert, bishop of Durham, and the dean and Chapter of Durham 1832.

Durham, John, Earl of (1792–1840) British statesman.

Durkheim, Emile (1858–1917) French sociologist.

Durrell, Lawrence [George] (1912–90) English poet, novelist and travel writer. His masterpiece is the series of sexual and linguistically elaborate novels comprising the 'Alexandria Quartet'. Other works include *Bitter Lemons* (1957).

Duse, Eleanora (1859–1924) Italian actress.

Dussek, Johann Ladislaus [Jan Ladislav Dusek] (1760–1812) Bohemian composer (*Elégie Harmonique*).

Dust wrappers for books first used in Britain 1832; came into general use *c.*1890.

Duveen, Sir Joseph Joel (1843–1908) Dutch-born American art dealer.

Dvorak, Antonin (1841-1904) Czech composer. Strongly influenced by Slavonic folk music, his work was widely praised and he was made a director of the New York Conservatory in 1891. His most famous work is *Symphony No. 9 from the New World* (1893).

Dyck, Sir Anthony van (1599-1641) Flemish painter. Renowned for his unique and influential style of portraiture, investing his sitters with character and refinement of detail, he became court painter to Charles I in 1632.

Dyfnwal I (d.934) king of Strathclyde (*c.*920–934) *see* Appendix.

Dyfnwal II (d.975) king of Strathclyde (934–*c.*973) *see* Appendix.

Dylan, Bob [Robert Allen Zimmerman] (1941–) American folk/rock singer and songwriter. He became the most prominent 'protest' folksinger in the 1960s and his lyrics are very highly regarded by some critics. His songs include 'Blowin' in the Wind' (1962). *See also* BAEZ.

Dynamite discovered 1867 by the Swedish manufacturer Alfred Nobel (1833–96).

Dynamo invented 1823 by the English electrician William Sturgeon (1783–1850).

Dynamometer electrical invented 1840 by the German physicist Wilhelm Eduard Weber (1804–91).

Dysentery bacillus first isolated by the Danish scientist C. Sonne 1915.

E

Eadbert (d.768) king of Northumbria (737–758) *see* Appendix.

Eadbert I (d.748) king of Kent (725–748) *see* Appendix.

Eadbert II (d.*c*.810) king of Kent (796–798) *see* Appendix.

Eadric (d.688) king of Kent (*c*.685–687) *see* Appendix.

Eadwig *see* Edwy and Appendix.

Ealing Studios established 1929 as Associated Talking Pictures, peaked 1946–58 with 'Ealing Comedies', dissolved late 1950s.

Eanfrith (d.634) king of Bernicia (633–634) *see* Appendix.

Eannatum king of Lagash: conquers Umma, Kish Opis, Erech, Ur; repels the Elamites 2900 BC.

Eanred (d.850) king of Northumbria (809–841).

Eardwulf (1) (d.762) king of Kent (747–762) *see* Appendix.

Eardwulf (2) king of Northumbria (796–809) *see* Appendix.

Earhart, Amelia (1898–1937) American aviator. She was the first woman to make a solo flight across the Atlantic (1932), after which she became a celebrity. She disappeared on a flight across the Pacific while attempting a round-the-world flight.

Earle, John (*c*.1601–1665) English divine and writer (*Microcosmographie* 1628).

Earth, circumference of the first calculated by Eratosthenes *c*.230 BC.

Earth, circumnavigation of the by Magellan's sailors September 1519–September 1522.

Earth, density of the calculated by the English mathematician Charles Hutton (1737–1823). Sir George Airy (1801–92), Astronomer-Royal, calculated the mean density of the earth to be 6.566 in 1954.

Earth, magnetism of the described 1600 by William Gilbert (1540–1603).

Earth, mass of the first calculated 1797 by Henry Cavendish (1731–1810).

Earth current discovered 1862 by the Scottish-born astronomer Johann von Lamont (1805–79).

East, Sir Alfred (1849–1913) English painter.

East Anglia a 6th-century Anglo-Saxon kingdom of eastern England (covering Norfolk and Suffolk) that was one of the Heptarchy but eventually became a dependency of Merica in the 8th century.

Easter Christian Feast of the Resurrection celebrated on the first Sunday after the first full moon after the Vernal Equinox.

Easter Island Pacific, discovered by the Dutch navigator Jakob Roggeveen 1722.

East India Company first chartered 1600, dissolved 1858.

Eastlake, Sir Charles Lock (1793–1865) English painter and president of the Royal Academy (1850–65).

East London South African port founded 1848.

Eastman, George (1854–1932) American inventor of photographic equipment and philanthropist. His invention of the Kodak roll-film camera revolutionized the photographic industry, as did his development of colour photography in the late 1920s.

East Prussia German *land* absorbed into Russia and Poland in 1945.

Eastwood, Clint (1930–) American screen actor and director (*The Unforgiven* 1992).

Eau de Cologne traditionally invented by the Italian Johann Maria Farina (1685–1766).

Eberlein, Gustav (1847–1926) German sculptor (*Boy Extracting a Thorn*).

Ebers, Georg (1837–98) German novelist (*Kleopatra* 1894).

Ebert, Friedrich (1871–1925) German statesman (president 1919–25).

Ebonite (vulcanized rubber) invented 1849 by the American inventor Charles Goodyear (1800–1860).

Ecbatana an ancient city and royal residence of Persia, on the site of Hamadan in west-central Iran. It was the capital of Media and royal residence of the Parthians. Alexander was at Ecbatana 330 BC.

Echegaray, José (1833–1916) Spanish playwright (Nobel prize 1904).

Echo, The British newspaper founded 1876 by John Passmore Edwards (1823–1911).

Eckermann, Johann Peter (1792–1854) German friend of Goethe.

Eckhardt, Meister Jean (*c*.1260–1327) German theologian and mystic.

Eclipse Stakes, Sandown Park, first run 1883.

Eco, Umberto (1932–) Italian critic and novelist. A leading literary critic, he is also highly regarded as a writer of fiction. His best-known work is the medieval philosophical whodunit, *The Name of the Rose*.

Ecole des Beaux Arts, Paris, founded 1648; adopted present name 1793.

Economist, The British periodical founded 1843 by the Scottish economist James Wilson (1805–60).

Ecu international currency unit adopted by the EC 1978.

Ecuador achieved independence by secession from Republic of Colombia 1830; granted new constitution 1945.

Edbald (d.640) king of Kent (616–640) *see* Appendix.

Eddington, Sir Arthur Stanley (1882–1944) British astronomer and writer (*The Expanding Universe* 1933).

Eddy, Mary Baker (1821–1910) American religious leader. A faith healer, she devised a system of healing based on the Bible which she called 'Christian Science', and founded the Church of Christ, Scientist, in Boston (1879).

Eddystone Lighthouse first structure erected by Henry Winstanley 1696–1700 and swept away 1703; second structure by John Rudyerd, completed 1709 and burnt December 1755; third, by John Smeaton, completed 1759; fourth, by J. N. Douglass, completed 1882.

Edelinck, Gérard (1640–1707) French engraver.

Eden, Sir [Robert] Anthony [1st Earl of Avon] (1897–1977) British Conservative statesman. He served several terms as foreign minister and was prime minister (1955–57). He resigned following the Suez Crisis, when British and French occupation of Egypt after Nasser's nationalization of the Suez Canal received worldwide condemnation.

Edgar (1) (944–975) king of Mercia and Northumbria (957–975) and of England (959–975) *see* Appendix.

Edgar (2) (1074–1107) king of Scots (1097–1107) *see* Appendix.

Edgar Atheling (*c.*1050–*c.*1125) English prince who was the great-nephew of Edward the Confessor but was passed over for the succession in favour of Harold II. He submitted to William I after the Norman Conquest, but a revolt was raised in his name and he had to flee. He made his peace in 1074.

Edgehill, Battle of a battle of the English Civil War between Charles I and the Parliamentary forces, 23 October 1642. Both sides claimed victory.

Edgeworth, Maria (1767–1849) Irish novelist (*Castle Rackrent* 1800).

Edict of Diocletian Roman measure to check speculation, issued 301.

Edict of Nantes, granting religious freedom to the Huguenots, signed by Henri IV 1598; revoked by Louis XIV 1685.

Edinburgh founded *c.*617 by Edwin, king of Northumbria.

Edinburgh, Treaty of enacting peace between England and Scotland, signed 1560.

Edinburgh Festival founded 1947.

Edinburgh Review British periodical, began publication October 1802.

Edinburgh University founded 1583.

Edison, Thomas [Alva] (1847–1931) American inventor. One of the most prolific and successful inventors of all time, he patented over a thousand inventions, including the gramophone, the incandescent electric light bulb and the microphone.

Edmund, Saint (1) (Edmund the Martyr) (*c.*840–870) king of East Anglia (*c.*855–870) *see* Appendix

Edmund, Saint (2) [Edmund Rich] (d.1240) English ecclesiastic and scholar.

Edmund I (921–946) king of England (939–946) *see* Appendix.

Edmund II Ironside (*c.*983–1016) king of England (1016) *see* Appendix.

Edmund Crouchback, Earl of Lancaster (1245–96) second son of Henry III. He accompanied his brother, Edward I, on crusade (1271) and helped him in his suppression of Wales.

Edred (923–955) king of England (946–955) *see* Appendix.

Education Acts 1870, 1944, 1992.

Edward (1) (Edward the Black Prince) (1330–76) the son of Edward III, during the Hundred Years' War he commanded part of the forces at Crécy, after whiche battle he adopted the motto, *Ich dien*, 'i serve', used ever since by the princes of Wales, and commanded a victory at Poitiers. He married Joan, the Maid of Kent, and was father of Richard II (*see* Appendix).

Edward (2) third son and fourth child of Elizabeth II (*see* Appendix).

Edward I ('Edward Longshanks', 'Hammer of the Scots') (1239–1307) king of England (1272–1307) and of Wales (1283–1307) *see* Appendix.

Edward II (1284–1327) king of England and Wales (1307–27) *see* Appendix.

Edward III (1312–77) king of England and Wales (1327–77) *see* Appendix.

Edward IV (1442–83) king of England and Wales (1461–83) *see* Appendix.

Edward V (1470–83) king of England and Wales (1483) *see* Appendix.

Edward VI (1537–53) king of England, Wales and Ireland (1547–53) *see* Appendix.

Edward VII (1841–1910) king of the United Kingdom and emperor of India (1901–10) *see* Appendix.

Edward VIII (1894–1972) king of the United Kingdom and emperor of India (1936) *see* Appendix.

Edward the Confessor, Saint (*c.*1003–1066) king of England (1042–66) *see* Appendix.

Edward the Elder (870–924) king of Wessex (899–924) *see* Appendix.

Edward the Martyr, Saint (*c*.963–978) king of England (975–978) *see* Appendix.

Edward, Lake a lake on the border between Uganda and Zaire, discovered 1889 by Sir Henry Morton Stanley (1841–1904).

Edwards, Jonathan American theologian (*Freedom of Will* 1754) (1703–58).

Edwin (*c*.585–633) king of Northumbria (617–633) *see* Appendix.

Edwy *or* **Eadwig** (940–959) king of England (955–959) *see* Appendix.

Egan, Pierce (1772–1849) English writer (*Life in London* 1821).

Egbert (775–.839) king of Kent (755–839, as Egbert III) and of Wessex (802–839) *see* Appendix.

Egbert I (d. 873) king of Bernicia (867–873) *see* Appendix.

Egbert II (d.878) king of Bernicia (876878) *see* Appendix.

Egbert I king of Kent (664 to 673) *see* Appendix.

Egbert II king of Kent (765–780) *see* Appendix.

Egbert III (755–839) king of Kent (755–839) *see* EGBERT and Appendix.

Egerton, Francis (1) [Duke of Bridgewater] (1736–1803) pioneer canal builder.

Egerton, Francis (2) [Earl of Ellesmere] (1800–1857) statesman and poet.

Egfrith (1) (d.685) king of Northumbria (670–685) *see* Appendix.

Egfrith (2) (d.796) king of Mercia (787–796) *see* Appendix.

Egmont, Lamoral, Count of (1522–68) Flemish soldier and statesman who became involved in the political and religious disputes that arose between the Netherlands and their ruler, Philip II of Spain and tried to bring about a peaceful settlement. He was tried and executed after a Spanish army was sent to quell the rebellion.

Egric (d.637) king of East Anglia (634–637) *see* Appendix.

Egypt approximate extent of ancient history (1st to 31st dynasties), 3188–332 BC: Fourth dynasty founded by Snefru 3000 BC; later kings of the dynasty built the Great Pyramids at Gizeh; Sixth dynasty ended the ancient empire 2600 BC; Twelfth dynasty 2000–1800 BC, all the rulers of which were great builders; Hyksos rule began 1800 BC; the Hyksos driven out and the New Empire founded by Amasis I; Palestine and Phoenicia conquered 1600 BC; Nubia conquered 1560 BC; Thutmosis III conquered Syria and penetrated to Assyria 1515 BC; Amenophis IV replaced the old religion by sun worship 1415 BC; Rameses I began Nineteenth dynasty 1355 BC; wars against Libyans, Syrians and Hittites 1350 BC; Rameses II waged long war with the Hittites, retained Palestine; greatest builder among the Egyptian kings 1340 BC; wars against Libyans and Asiatic pirates under Meneptah 1273 BC; Rameses III of Twentieth dynasty 1200 BC; throne seized 100 BC by Herihor, high priest of Ammon; deposed by a Tanite dynasty; Palestine conquered 950 BC by Sheshonk, Libyan king of Egypt; Psammetichus I, aided by Gyges of Lydia, made Egypt independent again 660 BC; Egyptian power in Syria overthrown by Babylon 605 BC at Battle of Carchemish; Persian conquest of Egypt 525 BC; Alexander entered Egypt 332 BC and founded Alexandria; Ptolemy I founded the dynasty of the Ptolemies and made Alexandria the intellectual centre of the Hellenic world; beginning of Egypt's decline in reign of Ptolemy IV 222 BC; period of anarchy in reign of Ptolemy V 205 BC; Caesar in Egypt, under the influence of Cleopatra 48-47 BC; suicide of Antony and Cleopatra; Egypt became a Roman province 30 BC; Arab conquest AD 640; Turkish conquest 1517; proclaimed an independent kingdom 1922, an independent republic 1953.

Egyptian Era (Cycle of Sothis) began 19 July 4241 BC.

Ehrenburg, Ilya Grigoryevich (1891–1967) Russian writer (*Julio Jurenito*).

Ehrlich, Paul (1854–1915) German bacteriologist. He did significant research into immunology and chemotherapy, and developed a cure for syphilis (1910). He was awarded the 1908 Nobel prize for physiology or medicine.

Eichmann, [Karl] Adolf (1906–62) Austrian Nazi leader and war criminal. He oversaw the 'Final Solution' (deportation of Jews to death camps) and escaped to Argentina at the end of the war but was captured and tried for crimes against humanity by the Israelis in 1960 and executed.

Eiffel Tower opened 1889, built by the French engineer Gustave Eiffel (1832–1923).

Eijkman, Christiaan (1858–1930) Dutch physician who discovered that beriberi is caused by nutritional deficiency. His research led to the discovery of 'essential food factors', i.e. vitamins. He shared the 1929 Nobel prize for physiology or medicine with Sir Frederick Hopkins.

Einstein, Albert (1879–1955) German-born physicist and mathematician. His formulations of the special theory of relativity (1906) and general theory of relativity (1916), and research into quantum theory, mark him as one of the greatest of all thinkers. He was awarded the 1921 Nobel prize for physics. Being Jewish and a pacifist, he was forced to flee Nazi Germany in 1933 and became a US citizen in 1940.

Eire established as Irish Free State 1921; renamed 'Eire' 1937; became Irish Republic (*Poblacht na h'Eireann*) and left British Commonwealth 1949.

Eisenhower, Dwight D[avid] (1890–1969) American general and Republican statesman known as 'Ike'. He became supreme commander of the Allied forces in 1943 and 34th president of the US (1953–61).

Eisenstaedt, Alfred (1898–) American photographer and pioneer photojournalist.

Eisenstein, Sergei Mikhailovich (1898–1948) Soviet film director. He served with the Red Army (1918–20) during the Civil War and became one of the most influential directors of all time with films such as *Battleship Potemkin* (1925), in which he deployed his theory of film montage.

Eisner, Kurt (1867–1919) German statesman. He was assassinated.

Eisteddfod Welsh national festival with a history of at least fourteen centuries, first so named in the twelfth century.

El Alamein Second World War, 8th Army offensive begun 23 October 1942; victorious 4 November 1942.

Elam an ancient kingdom east of the River Tigris; established before 4000 BC; overthrown 668 BC by Asurbanipal, king of Assyria.

Elasa, Battle of 161 BC Judas Maccabaeus killed; succeeded by his brother Jonathan.

Elastic first British patent issued 1832 to J. V. Desgrand.

Eldon, John Scott, Lord (1751–1838) English jurist.

Eleanor of Aquitaine (1122–1204) wife of Henry II of England.

Eleanor of Castile (d.1290) wife of Edward I of England.

Eleanor of Provence (d.1291) wife of Henry III of England.

Electors [*Kurfürsten*] of Holy Roman Empire, system established in 13th century, revised 1356; ended with Empire 1806.

Electrical Engineers, Institution of founded as The Society of Telegraph Engineers 1871.

Electric batteries invented 1800 by Italian scientist Alessandro Volta (1745–1827).

Electric lamps first publicly demonstrated by Sir Joseph Swan (1828–1914); invented simultaneously by Thomas Edison (1847–1931).

Electric light first produced 1800 by Sir Humphry Davy (1778–1829). First used domestically in Britain 1881.

Electric locomotives invented 1851 by American inventor Alfred Vail (1807–59).

Electric power station first English, opened at Godalming, Surrey, 1881.

Electrified railway first commercial line (City & South London Railway) opened 1890.

Electrocardiography study of heart action first developed by the Dutch physiologist Willem Einthoven (1860–1927).

Electrodynamics theory developed 1822 by French scientist André Marie Ampere (1775–1836).

Electroencephalography pioneered 1929.

Electrolysis investigated 1833 by Michael Faraday (1791–1867).

Electromagnet invented 1825 by the English electrician William Sturgeon (1783–1850).

Electromagnetic induction laws defined 1831 by the English chemist Michael Faraday (1791–1867).

Electromagnetic waves existence established 1864 by the Scottish physicist James Clerk Maxwell (1831–79).

Electromagnetism discovered 1819 by the Danish physicist Hans Christian Oersted (1777–1851).

Electron discovered 1897 by Sir Joseph John Thomson (1856–1940); first isolated *c.*1920 by the American physicist Robert Andrews Millikan (1868–1953).

Electron microscope constituted 1932 by Knoll and Ruska.

Electroplating invented 1832 by the English manufacturer George Richards Elkington (1801–65).

Eleutherius, Saint pope (175–189).

Elevated railway world's first, opened at Liverpool 1893.

Elfward (d.924) king of Wessex (924) *see* Appendix.

Elfwold (d.788) king of Northumbria (779–788) *see* Appendix.

Elgar, Sir Edward [William] (1857–1934) English composer. A master of many styles, he became recognized as the leading British composer with works such as the *Enigma Variations*, the oratorio *The Dream of Gerontius* and his famous *Cello Concerto*.

Elgin Marbles brought from the Parthenon to London 1801–03 by Lord Elgin (1766–1841).

El Greco [Domenikos Theotocopolous] (1541–1614) Cretan-born Spanish painter, sculptor and architect. He studied in Italy before settling in Toledo where he worked in an emotional and spiritually evocative style, using a palette of cold blues and greys at a time when the vogue was for warmer colours. His works include *The Burial of Count Orgaz*.

Elhred *see* ALCHRED and Appendix.

Eliot, George [pseud. of Mary Ann Evans] (1819–80) English novelist. Her novels, e.g. *The Mill on the Floss* and *Middlemarch*, deal with the problems of ethical choice in the rapidly changing rural environment of 19th-century England. She lived, unmarried, with her partner, the English writer **George Henry Lewes** (1817–78).

Eliot, John (1604–90) English missionary to the North American Indians.

Eliot, Sir John (1592–1632) English Parliamentarian. He died in prison.

Eliot, T[homas] S[tearns] (1888–1965) American-born English poet and critic. His early poetry, e.g. *The Waste Land*, is concerned with the breakdown of civilized values in the postwar 'Jazz Era'. He also wrote verse dramas and published critical works.

Elisabethville the name until 1966 of Lubumbashi.

Elizabeth, Saint (1207–31) daughter of Andrew II, king of Hungary.

Elizabeth (1) (1596–1662) English queen of Bohemia, daughter of James VI of Scotland. In 1613 she married Frederick V of the Palatinate came briefly to the throne of Bohemia in 1619. The family were expelled from the country and lived in exile in Holland.

Elizabeth (2) [Elizabeth Petrovna] (1709–61) empress of Russia (1741–61). Daughter of Peter the Great and Catherine I, she ascended the throe as the result of a conspiracy in which Ivan VI, a minor, was deposed. In 1748 she sent an army to assist Matria Theresa in the War of the Austrian Succession and joined in the Seven Years' War against Prussia but died before this war was concluded.

Elizabeth (3) (1837–98) empress of Austria. She was a Bavarian Princess who married the emperor Franz Joseph in 1854. She was assasinated by an anarchist at Geneva.

Elizabeth (4) (1843–1916) queen of Romania and author. She married Prince Charles of Hohenzollern, who became king of Romania in 1883. She was patron of Romanian writers and artists and wrote several books under the pseudonym Carmen Sylva.

Elizabeth (5) (Elizabeth, the Queen Mother) (1900–) consort of George VI and mother of Princess Margaret Rose (1930–) and Queen Elizabeth II (*see* Appendix).

Elizabeth I (1533–1603) queen of England and Ireland (1588–1603) *see* Appendix.

Elizabeth II (1926–) queen of the United Kingdom (1952–) *see* Appendix.

Ellington, Duke [Edward Kennedy Ellington] (1899–1974) American jazz composer, pianist and bandleader. Regarded as one of the finest jazz composers, his many works include 'Mood Indigo' and 'Sophisticated Lady'.

Elliptical functions discovered 1829 by Karl Gustav Jakob Jacobi (1804–51).

Ellis, Havelock (1859–1939) English physician (*The Psychology of Sex* 1901–10).

Ellis Island the principal immigration port for the US 1892–1943; restored and opened as Immigration Museum 1990.

Ellison, Ralph (1914–) Black American writer (*Invisible Man* 1952).

El Paso, Texas, first settled 1659.

Elphinstone, William (1431–1514) Scottish bishop.

El Salvador colonized by the Spanish from 1524; declared independence 1821; became a republic 1856; Civil War 1979–92.

Elssler, Fanny (1810–84) Austrian dancer.

Elssler, Thérèse (1808–78) Austrian dancer (and sister of Fanny).

Elton, Charles Sutherland (1900–) English ecologist. His field studies of animal communities in their environments raised awareness of the ability of animals to adapt to changing habitats.

Ely Cathedral built 11th to 14th centuries.

Elyot, Sir Thomas (*c.*1490–1546) diplomatist and writer.

Elzevir, Louis (1540–1617) Dutch publisher of the classics.

Emancipation of Catholics in Britain enacted 1829.

Emancipation of slaves in the USA proclaimed 1863.

Ember Days (in W. Christendom) fasts on Wednesday, Friday and Saturday after first Sunday in Lent, after Pentecost, after 14 September and after 13 December.

Emerson, Ralph Waldo (1803–82) American essayist, philosopher and poet who developed a philosophy of 'transcendentalism', based upon the authenticity of the individual conscience against both church and state.(*Essays* 1841–44).

Emin Pasha [Eduard Schnitzer] (1840–92) German explorer.

Emmet, Robert (1778–1803) Irish nationalist leader. Plotted to seize Dublin Castle. He was hanged on the 20th September 1803.

Emmett, Daniel Decatur (1815–1904) American composer (*Dixie* 1859).

Empedocles (*c.*494–*c.*434 BC) Greek philosopher.

Empire, French first: 1804–14, second: 1852–70.

Empire, German first: 962–1806, second: 1871–1918, third: 1933–45.

Empire State Building New York, built 1930–31.

Encyclopaedia Americana first published 1829–33.

Encyclopaedia Britannica first produced and published 1768–71 by Andrew Bell, Colin Macfarquhar and William Smellie.

Enderby Land, Antarctica, discovered 1831 by the British navigator John Biscoe (d.1848).

Enesco, Georges (1881–1955) Romanian violinist.

Enfrith (d.633) king of Bernicia (633) *see* Appendix.

Engels, Friedrich (1820–95) German Marxist *see* MARX, KARL.

Enghien, Louis, Duc d' (1772–1804) French Royalist shot in the castle moat at Vincennes in 1804 because

Napoleon chose to believe that he was part of the conspiracy against him.

English Folk Dance Society founded 1911 by Cecil Sharp (1859–1924); succeeded by English Folk Dance and Song Society 1932.

ENIAC (Electronic Numerical Integrator and Calculator) first electronic computer, first publicly demonstrated in February 1946.

Eniwetok Atoll an atoll in the Marshall Islands, scene of atom bomb tests started by the US Navy 1946.

Ennius, Quintus (239–170 BC) Roman poet and dramatist, only fragments of whose work remain. He invented the hexameter.

Enosis movement for the union of Cyprus with Greece had its origins in the Greek government's demand of 1912.

Enred (d.*c*.841) king of Northumbria (809–*c*.841) *see* Appendix.

Ensign infantry rank abolished 1871.

Entebbe raid freeing by Israeli commandos of Jewish passengers hijacked at Entebbe airport in Uganda by members of the Popular Front for the Liberation of Palestine, 3 July 1976.

Entente, Triple between England, France and Russia 1904–17; **Little,** between Czechoslovakia, Yugoslavia and Romania 1920–38.

Entropy the relation between the total amount of heat and temperature, discovered by the German physicist Rudolf Clausius (1822–88).

Envelope-making machine first invented 1851 by the British scientist Warren de la Rue (1815–89).

Enver Pasha (1881–1922) Turkish nationalist and leader in the revolution of 1908. Killed in action 1922.

Eocene Epoch Earth history, 60 million years ago.

Eocha (d.889) king of Scots (878–889) *see* Appendix.

Eoachaid I (d.*c*.629) king of Scots *see* Appendix.

Eochaid II (d.*c*.679) king of Scots *see* Appendix.

Eochaid III (d.*c*.733) king of Scos *see* Appendix.

Eochaid IV (d.*c*.737) king of Scots (733–737) *see* Appendix.

EOKA (National Organization of Cypriot Combatants) guerrilla and terrorist group organized in Cyprus 1954.

Eormenric (d.*c*.560) king of Kent (*c*.540–560) *see* Appendix.

Eorpwald (d.627) king of East Anglia (*c*.617–627) *see* Appendix.

Epaminondas (*c*.418–362 BC) Greek Theban general and statesman who, by defeating the Spartans at Leactra 371 and Mantinea 362 BC (during which he was killed) restored Greek power to Thebes.

Epée Charles Michel, Abbé de l' (1712–89) French priest and benefactor of the deaf and mute.

Ephesus a major city of ancient Greece; captured by Alexander 334 BC; sacked by the Goths AD 262.

Ephialtes (d.*c*.456 BC) Greek Athenian statesman and general. His democratic reform by limiting the powers of the Areopagus in 463 BC caused the enmity of the oligarchs and he was assassinated.

Epictetus (*c*.55–*c*.120) Greek Stoic philosopher who advocated self-denial and the brotherhood of man.

Epicurus (341–271 BC) Greek philosopher. He founded the Epicurean school of philosophy, which teaches that the highest good and proper study of mankind is pleasure, and that this can be attained through a life of simplicity and moderation.

Epicurus (341–270 BC) Greek philosopher.

Epinay, Louise, Marquise d' (1726–83) French writer.

Epiphany Christian Feast of the Manifestation of Christ to the Gentiles (connected with both the Nativity and the Baptism), celebrated 6 January.

Epirus a region of ancient Greece. In 278 BC Pyrrhus, its king, won a battle against the Romans that cost so many lives that it gave rise to the expression 'Pyrrhic victory'.

Eppilus (*fl* 1st century AD) king of the Atrebates tribe *see* Appendix.

Epsom races first run *c*.1620.

Epsom Salts discovered 1618.

Epstein, Sir Jacob (1880–1959) American-born sculptor (*Rima* 1925).

Equinox time at which day and night are of equal length; Vernal Equinox 21–22 March; Autumnal Equinox 21–22 September.

Erasmus, Desiderius (*c*.1466–1536) Dutch humanist, religious reformer and theologian. One of the leading scholars of the Renaissance, he was a strong advocate of tolerance in an intolerant age. His works include *Praise of Folly*, written partly in tribute to his friend Thomas More.

Erastus, Thomas [Thomas Lüber] (1524–83) German-Swiss theologian.

Eratosthenes (*c*.276–*c*.194 BC) Alexandrian philosopher.

Erbium chemical element first isolated 1843 by the Swedish chemist Karl Gustav Mosander (1797–1858).

Erckmann-Chatrian pen-name of the French writers Emile Erckmann (1822–99) and Alexandre Chatrian (1826–90) who worked in collaboration between 1847 and 1889.

Erconbert (d.664) king of Kent (*c*.660–664) *see* Appendix.

Erebus, Mount. volcanic mountain in the Antarctic discovered 1841 by Sir James Ross (1800–1862).

Eric (1) king of Denmark (814–854).

Eric (2) (d.918) king of East Anglia (900–902) *see* Appendix.

Eric I to V legendary kings of Sweden.

Eric VI (d.*c*.880) king of Sweden (*c*.850–*c*.880).

Eric VII king of Denmark (1396–1438), and **XIII** king of Sweden (1382–1459).

Eric VII (d.*c*.994) king of Sweden.

Eric VIII king of Sweden, reigned towards the end of the 11th century.

Eric IX, Saint (d.1160) king of Sweden and Denmark. He was beheaded.

Eric X (d.1216) king of Sweden (1210–16).

Eric XI (1216–52) king of Sweden (1222–52).

Eric XII (1339–59) king of Sweden.

Eric XIII (1382–1459) king of Sweden (1396–1438) and **VII** king of Denmark (1396–1438).

Eric XIV (1533–77) king of Sweden (1560–77).

Eric Eiggod (*c*.1056–1101) king of Denmark (1095–1101).

Eric Emune (d.1137) king of Denmark (1131–37). He was assassinated.

Eric Klipping (*c*.1249–1286) king of Denmark (1259–86). He was assassinated.

Eric Lam (d.1146) king of Denmark (1137–46).

Eric Menved (1274–1319) king of Denmark (1286–1319).

Eric Plogpenning (1216–50) king of Denmark (1241–50). He was beheaded.

Ericsson, John (1803–89) Swedish-born inventor.

Ericsson, Leif (*c*.971) Scandinavian discoverer (about 1000) of North America.

Eric the Red (*c*.949–*c*.1003) Norwegian discoverer (about 981) of Greenland.

Erie Canal, New York State, begun 1817, completed 1825.

Erie, Battle of Lake a naval battle of the War of 1812, 10 Septmber, when an American fleet defeated a British fleet.

Erigena, Johannes Scotus Irish philosopher and theologian in 9th century.

Erik Bloodaxe (d.954) king of York (947–954) *see* Appendix.

Eritrea conquered by Italy 1885–89; invaded by British forces 1941; sovereignty handed over by the British to Ethiopia 1952; Eritrean independence movement has fought against the government since 1961.

Erivan, Ivan Fyodorovich Paskevich, Count of (1782–1856) Russian field-marshal.

Erkel, Franz (1810–93) Hungarian composer (*Bánk Bán* 1861).

ERNIE (Electronic Random Number Indicating Equipment) used to select winning numbers in premium bonds, first issued by the Dept. of National Savings 1956.

Ernle, Rowland Edmund Prothero, Baron English agricultural historian (1851–1937).

Ernst, Max (1891–1976) German-born French painter. He was a leading member of both the Dada and Surrealist movements and pioneered the use of collage and photomontage.

Erskine, Ebenezer (1680–1754) Scottish church reformer.

Erskine, John, Earl of Mar (1675–1732). Jacobite supporter.

Erskine, John (1509–91) Scottish reformer.

Erskine, Thomas, Baron Erskine (1750–1823) Scottish lawyer.

Ervine, St John (1883–1971) Ulster-born playwright (*Jane Clegg* 1911).

Esarhaddon (d.669) king of Assyria (680–669 BC). He defeated Taharka, Ethiopian king of Egypt, and conquered Egypt (675–671), capturing Memphis in 670 BC.

Escalator first in England installed at Earls Court Station, London, in 1911.

Escorial, The Spain, palace built by King Philip II (1563–84).

Esparto grass first used for the manufacture of paper *c*.1855.

Esperanto universal language produced 1887 by the Polish scholar Lazarus Ludovic Zamenhof (1859–1917).

Essex, Robert Devereux, 2nd Earl of (1566–1601) English statesman and rebel. He was found guilty of treason against Elizabeth I and beheaded on 25 February.

Essex, Robert Devereux, 3rd Earl of (1591–1646) English statesman and general. Eldest son of Robert, 2nd Earl. The earldom was restored to him in 1604.

Essex, Walter Devereux, 1st Earl of (1541–76) [2nd Viscount Hereford] Earl marshal of Ireland.

Essex Anglo-Saxon kingdom of eastern England in the 7th century covering the modern county and parts of Hertfordshire and Surrey. By the late 8th century it had become a dependency of Mercia.

Este, Beatrice d' (1475–97) Italian diplomat and patron of the arts.

Esterházy, Prince Pál Antal (1786–1866) Austro-Hungarian diplomat.

Estienne, Henri (*c*.1531–1598) French printer and publisher.

Estienne, Robert (1503–59) French printer and publisher.

Estonia proclaimed an independent Republic 1918; incorporated in the Soviet Union 1940; independent since the dissolution of the Soviet Union, August 1991.

Estrées, Gabrielle d' (1573–99) mistress of King Henri IV of France.

ETA [Euzakadi Ta Askatasumar, 'Basque Homeland of Liberty'] radical terrorist group seeking Basque independence from Spain, split from the Basque Nationalist Party 1959.

Ethelbald (1) (d.757) king of Mercia (715–757) *see* Appendix.

Ethelbald (2) (834–860) king of Wessex (858–860) *see* Appendix.

Ethelbert (1) (d.792) king of East Anglia (792) *see* Appendix.

Ethelbert (2) (836–856) king of Wessex (857–865) *see* Appendix.

Ethelbert I, Saint (d.616) king of Kent (560–616) *see* Appendix.

Ethelbert II (d.762) king of Kent (725–762) *see* Appendix.

Ethelfrith (d.617) king of orthumbria (604–617) *see* Appendix.

Ethelheard (d.740) king of Wessex (726–*c*.740) *see* Appendix.

Ethelhere (d.654) king of East Anglia (654) *see* Appendix.

Ethelred king of Mercia (675–704) *see* Appendix.

Ethelred I (d.796) king of Northumbria (774–796) *see* Appendix.

Ethelred II king of Northumbria (841–850) *see* Appendix.

Ethelred I, Saint (840–871) king of Wessex (865–871) *see* Appendix.

Ethelred II (Ethelred the Unready) (*c*.968–1016) king of England (978–1016) *see* Appendix.

Ethelreda, Saint (630–679) daughter of King Anna of East Anglia (*see* Appendix) and founder of a monastery at Ely in 672 of which she was appointed abbess.

Ethelric king of Bernicia (568–572) *see* Appendix.

Ethelstan (895–939) king of Wessex and Mercia (928–939) *see* Appendix.

Ethelwalh king of Sussex (before 685) *see* Appendix.

Ethelweard king of Mercia (*c*.837–850).

Ethelwold (1) king of Mercia (654–663) *see* Appendix.

Ethelwold (2) king of Northumbria (759–765) *see* Appendix.

Ethelwulf (800–858) king of Wessex (839–858) *see* Appendix.

Ether a colourless, volatile flammable liquid, the soporific qualities of which were discovered 1818 by the English chemist Michael Faraday (1791–1867); first used as an anaesthetic 1846 by the American physician Crawford Williamson Long (1815–78).

Etherege, Sir George (*c*.1635–1692) English playwright (*She Would If She Could* 1667).

Ethiopia independence established 1906; conquered by Italy 1935–37; independence regained 1941; monarchy abolished 1975.

Etna [Mongibello] Sicilian volcano: main eruptions 125, 121 and 43 BC; AD 1169, 1669 and 1992.

Etruscans an ancient Italian people whose civilization greatly influenced the Romans. They and the Gauls were defeated by the Romans at Lake Vadimonian in 283 BC, leaving Rome as the ruler of northern Italy.

'Ettrick Shepherd', The [James Hogg] (1770–1835) Scottish poet.

Etty, William (1787–1849) English painter (*Youth at the Prow and Pleasure at the Helm*).

Euclid (*fl* 300 BC) Greek mathematician in Alexandria. He devised a a set of principles of geometry that was highly influential.

Eudocia (*c*.400–*c*.459) Byzantine empress.

Eudoxia (d.404) Byzantine empress.

Eugéne I, Saint pope (654–657).

Eugene II pope (824–827).

Eugene III [Bernardo Paganelli] pope (1145–53).

Eugene IV [Gabriel Condulmieri] pope (1431–47).

Eugene of Savoy, Prince (1663–1736) Austrian soldier, born in Paris.

Eugénie (1826–1920) wife of the Emperor Napoleon III.

Eulalius anti-pope (418).

Euler, Leonhard (1707–83) Swiss mathematician.

Eumenes [of Cardia] (*c*.360–316 BC) Greek general.

Euratom [European Atomic Energy Authority] established by Treaty of Rome 25 March 1957.

Eurhythmics, Dalcroze music educational system invented by the Swiss composer Emile Jaques-Dalcroze (1865–1950).

Euripides (480–406 BC) Greek dramatist. He was the youngest of the three great Greek tragedians, the others being Aeschylus and Sophocles. Nineteen of his plays are extant, the most notable including *Medea* and *The Trojan Women* (413 BC).

European Coal and Steel Community established by the Treaty of Paris 1951.

European Defence Community set up 27 May 1952.

European Economic Community established by Treaty of Rome 25 March 1957.

European Nuclear Energy Agency founded within OEEC 1 February 1958.

European Union established by Treaty February 1984; Single European Act signed February 1986.

Eurovision television link-up between European countries, first carried out on a large scale by the BBC 1954.

Eurymedon, Battle of the a naval and land battle of the third Persian invasion of Greece, 465 BC, when the Greeks under Cimon defeated the Persians.

Eusebius, Saint pope (309–311).

Eusebius of Caesarea (*c*.264–340) theologian, who wrote *History of the Christian Church*.

Eustachian tube in anatomy first described by the Italian anatomist Bartolommeo Eustachio (d.1574).

Eustathius (*c.*1196) Greek literary critic.

Euston Station, London, opened 1838.

Eutychian, Saint pope (275–283).

Evans, Sir Arthur [John] (1851–1941) English archaeologist. His excavations of the palace of Knossos in Crete resulted in the rediscovery of Minoan civilization.

Evans, Dame Edith [Mary Booth] (1888–1976) English actress, notable for her command of a wide variety of roles. She created the role of Lady Utterwood in Shaw's *Heartbreak House* and gave a definitive performance as Lady Bracknell in Wilde's *The Importance of Being Earnest.*

Evans, Sir John (1823–1908) English industrialist and archaeologist.

Evans, Oliver (1755–1819) American inventor of mining machinery.

Evaporated milk invented 1856 by the American surveyor Gail Borden (1801–74).

Evaristus, Saint pope (97–105).

Evelyn, John (1620–1706) English diarist.

Evening News, The British newspaper founded 1881; absorbed the *Star* 1960.

Evening Standard, The British newspaper founded 1827; absorbed the *St James's Gazette* 1905.

Everest, Mount the highest mountain in the world (8848 metres/29,028 feet), situated on the border between Nepal and China in the eastern Himalayas, summit first reached 29 May 1953 by the New Zealander Sir Edmund Hillary (1919–93) and Sherpa (Norgay) Tenzing (1914–86).

Everlasting League, The Swiss patriotic pact made 1291 between Schwyz, Uri and Unterwalden.

Evil-Merodach king of Babylon *c.*561 BC.

Evolution by natural selection, Darwinian theory first communicated to the Linnean Society of London 1 July 1858; Charles Darwin's *Origin of Species* first published 1859.

Ewart, William (1798–1869) English library pioneer.

Ewing, Sir James Alfred (1855–1935) Scottish scientist.

Ewing, Mrs Juliana Horatia (1841–85) English writer (*Jackanapes* 1884).

Exchange Rate Mechanism (ERM) stabilizing of currency (each valued in Ecus) in European Monetary System, Britain joined October 1990, withdrew September 1992.

Exclusion Struggle against the succession of James, Duke of York (later James II) (1678–81).

Excursion train world's first (Leicester-Loughborough return), organized by the English pioneer travel agent Thomas Cook (1808–92).

Exeter Cathedral constructed 1285–1367.

Exeter College, Oxford University, founded 1314 by Walter de Stapeldon, Bishop of Exeter (1261–1326).

Exmouth, Edward Pellew, Viscount English admiral (1757–1833).

Expanding universe theory developed by the Dutch scientist William de Sitter (1872–1934).

Explorer I first American satellite, launched 31 January 1958.

Exxon Valdez oil tanker that ran aground leaking 11 million gallons of crude oil into Prince William Sound, Alaska, 24 March 1989.

Eyck, Hubert van Flemish painter (*c.*1370–1426).

Eyck, Jan van Flemish painter (*c.*1389–1440).

Eyre, Edward John English explorer and statesman (1815–1901).

Eyre, Lake, South Australia, discovered 1840 by the English explorer Edward John Eyre (1815–1901).

Eysenck, Hans [Jürgen] (1916–) German-born British psychologist. He has been a notable critic of Freud's theory of psychoanalysis and holder of controversial views on the role of genetic factors in determining intelligence.

Ezekiel (*fl* 6th century BC) Old Testament prophet. When Jerusalem was taken by Nebuchadnezzar in 597 BC he was exiled to Babylon.

Ezra (*fl* 5th century BC) Jewish priest who returned with many Jews from Babylon to Jerusalem 458 BC after the captivity to re-establish the Jewish religion and law.

F

Faber, Frederick William (1814–63) English theologian and poet.

Fabian, Saint pope (236–250).

Fabian Society London, founded 1883 by the English writers Edward R. Pease and Frank Podmore (1855–1910).

Fabius Maximus, Quintus (d.203 BC) Roman statesman.

Fabre, Jean Henri (1823–1915) French entomologist (*Souvenirs Entomologiques* 1879–1907).

Fabriano, Gentile da (*c.*1370–1427) Italian painter.

Fabricius, Hieronymus (1533–1619) Italian anatomist.

Fabricius, Johann Christian (1745–1808) Danish entomologist.

Fabritius, Carel (1622–54) Dutch painter.

Fabyan, Robert (d.1513) English historian.

Factory Act first in England passed 1802.

Fahd (b.1933) king and prime minister of Saudi Arabia (since 1982).

Fahrenheit scale temperature invented *c.*1714 by the German physicist Gabriel Daniel Fahrenheit (1686–1736).

Fairbairn, Sir William (1789–1874) Scottish engineer and inventor.

Fairbanks, Douglas [Douglas Elton Ullman] (1883–1939) American film actor and producer who became one of the leading stars of silent films. His son, Douglas Fairbanks Jr (1909–), was also an actor. His first wife was Joan Crawford.(*The Thief of Baghdad* 1924).

Fairbanks, Douglas, Junior (1909–) American film actor (*The Prisoner of Zenda* 1937).

Fairbanks, Thaddeus(1796–1886) American inventor.

Fairey, Sir Charles Richard (1887–1956) British aviation pioneer.

Fairfax, Thomas (1612–71) English puritan general.

Faisal (1906–75) king of Saudi Arabia (1964–75), prime minister (1953–64).

Faithfull, Emily (1835–95) English champion of rights for women.

Falange Spanish Fascist Party founded 1933 by José Antonio Primo de Rivera; completed control of Spain in 1939; abolished 1977.

Faliero, Marino (1274–1355) doge of Venice (1354–55). He commanded the troops of the republic at the siege of Zara in Dalmatia, where he gained a brilliant victory over the king of Hungary. As doge, he was accused of attempting to overthrow the republic to make himself sovereign of the state, and he was beheaded. The last scenes of his life are depicted in Byron's tragedy, *Marino Faliero.*

Falkirk, Battle of (1) a battle of the Wars of Scottish Independence, 22 July 1298, when the English under Edward I defeated the Scots under William Wallace, who was forced to flee. (2) a battle of the Second Jacobite Rebellion, 17 January 1746, when the Highlanders under Charles Edward Stewart, the Young Pretender, were victorious over royal forces under General Hawley.

Falkland Islands, Battle of the a naval battle of the First World War, 8 December 1914, when the Royal Navy destroyed a German squadron.

Falklands War between Britain and Argentina over rival claims to sovereignty over the Falkland Islands (claimed by Britain as a Crown Colony since 1833): invaded by the Argentines April 1982, recaptured by British May–June 1982.

Falla, Manuel de (1876–1946) Spanish composer (*The Three-cornered Hat* 1919).

Fallopian tubes (*c.*1523–1562) physiological function first described by the Italian anatomist Gabriello Fallopio.

Family Allowances former name for Child Benefit, introduced into Britain 1945; general in France by 1932.

Fanshawe, Sir Richard (1608–66) English diplomat and translator.

Fantin-Latour, Ignace Henri Jean Théodore (1836–1904) French painter who is best known for his paintings of flowers and his group portraits, e.g. *Homage à Delacroix* (1864).

FAO, *see* **Food and Agricultural Organization.**

Faraday, Michael (1791–1867) English chemist and physicist. He was an assistant to Davy and discovered electromagnetic induction and investigated electrolysis.

Farel, Guillaume (1489–1565). Swiss religious reformer

Fargo, William George (1818–81) American partner in the Wells, Fargo & Co. express company.

Farinelli [Carlo Broschi] (1705–82) Italian castrato singer.

Farnese, Alessandro (1) (1468–1549) Italian cardinal and pope as Paul III (1534–49).

Farnese, Alessandro (2) (1546–92) Italian diplomat and soldier who worked in the service of Philip II of Spain and as governor of the Netherlands (1578–92) suppressed several rebellions against Spanish rule.

Farnese Palace, Rome, built *c.*1513–15.

Faroe Islands a group of eighteen islands in the North Atlantic, which came under Danish rule 1380; granted separate legislature and executive 1948.

Farouk, King (1920–65) the last king of Egypt (1936–52), who was deposed by a coup that included Nasser.

Farquhar, George (1678–1707) Irish dramatist. His lightly satirical plays, e.g. *The Beaux' Stratagem*, mark an important transitional stage between the bawdy world of Restoration comedy and the more decorous 18th-century stage.

Farr, William (1807–83) English pioneer in the study of vital statistics.

Farragut, David Glasgow (1801–70). American admiral

Fascist Party Italian, founded March 1919 by Mussolini; seized power 20 October 1922; dissolved 28 July 1943. Spanish (Falange) founded 1933; gained control of Spain 1936–39. English (British Union of Fascists) founded 1932 by Sir Oswald Mosley; revived (British Union Movement) in 1948.

Fashoda Incident, Egypt, between British and French 1898.

Fassbinder, Rainer Werner (1946–82) German film director and actor. His films, e.g. *The Bitter Tears of Petra Von Kant* (1972) and *Lola* (1981), are noted for their social comment, particularly on post-war Germany.

Fast breeder reactor first experimental, set up by the United Kingdom Atomic Energy Authority at Dounreay, Scotland, 1957.

Fast of Ab Jewish fast, Ab 9th.

Fastolf, Sir John (*c.*1378–1459) English soldier.

Father's Day 3rd Sun. in June.

Fatima (*c.*605–632) daughter of Mahomet.

Fatima, Miracle of (Portugal) occurred 13 October 1917.

Fatimids caliphs in North Africa 909–1171.

Faulkner, William [Harrison] (1897–1962) American novelist. Considered a master of the modern novel, his best-known work, *The Sound and the Fury*, deals with social tensions in the Old South. He was awarded the 1949 Nobel prize for literature.

Fauré, Gabriel (1845–1924) French composer (*Messe basse* 1907).

Faust, Johann *or* **Georg** (*c.*1480–*c.*1540). German magician

Fauvist movement French art group, first recognized 1905; disintegrated 1908.

Fawcett, Dame Millicent [Millicent Garrett] (1847–1929) English feminist and champion of women's rights. She became first president of the National Union of Women Suffrage Societies (1897–1919) and opposed the more militant tactics of Pankhurst.

Fawcett, Henry (1833–84) English economist.

Fawkes, Guy (1570–1606) English conspirator hanged for treason.

Feast of Tabernacles [*Sukkoth*] Jewish festival, 15th to 22nd Tishri inclusive.

Feast of Weeks [*Sharuoth*] Jewish festival, Sivan 6th.

Federal Reserve Bank Washington DC, founded 23 December 1913.

Feisal I (1883–1933) first king of Iraq (1921-1933).

Feisal II (1935–58) third and last king of Iraq (1939–58). He was assassinated.

Felix I, Saint pope (269–275).

Felix II (d.365) anti-pope (355–357).

Felix III pope (483–492).

Felix IV pope (526–530).

Felix V [Amadeus] (1383–1451). anti-pope (1440–49).

Fell, Dr John (1625–86) bishop of Oxford (1675–86).

Fellini, Federico (1920–93) Italian film director. The best known of his highly individual films is *La Dolce Vita* (1960), a cynical portrayal of Roman high society.

Fellowes, Edmund (1870–1951) English musicologist.

Felton, John (*c.*1595–1628) English assassin of the Duke of Buckingham. He was hanged.

Fénelon, François de Salignac de la Mothe (1651–1715) French theologian (*Télémaque* 1699).

Fenians (1816–77) (Irish Republican Brotherhood) Irish-American revolutionary movement founded 1858 in the USA by John O'Mahony.

Feodor I (1557–98) tsar of Russia (1584–98).

Feodor II (1589–1605) tsar of Russia. He was assassinated.

Feodor III (1656–82) tsar of Russia (1676–82).

Ferber, Edna (1887–1968) American writer (*Cimarron* 1929).

Ferdinand I (1503–64) Holy Roman emperor (1558–64).

Ferdinand II (1578–1637) Holy Roman emperor (1619–37).

Ferdinand III (1608–58) Holy Roman emperor (1637–58).

Ferdinand I (d.1065) king of Castile and Leon.

Ferdinand II king of Leon (1157–88).

Ferdinand III (1199–1212) king of Castile and Leon.

Ferdinand IV (d.1312) king of Castile and Leon (1296–1312).

Ferdinand V (1452–1516) king of Castile and Leon (1474–1516).

Ferdinand VI (1713–59) king of Spain (1746–59).

Ferdinand VII (1784–1833) king of Spain (1813–33).

Ferdinand I (1423–94) king of Naples (1458–94).

Ferdinand II (1469–96) king of Naples (1495–96).

Ferdinand I (1345–83) king of Portugal (1367–83).

Ferdinand II (1816–85) consort (1826–53) of Maria II of Portugal.

Fergus Mor (d.501) king of Scots *see* Appendix.

Ferguson, James (1710–76) Scottish astronomer.

Ferguson, Patrick (1744–80) Scottish inventor, killed at the battle of King's Mountain, South Carolina.

Fermat, Pierre de (1601–65) French mathematician. The founder of number theory, he initiated, with Pascal, the study of probability theory.

Fermi, Enrico (1901–54) Italian-born American atomic physicist. Awarded the Nobel prize for physics in 1938 for his work on radioactive substances and nuclear bombardment, he fled to the US. He built the first nuclear reactor at Chicago in 1942.

Fernandel [Fernand Contandin] (1903–71) French comedian.

Fernandez, Juan (*c.*1537–*c.*1603) Spanish explorer.

Fernando Po *see* BIOKO.

Fernel, Jean François (1497–1558) French scientist.

Ferrar, Nicholas (1592–1637) English religious leader.

Ferrara, Andrea Italian sword-maker active in the second half of the 16th century.

Ferrers, Laurence, Earl (1720–60) last nobleman who was executed in Britain.

Ferrier, Kathleen (1912–53) English contralto. A highly regarded singer whose tragically short career ended with her death from cancer, she created the title role in Britten's *Rape of Lucretia* and sang regularly with Bruno Walter.

Ferrier, Susan (1782–1854) Scottish novelist. Her works include *Marriage* (1818).

Ferris wheel invented for the World's Columbian Exposition 1892 by the American engineer George Washington Gale Ferris (1859–96).

Ferro, Canary Isles, prime meridian adopted by French in 17th century (after Arab usage); superseded by Paris and in 1911 by Greenwich.

Fersen, Hans Axel, Count (1755–1810) Swedish diplomat. He was murdered.

Fervidor French Revolutionary Calendar month, 19 July to 17 August.

Festival of Britain 3 May–30 September 1951.

Festival of Lights [Chanucah] Jewish festival, Kislev 25th.

Festival of the Purification of the Virgin [Candlemas] 2 February.

Feuchtwanger, Lion (1884–1958) German novelist [*Jud Süss* 1924].

Feuerbach, Ludwig Andreas (1804–72) German philosopher.

Feuillet, Octave (1821–90) French novelist (*Sibylle* 1862).

Féval, Paul (1817–87) French novelist (*Les Mystères de Londres* 1844).

Feydeau, Georges (1862–1921) French dramatist, noted for his many bedroom farces, e.g. *Hotel Paradise.*

Feynman, Richard (1918–88) American physicist. He shared the 1965 Nobel prize for physics for his work in quantum electrodynamics.

Fez, Treaty of concerning the establishment of a French protectorate (1912–56) in Morocco, concluded 30 March 1912; terminated 2 March 1956.

Fianna Fail ('Soldiers of destiny') Irish political party founded 1927 by statesman Eamon de Valera (1882–1975).

Fibreoptics, first suggested as a telecommunications medium by Charles Kao in 1966.

Fichte, Johann Gottlieb (1762–1814) German philosopher.

Fido airfield clearance method developed 1942 by the British engineer Arthur Clifford Hartley (1889–1960).

Field marshal military rank introduced into Britain in 1736.

Field of the Cloth of Gold *see* CLOTH OF GOLD.

Field, John (1782–1837) Irish composer and pianist who settled in Russia (1804–32) then in London. He is particularly noted for his 19 *Nocturnes*, and was an influence on Chopin.

Field, Marshall (1834–1906) American department store pioneer.

Fielding, Henry (1707–54) English novelist and dramatist. His early satirical plays, e.g. *Pasquin*, provoked the British government into passing strict censorship laws and his unconventional novels which followed caused similar controversy. His greatest work, *Tom Jones* (1748), surveys the whole of English society with masterly insight and compassion. He also wrote important tracts on social problems and worked tirelessly against legal corruption.

Fields, Dame Gracie (1898–1979) British singer.

Fields, W. C. [William Claude Dukenfield] (1880–1946) American comedian and film actor (*You Can't Cheat an Honest Man* 1939), noted for his hard drinking, red nose, gravel voice and antipathy to children and animals.

Fifth dimension existence affirmed 1929 by the British physicist Sir Owen Willans Richardson (1879–1959).

Fifth-monarchy Men English religious movement active 1642 to 1661.

Fifth Republic in France, constitution came into force 5 October 1958.

Fiji, Polynesia, discovered 1643 by Abel Janszoon Tasman (*c.*1603–1659); British colony 1874–1970; now an independent republic.

Fillmore, Millard (1800–1874) 13th US president (1850–53).

Film first flexible transparent, suitable for motion pictures, invented 1889 by the American inventor George Eastman (1854–1932).

Filmer, Sir Robert (d.1653) English political writer (*Patriarcha* 1680).

Films in colour (Kinemacolour) first shown 1906.

Finland ruled by Sweden until 1808, by Russia 1808–1918; independent republic since 1918.

Finney, Albert (1936–) British stage and film actor (*Under the Volcano* 1984).

Firdausi (*c.*940–1020) Persian poet.

Firearms used in Europe in late 14th century; wheellock introduced in early 16th century; flintlock in late 16th century; percussion detonator invented 1805 by the Scottish minister Alexander Forsyth (1768–1843).

Fire engines first acquired by London insurance company 1722.

Fire extinguisher (1765–1854) first portable, invented 1816 by the English barrack-master, George William Manby.

Fire insurance pioneered by Nicholas Barbon 1666.

Fireplaces in Britain removed from the centre of the hall to the side wall in the 14th century.

Fire plugs put into water mains in Britain 1667.

Fire rules drawn up by the City of London 1189.

First of June sea battle between French and British 1794.

First Republic, France, proclaimed 22 September 1792, ended 1804.

First Triumvirate the political alliance in Rome of Caesar, Pompey and Crassus formed 60 BC to rule the state. Their union lasted ten years, and then civil war ensued.

First Triumvirate, Wars of the 49 BC Battle of Bagradas between Roman supporters of Caesar and the Numidians who favoured Pompey. The Romans were defeated. Battle of Zela 47 BC Caesar defeated Pharnaces, king of Pontus.

Fischer, Bobby [Robert James Fischer] (1943–) American chess player. A grandmaster at 15 he became the first US player to win the world championship (1972) when he won against Spassky.

Fischer-Dieskau, Dietrich (1925–) German baritone.

Fisher, John, Admiral Lord (1841–1920) British sailor.

Fishmongers Company, London, origins uncertain, first extant charter granted by King Edward III 1364.

Fisk University, Nashville, Tennessee, American negro university founded 1866.

Fiske, John (1842–1901) American philosopher.

Fitzgerald, Edward (1809–83) English poet (*The Rubaiyat of Omar Khayyam* 1859).

Fitzgerald, Lord Edward (1763–98) Irish patriot.

Fitzgerald, Ella (1918–96) American jazz singer whose highly praised vocal range, rhythmic subtlety and clarity of tone made her one of the most popular singers of her day.

Fitzgerald, F[rancis] Scott [Key] (1896–1940) American novelist and short-story writer. His works are moralistic fables set in 1920s 'Jazz Age' High Society and include *The Great Gatsby* and *Tender is the Night*.

Fitzherbert, Mrs Maria (1756–1837, m.1785) wife of King George IV.

Fitzwilliam Collection (1745–1816) bequeathed to the University of Cambridge by Viscount Richard Fitzwilliam.

Fiume *see* RIJEKA-SUSAK.

Flag Day USA, celebrated 14 June.

Flagstad, Kirsten (1895–1962) Norwegian soprano noted for her roles in Wagner's operas. She is regarded as one of the finest Wagnerian singers of all time.

Flaherty, Robert [Joseph] (1884–1951) American documentary film director. His films, e.g. *Nanook of the North*, set high standards for all following documentary film makers.

Flambard, Ranulf (d.1128) English statesman.

Flaminian Way from north of Rome to Ariminum on Adriatic coast, built 220 BC by the tribune Flaminius Gaius.

Flaminius, Gaius (d.217 BC) Roman democratic leader. He was killed trying to halt Hannibal's invasion of Etruria.

Flammarion, Camille (1842–1925) French astronomer.

Flamsteed, John (1646–1719) first English Astronomer-Royal.

Flatman, Thomas (1637–88) English artist and poet.

Flaubert, Gustave (1821–80) French novelist. His masterpiece is his first published novel, *Madame Bovary* (1857), a study of self-deception, adultery and suicide in rural France. Flaubert is noted for his meticulously impersonal and objective narrative.

Flaxman, John (1755–1826) English sculptor (*Saint Michael*).

Flecker, James Elroy (1884–1915) English poet (*Hassan* 1922).

Fleet Prison, London, founded in Norman times; burnt down 1666; rebuilt, but again destroyed 1780; rebuilt 1782; pulled down 1844.

Fleming, Sir Alexander (1881–1955) Scottish bacteriologist. He discovered the antibacterial qualities of the enzyme lysozome, the substance he dubbed 'penicillin' (1928). He shared the 1945 Nobel prize for physiology or medicine with Chain and Florey.

Fleming, Ian [Lancaster] (1908–64) English novelist. His series of novels featuring the British secret agent James Bond, e.g. *Goldfinger*, were enormous successes and have all been filmed.

Fleming, Sir John Ambrose (1849–1945) English electrical engineer.

Fleming, Margaret (1803–11) Scottish child prodigy.

Fleming, Sir Sandford (1827–1915) Scottish-born Canadian engineer.

Fletcher, John (1579–1625) English dramatist. One of the most popular dramatists of his day, he frequently collaborated with other dramatists, such as Shakespeare, but most notably with Sir Francis Beaumont, from 1606 to 1613. Their best-known works are tragicomedies such as *The Maid's Tragedy*. He also wrote several plays on his own.

Fleury, André Hercule, Cardinal (1653–1743) French statesman.

Flintlocks invented *c.*1635.

Flodden, Battle of between English and Scots, 9 September 1513.

Flogging in the British Navy abolished through the efforts of the Irish politician John Gordon Swift Macneill (1849–1926).

Floral Games first held at Toulouse May 1324.

Floréal French Revolutionary calendar month, 20 April–19 May.

Florence of Worcester (d.1118) English historian (*Chronicon*).

Florey, Howard Walter, Baron (1898–1968) Australian pathologist. He shared the 1945 Nobel prize for physiology or medicine with Sir Alexander Fleming and Chain for their work on penicillin.

Florida discovered March 1512 by Juan Ponce de Leon (1460–1521). Ceded by Spain to USA 1819; granted statehood 1845.

Florio, John (*c.*1553–1625) English translator (Montaigne's *Essays* 1603).

Flotow, Friedrich, Freiherr von (1812–83) German composer (*Martha* 1847).

Flour mill first steam, erected by John Rennie (1761–1821) at Blackfriars, London, 1784–88; burnt down 1791.

Fluorescence in nature discovered by the Irish-born scientist Sir George Gabriel Stokes (1819–1903).

Fluorescent lighting low voltage, first marketed 1938.

Fluorine first isolated 1886 by Henri Moissan (1852–1907).

Fluorine in drinking water beneficial effects in preventing tooth decay first demonstrated by the American doctor Frederick S. McKay (1874–1959).

Flying boat invented 1912 by the American aviator Glenn Hammond Curtiss (1878–1930).

Flying bomb first used by the Germans against the Allies 12 June 1944.

Flying Doctor Service Australia, founded by the Australian Inland Mission of the Presbyterian Church of Australia 1928.

'Flying Saucers' first so named by the American Kenneth Arnold, June 1947.

Flynn, Errol [Leslie Thomas Flynn] (1909–59) Australian-born American film actor. His starring roles in the swashbuckling tradition, e.g. *Captain Blood*, earned him considerable popularity.

Foch, Ferdinand (1851–1929) French general and marshal of France (1918). He was Commander-in-Chief of the Allied forces in March 1918, and led the Allies to victory following the arrival of US troops in July 1918.

Fohi *see* FUHI.

Fokine, Michel (1880–1942) Russian-born American ballet dancer and choreographer. With Diaghilev in Paris, he created a new style of ballet in which all the elements, dance, music, costume and *mise en scène*, formed a coherent whole.

Fokker, Anton Hermann Gerard (1890–1939) Dutch aviation pioneer.

Folger Shakespeare Memorial Library, Washington DC, opened 1932.

Fonda, Henry (1905–82) American film actor, often seen as the epitome of 'decent' America, a man determined to set injustices right.

Fonda, Jane [Seymour] (1937-) daughter of Henry Fonda. American film actress (*Klute* 1971), won recognition as a fine actress, although her outspoken opposition to the Vietnam war was heavily criticized.

Fontainebleau, Palace of, France, origins unknown, oldest building erected in 12th century, additions being made up to 19th century.

Fontana, Domenico (1543–1607) Italian architect.

Fontane, Theodor (1819–98) German writer (*Stine* 1890).

Fontenelle, Bernard le Bouvier de (1657–1757) French writer (*La Pluralité des mondes* 1686).

Fontenoy, Battle of between French and English, 11 May 1745.

Fonteyn, Dame Margot [Margaret Hookham] (1919–91) English ballerina. Regarded as one of the finest classical ballerinas of the century, she partnered Nureyev at the age of 43.

Food and Agriculture Organization (FAO) UN agency established in Rome, 16 October 1945.

Foot, Michael [Mackintosh] (1913–) British Labour politician. A leading left-winger, pacifist and CND member, he was secretary of state of employment (1974–76) and leader of the House of Commons (1976–79), and succeeded Callaghan as leader of the Labour Party (1980–83). His many books include biographies of Swift and Bevan.

Football Association formed 1863.

Foote, Samuel (1720–77) English playwright (*The Nabob* 1772).

Footlights in British theatres first used 1672.

Foppa, Vincenzo (*c.*1429–*c.*1516) Italian painter.

Forbes-Robertson, Sir Johnston (1853–1937) English actor.

Ford, Ford Madox [Ford Hermann Hueffer] (1873–1939) English novelist, poet and critic. Writer of over 80 novels, e.g. *The Good Soldier, No More Parades*, he also founded the *Transatlantic Review* in 1924 and gave generous encouragement to many writers.

Ford, Gerald R[udolph] (1913–) American Republican statesman and 38th president of the US (1974–77). He replaced Agnew as Nixon's vice-president in 1973, becoming president the following year, after Nixon's impeachment and resignation.

Ford, Henry (1863–1947) American car designer and manufacturer. His Model T Ford, first introduced in 1908, was enormously successful and its production line manufacture became a role model for much of industry.

Ford, John (1586–*c.*1640) English dramatist, notable for such revenge tragedies as *'Tis Pity She's a Whore* (1633). His bleak, objective vision of human suffering and his command of blank verse were highly praised by T.S. Eliot.

Ford, John [Sean Aloysius O'Fearna] (1895–1973) American film director. He is regarded as one of the greatest directors for his epic and poetic vision of history, particularly that of the American West, e.g. *Stagecoach* and *The Searchers.*

Ford Motor Works, USA, founded 1903 by Henry Ford (1863–1947).

Forefathers' Day, USA, celebrating the landing (1620) of the Pilgrim Fathers at Plymouth Rock. Celebrated 21 December.

Forester, C[ecil] S[cott] (1899–1966) British writer, creator of the Hornblower series (*Ship of the Line* 1938).

Formosa *see* TAIWAN.

Forster, E[dward] M[organ] (1879–1970) English novelist and critic. His novels, e.g. *Howard's End, A Passage to India*, are mainly concerned with moral and ethical choices, and the personal relationships of educated, middle-class people.

Forsyth, Rev. Alexander John (1768–1843) British inventor 1805 of the percussion lock.

Fort Duquesne, Pennsylvania, built 1754, burnt 1758.

Fortescue, Sir John (*c.*1394–*c.*1476) Lord Chief Justice.

Forth and Clyde Canal begun 1768 by John Smeaton (1724–92); completed 1790.

Forth Rail Bridge Scotland, designed by Sir John Fowler (1817–98) and Sir Benjamin Baker (1840–1907); constructed 1883–90 by Sir William Arrol (1839–1913).

Forth Road Bridge construction begun 21 November 1958, completed 1964.

Fort Sumter, Battle of American Civil War battle fought 12–14 April 1861.

Foscolo, Ugo (1778–1827) Italian writer (*Sepolcri* 1807).

Fosse, Robert Louis (Bob) (1927–1987) American dancer, director and choreographer (*Cabaret*, 1973).

Fosse Way Lincoln to Exeter, Roman road begun as frontier line against raiding forces by Publius Ostorius Scapula AD 47.

Foster, Birket (1825–99) English artist.

Foster, Stephen Collins (1826–64) American songwriter (*Old Folks at Home*).

Foucault, Michel (1926–84) French philosopher, psychologist and social critic (*Madness and Civilization* 1961).

Foucault pendulum to measure rotation of the Earth constructed 1851 by the French scientist Jean Foucault (1819–68).

Foulis, Robert (1707–76) Scottish bookseller and printer.

Fountains Abbey Cistercian house in Yorkshire, founded 1132; building completed 1526.

Fouquet, Jean (*c.*1415–*c.*1481) French painter (miniatures in *Book of Hours*).

Fouquier-Tinville, Antoine Quentin (1747–95) French revolutionary leader executed by guillotine.

Fourier, François Marie Charles (1772–1837) French socialist.

Fourier, Jean Baptiste Joseph, Baron (1768–1830) French mathematician.

'Fournier, Alain' [Henri Fournier] (1886–1914) French writer (*Le Grand Meaulnes* 1913) killed in action in the First World War.

Fourth Republic in France, constitution came into force 1946; collapsed 1958.

Fowler, Henry Watson (1858–1933) expert on English usage.

Fowler, John (1826–64) English engineer and inventor.

Fowler, Sir John (1817–98) English engineer.

Fox, Charles James (1749–1806) English Whig statesman. A formidable orator, he was strongly opposed to the wars against the American and French revolutionaries and was a vigorous opponent of the slave trade.

Fox, George (1624–91) English religious leader. Brought up a Puritan, he preached opposition to established religion and advocated peace and toleration. He founded the Society of Friends (known popularly as 'Quakers') in 1647.

Foxe's *Book of Martyrs* (1554–59) written by the English historian John Foxe (1516–87).

Fra Angelico [Fra Giovanni da Fiesole] (*c.*1387–1455) Italian painter.

Fracastoro, Girolamo (1483–1553) Italian physician.

Fragonard, Jean-Honoré (1732–1806) French painter. One of the greatest exponents of Rococo art, his early works were historical scenes on a grand scale, but he is known for his smaller, picturesquely pretty canvases.

Frame, Janet (Janet Paterson Frame Cluthal) (b.1924) New Zealand novelist and poet (*An Angel at my Table* 1984).

Frampton, Sir George (1860–1928) English sculptor (*Peter Pan*).

'France, Anatole' [Jacques Anatole Thibault] (1844–1924) French novelist (*Penguin Island* 1908).

France: monarchy, Merovingian (481–751), Carolingian (751–987), Capetian (987–1328), Valois (1328–1589), (Bourbon (1589–1792); 1st republic 1793–1804; 1st empire 1804–14; restored monarchy 1814–48; 2nd republic 1848–52; 2nd empire 1852–70; 3rd republic 1871–1940; German occupation and Vichy regime 1940–44; 4th republic 1946–58; 5th republic since 1958.

Francesca, Piero della *see* PIERO DELLA FRANCESCA.

Francesca da Rimini (d.*c.*1285) Italian heroine, wife of Giovanni Malatesta. She was murdered.

Francis I (1708–65) Holy Roman emperor (1745–65).

Francis I (1494–1547) king of France (1515–47).

Francis II (1768–1835) Holy Roman emperor (1792–1806).

Francis II (1544–60) king of France (1559–60).

Francis Borgia, Saint (1510–72) general of the Society of Jesus.

Franciscan Order founded 1208 by Saint Francis of Assisi; constitution established 1209.

Francis de Sales, Saint (1567–1622) French Roman Catholic prelate and writer. Canonized in 1665

Francis of Assisi, Saint [Giovanni Bernardone] (1181–1226) Italian monk. He abandoned a military career to care for the poor and founded a 'brotherhood' of friars in 1210, and, in 1212, an order for women, the Poor Clares. He preached poverty, chastity and obedience to the Church, and received the stigmata in 1224. He was canonized in 1228.

Francis Xavier, Saint (1506–52) Spanish missionary who came under the influence of Ignatius Loyola and was one of the first members of the Society of Jesus. In 1542 he was appointed papal nuncio in the Indies, where he worked as a missionary, becoming known as the 'apostle of the Indies'. He proselytised in Ceylon (Sri Lanka), Malacca and the Moluccas, and visited Japan. He died while planning a mission to China and was canonized in 1622.

Franck, César [Auguste] (1822–90) Belgian-born French composer. His best works were written late in life, e.g. his string quartet, and his work received public acclaim only after his death. Le *Chasseur Maudit* 1882.

Franck, James (1882–1964) German-born American physicist. With the German physicist Gustav Ludwig Hertz (1887–1975), he shared the 1925 Nobel prize for physics for work on the quantum theory, notably the effects of bombarding atoms with electrons.

Franco [Bahamonde], Francisco (1892–1975) Spanish general and dictator. He led the right-wing rebellion against the Spanish Republican government during the Spanish Civil War (1936–39). He became leader of the Fascist Falange Party in 1937, and ruled Spain from 1939 until his death.

Franco-Prussian War began July 1870, ended February 1871.

Frank, Anne (1929–45) German-born Dutch Jewish girl. Her journal describing her family's experiences while hiding from the Nazis is one of the most moving accounts of the terrible suffering of the Jewish people during the World War II.

Frank, Bruno (1887–1945) German novelist (*Trenck* 1926).

Frank, Leonhard (1882–1961) German novelist (*Karl und Anna* 1928).

Frankenstein novel by Mary Shelley (1797-1851) written 1816–18; filmed in numerous versions since 1908, most memorably in the version by Hollywood director James Whale 1931.

Frankfurter, Felix (1882–1965) American Supreme Court judge.

Franklin, Benjamin (1706–90) American statesman and author. He helped draft the American Declaration of Independence, and played an active role in American political life for most of his long life. He published a highly entertaining *Autobiography* and also invented the lightning conductor.

Franklin, Sir John (1786–1847) Arctic explorer.

Franklin, Rosalind Elsie (1920–58) British chemist. Her X-ray crystallography research into DNA contributed to the discovery of its structure by James Watson and Crick.

Franz, Robert (1815–92) German composer.

Franz Ferdinand (1863–1914) Austrian archduke, assassinated by Serbian nationalists in 1914. Austria then attacked Serbia which resulted in the start of the First World War.

Franz Joseph (1830–1916) Austrian emperor (1848–1916).

Franz Joseph Land Arctic archipelago discovered 1873 by the German explorer Karl Weyprecht (1838–81).

Fraser, John Malcolm (1930–) Australian statesman (prime minister 1975–83).

Fraser, Simon (*c.*1776–1862) American-born explorer of Canada.

Fraser River British Columbia, discovered 1793 by the explorer Sir Alexander Mackenzie.

Fraunhofer lines in solar spectrum discovered by the English scientist William Wollaston (1766–1828), studied by German physicist Joseph von Fraunhofer (1787–1826).

Frayn, Michael (1933–) English dramatist and novelist noted for his dry, sardonic humour.

Frazer, Sir James George (1854–1941) Scottish scholar and anthropologist whose study of religious customs and myth influenced Freud and many 20th-century writers. (*The Golden Bough* 1890.)

Fréchette, Louis Honoré (1839–1908) French Canadian writer.

Fredegunde (*c.*546–*c.*598) Frankish queen.

Frederick I [Barbarossa] (*c.*1123–1190) Holy Roman emperor.

Frederick I (d.1533) king of Denmark (1523–33).

Frederick I (1657–1713) king of Prussia (1701–13).

Frederick II (1194–1250) Holy Roman emperor (1212–50).

Frederick II (1534–88) king of Denmark (1559–88).

Frederick II the Great (1712–86) king of Prussia (1740–86).

Frederick III (1831–88) emperor of Germany.

Frederick III (1415–93) Holy Roman emperor (1440–93).

Frederick III (1609–70) king of Denmark (1648–70).

Frederick IV (1671–1730) king of Denmark (1699–1730).

Frederick V (1723–66) king of Denmark (1746–66).

Frederick VI (1768–1839) king of Denmark (1808–39).

Frederick VII (1808–63) king of Denmark (1848–63).

Frederick VIII (1843–1912) king of Denmark (1906–12).

Frederick IX (1899–1972) king of Denmark (1947–72).

Frederick William I (1688–1740) king of Prussia (1713–40).

Frederick William II (1744–97) king of Prussia (1786–97).

Frederick William III (1770–1840) king of Prussia (1797–1840).

Frederick William IV (1795–1861) king of Prussia (1840–61).

Frederick William [the Great Elector] (1620–88) Elector of Brandenburg from 640.

Fredericksburg, Battle of American Civil War, 13 December 1862.

Free Church of Scotland formed 1843.

Freedom British periodical, began publication 1886.

Freeman, Edward Augustus (1823–92) English historian.

Freemasonry derived from Lodges of English and Scottish masons in the 17th century; Mother Grand Lodge inaugurated in London 1717.

Freetown, Sierra Leone capital, first settled 1787.

Frege, [Friedrich Ludwig] Gottlob (1848–1925) German mathematician and philosopher. He is regarded as having laid the foundations for both modern mathematical logic and the philosophy of language.

Freiligrath, Ferdinand (1810–76) German poet.

Fremont, John Charles (1813–90) American explorer.

French, Sir John [Denton Pinkstone] [1st Earl of Ypres] (1852–1925) English field marshal. He commanded the British Expeditionary Force in France (1914–15) and became Lord Lieutenant of Ireland (1918–21) during the Anglo-Irish War.

French Equatorial Africa former French Overseas Territories of Chad, Gabon, Middle Congo and Ubangi-Shari (1910–58); first settled 1839; assumed present name 1910.

French Foreign Legion first formed 1831.

French Guiana, South America, first settled 1604; became Department of France 1947.

French language earliest known document, the 'Strasbourg Oaths', dated 842.

French Revolution began June 1789; Consulate established November 1799.

French Revolutionary Calendar began 21–22 September 1792, ended 31 December 1805.

French Revolutionary Era, First 1792–1804.

French Revolutionary Wars 1792–1802.

French Somaliland *see* DJIBOUTI.

French West Africa former group of French Overseas Territories (1895–1958) comprising Senegal, Mauritania, French Sudan, Burkina-Faso, Niger, French Guinea, Ivory Coast, Dahomey.

Freneau, Philip (1752–1832) American poet.

Frenssen, Gustav (1863–1945) German novelist (*Jorn Uhl* 1901).

Frere, Sir Bartle (1815–84) Scottish-born statesman.

Frescobaldi, Girolamo (1583–1643) Italian organist and composer.

Freud, Anna (1895–1982) Austrian psychologist, daughter of Sigmund Freud. She pioneered child psychology in the UK.

Freud, Lucian (1922–) German-born British painter. The grandson of Sigmund Freud, he is renowned for his nudes and portraits, often painted from odd angles in an extreme-realist style.

Freud, Sigmund (1856–1939) Austrian psychiatrist who founded psychoanalysis. His writings have been enormously influential on 20th-century thought. The main tenet of Freudian theory is that neuroses and dreams are repressed manifestations of sexual desire. His stress on the importance of sex was rejected by Adler and Jung.

Freytag, Gustav (1816–95) German writer (*Soll und Haben* 1855).

Frick, Henry Clay (1849–1919) American industrialist.

Fricker, Racine (1920–90) English composer (*Rapsodia concertante* 1954).

Friedman, Milton (1912–) American economist. His controversial monetarist theory of economics, stressing the need for minimal government intervention, became the dominant economic theory of the 1980s. He was awarded the 1976 Nobel prize for economics.

Friedrich, Casper David (1774–1840) German Romantic painter. Largely uninfluenced by other artists or trends, his work was highly controversial in its treatment of landscape.

Friends, Society of [Quakers] founded 1647 by the Englishman George Fox (1624–90).

Frimaire French revolutionary calendar month, 21 November to 20 December.

Friml, Rudolf (1879–1972) Czech composer (*Katinka* 1915).

Frisch, Otto Robert (1904–79) Austrian-born British nuclear physicist. He and his aunt, Lise Meitner, discovered nuclear fission, and their work led directly to the invention of the atom bomb.

Frisch, Ragnar *see* TINBERGEN, JAN.

Frith, William (1819–1909) English painter (*Derby Day*).

Frobisher, Sir Martin (*c.*1535–1594). English navigator

Froebel System (1782–1852) of kindergarten education founded 1816 by the German educationalist Friedrich Wilhelm August Froebel (1782–1852).

Froissart, Jean (*c.*1337–1410) French historian (*Chroniques*).

Fromentin, Eugène (1820–76) French artist and writer.

Fronde, The French civil war begun 1648, ended 1653.

Frontenac, Louis de Buade, Comte de (1620–98) French statesman.

Fronto, Marcus Cornelius (*c.*100–*c.*166) Roman orator.

Frost, Robert [Lee] (1874–1963) American poet. His quiet, lyrical poems, e.g. 'Stopping by Woods on a Snow Evening', have been admired for their enigmatic use of symbolism.

Froude, James Anthony (1818–94) English historian (*History of England* 1856–70).

Fructidor French revolutionary calendar month, 18 August to 16 September.

Frumentius, Saint apostle of Ethiopia in 4th century; feast celebrated 27 October.

Fry, C[harles] B[urgess] (1872–1956) English sportsman, regarded as one of the greatest all-round sportsmen ever, representing England in athletics, cricket and soccer.

Fry, Christopher (1907–) English dramatist whose verse dramas, e.g. *The Lady's Not for Burning*, were popular with both critics and public.

Fry, Elizabeth (1780–1845) English social reformer. A Quaker and preacher, she campaigned for prison reform and founded hostels for the homeless.

Fry, Joseph (1728–87) English Quaker businessman.

Fry, Roger (1866–1934) English painter and art critic.

Fuad I (1868–1936) king of Egypt (1922–36).

Fuad II, Ahmed (1950–) king of Egypt (1952–54).

Fuchs, Klaus [Emil Julius] (1911–88) German-born British physicist. He began work on British atom-bomb research in 1941 and was jailed in 1950 for 14 years for passing details to the Soviet Union.

Fuchs, Sir Vivian Ernest (1908–) English explorer and scientist. He led the Commonwealth Trans-Antarctic Expedition (1955–58), which made the first overland crossing of Antarctica.

Fuentes, Carlos (1928–) Mexican writer and diplomat (*The Old Gringo* 1985).

Fugard, Athol (1932–) South African dramatist whose plays, e.g. *Boesman and Lena*, explore the tragedy of racial tension caused by apartheid in South Africa.

Fuhi *or* **Fohi** the first emperor of China, said to have founded China in 2850 BC and supposed to be the Noah of the Bible.

Fulk (1092–1143) count of Anjou and king of Jerusalem.

Fuller, [Richard] Buckminster (1895–1983) American architect and engineer. He invented the 'geodesic dome', a lightweight framework consisting of a set of polygons in the shape of a shell.

uller, Thomas (1608–61) English religious historian.

ulton, Robert (1765–1815) American inventor of the steamship.

ulvia (d.40 BC) wife of Marc Antony.

urfural solvent discovered by the German scientist Johann Wolfgang Döbereiner (1780–1849).

urness, Christopher, Baron Furness (1852–1912) British shipowner.

urniss, Harry (1854–1925) Irish-born humorous artist.

Furtwängler, Wilhelm (1886–1954) German conductor. He became one of the most popular conductors in Europe, particularly for his highly charged interpretations of Wagner's music.

Fuseli, Henry [Johann Heinrich Füssli] (1741–1825) Swiss-born British painter and illustrator. His paintings are mannered and Romantic with a sense of the grotesque and macabre.

Fustel de Coulanges, Numa Denis (1830–89) French historian.

Futurism art movement identified 1909 by the Italian poet Filippo Tommaso Marinetti (1878–); movement disintegrated *c.*1915).

G

Gabin, Jean [Jean Alexis Montgorgé] (1904–76) French actor (*Pépé le Moko* 1937).

Gable, [William] Clark (1901–60) American film actor. His rugged good looks, sardonic wit and easy-going charm made him one of the most popular film stars of his day. Among his films was *Gone with the Wind* (1939).

Gabon west central Africa; first settled by the French 1839; made part of the French Congo 1888; became independent 1960.

Gabor, Dennis (1900–1979) Hungarian-born British engineer. He was awarded the 1971 Nobel prize for physics for his invention (in 1947) of the hologram.

Gaboriau, Emile (1835–73) French novelist (*Monsieur Lecoq* 1869).

Gabriel, Jacques Ange (*c.*1698–1782) French architect.

Gaddafi *or* **Qaddafi, Moammar al-** (1942–) Libyan statesman and military dictator. He took power in a coup in 1969 and became president in 1977. Regarded almost universally as an unpredictable and often dangerous leader, Gaddafi has openly supported terrorist groups around the world.

Gaddi, Taddeo (d.1366) Italian painter (*Life of the Virgin*).

Gadolinium chemical element first isolated 1880 by the Swiss chemist Jean Charles Galissard de Marignac (1817–94).

Gaelic League founded in Dublin 1893.

Gagarin, Yuri [Alekseevich] (1934–68) Soviet cosmonaut, who became, on 12 April 1961, the first person in space, when his Vostok satellite circled the earth. He died in a plane crash.

Gage, Thomas (1721–87) English general.

Gainsborough, Thomas (1727–88) English painter. He worked as a portrait painter, but his keen interest in landscape painting pervades most of his work, his sitters often being portrayed out of doors. He developed a light, rapid painting style based on a delicate palette. His works include a portrait of Mrs Siddons.

Gaitskell, Hugh [Todd Naylor] (1906–63) British Labour politician. He was regarded as being on the right of his party, having introduced, as chancellor of the exchequer (1950–51), national health service charges. He was Labour Party leader (1955–63).

Galápagos Islands archipelago in the Pacific, discovered by the Spanish 1535; annexed by Ecuador 1832.

Galba (3 BC–AD 69) Roman emperor (68–69). He was assassinated.

Galbraith, John Kenneth (1908–) Canadian-born American economist, diplomat and author. He has been notably critical of the wastefulness of capitalist society. He was American ambassador to India (1961–63). His works include *The Affluent Society* (1958).

Galen, Claudius (*c.*130–*c.*201) Greek physician.

Galerius (d.311) Roman emperor (305–311).

Galiani, Ferdinando (1728–87) Italian economist.

Galicia ruled by Poland 1372–1772, by Austria 1772–1919, by Poland 1919–39, by Soviet Union 1945–91; now part of independent republic of Ukraine.

Galilei, Galileo (1564–1642) Italian astronomer, mathematician and natural philosopher. An innovative thinker and experimenter, he demonstrated the isochronism of the pendulum and showed that falling bodies of differing weight descend at the same rate. He also developed the refracting telescope and became convinced of the truth of Copernicus's theory that the earth revolved around the sun. He was unable to prove it and was forced to retract his support publicly.

Galle, Johann (1812–1910) German astronomer (observed the planet Neptune, 23 September 1846).

Gallegos, Rómulo (1884–1969) Venezuelan writer (*Dona Barbara* 1929).

Galli-Curci, Amelita (1882–1963) Italian operatic singer.

Gallic Wars 58–50 BC the eight campaigns by Julius Caesar to bring about the conquest of Gaul. Major battles included Bibract (58 BC) and Alesia (52 BC), when Vercingetorix, leader of the Gauls, was defeated and captured. Caesar's two unsuccessful invasions of Britain were part of the Gallic Wars.

Galliéni, Joseph Simon (1849–1916) French statesman.

Gallienus (d.268) Roman emperor (253–268). He was assassinated.

Gallipoli, Turkey, First World War, first Allied landings 25 April 1915; withdrawal 8 January 1916.

Gallitzin, Dmitri Augustin (1770–1840) Russian-born missionary in America.

Gallium chemical element first isolated 1875 by the

French scientist Paul Emile Lecoq de Boisbaudran (1838–1912).

Gallon Imperial standard measure legalized in Britain 1824.

Gallup, George Horace (1901–84) American statistician. He developed the opinion poll into a sophisticated device, the 'Gallup Poll', for testing public opinion, most notably on elections.

Gallus (d.253) Roman emperor (251–253). He was murdered.

Galsworthy, John (1867–1933) English novelist and dramatist. His plays, e.g. *Strife*, attacked social injustice. His novels include the Forsyte saga triology (1906–22). He was awarded the 1932 Nobel prize for literature.

Galt, Sir Alexander Tilloch (1817–93) British-born statesman in Canada.

Galt, John (1779–1839) Scottish novelist (*Annals of the Parish* 1821).

Galton, Sir Francis (1822–1911) English scientist and explorer. A cousin of Charles Darwin, he travelled widely in Africa and made significant contributions to meteorology and to heredity. He also developed the science of fingerprinting.

Galvani, Luigi (1737–98) Italian scientist.

Galvanometer mirror invented by Lord Kelvin (1824–1907).

Gama, Vasco da (*c*.1469–1525) Portuguese explorer and navigator. He discovered the route to India round the Cape of Good Hope (1497–99), reaching Calicut (India) on 23 May 1498. He became Portuguese viceroy in India in 1524.

Gambetta, Léon (1838–82) French statesman.

Gambia, The sold to English merchants by the Portuguese 1588; made an independent British Crown Colony 1843; incorporated in the West African settlements 1866; again made separate Crown Colony 1888; gained independence within the Commonwealth 1965; formed the Confederation of Senegambia with Senegal 1982.

Gamma rays discovered 1900 by Paul Villard.

Gandhi, Indira (1917–84) Indian stateswoman and prime minister. The daughter of Nehru, she became prime minister (1966–77, 1980–84) of India. Her second term of office saw much ethnic strife and she was assassinated by her Sikh bodyguards. Her son Rajiv Gandhi succeeded her.

Gandhi, Mahatma [Mohandas Karamchand Gandhi] (1869–1948) Indian nationalist statesman and spiritual leader ('Mahatma' means 'Great Soul'). A passionate advocate of non-violent resistance, Gandhi's long campaign (began 1 August 1920) against British rule in India, using tactics of civil disobedience through passive resistance and hunger strikes, had great influence on world public opinion. He also struggled for reconciliation between Hindus and Moslems, and championed the cause of the Hindu Harijan caste of 'untouchables'. He was assassinated 30 January 1948 by a Hindu extremist, in the wake of India's independence and partition.

Gandhi, Rajiv (1944–91) Indian politician. He succeeded his mother, Indira Gandhi, as prime minister (1984–90) but was assassinated in a suicide bomb attack.

Gantt Chart in industrial management devised by the American engineer Henry Lawrence Gantt (1861–1919).

Gapon, Georgy Apollonovich (1870–1906) Russian priest and politician. He was murdered.

Garamond, Claude (d.1561) French type designer.

Garbo, Greta [Greta Lovisa Gustafson] (1905–90) Swedish-born American film actress noted for her austere and remote beauty. Her films include *Mata Hari* (1931) and *Queen Christina* (1933).

García Lorca, Federigo *see* LORCA, FEDERIGO GARCÍA.

Garden cities idea introduced into England (1898) by Sir Ebenezer Howard (1850–1928); Letchworth begun 1903.

Gardiner, Samuel Rawson (1829–1902) English historian.

Gardiner, Stephen (*c*.1483–1555) bishop of Winchester.

Gardner, Ava [Lavinia] (1922–90) American film actress (*The Night of the Iguana* 1964).

Gardner, Erle Stanley (1889–1970) American detective-story writer (the Perry Mason series).

Garfield, James Abram (1831–81) 20th US president (1881). He was murdered.

Garibaldi, Giuseppe (1807–82) Italian patriot and leader. Forced into exile in 1834, he returned during the year of revolutions, 1848, and took part in the defence of Rome against the French, and, in 1860, with a force a thousand strong, he took Naples and Sicily for the newly united Italy. He is regarded as the most significant figure in the struggle for Italian independence. March to Rome 1862.

Garland, Judy [Frances Gumm] (1922–69) American film actress and singer. She became one of the most loved child stars of the cinema in *The Wizard of Oz* (1939) and later starred in such films as *Easter Parade* (1948) and *A Star is Born* (1954).

Garnard (d.635) king of Picts (631–635) *see* Appendix.

Garnett, David (1892–1981) English novelist (*Lady into Fox* 1922).

Garnett, Edward (1868–1937) English man of letters.

Garnier, Francis (1839–73) French explorer. He was killed.

'Garofalo, Il' (1481–1559) Italian painter.

Garrick, David (1717–79) English actor and dramatist. A pupil of Samuel Johnson at Lichfield, he accompanied him to London in 1737, soon making his mark as an actor. At home with tragedy, comedy or farce, he dominated the English stage for many years, and was actor-manager of Drury Lane Theatre 1747–76.

Garrison, William Lloyd (1805–79) American abolitionist.

Garter, Order of the founded by Edward III *c.*1348.

Garth, Sir Samuel (1661–1719) English poet (*The Dispensary* 1699).

Gartnart (d.597) king of Picts (657–663) *see* Appendix.

Garvin, James Louis (1868–1947) Irish-born journalist (edited *The Observer* 1908–42).

Gary, Indiana, founded 1905 by the US Steel Corporation and named after Elbert Henry Gary (1846–1927).

Gas, coal first produced in quantity by the Scottish inventor William Murdock (1754–1839).

Gas, poison first used in the First World War by Germans 22 April 1915; first used by British 25 September 1915.

Gascoigne, George (*c.*1525–1577) English poet (*Jocasta* 1575).

Gaskell, Mrs Elizabeth [Elizabeth Cleghorn Stevenson] (1810–65) English novelist. Her novels, e.g. *North and South*, are often concerned with the injustices of the 'two-nation' society of 19th-century England, although her most popular novel is *Cranford* (1853), a gentle study of life in a small village.

Gas Light and Coke Company first gas company, granted charter 1812.

Gas masks issued to civilians in Britain 1939.

Gassendi, Pierre (1592–1655) French scientist.

Gas-turbine-powered car first built by the British Rover Company 1950.

Gatling gun invented 1861–62 by the American engineer Richard Jordan Gatling (1818–1903).

GATT (General Agreement on Tariffs and Trade) signed 1947 by 23 nations; 96 nation members by 1990.

Gatty, Harold Charles (1903–57) Australian-born pioneer aviator.

Gauden, John (1605–1662) bishop of Worcester, theologian and probable author of *Eikon Basilike* (1649).

Gaudi, Antoni (1852–1926) Catalan architect.

Gaudier-Brzeska, Henri (1891–1915) French sculptor. He was killed in action in the First World War.

Gauguin, Paul (1848–1903) French painter. One of the greatest exponents of Postimpressionism, his interest in primitive art led to him settling in the South Pacific islands, where he painted some of his most important masterpieces.

Gaul the ancient name of France and Belgium. Its people, termed Galatae by the Greeks and Galli or Celtae by the Romans, came originally from Asia, and invading eastern Europe were driven westward and settled in Spain (in Gallicia), northern Italy (Cisalpine Gaul), France and Belgium (Transalpine Gaul) and the British Isles (the lands of the Cymry or Gaels). Rome burned down by Gauls under Brennus 390 BC; Roman defeat of Gauls and Etruscans at Lake Vadimonian 283 BC, Rome became ruler of northern Italy; Gauls invade Greece 280 BC; conquest of Cisalpine Gaul by Rome completed 222 BC; Roman province in Southern Gaul (hence Provence) established 120 BC; Gallic Wars of Caesar 58–50 BC; Roman conquest of Gaul complete 50 BC

Gaunt, John of, Duke of Lancaster (1340–1399).

Gauss, Karl Friedrich (1777–1855) German mathematician.

Gautier, Théophile(1811–72) French writer (*Mlle de Maupin* 1835).

'Gavarni, Paul' [Hippolyte Chevalier] (1804–66) French humorous artist.

Gaveston, Piers, Earl of Cornwall (d.1312) favourite of Edward II. He was executed.

Gay, John (1685–1732) English dramatist and poet. His masterpiece is *The Beggars' Opera* (1728), the ballad opera on which Brecht based his *Threepenny Opera*.

Gay-Lussac, Joseph Louis (1778–1850) French scientist.

Gaza a city and port at the southeastern corner of the Mediterranean. In Biblical times it was a Philistine city; capture by Alexander 332 BC; administered by Egypt 1949–67; occupied by Israel 1967.

Gdansk *see* DANZIG.

Ged, William (1690–1749) Scottish inventor 1725 of stereotyping.

Geddes, Andrew (1783–1839) Scottish painter.

Geddes, Sir Eric (1875–1937) British statesman.

Geertgen Van Haarlem [Geertgen tot Sint Jans] (*c.*1462–*c.*1490) Dutch painter (*The Bones of St John the Baptist*).

Geiger counter invented 1908 by the scientists Hans Geiger (1882–1945) and Lord Rutherford (1871–1937).

Geikie, Sir Archibald (1835–1924) Scottish geologist.

Geissler's tube invented by the German scientist Heinrich Geissler (1814–79).

Gelasius II [John of Gaeta] (d.1119) pope (1118–19).

Gelasius, St (d.496) pope (492–496).

Gell-Mann, Murray (1929–) American physicist. He

introduced the quark hypothesis into physics and was awarded the 1969 Nobel prize for physics for his research into particle physics.

General Agreement on Tariffs and Trade *see* GATT.

General Medical Council, London, held first meeting 23 November 1858.

General Strike, United Kingdom, 3–13 May 1926.

Genet, Jean (1910–86) French dramatist and novelist. His works are often based on his experiences in the criminal underworld where he spent much of his life and include *Les Bonnes* ('The Maids').

Geneva Convention establishing the International Red Cross held 1864.

Geneviève, Saint (d.512) patron saint of Paris.

Genghis Khan *or* **Jenghiz Khan** [originally Temujin] (*c.*1162–1227) Mongol leader who united the Mongol tribes and conquered China, establishing an empire that stretched from the Black Sea to the Pacific.

Genlis, Stéphanie Félicité Ducrest de St Aubin, Comtesse de (1746–1830) French writer (*Mémoires* 1825).

Genovesi, Antonio (1712–69) Italian philosopher.

Genseric (*c.*390–477) king of the Vandals (428–477) who seized large tracts of Roman lands in Gaul, Spain and North Africa and who sacked Rome in 455.

Gentile da Fabriano (*c.*1370–1427) Italian painter.

Gentleman's Magazine, The founded 1731 by 'Sylvanus Urban' (Edward Cave) (1691–1754).

Gentlemen-at-Arms the sovereign's personal bodyguard, established by King Henry VIII 1509.

Geoffrey of Monmouth (*c.*1100–1154) British divine and historian.

Geographical Society, Royal, London, founded 1830 by Sir John Barrow (1764–1848).

Geologists' Association, London, founded 17 December 1858.

Geometry, descriptive study founded 1771 by the French mathematician Gaspard Monge (1746–1818).

George, Henry (1839–97) American propounder of the 'single-tax' system (*Progress and Poverty* 1879).

George, Stefan (1868–1933) German poet.

George I (1660–1727) elector of Hanover (1698–1727) and king of Great Britain and Ireland (1714–27) *see* Appendix.

George II (1683–1760) elector of Hanover and king of Great Britain and Ireland (1727–60) *see* Appendix.

George III (1738–1820) elector of Hanover (1760–1815), king of Hanover (1815–20) and king of Great Britain and Ireland (1760–1820) *see* Appendix.

George IV (1762–1830) Prince Regent (1812–20), king of Hanover and king of Great Britain (1820–30) *see* Appendix.

George V (1865–1936) king of Great Britain and Ireland and emperor of India (1910–36) *see* Appendix.

George VI (1895–1952) king of Great Britain and last emperor of India (1936–52) *see* Appendix.

George I (1845–1913) king of Greece (1863–1913). He was assassinated.

George II (1890–1947) king of Greece (1922–23).

George Cross and George Medal British order instituted 23 September 1940.

George Washington Bridge, New York to New Jersey, constructed 1927–31.

Georgia (Gruzia, in Caucasus) acknowledged Russian suzerainty 1783; Soviet Socialist Republic, USSR, declared independent 1918; became a constituent republic of the USSR 1936; became independent republic on dissolution of the USSR April 1991.

Georgia, USA, founded as a colony 1733; entered Union 1788.

Gerard (d.1108) archbishop of York (1100–08).

Gerard, John (1545–1612) English herbalist.

Gerard, John (1564–1637) English Jesuit.

Gerhardie, William (1895–1977) English writer (*The Polyglots* 1925).

Géricault, Théodore (1791–1824) French Romantic painter. The realism and baroque dynamism of his work had a huge influence on many painters.

German, Sir Edward (1862–1936) English composer (*Merrie England* 1902).

Germanicus (15 BC– AD 19) Roman soldier.

Germanium chemical element first isolated 1886 by the German chemist Clemens Alexander Winkler (1838–1904).

German silver alloy discovered by the German scientist Ernst Augustus Geitner (1783–1852).

Germany separated from France by Treaty of Verdun (843); ruled by emperors, Saxon (919–1024), Salian (1024–1125), Welf and Hohenstaufen (1125–1254), Hapsburg and Luxemburg (1273–1457), Hapsburg (1457–1806); Confederation of Rhine (1806–12); German Confederation (1812–66); North German Confederation (1867–71); German Empire (Hohenzollern) (1871–1918); Weimar Republic (1919–33); 'Third Empire' (Nazi Regime) (1933–45); Allied Occupation after 1945; Bizonia 1946 and Trizonia 1947 became German Federal Republic 1949; Russian Zone became German Democratic Republic 1949; end of the Cold War and opening of the Berlin Wall 1989 led to German reunification 1 July 1990.

Gerry, Elbridge Thomas (1837–1927) American founder 1874 of the American Society for the Prevention of Cruelty to Children.

Gershwin, George (1898–1937) American composer and pianist (*Rhapsody in Blue* 1924). He and his brother, the lyricist **Ira Gershwin** (1896–1983), created several very popular musicals now considered masterpieces of American music.

Gerson, Jean Charlier de (1363–1429) French theologian to whom authorship of *The Imitation of Christ* is sometimes attributed instead of to Thomas à Kempis.

Gerstäcker, Friedrich (1816–72) German travel writer.

Gertrude, Saint (1256–*c.*1301).

Gervase of Canterbury (*fl* 1150–1200) English historian.

Gesenius, Heinrich Friedrich Wilhelm (1786–1842) Hebrew lexicographer.

Gesner, Konrad von (1516–65) Swiss bibliographer and naturalist.

Getty, J[ean] Paul (1892–1976) American industrialist and art collector, renowned for his wealth, miserliness and acquisition of works of art, now kep in a specially built museum in California.

Gettysburg, Battle of American Civil War battle, 1 to 3 July 1863; **Address of** delivered by Abraham Lincoln 19 November 1863.

Ghana (formerly Gold Coast) West Africa, settled by the Portuguese 1482; British colony established 1874; united with British Togoland 1957 and became republic within the Commonwealth 1960.

Ghazali, Abu Hamid Mohammed al [Algazel] (1058–1111) Muslim theologian.

Ghent Cathedral built 1274–1554 (crypt 941).

Ghent, Treaty of between the USA and Great Britain (ending the War of 1812), signed 24 December 1814.

Ghent, University of founded by King William of Württemberg 1816.

Ghiberti, Lorenzo (*c.*1378–1455) Italian sculptor.

Ghirlandaio, Domenico [Domenico Curradi] (1449–94) Florentine painter who ran a workshop with his brothers **Benedetto Ghirlandaio** (1458–97) and **Davide Ghirlandaio** (1452–1525), where he produced frescos and altarpieces for a number of churches in Florence. His son, **Ridolfo Ghirlandaio** (1483–1561), was Michelangelo's tutor. His works include *Adoration of the Shepherds*).

Giacometti, Alberto (1901–66) Swiss sculptor and painter. He became a Surrealist in 1930 and was influenced by Sartre's existentialism.

Giap, Vo Nguyen (1912–) Vietnamese general. He led the Viet Minh army against the French and commanded the North Vietnamese army against the US during the Vietnam War.

Gibbon, Edward (1737–94) English historian. His masterpiece is his *History of the Decline and Fall of the Roman Empire* (1776–88), a work that remains a great historical study.

Gibbons, Grinling (1648–1720) Dutch-born sculptor.

Gibbons, Orlando (1583–1625) English composer (*Fantasies* 1610).

Gibbs, James (1682–1754) Scottish architect.

Gibbs, Sir Vicary (1751–1820) English judge.

Gibraltar settled 711; conquered by Spain 1462; captured by British 1704 and ceded by Spain to Britain 1713; besieged by French and Spanish 1780–83.

Gibson, John (1790–1866) Welsh sculptor.

Gide, André (1869–1951) French writer (*Les Faux-Monnayeurs* 1926).

Gielgud, Sir [Arthur] John (1904–) English stage and film actor and producer. Regarded as one of the leading Shakespearian actors of the 20th century, he has also made appearances in several Hollywood films.

Gierek, Edward (1913–) Polish Communist statesman. He became leader of the Polish United Workers Party following Gomulka's resignation in 1971. He presided over increasing industrial unrest and the rise of the union Solidarity.

Gierke, Otto von (1841–1921) German legal and political thinker.

Gieseking, Walter (1895–1956) French pianist.

Gifford, William (1756–1826) English writer and editor.

Gigli, Beniamino (1890–1957) Italian operatic singer.

Gilbert, Sir Alfred (1854–1934) English sculptor (*Eros* in Piccadilly Circus).

Gilbert, Sir Humphrey (*c.*1539–1583). English explorer. He was drowned at sea.

Gilbert, William (*c.*1540–1603) English pioneer in magnetism (*De Magnete* 1600).

Gilbert, Sir W[illiam] S[chwenck] (1836–1911) English dramatist and librettist. His collaboration with the composer **Sir Arthur Sullivan** (1842–1900) resulted in the popular 'Savoy Operas', e.g. *Trial by Jury* (1875), *The Gondoliers* and *The Mikado*, of which there are 13 in all and which have retained their popularity.

Gilbert and Ellice Islands, Western Pacific, proclaimed a British protectorate 1892; annexed by Britain 1915 and remained a British colony until 1975; achieved full independence 1979.

Gilbertines English religious order founded at Sempringham (Lincs.) 1135 by St Gilbert (1083–1139).

Gildas, Saint (*c.*500–570) British historian.

Gill, [Arthur] Eric [Rowton] (1882–1940) English sculptor, engraver, typographer and writer. His work has been influential in several areas of art and design.

Gillespie, Dizzy [John Birks Gillespie] (1917–93) American jazz trumpeter, bandleader and composer, renowned as a virtuoso trumpeter.

Gillray, James (1757–1815) English political caricaturist.

Gilmore, Patrick Sarsfield (1829–92) Irish-born bandmaster and composer (*When Johnny Comes Marching Home* 1863).

Ginkel, or Ginckell, Godert de [1st Earl of Athlone] (1630-1703) Dutch-born British soldier who fought with William III at the Battle of the Boyne (1690) and became William's commander in chief in Ireland. He captured Ballymore and Athlone, defeated St Ruth at the battle of Aghrim and captured Limerick.

Ginkgo tree found in Japan (1690) by Kaempfer, introduced into Europe 1730.

Ginsberg, Allen (1926–) American poet, regarded as the leading poet of the Beat Generation, who had much influence on the hippy culture of the 1960s.

Giordano, Luca (1632–1705) Italian painter.

Giordano, Umberto (1867–1948) Italian composer (*Andrea Chénier* 1896).

Giorgione [Giorgio da Castelfranco] (*c.*1477–1510) Venetian painter. Little of his work has survived, although he is one of the most influential painters of his time, the importance of his work lying in his treatment of landscape, imbuing it with strong atmosphere and moods.

Giotto di Bondone (1267–1337) Florentine painter and architect who developed spatial perspective and fully rounded figures in a departure from the flat, decorative imagery of the Byzantine era.

Giraldus Cambrensis (*c.*1146–*c.*1220) Welsh historian.

Giraudoux, Jean (1882–1944) French writer (*Amphitryon 38* 1929).

Giric I (d.889) king of Scots (878–889) *see* Appendix.

Giric II (d.1005) king of Scots (997–1005) *see* Appendix.

Girl Guides and Girl Scouts, World Association of formed in London 1928.

Girl Guides Association movement formed in Britain 1910.

Girl Scouts, USA, founded 1912 by Mrs Juliette Gordon Low (1860–1927).

Girondins group in French Revolution 1791–94.

Girtin, Thomas (1775–1802) English artist *(Bolton Bridge* 1801).

Girton College, Cambridge University, founded by Miss Emily Davies and others 1866; College opened 16 October 1869, as the College for Women. Acquired present name and site 1872.

Giscard d'Estaing, Valéry (1926–) French statesman. He served as minister of finance under de Gaulle (1962–66) and Pompidou (1969–74) and was elected president (1974–81) following the latter's death.

Gish, Lillian (1896–1992) American film and stage actress (*Broken Blossoms* 1919).

Gissing, George (1857–1903) English novelist (*The Private Papers of Henry Ryecroft* 1903).

Giulio Romano (*c.*1496–1546) Italian artist.

Gjellerup, Karl Adolf (1857–1919) Danish writer (*Romulus* 1884).

Gladstone, Herbert John, Viscount (1854–1930) British statesman.

Gladstone, William Ewart (1809–98) British statesman. He became the leader of the Liberals in 1867, and was subsequently prime minister four times: 1868–74, 1880–85, 1886, and 1892–94. He had a long rivalry with his Tory opponent, Disraeli, whose imperialism he vehemently opposed.

Gland secretion discovered 1889 by Mauritius-born Charles Edouard Brown-Séquard (1817–94).

Glanvill, Joseph (1636–80) English theologian (*The Vanity of Dogmatising* 1661).

Glanvill, Ranulf (d.1190) English statesman.

Glasgow Chamber of Commerce oldest British chamber of commerce, founded 1783.

Glasgow University founded 1450.

Glashow, Sheldon *see* WEINBERG, STEVEN.

Glass blown glass discovered *c.*30 BC; English glass industry established *c.*1226; plate-glass first made commercially in France.

Glass, Philip (1937–) American composer. One of the leading avant-garde composers of the 1970s, he is noted for his deep interest in Eastern harmonies and use of repeated motifs. His works include *Einstein on the Beach* (1976).

Glauber's salts discovered by the German scientist Johann Rudolf Glauber (1604–68).

Glazunov, Aleksandr Konstantinovich (1865–1936) Russian composer (*Raymonda* 1898).

Glencoe, Massacre of Scotland, 13 February 1692.

Glidden, Joseph Farwell (1813–1906) American inventor 1873 of barbed wire.

Glinka, Mikhail Ivanovich (1804–57) Russian composer (*A Life for the Tsar* 1836).

'Glorious First of June' naval battle between English and French fought off Ushant 1794.

Gloucester, Humphrey, Duke of (1391–1447) statesman and soldier.

Gloucester, Statute of decreeing necessity of trial before the granting of the royal pardon, 1278.

Gloucester Cathedral built 1072–1104.

Glover, Sarah Ann (1785–1867) English inventor *c.*1845 of the tonic sol-fa system.

Glucinum chemical element first isolated 1828 by the German scientist Friedrich Wöhler (1800–1882).

Gluck, Christoph Willibald, Ritter von (1714–87) German composer. He is especially noted for his operas, e.g. *Orfeo and Eurydice* (1762) and *Alceste* (1767).

Glycerine discovered by the French chemist Charles Adolphe Wurtz (1817–84).

Glycogen discovered by Claude Bernard in 1857.

Glyndebourne Festival Opera founded 1934 by John Christie (1882–1962).

Glyndwr, Owain [Owen Glendower] (*c.*1350–*c.*1416) Welsh rebel leader.

Gmelin, Leopold (1788–1853) German scientist.

Gneisenau, August Wilhelm Anton, Graf Neithardt von (1760–1831) Prussian military commander.

Gnosticism philosophy founded by the philosopher Valentinus (d.*c.*160).

Goa on the southwest coast of India discovered by Vasco da Gama 1498; Portuguese overseas territory from 1510; annexed by India 1961.

Gobelins, The tapestry works near Paris founded 1601. First director (1662) Charles Le Brun, the painter (1619–90).

Gobineau, Joseph Arthur, Comte de (1816–62) French diplomat and writer.

Godard, Jean-Luc (1930–) French film director who is regarded as one of the most influential New Wave French film directors of the 1950s with such films as *A Bout de Souffle* (*Breathless*, 1959) and *Week-End* (1968).

Gödel, Kurt (1906–78) Austrian-born American logician and mathematician. 'Godel's theorem', shows the existence of undecidable elements in arithmetic systems.

Gödel's theory mathematical philosophy propounded 1931 by the Austrian-born US mathematician Kurt Gödel (1906–78).

Godfred (d.1095) king of the isle of Man (1079–95) *see* Appendix.

Godfrey, Sir Edmund Berry (1621–78) English justice of the peace. He was murdered.

Godfrey, Thomas (1736–63) America's first playwright (*The Prince of Parthia* 1765).

Godfrey de Bouillon (*c.*1060–1100) crusader and conqueror of Jerusalem. He led the First Crusade.

Godiva, Lady (*fl.* 1040–85) wife of Leofric, Earl of Mercia, traditionally rode naked through the streets of Coventry 1040.

Godolphin, Sidney, Earl of Godolphin (1645–1712) British statesman.

Godunov, Boris (1552–1605) tsar of Russia (1598–1605).

Godwin (d.1063) earl of the West Saxons. *See* Appendix.

Godwin, William (1756–1836) English novelist, philosopher and reformer. He questioned the validity of established goverment and institutions, notably marriage, and had a strong influence on many radicals, including Shelley, who married his daughter Mary. His works include *Political Justice* (1793).

Godwin-Austen, Robert Alfred Cloyne (1808–84) English geologist.

Godwin-Austen, Mt (K2) Himalayas climbed by an Italian expedition 31 July 1954.

Goebbels, [Paul] Joseph (1897–1945) German Nazi politician. Head of the Nazi Party propaganda section in 1929 and minister of enlightenment and propaganda (1933–45). He committed suicide after shooting his wife and children.

Goering, Hermann *see* GÖRING, HERMANN.

Goes, Hugo van der (d.1482) Flemish painter (*The Portinari Altarpiece*).

Goethals, George Washington (1858–1928) American builder (1907–14) of the Panama Canal and first governor (1914–17) of the Canal Zone.

Goethe, Johann Wolfgang von (1749–1832) German poet, dramatist, novelist, philosopher, scientist and statesman. He was one of the most learned and influential figures of his time. His works include *Werther* (1774) and his masterpiece, the verse drama *Faust* (1808, 1832).

Gogh, Vincent Van (1853–90) Dutch painter who studied theology before taking up painting in 1880. His art was thoroughly unacademic in its realistic subject matter and bold, expressionistic style, e.g. *The Potato Eaters*, but he was later influenced by the colours of Degas and Gauguin. He spent the last two years of his life in southern France, partly in an asylum, a period of intense creativity arising out of personal anguish, e.g. *The Cornfield*, painted at the scene where he shot himself.

Gogol, Nikolai Vasilievich (1809–52) Russian short-story writer, dramatist and novelist. His two greatest works are scathing satires on Russian bureaucracy and incompetence, the play *The Government Inspector* and the novel *Dead Souls* (1837).

Gold found in New Granada (South America) 1537; near Sacramento (California) 1847; on the Blue Hills (New South Wales) 12 February 1851, by Edmund Hammond Hargraves (1815–91); in Otago (New Zealand) June 1861; at Barberton (South Africa) 1882 and Witwatersrand (South Africa) 1884; in Rabbit Creek (Klondike) 16 August 1896 by George Washington Carmack.

Gold Coast *see* GHANA.

Golden Bull on German government promulgated by the Emperor Charles IV, 1356.

Golden Gate Bridge, San Francisco, opened 1937.

Golden Spurs, Battle of the *or* **Battle of Courtrai** between the Flemish and the French, 11 July 1302, which was a victory for the Flemish.

Golding, Louis (1895–1958) English writer (*Magnolia Street*).

Golding, Sir William [Gerald] (1911–93) English novelist. His first novel, *The Lord of the Flies* (1954), established him as a major modern novelist. He was awarded the Nobel prize for literature in 1983.

Goldman, Emma Russian-born anarchist (1869–1940).

Goldoni, Carlo (1707–93) Italian dramatist. Around 150 of his 250 plays are comedies, frequently featuring satirical attacks on the aristocracy and invariably set in his native Venice. They include *The Mistress of the Inn* (1753).

Gold rush California 1848; Australia 1851; South Africa 1886; Klondike 1897.

Goldsmith, Oliver (1728–74) Irish poet and essayist who settled in London in 1756. An entertaining essayist and one of the leading poets of his day, he did not receive acclaim until late in life. His two greatest works are the novel *The Vicar of Wakefield* (1766) and his hugely successful play *She Stoops to Conquer*.

Gold standard abandoned by Great Britain 21 September 1931.

Goldwyn, Samuel [Samuel Goldfish] (1882–1974) Polish-born American film producer. One of the founders of the Hollywood movie business, forming Metro-Goldwyn-Mayer with Louis B. Mayer in 1924, he was famous for his (mainly apocryphal) 'Goldwynisms', e.g. 'Include me out'.

Golf origins uncertain, earliest recorded allusion Scotland 1457. Introduced in the USA 1779.

Golf Club, earliest, the Honourable Company of Edinburgh Golfers, founded 1784.

Gollancz, Victor (1893–1967) English publisher and writer (*My Dear Timothy*).

Gompers, Samuel (1850–1924) English-born American labour leader.

Gomulka, Wladyslaw (1905–82) Communist leader of Poland 1956–71.

Goncharov, Ivan (1812–91) Russian novelist (*Oblomov* 1857).

Goncourt, Edmond de (1822–96) French writer (*La Fille Elisa* 1878).

Goncourt, Jules de (1830–70) French writer (with Edmond *Germinie Lacerteux* 1865).

Gondomar, Diego Sarmiento de Acuña, Count of (1567–1626) Spanish diplomat (English ambassador 1613–22).

Gongora [Luis de Gongora y Argote] (1561–1627) Spanish poet.

Gonville and Caius College, Cambridge University, founded as Gonville Hall 1348 by Edmund Gonville. Assumed present name by Royal Charter 1557.

Gonzaga, Federigo (1500–1540) duke of Mantua (1530–40).

Gooch, Sir Daniel (1816–89) English railway pioneer.

Good Friday Christian commemoration of the Crucifixion, the Friday before Easter.

Goodman, Benny [Benjamin David Goodman] (1909–86) American jazz clarinetist and bandleader. Known as the 'King of Swing', he was one of the first white jazz bandleaders to hire Black players.

Goodwin Sands off southeast coast of England, first mapped by the Dutch cartographer Lucas Janszon Waghenaer 1585.

Goodwood Cup, Goodwood, first run 1812.

Googe, Barnabe (1540–94) English poet.

'Goon Show, The' BBC radio comedy series 1949–60.

Goossens, Léon (1896–1988) English oboe player.

Gorbachev, Mikhail Sergeevich (1931–) Soviet Communist statesman. He became general secretary of the Soviet Communist party in 1985 and soon began instituting far-reaching social and political reforms. He became president in 1985 and 'executive president' in 1990, with wide-ranging powers, facing strong opposition from radicals such as Yeltsin and from hard-line Communists. His powers were insufficient to withstand the break-up of the USSR, and he resigned in December 1991.

Gorchakov, Prince Aleksandr Mikhailovich (1798–1883) Russian statesman.

Gordian I (*c.*158–238) Roman emperor (238). He committed suicide.

Gordian II (192–238) Roman emperor (238). He was killed.

Gordian III (*c.*224–244) Roman emperor (238–244). He was murdered.

Gordius legendary king of Phrygia who is said to have tied a knot so complicated that he who untied it would rule all Persia. Alexander the Great cut the Gordian knot 333 BC.

Gordon, Adam Lindsay (1833–70) British poet. He committed suicide.

Gordon, General Charles George (183385) governor of the Sudan (1877–80). He was killed.

Gordon, Lord George (1751–93) leader of the Gordon Riots (1780).

Gordon Highlanders raised by the Marquis of Huntly (later Duke of Gordon) 1794.

Gore, Al[bert] (1948–) American politician. A former investigative reporter, tobacco and livestock farmer, and developer, he became vice-president of the USA in 1992.

Gorges, Sir Ferdinando (*c.*1566–1647) pioneer in North America.

Gorgias (*c.*485 d.380 BC) Greek philosopher.

Göring *or* **Goering, Hermann [Wilhelm]** (1893–1946) German Nazi politician and military leader who served Hitler as Prussian prime minister, minister of the interior and air minister (1933–45), organizing the rebuilding of the Luftwaffe. He committed suicide.

Gorki *or* **Gorky, Maxim** [Aleksey Maximovich Peshkov] (1868–1936) Russian novelist, dramatist and short-story writer. A firm communist, he helped formulate the doctrine of socialist realism in the USSR in the 1930s. His works include *My Universities* (1923).

Gorky, Arshile [Vosdanig Manoog Adoian] (1904–48) Armenian-born American painter. Originally a surrealist, he developed an abstract approach that was influential on action painters.

Gort, John, Viscount (1886–1946) British soldier and administrator.

Gorton, John Grey (1911–) Australian statesman (prime minister 1968–71).

Goschen, George Joachim [Viscount Goschen] (1831–1907) British statesman.

Gosse, Sir Edmund (1845–1928) English writer (*Father and Son* 1907).

Gothic language first written by Bishop Wulfila (311–383); spoken in Crimea up to 1560.

Goths first attacked Romans 214, defeated Decius 251, became Christian *c.*340, attacked by Huns 363; **Visigoths** crossed Danube 376, defeated Valens 378, became *foederati* 382, attacked Greece 396, invaded Italy 401, sacked Rome 410, invaded Gaul 412–470, defeated by Arabs 711; **Ostrogoths** crossed Danube and became *foederati* 380, attacked Italy 405, occupied Italy 489–493, defeated by Byzantines 536–562.

Gottfried von Strassburg (*fl* late 12th and early 13th centuries) German poet (*Tristan und Isolde*).

Gottschalk (*c.*804–868) German theologian.

Gottsched, Johann Christoph (1700–1766) German critic and writer.

Götz von Berlichingen (1480–1562) German leader.

Goucher College in Baltimore, American women's college, founded 1885; assumed present name 1910.

Goudy, Frederick William (1865–1947) American type designer.

Gough Island probably discovered by the Portuguese navigator Pero d'Anhaya 1505.

Goujon, Jean (*fl* mid-16th century) French sculptor.

Gould, Jay (1836–92) American financier.

Gould, Sir Francis Carruthers (1844–1925) humorous artist.

Gounod, Charles (1818–93) French composer (*Faust* 1859).

Gourmont, Remy de (1858–1915) French writer (*Sixtine* 1890).

Gower, John (*c.*1325–1408) English poet (*Speculum Meditantis*).

Goya y Lucientes, Francisco de (1746–1828) Spanish painter and printmaker. His strong, free-flowing technique and powerful pictorial style are demonstated in early portraits of the royal family, to whom he was court painter, and in later works inspired by the behaviour of the French army in their invasion of Spain (*Charles IV*).

Gozzi, Count Carlo (1720–1806) Italian playwright (*Love for Three Oranges* 1761).

Gozzoli, Benozzo(*c.*1421–1497) Italian painter (*The Medici Family as the Magi*).

Gracchus, Gaius Sempromius (*c.*160–121 BC) Roman statesman and reformer and brother of Tiberius Gracchus. He became a tribune of the Plebs and furthered land reform 123 and 122 BC. He was refused a third tribuneship and the senate began to repeal his reforms. He was killed following a riot in the Forum, brought about by Gracchus attempting to oppose the senate.

Gracchus, Tiberius Sempronius (*c.*169–133 BC) Roman statesman and reformer and brother of Gaius Gracchus. He became tribune of the Plebs 133 BC and attempted to solve the land problem. He and many of his supporters were killed in a riot.

Grace, Princess [Grace Kelly] (1929–82) American film and stage actress (*Rear Window* 1954). She married Prince Rainier of Monaco 19 April 1956. She was killed in a car crash.

Grace, W[illiam] G[ilbert] (1848–1915) English cricketer and physician, one of the first English cricketers to become a national institution. He was also noted for his cunning gamesmanship.

Graetz, Heinrich (1817–91) German historian (*History of the Jews* 1853–76).

Graf, Urs (*c.*1485–1528) Swiss artist.

Graf Spee German warship trapped by the British in a naval action 13–17 December 1939 in the harbour at Montevideo in Uruguay; scuttled 17 December.

Grafton, Augustus, Duke of (1735–1811) English statesman.

Graf Zeppelin German airship that completed its first transatlantic flight 15 October 1928. Circumnavigated the world 15–29 August 1929.

Graham, Billy [William Franklin Graham] (1918–) American evangelist. His evangelical crusades go all over the world.

Graham, John, of Claverhouse [Viscount Dundee] (*c.*1649–1689) Scottish soldier who was killed in battle at Killiecrankie.

Graham, Martha (1894–1991) American dancer, choreographer and teacher who is regarded as one of the founders of modern dance.

Graham, Thomas [Baron Lynedoch] (1748–1843) Scottish soldier.

Grahame, Kenneth (1859–1932) Scottish author. His masterpiece, *The Wind in the Willows* (1908), is a children's classic.

Grahame-White, Claude (1879–1959) pioneer British aviator.

Graham's Law concerning the diffusion of gas formulated by the Scottish chemist Thomas Graham (1805–69).

Grainger, Percy [Aldridge] (1882–1961) Australian-born American pianist and composer who was a notable enthusiast for folk songs, on which many of his works are based. His works include *Spoon River* (1930).

Gramont, Philibert, Comte de (1621–1707) French courtier.

Gramophone (phonograph) invented 1876 by the American Thomas Alva Edison (1847–1931).

Gramsci, Antonio (1891–1937) Italian Marxist political theorist.

Granados, Enrique (1867–1916) Spanish composer (*Goyescas* 1916).

Grand Alliance war of between France and the Allies 1688–97.

Grand Canyon National Park, Arizona, established 1919.

Grand Central Station, New York, opened 1913.

Grand Junction Canal, England, built 1793–1805.

Grand National, Liverpool, first run 1837.

Grand Prix motor race first held at Le Mans 1906 (and won by M. Szisz in a Renault). First held in Britain at Brooklands August 1926.

Grand Trunk Canal, England, built 1766 onwards by the English engineer James Brindley (1716–72).

Granicus, Battle of the 334 BC a battle of Alexander's the Great's campaigns, when he defeated the Persians.

Granjon, Robert (*fl* mid-16th century) French type designer.

Grant, Cary [Archibald Alexander Leach] (1904–86) English-born American film actor who became one of Hollywood's leading stars in light comedy roles and thrillers. His films include *Bringing Up Baby* (1938), *The Philadelphia Story* (1941) and *To Catch a Thief* (1955).

Grant, Duncan (1885–1978) Scottish painter.

Grant, Ulysses S[impson] (1822–85) American soldier and 18th US President (1869–77). Commander of the Union forces in the Civil War, he was elected president in 1869. He established universal suffrage for all citizens, regardless of colour.

Granville, George, Earl (1815–91) English statesman.

Granville-Barker, Harley (1877–1946) English playwright and critic (*Waste* 1907).

Grape sugar discovered 1799 by the French scientist Joseph Louis Proust (1754–1826).

Grappelli, Stéphane (1908–) French jazz violinist. A founder of the Quintette de Hot Club de France, which became the leading European jazz group, he is still regarded as the finest jazz violinist ever.

Grass, Günter [Wilhelm] (1927–) German novelist, dramatist and poet. His works include the novel *Die Blechtrommel* (*The Tin Drum*, 1959), a grimly comic satire on the collapse of the Third Reich as seen through the eyes of a boy.

Grasse, François Joseph Paul, Comte de (1722–88) French admiral in the West Indies.

Gratian (359–383) Roman emperor (375–383). He was assassinated.

Grattan, Henry (1746–1820) Irish reformer.

Graves, Robert [Ranke] (1895–1985) English poet, novelist and critic. His works include his classic autobiographical account of World War I soldiering, *Goodbye to all That* (1929), several great love poems and popular historical novels, including *I, Claudius* (1934).

Gravity, Law of established 1684 by Sir Isaac Newton (1642–1727).

Gray, Elisha (1835–1901) American inventor.

'Gray, Maxwell' [Mary Glied Tuttiet] (1847–1923) English writer (*The Silence of Dean Maitland* 1886).

Gray, Thomas (1716–71) English poet. His best-known poem, 'Elegy Written in a Country Churchyard' (1751), is one of the most-quoted poems in the English Language.

Great Australian Basin largest artesian basin in the world, resources discovered in northwestern New South Wales 1878.

Great Exhibition, Crystal Palace, London, 1 May–15 October 1851.

Great Fire of London 2–6 September 1666.

Great Schism between Catholic and Orthodox churches 1054–1439 and since 1472.

Great Schism within Catholic Church 1378–1417.

Great Train Robbery of Glasgow to London mail train 8 August 1963 (£2.5 million); 12 of the gang were tried and convicted 1964.

Great Trek of Boers from Cape Colony to the Orange Free State area 1836.

Great Wall of China a defensive wall over 1500 miles (2400 kilometres) long, constructed 214 BC as a defence against the Mongols and rebuilt in the 15th century. Starting from a point on the Gulf of Pechili, it runs inland for a distance of about 1500 miles. It is from 20 to 30 feet high and provided with towers about 200 yards apart.

Great Yarmouth granted charter by King John 18 March 1208.

Greco, El [Domenico Theotocopuli] (1541–1614) Cretan-born Spanish painter (*El Espolio*).

Greece, Ancient Greek-speaking peoples entered Greece *c.*2000 BC; Mycenaen civilization 1700–1000 BC; Hellenic conquests 1300–1000 BC; first Olympiad 776 BC; Persians crossed Bosphorus 512; Greek victory over Persians at Marathon 490 BC; campaign of Xerxes 480; Persian victory over Greeks at Thermopylae 480 BC; Greek naval victory over the Persians at Mycale 479 BC; Greek victory over Persians at Plataea 479 BC; Confederacy of Delos 477; Greek victory over Persians at the Eurymedon 465 BC; Peloponnesian wars 431–404; Amphictyonic War 338 BC; Macedonian conquest completed 338; Alexander the Great elected supreme general of the Greeks 336 BC; Achaen League revived in Greece 280 BC; Romans proclaim freedom of Greece 196 BC; Greece became a Roman province 146 BC; Roman conquest completed 133; Constantinople founded AD 330.

Greece, Modern Turkish conquest completed 1466; achieved independence from Turkey 1821–27; monarchy 1833–1922; republic 1922–35; monarchy 1935–73; German occupation 1941–44.

Greek City States, Wars of battle of Cnidus 394 BC; peace of Antalcidas 387 BC; battle of Mantinea 362 BC; battle of Leactra 371 BC.

Greek Orthodox Era began 5509 BC.

Greeley, Horace (1811–72) American editor and politician.

Green, Charles (1785–1870) English balloonist.

Green, John Richard (1837–83) English historian.

Green, Thomas Hill (1836–82) English philosopher.

Greenaway, Kate (1846–1901) English illustrator of children's books (*Mother Goose*).

'Greenbacks' American legal tender notes first issued by Abraham Lincoln, 5 February 1862.

Green Belt Scheme approved by the London County Council 29 January 1935; came into operation 1 April 1935.

Greene, [Henry] Graham (1904–1991) English novelist. Regarded as one of the greatest modern novelists, he converted to Roman Catholicism in 1926 and his religious beliefs play an important part in work, e.g. *The Heart of the Matter*. Other novels include *Brighton Rock* (1938)

Greene, Hugh Carleton(1910–87) director-general of the BBC (1959–69).

Greene, Maurice(*c.*1695–1755) English organist and composer (*Jephthah* 1737).

Greene, Robert (*c.*1560–1592) English writer (*Friar Bacon and Friar Bungay* 1594).

Greenland discovered *c.*982 by the Norwegian explorer Eric the Red (b.*c.*949); resettled 1721; first crossed 1888 by the Norwegian explorer Fridtjof Nansen (1861–1930; declared a dependency of Denmark 1953; granted internal autonomy 1979.

Greenpeace international environment protection organization founded in Canada 1969.

Greenwich Mean Time made legal time for Great Britain 1880; made prime meridian of world 1884.

Greenwich Observatory established by Charles II 1675; moved to Herstmonceaux during 1950s.

Greer, Germaine (1939–) Australian feminist, writer and broadcaster who is best known for her controversial work, *The Female Eunuch* (1970).

Greg, Sir Walter Wilson (1875–1959) English bibliographer.

Gregg, Sir Cornelius (1888–1959) introducer (1944) of PAYE. in Britain.

Gregg, John Robert (1867–1948) Irish-born inventor 1888 of Gregg's shorthand.

Gregorovius, Ferdinand (1821–91) German historian.

Gregory, Lady Augusta (1852–1932) Irish patron and playwright (*Hyacinthe Halevy* 1909).

Gregory, Sir Augustus Charles (1819–1905) English explorer of Australia.

Gregory I, Saint (*c.*540–604) pope (590–604).

Gregory II, Saint (d.731) pope (715–731).

Gregory III, Saint (d.741) pope (731–741).

Gregory IV (d.844) pope (827–844).

Gregory V [Bruno] (*c.*971–999) pope (996–999).

Gregory VI [Johannes Gratianus] (d.1047) pope (1045–46).

Gregory VII, Saint [Hildebrand] (*c.*1035–1085) pope (1073–85).

Gregory VIII [Alberto de Mora] (d.1187) pope (1187).

Gregory VIII [Mauritius Burdinus] anti-pope (1118–21).

Gregory IX [Ugolino Conti de Segno] (d.1241) pope (1227–41).

Gregory X [Tebaldo Visconti] pope (1208–76) (1271–76).

Gregory XI [Pierre Roger de Beaufort] (1330–78) pope (1371–18).

Gregory XII [Angelo Coriaro] (*c.*1326–1417) pope (1406–15).

Gregory XII [Bartolommeo Alberto Cappellari] (1765–1846) pope (1831–46).

Gregory XIII [Ugo Buoncompagno] (1502–85) pope (1572–85).

Gregory XIV [Nicolo Sfondrato] (1535–91) pope (1590–91).

Gregory XV [Alessandro Ludovisi] (1554–1623) pope (1621–23).

Gregory Nazianzen, Saint (*c.*330–*c.*390).

Gregory of Tours, Saint historian (*c.*540–594).

Grenadier Guards organized on a permanent basis 1740.

Grenfell, Joyce (1910–79) English actress and entertainer.

Grenfell, Sir Wilfred (1865–1940) English medical missionary.

Grenville, George (1712–70) English statesman.

Grenville, Sir Richard (*c.*1541–1591) Captain of *The Revenge*. He died of wounds.

Gresham's Law on the question of coinage propounded by Sir Thomas Gresham (*c.*1519–1579).

Gretchaninov, Aleksandr (1864–1956) Russian-born composer (*Missa festiva* 1939).

Gretna Green, Scotland, scene of runaway marriages, particularly 1754 to 1856.

Grétry, André Ernest Modeste (1741–1813) Belgian composer (*Andromaque* 1780).

Greuze, Jean Baptiste (1725–1805) French painter (*The Broken Pitcher*).

Greville, Charles Cavendish Fulke (1794–1865) English political diarist (*Memoirs* 1875–87).

Greville, Sir Fulke (1554–1628) English poet. He was murdered.

Grey, Charles, Earl (1764–1845) British statesman (prime minister 1831–34).

Grey, Edward Viscount Grey of Fallodon (1862–1933) British statesman.

Grey, Lady Jane (*c.*1537–1554) claimant to the English throne (1553) *see* Appendix.

Grey, Zane (1875–1939) American writer (*The Last of the Plainsmen* 1908).

Greyhound racing in Britain began at White City 20 June 1927.

Grieg, Edvard [Hagerup] (1843–1907) Norwegian composer of Scottish descent. Strongly influenced by Norwegian folk music, his works include music for Ibsen's *Peer Gynt* (1874).

Grierson, John (1898–1972) Scottish documentary film director and producer, described as the 'father of British documentary'.

Grierson, Sir Robert (*c.*1655–1733) prototype of Scott's Sir Robert Redgauntlet.

Griffith, Arthur (1872–1922) Irish nationalist leader. He founded Sinn Fein in 1905, and (with Michael Collins) signed the Anglo-Irish Treaty of 1921. He was the first president of the Irish Free State (1922).

Griffith, D[avid] W[ark] (1875–1948) American film director and producer. His great technical skill was highly influential on other film-makers. In 1919, he founded United Artists with Chaplin, Fairbanks and Pickford. His films include *The Birth of a Nation* (1915).

Grillparzer, Frans (1791–1872) Austrian poet (*Sappho* 1819).

Grimald, Nicholas (1519–62) English writer (*Christus Redivivus* 1543).

Grimaldi, Joseph (1779–1837) English clown.

Grimbald, Saint (*c.*820–903) Flemish-born abbot at Winchester.

Grimm, Jakob Ludwig Karl (1785–1863) German philologist, folklorist and writer and brother of Wilhelm Karl Grimm, with whom he wrote *Fairy Tales*(1812–22). He also wrote *Deutsche Grammatik* (1819–37)

Grimm, Wilhelm Karl (1786–1859) German philologist, folklorist and writer who collaborated with his brother, Jakob Grimm, on *Fairy Tales* (1812–22).

Grimmelshausen, Hans Jacob Christoph von (*c.*1625–1676) German writer whose works include *Simplicissimus* (1669).

Grimond, Joseph (1913–93) British Liberal statesman.

Grimthorpe, Edmund Beckett, Baron (1816–1905) inventor and lawyer.

Grindal, Edmund (1519–1583) English divine.

Gringoire, Pierre (*c.*1475–1538) French poet.

Gris, Juan [José Victoriano Gonzàlez] (1887–1927) Spanish-born painter. He settled in Paris in 1906, where he became an associate of Picasso and Braque, and one of the leading Cubist painters.

Grisi, Giulia (1811–69) Italian operatic singer.

Grocers Company, London, origins uncertain but at least as early as 1231; Hall built 1427; first charter granted by King Edward III, 1345.

'Grock' [Adrien Wettach] (1880–1959) Swiss clown.

Grocyn, William (*c.*1446–1519) English scholar.

Grolier, Jean (1479–1565) French diplomat and book collector.

Gromyko, Andrei Andreyevich (1909–89) Soviet statesman and diplomat. He was Soviet foreign minister (1957–1985) and a Politburo member (1973–89) and adapted effortlessly to each stage of relations with the West, from Cold War through 1970s detente to the Gorbachev era.

Gropius, Walter (1883–1969) German-born architect.

Gros, Baron Antoine Jean (1771–1835) French painter (particularly of Napoleon). He committed suicide.

Grosseteste, Robert (*c.*1175–1253) English theologian.

Grossmith, George (1847–1912) English actor and writer (*Diary of a Nobody* 1892).

Grosz, Georg (1893–1959) German-born painter.

Grote, George (1794–1871) English historian.

Grotius, Hugo (1583–1645) Dutch jurist (*De jure belli et pacis* 1625).

Grouchy, Emmanuel, Marquis de (1766–1847) French general.

Groundnut scheme in Tanganyika begun 1947.

Grove, Sir George (1820–1900) English compiler of the *Dictionary of Music and Musicians* (first published 1879–89).

Grove cell electric battery invented 1839 by Sir William Robert Grove (1811–96).

Gruber, Franz Xaver (1787–1863) Austrian composer (*Silent Night* 1818).

Gruffyd ap Cynan (b.1055) king of Gwynedd (1081–1137) *see* Appendix.

Gruffyd ap Llywelyn (d.1062) king of Gwynedd (1039–63) *see* Appendix.

Grunewald, Matthias [Mathis Nithart] (*c.*1470–1528) German painter noted for his use of perspective, Gothic imagery, strong colour and an expressionistic style of distortion. His works include the Isenheim altarpiece.

Guadalcanal an island at the southern end of the Solomon Islands' achipelago, which was occupied 1942–43 by the Japanese in the Second World War. It was evacuated by the Japanese 9 February 1943 following a bitterly contested battle with the Americans.

Guam the largest of the Mariana Islands in the western Pacific, occupied in the Second World War by the Americans, 21 July 1944.

Guardi, Francesco (1712–93) Italian painter.

Guarneri, Giuseppe Antonio (1687–*c.*1745) Italian violin-maker.

Guatemala Central American republic conquered by the Spanish 1523; gained independence and annexed to Mexico 1821; became independent republic 1839.

Gucci, Guccio (1881–1953) Italian leatherworker and designer.

Gudea ruler of Lagash 2450 BC.

Guelphs German family founded by Welf (d.*c.*825).

Guericke, Otto (1602–1686) German scientist.

Guérin, Maurice de (1810–39) French poet (*Le Centaurel c.*1835).

Guernica Basque capital in northwest Spain, savagely bombed during the Spanish Civil War, 26 April 1937, by German forces.

Guernsey one of the Channel Islands, acquired 933 by William, Duke of Normandy (d.943) and attached to England since 1066.

Guesclin, Bertrand du (*c.*1320–1380) French leader.

Guest, Lady Charlotte [later Lady Charlotte Schreiber] (1812–95) translator of the *Mabinogion.*

Guevara, Che [Ernesto Guevara] (1928–67) Argentinian-born Communist revolutionary leader. He joined Fidel Castro's forces in the Cuban revolution (1956–59). He subsequently led a guerrilla group in Bolivia, where he was shot dead by government troops.

Guggenheim, Meyer (1828–1905) American financier.

Guiana, British *see* GUYANA.

Guiana, French *see* FRENCH GUIANA.

Guicciardini, Francesco (1483–1540) Italian diplomat and historian.

Guido d'Avezzo (*c.*995–1050) pioneer in musical instruction and notation.

Guido Reni (1575–1642) Italian painter (*Deeds of Hercules*).

Guilbert, Yvette (1869–1944) French actress.

Guild Socialism in Britain National Guilds League formed 1915; movement collapsed by 1924.

Guillotine introduced 1792 by the French doctor Joseph Guillotin (1738–1814).

Guinea colony of French Guinea from 1890; became independent republic 1958.

Guinea-Bissau formerly Portuguese Guinea, discovered 1446 by Nuno Tristão; made a separate colony of Portugal 1879; became an independent republic in 1974.

Guinegate, Battle of *see* BATTLE OF THE SPURS.

Guinness, Sir Alec (1914–) English stage and film actor. Regarded as one of the most versatile stage actors of his generation, he became a household name through his films, e.g. *Kind Hearts and Coronets* and *Star Wars*.

Guinness, Sir Benjamin Lee (1798–1868) Irish brewer.

Guise, François de Lorraine, Duc de (1519–63) French soldier and politician. He was assassinated.

Guise, Henri de Lorraine, Duc de (1550–88) French soldier. He was assassinated.

Guitry, Sacha (1885–1957) French actor and playwright (*Le Veilleur de nuit* 1911).

Guizot, François Pierre Guillaume (1787–1874) French statesman and historian.

Gulbenkian, Calouste Sarkis (1869–1955) Turkish Armenian-born British financier, industrialist, diplomat and philanthropist. He endowed the Gulbenkian Foundation for the arts and sciences. His son, **Nubar Sarkis Gulbenkian** (1896–1972), was an Iranian diplomat and a philanthropist.

Gun traditionally invented 1313 by Berthold Schwartz.

Gunpowder introduced into Europe by 1300.

Gunpowder Plot against the Houses of Parliament, 5 November 1605.

Gunter, Edmund (1581–1626) English mathematician.

Gurney, Sir Goldsworthy (1793–1875) English inventor.

Gustavus I (1496–1560) king of Sweden (1523–60).

Gustavus II (1594–1632) king of Sweden (1611–32). He was killed in battle.

Gustavus III(1746–92) king of Sweden (1771–92). He was assassinated 1792).

Gustavus IV (1778–1837) king of Sweden (1792–1809).

Gustavus V (1858–1950) king of Sweden (1907–50).

Gustavus VI (1882–1973) king of Sweden (1950–73).

Gutenberg, Johannes (*c.*1397–1468) German founder *c.*1440 of Western printing.

Guthrie, Thomas (1803–73). Scottish reformer

Guthrie, Sir [William] Tyrone (1900–71) Irish actor and theatrical producer. His productions included a controversial Hamlet in modern dress and several important Shakespeare productions.

Guthrie, Woody [Woodrow Wilson Guthrie] (1912–67) American folksinger and political activist. His songs, which attack racial bigotry and the economic exploitation of the poor and immigrants, were a strong influence on 1960s 'protest' singers.

Guthrum (d.890) king of East Anglia (880–890) *see* Appendix.

Guyana (formerly British Guiana) northeast South America became a British colony 1831 and an independent republic within the Commonwealth 1966.

Guy de Lusignan (d.1194) king of Jerusalem (1186–92).

Guy Fawkes Day 5 November, commemorating the attempt on the Houses of Parliament by the English conspirator Guy Fawkes (1570 executed 1606).

Guyon, Jeanne (1648–1717) French mystic.

Guyot, Arnold (1807–84) Swiss geographer.

Guys, Constantin (1802–92) French artist.

Guy's Hospital, London, founded 1722 by the English philanthropist Thomas Guy (*c.*1644–1724).

Gwyn, Nell (1650–87) mistress of King Charles II.

Gyges king of Lydia (716–678 BC) who dethroned a previous dynasty and founded his own. The Lydians were disinclined to submit to him but an oracle from Delphi established his authority, in gratitude for which he sent magnificent presents to the temple.

Gyrocompass invented 1915 by the American inventor Elmer Ambrose Sperry (1860–1930).

Gyroscope invented 1852 by the French scientist Jean Bernard Leon Foucault (1819–68).

H

Haakon I the Good (d.961) king of Norway (935–961). He was killed in battle.

Haakon II the Broadshouldered (1047–1162) king of Norway (1161–62).

Haakon III king of Norway (1202–1204).

Haakon IV the Old (1204–1263) king of Norway (1217–63).

Haakon V king of Norway (1299–1319).

Haakon VI (1340–1386) king of Norway (1343–80).

Haakon VII (1872–1957) king of Norway (1905–57).

Habberton, John (1842–1921) American writer (*Helen's Babies* 1876).

Habeas Corpus Act principle stated in Magna Carta 1215, confirmed by Petition of Right 1628; became law in England 27 May 1679.

Haberdashers' Company, London, origins uncertain; bye-laws drawn up 1371; granted first charter by Henry VI 1448.

Hackney carriages used at least as early as 1636 in London; regularized by the Carriage Act 1831.

Haden, Sir Francis Seymour (1818–1910) English surgeon and etcher.

Hadow, Sir William Henry (1859–1937) English musicologist (*William Byrd* 1923).

Hadrian [Publius Aelius Hadrianus] (76–138) Roman soldier and emperor (117–138). He spent much of his reign travelling, visiting all he provinces of the empire, the boundaries of which he was concerned to make firm. He abandoned Trajan's conquests beyond the Euphrates and built Hadrian's Wall in the north of England.

Hadrian's Wall Roman wall across northern England built under the governorship of Aulus Platorius Nepos, 122–126. Strengthened by Severus Septimius 210.

Haeckel, Ernst Heinrich (1834–1919) German naturalist.

Hafiz [Shams ad-Din Mohammed] (*c.*1320–*c.*1389) Persian poet.

Hafnium a metal first isolated by the Norwegian scientist Dirk Coster and the Hungarian scientist Georg von Hevesy 1922.

Hagedorn, Friedrich von (1708–54) German poet.

Haggard, Sir Rider (1856–1925) English novelist (*King Solomon's Mines* 1885).

Hahn, Otto (1879–1968) German physical chemist. With Meitner and others, he undertook significant research which led to the discovery of nuclear fission. He was awarded the 1944 Nobel prize for chemistry.

Hahn, Reynaldo (1875–1947) Venezuelan composer (*Concerto provençal* 1930).

Haidar Ali *see* HYDER ALI.

Haig, Douglas, 1st Earl (1861–1928) British field marshal. In World War I he was appointed commander in chief of the British forces on the western front (1915–18). The terrible losses of soldiers under his command led to fierce criticism of his tactics. He founded the British Legion.

Haile Selassie [title of Ras Tafari Makonnen] (1892–1975) emperor of Ethiopia (1930–36, 1941–74). He lived in Britain during the occupation of his country by Italy (1936–41). In the early 1960s he helped establish the Organization of African Unity. The famine of 1973 created unrest which led to his deposition in a military coup. He is worshipped as a god by the Rastafarian cult.

Haiti discovered by Christopher Columbus 6 December 1492; ruled by French 1697–1792; independence proclaimed 1803; ruled by USA 1915–41; under dictatorships of Francois Duvalier ('Papa Doc') 1957–71 and Jean-Claude Duvalier 1971–86.

Haitink, Bernard [Johann Herman] (1929–) Dutch conductor, renowned as an interpreter of Bruckner and Mahler.

Hakluyt, Richard (*c.*1552–1616) English historian (*Voyages* 1598–1600).

Haldane, John Burdon Sanderson (1892–1964) British scientist.

Haldane, John Scott (1860–1936) Scottish physiologist.

Haldane, Richard Burdon [Viscount Haldane of Cloan] (1856–1928) British statesman and reformer.

Hale, Edward Everett (1822–1909) American storyteller (*The Man Without a Country* 1863), poet and Unitarian minister.

Hale, Sir Matthew (1609–76) English jurist and writer.

Hale, Nathan (1755–76) American patriot. He was hanged.

Halévy, Jacques François Fromental Elie (1799–1862) French composer (*La Juive* 1835).

Haley, Bill (1927–81) American guitarist, singer and

pioneer of rock 'n' roll ('Rock around the Clock' 1955).

Halfpenny postage introduced in Britain 1 October 1870.

Halfran (d.895) king of York (875–883) *see* Appendix.

Halftone engraving first practical process invented 1878 by the American pioneer in photography Frederick Eugene Ives (1856–1937).

Halicarnassus (modern name Bodrum) an ancient port on the southeastern Mediterranean coast of Turkey, the Mausoleum at which was one of the Seven Wonders of the World. It was besieged and captured by Alexander the Great 334 BC.

Halifax, Charles Montagu, Earl of (1661–1715) British statesman and writer.

Halifax, Earl of (1881–1959) viceroy and governor-general of India (1926–31).

Halifax, Nova Scotia, founded 1749.

Hall, Sir Edward Marshall (1858–1929) English lawyer.

Hall, Joseph (1574–1656) English theologian and writer.

Hall, Marshall (1790–1857) English physiologist.

Hall, Sir Peter [Reginald Frederick] (1930–) English stage director and theatre manager. He was director of the Royal Shakespeare Company (1960–68) and the National Theatre (1973–88).

Hallam, Henry (1777–1859) English historian.

Halle, Adam de la (*c.*1240–1287) French troubadour.

Hallé Orchestra, Manchester, established 1857 by Sir Charles Hallé (1819–95). First regular public concert 30 January 1858.

Halley, Edmund (1656–1742) English astronomer and mathematician. In 1583, he calculated the orbit of the comet now named after him, and correctly predicted its return in following years.

Halley's Comet named after Edmund Halley; appeared 1456, 1531, 1607, 1682, 1758, 1835, 1910, 1986. First photographed by astronomers 1910.

Hall of Fame, New York, US national shrine established 1900.

Hallowe'en (All-Hallows Eve) celebrated 31 October.

Hall's effect electromagnetism discovered 1879 by the American scientist Edwin Herbert Hall (1853–1921).

Hals, Frans (*c.*1581–1666) Dutch painter. Noted for his lively and innovative group portraiture that moved away from formal trends. His most famous work is *The Laughing Cavalier* (1624), now in the Wallace Collection, London.

Mithridatic War, Second 83–82 BC between Rome and Mithradates VI, king of Pontus. The Roman commander was Murena who broached the peace treaty:

Halys, Battle of the 82 BC a battle of the Second Mithridatic War when Mithridates was successful and the Roman commander, Murena, was forced to retreat into Phrygia.

Hamburg-Amerika Line founded 1847.

Hamilcar Barca (d.229 BC) Carthaginian general who assumed command in Sicily 247–241 BC during the First Punic War and established Carthaginian influence in Spain 238–229, where he died in battle. He was the father of Hannibal.

Hamilton, Alexander (1757–1804) American statesman. He founded the Federalist party in 1787 and, as first secretary of the Treasury (1789–95), founded the US federal bank. He was killed in a duel.

Hamilton, Emma, Lady (*c.*1765–1815) mistress of Lord Nelson.

Hamilton, Patrick (*c.*1504–1528) Scottish martyr. He was burnt at the stake.

Hamilton, Sir Robert (1836–95) governor of Tasmania (1886–93).

Hamilton, Sir William (1730–1803) diplomat, archeologist (purchaser of the Portland Vase).

Hamlet story of in existence in 12th century.

Hammarskjöld, Dag [Hjalmar Agne Carl] (1905–61) Swedish-born secretary-general of the the United Nations (1953–61). His period of office was a turbulent one, and he died in a plane crash during the Congo crisis. He was posthumously awarded the 1961 Nobel Peace Prize.

Hammer action in modern pianos invented *c.*1710 by the Italian harpsichord-maker Bartolommeo Cristofori (1655–173.

Hammerstein, Oscar American impresario (1848–1919).

Hammerstein II, Oscar (1895–60) American songwriter and librettist, best known for his musicals written with Richard Rodgers, e.g. *South Pacific* and *The Sound of Music*.

Hammett, [Samuel] Dashiell (1894–1961) American novelist. He wrote realistic crime novels based on his own experiences as a Pinkerton detective. His best known are *The Maltese Falcon* and *The Thin Man*. He also wrote *Red Harvest* (1929).

Hammond, Joan (1912–) Australian operatic singer.

Hammond, John (1872–1949) English social historian.

Hammurabi (*fl* 21 century BC) king of Babylonia. He was the greatest king of the first Babylon dynasty and his reign was noted for agricultural improvements and law reform.

Hampden, John (1594–1643) English parliamentarian. Prosecuted in 1637 for refusing to pay Charles I's unpopular ship-money tax (1636–37). He raised a regiment for Parliament during the Civil War and died of wounds received in battle.

Hampton Court, Treaty of alliance between Queen Elizabeth I and the Prince de Condé, signed 21 September 1562.

Hampton Court Conference of English clergy held 1604.

Hamsun, Knut (1859–1952) Norwegian writer (*Hunger* 1888).

Han dynasty in China 206 BC to 220 AD.

Hancock, Tony [Anthony John Hancock] (1924–68) English comedian. His popular BBC radio and TV series, *Hancock's Half Hour*, established his well-known comic persona of the belligerent misfit. He committed suicide.

Handel, George Frederick [Georg Friedrich Händel] (1685–1759) German-born English composer. He became court composer to the Hanover court in 1710 and wrote over 40 operas, e.g. *Semele*, and many concertos and oratorios, e.g. *The Messiah* (1742), as well as chamber and orchestral music, e.g. *Water Music*.

Hannibal, (247–182 BC) Carthaginian general who became commander in chief of the Carthaginian army in 221 BC at the age of twenty-six. During the Second Punic War with Rome (218–202), he invaded Italy in 218 and crossed the Alps. For years he campaigned in Italy but was finally defeated at Zama in 202. He later lived in exile and committed suicide to avoid falling captive to the Romans.

Hannington, James (1847–85) first bishop of Eastern Equatorial Africa. He was murdered.

Hanno Carthaginian navigator explored West African coast *c.*450 BC.

Hansard record of parliamentary debates begun 1774 by Luke Hansard (1752–1828); present series founded 1803 by William Cobbett (1763–1835).

Hanseatic League North German and Baltic commercial alliance, origins *c.*1140; formal alliance 1241; last meeting 1669.

Hansen, Gerhard (1841–1912) Norwegian scientist.

Hansom cab idea patented 1834 by the English architect Joseph Aloysius Hansom (1803–82).

Hapsburg dynasty ruled Austria 1278–1918, Netherlands 1482–1700 (and Belgium 1713–94), Spain 1516–1700, Bohemia 1526–1918.

Hara-kiri Japanese obligatory suicide abolished officially 1868.

Harald I Haarfager (850–933) king of Norway (860–933).

Harald II Graafeld (d.969) king of Norway (961–969). He was murdered.

Harald III Haardraade (d.1066) king of Norway (1048–66). He was killed in battle.

Harald IV Gylle (d.1136) king of Norway (1134–36). He was murdered.

Harcourt, Sir William (1827–1904) British statesman.

Hardicanute (1018–1042) king of England (1040–42) *see* Appendix.

Hardie, [James] Keir (1856–1915) Scottish Labour politician. He was the first leader of the parliamentary Labour Party (1906–7). A committed pacifist, he withdrew from politics following the failure of parties of the Left in Europe to oppose World War I.

Harding, Stephen, Saint (d.1134).

Harding, Warren Gamaliel 29th US president (1921–23) (1865–1923).

Hardinge, Henry [Viscount Hardinge] (1785–1856) statesman and soldier.

Hardwicke, Sir Cedric (1893–1964) English actor.

Hardwicke, Philip Yorke, Earl of (1690–1764) Lord Chancellor.

Hardy, Godfrey Harold (1877–1947) English mathematician, noted for his work on analytic number theory.

Hardy, Oliver *see* LAUREL, STAN.

Hardy, Thomas (1840–1928) English novelist, short-story writer and poet. As well known for his influential novels, e.g. *Tess of the D'Urbevilles* (1891) and *Far from the Madding Crowd*, as for his poetry, he is now ranked, with Eliot and Yeats, as one of the three great modern poets in English.

Hare, Augustus (1834–1903) English writer (*The Story of My Life* 1896–1900).

Hare, William (d.*c.*1865) Irish murderer in the Burke and Hare case.

Hargreaves' Spinning Jenny invented *c.*1764 by the English weaver James Hargreaves (d.1778).

Harington, Sir John (1561–1612) English writer (*Metamorphosis of Ajax* 1596).

Harleian Library, British Museum, formed by Robert Harley, Earl of Oxford (1661–1724).

Harley, Robert, Earl of Oxford (1661–1724) English statesman and book collector.

Harlow, Jean [Harlean Carpentier] (1911–37) American film actress who became one of the screen's main sex symbols of the 1930s, with her tough, wise-cracking 'platinum blonde bombshell' image. Her films include *Red Dust* (1932).

Harmonium invented 1840 by the French organ manufacturer Alexandre François Debain (1809–77).

Harold I Harefoot (1016–40) king of England (1035–40) *see* Appendix.

Harold II (1020–66) king of England (1066) *see* Appendix.

Harper's Ferry, Virginia, captured by John Brown, 16 October 1859.

Harpignies, Henri (1819–1916) French painter (*View of Capri*).

Harriman, W[illiam] Averell (1891–1986) American diplomat. He was the main negotiator of the nuclear test-ban treaty of 1963, between the US, UK and USSR. He was also governor of New York (1955–58).

Harris, Sir Arthur Travers (1892–1984) English air force officer, nicknamed 'Bomber Harris' for his advocacy of heavy bombing raids on German cities during the Second World War. The policy lasted from 1942 to the firebombing of Dresden in 1944.

Harris, Frank (1856–1931) Irish-born writer (*My Life and Loves* 1923–27).

Harris, Joel Chandler (1848–1908) American writer (*Uncle Remus* 1880).

Harris, Thomas Lake (1823–1906) British-born founder of the Brotherhood of the New Life (1823–1906).

Harrison, Benjamin (1833–1901) 23rd US president (1889–93) (1833–1901).

Harrison, George (1943–) English singer-songwriter. He played lead guitar for the Beatles (1962–70).

Harrison, Sir Rex [Reginald Carey Harrison] (1908–90) English stage and film actor (*My Fair Lady* 1964).

Harrison, William (1534–93) English topographer (*Description of England* 1577).

Harrison, William Henry (1773–1841) 9th US president (1841).

Hart, Lorenz [Milton] (1895–1943) American lyricist who is best known for his collaborations with the composer Richard Rodgers, e.g. *The Boys from Syracuse* and *Pal Joey*. His songs include 'With a Song in My Heart'.

Harte, Bret (1839–1902) American writer (*The Luck of Roaring Camp* 1870).

Hartley, Arthur Clifford (1889–1960) British inventor of 'Pluto' and 'Fido'.

Hartley, L[eslie] P[oles] (1895–1972) English novelist, whose best-known works are subtle portrayals of social and sexual intrigue in Edwardian England, e.g. *The Go-Between*, *The Shrimp and the Anemone*.

Hartmann von Aue (*c.*1168–*c.*1217) German minnesinger.

Harty, Sir Hamilton (1879–1941) English conductor and composer.

Harun-al-Rashid (*c.*763–809) caliph.

Harunobu, Suzuki (*c.*1720–*c.*1770) Japanese artist (*The Broken Shoestring*).

Harvard University founded 1636, named after the Puritan minister John Harvard (1607–38).

Harvard University Observatory built 1843–47.

Harvest moon the full moon within a fortnight of 22 or 23 September.

Harvester mechanical invented 1831 by the American manufacturer Cyrus Hall McCormick (1809–84).

Harvey, Gabriel (*c.*1545–1630) English poet.

Harvey, Thomas (1812–84) Quaker relief worker and theologian.

Harvey, William (1578–1657) English physician. Court physician to both James VI and Charles I, he published his discovery of the circulation of the blood in 1628 in *De Motu Cordis*.

Hasdrubal (d.207 BC) Carthaginian general (brother of Hannibal) and commander in chief of the Carthaginian army in Spain 218–211 BC. He crossed the Alps into Italy 207 BC to join his brother, but was defeated and killed in battle at Metaurus during the Second Punic War.

Hasek, Jaroslav (1883–1923) Czech novelist and short-story writer. His masterpiece is *The Good Soldier Svejk* (1925) (*The Good Soldier Schweik* 1920–23) , based on his own experiences in the Austro-Hungarian army.

Hastings, Battle of fought at Battle between the Normans and the English 14 October 1066.

Hastings, Warren (1732–1818) British administrator in India. He was the first governor-general of Bengal (1773–85) and established the East India Company as one of the most powerful forces in India. He resigned office in 1784 and was impeached before the House of Commons 1788–95 for corruption.

Hathaway, Anne (*c.*1556–1623) wife of William Shakespeare.

Hatton, Sir Christopher (1540–91) lord chancellor.

Haughey, Charles [James] (1925–) Irish Fianna Fáil politician. He was prime minister of the Republic of Ireland (1979–81, 1982, 1988–92) but was forced to resign after several scandals.

Hauptmann, Gerhart (1862–1946) German playwright (*Rose Bernd* 1903).

Haussmann, Georges Eugène, Baron (1809–91) French town planner.

Havas Agency French press agency founded 1835 by the Frenchman Charles Havas (d.1850).

Havel, Vaclav Czech writer, also president of Czechoslovakia (1989–92) (1936–).

Havel, Vàclav (1936–) Czech dramatist and statesman. His plays satirized the brutality and corruption of Czech communism and he was imprisoned for several years after the Soviet invasion of 1968. He was president of Czechoslovakia (1989–92) and of the Czech Republic.

Havelock, Sir Henry (1795–1857) general in India.

Havelock the Dane early 14th-century Anglo-Danish epic.

Hawaii (formerly Sandwich Islands), Pacific, discovered 1778 by Captain James Cook; formally annexed by the USA 1898; admitted to the Union 1959.

Hawes, Stephen (d.*c.*1523) English poet (*Passetyme of Pleasure* 1509).

Hawke, Robert [James Lee] (1929–) Australian trades unionist and Labor statesman. He was prime minister (1983-92 or 1983–91).

Hawker, Robert Stephen (1803–75) English poet ('And shall Trelawny die?').

Hawking, Stephen William (1942–) English astrophysicist and author. Widely regarded as perhaps the greatest physicist since Einstein, his research into the theory of black holes has been highly acclaimed. He has suffered from a rare crippling nervous disease since the early 1960s and is confined to a wheelchair. His book, *A Brief History of Time* (1988), has been a worldwide best-seller.

Hawkins, Sir John (1532–95) English naval reformer and slave-trader.

Hawkins, Sir Richard (*c.*1562–1622) English admiral.

Hawks, Howard (1896–1977) American film director and producer. His films include several classics starring Bogart and Bacall, e.g. *The Big Sleep*, John Wayne, and Marilyn Monroe.

Hawksmoor, Nicholas (1661–1736) English architect.

Hawthorne, Nathaniel (1804–64) American novelist and short-story writer. New England Puritanism profoundly shaped his life and work, as in his masterpiece, *The Scarlet Letter* (1850).

Haydn, Franz Joseph (1732–1809) Austrian composer. An innovative composer, he established the form of both the symphony and the string quartet. His huge oeuvre includes over 100 symphonies, 84 string quartets and the oratorio *The Creation* (1798).

Haydn, Joseph (d.1856) English compiler of the *Dictionary of Dates* (1841).

Haydon, Benjamin Robert (1786–1846) English painter (*Lazarus*). He committed suicide.

Hayek, Friedrich August von (1899–1992) Austrian-born British economist. A supporter of free-market policies and against government economic management, he shared the 1974 Nobel prize for economics with Myrdal.

Hayes, Rutherford Birchard (1822–93) 19th US president (1877–81).

Hays, William Harrison (1879–1954) American film administrator. He devised the Hays Code to censor films. It remained in operation until 1966.

Hayworth, Rita [Margarita Carmen Cansino] (1918–87) American film actress (*Gilda* 1946).

Hazlitt, William (1778–1830) English essayist and critic. Highly influential in his own day, he remains one of the most important literary critics, especially for his essays on his contemporaries. His works include *Table Talk* (1821).

H-bomb first exploded by the Americans in the Pacific 21 November 1952; first Russian explosion (USSR) 12 August 1953.

Healey, Denis [Winston] (1917–) English Labour politician. Chancellor of the exchequer (1974–79) and deputy leader of his party (1980–83), he is widely regarded as one of the most impressive modern British politicians.

Healy, Timothy Michael (1855–1931) Irish Free State governor-general (1922–28).

Heaney, Seamus [Justin] (1939–) Irish poet, critic and teacher who is regarded by many critics as the finest Irish poet since Yeats. He was awarded the 1995 Nobel prize for literature.

Heaphy, Charles (1820–81) explorer in New Zealand, awarded New Zealand's first (1867) Victoria Cross.

Hearn, Lafcadio (1850–1904) naturalized Japanese writer (*Japan* 1904).

Hearst, William Randolph (1863–1951) American newspaper publisher and politician. In the late 1920s he owned more than 25 daily newspapers and built a spectacular castle at San Simeon in California. He was congressman for New York (1903–7). Welles' film, *Citizen Kane*, is a thinly disguised account of his life.

Heart surgery pioneered by Rehn of Frankfurt in 1896.

Heart transplant first performed by Christiaan Barnard 1957.

Heat existence of latent heat established *c.*1765 by the British scientist Joseph Black (1728–99); dynamical theory of heat suggested by experiments of Count Rumford at Munich in 1798 and postulated 1841 by James Joule (1818–89).

Heath, Sir Edward [Richard George] (1916–) British Conservative statesman and prime minister (1970–74). A fervent pro-European, he negotiated Britain's entry into the Common Market in 1973. He has also been active and influential in world politics.

Heath, Neville (1917–46) English murderer. He was hanged.

Heavier-than-air machine first flight made by the American brothers, Orville and Wilbur Wright, 17 December 1903.

Heaviside, Oliver (1850–1925) English scientist.

Heavy hydrogen (deuterium) discovered 1931 by the American chemist Harold Clayton Urey (1893–1981).

Heavy-oil engine first used in Britain, invented by William Priestman 1885.

Heavy water discovered 1931 by the American chemist Harold Clayton Urey (1893–1981).

Hebbel, Friedrich (1813–63) German writer (*Agnes Bernauer* 1852).

Heber, Reginald (1783–1826) English hymn-writer ('From Greenland's icy mountains').

Hébert, Jacques René (1757–94) French revolutionary leader. He was guillotined.

Hectograph duplicating process invented 1780 by the Scottish engineer James Watt (1736–1819).

Hedin, Sven (1865–1952) Swedish explorer.

Hegel, Georg Wilhelm Friedrich (1770–1831) German philosopher. His highly influential works, which describe how the Absolute is being reached by man's evolving powers of consciousness, influenced Karl Marx.

Hegira Mahommed's flight from Mecca to Medina, 13 September 622).

Heidegger, Martin (1889–1976) German philosopher. He is usually described as an existentialist, despite his disclaimer of the label, and his concepts, such as 'angst', had a great deal of influence on existentialists such as Sartre.

Heidelberg Catechism instigated by the Elector Frederick III; published 19 January 1563 by Zacharias Ursinus (1536–83) and Caspar Olevianus (1536–87).

Heidelberg University, Germany, founded 1385.

Heifetz, Jascha (1901–87) Lithuanian-born American violinist. His flamboyant and expressive interpretation of music from Bach to Walton has been widely acclaimed.

Heine, Heinrich (1797–1856) German poet and critic. His masterpiece is his *Book of Songs* (1827), which includes some of the finest lyric poems ever written.

Heinsius, Daniel (1580–1655) Dutch classical scholar.

Heisenberg, Werner Karl (1901–76) German theoretical physicist. He was awarded the 1932 Nobel prize for physics for his work on quantum theory.

Hejaz proclaimed independent kingdom 1916; conquered by and annexed to the kingdom of Saudi Arabia 1925–26.

Helena, Saint (*c*.248–*c*.328).

Helena, St island in the South Atlantic discovered by the Portuguese navigator João de Nova 1502; appropriated by the British East India Company 1661; vested in the Crown 1833.

Helicopter first successful model built 1918 by the Americans Peter Cooper Hewitt (1861–1921) and F. B. Crocker.

Heliogabalus [Elagabalus] (*c*.204–222) Roman emperor (218–222). He was assassinated.

Heliograph invented by the German mathematician and astronomer Johann Karl Friedrich Gauss (1777–1855).

Heliometer modern form invented 1754 by the English optician John Dollond (1706–61).

Helioscope instrument for observing the sun invented by the American engineer Herschel Clifford Parker (b.1867).

Heliport Britain's first opened in London 23 April 1959.

Helium discovered spectroscopically in sun 1868 by Sir Joseph Norman Lockyer (1836–1920); obtained 1895 by Sir William Ramsay (1852–1916).

Helium liquid obtained 1913 by the Dutch scientist Heike Kamerlingh Onnes (1853–1926).

Heller, Joseph (1923–) American novelist. His most popular novel, *Catch–22* (1961), is a grim, surrealist satire on military life and logic.

Hellespont (modern Dardanelles) the narrow ribbon of water in Turkey that connects the Aegean Sea to the Sea of Marmara and from thence the Black Sea. It was crossed by Alexander the Great in 334 BC en route for Asia.

Hellgate Bridge, New York, built 1902–1903 by Austrian-born engineer Gustav Lindenthal (1850–1935).

Hellman, Lillian Florence (1905–84) American playwright (*The Little Foxes* 1939).

Helmholtz, Hermann von (1821–94) German scientist.

Helsinki capital of Finland since 1812.

Helvétius, Claude Adrien(1715–71) French writer (*De l'Esprit* 1758).

Hemans, Mrs Felicia Dorothea (1793–1835) English hymn-writer and poet (*Casabianca* 1829).

Hematin artificial blood pigment discovered 1928 by the German scientist Hans Fischer (1881–1945).

Heming, John (d.1630) English actor-manager.

Hemingway, Ernest [Millar] (1899–1961) American novelist and short-story writer, whose laconic narrative style made a big impression on his contemporaries. Major novels include *A Farewell to Arms* (1929) and *For Whom the Bell Tolls*. He was awarded the Nobel prize for literature in 1954. He committed suicide.

Hémon, Louis (1880–1913) French-Canadian novelist (*Marie Chapdelaine* 1913).

Henderson, Alexander (*c*.1583–1646) Scottish religious leader.

Henderson, Arthur (1863–1935) British statesman.

Hendrix, Jimi [James Marshall Hendrix] (1942–70) American rock guitarist, singer and songwriter. With his trio, the Jimi Hendrix Experience, he became perhaps the most influential of all rock guitarists. He died of alcohol and drug abuse.

Hengest king of Kent (455–488) *see* Appendix.

Henley, William Ernest English poet (*For England's Sake* 1900) (1849–1903).

Henley regatta, Henley-on-Thames, founded 1839.

Henri I (*c*.1008–1060) king of France (1031–60).

Henri II (1519–59) king of France (1547–59).

Henri III (1551–89) king of France (1574–89). He was assassinated.

Henri IV (1553–1610) king of France (1589–1610). He was assassinated.

'Henri V' [Henri, Comte de Chambord] (1820–83) claimant to the French throne.

Henrietta (1644–70) daughter of King Charles I and Duchess of Orleans.

Henrietta Maria (1609–69) wife of King Charles I.

Henry, Patrick (1736–99) governor of Virginia.

Henry, William (1774–1836) English chemist.

Henry Christophe (1767–1820) king of Haiti . He committed suicide.

'Henry, O' [William Sydney Porter] (1862–1910) American writer (*Cabbages and Kings* 1904).

Henry II (973–1024) Holy Roman emperor (1002–24).

Henry III (1017–56) Holy Roman emperor (1039–56).

Henry IV (1050–1106) Holy Roman emperor (1056–1106).

Henry V (1081–1125) Holy Roman emperor (1106–25).

Henry VI (1165–97) Holy Roman emperor (1190–97).

Henry VII (1269–1313) Holy Roman emperor (1308–13).

Henry I (1068–1135) king of England (1100–35) *see* Appendix.

Henry II (1133–89) king of England (1154–89) *see* Appendix.

Henry III (1207–72) king of England (1216–72) *see* Appendix.

Henry IV (1367–1413) king of England and Wales (1399–1413) *see* Appendix.

Henry V (1387–1422) king of England and Wales (1413–22) *see* Appendix.

Henry VI (1421–71) king of England and Wales (1422–61, 1470–71) *see* Appendix

Henry VII (1457–1509) king of England and Wales (1485–1509) *see* Appendix.

Henry VIII (1491–1547) king of England and Wales (1509–47) and of Ireland (1542–47) *see* Appendix.

Henry the Fowler (*c.*875–936) German king (919–936).

Henry the Navigator (1394–1460) Portuguese prince.

Henryson, Robert (*c.*1430–*c.*1508) Scottish poet (*Testament of Cresseid*).

Henschel, Sir George (1850–1934) German-born composer and conductor.

Henslowe, Philip (d.1616) English theatre manager.

Henson, Jim [James Maury Henson] (1936–90) American puppeteer and film producer who created the engaging cast of 'muppets', including Kermit the Frog and Miss Piggy.

Henty, George Alfred (1832–1902) English writer for boys.

Henze, Hans Werner (1926–) German composer. His works, which often reflect his enthusiasm for left-wing causes, include the opera *Elegy for Young Lovers* with a libretto by Auden.

Hepburn, Katharine (1907–) American film and stage actress, noted for her wit and versatility. She had a long personal and acting relationship with Spencer Tracy. Her films include The African Queen (1952), *Guess Who's Coming to Dinner* (1967) and On Golden Pond (1981), the last two bringing her Oscars.

Hepplewhite, George (d.1786) English cabinet-maker.

Heptarchy the seven kingdoms into which Anglo-Saxon England was divided from about the 7th to the 9th centuries: East Anglia, Essex, Kent, Mercia, Northumbria, Sussex and Wessex.

Hepworth, Dame [Jocelyn] Barbara (1903–75) English sculptor. She became one of Britain's leading abstract sculptors in the 1930s, noted for her strong, often monumental carving.

Heraclea, Battle of 280 BC during the invasion of Italy by Pyrrhus, king of Epirus, when he defeated the Romans.

Heraclitus (*c.*540–475 BC) Greek philosopher who held that fire was the physical principle inherent in all phenomena.

Heraclius (*c.*575–641) Roman emperor of the East (610–641). He crushed Persia, the hereditary enemy of Rome 622–628, and received from the Persians the Holy Cross, which he presented to the holy sepulchrre in Jerusalem in 629 BC. By the end of his reign, however, Syria, Palestine and Jerusalem, Mesopotamia and Egypt had all been annexed by Mohammed and his successors and the Roman empire in the East was at an end.

Heralds College, London, founded 1461 by King Edward IV, chartered 1483.

Herbart, Johann Friedrich (1776–1841) German philosopher.

Herbert, George (1593–1633) Welsh-born English Anglican priest and poet. His poems are among the greatest devotional poems in the language, and are characteristic of metaphysical poetry in their subtle, paradoxical exploration of spiritual themes. His works include *The Temple* (1633).

Herbert of Cherbury, Edward Herbert, Baron (1583–1648) English philosopher and historian.

Herder, Johann Gottfried (1744–1803) German writer (*Der Cid* 1805).

Heredia, José Maria de (1842–1905) Cuba-born poet (*Les Trophées* 1893).

Heredity principles of postulated 1865 by the Austrian biologist and monk Gregor Johann Mendel (1822–84).

Hereford Cathedral, England, constructed 1079–1148 (crypt Anglo-Saxon).

Hereward the Wake English outlaw lived in second half of 11th century.

Hergesheimer, Joseph (1880–1954) American novelist (*Java Head* 1919).

Herihor Egyptian high priest of Ammon, who seized the throne 1100 BC. He was deposed by a Tanite Dynasty.

Heriot, George (1563–1624) Scottish goldsmith and royal banker.

Herkomer, Sir Hubert von (1849–1914) German-born painter.

Hero of Alexandria Greek mathematician in 1st century.

Herod (Herod the Great) (*c.*68–4 BC) king of Judaea (37–4 BC) who conquered Galilee, raised the siege of Masada and laid siege to Jerusalem, in 20 BC beginning the Great Restoration of the Temple at Jerusalem. His reign was marked by cruel acts, and according to the New Testament he ordered the Massacre of the Innocents at Bethlehem.

Herod Agrippa I (10 BC– AD 44) tetrarch of Galilee and Peraea, later of Judaea and Samaria, he was recognized as king of Judaea and Samaria in 41. Following his death Judaea was governed by Roman procurators.

Herod Antipas (d.*c.*39) tetrarch of Galilee and Peraea (4 BC–AD 39). He married as his second wife his niece Herodias, infuriated the Jews and, according to the Gospels, brought a rebuke from John the Baptist. It was herold Antipas who had John put to death.

Herod Archelaus son of Herod, brother of Herod Antipas and ethnarch ('leader of the people') of Judaea, Samaria and Idumea (4 BC–AD 6). Like his father, he was notorious for his cruelty. The Jews and Samaritans untied to complain to the emperor about him and he was removed from power and exiled and a Roman governor put in his place.

Herodotus (*c.*485–*c.*431 BC) Greek historian who chronicled the the wars between the Greeks and the Persians.

Hérold, Louis Joseph Ferdinand (1791–1833) French composer (*Zampa* 1831).

Herrera, Ferdinando (*c.*1534–1597) Spanish poet.

Herrick, Robert (1591–1674) English Anglican priest and poet. Many of the poems, which are often delicately sensual, are surprisingly direct in their sympathy for the traditional (virtually pagan) customs of English country life. His works include *Hesperides* (1648).

Herrings, Battle of the (Battle of Rouvray) between the English and the French, 1429.

Herriot, Édouard (1872–1957) French statesman.

Herschel, Sir John Frederick William (1792–1871) English astronomer.

Herschel, Sir William (1738–1822) German-born astronomer.

Hertford College, Oxford University, founded as Hertford Hall 1282 by Elias de Hertford; incorporated as Hertford College 1740; reincorporated 1874.

Hertz, Gustav Ludwig *see* FRANCK, JAMES.

Hertzog, James Barry Munnik (1866–1942) South African statesman. He founded the Nationalist Party (1913) and advocated non-cooperation with Britain during World War I. He became prime minister (1924–39) and founded the Afrikaner Party in 1941.

Herzen, Aleksandr (1812–70) Russian revolutionary leader.

Herzl, Theodor (1860–1904) Hungarian-born founder of Zionism (*Der Judenstaat* 1896).

Herzog, Werner (1942–) German film director. Bizarre enterprises, e.g. the building of an opera house up the Amazon in *Fitzcarraldo* (1982), are a notable feature of his films.

Heseltine, Michael *see* THATCHER, MARGARET HILDA.

Heseltine, Philip ('Peter Warlock') (1894–1930) English composer (*Capriol Suite* 1926). He committed suicide.

Hesiod Greek poet of the 8th century BC.

Hesperia an asteroid discovered 1861 by the Italian astronomer Giovanni Virginio Schiaparelli (1835–1910).

Hess, Dame Myra (1890–1965) English pianist. She was also a much acclaimed concert pianist and an influential teacher.

Hess, [Walter Richard] Rudolf (1894–1987) German Nazi politician. Deputy leader of Nazi party (1934–41). On the eve of Hitler's invasion of Russia, he flew to Scotland, apparently in the hope of negotiating peace terms with Britain. He spent the rest of his life in prison in Berlin, where he committed suicide.

Hess, Victor Francis (1883–1964) Austrian-born American physicist. He shared the 1936 Nobel prize for physics with the American physicist Carl David Anderson (1905–) for his research into cosmic rays.

Hesse, Hermann (1877–1962) German-born Swiss novelist, short-story writer and poet. His fiction reflects his fascination with oriental mysticism, spiritual alienation and worldly detachment. He was awarded the Nobel prize for literature in 1946. His works include *Peter Camenzind* (1904).

Heston, Charlton [John Charlton Carter] (1923–) American film and stage actor, renowned principally for his physique, noble profile and commanding presence in religious epics. His films include *Ben Hur* (1959).

Hesychasts Greek mystic movement in 14th century.

Hetton line, Co. Durham, oldest mineral railway in Britain and first real railway on a prepared surface, built 1819–22 by George Stephenson (1781–1848; opened 1822; closed 1959.

Heuristic method of education suggested 1884 by Professor Meiklejohn.

Heuss, Dr Theodor (1884–1963) president of West Germany (1949–59).

Hevelius, Johannes (1611–87) Polish astronomer.

Hewlett, Maurice (1861–1923) English writer (*The Forest Lovers* 1897).

Heyerdahl, Thor (1914–) Norwegian anthropologist. His practical demonstration of his theory that South Americans emigrated to Polynesia on rafts of balsa wood caught the public imagination and he subsequently launched similar expeditions.

Heyward, DuBose (1885–1940) American writer (*Porgy* 1925).

Heywood, John (*c.*1497–*c.*1580) English writer (*The Four P's* 1569).

Heywood, Thomas (*c.*1574–1641) English writer (A *Woman Killed with Kindness*).

Hezekiah king of Judah (720–687 BC) who was a noted religious reformer and skilful leader.

Hibbert Trust originally for the elevation of the Unitarian ministry founded 1847 by the British merchant Robert Hibbert (1770–1849).

'Hickock, Wild Bill' [James Butler Hickock] (1837–76) American pioneer. He was murdered.

Hiero I (d.467 BC) king of Syracuse (478–467 BC).

Hiero II (d.215 BC) king of Syracuse (270–215 BC).

Higden, Ranulf (d.1364)) English historian (*Polychronicon*).

High-pressure steam pioneered 1800 by the English engineer Richard Trevithick (1771–1833).

Highsmith, Patricia (1921–95) American thriller writer (*Strangers on a Train* 1950).

Hilarius, Saint (*c.*300–367).

Hilary, Saint (d.467) pope (461–467).

Hilary Term legal term beginning 11 January, ending Wednesday before Easter.

Hilda, Saint (614–680).

Hildebert (*c.*1055–1133) French ecclesiastic and writer.

Hildebrand, Adolf von (1847–1921) German sculptor.

Hildegard, Saint (1098–1179).

Hill, Octavia (1838–1912) English social reformer.

Hill, Sir Rowland (1795–1879) English pioneer in postal services.

Hillary, Sir Edmund [Percival] (1919–) New Zealand explorer and mountaineer. He and the Tibetan sherpa, **Tenzing Norgay** (1914–86), made the first ascent of Mount Everest in 1953. His other exploits include an overland trek to the South Pole in 1958.

Hilliard, Nicholas (*c.*1547–1619) English painter (particularly of miniatures).

Hillsborough stadium disaster 95 football fans crushed to death at Liverpool vs Nottingham Forest match, Sheffield, 15 April 1989.

Himera, Battle of 480 BC a Carthaginian attack on Sicily which was repelled by Sicilian Greeks.

Himmler, Heinrich (1900–1945) German Nazi leader. He was chosen by Hitler to head the SS in 1929, and by 1936 was in command of the German police structure. Through his secret police, the Gestapo, he organized repression first in Germany then in occupied Europe, and oversaw the construction of the Nazi concentration and death camp system and the genocide of the Jews. He committed suicide.

Hindemith, Paul (1895–1963) German composer and violist. The Nazis banned his works for their 'impropriety', and he settled in the US in 1939. Highly prolific, he wrote operas (e.g.*Mathis der Maler* 1938), symphonies, song cycles, ballet and chamber music.

Hindenburg, Paul von Beneckendorff und von (1847–1934) German field marshal and statesman. He shared command of the German forces in World War I (1916–18), and became president of Germany (1925–34). He defeated Hitler in the presidential election of 1932 but was persuaded to appoint Hitler chancellor in 1933.

Hines, Earl [Kenneth] 'Fatha' (1903–83) American jazz pianist, bandleader and songwriter. He became one of the most influential jazz pianists of the 1930s and 1940s.

Hinton, Dr William Augustus (1884–1959) first black American to hold a professorship Harvard University.

Hipparchus (d.514 BC) Greek tyrant of Athens (527–514), son of Pisistratus, who ruled with his brother Hippias.

Hipparchus (*c.*160–*c.*125 BC) Greek astronomer who constructed a catalogue of the stars, numbering them and assigning them their places and magnitudes.

Hippias (d.*c.*490) Greek tyrant of Athens (527–510 BC), son of Pisistratus, who ruled with his brother Hipparchus until 514 and thereafter alone. He was overthrown and expelled from Athens 510 BC.

Hippocrates (*c.*460–*c.*370 BC) Greek physician and writer. Born on the island of Cos, he practised there and also travelled throughout Greece. Regarded as the 'father of medicine', the Hippocratic Oath is named after him.

Hippolytus (*fl* early 3rd century) Roman ecclesiastical writer who may have been martyred by being drowned in the River Tiber.

Hirohito (1901–89) Japanese emperor (1926–89). He ruled Japan as a divinity until her defeat in 1945, after which he became a constitutional monarch, known primarily for his marine biology research. He was succeeded by his son **Akihito** (1933–).

Hiroshige, Ando (1797–1858) Japanese artist.

Hiroshima Japanese city destroyed by an atom bomb, 6 August 1945.

Hirsch Music Library, British Museum, founded by Paul Adolf Hirsch (1881–1951).

Hirsch, Samson Raphael (1808–88) German Jewish scholar.

Hispanic and Luso-Brazilian Councils, London, incorporated 1943.

Hispanic Society of America, New York, founded 1904.

Hiss, Alger (1904–) American state department official. A highly respected public servant, he was jailed (1950–54) for spying for the USSR.

Hitchcock, Sir Alfred (1899–1980) English-born film director, based in Hollywood from 1940, whose suspenseful thrillers, e.g. *The Thirty-Nine Steps* (1935), have long been regarded as masterpieces.

Hitler, Adolf (1889–1945) Austrian-born German dictator. He co-founded the National Socialist Workers' Party in 1919, and was jailed for nine months following his part in the failed Munich coup of 1923, during which time he wrote *Mein Kampf* ('my struggle'), an anti-semitic 'testament' of his belief in the superiority of the Aryan race. He was appointed chancellor by Hindenburg in 1933 and consolidated his brutal regime through Himmler's Gestapo, becoming Reichsführer in 1934. He allied himself temporarily with Stalin in 1939, in which year he invaded Poland, beginning World War II. He invaded Russia in 1941 and survived an attempted assassination in 1944. He killed himself in Berlin in 1945. Hitler's war resulted in *c.*40 million dead.

Hittites an ancient people of Anatolia who, in the second millenium BC, built an empire in northern Syria and Asia Minor. They waged a long war against Rameses II, king of Egypt.

HIV (human immuno-deficiency virus) discovered as cause of Aids 1984.

Hlothere (d.685) king of Kent 9673–685) *see* Appendix.

Hoadly, Benjamin (1676–1761) English theologian.

Hoban, James (*c.*1762–1831) Irish-born architect (the White House, Washington DC).

Hobart capital of Tasmania, founded 1804.

Hobbema, Meindert (1638–1709) Dutch painter (*The Water Mill*).

Hobbes, Thomas (1588–1679) English philosopher and historian (*The Leviathan* 1651).

Hobhouse, Leonard Trelawney (1864–1929) English sociologist.

Hoccleve, Thomas (*c.*1369–*c.*1450) English poet (*De Regimine Principum* 1411–12).

Hoche, Lazare (1768–97) French revolutionary general.

Ho Chi Minh [Nguyen That Tan] (1890–1969) Vietnamese communist leader. A Marxist nationalist, he led the Viet Minh forces, with US help, against the occupying Japanese during World War II and became president of Vietnam (1945–54), during which time he led his forces to victory against French colonial rule. He became president of North Vietnam (1954–69) after the country's partition at the 1954 Geneva conference.

Hockey Association present body formed 1886.

Hockney, David (1937–) English painter and etcher. Associated with the Pop Art movement in his early work, he is now regarded as one of the world's leading representational painters.

Hodgkin, Dorothy [Dorothy Mary Crowfoot] (1910–) English chemist. She was awarded the 1964 Nobel prize for chemistry for her work on the molecular structures of penicillin, insulin and vitamin B12.

Hodgkin, Sir Alan Lloyd (1914–) English physiologist. With Sir Andrew Fielding Huxley (1917–) and Sir John Carew Eccles, he shared the 1963 Nobel prize for physiology or medicine for research into nerve impulses.

Hodgson, Ralph (1871–1962) English poet (*The Last Blackbird* 1907).

Hodler, Ferdinand (1853–1918) Swiss artist.

Hoe, Richard Marsh (1812–86) American inventor (1846) of the rotary printing press.

Hoe, horse-drawn invented 1731 by the English farmer Jethro Tull (1674–1714).

Hofer, Andreas (1767–1810) Tyrolese patriot. He was executed.

Hoffman, Dustin (1937–) American stage and film actor (*The Graduate* 1967).

Hoffmann, Ernst Theodor Amadeus (1776–1822) German poet.

Hoffmann, Heinrich (1809–94) German humorous writer (*Struwwelpeter* 1847).

Hoffnung, Gerard (1925–59) English caricaturist, musician and social reformer.

Hofmannsthal, Hugo von (1874–1929) Austrian poet (*Ariadne auf Naxos* 1912).

Hofmeyr, Jan Hendrik (1845–1909) South African statesman.

Hofstadter, Robert *see* MOSSBAUER, RUDOLF LUDWIG.

Hogarth, David George (1862–1929) English archaeologist.

Hogarth, William (1697–1764) English artist. Trained as an engraver in the rococo tradition, by 1720 he had established his own illustration business. He then began his series of 'conversation pieces' and was executing some fine portraits. He also produced a remarkable series of paintings following a sequential narrative, the best known of which are *Marriage à la* Mode and *The Rake's Progress* (1735). He wrote a treatise on aesthetic principles entitled *The Analysis of Beauty*.

Hogg, James ('The Ettrick Shepherd') (1770–1835) Scottish poet.

Hogg, Quintin (1845–1903) English founder (1882) of The (London) Polytechnic.

Hohenlinden, Battle of Wars of the French Revolution between the French and the Austrians, 3 December 1800.

Hohenstaufen dynasty emperors of Germany 1138–1254.

Hohenzollern dynasty ruled Brandenburg 1411–1701, Prussia 1701–1871, Germany 1871–1918.

Hokusai (1760–1849) Japanese painter.

Holbach, Paul Heinrich Dietrich, Baron d' (1723–89) French philosopher (*Système de la Nature* 1770).

Holbein, Hans (the Elder) (*c.*1465–1524) German painter.

Holbein, Hans (the Younger) (1497–1543) German painter. He painted mainly portraits and religious paintings, the most memorable of the latter being the *The Death of Christ* (1521). He became court painter to Henry VIII.

Holbrooke, Josef (1878–1958) English composer (*Queen Mab* 1904).

Holcombe, Henry (*c.*1690–*c.*1750) English composer.

Holcroft, Thomas (1745–1809) English playwright (*The Road to Ruin* 1792).

Hölderlin, Johann Christian Friedrich (1770–1843) German poet.

Holgate, Robert (*c.*1481–1555) archbishop of York (1545–54).

Holiday, Billie 'Lady Day' [Eleanora] (1915–59) American jazz and blues singer. She became one of the most influential jazz singers of her time, with her sad, elegiac and subtle interpretations of popular songs.

Holidays with pay enforced by law in Britain since 1938.

Holinshed, Raphael (d.*c.*1580) English historian (*Chronicles* 1578).

Holland, Henry (*c.*1746–1806) English architect (Battersea Bridge 1771–72).

Holland, Henry Richard Vassal Fox, Baron (1773–1840) British statesman.

Holland, John (d.1722) founder and first governor (1695) of the Bank of Scotland.

Hollar, Wenceslaus (1607–77) Bohemian artist.

Holles, Denzil, Baron (1599–1680) Puritan leader.

Holly, Buddy [Charles Hardin Holley] (1936–59) American rock singer, songwriter and guitarist. He was one of the first rock singers to use the back-up of lead, rhythm and bass guitars, with drums. He died in a plane crash.

Hollywood, California, founded 1887, incorporated 1903.

Holmes, Oliver Wendell (1809–94) American writer (*The Autocrat of the Breakfast Table* 1831–58).

Holmes, Oliver Wendell (1841–1935) US Supreme Court judge.

Holmium chemical element discovered 1879 by Per Teodor Cleve.

Holocene Epoch the time from *c.*8000 BC to the present day.

Holst, Gustav [Theodore] (1874–1934) English composer of Swedish descent. His best-known compositions are *The Planets* (1917) and *The Perfect Fool* (1923). Much of his music was inspired by the English landscape and by Thomas Hardy.

Holstein, Friedrich von (1837–1909) German statesman.

Holy Alliance an alliance made in Paris between the emperors of Russia and Austria and the king of Prussia, 26 September 1815.

Holy Island (Lindisfarne), England, chosen for the site of his church and monastery by St Aidan 635.

Holyoake, George Jacob (1817–1906) English pioneer in co-operation.

Holyoke, Samuel (1762–1820) American hymn-writer (*Arnheim* 1778).

Holy Roman Empire crown first held 800 by Charlemagne; renounced by Francis II, 1806.

Holyrood Abbey, Scotland, founded by King David I, 1128; Palace begun 1498.

Holy Spirit dogma of procession from the Father and the Son ('Filioque') added to Catholic doctrine 589.

Holy Thursday (Ascension Day), 40th day after Easter Sunday.

Holy Week the week from Palm Sunday to Easter Saturday.

Home, John (1722–1808) Scottish playwright (*Douglas* 1756).

Home Guard founded May 1940 as LDV, adopted new name July 1940, disbanded December 1945.

Home Office, Great Britain, founded by 1785.

Homer (*fl* 8th century BC) Greek poet, author of the two great epic poems *The Iliad*, the story of the Greek war against Troy, and *The Odyssey*, which describes the adventures of the Greek hero Odysseus (known to the Romans as Ulysses) on his voyage home from the war. Little is known of Homer but the characters and events of the poems have had a profound influence upon western literature.

Homer, Winslow (1836–1910) American painter.

Home Rule for Ireland League founded 1870 by Isaac Butt; first Bill 1886, second Bill 1893, third Bill 1912–14; Government of Ireland Bill 1919–20.

Homoeopathic physician first to practice in England Dr Frederic Hervey Foster Quin (1799–1878).

Homoeopathy principles first enunciated 1796 by the German physician Samuel Hahnemann (1755–1843).

Homology principle declared 1818 by the French naturalist Etienne St Hilaire.

Honduras Central American republic discovered by Christopher Columbus 1502; colonized by Spanish from 1524; gained independence 1821.

Honduras, British *see* BELIZE.

Honecker, Erich (1912–94) East German Communist politician. Appointed head of state in 1976, he fell from power in 1989 following the wide social unrest that followed Gorbachev's statement that the USSR would no longer intervene in East German affairs. He was charged in 1990 with treason and corruption following the re-unification of Germany.

Honegger, Arthur (1892–1955) French-born Swiss composer. One of the group of Parisian composers dubbed 'Les Six' his works include ballet music, symphonies, film scorces and *Pacific 231*, a musical portrait of a train. (*King David* 1921).

Hong Kong leased to Britain by China 1842 (New Territories, Kowloon and Stonecutters Island, 1898); occupied by the Japanese 1941–45; to be returned to Chinese control 1997.

Honorius I pope (625–638).

Honorius II [Lamberto Scannabecchi] (d.1130) pope (1124–30).

Honorius II [Pietro Cadalo] (d.1072) antipope (1061–64).

Honorius III [Cencio Savelli] (d.1227) pope (1216–27).

Honorius IV [Giacomo Savelli] (d.1287) pope (1285–87).

Honourable Corps of Gentlemen at Arms the queen's personal bodyguard, founded 1559.

Honthorst, Gerard van (1590–1656) Dutch painter (*Christ before Pilate*).

Hooch, Pieter de (1629–*c.*1685) Dutch painter (*Scene in a Courtyard*).

Hood, Samuel [Viscount Hood] (1724–1816) admiral.

Hood, Thomas (1799–1845) English poet (*Eugene Aram's Dream* 1829).

Hook, Theodore (1788–1841) English writer (*Maxwell* 1830).

Hooke, Robert (1635–1703) English clockmaker and inventor of the anchor escapement.

Hooker, Richard (*c.*1554–1600) English theologian (*Ecclesiasticall Politie* 1594–1648).

Hooker, Sir William Jackson (1785–1865) English botanist.

Hooper, John (d.1555) English religious reformer. He was burnt at the stake.

Hoover, Herbert [Clark] (1874–1964) American Republican statesman and 31st president of the US (1929–33). He succeeded Coolidge as president in 1929, and was widely perceived as failing to cope with the crisis of the Great Depression.

Hoover, J[ohn] Edgar (1895–1972) American public servant and founder of the Federal Bureau of Investigation (1924–1972). He made the FBI into a highly effective federal crime-fighting force in the 1930s, but also used his organization's considerable powers against anyone perceived as 'radical' in politics.

'Hope, Anthony' [Sir Anthony Hope Hawkins] (1863–1933) English novelist (*The Prisoner of Zenda* 1894).

Hope, Bob [Leslie Townes Hope] (1903–) English-born American comedian and film actor, known for his snappy wisecracks. He starred in the 'Road' films with Bing Crosby.

Hope, Thomas (1709–1831) English designer (*Household Furniture* 1807).

Hopkins, Sir Frederick Gowland (1861–1947) English biochemist. He shared the 1929 Nobel prize for physiology or medicine with Eijkman for his discovery of 'accessory food factors', which came to be called vitamins.

Hopkins, Gerard Manley (1844–89) English Jesuit priest and poet. A convert, he frequently expressed in his poems the keen conflict he felt between his desire to serve God as both priest and poet. None of his work was published in his lifetime. *Poems* was published in 1918).

Hopkins, Johns (1795–1873) American merchant and philanthropist.

Hopkins, Stephen (1707–85) governor of Rhode Island.

Hopkinson, Joseph (1770–1842) American lawyer and writer of 'Hail, Columbia' (1798).

Hopper, Edward (1882–1967) American artist. Regarded as the foremost realist American painter, his paintings have a still, introspective and often mysterious quality.

Hoppner, John (1758–1810) English painter (*The Countess of Oxford*).

Horace [Quintus Horatius Flaccus] (65–8 BC) Roman poet and satirist. He looked to the literature of Greece for inspiration, but his sardonic, realistic and tightly controlled language is wholly Roman. His *Odes* (*c.*24 BC), *Satires* and *Epistles* have been much imitated.

Hormisdas, Saint pope (514–523).

Hormones internal secretions discovered 1902–1903 by the English physiologists Sir William Bayliss (1866–1924) and Ernest Henry Starling (1866–1927).

Hornung, Ernest William (1866–1921) English author of the 'Raffles' stories.

Horowitz, Vladimir (1904–89) Russian-born pianist.

Horrocks, Jeremiah (*c.*1617–1641) English astronomer.

Horsa (d.455) king of Kent (455) *see* Appendix.

Horsley, Samuel (1733–1806) English theologian.

Hortensius, Quintus (114–50 BC) Roman orator.

Horthy of Nagybanya, Admiral Miklos (1868–1957) regent of Hungary (1920–44).

Hot blast, in smelting process, invented 1825–28 by the Scottish engineer James Beaumont Neilson (1792–1865).

Hotchkiss machine gun invented 1872 by the American Benjamin Berkeley Hotchkiss (1826–85).

Hot Springs Conference Second World War conference held 18 May–1 June 1943.

'Hotspur' [Sir Henry Percy] (1364–1403). He was killed in battle.

'Houdini, Harry' [Erich Weiss] (1874–1926) Hungarian-born magician and conjurer.

Houdon, Jean Antoine (1741–1828) French sculptor (*Morpheus* 1777).

House, Colonel Edward Mandell (1858–1938) American statesman.

House of Commons, Great Britain, origins in 13th century.

House of Lords, Great Britain, origins in 13th century.

House of Representatives, US Congress, instituted 1787.

Housman, A[lfred] E[dward] (1859–1936) English poet and scholar. A distinguished classical scholar, his few works of poetry were published posthumously, e.g. *A Shropshire Lad* (written 1896).

Housman, Laurence (1865–1959) English writer (*Palace Plays* 1930).

Houston, Samuel (1793–1863) first Texas president (1836–44).

Hovercraft started as a private venture 1953 by its English inventor, Christopher S. Cockerell (1910–); development and manufacture undertaken 1958; first Dover-Calais crossing 1959.

Howard League for Penal Reform founded 1866.

Howard, Catherine (1521–42) fifth wife of Henry VIII, whom she married in 1540. She was beheaded.

Howard, Henry, Earl of Surrey (1517–47) English politician and poet. He was beheaded.

Howard, John (1726–90) English prison reformer.

Howard, Sidney (1891–1939) American playwright (*Alien Corn* 1933).

Howard, Trevor (1916–88) British film and stage actor (*Brief Encounter* 1946).

Howe, Elias(1819–67) American inventor of the sewing-machine (1846).

Howe, Sir Geoffrey *see* MAJOR, JOHN.

Howe, Admiral Richard (1726–99) of 'The Glorious First of June' 1794.

Howell, James (d.*c.*1594) Welsh writer (*Epistolae Ho-Elianae* 1655).

Howells, Herbert (1892–1983) English composer.

Howells, William Dean (1837–1920) American writer and editor.

Howrah Bridge, Calcutta, opened 1943.

Hoyle, Edmond (1672–1769) English whist expert.

Hoyle, Sir Fred (1915–) English astronomer, mathematician, broadcaster and writer. He became the main proponent of the theory of the universe which holds that the universe is basically unchanging (as opposed to the big-bang theory).

Hsüan Tê Period, China, 1426–35.

Hubbard, L. Ron (1911–86) American writer and founder of Scientology.

Hubble, Edwin Powell (1889–1953) American astronomer and cosmologist. His discovery of galactic 'red shift' and other research established the theory of the expanding universe.

Hubert, Saint (*c.*656–*c.*727).

Hubert de Burgh (d.1243) Chief Justiciar of England.

Huc, Evariste Régis (1813–60) French missionary to Tibet.

Huch, Ricarda (1864–1947) German writer (*Ludolf Urslev* 1883).

Hudson, Henry (d.1611) English navigator.

Hudson, Rock (1925–85) American film and TV actor (*Giant* 1956). He died of Aids.

Hudson, William Henry (1841–1922) Argentine-born naturalist and writer (*Green Mansions* 1904).

Hudson's Bay discovered 1610 by the English navigator Henry Hudson (d.1611).

Hudson's Bay Company formed by Prince Rupert, chartered by King Charles II, 1670.

Hughes, Howard [Robard] (1905–76) American industrialist, aviator and film producer. He greatly extended his inherited oil wealth and made several epic flights, including a record round-the-world trip. He became increasingly eccentric and went into seclusion in 1966.

Hughes, Ted [Edward James Hughes] (1930–) English poet, noted for his violent poetic imagery drawn from the natural world. He was married (1956–63) to Sylvia Plath. He was appointed poet laureate in 1984.

Hughes, Thomas (1822–96) English writer (*Tom Brown's Schooldays* 1856).

Hugo, Victor (1802–85) French novelist, dramatist and poet. His socially challenging dramas established Hugo as the leader of the French literary Romantics. His novels include *The Hunchback of Notre Dame* and *Les Misérables* (1862).

Huguenots French Protestants, so called from the middle of 16th century.

Hugues Capet (*c.*938–996) king of France (987–996).

Huli, Feast of Indian custom similar to April Fools' Day, celebrated 31 March.

Hull, Cordell (1871–1955) American statesman.

Hulme, Thomas Ernest (1883–1917) English writer (*Speculations* 1924).

Human experiment first planned to test an hypothesis based on observation, undertaken 1798 by the English physician Edward Jenner (1749–1823).

Human Rights, Declaration of adopted by the United Nations General Assembly 10 December 1948.

Humboldt, Alexander von (1769–1859) German naturalist and explorer.

Hume, David (1711–76) Scottish philosopher, economist and historian. An empiricist and sceptic, Hume disallowed human speculation much beyond what could be perceived by the senses. His works include *Political Discourses* (1752) and *A Treatise of Human Nature*. He has been claimed by some modern economics to have been a pro-monetarist for his discussion of the 'hidden hand' guiding market forces.

Humperdinck, Engelbert (1854–1921) German composer (*Hansel and Gretel* 1893).

Hundred Days, The Napoleon's return from Elba, 20 March 1815 to 28 June 1815.

Hundred Years' War, The between England and France, 1337–1453.

Hungary traditionally conquered by Magyars 896; independent kingdom from 1001; Hapsburg rule 1526–1918; republic and communist regime 1918–19; Horthy's dictatorship 1920–44; republic proclaimed 1946; Communist regime began 1949; popular revolt crushed by Soviet forces October–November 1956; democracy established 1989.

Hung Chih Period, China, 1488–1505.

Hung Wu Period, China, 1368–98.

Huns invaded Europe 363; defeated 454.

Hunt, Leigh (1784–1859) English essayist (*Imagination and Fancy* 1844) and friend of Keats.

Hunt, William Holman (1827–1910) English painter. A founder of the Pre-Raphaelite movement, he sought inspiration in direct study from nature and natural composition. His works include *The Light of the World* (1854).

Hunt, Wilson Price (*c.*1782–1842) American explorer.

Hunter, John Scottish surgeon (1728–93).

Hunter, William (1718–83) Scottish anatomist.

Hunter, Sir William Wilson (1840–1900) Scottish administrator in India.

Hunters' moon the first full moon after the Harvest Moon.

Huntingdon, Selina Hastings, Countess of (1707–91) founder of the Calvinist-Methodist 'Countess of Huntingdon's Connexion'.

Huntington, Henry Edwards (1850–1927) American railway promoter.

Hunyadi, János (*c.*1387–1456) Hungarian patriot.

Hurricane aeroplane, last flypast over London commemorating the Battle of Britain, Sunday, 20 September 1959.

Hurst, Fannie (1889–1968) American novelist (*Back Street* 1931).

Hus, Jan (*c.*1369–1415) Bohemian religious reformer. He was burnt at the stake.

Huskisson, William (1770–1830) British statesman.

Hussein [Ibn Talal] (1935–) king of Jordan (1952–). He lost the West Bank of his country to Israel after the Six Day War of 1967, and has trod an uneasy diplomatic line between friendship with the West and his efforts on behalf of the Palestinians.

Hussein ibn Ali (1856–1931) king of the Hejaz (1916–24).

Hussein, Saddam (1937–) Iraqi dictator. He became president of Iraq in 1979, and established a reputation for ruthlessness in the suppression of his opponents. After his invasion of Kuwait in 1990, UN forces forced his withdrawal in the Gulf War of 1991.

Husserl, Edmund (1859–1938) Austrian philosopher.

Huston, John [Marcellus] (1906–87) American film director. His films include several classics, e.g. *The Maltese Falcon* (1941), from a story by Hammet. His last film, *The Dead*, from a short story by Joyce, starred his daughter, the actress **Anjelica Huston** (1951–).

Hutcheson, Francis (1694–1746) Irish philosopher (*System of Moral Philosophy* 1755).

Hutchinson, Anne (1590–1643) English-born religious leader. She was killed.

Hutchinson, Thomas (1711–80) governor of Massachusetts Bay.

Hutton, James (1726–97) Scottish pioneer in the study of geology.

Hutton, Sir Leonard ('Len') (1916–90) English cricketer. A Yorkshire player throughout his long career, he became the first professional player to captain England regularly (1952–54).

Huxley, Aldous [Leonard] (1894–1963) English novelist, short-story writer and essayist. His early work depicted the brittle word of 1920s English intellectual life (e.g. *Point Counter Point* (1928), but his masterpiece is *Brave New World*, a chilling fable of a future totalitarian state. His brother was Julian Huxley.

Huxley, Sir Andrew Fielding *see* HODGKIN, SIR ALAN LLOYD

Huxley, Sir Julian [Sorell] (1887–1975) English biologist. He became one of Britain's best-known scientists and humanists and was the first director-general of UNESCO (1946–48). His brother was Aldous Huxley.

Huxley, Thomas Henry (1825–95) English biologist. He became the most prominent scientific defender of Darwin's theory of evolution. He gradually lost his belief in a deity and coined the term 'agnostic'. His works include *Lay Sermons* (1870).

Huygens, Christiaan (1629–95) Dutch scientist.

Huysmans, Cornelis (1648–1727) Flemish painter.

Huysmans, Joris Karl (1848–1907) French novelist (*A Rebours* 1884).

Huysum, Jan van (1682–1749) Dutch painter (particularly of flower-pieces).

Hydaspes, Battle of the 326 BC a battle of Alexander the Great's campaigns, when he conquered the Punjab.

Hyder *or* **Haidar Ali** (*c.*1728–1782) Indian leader.

Hyderabad, India, founded 1589; absorbed into India 1948.

Hydraulic crane invented *c.*1845 by William George Armstrong (later Baron Armstrong) (1810–1900).

Hydraulic press invented 1796 by the English inventor Joseph Bramah (1748–1814).

Hydraulic pressure accumulator invented 1850 by William George Armstrong (later Baron Armstrong) (1810–1900).

Hydroelectric station first example begun in Northern Ireland 1883.

Hydroelectricity discovered 1843 by the English scientist Michael Faraday (1791–1867).

Hydrogen properties discovered 1776 by the British scientist Henry Cavendish (1731–1810).

Hydrogen bomb first American exploded over Bikini Atoll, 1 March 1954.

Hydrogen bomb first Russian exploded in the Pacific, 12 August 1953.

Hydrogen peroxide obtained 1810 by the French chemist Louis Jacques Thénard (1777–1857).

Hydrophobia effective vaccine treatment developed 1885 by the French scientist Louis Pasteur (1822–95).

Hygiene modern practice developed by the English physician Edmund Alexander Parkes (1819–76).

Hyginus, St pope (136–140).

Hygrometer invented 1783 by the Swiss scientist Horace Benédict de Saussure (1740–99).

Hyksos a nomadic people originally from Palestine who ruled in Egypt from 1800 to 1600 BC, forming the fifteenth dynasty.

Hyndman, Henry Mayers (1842–1921) English socialist leader.

Hypatia (d.415) Alexandrian scholar. He was murdered.

Hypnotism term first introduced 1841 by the Scottish scholar James Braid (1796–1860).

Hyppolytus, Saint anti-pope (217).

Hysterisis, Law of discovered by the German-born engineer Charles Proteus Steinmetz (1865–1923).

Hywel ab Idwal king of Gwynedd (979–985) *see* Appendix.

Hywel Dda (d.950) king of Gwynedd (904–950) *see* Appendix.

I

áñez, Vicente Blasco (1867–1928) Spanish novelist (*The Four Horsemen of the Apocalypse*).

go I ab Idwal (d.*c.*980) king of Gwynedd (950–979) *see* Appendix.

go II ab Idwal (d.*c.*1040) king of Gwynedd (1023–39) *see* Appendix.

3M (International Business Machines) the world's largest computer manufacturer, founded 1914.

n Battutah (1304–68) Arab traveller.

n Khaldun (1332–1406) Arab historian (*Kitab al 'Ibar*).

n Saud, Abdul Aziz (1880–1953) king of Saudi Arabia. He became the first king of Saudi Arabia (1932–53) and negotiated terms with American oil companies after the discovery of oil in his country (1938).

rahim Pasha (1789–1848) viceroy of Egypt (1844).

sen, Henrik (1828–1906) Norwegian dramatist. His early verse dramas (e.g. *Peer Gynt* 1867), plays of social realism (e.g. *Ghosts*), and later symbolic plays were all hugely influential on later dramatists, e.g. SHAW.

CAO (International Civil Aviation Organization), Montreal, proposed at an international conference at Chicago 1944; came into being 1947; 168 members in 1992.

eland first settled 874; independent republic 930–1262; ruled by Denmark 1381–1918; sovereign state 1918–44; independent republic since 1944.

eni a people of ancient Britain who occupied the modern counties of Suffolk, Norfolk, Cambridge and Huntingdon. They fought against the Romans under their queen, Boudicca.

hthyosaurus first brought to scientific notice 1811 by the English fossil collector Mary Anning (1799–1847).

knield Way from Berkshire Down to the Fens, England, natural road of Celtic origin, first recorded mention 45.

onoclast Controversy in Byzantine Empire, 726–843.

a (d.*c.*568) king of Bernicia (547–568) *see* Appendix.

aho a state of the USA, first permanently settled 1860; organized as a Territory 1863; admitted to the Union 1890.

entity cards introduced in Britain 1939; abolished 21 February 1952.

Ido revision of Esperanto produced 1907 by Marquis de Beaufront.

Idrisi (*c.*1099–*c.*1155) Arab geographer.

Idwal Foel king of Gwynedd (916–942) *see* Appendix.

Ifni former Spanish province administered from Madrid ceded by Morocco to Spain 1860; returned to Morocco 1969.

Ignatius Loyola, St (1491–1556) Spanish saint. A former solder who was severely wounded in action, he had a spiritual conversion and founded the Society of Jesus (the Jesuits) in 1534.

Ignatius of Antioch, Saint lived in the 1st century.

Ignatius of Constantinople, Saint (*c.*800–*c.*878).

Ikhnaton (d.*c.*1357 BC) pharaoh of Egypt.

Illinium chemical element discovered 1926 by the American scientist B. Smith Hopkins (1873–1952).

Illinois University, Urbana, founded 1867.

Illinois state of the USA, discovered by the French 1673; settled 1720; ceded by France to Britain 1763; organized as a Territory 1809; admitted to the Union 1818.

Illium an alloy discovered by the American chemist Samuel Wilson Parr (1857–1931).

Illuminati German rationalist society founded 1776 by the German philosopher Adam Weishaupt (1748–1830); officially proscribed and dissolved 1785.

Illustrated London News British periodical that began publication 1842.

Illyria an ancient region on the eastern shore of the Adriatic Sea. Alexander the Great visited there in his campaign in Thrace and Illyria 335 BC

Immaculate Conception of the Virgin Mary, Catholic dogma defined 1854.

Imperial Defence College, London, for senior army, navy and air force officers, founded 1926.

Inauguration Day, USA, 20 January, on which American presidents take the oath of office every four years.

Incandescent electric lamp invented 1878 by Thomas Alva Edison (1847–1931) and Sir Joseph Wilson Swan (1828–1914).

Incandescent gas mantles invented 1886 by the Austrian chemist Baron Auer von Welsbach (1858–1929).

Inchbald, Mrs Elizabeth English actress and novelist (1753–1821).

Income tax introduced in Britain 1799.

Incunabula books printed in Europe before 1500.

Independence Day commemorating the Declaration of Independence 4 July 1776; celebrated in the USA 4 July each year.

Independent Labour Party founded 1893 by the Scottish socialist James Keir Hardie (1856–1915); seceded from Labour Party 1932 under James Maxton (1885–1946); ceased to have parliamentary representation 1948.

Index Vaticanus (*Index librorum prohibitorum*) the list of books condemned by the Catholic Church, first issued 1559.

India entered by Alexander the Great 327 BC; government of India transferred from East India Company to British Crown 1858; Indian Empire proclaimed 1877; gained independence within the Commonwealth and divided into separate dominions of Pakistan (Muslim) and India (Hindu); India became a republic 1950.

Indiana state of the USA, first settled 1732; organized as a Territory 1800; admitted to the Union 1816.

Indianapolis state capital of Indiana, first settled 1819.

Indian Mutiny against the British 1857–58.

Indian National Congress founded 1885 by Wedderburn and Hume.

Indian Post Office established 24 July 1837.

India Office Library, London, founded by the East India Company 1801.

India rubber discovered *c.*1740 by the French traveller Charles Marie de la Condamine (1701–74).

Indium metallic element discovered by the German scientists F. Reich and T. Richter 1863.

Indo China former collective name for Cambodia, Laos and Vietnam, occupied by French 1859–85; French protectorates until Japanese occupation 1940–45; Laos and Cambodia achieved independence after World War II; French re-established colonial rule in Vietnam which led to the war against the French 1946–54; Vietnam partitioned between North and South 1954; American supported the South 1965–73 in the Vietnam War, with North Vietnam gaining control over the whole country 1975.

Indo-European Language existence postulated 1786 by Sir William Jones.

Indonesia settled by the Portuguese *c.*1545; ruled by the Netherlands East India Company from 1602; became Dutch East Indies 1798; declared independence 1945; became a republic 1950.

Induction principles discovered 1830 by the English scientist Michael Faraday (1791–1867).

Indulf king of Scots (954–962) *see* Appendix.

Industrial Revolution in Britain occurred roughly 1760–1840; name first applied 1884 by Arnold Toynbee.

Industrial Workers of the World labour organization founded in USA in 1905.

Indy, Vincent d' (1851–1931) French composer (*Istar* 1896).

Ine (d.*c.*728) king of Wessex (688–726) *see* Appendix.

Infallibility, Papal Catholic dogma defined 1870.

Influenza pandemics 1889–90, 1918–19.

Information, Ministry of existed in Britain 1939–46.

Inge, Dean Ralph (1880–1945) English writer and divine.

Inglis, James (d.1531) abbot of Culross. He was murdered.

Ingoldsby, Thomas [Richard Harris Barham] (1788–1845) English writer.

Ingres, Jean Auguste Dominique (1780–1867) French painter. One of the greatest exponents of neoclassical art, his excellent draughtsmanship influenced DEGAS, MATISSE and PICASSO. His works include *Apotheosis of Homer*.

Inkatha Zulu nationalist movement in South Africa led by Chief Mangosuthu Buthelezi since 1975.

Inkerman, Battle of between the Russians and British in the Crimean War, 5 November 1854.

Inman, Henry (1801–46) American painter (*William Penn*).

Inness, George (1825–94) American painter (*Georgia Pines*).

Innocent I, St pope (401–417–417).

Innocent II [Gregorio Papareschi dei Guideni] (d.1143) pope (1130–43).

Innocent III [Lando da Sezza] anti-pope (1179–80).

Innocent III [Lotario de' Conti di Segni] (*c.*1160–1216) pope (1198–1216).

Innocent IV [Sinibaldo Fiesco] (d.1254) pope (1243–54).

Innocent V [Pierre de Champagni] (*c.*1225–1276) pope (1276).

Innocent VI [Etienne Aubert] pope (d.1362) (1352–62).

Innocent VII [Cosimo dei Migliorati] (1339–1406) pope (1404–1406).

Innocent VIII [Giovanni Battista Cibo] (1432–92) pope (1484–92).

Innocent IX [Giovanni Antonio Fachinetti] (1519–91) pope (1591).

Innocent X [Giovanni Battista Pamfili] (1574–1655) pope (1644–55).

Innocent XI [Benedetto Odescalchi] pope (1611–89) (1676–89).

Innocent XII [Antonio Pignatelli] (1615–1700) pope (1691–1700).

Innocent XIII [Michele Angelo Conti] (1655–1724) pope (1721–24).

Inoculation for smallpox introduced *c.*1718 into England from Constantinople by Lady Mary Wortley Montagu (1689–1762).

Inquisition, Holy office of the founded 1231; Spanish Inquisition reorganized 1478, abolished 1820.

Institute of Contemporary Arts, London, founded 1948.

Institute of International Law, Ghent, founded 1873 by the Swiss jurist Johann Kaspar Bluntschli (1808–81).

Insulin isolated 1921 by the Canadian scientists Sir Frederick Grant Banting (1891–1941) and Charles Herbert Best (1899–1978).

Insurance earliest recorded policy 1523; fire insurance pioneered 1666 by Nicolas Barbon; earliest recorded life assurance bond 1228.

Intelligence test IQ scale devised by Binet and Simon in 1905; Stanford-Binet scale introduced 1916.

Interdict, Papal on England 1208–13.

Interferometry study pioneered 1861 by the French physicist Armand Fizeau (1819–96).

Internal combustion engine first constructed 1860 by Lenoir.

International: *First* ('International Working Men's Association', Marxist and Anarchist), 1864–76; *Second* (Socialist) 1889–1914, revived 1918–46 (as so-called '$2^1/_2$th International') and again in 1948 (as 'Comisco'); *Third* ('Comintern', Communist) 1919–43, revived in 1947 (as 'Cominform'); *Fourth* (Trotskyist) formed in 1928.

International Atomic Energy Agency (IAEA) Vienna, established 1956.

International Bank for Reconstruction and Development (IBRD) *see* WORLD BANK.

International Civil Aviation Organization (ICAO), Montreal, proposed at an international conference at Chicago 1944; came into being 1947.

International Code of Signals devised by the British Government 1857; amended 1901.

International Criminal Police Commission (Interpol) formed in Vienna 1923.

International Date Line in Pacific Ocean represented by the meridian of 180° for the convenience of adjusting the loss or gain of one day; established 1883.

International Labour Organization, Geneva, set up 1919.

International Monetary Fund established 27 December 1945.

International Postal Union founded at Berne 9 October 1875.

International Red Cross founded at Geneva 22 August 1864.

International Statistical Congress first convened 1853 at Brussels by the Belgian scientist Lambert Adolphe Jacques Quetelet (1796–1874).

International Telecommunication Union founded 1865, reorganized 1947.

Intifada Palestinian popular uprising against Israeli authority in the West Bank began 9 December 1987.

Invar alloy discovered 1920 by the Swiss scientist Charles Edouard Guillaume (1861–1938).

In vitro fertilization technique to treat infertility first used successfully 1978.

Iodine discovered 1811 in the ashes of seaweed by the French chemist Bernard Courtois (1777–1838).

Iona home of Saint Columba from 563 AD.

Iona Community founded 1938 by the Rev. George Macleod (1895–1991).

Ionesco, Eugène (1912–94) Romanian-born French dramatist. His plays, regarded as masterpieces of the Theatre of the Absurd, include *The Bald Prima Donna* and *The Lesson*.

Ionium discovered 1907 by the American chemist Bertram Borden Boltwood (1870–1927).

Ionization theory developed 1887 by Swedish chemist Svante August Arrhenius (1859–1927).

Iowa state of the USA, first settled 1788; organized as a Territory 1838; admitted to the Union 1846.

Ipsus, Battle of a battle of the Wars of Alexander's Successors, when the distribution of Alexander's empire among his generals was decided, 301 BC.

IRA *see* IRISH REPUBLICAN ARMY.

Iran ruled by Achaemenids (*c*.550–330 BC), Arsacids (227 BC–AD 224), Sassanids (226–651), Muslims (651–1231), Mongols and Turks (1231–1502), Safavids (1502–1722), Turks (1722–79), Kajars (1779–1925); by Pahlavis 1925–79; Ayatollah Khomeini returned from exile to head new Islamic republic 1979.

Iran-Iraq War 21–22 September 1980–August 1988.

Iraq conquered by British from Turkey 1914–18; British mandate 1919–21; Hashemite kingdom 1921–58; military republic since 1958.

Iraq-Mediterranean oil pipeline, Kirkuk to Haifa, inaugurated 14 January 1935.

Ireland first invaded by Norsemen 795, by English 1167; Act of Union 1800; Easter Rising 1916; Irish Free State recognized 1921 (*see* EIRE).

Ireland, John (1879–1962) English composer (*The Forgotten Rite* 1915).

Ireland, William Henry (1777–1835) English literary forger.

Irenaeus, Saint (*fl* 2nd century) bishop of Lyons.

Irene (752–803) Byzantine empress (797–802).

Ireton, Henry (1611–51) English Puritan leader.

Iriarte, Ignacio (1620–85) Spanish painter.

Iridium discovered 1804 by the English chemist Smithson Tennant (1761–1815).

Irish Free State title of Southern Ireland 1922–37.

Irish Land League founded 1879 by Michael Davitt (1846–1906).

Irish Republican Army (IRA) formed 1919.

Irish Treaty 1922.

Irish Volunteers first formed 1779; second formed 1913 and merged with IRA in 1919.

Iron Age the period of history characterized by the spread of iron tools and weapons, which began in the Middle East 1000 BC. It followed the Bronze Age.

Iron bridge first example constructed at Coalbrookdale 1773–79.

Ironclad ships first battle of took place in the American Civil War between *Monitor* and *Merrimac* 9 March 1862.

'Iron Curtain' term describing former barrier between the USSR and Western Europe, first popularized by Sir Winston Churchill 5 March 1946; had been used earlier in the sense of protection by *Pravda* 11 October 1939.

Ironmongers Company, London, origins uncertain; first recorded mention 1300; grant of arms 1455; royal charter 1463.

Irving, Sir Henry [John Henry Brodribb] (1838–1905) English actor.

Irving, Washington (1783–1859) American essayist and historian. His best-known stories are 'Rip Van Winkle' (1819) and 'The Legend of Sleepy Hollow'. He wrote a biography of WASHINGTON.

Irvingites Catholic Apostolic Church founded 1829 by the Scottish preacher Edward Irving (1792–1834).

Isaac I (d.1061) Byzantine emperor (1057–59).

Isaac II (d.1204) Byzantine emperor (1185–95, 1203–1204) He was executed.

Isabella (1214–1241) wife of the Emperor Frederick II.

Isabella I (1451–1504) queen of Castile and Leon.

Isabella II (1830–1904) queen of Spain.

Isabella of Angoulême (d.1246) queen of England.

Isabella of France (1292–1358) queen of England.

Isabey, Jean Baptiste (1767–1855) French painter (*The Empress Josephine*).

Isherwood, Christopher [William Bradshaw] (1904–86) English-born American novelist and dramatist. His best-known works are set in pre-World War II Berlin (*Goodbye to Berlin* 1939).

Isidore, Saint (*c.*560–636) bishop of Seville (*Etymologies*).

Isin a dynasty in Sumeria 2300–2100 BC, established by Ishbi-Ura.

Islam religious movement founded *c.*610 by Mahommed (*c.*570–632).

Ismail Pasha (1830–95) khedive of Egypt.

Ismailis Muslim sect formed in 8th century.

Ismi-Dagan (*fl* 2nd millenium BC) oldest known ruler of Assyria.

Isocrates (436–338 BC) Greek orator.

Isomorphism chemical relationship, principle defined 1820 by the German scientist Eilhard Mitscherlich (1794–1863).

Isotopes theory developed 1912 by the English scientist Frederick Soddy (1877–1956); first identified 1910 by Sir Joseph John Thomson (1856–1940).

Israel united as a kingdom in the reign of David (1000–967 BC) with Jerusalem as the capital; kingdom divided on the death of Solomon 930 BC, Jeroboam I becomes king of Israel in the north; Rehoboam becomes king of Judah in the south; at the battle of Karkar 854 BC Benhadad of Damascus and Ahab of Israel withstood the might of Assyria; Syrian attacks 797 BC successfully repelled by Jehoash, king of Israel; Syria defeated and Israel's prestige increased by Jeroboam II, king of Israel 782 BC; Sargon, king of Assyria, takes Samaria and transports a large number of the Israelites to Mesopotamia and Media; the northern kingdom of Israel never revives 721 BC.

Israel modern state of Israel proclaimed 14 May 1948.

Israëls, Jozef (1824–1911) Dutch painter (*Toilers of the Sea*).

Istanbul founded (as Byzantium) 658 BC; capital of Byzantine Empire (as Constantinople) 330–1453; of Ottoman Empire (as Istanbul) 1453–1923.

Issus, Battle of 333 BC a battle of Alexander the Great's Asiatic campaigns when he defeated the Persians under Darius.

Isthmian games held in Ancient Greece began 581 BC.

Italian language earliest known document the *Placito Capuano*, dated March 960.

Italian Parliament opened 18 February 1861.

Italian Somaliland *see* SOMALIA.

Italy kingdom 1861–1946; Fascist regime 1922–43; democratic republic since 1946.

Ito, Prince Hirobumi (1841–1909) Japanese statesman and reformer. He was assassinated.

Itúrbide, Agustin de (1783–1824) emperor of Mexico (1822–23). He was shot.

Ivan I (d.1341) grand duke of Vladimir.

Ivan II (1326–59) grand duke of Vladimir (1353–59).

Ivan III the Great (1440–1505) grand duke of Muscovy (1462–1505).

Ivan IV the Terrible (1530–84) tsar of Muscovy (1547–84).

Ivan V (1666–96) tsar of Russia (1682–96).

Ivan VI (1740–64) emperor of Russia (1740–41). He was murdered.

Ives, Saint (1253–1303).

Ives, Charles Edward (1874–1954) American composer. His works are frequently experimental but based firmly within the American tradition.

Ivo, Saint (*c.*1040–1116) bishop of Chartres.

Ivory Coast *see* CÔTE D'IVOIRE.

J

'Jack of Tilbury' [Sir John Arundell] (1495–1561).

Jackson, Andrew (1767–1845) 7th US president (1829–37).

Jackson, Sir Barry (1879–1961) English theatre manager and director.

Jackson, Frederick George (1860–1938) British Arctic explorer.

Jackson, Glenda (1936–) English actress. Highly regarded on film and stage, she became a Labour MP in 1992. Her films include *Women in Love* (1969).

Jackson, Jesse Louis (1941–) American civil rights leader and Democrat politician. A Baptist minister and one of Martin Luther King's aides, he campaigned twice for the Democratic presidential nomination.

Jackson, Michael [Joe] (1958–) American pop singer. The youngest of five brothers who as children formed the Jackson 5, he became a solo performer in the late 1970s ('Thriller' 1982).

Jackson, 'Stonewall' [Thomas Jonathan Jackson] (1824–63) American Confederate general. He was killed.

'Jack the Ripper' perpetrator of series of unsolved murders of women in London 1888.

Jacobin Club founded in France 1789. Movement ended 1794 but was revived during the 1848 Revolution.

Jacobite glass manufactured mainly 1745–65.

Jacobites supporters of James II and his descendants 1688–1760.

Jacobs, William Wymark (1863–1943) English writer (*The Skipper's Wooing* 1897).

Jacobus de Voragine (*fl.* 13th century) Italian writer (*The Golden Legend*).

Jacopone da Todi (*c.*1240–1306) Italian poet (*Stabat Mater*).

Jacquard loom first to weave patterns invented 1801 by the French inventor Joseph Marie Jacquard (1752–1834).

Jacquerie, The insurrection of French peasants May 1358.

Jadassohn, Solomon (1831–1902) German composer.

Jadwiga (*c.*1372–1399) Polish queen.

Jaggard, William (*c.*1568–1623) English publisher of Shakespeare.

Jagger, Mick [Michael Philip Jagger] (1943–) English singer and songwriter, and lead singer with the Rolling Stones rock group, the original members of which, with Jagger, were the guitarist and co-writer with Jagger of many of their songs, **Keith Richard** (1943–), bass guitarist **Bill Wyman** (1936–), drummer **Charlie Watts** (1941–) and guitarist **Brian Jones** (1944–69).

Jagiellon dynasty Lithuanian dynasty ruled Poland 1386–1572.

Jahangir (1569–1627) Mogul emperor of India (1605–27).

Jainism Indian religious movement had its beginnings in the 6th century BC.

Jalal Ad-din Rumi, Mohammed (1207–73) Persian mystical poet.

Jalalian *or* **Seljuk Era** began 15 March 1079.

Jamaica an island in the Caribbean Sea, discovered by Christopher Columbus 1494; under Spanish rule until 1655; captured by the British 1655 and established as a colony 1866; included in the British Caribbean Federation 1956; gained independence 1962.

Jamboree, World of Boy Scouts first held London 1920.

James, the Old Pretender (James Francis Edward Stewart) (1688–1766).

James, Henry (1) (1811–82) American theologian.

James, Henry (2) (1843–1916) American-born British novelist, short-story writer and critic. Much of his work is concerned with the contrast between American innocence and the older, wiser European culture, e.g. *Daisy Miller*, *The Ambassadors* (1903).

James, Jesse (1847–82) American outlaw. He was killed.

James, M[ontague] R[hodes] (1862–1936) English scholar and ghost-story writer. His stories are a mix of dry, scholarly wit with a horrifically reticent undertone of supernatural terror.

James, Dame P. D. [Phyllis Dorothy White] (1920–) English novelist. Her crime novels have been much admired for their wit.

James, William (1842–1910) American philosopher and psychologist. His works include *The Varieties of Religious Experience*, in which he coined the term 'stream of consciousness'.

James I (1566–1625) king of Scotland (1567–1625 as James VI) and of Great Britain and Ireland (1603–25) *see* Appendix.

James II (1633–1701) king of Great Britain and Ireland (1685–88) *see* Appendix.

James I (1394–1437) king of Scotland (1406–37) *see* Appendix.

James II (1430–60) king of Scotland (1437–60) *see* Appendix.

James III (1451–88) king of Scotland (1460–88) *see* Appendix.

James IV (1473–1513) king of Scotland (1488–1513) *see* Appendix.

James V (1512–42) king of Scotland (1513–42) *see* Appendix.

James VI king of Scotland (1567–1603) and of Great Britain and Ireland (1603–25 as James I) *see* Appendix: James I.

James VII title of James ii of Great Britain as king of Scotland.

Jameson, Mrs Anna (1794–1860) Irish-born popular writer (*Legend of the Madonna* 1852).

Jameson Raid, Transvaal, led 29 December 1895 to 2 January 1896 by the Scottish pioneer in South Africa, Sir Leander Starr Jameson (1853–1917).

Jammes, Francis (1868–1938) French writer (*Le Roman du lièvre* 1903).

Jan Mayen Island, Arctic, discovered 1607 by the English explorer Henry Hudson (d.1611); annexed by Norway 1929.

Janácek, Leos (1854–1928) Czech composer. His works, heavily influenced by Czech folk music and culture, include the operas *The Cunning Little Vixen*, *The House of the Dead*, *Jenufa* (1902), and two highly regarded string quartets.

Jane, Queen (Lady Jane Grey) (*c*.1537–1554) proclaimed queen of England (1553) *see* Appendix.

Janin, Jules Gabriel (1804–74) French writer (*L'Ane mort et la femme guillotiné* 1829).

Janissaries Turkish troops first levied 1330, abolished 1826.

Jansenism religious movement deriving from the posthumous publication of *Augustinus* (1640) by the Dutch theologian Cornelis Jansen (1585–1638).

Janssens Van Nuyssen, Abraham (*c*.1575–1632) Flemish painter (*Ecce Homo!*).

Japan empire for at least 2000 years; Togukawa Shogunate 1600–1867; feudal system abolished 1871; American occupation 1945–52; new constitution granted 1947.

Jaques-Dalcroze, Émile (1865–1950) Swiss composer.

Jarry, Alfred (1873–1907) French writer (*Ubu Roi* 1896).

Jarvis, John Wesley (*c*.1781–1839) English-born painter (*Alexander Anderson*).

Jasper National Park, Canada, established 1907.

Jaurès, Jean Léon (1859–1914) French socialist leader. He was assassinated.

Jay, John (1745–1829) American statesman.

Jazz began to develop in New Orleans *c*.1893–95; first so named 1910.

Jean de Meung (d.*c*.1305) French writer (second part of the *Roman de la rose*).

Jeanne d'Albret (1528–1572) queen of Navarre.

Jeanne d'Arc, Sainte *see* JOAN OF ARC.

Jeans, Sir James (1877–1946) English scientist (*The Stars in Their Courses* 1931).

Jefferies, Richard (1848–87) English writer (*The Story of My Heart* 1883).

Jeffers, Robinson (1887–1962) American poet (*Flagons and Apples* 1912).

Jefferson, Thomas (1743–1826) American statesman. He was the main creator of the Declaration of Independence in 1776 and became secretary of state (1790–93) under Washington. He was elected the 3rd president of the United States (1801–1809).

Jeffreys, George, Baron (1648–1689) judge of the 'Bloody Assizes'.

Jehoash king of Israel who successfully repelled Syrian attacks 797 BC.

Jehoiachin (*c*.615–560) second last king of Judah who reigned for three months (597 BC). When Judah was conquered by Nebuchadnezzar, Jehoiachin was taken into exile in Babylon and a puppet king, Zedekiah, made king of Judah.

Jehovah's Witnesses founded 1872 in Pennsylvania by Charles Taze Russell (1852–1916).

Jehu king of Israel (842–814). An army commander, he gained the throne by order of Elisha by killing the sons of Ahab as well as Jezebel and Ahab's advisers and priests. He also rid the country of the worship of Baal and slaughtered the worshippers.

Jellicoe, Admiral John, Earl Jellicoe (1859–1935) governor-general of New Zealand (1920–24).

Jemison, Mrs Mary ('The White Woman of the Genesee') (1743–1833).

Jena University, Germany, founded 1558.

Jena, Battle of a battle between Napoleon and the Prussians, 14 October 1806.

Jenghiz Khan *see* GENGHIS KHAN.

Jenkins, Roy [Baron Jenkins of Hillhead] (1920–) Welsh Labour and Social Democrat politician. He resigned from the Labour Party in 1981 to co-found the Social Democratic Party. He was SDP MP for Glasgow Hillhead (1982–87).

Jenkins's Ear, War of between Britain and Spain 1739–41.

Jenner, Edward (1749–1823) English physician. He investigated the traditional belief that catching cowpox gave protection against smallpox and discovered that vaccination was efficacious in preventing smallpox (1796).

Jenson, Nicolas (d.*c.*1480) French pioneer printer in Italy.

Jenyns, Soame (1704–87) English writer (*Free Enquiry into the Nature and Origin of Evil* 1756).

Jeroboam I first king of the northern kingdom of Israel (10th century BC who, according to the Old Testament, introduced pagan practices.

Jeroboam II king of Israel (782–741 BC). He defeated Syria and increased the prestige of Israel 782 BC with his capital at Samaria

Jerome, Saint (*c.*340–420) (produced *Vulgate* 382–405).

Jerome, Jerome Klapka (1859–1927) English humorous writer (*Three Men in a Boat* 1889).

Jerome of Prague (*c.*1365–1416) Czech religious reformer.

Jerrold, Douglas (1803–57) English writer (*Mrs Caudle's Curtain Lectures* 1846).

Jerusalem failure of attack by Sennacherib, king of Assyria 701 BC; destroyed by Nebuchadnezzar 587–586 BC; rebuilt 536–516 BC; return of Ezra with many Jews from Babylon 458 BC; rebuilding of walls begun by Nehemiah 445 BC; razed 168 BC by Antiochus Epiphanes; Syrian garrison expelled 142 BC; taken by Pompey 63 BC; restoration of Temple begun by Herod the Great 20 BC; destroyed AD 70 by Titus; sacked by the Persians 615; captured by the Crusaders 1099; recovered by Saladin 1187; taken by the British 1917; divided between Jordan and Israel 1949; unified after the Six Day War (1967) under the Israelis.

Jervis, John [Earl St Vincent] (1735–1823) British admiral who commanded a squadron in the West Indies, capturing Martinique, Guadeloupe and St Lucia. In 1797 he defeated a Spanish fleet off Cape St Vincent.

Jesus, Society of founded 1534 by St Ignatius Loyola (1491–1556; dissolved 1773 by Pope Clement XIV; re-established by Pope Pius VII 1814.

Jesus Christ *or* **Jesus of Nazareth** (*c.*6 BC–*c.*30 AD) founder of Christianity. The New Testament records that he was born in Bethlehem, the son of Joseph and Mary, and Christians have traditionally believed that he is the Son of God. The Book of Acts describes how Christianity was spread through the Mediterranean world by his disciples, notably Paul and Peter, the latter being recognized as the founder of the Roman Catholic church.

Jesus College, Cambridge University, founded 1496 by John Alcock, bishop of Ely (1430–1500).

Jesus College, Oxford University, founded by Queen Elizabeth I, 1571.

Jet aircraft engine developed by Sir Frank Whittle (1907–91) first ran on test-bed 1937.

Jewel, John (1522–71) English divine and writer (*Apologia Ecclesiae Anglicanae* 1562).

Jewett, Sarah Orne (1849–1909) American writer (*The Country of the Painted Firs* 1896).

Jewish calendar calculated from 3761 BC; fixed AD 358.

Jewish Diaspora dispersal of the Jews, began with deportations by Assyrians 721 BC.

Jewish Disabilities Removal Act, Great Britain, passed 1858.

Jewish Era began 7 October 3761 BC.

Jex-Blake, Sophia Louisa (1840–1912) English physician, mathematician and champion of women's right.

Jhabvala, Ruth Prawer (1927–) British novelist and screenwriter (*Heat and Dust* 1975).

Jiang Jie Shi *see* CHIANG KAI-SHEK.

Jiang Qing *see* CHIANG CH'ING.

Jiménez de Cisneros, Francisco (1436–1517) Spanish divine and statesman.

Jinnah, Mohammed Ali (1876–1948) Pakistani statesman. An early member of the Indian Muslim League, he became convinced of the need for Indian partition into Hindu and Muslim states and was the first governor-general of Pakistan (1947–48).

Joachim, Joseph (1831–1907) Bohemian violinist.

Joan [Fair Maid of Kent] (1328–1385) wife of Edward, the Black Prince.

Joan, Pope (*c.*855–858) mythical female pope.

Joanna I (*c.*1327–1382) queen of Naples (1343–82). She was executed.

Joanna II (1371–1435) queen of Naples (1414–35).

Joan of Arc [Sainte Jeanne d'Arc] (*c.*1412–1431) French patriot. From a peasant family, she had a vision when she was thirteen, urging her to free France from the invading English. She helped raise the siege of Orléans in 1429, and brought Charles VII to Rheims to be crowned king of France. Captured by the English in 1430, she was condemned for witchcraft and burned at the stake. She was canonized in 1920.

Jocelin de Brakelond (*fl* end of 12th and beginning of 13th centuries) English historian.

Jodelle, Étienne (1532–73) French playwright (*Cléopatre captive* 1552).

Joffre, Joseph Jacques Césaire (1852–1931) French soldier.

Johannesburg, South Africa, founded 1886.

John (1167–1216) king of England (1199-1216) *see* Appendix.

John, Augustus [Edwin] (1878–1961) Welsh painter who was a superb draughtsman and portraitist. His works include *Bella*. His sister, **Gwen John** (1876–1939), was also a painter.

John I, Saint (d.526) pope (523–526). He died in prison.

John II pope (533–535).

John III pope (561–574).

John IV pope (640–642).

John V pope (685–686).

John VI pope (701–705).

John VII pope (705–707).

John VIII pope (872–882 murdered 882).

John IX pope (898–900).

John X pope (914–928).

John XI pope (931–935).

John XII [Octavian] pope (955–963 (*c*.938–963).

John XIII pope (965–972).

John XIV (d.984) pope (983–984). He died in prison.

John XV pope (985–996).

John XVI [Philagathus] anti-pope (997–998).

John XVII [Sicco] pope (1003).

John XVIII pope (1004–1009).

John XIX pope (1024–32).

John XX (non-existent: a fault in numbering).

John XXI [Pedro Giuliamo Rebulo] pope (1276–77).

John XXII [Jacques Duèse] (1249–1334) pope (1316–34).

John XXIII [Baldassare Cossa] (d.1419) anti-pope (1410–15).

John XXIII [Angelo Roncalli] (1881–1963) pope (1958–63).

John I [Tzimisces] (925–976) Byzantine emperor (969–976).

John II [Comnenus] (1088–1143) Byzantine emperor (1118–43).

John III [Vatatzes] (1193–1254) Byzantine emperor (1222–54).

John IV [Lascaris] (*c*.1250–*c*.1300) Byzantine emperor (1258–61).

John V [Palaeologus] (1332–91) Byzantine emperor (1341–47).

John VI [Cantacuzene] (*c*.1292–1383) Byzantine emperor (1347–55).

John VII Byzantine emperor (1390).

John VIII (1390–1448) Byzantine emperor (1425–48).

John I king of Poland (1492–1501).

John II [Casimir] (1609–72) king of Poland (1648–68).

John III [Sobieski] (1624–96) king of Poland (1674–96).

John I (1357–1433) king of Portugal (1385–1433).

John II (1455–95) king of Portugal (1481–95).

John III (1502–57) king of Portugal (1521–57).

John IV (1603–56) king of Portugal (1640–56).

John V (1689–1750) king of Portugal (1706–50).

John VI (1769–1826) king of Portugal.

John Chrysostom, Saint (*c*.357–407).

John of Austria, Don (1545–1578) Austrian soldier and administrator.

John of Beverley, Saint (687–721).

John of Damascus, Saint theologian *fl* late 7th and first half of 8th centuries.

John of Fornsete (d.1239) English monk and reputed composer of *Sumer is icumen in*.

John of Gaunt, Duke of Lancaster (1340–1399).

John of Lancaster, Duke of Bedford (1389–1435).

John of Leyden [John Beuckelszoon] (1509–36) Dutch anabaptist. He was killed.

John of Nepomuk, Saint (d.1393) national saint of Bohemia. He was killed.

John of Salisbury (*c*.1115–1180) English scholar and divine.

John of the Cross, Saint (1542–1591).

John of Trevisa (1326–1412) English translator (of Higden's *Polychronicon* 1387).

John O'London's Weekly British periodical published 1919–54, revived 1959.

John Paul I (1912–78) pope (1978).

John Paul II [Karel Jozef Wojtyla] (1920–) Polish pope (1978–) The first Polish pope and first non-Italian pope for 450 years. His primacy has been notable for his conservatism in matters such as abortion and the celibacy of the priesthood.

John Rylands Library, Manchester, founded 1899 by his widow in memory of John Rylands (1801–88).

Johns, Jasper (1930–) American painter, sculptor and printmaker. His work, especially his use of everyday images such as the stars and stripes, was very influential on later Pop Artists and includes *Target with Four Faces* (1955).

Johns Hopkins University, Baltimore, founded 1867 by bequest of the American philanthropist Johns Hopkins (1795–1873. Opened 1876.

Johnson, Amy (1903–41) English aviator. She was the first woman to fly solo from England to Australia (1930). Her other records include a solo flight from London to Cape Town (1936). She was presumed drowned, after baling out over the Thames Estuary while serving as a transport pilot in World War II.

Johnson, Andrew 17th US president (1865–69) (1808–75).

Johnson, Dame Celia (1908–82) British stage and screen actress (*Brief Encounter* 1945).

Johnson, Dr John (1794–1848) first colonial-surgeon in New Zealand.

Johnson, Dr Samuel (1709–84) English critic, lexicographer and poet. One of the greatest literary figures of the 18th century who wrote on many subjects and was considered the moralist of the age. His works include the *Dictionary of the English Language* (1755), an important edition of Shakespeare, several essays and one novel. In 1763 he met James Boswell (1740–95) with whom he toured the Western Isles. Boswell's biography of Johnson is considered to be the finest in the language.

Johnson, Lyndon B[aines] (1908–73) American Democrat statesman. Following John F. Kennedy's assassination in 1963, he became the 36th president of the US (1963–69). With Civil Rights agitation and the increasing unpopularity of the Vietnam War his time in office was a troubled one.

Johnston, Joseph (1807–91) American soldier.

Joinville, Jean, Sire de (*c.*1224–1319) crusader and historian.

Joliot-Curie, Professor Frédéric (1900–1958) French physicist.

Jolliet, Louis (1645–1700) French explorer.

Jolson, Al [Asa Yoelson] (1886–1950) American stage and screen actor and singer (*The Jazz Singer* 1927).

Jonathan Maccabaeus *see* JUDAS MACCABAEUS.

Jones, Brian *see* JAGGER, MICK.

Jones, Ernest (1879–1958) first British psychoanalyst.

Jones, Henry Arthur (1851–1929) English playwright (*Judah* 1890).

Jones, Inigo (1573–1652) English architect.

Jones, John Luther ('Casey') (1864–1900) American railway hero. He was killed.

Jones, John Paul (1747–92) Scottish-born American naval adventurer.

Jones, Owen (1809–74) British architect (*Grammar of Ornament* 1856).

Jonestown Massacre mass suicide by members of Jim Jones's People's Temple religious cult, 18 November 1978.

Jonson, Benjamin (1572–1637) English dramatist. After a turbulent early life, during which he served as a soldier and killed a fellow soldier in a duel, he began writing comedies which are particularly noted for their satirical dialogue and use of the 'Theory of Humours' and which established him as a great dramatist. His plays include *Bartholomew Fair (*1614), *Volpone* (1616) and *The Alchemist* (1610). He became the first poet laureate in 1616.

Jonson, Cornelis (1593–1661) English painter (*Charles I*).

Jooss, Kurt (1901–79) German-born choreographer.

Joplin, Janis (1945–70) American rock singer.

Joplin, Scott (1868–1917) American pianist and composer. His ragtime compositions, e.g. *Maple Leaf Rag*, were enormously popular in the USA, selling over a million copies of sheet music.

Jordaens, Jacob (1593–1678) Flemish painter (*Triumph of Bacchus*).

Jordan, Hashemite Kingdom of came under British control 1922; became independent kingdom 1946; former name Trans-Jordan 1922–49.

Jordan, Mrs Dorothy (1762–1816) Irish actress and mistress of William IV.

Joseph, Chief (d.1904) American Indian leader.

Joseph I (1678–1711) Holy Roman emperor (1705–11).

Joseph II (1741–90) Holy Roman emperor (1765–90).

Josephine (1763–1814) empress of the French, wife of Napoleon I.

Josephus, Flavius (*c.*37–*c.*95) Jewish historian.

Josiah king of Judah (637–608 BC) who succeeded to the throne at the age of eight. He was a noted religious and political reformer. At the battle of Megiddo he was defeated and killed by Necho of Egypt.

Joubert, Joseph (1754–1824) French writer.

Joule's Law of electrical energy pronounced 1841 by the English scientist James Prescott Joule (1818–89).

Jouvenet, Jean (1647–1717) French painter.

Jovian (*c.*331–364) Roman emperor (363–364).

Jowett, Benjamin (1817–93) English scholar and educationist.

Joyce, James [Augustine Aloysius] (1882–1941) Irish novelist and short-story writer. He left Ireland in 1902, returning briefly twice. His works include athe short-story collection *Dubliners* (1914), and two great novels, *Portrait of the Artist as a Young Man* (1914–15) and *Ulysses* (1922), the latter one of the key novels of the 20th century.

Joyce, William (1906–46) American-born British traitor (of Anglo-Irish descent). Dubbed 'Lord Haw-Haw' by the British public, he broadcast rabid Nazi propaganda to Britain during World War II and was executed by hanging for treason in 1946.

Juan Carlos (1938–) king of Spain (1975–). Nominated by Franco in 1969 as his successor, Juan Carlos carefully steered his country towards democracy after Franco's death in 1975.

Juan Fernández Islands discovered *c.*1564 by the navigator Juan Fernández–*c.*1603.

Juárez, Benito (1806–72) Mexican president (1861–62, 1867–72).

Judah the southern kingdom formed 930 BC after the death of Solomon when the Hebrew kingdom was divided, Rehoboam became king; religious reforms under Hezekiah 720 BC and Josiah 637–608 BC; Josiah of Judah defeated and killed by Necho of Egypt at battle of Megiddo 608 BC; conquest of Judah by Nebuchadnezzar 597 BC, Zedekiah made puppet king; revolt by Zedekiah against Babylonian rule 587 BC and destruction of Jerusalem by Nebuchadnezzar.

Judas Maccabaeus (d.161 BC) Jewish rebel leader. The

son of Mattathias, he succeeded his father as leader of the revolt against Antiochus Epiphanes on his father's death in 166 BC. The revolt led to the recapture of Jerusalem and rededication of the Temple. He was killed at Elasa and was succeeded by his brother Jonathan.

Jugurtha (d.104 BC) king of Numidia (113–106 BC) who waged war with the Romans. He was defeated and captured by Marius 106 BC and died in prison.

Julian calendar introduced in Rome by Julius Caesar 46 BC.

Juliana (1909–) queen of the Netherlands (1948–80). She married Prince Bernhard zur Lippe-Biesterfeld in 1937 and succeeded to the throne on the abdication of her mother, Queen Wilhelmina. In turn she abdicated in favour of her daughter Beatrix.

Juliana of Norwich (1343–1443) English mystic.

Julian the Apostate (*c.*331–363) Roman emperor (361–363).

Jülich-Cleves dispute over succession 1609–14.

Julius I, Saint pope (337–352).

Julius II [Giuliano della Rovere] (1443–1513) pope (1503–13).

Julius III [Giovanni Maria del Monte] (1487–1555) pope (1550–55).

Julius Caesar *see* CAESAR, JULIUS.

July Revolution provoked by the reactionary measures of Charles X of France, 27 July to August 1830.

Juneau, Solomon Laurent (1793–1856) French-American founder 1846 of Milwaukee.

Jung, Carl Gustav (1875–1961) Swiss psychiatrist who began as a follower of Freud, but split with him after challenging his concentration on sex. His theory of the 'collective unconscious', and his use of the term 'archetype' to denote an image or symbol drawn from this store, have been highly influential.

Jungfrau Swiss mountain (13,699 feet) first climbed 1811 on the east side by the Swiss brothers Meyer of Aaravi, first climbed on the west side by Sir George Young and the Rev. H. B. George 1865.

Jungfrau railway the highest railway in Europe, constructed 1896–1912.

'Junius' writer of political letters published 1769–72. Pseudonym believed to conceal the authorship of Sir Philip Francis (1740–1818).

Jupiter satellites first discovered 1610 by Galileo; Red Spot first observed 1831

Jurassic Period 170 million years ago.

Jusserand, Jean Antoine Jules (1855–1932) French diplomat and historian.

Justice of the peace English judicial and administrative post, first recorded reference 1264.

Justiciar official of Anglo-Norman kings until 1234.

Justin, Saint (b.*c.*100–*c.*165) he was martyred.

Justin I (450–527) Byzantine emperor (518–527).

Justin II (d.578) Byzantine emperor (565–578).

Justinian I (483–565) Byzantine emperor (527–565).

Justinian II (669–711) Byzantine emperor (685–695, 704–711). He was assassinated.

Jutes a Germanic people who invaded England in the 6th century, settling in Kent.

Jutland, Battle of a naval battle of the First World War, 31 May 1916, between the British and German fleets. It was the major naval battle of the war, victory being claimed by both sides, but it had the effect of keeping the German fleet off the seas for the rest of the war.

Juvenal [Decimus Junius Juvenalis] (*c.*55–*c.*140) Roman satirical poet. His works include *The legend of Bad Women*.

Juxon, William (1582–1663) English divine.

K

K2 (Mt Godwin-Austen), Himalayas, climbed by an Italian expedition 31 July 1954.

Kabalevsky, Dimitri (1904–87) Russian composer (*Master of Clamecy* 1937).

Kabul capital of Afghanistan since 1774.

Kafka, Franz (1883–1924) Czech-born German novelist and short-story writer. His novels, *The Trial* and *The Castle*, and several of his short stories, notably 'Metamorphosis', are established classics of 20th-century literature.

Kagawa, Toyohiko (1888–1960) Japanese writer (*The Psychology of the Poor* 1915).

Kaiser Wilhelm II Land Antarctica, discovered 1903 by the German explorer Erich von Drygalski (1865–1949).

Kaiser, Georg (1878–1945) German dramatist (*Die Bürger von Calais* 1913).

KAL 007 Korean Airlines Boeing 707 passenger jet shot down by Soviet fighters for straying from flight path, 1 September 1983.

Kaleidoscope invented 1816 by Sir David Brewster (1781–1868).

Kalevala Finnish folk epic, first published 1822 onwards.

Kalidása (*fl* 4th century) Indian writer (*The Sakuntala*).

Kalinin, Mikhail Ivanovich (1875–1946) Russian Bolshevik leader.

Kalium (potassium) discovered 1817 by the English chemist Sir Humphrey Davy (1778–1829).

Kamenev, Lev Borisovich (Rosenfeld) (1883–1936) Russian Bolshevik leader. He was executed.

Kamerlingh Onnes, Heike (1853–1926) Dutch scientist.

Kanchenjunga, Himalayas, climbed by a British expedition 25 May 1955.

Kandinsky, Wassily (1866–1944) Russian-born French painter. He co-founded (with Klee and Marc) the *Blaue Reiter* group in 1912 and is regarded as the first major abstract artist.

K'ang Hsi Period, China, 1662–1722.

Kansas, USA, formed into a Territory 1854; admitted to the Union 1861.

Kansas University, Lawrence, Kansas, founded 1864.

Kant, Immanuel (1724–1804) German philosopher. His works include *The Critique of Pure Reason* (1781), in which he adopts (in response to Hume's empiricism) an idealist position, arguing that our knowledge is limited by our capacity for perception, and *The Critique of Practical Reason* (1788), in which he expounds his theory of ethics based upon 'categorical imperatives'.

Kapitza, Pyotr Leonidovich (1894–1984) Russian physicist.

Karajan, Herbert von (1908–89) Austrian-born conductor. His recordings with the Berlin Symphony Orchestra, notably of Beethoven's symphonies, are held by some critics to be definitive.

Kara Mustafa (d.1683) Turkish grand vizier (1676-83). In 1682 he conquered the whole of upper Hungary. An attack was also planned on Vienna but the Austrian forces were backed up by those of the Polish king, John Sobieski, and the Ottoman attack failed. Kara Mustafa was dismissed and executed.

Karg-Elert, Siegfried (1877–1933) German composer.

Kariba Hydroelectric Project High Dam, Zambezi River, construction began 6 November 1956, opened 18 May 1960.

Karkar *or* **Qarqar, Battle of** 854 BC a battle at which Benhadad of Damascus and Ahab of Israel withstood the Assyrians under Shalmaneser III.

Karloff, Boris [William Pratt] (1887–1969) British-born (horror) film and stage actor (*Frankenstein* 1931).

Karlsefni, Thorfinn (*fl.* late 10th and first half of the 11th centuries) Icelandic navigator.

Karsavina, Tamara (1885–1978) Russian-born ballet dancer.

Karsh, Yousuf (1908–) Armenian-born Canadian photographer (*Sir Winston Churchill*).

Kashmir, Jammu and became part of the Mogul Empire 1586; British supremacy recognized 1846; the Maharajah acceded to the dominion of India 1947; disputed between India, Pakistan and China since 1947; Indian-held territory became a state 1956.

Kasparov, Gary [Garik Weinstein] (1963–) Russian chess master.

Kassem, Abdul Karim (1914–63) ruler of Iraq (1958–63). He was killed in a coup.

Kate Greenaway Medal British award for the most distinguished work in the illustration of children's books, awarded annually by the British Library Association since 1956.

Kauffmann, Angelica (1741–1807) Swiss-born painter. Influenced by neoclassicism, she settled in London in 1776 where she was noted for her portraits (of Reynolds and Goethe among others) and history paintings. She was a founder of the Royal Academy.

Kaufman, George Simon (1889–1961) American writer (*Of Thee I Sing* 1931).

Kaulbach, Wilhelm von (1805–74) German painter (*Narrenhaus*).

Kaunda, Kenneth [David] (1924–) Zambian politician, president of Zambia (1964–91). He became president of Zambia when his country became independent.

Kautsky, Karl (1854–1938) German socialist .

Kaye, Danny [Daniel Kominski] (1913–87) American comic actor and entertainer (*The Secret Life of Walter Mitty* 1947).

Kay's flying shuttle invented 1733 by the English clockmaker John Kay (1704–64).

Kazan, Elia (1909–) American stage and film director (*A Streetcar Named Desire* 1951).

Kazantzakis, Nikos (1883–1957) Greek author (*Zorba the Greek* 1946).

Kean, Charles John (*c.*1811–1868) English actor.

Kean, Edmund (1787–1833) English actor.

Keating, Paul (1945–) Australian statesman (prime minister 1991–96).

Keaton, Buster [Joseph Francis Keaton] (1895–1966) American silent film comedian, director and producer. Widely regarded as one of the all-time great comedians of the cinema, with his 'deadpan' expression and remarkable acrobatic skill, his silent comedy films include *The Navigator* (1924) and *The General* (1926).

Keats, John (1795–1821) English poet. His first sonnets were published by Leigh Hunt (1784–1859) in *The Examiner*, the weekly paper Hunt founded in 1808 with his brother James Hunt (1774–1848). Although savagely criticised early in his career, Keats went on to write some of the greatest works of English romantic literature, e.g. *Endymion* (1818). He died to tuberculosis in Rome.

Keble, John (1792–1866) English divine (*Christian Year* 1827).

Keble College, Oxford University, erected 1870 as a memorial to the English divine John Keble (1792–1866).

Keene, Charles (1823–91) English artist and illustrator.

Keir Hardie, James (1856–1915) Scottish socialist leader.

Keller, Gottfried (1819–90) Swiss novelist (*Der grüne Heinrich* 1851–53).

Keller, Helen [Adams] (1880–1968) American writer. She became deaf and blind when 19 months old, and was taught to read and write by the partially sighted Anne Sullivan. She wrote an autobiography, *The Story of My Life* (1903).

Kellogg-Briand Pact (The Pact of Paris) renouncing war, signed 27 August 1928.

Kelly, Gene [Eugene Curran Kelly] (1912–96) American dancer, choreographer, actor and film director, who was noted for his athleticism and witty dancing style. His films include *Singin' in the Rain* (1952)

Kelly, Grace [Patricia] (1929–82) American film actress. She married Prince Rainier III (1923–) of Monaco in 1956, and gave up her career.

Kelmscott Press private press founded and operated (1891–98) by William Morris (1834–96).

Kelvin, William Thomson, Baron (1824–1907) British physicist who made important contributions to our knowledge of electricity, magnetism and heat. Among his many inventions were a deep-sea-sounding machine and an improved form of mariner's compass.

Kemal Atatürk [Mustafa Kemal] (*c.*1880–1938) Turkish soldier and statesman (president 1923–38).

Kemble, Fanny (1809–93) English actress.

Kemény, Zsigmond, Baron (1814–75) Hungarian politician and writer.

Kempis, Thomas à *see* THOMAS À KEMPIS.

Ken, Thomas (1637–1711) bishop of Bath and Wells and hymn-writer ('Praise God from Whom All Blessings Flow').

Kennedy, Edward [Moore] (1932–) American Democratic politician, brother of John Fitzgerald Kennedy. He became a senator in 1962 and was widely regarded as a future president until the 'Chappaquidick' incident of 1969, in which a girl passenger in his car was drowned.

Kennedy, John Fitzgerald (1917–63) American Democratic politician, who became 35th president of the US (1961–63). He was the first Roman Catholic and the youngest man elected to the presidency. His period of office, cut short by his assassination in Dallas, 22 November 1963, was subsequently seen by many as a period of hope and social reform, with most of his 'New Frontier' legislation being implemented by Lyndon Johnson.

Kennedy, Robert Francis ('Bobby') (1925–68) American Democratic politician, brother of John Fitzgerald Kennedy. He was attorney general (1961–64) in his brother's administration and senator for New York (1965–68). He furthered civil rights legislation and was assassinated, 5 June 1968.

Kenneth I (d.858) king of Scots (841–858) *see* Appendix.

Kenneth II (d.995) king of Scots (971–995) *see* Appendix.

Kenneth III (d.1005) king of Scots (997–1005) *see* Appendix.

Kensington Gardens, London, became generally accessible to the public at the beginning of the 19th century.

Kensington Palace, London, acquired 1661 by the Earl of Nottingham (1621–1682), purchased by King William III 1689.

Kent, Rockwell (1882–1971) American artist writer (*Salamina* 1935).

Kent, William (1684–1748) English architect.

Kent an Anglo-Saxon kingdom in southeast England that became one of the Heptarchy but was absorbed by Wessex in the 9th century.

Kentucky a state of the USA, first settled 1765; admitted to the Union 1792.

Kentucky Derby, USA, first run 17 May 1875.

Kenya annexed to the British Crown as a colony 1920; gained independence 1963; member of the Commonwealth.

Kenyatta, Jomo (*c.*1893–1978) Kenyan nationalist politician. He was jailed for six years (1952–58) for his leadership of the Mau-Mau rebellion. He became prime minister of Kenya on independence in 1963 and its first president (1964–78).

Keokuk (*c.*1780–1848) American Indian chief.

Kepler, Johannes (1571–1630) German mathematician and astronomer.

Ker, William Paton (1855–1923) Scottish literary critic (*Epic and Romance* 1897).

Kerenski *or* **Kerensky, Alexsandr Feodorovich** (1881–1970) Russian revolutionary leader. A member of the Social Democratic Party's liberal wing, he became prime minister of the Russian provisional government of 1917 (July-November) but was deposed by Lenin's Bolsheviks.

Kerguélen Archipelago a remote group of some 300 islands in the southern Indian Ocean, discovered 1772 by the French explorer Yves Kerguélen Trémarec (1745–97).

Kern, Jerome [David] (1885–1945) American composer and songwriter. A highly prolific writer of music and songs, he had a huge influence on the American musical tradition. His works include *Sally* (1920).

Kerosene oil discovered 1852 by the Canadian geologist Abraham Gesner (1797–1864).

Kerouac, Jack [Jean-Louis Lebris de Kérouac] (1922–69) American novelist and poet who was a much imitated central figure of the Beat Generation of poets and writers in the 1950s. His most influential work was *On the Road* (1957).

Kerschensteiner, Georg (1854–1932) German educationist.

Kesey, Ken (1935–) American writer (*One Flew Over the Cuckoo's Nest* 1962).

Ketch, Jack (d.1686) official executioner (1663–86).

Ketelby, Albert William (1880–1959) English composer (*In a Monastery Garden* 1912).

Kett's Rebellion, 1549, led by the English landowner Robert Kett (d.1549) who was hanged.

Kew Gardens established by Princess Augusta, Dowager Princess of Wales, 1759.

Kew Palace, the Dutch House, purchased by King George III, 1781.

Key, Francis Scott (1779–1843) American lawyer and poet (*The Star-spangled Banner* 1814).

Keyes, Roger, Baron of Zeebrugge (1872–1945) sailor and politician.

Keynes, John Maynard, 1st Baron (1883–1946) English economist. He argued that unemployment was curable through macroeconomic management of monetary and fiscal policies and advocated the creation of employment through government schemes. His works include *General Theory of Employment, Interest and Money* (1936)

KGB [Komitet Gosudarstvennoye Bezhopaznosti] Soviet Committee for State Security in charge of frontier and general security from 1953.

Khachaturiyan, Aram Ilich (1903–78) Armenian-born Russian composer (*Masquerade Suite* 1944).

Khaki first worn 1843, introduced by Colonel Sir Harry Burnett Lumsden (1821–96) of the Queen's Own Corps of Scouts and Guides, became general in the 2nd Afghan War.

Khaki Election, Great Britain, won by Conservatives, 28 September to 16 October 1900.

Khartoum capital of the Sudan, founded *c.*1823. A siege by the Mahdi began 16 April 1884, just a month after General Gordon had reached the city and lasted ten months. Lord Wolseley's relief forced arrived two days after the city had fallen (26 January 1885) and Gordon had been killed.

Khayyam, Omar (*fl* 11th century) Persian poet (*The Rubaiyat*).

Khedive of Egypt the last Abbas Hilmi II, deposed 1914.

Khmer Rouge revolutionary Cambodian political movement, captured Phnom Penh 1975; leader Pol Pot ruled Cambodia (renamed Kampuchea) 1975–79, perpetrating mass killings ('Year Zero').

Khomeini, Ayatollah [Ruhollah] [Sayyid Ruhollah Moussari] (*c.*1900–1989) Iranian Shi'ite Muslim religious leader who established a theocratic dictatorship (1979–89) that crushed all dissent and declared his intention of 'exporting' the Shiite revolution to other Islamic countries. He aroused Western anger by proclaiming a death sentence against Salman Rushdie in 1989, shortly before his death.

Khosru I (d.579) Persian ruler (531–579).

Khosru II (d.628) Persian ruler (591–628). He was murdered.

Khrushchev, Nikita Sergeyevich (1894–1971) Soviet politician. He was first secretary of the Communist Party (1953–64) and prime minister (1958–64). He promoted peaceful co-existence with the West and was deposed in 1964 in the Kremlin coup that brought Brezhnev to power.

Khufu (Cheops) (*fl. c.*2900 BC) Egyptian king.

Kidd, Captain William (*c.*1645–1701) Scottish pirate. He was hanged.

Kiel canal first opened 1784; second opened 21 June 1895.

Kiel mutiny of the German Navy World War I, 3 November 1918.

Kierkegaard, Søren Aabye (1813–55) Danish theologian and philosopher. Regarded as the founder of existentialism, he rejected the spiritual authority of organized religion and emphasized the centrality of individual choice.

Kilimanjaro highest African mountain (19,710 ft), first climbed 1889 by the German geographer Hans Meyer (1858–1929).

Killiecrankie, Battle of between the Jacobites and the Royal force, 27 July 1689. It was a Jacobite victory but their leader was killed.

Killigrew, Thomas (1612–83) English playwright (*The Parson's Wedding* 1637).

'Kilmainham Treaty' between Gladstone and Parnell, May 1882.

Kilogram national standard established in Britain 1897.

Kim Il Sung (1912–94) North Korean marshal and Communist politician. He became prime minister (1948–72) and president (1972–94) of North Korea, establishing a Stalinist dictatorship based on a personality cult of himself as the 'great leader'. His son, **Kim Jong Il** (1942–), succeeded him as president.

Kindergarten first American opened by the American educationalist Elizabeth Peabody (1804–94) at Boston 1860.

Kindergarten first English opened *c.*1850 by Johannes Ronge.

Kindergarten first Froebel started at Blankenburg, Switzerland, 1837–45, by the German educationalist Friedrich Wilhelm August Froebel (1782–1852).

Kineth (d.843) king of the Picts (842–843) *see* Appendix.

Kinetic theory of gases postulated 1859 by the Scottish physicist James Clerk Maxwell (1831–79).

Kinetoscope invented 1887 by the American inventor Thomas Alva Edison (1847–1931).

King, Billie Jean (1943–) American tennis player. Regarded as one of the finest women players ever, she won twenty Wimbledon titles between between 1965 and 1980.

King, Henry (1592–1669) English divine and poet.

King, Martin Luther, Jr (1929–68) American civil rights leader and Baptist minister. Influenced by Gandhi's policy of nonviolent resistance, he organized opposition to segregationist policies in the Southern US. He was awarded the 1964 Nobel Peace Prize and was assassinated 4 April 1968.

King, Stephen (1947–) American horror novelist (*The Shining* 1977).

King, William Mackenzie (1874–1950) Canadian prime minister (1921–30, 1935–48).

King Charles the Martyr anniversary of, commemorating his execution 1649, held 30 January.

King Edward VII Land, Antarctica, sighted 1842 by Sir James Clark Ross (1800–1862; identified 1902 by the English explorer Robert Scott (1868–1912).

King George V Dock, Glasgow, opened 10 July 1931.

King George V Dock, London, opened 1921.

King George V Land, Antarctica, discovered 1912–13 by the Australian explorer Sir Douglas Mawson (1882–1958).

King George's War waged by Britain and France in North America 1745–54.

Kinglake, Alexander William (1809–91) English traveller (*Eothen* 1844) and historian.

King Philip's War waged 1675–76 by the American Indian chief Philip (killed 1676).

King's College, Cambridge University, founded by King Henry VI, 1441.

King's College, London University, founded 1829; reincorporated 1882.

King's College, New York (now Columbia University), founded by grant of King George II, 1754.

Kingsley, Charles (1819–75) English writer (*Westward Ho!* 1855).

Kingsley, Henry (1830–76) English writer (*Ravenshoe* 1861).

Kingsley, Mary (1862–1900) English traveller and writer (*Travels in West Africa* 1897).

King's Police Medal instituted by royal warrant 1909.

Kingsway, London, opened 18 October 1905.

King William Island, Arctic, discovered 1831 by the Scottish explorer Sir James Clark Ross (1800–1862).

Kinnock, Neil [Gordon] (1942–) Welsh Labour politician. Elected leader of the Labour Party in 1983 in succession to Foot, he gradually moderated the Party's policies and had great success in marginalizing the hard left of the party. He resigned as leader following his party's defeat in the 1992 general election and became a commissioner with the European Union.

Kinsey, Alfred (1894–1956) American sexologist (the Kinsey Reports 1948, 1953).

Kinshasa *see* LÉOPOLDVILLE.

Kipling, John Lockwood (1837–1911) British artist.

Kipling, [Joseph] Rudyard (1865–1936) Indian-born English short-story writer, poet and novelist. Although best known for his stories for children, e.g. *Kim* (1911) and *The Jungle Book*, he was also a caustic observer of Anglo-Indian society and critical of many aspects of colonialism in his writing.

Kircher, Athanasius (1601–80) German inventor of the magic lantern (1646).

Kiritimati *see* CHRISTMAS ISLAND.

Kirke's Lambs' British soldiers led at the Battle of Sedgemoor (1685) by the English brigadier Percy Kirke (*c.*1646–1691).

Kissinger, Henry [Alfred] (1923–) German-born American statesman, diplomat, foreign policy adviser and analyst. He shared the 1973 Nobel Peace Prize with the North Vietnamese negotiator Le Duc Tho (1911–) for the treaty ending US involvement in Vietnam. As secretary of state (1973–76) he fostered détente with the Soviet Union and China, and helped negotiate peace between Israel and Egypt in 1973.

Kit-Cat Club, London, anti-Jacobite dining club of writers, politicians, etc., existed roughly 1700–1720.

Kitchener of Khartoum, [Horatio] Herbert, 1st Earl (1850–1916) Anglo-Irish field marshal. Commander in chief of the British forces during the Boer War of 1901–2, and of the British forces in India (1902–9), he was appointed secretary for war in 1914 and had mobilized Britain's largest-yet army by the time of his death by drowning when his ship hit a mine.

Kléber, Jean Baptiste (1755–1800) French general. He was assassinated.

Klee, Paul (1879–1940) Swiss painter and etcher who developed a style of mainly abstract work characterized by doodle-like drawings. He was a member of the *Blaue Reiter* group. His works include *High Spirits* (1939).

Klein, Calvin (1942–) American fashion designer.

Kleist, Heinrich von (1777–1811) German poet and playwright (*Prinz Friedrich von Homburg* 1811).

Klemperer, Otto (1885–1973) German-born conductor. A great interpreter of both classical and contemporary works, he became director of the Los Angeles Symphony Orchestra in 1936 and director of the Budapest Opera (1947–50).

Klimt, Gustav (1862–1918) Austrian painter. An excellent draughtsman, his early works were influenced by Impressionism, Symbolism and Art Nouveau. He was a founder of the Vienna Sezession and had a great influence on younger artists.

Klondike gold rush gold discovered 1896; rush began 1897.

Klopstock, Friedrich Gottlieb (1724–1803) German poet (*Messias* 1748–73).

Kneller, Sir Godfrey (*c.*1648–1723) German-born portrait painter.

Knight, Dame Laura [née Johnson] (1877–1970) English painter.

Knight, William Angus (1836–1916) Scottish philosopher.

Knights, Teutonic order formed 1190, recognized by papacy 1191, went to Prussia *c.*1225.

Knights Hospitallers of St John of Jerusalem order founded during the First Crusade, recognized by papacy 1113.

Knights of Malta Order of St John of Jerusalem 1529–1798.

Knights of Rhodes Order of St John of Jerusalem 1309–1522.

Knights Templars *see* TEMPLAR, ORDER OF THE KNIGHTS.

Knitting Frame, Cotton's invented 1864 by the merchant William Cotton (1786–1866).

Knossos Excavations started 1900 by the English archaeologist Sir John Evans (1851–1941).

Knowles, James (1831–1908) English architect and founder (1877) of the *Nineteenth Century*.

Knowles, Sir James Sheridan (1784–1862) Irish-born playwright (*Virginius* 1820).

Knox, John (*c.*1513-1572) Scottish Protestant reformer. He was noted for his antagonistic relationship with Mary Queen of Scots and for his single-minded determination in the pursuit of religious reformation.

Knox, Ronald English writer (1888–1957).

Knut II the Great *see* CANUTE.

Knut III *see* HARDEKNUT.

Knut IV, Saint (d.1086) king of Denmark (1080–86). He was killed.

Knut V (d.1157) king of Denmark (1147–57). He was assassinated.

Knut VI (1163–1202) king of Denmark (1182–1202).

Koberger, Anton (*c.*1445–1513) German pioneer printer and publisher.

Koch, Charles Henri Emmanuel (1809–79) German traveller and naturalist.

Koch, Robert (1843–1910) German bacteriologist and discoverer 1882 of the TB bacillus.

'Kodak' folding cameras first marketed 1898 by the

American inventor George Eastman (1854–1932).

Kodály, Zoltán (1882–1967) Hungarian composer. Like his friend Bartók, he was much influenced by the traditional music of his country. He wrote chamber music, choral works and operas, including the comic opera *Háry János* (1926).

Kodiak Island, Alaska, discovered 1764 by the Russian fur-trader Stephen Glotov.

Koestler, Arthur (1905–83) Hungarian-born British author and journalist (*Darkness at Noon* 1940). He and his wife committed suicide.

Koh-I-Noor Indian diamond known since 1304; acquired by East India Company and presented to British regalia 1850.

Kohl, Helmut (1930–) German Christian Democrat statesman. He became chancellor of West Germany (1982–90) and the first chancellor of reunited Germany in 1990.

Kokoschka, Oskar (1886–1980) Austrian-born painter and dramatist. A leading Expressionist painter, noted particularly for his landscapes and portraits, he fled to Britain in 1938.

Kollwitz, Käthe (1867–1945) German artist.

Königsmark, Otto Wilhelm, Freiherr von (1639–1688) German general.

Koninck, Laurent Guillaume de(1809–87) Belgian palaeontologist .

Konrad von Würzburg (d.1287) German poet (*Trojanerkrieg* 1280–87).

Koran sacred book of Islam, written approximately 620 to 632.

Korda, Sir Alexander [Sandor Kellner] (1893–1956) Hungarian-born British film director and producer. His films include *The Private Life of Henry VIII* and *The Third Man*.

Korea occupied by Japan 1905 and formally annexed to that country 22 August 1910; occupied and partitioned by USA and USSR 1945, becoming North Korea and South Korea in 1948.

Korean Truce between the United Nations and North Korea, signed 27 July 1953.

Korean War between the United Nations and North Korean and Chinese forces, June 1950 to June 1951.

Kosciuszko, Tadeusz (1746–1817) Polish leader.

Kossuth, Lajos (1802–94) Hungarian patriot.

Kotzebue, August Friedrich Ferdinand von (1761–1819) German playwright (*Adelheid von Wulfingen* 1789). He was killed.

Koussevitsky, Sergei (1874–1951) Russian-born conductor.

Krafft-Ebing, Richard, Freiherr von (1840–1902) German expert in mental disorders.

Kreisler, Fritz (1875–1962) Austrian-born American violinist and composer. Elgar's violin concerto was dedicated to him, and he became one of the most popular violinists of his day.

Kreuger, Nils Edvard (1858–1930) Swedish painter.

Kreutzer, Rodolphe (1766–1831) French-born violinist to whom Beethoven dedicated his Kreuzer Sonata, a sonata for violin and piano.

Krishnamurti, Jiddu (1895–1986) Indian mystic.

Kronstadt Russian naval base founded 1710; scene of mutiny March 1921.

Kropotkin, Prince Peter (1842–1921) Russian scientist and anarchist (*Mutual Aid* 1902).

Kruger, Stephanus Johannes Paulus (1825–1904) Boer leader and president of South Africa (1883–1900).

Krupp Works founded 1810 at Essen, Germany, by Friedrich Krupp (1787–1826) and developed by his son Alfred Krupp (1812–87).

Krusenstern, Adam Ivan (1770–1846) circumnavigator (1803–1806) of the world.

Krylov, Ivan Andreievich (1786–1844) Russian writer of fables.

Krypton inert gas first obtained 1898 from the atmosphere by the British scientists Sir William Ramsay (1852–1916) and Morris William Travers (1872–1961).

Ku Klux Klan American secret society founded 1865 at Polask, Tennessee; revived 1915 by William J. Simmons and again in 1945 by Dr Samuel Green.

Kubelik, Jan (1880–1940) Czech violinist.

Kublai Khan (1216–94) Mongolian emperor (1276–94).

Kubrick, Stanley (1928–) American film director and producer. His films include the anti-war classic *Paths of Glory* (1957), the black nuclear war comedy *Dr Strangelove* (1963), the innovative science fiction classic *2001: A Space Odyssey* (1968), the still highly controversial *A Clockwork Orange* (1971) and *Full Metal Jacket*, about the Vietnam War.

Kulturkampf Bismarck's struggle with Catholic Church in Germany 1871–87).

Kun, Béla (1886–*c*.1919) Communist leader in Hungary March–August 1919. He disappeared in Russia after 1919.

Kundera, Milan (1929–) Czech novelist. His masterpiece is *The Unbearable Lightness of Being*, a love story set against the background of repression following the Russian invasion of Czechoslovakia in 1968. Other works include *The Book of Laughter and Forgetting* (1980).

Kung, Hans (1928–) Swiss Roman Catholic theologian (*Does God Exist?* 1978).

Kuomintang Chinese national republic party founded at the beginning of 20th century.

Kuprin, Aleksandr (1870–1938) Russian novelist

whose works include *Yama, the Pit* (1909).

Kuropatkin, Alexei Nikolaievich (1848–1925) Russian general.

Kurosawa, Akira (1910–) Japanese film director. His films include the samurai classics *The Seven Samurai* (1954) and *Yojimbo* (1961) (remade in the west as *The Magnificent Seven* and *A Fistful of Dollars*), and samurai versions of *Macbeth*, titled *Throne of* Blood (1957), and *King Lear*, titled *Ran* (1985). Kurosawa was happiest with the epic form, and also had a 'family' of actors he used regularly.

Kut, Mesopotamia, in the First World War captured by the British 1915; surrendered to the Turks 1916, retaken by the British 1917.

Kutuzov, Mikhael Ilarionovich (1743–1813) Russian diplomat, administrator and soldier.

Kuwait, Gulf state, became British protectorate 1899; recognized as independent under British protection 1914; complete independence 1961.

Kyd, Thomas (1558–94) English dramatist. His most important work is his revenge tragedy, *The Spanish Tragedy* (1586), which served as a model for Shakespeare's *Titus Andronicus*. A close associate of Christopher Marlowe, he died in poverty after being accused of denying the divinity of Christ.

Kynaston, Edward (*c.*1640–1706) English actor (possibly the last to take female parts).

Kyoto capital of Japan until 1868.

L

Labé, Louise (La Belle Cordière) (*c.*1525–1566). French poet (*Sonnets* 1555)

Labiche, Eugène Marin (1815–88) French playwright (*Le Voyage de M. Perrichon* 1860).

Labienus, Titus Roman tribune, killed 45.

Labor Day public holiday in USA and Canada, first Monday in September. Inaugurated 1882; officially adopted 1894.

Labouchère, Henry (1831–1912) English politician and journalist (founded *Truth* 1877).

Labour Day 1 May.

Labour Party origins in the Labour Representation League, organized 1869, and the Labour Electoral Association, formed by the TUC in 1887; founded (as Labour Representation Committee) at a conference in London 27–28 February 1900; present name adopted 1906; constitution adopted 1918.

La Bruyère, Jean de (1645–96) French writer (*Characters* 1688).

Labuan, Malay Archipelago, island off northwest Borneo, ceded to Britain by the Sultan of Brunei 1846; part of Straits Settlements until 1946 when transferred to North Borneo.

La Calprenède, Gauthier de Costes de (1614–63) French writer (*Cassandre* 1642–50).

Laccadive, Minicoy and Amindivi Islands *see* LAKSHADWEEP ISLANDS.

Lace-making, pillow introduced 1561 into Germany by the German Barbara Uttman (1514–75).

La Chaise, François de (1624–1709) father confessor to Louis XIV.

Lactantius Firmianus (*c.*260–*c.*340) early Christian Father.

'Ladies of Llangollen' Lady Eleanor Butler (1778–1829) and Sarah Ponsonby (1778–1831).

'Ladies' Peace' the Treaty of Cambrai, renewing the Treaty of Madrid, signed 1529.

Ladislaus I, Saint [Laszlo] (1040–95) king of Hungary (1077–95).

Ladislaus II (*c.*1134–1162) king of Hungary (1161).

Ladislaus III (1199–1205) king of Hungary (1204–1205).

Ladislaus IV (1272–90) king of Hungary (1262–90). He was murdered.

Ladislaus V (1440–57) king of Hungary (1444–57).

Lady Day (Annunciation of the Virgin) 25 March.

Lady Margaret Hall, Oxford University, founded 1879.

Ladysmith, Siege of Boer War, October 1899, relieved 28 February 1900.

Laetare Sunday the fourth Sunday in Lent.

La Fayette, Marie Joseph Paul Yves Roch Gilbert du Motier, Marquis de French political reformer (1757–1834).

La Fayette, Marie Madeleine, Comtesse de (1634–93) French writer.

Laffitte, Jacques (1767–1844) French financier.

La Follette, Robert (1855–1925) American senator.

La Fontaine, Jean de (1621–95) French writer (*Fables* 1668–90).

Laforgue, Jules (1860–87) French poet (*Complaintes* 1885).

Lagash ancient city in Sumeria; dynasty founded 3000 BC by Ur-Nina, which built temples and canals; Umma, Kish, Opis, Erech and Ur conquered by Eannatum, king of Lagash, and the Elamites repelled 2900 BC; defeated and destroyed 2800 BC by Lugai-Zaggisi, ruler of Umma and king of Erech, who became overlord of all Sumeria.

Lagerlöf, Selma (1858–1940) Swedish novelist (*Gösta Berling* 1894).

Lagrange, Joseph Louis Italian-born scientist (1736–1813).

La Guardia, Fiorello (1882–1947) American lawyer and politician (reformist mayor of New York City 1933–45).

Laing, R[onald] D[avid] (1927–89) Scottish psychiatrist. He became a counterculture guru in the 1960s for his revolutionary ideas about mental disorders.

Lake Trasimene, Battle of 217 BC a battle of the Second Punic War in which Hannibal was victorious over the Romans.

Lakshadweep Islands a group of small islands in the Indian Ocean discovered by the Portuguese 1498; sequestrated by Britain 1877; now a territory of India.

Lalande, Joseph Jérome Lefrançais de French astronomer (1732–1807).

Lalo, Edouard (1823–92) French composer (*Symphonie espagnole* 1875).

Lamarck, Jean [Baptiste Pierre Antoine de Monet, Chevalier de] (1744–1829) French naturalist. His theory of the evolution of species through the acquisition of inherited characteristics prepared the ground for Darwin's theory of evolution.

Lamartine, Alphonse Marie Louis de (1790–1869) French writer (*Meditation* 1820).

Lamb, Charles (1775–1834) English essayist and critic. A friend of Hazlitt, Wordsworth and Coleridge, his writings display the great charm his friends describe. With his sister, **Mary Anne Lamb** (1764–1847), he adapted several of Shakespeare's plays to prose form. In 1796, in a fit of insanity, Mary killed their mother, and Charles looked after her until his death.

Lamb, John (1890–1958) British pioneer in the development of gas turbine propulsion.

Lambert, Constant (1905–51) English composer (*Rio Grande* 1929).

Lambert, John (1619–84) English Puritan general.

Lambeth Articles (*c.*1530–1604) concerning predestination and election drawn up 1595 by John Whitgift, archbishop of Canterbury.

Lambeth Bridge, London, opened 1862, pulled down 1929, new bridge opened 1932.

Lambeth Conference Anglican bishops' assembly, first convened 1867.

Lambeth Palace origin uncertain, chapel built 1245–70, Water Tower built *c.*1430.

Lamennais, Fèlicité Robert de (1782–1854) French church reformer (*Paroles d'un croyant* 1834).

Lamian War 323–322 BC a war following the death of Alexander the Great between Antipater of Macedonia and a strong confederacy of Greek states with Athens at the head. At first unsuccessful, he defeated the insurgent Greeks at Crannon 322 BC.

Lammas Day 1 August.

Lamond, Frederick (1868–1948) Scottish pianist.

La Motte-Fouqué, Friedrich, Freiherr de (1777–1843) German writer (*Undine* 1811).

L'Amour, Louis (1908–88) American writer of western novels (*Hondo* 1953).

Lamp (1828–1914) electric, first public demonstration 1879 by the inventor Sir Joseph Swan.

Lampedusa, Giuseppi Tomasi Di (1896–1957) Italian writer (*The Leopard* 1955–56).

Lancashire witch the last, Mary Nutter (1856–1928).

Lancaster, Burt (Burton Stephen Lancaster) (1913–95) American film actor (*The Swimmer* 1968).

Lancaster, Duchy of established 1265; attached to the Crown since 1399.

Lancers form of quadrille, came into fashion in Britain *c.*1850.

Lancet, The British medical journal founded 1823 by the English surgeon Thomas Wakley (1795–1862).

Lancret, Nicolas (1660–1743) French painter (*Les cinq sens*).

Land Registry British, established 1862, reformed 1875; now operates under Land Registration Acts 1925–88.

Land, Edwin (1909–91) American inventor of the Polaroid camera 1948, colour version 1963.

Landor, Walter Savage (1775–1864) English writer (*Imaginary Conversation* 1824–46).

Landowska, Wanda (1877–1959) Polish-born harpsichord player.

Landseer, Sir Edwin Henry (1802–73) English painter. Highly regarded for his animal studies, his notable works include *The Monarch of the Glen* (1850) and the lions modelled for Trafalgar Square, London, in 1867.

Landseer, Sir Edwin (1804–75) English painter (*Suspense* 1834).

Landus pope 913–914.

Lane Bequest of modern paintings bequeathed by Sir Hugh Lane, shared by Britain with Eire 1959.

Lane, Sir Hugh (1875–1915) Irish art collector. Drowned at sea when the *Lusitania* was torpedoed

Lanfranc (*c.*1005–1089) archbishop of Canterbury (1070–89).

Lang, Andrew (1844–1912) Scottish writer and translator (*Myth, Ritual and Religion* 1887).

Lang, Fritz (1890–1976) German-born film director (*Metropolis* 1927).

Lange, David (1942–) New Zealand politician (prime minister 1984–89).

Langham, Simon (d.1376) archbishop of Canterbury (1366–68).

Langland, William (*c.* 1330–*c.*1400) English poet whose only surviving work is the *Vision of Piers Plowman* which exists in three versions (*c.*1362, 1377 and 1393–98).

Langton, Stephen (*c.*1150–1228) archbishop of Canterbury (1207–28).

Langtry, Lillie ('The Jersey Lily') (1852–1929) actress.

Lanier, Sidney (1842–81) American poet (*Florida* 1875).

Lansbury, George (1859–1940) English Labour politician. Noted for his support for women's suffrage and pacifism, he became leader of his party (1931–35) when MacDonald joined the National Government. His daughter, **Angela Lansbury** (1925–) became a popular film actress in the 1940s.

Lansdowne, William Petty Fitzmaurice, Marquess of (1737–1805) Irish-born secretary of state.

Lansky, Meyer (1902–83) American Mafia figure.

Lanthanum a silvery white metallic element discovered 1839 by the Swedish scientist Karl Gustav Mosander (1797–1858).

Laos French protectorate 1893, became independent

sovereign state, within the French Union, 1949; became a republic in 1975.

Lâo-tse (*c.*604 BC) Chinese founder of Taoism.

La Paz capital of Bolivia, founded 1548 by the 16th-century Spanish explorer Alfonso de Mendoza.

La Pérouse, Jean François de Galaup, Comte de (1741–88) French navigator and explorer. In February of 1788 his two ships sailed from Botany Bay in Australia and were never seen again

Laplace, Pierre Simon, Marquis de (1749–1827) French astronomer and mathematician (*Méchanique céleste* 1799-1825).

Laporte, Pierre de (1603–50) valet to Louis XIV and intriguer.

Larbaud, Valéry (1881–1957) French writer (*Enfantines* 1918).

Lardner, Ring [Ringgold Wilmer Lardner] (1885–1933) American journalist and short-story writer whose stories of American low life are noted for their cynical wit. (*Gullible's Travels* 1917)

Largillière, Nicolas de (1656–1746) French painter (*Mlle Duclos*).

Larissa, Battle of 171 BC a battle of the Third Macedonian War, when the Macedonians under Perseus were victorious over the Romans.

Larkin, Philip [Arthur] (1922–85) English poet, jazz critic and librarian. Known for his dark, sardonic lyricism, he is regarded as one of the greatest of all modern English poets. He also wrote two novels and a collection of essays on jazz (*High Windows* 1974).

Laroche, Raymonde, Baronne de French aviator, first woman in the world (1910) to qualify for a pilot's certificate.

La Rochefoucald, François de (1613–80) French writer (*Maxims* 1665).

Larousse, Pierre Athanase French encyclopaedist (1817–75).

Larwood, Harold (1904–95) English cricketer. His use of 'bodyline' tactics in the 1932–33 tour of Australia created great controversy, causing diplomatic tension in relations between Australia and the UK.

Laryngoscope use introduced 1861 by the American physician Louis Elsberg (1836–85).

Laryngoscopy study founded by the Bohemian scientist Johann Nepomuk Czermak (1828–73).

Las Casas, Bartolomé de Spanish prelate (1474–1566).

La Salle, Robert Cavelier, Sieur de (1643–87) French explorer and navigator (the Mississippi 1682). He was assassinated.

Lascaux caves southwest France, painted caves discovered by five boys from Montignac 1940.

Lasdun, Sir Denys Louis (1914–) English architect. Influenced by Le Corbusier, his buildings include the University of East Anglia and the National Theatre in London.

Lasker, Emanuel (1868–1941) German chess player. His reign as world champion (1894–1921) is still a record.

Laski, Harold [Joseph] (1893–1950) English political scientist and socialist propagandist. He was a highly influential spokesman for Marxism through his position as teacher, writer and Labour Party power-broker (he was party chairman 1945–46), and through his friendships with politicians such as Roosevelt.

Lassalle, Ferdinand (1825–64) German socialist. Died in a duel for the hand of Helene von Dönniges. (*System of Acquired Rights* 1860).

Lassie collie dog film star, first appeared in *Lassie Come Home* 1943.

Lasso, Orlando di (*c.*1531–1594) Dutch composer (*Psalma Davidis poenitentiale*).

László, Philip (1869–1937) Hungarian painter.

Latent heat nature defined *c.*1765 by the British scientist Joseph Black (1728–99).

Lateran Councils, First 18 March 1123 onwards; **Second,** April 1139; **Third,** March 1179; **Fourth,** 1215; **Fifth,** 3 May 1512 to 16 March 1517.

Lateran Treaty between the Holy See and the kingdom of Italy 1929.

Latimer, Hugh (*c.*1485–1555) English religious reformer. He was burnt at the stake.

Latium (modern Lazio) an ancient territory of the central western coast of Italy which was occupied by the Latin people until it was conquered by Rome 340–338 BC.

La Tour, Maurice Quentin de (1704–88) French artist (*Louis XV*).

Latrobe, Charles Joseph (1801–75) lieutenant governor of Victoria, Australia.

Latterday Saints, Church of Jesus Christ of the (Mormons) founded 1827 by the American Joseph Smith (1805–44).

Latvia ruled by Russia 1795–1918; independence declared 1919; occupied by the Russians June 1940 and admitted to the Soviet Union August 1940; gained independence from the former Soviet Union 21 August 1991.

Latvian language earliest known text dated 1585.

Laud, William (1573–1645) archbishop of Canterbury (1633–45) beheaded for treason.

Lauda, Niki [Nikolas Andreas Lauda] (1949–) Austrian racing driver. World champion in 1975, 1977 and 1984, he suffered dreadful injuries in the 1976 German Grand Prix. He retired in 1985.

Laudanum alcoholic tincture of opium, formula developed *c.*1660 by the English physician Thomas Sydenham (1624–89).

Lauder, Sir Harry [Hugh MacLennan] (1870–1950) Scottish music-hall comedian and singer, who made an international career out of his Scottish comedy routines and songs.

Lauderdale, John Maitland, Duke of (1616–82) Scottish statesman.

Laughing gas (nitrous oxide) discovered 1772 by the English scientist Joseph Priestley (1733–1804). First used 1844 as an anaesthetic in dentistry by the American dentist Horace Wells (1815–48).

Laughton, Charles (1899–1962) English-born American stage and film actor, renowned for his larger-than-life performances in many memorable films, e.g. *The Private Life of Henry VIII.*

Laurel, Stan [Arthur Stanley Jefferson] (1890–1965), English-born American comedian, and Oliver Hardy (1892–1957) American comedian. Laurel began his career on the English music-hall stage (understudying Chaplin at one point), and Hardy performed with a minstrel troupe before going into films. They formed their Laurel (thin, vacant and bemused one) and Hardy (fat, blustering one) partnership in 1929 and made some very funny films, e.g. *Another Fine Mess* (1930).

Laurel and Hardy comedy duo of silent and talking pictures: Stan Laurel (1890–1965) and Oliver Hardy (1892–1957).

Laurie, Annie [Mrs Alexander Ferguson] (1682–1764).

Laurier, Sir Wilfrid (1841–1919) first French-Canadian premier of Canada (1896–1911).

Lausanne Pact between the Allies and Germany, signed 1932.

Lausanne, Treaty of concerning Turkey, signed 24 July 1923.

Lautrec, Henri Marie Raymond de Toulouse *see* TOULOUSE-LAUTREC, HENRI [MARIE RAYMOND] DE

Laval, Pierre (1883–1945) French statesman. Prime minister (1931–32, 1935–36, 1942–44), he sided openly during the occupation with the Germans and was executed for treason in 1945 by the victorious Free French.

La Vallière, Louise de (1644–1710) mistress of Louis XIV.

Lavater, Johann Kaspar (1741–1801) Swiss theologian and physiognomist.

Lavery, Sir John (1856–1941) Ulster painter.

Lavoisier, Antoine Laurent (1743–94) French chemist. Regarded as the founder of modern chemistry, he discovered oxygen and established its role in combustion and respiration. He was guillotined in 1794 despite being politically liberal.

Law, John (1671–1729). Scottish controller-general of finance in France. In 1694 he was imprisoned for killing a man in a duel over a woman. The following year he escaped and fled to the continent. He and his brother William set up a private bank in1716 in Paris. Left for Venice when his unpopularity grew in France, where he died in 1729.

Law, William (1686–1761) English theologian (*Serious Call* 1729).

Lawes, William (1582–1645) English composer ('Gather ye rosebuds while ye may'). He was killed.

Lawrence anti-pope (498).

Lawrence, Kansas, sacked by Quantrill Gang 1863.

Lawrence, D[avid] H[erbert] (1885–1930) English novelist, poet and short-story writer. His novels caused much controversy for their frank treatment of sex. *Lady Chatterley's Lover* (1928) was not published in its full form until 1960.

Lawrence, Dr Ernest Orlando(1901–58) American physicist who invented a machine called a cyclotron that accelerated atomic particles to enormous speeds and then used them to bombard atoms, producing artificial radioactivity. He won the Nobel Prize for Physics(1939).

Lawrence, Gertrude [Gertrud Alexandra Dagmar Lawrence-Klasen] (1898–1952) English actress noted for her professional relationship with Noel Coward, many of whose plays had parts written especially for her.

Lawrence, John Laird Mair, Baron Lawrence (1811–79) viceroy and governor-general of India (1864–69).

Lawrence, Sir Thomas (1769–1830) English painter. The leading portraitist of his time, he was made court painter in 1792. (*Mrs Siddons*)

Lawrence, T[homas] E[dward] (1888–1935) Welsh-born Anglo-Irish soldier, explorer and author, known as 'Lawrence of Arabia'. In the First World War he helped the Arab revolt against the Turks and was instrumental in the conquest of Palestine (1918) (*Seven Pillars of Wisdom* 1926).

Lawson, Nigel *see* MAJOR, JOHN.

Layamon English priest and historian (*The Brut*), lived in the late 12th and early 13th centuries.

Layard, Sir Austen Henry (1817–94) archaeologist and diplomat.

LDV (Local Defence Volunteers) formed May 1940, became Home Guard July 1940; disbanded 1 November 1944.

Leach, Bernard Howell (1887–1979) English potter who revolutionized the production of pottery by creating reasonably priced, attractively designed studio pottery.

Leacock, Stephen (1869–1944) English-born Canadian humorist (*Nonsense Novels* 1911).

Leactra, Battle of a battle of the Wars of the Greek

City States, 371 BC, when Sparta was defeated by Thebes under Epaminondas.

Leadbelly [Huddie Ledbetter] (1888–1949) American blues singer. Discovered in a Louisiana prison in 1933, he later recorded several songs that soon became recognized as blues/folk classics, e.g. 'Rock Island Line' and 'Goodnight, Irene'.

League of Nations founded 28 April 1919; superseded by the UN 8 April 1946.

Leakey, Louis Seymour Bazett (1903–72) Kenyan-born British archaeologist and anthropologist, and **Mary Douglas Leakey** (1913–) English archaeologist. Married in 1936, the Leakeys made several important discoveries about humanity's origins eg early primate fossil remains in Olduvai Gorge, East Africa, 1959. Their son, **Richard Erskine Frere Leakey** (1944–), is also a prominent (Kenyan) archaeologist.

Lean, Sir David (1908–91) English film director. Highly regarded for his compositional skill and craftsmanship, his films include many classics, e.g. *Brief Encounter* and *Great Expectations*.

Leaning Tower of Pisa built 1174–1350.

Leap year the system by which every fourth year comprises 366 days, the extra day being 29 February.

Lear, Edward (1812–88) English artist and humorist (*Book of Nonsense* 1846).

Leary, Timothy (192096) American psychologist and experimental drugs guru.

Lease-Lend US aid to Britain programme proposed by President Roosevelt 1940; put into action 1941; made reciprocal 1942.

Leather hose for fire fighting invented 1672.

Leather, artificial, first manufactured in Britain 1884.

Leavis, F[rank] R[aymond] (1895–1978) English literary critic. With his wife, **Queenie Dorothy Leavis** (1906–81), he made a major impact on literary criticism from the 1930s attacking the modern age of mass culture and advertising. (*The Great Tradition* 1948, *The Common Pursuit* 1952).

Lebanon part of the Ottoman Empire 1516–1919; under French mandatory rule 1920–41; independence proclaimed 1941; French withdrawal completed 1946; intermittent civil war between Christian and Muslim factions 1975–76; Israeli occupations 1978, 1980, 1982–85 in reprisal for Lebanon-based Palestinian attacks on Israeli border settlements; Lebanese government authority over rival militias restored 1990–92.

Leblanc, Nicolas (1742–1806) French chemist who devised a cheap method of making soda (sodium carbonate) but never managed to get it into production and commited suicide. His method of making soda was used widely in France for a century.

Le Brun, Charles (1619–90) French painter influenced by Poussin. Regarded as the creator of the Louis XIV style. Much of his work is to be found in the Palace of Versailles (*La Famille de Darius*).

Le Carré, John [David John Moore Cornwell] (1931–) English novelist. His popular novels are sombre anti-romantic narratives of Cold War espionage, e.g. *The Spy Who Came in from the Cold*.

Lecky, William Edward Hartpole (1838–1903) Irish historian. His greatest achievement was the eight-volume work, *A History of England in the Eighteenth Century* (1878-1890).

Lecocq, Charles (1832–1918) French composer of comic operas and operettas. His more serious music was never appreciated (*Giroflé-Girofla* 1874).

Leconte de Lisle, Charles Marie (1818–94) French poet. He was part of the revolution of 1848 but was unhappy with its result and so left politics and devoted himself to a literary life. Leader of the Parnassian group of poets (*Poèmes antiques* 1852).

Le Corbusier [Charles Edouard Jeanneret] (1887–1965) Swiss-born French architect and town planner. One of the most influential (and most praised and reviled) architects and planners of the century, his work is characterized by use of reinforced concrete and modular, standardized units of construction (based upon the proportions of the human figure), with the house famously defined as a 'machine for living in'.

Lecouvreur, Adrienne (1692–1730) French actress who made her first performanc ea t he Comédie Français in 1717. It is said that her death may be due to poisoning by a rival.

Le Despenser, Hugh, Earl of Winchester (1262–1326) royal favourite whose fortune turned and who was hanged in 1326.

Lederberg, Joshua (1925–) American geneticist. He shared the 1958 Nobel prize for physiology or medicine (with George Beadle and Edward Tatum) for his bacterial research.

Le Duc Tho *see* KISSINGER, HENRY.

Lee, Ann (Mother Ann) (1736–1784) English founder (1758) of the religious movement the Society of Shakers. Emigrated to the USA in 1774 and founded a Shaker settlement in 1776.

Lee, Laurie (1914–) English poet and author whose work is often autobiographical (*Cider with Rosie* 1959).

Lee, Nathaniel (*c.*1653–1692) English playwright (*The Rival Queens* 1677).

Lee, Robert E[dward] (1807–70) American Confederate general who is said to have been one of the greatest of the confederate generals particularly in tactical and strategic manoeuvres.

Lee, Sir Sidney (1859–1926) English editor of the *Dictionary of National Biography*.

Leech, John (1817–64) English engraver.

Leeds University England, founded 1874, granted university status 1904.

Lee Kuan Yew (1923–) Singaporean politician. He became Singapore's first prime minister (1959–), establishing a strict regime noted for its economic achievements and authoritarianism.

Leeuwenhoek, Anton van (1632–1723) Dutch self-taught naturalist and microscopist. He made significant discoveries in both his biological and zoological work.

Le Fanu, Sheridan (1814–73) Irish writer who wrote stories of mystery and horror (*Uncle Silas* 1864, *In a Glass Darkly* 1872).

Le Gallienne, Richard (1866–1947) English writer of both prose and verse born in Liverpool, becoming a journalist in London and later living in New York (*English Poems* 1892).

Legal memory in England dates back to accession of Richard I, 1 September

Léger, Fernand (1881–1955) French painter. A leading Cubist, he was much influenced by industrial imagery and machinery.

Legion of Honour (La Légion d'Honneur) created by the French Consular law of 19 May 1802.

Legitimacy by marriage of parents made legal in England 1926.

Lego®, construction toy using plastic bricks developed in Denmark 1947.

Legros, Alphonse (1837–1911) French artist (*Ex voto* 1861).

Lehár, Franz (1870–1948) Hungarian composer and conductor noted for his operettas, e.g. *The Merry Widow* (1905).

Lehmann, Beatrix (1903–79) English actress, sister of John and Rosamund Lehmann.

Lehmann, John Frederick(1907–87) English writer and editor.

Lehmann, Lilli German operatic singer (1848–1929).

Lehmann, Lotte German-born operatic singer (1888–1976).

Lehmann, Rosamund English novelist (*Dusty Answer* 1927) (1903–90).

Leibnitz *or* **Leibniz, Gottfried Wilhelm** (1646–1716) German philosopher and mathematician. Renowned for the range and depth of his intellect, he made important contributions to many different scientific fields.

Leicester, Robert Dudley, Earl of (*c.*1531–1588) Elizabethan courtier who became a favourite of Elizabeth I. He is rumoured to have had his wife Amy Robsart poisoned in order to be free to marry the Queen. He also had a bigamous marriage and died suddenly in 1588 of a poison that was said to have been intended for his wife

Leicester University England, founded 1918 as the Leicester, Leicestershire and Rutland College; became University College, Leicester, 1927; gained university status 1957.

Leif Ericsson (*c.*1000) Icelandic discoverer of North America, son of Eric the Red and reputedly the first European to discover America.

Leigh, Vivien [Vivien Mary Hartley] (1913–67) Indian-born English stage and film actress. She became an international star with *Gone With the Wind* (1939), in which she co-starred with Clark Gable.

Leighton, Frederick, Lord (1830–96) English painter. A leading neo-classical painter of Victorian times (*Andromache* 1888).

Leipzig University Germany, founded 1409.

Lekeu, Guillaume (1870–94) French composer (*Andromède* 1891).

Leland, John (*c.*1506–1552) English antiquary whose papers are chiefly to be found in the Bodleian and British museums(*Itinerary* 1710–12)

Lely, Cornelis Dutch statesman, engineer and planner of the Zuider Zee (1854–1929).

Lely, Sir Peter (1618–80) German-born painter (*Nell Gwynn*).

Lemmon, Jack [John Uhler Lemmon III] (1925–) American film actor. With the film *Some Like it Hot* (1959) he began a successful collaboration with the director Billy Wilder in seven films(*The Apartment* 1960).

Lemon, Mark (1809–70) English writer and editor *of Punch.*

Lemonnier, Pierre Charles (1715–99) French astronomer.

Le Moyne, François (1688–1737) French painter who specialized in mythological subjects. Committed suicide 1737 (*Ruth et Boaz* 1711).

Le Nain, The brothers French painters of scenes of peasant life: Antoine (1588–1648), Louis (1593–1648), and Mathieu (1607–77). Founder members of the French Académie.

Lenbach, Franz German painter (*Bismarck*) (1836–1904).

'Lenclos, Ninon de' [Anne Lenclos] (1620–1705) French courtesan.

L'Enfant, Pierre Charles (1754–1825) French architect and town planner in the USA.

Lenin, Vladimir Ilyich [Vladimir Ilyich Ulyanov] (1870–1924) Russian revolutionary leader and Marxist philosopher. He was instigator of the Bolshevik October Revolution which overthrew Kerenski's government and leader of the Bolsheviks in the Civil War (1918–21). The failure of his economic policy after the war led to the institution of the New Economic Policy of 1921, which fostered limited private enterprise. He was a brilliant demagogue and an influential philosopher.

Leningrad former name for St Petersburg 1924–91 (previously St Petersburg 1703–1914, Petrograd 1914–1924) named after Lenin 1924.

Leningrad, Siege of by the Germans, relieved after 16 months by the Russians, 18 January 1943.

Lennon, John [Winston] (1940–80) English rock guitarist, singer and songwriter. With Paul McCartney, George Harrison and Ringo Starr, he formed the Beatles, the most popular rock group ever. The success of the band was based on the songwriting partnership of Lennon/McCartney, whose songs achieved phenomenal popularity. He married Yoko Ono (1933–) and pursued a solo career after the Beatles split in 1969. He was assassinated in New York.

Lennox, Charlotte (1720–1804) American-born writer (*The Female Quixote* 1752).

'Leno, Dan' [George Galvin] (1861–1904) English comedian famous his pantomime dames.

Le Normand, Henri René (1882–1951) French playwright (*Le Lâche* 1925).

Le Nôtre, André (1613–1700) French landscape architect who designed the gardens at Versailles (with Louis Le Vau), Fontainbleau and St James's Park, London.

Lens first referred to by Meisner in 13th century.

Lent period of 40 days of fasting preceding Easter.

Leo I, Saint [Leo the Great] pope (440–461) who persuaded Attila the Hun to spare Rome but he could not save the city from the Vandals in 455.

Leo II, Saint pope (682–683).

Leo III, Saint (*c*.750816) pope (795–816).

Leo IV, Saint pope (847–855).

Leo V pope (903).

Leo VI pope (928).

Leo VII pope (936–939).

Leo VIII pope (963–964).

Leo IX [Bruno] (1002–54) pope (1049–54).

Leo X [Giovanni de Medici] (1475–1521) pope (1513–21), best remembered as a patron of art and learning.

Leo XI [Alessandro de Medici] (*c*.1535–1605) pope (1605).

Leo XII [Annibale della Genga] (1760–1829) pope (1823–29).

Leo XIII [Vincenżo Gioacchino Pecci] (1810–1903) pope (1878–1903), was greatly responsible for the modernization of the papacy.

León, Juan Ponce de *see* PONCE DE LEÓN, JUAN.

León, Luis Ponce de *see* PONCE DE LEÓN, LUIS.

Leonardo da Vinci (1452–1519) Florentine painter, draughtsman, engineer, musician and thinker. The outstanding genius of his time, his greatest paintings include *The Last Supper* (1489) and his portrait of *Mona Lisa* (1504). His later years were devoted to scientific studies, and his work in mechanics, aeronautics, physiology and anatomy displays an understanding far beyond his times.

Leone, Sergio (1921–89) Italian director of spaghetti westerns (*A Fistful of Dollars* 1964).

Leonidas (d.480 BC) king of Sparta (*c*.491–480 BC) who took part in the Greek resistance to the Persian invasion. He and his army bravely held the pass at Thermopylae, allowing the Greeks to retreat. Leonidas was killed in the battle.

Leopardi, Giacomo (1798–1837) Italian poet (*Operette Morali* 1827).

Leopold I (1640–1705). Holy Roman emperor (1658–1705), most of whose reign was spent in battle with the Turks.

Leopold II (1747–92) Holy Roman emperor (1790–92) brother of Marie Antoinette. Among the reforms he made before his death was the abolition of torture.

Leopold I (1790–1865) first king of the Belgians (1831–65), under whose reign Belgium escaped the revolution of 1848.

Leopold II (1835–1909) king of the Belgians (1865–1909). Although he was not a popular monarch, Belgium flourished commercially and industrially under his reign.

Leopold III (1901–83) king of the Belgians (1934–51) who surrendered his army to the Nazis during the Second World War despite the opposition of the government.

Léopoldville, now Kinshasa, capital of the former Belgian Congo, now Zaire; founded 1881 by the Welsh explorer Sir Henry Morton Stanley (1841–1904).

Lepanto, Battle of a naval battle fought between the Holy League under Don John and the Turks, 7 October 1571, which was won by the League and prevented further Turkish encroachment into Europe.

Le Pen, Jean-Marie (1928–) French politician. He founded the right-wing National Front in 1972, a crypto–fascist party with anti-immigrant policies.

Lepidus, Marcus Aemilius (d.13) Roman statesman who was part of the Second Triumvirate (43–36 BC) with Octavian and Antony. He attempted to take Sicily for himself, and Octavian deprived him of his triumvirate.

Le Play, Pierre Guillaume Frédéric (1806–82) French engineer and economist whose theories on the importance of sociology and its effect in economics were among the first of their kind.

Leprosy mentioned in India 1400 and in Egypt 1350

BC; bacillus discovered 1872 by the Norwegian physician Gerhard Hansen (1841–1912).

Lermontov, Mikhail Yurievich (1814–41) Russian novelist and poet. His masterpiece is the novel *A Hero of our Time* (1840), a brilliant study of a disaffected, Byronic young aristocrat. He was killed in a duel in 1841.

Le Sage, Alain René (1668–1747) French writer, started as a translator of Latin, Greek and Spanish works of literature. His first original work was a satirical comedy *Turcaret* (1707).(*Gil Blas* 1715–35).

Leschetizky, Theodor (1830–1915) Polish-born pianist.

Lespinasse, Jeanne Julie Eléonore de (1732–76) French writer (*Lettres* 1809).

Lesseps, Ferdinand de (1805–94) French canal builder.

Lessing, Doris [May] (1919–) Iranian-born English novelist and short-story writer. Her novels include the 'Children of Violence' quintet series which explores the social and political undercurrents of modern society (*The Golden Notebook* 1962).

Lessing, Gotthold Ephraim (1729–81) German writer (*Laokoon* 1766).

L'Estrange, Sir Roger (1616–1704) English pamphleteer, journalist and translator.

Le Sueur, Eustache (1617–55) French painter (*Vie de St Bruno* 1645–48).

Lesueur, Jean François (1760–1837) French composer (*Paul et Virginie* 1794).

Letchworth England's first garden city founded 1903.

Letter Office, General first established in England by Act of Parliament 1660.

Letters of Marque licences granted to private persons to fit out armed ships in time of war, abolished by the Declaration of Paris 1855.

Leukaemia disease of the blood, treatment developed by the American physician Edward Gamaliel Janeway (1841–1911).

Levant Company English trading venture founded 1581; chartered 1592.

Le Vau, Louis (1612–70) French baroque architect among whose designs is the Palace of Versailles (with André Le Nôtre).

Levellers English republican and democratic group; appeared 1647, crushed by Cromwell 1649, disappeared after Restoration 1660.

Lever, Charles (1806–72). Irish-born novelist (*Harry Lorrequer* 1837)

Leverhulme, William Lever, 1st Viscount (1851–1925) English manufacturer of soap from vegetable oils. Eventually the business expanded to become the international company Unilever.

Leverrier, Urbain (1811–77) French astronomer who predicted the position of the planet Neptune 1846.

Levi, Primo (1919–87) Italian author, survivor of Auschwitz (*The Periodic Table* 1975). He committed suicide.

Levi-Strauss, Claude (1908–) French anthropologist and founder of structuralism.

Lewes, Battle of between Henry III and barons 1265.

Lewes, George Henry *see* ELIOT, GEORGE.

Lewis machine gun invented 1911 by the American Isaac Newton Lewis (1858–1931).

Lewis, C[live] S[taples] (1898–1963) English novelist and critic. His works include studies of medieval literature (e.g. *The Allegory of Love*) works of Christian apologetics (e.g. *The Problem of Pain*), and science fiction novels (e.g. *Out of the Silent Planet*). He is best remembered for his enchanting Narnia stories for children (e.g. *The Lion, the Witch and the Wardrobe*).

Lewis, Jerry Lee (1935-) American rock singer and pianist noted for his flamboyant playing style and primitive rock 'n' roll lyrics.

Lewis, Meriwether (1774–1809) American explorer of the far West, died in a shooting incident in a cabin in Tennessee which may have been suicide.

Lewis, 'Monk' [Mathew Gregory Lewis] (1775–1818) English writer (*The Monk* 1796).

Lewis, [Harry] Sinclair (1885–1951) American novelist. His work is particularly noted for its satirical view of small-town American life. He was the first American to win the Nobel prize for literature, in 1930 (*Babbitt* 1922).

Lewis, [Percy] Wyndham (1884–1957) English painter, novelist and critic. An influential writer with unfashionable right-wing views, he was also a leading member of the Vorticist group of artists. His best-known fictional work is the novel *The Apes of* God (1930).

Lewisite poison gas invented 1916 by the American chemist Gilbert Newton Lewis (1875–1946).

Lex the Latin word for a law or a body of laws. In Roman history the Lex Publilia (471 BC) required that tribunes be chosen by the Comitia Tributa (popular assembly); the Lex Canuleia (445 BC) legalized marriage between patricians and plebieans; the Licinian Laws (366 BC) legislated for the first plebeian consul; the Lex Ogulnia (300 BC) provided for plebeian pontiffs and augurs; the Lex Hortensia (286 BC) made the Comitia Tributa the supreme legislative power.

Leyden jar electric condenser first made 1746 by the Dutch scientist Pieter van Musschenbroek (1692–1761) and his pupil Cunaeus in Leyden; and simultaneously by the German divine Ewald von Kleist at Cammin in Pomerania.

Leyden University Netherlands, founded 1575.

Liadov, Anatol Constantinovich Russian composer (*Danse de l'Amazone*) (1855–1914).

Liao dynasty China, 907–1125.

Liberace [Wladziu Valentino Liberace] (1919–87) American pianist and entertainer.

Liberal Party British origins in the Whigs (so named *c.*1679); present name used from *c.*1816, adopted officially during 1830s; merged with the Social Democratic Party to form the Social and Liberal Democratic Party in 1988.

Liberals Spanish supporters of 1812 constitution; French opponents of 'Ultras' in 1815 and 1820–30; Italian opponents of Austrian rule after 1815; European supporters of 1848 revolts.

Liberia West African country founded by freed slaves brought (1820) from the USA to Liberia on board the *Elizabeth* by American Colonization Society; became a Commonwealth 1838, declared independent republic 26 July 1847.

Liberius pope (352–366).

Liberty Bell Independence Hall, Philadelphia, hung 1753, replaced 1781, cracked 1835.

Library first public library built in Rome by C. Asinius Pollio 39 BC; Vatican Library begun by pope Nicolas V, 1447; Bodleian Library opened 1602; Advocates' Library, Edinburgh, founded 1682 (now National Library of Scotland); British Museum founded 1753; Library of Congress in US established 1800; London Library founded 1840; British Library established 1973.

Library Act first British Public, passed 1850; after several amendments, superseded by the Act of 1919.

Library Association, American established 1876.

Library Association of the United Kingdom established 1877.

Libreville capital of Gabon, founded 1843–48.

Libya North African country conquered by Italians 1911–30; became an independent state 24 December 1951; People's Republic 1969.

Lichfield Cathedral, England, constructed 13th–14th centuries.

Lichtenstein, Roy (1923–) American painter and sculptor. He became the leading Pop Art painter of the 1960s with his highly coloured reproductions of sections of advertisements and cartoon strips.

Licinius (*c.*250–324) Roman emperor (307–323). He was executed.

Lick Observatory, Mount Hamilton, USA, founded 1876–88 by the legacy of James Lick (1796–1876).

Liddell, Eric Henry (1902–45) Scottish athlete, nicknamed the 'Flying Scot', who refused to compromise his Sabbatarian principles by running on a Sunday during the 1924 Olympic Games (the subject of the award-winning film *Chariots of Fire* 1981). He became a missionary and died in a Japanese prisoner-of-war camp.

Liddell Hart, Sir Basil Henry (1895–1970) English soldier and military historian, noted for his persistent advocacy of mechanized warfare and the development of air power after the First World War.

Lie, Jonas (1833–1908) Norwegian novelist (*The Pilot and His Wife* 1874).

Lie, Trygve Halvdan (1896–1968) Norwegian-born secretary general of the United Nations (1946–53).

Lieber, Francis (1800–1872) German-born founder (1829–33) of the *Encyclopaedia Americana*.

Liebermann, Max (1848–1935) German painter (*Knöpflerinnen*).

Liebig, Justus Freiherr von (1803–73) German chemist.

Liebknecht, Karl (1871–1919) German socialist leader, founder member of the German Communist Party. In 1919 he led a revolt in Berlin and was killed *see also* LUXEMBOURG, ROSA.

Liebknecht, Wilhelm (1826–1900) German socialist leader, took part in the Baden insurrection of 1848–49, for which he had to live in exile in Switzerland and England.

Liechtenstein formed (as the Principality of Vaduz) 1342; enlarged to present size 1434; constituted as the Principality of Liechtenstein 1719; independent since 1866.

Lie detector principle stated and first apparatus constructed by Cesare Lombroso (1836–1909).

Liege Cathedral, Belgium, first cathedral destroyed 1794, second, constructed 10th century, rebuilt 13th century.

Life Magazine American periodical founded 1936; folded in 1970 but later revived.

Lifeboat first, designed by the English coach-builder Lionel Lukin 1785.

Lifeline fired by mortar from shore to ship invented 1807 by the English barrack-master George William Manby (1765–1854).

Lift first hydraulic passenger, installed in New York 1857 by the American inventor Elisha Graves Otis (1811–61); electric lifts developed in USA and Britain during 1880s.

Ligature use in amputations introduced by the French surgeon Ambroise Paré (*c.*1510–1590).

Ligeti, György Sándor (1923–) Hungarian composer. He fled to Vienna in 1956, where he soon became established as one of Europe's leading avant-garde composers.

Light composition of, discovered 1660 by Sir Isaac Newton (1642–1727).

Light refraction of, law postulated 1621 by the Dutch scientist Willebrord Snell (1591–1626).

Light velocity of, first calculated 1675 by Olaus Roemer (1644–1710); also measured by Jean Bernard Léon Foucault (1819–68).

Light Brigade, Charge of the *see* BALAKLAVA, BATTLE OF.

Lightfoot, Joseph Barber (1828–89) English theologian and textual critic.

Lighthouse, Pharos Alexandria, built *c.*280 BC; Eddystone built 1698, 1708, 1759, 1879–81; Bell Rock 1807–10; Bishop Rock 1858.

Lightning conductor principle discovered 1747 by the American statesman Benjamin Franklin (1706–90).

Light year distance (nearly 6 million million miles) travelled by light in one year.

Ligne, Charles Joseph, Prince de (1735–1814) Belgian field marshal and skilful diplomat.

Liguori, Alfonso Maria dei, Saint (1696–1787) Italian theologian.

Lilburne, John ('Freeborn John') (*c.*1614–1657) English pamphleteer and Leveller leader.

Liliencron, Detlev von (1844–1909) German writer (*Krieg und Frieden* 1891).

Lilienthal, Otto (1848–96) German engineer.

Liliuokalani (1838–1917) last queen of Hawaii (1891–93).

Lilliput British periodical founded 1937 by the Hungarian journalist Stefan Lorant (1901–).

Lillo, George (1693–1739) English dramatist (*The London Merchant* 1731).

Lilly, William (1602–81) English astrologer.

Lima, Peru, founded *c.*1541 by the Spanish conquistador Francisco Pizarro (1478–1541).

Limbourg *or* **Limburg, Jean, Paul and Herman de** (all *fl.* 1400–16) Dutch illuminators. Their masterpiece, the unfinished *Les Tres Riches Heures*, is one of the greatest illuminated manuscripts of all time.

Lime juice made compulsory in the Royal Navy as a preventative of scurvy 1795. Its use introduced for this purpose by Sir Gilbert Blane (1749–1834).

Limelight (Drummond Light) invented by Sir Goldsworthy Gurney (1793–1875); introduced by Thomas Drummond (1797–1840).

Limitation of Armaments Conference held at Washington 12 November 1921 to 6 February 1922.

Limousin, Léonard (*c.*1505–*c.*1577) French painter in enamel (*Marguérite de Valois*).

Linacre, Thomas (*c.*1460–1524) English founder 1518 of the (Royal) College of Physicians.

Lincoln Cathedral England, construction began 1086, consecrated 1092.

Lincoln, Abraham (1809–65) American statesman. From a poor background, he trained as a lawyer and became an Illinois congressman in 1846. He became the 16th president of the United States in 1861 and led the Union to victory in 1865. Firmly opposed to slavery, he finally declared emancipation 1863. He was assassinated while attending the theatre.

Lincolnshire Insurrection largely against religious and fiscal oppression arose 1536, suppressed 1536–37.

Lind, Jenny (The 'Swedish Nightingale') (1820–87) operatic singer.

Lindbergh, Charles Augustus (1902–74) American aviator. He became the first man to fly the Atlantic solo and nonstop with his 1927 flight in the monoplane *Spirit of St Louis*. The kidnap and murder of his infant son in 1932 made world headlines.

Lindbergh, Charles (1902–74) American aviator crossed the Atlantic 20–21 May 1927.

Lindisfarne (Holy Island) chosen as the site of his church and monastery by St Aidan 635.

Lindley, John English botanist (1799–1865).

Lindsay, Lady Anne (1750–1825) Scottish poet (*Auld Robin Gray* 1771).

Lindsay, Vachel (1879–1931) American poet (*The Congo* 1914).

Line coordinates geometry introduced 1868–69 by the German mathematician and physician Julius Plücker (1801–68).

Ling, Pehr Henrik Swedish pioneer in gymnastics (1776–1839).

Lingard, John English historian (1771–1851).

Linklater, Eric (1899–1974) British writer (*Poet's Pub* 1929).

Linnaeus, Carl Swedish botanist (1707–78).

Linnean Society London, founded 1788 by the botanist Sir James Edward Smith (1759–1828).

Linoleum invented by the Englishman Frederick Walton 1860.

Linotype invented 1884 by the German-born Ottmar Mergenthaler (1854–99). First made in England 1892.

Linton, Sir Richard (1879–1959) New Zealand-born founder of the Big Brother Movement.

Linus, Saint pope 67–76.

Liotard, Jean Etienne (1702–89) French painter (*Général Hérault*).

Lippershey, Hans (d.1619) Dutch optician and inventor 1608 of the telescope.

Lippi, Fra Filippo [Lippo] (*c.*1406–69) Florentine painter. He took up painting while a monk and later forsook his vows to marry the mother of his son, Lucrezia Buti, who was a nun. His son Filippino Lippi (1457–1504), also became a painter. His lyrical and fluid style invest his paintings with a wistful melancholy. An innovative painter, he was one of the first artists to explore and develop the *Madonna and Child* theme.

Lippmann, Walter American political commentator and writer (1889–1974).

Lipton, Sir Thomas Scottish-born merchant and sportsman (1850–1931).

Liquefaction of gas principle discovered 1878 by the French chemist Louis Paul Cailletet (1832–1913).

Lisbon earthquake (greatest of many suffered by the city), 1 November 1755.

List, Friedrich (1789–1846) German economist and follower of Adam Smith. He committed suicide.

Listener, The first published 16 January 1929, ceased publication 1991.

Lister, Joseph Lister, 1st Baron (1827–1912) English surgeon whose great achievement was the introduction of antiseptic surgery.

Liszt, Franz *or* **Ferencz** (1811–86) Hungarian pianist and composer. Recognized as one of the greatest pianists of his day, he made several important contributions to musical form and was influential in his experimentation.(*Piano concertos* 1857 and 1863)

Lithium an alkali metal discovered 1817 by the Swedish chemist Johann August Arfvedson (1792–1841).

Lithography invented 1798 by the German inventor Alois Senefelder (1771–1834).

Lithuania ruled by Russia 1795–1918; proclaimed an independent republic 16 February 1918; occupied by the Russians and admitted to the Soviet Union 1940; became independent republic 10 September 1991.

Lithuanian language earliest known text dated 1547.

Litolff, Henry Charles English pioneer 1851 in the publication of cheap editions of music (1818–91).

Little Entente Permanent Council founded on Czech-Yugoslav Treaty of 14 August 1920; created 16 February 1933; collapsed 1938.

Little Rock Arkansas, USA, scene of racial conflict 1957.

Littleton, Sir Thomas (1422–81) English jurist.

Littlewood, Joan (1914–91) English theatre director. Her theatre company, Theatre Workshop, formed in 1945, became one of the major left-wing companies.

Littré, Maximilien Paul Emile (1801–81) French compiler of a French dictionary.

Litvinov, Maksim Maksimovich (1876–1951) Russian diplomat.

Liutprand (*c.*921–972) Lombard divine and chronicler.

Liverpool Cathedral first stone laid 19 July 1904, consecrated 19 July 1924.

Liverpool University civic inauguration 7 November 1903.

Liverpool, Robert Banks Jenkinson, Earl (1770–1828) British statesman (prime minister 1812–27).

Livery companies London, *see* under individual names—*Skinners*, *Vintners*, *etc.*

Livia, Drusilla (*c.*55 BC– AD 29) Roman empress, third wife of the Emperor Augustus and who is said to have had a great deal of influence over her husband's rule.

Livingston, Edward American statesman (1764–1836).

Livingston, Robert Scottish-born administrator in New York (1654–1728).

Livingstone, David (1813–73) Scottish missionary and explorer. His discoveries during his African expeditions include Lake Ngami (1849) and the Victoria Falls (1855). He was also a vigorous campaigner against the slave trade. His last expedition was a search for the source of the Nile, in the course of which he himself was 'discovered' by the Welsh-American adventurer Henry Morton Stanley (1841–1904).

Livius Andronicus (fl. 3rd century BC) Roman poet, probably Greek by birth, whose writing reflected the Greek tradition.

Livonia ruled by Russia 1710–1918 absorbed into Latvia 1918.

Livy [Titus Livius] (59 BC– AD 17) Roman historian who wrote a history of Rome from its foundation to the death of Augustus's stepson Nero Claudius Drusus (39–9 BC).

Llandaff Cathedral original building opened 1120; second, 18th century; third, built 1844–69.

Llangollen, Ladies of Lady Eleanor Butler (1778–1829) and Sarah Ponsonby (1778–1831).

Llewelyn *see* LLYWELYN.

Lloyd, Clive Hubert (1944–) Guyanian-born West Indian cricketer. A very fine batsman and fielder, he captained the West Indies team (1974–78, 1979–85).

Lloyd, Harold [Clayton] (1893–1971) American film comedian. He made hundreds of short silent films and is noted for his dangerous stunts.

'Lloyd, Marie' [Matilda Alice Victoria Wood] (1870–1922) English music-hall comedian, she became one of the most popular music-hall performers of all time.

Lloyd George, David, 1st Earl Lloyd George of Dwyfor (1863–1945) Welsh Liberal statesman. As chancellor of the exchequer (1908–15), he introduced far-reaching reforms in British society, notably the introduction of old-age pensions (1908) and the National Insurance Act (1911). Formerly a pacifist, he became minister of munitions (1915–16) and prime minister (1916–22) of coalition governments.

Lloyd's List and Shipping Gazette London, founded 1734.

Lloyd's of London first known allusion as Edward Lloyd's Coffee House, Tower St, London, February 1688.

Lloyd's Register of shipping first prepared *c.*1764.

Lloyd Webber, Sir Andrew (1948–) English composer. With the librettist Tim Rice (1944–), he composed several highly successful musicals, notably *Joseph and the Amazing Technicolour Dreamcoat*, *Jesus Christ Superstar* and *Evita*. Other successes were *Cats*, adapted from T. S. Eliot's *Old Possum's Book of Practical Cats*, *Starlight Express* and *Phantom of the Opera*.

Llywelyn ap Gruffydd [Llewelyn the Last] (d.1282) king of Gwynedd (*c.*1260–1282).

Llywelyn ap Iorwerth [Llewelyn the Great] (d.1240) king of Gwynedd (1202–40) *see* Appendix.

Loanda *or* **Luanda** capital of Angola, oldest extant European settlement in Africa, founded 1576.

Lobachevsky, Nikolai Ivanovich (1793–1856) Russian mathematician.

Lobel, Matthias de French botanist and physician, lived early in the 17th century.

Locarno Pact guaranteeing peace and frontiers in Europe, signed 16 October 1925.

Loch Lomond Scotland, first swum (22 miles) by Commander Gerald Forsberg (1912–) in 1959).

Lochner, Stephen (*c.*1401–1451) German painter (*The Last Judgment*).

Locke, John (1632–1704) English philosopher. His influential theory of the political nature of man saw the social contract as resting on a 'natural law', which, if ignored by rulers, allowed them to be overthrown (*Essay Concerning Human Understanding* 1690).

Locke, Joseph (1805–60) English civil engineer, worked for George Stephenson for ten years and developed a keen interest in railway civil engineering.

Lockerbie Disaster terrorist bomb destroyed Pan Am flight 103 which crashed onto the Scottish village killing 244 passengers, 15 crew and 11 on the ground, 21 December 1988.

Lockhart, John Gibson (1794–1854) Scottish writer (*Ancient Spanish Ballads* 1823).

Lockwood, James Booth American Polar explorer (1852–84).

Lockwood, Margaret British actress (*The Lady Vanishes* 1938) (1916–90).

Lockyer, Sir Joseph Norman (1836–1920) English astronomer.

Locomotives early models constructed 1803 by the English engineer Richard Trevithick and 1814 by the English civil engineer George Stephenson.

Lodge, David (1935–) English novelist and critic. His best-known novels are entertaining satires on academic life, e.g. *Small World*, and his novel *Nice Work* is a hybrid of the campus novel with the 19th-century 'condition of England' tradition.

Lodge, Sir Oliver (1851–1940) British physicist.

Lodge, Thomas (*c.*1558–1625) English writer (*Rosalynde* 1590).

Loeb, James (1867–1933) American banker and philanthropist.

Loeb Classical Library authoritative texts and translations, series founded by James Loeb 1912.

Loeffler, Charles Martin (1861–1935) American composer (*A Pagan Poem* 1909).

Loewe, Carl (1796–1869) German composer (*Erlkönig*).

Löffler, Friedrich (1852–1915) German bacteriologist.

Lofting, Hugh (1896–1947) English-born writer (*Dr Dolittle* 1920).

Logan, Benjamin (*c.*1743–1802) American pioneer.

Logarithms (1550–1617) invented 1614 by the Scottish inventor John Napier.

Logic (384–322 BC) study founded by the Greek philosopher Aristotle.

Logical positivism philosophical movement originating in Vienna in 1920s.

Logue, Cardinal Michael (1840–1924) archbishop of Armagh.

Lollards English church reformers (followers of John Wyclif) after 1382, active during early 15th century.

Lombard, Peter(*c.*1100–*c.*1160) Italian theologian (*Sententiae* 1145–50).

Lombard League of cities in Lombardy founded 1167.

Lombardo, Pietro (*c.*1435–1515) Italian sculptor.

Lombards invaded Italy 568; conquered by Franks 774.

Lombroso, Cesare (1836–1909) Italian pioneer criminologist.

Lomonosov, Mikhail Vasilievich (1711–65) Russian scientist and writer.

London, Jack [John Griffith] (1876–1916) American novelist (*The Call of the Wild* 1903).

London Bridge, New (1794–1874) constructed 1824–31 by Sir John Rennie.

London Bridge, Old built by Peter, chaplain of St Mary's Colechurch, 1176–1209.

London Company formed to colonize part of Virginia, chartered 1606.

London County Hall foundation stone laid 9 March 1912.

Londonderry, Siege of lasted from 20 April to 1 August 1689. The Protestant garrison held out until relieved but lost 3000 out of a total of 7000 men.

London Gazette founded 1665.

London Irish Volunteer Rifles now the only Irish territorial infantry regiment in Britain, formed 25 November 1859.

London Library London subscription library founded 1840, opened 1841.

London Naval Conference concerning war at sea held 1908–1909.

London Naval Treaty ratified 1930.

London Oratory established 1849 by the English theologian and poet Frederick William Faber (1814–63).

London Salvage Corps founded 1866.

London Symphony Orchestra first concert given 9 June 1904.

London University founded 1828, chartered 1836.

London, Declaration of concerning maritime law, signed 1909.

London Metropolitan Police Force set up 1829; London divided into postal districts 1858; Port of London Authority established 1909.

London, Tower of built mainly at the end of the 11th century, additions made in the late 17th century.

London-Paris daily air service inaugurated 25 August 1919.

London-Paris phone service opened 1891.

Londonderry, Edith Helen, Marchioness of (1879–1959) founder and director of the Women's Legion, first to be created (1917) a DBE (military).

Long Island first settled *c.*1640; annexed to New York 1664.

Long Parliament called 1640, purged 1648, expelled 1653, recalled 1659, dissolved 1660.

Long, Huey (1893–1935) US Senator and governor of Louisiana. The unfair tactics with which he won the election and his dictatorial style of ruling led to his assassination.

Long, John Luther (1861–1927) American writer (*Madame Butterfly* 1898).

Longchamp, William of (d.1197) bishop of Ely and statesman.

Longfellow, Henry Wadsworth (1807–82) American poet. His narrative poems based on American legends and folk tales were among the most popular of the 19th century, e.g. *The Song of Hiawatha* (1855) the hypnotic unrhymed rhythms of which were much parodied by later writers e.g. Carroll.

Longhi, Pietro (1702–85) Italian painter (*Exhibition of a Rhinoceros*).

Longinus (*c.*213–273) Greek philosopher who was beheaded.

Longman, Thomas (1699–1755) English publisher.

Longomontanus, Christian Sorensen (1562–1647) Dutch astronomer.

Longueuil, Charles le Moyne, Sieur de (1626–85) French pioneer in Canada.

Longus (*c.*4th or 5th century) Greek writer (*Daphnis and Chloë*).

Longworth, Nicholas (1782–1863) American pioneer in viticulture.

Lönnrot, Elias (1802–84) Finnish collector of folk material.

Löns, Hermann (1866–1914) German writer. He was killed in battle (*Mein grunes Buch*).

Lonsdale Boxing Belt founded 1909 by the English sportsman Lord Lonsdale (1857–1944).

Lonsdale, Dame Kathleen (1903–71) Irish physicist noted for innovative work in X-ray crystallography. She was the first woman to be elected a fellow of the Royal Society (1945).

Loomis, Mahlon (1826–86) American radio pioneer.

Loop first aeronautic, performed 27 August 1913 by the Russian pilot Peter Nesterov.

Lope de Vega (1562–1635) Spanish playwright (*Pedro en Madrid*).

Lopez, Carlos Antonio (1790–1862) president of Paraguay (1844–62).

Lopez, Francisco Solano (1827–70) president of Paraguay (1862–70). He was killed in battle.

Lorca, Federigo García (1899–1936) Spanish poet and dramatist. His dramatic masterpiece is his trilogy of tragedies on the plight of oppressed Spanish women, *Blood Wedding*, *Yarma* and *The House of Bernarda Alba*. He was killed by Fascist forces near the beginning of the Spanish Civil War.

Lord Howe Island an island in the South Pacific discovered by Lt H. L. Ball 1778.

Lord Mayor of London office traditionally held to have been founded 1189.

Lord Mayor's Show London, first held 1215, first organized, Sir Christopher Drape's pageant 1566.

Lords Appellants group of English nobles held power 1388–97.

Lords Ordainers group of English nobles held power 1310–16.

Lords, House of absolute power of veto abolished by Act of Parliament 1911.

Loren, Sophia [Sofia Scicolone] (1934–) Italian film actress (*The Millionairess* 1961).

Lorentz, Hendrik Antoon (1853–1928) Dutch physicist.

Lorenz, Adolf (1854–1946) Austrian surgeon.

Lorenz, Konrad [Zacharias] (1903–89) Austrian ethologist and zoologist. He shared the 1973 Nobel prize for physiology or medicine (with Niko Tinbergen and Karl von Frisch) for his work on animal behaviour.

Lorenzetti, Ambrogio (before 1319–after 1347) Italian painter.

Lorenzetti, Pietro Italian painter born before 1320, died after 1345.

Lorenzo di Pietro (*c.*1412–1480) Italian artist.

Loreto Italy, reputed site of the house of the Virgin Mary, miraculously deposited in 1295.

Lorimer, George Horace (1868–1937) American writer (*Letters from a Self-made Merchant* 1902).

Loring, William Wing (1818–86) American military commander and adviser.

Lorne, John Douglas Sutherland Campbell, Marquess of (1845–1914) governor general of Canada (1878–83).

Lorraine, Claude (*c.*1600–1682) French painter (*Liber veritatis*).

Lorraine ruled by France 1766–1870, by Germany 1871–1918, by France 1918–40, by Germany 1940–44, by France since 1944.

Lorre, Peter [Laszlo Lowenstein] (1904–64) Hungarian-born stage and film actor. His first major film part, as the pathetic child-murderer, in Lang's *M* (1931) established him as a star. Other films include *Casablanca* and *The Maltese Falcon* (1941).

Lorris, Guillaume de French poet (part of the *Roman de la Rose*) lived in the first half of the 13th century.

Lortzing, Albert (1801–51) German composer (*Der Wildschütz* 1842).

Los Angeles American city in California, founded 1781.

Losey, Joseph (1909–84) American film director. Blacklisted during the McCarthy era, he came to work in England and had a great influence on the British film industry with films such as *The Servant*, *Accident* and *The Go-Between.*

Lothair I (795–855) Holy Roman emperor (817–855).

Lothair II (*c.*1070–1137) Holy Roman emperor (1075–1137).

Lothair III (941–986) king of France (954–986).

Lotharingia created by Treaty of Verdun 843.

'Loti, Pierre' [Julian Viaud] (1850–1923) French writer (*Pécheur d' Islande* 1886).

Lotto, Lorenzo (*c.*1480–1556) Italian painter (*St Jerome*).

Lotze, Rudolf Hermann (1817–81) German philosopher.

Loudon, John Claudius (1783–1843) Scottish horticulturist.

Louis, Joe [Joseph Louis Barrow] (1914–81) American boxer, nicknamed the 'Brown Bomber'. He was world heavyweight champion for a record 12 years.

Louis I (Louis the Pious) (778–840) emperor and king of France.

Louis II (846–879) king of France (877–879).

Louis III (*c.*863–882) king of France (879–882).

Louis IV (921–954) king of France (936–954).

Louis V (967–987) king of France (986–987).

Louis VI (1081–1137) king of France (1108–37).

Louis VII (*c.*1121–1180) king of France (1137–80).

Louis VIII (Louis the Lion) (1187–1226) king of France (1223–26). Son of Philip II, he was offered the English crown by a group of barons whose aim was to depose John, but he was forced to return to France when, with John's death, the plan lacked the necessary support. The cause of his death is unclear.

Louis IX (Saint Louis) (1214–70) king of France (1226–70) He led the sixth Crusade (1248–54) against Egypt, where he was captured by the Saracens. He returned to France after two years imprisonment and his reign brought great prosperity to the nation. On another crusade he and his army were exposed to a plague that caused his death. He was canonized in 1297.

Louis X (Louis the Quarrelsome) (1289–1316) king of France (1314–16) and son of Philip IV.

Louis XI (1423–83) king of France (1461–83) and son of Charles VII.

Louis XII (1462–1515) king of France (1499–1515). Son of Charles, Duc d'Orléans, he married his brother-in-law Charles's widow, Ann, in order to retain the kingdom of Brittany. With Ann's death in 1514 he married Mary Tudor, but he died a short time afterwards.

Louis XIII (1601–43) king of France (1610–43) and son of Henry IV.

Louis XIV ('le Roi Soleil') (1638–1715) king of France (1643–1715). Son of Louis XIII, he succeeded to the throne at the age of five, and his mother and her lover, Cardinal Mazarin, controlled government. Once in power himself he was a pious and conservative ruler. The high tax levels he enforced allowed him to build the palace of Versailles. He began a long war with Holland in 1672 but never seized the country. He attacked Spain in the War of the Spanish Succession (1702–13) and managed to ruin France's finances entirely.

Louis XV (1710–74) king of France (1715–74) and great-grandson of Louis XIV.

Louis XVI (1754–93). king of France (1774–92) and grandson of Louis XV. He was a well-meaning ruler who took over the reign when the treasury was in a much depleted state and taxes were high. The extravagant spending of his wife, Marie Antoinette, caused his political image severe damage in a period when revolutionary changes were taking place. In 1792 France was at war with Prussia and Austria, and Louis's involvement was suspected. In August of that year the palace was stormed by a mob, and the royal family was imprisoned. Louis was sentenced to death on 20 January 1793 and guillotined the following day.

Louis XVII (1785–95) titular king of France (1793–95). The son of Louis XVI, he is said to have died in prison at the age of eleven.

Louis XVIII (1755–1824) king of France (1814–24).

Younger brother of Louis XVI, he fled during the revolution in 1791. He took up the kingship when Napoleon fell in 1814. A weak monarch, he was deposed by his brother, Charles X.

Louis Ferdinand (1772–1806) prince of Prussia, killed in battle.

Louis Napoleon [Napoleon III] (1808–73) emperor of the French (1852–70).

Louis Philippe (1773–1850) king of France (1830–48). In its early stages he supported the revolution of 1830 but later had to live in exile in England for a time. He returned to France and replaced the deposed Charles X, and was known as the 'citizen king' because of his informal way of behaving. With the revolution of 1848 and the king becoming more unpopular, with several attempts on his life, he took refuge in England and Louis Napoleon [III] came to power.

Louisiana state of the USA, first settled 1699; admitted to the Union 1812.

Louisiana Purchase from France, of territory west of the Mississippi, completed by the USA 1803.

Lourdes a place of pilgrimage in the foothills of the central Pyrenees, France, where Bernadette Soubirous first saw visions of the Virgin Mary, 1858. The Festival of Our Lady is celebrated 11 February at Lourdes.

Loutherbourg, Philip James (1740–1812) French-born artist.

Louvre, Paris, designed 1546–78 by the French architect, Pierre Lescot (*c.*1510–1578).

Louÿs, Pierre (1870–1925) French writer (*Aphrodite* 1896).

Lovejoy, Owen (1811–64) American abolitionist.

Lovelace, Richard (1618–58) English poet, one of the Cavalier poets, a loose grouping associated with the court or cause of Charles i during his clashes with parliament and the ensuing Civil War. His poem, 'To Althea', is perhaps the best loved of the Cavalier poems.

Loveless, George (1792–1874) British trade union pioneer ('Tolpuddle martyr' 1834).

Lover, Samuel (1797–1868) Irish novelist (*Rory O'More* 1836).

Low, Sir David (1891–1963) New Zealand-born cartoonist.

Low, Juliette Gordon (1860–1927) founder of the Girl Scouts in America.

Low, Sampson (1797–1886) English publisher.

Lowe, Sir Hudson (1769–1844) Irish-born governor of St Helena (1815–21).

Lowei, Otto *see* DALE, SIR HENRY HALLETT.

Lowell, Amy (1874–1925) American poet.

Lowell, James Russell (1819–91) American poet, essayist and diplomat. His best-known verse was written in 'Yankee' dialect and inspired by his fervent abolitionism. His works include *Bigelow Papers* (1848 and 1867).

Lowell, Robert [Traill Spence] (1917–77) American poet. His verse is intensely personal and marked by private symbolism.

Lowell Observatory Arizona, founded 1894 by the American astronomer Percival Lowell (1855–1916).

Lowestoft, Battle of a naval battle between the English and the Dutch, 3 June 1665, which was an English victory.

Lowie, Robert Heinrich (1883–1957) Austrian-born American anthropologist.

Lowndes, William Thomas (*c.*1798–1843) English bibliographer.

Lowry, L[aurence] S[tephen] (1887–1976) English painter. His paintings, which depict thin, dark 'matchstick' figures against a background of Northern Industrial life, became very popular in the mid-1960s.

Lowry, [Clarence] Malcolm (1909–57) English novelist and poet. His novels, e.g. *Under the Volcano* (1947), often feature thinly veiled accounts of incidents from his own adventurous life.

Low Sunday first Sunday after Easter.

Loyola, Saint Ignatius *see* IGNATIUS LOYOLA, ST.

Loyola University, Chicago, founded as St Ignatius College 1870; established with present status and title 1907.

Lubbock, Sir John, Baron Avebury (1834–1913) English writer and naturalist.

Lubin, David (1849–1919) American merchant and founder of the International Institute of Agriculture.

Lubitsch, Ernst (1892–1947) German film director.

Lubumbashi the principal mining town of Zaire, founded 1910 as Elisabethville; name changed 1966.

Lucan, Marcus Annaeus (39–65), Roman poet (*Pharsalia*), who committed suicide.

Lucaris, Cyril (1572–1637) Greek theologian.

Lucas, Edward Verrall (1868–1938) English writer (*Over Bemerton's* 1908).

Lucas, Frank Laurence (1894–1967) English writer (*Poems* 1935).

Lucas, George (1944–) American film director and producer (*Star Wars* 1977).

Lucas van Leyden (*c.*1494–1533) Dutch painter (*The Last Judgment*).

Luce, Henry Robinson (1898–1967) American publisher.

Lucian (*c.*120–180) Greek writer (*Dialogues*).

Lucifer matches (*c.*1781–1859) invented 1827 by the English chemist John Walker.

Lucius I, Saint pope 253–254.

Lucius II [Gherardo Caccianemici dal Orso] pope 1144–45.

Lucius III [Ubaldo Allucingoli] pope 1181–85.

Lucknow residency defended by the Duke of Cornwall's Light Infantry 1857.

Lucrece *or* **Lucretia** (d.510 BC) victim of Tarquin [Tarquinius Superbus], who committed suicide.

Lucretius Roman poet (*c*.96–*c*.55 BC) (*De Rerum Natura*).

Lucullus, Lucius Licinius (*c*.110–57 BC) Roman general and statesman. With Pompey he led the Roman army in the Third Mithradatic War 74 BC. He won a victory over Tigranes of Armenia at Tigranocerta 69 BC and allowed Antiochus XIII to take possession of Syria, and was victorious over Pontus at Cabria 72 BC.

Lucy, Saint *c*.305 martyred.

Lucy, Sir Thomas (1532–1600) prototype of Shakespeare's 'Justice Shallow'.

Luddites English machine wreckers active 1810–18.

Ludendorff, Erich von (1865–1937) German general.

Ludlow, Edmund (*c*.1617–1692) English Puritan soldier and regicide.

Ludwig, Emil (1881–1948) German writer (*Napoleon* 1924).

Ludwig I (1786–1868) king of Bavaria (1825–48).

Ludwig II (1845–86) king of Bavaria (1864–86).

Ludwig III (1845–1921) king of Bavaria (1913–18).

Lugard, Frederick John Dealtry Lugard, Baron (1858–1945) pioneer administrator in East Africa.

Luini, Bernardino (*c*.1481–1532) Italian painter (*Madonna*).

Lulach (1032–58) king of Scots (1057–58) *see* Appendix.

Lull, Ramón (*c*.1236–1315) Catalan mystic.

Lully, Jean-Baptiste [Giambattista Lulli] (1632–87) French composer of Italian origin. He worked in the French court, where he composed many operas and comedy ballets. He died from an abscess after striking his foot with his conductor's baton. His works include *Alceste* (1674).

Lumet, Sidney (1924–) American film and TV director (*Serpico* 1974).

Lumière, Auguste Marie Louis Nicolas (1862–1954) and **Louis Jean Lumière** (1864–1948) French chemists and cinematographers. They invented the first operational cine camera and projector and a colour photography process.

Lundy, Benjamin (1789–1839) American abolitionist.

Luneville, Peace of between France and Austria, signed 1801.

Lunik I Russian lunar rocket launched 11 October 1958.

Lunik II Russian lunar rocket hit the moon 10.00 hrs BST, 13 September 1959.

Lusaka former capital of Northern Rhodesia, now Zambia, 1964.

Lusitania (modern Portugal) the Latin name for a region of the Iberian peninsula, conquered by Rome 140 BC; Roman province 27 BC–late 4th century AD.

Lusitania Atlantic passenger liner launched 7 June 1906; torpedoed by the Germans 7 May 1915.

Lutecium a rare earth metal discovered independently 1907 by the Austrian chemist Baron von Welsbach (1858–1929) and 1906 by Georges Urbain.

Luther, Martin (1483–1546) German religious reformer. An Augustinian monk who suffered a crisis of faith that led to his proclaiming a break with Rome following the nailing of his '95 theses' on the church door of Wittenberg. The Lutheran Reformation spread rapidly throughout Germany. Calvin, Zwingli and others subsequently preached their variants of the new religion.

Lutheran Church organized 1522.

Luthuli *or* **Lutuli, Chief Albert John** (1898–1967) South African nationalist. He became president of the African National Congress (1952–60) and was awarded the 1961 Nobel Peace Prize for his advocacy of nonviolent resistance to apartheid.

Lutoslawski, Witold (1913–) Polish composer and teacher. He has written extensively, including chamber, piano and vocal music, but is best known for his orchestral works, e.g. *Concerto for Orchestra*.

Luttrell Psalter illuminated manuscript in the British Museum, dated *c*.1340.

Lutyens, Sir Edwin Landseer English architect (1869–1944).

Lützen, Battle of between the Swedes and the Imperialists in the Thirty Years' War, 16 November 1632.

Lützow, Adolf, Freiherr von German military leader (1782–1834).

Luxembourg grand duchy created by the Congress of Vienna 1814–15; neutrality guaranteed 1817; constitution granted 1868 and revised 1919 and 1948.

Luxembourg, Palace of Paris, built 1615–20.

Luxemburg, Rosa (1871–1919) Polish-born German revolutionary and socialist theorist. With Karl Liebknecht (1871–1919) she founded the revolutionary Spartacus League in Berlin on the outbreak of World War I and later the German Communist Party. She and Liebknecht were killed after the failed revolt of 1919.

Luxorius (*fl.* early 6th century) Roman epigrammatist.

Luynes, Charles d'Albert, Duc de (1578–1621) constable of France.

Lvov, Alexis von (1798–1870) composer of the Russian national anthem ('God save the Czar' 1833).

'Lyall, Edna' [Ada Ellen Bayly] (1857–1903) English novelist (*Donovan* 1882).

Lyautey, Louis Hubert Gonsalve (1854–1934) French commissary-general in Morocco (1912–25).

Lycurgus (*fl* 7th or 8th century BC) Spartan reformer who is said to have been the instigator of the harsh Spartan laws of obedience and self-discipline.

Lydekker, Richard (1849–1915) English naturalist.

Lydgate, John (*c.*1370–*c.*1451) English poet (*Troy Book* 1412–20).

Lydia an ancient kingdom in western Asia Minor with its capital at Sardis. It was a powerful kingdom, subduing various Greek cities under Croesus 560 BC, until it was conquered by the Persians under Cyrus. Alexander the Great captured Sardis and conquered Lydia 334 BC.

Lyell, Sir Charles (1797–1875) Scottish geologist.

Lyly, John (*c.*1554–1606) English writer (*Euphues* 1578).

Lyman, Theodore (1833–97) American naturalist.

Lynching term believed to derive from the American military leader Charles Lynch (1736–96).

Lyndhurst, John Singleton Copley, Baron statesman (1772–1863).

Lyndsay, Sir David Scottish poet (*The Three Estaits* 1540) (1490–1555).

Lyon, Mary (1797–1849) American advocate of advanced education for women.

Lyon, Nathaniel (1818–61) American military commander. He was killed in battle.

Lyons, Joseph Aloysius (1879–1939) Australian statesman (prime minister 1932–39).

Lyons French city, founded 43 BC by Lucius Plancus.

Lyons, Ecumenical Councils of first: 1245; second: 1274.

Lysander (d.395 BC) Spartan commander whose victory over Athens at Aegospotami 405 BC secured Spartan domination throughout Greece.

Lysenko, Trofim Denisovich (1898–1976) Russian scientist.

Lysimachus (*c.*355–281 BC) Greek general who was killed in battle at Koroupedion by Seleucus.

Lysippus (4th century BC) Greek sculptor.

Lysistratus (4th century BC) Greek sculptor.

Lyte, Henry Francis (1793–1847) British hymnwriter (*Abide with me* 1833).

Lytle, William Haines (1826–63) American poet. He was killed in battle.

Lyttleton, George, 1st Baron (1709–73) English politician and writer.

Lytton, Bulwer, Lord Lytton (1803–73) English novelist (*The Last Days of Pompeii* 1834).

Lytton, Edward Robert Bulwer, Earl Lytton (1831–91) viceroy of India (1876–80) and writer.

M

M1 London-Birmingham motorway, main section officially opened 2 November 1959.

'Maartens, Maarten' [Joost Marius William van der Poerten-Schwartz] (1858–1915) Dutch-born novelist (*God's Fool* 1893).

Maastricht, Treaty of provides timetable for European political, economic and monetary union, ratified July 1993.

Mabillon, Jean (1632–1707) French monk and writer.

Mabinogion Welsh epic collection compiled 14th-15th centuries.

Mabuse, Jan de (*c.*1470–*c.*1533) Flemish painter (*Madonna and Child*).

Macadamized roads invented 1816 by the Scottish surveyor John Loudon Macadam (1756–1836).

McAdoo, William Gibbs (1863–1941) American politician.

Macao, China, first settled by the Portuguese 1557; Portuguese suzerainty recognized by China by treaty of 1887; attained partial autonomy 1976; sovereignty to pass to China 1999.

MacArthur, Douglas (1880–1964) American general. He was commander of the US Far East forces in 1941. When the Japanese forced him to withdraw from the Philippines in 1942, he pledged 'I shall return'. He was appointed supreme Allied commander in the southwest Pacific in 1942 and gradually rolled back the Japanese forces, accepting their surrender in 1945. He also commanded the UN forces at the beginning of the Korean War (1950–51), being dismissed his command by Truman.

McArthur, John (1767–1834) English pioneer in New South Wales.

Macaulay, Dame Rose (1887–1958) English novelist (*Potterism* 1920).

Macaulay, Thomas Babington, Lord (1800–1859) historian (*History of England* 1849–61).

Macbeth (1005–57) king of the Scots (1040–57) *see* Appendix.

Maccabees a family of Jewish leaders who freed Judaea from Syrian oppression *c.*170 BC and were rulers until 63 BC. They included Mattathias, Judas Maccabaeus and Simon Maccabaeus.

McCarthy, Joseph R[aymond] (1909–57) American lawyer and politician He became a Republican senator in 1946 and embarked upon a crusade against supposed communist sympathizers in public life (1950–54). His wide and increasingly bizarre accusations against innocent people came to an end shortly after he was accused, during a televised hearing, of having no shame.

McCarthy, Justin (1830–1912) Irish politician and historian.

McCartney, Paul (1942–) English rock guitarist, singer and songwriter. He was a member of the Beatles (1961–70) with John Lennon, George Harrison and Ringo Starr. With Lennon, he formed one of the most successful songwriting partnerships of the century. After the band's break-up, he formed the group Wings.

McClellan, George Brinton (1826–85) American general.

McClintock, Admiral Sir Francis Leopold (1819–1907) Irish-born explorer.

McClure, Sir Robert John le Mesurier (1807–73) British navigator.

McCook, Alexander McDowell (1831–1903) American general.

McCormack, Count John (1884–1945) Irish tenor.

McCormick, Cyrus Hall (1809–84) American inventor 1831 of the reaper.

McCoy, Sir Frederick (1823–99) Irish-born palaeontologist.

McCullers, Carson [Smith] (1917–67) American novelist and short-story writer. Her works, many of them filmed, usually centre on loners and misfits and include *The Heart is a Lonely Hunter* and *The Ballad of the Sad Café*.

MacCunn, Hamish (1868–1916) Scottish composer (*Cior Mhor* 1887).

MacDiarmid, Hugh [Christopher Murray Grieve] (1892–1978) Scottish poet and critic. Noted for his Communist and Nationalist sympathies, he influenced many Scottish writers, particularly with his masterpiece, *A Drunk Man Looks at the Thistle* (1926).

MacDonald, George (1824–1905) Scottish writer (*At the Back of the North Wind* 1871).

Macdonald, Flora (1722–90) Scottish rescuer 1746 of the Young Pretender.

MacDonald, [James] Ramsay (1866–1937) Scottish statesman. He became the first British Labour prime minister (1924, 1929–31) and was prime minister of the (mostly Conservative) coalition government of 1931–35.

Macdonough, Thomas (1786–1825) American naval officer.

McDougall, William (1871–1938) English-born psychologist (*Introduction to Social Psychology* 1908).

MacDowell, Edward Alexander (1861–1908) American composer (*Sea Pieces* 1898).

Macedonia an ancient kingdom of southeastern Europe; Persian conquest 492 BC; Philip II king of Macedonia 359–336 BC; his victory over Athens and Thebes at Chaeronea made Macedonia supreme in Greece 338–306 BC; Alexander the Great king of Macedon 336–323 BC after assassination of Philip; Spartans defeated by Macedonian regent Antipater at Megalopolis 331 BC; Antipater wins Lamian War 322 BC; First Macedonian War 214–205 BC; Second Macedonian War 200–197 BC; Third Macedonian War begins 171–168 BC; Fourth Macedonian War 149–147 BC; Roman victory at Corinth and Macedonia made a Roman province 147 BC.

Macedonian War, First 214–205 BC between Macedonia and Romans. Romans victorious over Philip V.

Macedonian War, Second 200–197 BC: battle of Avus 198 BC Roman victory; battle of Cynoscephaloe Roman victory ended Second Macedonian War 197 BC.

Macedonian War, Third 171–168 BC: battle of Larissa 171 BC Macedonians under Perseus victorious over Romans; battle of Pydna 168 BC Perseus of Macedonia crushed by Romans.

Macedonian War, Fourth 149–147 BC: Roman victory under Mummius at Corinth.

MacEwen, Sir William (1848–1924) Scottish surgeon.

McGill University, Montreal, chartered 1821, opened 1829. Named after the Scottish benefactor James McGill (1744–1813).

McGillivray, Alexander (*c.*1739–1793) American Indian chief.

MacGonagall, William (*c.*1830–*c.*1902) Scottish poet, renowned for his memorably awful doggerel verse.

Macgregor, Robert ('Rob Roy') (1671–1734) Scottish rebel.

Machaut, Guillaume de (*c.*1300–1377) French poet.

Machen, Arthur (1863–1947) English writer (*The Great Return* 1915).

Machiavelli, Niccolò di Bernardo dei (1469–1527) Italian statesman and political theorist. His treatise on the art of ruling, *The Prince* (1532), takes a dim view of human nature, seeing humanity as essentially corrupt and therefore best ruled by whatever method ensures the stability of the state, even if the method entails merciless cruelty.

McIndoe, Sir Archibald [Hector] (1900–1960) New Zealand plastic surgeon. One of the world's leading plastic surgeons, he pioneered facial surgery on burns victims.

Machine gun models made by Drummond 1626, Palmer 1663, Puckle 1718, Gatling 1862, Nordenfeldt 1873, Hotchkiss 1878, Maxim 1884.

Macintosh, Charles (1766–1843) Scottish chemist and inventor (1823) of waterproofs.

McKay, Charles (1814–89) Scottish singer (*Cheer, Boys, Cheer*).

McKaye, Steele (1842–94) American playwright (*Hazel Kirke* 1880).

Macke, August (1887–1914) German painter (*Franz Marc*). He was killed.

Mackensen, August von (1849–1945) German field-marshal.

Mackenzie, Sir [Edward Montague] Compton (1883–1972) English novelist, best known for his series of very popular comic novels set in the Scottish Western Isles, e.g. *Whisky Galore*.

Mackenzie, Henry (1745–1831) Scottish writer (*The Man of Feeling* 1771).

Mackenzie, William Lyon (1795–1861) Canadian politician and lawyer.

Mackintosh, Charles Rennie (1868–1928) Scottish architect and designer.

Mackintosh, Sir James (1765–1832) Scottish historian and lawyer.

Macklin, Charles (*c.*1697–1797) British actor.

McKinley, William (1843–1901) 25th US president (1897–1901). He was assassinated.

McKinley, Mount, Alaska, first climbed 1913 by the American missionary Hudson Stock (1863–1920).

'Maclaren, Ian' [John Watson] (1850–1907) Scottish novelist (*Beside the Bonnie Brier Bush* 1894).

Maclean, Donald *see* BURGESS, GUY.

McLean, Sir Donald (1820–77) New Zealand statesman.

Macleish, Archibald (1892–1982) American poet (*Conquistador* 1932).

'Macleod, Fiona' [William Sharp] (1855–1905) Scottish novelist (*The Immortal Hour* 1900).

Maclise, Daniel (1806–70) Irish-born painter (*The Death of Nelson* 1857–66).

McLoughlin, John (1784–1857) American fur trader and explorer.

McLuhan, [Herbert] Marshall (1911–80) Canadian critic and educator. His studies of mass culture and communication include the influential *The Medium is the Message*.

Maclure, William (1763–1840) American geologist.

McMahon Line delineating the northeast frontier of India agreed by British, Chinese and Tibetan representatives at the 1914 Simla Conference. Named after the British representative Sir Henry McMahon (1862–1949).

Macmanus, Terence Bellew (*c*.1823–1860) Irish patriot.

McMaster, John Bach (1852–1932) American historian.

Macmillan, Daniel (1813–57) Scottish publisher.

Macmillan, Sir [Maurice] Harold [1st Earl of Stockton] (1894–1986) English Conservative statesman and prime minister (1957–63) in succession to Eden. Christened 'Supermac' by the cartoonist Vicky, he won the General Election of 1959 on the slogan 'You've never had it so good' and gained much international respect for his 'wind of change' speech in South Africa in 1958. His later years as premier were darkened by the Profumo scandal, and his manoeuvres against Rab Butler cost the latter the Tory leadership, which went to Douglas-Home. At the end of his life, he made a notably cutting speech in the House of Lords against Thatcher's privatization policies, 'selling the family silver'.

MacMillan, Sir Kenneth (1929–92) Scottish choreographer. He became the Royal Ballet's principal choreographer in 1977. He was also director of the Royal Ballet (1970–77).

McMillan, Margaret (1860–1931) American-born pioneer in British school clinics.

McMillan, Rachel (1859–1917) American-born pioneer in British nursery school work.

MacNaghten Rules legal definition of insanity formulated after the trial for murder of Daniel MacNaghten, 1843.

MacNeice, [Frederick] Louis (1907–63) Irish poet and scholar. He was one of the leading Auden generation of poets, and his collections include *Letters from Iceland* (1937, written with Auden).

Macon, Nathaniel (*c*.1757–1837) American statesman.

Maconchy, Dame Elizabeth (1907–) English composer (*Great Agrippa* 1935).

Maconochie, Captain Alexander (1787–1860) Scottish geographer and prison reformer, first secretary of the Royal Geographical Society.

McPherson, Aimée Semple (1890–1944) American evangelist.

Macpherson, James (1736–96) Scottish 'editor' of Ossian.

Macpherson, Samuel Charters (1806–60) Scottish administrator in India.

Macready, William Charles (1793–1873) English actor.

Macrinus (164–218) Roman emperor (217–218). He was killed.

MacSwiney, Terence James (1880–1920) Irish patriot. He starved himself to death in prison.

McTaggart John McTaggart Ellis (1866–1925) English philosopher.

MacVeagh, Wayne (1833–1917) American lawyer and diplomat.

Macy, Mrs Anne Sullivan (1866–1936) American teacher of Helen Keller.

Madagascar discovered by the Portuguese navigator Diego Diaz 1500; annexed by France 1895; became autonomous 1958 and fully independent 1960.

Madame Tussaud's Waxworks, London, founded by the Swiss showperson Mme Marie Tussaud (1760–1850); new building opened 1928.

Madariaga, Don Salvador de (1886–1978) Spanish-born writer (*Don Quixote; A Psychological Study* 1934).

Madden, Sir Frederic (1801–73) English antiquary and palaeographer.

Madeira Islands discovered 1418 by pupils of Prince Henry the Navigator (1394–1460).

Madeira Pet British-owned ship, made first voyage (51 days) from Liverpool to Chicago, arriving 14 July 1857.

Madeleine, Paris, construction begun 1764, completed 1842.

Madison, James (1751–1836) 4th US president (1809–17).

Madoc reputed Welsh discoverer of America, lived in the second half of 12th century.

Mad Parliament held in Oxford 1258.

Madras State, India, trading begun by the British 1611; brought under British rule by 1801; reorganized and made smaller 1956 and 1960; renamed Tamil Nandu 1968.

Madrid University, Spain, founded 1508.

Maecenas, Gaius Cilnius (*c*.70–8 BC) Roman statesman and patron of letters.

Mael Sechnaill I (d.862) high king of Ireland *see* Appendix.

Mael Sechnaill II (d.1023) high king of Ireland (1002–23) *see* Appendix.

Maes, Nicolas (1632–93) Dutch painter (*The Card Players*).

Maeterlinck, [Count] Maurice (1862–1949) Belgian poet, writer and playwright. Trained as a lawyer, he turned to writing poetry under the influence of the Symbolist poets (*The Blue Bird* 1909). His masterpiece is *Pelléas et Mélisande* (1892), the basis for the opera by Debussy. He was awarded the Nobel prize for literature in 1911.

Mafeking, Cape Province, besieged by the Boers 12 October 1899; relieved by the British 17 May 1900.

Magdalen College, Oxford University, founded 1458

by William of Wayneflete (1395–1486).

Magdalene College, Cambridge University, founded by Thomas, Baron Audley of Walden, 1542.

Magdeburg hemispheres demonstrating air pressure invented 1654 by the German scientist Otto von Guericke (1602–86).

Magellan, Ferdinand [Fernão Magalhães] (*c.*1480–1521) Portuguese navigator whose ship first circumnavigated the world (1519–22). He was killed before the voyage was completed.

Magendie, François (1783–1855) French scientist.

Magenta, Battle of between the Italian and the Austrians, 4 June 1859.

Magic lantern invented 1646 by the German scientist Athanasius Kircher (1601–80).

Maginn, William (1793–1842) Irish writer (*Homeric Ballads* 1849).

Maginot Line French defence system, construction began 1928, handed over to the Germans 1940.

Magistrate first British stipendiary, Henry Fielding, appointed 1748; first British woman, Emily Duncan, appointed 26 May 1913.

Magliabechi, Antonio (1633–1714) Italian librarian.

Magna Carta *or* **Charta** sealed by King John at Runnymede, 15 June 1215.

Magnesia, Battle of 190 BC Roman defeat of Antiochus the Great of Syria.

Magnesium discovered 1808 by the English chemist Sir Humphry Davy (1778–1829).

Magnetic clutch, eliminating spring action, invented 1900 by the American engineer Bion Joseph Arnold (1861–1942).

Magnetic compass used by Chinese before 1200; variations of it discovered 1622 by the English scientist Edmund Gunter (1581–1626).

Magnetic pole, North, located 1831 by Sir James Clark Ross (1800–1862).

Magnetic pole, South, reached by the Shackleton Expedition, 16 January 1909.

Magnetism by electricity achieved 1820 by the French physicist Dominique François Arago (1786–1853).

Magnetism defined 1600 by the English physician William Gilbert (1540–1603).

Magnus I the Good (1024–47) king of Norway and Denmark (1035–47).

Magnus II (d.1069) king of Norway (1067–69).

Magnus III (d.1103) king of Norway (1093–1103).

Magnus IV (d.1135) king of Norway (1130–35).

Magnus V (d.1184) king of Norway (1162–84). He was killed in battle.

Magnus VI (1238–80) king of Norway (1263–80).

Magnus VII (1316–74) king of Norway (1319–43).

Magritte, René (1898–1967) Belgian painter. He became a major Surrealist painter in Paris in the 1930s, devising a style dubbed 'magic realism' for its incongruous, dreamlike juxtaposition of carefully detailed everyday objects in dreamlike situations, e.g. men in bowler hats raining from the sky.

Magsaysay, Ramón (1907–57) Philippines statesman.

'Mahabharata' Indian epic composed about the 6th century BC.

Mahan, Alfred Thayer (1840–1914) American naval historian.

'Mahdi, The' name applied to several Muslim leaders, especially the Sudanese rebel, Mohammed Ahmed (b.*c.*1843) who rose against Anglo-Egyptian government–1885.

Mahler, Gustav (1860–1911) Austrian composer and conductor. Of Jewish birth, he became a Roman Catholic but remained subject to anti-semitic gibes while conductor of the Vienna State Opera (1897–1907). Regarded as both the last of the great Romantic composers of the 19th century and the first great composer of the modern era, his works include nine symphonies (1891–1913), song cycles, and the great symphonic song cycle, *The Song of the Earth* (1908).

Mahmud I (1696–1754) sultan of Turkey (1730–54).

Mahmud II (1785–1839) sultan of Turkey (1808–39).

Mahommed *or* **Mahomet** *see* MOHAMMED.

Maiden Castle, Dorset, developed in the Iron Age, turned into a camp 250 BC; destroyed *c.*AD 70; excavated 1934.

Mail coaches first ran between Bristol and London 1784.

Mailer, Norman (1923–) American novelist (*The Naked and the Dead* 1948).

Maillol, Aristide (1861–1944) French sculptor.

Maimonides [Moses ben Maimon] (1135–1204) Jewish theologian (*Mishna Torah*).

Maine, Sir Henry James Sumner (1822–88) English jurist and historian.

Maine US battleship blown up in Havana Harbour 1898.

Maine, USA, first successful settlement 1623, admitted to the Union 1820.

Maintenon, Françoise d'Aubigné, Mme, de (1635–1719) wife of Louis XIV.

Maitland, Frederick William (1850–1906) English jurist.

Maitland, William (*c.*1528–1575) Scottish statesman.

Major, John (1943–) English Conservative politician. He became an MP in 1979 and was appointed a junior minister by Thatcher in 1981. His rise in the late 1980s was spectacular: he replaced **Sir Geoffrey Howe** (1926–) as foreign secretary in 1989, and later that year replaced **Nigel Lawson** (1932–) as chancellor. After Thatcher's resignation in late 1990, he was selected as Tory leader and prime minister. He called a general election in 1992, which he won.

Majorca *or* **Mallorca** conquered by James I of Aragon 1229.

Majorian (d.461) Roman emperor (457–461).

Makarios III [Mikhail Khristodoulou Mouskos] (1913–77) Cypriot archbishop and statesman. Archbishop of the Orthodox Church in Cyprus, he became first president of Cyprus (1960–74) after independence and again (1974–77).

Malacca settled by the Portuguese 1511, came under British rule 1824; incorporated in the Malayan Union 1946.

Malachy, Saint (*c.*1094–1148).

Malamud, Bernard (1914–86) Jewish American author (*The Natural* 1952).

Malan, Daniel F[rançois] (1874–1959) South African politician. A fervent believer in a racially divided society, he was prime minister (1948–54) and was responsible for the apartheid legislation.

Malaria parasite discovered 1895–98 by the Indian-born physician Sir Ronald Ross (1857–1932).

Malatesta, Enrico (1853–1932) Italian anarchist.

Malawi (formerly Nyasaland) constituted 1891 as the British Central Africa Protectorate; federated with Southern and Northern Rhodesia 1953; became an independent republic 6 July 1964.

Malawi, Lake (formerly Lake Nyasa) discovered 1859 by the Scottish explorer David Livingstone (1813–73).

Malaya Straits Settlements formed 1826; Federation of Malaya formed 1895, occupied by Japanese 1942–45, became a sovereign member state of the British Commonwealth 1957; joined Malaysia in 1963.

Malcolm I (d.954) king of Scots (943–954) *see* Appendix.

Malcolm II (*c.*954–1034) king of Scots (1005–34) *see* Appendix.

Malcolm III (1031–93) king of Scots (1058–93) *see* Appendix.

Malcolm IV (1141–65) king of Scots (1153–65) *see* Appendix.

Malcolm X [Malcolm Little] (1925–65) American black nationalist leader. A convert to Islam, he became an advocate of violence in response to racism only if used in self-defence. He was assassinated in February 1965.

Malcontents, Treaty of the signed with the Prince of Parma, 19 May 1579.

Maldives, Indian Ocean, came under British protection 1887; became independent 1965, and a republic in 1968.

Maldon, Battle of between the Danes and the East Saxons 991.

Mâle, Emile (1862–1954) French art critic and historian (*L'An Mil*).

Malebranche, Nicolas (1638–1715) French philosopher.

Malesherbes, Chrétien Guillaume de Lamoignon (1721–94) French statesman. He was guillotined.

Malherbe, François de (1555–1628) French poet (*Larmes de St Pierre* 1587).

Mali conquered by French 1898 and incorporated (as French Sudan) into French West Africa; gained independence 1960.

Malinowski, Bronislaw (1884–1942) Polish-born anthropologist.

Malipiero, Francesco (1882–1973) Italian composer (*I Corvi di San Marco* 1932).

Mallarmé, Stéphane (1842–98) French Symbolist poet. His impressionistic free-verse works and literary theorizing had a strong influence on the development of the Symbolist movement. His works include *L'Après-midi d'un faune* (1876).

Malle, Louis (1932–) French film director (*Au Revoir, Les Enfants* 1988).

Mallet, David (*c.*1705–1765) Scottish poet (*William and Margaret* 1723).

Mallorca *see* MAJORCA.

Malmö, Treaty of between Gustavus Vasa and the Danes, signed 1523.

Malone, Edmond (1741–1812) Irish literary critic.

Malory, Sir Thomas (*fl.*15th century) translator, largely from French sources, of *Le Morte Darthur* (printed 1485), a collection of Arthurian legends. The work includes several episodes, e.g. the quest for the Holy Grail, that have been recycled by generations of writers.

Malpighi, Marcello (1628–94) Italian biologist.

Malplaquet, Battle of between the Allies and the French, 11 September 1709.

Malraux, André (1901–76) French writer (*La Condition humaine* 1933).

Malta ruled by Knights of St John of Jerusalem (1530–1798); conquered from French by English 1800; annexed to the British Crown by the Treaty of Paris 1814. Awarded the George Cross by King George VI, 15 April 1942. Became independent in 1964, and a republic in 1974.

Malta, Knights of order of St John of Jerusalem 1529–1798.

Malthus, Thomas Robert (1766–1834) English economist and population expert (*Essay on the Principle of Population* 1798).

Malvern Festival of English drama instituted 1928.

Malvern Hill, Battle of American Civil War 1 July 1862.

Mamluks ruled Egypt 1250–1517, Iraq 1749–1831.

Man, Isle of ceded to Scotland 1266; came under English government 1290; ruled by Stanley family 1405–1651, 1660–1736; by Duke of Atholl 1736–66; Crown colony 1766–1866; home rule since 1866.

Manasseh ben Israel (1604–57) Portuguese-born Jewish scholar who successfully interceded with Cromwell for the readmission of Jews to England.

Manchester Guardian founded 1821, changed its name to *The Guardian* 1959.

Manchester-Liverpool Railway opened 15 September 1830.

Manchester November Handicap first run 1876.

Manchester Ship Canal construction began 1887; opened 1894.

Manchester University founded 1846 as Owens College by the English philanthropist John Owens (1790–1846); first session formally opened 6 October 1903.

Manchu dynasty, China, 1644–1912.

Mandela, Nelson [Rolihlahla] (1918–) South African lawyer and nationalist leader. Leader of the banned African National Congress, he was imprisoned in 1964 for life by the South African government. Upon his release in 1990, he helped to dismantle apartheid and was elected president in the first free elections in 1994. He seperated from his second wife, Winnie Mandela (1934–) in 1992.

Mandelstam, Osip (1891–1938) Russian poet whose works include *Karmen* (1913). Denounced for reading a satirical poem about Stalin, he and his wife, Nadezhda Mandelstam (1899–1980), were sent into exile in Siberia, where he died. Nadezhda later wrote accounts of their life together.

Mandeville, Bernard de (1670–1733) Dutch-born physician and writer (*A Fable of the Bees* 1714).

Manet, Edouard (1832–83) French painter. His direct approach and fresh, painterly style was influenced by the Impressionists, although he never exhibited with them. His works include *Olympia* (1865).

Manetho (*fl* 4th century BC) Egyptian historian.

Manfred (*c.*1232–1266) king of Sicily (1255–66). He was killed in battle.

Manganese steel discovered 1885 by the British metallurgist Sir Robert Abbott Hadfield (1859–1940).

Manganese metallic chemical element isolated by J. G. Gahn 1774.

Manhattan Bridge, NY, construction began 1901; officially opened 1909.

Manhattan Island bought (1626) from the Indians by Peter Minuit (*c.*1580–1638).

Manhattan Project codename for the top secret US programme to develop the atomic bomb during the Second World War.

Mani (*c.*215–*c.*276) Persian founder of Manichaeism. He was crucified.

Manila Conference on South East Asia defence held 6–8 September 1954.

Manilius (*fl* 1st century) Roman poet.

Manin, Daniele (1804–57) Italian statesman.

Manitoba organized as the Red River Settlement 1812, admitted to the Dominion of Canada 1870.

Manley, Mary de la Riviere (*c.*1663–1724) English writer (*Secret Memoirs* 1709).

Manley, Michael [Norman] (1923–) Jamaican statesman. He became leader of the socialist People's National Party in 1969, and prime minister (1972–80). He lost two subsequent elections but won the 1989 election with a much less radical policy programme. He is regarded as a spokesman for the Third World.

Manley, Norman (1893–) Jamaican statesman.

Manlius, Titus (*fl.* 363–340 BC) Roman statesman.

Manmade fibres industry established *c.*1885 by the French scientist Hilaire, Comte de Chardonnet (1839–1924).

Mann Act (White Slave Act) brought into being 1910 by the American politician James Robert Mann (1856–1922).

Mann, Heinrich (1871–1950) German novelist (*Professor Unrat* 1904).

Mann, Thomas (1875–1955) German novelist and critic, primarily concerned with the role of the artist and the purpose of artistic creation in modern society. His works include *Buddenbrooks* (1901), *Death in Venice* (1912), *The Magic Mountain* (1930), and *The Confessions of the Confidence Trickster Felix Krull* (1954), a comedy. He was awarded the Nobel prize for literature in 1929 and fled Nazi Germany in 1933.

Manning, Cardinal Henry Edward (1808–92) English convert (6 April 1851) to Catholicism.

Manning, Olivia (1908–80) British author (*Fortunes of War* series 1960–80).

Mannyng, Robert (*c.*1264–*c.*1340) English poet (*Handlyng Synne*).

Manoel I (1469–1521) king of Portugal (1495–1521).

Manoel II (1889–1932) king of Portugal (1908–10).

Mansard, François Nicolas (1598–1666) French architect.

Mansard, Jules Hardouin (1645–1708) French architect.

'Mansfield, Katherine' [Katherine Beauchamp] (1888–1923) New Zealand short-story writer (*The Dove's Nest* 1923).

Mansfield College, Oxford University (formerly Spring Hill College, Birmingham), refounded at Oxford 1886).

Manship, Paul (1885–1966) American sculptor.

Mansion House, London, designed 1739 by the English architect George Dance (1700–1768).

Manson, Charles (1934–) American mass murderer.

Mansur, Abu Ja'far al- (d.775) caliph and founder (762) of Baghdad.

Mantegna, Andrea (1431–1506) Italian painter (*St Euphemia*).

Mantell, Gideon Algernon (1790–1852) English geologist.

Mantinea, Battle of (1) 418 BC a battle of the Peloponnesian War, when Athenians were defeated by the Spartans. (2) 362 BC a battle of the Wars of the Greek City States, when Sparta was defeated by Thebes under Epaminondas, who was killed in the battle. (3) 208 BC a battle between the Achaean League led by Philopoemen and the Spartans. It was an Achaean victory.

Manu, Laws of Brahman code composed before 3rd century BC.

Manuel I [Commenus] (*c.*1120–1180) Byzantine emperor (1143–80).

Manuel II [Palaeologus] (1350–1425) Byzantine emperor (1391–1425).

Manutius, Aldus (1449–1515) Venetian printer.

Manzoni, Alessandro (1785–1873) Italian writer (*I Promessi sposi* 1825–27).

Maori Wars, New Zealand, began 1860, ended 1870.

Mao Tse-tung *or* **Mao Ze Dong** (1893–1976) Chinese Communist statesman and Marxist philosopher. He was a founder of the Chinese Communist Party (1922). Following the Japanese occupation (1937–45), during which Nationalists and Communists collaborated against the Japanese, the Communists won the resumed civil war and Mao established his People's Republic (1949). His dictatorship became murderous as he sought to break traditional patterns of Chinese family life and launched his 'Cultural Revolution' (1966–69).

Map, Walter (*c.*1138–1209) Welsh writer (*De nugis curialium*).

Mapplethorpe, Robert (1946–89) American photographer.

Mapungubwe, Zimbabwe, ruins of remarkable buildings erected 12th to 16th centuries.

Mar, John, Earl of (1675–1732) Jacobite leader.

Marat, Jean Paul (1743–93) French revolutionary and journalist. A prominent supporter of Danton and Robespierre, he made repeated calls for increased executions during the establishment of the Revolution and was stabbed to death in his bath by the Girondist aristocrat Charlotte Corday (1768–93).

Marathon, Battle of 490 BC a battle between the Greeks and the Persians, when the Persians were defeated by the Greeks under Miltiades.

Marbeck, John (1523–85) English composer and organist.

Marble Arch, London, built 1828; re-erected at Cumberland Gate, Hyde Park, 1851.

Marbling printing process came into use in England late in the 17th century.

Marburg Colloquy Protestant conference held 1529.

Marc, Franz (1880–1916) German painter. With Kandinsky he founded the *Blaue Reiter* group of expressionist artists. His works include *La Tour des chevaux bleux*). He was killed in battle.

Marc Antony *see* ANTONY, MARK.

Marceau, Marcel (1923–) French mime artist, regarded as the world's leading mime artist.

Marcellinus, Saint pope (296–308).

Marcellus II pope (1555).

Marcellus, Saint pope (308–309).

Marcellus, Marcus Claudius (*c.*268–208 BC) Roman general and statesman who blockaded and captured Syracuse in 212 BC during the Second Punic War.

March, Roger de Mortimer, Earl of (1374–98) lieutenant of Ireland. He was killed in battle.

March, Roger de Mortimer, Earl of (*c.*1287–1330) statesman. He was hanged.

Marchmont, Patrick Hume, Earl of (1641–1724) statesman.

Marcian [Martianus Capella] (*fl* 5th century) North African writer.

Marciano, Rocky [Rocco Francis Marchegiano] (1923–69) American boxer. He became world heavyweight champion (1952–56) and never lost a professional fight.

Marcion of Sinope (*c.*100–*c.*165) shipowner and founder of the sect of Marcionites.

Marconi, Guglielmo, Marchese (1874–1937) Italian physicist, electrical engineer and radio pioneer. He shared the 1909 Nobel prize for physics for his development of wireless telegraphy and later developed short-wave radio transmissions.

Marconi Transatlantic Wireless Service inaugurated 1907.

Marco Polo (1254–1324) Italian explorer.

Marcos, Ferdinand [Edralin] (1917–89) Philippines politician. He was president of the Philippines (1965–86). An autocratic ruler, he declared martial law in 1972, after which he ruled by oppressive and idiosyncratic decree. He was deposed in 1986 after the popular unrest that brought Aquino to power, and lived in exile in Hawaii with his wife, Imelda. After his death his wife returned to the Philippines.

Marcus Aurelius (121–180) Roman emperor (161–180) and philosopher. Renowned by his contemporaries for his nobility and learning, he spent much of his reign in war against the incoming 'barbarians' in the eastern part of the Empire. His *Meditations* outlines his Stoic philosophy.

Marcuse, Herbert (1898–1979) German-born political philosopher and critic.

Mardi Gras the last day of carnival, celebrated on Shrove Tuesday.

Marengo, Battle of between Napoleon and the Austrians, 4 June 1800.

Margaret, Saint (*c.*1045–1093) queen of Scotland, wife of Malcolm III (*see* Appendix).

Margaret (Maid of Norway) (1283–90) queen of Scots (1285–90) *see* Appendix.

Margaret (1492–1549) queen of Navarre and writer (*The Heptameron*).

Margaret, Mary Alacoque, Saint (1647–90) French visionary (Sacred Heart 1673–75).

Margaret Tudor (1489–1541) queen of Scotland.

Margarine invented by the French chemist Hippolyte Mège-Mouriés (1817–80).

Marggraf, Andreas (1709–82) German chemist.

Maria I (1734–1816) queen of Portugal (1777–86).

Mariana Islands, Pacific, passed into US trusteeship 1947; except Guam, which was ceded by Spain to the USA 1898.

Marianus Scotus (1028–82) Irish historian.

Maria Theresa (1717–80) Austrian empress.

Marie Amélie (1782–1866) queen of France.

Marie Antoinette (1755–93) queen of France. She was guillotined.

Marie Byrd Land, Antarctica, discovered 1929 by the American admiral Richard Evelyn Byrd (1888–1957).

Marie Leszczynska (1703–68) queen of France.

Mariette, Auguste Ferdinand François (1821–81) French Egyptologist.

Marignan, Battle of between the French and the Swiss, 13–14 September 1515.

Marine steam turbines first installed in the *Turbinia* 1894.

Marini, Marino (1901–80) Italian sculptor.

Marinus I pope (882–884).

Marinus II pope (942–946).

'Mario, Giuseppe' [Giovanni de Candia] (1810–83) Italian operatic singer.

Mariotte, Edme (*c.*1620–1684) French physician.

Maris, William (1844–1910) Dutch painter, principally of landscapes and animals.

Marischal College, Aberdeen, founded 1593 by George Keith, Earl Marischal (*c.*1553–1623).

Marists Catholic orders, Fathers founded 1816, Brothers founded 1817, Sisters founded 1834.

Maritain, Jacques (1882–1973) French philosopher.

Marius, Gaius (*c.*155–86 BC) Roman general and consul seven times. He served in Spain and, with Metellus Numidicus, commanded the army in the war between Rome and Jugurtha, king of Numidia, in Africa 111–106 BC, Marius defeating and capturing Jugurtha in 106. He reorganized the Roman army and defeated the barbarian Teutone and Cimbri tribes who were moving to invade Italy at Aix, in France, in 102 BC and Vercellae, west of Milan, in 101 BC. In 100 BC he conspired against Metellus to have him banished and growing rivalry with Sulla for the command in Asia against Mithridates culminated 88 BC in civil war in Rome, of which Sulla was the victor. Marius fled Rome but returned the following year, when he and Cinna engaged in a power struggle with the senate, leading to massacres in the city 87 BC. Marius and Cinna named themselves consuls for 86 BC, but Marius died very shortly afterwards.

Marivaux, Pierre Carlet de (1688–1763) French writer (*L'Amour et la Verité* 1720).

Mark, Saint pope (336–337).

Markham, Gervase (*c.*1568–1637) English scholar and agricultural reformer.

Markham, Sir Clements Robert (1830–1916) English geographer and historian.

Markiewicz, [Constance Georgine] Countess (1868–1927) Irish nationalist. A member of Sinn Fein involved in the Easter Rising of 1916, she became the first woman to be elected to the British Parliament in 1918 but refused to take her seat.

Markova, Dame Alicia [Lilian Alicia Marks] (1910–) English ballerina. She was a member of Diaghilev's Ballet Russe (1924–29) and then of the Vic-Wells Ballet, where she became prima ballerina (1933–35).

Marks, Simon [1st Baron Marks of Broughton] (1888–1964) English businessman. He inherited the Marks and Spencer chain of shops and helped build it into a respected retail empire.

Marlborough, John Churchill, Duke of (1650–1722) English soldier who was given command of the British army in 1702 and succeeding years won great victories in Austria and the Netherlands, including Blenheim (1704).

Marlborough, Sarah, Duchess of (1660–1744) wife of the Duke of Marlborough.

Marley, Bob [Robert Nesta Marley] (1945–81) Jamaican singer and songwriter. With his group, the Wailers, he became the world's leading reggae singer.

Marlowe, Christopher (1564–93) English dramatist and poet. He was one of the first English dramatists to use blank verse to great dramatic and poetic effect in his plays, the most famous of which are *Tamburlaine the Great* and his masterpiece, *Doctor Faustus* (1588). He was probably a secret agent in the employ of the Elizabethan government and was killed in a tavern brawl.

Marmont, August Viesse de, Duc de Raguse (1774–1852) marshal of France.

Marmontel, Jean François (1723–99) French writer (*Aristomène* 1749).

Marne, Battle of the First World War battle, 6–12 September 1914.

Maronites Christian heretical sect, appeared in the Lebanon *c.*681, reconciled to Rome 1182; massacre by Druses 1860.

'Marprelate, Martin' unidentified writer of Puritan pamphlets issued 1588–89.

Marquesas Islands, French Polynesia, formally annexed by France 1842.

Marquette, Jacques (1637–75) French missionary and explorer in America.

Marquis, Don (1878–1937) American humorous writer (*Archy and Mehitabel* 1927).

Marriages, clandestine, abolished in England 1754; non-religious, made legal 1836.

Married Women's Property Act, Britain, became law 1883.

Marryat, Frederick (1792–1848) English sailor and novelist (*Mr Midshipman Easy* 1836).

Mars the fourth planet from the sun, 'canals' on which were observed 1877 by the Italian astronomer Giovanni Schiaparelli (1835–1910).

Marsalis, Wynton (1961–) American jazz trumpeter and composer.

'Marseillaise, La' composed and written 1792 by the Frenchman Claude Joseph Rouget de l'Isle (1760–1836).

Marsh, James (1794–1846) English pioneer in electromagnetism.

Marshal, William, Earl of Pembroke (d.1219) regent of England.

Marshall, Alfred (1842–1924) English economist. His works have been of great influence on modern economics. He devised concepts such as 'elasticity', 'consumer surplus' and 'time analysis'.

Marshall, George C[atlett] (1880–1959) American general and statesman. He was chief of staff of the US army during World War II, and, as US secretary of state, oversaw the Marshall Aid Plan, for which he was awarded the 1953 Nobel Peace Prize.

Marshall Islands a scattered group of some 1250 islands in the western Pacific Ocean, which passed into US trusteeship 1947–87; now a self-governing republic.

Marshall Plan for European post-war recovery devised 1947 by the American General George Catlett Marshall (1880–1959).

Marshalsea Prison, London, established by King Edward II's reign; abolished 1849.

Marsilius of Padua (*fl* 2nd half of the 13th and 1st half of the 14th centuries) Italian writer (*Defensor Pacis* 1324).

Marston, John (*c.*1575–1634) English playwright (*Antonio and Mellida* 1602).

Marston Moor, Battle of a battle of the English Civil War between the Parliamentarians and the Royalists, 2 July 1644. It was a Parliamentary victory.

Martello towers English coastal defences built at the turn of the 18th century.

Martha's Vineyard, Mass., discovered 1602 by the English navigator Captain Bartholomew Gosnold (d.1607).

Marti, José Maria (1853–95) Cuban patriot. He was killed in battle.

Martial (*c.*40–104) Latin poet (*Epigrams*).

Martin, Saint (*c.*316–397) bishop of Tours.

Martin, John (1789–1854) English painter (*Belshazzar's Feast* 1821).

Martin I, Saint (d.655) pope (649–653).

Martin II, Martin III (non-existent; numbering confused with Popes Marinus I and II).

Martin IV [Simon Monpitié de Brion] (*c.*1210–1285) pope (1281–85).

Martin V [Otto Colonna] (d.1431) pope (1417–31).

Martin du Gard, Roger (1881–1958) French writer (*Les Thibault* 1922–40).

Martineau, Harriet (1802–76) English writer (*Feats on the Fjord* 1841).

Martini, Padre [Giambattista Martini] (1706–84) Italian composer.

Martinique a large island in the southern Caribbean, discovered 1502 by Christopher Columbus; colonized by the French from 1625.

Martinmas Feast of St Martin, celebrated 11 November.

Martinu, Bohuslav (1890–1959) Czech composer (*The Judgment of Paris* 1935).

Martyn, Henry (1781–1812) English missionary.

Marvell, Andrew (1621–78) English poet. A (passive) supporter of Parliament during the English Civil War, he became member of parliament for Hull in 1659, a position he held until his death. His verse satires were much enjoyed by the wits of the day, even by those whose vices were attacked. His strange, metaphysical poems, e.g. 'The Garden' and 'Upon Appleton House', display a talent for symbolism and metaphor. His poem celebrating Oliver Cromwell's suppression of the Irish rebellion, 'An Horatian Ode upon Cromwell's Return from Nature', is a great political poem, with its cool, restrained appreciation of Cromwell's stature.

Marx, Karl [Heinrich] (1818–83) German philosopher. His theories on class struggle dominated 20th-century political thought from the Bolshevik Revolution to the collapse of the communist regimes of eastern Europe in 1989–91. *Das Kapital*, his study of the economics of capitalism, appeared in 1867; subsequent volumes, edited by Friedrich Engels (1820–95), appeared in 1885 and 1895. He also wrote *The Communist Manifesto* with Engels in 1848, and was one of the founders of the 'First International' in 1864.

Marx Brothers American comedy group of brothers consisting of Arthur Marx (Harpo) (1888–1964), Milton (Gummo) (1893–1977), Herbert Marx (Zeppo) (1901–79), Julius Marx (Groucho) (1890–1977) and Leonard Marx (Chico) (1886–1961). The anarchic humour of the Marx Brothers' films, e.g. *Duck Soup* (1933), was enormously popular with both critics and public, with Groucho in particular enjoying a cult status among intellectuals.

Mary, Queen (1867–1953) wife of George V (*see* Appendix).

Mary I (1516–58) queen of England (1553–58) *see* Appendix.

Mary II (1662–94) queen of England, Scotland and Ireland (1689–94) *see* Appendix.

Mary Celeste derelict ship found 5 December 1872.

Maryland, state of the USA, first settled 1634, one of the 13 original states of the Union.

Maryland University, Baltimore, founded 1807.

Marylebone Cricket Club founded 1787; first match 1788; present ground opened 1814.

Mary of Modena (1658–1718) queen of King James II (*see* Appendix).

Mary, Queen of Scots (1542–87) queen of Scotland (1542–67) *see* Appendix.

Masaccio [Tommaso di Ser Giovanni di Mone] (1401–*c.*1428) Florentine painter who was a key figure of the early Renaissance and in the development of perspective.

Masaniello [Tommaso Aniello] (1623–47) Italian patriot. He was murdered.

Masaryk, Jan (1886–1948) Czech statesman.

Masaryk, Thomas Garrigue (1850–1937) Czech president (1918–35).

Mascagni, Pietro (1863–1945) Italian composer. His works include the perennial favourite, the one-act *Cavalleria Rusticana* (1890).

Masefield, John [Edward] (1878–1967) English poet whose best-known poem, from *Salt-Water Ballads* (1902) is 'I must go down to the sea again'. Many later poems, e.g. *The Everlasting Mercy* (1911), caused scandal with their frank treatment of rural themes. He was appointed poet laureate in 1930.

Masham, Abigail [Lady Masham] (d.1734) court favourite.

Maskelyne, John Nevil (1839–1917) English conjuror.

Masolino (*c.*1383–*c.*1447) Italian painter (*Madonna*).

Mason, John (1586–1635) English founder 1631 of New Hampshire, USA.

Mason, Lowell (1792–1872) American composer (*From Greenland's Icy Mountains*).

Mason-Dixon Line boundary between Pennsylvania and Maryland (and so between free and slave regions), fixed 1763–67.

Maspero, Gaston (1846–1916) French Egyptologist.

Massachusetts, USA, first settled 1620; one of the 13 original states of the Union.

Massachusetts Bay Company granted territory 1628 by the Council of New England; grant ratified by royal charter 1629.

Massachusetts Institute of Technology founded in Boston 1859; moved to Cambridge, Mass., 1915.

Masséna, Marshal André (1756–1817) Italian-born French army leader.

Massenet, Jules (1842–1912) French composer (*Manon Lescaut* 1884).

Massey, Vincent (1887–1967) first Canadian governor-general of Canada (1952–59).

Massinger, Philip (1583–1640) English dramatist (*The City Madam* 1632).

Masson, David (1822–1907) Scottish historian.

Master Gunner of England office last held (from 1709) by Colonel James Pendlebury (d.*c.*1758).

Master of the King's Musick title originated *c.*1625; first Master, Nicholas Lanier (1588–1666).

Masters, Edgar Lee (1869–1950) American poet (*Spoon River Anthology* 1915).

Mastoid operation first successfully performed in 1774 by the French surgeon Jean Louis Petit.

Masurian Lakes, Battles of the two battles of the First World War between the German and the Russians 1914–15.

Masurium (technetium) chemical element discovered 1925 by I. and W. Noddack. Confirmed by C. Perrier and E. Segré 1937.

Mata Hari [Margarethe Geertruida Zelle] (1876–1917) Dutch spy. A dancer in Paris with many lovers, she became a German spy and was shot for treason.

Matapan, Battle of a naval battle of the Second World War, 28 March 1941, when a British fleet destroyed an Italian fleet, ensuring Allied superiority in the Mediterranean.

Matches book of matches invented 1892 by the American attorney John Pusey.

Matches friction wooden matches invented 1827 by the English chemist John Walker (*c.*1781–1859).

Matches safety matches invented 1855 by the Swedish inventor Johan Edvard Lundström.

Mather, Cotton (1663–1728) American witch-hunting writer (*Memorable Providences Relating to Witchcraft* 1685).

Mather, Increase (1639–1723) American president of Harvard College.

Mathews, Charles James (1803–78) English actor and playwright.

Matilda (1102–67) queen of England (1141) *see* Appendix.

Matisse, Henri (1869–1954) French painter and sculptor. In the period before the First World War he became a leading Fauvist.. A superb draughtsman, he also designed ballet sets for Diaghilev. He continued to paint more abstract and decorative works, and made use of cut-outs and collages in simple compositions. His works include *Odalisque* (1910).

Matsys, Quentin (*c.*1466–1530) Flemish painter (*Burial of Christ*).

Mattathias (d.166 BC) Jewish priest who began a revolt of the Jews against the Hellenizing policy of Antiochus Epiphanes (166–161 BC). On his death, he was succeeded by his son, Judas Maccabaeus.

Matterhorn mountain on the Swiss-Italian frontier, first climbed 1865 by the English mountaineer Edward Whymper (1840–1911).

Matthay, Tobias (1858–1945) English musician.

Matthew, Tobie (1546–1628) archbishop of York (1606–28).

Matthew of Paris (d.1259) English historian (*Chronica majora*).

Matthews, Sir Stanley (1915–) English footballer. Regarded as one of the greatest wingers of all time (the 'Wizard of Dribble'), he won 54 international caps in a career that spanned 22 years.

Matthias (1557–1619) Holy Roman emperor (1612–19).

Matthias Corvinus (1440–90) king of Hungary (1458–90).

Maturin, Charles Robert (1782–1824) Irish writer (*Melmoth* 1820).

Maud (1080–1118) wife of King Henry I of England. *See* Appendix.

Maugham, W[illiam] Somerset (1874–1965) English novelist and dramatist. Trained as a doctor, he used his experiences working in the London slums for his first novel, *Liza of Lambeth* (1897). His best-known novels are *Of Human Bondage* (1915) and *The Moon and Sixpence* (1919), the latter based on the life of the painter Paul Gauguin. He was a British secret agent during World War I, and his experiences then form the basis of his spy novel, *Ashenden* (1928).

Mau Mau nationalist rebel movement in Kenya 1952–57.

Maundy Thursday commemoration on the Thursday before Easter of Christ's washing the Apostles' feet.

Maupassant, Guy de (1850–93) French writer (*Boule de suif* 1880).

Maupertuis, Pierre Louis (1698–1759) French mathematician.

Maurepas, Jean Frédéric Phélipeaux, Comte de (1701–81) French statesman.

Mauretania Atlantic passenger liner launched 20 September 1906.

Mauriac, François (1885–1970) French novelist (*Le Baiser aux Lépreux* 1922).

Maurice (*c.*540–602) Byzantine emperor (582–602). He was assassinated.

Mauritania West African republic, French protectorate from 1903, colony from 1920; gained full independence 1960.

Mauritius settled by the Dutch 1638–1710; taken by the French 1715, and British 1810; independent member of the Commonwealth since 1968.

Maurois, André [Emile Herzog] (1885–1967) French writer (*Vie de Disraeli* 1927).

Maurras, Charles (1868–1952) French writer (*Les Amants de Venise* 1902).

Maury, Jean Siffrein (1746–1817) French cardinal and political writer.

Mauve, Anton (1838–88) Dutch painter (*Watering Horses*).

Mauveine first synthetic organic dye discovered 1856 by the English chemist Sir William Henry Perkin (1838–1907).

Mawson, Professor Sir Douglas (1882–1958) Antarctic explorer.

Maxentius (d.312) Roman emperor (306–312). He was drowned.

Maximian (d.310) Roman emperor (286–305). He committed suicide.

Maximilian (1832–67) Austrian-born emperor of Mexico (1864–67). He was shot.

Maximilian I (1459–1519) Holy Roman emperor (1493–1519).

Maximilian II (1527–76) Holy Roman emperor (1564–76).

Maximilian I (1756–1825) king of Bavaria (1806–25).

Maximilian II (1811–64) king of Bavaria (1848–64).

Maximin (d.238) Roman emperor (235–238). He was murdered.

Maximin (d.313) Roman emperor (308–313).

Maxim machine gun invented 1884 by the American-born inventor Sir Hiram Stevens Maxim (1840–1916).

Maximus (d.388) Roman emperor (383–388). He was executed.

Maximus, Saint the Confessor (*c.*580–662).

Maxton, James (1885–1946) Scottish socialist.

Maxwell, James Clerk (1831–79) Scottish physicist.

Maxwell, [Ian] Robert [Robert Hoch] (1923–91) Czech-born British newspaper proprietor, publisher and politician. His mysterious death by drowning off the Canary Islands was followed by revelations of his mishandling of his companies' assets.

May, Phil (1864–1903) humorous artist.

May, Thomas (1595–1650) English writer (*History of the Long Parliament* 1647).

Mayakovsky, Vladimir Vladimirovich (1894–1930) Russian poet. He committed suicide.

Mayan empire in Mexico flourished 3rd to 15th centuries AD.

May Day day of celebration connected with vegetation and labour.

Mayenne, Charles de Lorraine, Duc de (1554–1611) French king-maker (1554–1611).

Mayer, Joseph (1803–86) English antiquary and philanthropist.

Mayer, Louis B[urt] [Eliezer Mayer] (1885–1957) Russian-born American film producer. He joined with Goldwyn to form Metro-Goldwyn-Mayer in 1924 and became one of the most powerful of the Hollywood film-makers.

Mayerling Tragedy, in which the Crown Prince Rudolf of Austria and Mary Vetsera committed suicide, 30 January 1889.

Mayflower Pilgrims set sail from Plymouth for New England, 6 September 1620; arrived Plymouth Rock, Massachusetts, 16 December 1620 (OS).

Mayhew, Henry (1812–87) English writer on social subjects (particularly London).

Maynooth Irish seminary for Catholic priesthood founded 1795.

Mayor first English woman mayor, Elizabeth Garrett Anderson (1836–1917) elected mayor of Aldeburgh 1908.

Mayow, John (1640–79) English physiologist.

Mazarin, Jules, Cardinal (1602–61) Italian-born French statesman (regent 1642–61).

Mazarine public library of Paris opened 1643; absorbed by the Bibliothèque Nationale 1930.

Mazeppa, Ivan Stepanovich (*c.*1644–1709) Cossack leader.

Mazzini, Giuseppe (1805–72) Italian leader who worked with Garibaldi for a united Italy.

MCC (Marylebone Cricket Club) founded 1787; first match 1788; present ground opened 1814.

Mead, Margaret (1901–78) American anthropologist. Her works, which include *Coming of Age in Samoa*, argue that cultural conditioning rather than heredity shapes personality.

Mead, Richard (1673–1754) English Royal physician.

Meagher, Thomas Francis (1823–67) Irish patriot. He was drowned.

Meal Tub Plot 1679 conceived by the English adventurer Thomas Dangerfield (1650–85).

Mecca Muslim holy city, captured by Mohammed 630; by Ibn Sa'ud 1924.

Mechnikov, Ilya *see* METCHNIKOFF, ELIE.

Mecklenburg Declaration of American independence made 1775.

Medal first English medal struck by King Charles I 1643. The first medal given to all ranks: King George II's 1745–46.

Medawar, Sir Peter Brian (1915–87) Brazilian-born British zoologist and immunologist. He shared the 1960 Nobel prize for physiology or medicine with the Australian virologist **Sir Frank Macfarlane Burnet** (1899–1985) for his work on immunological tolerance.

Media an ancient country of southwest Asia, which was inhabited by the Medes; monarchy founded by Deioces 700 BC; Cyaxares became king of Media 624 BC; Nineveh captured and destroyed by Nabopolassar of Babylon and Cyaxares of Media 612 BC, ending the Assyrian Empire; battle between Cyaxares of Media and Alyattes of Lydia stopped by eclipse of the sun 585 BC; Media conquered by Cyrus in the course of founding the Persian Empire 550 BC.

Medical inspection of schoolchildren first British inspection held at Bradford 1899.

Medical profession British medical profession opened 1876 to women by the efforts of the English physician and mathematician Sophia Louisa Jex-Blake (1840–1912).

Medici, Catherine de' (1519–89) queen of France, wife of Henri II. She was the only daughter of Lorenzo de' Medici. She had little influence in France until the minority of her son, Charles IX, when she was regent (1560–72), playing off the Guise faction against Condé and Coligny. The St Bartholomew's Day massacre was largely at her instigation.

Medici, Cosimo de' (1389–1464) Florentine leader who was for thirty-four years sole arbitator of the republic and the adviser of the kings of Italy. He was wealthy, liberal and a clever statesman.

Medici, Ferdinand de' (1549–1609) grand duke of Tuscany (1587–1609).

Medici, Giovanni de' (1498–1526) Italian military commander. He was mortally wounded.

Medici, Lorenzo de' (1449–92) Florentine aristocrat and statesman. Styled 'The Magnificent', he was a poet and a noted patron of the arts. His tomb in Florence was designed by Michelangelo.

Medici, Maria de' (1573–1642) queen of France as wife of Henri IV. After his assassination she was regent (1610–17) for her son, Louis XIII.

Medici family ruled Florence 1434–94, 1512–27, 1530–1737.

Medina Arabian city, home of Mohammed after *hegira* 622.

Medina-Sidonia, Alonso Pérez de Guzman el Bueno, Duke of (1550–1615) Spanish Armada commander.

Medtner, Nikolai (1880–1951) Russian-born composer (*Märchen*).

Meer, Jan van der (1628–91) Dutch painter (*The Astronomer*).

Meerut place of outbreak of Indian Mutiny, 10 May 1857.

Megalopolis, Battle of 331 BC a battle of the Macedonian Wars, when the Spartans under Agis were defeated by the Macedonian regent, Antipater.

Mège-Mouriés, Hippolyte (1817–80) French chemist and inventor 1869 of margarine.

Megiddo, Battle of a battle in 608 BC, when Josiah, king of Judah, was defeated and killed by Neco of Egypt at the ancient fortress city of Megiddo in northern Palestine.

Mèhul, Étienne Nicolas (1763–1817) French composer (*Joseph* 1807).

Meilhac, Henri (1831–97) French playwright (with Halévy *Barbe-Bleue* 1866).

Meillet, Antoine (1866–1936) French philologist.

Meinhoff, Ulrike (1934–76) German terrorist. With Andreas Baader and others, she founded the 'Red Army Faction' in 1970, an ultra-leftist terrorist organization dedicated to using violence to bring about the collapse of West German 'capitalist tyranny'. She committed suicide in prison.

Meir, Golda [Golda Mabovitz] (1898–1978) Russian-born Israeli stateswoman. Active in the fight for a Jewish state, she was minister of labour (1949–56) and of foreign affairs (1956–66) before becoming Israel's first female prime minister (1969–74).

Meissonier, Jean Ernest (1815–91) French painter (*Napoleon with His Staff*).

Meitner, Lise (1878–1968) Austrian-born Swedish physicist. She and Otto Hahn discovered the radioactive element protactinium (1918). With her nephew, Otto Frisch, and others, she discovered the process of nuclear fission in the late 1930s.

Melanchthon, Philipp [Schwartzerd] (1497–1560) German religious reformer.

Melba, Dame Nellie [Helen Porter Mitchell] (1861–1931) Australian soprano. Renowned for her light, pure voice, she became one of the world's leading prima donnas in the late 1880s.

Melbourne, William Lamb, Viscount British statesman (prime minister 1834, 1835—41) (1779–1848).

Melbourne University, Victoria, Australia, founded 1854; opened 1855.

Melchett, Alfred Moritz Mond, Baron (1868–1930) English industrialist.

Melchiades, Saint pope (311–314).

Melchior, Lauritz (1890–1973) Danish operatic singer.

Melkites name given to orthodox Christians after 451, and again to Catholics after 1724, in the Levant.

Mellon, Andrew William (1855–1937) American financier.

'Melmoth, Sebastian' (Oscar Wilde) Irish writer (1856–1900).

Melrose Abbey, Scotland, founded by King David I in 1136.

Melville, Herman (1819–91) American novelist, short-story writer and poet. His masterpiece is the novel *Moby Dick* (1851), a complex and symbolic narrative featuring the revengeful Captain Ahab. His short novel *Billy Budd, Foretopman* was made into an opera by Britten.

Melville, James (1556–1614) Scottish reformer.

Member of Parliament first woman elected, Countess Markiewicz in 1918, but she refused to take her seat; first woman to take her seat in the House of Commons, Lady Astor, 1 December 1919.

Memling *or* **Memlinc, Hans** (*c.*1430–1494) German-born Dutch painter. He was a prolific and popular artist, and was a successful portraitist. His works include *The Marriage of St Catherine.*

Memnon of Rhodes (d.333 BC) Greek military commander who led Persian opposition to Alexander the Great in Asia Minor 335 BC and at Halicarnassus 334 BC.

Memorial Day (Decoration Day), USA, 30 May; first observed 1869.

Memphis an ancient city of Egypt situated on the Nile. It was taken by Antiochus Epiphanes at the battle of Pelusium 171 BC.

Menahem king of Israel 738 BC.

Menai suspension bridge built 1818–26 by the Scottish engineer Thomas Telford (1757–1834).

Menander (342–*c.*291 BC) Greek playwright (*Diskolos*).

Mencius (372–*c.*289 BC) Chinese philosopher.

Mencken, Henry Louis (1880–1956) first editor (1924–33) of the *American Mercury.*

Mendel, Gregor Johann (1822–84) Austrian monk who was also a biologist and botanist. He discovered that traits such as colour or height had two factors (hereditary units) and that these factors do not blend but can be either dominant or recessive.

'Mendele Moichersforim' [Shalom Abramovich] (1835–1917) Yiddish writer.

Mendeleyev, Dmitri Ivanovich (1834–1907) Russian chemist.

Mendelian principles of heredity postulated 1865 by the Austrian scientist and monk Gregor Johann Mendel.

Mendelsohn, Erich (1887–1953) German-born architect whose buildings included Potsdam Observatory and the Columbushaus in Berlin.

Mendelssohn, Felix [Jakob Ludwig Felix Mendelssohn-Bartholdy] (1809–47) German composer. The grandson of the philosopher Moses Mendelssohn (1729–86), he became one of the leading Romantic composers. His works include five symphonies, the opera *Elijah* (1846), songs and the overtures *A Midsummer Night's Dream* (1826) and *Fingal's Cave* (1832). His performance of Bach's *St Matthew Passion* resulted in a resurgence of interest in the composer.

Mendelssohn, Moses (1729–86) German Jewish philosopher.

Mendès, Catulle (1841–1909) French poet (*Philomela* 1864). He was killed in an accident.

Mendès-France, Pierre (1907–82) French statesman (prime minister 1954–55).

Mendoza, Antonio de (*c.*1590–1644) Spanish poet (*La Celestina*).

Menelik I (*fl* 13th century BC) emperor of Ethiopia, son of Solomon and Sheba.

Menelik II (1844–1913) emperor of Ethiopia (1889–1913).

Menendez Pidal, Ramón (1869–1968) Spanish philologist.

Meneptah king of Egypt who conducted wars against Libyans and Asiatic pirates 1273 BC.

Mengistu, Mariam Haile (1937–) Ethiopian dictator. He participated in the 1974 coup that toppled Haile Selassie and established a brutal dictatorship after a further coup in 1977.

Mengs, Anton Raffael (1728–79) German painter (*Mount Parnassus* 1861).

Menin Gate, Belgium, memorial to the British who fell in the Ypres salient, World War I; unveiled 1927.

Menken, Adah Isaacs (1835–68) American actress.

Mennonites religious movement originating among Anabaptists 1525, founded 1537 by the Dutch religious leader Menno Simons (1492–1559).

Menorca *or* **Minorca** captured by British 1708, returned to Spain 1802.

Menotti, Gian Carlo (1911–) Italian-born American composer. His operas, for which he also wrote the librettos, employ a number of musical styles and include *The Medium* (1946).

Menpes, Mortimer (1859–1938) Australian-born painter (*Head of Cecil Rhodes*).

Mensheviks minority faction of Russian Social-Democrat Party at Congress in Brussels and London 1903; expelled from Party by Bolsheviks in 1912.

Menshikov, Prince Aleksandr Danilovich (1672–1729) Russian statesman.

Menton elected by plebiscite to be annexed to France 1860.

Menuhin, Sir Yehudi (1916–) American-born British violinist. An infant prodigy, he became one of the world's leading virtuosos and founded a school (in 1962) for musically gifted children.

Menzies, Sir Robert (1894–1978) Australian statesman (prime minister 1939–41, 1949–66).

Merbecke, John (1523–85) English composer and organist.

Mercator, Gerardus (1512–94) Flemish geographer (first world map 1538; first atlas published 1595).

Mercer, John (1791–1866) English chemist and inventor 1850 of mercerizing.

Mercers' Company, London livery company, first recorded reference 1172; chartered 1393.

Merchant Taylors Company, London livery company, origins uncertain; first chartered by King Edward III in 1327; again chartered by King Henry VII in 1503.

Mercia the largest of the Anglo-Saxon kingdoms, comprising all the middle counties of England and founded by Creoda in 585. In 827 it was conquered by Egbert, who united the different kingdoms of England into one. After this time it was repeatedly overrun by the Danes.

Merciless Parliament which condemned friends of Richard II to death, February-May 1388.

Mercury the smallest planet and the one nearest to the sun, the transit of which was first observed 1631 by the French scientist Pierre Gassendi (1592–1655).

Mercury vapour lamp invented 1901 by the American scientist Peter Cooper-Hewitt (1861–1921).

Meredith, George (1828–1909) English writer (*The Egoist* 1879).

'Meredith, Owen' [Edward Robert Bulwer Lytton, Earl Lytton] (1831–91) English poet (*The Wanderer* 1857).

Merezhkovsky, Dmitri Sergeivich (1865–1941) Russian writer (*Leonardo da Vinci* 1901).

Mergenthaler, Ottmar (1854–99) German-born inventor of Linotype.

Meridian first measured 1735–36 by the Frenchmen Charles Marie la Condamine (1701–74) and Pierre Louis Moreau de Maupertuis (1698–1759).

Merimée, Prosper (1803–70) French novelist (*Carmen* 1845).

Merit, Order of, Great Britain, founded 1902.

Mermaid Theatre first English theatre opened in the City of London since The Restoration, opened 1959.

Merodachbaladan Babylonian king (721–709) who ended Assyrian power in Babylon and reigned for twelve years.

Merovingian dynasty ruled France 481–751.

Mersen, Treaty of a treaty that divided the kingdom of Lothair II between Charles the Bald and Louis the German, signed 8 August 870.

Mersey Tunnel, Liverpool-Birkenhead, construction began 1925; opened 1934.

Merton, Walter de (d.1277) bishop of Rochester (1274–77).

Merton College, Oxford University, founded 1264–74 by Walter de Merton.

Meryon, Charles (1821–68) French engraver (*La Vieille Morgue*).

Meslim (*fl* 5th milennium BC) king of Kish who became overlord of Sumeria (southern Babylonia).

Mesmerism founded 1776 by the German physician Friedrich Franz Mesmer (1734–1815).

Mesopotamia an ancient region of southwest Asia between the Rivers Tigris and Euphrates. An Akkadian empire was founded here by Sargon 2650 BC.

Mesozoic Era Earth history between 70 and 200 million years ago.

Messager, André (1853–1929) French composer (*Véronique* 1898).

Messalina, Valeria (d.48) Roman empress. She was executed.

Messene an ancient city founded 369 BC as the capital of Messenia.

Messenia an ancient region of southwest Greece which was conquered by Sparta 740 BC and 685 BC.

Messerschmitt, Willy [Wilhelm Messerschmitt] (1898–1978) German aircraft designer and manufacturer. His planes include the first jet combat aircraft.

Messiaen, Olivier (1908–92) French composer and organist. His rhythmically complex works were often heavily influenced by religious mysticism and include *L'Ascension* (1933).

Messmer, Otto (1894–1985) American cartoonist. His 'Felix the Cat' became the first cartoon superstar.

Mestrovic, Ivan (1883–1962) Yugoslav sculptor.

Metaphysical Society founded in London 1869 by the English architect Sir James Knowles (1831–1908).

Metastasio, Pietro (1698–1782) Italian writer (*Olimpiade* 1733).

Metaurus, Battle of a battle of the Second Punic War, 207 BC, between the Romans and the Carthaginians after Hasdrubal, brother of Hannibal, had crossed the Alps into Italy. Hasdrubal was defeated and killed.

Metcalf, John ('Blind Jack of Knaresborough') (1717–1810) English horse dealer and racer, athlete, soldier, road and bridge builder.

Metchnikoff, Elie (1845–1916) Russian-born bacteriologist (Nobel prize 1908).

Metellus Macedonicus, Quintus Caecilius (d.115 BC) Roman soldier and statesman who fought fought in Greece and Spain.

Metellus Numidicus, Quintus Caecilius (*fl* 2nd century BC) Roman general and statesman, In the war between Rome and Jugurtha, king of Numidia, in Africa, he commanded the army with Marius 111–106 BC. The machinations of Marius later led to his expulsion from the senate in 100 BC and he retired to Rhodes. His reputation was restored the following year.

Marius, Gaius (*c*.155–86 BC) Roman general and consul seven times. He served in Spain and, with Metellus Numidicus, commanded the army in the war between Rome and Jugurtha, king of Numidia, in Africa 111–106 BC, Marius defeating and capturing Jugurtha in 106. He reorganized the Roman army and defeated the barbarian Teutone and Cimbri tribes who were moving to invade Italy at Aix, in France, in 102 BC and Vercellae, west of Milan, in 101 BC. In 100 BC he conspired against Metellus to have him banished and growing rivalry with Sulla for the command in Asia against Mithridates culminated 88 BC in civil war in Rome, of which Sulla was the victor. Marius fled Rome but returned the following year, when he and Cinna engaged in a power struggle with the senate, leading to massacres in Rin the city 87 BC. Marius and Cinna named themselves consuls for 86 BC, but Marius died very shortly afterwards.

Meteorological Office founded 1850 in London by the English meteorologist James Glaisher (1809–1903).

Meteors, Leonid great shower recorded 12 November 1833

Methodism John Wesley (1703–91) founded the first Methodist association May 1738. First General Conference of Methodists 1744. The Methodist Church of Great Britain and Ireland, uniting the Wesleyan, Primitive and United Methodist Churches, founded 20 September 1932.

Methodists, Primitive Methodist sect appeared 1811.

Methodists, United group of Methodist sects merged 1857, joined by other sects 1907.

Methuen Treaty concerning British trade with Portugal negotiated 1703 by the British statesman and diplomat John Methuen (*c*.1650–1706).

Metre national standard established in Britain 1897.

Metric system introduced and legally adopted in France 1 August 1793; new standards adopted 1889.

Metronome invented 1812 by the mechanician Winkel of Amsterdam.

Metropolitan District Railway, London, opened 24 December 1868 between Mansion House and South Kensington.

Metropolitan drainage system, London, planned and carried out 1855–65 by the English engineer Sir Joseph William Bazalgette (1819–91).

Metropolitan Museum of Art, New York, opened 1871.

Metropolitan Opera Company, New York, founded as Abbey's Italian Opera Company 1883.

Met opolitan Opera House, New York, opened 22 October 1883; gold curtain installed 1905.

Metropolitan Police, London, established 1829.

Metropolitan Railway, London, opened 10 January 1863 between Paddington and Farringdon Street; electrified between Baker Street and Harrow 1904; Paris, opened 1900.

Metropolite, The London's oldest music hall, opened 1861; renamed London's Irish Music Hall 1959.

Metsu, Gabriel (1629–67) Dutch painter (*The Music Lesson*).

Metternich, Clemens, Prince (1773–1859) Austrian diplomat and statesman.

Metz, Siege of Franco-Prussian War, 27 August to October 1870.

Meulen, Adams Frans van der (1632–90) Flemish painter (*Nancy and Arras*).

Meung, Jean de (*c.*1250–*c.*1305) French writer (part of the *Roman de la Rose*).

Mexican War between the USA and Mexico 1846–48.

Mexico conquered by the Spanish 1520; Spanish viceroyalty 1535–1821; war of independence 1810–21; period of national formation 1810–1910; social revolution 1911–21.

Meyer, George W. (1884–1959) American composer (*For Me and My Girl*).

Meyerbeer, Giacomo [Jakob Beer] (1791–1864) German-born composer who visited Italy and wrote operas in the style of Rossini. His best-known work is *L'Africaine*, but he also wrote *The Huguenots* (1836).

Meyerhof, Otto (1884–1951) German physiologist.

Meyerling Tragedy *see* MAYERLING TRAGEDY.

Meynell, Alice (1847–1922) English writer (*The Children* 1896).

Meyrink, Gustav (1868–1932) Austrian writer (*The Golem* 1915).

Mezzotint process invented 1642 by the Dutch-born engraver Ludwig von Siegen (*c.*1609–1680).

Miami, University of, Florida, founded 1925; opened 1926.

Michael, Sir John (1804–86) British field marshal.

Michael (1) (1596–1645) tsar of Russia (1613–45).

Michael (2) king of Poland (1669-77).

Michael (3) (1921–) king of Romania (1927–30) .

Michael I (d.845) Byzantine emperor (811–813).

Michael II (d.829) Byzantine emperor (820–829).

Michael III (d.867) Byzantine emperor (842–867). In 866 he appointed Basil I co-emperor and the following year he was assassinated.

Michael IV (d.1041) Byzantine emperor (1034–41).

Michael V Byzantine emperor (1041–42).

Michael VI Byzantine emperor (1056–57).

Michael VII (d.1078) Byzantine emperor (1071–78).

Michael VIII (1234–82) Byzantine emperor (1260–82).

Michaelis, Johann David (1717–91) German theologian.

Michaelmas (Feast of St Michael the Archangel) celebrated 29 September.

Michaud, Joseph François (1767–1839) French historian (*Biographie Universelle* 1811–28).

Michelangelo Buonarotti (1475–1564) Florentine painter, sculptor, draughtsman, architect and poet, an outstanding figure of the Renaissance. His masterpiece was the ceiling paintings for the Sistine Chapel (1508–12). He also worked on the tombs of Lorenzo and Giuliano de Medici, and on the rebuilding of St Peter's. He was an accomplished poet, and wrote fine sonnets.

Michelet, Jules (1798–1874) French historian.

Michelozzi, Michelozzo (1396–1472) Italian artist.

Michelson, Albert Abraham (1852–1931) American scientist.

Michigan, USA, first settled 1668; admitted to the Union 1837.

Michigan University, Ann Arbor, founded 1839; opened 1841.

Mickiewicz, Adam (1798–1855) Polish poet (*Konrad Wallenrod* 1827).

Microbes as agents of disease postulated 1546 by the Italian physician Fracastoro (1483–1553).

Microphone invented 1877 by the German-born inventor Emile Berliner (1851–1929; and 1878 by the American inventor David Edward Hughes (1831–1900).

Microscope traditionally invented by the Dutch opticians Johann and Zacharias Janssen *c.*1590; used by Galileo 1610 and Hooke 1665.

Microwave telecommunication system first publicly demonstrated 1931; first commercial service 1934.

Midas possibly legendary king of Phrygia whose touch was supposed to turn everything to gold 700 BC.

Middle Ages in western Europe roughly 5th century to 15th century; in eastern Europe 330–1453; in Arab world 622–1517.

Middle English in use from the 12th century to *c.*1500.

Middleton, Conyers (1683–1750) English scholar (*Life of Cicero* 1741).

Middleton, Thomas (*c.*1570–1627) English dramatist. His two powerful tragedies, *The Changeling* and *Women Beware Women*, are now highly regarded. Other works include the satirical comedy *A Trick to Catch the Old One* and a political satire, *A Game at Chesse* (1624), which almost resulted in his imprisonment. He collaborated with many other dramatists.

Midrash Rabbinical commentary or the Holy Scriptures compiled 1st to 12th centuries.

Midsummer Day (Feast of the Nativity of St John the Baptist) 24 June; summer solstice, 21 or 22 June.

Midsummer Night: 23 June.

Midway, Battle of World War II between the Americans and the Japanese, 5–6 June 1942.

Midwinter winter solstice, 21 or 22 December.

Mieris, Frans van (1635–81) Dutch painter (*The Lute Player*).

Miës van der Rohe, Ludwig (1886–1969) German-born architect.

Mignard, Pierre (1612–95) French painter (*Le Printemps*).

Migne, Jacques Paul (1800–1875) French theologian (*De la Liberté*).

Mignet, François Auguste Marie (1796–1884) French historian (*Charles-Quint* 1854).

Migraine described by Aretaeus of Cappadocia in *c.*131.

Milan Cathedral, Italy, constructed 1386–1813; consecrated 1577.

Milan Decree extending ban on British goods issued by Napoleon 1807.

Mildenhall Treasure Roman silver tableware discovered near Mildenhall, Suffolk, 1942–43.

Mile, British Statute, established by law 1593.

Miletopolis, Battle of 86 BC a battle of the First Mithridatic War, when the Romans under Sulla were victorious over Mithridates.

Miletus an ancient city on the west coast of Asia Minor which was besieged and captured by Alexander the Great in 334 BC.

Milhaud, Darius (1892–1974) French composer. A member of 'Les Six', he was a highly prolific composer. His works were mostly polytonal and often influenced by jazz and include *David* (1954).

Military Cross Great Britain instituted 1 January 1915.

Milk evaporated process invented 1856 by the American Gail Borden (1801–74).

Milky Way constitution discovered by the German-born astronomer Sir William Herschel (1738–1822).

Mill, James (1773–1836) British philosopher.

Mill, John Stuart (1806–73) English philosopher and economist. A follower of Bentham, he elaborated the philosophy of the 'greater good' in his philosophy of utilitarianism. His most popular work is the defence of personal freedom *On Liberty* (1859).

Millais, Sir John Everett (1829–96) English painter. Along with Holman Hunt and Rossetti, he founded the Pre-Raphaelite Brotherhood and was known for his posed, studied tableaux in clashing colours. His works include *Eve of St Agnes* (1862).

Millay, Edna St Vincent (1892–1950) American writer (*Poems* 1929).

Millenium period of 1,000 years, particularly that of Christ's reign in person on Earth.

Miller, Arthur (1915–) American dramatist. His tragedies include three classics of the American stage: *Death of a Salesman* (1949), *The Crucible*, a comment on McCarthyism in the USA, and *A View from the Bridge*, inspired by Greek drama. He was married to Marilyn Monroe (1955–61) for whom he wrote the screenplay for her last film, *The Misfits* (1961).

Miller, [Alton] Glen (1904–44) American jazz trombonist, arranger and bandleader. His dance band became one of the most popular in the world. He died in plane crash.

Miller, Henry (1891–1980) American writer (*Tropic of Cancer* 1931).

Miller, Joe English comedian (1684–1738).

Millerand, Alexandre (1859–1943) French statesman.

Millet, Jean-François (1814–75) French painter. He earned his living as a portraitist, and exhibited his first major genre painting, *The Winnower*, in 1848. He was labelled a social-realist although his work had no direct political import.

Millett, Kate (1934–) American feminist. Her works are cornerstones of feminist fundamentalism.

Milligan, Spike [Terence Allan Milligan] (1918–) Anglo-Irish comedian and writer. With Peter Sellers, the Welsh comedian and singer **Harry Secombe** (1921–) and the Anglo-Peruvian comedian **Michael Bentine** (1921–), he co-wrote and performed in the radio comedy series *The Goon Show* (1951–59), which became a highly influential comedy series, with its manic wit and surreal invention.

Millikan, Robert Andrews (1868–1953) American physicist. He was awarded the 1923 Nobel prize for physics for his determination of the charge on the electron.

Mills, George (1808–81) British shipbuilder.

Milman, Henry Hart (1791–1868) dean of St Paul's and historian.

Milne, A[lan] A[lexander] (1882–1956) British writer and dramatist. His children's books featuring Winnie the Pooh (first published 1926) are much loved classics of children's literature.

Milner, Alfred, Lord (1854–1925) colonial secretary (1919–21).

Miltiades (d.489 BC) Greek general who commanded the Greeks at the battle of Marathon 490 BC when they defeated the Persians

Milton, John (1608–74) English poet. One of the most formidably learned of all English poets, he had a European-wide reputation by his late twenties. His early poems, e.g. the elegy *Lycidas (*1637), are steeped in the humanist tradition, which looked to classical literature for ethical principles and modes of expression, and to Scripture and the Christian tradition for faith. He supported Parliament during the Civil War and wrote tracts attacking royalty and episcopacy. His most famous prose work is the tract *Aeropagitica* (1644), a rousing defence of the liberty of free speech. His masterpiece is the great epic poem on the Fall of Man, *Paradise Lost (*1667–74). Other notable works include the verse drama *Samson Agonistes* (1671), in which the blind hero represents Milton himself in Restoration England.

Milwaukee a port in Wisconsin, USA, founded by the French-American fur-trader Solomon Laurent Juneau (1793–1856).

Milyukov, Paul Nikdayevich (1859–1943) Russian politician and historian.

Mindanao in the Second World War reconquered by the Americans 23 June 1945.

Minden, Battle of between the English and the French, 1 August 1759.

Mines explosive first used by Russians at Kronstadt between 1853 and 1856.

Ming Dynasty, China, 1368–1644.

Ministries *see under significant word of title:* **Agriculture**, etc.

Minnesota state of the USA, organized as a Territory 1849; granted statehood 1858.

Minoan Age of Cretan civilization dating from the late Neolithic age to 1100 BC: Early Minoan Age began 3000 BC; Middle Minoan Age in Crete 2000–1850 BC; Late Minoan Age 1800–1100 BC

Minoan Civilization discovered 1900 by the English archaeologist Sir John Evans (1851–1941).

Minoan Script B Mycenaean Greek, first deciphered 1952 by the English architect Michael Ventris (1922–56).

Minorca *see* MENORCA.

Mint, The Royal, London, origins uncertain; first recorded mention 1229.

Minto, Gilbert John Elliot-Murray-Kynynmond, Earl of (1845–1914) governor general of Canada (1898–1904) and viceroy of India (1905–10).

Minuit, Peter (*c.*1580–1638) purchaser 1626 of Manhattan Island.

Miocene Epoch, Earth history, 35 million years ago.

Mirabeau, Honoré Gabriel Riquetti, Comte de (1749–91) French political writer.

Miracle Plays originated in France; first played in England about the beginning of the 14th century and continued into the 16th century.

Mirage of Hastings occurred July 1798.

Miró, Joan (1893–1983) Spanish painter. Influenced by Picasso, his work became increasingly abstract over the years and was influential on the abstract expressionist painters. His works include *The Horse*).

Mishima, Yukio [Hiraoka Kimitake] (1925–70) Japanese writer (*Sea of Fertility* 1965–70). He committed ritual suicide.

Missionary Ridge, Battle of American Civil War battle, 24–25 November 1863.

Mississippi River navigated 1682 by Robert Cavelier, Sieur de La Salle (1643–87). He was assassinated.

Mississippi Scheme inaugurated as the 'Western Company' 1717 by the Scottish financier John Law (1671–1729).

Missouri state of the USA, first settled 1735; made a Territory 1812; admitted to the Union 1821.

Mistral, Frédéric (1830–1914) Provençal poet (*Mirèio* 1859).

'Mistral, Gabriela' [Lucila Gedoy Alcayaga] (1889–1957) Chilean poet (*Tala* 1938).

MIT [Massachusetts Institute of Technology] founded Boston 1859, moved to Cambridge, Mass., 1915.

Mitchel, John (1818–75) Irish patriot.

Mitchell, R[eginald] J[oseph] (1895–1937) English aircraft designer. He designed the Supermarine Spitfire (1934–36).

Mitchell, Sir Thomas Livingston (1792–1855) Australian explorer.

Mitchum, Robert (1917–) American film actor (*The Night of the Hunter* 1955).

Mitford, Mary Russell (1787–1855) English writer (*Our Village* 1824–32).

Mithridates I satrap of Pontus (402–363 BC) under the Persian king.

Mithridates II (d.302 BC) king of Pontus (337–302 BC) who founded the kingdom and extended it over neighbouring countries.

Mithridates III king of Pontus (302–266 BC) who succeeded his father, Mithridates II, and extended the kingdom still farther. In 281 BC he made an alliancre withthe Heracleans to protect them against Seleucus and also employed the Gauls, who had lately settled in Asia, to overthrow a force sent against him by Ptolemy, king of Egypt.

Mithridates IV (d.*c.*222 BC) king of Pontus (*c.*240–*c.*222 BC). Shortly after his accession his kingdom was invaded by the Gauls who were, however, repulsed. In 220 BC he made war on the city of Sinope but was unable to take it.

Mithridates V king of Pontus (*c.*154–120 BC) who entered into a regular alliance with the Romans, whom he supported in the Third Punic War with a small auxiliary fleet. He was assassinated by a conspiracy among his attendants.

Mithridates VI (Mithridates the Great) (*c.*131–63 BC

king of Pontus (120–63) who succeeded his father, Mithridaes V, at a very young age. He waged three Mithridatic Wars on Rome (88–84 BC, 83–82 BC, 74–64 BC), finally being defeated by Pompey and forced to flee. His son, Pharnaces, organized an insurrection against him and he committed suicide by poisoning himself.

Mithridatic War, First 88–84 between Rome and Mithradates VI, king of Pontus in Asia Minor. Sulla was the Roman general: battle of Cyzicus 88 BC Roman victory; battle of Chaeronea 86 BC Roman victory; Miletopolis 86 BC Roman victory; battle of Orchomenus 85 BC Roman victory. Peace treaty negotiated at Dardanus.

Mithridatic War, Second 83–82 BC between Rome and Mithradates VI, king of Pontus. The Roman commander was Murena who broached the peace treaty: battle of the Halys 82 BC Pontic victory; peace resumed.

Mithridatic War, Third 74–64 BC between Rome and Mithradates VI, king of Pontus. The Roman leaders were Lucullus and Pompey: naval battle of Chalcedon 74 BC Pontic fleet destroyed the Roman fleet; battle of Cabria 72 BC Roman victory under Lucullus; battle of Tigranocerta 69 BC Roman victory under Lucullus; battle of Zela 67 BC Pontic victory but Mithridates was wounded; Nicopolis 66 BC Roman victory under Pompey.

Mitscherlich, Eilhard German scientist (1794–1863).

Mitterrand, François [Maurice Marie] (1916–96) French statesman. He became leader of the Socialist Party in 1971 and the first socialist president of France (1981–95).

Mivart, St George Jackson (1827–1900) English biologist.

Moabite Stone discovered at Dibon by the German missionary F. Klein 1868.

Mobuto, Sese Seko Kuku Ngbendu Wa Za Banga [Joseph Désiré Mobuto] (1930–) Zairean dictator. He assumed complete power over the Congo in 1965, changing the country's name to Zaire in 1971.

Modern face type design introduced *c.*1788 by the English bookseller John Bell (1745–1831).

Modigliani, Amadeo Italian-born artist (1884–1920).

Modigliani, Amedeo (1884–1920) Italian painter and sculptor. His best-known works are his African-influenced sculptures of elongated figures, e.g. *Woman with Cigarette* (1911).

Modjeska, Helena (1844–1909) Polish actress.

Moe, Jörgen Engebretsen (1813–82) Norwegian poet.

Moeran, Ernest John (1894–1950) English composer (*Rhapsody* 1924).

Moguls ruled India 1525–1707.

Mohammed *or* **Muhammad** (*c.*570–*c.*632) (Mohammed the Prophet) Arab prophet and founder of Islam. Born in Mecca, the son of a merchant, he began having revelations, sometime after 600, that he was the last prophet of Allah and His channel of communication with the world. He gathered together a band of followers and established himself at Medina in 622, from where, after several battles, his forces conquered Mecca in 629, and shortly after all Arabia.

Mohammed I (1387–1421) Ottoman emperor (1413–21).

Mohammed II (1430–81) sultan of Turkey (1451–81).

Mohammed III (1566–1603) sultan of Turkey (1595–1603).

Mohammed IV (1638–92) sultan of Turkey (1648–87).

Mohammed V (1844–1918) sultan of Turkey (1909–18).

Mohammed VI (1861–1926) sultan of Turkey (1918–22).

Mohammed Ali (1769–1849) viceroy of Egypt (1805–49).

Mohl, Hugo von (1805–72) German botanist.

Mohr, Charles Theodor (1824–1901) German-born botanist.

Moir, David Macbeth (1798–1851) Scottish physician and writer.

Moiseiwitsch, Benno (1890–1963) Russian-born pianist.

Moissan, Henri (1852–1907) French scientist.

Moivre, Abraham de (1667–1754) French-born mathematician.

Moldavia *see* MOLDOVA.

Moldova (formerly **Moldavia**) formed 1940 from land ceded by Romania to the Soviet Union and from parts of Ukraine; independence declared from former USSR August 1991.

Molesworth, Mrs [Mary Louisa Stewart] (1839–1921) British writer (*Robin Redbreast* 1892).

Molière [pseud. of Jean-Baptiste Poquelin] (1622–73) French dramatist. His great comedies are as popular now as when they were first performed; only Shakespeare's plays have been more widely performed. The plays include *Tartuffe*, a satire on religious hypocrisy, *The Misanthrope*, a study of a cynic in love, and *The Imaginary Invalid* (1673), a hilarious depiction of hypochondria and quack medicine.

Molinism Jesuit reconciliation of predestination and free will, postulated in his *Concordia* (1588) by Luis de Molina (1535–1600).

Molinos, Miguel de (1640–97) Spanish founder (in his *Guida Spirituale* 1675) of the Quietist movement, condemned 1687 by the Inquisition.

Mollison, James Allan (1906–59) British aviator.

Molly Maguires Irish-American secret labour organization flourished in Pennsylvania *c.*1865–75; also Irish secret society of the 1840s.

Molnar, Ferenc (1878–1952) Hungarian writer (*Liliom* 1909).

Molotov, Vyacheslav Mikhailovich [Vyacheslav Mikhailovich Scriabin] (1890–1986) Russian statesman. He negotiated the non-aggression pact with Nazi Germany and became minister for foreign affairs (1953–56).

Moltke, Helmut, Graf von (1800–1891) German field marshal.

Molybdenum metal discovered 1778 by the Swedish chemist Carl Wilhelm Scheele (1742–86).

Mommsen, Theodor (1817–1903) German historian.

Mompou, Federico (1893–1987) Spanish composer (*Dialogues* 1923).

Monaco independence recognized by Savoy 1489, by France 1512, by Papacy and Spain 1524; alliance with France since 1641; constitutional monarchy established 1911; reign of Prince Rainier since 1949.

Monasteries, English, dissolved 1536–39.

Monastery, first Christian, founded *c.*315 by the Egyptian Pachomius on an island in the Nile.

Monck *or* **Monk, George** [1st Duke of Albemarle] (1608–70) English soldier who at first joined the royalist side in the English Civil War and in 1644 was taken prisoner and imprisoned in the Tower of London. In 1646 he switched his support to the Commonwealth and was released. Under Parliament he served in Ireland and with Cromwell in Scotland, in 1650 reducing that country to obedience within a few weeks. In 1653 he assisted in inflicting two severe naval defeats on the Dutch. After Cromwell's death he was instrumental in the restoration of Charles II.

Mond, Ludwig (1839–1909) German-born chemist and businessman.

Mondrian, Piet [Pieter Cornelis Mondriaan] (1872–1944) Dutch painter. He developed a style of painting based on grids of lines against strong colours and co-founded the De Stijl group.

Monet, Claude Oscar (1840–1926) French Impressionist painter whose *Impression: Sunrise* gave the movement its name. With Renoir and Sisley, he began the direct studies of nature and changing light that were to characterize their works. His works include the *Haystacks* (1891) and *Rouen Cathedral* (1894) series.

Monge, Gaspard, Comte de Péluse (1746–1818) French mathematician.

Mongolia recognized Chinese suzerainty in 1636 (Inner) and 1688 (Outer); Soviet-controlled Mongolian People's Republic established 1924; achieved independence 1945; new democratic constitution adopted 1992.

Mongols invaded China 1210, Transoxiana 1219, Caucasia 1221, Persia 1222, Russia 1224, Central Europe 1241, Mesopotamia 1258. Ruled China 1280–1368, Persia 1225–1386, Russia 1242–1380.

Monk, George *see* MONCK, GEORGE.

Monk, Maria (*c.*1817–1850) fraudulent exposer of convent life.

Monk, Thelonius [Sphere] (1917–82) American jazz pianist and composer. His compositions include the classic 'Round Midnight'.

Monkey gland (1866–1951) transplantation for rejuvenation introduced by the Russian-born surgeon Serge Voronov.

Monmouth, Battle of a battle of the American War of Independence in New Jersey, 28 June 1778, when the British were defeated by Washington.

Monmouth's Rebellion led 11 June to 6 July 1685 by James, Duke of Monmouth (1649–85), illegitimate son of Charles II. He was beheaded.

Monocacy, Battle of American Civil War battle, 8 July 1864.

Monophysitism Christian heresy condemned at Council of Chalcedon 451.

Monotheletism Christian heresy similar to monophysitism, condemned at Council of Constantinople 680.

Monotype invented 1887 by the American inventor Tolbert Lanston (1844–1913).

Monroe, James (1758–1831) 5th US president (1817–25).

Monroe, Marilyn [Norma Jean Baker *or* Mortenson] (1926–62) American film actress. She became the leading "dumb blonde" sex symbol in the movies with such films as *Gentleman Prefer Blondes* (1953). Her other films include *Bus Stop* (1956) and the classic comedy *Some Like It Hot* (1959). Her last film, *The Misfits* (1961), was written by her third husband, Arthur Miller. Her death was apparently due to an overdose of sleeping pills.

Monroe Doctrine concerning American foreign policy announced by President James Monroe 1823.

Mons, Retreat from in First World War, August 1914.

Mons Graupius, Battle of *or* **Battle of the Grampians** a battle during the Roman conquest of Britain, AD 84, when the Romans under Agricola defeated the Caledonians, completing the conquest.

Montagna, Bartolommeo (*c.*1450–1523) Italian painter (*Presentation of Christ in the Temple*).

Montagu, Lady Mary Wortley (1689–1762) English writer and traveller.

Montague, Charles Edward (1867–1928) English writer (*Fiery Particles*).

Montaigne, Michel Eyquem de (1533–92) French essayist. The dominant theme in his work was antidogmatic scepticism and he did much to establish the essay as a literary form .

Montalembert, Marc René, Marquis de (1714–1800) French engineer and soldier.

Montana state of the USA, first settled 1809; made a Territory 1864; admitted to the Union 1889.

Montanism Christian heresy prominent in Asia Minor; in 2nd century.

Mont Blanc *see* BLANC, MONT.

Mont Blanc Tunnel construction began 1959; completed 1961.

Montcalm, Louis Joseph, Marquis de (1712–59) French general. He was mortally wounded in battle.

Mont Cenis Pass between France and Italy completed 1806; tunnel opened 1871.

Montefiore, Sir Moses Haim (1784–1885) Italian-born champion of Jewish freedom.

Montemayor, Jorge de (*c.*1520–1561) Spanish poet (*La Diana Enamorada c.* 1550). He was assassinated.

Montenegro independent since 14th century; monarchy since 1910; occupied by Austrians 1916–18; part of the former Yugoslavia 1919–91.

Montespan, Françoise Athénaïs, Mme de (1641–1707) mistress of Louis XIV.

Montesquieu, Charles de Secondat, Baron de la Brède et de (1689–1755) French writer (*Lettres Persanes* 1721).

Montessori, Maria (1870–1952) Italian educationalist. Her method of encouraging the child to learn at her or his own pace without restraint, was very influential on modern pedagogy.

Montessori method in education founded *c.*1909 by the Italian educationalist Maria Montessori (1870–1952).

Monteux, Pierre (1875–1964) French conductor.

Monteverdi, Claudio Giovanni Antonio (1567–1643) Italian composer. He introduced many new elements to the opera form and is regarded as the first major opera composer. His works include *Orfeo* (1608) and *The Coronation of Poppea*.

Montez, Lola' [Marie Dolores Eliza Rosanna Gilbert] (1818–61) adventuress.

Montezuma I (1390–1464) Aztec emperor (1436–64).

Montezuma II (*c.*1480–1520) last Aztec emperor (1502–20). He was killed.

Montfort, Simon de English crusader and baronial leader (*c.*1208 killed in battle 1265).

Montfort, Simon de English soldier and rebel (1240–71).

Montgolfier, Joseph Michel (1740–1810) French balloonist.

Montgomerie, Alexander (*c.*1556–*c.*1610) Scottish poet (*The Cherry and the Slae*).

Montgomery of Alamein, Bernard Law, 1st Viscount (1887–1976) English soldier. In World War II he was given command of the 8th Army in Egypt in 1942, and won the Battle of Alamein, a victory recognized by Churchill as a turning point in the war. He later commanded the Allied land forces on D-Day.

Month in astronomy 29.53 days; in calendar 28, 29, 30 or 31 days; in law 28 days.

Montholon, Charles Tristan, Comte de (1783–1853) French general.

Monticelli, Adolphe (1824–86) French painter (*Baigneuses*).

Montmorency, Anne, Duc de (1493–1567) French statesman and soldier.

Montpensier, Anne Marie Louise d'Orléans, Duchesse de ('Grande Mademoiselle') (1627–93).

Montreal, Canada, founded 1642.

Montreal University founded 1876; opened 1878.

Montrose, James Graham, Marquis of (1612–50) Royalist supporter. He was hanged.

Mont Saint Michel, France, monastery founded by Aubert, bishop of Avranches 708.

Moody, Dwight Lyman (1837–99) American revivalist who led a religious revival in the USA and UK with I. D. Sankey.

Moody, Richard Clement (1813–87) first governor (1841–49) of the Falkland Islands.

Moon, Sun Myung (1920–) South Korean founder of the Unification Church ('Moonies') in 1954.

Moon alphabet for the blind invented 1845 by the English Dr William Moon (1818–94).

Moorcroft, William (1765–1825) English veterinary surgeon and explorer.

Moore, Brian (1921–) Irish-born novelist (*Black Robe* 1985).

Moore, George (1852–1933) Irish writer (*Esther Waters* 1894).

Moore, Henry [Spencer] (1898–1986) English sculptor. His monumental sculptures, often semi-abstract in style but always based on organic form, resulted in him becoming the best known of modern sculptors. They include *Madonna*) (1898–1986).

Moore, Sir John (1761–1809) Scottish soldier. He died of wounds sustained at the Battle of Corunna.

Moore, Thomas (1779–1852) Irish poet (*Lalla Rookh* 1817).

Moraes Barros, Prudente de (1841–1902) president of Brazil (1894–98).

Morality plays played mainly in the 15th and 16th centuries.

Moral Rearmament religious movement founded 1921 by the American religious leader Frank Buchman (1878–1961).

Moran, Edward (1829–1901) English-born painter (*Outward Bound*).

Morand, Paul (1888–1975) French novelist (*Fermé la Nuit* 1922).

Moravian Brethren Christian sect appeared 1457 among followers of Hus, regathered 1722, began mission work 1732.

Moravian Church in America founded 1739 by Bishop August Gottlieb Spangenberg (1704–92).

More, Hannah (1745–1833) English writer (*Coelebs in Search of a Wife* 1809).

More, Paul Elmer (1864–1937) American writer (*Pages from an Oxford Diary* 1937).

More, Sir Thomas (1478–1535) English statesman and Roman Catholic saint. He was Henry VIII's Lord Chancellor (1529–32), and his refusal to recognize the annulment of Henry's marriage to Catherine of Aragon and declaration of supremacy over the Church in England led to his execution for treason. He was widely recognized as an honourable man, and his execution revulsed moderate opinion throughout Europe. His greatest work is his fantasy of a supposedly ideally organized state, *Utopia* (1516). More was canonized in 1835, and has always been admired for his firm principles. His involvement in heresy trials, however, and his dispute with William Tyndale, English translator of the Bible, show a less attractive side of his character.

Moreau, Gustave (1826–98) French painter ((*Oedipe et le Sphinx* 1868).

Morgan, Charles (1894–1958) English novelist (*Portrait in a Mirror* 1929).

Morgan, Sir Henry (*c.*1635–1688) Welsh buccaneer.

Morgan, John Pierpont (1837–1913) American financier.

Morgan, Thomas Hunt (1866–1945) American geneticist and biologist. He was awarded the 1933 Nobel prize for physiology or medicine for his research into chromosomes and heredity.

Morgan, William de (1839–1917) English writer (*Joseph Vance* 1906).

Morgenthau, Henry (1856–1946) German-born financier.

Morier, James (*c.*1780–1849) British traveller and writer (*Hajji Baba* 1824).

Mörike, Eduard Friedrich (1804–75) German poet.

Morison, James (1816–93) Scottish founder 1843 of the Evangelical Union.

Morisot, Berthe (1841–95) French painter who exhibited in all but one of the Impressionist shows. Her works include *Le Berceau* (1873).

Morland, George (1763–1804) English painter (*The Angler's Repast*).

Morley, Henry (1822–94) English writer and editor.

Morley, John, Viscount Morley (1838–1923) English statesman and writer (*Edmund Burke* 1867).

Mormon movement founded 1827 in Fayette, NY, by the American religious leader Joseph Smith (1805–44). He was murdered.

Mornay, Philippe de (Duplessis-Mornay) 'the Pope of the Huguenots' (1549–1623).

Moro, Aldo (1916–78) Italian Christian democrat statesman. He was prime minister (1963–68, 1974–76) and brought the Communist Party into close co-operation with his centre-left coalition shortly before his abduction and murder by the Red Brigade.

Moro, Antonio (*c.*1520–*c.*1576) Flemish painter (*Mary Tudor*).

Morocco arrival of the first Arabs under Okbar ben Nafi' 682; first invasion of Spain under Ibn Tariq 711; dynastic governments 788 to 1911; French protectorate 1912–56; independence 2 March 1956.

Moroni, Giambattista (*c.*1525–1578) Italian painter (*Ludovico di Terzi*).

Morris, Desmond [John] (1928–) English zoologist. His studies of animal and human behaviour have been bestsellers.

Morris, Gouverneur (1752–1816) American diplomat and statesman.

Morris, William (1834–96) English poet, romance writer and artist. His influence on the arts and crafts movement was immense, as was his influence on the development and character of British socialism. his Works include *News from Nowhere* (1891). He founded the Kelmscott Press 1891–98.

Morris dancing revived in England as a result of Cecil Sharp's first seeing Morris dancing under the leadership of William Kimber (b.1873) at Headington, Oxford, 26 December 1899.

Morrison, Jim (1943–71) American rock singer and songwriter. His band, The Doors, became a huge cult after his death (from alcohol and drug abuse).

Morrow, Dwight Whitney (1873–1931) American financier.

Morse, Henry (1595–1645) English Jesuit missionary in England. He was executed.

Morse code (1791–1872) invented *c.*1832 by the American inventor Samuel Finley Breese Morse.

Mortar developed 1756 by the English architect John Smeaton (1724–92).

Mortimer, Edmund, Earl of March (1391–1425) lieutenant of Ireland.

Mortimer, Roger, Earl of March (*c.*1287–1330) royal adviser. He was hanged.

Morton, Jelly Roll [Ferdinand Joseph Lemott] (1885–1941) American jazz pianist, composer and bandleader who is regarded as one of the founders of New Orleans jazz.

Morton, Cardinal John (*c.*1420–1500) archbishop of Canterbury (1486–1500).

Morton, Thomas (1781–1832) Scottish shipwright and inventor.

Moscheles, Ignaz (1794–1870) Austrian pianist and composer.

Moschus (*fl* 2nd century BC) Greek poet of Syracuse.

Moscow Russian capital burnt and pillaged by the Mongols 1382; taken and burnt by the French September 1812; battle of Moscow 5–7 September 1812.

Moscow Conference of Second World War, 9–21 November 1944.

Moseley, Henry Gwyn Jeffreys (1887–1915) British physicist. He was killed in battle.

'Moses, Grandma' [Mrs Anna Mary Robertson Moses] (1860–1961) American primitive painter.

Moslem League founded in India 1906.

Mosley, Sir Oswald [Ernald] (1896–1980) English Fascist leader. First elected to Parliament as a Conservative (1918–22), he became an Independent (1922–24), then a Labour MP (1924, 1929–31), and finally founder and leader of the New Party (1931) and the British Union of Fascists (1932–36). The thuggery and demagoguery of his movement failed to attract much support, and he was interned during the Second World War. He established the British Union Movement in 1948.

Mossbauer, Rudolf Ludwig (1929–) German physicist. He shared the 1961 Nobel prize for physics with the American physicist **Robert Hofstadter** (1915–) for his discovery of the 'Mossbauer effect', involving gamma radiation in crystals.

Moszkowski, Moritz (1854–1925) German-born pianist and composer (*Spanish Dances*).

Mother's Day second Sunday in May (USA); second Sunday in March (UK).

Motherwell, William (1797–1835) Scottish poet (*Jeannie Morrison* 1832).

Motion, planetary, Kepler's Laws of, 1609 and 1619.

Motley, John Lothrop (1814–77) American diplomat and historian (*The Rise of the Dutch Republic* 1856).

Motorcar invented 1890–95.

Motorcycle three-wheeled model built 1884 by Edward Butler; two-wheeled model built in Paris 1900 by the Werner Frères.

Motor scooter, first, invented 1919 by Greville Bradshaw.

Mott, Lucretia (1793–1880) American anti-slavery worker.

Mountains of the Moon *see* RUWENZORI.

Mountbatten, Louis [Francis Victor Albert Nicholas] [1st Earl Mountbatten of Burma] (1900–1979) British naval commander and statesman. Supreme Allied Commander in South-East Asia (1943–45) and viceroy of India (1947), he oversaw the transfer of power to the independent governments of India and Pakistan. He was assassinated by the IRA while on holiday in Ireland.

'Mounties' Royal Canadian Mounted Police formed as the North-West Mounted Police 1873; assumed present title 1920.

Mount Palomar, California, site of observatory selected 1934, observatory opened 1949.

Mount Wilson Observatory, California, opened 1904.

Moussorgsky, Modest *see* MUSSORGSKY, MODEST.

Mowbray, Thomas, Duke of Norfolk (*c.*1366–1399) warden of the Scottish Marches.

Mozambique (formerly Portuguese East Africa) discovered by Vasco da Gama's fleet 1498; first colonized 1505; created an overseas territory of Portugal 1951; became an independent republic 1975.

Mozart, Wolfgang Amadeus (1756–91) Austrian musician and composer. A child prodigy, he began composing at the age of 5. One of the most lyrical of all composers, his works include the operas *The Marriage of Figaro*, *Don Giovanni* (1787), *Cosi fan tutte* and *The Magic Flute*, over 40 symphonies, concertos, string quartets, sonatas, 18 masses, and the unfinished *Requiem*.

Mubarak, Hosni (1928–) Egyptian politician (president 1981–).

Mudie, Charles Edward (1818–90) founder of Mudie's library (1842–1937).

Mugabe, Robert [Gabriel] (1924–) Zimbabwean statesman. He became leader of the Zimbabwe African National Union and prime minister (1980–) following the end of white minority rule. He merged his ruling party with the Zimbabwe African People's Union in 1988 to form a one-party state.

Muggeridge, Malcolm (1903–90) British journalist, writer and TV personality.

Muggletonians religious sect founded *c.*1651 by the English journeyman tailors Lodowicke Muggleton (1609–98) and John Reeve (1608–58).

Mühlenberg, Heinrich Melchior (1711–87) German-born pioneer of American Lutheranism.

Mukden, Battle of between Russians and Japanese fought February–March 1905.

'Mulberry' artificial harbour used at Arromanches, Normandy, in 1944.

Muldoon, Robert David (1921–) New Zealand statesman (prime minister 1974–84).

Mullan, John (1830–1909) American soldier and surveyor.

Müller, Fritz (1827–97) German naturalist.

Müller, Wilhelm (1794–1827) German poet.

Mulliken, Robert Sanderson (1896–1986) American chemist and physicist. He was awarded the 1986

Nobel prize for chemistry for his work on molecular structure and on chemical bonding.

Mulock, Dinah Maria [Mrs Craik] (1826–87) English writer (*John Halifax, Gentleman* 1857).

Mulready, William (1786–1863) Irish painter.

Mulroney, Martin Brian (1939–) Canadian statesman (prime minister 1984–93).

Mumbles Railway, Swansea, Britain's oldest passenger railway, first recorded journey 1807; closed 1 January 1960.

Mumford, Lewis (1895–1990) American writer (*The Culture of Cities* 1938).

Mummius, Lucius (*fl* 2nd century BC) Roman military commander who won the battle of Corinth in the Fourth Macedonian War 147 BC and established Macedonia as a Roman province 146–145 BC.

Munch, Edvard (1863–1944) Norwegian painter. An Expressionist, his works, e.g. *The Scream*, are noted for their strong use of primary colours and emotions.

Münchhausen, Karl Friedrich Hieronymus, Baron von (1720–97) German cavalry officer.

Munda, Battle of 45 BC a battle of the civil war between Julius Caesar and Pompey, when Pompey's sons were defeated in Spain by Caesar.

Munday, Anthony (1553–1633) English writer and spy.

Munich Pact determining the fate of Sudetenland made 29 September 1938.

Munich Putsch unsuccessfully attempted by Hitler, 8 November 1923.

Munkácsy, Michael (1844–1900) Hungarian painter (*The Blind Milton* 1878).

Munnings, Sir Alfred (1878–1959) English painter (*The Prince of Wales on Forest Witch* 1921).

Munro, Hector Hugh ('Saki') (1870–1916) British writer (*Chronicles of Clovis* 1911). He was killed in battle.

Munro, Sir Thomas (1761–1827) governor of Madras.

Münster, Treaty of concluding Thirty Years' War 1649.

Munthe, Axel [Martin Frederik] (1857–1949) Swedish physicist and psychiatrist. His autobiographal book, *The Story of San Michele*, describing his experiences while practising medicine, became a world bestseller.

Murad I (1319–89) Turkish sultan (1350–89). He was assassinated.

Murad II (d.1451) Turkish sultan (1421–51).

Murad III (d.1596) Turkish sultan (1574–96).

Murad IV (*c.*1611–1640) Turkish sultan (1623–40).

Murad V (1840–1904) Turkish sultan (1876).

Murasaki, Lady (*fl* 10th century) Japanese novelist (*Tale of Genji*).

Murat, Achille, Prince (1801–41) French writer (*Letters of a United States Citizen* 1830).

Murat, Joachim (1767–1815) French soldier and king of Naples. He was shot.

Murchison, Sir Roderick Impey (1792–1871) Scottish geologist.

Murdoch, Dame Iris (1919–) Anglo-Irish writer (*The Sea, The Sea* 1978).

Murdoch, [Keith] Rupert (1931–) Australian-born American newspaper and media tycoon. He inherited an Australian newspaper group from his father and expanded his media empire in Britain and America. His expansion into the US market necessitated his acquisition of US citizenship in 1985.

Murdock, William (1754–1839) Scottish engineer and inventor 1792 of coal-gas lighting.

Murena, Lucius Licinius (d.*c.*81) Roman military commander who took part in the battle of Chaeronea in the First Mithridatic War but then broached the peace treaty with Mithridates and brought about the Second Mithridatic War. He was defeated by Mithridates at the Halys 82 BC and forced to flee to Phrygia.

Murfreesboro, Battle of American Civil War battle, 31 December 1862 to 2 January 1863.

Murger, Henri (1822–61) French novelist (*Scènes de la vie de Bohème* 1848).

Murillo, Bartolomé (1617–82) Spanish painter (*Vision of St Anthony*).

Murmansk Russian port on the Kola peninsula founded 1915.

Murphy, Jeremiah Daniel (1806–24) Irish boy linguist.

Murray, Gilbert (1866–1957) Australian-born classical scholar.

Murray, Sir James (1837–1915) British editor of the *Oxford English Dictionary* (1879–1928).

Murray, John (1778–1843) Scottish publisher and founder 1809 of the *Quarterly Review*.

Murray, Sir John (1841–1914) Canadian oceanographer.

Murry, John Middleton (1889–1957) English critic (*Aspects of Literature* 1920).

Museum of Modern Art, New York, established 1929.

Museums Association, London, founded 1889.

Musgrave, Thea (1928–) Scottish composer. Her early works were often on Scottish themes. Later compositions, often in serial form, include choral works and concertos.

Music printing first complete collection of part-songs printed from movable type issued *c.*1498 by Ottaviano dei Petrucci (1466–1539).

Musil, Robert (1880–1942) Austrian writer (*The Man Without Qualities* 1930–42).

Muslim Era began 16 July 622.

Musset, Alfred de (1810–57) French playwright (*Les Nuits* 1835–36).

Mussolini, Benito [Amilcare Andrea] (1883–1945) Italian dictator. Originally a socialist, he founded his fascist 'Blackshirt' party in 1919, and was elected to parliament in 1921, establishing himself as dictator ('Il Duce') in 1922. He formed the Axis with Hitler in 1937 and declared war on the Allies in 1940. He was deposed in 1943 and arrested. He was rescued by the Germans 1943 and later executed by partisans.

Mussorgsky *or* **Moussorgsky, Modest Petrovich** (1839–81) Russian composer. His best-known works include the opera *Boris Godunov* (1874) and the piano piece 'Pictures at an Exhibition'.

Mustafa Kemal [Kemal Atatürk] (1880–1938) Turkish soldier and statesman (prime minister 1923–38).

Mustapha I (1591–1639) Turkish sultan (1617–18, 1622–23). He was strangled.

Mustapha II (1664–1703) Turkish sultan (1695–1703).

Mustapha III (1717–74) Turkish sultan (1757–74).

Mustapha IV (1779–1808) Turkish sultan (1807–1808). He was put to death.

Mustard gas first used by the Germans in the First World War, July 1917.

Mutation biological variation study first developed 1901 by the Dutch botanist Hugo de Vries (1848–1935).

Mutiny *Bounty* 1789, Nore 1797, *Danaë* 1800, Indian 1857–58, Curragh 1914.

Muybridge, Eadweard (1830–1904) English pioneer in the study of human and animal movement.

Muzaffar-ed-Din (1853–1907) shah of Persia (1896–1907).

Muziano, Girolamo (1530–90) Italian painter (*St Jerome*).

Muzorewa, Bishop Abel *see* SMITH, IAN.

Mycale, Battle of 479 BC a naval battle between the Greeks and the Persians, which was a victory for the Greeks.

Mycenaen Civilization in Greece 1700–1000 BC; proto-Mycenean civilization of the island of Thera (modern Santorini) destroyed by volcanic upheaval 2000–1700 BC.

Myddleton, Sir Hugh (*c.*1560–1631) English builder of 'New River'.

Myers, Frederick William Henry (1843–1901) English writer and joint-founder 1882 of the Society for Psychical Research.

Mylae, Battle of 260 BC a naval battle of the First Punic War, which was a Roman victory.

My Lai Massacre slaughter of South Vietnamese women and children by American soldiers in the hamlet of My Lai during the Vietnam War, 16 May 1968.

Myrdal, [Karl] Gunnar (1898–1987) Swedish economist. He shared the 1974 Nobel prize for economics with Hayek, largely for his work on the application of economic theory to the economies of the Third World.

Mytilene a port on the island of Lesbos in Greece. During the Peloponnesian War it was twice the scene of action. Athenians laid siege to it in 428 BC BC and the city surrendered 427 BC, and the naval battle of Mytilene 406 BC, which was an Athenian defeat, took place here.

Mytens, Daniel (*c.*1590–*c.*1647) Dutch painter (*Duke of Hamilton* 1629).

Myxomatosis first used to destroy rabbits in Australia 1950; in Britain 1952.

N

Nabokov, Vladimir Vladimirovich (1899–1977) Russian-born American novelist, who wrote in both Russian and English. His most famous novel is *Lolita* (1955).

Nabonassar, Era of (Babylonian chronology) began 26 February 747 BC, used by the Babylonian astronomers as the era from which they began their calculations. It serves in astronomical history the same purpose as the Olympiads in civil history. It was the starting point of Babylonian chronology and was adopted by the Greeks of Alexandria.

Nabonidus (d.539 BC) king of Babylon (555–539 BC). He was the last king of Babylon before its capture by Cyrus.

Nabopolassar king of Babylon (625– BC) who, with Cyaxares of Media, captured and destroyed Nineveh in 612 BC, thus ending the Assyrian Empire.

Nachtigal, Gustav (1834–85) German explorer.

Nader, Ralph (1934–) American lawyer and consumer protectionist. Nader and his followers ('Nader's Raiders') publicized many such cases of consumer abuse in the late 1960s and 70s.

Nagasaki, Japan, bombed by the Allies' second atomic bomb August 1945.

Nagy, Imre (1895–1958) Hungarian Communist statesman. He was appointed prime minister (1953–55) and forced to resign after attempting to liberalize communist policies. He became premier again in 1956, but was replaced after the Soviet invasion of that year. He was executed.

Naidu, Sarajini (1879–1949) Indian politician.

Naipaul, Vidiadhar Surajprasad (1932–) British Trinidad-born writer of Indian descent (*A House for Mr Biswas* 1961).

Nairne, Caroline, Baroness Nairne (1766–1845) Scottish ballad writer (*Charlie is My Darling*).

Namier, Lewis (1888–1960) Polish-born historian.

Nanak (1469–1538) Indian religious leader, founder of the Sikh religion.

Nancy, Battle of a battle between the Duke of Lorraine and Charles the Bold, 5 January 1477.

Nanga Parbat, Himalayas, climbed by a German Austrian expedition 3 July 1953.

Nansen, Fridtjof (1861–1930) Norwegian explorer, scientist and statesman. He traversed Greenland (1888–89) and almost reached the North Pole in 1895, achieving a record latitude. He was appointed commissioner for refugees (1920–22) by the League of Nations and awarded the 1922 Nobel Peace Prize.

Nantes, Edict of a treaty, signed by Henri IV of France 1598, that gave recognition and legal status to the Protestant Huguenots. it was revoked by Louis XIV, 20 October 1685, whereupon about 400,000 Huguenots took refuge in Britain or Holland. The rise of the textile industries in England dates from this influx of skilled workers.

Napier, Sir Charles (1786–1860) naval strategist and politician.

Napier, John (1550–1617) Scottish inventor 1614 of logarithms.

Napier, Sir William (1785–1860) Irish-born historian of the Peninsular War.

Naples ruled by Normans 1139–94, by Angevins 1265–1382, by Aragonese 1442–1501, by Spain 1503–1707, by Austria 1707–34, by Bourbons 1734–99, 1815–60.

Napoleon Buonaparte emperor of France (consul 1799; emperor 1804; king of Italy 1805; abdicated 1814; defeated at Waterloo and banished to St Helena 1815).

Napoleon I [Napoleon Bonaparte] (1769–1821) (consul 1799; emperor 1804; king of Italy 1805; abdicated 1814) emperor of France (1804–15). A brilliant and ruthless military leader, he established an empire throughout Europe, defeating coalitions of the other major powers. His invasion of Russia in 1812, and the murderous campaign in the Pyrenees against Wellington's forces, led to the defeat of his armies at Leipzig in 1813 and Allied victory in 1814. Napoleon retired to Elba, from whence, in 1815, he came back to France, beginning the 'Hundred Days' campaign which resulted in his defeat at Waterloo, and subsequent banishment to St Helena, where he died.

Napoleon II (1811–32) king of Rome, duke of Reichstadt and son of Napoleon and his second wife, Marie Louise.

Napoleon III (1808–73) president of France (1848–51) and emperor (1852–70). Nephew of Napoleon I, he was elected president after the revolution of 1848 and took the oath of allegiance to the republic, but in 1852 he revived the National Guard and a few months later was proclaimed Emperor. He joined in the Crimean War against Russia and helped Italy against Austria in 1859, but surrendered to the Prussians at Sedan in 1870.

Napoleonic Wars waged between the Allies and the French 1799 to 1815.

Naram-Sin 2600 BC son of Sargon, founder of the Akkadian Empire in Mesopotamia.

Narses (*c.*478–*c.* 573) Byzantine general.

Narvik, Norway, scene of unsuccessful Allied expedition, World War II, 28 May–9 June 1940.

NASA (National Aeronautics and Space Administration) US government agency that coordinates the US space programme, founded 1958.

Naseby, Battle of a battle of the English Civil War, 14 June 1645, when the Parliamentarians under Cromell and Fairfax were victorious over the Royalists under Charles I and Prince Rupert.

Nash, 'Beau' [Richard Nash] (1674–1762) master of ceremonies at Bath.

Nash, John (1752–1835) English architect.

Nash, Paul (1889–1946) English painter.

Nashe, Thomas (1567–1601) English writer of pamphlets and tracts on various subjects, which were usually satirical and often contained barbs directed against his many literary and religious enemies. He was particularly virulent against the Puritans. His works include *Pierce Penilesse* (1592).

Nasmyth, James (1808–90) Scottish engineer.

Nasr-ed-Nir (*c.*1831–1896) shah of Persia (1848–96). He was assassinated.

Nasser, Gamal Abdel (1918–70) Egyptian soldier and statesman. He took a leading part in the coup that deposed King Farouk (1920–65) in 1952, and became prime minister in 1954. He became president (1956–70) and precipitated the Suez Crisis by nationalizing the Suez Canal (1956).

Natal annexed to Cape Colony 1844; made a British colony 1856; merged in the Union of South Africa 1910.

Nathan's theatrical costumiers established in London 1790.

Nation, Carry (1846–1911) American temperance advocate.

Nation, The British periodical founded 1907; absorbed into the *New Statesman* 1931.

National Assembly of France formed 1789; renamed Constituent Assembly 1789; replaced by the Legislative Assembly 1791.

National Debt the money borrowed by the government for national purposes for which ordinary revenue does to suffice. It began definitely 1694.

National Farmer's Union, London, founded 10 December 1908.

National Gallery, London, founded 1824.

National Guard, USA, founded 1903.

National Health Service, Great Britain, came into effect 5 July 1948.

Nationalization of the Bank of England 1946.

National Park, Britain's first, started by a gift of 300 acres near Snowdon 1935.

National Physical Laboratory, Great Britain, founded 1899.

National Playing Fields Association, Great Britain, granted charter 3 January 1933.

National Portrait Gallery, London, founded 1857; opened 1859.

National Rifle Association founded 1860 in Wimbledon; moved to Bisley 1890.

National Rifle Association of America powerful pro-gun lobby established in 1871.

National Savings Movement, Great Britain, founded 1916.

National Socialism, Germany, founded 1919.

National Socialist German Workers Party (Nazis) founded by Adolf Hitler 1919.

National Socialist Party, Germany, founded 1843.

National Society for the Prevention of Cruelty to Children, London, founded 1884.

National Sporting Club, Great Britain, founded 1891.

National Theatre *see* ROYAL NATIONAL THEATRE.

National Trust for places of historic interest or natural beauty, Great Britain, founded 1895.

National Trust for Scotland for places of historic interest or natural beauty, founded 1931.

National University of Ireland, Dublin, came into being 31 October 1909. Previously Royal University of Ireland, founded 1882, superseding the Queen's University in Ireland, founded 1849.

NATO (North Atlantic Treaty Organization) mutual defence pact between 13 European nations and the USA, signed 4 April 1949.

Nattier, Jean Marc (1685–1766) French painter (*Portrait a Lady of in Blue*).

Nature British periodical began publication 1869 under the editorship of Sir Joseph Norman Lockyer (1836–1920.

Nature Conservancy, Great Britain, set up 1949.

Naundorff, Karl Wilhelm (d.1845) pretender to the throne of France.

Naupactus, Battle of 429 BC a naval battle of the Peloponnesian War, which was an Athenian victory.

'Nautical Almanac' a volume of tables and calcuations for the use of sailors and astronomers, published yearly since 1767.

Nautilus, USS first atomic-powered submarine launched January 1954.

Naval Architects, Institution of, London, founded 1860.

Naval Limitation Conference, Washington DC, held 1921–22.

Navarino, Battle of between the Allied and Egyptian fleets, 20 October 1827.

Navarrete, Battle of between the Black Prince and Spanish rebels, 13 April 1367.

Navratilova, Martina (1956–) Czech-born American tennis player. Regarded as the one of the world's greatest tennis players, she defected to the US in 1975.

Nayler, James (*c.*1617–1660) English Quaker.

Nazianzen, Saint Gregory (*c.*330–390).

Nazis German National Socialists movement founded 1919.

NBC (National Broadcasting Company) American radio and TV network (one of the 'Big Three' with CBS and ABC), established 1926.

Neal, Daniel (1678–1743) English historian of New England.

Neale, John Mason (1818–66) English hymn-writer (*Jerusalem the Golden* 1865).

Neander, Johnson August Wilhelm (1789–1850) German theologian.

Neanderthal Man remains discovered near Dusseldorf 1856.

Nebraska state of the USA, discovered by Francisco Vasquez de Coronado 1541; sold to the USA by France 1803; first settled 1847; admitted to the Union 1867.

Nebraska University, Lincoln, founded 1867; opened 1871.

Nebuchadnezzar *or* **Nebuchadrezzar** king of Babylon (605–562 BC) and the most famous ruler of his day. He defeated the Egyptian army at Carchemish in 605 BC, gaining power over the whole of the Middle East. He conquered Judah 597 BC and made it a vassal state with Zedekiah as puppet king and took Jehoiachin, the king, Ezekiel and others into exile in Babylon. Because of Jewish rebellion, he again attacked Jerusalem, looting the Temple and exiling many more of its leading people. The final siege in 586 BC was long, ruthless and thorough. When the city fell, his army broke down the walls, razed the Temple and other buildings, plundered all that was of value and carried off the remaining citizens to exile in Babylon. It is regarded as the darkest day in Jewish history. He took Tyre in 585 BC.

Nebula in Andromeda described by the Arab astronomer Al Sufi before 1000.

Necker, Jacques (1732–1804) Swiss-born French financier who began as a bank clerk and accumulated a fortune as a banker. He was appointed to the French treasury in 1776 and his exposure of abuses made him so many enemies that he retired to Switzerland but he was recalled in 1788. His removal in the following year led to the storming of the Bastille and he was again recalled.

Nechton (d.*c.*724) king of picts (706–724) *see* Appendix.

Neco *or* **Necho** (1) king of Egypt (*c.*750 BC) who was dethroned by Sabacon, the Ethiopian usurper. His son, Psammetichus, fled to Egypt and subsequently regained the throne. (2) (d.601) king of Egypt (617–601 BC) During his reign he authorized a circumnavigation of Africa that took two years to complete, sailing from the Arabian Gulf and returning through the Straits of Gibraltar. He followed the career of conquests towares the northeast for which his father had opened the way and formed a navy. He defeated and killed Josiah of Judah at Megiddo 608 BC but in turn was defeated by Nebuchadnezzar at Carchemish 605 BC.

Necker, Jacques (1732–1804) French statesman and financier.

Needle and Thread Ceremony, Queen's College, Oxford University, 1 January each year.

Negus a drink of hot, sweet wine and water, invented 1704 by the English soldier Colonel Francis Negus (*c.*1665–1732).

Nehemiah (*fl* 5th century BC) Jewish exile from Jerusalem who became caupbearer to Artaxerxes I of Persia. He was appointed governor of Judah and began the rebuilding of the walls of Jerusalem 445 BC.

Nehru, Pandit Jawaharlal (1889–1964) Indian nationalist leader and statesman. The son of the nationalist lawyer, Motilal Nehru ('Pandit' Nehru) (1861–1931), he joined the Indian National Congress in 1919 and was imprisoned many times in the 1930s and 40s for his nationalist views. He became the first prime minister of India (1947–64) following independence and the partition of the subcontinent into India and Pakistan. His daughter Indira Gandhi became prime minister in 1966.

Nekrasov, Nikolai Alekseievich (1821–77) Russian poet.

Nelson, Horatio, Lord [Viscount Nelson] (1758–1805) English naval commander. Renowned for his tactics, he became rear-admiral in 1797 after defeating the Spanish fleet at the battle of Cape St Vincent. The following year, he won a striking victory over the French at the battle of the Nile, and was killed by a sniper during his defeat of the French at Trafalgar in 1805.

Nemours, Louis, Duc de (1814–96) French soldier.

Nennius (*fl* 8th century) Welsh writer (*Historia Britonum*).

Neodymium metallic element discovered 1885 by the Austrian chemist Baron von Welsbach (1858–1929).

Neon a gaseous element discovered 1898 as existing in the atmosphere by the Scottish scientist Sir William Ramsay (1852–1916).

Nepal independent kingdom, conquered by the Gurkhas 1768; constitutional monarchy since 1951.

Nepomuk, Saint John of (d.1393) national hero of Bohemia. He was killed.

Nepos, Cornelius (*c.*100–*c.*25 BC) Roman biographer.

Nepos, Julius (d. 480) Roman emperor (474–475).

Neptune the eighth planet from the sun, the position of which was predicted 1845 by the English astronomer John Couch Adams (1819–92) and 1846 by the French astronomer Urbain Leverrier (1811–77); observed 23 September 1846 by the German astronomer Johann Gottfried Galle (1812–1910).

Neri, Saint Filippo (1515–95).

Nernst, Walther(1864–1941) German physicist.

Nero, Tiberias Claudius (37–68) Roman emperor (54–68). He succeeded Claudius and soon became infamous for his debauchery, vanity and paranoia. He had many people put to death or forced to kill themselves. He committed suicide.

Neruda, Jan (1834–91) Czech writer (*Mala Strana* 1878).

Nerva (*c.*30–98) Roman emperor (96–98).

Nerval, Gérard de [Gérard Labrunie] (1808–55) French writer (*Voyage en Orient* 1848–50).

Nervi, Pier Luigi (1891–1979) Italian architect and engineer. An exponent of the virtues of reinforced concrete, his designs include the Pirellie skyscraper in Milan.

Nesbit, Edith (1858–1924) English children's writer (*The Treasure Seekers* 1899).

Nesselrode, Karl Robert, Count (1780–1862) Russian statesman.

Nestorian Church Middle Eastern religious movement dating from the deposition 431 of Nestorius (d.*c.*451), patriarch of Constantinople (428–431).

Netherlands, The revolt against Spain (1572–1609), war with Spain (1621–48); republic 1650–72, 1702–47; French domination 1795–1813; restored as an independent monarchy 1814; Belgian provinces seceded 1830; new constitution granted 1848, revised constitution granted 1917.

Neuhof, Theodor, Baron von (1686–1756) German king of Corsica (1736–43).

Neuilly, Treaty of between the Allies and Bulgaria, signed 1919.

Neumann, Alfred (1895–1952) German writer (*Alfred de Musset* 1925).

Neutrons nuclear particles discovered 1932 by the English scientist Sir James Chadwick (1891–1974).

Nevada state of the USA, first settled 1849; created a Territory 1861; admitted to the Union 1864.

Nevada University, Reno, founded 1873; opened 1874.

Neville, George (*c.*1433–1476) archbishop of York and chancellor of England.

Neville's Cross, Battle of between the Northern Levies and the Scottish armies, 17 October 1346.

Nevin, Ethelbert Woodbridge (1862–1901) American composer (*Narcissus* 1891).

Nevinson, Henry Woodd (1856–1941) English journalist.

New Amsterdam early name of New York City until 1664.

Newberry Library, Chicago, founded by the will of the American financier Walter Loomis Newberry (1804–68).

Newbolt, Sir Henry (1862–1938) English writer (*Drake's Drum* 1914).

New Caledonia, South Pacific, discovered by Captain James Cook 1774; annexed by France 1853.

Newcastle, William Cavendish, Duke of (1592–1676) Royalist supporter.

New College, Oxford University, founded 1379 by William of Wykeham (1324–1404).

Newcomen, Thomas (1663–1729) English engineer and inventor who invented the earliest practical type of steam engine, which was used for pumping water from mines.

New Daily, The British newspaper founded 1960.

New Deal, USA, President Roosevelt's legislative policy 1933 onwards.

New Delhi Indian capital, construction began 1911; opened officially 10 February 1931.

Newdigate Prize, Oxford University, for English verse endowed 1805 by Sir Roger Newdigate (1719–1806).

New England Confederation formed 1643; dissolved 1684.

New Forest, England, named by William the Conqueror 1079; scheduled as a National Park 1877.

Newfoundland discovered by John Cabot 1497; annexed by England 1583; constituted a Dominion 1917; created a Province of Canada 1949.

Newgate London prison, rebuilt 1770–83 by the English architect George Dance the younger (1741–1825); demolished 1902–1903.

New Guinea *see* PAPUA NEW GUINEA.

New Hampshire state of the USA, first settled 1623; entered the Union 1788.

New Hebrides *see* VANUATU.

New Jersey state of the USA, first settled in the early 17th century; entered the Union 1787.

Newman, Ernest (1868–1959) English music critic (*The Life of Richard Wagner* 1933–37).

Newman, Cardinal John Henry (1801–90) English

theologian and writer. His spirited defence of his faith, *Apologia pro Vita Sua* (1864), was much admired by believers and non-believers alike. Converted to Catholicism in 1845, he became a cardinal in 1879.

Newman, Paul (1925–) American film actor. His films include *Hud* (1963), *Cool Hand Luke* (1967), *Butch Cassidy and the Sundance Kid* (1969) and *The Color of Money* (1986), the last earning him an Oscar. A political activist of the moderate left, he has also raised considerable sums of money for charity through sales of his own-name salad dressing.

Newmarch, Mrs Rosa (1857–1940) English music critic (*Promenade Concert Notes*).

Newmarket English racing centre, first developed as such by King Charles I.

New Mexico state of the USA, first settled 1598; annexed to NewSpain 1771; made a Territory 1850; admitted to the Union 1912.

Newnes, Sir George English newspaper and magazine publisher (1851–1910).

New Orleans, Louisiana, founded *c.*1718 by the French Canadian explorer Jean Baptiste le Mayne, Sieur de Bienville (1680–1768).

Newport, Rhode Island, USA, first settled 1639.

'New River', London, built between 1609 and 1613 by the English goldsmith Sir Hugh Myddleton (*c.*1560–1631).

News Chronicle formed by amalgamation of the *Daily News* and the *Daily Chronicle* 1930. Incorporated in the *Daily Mail* 1960.

News of the World founded 1 October 1843.

Newsfilms introduced 1911 by the French photographer Charles Pathé (1873–1957).

New South Wales, Australia, declared British by Cook on 23 August 1770; first free settlers arrived 1793.

Newspaper advertisement duty abolished in Britain 1853.

Newspaper stamp tax introduced in Britain 1712; abolished 1855.

Newspaper, first British daily, the *Daily Courant*, began 11 March 1702.

Newspapers first printed on a train (the *Grand Trunk Herald*), produced by the American inventor Thomas Alva Edison (1847–1931).

New Statesman British periodical founded 1913; absorbed *The Nation* 1931; now called *New Statesman and Society*.

New Stone Age six to eight thousand years ago.

New Style British calendar (Gregorian) introduced September 1752.

Newton, Huey (1942–89) American black activist, cofounder of the Black Panther Party. He was assassinated.

Newton, Sir Isaac (1642–1727) English scientist, philosopher and mathematician. According to legend, observing the fall of an apple inspired him to discover the law of gravity. He also discovered (independently of Leibnitz) the differential calculus, the reflecting telescope, and devised the three laws of motion. His works include *Principia* (1687).

Newton, Thomas (1704–82) English divine.

New Year's Day 1 January.

New York City founded as New Amsterdam 1626.

New York Herald Tribune American newspaper founded as *The New York Tribune* 1841 by the American editor Horace Greeley (1811–72).

New York Public Library founded 1895.

New York State, USA, first settled by the Dutch 1614; came under English rule 1664; entered the Union 1788.

New York Times American newspaper founded 1851 by the American editor and politician Henry Jarvis Raymond (1820–69) called the *New York Daily Times* 1851–57.

New York University founded 1831.

New Yorker, The American literary magazine founded in 1925 by editor Harold Ross (1892–1951).

New Zealand discovered 925 by the Polynesian explorer Kupe; rediscovered 1642 by the Dutch navigator Abel Janszoon Tasman (1603–59; declared a dominion 1907; national day 6 February, celebrating the signing with the Maoris of the Treaty of Waitangi 1840.

Nexö, Martin Andersen (1869–1954) Danish novelist (*Ditte* 1917–21).

Ney, Michel [Duc d'Elchingen, Prince de la Moskova] (1769–1815) marshal of France who was a prominent commander in the Napoleonic Wars. He won the battle of Lutzen and had five horses shot from under him at Waterloo. He was executed for treason, having taken the oath of allegiance to the Bourbon dynasty after the abdication of Napoleon.

Niagara Falls first crossed on a tightrope 30 June 1859 by the French acrobat Charles Blondin (1824–97) who crossed it again on stilts in 1860. He also walked across in a sack, wheeled a barrow across, turned somersaults, cooked his dinner and carried a man over on his back.

Niall of the Nine Hostages (d.405) high king of Ireland (379–405) *see* Appendix.

Nibelungenlied German epic poem compiled *c.*1160.

Nicaea, First Council of ecumenical council convened 325.

Nicaea, Second Council of ecumenical council convened 787.

Nicaragua colonized by the Spanish from 1520s; achieved independence from Spain 1821; became an independent republic 1838; guerilla war led by Augusto Cesar Sandino against American occupation 1927–33; Anastasio Somoza assumed presidency 1936, followed by his sons; 1979 Somoza dynasty overthrown by Sandinista Liberation Front; Sandinistas lost parliamentary majority in free elections 1990.

Niccoli, Niccolò (1364–1437) Italian humanist and book collector.

Nice (Nizza) elected by plebiscite to be annexed to France 1860.

Nicene Creed believed to be fundamentally the work of St Cyril of Jerusalem (*c.*315–386); promulgated at Nicaea 325.

Nicephorus, Saint (190–258). He was martyred.

Nicephorus I (d.811) Byzantine emperor (802–811). He was killed in battle.

Nicephorus II [Phocas] (*c.*912–969) Byzantine emperor (963–969). He was assassinated.

Nicephorus III [Botaniates] Byzantine emperor 1078–81).

Nicholas I, Saint (d.867) pope (858–867).

Nicholas II [Gerard] pope (1059–61).

Nicholas III [Giovanni Guetano Orsini] (d.1280) pope (1277–80).

Nicholas IV [Girolamo Masci] (d.1293) pope (1288–93).

Nicholas IV [Pietro Rainalducci] (d.1333) anti-pope (1328–30).

Nicholas V [Tomaso Parentucelli] (1398–1455) pope (1447–55).

Nicholas I (1796–1855) emperor of Russia (1825–55).

Nicholas II (1868–1918) Russian tsar (1895–1917). A weak ruler, alternating between bursts of liberalization and repression, his authority was seriously weakened by Russia's defeat in the war with Japan (1904–5). He was deposed by the Bolsheviks in 1917, who later murdered him and his family.

Nicholson, Jack (1937–) American film star and director (*One Flew Over the Cuckoo's Nest* 1975).

Nicholson, John (1812–57) Irish-born general in India. He died of wounds.

Nicholson, Sir William (1872–1949) English artist (*W. E. Henley*).

Nicias, Peace of 421 BC between Athens and Sparta, ending the first part of the Peloponnesian War, effected by the Greek statesman Nicias (executed 413 BC).

Nickel carbonyl a gas discovered 1899 by the German-born chemist Ludwig Mond (1839–1909).

Nickel discovered 1754 by the Swedish scientist Baron Cronstedt (1722–65).

Nicklaus, Jack [William] (1940–) American golfer. One of the greatest golfers of all time, he won more major tournaments than any other player in history.

Nicobar Islands, Bay of Bengal, annexed by Britain 1869; centrally administered by the government of India from 1956 to date.

Nicolai, Otto (1810–49) German composer (*The Merry Wives of Windsor* 1849).

Nicolls, Richard (1624–72) first English governor (1664–67) of New York. He was killed.

Nicol prism polarization of light invented 1828 by the Scottish physicist William Nicol (*c.*1768–1851).

Nicopolis, Battle of (1) 66 BC a battle of the Third Mithridatic War, which was a victory for the Romans under Pompey. (2) 47 BC a battle between a Roman force and Pharnaces II, which was a victory for Pharnaces.

Nicot, Jean (*c.*1530–1600) French diplomat, introduced tobacco into France.

Niebuhr, Reinhold (1892–1971) American theologian.

Nielsen, Carl [August] (1865–1931) Danish composer. The first prominent polytonal Danish composer, his works include six symphonies, two operas and concertos.

Niemöller, Martin (1892–1984) German Lutheran pastor. An outspoken opponent of Hitler and Nazi ideology, he was imprisoned in concentration camps (1937–45). He was president of the World Council of Churches (1961–68) and a prominent pacifist.

Niepce, Nicéphore (1765–1833) French physician and pioneer in photography.

Nietzsche, Friedrich Wilhelm (1844–1900) German philosopher and poet, whose works were highly critical of traditional morality and Christianity and proclaimed the advent of the superman. He has been very influential on many 20th-century writers and was claimed by Hitler to be a spiritual forebear of Nazism, but Nietzsche, who despised anti-Semitism, would have rejected this. His works include *Also Sprach Zarathustra* (1883–85).

Niger navigated by Mungo Park 1795.

Niger, West Africa, made a French colony 1922; became fully independent republic 1960.

Nigeria former British colony, achieved independence within the Commonwealth 1960.

Nightingale, Florence (1820–1910) English pioneer in the training of nurses.

Nightingale Training School first British training school for nurses founded by Florence Nightingale at St Thomas's Hospital, London, 1860.

'Night of the Long Knives' Nazi purge in Germany, 30 June 1934.

Nihilism Russian revolutionary movement founded *c.*1860.

Nijinsky, Vaslav (1890–1950) Russian ballet dancer and choreographer. He became a protégé of

Diaghilev and is regarded as one of the greatest ballet dancers of all time.

Nikisch, Artur (1855–1922) Hungarian conductor.

Nile, Battle of the (Battle of Aboukir Bay) between the British and the French, 1 August 1798.

Nile Bridge, Cairo, built by the British engineer Sir William Arrol (1839–1913).

Nile, Source of the discovered 1862 by the English explorer John Hanning Speke (1827–64 and Colonel James Augustus Grant (1827–92).

Nine Lessons and Nine Carols festival held at King's College Chapel, Cambridge, each year on Christmas Eve.

Nineveh an ancient city of the Middle East and capital of Assyria; captured and destroyed 612 BC by Nabopolassar of Babylon and Cyaxares of Media, ending the Assyrian empire; excavated 1845–47 by the archaeologist and diplomat Sir Austen Henry Layard (1817–94).

Ninian, Saint (*c.*360–432).

'Ninon de Lenclos' [Anne Lenclos] (1620–1705) French courtesan.

Niobium (columbium) chemical element isolated 1801 by the English chemist Charles Hatchett (*c.*1765–1847).

Nitrogen discovered 1772 by the Scottish physician Daniel Rutherford (1749–1819).

Nitrogen trichloride discovered 1811 by the French scientist Pierre Louis Dulon (1785–1838).

Nitroglycerine manufacture perfected *c.*1860 by the Swedish chemist Alfred Nobel (1833–96).

Nitroprussides discovered 1841 by the Scottish chemist Lord Playfair (1818–98).

Nitrous oxide first used 1844 as an anaesthetic in dentistry by the American dentist Horace Wells (1815–48).

Niven, David [James David Graham Nevins] (1909–83) Scottish film actor who established himself as the model urbane Englishman in many Hollywood productions.

Nixon, Richard Milhous (1913–94) American Republican politician. The 37th president of the US (1969-74) he became the first president to resign from office, in 1974, following the 'Watergate' scandal. He was pardoned in 1974. While in office, he ended the Vietnam war and established rapprochement with China.

Nkrumah, Kwame (1909–72) Ghanaian statesman. He was the first president of Ghana (1957–66) after independence.

Noailles, Adrien Maurice, Duc de (1678–1766) French soldier.

Nobel, Alfred (1833–96) Swedish chemist and philanthropist.

Nobel Peace Prize founded by Alfred Nobel 1895.

Nobile, Umberto (1885–1978) Italian explorer.

Noguchi, Hideyo (1876–1928) Japanese bacteriologist.

Nolan, Sir Sidney [Robert] (1917–92) Australian painter. His paintings draw heavily upon Australian history and folklore.

Nollekens, Joseph (1737–1823) British sculptor (*King George III*).

Non-Euclidean geometry founded 1829 by the Russian mathematician Nicholas Lobachevsky (1793–1856).

Nonjurors British clergymen who refused to take the oath of allegiance 1689–1805.

No Plays Japanese traditional plays dating from 15th century.

Nordenskjöld, Otto (1869–1928) Swedish explorer and scholar.

Norfolk, Hugh Bigod, Earl of (d.*c.*1177) crusader.

Norfolk Island, South Pacific, discovered by Captain James Cook 1774; settled 1856; made an external territory of Australia 1913.

Norham, Peace of between Scotland and England, held 1209.

Norman Conquest of England by William the Conqueror 1066.

Norman, Conolly (1853–1908) Irish alienist and reformer.

Norman, Montagu Collet, Baron Norman (1871–1950) governor of the Bank of England (1920–44).

Normandy founded 911.

Normandy, Alphonse René le Mire de (1809–64) French-born chemist and inventor 1851 of a distiller for sea water.

Normandy Offensive World War II began 6 June 1944.

Norris, Frank (1870–1902) American novelist (*The Pit* 1903).

Norroy King of Arms post established in the 13th century.

Norsemen *see* VIKINGS.

'North, Christopher' [John Wilson] (1785–1854) Scottish writer (*Recreations* 1842).

North, Frederick, 8th Lord North [2nd Earl of Guilford] (1732–92) English statesman. As prime minister (1770–82) during the reign of George III, he implemented the king's policy that led to the loss of the American colony.

North, Sir Thomas (*c.*1525–*c.*1601) English translator (Plutarch's *Lives* 1579).

Northampton, Treaty of recognizing the independence of Scotland, signed 1328.

North Atlantic Treaty signed at Washington DC, 4 April 1949; amended in London by protocol 17 October 1951.

North Carolina state of the USA, first settled 1585; permanently settled 1663; entered the Union 1789.

North Channel between Scotland and Northern Ireland swum 1947 for the first time by Tom Blower of Nottingham.

Northcliffe, Alfred Charles William Harmsworth, Viscount (1865–1922) Irish-born newspaper owner.

Northcote, Henry Stafford Northcote, Baron (1846–1911) governor-general (1903–1907) of Australia.

North Dakota state of the USA, first settled 1766; formed part of the Dakota Territory 1861; admitted to the Union 1889.

Northeast Passage a shipping route between the Atlantic and Pacific Oceans, along the Arctic coasts of Europe and Asia, first navigated 1878–79 by the Swedish explorer Nils Adolf Erik Nordenskiöld (1832–1901).

Northern Ireland administration by separate parliament and executive government established by the Government of Ireland Act, 1920; 1969–70 violence between Protestant and Catholic communities erupted, British troops eventually stationed to prevent bloodshed, provoking terrorist campaign from IRA; Northern Irish parliament suspended 1972 and replaced by Direct Rule from London.

Northern Territory, Australia, formerly part of New South Wales, annexed to South Australia 1863; placed under the control of a Commonwealth Administrator 1931; now an administrative division of northern central Australia.

Northern Underground Line London, opened 1904 as the Great Northern and City Railway.

Northern Wei Dynasty, China, 386.

Northmen *see* VIKINGS.

North Pole first reached 6 April 1909 by the American explorer Robert Edwin Peary (1856–1920; first flown over 1926 by the American aviator Richard E. Byrd (1888–1957; atomic-powered *Nautilus*, first submarine to reach it underwater 1958; first successful dogsled expedition 1968–69; first person to reach it alone by dogsled, Japanese Naomi Uemura, 1978.

North Staffordshire, University College of, Keele, founded 1949.

Northumberland, Henry Percy, Earl of (1342–1408) marshal of England. He was killed in battle.

Northumberland, Thomas Percy, Earl of (1528–72) rebel. He was beheaded.

Northumbria an Anglo-Saxon kingdom that stretched from the River Humber to the Firth of Forth, which was formed in the 7th century and lasted until 876.

Northwest Frontier Province, northern Pakistan, part of British India 1901–47.

Northwest Mounted Police, Canada, formed 1873; renamed the Royal Canadian Mounted Police 1920.

Northwest Ordinance for the government of US Western territories passed 1787.

Northwest Passage discovered 1850–54 by the British navigator Sir Robert John le Mesurier McClure (1807–73).

Northwest Territories, Canada, administered by a commissioner since 1952.

Northwestern University, Illinois, founded 1851.

Norton, Thomas (1532–84) English poet (with Sackville *Gorboduc* 1561).

Norway united with Sweden 1319–55, with Denmark 1380–89, with Sweden and Denmark 1389–1450, with Denmark 1450–1814, with Sweden 1814–1905; independent kingdom since 1905; German occupation 1940–45.

Norwich granted first charter by King Henry II 1158.

Norwich Cathedral constructed 1096 to *c.*1150.

Nostradamus [Michel de Notredame] (1503–66) French astrologer and physician. In 1555 he published the first of two books of cryptic prophecies in rhymed quatrains ('centuries') which enjoyed a huge vogue.

Notium, Battle of 407 BC a naval battle of the Peloponnesian War which was an Athenian defeat.

Notke, Bernt (*c.*1440–1509) German artist (*St George and the Dragon* 1489).

Notre Dame de Paris constructed 1163–82.

Nottingham, Charles Howard, Earl of (1536–1624) Lord High Admiral.

Nottingham University opened as University College 1881; achieved university status 1948.

'Novalis' [Friedrich von Hardenberg] (1772–1801) German poet (*Hymnen an die Nacht* 1798–1800).

Nova Scotia first settled by the French in the early century; ceded to Britain 1713; became a province of Canada 1867.

Novatian anti-pope (251).

Novello, Ivor [Ivor Novello Davies] (1893–1951) Welsh songwriter, composer and actor. His songs include 'Keep the Home Fires Burning', which was hugely popular with British soldiers during World War I, and 'We'll Gather Lilacs'.

Novello, Vincent (1781–1861) English music publisher.

Noverre, Jean-Georges (1727–1810) French pioneer ballet-master at the Opéra-Comique.

Novi, Battle of a battle between the Allies and the French, 15 August 1799. The French were defeated.

Noyes, Alfred (1880–1958) English poet (*Drake* 1908).

Noyes, John Humphrey (1811–86) American founder 1848 of the Oneida Community.

Noyon, Treaty of between France and Spain, signed 1516.

Nuclear disintegration in nitrogen atoms first observed by Rutherford in 1919.
Nuclear fission in uranium atoms first observed by Hahn and Strassman in 1939.
Nuclear reactor, first American, built at Chicago University December 1942 by the Italian atomic physicist Enrico Fermi (1901–54).
Nuclear reactor, first British, built at Harwell 1947.
Nuffield, William Richard Morris, 1st Viscount (1877–1963) English car manufacturer and philanthropist. He developed a Henry Ford-like system of mass production of cars, notably the Morris Oxford and the Morris Minor.
Nuffield College, Oxford University, founded 1937.
Nuffield Foundation formed 1943.
Numidia an ancient country of northern Africa; Roman victory over Jugurtha, king of Numidia 111 BC; Jugurtha captured and killed 106 BC; Roman province 46 BC; invaded by Vandals 429.
Nunez, Alvar (d.1564) Spanish navigator and discoverer 1528 of Florida.
Nunez, Pedro (1601–54) Spanish painter (*Philip IV*).
Nunna king of Sussex (*c.*710–*c.*725) see Appendix.
Nuremberg, War Crimes Tribunal Second World War held November 1945–October 1946.
Nureyev, Rudolf (1939–93) Russian ballet dancer and choreographer. Regarded as the successor to Nijinsky, he formed a famous partnership with Fonteyn in 1962.
Nuri-es-Said (1888–1958) Iraqi general and prime minister of the Arab Federation. He was assassinated.
Nurses, training of, organized by the English pioneer Florence Nightingale (1820–1910).
Nuttall, Enos (1842–1916) first archbishop of the West Indies.
Nutter, Mary (1856–1928) the last Lancashire witch.
Nyasa, Lake *see* MALAWI, LAKE.
Nyasaland *see* MALAWI.
Nyerere, Julius [Kambarage] (*c.*1922–) Tanzanian statesman. He became president (1962–85) and negotiated the union of Tanganyika and Zanzibar (1964), which formed Tanzania. Widely regarded as Africa's leading statesman, his invasion of Uganda in 1978 brought Amin's dictatorship to an end.
Nylon discovered 1927 by research workers of the American firm Du Pont de Nemours.
Nylon shirts first introduced in the USA 1939.
Nymphenburg Bavarian chateau constructed 1664; porcelain manufactured since 1747.
Nyon Conference on the suppression of Mediterranean submarine piracy held 1937.

O

Oak Apple Day 29 May, celebrating the Restoration of King Charles II, 1660.

'Oaks, The', Epsom, first run 1779.

Oates, Titus (1649–1705) English conspirator (1678).

Oath of Strasbourg sworn between Charles the Bold and Louis the German against Lothair 1842.

Oath of the Tennis Court, French Revolution, 20 June 1789.

Oberammergau, Germany, scene of the decennial presentation of the Passion Play since 1634.

Oberlin, Johann Friedrich (1740–1826) German reformer.

Obote, [Apollo] Milton (1924–) Ugandan politician. He became Uganda's first prime minister (1962–66) after independence, and became president (1966–71) after deposing King Mutesa II. He was in turn deposed by Amin and became president again (1980–85) after Amin's overthrow. He was deposed again in 1985.

O'Brien, Conor Cruise (1917–) Irish diplomat, journalist, writer and critic.

O'Brien, William Smith (1803–64) Irish patriot.

Observer*, *The British newspaper, began publication 1791.

O'Casey, Sean (1884–1964) Irish dramatist. His early plays, e.g. *Juno and Paycock* (1924), reflect the patriotism that followed the Easter Rising of 1916.

Occleve, Thomas (*c.*1369–*c.*1450) English poet (*De Regimine Principum*).

Ockham, William of (*c.*1280–*c.*1349) English-born philosopher.

O'Clery, Michael (1575–1643) Irish historian (*Annals of the Four Masters* 1632–36).

O'Connell, Daniel (1775–1847) Irish nationalist leader.

O'Connor, Cathal *see* CATHAL O'CONNOR and Appendix.

O'Connor, Rory *see* RORY O'CONNOR and Appendix.

Octa (d.*c.*540) king of Kent (*c.*512–*c.*540) *see* Appendix.

Octavia (1) (d.11 BC) wife of Mark Antony.

Octavia (2) (d.62 BC) wife of the Roman Emperor Nero. She was killed.

Octavian [Gaius Octavianus] (Augustus) (63 BC–14 AD) first emperor of Rome (27 BC–AD 14). After adoption by his uncle Julius Caesar in 44 BC, he took the name Gaius Julius Caesar Octavianus. He formed the Second Triumvirate with Antony (43–31 BC) and Lepidus (43–36 BC). A rupture between Octavian and Mark Antony was largely brought about by the ambition of the Egyptian queen, Cleopatra, with whom Antony was infatuated. Octavian defeated Mark Antony at the naval battle of Actium 31 BC. He became first emperor of Rome in 27 BC when the senate gave him the title of Augustus. A cultured tyrant, he cultivated the arts and was the patron of Virgil. He was succeeded by his stepson Tiberius.

October Revolution, Russia, 7 November 1917 (New Style).

Oddfellows, Independent Order of a temperance society founded in Manchester 1810; in the USA 1819.

Odenathus (d.266) king of Palmyra and husband of Zenobia, who was an important ally of Rome and was appointed by Gallienus governor of the East. He was murdered, probably by a nephew.

Odode Clugny, Saint (d.942) pioneer in the development of musical theory.

Odovacar (d.493) Scirian king of Italy (476–493). He was killed.

Odyssey Greek epic attributed to Homer, believed to have lived in the 11th, 10th or 9th century BC.

Oecolampadius, Johannes (1482–1531) German religious reformer.

OEEC [(Organization for European Economic Cooperation] set up 16 April 1948.

Oengas (d.761) king of Picts (728–761) *see* Appendix.

Oenoparas, Battle of 146 BC a battle between Alexander Balas and his father-in-law, Ptolemy VI, when Ptolemy defeated Alexander but was thrown from h9is horse and died a few days later.

Oersted, Hans Christian (1777–1851) Danish pioneer in electromagnetism.

Offa (1) (d.*c.*720) king of Essex (709) *see* Appendix.

Offa (2) (d.7910 king of Mercia (757–796) *see* Appendix.

Offa's Dyke Welsh border defence constructed 779 by Offa, king of Mercia.

Offenbach, Jacques [Jakdo Levy Eberst] (1819–80) German-born composer (*Tales of Hoffman* 1881).

O'Flaherty, Liam (1897–1984) Irish novelist (*The Informer* 1925).

Oglethorpe, James Edward (1696–1785) English founder (1732) of Georgia, USA.

'O Henry' *see* PORTER, WILLIAM SYDNEY.

O'Higgins, Bernardo (1776–1842) Chilean leader.

Ohio state of the USA, first settled 1788; entered the Union 1803.

Ohio Company English colonizing organization, chartered 1749.

Ohm's law of electrical resistance pronounced 1827 by the German physicist George Simon Ohm (1787–1854). His law of sound vibrations, 1843.

Ohnet, Georges (1848–1918) French writer (*Serge Panine* 1881).

Ohthere (*fl* 9th century) Norse explorer.

Oil distilled from coal and shale 1847–50 by the Scottish chemist James 'Paraffin' Young (1811–83).

Oil struck 1859 in Pennsylvania (first known drilling in the world) by the American oil prospector Colonel Edwin Laurentine Drake (1819–80).

Oil drilling rotary method first adopted in Texas *c.*1900.

Oil lighting first used for London streets 1681.

Oil tanker first 100,000 dead weight tonnage, built 1958.

Oil tanker prototype (*The Gluckauf*) built on Tyneside 1886.

Oil tanker world's first gas turbine-powered, the British GTS *Auris*, made maiden voyage 1959.

Oil well first drilled at Titusville, Pennsylvania, 1859.

Oireachtas National Parliament of the Irish Republic, founded 1937.

Oistrakh, David Feodorovitch (1908–74) Russian violinist. A widely admired virtuoso whose son, **Igor Davidovitch Oistrakh** (1931–), also has an international reputation as a violinist.

Okapi first noted 1878 by the Russian-born explorer Wilhelm Junker (1840–92).

O'Keefe, Georgia (1887–1986) American artist.

Okhotsk, East Siberia, founded 1649.

Okinawa, Battle of a battle of the Second World War, 1 April–22 June 1945.

Oklahoma a state of the USA, first settled 1887; created a Territory 1890; admitted to the Union 1907.

Olaf I (969–1000) king of Norway (995–1000). He was drowned.

Olaf II, Saint (995–1030) king of Norway (1016–29). He was killed in battle.

Olaf III (d.1093) king of Norway (1067–93).

Olaf IV (d.1116) king of Norway (1103–16).

Olaf V (d.1387) king of Norway (1381–87).

Olaf Guthfrithson (d.941) king of Dublin *see* Appendix.

Olaf the White king of Dublin (853–*c.*854) *see* Appendix.

Olaf the Red (b.*c.*920) king of Dublin (*c.*945–980) *see* Appendix.

Olav V (1903–91) king of Norway (1957–91).

Olbers, Heinrich Wilhelm Mathias (1758–1840) German astronomer.

Old Age Pensions Act, Great Britain, came into force 1 January 1909.

Oldcastle, Sir John (d.1417) English leader of the Lollards. He was executed.

Old Catholics religious movement formed 1870–71.

Oldenbarneveldt, John van (1547–1619) Dutch statesman. He was executed.

Old Pretender, The' (James Francis Edward Stewart) (1688–1766).

Old Style British calendar (Julian), superseded by New Style 1752.

Old Vic London theatre built 1818, assumed its present role 1914.

Oldys, William (1696–1761) English antiquary.

Oleic acid fat-forming acid discovered 1815 by the French scientist Michel Eugene Chevreul (1786–1889).

Olga, Saint (d.*c.*969).

Oligocene Epoch, Earth history, 45 million years ago.

Oliphant, Laurence (1829–88) South African-born writer and journalist.

Olivares, Gaspar (1587–1645) Spanish statesman.

Oliver, Isaac (*c.*1556–1617) French-born miniature painter (*James I*).

Olivier, Laurence [Kerr], [Baron Olivier of Brighton] (1907–89) English stage and film actor and director. Regarded as the leading British actor of the modern era, he played all the major Shakespeare roles and became an international film star. He was director of the National Theatre (1962–73). His second wife (of three) was Vivien Leigh.

Olmsted, Denison (1791–1859) American scientist.

Olpae, Battle of 426 BC a battle of the Peloponnesian War which was an Athenian victory.

Olympiad ancient Greek four-year period calculated by the Olympian games. The first Olympiad was held 776 BC.

Olympias (d.316 BC) wife of Philip II of Macedonia and mother of Alexander the Great. When Philip took another wife, she left Macedonia but returned on his death and the accession of Alexander. She feuded with Antipater, the regent in Alexander's absence campaigning, and subsequently with his son, Cassander, who had her put to death.

Olympic Cup instituted 1906 by Baron Pierre de Coubertin (1863–1937).

Olympic Era began 1 July 776 BC.

Olympic Games idea of revival introduced 1892 by Baron Pierre de Coubertin (1863–1937.

Olympic Games, ancient, held 776 BC to AD 394.

Olympic Games, modern, 1st Athens, Greece 1896; 2nd Paris, France 1900; 3rd St Louis, USA 1904; 4th

London, England 1908; 5th Stockholm, Sweden 1912; 6th Berlin, Germany 1916 (cancelled); 7th Antwerp, Belgium 1920; 8th Paris, France 1924; 9th Amsterdam, Netherlands 1928; 10th Los Angeles, USA 1932; 11th Berlin, Germany 1936; 12th Tokyo, Japan, and Helsinki, Finland 1940 (cancelled.); 13th London, England 1944 (cancelled); 14th London, England 1948; 15th Helsinki, Finland 1952; 16th Melbourne, Australia 1956 (equestrian sports at Stockholm); 17th Rome, Italy 1960; 18th Tokyo, Japan 1964; 19th Mexico City, Mexico 1968; 20th Munich, Germany 1972; 21st Montreal, Canada 1976; 22nd Moscow, USSR 1980 (boycotted); 23rd Los Angeles, USA 1984 (boycotted); 24th Seoul, South Korea 1988; 25th Barcelona, Spain 1992; 26th Atlanta, USA 1996.

•lympic Winter Games, official, 1st Chamonix, France 1924; 2nd St Moritz, Switzerland 1928; 3rd Lake Placid, USA 1932; 4th Garmisch-Partenkirchen, Germany 1936; 5th St Moritz, Switzerland 1948; 6th Oslo, Norway 1952; 7th Cortina d'Ampezzo, Italy 1956; 8th Squaw Valley, USA 1960; 9th Innsbruck, Austria 1964; 10th Grenoble, France 1968; 11th Sapporo, Japan 1972; 12th Innsbruck, Austria 1976; 13th Lake Placid, USA 1980; 14th Sarajevo, Yugoslavia 1984; 15th Calgary, Canada 1988; 16th Albertville, France 1992; 17th Lillehammer, Norway 1996.

•lympic Winter Games, unofficial, first London 1908; second Antwerp 1920).

•'Mahony, John (1816–77) Irish patriot.

•man, Sir Charles (1860–1946) historian.

•mar (*c.*581–644) second of the Mahommedan Caliphs. He was assassinated.

•mar Khayyam (*fl* 11th century) Persian poet (*Rubaiyat*).

•mar Pasha (1806–71) Turkish soldier and statesman.

•'Meara, Barry Edward (1786–1836) Napoleon's surgeon at St Helena.

•mpteda, Georg von (1863–1931) German novelist (*Herzeloyde* 1905).

•nassis, Aristotle Socrates (1906–75) Argentine shipowner. He married Jacqueline Bouvier Kennedy (1929–95), widow of John F. Kennedy, in 1968.

•neida Community, NY, founded 1848 by the American reformer John Humphrey Noyes (1811–86).

'Neill, Eugene [Gladstone] (1888–1953) American dramatist. His greatest play is *Long Day's Journey into Night* (1940–41), a study of family breakdown. Other works include*Strange Interlude* (1928). He was awarded the Nobel prize for literature in 1936.

'Neill, Peggy (*c.*1796–1879) American socialite.

no, Yoko *see* LENNON, JOHN.

•ntario, Canada, settled by the French; British territory from 1763; organized as Upper Canada 1791; made a province of Canada 1867.

OPEC *see* ORGANIZATION OF PETROLEUM EXPORTING COUNTRIES.

Open-hearth method of making Bessemer steel invented *c.*1866 by the electrical engineers Sir William Siemens (1823–83) and Ernst Werner von Siemens (1816–92).

Opera first real opera *La Dafne* (1597) by Rinuccini and Peri.

Operation Desert Shield, military operation by US and UN allies in Kuwait to deter further Iraq attacks on Kuwait after the Iraqi invasion of Kuwait August 1990.

Operation Desert Storm, massive air bombardment of Iraqi forces in Kuwait by US and allies during the Persian Gulf War January 1991.

Operation Overlord, codename for the Allied invasion of Normandy, 6 June 1944.

Ophthalmoscope invented 1851 by the German scientist Hermann von Helmholtz (1821–94).

Opie, Amelia Alderson (1769–1853) English writer (*Father and Daughter* 1801).

Opie, John English painter (*The Assassination of Rizzio* 1787) (1761–1807).

Opium War, China, between Britain and China, waged 1840–42.

Oppenheimer, J[ulius] Robert (1904–67) American nuclear physicist, 'father of the atomic bomb'. He resigned from the Los Alamos atom bomb project after the dropping of the bombs on Hiroshima and Nagasaki, and argued for cooperation with the USSR on the control of nuclear weapons.

Orange, William I, Prince of (William the Silent) (1533–84).

Orange, William II, Prince of (1626–50).

Orange, William III, Prince of (William III, king of England) (1650–1702).

Orange Free State, South Africa, first settled *c.*1810; proclaimed British Territory 1848; independence recognized 1854; finally created a Province of the Union of South Africa 1910.

Orangemen Irish Protestant association formed by 1795.

Oratorians religious order founded 1575 by St Filippo Neri (1515–95).

Oratorio, first, deemed to have been composed 1600 by the Italian composer Emilio del Cavalieri (*c.*1550–1602).

Oratory, The, Birmingham, founded 1847.

Oratory, The (Brompton Oratory), London, founded 1850.

Orcagna (*c.*1308–1368) Italian artist whose masterpiece and only certain dated work is the altarpiece,

The Redeemer with the Madonna and Saints (1354–57), in the Church of Santa Maria Novella in Florence.

Orchardson, Sir William (1832–1910) Scottish painter (*Napoleon on board the* Bellerophon 1880).

Orchomenus, Battle of 85 BC a battle of the First Mithridatic War when the Roman army under Sulla was victorious over Mithridates.

Ordericus Vitalis (1075–*c.*1143) English historian.

Ordinance of 1787 for the government of US western territories.

Ordnance Survey of Great Britain set up 1791.

Ordovician Period, Earth history, 420 million years ago.

Oregon state of the USA, first settled *c.*1830; made a Territory 1848; admitted to the Union 1859.

Oregon Trail, Missouri to Oregon, first travelled 1811.

Oregon University founded 1876.

Orff, Carl (1895–1982) German composer. His best-known work is the popular *Carmina Burana* (1937), a 'secular oratorio' based on medieval poems.

Orford, Robert Walpole, Earl of (1676–1745) English statesman.

Organization for Economic Cooperation and Development (OECD) international organization based in Paris, succeeded OEEC 1960.

Organization for European Economic Cooperation (OEEC), established 1948; superseded by OECD 1960.

Organization of American States formed 1948.

Organization of Petroleum Exporting Countries (OPEC) established 1961 to coordinate petroleum supply policies and prices.

Orgetorix (d*c.*60 BC) leader of the Helvetii against Julius Caesar.

Oriel College, Oxford University, founded by King Edward II 1326.

Origen (185–254) Alexandrean theologian.

Orinoco South American river discovered 1498 by Christopher Columbus; first explored by the Spaniard Diego de Ordaz (1531–32).

Orissa, India, conquered by the British 1803; constituted a separate Province 1936; the independent princely states merged with the State of Orissa 1949.

Orkneys passed (by default) from Danish to Scottish ownership 1468; formally annexed to the Scottish crown 1471.

Orlando, Vittorio Emanuele (1860–1952) Italian statesman.

Orleanists French political party arose *c.*1790; ceased to exist *c.*1874

Orleans relieved by Jeanne d'Arc 1429.

Orléans, Charles, Duc d' (1391–1465) French poet.

Orléans, Henri, Prince d' (1867–1901) explorer.

Orley, Bernard (*c.*1488–1541) Flemish painter (*Charles V*).

Orlov, Aleksei Feodorovich, Prince (1787–1862) Russian statesman.

Orm *or* **Ormin** (*fl.* 13th century) English poet (*Ormulum*).

Ormonde, Sir James ('Black James') (d.1497) Lord Treasurer of Ireland. He was killed.

Orosius (*fl* late 4th and early 5th centuries) Spanish historian (*Historia adversus Paganos*).

Orozco, José Clemente (1883–1949) Mexican painter.

Orpen, Sir William (1878–1931) Irish painter (*In the Wicklow Mountains*).

Orrery, Roger Boyle, Earl of (1621–79) statesman and soldier.

Orsini, Felice (1819–58) Italian patriot. After an unsuccessful attempt on the life of Napoleon III in 1858, he was executed.

Ortega [Saavedra], Daniel (1945–) Nicaraguan politician. A leader of the Sandinista resistance movement that overthrew the dictatorship in 1979, he became president (1981–90). The Reagan administration gave backing to the right-wing 'Contra' forces in their guerrilla war against the Sandinistas, and Ortega was defeated in the 1989 election.

Ortega y Gasset, José (1883–1955) Spanish philosopher who argued that democracy in the modern era could easily lead to tyrannies of either the left or right. His works include *La Rebelión de las Masas* (1930).

Orthodox Eastern Church finally separated from the Western Church 1054.

Orton, Arthur (1834–98) English pretender to the Tichbourne title.

Orton, Joe [Kingsley Orton] (1933–67) British playwright (*Entertaining Mr Sloane* 1964). He was murdered by his lover, Kenneth Halliwell, who then committed suicide.

Orwell, George [Eric Arthur Blair] (1903–50) Indian-born English novelist and essayist. His two greatest novels have become classics: *Animal Farm* (1945), a grim allegory of the history of the Soviet Union, and *Nineteen Eighty-Four* (1949), an even grimmer picture of a totalitarian world.

Osbald (d.796) king of Northumbria (796) *see* Appendix.

Osbert (d.867) king of Northumbria (850–865) *see* Appendix.

Osborne, Dorothy, Lady Temple (1627–95) wife of Sir William Temple (1628–99).

Osborne, John [James] (1929–94) English dramatist and actor. His first play, *Look Back in Anger* (1956), gave its name to the 'Angry Young Men', a group of young playwrights who replaced the drawing-room comedies of 1950s British theatre with realistic dramas of working-class life.

Oscar I (1799–1859) king of Sweden and Norway (1844–59).

Oscar II (1829–1907) king of Sweden (1872–1907) and Norway (1872–1905).

Oscillograph first devised (ondograph) by Hospitalier in 1903.

Osiander, Andreas (1498–1552) German religious reformer.

Osler, Sir William (1848–1919) Canadian professor of medicine.

Oslo, Convention of electing the Norwegian King Magnus king of Sweden, 1319.

Osman Pasha (1832–1900) Turkish field-marshal.

Osmium metallic element discovered 1803 by the English chemist Smithson Tennant (1761–1815).

Osmund king of Sussex (*c.*765–770) *see* Appendix.

Osred I (d.716) king of Northumbria (705–716) *see* Appendix.

Osred II king of Northumbria (788–790) *see* Appendix.

Osric (d.729) king of Northumbria (718–729) *see* Appendix.

'Ossian' [James Macpherson] (1736–96) Scottish poet.

Ossory, Cearbhall, Lord of (d.888) king of Dublin (875).

Ostend Manifesto concerning the future of Cuba drawn up 1854 (but was implemented).

Osteopathy founded 1874 by the American surgeon Andrew Taylor Still (1828–1917).

Ostrog Bible first Russian Bible (printed in Church Slavonic), published 1580–81 by order of Konstantin, Prince of Ostrog.

Ostwald Process for the preparation of nitric acid invented 1900 by the German scientist Wilhelm Ostwald (1853–1932).

Oswald, Saint (1) (605–642) king of Northumbria (634–642) *see* Appendix.

Oswald, Saint (2) (d.992) archbishop of York (972–992).

Oswald, Lee Harvey (1939–63) American alleged assassin of President Kennedy, 22 November 1963. He was arrested shortly after Kennedy's murder in Dallas, and was himself shot dead by **Jack Ruby** (1911–64) while in police custody, 24 November 1963, before he could come to trial.

Oswiecim *see* AUSCHWITZ.

Oswin (d.651) king of Deira (642–651) *see* Appendix.

Oswini (d.690) king of Kent (688–690) *see* Appendix.

Oswulf (d.759) king of Northumbria (759) *see* Appendix.

Oswy (602–670) king of Northumbria (651–670) *see* Appendix.

Otago New Zealand province, shore stations established 1832; first officially organized band of settlers landed 1848.

Otho (32–69) Roman emperor (69). He committed suicide.

Otis, Elisha Graves (1811–61) American inventor (particularly of lift machinery).

Ottawa, Canada, founded 1827 as Bytown by the English engineer John By (1781–1836).

Ottawa Conference Imperial Economic Conference held 21 July–20 August 1932.

Otto I (Otto the Great) (912–973) Holy Roman emperor (962–973).

Otto II (955–983) Holy Roman emperor (973–983).

Otto III (980–1002) Holy Roman emperor (996–1002).

Otto IV (*c.*1182–1218) Holy Roman emperor (1209–18).

Otto I (1815–67) king of Greece (1832–62).

Ottocar I (d.1230) king of Bohemia (1198–1230).

Ottocar II (*c.*1230–1278) king of Bohemia (1253–78). He was killed in battle.

Ottoman Empire began 1288; ended 1923 when Turkey became a republic.

Otway, Thomas (1652–85) English playwright (*Venice Preserved* 1682).

Ouchy, Treaty of by which Turkey recognized Italian sovereignty in Tripoli, signed 19 October 1912.

Oudenarde, Battle of between British and French, 11 July 1708.

'Ouida' [Marie Louise de la Ramée] (1839–1908) English novelist (*Under Two Flags* 1867).

Outlawry abolished in Britain 1879.

Outram, Benjamin (1764–1805) English civil engineer.

Outward Bound Mountain School, Eskdale, opened 1950.

Outward Bound Sea School, Aberdovey, opened autumn 1941.

Ovaries, human, nature discovered 1672 by the Dutch naturalist Jan Swammerdam (1637–80).

Overbeck, Johann Friedrich (1789–1869) German painter (*Pietà* 1846).

Overbury, Sir Thomas (1581–1613) English courtier and writer (*Characters*). He was poisoned.

Overland mail, USA, from the Mississippi River to California, authorized by Act of Congress 1857; inaugurated 15 September 1858.

Overland telegraph line completed from Darwin to Adelaide 1872.

Ovid [Publius Ovidius Naso] (43 BC–AD *c.*17) Roman poet. His sensual, witty love poems have always been admired, but his long narrative poem *Metamorphoses*, which describes myths in which characters change their forms, is of greater significance. It was used as a source book by many, e.g. Shakespeare.

Owain Gwynedd (1100–1170) king of Gwynedd (1137–70) *see* Appendix.

Owen (d.*c*.1018) king of Strathclyde *see* Appendix.

Owen, David [Anthony Llewellyn] [Baron Owen of the City of Plymouth] (1938–) English doctor and politician. Founder of the Social Democratic Party with Jenkins and others, he refused to accept the merger of the SDP with the Liberal Party in 1987, but dissolved the SDP in 1990. He was made a life peer and worked as a UN peace negotiator in the Bosnian conflict of the early 1990s.

Owen, Sir Richard (1804–92) English naturalist.

Owen, Robert (1771–1858) Welsh social reformer and pioneer of infant schools. Successful in business, he became a prominent exponent of socialist doctrines in Britain and the USA and founded many cooperative societies.

Owen, Wilfred (1893–1918) British poet and war hero ('Anthem for Doomed Youth').

Owen Falls Dam at Jinja, Uganda, opened 1954.

Owen Glendower [Owain Glyndwr] (*c*.1350–*c*.1416) Welsh rebel leader.

Owens, Jesse [James Cleveland Owens] (1913–80) American athlete. One of the finest athletes of his generation, he won four gold medals in the 1936 Berlin Olympics. Adolf Hitler left the stadium to avoid congratulating the black, non-Aryan athlete.

Owens College, now Manchester University, founded 1846 (opened 1851) by the bequest of the English merchant John Owens (1790–1846).

Oxenstierna, Count Axel Gustafsson (1583–1654) chancellor of Sweden.

OXFAM (Oxford Committee for Famine Relief) charitable Thirld World relief agency founded 1942.

Oxford, Edward de Vere, Earl of (1550–1604) English poet (to whom Shakespeare's works have been attributed).

Oxford, Robert de Vere, Earl of (1362–92) court favourite.

Oxford and Cambridge Boat Race first held 10 June 1829. First broadcast 2 April 1927.

Oxford English Dictionary (New English Dictionary) published 1884–1928; updated at regular intervals ever since.

Oxford Group religious movement founded 1921 by the American evangelist Frank Buchman (1878–1961); first so named 1929.

Oxford India paper first made at the OUP's Wolvercote Mill 1875; copied from an Indian paper brought to Oxford 1841.

Oxford Movement launched by the English divine John Keble (1792–1866) on 14 July 1833.

Oxford tracts (*Tracts for the Times*) issued in defence of the Church of England as a Divine institution 1833 onwards.

Oxford Union Society founded 1625.

Oxford University in existence before 1200; granted charter by King Henry III 1248; incorporated by Queen Elizabeth I 1570; religious tests abolished 1871; Rhodes Scholarships founded 1902; women admitted to degrees 1920.

Oxford University Observatory founded 1873.

Oxford University Press founded 1585.

Oxygen isolated 1773 by the Swedish scientist Karl Scheele (1742–86); 1774 by the English scientist Joseph Priestley (1733–1804).

Oxyhydrogen blowpipe, invented 1801 by the American chemist Robert Hare (1781–1858).

Ozone discovered 1840 by the German scientist Christian Friedrich Schönbein (1799–1868).

P

Pablos, Juan (d.*c.*1561) Italian-born first printer in the western hemisphere.

Pachmann, Vladimir de (1848–1953) Russian pianist.

Pachomius, Saint (*c.*292–*c.*346) pioneer of coenobitic monasticism.

Pacific Cable completed at Suva 31 October 1902.

Pacific Ocean first sighted September 1513 by the Spanish navigator Basco Nuñez de Balboa (*c.*1475–*c.*1517).

Pacific, War of the between Chile and Peru and Bolivia 1879 to 1884.

Packard, Alpheus Spring (1839–1905) American scientist.

Padarewski, Ignace Jan (1860–1941) Polish pianist, composer and statesman. Widely regarded as the greatest pianist of his day, he served as prime minister for ten months in 1919 and was president of the provisional Polish government (1940–41).

Padua, University of founded 1222.

Paganini, Nicolò (1782–1840) Italian violinist.

Paget, Sir James (1814–99) English surgeon.

Paget, William, Baron Paget (1505–63) British statesman and diplomat.

Pahang Peninsular Malaysia state, entered into treaty relations with Britain 1874–95; agreed with three other states to form a federation 1895; federal council of these states constituted 1909.

Pahlavi, Mohammed Reza (1919–80) shah of Iran (1941–79). He succeeded his father, Reza Pahlavi, and gradually established a dictatorship that was undermined by religious fundamentalists led by Khomeini and forced to flee his country in 1979.

Pahlavi, Reza (1877–1944) ruler of Persia from 1921 and shah (1925–41).

Paine, Thomas (1737–1809) English-born American political theorist and pamphleteer. His highly influential pamphlet *Common Sense* (1776), which argued for American independence, was recognized by Washington as being a significant contribution to the Revolution. Paine returned to England in 1787 and published a defence of democratic principles, *The Rights of Man* (1791–92), in reply to Edmund Burke's *Reflections on the Revolution in France*. In danger of arrest, he moved to France where he was elected to the National Convention. He sided with the moderates, was imprisoned by Robespierre's faction, and released after 11 months, having narrowly escaped execution. He remained in France until 1802 before returning to the USA.

Painlevé, Paul (1863–1933) French statesman and pioneer in aviation.

Painter, William (*c.*1540–1594) English translator (*Palace of Pleasure* 1566–67).

Paisley, Ian [Richard Kyle] (1926–) Northern Ireland Protestant clergyman and Unionist politician. A highly vocal opponent of Irish nationalism and Roman Catholicism.

Pakistan established as a dominion and separated from India 1947, as East Pakistan and West Pakistan; proclaimed an Islamic republic 1956; East Pakistan gained independence as Bangladesh 1971.

Palaeocene Epoch, Earth history, 70 million years ago.

Palaeozoic Era, Earth history, between 200 and 520 million years ago.

Palafox y Melzi, José de duke of Saragossa (1780–1847).

Palestine conquered from Turks by British 1917–18; British mandate proclaimed 1922, ended 1948; partitioned between Jordan and new state of Israel 14 May 1948.

Palestine Liberation Organization (PLO), formed 1964 to bring about an independent state of Palestine.

Palestrina, Giovanni Pierluigi da (*c.*1525–1594) Italian composer. One of the greatest Renaissance composers, his compositions are practically all choral church works, including more than 90 masses, hymns, motets and madrigals.

Paley, William (1743–1805) English philosopher and theologian.

Palgrave, Francis Turner (1824–97) English compiler of *The Golden Treasury* (1861).

Palissy, Bernard (1509–89) French potter (invented Palissy Ware *c.*1545).

Palladio, Andrea (1518–80) Italian architect.

Palladium metallic element discovered 1803 by the English scientist William Hyde Wollaston (1766–1828).

Pallavicino, Pietro Sforza (1607–67) Italian cardinal and writer.

Palm Sunday the Sunday before Easter.

Palma, Jacopo (*c.*1480–1528) Italian painter (*Epiphany*).

Palmer, Edward Henry (1840–82) English expert in

Middle East languages and politics. He was murdered.

Palmer, George (1818–97) English biscuit manufacturer.

Palmer, Samuel (1805–81) English painter and engraver, noted for his pastoral landscapes. He was a follower of Blake, who deeply influenced the visionary mysticism of his work.

Palmer, William (1824–56) English murderer. He was hanged.

Palmerston, Henry John Temple, Viscount (1784–1865) British statesman (prime minister 1855–58, 1859–65). His great concern was to increase the prestige of England, and in this he succeeded, although on several occasions his actions were decidedly high-handed.

Palmgren, Selim (1878–1951) Finnish composer (*Peter Schlemihl*).

Palmyra an ancient city in Syra, said to have been founded by Solomon, of which Zenobia was queen (*c.*267–273).

Palomar, Mount, California, site of observatory selected 1934; observatory opened 1949.

Panama proclaimed an independent republic 1903; new constitution adopted 1946.

Panama Canal preliminary work 1881–89; construction began again 1904; opened 15 August 1914.

Panama Canal Zone treaty defining government and use signed by USA and Panama 18 November 1903; zone disestablished October 1979.

Pan-American Union, Washington DC, founded 1890.

Panchatantra Sanskrit collection of fables assembled *c.*5th century.

Panchen Lama deputy temporal and spiritual leader of Tibet, office dating from 1640.

Pancras, St (290 martyred 304).

Pandulf (d.1226) Italian-born bishop of Norwich and papal legate.

Paneth, Professor Friedrich Adolf(1887–1958) Austrian scientist.

Pan-German League (*Alldeutschen Verband*) German nationalist organization founded 1891, superseded by nationalist parties after 1918.

Panizzi, Sir Anthony (1797–1879) Italian-born librarian of the British Museum (1856–66).

Pankhurst, Dame Christabel Harriette (1880–1958) English suffragette leader and feminist who, with her mother, Emmeline Pankhurst, founded the Women's Social and Political Union in 1903, a campaigning organization for women's suffrage.

Pankhurst, Emmeline (1858–1928) English suffragette and feminist. She and her daughter Christabel Harriette Pankhurst, founded the Women's Social and Political Union in 1903, a campaigning organization for women's suffrage.

Pankhurst, Sylvia (1882–1960) English suffragette and pacifist, the daughter of Emmeline Pankhurst and sister of Christabel Pankhurst.

Panormus, Battle of 251 BC a battle of the First Punic War when the Romans defeated the Carthaginians.

Pantheon, Rome, built by Agrippa *c.*25 BC; rebuilt *c.*120 by Hadrian; transformed into a Christian church 609.

Panthéon, Paris, designed by the French architect Jacques Germain Soufflot (1709–80; built 1754–80 as a church; secularized 1789.

Pantomimes introduced into England by the English dancing-master John Weaver (1673–1760).

Paoli, Pascal (1725–1807) Corsican patriot.

Papadopoulos, George (1919–) military ruler of Greece (1967–73).

Papagos, Alexander (1883–1955) Greek soldier.

Papal States finally incorporated with the Italian kingdom 1859–60 and 1870.

Papandreou, Andreas George (1919–) Greek socialist politician and Greece's first socialist prime minister (1981–89).

Papandreou, George (1888–1968) Greek politician (prime minister 1944–45, 1964–65).

Papen, Franz von (1879–1969) German statesman (chancellor 1932, vice chancellor 1933–34).

Paper traditionally invented by the Chinese Tsai-Lun 105.

Papini, Giovanni (1881–1956) Italian writer (*Storia di Cristo* 1921).

Papinian (d.212) Roman jurist. He was killed.

Papua New Guinea New Guinea first sighted by Spanish and Portuguse navigators in the 16th century; 1884 British protectorate established over southern area (Papua) and Germany took possession of the northern area (New Guinea); German areas came under Australian control 1914, and remained under Australian supervision 1921–70; self-government established over the whole territory December 1973; complete independence September 1975.

Paracelsus [Theophrastus Bombastus von Hohenheim] (1493–1541) Swiss physician.

Parachutes believed to have been invented 1785 by the French balloonist Jean Pierre Blanchard (1753–1809); first used 1802 by the Frenchman André Garnevin (1769–1823).

Paraffin discovered 1830 by the German inventor Baron von Reichenbach (1788–1869).

Paraffin industry, originated in England 1856 by the Scottish chemist James 'Paraffin' Young (1811–83).

Paraguay declared independent of Spanish rule 1811.

Paratroops first developed by the Russians *c.*1925; first used in war by the Germans in 1940.

Parcel post, inland, began in Britain 1883.

Parchment traditionally invented by Eumenes II of Pergamon in the 2nd century BC.

Paré, Ambroise (1510–90) French surgeon.

Pareto, Vilfredo (1848–1923) Italian economist and sociologist.

Paris, Matthew (d.1259) English historian (*Chronica Majora*).

Paris, Treaty of adjusting the claims of King Henry III of England, ratified December 1259; ending the Seven Years' War 1763; ending War of American Independence 1783; ending the Napoleonic Wars 1814 and 1815; ending Crimean War 1856.

Paris, University of founded 1120.

Paris Observatory founded 1667–1771.

Paris Peace Accords, ceasefire agreement intended to end the Vietnam War, signed by North Vietnam, South Vietnam and USA, 27 January 1973.

Park, Mungo (1771–*c.*1805) Scottish explorer (explored Niger 1796).

Parker, Charlie *or* **Bird** [Charles Christopher Parker] (1920–55) American jazz alto saxophonist. He became the leading exponent of 'bop' jazz in the 1940s and worked with Dizzy Gillespie.

Parker, Dorothy [Rothschild] (1893–1967) American journalist, poet and short-story writer, noted for her dry wit and sharply ironic epigrams and satires.

Parker, Matthew (d. 1575) archbishop of Canterbury (1559–75).

Parker, Richard(*c.*1767–1797) leader of the mutineers (1797) at the Nore. He was hanged.

Parkes, Alexander (1813–90) English scientist and inventor (1855) of celluloid.

Parkhurst, John (*c.*1512–1575) bishop of Norwich (1560–75).

Parking meters first introduced in Britain in Westminster, London, in 1958.

Parkman, Francis (1823–93) American historian.

'Parley, Peter' pseudonym adopted by both the English writers William Martin (1801–67) and George Mogridge (1787–1854).

Parliament first called as advisory body by King John in 1213.

Parliament of Dunces in the reign of King Henry IV met at Coventry 1404.

Parliament, Addled held 1614.

Parliament, Cavalier held 1660 to 1678.

Parliament, Long held 1640 to 1653, 1659 to 1660.

Parliament, Mad held in Oxford 1256.

Parliament, Merciless which condemned friends of Richard II to death, 1388.

Parliament, Rump held 1648 to 1653 and 1659.

Parliament, Short held 1640.

Parmenides (*fl* 6th and 5th centuries BC) Greek philosopher born in Italy who held that the universe is unchanging. He expounded his convictions in a didactic poem, On Nature.

Parmenion (*c.*400–330 BC) Macedonian general who served Philip II and Alexander the Great. He carried out military operations in the Troad in Asia Minor where he was opposed by Memnon of Rhodes 335 BC. He acted as military adviser to Alexander and second in command at several battles on the campaign in Asia. His son was implicated in a plot against Alexander's Life, which resulted in his execution.

Parmigianino, Francesco (1503–40) Italian painter (*St Jerome*).

Parnell, Charles Stewart (1846–91) Irish politician. An ardent Home Ruler, he became MP for Cork in 1880 and organized in parliament a masterly campaign of obstruction with the aim of disrupting Parliament and ultimately gaining Home Rule for Ireland. Gladstone became a convert to the cause, but in 1890, his career began to crumble after he was cited in a divorce case (1889).

Parr, Catherine (1512–48) queen of Henry VIII.

Parr, Thomas ('Old Parr') (*c.*1483–1635) probably the longest-lived Englishman.

Parry, Sir Charles Hubert Hastings (1848–1918) English composer (*De Profundis* 1891).

Parsees Indian followers of Zoroaster (*c.*659–*c.*582 BC).

Parsons, Elizabeth the 'Cock Lane ghost' (1749–1807).

Parsons, Robert (1546–1610) Jesuit missionary in England.

Parthenogenesis first recognized by the Greek philosopher Aristotle (384–322 BC).

Parthenon the temple on the Acropolis in Athens, built by Pericles *c.*447–436 BC; wrecked by an explosion 1687.

Parthia an ancient country of southeast Asia which became an empire, in existence 227 BC to AD 224, when it was destroyed by the Seleucids.

Parthian War a war between Rome and the Parthians, the principal battle of which was Carrhae 53 BC.

Parton, James (1822–91) English-born writer (*Aaron Burr* 1857).

Partridge, John (1644–1715) English astrologer.

Pascal, Blaise (1623–62) French theologian, mathematician and physicist. He made important discoveries in hydraulics and invented a calculating machine. His writings include *Lettres Provinciales* (1656–57).

Paschal I, Saint (d.824) pope (817–824).

Paschal II [Ronieri] (d.1118) pope (1099–1118).

Paschal III [Guido] anti-pope (1164–68).

Pasquier, Etienne (1529–1615) French writer (*Recherches de la France* 1560–1615).

Passchendaele, Battle of a battle of the First World War in Belgium, 28 September 1918.

Passion Play, Oberammergau, Germany, acted every ten years since 1634.

Passover (*Peisach*) Jewish feast, begins on evening of the 14th day of Nisan.

Passy, Frédéric (1822–1912) French economist.

Pasternak, Boris [Leonidovich] (1890–1960) Russian poet and novelist. A highly original and passionate lyric poet in a regime that demanded safe verse praising its achievements forced him to turn to translation for a living; his translations of Shakespeare's plays are still highly valued. His great novel *Dr Zhivago* was first published in Italy in 1958. He was awarded the Nobel prize for literature but was forced to decline it by the Soviet authorities.

Pasteur, Louis (1822–95) French chemist who discovered that fermentation is due to the presence of microorganisms and developed the process of pasteurization to destroy them. He also developed immunization processes against rabies and anthrax.

Paston, John (1421–66) English country gentleman.

Pastor, Ludwig, Freiherr von (1854–1928) German historian of the popes.

Patent, world's first, granted in Venice to the German printer John of Speyer 1469.

Pater, Walter Horatio (1839–94) English writer and critic (*Marius the Epicurean* 1885).

Paterson, Mrs Emma Anne (1848–86) first woman admitted (1875) to the Trade Union Congress.

Pathé, Charles (1873–1957) French pioneer film producer (*The Dancing Years*).

Pathé News Reel founded 1911 by the French photographer Charles Pathé.

Pathology (1821–1902) modern practice founded by Rudolf Virchow.

Patmore, Coventry (1823–96) English writer (*The Angel in the House* 1854–62).

Patrician *see* PLEBEIAN.

Patrick, Saint (*fl*. 5th century) British missionary. He was sold into slavery in Ireland as a youth, escaped to France and became a monk. He returned to Ireland as a missionary and converted many to his faith, and became the patron saint of Ireland.

Patrick, Order of St founded by George III in 1783.

Patti, Adelina (1843–1919) operatic singer.

Pattinson, Hugh Lee (1796–1858) English metallurgical chemist and inventor.

Patton, George S[mith] (1885–1945) American general. In the Second World War he commanded the Allied invasion of North Africa (1942–43), and led the 3rd US army across France and Germany to the Czech border (1944–45).

'Paul, Jean' [Johann Paul Friedrich Richter] (1763–1825) German humorous writer (*Hesperus* 1795).

Paul, Saint (St Paul the Apostle) (d. *c*.67 AD) Christian apostle and missionary to the Gentiles. A pharisee, he was a notable persecutor of Christians before his 'Damascus Road' conversion. Many of the Epistles in the New Testament are his. According to tradition, he was beheaded during the reign of Nero.

Paul I (1754–1801) tsar of Russia (1799–1801). He was murdered 1801).

Paul I, Saint (d.767) pope (757–767).

Paul II [Pietro Barbo] (1417–71) pope (1464–71).

Paul III [Alessandro Farnese] (1468–1549) pope (1534–49).

Paul IV [Giovanni Pietro Caraffa] (1476–1559) pope (1555–59).

Paul V [Camillo Borghese] (1552–1621) pope (1605–21).

Paul of the Cross, Saint (1694–1775) Italian founder (1720–25) of the Passionists.

Paul the Deacon (*fl* 8th century) Italian historian.

Pauli, Professor Wolfgang (1900–1958) Austrian physicist.

Pauling, Linus Carl (1901–94) American chemist. He was awarded the 1954 Nobel prize for physics for his research into chemical bonding and molecular structure, and the 1962 Nobel Peace Prize for his criticisms of nuclear testing and deterrence.

Paulinus (d.644) Roman bishop of York.

Paulus Lucius Aemilius (*c*.229–160 BC) Roman general.

Pausanias (*fl* 2nd century) Greek writer who travelled extensively in Greece and elsewhere. His *Description of Greece* is an account of the topography of the country at the time. At the time of his travels Greece was still rich in works of art, and his factual descriptions of these are an important record.

Pausanias (d.470 BC) Spartan regent (479–470) and military commander who led an allied Greek force against the Persians at the battle of Plataea 479 BC at which the Persians were defeated. In 477 he command a fleet to drive the Persians out of the Greek islands and Cyprus and then conquered Byzantium. He enlisted Persian help in an attempt to take power for himself and when this was discovered he took sanctuary in the temple of Athene Chalcioecus, where he was walled up until he was practically dead.

Pausanias (*fl* 2nd century) Greek writer who travelled extensively in Greece and elsewhere. His *Description of Greece* is an account of the topography of the country at the time. At the time of his travels Greece was still rich in works of art, and his factual descriptions of these are an important record.

Pavarotti, Luciano (1935–) Italian tenor. He is regarded as one of the most powerful tenor singers of the modern era.

Pavlov, Ivan Petrovich (1849–1936) Russian physiologist. He was awarded the 1904 Nobel prize for physiology or medicine for his work on the physiology of digestion.

Pavlova, Anna (1885–1931) Russian ballerina. Fokine choreographed *The Dying Swan* for her. She also worked with Diaghilev, and became one of the most famous ballerinas in the world.

Paxton, Sir Joseph (1801–65) English designer (1850) of the Crystal Palace.

PAYE (Pay As You Earn) British income-tax system introduced 1944.

Payne, John Howard (1791–1852) American writer (*Home, Sweet Home* 1823).

Pazzi Assassination of Giuliano de' Medici, 26 April 1478.

Peabody, Elizabeth Palmer (1804–94) American pioneer in kindergarten provision.

Peabody, George (1795–1869) American merchant and philanthropist.

Peace, Charles (*c.*1832–1879) English murderer. He was hanged.

Peace Congress, First International, held in London 1843.

Peace Corps, US agency established by President J. F. Kennedy 1961 to provide volunteers to work in Third World countries.

Peace Pledge initiated 1934 by the Rev. Dick Sheppard (d.1937).

Peacock, Thomas Love (1785–1866) English writer (*Headlong Hall* 1816).

Peada (d.656) king of Middle Anglia (653–656) *see* Appendix.

Peake, Mervyn Laurence (1911–68) British writer and artist (*Gormenghast Trilogy* 1946–59).

Peale, Charles Willson (1741–1826) American painter (*George Washington* 1772).

Pearl Harbour attack Second World War attack made by the Japanese on the Honolulu naval base, 7 December 1941.

Pears, Sir Peter (1910–86) English tenor. A close associate of Benjamin Britten, several of whose tenor opera roles were written for him.

Pearse, Pádraic (1879–1916) Irish nationalist leader. He was shot.

Pearson, Sir Arthur (1866–1921) English newspaper owner and philanthropist (founded *Pearson's Weekly* 1890).

Pearson, John (1613–86) English theologian (*Exposition of the Creed* 1659).

Pearson, Lester Bowles (1897–1972) Canadian statesman (prime minister 1963–68).

Pearson, William (1767–1847) English astronomer.

Peary, Robert Edwin (1856–1920) American naval commander and Arctic explorer. He is credited with being the first man to reach the North Pole (1909).

Peasants' Revolt led by the English rebel Wat Tyler 1381.

Peasants' War in South Germany 1525.

Peck, Francis (1692–1743) English antiquary (*Desiderata Curiosa* 1732–35).

Peckham, John (d.1292) archbishop of Canterbury (1279–92).

Pecock, Reginald (*c.*1395–*c.*1460) Welsh theologian (*Book of Faith* 1466).

Peculiar People religious movement founded in London 1838 by John Banyard.

Pedal bicycle, first, built 1838 by Kirkpatrick Macmillan.

Pedro the Cruel (1334–69) king of Castile and Leon (1350–69). He was killed in combat.

Pedro I (1798–1834) emperor of Brazil (1822–31).

Pedro II (1825–91) emperor of Brazil (1831–89).

Peel, Sir Robert (1788–1850) British statesman. He became Home Secretary in 1828 and founded the Metropolitan police. He was prime minister twice (1834–35, 1841–6). By his last year of office he had accepted and promoted the free-trade principles that disrupted the Tory party.

Peele, George (*c.*1558–*c.*1597) English writer (*David and Bethsabe* 1599).

Peep-of-Day Boys Irish Protestant secret society flourishing at the end of the 18th century.

Péguy, Charles (1873–1914) French writer (*Jeanne d'Arc* 1897).

Peierls, Sir Rudolf Ernst (1907–) German-born British physicist. With Otto Frisch, he demonstrated the feasibility of an atom bomb during World War II.

Peine Forte et Dure used in England as late as 1741.

Peirce, Benjamin (1809–80) American scientist.

Peisistratus *see* PISISTRATUS.

Peking Man early Pleistocene period remains discovered near Peking 1927.

Pelagius (*c.*360–*c.*420) British theologian.

Pelagius I (d.561) pope (555–561).

Pelagius II (d.590) pope (579–590).

Pelé [Edson Arantes do Nascimento] (1940–) Brazilian footballer, universally recognized as one of the most skilful and entertaining players of all time.

Pellegrini, Carlo (1839–89) Italian-born caricaturist ('Ape' in *Vanity Fair*).

Pelletier, Pierre Joseph (1788–1842) French chemist.

Pelopidas (d.364 BC) Greek statesman and general. He was killed in battle.

Peloponnesian League organized by Sparta *c.*550 BC; Athens joined 510 BC; ended in the 4th century BC.

Peloponnesian War Sparta against Athens and allies 431–404 BC; Thucydides its historian: naval battle of Sybota 433 BC both sides claimed victory; naval battle of Corinth 429 BC Athenian victory; naval battle of Naupactus 429 BC Athenian victory; Spartans besieged Plataea 429–427 and the city surrendered; Athenians laid siege to Mytilene 428–427 BC and the city surrendered; battle of Olpae 426 BC Athenian victory; Athenians besieged at Pylos 425 BC by the Spartans based at Sphacteria but the siege at Pylos was lifted by an Athenian fleet which mounted a counter-siege of Sphacteria, which surrendered; battle of Delium 424 BC Athenian defeat; battle of Amphipolis 422 BC Athenians defeated; Peace of Nicias ends first part of war 421 BC; battle of Mantinea 418 BC, Athenians defeated; Athenians laid siege to Syracuse 415 BC but forced to lift it when they were defeated in a naval battle at Syracuse 413 BC; naval battle of Cynossema 411 BC Athenian victory; naval battle of Cyzicus 410 BC Athenian victory; naval battle of Notium 407 BC Athenian defeat; naval battle of Arginusae 406 BC Athenian victory; naval battle of Mytilene 406 BC Athenian defeat; naval battle of Aegospotami 405 BC, victory of Sparta under Lysander over Athens; end of the war 404 BC, Spartans enter Athens and set up the Thirty Tyrants.

Peloponnesus *or* **Peloponnese** a broad peninsula of souther Greece, joined to the northern part of the country of the isthmus of Corinth. In history its main cities were Sparta and Corinth (modern Patras). Sparta became supreme in the Peloponnesus 550 BC.

Peltier effect heat properties of electric currents discovered 1834 by the French scientist Jean Charles Athanase Peltier (1785–1845).

Pelusium, Battle of 171 BC a battle in the war between Egypt and an invading Syran army under Antiochus Epiphanes. It was a victory for the Syrians and enabled them to take Memphis.

Pembroke, Mary Herbert, Countess of (1561–1621) patron of poets.

Pembroke, William Herbert, Earl of (*c.*1501–1570) governor of Calais.

Pembroke, Richard de Clare, 2nd Earl of Pembroke and Strigul *see* STRONGBOW, RICHARD.

Pembroke College, Cambridge University, founded as the Hall or House of Valence-Mary by Mary de St Paul, widow of the Earl of Pembroke, 1347.

Pembroke College, Oxford University, founded 1624; previously known as Broadgates Hall.

Penang state of Peninsula Malaysia consisting of the island of Penang (formerly Prince of Wales' Island) and the province of Wellesley; first British settlement in the Malay Peninsula, ceded by the Sultan of Kedah to the East India Company 1786, Province Wellesley being added 1800; incorporated with Malacca and Singapore 1826 under a single government; known as the Straits Settlements 1867–1946.

Pencils possibly invented much earlier but certainly in use by the mid-16th century.

Penda (577–655) king of Mercia (626–655) *see* Appendix.

Pendleton, Edmund (1721–1803) Federalist Party leader in Virginia.

Pendulum isochronism observed 1582 and time-keeping mechanism devised 1641 by Galileo Galilei; pendulum clocks constructed 1649 by Vincenzio Galilei, and 1658 by the Dutch scientist Christiaan Huygens (who described the principles in his *Horologium Oscillatorium* 1673) (1629–95; compensated pendulum constructed 1722 by the English mechanician George Graham (1675–1751).

Penicillin discovered 1928 by Sir Alexander Fleming (1881–1955).

Peninsular War between the Allies and Napoleon 1808–1814.

PEN International, London, world association of writers, founded 1921.

Penn, William (1644–1718) English Quaker, founder (1682) of Pennsylvania.

Pennell, Joseph (1860–1926) American artist.

Penney, William George (1909–91) British physicist, creator of the British atomic bomb (1952).

Pen nibs, steel, manufacture perfected 1829 by the English industrialists Sir Josiah Mason (1795–1881) and Joseph Gillott (1797–1873).

Pennsylvania, USA, first settled 1682; ratified US Constitution 1787.

Pennsylvania University, Philadelphia, founded 1740.

Penny postage invented 1837 and put into effect 1840 by Sir Rowland Hill (1795–1879).

Penrose, Francis Cranmer (1817–1903) English archaeologist and astronomer.

Pentecost Christian feast of the Holy Spirit celebrated on Whit-Sunday.

Pepin I (d.640) Frankish ruler.

Pepin II (d.714) Frankish ruler.

Pepin III (d.768) king of the Franks (751–768).

Pepper, John Henry (1821–1900) English illusionist ('Pepper's Ghost').

Pepsin first described 1836 by the German physiologist Theodor Schwann (1810–82).

Pepusch, Dr John Christopher (1667–1752) German-born composer (*The Beggar's Opera* 1728).

Pepys, Samuel (1633–1703) English diarist and Admiralty official. His diary (written in code) covers the years 1660–69 and was first published in 1825. The full uncensored version was published in 11 volumes (1970–83).

Perak state of peninsula Malaysia; entered into treaty relations 1874–95 with Britain; agreed 1895 with three other Malay states to form a federation; federal council of these states formed 1909.

Perceval, Spencer (1762–1812) prime minister of Great Britain (1809–12). He was assassinated.

Percier, Charles (1764–1838) French architect.

Percussion cap in gunmaking introduced into the British Army 1842.

Percussion lock in gunmaking invented 1805 by the Scottish minister the Rev. Alexander John Forsyth (1768–1843).

Percy, Sir Henry ('Hotspur') (1364–1403). He was killed in battle.

Percy, John (1817–89) English physician and metallurgist.

Percy, Lord, of Newcastle (1887–1958) pioneer in English education.

Perdiccas (d.321 BC) regent of the Macedonian Empire (323–321 BC). He was assassinated.

'Perdita' [Mary Robinson] (1758–1800) English actress and mistress of Prince of Wales.

Peres, Shimon (1923–) Israeli politician (prime minister 1984–86).

Peretz, Isaac (1852–1915) Yiddish writer.

Pérez de Ayala, Ramón (1881–1962) Spanish writer (*Belarmino y Apolonio* 1921).

Pérez de Cuellar, Javier (1920–) Peruvian diplomat and UN secretary general (1982–92).

Pérez Galdos, Benito (1843–1920) Spanish (*Gloria* 1877).

Pergamom an ancient city of northwest Asia Minor. Attalus III, king of Pergamom, bequeathed his dominions to Rome and it became the Roman province of Asia 133 BC.

Pergolesi, Giovanni Battista (1710–36) Italian composer (*La Serva Padrona* 1733).

Pericles (b.*c*.492–429 BC) Greek statesman whose influence on the government of Athens began 462 BC and by 449 BC he was virtual ruler. He was commander in chief during the Peloponnesian War and was responsible for the building of the Parthenon.

Perim island off Aden, permanently occupied by the British 1857.

Periodic law relating to chemical elements developed 1869 from a paper published 1864 of the English chemist John Newlands (1837–98), by the Russian chemist Dmitri Ivanovich Mendeleieff (1834–1907).

Periwig use general in western Europe approximately 1660–1800.

Perkin, Sir William Henry (1838–1907) English chemist and discoverer (1856) of mauveine.

Perkins, Loftus (1834–91) English engineer and pioneer in refrigeration.

Perkins, William (1558–1602) English theologian (*Armilla Aurea* 1590).

Perlman, Itzhak (1945–) Israeli-born concert violinist.

Permanent Court of Arbitration, The Hague, established 1899.

Permanganate acid first obtained 1830 by the German chemist Eilhard Mitscherlich (1794–1863).

Permian Period, Earth history, 220 million years ago.

Perón, Juan Domingo (1895–1974) Argentinian dictator. He was president (1946–55), was deposed by the army and lived in exile until re-elected president (1973–74). His success was based to a large extent on his first wife, Eva [Duarte] Perón (1919–52), an ex-actress nicknamed 'Evita'.

Perrault, Charles (1628–1703) French collector of fairy tales (*Contes de ma Mère l'Oie* 1697).

Perrers, Alice (d.1400) royal mistress.

Perret, Auguste (1874–1954) French architect and pioneer in the use of modern concrete construction.

Perronet, Edward (1721–92) English hymn-writer (*All Hail the Power of Jesu's Name* 1780).

Perronneau, Jean Baptiste (1715–83) French painter.

Perrot, Sir John (*c*.1527–1592) Lord Deputy of Ireland (1584–88).

Perry, Fred[erick John] (1909–95) English-born American tennis and table-tennis player. He was one of the most successful lawn tennis players of the 1930s, winning every major tournament.

Perry, John (1670–1732) English traveller and canal builder.

Perry, Stephen Joseph (1833–89) English astronomer.

Persepolis the capital of ancient Persia, southeast of modern Tehran. It was destroyed by Alexander the Great in 330 BC

Perseus (d.*c*.163) last king of Macedonia (179–168 BC). He tried to placate Rome, but the senate declared war on him 171 BC (Third Macedonian War 171–168 BC). He was victorious over the Romans at Larissa 171 BC but was crushed at the battle of Pydna 168 BC. He fled to the sacred island of Samothrace where he was blockaded by a Roman fleet and compelled to surrender. In 167 he was taken to Rome and then kept captive at Alba until his death.

Pershing, John Joseph (1860–1948) American general who was commander in chief of the American Expeditionary Force in France in the First World War 1917–18.

Persia *see* IRAN.

Persia conquest of Media by Cyrus and foundation of the Persian empire 550 BC; Asiatic Greek cities conquered 546 BC; Lydia conquered 546 BC; Babylon conquered by Cyrus 538 BC; Cambyses, king of Persia 529–522 BC; Persian conquest of Egypt 525 BC;

Darius I (Darius the Great) king of Persia 521–486 BC; Persian conquest of Babylon 520 BC and Thrace 512 BC; revolt Asiatic Greeks revolt from Persia 499 BC; Persian conquest Thrace and Macedonia 492 BC; Persians defeated by Greeks at Marathon 490 BC; Xerxes king of Persia 485 BC; Persians defeated at Salamis 480 BC; Persians victorious at Thermopylae 480 BC; Persians defeated at Plataea and Mycale 479 BC; Persians defeated at Eurymedon 465 BC; Artaxerxes I, king of Persia 465–425 BC; Darius II, king of Persia 424–404 BC; Artaxerxes II, king of Persia (404–358 BC); Wars of the Greek City States 394–387 BC; Persian-Athenian fleet victorious at Cnidus 394 BC; peace of Antalcidas between Sparta and Persia 387 BC; Artaxerxes III, king of Persia 358–338 BC; Arses, king of Persia 338–336 BC); Darius III, king of Persia 336–330 BC; Persians defeated by Alexander the Great at Granicus 334 BC, Issus 333 BC and Arbela 331 BC; death of Darius III and end of the Persian empire 330 BC.

Persian Gulf States *see* BAHRAIN, KUWAIT, QATAR.

Persian Gulf War between Iraq and allied coalition sponsored by the UN, January–March 1991; triggered by the Iraqi invasion of Kuwait, 2 August 1990.

Persian Wars with the Greek city-states 500–449 BC.

Persigny, Jean Gilbert Victor Fialin, Duc de (1808–72) French diplomat and statesman.

Persius (34–62) Latin writer (*Satires*).

Perthes, Justus (1749–1816) German publisher.

Pertinax (126–193) Roman emperor (193). He was assassinated.

Peru declared an independent republic 1821.

Perugino [Pietro Vannucci] (1446–1524) Italian painter (*The Assumption*).

Peruzzi, Baldassare (1481–1536) Italian architect.

Pervigilium Veneris anonymous Latin poem written probably in the 2nd century.

Pestalozzi, Johann Heinrich (1746–1827) Swiss educationalist (opened his first orphan school 1798).

Pétain, Henri Philippe Omer (1856–1951) French soldier and statesman. Appointed marshal of France in 1918 in recognition of his generalship during World War I, he was prime minister of the collaborationist Vichy government (1940–44) and was sentenced to death at the end of World War II (later commuted to life imprisonment).

Peter, Saint (St Peter the Apostle) (died *c.*67 AD) Disciple of Jesus Christ and Christian apostle. A fisherman, he became one of Jesus's leading disciples and played an equally prominent role in establishing Christianity after the crucifixion and is regarded by Roman Catholics as the first pope. He is believed to have been martyred in Rome.

Peter I the Great (1672–1725) tsar of Russia (1689–1725).

Peter I Land Antarctic island discovered 1821 by the Russian Admiral von Bellingshausen; annexed by Norway 1929–31.

Peter II (1715–30) tsar of Russia (1728–30).

Peter III (1728–62) tsar of Russia (1762). He was murdered.

Peterborough Cathedral, England, present building begun 1117; consecrated 1238.

Peterborough, Charles Mordaunt, Earl of (1658–1735) admiral and diplomat.

Peterhouse, Cambridge, founded by Hugh de Balsham, bishop of Ely, 1284.

Peter Lombard (*c.*1100–*c.*1160) Italian theologian (*Sententiae* 1145–50).

Peterloo massacre at reform meeting at St Peter's Field, Manchester 16 August 1819.

Petermann, August Heinrich (1822–78) German cartographer. He committed suicide.

PeterMartyr (1500–1555) Italian Protestant leader.

PeterMartyr, Saint (d.1252) Italian inquisitor. He was killed.

Peters, Carl Friedrich (1779–1827) German music publisher.

Petersen, Wilhelm (1890–1957) Greek-born composer (*Grosse Messe* 1930).

Peterson, Oscar [Emmanuel] (1925–) Canadian jazz pianist and composer. His Oscar Peterson Trio became one of the best-known small jazz groups of the 1950s.

Peter's Pence annual English offering to the pope, first sent 787; abolished 1534.

Peterthe Hermit (d.*c.*1115) French Crusader.

Peterthe Wild Boy (*c.*1712–1785).

Petipa, Marius (1822–1910) French dancer and choreographer.

Petition of Right submitted by the House of Commons to King Charles I and accepted by him 1628.

Petitioners political group (connected with Whigs) that became prominent 1680.

Petit Trianon, Versailles, constructed 1762–68 by the French architect Jacques Ange Gabriel (*c.*1698–1782).

Petöfi, Sandor (1823–49) Hungarian national poet. He was killed in battle.

Petra ruins of Nabataean and Graeco-Roman settlements in the present territory of Jordan, built mainly 6th century BC to 3rd century AD.

Petrarch [Francesco Petrarca] (1304–74) Italian lyric poet and humanist. His work popularized the sonnet form, and he is recognized as the first major poet of the Renaissance. His works include (*Rime in Vita e Morte*).

Petre, Edward (1631–99) English Jesuit missionary to England.

Petrie, Sir William Flinders (1853–1942) English archaeologist.

Petrified Forest, Arizona, established as a national monument 1906.

Petrol engine first constructed 1883 by the German engineer Gottlieb Daimler (1834–1900).

Petroleum first transported in the brig *Elizabeth Watts* from the USA to Europe, arriving at the Port of London 1861.

Petroleum flashpoint apparatus for its determination (the Abel close-test instrument) invented *c.*1879 by the English chemist Sir Frederick Augustus Abel (1827–1902).

Petronius 'Arbiter' (d.*c.*66) Roman writer (*The Satyricon*). He committed suicide.

Petronius [Gaius Petronius Arbiter] (d. AD *c.*66) Roman courtier and satirist. His great satirical novel, the *Satyricon*, is an important landmark in Western literature.

Petrucci, Ottaviano dei (1466–1539) Italian pioneer music printer.

Petty, Sir William (1623–87) English economist.

Petunia, double, first grown (in France) *c.*1855.

Pfister, Albrecht (*c.*1420–*c.*1470) German pioneer printer.

Phalaris (*c.*570–*c.*554 BC) tyrant of Acragas. He was killed.

Pharmaceutical Society of Great Britain founded 1841, incorporated by Royal Charter 1843.

Pharnaces I first king of Pontus (190–156 BC) who conducted wars against Rhodes and Pergamom and was compelled to sue for peace 179 BC.

Pharnaces II (d.47 BC) king of the Bosphorus (63–). The son of Mithridates VI, he organized an insurrection against his father, who poisoned himself. He made peace with Pompey, who granted him the kingdom of the Bosphorus, but took advantage of the civil war between Caesar and Pompey to seize back territories lost in the Mithridatic Wars. He won a victory over Rome at Nicopolis 47 BC and occupied the whole of Pontus, but was soon defeated by Caesar at Zela. He fled to the Bosphorus but was killed.

Pharos, near Alexandria, site of the world-famous lighthouse, built *c.*280 BC and demolished in the 14th century.

Pharsalia, Battle of 48 BC a battle of the civil war between Caesar and Pompey, which was a victory for Caesar. Pompey was murdered soon afterwards in Egypt.

Phelps, Samuel (1804–78) English actor-manager.

Phelps, Thomas (1694–after 1776) English astronomer.

Phidias (*c.*490–*c.*432 BC) Greek sculptor.

Philadelphia, Pennsylvania, founded under a patent from King Charles II 1681.

Philby, Kim [Harold Adrian Russell Philby] (1911–88) English diplomat, journalist and secret-service double agent. He became a Soviet agent in 1933 and was recruited to the British Secret Service in 1940. He became head of anti-communist espionage (1944–46) and worked in the British embassy in Washington DC (1949–51). He worked as a foreign correspondent (1956–63) before fleeing to the USSR.

Philemon (*c.*360–263 BC) Greek playwright (*The Treasure*).

Philidor, François André Danican (1726–95) French chess champion.

Philip, Prince [Duke of Edinburgh] (1921–) Greek-born British naval officer and prince consort. The nephew of Mountbatten, he married the then Princess Elizabeth in 1947.

Philip anti-pope (768).

Philip I (1052–1108) king of France (1059–1108).

Philip II (1165–1223) king of France (1180–1223).

Philip III the Bold (1245–85) king of France (1270–85).

Philip IV the Fair (1268–1314) king of France (1285–1314).

Philip V the Tall (*c.*1294–1322) king of France (1317–22).

Philip VI (1293–1350) king of France (1328–50).

Philip I possibly mythical early king of Macedonia.

Philip II (Philip of Macedon) (*c.*382–336 BC) king of Macedonia (359–336 BC) and father of Alexander the Great. A man of few scruples, he had great talents for war and diplomacy and soon reorganized the army and extended his kingdom. By 352 he had made himself master of Thessaly and then equipped a navy to harass Athenian trade. He defeated the Athenians and Thebans at Chaeronea 338 BC and became supreme in Greece. He drew up plans for an invasion of Asia but was assassinated before he could do this.

Philip III [Arrhidaeus] (d. 317 BC) king of Macedonia (323–317 BC). A bastard son of Philip II and half-brother of Alexander the Great who had sent him abroad. He was in Babylon at the time of Alexander's death and was elected king under the name of Philip. He returned to Macedonia with his wife, Eurydice, who entered into a power struggle. They were put to death by Olympias.

Philip IV king of Macedonia (297–296 BC). The son of Cassander, he reigned only a few months before dying of a comsumptive disease.

Philip V (*c.*237–179 BC) king of Macedonia (220–179 BC) who took the part of Hannibal in the Second Punic War. As a result, in 211 BC the Romans began a campaign against him, which they won. By the peace finally granted to Philip in 196 BC, he was compelled to withdraw his garrisons from all Greek cities, surrender his fleet and limit his army.

Philip I (Philip the Handsome) (1478–1506) king of Spain (1506).

Philip II (1527–98) king of Spain (1556–98) who married Mary of England in 1554, her troops helping to win the battle of St Quentin against the French in 1557. In 1566 the revolt of the Netherlands led to their separation from the Spanish crown and the formation of the Dutch Republic, but in 1580 his troops, under Alva, subdued Portugal, of which Philip became king. In 1586 he declared war against England, and in 1588 his Armada was destroyed.

Philip III (1578–1621) king of Spain (1598–1621).

Philip IV (1605–65) king of Spain (1621–65).

Philip V (1683–1746) king of Spain (1700–46).

Philip Neri, Saint (1515–95).

'Philippe Egalité' (Louis-Philippe, Duc d'Orléans) (1747–93). He was guillotined.

Philippi, Battle of 42 BC between Octavian and Antony and the Senate party of Brutus and Cassius, the leaders of the revolt against Caesar. Brutus and Cassius were defeated and committed suicide.

Philippines a group of islands in the western Pacific, discovered by the Portuguese navigator Ferdinand Magellan 1521; ceded by Spain to the USA. 1898; became an independent republic 1946.

Philippus king of Syria (95–83) son of Antiochus VIII and grandson of Demetrius II and one of the royal princes who took part in the civil wars that followed the death of Antiochus VIII. For a time he and his brother Demetrius III held the whole of Syria, at first ruling jointly, but war broke out between them and Demetrius was blockaded in his camp and forced to surrender.

Philips, John (1676–1709) English poet (*Cyder* 1708).

Philips, Richard (1661–1751) governor of Nova Scotia (1720–49).

Phillipps, Sir Thomas (1792–1872) English book and MSS. collector.

Phillpotts, Eden (1862–1960) Indian-born writer (*The Girl and the Faun* 1916).

Philo Judaeus (*c.*15 BC–*c.*AD 50) Jewish philosopher of Alexandria.

Philopoemen (*c.*253–184 BC) Greek general who became leader of the Achaean League 208 BC and defeated the Spartans at Mantinea. He was elected general of the league for the eighth time in 183 BC and led an expedition against Messenia, but he was captured and poisoned by the Messenians.

Phipps, Charles John (1835–97) English theatre architect.

'Phiz' [Hablot Knight Browne] (1815–82) English artist and illustrator.

Phlogiston theory propounded 1731 by the German scientist Georg Ernst Stahl (1660–1734).

Phocion (*c.*402–317 BC) Greek statesman and general.

Phoenix Park Murders, Dublin, the murder of Lord Frederick Cavendish and Thomas Henry Burke by Irish patriots, 6 May 1882.

'Phoney War' at beginning of the Second World War, October 1939–March 1940.

Phonograph first sound recording machine invented 1876 by the American inventor Thomas Alva Edison (1847–1931).

Phosphorus discovered 1669 by the German alchemist Henning Brandt.

Photius (*c.*820–891) patriarch of Constantinople.

Photochromolithography process invented 1868 by the British photolithographer William Griggs (1832–1911).

Photoelectric property of selenium first observed 1875 by the English scientist Willoughby Smith (1828–91).

Photoengraving invented in France 1827.

Photograph earliest surviving taken 1835 by William Fox Talbot (1800–1877).

Photographer, the first, the English inventor Thomas Wedgwood (1771–1805).

Photographic roll film invented 1884 by the American inventor George Eastman (1854–1932).

Photography principle discovered 1823 by the French physician Joseph Nicéphore Niepce (1765–1833).

Photography, colour, invented 1907 by the French inventor Auguste Lumière (1862–1954).

Photogravure invented 1895 by the Czech-born manufacturer Karl Klietsch [Karel Klic] (1841–1926).

Phraates I king of Parthia (175–170 BC).

Phraates II (d.127 BC) king of Parthia (138–127 BC). He was killed.

Phraates III (d.57 BC) king of Parthia (70–57 BC). He was murdered.

Phraates IV (d.AD 2) king of Parthia (37 BC-AD 2). He was murdered.

Phraates V (d.5) king of Parthia (2–5). He was killed.

Phraortes (d.624 BC) king of Media (647–624 BC) He conquered the Persians and then subdued the greater part of Asia, but he was defeated and killed while besieging Nineveh, the capital of the Assyrian empire. He was succeeded by his son Cyaxares.

Phrenology study founded by the German physician Franz Joseph Gall (1758–1828).

Phthisis bacillus discovered 1890 by the German bacteriologist Robert Koch (1843–1910).

Physick, Philip Synge (1768–1837) American pioneer surgeon.

Piaf, Edith [Edith Giovanna Gassion] (1915–63) French singer and songwriter. Nicknamed 'Little Sparrow' for her small size and frail appearance, her songs include '*Non, je ne regrette rien*'.

Piaget, Jean (1896–1980) Swiss psychologist. His studies of children's intelligence and perception have been highly influential on modern educationalists.

Pianoforte first practical model invented *c.*1710 by the Italian harpsichord-maker Bartolommeo Cristofori (1655–1731).

Piatigorsky, Gregor (1903–76) Russian-born cellist.

Piazzi, Giuseppe (1746–1826) Italian astronomer.

Picard, Jean (1620–82) French astronomer.

Picasso, Pablo (1881–1973) Spanish Catalan painter and sculptor. Regarded as the most influential artist of the modern era, with Braque, he was the founder of Cubism. His 'blue period' (1901–4) works include *The Blue Room* (1901); Cubist works include *Les Demoiselles d'Avignon* (1906–7). He designed costumes and scenery for Diaghilev from 1917, exhibited with the Surrealists in the mid–1920s, and created his strongest and perhaps best-known image *Guernica* (1937) in response to the fascist bombing of that Basque town during the Spanish Civil War.

Piccadilly Circus, London, new underground station opened 1928; first lit by electricity 1932.

Piccard, Auguste (1884–1962) Belgian physicist and explorer of the stratosphere and the bathysphere.

Piccolomini, Prince Octavio (1599–1656) military commander who brought to an end the Thirty Years' War.

Pickens, Andrew (1739–1817) American soldier and politician.

Pickering, John (d.1537) leader in the Pilgrimage of Grace (1536). He was executed.

Pickering, Timothy (1745–1829) American statesman.

Pickering, William (1796–1854) British publisher who introduced cloth bindings.

Pickford, Mary [Gladys Mary Smith] (1893–1979) Canadian-born American film star. Known for her silent roles and as co-founder of the United Artists film studio (1919) with Charlie Chaplin and D. W. Griffith.

Pico della Mirandola, Count Giovanni (1463–94) Italian philosopher (*Heptaplus* 1490).

Picric acid (trinitrophenol) known since 1771; effective use dates from 1885 when Turpin patented its use as a charge for shells.

Picts a people who lived in Britain north of the Forth and Clyde at the time of the Roman invasion and by the 4th century had become the dominant people of Caledonia. By the middle of the 6th century the Pictish capital was at Inverness and in the 9th century the Picts and Scots were united under Kenneth mac-Alpin, whose mother ws a Pict.

Picture Post British periodical published 1938–58.

Pierce, Franklin (1804–69) 14th US president (1853–57).

Pierné, Gabriel (1863–1937) French composer (*La Croisade des enfants* 1902).

Piero della Francesca (*c.*1416–92) Italian early Renaissance painter. While working in Florence he was deeply influenced by Masaccio, who inspired the monumental grandeur of his subsequent works. From *c.*1460 he was working at the Urbino court, where he painted some of his finest works, e.g. (*The Baptism of Christ*).

Piero di Cosimo (1462–*c.*1521) Italian painter (*Death of Procris*).

Pierrot role created by the French actor Jean Gaspard Debureau (1796–1846).

Pietermaritzburg South African city, capital of Natal province, founded 1839.

Pigalle, Jean Baptiste (1714–85) French sculptor (*Love and Friendship*).

Piggot, Lester (1935–) British champion jockey.

Pig iron process of production improved 1709 by the English iron-master Abraham Darby (1677–1717).

Pike, Zebulon Montgomery (1779–1813) American soldier and explorer. He was killed in battle.

Pilate, Pontius Roman procurator in Judea (26–36).

Pilgrimage of Grace 1536 insurrection in Yorkshire and Lincolnshire provoked by the dissolution of the monasteries by Henry VIII and led by the English attorney Robert Aske. The rebels marched on Doncaster, were defeated, rose again in 1537 and were suppressed finally the same year. Aske was executed in 1537.

Pilgrim Fathers set sail in the *Mayflower* from Plymouth, 6 September 1620; arrived Plymouth Rock, Massachusetts, 16 December 1620 (OS).

Pilgrim Trust established 1930 by the American philanthropist Edward Stephen Harkness (1874–1940).

Pill, the oral contraceptive, first became widely available 1961.

Pilsudski, Józef (1867–1935) Polish statesman (premier 1926–28, 1930–35).

Piltdown Skull discovered 1912; exposed as a fraud 1955.

Pinchbeck alloy of copper and zinc invented 1732 by the English clockmaker Christopher Pinchbeck (1670–1732).

Pinckney, Charles Cotesworth (1746–1825) American statesman and diplomat.

Pindar (*c.*518–*c.*438 BC) Greek lyric poet, noted for his odes and carefully constructed, elaborate poems which became influential in late-17th century England.

'Pindar, Peter' [John Wolcot] (1738–1819) English writer (*The Lousiad* 1785).

Pinero, Sir Arthur (1855–1934) English playwright (*The Second Mrs Tanqueray* 1893).

Pinkerton Detective Agency, USA, founded *c.*1852 by the Scottish-born American detective Allan Pinkerton (1819–84).

Pinkie, Battle of between the English and the Scots, 10 September 1547.

Pinochet [Ugarte], Augusto (1915–) Chilean general and dictator. He led the 1973 coup that deposed Allende and became president (1974–90). He ruthlessly suppressed dissent and instituted monetarist economic polities.

Pinter, Harold [Harold Da Pinta] (1930–) English dramatist and screenwriter, known for his halting, menacing dialogue and sinister pauses, e.g. *The Caretaker, Betrayal* 1978, 1982) (1930–).

Pinturicchio, Bernardino (1454–1513) Italian painter (*Dispute of St Catherine*).

Pinza, Ezio (1892–1957) Italian opera singer.

Pinzon, Martin Alonso (*c.*1440–1493) Spanish navigator.

Pinzon, Vicente Yañez (*c.*1460–*c.*1524) Spanish navigator.

Piozzi, Mrs Hester Lynch (Mrs Thrale) (1741–1821) friend of Dr Samuel Johnson.

Piper, John (1903–92) English painter and designer for opera and ballet.

Pipe Rolls of English Exchequer, annual rolls introduced 1110 by Roger, bishop of Salisbury; discontinued 1834.

Piraeus the main port of Athens in Greece, founded in the 5th century BC when the Long Walls to Piraeus were built 458 BC.

Pirandello, Luigi (1867–1936) Italian dramatist and novelist. His two best-known plays are *Six Characters in Search of an Author* (1921) and *Henry IV*, both of which question theatrical conventions. He was awarded the Nobel prize for literature in 1934.

Piranesi, Giambattista (1720–78) Italian artist (*Carceri d' Invenzione*).

Pisa, Council of assembled 25 March to unite Christendom under a new pope, dissolved 7 August 1409.

Pisa, Leaning Tower of *see* LEANING TOWER OF PISA.

Pisa, University of founded 1343 by the Florentine leader Lorenzo de' Medici (1449–92).

Pisanello, Vittore Italian artist (*c.*1380–1456) (*The Miraculous Stag Appearing to St Eustace*).

Pisano, Andrea (*c.*1290–1348) Italian sculptor.

Pisano, Giovanni (*c.*1245–*c.*1314) Pisan sculptor. A leading sculptor of his time, his works are expressive and elegant in the Gothic tradition. His father was Nicola Pisano.

Pisano, Nicola (*c.*1220–*c.*1284) Pisan sculptor. He was instrumental in the development of Christian art towards Roman rather than Gothic influences.

Pisistratus *or* **Peisistratus** (*c.*605–527 BC) Greek statesman. He was Tyrant, or absolute ruler, of Athens (560–555, 550–549, 540–527 BC), being expelled twice before gaining power a third time and ruling until his death. He was a wise ruler who advocated civil equality and a democratic constitution. He was succeeded by his sons Hippias and Hipparchus (the Pisistratae).

Piso Caesoninus, Lucius Calpurnius (d.*c.*40 BC) Roman statesman.

Pissarro, Camille (1830–1903) West Indian-born French Impressionist painter. Influenced by both Constable and Turner, he exhibited in all eight Impressionist exhibitions. His works include *Paysanne Assise*).

Pissarro, Lucien (1863–1944) French-born painter (*Chrysanthèmes*).

Pistols first manufactured by Camillo Vetelli, *c.*1540.

Piston, Walter (1894–1976) American composer (*Violin concerto* 1939).

Pistrucci, Benedetto (1784–1855) Italian-born gem engraver and medallist.

Pitcairn Island an island in the Pacific discovered 1767 by the English navigator Philip Carteret (d.1796). It was settled by mutineers from the *Bounty* 1790.

Pitman, Sir Isaac (1813–97) English shorthand pioneer who introduced 1837 a phonetic system of shorthand that had been so well thought out that it still has a wide vogue.

Pitt, William ('The Younger') (1759–1806) British statesman (prime minister 1783–1801, 1804–1805).

Pitt, William ('The Elder') [1st Earl of Chatham] (1707–78) English statesman (prime minister 1756–57, 1766–67). He led Britain to victory in the Seven Years War (1756–63) with France. He resigned in 1761, and served again 1766–68. His son was William Pitt (the Younger).

Pius I, Saint pope (141–154).

Pius II [Aeneas Silvius] pope (1405–64) (1458–64).

Pius III [Francesco Nanni-Todeschini-Piccolomini] (1439–1503) pope (1503).

Pius IV [Giovanni Angelo Medici] (1499–1565) pope (1559–65).

Pius IX [Giovanni Maria Mastai-Ferretti] (1792–1878) pope (1846–78).

Pius V, Saint [Michele Ghislieri] (1504–72) pope (1566–72).

Pius VI [Giovanni Angelo Braschi] (1717–99) pope (1775–99).

Pius VII [Luigi Barnaba Chiaramonti] (1740–1823) pope (1800–1823).

Pius VIII [Francesco Xaviero Castiglioni] (1761–1830) pope (1829–30).

Pius X, Saint [Giuseppe Sarto] (1835–1914) pope (1903–14).

Pius XI [Achille Ratti] (1857–1939) pope (1922–39).

Pius XII [Eugenio Pacelli] (1876–1958) pope (1939–58).

Pizarro, Francisco (*c.*1478–1541) Spanish *conquistador* of Peru. He was assassinated.

Pizarro, Gonzalo (d.1548) Spanish *conquistador*. He was executed.

Place, Francis (1771–1854) English radical reformer.

Plague bacillus discovered 1894 independently by the Swiss scientist Alexander Emile John Yersin (1863–1943) and the Japanese doctor Shibasaburo Kitasato (1856–1931); last pandemic 1894–1901).

Plague of London (The Great Plague) 1664–65.

Planck, Max [Karl Ernst Ludwig] (1858–1947) German physicist. He formulated the quantum theory in 1900 and was awarded the 1918 Nobel prize for physics.

Planetary motion, Kepler's laws of, 1609, 1609 and 1619.

Plankton term introduced 1886 by Henson.

Planquette, Robert (1848–1903) French composer (*Les Cloches de Corneville* 1877).

Plantin, Christopher (1514–89) French printer.

Plassey, Battle of a battle of the Seven Years' War between Clive and Indian rebel forces, 23 June 1757, which was a victory for Clive.

Plataea an ancient city state in Greece. It was the scene in 479 BC of a battle in which the Persians were defeated by the Greeks under Pausanias. The city was besieged by Sparta 429–427 BC and surrendered.

Platform scales invented 1831 by the American engineer Thaddeus Fairbanks (1796–1886).

Plath, Sylvia (1932–63) American poet and novelist. Her intense and highly expressive style has been very influential. She was married to Ted Hughes (1956–63). She committed suicide. Her works include the novel *The Bell Jar* (1961).

Platinite alloy discovered by the French scientist Charles Edouard Guillaume (1861–1938).

Platinum found in Spain at least as early as 1538; discovered in England 1741 by the English chemist William Brownrigg (1711–1800).

Plato (*c.*427–*c.*347 BC) Greek philosopher, regarded as the main founder of Western philosophy. Taught by Socrates, he was in turn Aristotle's tutor. His many works, which take the form of dialogues, notably the *Symposium, Phaedo* and *The Republic*, have influenced almost every subsequent age and tradition.

Platt Amendment American measure concerning Cuba framed 1901 by the American politician Orville Hitchcock Platt (1827–1905). Abolished 1934.

Plautus, Titus Maccius (*c.*254–184 BC) Roman comic playwright who borrowed his plots from Greek sources. He was the earliest of Roman writers whose works have survived complete, no fewer than 20 of his plays being extant. His play *Menaechmi* provided Shakespeare with the plot of *The Comedy of Errors.*

Playfair, Sir Nigel (1874–1934) English actor-manager.

Playfair, William Henry (1789–1857) Scottish architect.

Playford, John (1623–86) English music publisher.

Plebeian in early Rome, a citizen who was not a member of the patrician ruling elite. Gradually the plebeians (or plebs) gained a footing in the power system: first secession of plebeians at Rome and tribunes of the Plebs first appointed 493 BC; second secession of the plebeians and a great increase in the powers of Comitia Tributa 448 BC; Lex Canuleia legalized marriage between patricians and plebeians 445 BC; Licinian Laws passed at Rome and first plebeian consul 366 BC; Publilian Laws at Rome allowed decrees of Comitia Tributa to bind whole people; one Censor to be a plebeian 339 BC; Praetorship thrown open to plebeians 336 BC; Lex Ogulnia provided for plebeian pontiffs and augurs 300 BC; third secession of the plebs 287 BC; Tiberius Gracchus became tribune of the plebs and attempted to solve the land problem 133 BC; Cais Gracchus, brother of Tiberius, became tribune of the plebs and promoted further land reform 123 BC; Caius Gracchus killed in a riot 121 BC.

Pléiade, The French literary movement launched 1549.

Pleistocene Epoch The Great Ice Age between 20,000 and one million years ago.

Plekhanov, Georgi Valentinovich (1857–1918) Russian socialist leader.

Plesiosaurus remains first discovered 1821 by the English fossil collector Mary Anning (1799–1847).

Plimsoll Line limit to which a ship may be loaded brought into force 1876 by the efforts of the coal merchant and politician Samuel Plimsoll (1824–98).

Pliny the Elder (23–79) Latin writer (*Historia Naturalis* 77).

Pliny the Younger (62–114) Latin writer (*Epistles*).

Pliocene Epoch Earth history 15 million years ago.

Plotinus (205–270) Egyptian-born philosopher.

Plücker, Julius (1801–68) German scientist.

Plumptre, Edward Hayes (1821–91) English theologian and classical scholar.

Plunkett, Sir Horace (1854–1932) Irish statesman and pioneer in agricultural cooperation.

Plural voting discontinued in Britain by Act of Parliament 1948.

Plutarch (50–*c.* 120) Greek philosopher and historian.

Pluto, planet, discovered 1930 by the American astronomer Clyde William Tombaugh (1906.

Pluto Channel underwater oil pipeline ('Pipeline Under The Ocean') first in action 12 August 1944; proposed by the British engineer Arthur Clifford Hartley (1889–1960).

Plutonium transuranic element produced in the USA 1940.

Plymouth breakwater constructed 1811–41 by the Scottish civil engineer John Rennie (1761–1821).

Plymouth Brethren religious movement founded 1830 by the Rev. John Nelson Darby (1800–1882).

Plymouth Colony, Massachusetts, first settled permanently by the Pilgrim Fathers 1620.

Pneumatic tyre invented 1845 by the Scottish engineer Robert William Thomson (1822–73; perfected 1888 by the Scottish inventor John Boyd Dunlop (1840–1921).

Pocahontas (1595–1617) American Indian chieftain's daughter and wife of John Rolfe (1595–1622). She was brought to England in 1616.

Pococke, Edward (1604–91) English orientalist.

Poe, Edgar Allan (1809–49) American short-story writer, poet and critic. His macabre, highly Gothic horror stories are studies in pathological obsession, and his detective stories, e.g. 'The Murders in the Rue Morgue', have been highly influential. Other works include *The Gold Bug* (1843).

Pogany, Willy (1882–1955) Hungarian-born painter and illustrator.

Poggendorff, Johann Christian (1796–1877) German scientist.

Poggio, Gian Francesco (1380–1459) Italian scholar and writer (*Facetiae*).

Poincaré, Raymond (1860–1934) French statesman.

Poindexter, George (1879–1953) American politician.

Point Pleasant, Battle of between the Virginia militia and the Indians, 10 October 1774.

Poison gas first used in the First World War by the Germans, 22 April 1915; first used by the British 25 September 1915.

Poissy, Colloquy of to reconcile French Catholics and Protestants held 1561.

Poitier, Sidney (1924–) black American film star (*In the Heat of the Night* 1967).

Poitiers, Battle of between the English and the French, 19 September 1356.

Pol Pot (Saloth Sar) Cambodian politician, head of the Khmer Rouge which ruled Cambodia 1975–79.

Pol Pot *or* **Saloth Sar** [Kompong Thom] (1929–1996?) Cambodian Communist politician, head of the Khmer Rouge. The establishment of his Maoist dictatorship (1975–79) cost the lives of up to three million people. The Khmer Rouge regime was overthrown by the Russian-backed Vietnamese invasion of 1979 but he remained a powerful figure. His death from malaria was reported in 1996 but not confirmed.

Poland independent kingdom since 1025; first partition (Prussia, Russia and Austria) 1772–93; second (Prussia and Russia) 1793–95; third (Prussia, Russia and Austria) 1795–1918; independent republic 1919–39; German occupation 1939–44; communist regime 1947–89; democratic constitution adopted 1989.

Polarization of heat discovered 1837 by the Scottish scientist James David Forbes (1809–68).

Polarization of light discovered by the Dutch scientist Christiaan Huygens (1629–95). Experiments on polarization carried out 1845 by the English scientist Michael Faraday (1791–1867).

Polders arable land created in the Zuyder Zee; first undertaken on a large scale 1930.

Pole, Cardinal Reginald (1500–1558) archbishop of Canterbury.

Pole, Margaret, Countess of Salisbury (1473–1541). She was beheaded.

Police, London, reorganized 1829 by the English statesman Sir Robert Peel (1788–1850).

Polignac, Prince Jules de (1780–1847) French diplomat and statesman.

Poliomyelitis vaccine discovered 1934 by the American bacteriologist William Hallock Park (1863–1939); Salk vaccine developed 1954 by the American scientist Jonas Edward Salk (1914–).

Polish Succession, War of the concerning the succession to the throne of Poland 1733–35.

Politian [Angelo Ambrogini] (1454–94) Italian scholar and poet (*La Giostra*).

Polk, James Knox (1795–1849) 11th US president (1845–49).

Pollajuolo, Antonio (*c.* 1432–1498) Italian artist.

Pollard, Alfred Frederick (1869–1948) English historian.

Pollitt, Harry (1890–1960) English Communist leader.

Pollock, Sir Frederick (1845–1937) English jurist.

Pollock, [Paul] Jackson (1912–56) American painter. He became the leading exponent of action painting, a development of Abstract Expressionism, in the late 1940s.

Poll tax first levied in England 1380; abolished 1689; revived April 1990 (as Community Charge), re-abolished 1992.

Polo, Marco (1254–1324) Italian explorer.

Polonium radioactive element discovered 1898 by the French scientists Pierre and Marie Curie.

Polybius (*c.*205–123 BC) Greek historian.

Polycarp, Saint (d.155) bishop of Smyrna and martyr.

Polycrates (d.522 BC) tyrant of Samos. He was crucified.

Polyglot Bible Complutensian first polyglot Bible prepared 1514–22.

Polythene discovered by Imperial Chemical Industries' chemists 1933.

Pombal, Sebastião José de Carvalho e Mello, Marquess of (1699–1782) Portuguese statesman.

Pompadour, Mme de (1721–64) mistress of Louis XV.

Pompeii, Italy, devastated by the eruptions of Mount Vesuvius 63 and 79; ruins discovered 1748.

Pompey [Gnaeus Pompeius Magnus] (106–48 BC) Roman general and statesman who first made his name in fighting for Sulla against Marius. After Sulla's death he put down the revolt of Sertorius in Spain 76–71 BC, cleared the pirates out of the Mediterranean, commanded in the Third Mithridatic War, conquered Syria, depriving Antiochus XIII of the throne and making it a Roman province 65 BC, and took Jerusalem 63 BC. On his return to Rome he married Caesar's daughter and with Caesar and Crassus formed the First Triumvirate 60 BC. Relations soon became strained, however, and in 52 BC civil war broke out between Pompey at the head of the senatorial party and Caesar as leader of the popular party. In 48 BC Pompey was crushingly defeated at Pharsalia in Epirus and fled to Egypt, where he was murdered. His sons were defeated at Munda in Spain by Caesar 45 BC.

Pompidou, Georges [Jean Raymond] (1911–74) French statesman. He was prime minister (1962–68), but was dismissed in 1968 by de Gaulle following the May student riots in Paris but elected president (1969–74).

Ponce de Léon, Juan (1460–1521) Spanish colonial administrator. He was killed.

Ponce de Léon, Luis (*c.*1527–1591) Spanish poet.

Pond, John (1767–1836) English astronomer.

Pondicherry, India, settled by the French 1674; administration transferred to the government of India 1954; made a Union Territory in 1962.

Pons, Lily (1904–76) French operatic singer.

Pontiac's Rebellion 1763–64 led by the American Indian chief Pontiac (*c.*1720–1769). He was reputed to have been murdered.

Pontian, Saint pope (230–235).

Pontius Pilate Roman procurator of Judea (26–36).

Pontormo, Jacopo (1494–1556) Italian painter (*The Deposition*).

Pontus an ancient region on the Black Sea. It became a kingdom in the 4th century BC and reached its height during the reign of Mithradates VI, controlling all Asia Minor, but was defeated by Rome in the reign of Pharnaces.

Pony Express, USA, began 1860, ended 1861.

Poole, William Frederick (1821–94) American bibliographer and historian.

Poor Clares Order of Franciscan nuns organized by St Clare (*c.*1193–1253).

Poore, Richard (d.1237) English bishop and builder of Salisbury Cathedral.

Poor Law System begun in Britain 1601, reformed 1834, abolished 1929.

Pope, Alexander (1688–1744) English poet. His mastery of the rhymed couplet, his deadly satire and gift for sustaining metaphor place him as one of the greatest English poets. His works include *The Rape of the Lock* (1714).

Pope, Sir Thomas (*c.*1507–1559) privy councillor and philanthropist.

'Popish Plot' to murder King Charles II invented 1678 by Titus Oates (1649–1705); agitation 1678–81.

Poppaea Sabina (d.65) wife of Nero, killed by Nero.

Popper, Sir Karl [Raimund] (1902–94) Austrian-born British philosopher. He established the concept of 'falsifiability' as the criterion by which to judge whether or not a particular proposition can be said to be scientific.

Popular Front policy of cooperation of left-wing parties against Fascism between 1933 and 1939.

Porcelain, printing on, first achieved in Liverpool and Worcester 1756–57; introduced into France 1789 by Christopher Potter (d.1817).

Pordenone, Giovanni Antonio (*c.*1483–1539) Italian painter (*Le Mariage de Ste Catherine*).

Porphyry (233–*c.*304) Greek philosopher.

Porson, Richard (1759–1808) English classical scholar.

Porta, Giovanni Battista della (1542–97) Italian sculptor.

Port Elizabeth South African city, founded 1820.

Porteous Riots, Edinburgh, occasioned at a public execution by the hasty action of the captain of the City Guard, John Porteous, hanged by the mob 1736.

Porter, Cole American composer (1893–1964).

Porter, Cole [Albert] (1893–1964) American songwriter and composer. His highly popular songs, admired for their wit and lyricism, include 'Begin the Beguine' and 'Night and Day'. *Anything Goes* (1934)

Porter, William Sydney ('O Henry') (1862–1910) American writer (*The Gentle Grafter* 1908).

Portland American city in Maine, first settled 1633; assumed present name 1786.

Portland American city in Oregon, founded 1845; chartered 1851.

Portland cement invented 1824 by the English stonemason Joseph Aspdin (1779–1855).

Portland vase Roman glass funerary urn now in British Museum, probably made in the 1st century BC; bought 1770 by Sir William Hamilton, lent by the Duke of Portland to the British Museum (smashed 1845).

Porto Rico,*see* PUERTO RICO.

Port radar system, world's first, opened at Gladstone Dock, Liverpool, 30 July 1948.

Port Royal French abbey near Paris founded 1204; transferred to Paris 1626; suppressed 1704.

Port Said Egyptian city, founded 1859.

Portsmouth English city, granted a charter by Richard I 1194.

Portsmouth, Treaty of ending the Russo-Japanese war (1904–1905), signed 5 September 1905.

Portugal conquered by Rome 140 BC; declared an independent monarchy 1143; ruled by Spain 1581–1640; Bragança monarchy 1640–1910; proclaimed a republic 1910; ruled by prime minister Dr Salazar 1932–68; military coup 1974; constitutional reform and democratization 1982–89.

Portuguese East Africa *see* MOZAMBIQUE.

Portuguese Guinea *see* GUINEA-BISSAU.

Portuguese India former Portuguese overseas province discovered 1498 by the Portuguese navigator Vasco da Gama; first colonized 1505; status changed to overseas territory 1951; annexed by India 1961.

Portuguese Timor former Portuguese overseas province first colonized 1586; created an independent province 1896; overseas territory 1951; annexed by Indonesia 1975.

Portuguese West Africa *see* ANGOLA.

Positivism philosophical system developed 1822 by the French philosopher Auguste Comte (1798–1857).

Positrons positive particles discovered 1932 by the American scientist Carl David Anderson (1905–91).

Post, Wiley American pioneer aviator (1899 died in an air crash 1935).

Postage stamps, adhesive, first used in Britain 6 May 1840.

Postage stamps, hand-struck, first used in Britain 1661.

Postal orders first used in Britain 1 January 1881.

Postcards, stamped, introduced in Britain 1870.

Postcards with adhesive stamps, use permitted in Britain from 1894.

Post Office Savings Bank system introduced in Britain 1861.

Potassium discovered 1807 by the English chemist Sir Humphry Davy (1778–1829).

Potato famine in Ireland 1845 to 1849.

Potatoes introduced into England 1587 by Sir Walter Raleigh (1552–1618).

Potemkin, Gregory Alexandrovich (1739–91) Russian statesman.

Potgieter, Everhardes Johannes (1808–75) Dutch poet (*Florence* 1868).

Potsdam Agreement Second World War, 17 July to 2 August 1945.

Pott, Percivall (1714–88) English pioneer in modern surgery.

Potter, Beatrix (1866–1943) English writer and illustrator of children's books (*Jemima Puddleduck*).

Potter, Dennis (1935–95) British film and TV writer and novelist (*Pennies from Heaven* 1978).

Potter, Sir Thomas (1773–1845) joint-founder of the *Manchester Guardian*.

Poulenc, Francis (1899–1963) French composer. A member of 'Les Six', he is particularly noted for his his settings of verses from poetry. His works include *Mouvement perpetuel*.

Pound Imperial standard weight established in Britain 1844.

Pound, Ezra [Weston Loomis] (1885–1972) American-born poet and critic. A generous supporter of younger writers, e.g. T. S. Eliot, Hemingway, he lived in Italy from 1925 and broadcast propaganda against the Allies during the Second World War. He was committed to a US asylum after the war until 1958, when he returned to Italy. His works include (*Cantos* 1925 onwards).

Pourtalès, Louis François de (1824–80) Swiss-born naturalist.

Poussin, Nicolas (1594–1665) French painter who is noted for his carefully composed pictures in a classical style, e.g. *Venus and Adonis*.

Powell, Anthony (1905–) British novelist (*A Dance to the Music of Time* 12 vols 1951–75).

Powell, [John] Enoch (1912–) English Conservative politician. An outspoken opponent of immigration into Britain and of the Common Market. He was an Ulster Unionist MP (1974–87).

Powell, Humphrey (d. after 1556) English printer who established (1551) Ireland's first printing press at Dublin.

Powell, Michael (1905–90) English film producer, director and writer. With the screenwriter **Emeric Pressburger** (1902–88), he made several films that have subsequently been hailed as important works, e.g. *The Life and Death of Colonel Blimp* (1943).

Powell, Vavasour (1617–70) Welsh itinerant preacher.

Power loom, Cartwright's, invented 1785 by Edmund Cartwright (1743–1823).

Powys, John Cowper (1872–1963) English writer (*A Glastonbury Romance* 1933).

Powys, Llewellyn (1884–1939) English author (*Apples be Ripe* 1930).

Powys, Theodore Francis (1875–1953) English novelist (*Mr Tasker's Gods* 1925).

Poynings' Law regulating Irish government passed 1495 by Sir Edward Poynings (1459–1521), Lord Deputy of Ireland.

Prado, Spain, national museum of paintings and sculpture founded 1819.

Praed, Winthrop Mackworth (1802–39) English poet (*Molly Mog*).

Pragmatism idea introduced 1878 by the American scientist Charles Sanders Peirce (1839–1914).

Prague Czech capital, in existence by 600.

Prague, Treaty of ending the war between Austria and Prussia, signed 23 August 1866.

Prague University founded by the Emperor Charles IV in 1348.

Praseodymium rare earth element discovered 1885 by the Austrian chemist Baron von Welsbach (1858–1929).

Prasutagus (d.60) king of the Iceni *see* Appendix.

Pratt, Charles [Earl Camden] (1714–94) Lord Chancellor.

Pratt, Silas Gamaliel (1846–1916) American composer (*Zenobia* 1882).

Pratt Institute, New York, founded 1887.

Pratt Institute, Pittsburg, founded 1906 by Silas Gamaliel Pratt.

Praxiteles (*c*.390–*c*.332 BC) Greek sculptor.

Prayer Book *see* BOOK OF COMMON PRAYER.

Pre-Cambrian Period Earth history more than 520 million years ago.

Prefabricated house, first, a toll house created on the West Bromwich to Birmingham highway *c*.1830; dismantled 1926.

Premium Bonds first issued in Britain 1956.

Premonstratensian Canons founded 1120 by St Norbert (*c*.1080–1134).

Pre-Raphaelites English art movement flourished in the mid-19th century.

Presbyterianism modern founder John Calvin (1509–64); introduced to Scotland 1559–60 by John Knox (*c*.1505–1572); established again 1638–41, established finally 1690.

Prescott, William Hickling (1796–1859) American historian (*The Conquest of Mexico* 1843).

Presley, Elvis [Aaron] (1935–77) American rock singer. He became one of the most popular singers in the world in the mid-1950s and was an outstanding interpreter of ballads.

Press Association, London, founded 1868.

Pressburg, Treaty of between France and Austria, signed 26 December 1805.

Prester John mythical medieval monarch of Asia.

Prestonpans, Battle of between the Jacobites and government forces, 21 September 1745.

Pretoria capital of the Union of South Africa, founded 1855.

Pretorius, Andries Wilhelmus Jacobus (1799–1853) founder of the Transvaal.

Prevost, Sir George (1767–1816) governor-general of Canada (1811–16).

Prévost, Marcel (1862–1941) French novelist (*Les Demi-vièrges* 1894).

Prévost, The Abbé [Antoine François Prévost d'Exiles] (1697–1763) French novelist (*Manon Lescaut* 1731).

Price, Hugh (*c*.1495–1574) founder (1571) of Jesus College, Oxford.

Prideaux, Humphrey (1648–1724) English theologian and scholar.

Pride's Purge the expulsion from the Long Parliament of over 100 Presbyterian royalist members, carried out 1648 by the Parliamentary general Thomas Pride (d.1658). The remaining 80 members sealed the fate of Charles I and brought about his execution.

Priestley, J[ohn] B[oynton] (1894–1984) English novelist and dramatist. His astute social commentaries made him one of the best-known literary figures of the day. His huge output includes the play *An Inspector Calls* and the novel, *The Good Companions* (1929).

Priestley, Joseph (1733–1804) English scientist.

Primaticcio, Francesco (1504–70) Italian painter (*Diane de Poitiers*).

Prime minister office introduced in Britain 1721–42 but not legally recognized until 1905.

Primitive Methodists movement founded 1811 by the English Methodist Hugh Bourne (1772–1852).

Primrose League British Conservative organization founded in 1883 by Lord Randolph Churchill (1849–94).

Prince, Thomas (1600–1673) English governor of Massachusetts.

Prince Edward Island, Canada, discovered 1534 by the French navigator Jacques Cartier (1491–1557).

Princeton American city in New Jersey, first settled 1696.

Princeton, Battle of American War of Independence battle, 3 January 1777.

Principe former Portuguese overseas territory discovered by the Portuguese 1471; part of São Tomé and Principe.

Printer's device first known example printed in Fust and Schoeffer's Mainz Psalter 1484.

Printing known in China and Japan by 8th century, movable type invented 1041; invented (in Europe) at

Mainz *c.*1440; movable type used by Gutenberg in 1454; steam press (1810) and cylinder press (1811) invented by the German inventor Friedrich Koenig (1774–1833).

Printing offices, provincial, suppressed by order of the Star Chamber 23 June 1585.

Prior, Matthew (1664–1721) English poet (*To a Child of Quality*).

Priscian (*fl* late 5th and early 6th centuries) Roman grammarian.

Priscillian (d.385) Spanish theologian. He was burnt at the stake.

Prisons first used in England for punishment during 16th century.

Privy councillor, first woman, Miss Margaret Bondfield (1873–1953), appointed 1929.

Prize fight last held in England between Sayers and Heenan, 17 April 1860.

Probabilities, theory of modern approach founded by the French philosopher Blaise Pascal (1623–62).

Probus (d.282) Roman emperor (276–282). He was killed.

Proclus (*c.*410–485) Greek philosopher.

Procopius (d.*c.*562) Byzantine historian.

Proctor, Richard Anthony (1837–88) English astronomer.

Profumo, John Dennis (1915–) English Conservative politician. Secretary of state for war (1960–63), he resigned after admitting misleading the House of Commons about a sexual affair.

Profumo Affair resignation of Tory cabinet minister John Profumo (1915–92) for affair with call girl Christine Keeler (who was also involved with a Russian diplomat) 1963.

Prohibition came into effect nationally in the USA, 17 January 1920; repealed 1933.

Prokofiev, Sergei Sergeyevich (1891–1953) Russian composer and pianist. His works include seven symphonies, ballets, piano and violin concertos, and the well-known orchestral 'fairy tale', *Peter and the Wolf* (1936).

Promenade Concerts, London, founded 1895 by the English composer and conductor Sir Henry Wood (1869–1944).

Prontosil sulphonamide drug, curative powers discovered 1935 by the German bacteriologist Gerhard Domagk (1895

Propertius, Sextus Aurelius (*c.*48–*c.*14 BC) Roman poet from Umbria who was influenced by the Greek poets. From a love affair came his poem *Cynthia* (25 BC).

Protagoras (*fl* 5th century BC) Greek philosopher born at Abdera who went to Athens and Sicily. He was impeached after he wrote a book on the gods, which began, 'Respecting the gods, I am unable to know whether they exist or do not exist.' He was the first philosopher to charge fees for teaching, leaving it to his pupils to fix the amount in proportion to the profit they considered thermselves to have derived from his lessons. He is famous for the dictum, 'Man is the measure of all things.'

Proterozoic Era earth history more than 520 million years ago.

Protestant Episcopal Church, USA, founded 1789.

Protogenes (*fl* late 4th century BC) Greek Rhodian painter who was befriended by Apelles and whose work was much praised by Pliny.

Proton unit of positive charge, the hydrogen nucleus of the atom, identified 1912 by the New Zealand-born scientist Lord Rutherford (1871–1937).

Protoplasm discovered in the 18th century; first so named 1846 by the German botanist Hugo von Mohl (1805–72).

Protozoa unicellular animals discovered 1674 by the Dutch scientist Antony van Leeuwenhoek (1632–1723).

Proudhon, Pierre Joseph (1809–65) French social reformer.

Proust, Marcel (1871-1922) French novelist, essayist and critic, known for his long semi-autogiographic novel, *A la recherche du temps perdu* (1913–27). By subjecting a mass of detail to an analytical eye and by using a circular form, Proust broke new ground in conveying the complexity of life and time and the importance ofmemory

Prout, Ebenezer (1835–1909) English music theorist (*Harmony* 1889).

Provence a historical Mediterranean region of southeast France which became a Roman province in Southern Gaul in 120 BC, hence its name.

Proxima Centauri star nearest to the Earth discovered 1916 by the Scottish astronomer Robert T. A. Innes (1861–1933).

Prudentius, Aurelius Clemens (348–410) Spanish poet (*Contra Symmachum*).

Prud'hon, Pierre Paul (1758–1823) French painter (*L'Assomption* 1816).

Prussia kingdom 1701–1918.

Prussian blue discovered by the German scientist Johann Konrad Dippel (1673–1734).

Prussic acid discovered 1782 by the Swedish chemist Karl Scheele (1742–86).

Prynne, William (1600–1669) Puritan champion and pamphleteer.

Pryor, Roger Atkinson (1828–1919) New York Supreme Court judge and Confederate general.

'Psalmanazar, George' (*c.*1679–1763) French-born imposter.

Psammetichus king of Egypt (*c.*671–617 BC) and founder of the Saitic dynasty. After his father, Neco (1), had been put to death by Sabacon, the Ethiopian usurper of the Egyptian throne, he fled to Syria and was restored when Sabacon abandoned Egypt in consequence of a dream. During his reign the Greeks were first introduced into Egypt, primarily as mercenaries who helped him defeat gain territory in Syria and Phoenicia. He was succeded by his son, Neco (2).

Psammis king of Egypt (601-595 BC) who succeeded his father Neco. He carried on war against Ethiopia and died immediately after his return from the latter country. He was succeeded by Apries.

Psychoanalysis study founded by the Austrian psychoanalyst Sigmund Freud (1856–1939).

Ptolemy, Claudius (*fl* 2nd century ad) Alexandrian geographer who invented the astronomical theory called after him *c.*140. The Ptolemaic theory regarded the earth as the centre of the universe around which the moon, sun and planets revolved in true circles. It was generally accepted until superseded by the Copernican theory *c.*1540..

Ptolemy I [Soter] (d.283 BC) Macedonian general and king of Egypt (323–285 BC) who accompanied Alexander the Great on his Asian campaign. After Alexander's death his lands were divided up among his generals and Ptolemy acquired Egypt and founded the Ptolemy dynasty. He made Alexandria, his capital, the intellectual centre of the Hellenic world. He abdicated in favour of his son, Ptolemy II.

Ptolemy II [Philadelphus] (309–246 BC) king of Egypt (285–*c.*246 BC) who consolidated and extended the kingdom. During his reign Egypt reached its height in terms of power, wealth and culture.

Ptolemy III [Euergetes] (d.222 BC) king of Egypt (246–222 BC) who succeeded his father and in whose reign the kingdom continued to flourish. He greatly extended the library at Alexandria.

Ptolemy IV [Philopator] (d.205 BC) king of Egypt (222–205 BC) who put to death his mother, his brother and his uncle to secure his position. He managed to contain a Syrian invasion of Egypt's territories but withdrew from the Jews of Alexandria the privileges they had enjoyed under his predecessors and persecuted them. In his reign Egypt began its decline.

Ptolemy V [Epiphanes] (*c.*210–181 BC) king of Egypt (205–181 BC) who succeeded his father, Ptolemy IV, at the age of four or five. During his reign Egypt was invaded by Macedonian and Syrian armies and there were revolts in Lower Egypt.

Ptolemy VI [Philometor] (d.146 BC) king of Egypt (181–146 BC) who was a child when he succeeded his father, his mother acting as regent. Following the battle of Pelusium in 171 BC, he was captured by the Syrians, and his brother, Ptolemy VII, proclaimed himself king. The Syrians supported Ptolemy Philometor and established him as king at Memphis but he made peace with his brother and they agreed to rule jointly, but in 164 BC Ptolemy VII expelled his brother from Alexandria and he went to Rome to seek support. It was agreed that the monarchy should be divided but VII tried to add Cyprus to his share and was defeated by VI 154 BC. Philometor married his daughter to the Syrian usuper Alexander Balas, who later plotted against his father-in-law's life. Philometor was killed as a result of being thrown from his horse at Oenoparas, when he defeated Alexander.

Ptolemy VII [Euergetes II or Physcon] (d.117 BC) king of Egypt (146–117 BC) and brother of Ptolemy VI. After his defeat in Cyprus he remaind within his own part of the kingdom, but on the death of his brother, he married his widow (and sister) and put to death Ptolemy VI's son so that he could regain the whole of the kingdom. A bloodthirsty king, his activities provoked a revolt in Alexandria in 130 BC. Ptolemy fled to Cyprus, and Cleopatra (3), his sister (and former wife), was proclaimed queen, but when she sought help from Syria she was compelled to flee from Alexandria and Ptolemy was reinstated 127 BC.

Ptolemy VIII [Lathyros or Soter II] (d.81 BC) king of Egypt (117–107, 89–81 BC) and son of Ptolemy VII and Cleopatra (4). On his father's death he ruled jointly with his mother before she provoked an insurrection against him in favour of his brother, Ptolemy IX, and he was forced to flee to Cyprus where he remained while his mother and brother reigned in Egypt. After Cleopatra's death in 90 BC and the expulsion of Ptolemy IX in 89 BC, he was recalled and reigned until his death.

Ptolemy IX [Alexander I] (d.89 BC) king of Egypt (107–89 BC) and son of Ptolemy VII and Cleopatra (4). He was his mother's preferred choice as joint ruler on his father's death, but the Alexandrians compelled her choose his brother, Ptolemy VIII. He governed Cyprus until 107 BC, when his mother expelled Ptolemy VIII and recalled him to fill the vacant throne. He was killed. Terrified by his mother's cruelty and violence, he secretly left Alexandria. Fearing that her sons would plot against her, Cleopatra entreated him to return, secretly planning to assassinate him. He soon found reasons to suspect her and immediately decided to anticipate them by causing her to be assassinated in 90 BC. He did not rule long alone, however, as Cleopatra had been popular with the army and he was compelled by an army rebellion to leave Alexandria. He raised an army but was defeated in a naval action in which he was killed.

Ptolemy X [Alexander II] (d.81 BC) king of Egypt (81 BC) and son of Ptolemy IX. He was brought up on the island of Cos, which was taken by Mithridates the Great in 88 BC. Ptolemy took refuge with Sulla, whom he accompanied to Rome where he remained until 81 BC and the death of Ptolemy VIII when he returned to Egypt. He married Cleopatra (5), the daughter of Ptolemy VIII, but caused her to be murdered nineteen days later. The Alexandrians rose against him and he was killed.

Ptolemy XI [Auletes] (d.51 BC) king of Egypt (81–58, 55–51 BC). An illegitimate son of Ptolemy VIII, he succeeded to the throne on the death of Cleopatra (5) and Ptolemy X. He spent large amounts of money in attempting to bribe Rome to ratify his title to the crown and the taxes that he demanded to pay for this led to a revolt and he was expelled in 58 BC. His bribes were ultimately successful, however, and he obtained Rome's support, defeated his daughter Berenice in battle and regained the throne. One of his first acts was to have his daughter put to death.

Ptolemy XII (d.*c.*47 BC) king of Egypt (51–47 BC) who ruled jointly with his sister, Cleopatra (6), (51–48 BC) before expelling her. She took refuge in Syria where she assembled an army and invaded Egypt. Before the need for war, however, Caesar arrived in Egypt in pursuit of Pompey and took it upon himself to to arrange matters between Cleopatra and her brother. Cleopatra soon obtained so powerful a hold over Caesar that it was evident that he would decide the controversy in her favour. Ptolemy rebelled against Caesar, who attacked and defeated him neart the mouth of the River Nile. Ptolemy was drowned while attempting to escape.

Ptolemy XIII (d.44 BC) king of Egypt (47–43 BC). The youngest son of Ptolemy XI, he was declared king by Caesar after the death of Ptolemy XII and was nominally married to his sister, Cleopatra (6). Cleopatra took him with her to Rome, but shortly after the death of Caesar she put him to death.

Public Libraries Act, first, permitting the establishment of English public libraries, passed 1850.

Public Safety, Committee of, French Revolution, established 1793.

Public Trustee Office, London, opened 1908.

Publilian Laws in ancient Rome decrees of the Comitia Tributa passed in 339 BC to bind the people together, with one Censor to be a plebeian.

Publishers' cloth introduced into Britain 1820 by the British publisher William Pickering (1796–1854).

Puccini, Giacomo (1858–1924) Italian composer. His operas, e.g. *La Bohème*, *Tosca* (1900), *Madama Butterfly*, are regarded as the last great lyrical and dramatic works in the Italian tradition.

Puddling furnace invented 1784 by the British ironmaster Henry Cort (1740–1800).

Puerto Rico (formerly Porto Rico) discovered by Christopher Columbus 1493; ceded by Spain to the USA 1898.

'Puffing Billy' pioneer locomotive invented 1813 by the inventor William Hedley (1779–1843).

Puget, Pierre (1622–94) French artist (*Milo of Crotona* 1683).

Pulaski, Count Casimir (1748–79) Polish soldier in Washington's army. He died of wounds.

Pulcheria (399–453) Byzantine empress (450–453).

Pulitzer Prizes for American writing founded 1917 through the philanthropy of the Hungarian-born newspaper owner Joseph Pulitzer (1847–1912).

Pullman sleeping car invented 1864 by the American financier George Mortimer Pullman (1831–97).

Pultava, Battle of between the Russians and the Swedes 8 July 1709.

Pumping engine, atmospheric, invented *c.*1708 by the English engineer Thomas Newcomen (1663–1729).

Punch British periodical founded 17 July 1841 by the English engraver Ebenezer Landells (1808–50) and the English writer Mark Lemon (1809–70). Ceased publication 1992.

Punch and Judy puppet play origins (probably Italian) uncertain; introduced into England via France in the 17th century.

Punic War any war involving Carthage. Dionysius of Syracuse conducted a Punic War in 398 BC, but the most famous Punic Wars were three wars between Rome and Carthage: First Punic War 264–241 BC; Second Punic War 218–202 BC; Third Punic War 149–146 BC.

Punic War, First (264–241 BC) 262 BC battle of Agrigentum, Roman victory; 260 BC naval battle of Mylae Roman victory; 257 BC naval battle of the Liparaean Islands Roman victory; 256 BC naval battle of Ecnomus Roman victory; Romans invaded Africa; 255 BC Romans under Regulus heavily defeated by Carthaginians at Tunis in Africa; 251 BC battle of Panormus in Sicily Carthaginian defeat; 250–241 BC Carthaginians withstood Roman siege of the Sicilian fortress of Lilybaeum; 249 BC naval battle of Drepanum Carthaginian victory; 247 BC Hamilcar Barca assumed Carthaginian command; 241 BC naval battle of the Aegates Islands Roman victory; cession of Sicily to Rome.

Punic War, Second (218–202 BC) 218 BC Hannibal crossed the Alps into Italy; 218 BC battle of Ticinus, Hannibal victorious; 218 BC battle of Trebbia, Hannibal victorious; 217 BC battle of Lake

Trasimene, Hannibal victorious; 216 BC battle of Cannae, Hannibal victorious; 214 BC battle of Beneventum, Roman victory; 213–212 BC Romans under Marcellus besieged and captured Syracuse; 212 BC Roman siege of Capua successful; 212 BC second battle at Beneventum, Roman victory; 210 BC battle of Herdonea, Hannibal victorious; 211 BC city of Leontini in Sicily taken by Romans under Marcellus; 209 BC Nova Carthago taken by Romans; 207 BC Hasdrubal, brother of Hannibal, crossed the Alps into Italy but was defeated and killed at Metaurus; 206 BC battle of Elinga in Spain, Roman victory under Scipio and Spain conquered; 204 BC war carried into Africa by Scipio; 202 BC battle of Zama, when Hannibal was completely defeated near Carthage by the younger Scipio.

Punic War, Third (149–146 BC) 146 Carthage besieged by the Romans and destroyed; Roman province of Africa formed.

Punjab in India conquered by Alexander the Great at battle of the Hydaspes 326 BC; annexed by Britain 1849; constituted an autonomous province 1937; partitioned between India and Pakistan 1947.

Purcell, Henry (*c.*1659–1695) English composer and organist of Westminster Abbey. His works include incidental music for the theatre, songs, church music and six operas, notably *Dido and Aeneas* (1689) and *The Fairy Queen*.

Purchas, Samuel (*c.*1575–1626) English compiler (*Purchas, His Pilgrimage* 1613).

Purdue University, Lafayette, Indiana, founded 1874.

Purim Jewish festival celebrated 14th and 15th days of Adar.

Pusey, Edward Bouverie (1800–1882) English theologian. He was not prominently connected with the Oxford Movement until he wrote a tract on baptism (1835–36). In 1843 he was suspended from preaching for two years, and this brought his name prominently before the public. When Newman converted to Roman Catholicism, he became the head of the Movement.

Pushkin, Aleksandr Sergeyevich (1799–1837) Russian poet, novelist and dramatist. Widely regarded as Russia's greatest poet, the best known of his works are the verse novel *Eugene Onegin* and the historical tragedy *Boris Gudonov*. He died in a duel.

Putnam, Frederick Ward (1839–1915) American anthropologist.

Putnam, George Palmer (1814–72) American publisher.

Puvis de Chavannes, Pierre (1824–98) French painter (*St Geneviève*).

Pu Yi, Henry (1905–67) last emperor of China (1908–12), first emperor of Manchukuo (1934–45).

Pybba (d.*c.*606) king of Mercia (*c.*593–*c.*606) *see* Appendix.

Pydna, Battle of a battle of the Third Macedonian War, 168 BC, when Perseus of Macedonia was crushed; end of the war.

Pygmies, African, first discovered 1870 by the German ethnologist Georg August Schweinfurth (1836–1925).

Pylos (modern Pilos) a port in southwest Greece where, during the Peloponnesian War, the Athenians were besieged 425 BC by the Spartans based at Sphacteria but the siege at Pylos was lifted by an Athenian fleet which mounted a counter-siege of Sphacteria, which surrendered

Pym, John (1584–1643) English Puritan leader.

Pynson, Richard (d.1530) French-born pioneer printer in England.

Pyramids, Battle of the between Napoleon and the Mamelukes, 21 July 1798

Pyrenees, Peace of the ending war between France and Spain November 1659.

Pyridine organic base discovered 1851 by the Scottish chemist Thomas Anderson (1819–74).

Pyroscope invented by the Scottish mathematician Sir John Leslie (1766–1832).

Pyrrho of Elis (*c.*360–270 BC) Greek philosopher who founded scepticism and accompanied Alexander the Great on as Asian campaign.

Pyrrhus (*c.*318–272 BC) Greek king of Epirus (295–272 BC) who invaded Italy 280 BC and defeated the Romans at Heraclea and Asculum 279 BC but at the latter with such a loss of his own troops that it gave rise to the term 'Pyrrhic victory'. He was finally defeated at Beneventum in 275 BC and soon afterwards left Italy.

Pyruvic acid organic acid first obtained 1835 by the Swedish chemist Baron Berzelius (1779–1848).

Pythagoras (*c.*582–500 BC) Greek philosopher and mathematician who founded a school of philosophy. He believed in the transmigration of souls and impressed on his disciples the need to live a pure and self-denying life. His followers regarded themselves into clubs with secret religious rites. These clubs became so powerful that eventually they were suppressed.

Q

Qaddafi, Moammar al- *see* GADDAFI, MOAMMAR AL-.

Qatar Persian Gulf State, became a British protectorate 1916; declared independence 1971.

Q-ship a merchant ship converted into a warship and armed with carefully concealed guns used by the British navy in the First World War to decoy and sink German submarines.

Quadragesima the forty days of Lent; sometimes restricted to the first Sunday in Lent.

Quadrant, reflecting, invented 1731 by the English mathematician John Hadley (1682–1744).

Quadrille first introduced into Britain 1815.

Quadruple Alliance an alliance of four parties. One was concluded in 1718 by Britain, France, Austria and Holland to maintain the Peace of Utrecht. Another was concluded by Britain, Austria, Russia and Prussia against Napoleon 1814–15.

Quadruple Treaty guaranteeing the constitutional monarchies of Spain and Portugal, signed by France and Britain 1834.

Quaestor an official of ancient Rome who originally had judicial powers but later was an army paymaster or had charge of the finances of a province. As the empire expanded the number of quastors was gradually increased.

Quakers [Society of Friends] founded 1647 by the English shoemaker George Fox (1624–90); first Quaker MP elected 1833.

Quant, Mary (1934–) English fashion designer. Her most famous design was the miniskirt, which became the symbol of 'swinging sixties' London.

Quantitive analysis theory developed 1754 by the British scientist Joseph Black (1728–99).

Quantum theory formulated 1900 by the German physicist Max Planck (1858–1947).

Quare, Daniel (1648–1724) English clockmaker and inventor 1687 of repeating watches.

Quark subatomic (smallest elementary) particle, existence first suggested 1964 by Murray Gell-Mann and George Zweig.

Quarles, Francis (1592–1644) English poet (*Emblems* 1635).

Quarterdays in England and Ireland 25 March, 24 June, 29 September, 25 December; in Scotland 2 February, 15 May, 1 August, 11 November.

Quarterly Review a periodical that was started in 1809 by the publisher John Murray (1778–1843) in opposition to the Edinburgh Review and was supported by Canning and other Tories. The first; first editor was William Gifford (1756–1826).

Quarter Sessions British court of record, held four times a year by statute since 1363.

Quaternary Period the last million years of Earth history.

Quaternions in vector analysis invented 1852 by the Scottish mathematician Sir William Rowan Hamilton (1805–65).

Quatre Bras, Battle of a battle of Napoleon's Hundred Days at the village of Quatre Bras in Belgium between British, Belgian and German forces under Wellington and the French under Marshal Ney, 16 June 1815, in which the French were driven back. Waterloo was fought two days later.

Quayle, Sir [John] Anthony (1913–89) English actor and director. He appeared in several films but was principally a stage actor, founding his own classical touring company, Compass.

Quebec city in Canada founded 3 July 1608 by the French navigator Samuel de Champlain (1557–1635).

Quebec Act concerning the government and territory of the Province of Quebec 1774.

Quebec Conference Second World War conference held 11–24 August 1943.

'Queen, Ellery' [Frederic Dannay and Manfred B. Lee] American detective fiction writers (*The Roman Hat Mystery* 1929); *Ellery Queen Mystery Magazine* began 1941.

Queen Alexandra's Day first held 26 June 1912. The emblem was then an artificial rose.

Queen Anne's Bounty an ecclesiastical fund founded in England 1704 by Queen Anne with the consent of parliament to receive the fees (called 'first fruits' and 'tenths') paid by high dignitaries of the church on being appointed to bishoprics, etc. These fees were originally paid to the pope, but Henry VIII appropriated them to the sovereign. Anne restored them to the church to increase the income of poor livings and assist in others ways. The payment of first fruits and tenths was abolished in 1926 but the fund continues.

Queen Elizabeth Atlantic passenger liner launched 27 September 1938.

Queen Elizabeth II Atlantic passenger liner launched 1968.

Queen Mary Atlantic passenger liner launched 26 September 1934.

Queen Mary Land, Antarctica, discovered 1912 by the English Captain John King Davis (b.1884–).

Queen Maud Land, Antarctica, placed under Norwegian sovereignty 1939.

Queensberry Rules for glove-fighting initiated 1867 by Lord Queensberry (1844–1900).

Queen's College, The of Oxford University founded by Robert de Eglesfield 1340–41.

Queens' College, Cambridge University, founded 1448 by Queen Margaret of Anjou; refounded by Elizabeth Widville, consort of King Edward IV, 1465.

Queensland Australia, formed into separate colony 1859.

Queen's University, Belfast, came into being 1909. Previously Queen's College, Belfast.

Quetta city in west-central Pakistan founded 1876.

Quetta Earthquake 31 May 1935.

Quevedo, Francisco Gomez de (1580–1645) Spanish writer (*Sueños* 1627).

Quiberon Bay, Battle of between English and French fleets, 20 November 1759.

Quietism contemplative mystical movement founded 1675 by the Spanish theologian Miguel de Molinos (1640–97).

Quiller-Couch, Sir Arthur ('Q') (1863–1944) English writer (*Troy Town* 1888).

Quilter, Roger (1877–1953) English composer (*Where the Rainbow Ends* 1911).

Quin, James (1693–1766) London-born Irish actor.

Quincey, Thomas de (1785–1859) English writer (*Confessions of an Opium-eater* 1821).

Quinet, Edgar (1803–75) French historian.

Quinine discovered 1820 by the French scientists Pierre Joseph Pelletier (1788–1842) and Joseph Bienaimé Caventou (1795–1877).

Quinquagesima the 50 days immediately preceding Easter; or the Sunday before Ash Wednesday.

Quintana, Manuel José (1772–1857) Spanish writer (*Pelayo* 1805).

Quintilian (*c*.35–95) Roman orator (*Institutio Oratoria*).

Quirinal Palace in Rome designed 1574 by the Italian architect Domenico Fontana (1543–1607).

Quisling, Vidkun (1887–1945) Norwegian Fascist leader. He was installed as prime minister (1942–45) by the Nazis and was executed for treason after the war.

Quito capital of Ecuador, annexed by the Spaniards 1533, created a city 1541.

Quiz programme first British, the Inter-Regional Spelling Competition (later Regional Round) broadcast 25 November 1937.

Quiz programme, first, broadcast in Canada 15 May 1935.

Qumran Palestinian village, site of Dead Sea Scrolls, found by shepherd 1947.

Quorn Hunt, predominantly Leicestershire, county first hunted 1698–1753 by Thomas Boothby; first Master Hugo Meynell from 1753 to 1800.

R

R 101 British dirigible that had its first trials 14 October 1929 and flew the Atlantic 30 July 1930. It crashed at Beauvais in France 5 October 1930 while on her way to India. Out of the 54 people aboad, 48 died. The diaster caused the government to discontinue the construction of airships.

Raabe, Peter (1872–1945) German music historian (*Franz Liszt* 1931).

Rabbi ben Ezra [Abraham ben Meir ibn Ezra] (*c.*1092–1167) Spanish Jewish scholar.

Rabbinical Bible (d.1549) first published 1516–17 by the Christian printer Daniel Bomberg.

Rabelais, François (*c.*1494–*c.*1553) French monk, physician and satirist, noted for his huge, rambling and often licentious prose fantasy *Gargantua and Pantagruel*. The adjective 'Rabelaisian' is used to denote language that is robustly bawdy.

Rabies (1822–95) effective treatment developed 1885 by the French scientist Louis Pasteur.

Rabin, Yitzhak (1921-95) Israeli politician (prime minister 1974–77). He was assassinated.

Rachel, Elisa [Elisa Rachel Félix] (1821–58) Swiss-born actress who specialized in tragedy roles and won great triumphs in all the capitals of Europe.

Rachmaninov, Sergei (1873–1943) Russian composer and pianist. Influenced by Tchaikovsky, his music was very much in the 19th-century romantic tradition. His works include three symphonies, four piano concertos, the *Rhapsody on a Theme by Paganini* (1934) and many songs.

Racine, Jean (1639–99) French playwright who is regarded as the finest of the French tragedians. Several of his plays, eg Andromache (1667) and *Phèdre* (1677) have been performed in English translations from the late 17th century onwards.

Rackham, Arthur (1867–1939) English artist and illustrator.

Radar first practical demonstration made 1935 by a team led by the British scientist Sir Robert Watson-Watt (1892–1973).

Radcliffe Observatory, Oxford University, founded 1771, through the benefaction of the executors of the English physician John Radcliffe (1650–1714).

Radcliffe, Anne (1764–1823) English novelist (*The Mysteries of Udolpho* 1794).

Radek, Karl [Karl Sobelsohn] (1885–*c.*1939) Russian Bolshevik leader.

Radetzky, Josef (1766–1858) Count of Radetz, Austrian field-marshal.

Radiation theory developed 1900 by the German physicist Max Planck (1858–1947); and also 1896 by the German physicist Wilhelm Wien (1864–1938).

Radioactivity the property possessed by thorium, uranium and their compounds of emitting rays able to pass through substances that are opaque to light. It was discovered 1896 by the French scientist Antoine Henri Becquerel (1852–1908).

Radiometer an instrument used to detect or measure radiant energy. It was invented 1873–76 by the English scientist Sir William Crookes (1832–1919) *see also* CROOKES TUBE.

Radio photographs first transmitted from Britain to the USA 1924).

Radio signals first detected 1888; first sent across the Atlantic (Cornwall to Newfoundland) 1901 by the Italian inventor Guglielmo Marconi (1874–1937).

Radiotelegraphy *or* **wireless telegraphy** a form of telegraphy in which messages are transmitted by radio waves, brought into being 1895 by the Italian inventor Guglielmo Marconi (1874–1937).

Radio telephone service first, initiated 1927.

Radio Times British periodical first published 28 September 1923.

Radio tuning selective, basic principles of the method defined 1898 by the British physicist Sir Oliver Lodge (1851–1940).

Radio waves discovered 1888 by the German physicist Heinrich Rudolf Hertz (1857–94); theory developed 1868 by the Scottish physicist James Clerk Maxwell (1831–79).

Radisson, Pierre Esprit French explorer (*c.*1632–*c.*1710).

Radium discovered 1898 by the French scientist Pierre Curie; isolated 1902 by Marie Curie.

Radon radioactive element discovered 1900 by the German scientist F. E. Dorn.

Raeburn, Sir Henry (1756–1823) Scottish painter (*The Macnab*).

Raemaekers, Louis (1869–1956) Dutch cartoonist.

RAF (Royal Air Force) established 1918.

Raff, Joseph Joachim (1822–81) Swiss-born composer (*Im Walde*).

Raffles, Sir Stamford (1781–1826) British founder (1819) of Singapore.

Ragged Schools free elementary schools for poor children started by Robert Raikes and others at the end of the 18th century and the beginning of the 19th. They were converted into day schools by the Education Acts of 1870–72.

Raglan, Fitzroy James Henry Somerset, Baron (1788–1855) commanded the British troops at the Crimea.

Rahere (d.1144) founder 1123 of St Bartholomew's Hospital, London.

Raikes, Robert (1735–1811) English founder (1780) of Sunday schools.

Railway letter stamps first issued in Britain 1891.

Railway ticket dating machine, first, invented 1837 by the British inventor Thomas Edmondson (1792–1851).

Railway mining railways in use in Europe in 16th century; first public railway (Wandsworth to Croydon) opened 1803; first recorded journey (Mumbles) 1807; first public steam railway (Stockton to Darlington) opened 1825; first in USA 1829, France 1828, German 1835, Austria 1828, Spain 1848; first public electric (City and South London) opened 1890.

Raimondi, Marcantonio (*c.*1480–*c.*1534) Italian engraver.

Raines Law 1896, relating to liquor sales in New York State, framed by the American politician John Raines (1840–1909).

Rainier III (1923–) Prince of Monaco (1949–), head of the house of Grimaldi, rulers of Monaco since the Middle Ages. Married Grace Kelly 19 April 1956.

Rákóczy, Francis II (1676–1735) prince of Transylvania.

Raleigh, Sir Walter (1552–1618) English courtier, poet and explorer. He became a favourite of Elizabeth I after returning from a punitive expedition to punish Irish rebels in 1580, and organized unsuccessful attempts to colonize Virginia with English settlers in the 1580s. In 1595, he travelled to the Orinoco and participated in the English raid on Cadiz in 1596. He was imprisoned in the Tower after Elizabeth's death, was released to search for treasure on the Orinoco in 1616, and was executed on his return.

Ramadan Islamic month (depending on moon) of fasting during the day.

Raman Effect in physics, discovered 1928 by Sir Chandrasekhara Venkata Raman (1888–1970).

Rambert, Dame Marie [Cyvia Rambam] (1888–1982) Polish-born British ballet dancer, teacher and producer. After working with Diaghilev and Nijinsky, she settled in Britain in 1917. She formed the Ballet Club in 1931, which, renamed Ballet Rambert in 1935, became the most influential ballet company in Britain.

Rambouillet, Catherine de Vivonne, Marquise de (1588–1665) French patron of men of letters.

Rameau, Jean Philippe (1683–1764) French composer, organist and harpsichordist. He published an influential textbook on harmony and composed motets and cantatas. When he was 50, he started to write operas, with Voltaire contributing several libretti.

Rameses I (d.*c.*1314 BC) king of Egypt who founded the Nineteenth Dynasty in 1355 BC.

Rameses II (d *c.*1225 BC) king of Egypt (*c.*1304–1225 BC), the third of the Nineteenth Dynasty. The most celebrated king of Egypt, he waged a long war with the Hittites *c.*1300 BC, retained Palestine and was the greatest builder among the Egyptian kings, his works including the rock temple at Abu Simbel.

Rameses III (d *c.*1167 BC) king of Egypt (*c.*1200–1167 BC), the second king of the Twentieth Dynasty. He conducted a war against Syria and reconquered Ethiopia.

Ramillies, Battle of between the British and the French, 23 May 1706).

Ramsay, Allan (1686–1758) Scottish poet (*The Gentle Shepherd* 1725).

Ramsay, Sir William (1852–1916) Scottish scientist.

Ramsden, Jesse (1735–1800) English instrument maker.

Ramus, Petrus [Pierre de la Ramée] (1515–72), French philosopher. He died in the massacre of St Bartholomew

Ramuz, Charles Ferdinand (1878–1947) Swiss novelist.

Ranavalona III (1861–1916) last queen of Madagascar (1883–1916).

Randall, John (1755–1802) English shipbuilder

Randolph, Sir Thomas (d.1332) Earl of Moray, regent of Scotland.

Randolph, Thomas (1605–35) English writer (*Amyntas* 1638).

Randolph, William (1650–1711) English founder (1693) of William and Mary College, Virginia.

Ranelagh London pleasure gardens, opened to the public 1742; closed 1803.

Ranjit Singh (1799–1838) Sikh ruler.

Ranjitsinhji, Prince [Maharaja Jam Sahib of Nawanagar] (1872–1933) Indian cricketer who was the first to scorce over 3,000 runs in first-class cricket in a season.

Ranke, Leopold von (1795–1886) German historian.

Rankin, Thomas (1738–1810) Scottish Methodist reformer.

Rankine, William John Macquorn (1820–72) Scottish civil engineer and molecular physicist.

Rapallo, Treaties of settling the frontiers between Yugoslavia and Italy, signed 1920; between Germany and Russia, signed 1922.

Raphael [Raffaello Sanzio] (1483–1520) Italian painter. A leading figure of the High Renaissance, his portrayals of the Madonna and Holy Family combined Christian ideals with the grace and grandeur of classical antiquity *(St Catherine)*.

Rapin du Thoyras, Paul de (1661–1725) French historian.

Rappard, Professor William (1883–1958) Swiss political scientist.

Rasmussen, Knud Johan Victor (1879–1933) Danish Polar explorer.

Raspe, Rudolf Eric (1737–94) German-born writer (*Baron Munchhausen* 1785).

Rasputin, Grigori Efimovich (*c.*1871–1916) Russian monk. Claiming to having healing powers, he became a cult figure among the Russian aristocracy and an influential member of the royal household. He was assassinated.

Ratcliffe, Samuel Kerkham (1868–1958) English journalist.

Ratdolt, Erhard (*c.*1443–*c.*1528) German pioneer printer.

Rathbone, William (1819–1902) English founder (1859) of the District Nurse movement.

Rathenau, Walter (1867–1922) German statesman born in Berlin of Jewish parents, assassinated by nationalist fanatics soon after becoming foreign minister.

Rationing, 'points' Second World War, began in Britain 1 December 1941.

Rationing, food in Britain, First World War, 1916–18; Second World War, began 8 January 1940, ended 1953). In Germany, Second World War, began 27 August 1939.

Rattigan, Sir Terence (1892–1967) British playwright (*The Winslow Boy* 1935).

Rauschenberg, Robert American painter (1925).

Ravel, Maurice (1875–1937) French composer. He was one of the leading impressionist composers of his time. His works include the small orchestral apiece *Boléro* and*Tombeau de Couperin* 1917.

Ravenna chief residence of the Roman emperors 404–476 and of Byzantine exarchs 540–751; ceded to Papacy 756; recovered from Venetians 1509.

Ravi Shankar (1920–) Indian sitar player and composer. Regarded as one of India's greatest modern musicians, he became world-famous after teaching George Harrison to play the sitar.

Rawalpindi, Treaty of concluding the 3rd Afghan War, signed 8 August 1919.

Rawlins, Thomas (*c.*1620–1670) English medallist and playwright.

Rawlinson, Sir Henry Crewicke (1810–95) English Assyriologist.

Rawsthorne, Alan (1905–71) English composer (*Cortège* 1945).

Ray, John (1627–1705) English naturalist.

Ray, Man (1890–1976) American photographer and painter, he was a leading exponent of Surrealist photography.

Ray, Satyajit (1921–92) Indian film director. His films, popular in art houses the world over, include the *Apu* trilogy of life in rural India, i.e. *Pather Panchali* (1955), *Aparajito* (1956) and *Apu Sansar* (1959), and *The Chess Players* (1977).

Rayleigh, John William Strutt, Baron (1842–1919) English scientist.

Raymond I count of Toulouse 852–864).

Raymond II count of Toulouse 918–924).

Raymond III count of Toulouse 924–950).

Raymond IV (d.1105) count of Toulouse (1093–1105) and crusader.

Raymond V count of Toulouse (1148–94).

Raymond VI (d.1222) count of Toulouse (1194–1222).

Raymond VII (d.1249) count of Toulouse (1222–49).

Raymond le Gros [Raymond Fitzgerald] (d.*c.*1182) English ruler of Ireland.

Rayon first successfully manufactured 1889 by the French chemist Hilaire, Comte de Chardonnet (1839–1924).

Razor, Safety invented 1901 by the American manufacturer King Camp Gillette (1855–1932).

Read, Sir Herbert (1893–1968) English poet and critic.

Reade, Charles (1814–84) English novelist. His best-known work is *The Cloister and the Hearth* (1861), a semi-historical representation of life in the 15th century.

Reade's kettledrum condenser for the microscope invented 1861 by the chemist Joseph Bancroft Reade (1801–70).

Reader's Digest American periodical began in 1922 by DeWitt Wallace.

Reading, Rufus Daniel Isaacs, Marquess of (1860–1935) British lawyer and statesman. He was appointed Solicitor General in 1910, Lord Chief Justice in 1913 and was British ambassador in the USA 1918–19 and viceroy of India 1921–26.

Reading University founded 1892 as the University Extension College; university status 1926.

Reagan, John Henninger (1818–1905) American statesman.

Reagan, Ronald [Wilson] (1911–) American film actor, Republican statesman and 40th president of the US (1981–89). He appeared in around fifty films and was president of the Screen Actors Guild (1947–52, 1959–60). As US president he pursued strong monetarist economic policies and a strong anti-communist foreign policy.

Real Academia Español founded at Madrid July 1713.

Reaper invented 1826 by the Scottish inventor Patrick Bell (1799–1869). First practical machine invented 1831 by the American Cyrus Hall McCormick (1809–84).

Réaumur scale temperature invented by the French scientist René Antoine Ferchault de Réaumur (1683–1757).

Rebecca Riots in Wales 1839 and 1843.

Recamier, Mme (1777–1849) French leader of society.

Rechabites, Independent Order of temperance society founded at Salford 1835.

Recife city in Brazil founded 1536.

Reclus, Jean-Jacques (1830–1905) French geographer and anarchist.

Record Office first British local, established at Bedford 1923.

Records, Public first brought under the superintendence of the Master of the Rolls in Britain by Act of Parliament 1838.

Red Cross, International founded at Geneva 1864.

Redding, Otis (1941–67) American soul singer, killed in a plane crash ('Sittin' on the Dock of the Bay' 1967).

Redford, Robert (1937–) American film actor and director (*The Natural* 1984).

Redgrave, Sir Michael [Scudamore] (1908–85) English stage and film actor. One of the finest actors of his generation, with a distinctively intellectual approach to his craft (*The Lady Vanishes* 1938). He was knighted in 1959. All of his three children, Vanessa, Corin and Lynn, became successful performers. His daughter, **Vanessa Redgrave** (1937–), became a highly renowned and successful stage and film actress, and is well known for her interest in left-wing and humanitarian causes. **Corin** (1939–) became a character actor. **Lynn** became famous for her role in *Georgy Girl* (1966).

Redmond, John Edward (1856–1918) Irish patriot.

Redouté, Pierre Joseph (1759–1840) French botanical artist.

'Red Sunday' Russian revolt that took place at St Petersburg, 22 January 1905.

Redwald king of East Anglia (*c.*593–*c.*617) *see* Appendix.

Reed, Sir Carol (1906–76) English film director. His films include *The Third Man* (1949), written by Graham Greene and starring Orson Welles, a bleak thriller set in postwar Vienna that is one of the most highly praised films ever made.

Reed, Talbot Baines (1852–1903) English writer of books for boys.

Reed, Walter (1851–1902) American bacteriologist.

Reflex and voluntary action (1790–1857) distinguished 1833–37 by the English physiologist Marshall Hall.

Reformation the great religious revolution of the 16th century against the supreme authority of the pope in all matters of religion and against certain practices of the Church. It started in 1517 with the attack on indulgences and abuses by the German reformer Martin Luther (1483–1546). From Germany to spread to other countries and in England resulted in the dissolution of the monasteries, the translation of the Bible into England, the severance of the Church of England from papal control and the issue of a Book of Common Prayer.

Reformatory first British, opened at Redhill 1850.

Refraction of light law postulated 1621 by the Dutch scientist Willebrord Snell (1591–1626).

Refraction, Double theory made public 1810 by the French physicist Etienne Louis Malus (1775–1812).

Refrigerated railway waggons first used in the USA 1877).

Refrigerator invented 1867 by the French inventor Charles Tellier (1828–1913).

Regency period in Britain approximately 1810 to 1820, pertaining to the regency of the then Prince of Wales who was later to become George IV. In France it refers to the regency of Philip, Duke of Orléans.

Reger, Max (1873–1916) German composer (*Sinfonietta*).

Regiomontanus [Johannes Müller] (1436–76) German astronomer.

Regional broadcasting in Britain began with the opening of the transmitting station at Brookmans Park 21 October 1929.

Registered trademark, first the Red Badge of Messrs Bass & Co.'s Pale Ale, created 1855.

Registrar-General, first British Thomas Henry Lister (1800–1842) (appointed 1836).

Registration of births, marriages and deaths, instituted in Britain by Thomas Cromwell (*c.*14851540); made compulsory 1837.

Regnault, Alexandre Georges Henri (1843–71) French painter killed in the Franco-Prussian War (*Salome* 1870).

Régnier, Mathurin (1573–1613) French satirical writer (*Macette*).

Regulus, Marcus Atilius (3rd century BC) Roman hero.

Rehan, Ada (1860–1916) Irish-born actress.

Reichenbach, Hans (1891–1953) German-born exponent of the philosophy of science.

Reichstadt, Napoléon Francis Joseph Charles, Duc de *see* NAPOLEON II.

Reichstag German parliament reconstituted 1867–71; building burnt 27 February 1933; trial began at Leipzig 21 September 1933).

Reid, Sir William (1791–1858) governor of the Bermudas (1839–46).

Reign of Terror the period of the French Revolution (1793–94) during which the infamous Committee of Public Safety sent more than 30,000 people to the guillotine.

Reinach, Salomon (1858–1932) French archaeologist (*Apollo* 1902–1903).

Reinhardt, Django [Jean Baptiste Reinhardt] (1910–53) Belgian guitarist, he formed the influential Quintette de Hot Club de Paris with Grappelli.

Reinhardt, Max Austrian pioneer of the Modern Theatre (1873–1943).

Réjane, Gabrielle (1857–1920) French actress.

Relativity, Special Theory of propounded 1905; **General Theory of** propounded 1916: both by the German-born scientist Albert Einstein (1879–1955).

Relief map, earliest (of Peru), prepared for the 9th Inca (d.1191).

Remarque, Erich Maria (1898–1970) German-born novelist (*All Quiet on the Western Front* 1929).

Rembrandt Harmensz, van Rijn (1606–69) Dutch painter, draughtsman and etcher. His remarkable series of self-portraits, painted over 40 years, reveal the depth and spiritual development of his work. His works include *Woman Taken in Adultery* (1644).

Remington, Frederick (1861–1909) American artist.

Remonstrance, Grand parliamentary indictment of Charles I, November 1641.

Remonstrants Dutch religious movement founded 1609.

Rémusat, Charles François Marie, Comte de (1797–1875) French writer and politician.

Renaissance the name applied to the awakening of Europe between 14th and 16th centuries from the moral, mental and material slumber of the Middle Ages in which the creed of the Church, the prevalence of Latin and the bonds of feudalism had kept minds and bodies stagnant. The Crusades, in spite of the blessing of various popes, had been a failure, and in retaliation the Turks invaded Euopre and took Constantinope in 1453. This involved the dispersal of various learned schools, the members of which carried science and literature into western Europe. It had enturing effects on western scholarship, literature, architecture and religion, and in Spain and Portgual created the desire for exploration, which opened to Europe many other parts of the world. It began with the revival of Italian art.

Renan, Ernest (1823–92) French theologian and Orientalist. He became professor of Oriental Languages in the Collège de France in 1862 but after publication of *La Vie de Jesus* (1863) he was removed from his chair, which he recovered in 1871.

Reni, Guido (1575–1642) Italian painter (*Deeds of Hercules* 1617–21).

Rennie, John (1761–1821) Scottish civil engineer who became the most famous builder of his age. Among his chief works were Southwark, Waterloo and London bridges across the Thames, the Crinan, Avon and Kennet canals, harbours, docks and dockyards.

Renoir, Pierre Auguste (1841–1919) French Impressionist painter. His form of Impressionism developed the use of perspective, solidity of form and preliminary sketches (*Les Grands Boulevards*). His son, **Jean Renoir** (1894–1979), was a film director. His memorable films, e.g. *La Grande Illusion* and *La Règle du Jeu*, are often described as 'humanist' for their compassion and sense of human unity.

Renwick, James (1662–88) Scottish Covenanter who proclaimed the Lanark Declaration in 1682, and was outlawed for his *Apologetic Declaration*. He was executed after his public rejection of James VII and II meant there was a reward for his capture.

Reparations, German, after the Second World War, paid 1921–31.

Repeating watch invented 1687 by the English clockmaker Daniel Quare (1648–1724).

Repington, Cardinal Philip (d.1424) bishop of Lincoln.

Repplier, Agnes (1858–1950) American essayist (*To Think of Tea* 1932).

Republic, French First 1793–1804, Second 1848–52, Third 1875–1940, Fourth 1946–58, Fifth since 1958; English 1649–60; Spanish 1873–74, 1931–39; Portuguese since 1910; Italian since 1946; German 1918–33, 1949 to date.

Republican Party USA, present-day party formed 1854.

Resnais, Alain (1922–) French film director. One of the best known of the French 'New Wave' directors, his films include the romance *Hiroshima mon amour* (1959) and the experimental, "Surrealist" *Last Year in Marienbad* (1961).

Respighi, Ottorino (1879–1936) Italian composer (*La Boutique Fantasque* 1919).

Restif de la Bretonne, Nicolas Edmé (1734–1806) French writer (*Monsieur Nicolas* 1794–97).

Restoration, English, of King Charles II, 29 May 1660.

Restoration, French, of King Louis XVIII, 1814.

Reszke, Jean de (1850–1925) Polish operatic singer.

Retarded potentials relativity theory made public 1867 by the German scientist Ludwig Lorenz (1829–91)

Retreat from Mons First World War retreat, August 1914.

Retz, Jean François Paul de, Cardinal de (1614–79) abbot of St Denis and politician.

Reuchlin, Johann (1455–1522) German scholar and pioneer in Hebrew grammar.

Reunion island in the Indian Ocean discovered 1507 by the Portuguese navigator Diego Fernandes Pereira; formally annexed by France 1643; an overseas department of France since 1946.

Reuter, Paul Julius (Josephat), Baron de [Israel Beer Josaphat] (1816–99) German-born telegrapher and pioneer in the speedy transmission of news.

Reuters press agency founded by the German-born Paul Julius Reuter 1849 at Aix-la-Chapelle but transferred to London ater the laying of the Calais-Dover cable in 1851.

Revere, Paul (1735–1818) American revolutionary who took part in the 'Boston Tea Party', the destruction of the tea in Boston Harbour (1773). The story of his ride from Charleston to Lexington and Concord is told in the poem by Longfellow, *The Midnight Ride of Paul Revere.*

Revised Version of the Bible a revision of the Authorized Version of the Bible which was begun in 1870 and completed 1884. The committee consisted originally of 16 members but was afterwards increased to 79 members. The New Testament appeared 1881, four years before the Old Testament, 1885.

Rexists Belgian Fascist party founded 1935 by Léon Degrelle.

Reykjavik the capital of Iceland, founded *c.*875.

Reymont, Wladislaw Stanislaw (1868–1925) Polish novelist (*The Promised Land* 1898).

Reynolds, Albert (1933–) Irish politician. Elected in 1977 as a Fianna Fáil member, he held several posts under Haughey but was sacked by him (1991) before succeeding as *taoiseach* (prime minister) (1992–94).

Reynolds, George Nugent (*c.*1770–1802) Irish poet (*Kathleen O'More* 1800).

Reynolds, Sir Joshua (1723–92) English painter and art theorist. A portraitist, influenced by his studies of Renaissance and Baroque painting and classical sculpture, he became first president of the Royal Academy. He painted most of the beautiful and famous women of his age, e.g. the Duchess of hamilton, Sarah Siddons, and was a friend of Goldsmith, Garrick and Dr Johnson.

Rhankaves, Alexandres (1810–92) Greek statesman.

Rhee, Syngman [Li Sung-man] (1875–1965) ruler of South Korea (1948–60).

Rheims Cathedral construction began 1210, mostly completed by 1298; west front erected in the 14th century.

Rheinberger, Josef (1839–1901) Liechtenstein composer of organ sonatas.

Rhenium metallic element discovered 1925.

Rhine, Confederation of the, of German states, formed by Napoleon 1806; collapsed 1813.

Rhineland occupied by French 1792–1813; by Allies 1918–30; taken over by Hitler 7 March 1936.

Rhode Island state of the USA, first settled 1636; entered the Union 1790.

Rhodes, Cecil John (1853–1902) English-born Central African pioneer who made a fortune at the age of seventeen by joining the rush for diamonds at Kimberley in South Africa, where he had been sent because of ill health. He was an undergraduate at Oxford 1873–81 and returned to South Africa where amalgamated the many mines at Kimberley and in 1881 was elected to the Cape parliament. He then entered on a policy of expanding British territory northwards, which ended in the large area, named Rhodesia after him, being added to the B ritish empire. He formed the British South Africa Company in 1889, was prime minister of Cape Colony 1890–96, resigning after the Jameson Raid. He was besieged in Kimberley during the Boer War. He left practically the whole of his vast fortune to public objects, including the funding for endowing scholarships at Oxford.

Rhodes, Colossus of statue built *c.*285 BC; destroyed by an earthquake 224 BC.

Rhodes, Island of seized by the Knights Hospitallers 1309; ceded to the Turks 1522; seized by the Italians 1912; ceded to Greece 1947.

Rhodesia *see* ZIMBABWE.

Rhodesia, Northern *see* ZAMBIA.

Rhodesia, Southern, *see* ZIMBABWE.

Rhodesia and Nyasaland, Federation of consisting of Northern Rhodesia, Southern Rhodesia and Nyasaland 1953–63.

Rhodesia University multi-racial, foundation stone laid 1953.

Rhodes Scholarships for the education at Oxford of overseas students, set up 1902 by the will of Cecil John Rhodes (1853–1902).

Rhodi Mawr king of Gwynedd (844)878) *see* Appendix.

Rhodium metallic element discovered 1803 by the English scientist William Hyde Wollaston (1766–1828).

Rhondda, Margaret Haig Thomas, Viscountess (1883–1958) founder and editor (1920–58) of *Time and Tide* .

Ribauit, Jean (*c.*1520–1565) French navigator and pioneer colonist in North America. He was killed.

Ribbentrop, Joachim von (1893–1946) German Nazi

leader, foreign minister (1938–45), captured by the British and hanged at Nuremberg 1946.

Ribbing machine for stocking manufacture invented 1759 by the English manufacturer Jedediah Strutt (1726–97).

Ribera, Jusepe de Spanish-born painter (*St Sebastian*) (1591–1652).

Ricardo, David (Israel) (1772–1823) English economist (*Principles of Political Economy* 1817).

Ricci, Matteo Italian missionary in China (1552–1610).

Rice, Elmer [Elmer Reizenstein] (1892–1967) American playwright (*Counsellor-at-law* 1931).

Rice, Tim *see* LLOYD WEBBER, ANDREW.

Rich, Richard (*fl.* late 16th and early 17th centuries) English traveller and writer (*Newes from Virginia* 1610).

Richard, Sir Cliff [Harry Roger Webb] (1940–) Indian-born English singer and film actor, and an institution in British popular music.

Richard, Keith *see* JAGGER, MICK.

Richard I [Coeur de Lion or the Lionheart] (1157–99) king of England (1189–99) *see* Appendix.

Richard II (1367–1400) king of England (1377–99) *see* Appendix.

Richard III (1452–85) king of England (1483–85) *see* Appendix.

Richard de Bury (1281–1345) English divine and book collector (*Philobiblon*).

Richard of Cirencester (d.*c.*1401) English historian (*Speculum Historiale*)

Richard of Devizes English historian of the late 12th century.

Richards, Alfred Bate (1820–76) English writer and first editor (1855) of the *Daily Telegraph*.

Richards, Frank (1875–1961) English writer of the 'Billy Bunter' series for boys.

Richards, Viv (1952–) Antiguan-born West Indian cricketer. One of the best batsmen and fielders in modern cricket, he was captain of the West Indies (1985–91).

Richardson, Dorothy English novelist (*Pilgrimage*) (1873–1957).

Richardson, Jonathan English painter (*Matthew Prior*) (1665–1745).

Richardson, Sir Ralph [David] (1902–83) English stage and film actor. Ranked with Gielgud and Olivier as among the finest British actors of the 20th century, he was equally at home with the classics and modern roles. Notable film roles include Buckingham in Olivier's film of *Richard III*, the head of the secret service in *Our Man in Havana* and God in *Time Bandits* (1981).

Richardson, Samuel (1689–1761) English novelist. All his novels were written in epistolary form and all were hugely popular. The first was *Pamela; or Virtue Rewarded* (1740), in which a servant girl achieves an upwardly mobile marriage by resisting seduction (the work was attacked by Fielding in his parody *Shamela* for its dubious morality). Richardson subsequently published *Clarissa Harlowe* (1748) and *Sir Charles Grandison*.

Richelieu, Cardinal Armand Jean du Plessis, Duc de (1585–1642) French statesman. He was nominated bishop of Luçon at the age of twenty-one. He was adviser to Marie de' Medici in 1614, and secretary for war and for foreign affairs in 1616. In 1622 he was named cardinal and, two years later, he became minister of state to Louis XIII, and for the rest of his life held much of the ruling power in France.

Richemont, Henri Louis Victor Hébert, Comte de (d.1853) pretender to the throne of France.

Richepin, Jean (1845–1926) French writer (*Monsieur Scapin* 1886).

Richmond, George (1809–96) English painter (*William Wilberforce*).

Richter, Ernst Friedrich (1808–79) German composer and writer on harmony.

Richter, Hans (1843–1916) Hungarian-born conductor (particularly of Wagner's works).

Richthofen, Manfred, Baron von (1892–1918) German fighter pilot, nicknamed the 'Red Baron'. He was credited with shooting down 80 allied aircraft in the First World War.

Ricordi, Giovanni (1785–1853) Italian music publisher.

Riddell, George Allardice, Baron (1865–1934) Scottish lawyer and newspaper proprietor, who became chairman of *News of the World*.

Ridley, Nicholas (*c.*1500–1555) bishop of London. On the death of Edward VI he denounced Elizabeth and Mary I as illegitimate and supported the cause of Lady Jane Grey. He was sent to the Tower of London when Mary came to the throne and was burnt at the stake 18 months later.

Ridolfo, Roberto di (1531–1612) Italian intriguer in England.

Ridpath, George (d.1726) Scottish writer and journalist .

Riefenstahl, Leni (1902–) German film director and Nazi propagandist. Her films include *Triumph of the Will* (1934).

Riemann, Hugo (1849–1919) German music historian.

Riemenschneider, Tilman (*c.*1468–1531) German sculptor (*Adam and Eve*)

Rienzi, Cola di (*c.*1313–1354) Italian reformer whose aim was to restore Rome to its former glory, but who succeeded in only creating unease and resentment. In the end he was killed by a mob on his return to Rome.

Rifle a firearm with a long barrel that imparts a spinning motion to bullets and allows greater accuracy over a longer range. Rifles were adopted generally for miliary purposes in the 1860s when breech-loading rifles came into use. The Enfield rifle was invented by the Frenchman Claude Minié (1814–79); Lee-Enfield introduced in Britain 1895; the Belgian FN. 30 adopted by Britain 19 January 1954.

Riga Baltic port and capital of Latvia, founded 1200.

Rigaud, Hyacinthe (1659–1743) French painter (*Louis XIV*).

Rigaud, Stephen Peter (1774–1839) English mathematician and astronomer.

Rights, Declaration (February) **and Bill** (October) **of** 1689.

Rights of Man, Declaration of issued by the French Constituent Assembly 1789.

Rigveda a collection of Hindu poems compiled in India *c.*1000 BC.

Rijeka-Susak (formerly Fiume) a port on the Adriatic Sea, seized by d'Annunzio 1919; ruled by Italy 1924–47; part of Croatia since 1947.

Riley, Bridget [Louise] (1931–) English painter and exponent of Op Art paintings that use precise hard-edged patterns in strong colours.

Riley, James Whitcomb (1853–1916) American poet (*Love Lyrics* 1899).

Riley, John (1646–91) English painter to the court.

Rilke, Rainer Maria (1875–1926) German poet (*Duinese Elegies* 1923).

Rimbaud, Arthur (1854–91) French poet. An early Symbolist, he stopped writing poetry at the age of nineteen. Some of the pieces in his collection of hallucinatory, vivid prose poems, *Les Illuminations* (1886), were set to music by Britten.

Rimini, Francesca da (d.*c.*1285) Italian heroine, wife of Giovanni Malatesta and mistress of Paolo il Bello. She was murdered.

Rimmer, William (1816–79) English-born artist (*A Dying Centaur*).

Rimsky-Korsakov, Nikolay Andreyevich (1844–1908) Russian composer. His music is typically Russian and he freely used local history, folk tunes, legends and myths as sources of inspiration. His works include 16 operas (e.g. *The Golden Cockerel* 1910), three symphonies and numerous orchestral pieces.

Rinehart, William Henry (1825–74) American sculptor.

Ring, wedding changed from right to left hand in English Prayer Book of 1549, and in *Rituale Romanum* of 1614.

Rio de Janeiro capital of Brazil, site believed to have been discovered by the Portuguese navigator André Gonçalves 1502.

Rio de Oro former region of West Africa comprising south of Spanish Sahara (now Western Sahara); annexed by Spain 1885.

Ripley, Thomas (*c.*1683–1758) English architect.

Ripon, George Frederick Samuel Robinson, Marquess of (1827–1909) statesman.

Risorgimento movement for Italian unity in 19th century.

Ritchie, Charles Thomas, Baron Ritchie (1838–1906) British statesman.

Ritschl, Albrecht (1822–89) German theologian.

Ritson, Joseph (1752–1803) English antiquary (*Bibliographia Poetica* 1802).

Rittenhouse, David (1732–96) American astronomer.

Ritter, Hermann (1849–1926) German inventor (1876) of the viola alta.

River Plate, Battle of the a naval battle between British cruisers and the German *Graf Spee*, 13–17 December 1939. The *Graf Spee* was trapped in Montevideo harbour in Uruguay and scuttled by her crew.

Rivera, Diego (1886–1957) Mexican painter of murals who developed a style derived from Aztec art.

Rivers, Richard Woodville, Earl (d.1469) High Constable of England. He was executed.

Rizzio, David (*c.*1533–1566) Italian secretary to Mary Queen of Scots, murdered at the palace of Holyrood when the Queen's husband, Lord Darnley, became jealous of Rizzio's influence over Mary.

Robbia, Luca della (*c.*1400–1482) Italian sculptor.

Robert I (d.923) king of France (922–923). He was killed in battle.

Robert II (d.1031) king of France (996–1031).

Robert I (Robert the Bruce) (1274–1329) king of Scotland (1306–29) *see* Appendix.

Robert II (1316–90) king of Scotland (1371–90) *see* Appendix.

Robert III (*c.*1340–1406) king of Scotland (1390–1406) *see* Appendix.

Robert Gordon University a college in Aberdeen, founded 1729 as Robert Gordon's College, which became the Robert Gordon Institute of Technology then the Robert Gordon University 1992.

Robert of Gloucester English historian, probably lived in the 13th and 14th centuries.

Roberts [of Kandahar], Frederick Sleigh, Earl (1832–1914) British soldier who took part in the suppression of the Indian Mutiny, when he won the VC. As commander of the Kuram field force in the Afghan War of 1879 he marched on Kabul and during his return routed the Afghans. He was commander-in-chief of the Indian army 1885–93. After his retirement he devoted his energies to warning of the need for universal military training as he foresaw clearly the coming struggle with Germany. He died in France, within the sound of the guns, while visiting Indian troops.

Roberts, Richard (1789–1864) Welsh inventor.

Robertson, James (*c.*1720–1788) Scottish governor of New York.

Robertson, Sir John (1816–91) Australian statesman.

Robertson, Thomas William (1829–71) English playwright (*Caste* 1867).

Robeson, Paul [Le Roy] (1898–1976) American bass singer and actor. He qualified as a lawyer before becoming a highly popular stage actor in the 1920s. Notable performances include *Showboat* (1927) and *Othello* (1940). His warm, sensitive recordings of spirituals and folk songs were also very popular. A noted advocate of civil rights for Blacks, he came under strident attack in the US for supposed Communist sympathies and spent much of his life from the early 1960s in seclusion.

Robespierre, Maximilien Marie Isidore de (1758–94) French lawyer and revolutionary. He was elected to the National Assembly (1789) at the beginning of the French Revolution and became leader of the Jacobin group. He launched the infamous Reign of Terror, but was eventually guillotined himself.

Robin Hood legendary English hero famous for stealing from the rich to give to the poor. May have lived *c.*1200, or possibly a century later, but there is no evidence that he is anything more than a character of folk legend.

Robinson, Edward G. [Emmanuel Goldenberg] (1893–1973) Romanian-born American film actor who specialized in gangster roles. His films include *Little Caesar* (1930).

Robinson, Henry Crabb (1775–1867) English diarist.

Robinson, Mary ('Perdita') (1758–1800) English actress and mistress of the Prince of Wales.

Robinson, Mary (1944–) Irish barrister, politician and president (1990–) of the Republic of Ireland. Notably liberal in her policies, she won wide support from parties opposed to her opponent.

Rob Roy [Robert Macgregor] (1671–1734) Scottish outlaw who gathered together a group of followers to protect his herds and those of his neighbours from plunderers from the North. His life has been romanticized in many stories of him robbing the rich to give to the poor. Undoubtedly, however, there was an element of personal gain involved, e.g. in receiving money from his neighbours for the protection of their herds, in regaining his land from the Duke of Montrose and in seeking to become the chief of the clan Macgregor.

Robsart, Amy (*c.*1532–1560) wife of Robert Dudley, Earl of Leicester.

Robson, Dame Flora (1902–84) English actress. She was made a dame in 1960. her films included *Catherine the Great* (1934).

Rochambeau, Jean Baptiste Donatien de Vimeur, Comte de (1725–1807) French soldier in Washington's army.

Rochdale canal (1761–1821) constructed (opened 1804) by the Scottish civil engineer John Rennie.

Rochester, John Wilmot, 2nd Earl of (1647–80) English poet and courtier. Renowned for his savage wit and depravity, his verse is among the most sexually explicit in English (*Poems on Several Occasions* 1680).

Rock drill invented 1871 by the American inventor Simon Ingersoll (1818–94).

Rockall Island in the Outer Hebrides, first British landing 1810; formally annexed by the Royal Navy 1955.

Rockefeller Foundation established 1913 through the philanthropy of the American financier John Davison Rockefeller (1839–1937) who made his fortune by absorbing rival concerns in his Standard Oil Company.

Rocker, Rudolf (1873–1958) German-born anarchist leader.

'Rocket, The' the first successful high-speed locomotive, built 1829 by George Stephenson (1781–1848) and Robert Stephenson (1803–59).

Rockingham, Charles Watson Wentworth, Marquess of (1730–82) prime minister (1765–66, 1782).

Rocroi, Battle of a battle of the Thirty Years' War between the French and the Spaniards, 19 May 1643. It was a French victory.

Roddick, Anita (1943–) British entrepreneur who founded the Body Shop chain of shops 1976.

Roderick O'Connor *see* Appendix: Rory O'Connor.

Rodgers, Richard [Charles] (1902–79) American composer. With the librettist Lorenz Hart, he created musicals such as *The Pal Joey*. After Hart died, Rodgers collaborated with Hammerstein on several more successful musicals, e.g. *Oklahoma* (1943).

Rodin, Auguste (1840–1917) French sculptor. He was responsible for reviving sculpture as an independent form rather than as an embellishment or decoration with works such as *The Thinker* or *Le Baiser* (1898)

Rodney, Admiral George Brydges Rodney, 1st Baron (1719–92) British sailor who defeated the Spanish fleet off Cape St Vincent in 1780 and two subsequent victories over the French.

Rodrigues an island in the Indian Ocean, discovered by the Portuguese 1645; formally ceded to Britain 1814 and governed as a dependency of Mauritius.

Roebling, John Augustus (1806–69) German-born civil engineeer.

Rogation Days the three days before Ascension Day.

Roger de Wendover (d.1236) English historian (*Flores Historiarum*).

Roger I (1031–1101) king of Sicily

Roger II (1093–1154) king of Sicily (1112–54).

Roger the Great (d.1139) bishop of Salisbury (1102–39).

Rogers, Ginger *see* ASTAIRE, FRED.

Rogers, Richard (1933–) Italian-born English architect. His designs include the Lloyds building (1979) in London, a steel and glass confection that typifies the controversial nature of his work.

Rogers, Samuel (1763–1855) English poet (*Italy* 1822–28).

Rogers, Will (1879–1935) American humorist, died in an air crash.

Rogers, William (1819–96) English educationalist.

Roget's Thesaurus compiled 1852 by the English scholar Peter Mark Roget (1779–1869).

Roland (Orlando) (*fl* 8th century) one of Charlemagne's knights, who became the hero of the great national epic poem of France, *The Song of Roland*. He died while fighting a reargauard action at Roncesvalles against an overwhelming Saracen force.

Roland, Chanson de French version of the Roland epic dating from the 11th century; Roland traditionally died fighting on 15 August 778.

Rolfe, Frederick ('Baron Corvo') (1860–1913) English novelist (*Hadrian the Seventh* 1904).

Rolfe, John (1585–1622) English colonist in Virginia.

Rolland, Romain (1866–1944) French writer (*Jean Christophe* 1904).

Rolle, Richard (*c.*1290–1349) English writer (*The Pricke of Conscience*).

Rollo, Sir William (d.1645) Royalist soldier. He was executed.

Rolls, Charles Stewart (1877–1910) English motor car manufacturer and aviator. He joined Henry Royce in car manufacture in 1906.

Rolvaag, Ole Edvart (1876–1931) Norwegian-born novelist.

'Romains, Jules' [Louis Farigoule] (1885–1972) French writer (*Les Hommes du bon volonté* 1932–46).

Roman era traditional date of foundation 21 April 753 BC.

Roman type first used in England by the French-born printer Richard Pynson (d.1530).

Romanes Lectures at Oxford University founded 1891 by the Canadian-born scientist George John Romanes (1848–94).

Romania a country of southeast Europe formed when Wallachia and Moldavia were united 1856; principality 1866–81; monarchy 1881–1947; communist regime 1948–89; new constitution and multi-party democracy introduced 1991.

Romanus pope (897).

Romanus I (d.948) Byzantine emperor (919–944).

Romanus II (d.963) Byzantine emperor (959–963) who was succeeded by his sons Basil II and Constantine.

Romanus III (d.1034) Byzantine emperor (1028–34).

Romanus IV (d.1071) Byzantine emperor (1068–71).

Romberg, Sigmund (1887–1951) Hungarian-born composer of operattas, e.g. *The Student Prince* (1924) and *The Desert Song* (1926).

Rome legendary date of the foundation of Rome by Romulus 753 BC; treaty between Rome and Carthage 508 BC; end of monarchy, republic founded 500 BC; first secession of plebeians and tribunes of the Plebs first appointed 493 BC; first Agrarian Law (Land Reform) passed by Spurius Cassius 486 BC; Lex Publilia passed, allowing for tribunes to be chosen by the Comitia Tributa (popular assembly) 471 BC; Decemvirs drew up laws of the Twelve Tables 452 BC; second secession of the plebeians and great increase in the powers of the Comitia Tributa 448 BC; Lex Canuleia legalized marriage between patricians and plebieans 445 BC; Etruscan city of Veii captured 400 BC; Rome burned down by Gauls under Brennus 390 BC; Licinian Laws passed allowing for first plebeian consul 366 BC; First Saminite War 343–340 BC; Latium conquered 340–338 BC; Publilian Laws allowed one censor to be a plebeian 339 BC; praetorship opened to plebeians 336 BC; Lex Ogulnia provided for plebeian pontiffs and augurs 300 BC; Second Samnite War 326–304 BC; Third Samnite War 298–290 BC, Rome ruler of central Italy 290 BC; third secession of the plebs 287 BC resulted in Lex Hortensia making the Comitia Tributa the supreme legislative power 286 BC; Romans defeat Gauls and Etruscans at Lake Vadimonian, Rome ruler of northern Italy 283 BC; Pyrrhus of Epirus invaded Italy 280 BC; Pyrrhus driven from Italy 275 BC, Rome ruler of all Italy 266 BC; First Punic War 264–241 BC; Rome seized Sardinia and made it a province 239 BC; conquest of Cisalpine Gaul completed 222 BC; Second Punic War 218–202 BC; First Macedonian War 214–205 BC; Second Macedonian War 200–197 BC; Romans proclaimed freedom of Greece 196 BC; Romans defeated Antiochus the Great of Syria at Magnesia 190 BC; Third Macedonian War 171–168 BC; Fourth Macedonian War 149 BC; Third Punic War 149–146 BC, Greece a Roman province 146 BC; Carthage destroyed and Roman province of Africa formed 146

BC; Roman conquest of Lusitania (Portugal) 140 BC; Roman provinces formed in Spain 133 BC and in Asia when Attalus III bequeathed Pergamom to Rome; Tiberius Gracchus, tribune of the plebs, attempted to solve the land problem 133 BC; Cais Gracchus, tribune of the plebs, attempted further land reform 123 BC; Roman province in southern Gaul (hence Provence) 120 BC; war against Jugurtha, king of Numidia, 111 BC; Social War 90 BC, Roman franchise granted to some Italians and soon afterwards to all 89 BC; civil war in Rome between Marius and Sulla, immediate occasion being rivalry for the command in Asia 88 BC; First Mithradatic War 88–84 BC; massacres in Rome by Marius and Cinna 87 BC; Second Mithradatic War 83–82 BC; Sulla returned to Rome and many citizens proscribed and executed 83 BC; Sulla made dictator of Rome 82 BC; Third Mithradatic War 74– 64 BC; revolt of gladiators and slaves under Spartacus 73–71 BC; conspiracy of Catiline exposed and foiled by Cicero 63 BC; beginning of First Triumvirate 60 BC; conquest of Gaul completed 50 BC; civil war between Caesar and Pompey 48–45 BC, Pompey defeated at Pharsalia 48 BC; Zela, Battle of: Caesar defeats Pharnaces, king of Pontus, defeated at Zela 47 BC; republicans defeated by Caesar at Thapsus in Africa 46 BC; Pompey's sons defeated at Munda in Spain by Caesar 45 BC; Caesar made perpetual dictator 44 BC; Assassination of Caesar 44 BC; Second Triumvirate constituted and Cicero executed 43 BC; Brutus and Cassius, leaders of the revolt against Caesar, defeated at Philippi 42 BC; Antony and Cleopatra defeated in naval battle of Actium by Octavian 31 BC; temple of Janus in Rome closed, denoting a world at peace—the first time for 200 years; Octavian given the titles of Augustus and Princeps of the Roman State by the senate, beginning of the Principate, an empire under the forms of the old republic 27 BC; readjustment of the authority of Augustus 23 BC.

Rome, University of founded 1244.

Romer, Carl Ferdinand von German geologist (1818–91)

Römer, Olaus (1644–1710) Danish astronomer who calculated the velocity of light in 1675.

Romilly, Sir Samuel (1757–1818) English legal reformer. He committed suicide.

Rommel, Erwin (1891–1944) German soldier. During the Second World War, he commanded the Afrika Korps in North Africa, earning the nickname the 'Desert Fox' for his brilliant tactics. He committed suicide after the discovery of his complicity in an assassination attempt on Hitler.

Romney, George (1734–1802) English painter who was the son of a carpenter. At his best he was a worthy rival of Reynolds and Gainsborough. His portraits of Lady Hamilton are mong his most famous pictures.

Romulus the legendary founder of the city of Rome 753 BC. He was reputed to be the son of Mars and Rhea Sylvia and twin brother of Remus. When their mother was turned into a goddess he and his twin were suckled by a wolf.

Romulus Augustulus Roman emperor (475–476) (last in West).

Ronald, Sir Landon (1873–1938) English conductor.

Ronsard, Pierre de (1524–85) French poet (*Hymne de la France* 1549).

Röntgen, Konrad Wilhelm (1845–1923) German physicist who discovered the rays named after him but which he termed 'X-rays' as their nature was not then fully understood. He was awarded the Nobel prize for physics in 1901.

Röntgen rays (1845–1923) discovered *c.*1895 by the German scientist Wilhelm Konrad Röntgen.

Rooftop landing first successfully made in Paris 1913 by the French aviator Jules Vedrines (1881–1919).

Roosevelt, Franklin D[elano] (1882–1945) American Democratic statesman. He became 32nd president of the US (1933–45) and, in order to deal with the crisis of economic collapse, instituted far-reaching 'New Deal' reforms. He was a popular and highly effective leader during the Second World War, dying shortly after the Yalta summit meeting with Churchill and Stalin. His wife, **[Anna] Eleanor Roosevelt** (1884–1962), was an active and popular First Lady, supporting her husband during his illness with polio. After his death she worked with the UN as US representative to the General Assembly (1946–52).

Roosevelt, Theodore (1858–1919) American Republican statesman. 26th president of the US (1901–1909). He legislated against big business monopolies, intervened forcefully during the Panama civil war to protect the construction of the Panama Canal and won the 1906 Nobel Peace Prize for mediating the end of the Russo-Japanese war.

Root, Elihu (1845–1937) American statesman.

Roper, Margaret (1505–44) scholar and daughter of Sir Thomas More.

Rops, Félicien (1833–98) Belgian artist (*Buveuse d'absinthe* 1865).

Rorschach test (1884–1922) devised in 1942 by the Swiss psychiatrist Hermann Rorschach.

Rory *or* **Roderick O'Connor** (*c.*1116–1198) king of Connaught and high king of Ireland *see* Appendix.

Rosa, Carl (1843–89) German-born founder of the Carl Rosa Opera Company.

Rosa, Salvator (1615–73) Italian painter and poet who his best known for his studies of nature, especially along the Neapolitan coast. His poems were biting satires.

'Rosamund, Fair' [Rosamund Clifford] (d.*c.*1176) the daughter of Lord Clifford who became mistress of Henry II.

Rosaniline (1818–92) red dye discovered 1858 by the German scientist August Wilhelm von Hofmann.

Roscius Gallus, Quintus (*c.*126–62 BC) Roman actor.

Roscoe, William (1753–1831) English writer (*Lorenzo de' Medici* 1796).

Rose of Lima, Saint (1586–1617) first canonized saint in the New World.

Rosebery, Archibald Philip Primrose, Earl of (1847–1929) British Liberal statesman who became Foreign Secretary (1886, 1892–94) and prime minister (1894–96). He resigned his leadership of the Liberal Party in 1896.

Rosegger, Peter (1843–1918) Austrian writer (*Mann und Weib* 1879).

Rosenberg, Isaac (1890–1918) English poet killed in action in the First World War.

Roses, Wars of the between the houses of Lancaster and York, 1455–85, lasting from the battle of St Albans to that of Bosworth. The Lancastrians wore red and the Yorkists—who were ultimately victorious—wore white roses.

Rosetta Stone a slab of black basalt that bears an inscription in three different languages—Egyptian hieroglyphic, demotic and Greek— that was discovered in 1799 at Rosetta and deciphered 1821–28 by the French Orientalist Jean François Champollion (1790–1832), providing a key to hieroglyphics.

Rosh ha-Shanah [Feast of the Trumpets] the Jewish New Year, 1st day of Tishri.

Rosicrucians occult society in 17th century, revived in 18th century and several times since.

Ross, Sir James Clark (1800–1862) Scottish explorer who accompanied his uncle, Sir John Ross, and Captain Parry on expeditions before making his name by discovering the north magnetic pole in 1831. He commanded the *Erebus* and *Terror* expedition to the Antarctic 1839–43. The Ross Sea is named after him, and his ships gave their names to the volcanoes, Mt Erebus and Mt Terror, on its shores.

Ross, Sir John (1777–1856) Scottish explorer who fought as a sailor in the Napoleonic Wars before becoming an Arctic explorer. He took part in two expeditions with his nephew, James Clark Ross, to find the northwest passage.

Ross, Sir Ronald (1857–1932) Indian-born pioneer in the cure of malaria.

Rosse, William Parsons, Earl of (1800–1867) astronomer.

Rossellino, Antonio (1427–*c.*1479) Italian sculptor.

Rossetti, Christina Georgina (1830–94) English poet noted for her reflective, occasionally melancholic religious poems (*Goblin Market* 1862). She also wrote for children. Her brother was Dante Gabriel Rossetti.

Rossetti, Dante Gabriel (1828–82) English painter (*Dante's Dream*) and poet, brother of Christina Rossetti. He was a founder of the Pre-Raphaelite school of painting.

Rossi, Charles (1762–1839) English sculptor (*James Wyatt*).

Rossini, Gioacchino Antonio (1792–1868) Italian composer, noted especially for his light operas, e.g. *The Barber of Seville*, *The Thieving Magpie*. His other works include the opera *William Tell* (1829) and a *Stabat Mater*.

Rostand, Edmond (1868–1918) French dramatist and poet. His best-known work is the verse drama *Cyrano de Bergerac* (1897).

Rostropovich, Mstislav (1927–) Russian cellist. One of the outstanding cellists of modern times, he has also given many recitals as a pianist, often accompanying his wife, the soprano **Galina Vishnevskaya** (1926–), in song recitals.

Rosyth naval base in Scotland, construction begun 1909.

Rotary International an international association of businessmen and professional men founded in the USA 1905 and in Britain 1914 to promote community service.

Rotary printing press invented 1846 by the American inventor Richard March Hoe (1812–86).

Roth, Philip (1933–) American novelist, much of whose fiction is concerned with the problems (often sexual) of Jewish family life, e.g. *Goodbye Columbus* (1959).

Rothamsted experimental station world's first agricultural experimental station founded 1843 by the English agriculturist Sir John Bennet Lawes (1814–1900).

Rothenstein, Sir John (1901–) director of the Tate Gallery (1938–64).

Rothenstein, Sir William (1872–1945) English painter (*T. E. Lawrence*).

Rotherhithe-Stepney tunnel in London opened 12 June 1908.

Rothermere, Harold Sidney Harmsworth, Viscount (1868–1940) British newspaper publisher.

Rothko, Mark [Marcus Rothkovitch] (1903–70) Russian-born American painter. Having passed through Expressionism and Surrealism, he adopted the abstract expressionist style of painting, creating large canvases with almost luminous rectangles of colour.

Rothschild, Meyer Amshel (1743–1812) German financier.

Rouault, Georges (1871–1958) French painter who trained as a stained glass designer, which later influenced his paintings. His subject matter was concerned with human frailty, depicted in images of judges, prostitutes and sad clows, e.g. *Little Olympia* (1906).

Roubillac, Louis François (1695–1762) French-born sculptor (*Handel* 1738).

Rouen, Siege of by King Henry V of England, 1418–19.

Rouen Cathedral construction began 1206.

Rouget de l'Isle, Claude Joseph (1760–1836) French composer of the *Marseillaise* (1792).

Roundheads nickname of Parliamentary supporters during the English Civil War period of the mid-17th century.

Rousseau, Henri Julien ('Le Douanier') (1844–1910) French painter. His naive style remained unaffected by all trends, and he defied conventions of colour and perspective in his exotic imaginary landscapes and painted dreams (*La Chasse au tigre*).

Rousseau, Jean-Jacques (1712–78) Swiss-born French philosopher. His most notable fictional works are the novels *Julie, or the New Héloïse* (1761) and *Emile* (1762), the former describing a highly improbable menage à trois, the latter a didactic work on how to educate children (whom he saw as naturally good). These works and others, notably the political tract *The Social Contract* (1762), which begins with the famous statement 'Man is born free, and is everywhere in chains', were profoundly influential on the intellectual ferment that led to the French Revolution. His very frank autobiography, *Confessions*, was published posthumously and set a fashion for this style of reminiscence.

Routledge, George (1812–88) English publisher.

Rouvray, Battle of or Battle of the Herrings a battle of the Hundred Years' War between the English and the French, 12 February 1429, when a French attack was defeated by the English.

Roux, Pierre Paul Emile (1853–1933) French bacteriologist.

Rover Scouts movement formed in Britain 1919.

Rowan, Archibald Hamilton (1751–1834) United Irishman.

Rowe, Nicholas (1674–1718) English writer (*Tamerlane* 1702).

Rowlandson, Thomas (1756–1827) English artist (*Dance of Death* 1814–16).

Rowley, William English playwright (*c.*1585–*c.*1642) (*A Woman Never Vext* 1632).

Rowley Poems '15th-century poems' written 1765 onwards by the English poet Thomas Chatterton (1752–70).

Rowntree, Joseph (1801–59) English Quaker educationist.

Rowton Houses poor men's hotels in London founded 1892 onwards by the philanthropist Baron Rowton (1838–1903).

Roxana (killed 311 BC) wife of Alexander the Great.

Roy, Rob *see* ROB ROY.

Royal Academy of Arts founded in Somerset House in London 1768 by George III; moved to Trafalgar Square 1834; to Burlington House 1869. Its two objects were to establish a school of design and to hold an annual exhibition. Its first president was Sir Joshua Reynolds.

Royal Academy of Music was founded in London in 1822 and reconstituted in 1868.

Royal Aeronautical Society, founded 1866 as the Aeronautical Society of Great Britain; present name since 1919.

Royal Agricultural Society was founded in 1840. It holds annual shows and maintains a staff to experts to make chemical, botantical, zoological and other scientific experiments.

Royal Air Force formed 1918.

Royal Albert Hall, London, opened by Queen Victoria, 29 March 1871.

Royal and Ancient Golf Club of St Andrews founded 1754.

Royal Astronomical Society London, founded 1820, chartered 1831.

Royal Automobile Club founded 1897.

Royal Canadian Mounted Police founded as the North-West Mounted Police 1873; assumed present title 1920.

Royal College of Physicians, London, founded 1518.

Royal College of Surgeons founded 1800 in London as the Royal College of Surgeons of London but obtained a royal charter in 1843 as the Royal College of Surgeons of England.

Royal Dutch Petroleum Company established at The Hague 16 June 1890.

Royal Exchange, London, founded 1566–71 by the English financier Sir Thomas Gresham (1519–79).

Royal Flying Corps, approved by King George V as title for the aeronautical branch of the Armed Forces 1912; superseded by R.A.F. in 1918.

Royal George, The, sank at Portsmouth 1782.

Royal Hospital, Chelsea, built 1682–92 by the English architect Sir Christopher Wren (1632–1723); opened 1694.

Royal Hunt Cup Ascot, first run 1843.

Royal Institute of International Affairs founded in London 1920.

Royal Institution of Great Britain founded in London 1799.

Royal London Homoeopathic Hospital, founded 1849 by Dr Frederick Hervey Foster Quin (1799–1878).

Royal Marine Corps constituted 1664 as the Duke of York and Albany's Maritime Regiment of Foot.

Royal Marriage Act passed 1772.

Royal Military Academy, Sandhurst (combining Sandhurst and Woolwich), came into being 2 April 1946.

Royal National Theatre, established as National Theatre in 1962 with Sir Laurence Olivier as director; 'Royal' added to name in 1988.

Royal Naval Reserve, formed in Britain under the Royal Naval Reserve (Volunteers) Act of 1859.

Royal Oak torpedoed by the Germans in World War II, 14 October 1939.

Royal Observatory, Greenwich, founded 1675. It was built by Charles II on the site of Duke Humphrey of Floucester's castle because the great increase in British commerce had made the determination of longitude at sea an absolute necessity.

Royal Opera House, Covent Garden, London, opened 15 May 1858). Preceded by two other opera houses, both destroyed by fire.

Royal Shakespeare Company founded 1960.

Royal Society, The founded in 1662 to promite the advancement of scientific knowledge and given a royal charter by Charles II.

Royal Society for the Prevention of Cruelty to Animals, London, founded 1824.

Royal Society of Arts, London, founded 1754.

Royal Society of British Artists, London, founded 1823.

Royal Society of London, organized 1660; constituted by Royal Charter 1662.

Royal Society of Painters in Watercolours, London, founded 1804.

Royce, Sir [Frederick] Henry (1863–1933) English engineer. In partnership with Charles Rolls, he founded the car firm Rolls-Royce in 1906).

Royce, Josiah (1855–1916) American philosopher.

Royden, Maude (1876–1956) English leader of the women's movement and preacher.

Ruanda-Urundi former territory of central Africa, ceded 1919 to Belgium as a mandatory of the League of Nations; trusteeship territory by United Nations' agreement 1946; divided into the independent states of Rwanda and Burundi 1962.

Rubber, synthetic first produced 1891 by the English chemist, Sir William Tilden (1842–1926).

Rubber, vulcanization of patented by the English merchant Thomas Hancock (1786–1865); pioneered 1839 by the American manufacturer Charles Goodyear (1800–1860).

Rubber factory first, built 1819 in London by the English merchant Thomas Hancock (1786–1865).

Rubber tree first cultivated at the Royal Botanic Gardens, Kew; introduced by Sir Henry Wickham (1846–1928) into the Far East *c.*1885.

Rubbra, Edmund (1901–86) English composer and conductor.

Rubens, Sir Peter Paul (1577–1640) Flemish painter and diplomat. He entered the service of the Duke of Mantua in Italy and became court painter to the Spanish viceroys in Antwerp. His masterpiece is the triptych *Descent from the Cross* (1614). In 1629 he was sent to England to negotiate peace with Charles I, who knighted him.

Rubidium a radioactive chemical element discovered by the German scientists Bunsen (1791–1860) and Gustav Robert Kirchhoff (1824–87).

Rubinstein, Anton (1829–94) Russian pianist and composer (*Dmitri Donskoi in* 1851).

Rubinstein, Artur (1888–1982) Polish-born American pianist. An outstanding concert pianist, he was particularly noted for his Chopin recitals.

Rubinstein, Nikolai (1835–81) Russian pianist.

Ruby, Jack [Jacob Rubinstein] (1911–67) nightclub owner and assassin of Lee Harvey Oswald (assassin of J. F. Kennedy).

Rude, François (1784–1855) French sculptor (*Jeanne d'Arc in* 1852).

Rudolf I (1218–91) German king (1273–91).

Rudolf II (1552–1612) Holy Roman emperor (1576–1612).

Rueda, Lope de (*c.*1510–*c.*1565) Spanish playwright (*Medora*).

Rufinus, Tyrannius (*c.*342–410) Italian theologian.

Rugby football started by William Webb Ellis of Rugby School 1823; legalized 1846.

Rugby league seceded from Rugby Union 1895 as Northern Union; adopted present name 1922.

Rugby union British, founded 1871.

Ruhmkorff, Heinrich Daniel (1803–77) German physicist.

Rule Britannia first published 1740; words by the Scottish poet James Thomson (1700–1748); music by the English composer Thomas Arne (1710–78).

Rumania *see* ROMANIA.

Rumelia, Eastern ruled by Bulgaria since 1878.

Rumford, Benjamin Thompson, Count von (1753–1814) American-born scientist.

Rump Parliament in England, 6 December 1648 to 20 April 1653, and 1659.

Run (d.*c.*878) king of Strathclyde *see* Appendix.

Runcie, Robert (1921–) archbishop of Canterbury (1979–90).

Runciman, Walter, Baron Runciman (1847–1937) British shipowner.

Rupert (1352–1410) German king (1400–1410).

Rupert of the Rhine, Prince (1619–82) English cavalry officer.

Rush, Benjamin (1745–1813) American physician and abolitionist.

Rush-Bagot Convention providing for an unarmed frontier between the USA and Canada, signed 1817.

Rushdie, [Ahmed] Salman (1947–) Indian-born British novelist (*Midnight's Children,* 1981). After the publication of *Satanic Verses* (1988), Islamic fundamentalist leader Ayatollah Khomeini pronounced a death sentence, *fatwa,* for the supposedly blasphemous content of the novel.

Rushworth, John (1669–1736) English surgeon and promoter of dispensaries.

Ruskin, John (1819–1900) English writer, artist and influential art critic. His works, which include *Modern Painters,* dictated Victorian taste for over half a century. He was an enthusiast for Gothic art, the Pre-Raphaelite movement and Turner, and was a strong critic of the values and ugliness of Industrial England(*The Stones of Venice* 1851–53).

Russell, Bertrand [Arthur William] 3rd Earl Russell (1872–1970) British philosopher (*History of Western Philosophy* 1946). He made notable contributions to mathematical and philosophical theory and, with the help of his student, Wittgenstein, logical positivism. He was awarded the 1950 Nobel prize for literature.

Russell, George ('AE') (1867–1935) Irish writer.

Russell, John Scott (1808–82) Scottish naval architect (the *Great Eastern*).

Russell, Ken (1927–) English film director. He is especially noted for his film biographies of musicians, e.g. *Lisztomania.*

Russell, Lord John, 3rd Earl Russell (1792–1878) British statesman (prime minister 1846–52, 1865–66).

Russell, William Howard British war correspondent (1820–1907).

Russia Mongol domination 1242–1368, Muscovite ascendancy 1328–1613; Romanov Empire 1613–1917; revolutionary period 1917–22; largest constituent of the USSR 1922–91.

Russian Navy founded by Count Feodor Apraksin (1671–1728).

Russian Revolutions abortive revolution January-October 1905; February Revolution 8–14 March 1917; October Revolution 7 November 1917; Civil War 1917–22; USSR formed December 1922.

Russo-Japanese War began 1904; ended 1905.

Russo-Turkish Wars 1696; 1768–74; 1787–91; 1806–12; 1828–29; 1853–55; 1877–78.

Rutebeuf French troubadour lived in the 13th century.

Rutgers University, New Jersey, USA, founded as Queen's College 1766; became Rutger's College 1825.

Ruth, 'Babe' [George Herman Ruth] (1895–1948) American champion baseball player.

Ruthenium a hard white metallic element discovered 1845 by the German chemist Karl Ernst Claus (1796–1864).

Rutherford, Daniel (1749–1819) Scottish physician and discoverer (1772) of nitrogen.

Rutherford, Ernest [1st Baron Rutherford of Nelson] (1871–1937) New Zealand-born physicist. He was awarded the 1908 Nobel prize for chemistry. In 1911 he deduced the existence of the atom's structure and was the first scientist to split the atom.

Rutherford, Mark [William Hale White] (1831–1913) English writer (*The Revolution in Tanner's Lane* 1887).

Rutherford, Samuel (*c.*1600–1661) Scottish Covenanter.

Ruthven, Raid of a Presbyterian political coup, 22 August 1582, named after one of the conspirators William Ruthven, Baron Ruthven (b.*c.*1541), when the young James Vi of Scotland was made a prisoner of the English in Ruthven Castle to keep him from the influence of Catholic courtiers. James escaped in June 1583 and a year later Ruthven was beheaded.

Ruwenzori *or* **Mountains of the Moon** a mountain range on the border between Zaire and Uganda, first climbed by the Duke of Abruzzi in 1906.

Ruysbroek, Johannes (1293–1381) Dutch mystical writer (*De Vera Contemplatione*)

Ruysdael, Jakob (1628–81) Dutch painter (*Dutch Dunes*)

Ruyter, Michael Adriaanszoon de (1607–76) Dutch admiral.

Rye House Plot conspiracy of Whigs to assassinate King Charles II, April 1683.

Rylands, John (1801–88) English textile manufacturer whose widow founded the John Rylands library in Manchester1899 in his memory.

Rymer, Thomas (1641–1713) English archaeologist and compiler (*Foedera* 1704–35).

Rysbrack, John Michael (*c.*1693–1770) Flemish sculptor (*John Howard*) .

Ryswick, Treaty of the treat that ended the War of the Grand Alliance between France and the Allies, signed September 1697.

S

aar Offensive Second World War attack, 9–30 September 1939.

aarinen, Eero (1910–61) Finnish architect whose works include the US Embassy in London.

aarinen, Eliel (1873–1950) Finnish-born architect and town planner whose works include Helsinki Railway Station.

aarland an area of southwest Germany on the border with the French region of Lorraine. Since the 17th century it has been fought over by France and Germany; placed under the control of the League of Nations 1919; reverted to Germany 1935; administered by France 1945–57; returned to Germany 1957–59 following a plebiscite.

abacon an Enthiopian king who invaded Egypt in the reign of Neco (1) and usurped the throne. He abandoned Egypt in consequence of a dream. Neco's son, Psammetichus, regained the thrown.

abata, Victor de (1892–1967) Italian conductor and composer (*Gethsemani* 1925).

abatier, Louis Auguste (1837–1901) French theologian.

abatini, Rafael (1875–1950) Italian writer (*Scaramouche* 1921).

abbath Jewish day of rest, seventh day of week; Christian day of rest, first day of week (Lord's Day) since 4th century.

abin, Albert Bruce (1906–) Polish-born American micro- biologist. He developed the Sabin polio vaccine in the mid–1950s.

abinian pope (604–607).

accharin discovered 1879 by the American scientist Ira Remsen (1846–1927) and C. Fahlberg.

acheverell, Henry (*c.*1674–1724) English clergyman and pamphleteer.

achs, Hans (1494–1576) German writer of *Meisterlieder.*

ackville, Charles, Earl of Dorset (1638–1706) English poet.

ackville, Thomas, Earl of Dorset (1536–1608) English playwright (with Norton, *Gorboduc* 1561).

ackville-West, Victoria (1892–1962) English writer (*All Passion Spent* 1931).

adat, [Mohammed] Anwar El (1918–81) Egyptian statesman. He succeeded Nasser as president in 1970. After the 1973 war with Israel, he signed a peace treaty with Begin, for which they were awarded the 1978 Nobel Peace Prize. He was assassinated by Islamic fundamentalist soldiers during a military parade.

Sade, Donatien Alphonse François, Marquis de (1740–1814) French soldier and novelist. His highly licentious works include several novels, e.g. *Justine* (1791). The term 'sadism' derives from the dominant theme in his life and work.

Sadi (*c.*1184–1292) Persian poet (*Gulistan* 1258).

Sadleir, Michael (1888–1957) English publisher and writer (*Fanny by Gaslight* 1940).

Sadler's Wells London theatre opened in 1765; reconstructed 1879; closed 1916; reopened 1931.

Sadowa, Battle of (Königgrätz) a battle between Austrians and Prussians, 3 July 1866, which was a Prussian victory.

Saebert (d.616) king of Essex (605–616) *see* Appendix.

Saelred (d.746) king of Essex (709–746) *see* Appendix.

Saeward (d.616) king of Essex (616) *see* Appendix.

Safety bicycle invented 1874 by the English inventor H. J. Lawson at Brighton.

Safety lamp a lamp used by miners, which operates by admitting air to the flame through a wire gauze that prevents the flame igniting gas outside the lamp since it radiates heat too fast to become hot enough to cause ignition. It was invented independently in 1815 by the English scientist Sir Humphry Davy (1778–1829) and the English civil engineer and inventor George Stephenson (1781–1848).

Safety razor invented 1901 by the American manufacturer King Camp Gillette (1855–1932).

Sagan, Carl (1934–) American astronomer and sci-fi novelist.

Sagan, Françoise [Françoise Quoirez] (1935–) French writer, the best-known of whose novels is *Bonjour tristesse* (1956).

Saguntum (modern Sagunto) a town in eastern Spain that was allied to Rome and was attacked and captured by the Carthiginians under Hannibal 219 BC.

Sahagun, Bernardino de (*c.*1499–1590) Spanish missionary and historian of Mexico.

Sailors' Rests founded by the English philanthropist Agnes Elizabeth Weston (1840–1918).

St Albans' Abbey, England, original church built 303; construction of abbey begun 1077; abbey consecrated 1115.

St Andrew's Day 30 November.

St Andrews Cathedral, Scotland, built 1159–1318.

St Andrews University, Scotland, founded by Bishop Wardlaw 1411.

St Anne's College, Oxford University, founded 1879.

St Anthony's College, Oxford University, founded 1950.

St Bartholomew's Day Massacre the slaughter of Huguenots, 24 August–17 September 1572, which was instigated by Catherine de' Medici and began in Paris on the night of St Bartholomew's Day, when many Huguenots were in Paris for the wedding of Catherine's daughter to Henri of Navarre, later Henri IV. At least 4000 people were murdered in Paris, one of whom was Coligny, and probably 30,000 in the provinces, but the provincial officials were less thorough in carrying out the infamous order.

St Bartholomew's Hospital a hospital in London founded 1123 by an Augustine prior. The original structure was rebuilt 1730–66.

St Benet's Hall, Oxford University, founded 1947.

St Catharine's College, Cambridge University, founded by Robert Woodlark, Provost of King's College, 1473.

St Catherine's Society, Oxford University, founded 1868.

St Cyr French military training school founded 1686.

St David's Cathedral, Wales, constructed 1176–98.

St David's Day 1 March.

St Dunstan's, Regent's Park, London, home for blinded soldiers and sailors founded 1915 by the English newspaper owner and philanthropist Sir Arthur Pearson (1866–1921).

Ste-Beuve, Charles Augustin (1804–69) French writer and critic (*Causeries du Lundi* 1863–70).

Ste-Chapelle, Paris, constructed 1245–48.

St Edmund Hall, Oxford University, reputed to have been founded 1226.

St Évremond, Charles (*c.*1613–1703) French soldier and poet.

St Exupéry, Antoine de (1900–1944) French writer (*Vol de nuit* 1931) and aviator. He was killed in battle.

St Gaudens, Augustus (1848–1907) American sculptor (*Abraham Lincoln* 1887).

St George patron saint of England, formally adopted as such in 1349. His history is obscure, but he is believed to have been a Christian noble of Cappadocia in Asia Minor who was put to death for his faith in 303 during the Diocletian persecution. He is also the patron saint of Portugal, and during the Middle Ages was regarded generally in Europe as the patron of chivalry.

St George's Day 23 April.

St-Germain, Treaty of settling with Austria, signed 10 September 1919.

St Gotthard Pass carriage road constructed 1820–30.

St Gotthard Tunnel construction began 1872; completed 1880; railway opened 1882.

St Helena island in the South Atlantic, discovered by the Portuguese navigator João de Nova 1502; formally annexed by the British East India Company 1661; Crown Colony since 1834.

St Hilda's College, Oxford University, founded 1893.

St James's Gazette British newspaper founded 1880, absorbed into the *Evening Standard* 1905.

St James's Palace, London, built by King Henry VIII 1532–33. It was the London residence of many monarchs until the 19th century, when Buckingham Palace took its place. Little of the original building remains.

St John's College, Cambridge University, founded by Lady Margaret, Countess of Richmond and Derby, 1511.

St John's College, Oxford University, founded 1555 by Alderman Sir Thomas White (1492–1567).

St John, Henry [Viscount Bolingbroke] (1678–1751) statesman.

St Just, Louis de (1767–94) French Revolutionary leader. He was guillotined.

St Katharine's Dock, Port of London, built by the Scottish engineer Thomas Telford (1757–1834) between 1826 and 1829.

St Kitts-Nevis island in the West Indies, discovered by Christopher Columbus 1493; ceded to the British 1713; with Anguilla formed British colony 1882–1967; British Associated State 1967–83; Anguilla separated 1983; gained full independence 1983.

St Laurent, Louis Stephen (1882–1973) Canadian statesman (prime minister 1948–57).

Saint Laurent, Yves (1936–) French fashion designer.

St Lawrence River, North America, explored 1535–36 by the French navigator Jacques Cartier (1491–1557).

St Lawrence Seaway Project officially launched 1954; opened to deep-draught merchant shipping 25 April 1959; officially opened 26 June 1959.

St Leger, Doncaster, first run 1776.

St Lucia island in the West Indies, believed to have been discovered 1502 by Christopher Columbus; ceded to Britain by France 1814; gained self-government as British Associated State 1967; full independence within the Commonwealth 1979.

St Mark's Church in Venice, reconstructed 1437–52 by the Italian Michelozzo (1396–1472).

St Martin-in-the-Fields London church built 1722–26 by the Scottish architect James Gibbs (1682–1754).

St Mary Redcliffe Bristol church built 1325–1475.

St Patrick's Cathedral New York cathedral constructed 1858–79.

St Patrick's Day 17 March.

St Paul's Cathedral London cathedral constructed 1675–1710 by Sir Christopher Wren (1632–1723).

St Peter's Hall, Oxford University, founded 1929.

St Peter's cathedral in Rome constructed 1445–1626.

St Pierre, Charles (1658–1743) French writer and reformer.

St Pierre, Jacques Henri Bernardin de (1737–1814) French writer (*Paul et Virginie* 1787).

St Saëns, Camille (1835–1921) French composer (*Samson and Delilah* 1877).

Saint-Simon, Claude Henri, Comte de (1760–1825) French political reformer.

Saint-Simon, Louis de Rouvroy, Duc de (1675–1755) French writer (*Memoirs* 1752).

St Swithin's Day 15 July.

St Valentine's Day (Old Candlemas) 14 February.

St Valentine's Day Massacre machine-gunnning of 'Bugs' Moran's gang members by henchmen of Al Capone in a Chicago garage, 14 February 1927.

St Vincent, Earl *see* JERVIS, JOHN.

St Vincent island in the West Indies, believed to have been discovered by Christopher Columbus 1498; ceded to Britain by France 1783; with the Grenadines, formed a British Associated State 1969–79; gained full independence 1979.

Saintsbury, George (1845–1933) English literary historian and critic.

Sakharov, Andrei Dimitrievich (1921–89) Russian nuclear physicist and political dissident. He developed the Russian hydrogen bomb in the 1950s and subsequently campaigned for international control of nuclear weapons. He was awarded the 1975 Nobel Peace Prize.

Saki *see* MUNRO, HECTOR HUGH.

Saladin [Salah al-Din al-Ayyubi] (1137–93) sultan of Egypt and Syria and the leader of the Arab world during the Crusades. He was vizier to the last of the Fatimite caliphs and, at the latter's death, usurped his wealth and authority. In 1174 he succeeded the sultan of Damascus and, extending his conquests over Syria, came in contact with the Crusaders in the Third Crusade. In 1187 he gained victory of Tiberias, after which Jerusalem surrendered to him, but the conquests of Richard I compelled him to make a truce. He was a skilful general and an astute ruler.

Salam, Abdus *see* WEINBERG, STEVEN.

Salamis (1) an ancient Greek city on the east coast of Cyprus which was the scene of a naval victory for the Greeks over the Egyptians 306 BC. (2) an island in the Saronic gulf that was conquered by Athens 570 BC and was the scene of a naval battle when the Athenians under Themistocles defeated the Persians 480 BC.

Salazar, Antonio de Oliveira (1889–1970) Portuguese dictator 1932–68.

Sale, George (*c.*1697–1736) English translator (1734) of the Koran.

Salicylic acid discovered 1838 by the Italian chemist Rafaelle Piria (1815–65).

Salinas (Serrano), Pedro (1891–1951) Spanish poet and literary critic (*Jorge Manrique* 1947).

Salinger, Jerome David (1916–) American author (*A Catcher in the Rye* 1951).

Salisbury, John de Montacute, Earl of (*c.*1350–1400) diplomat and soldier. He was beheaded.

Salisbury, Robert Arthur Talbot Gascoyne-Cecil, Marquess of (1830–1903) British statesman. He entered parliament in 1858 and the House of Lords in 1868. In 1878 he accompanied Disraeli to the Congress at Berlin, and at the latter's death became leader of the Conservate party. He was prime minister 1885–86, 1886–92, 1895–1902.

Salisbury Cathedral, England, construction began 1220; consecrated 1258.

Saliva digestive action of discovered by the Italian scientist Lazaro Spallanzani (1729–99).

Salk, Jonas Edward (1914–95) American physician and microbiologist. He developed the Salk vaccine against polio.

Salk vaccine against poliomyelitis developed 1954 by the American scientist Jonas Edward Salk.

Sallust [Gaius Sallustius Crispius] (86–34 BC) Roman historian who accompanied Julius Caesar to Africa, where he was appointed governor of Numidia. He wrote *Bellum Catilinarium* (the history of the Catiline Conspiracy) and *Jugurtha* or *Bellum Jugurthinum* (the history of the war against Jugurtha).

Salmasius, Claudius [Claude de Saumaise] (1588–1653) French scholar.

Salomon, Dr Erich (1886–1944?) German pioneer in the use of the miniature camera and in candid-camera technique. He was probably killed at Auschwitz.

Saloth Sar *see* POL POT.

Salt, Sir Titus (1803–76) English wool manufacturer.

SALT (Strategic Arms Limitation Talks) between US and USSR, Salt I signed 26 May 1972; Salt II signed 18 June 1979.

Salten, Felix (1869–1945) Austrian writer (*Bambi* 1923).

Salters Company London livery company, origins uncertain; chartered by King Edward III 1377.

Salt Lake City American city in Utah, USA, founded 1847.

Saltykov, Mikhail [Evgrafovich Shchedrin] (1826–89) Russian writer (*Fables* 1885).

Salvador, El South American country colonized by Spanish 1524; became independent 1841; became a republic 1856; 12-year civil war between government and leftist rebels ended 1992.

Salvarsan a drug curing syphilis discovered 1908 by the German bacteriologist Paul Ehrlich (1854–1915).

Salvation Army a religious movement founded 1865 in London by William Booth (1829–1912), a Methodist minister. It received its name in 1877, when its founder took the title of general, and its organization adopted military nomenclature. Its object is to care for the souls and bodies of those who find life very hard. Official members have to abstain from alcohol and tobacco and generally lead a self-denying life. In its early days it met with opposition, abuse and even violence, but the good done by it eventually won tolerance and then approval, on which the seal was set by Edward VII's personals thanks, in 1904, to General Booth..

Salvator Rosa (1615–73) Italian painter (*Death of Socrates*).

Salyut first orbital space station (USSR), launched April 1971.

Salzburg Festival in honour of Mozart founded 1877.

Samaria the name of the central region of ancient Palestine, situated between the Mediterranean and the River Jordan, that formed the northern kingdom of Israel and also the name of its capital. It was conquered 721 BC by Sargon, king of Assyria, who transported a large number of the Israelites to Mesopotamia and Media and brought in people from Babylonia and elsewhere. The city was rebuilt by Herod the Great and renamed Sebaste.

Samarium metallic element discovered 1879 by the French scientist Paul Emile Lecoq de Boisbaudran (1838–1912).

Samnites a tribe of the Appenine mountains of Italy who waged war on Rome three times (343–340 BC, 326–304 BC, 298–290 BC), leaving Rome ruler of central Italy.

Samnite War, First 343–340 BC.

Samnite War, Second 326–304 BC: Roman army captured by the Samnites at the Caudine Forks 321 BC; battle of Lautulae 316 BC when the Romans were defeated by the Samnites; battle of Bovianum 305 BC, when a Samnite attempt to break a Roman siege of the town was defeated.

Samnite War, Third 298–290 BC: battle of Camerinum 298 BC when the Romans were defeated by the Samnites and allies; battle of Sentinum 295 BC when the Samnites and allies were defeated by the Romans.

Samoa, American discovered 1722; created neutral territory 1889; ceded to the USA 1899–1904 and 1925.

Samoa, Western mandated to New Zealand 1919; achieved full independence 1962.

Samuel, Herbert [1st Viscount Samuel] (1870–1963) British statesman.

Sancho I (d.1211) king of Portugal (1185–1211).

Sancho II (*c.*1210–1248) king of Portugal (1223–48).

Sanctuary, Right of abolished in England 1623–24.

Sand, George [Armandine Dupin] (1804–76) French writer (*Lélia* 1833).

Sand River Convention recognizing the establishment of the independent South African Republic (The Transvaal), signed by Britain 17 January 1852.

Sandburg, Carl (1878–1967) American poet (*Cornhuskers* 1918).

Sandby, Paul (1725–1809) English artist.

Sandhurst Royal Military College founded 1799 by the Duke of York as a training college for cadets about to enter the army; occupied present site 1812.

Sandino, Augusto Cesar (1893–1934) Nicaraguan rebel leader (inspiration of the Sandinista rebels in the 1970s).

Sandow, Eugene (1867–1925) strong man and wrestler.

Sandringham House, Norfolk, British royal residence purchased by King Edward VII 1861; rebuilt 1871.

Sandwich, Edward Montagu, Earl of (1625–72) admiral. He was killed in battle.

Sandwich Islands *see* HAWAII.

Sandys, Sir Edwin (1561–1629) organizer of the colony of Virginia.

Sandys, George (1578–1644) English poet (*Hymn to my Redeemer*) and translator.

San Francisco Conference Second World War conference held 25 April–26 June 1945.

San Francisco Earthquake took place 18–19 April 1906.

Sangallo, Antonio di (*c.*1485–1546) Italian architect.

Sanger, Frederick (1918–) British biochemist awarded Nobel prize for chemistry 1958 and 1977.

Sanger, 'Lord' George (1825–1911) English circus manager. He was murdered.

Sanger, John (1816–89) English circus manager.

Sanhedrin the supreme judicial tribunal of the Jews, existing in the time of the Maccabees and in New Testament times. According to the Talmud, Moses founded it when he elected 70 elders to assist him as judge in the wilderness, but this idea is now rejected.

Sankey, Ira David (1840–1908) American hymn-writer and evangelist who led a religious revival in the UK and USA 1873–74 with D. L. Moody.

San Marino the world's smallest republic; founded 9th to 10th centuries; independence recognized by the papacy 1631; under Italian protection since 1860.

San Martin, José de (1778–1850) South American liberator.

San Nicandro, Italy, place of Judaic sect, led by Donato Manduzio (1885–1948) who was converted in 1930.

San Quentin, California, state prison opened 1852.

Sansovino, Jacopo (1486–1570) Italian sculptor and architect.

Santa Anna, Antonio López de (1795–1876) Mexican statesman and soldier.

Santa Claus (Saint Nicholas) (*fl.* 11th century) bishop of Myra in Lycia.

Santa Fe Trail USA-Mexican trading route mainly used 1822 to 1861.

Santa Sophia place of worship in Istanbul, built 532–537 on the site of two previous churches; converted into a mosque 1453.

Santayana, George (1863–1952) Spanish-born philosopher and writer.

Santillana, Iñigo Lopez de Mendoza, Marquis of (1398–1458) Spanish poet (*Comedieta de Ponza*).

Santos-Dumont, Alberto (1873–1932) Brazil-born pioneer aviator.

São Paulo city in Brazil founded by the Portuguese 1554.

São Tomé Portuguese colony from 1521; gained independence 1974.

Sappho (b.*c*.650 BC) Greek poet. The Greeks regarded her as one of the greatest of all lyric poets, but only short fragments of her work survive.

Sarajevo capital of Bosnia-Herzegavina; scene of the murder of the Archduke Franz Ferdinand 28 June 1914; 1991–93 besieged by Serbian forces after disintegration of the former Yugoslavia.

Sarasate, Pablo de (1844–1908) Spanish violinist.

Saratoga, Battle of between the Americans and the British, 17 October 1777.

Sardinia second larges island of the Mediterranean. It became a province of Rome 239 BC; ruled by Spain 1592–1713; ruled by Savoy from 1720; became part of Italy 1861.

Sardis an ancient city in western Asia Minor and capital of Lydia. It was burned by the Athenians 497 BC and captured by Alexander the Great in his conquest of Lydia 334 BC.

Sardou, Victorien (1831–1908) French playwright (*Madame Sans Gene* 1893).

Sargent, John (1856–1925) Italian-born painter of American descent (*Suggia*).

Sargent, Sir Malcolm (1895–1967) English conductor.

Sargon (d.705 BC) king of Assyria (722–705 BC). In 721 BC he took Samaria and transported a large number of the Israelites to Mesopotamia and Media. He was murdered.

Sargon of Akkad (*fl* 37th century BC) possibly legendary ruler who founded the Akkadian Empire in Mesopotamia 2650 BC.

Sarmiento, Domingo Faustino (1811–88) president of Argentina (1868–74).

Saroyan, William (1908–81) American writer (*The Daring Young Man on the Flying Trapeze* 1934).

Sarto, Andrea del (1486–1531) Italian painter (*Birth of the Virgin* 1514).

Sartre, Jean-Paul (1905–80) French philosopher, novelist and dramatist. His attempts at reconciling Existentialist philosophy with Marxism are now of historical interest. His novels, however, e.g. *Nausea* (1938), are highly readable. Several of his plays, e.g. *Huis clos* (1944), are frequently performed.

Saskatchewan, Canada, created a separate province 1905.

Sassanids ruled Persia 226–651.

Sassoon, Siegfried(1886–1967) English writer (*Memoirs of a Fox-hunting Man* 1928).

Satellite first American (Explorer I), successfully launched from Cape Canaveral, Florida, 31 January 1958; first Russian (Sputnik I), successfully launched 4 October 1957; second Russian, 3 November 1957.

Satie, Erik [Alfred Leslie] (1866–1925) French composer (his mother was a Scottish composer). His simple, classically inspired compositions were influential on Debussy and Ravel, e.g. *Gymnopédies* (1888).

Saturn the second largest of the planets and sixth in distance from the sun. Its year is equal in lenth to 28.5 earth years. Its rings were first described 1655 by the Dutch astronomer Christiaan Huygens (1629–95).

Saud, Ibn (*c*.1880–1953) king of Saudi Arabia (1926–53).

Saudi Arabia a country of the Arabian Peninsual, formally proclaimed a kingdom 1932.

Saumarez, James Saumarez, Baron de (1757–1836) British admiral.

Saussure, Ferdinand de (1857–1913) Swiss linguist. Regarded as one of the founders of modern linguistics, he established the 'structuralist' approach to language as a social phenomenon, focusing on the arbitrary relationship between the word as 'linguistic sign' and the thing it signifies.

Saussure, Horace Benedict de (1740–99) Swiss physicist and alpinist.

Savage, Edward (1761–1817) American artist (*The Washington Family*).

Savage, Richard (*c.*1697–1743) English poet (*The Wanderer* 1729).

Savak Persian secret police under the shah, disbanded 1977.

Savannah first steam-propelled ship, crossed the Atlantic 1819.

Savary, Anne Jean Marie René, Duke of Rovigo (1774–1833) French general and diplomat.

Savery, Thomas (*c.*1650–1715) English military engineer and inventor.

Savigny, Friedrich Karl von (1779–1861) German jurist (*Das Recht des Besitzes* 1803).

Savile, Sir Henry (1549–1622) English classical scholar and philanthropist.

Savings bank first examples established by Priscilla Wakefield at Rotherham 1804 and by Henry Duncan at Ruthwell, Scotland, 1810.

Savonarola, Girolamo (1452–98) Italian ecclesiastical reformer who was educated for the medical profession but secretly joined the Dominican order at Bologna in 1475. He began preaching at Florence in 1483. He eventually became so powerful in his influence that after the death of Lorenzo de' Medici he organized the city into a republic and wrote to the Christian princes that the Church was corrupt, for which the pope excommunicated him in 1497. He was executed.

Savoy elected by plebiscite to be annexed to France 1860; dukes of Savoy ruled Sardinia from 1720 and Italy from 1860–1946.

Saxaphone, invented 1846 by the Belgian musical instrument-maker Adolphe Sax (1814–94).

Saxe, Maurice, Comte (1696–1750) marshal of France.

Saxhorn invented 1843–45 by the Belgian musical instrument-maker Adolphe Sax (1814–94).

Saxo-Grammaticus (*c.*1150–*c.*1205) Danish historian.

Saxton, Christopher (*fl* late 16th century) English map designer.

Sayers, Tom (1826–65) English pugilist.

Scaliger, Joseph Justus (1540–1609) French scholar and critic.

Scaliger, Julius Caesar (1484–1558) Italian-born philosopher and scientist.

Scapa Flow a large sheet of water almost surrounded by the islands of Orkney, north of Scotland. It was the British naval base in the First World War and the scene of the scuttling by their crews of the vessels of the surrendered German Grand Fleet, 23 June 1919. It was the British naval base durig the Second World War, when causeway joining the islands down its eastern side was built by Italian prisoners or war.

Scarlatti, Alessandro (1659–1725) Italian composer.

Scarlatti, Domenico (1685–1757) Italian composer.

Scarron, Paul (1610–60) French writer (and husband of Mme de Maintenon).

Schacht, Hjalmar (1877–1970) German statesman and banker.

Schadow, Johann Gottfried (1764–1850) German sculptor (*Frederick the Great*).

Scharnhorst German battleship sunk by the British Navy off North Cape 26 December 1943.

Scharnhorst, Gerhard Johann David von (1755–1813) German general.

Scharwenka, Xaver (1850–1924) German composer (*Meisterschule des Klavierspiels*).

Scheele, Carl Wilhelm (1742–86) Swedish chemist.

Scheer, Admiral Reinhard (1863–1928) German naval chief.

Scheffer, Ary (1795–1858) Dutch-born painter (*Mignon* 1836).

Schelling, Friedrich Wilhelm Joseph von (1775–1854) German philosopher.

Scherer, Wilhelm (1841–86) German historian of language and literature.

Schiaparelli, Giovanni (1835–1910) Italian astronomer.

Schick test for immunity from diphtheria discovered 1913 by the Hungarian-born scientist Bela Schick (1877–1967).

Schiele, Egon (1890–1918) Austrian expressionist painter.

Schiller, Friedrich von (1759–1805) German poet, dramatist and historian who was a man of high character and strove after ideals. He wrote ballads and some very fine plays, e.g. *Maria Stuart*, and his *History of the Netherlands* and *The History of the Thirty Years' War* are classics.

Schirmer, Gustav (1829–93) German-born music publisher.

Schism, Great between Western and Eastern Churches, complete 1054.

Schism, Papal 1378–1417.

Schism of Photius, from which arose *c.*880 the Eastern Orthodox Church, occasioned by the actions of the Patriarch Photius (*c.*820–*c.*891).

Schlegel, August (1767–1829) German critic and writer.

Schlegel, Friedrich (1772–1829) German poet.

Schleswig-Holstein northwest German state under Danish rule 1460–1864, under Prussian rule from 1864.

Schlieffen, Alfred, Graf von (1833–1913) German soldier and strategist.

Schliemann, Heinrich (1822–90) German archaeologist who is famous for his excavations at Mycenae in 1876 and Troy 1870–82.

Schmidt, Helmut (1918–) German politician (chancellor of West Germany 1974–82).

Schnabel, Artur (1882–1951) Austrian-born pianist.

Schnitger, Arp (1648–1720) German organ-builder.

Schnitzer, Eduard (Emin Pasha) (1840–92) German-born doctor and administrator in Turkey, Egypt and Central Africa.

Schnitzler, Arthur (1862–1931) Austrian writer (*Professor Bernhardi* 1912).

Schoenberg *or* **Schönberg, Arnold [Franz Walter]** (1874–1951) Austrian composer (US citizen from 1941). His early works, e.g. *Gurrelieder* (1900), are lush chromatic compositions in the late Romantic tradition. He then began composing atonal works and eventually developed his serial or 'twelve-tone' method. His works include *Pierrot Lunaire* (1912).

Scholes, Percy (1877–1958) English musicologist.

Schomberg, Frederick Herman Schomberg, Duke of (1615–90) German-born commander-in-chief of British forces in Ireland (1689–90). He was killed in battle.

Schomburgk, Richard (1811–90) German-born botanist in Australia.

Schönberg, Arnold *see* SCHOENBERG, ARNOLD.

Schopenhauer, Arthur (1788–1860) German philosopher. Renowned for his pessimistic outlook on life, he emphasized the active role of the will as the creative force in human thought. His works include *The World as Will and Idea* (1819).

Schott, Bernhard (d.1817) German music publisher.

Schreiner, Olive (1859–1922) South African writer (*Story of an African Farm* 1883).

Schrödringer, Erwin (1887–1961) Austrian-born scientist. He was awarded the Nobel prize for physics 1933.

Schubert, Franz [Peter] (1797–1828) Austrian composer. His works include nine symphonies, the eighth (in B minor) being the 'Unfinished', string quartets, and other chamber music. His songs, as in the song cycles *Die schöne Müllerin* and *Die Winterreise*, are regarded as some of the finest ever written, include settings of lyrics by Heine and Goethe (*Erlkönig* 1815), and others.

Schumacher, Ernst Friedrich (1911–77) German-born British economist. His book, *Small is Beautiful* (1973), became a founding text of the conservationist movement.

Schumann, Elizabeth (1891–1952) German-born operatic singer.

Schumann, Robert Alexander (1810–56) German composer. Noted for his espousal of Romantic values in music, his works include four symphonies, songs, and much fine piano music. His wife, **Clara Schumann** (*née* Wieck) (1819–96), was also a pianist and composer.

Schuschnigg, Kurt von (1897–1977) Austrian statesman. A staunch opponent of Hitler, he became chancellor in 1934 and was imprisoned by the Nazis (1938–45).

Schuyler, General Philip John (1733–1804) American Revolutionary leader.

Schwann, Theodor (1810–82) German physiologist.

Schwarzenburg, Felix (1800–1852) Austrian statesman.

Schweitzer, Dr Albert (1875–1965) Alsatian musician, theologian and medical missionary.

Sciascia, Leonardo (1921–89) Italian novelist (*Salt in the Wound* 1956).

Scientist term first introduced 1840 by the Master of Trinity College, Cambridge, William Whewell.

Scientology, Church of quasi-religious movement founded 1952 by L. Ron Hubbard.

'Scinde Dawk' first Indian postage stamp issued 1 July 1852.

Scipio Africanus (the Elder) [Publius Cornelius Scipio] (*c.*236–183 BC) Roman general who, during the Second Punic War, escaped the massacre at Cannae, drove the Carthaginians out of Spain 206 BC, carried the war into Africa 204 BC and utterly defeated the Carthaginians at the battle of Zama (202 BC), thus ending the war and bringing about the surrender of Carthage.

Scipio Africanus (the Younger) [Publius Cornelius Scipio Aemilianus Africanus Minor] (185–129 BC) Roman general and statesman, a Scipio by adoption, who captured and completely destroyed Carthage in 146 BC, thus finally ending the Punic Wars and ridding Rome of a dangerous rival.

Scipio, Quintus Caecilius Metellus Pius (d.46 BC) Roman consul and colonial administrator. He committed suicide.

Scopas (*fl* 4th century BC) Greek sculptor.

Scopes trial of local teacher accused of teaching Darwinian theories in Dayton, Tennessee, held 1925.

Scoresby, William (1760–1829) English navigator in Arctic regions.

Scorsese, Martin (1942–) American film director. His films include *Taxi Driver* (1976), *Raging Bull* (1980) and *Goodfellas* (1990), these three films starring the actor most associated with Scorsese's work, Robert De Niro.

Scot, Michael (*c.*1175–*c.*1234) Scottish astronomer and alchemist.

Scotland a country of the united Kingdom, occupying the northern part of Great Britain; independent until the crown was united with that of England 1603;

kingdoms and parliaments united 1707 under Treaty of Union; unsuccessful Jacobite rebellions 1715 and 1745; devolution referendum 1979.

Scotland Yard, New designed 1891 by the Scottish architect Richard Norman Shaw (1831–1912) and built on the Victoria Embankment in London, the 'New' being used to distinguish it from the original Scotland Yard in Whitehall.

Scots a Celtic people from Ireland who settled in northern Britain in the 5th and 6th centuries.

Scott, Charles Prestwich (1846–1932) English editor (of *Manchester Guardian* 1872–1929) and politician.

Scott, Cyril (1879–1970) English composer (*Oboe Concerto* 1948).

Scott, Robert Falcon (1868–1912) English explorer who led two Antarctic expeditions (1901–4, 1910–12). He died with four companions on the latter, returning from the South Pole after having reached it a month after Amundsen. His son was Sir Peter Scott.

Scott, Sir Peter Markham (1909–89) British naturalist, artist, writer and TV wildlife presenter whose television documentaries and many books were notably influential in promoting conservation.

Scott, Sir Walter (1771–1832) Scottish novelist and poet. His early, highly Romantic narrative poems, set in the Scottish past, e.g. *The Lady of the Lake*, established his popularity with both the reading public and the literary world, Byron being particularly generous in his praise. His historical novels (a genre he refined and made into an art form), particularly *Waverley* (1814), *The Heart of Midlothian* (1818) and *Ivanhoe* (1819), were enormously influential and spawned a host of imitators. He was a prolific writer, partly because the failure of publishing houses with which he was connected in 1826 reduced him to poverty and left him with great debts that he had largely paid off by the time of his death.

Scottish Labour Party founded 1888 by the Scottish socialist Keir Hardie (1856–1915).

Scotus, Duns (*c.*1266–1308) Scottish philosopher.

Scouts, Boy *see* BOY SCOUTS.

Screw propeller invented 1836 by the English inventor Sir Francis Pettit Smith (1808–74).

Screw threads standardized 1841 by the English mechanical engineer Sir Joseph Whitworth (1803–87).

Scriabin *or* **Skryabin, Alexander Nikolayevich** (1872–1915) Russian composer and pianist. His compositions often involved extra-musical effects, e.g. *Prometheus*, a piece for piano accompanied by coloured light projected on a screen. He envisaged all the arts coming together in one great performance.

Scribe, Eugène (1791–1861) French playwright (*Valérie* 1822).

Scribner, Charles (1821–71) American publisher.

Scripps, Edward Wyllis (1854–1926) American newspaper publisher.

Scroggs, Sir William (*c.*1623–1683) Lord Chief Justice of England.

Scrope, Richard le (*c.*1350–1405) archbishop of York (1398–1405). He was executed.

Scudéry, Madeleine de (1607–1701) French writer (*Clélie* 1654–61).

Scurvy, fruit juice first used against, in 1601 by Sir James Lancaster (d.1618).

Scuttling of German Grand Fleet 21 June 1919; of *Graf Spee* 17 December 1939.

Seaplane first invented 1911 by the American aviation pioneer and inventor Glenn Hammond Curtiss (1878–1930).

Searchlights, pioneer model invented 1763 by the Liverpool dockmaster William Hutchison (1715–1801).

Searle, Ronald [William Fordham] (1920–) English cartoonist and writer. Known primarily as the creator of the monstrous St Trinian's schoolgirls, who feature in several of his works, he is regarded, particularly in the US and France, as one of the finest graphic artists of the 20th century. His haunting book *To the Kwai—and Back: War Drawings 1939–45* is a record of his experiences as a Japanese prisoner of war.

Sea Scouts movement started in Britain 1908.

Sea serpent sighted in the South Atlantic by the crew of HM corvette *Daedalus* 1848.

Seaton, Edward Cator (1815–80) English promoter of vaccination.

Seaweed propagation method discovered 1886 by the French botanists Edouard Bornet (1828–1911) and Gustave Adolphe Thuret (1817–75).

Sebastian (1554–78) king of Portugal (1557–78). He was killed in battle.

Sebastiano del Piombo (*c.*1485–1547) Italian painter (*Raising of Lazarus*).

Sebbi king of Essex (665–695) *see* Appendix.

Secombe, Harry *see* MILLIGAN, SPIKE.

Second Triumvirate the political alliance in Rome of Octavian, Antony and Lepidus formed 43 BC to rule the state in the wake of the death of Caesar and to stop the disputes between Octavian and Antony. Each governed a separate part of the Roman world. They executed Cicero, and Antony and Octavian took an army into Macedonia where they defeated Brutus and Cassius at Philippi in 42 BC. Octavian disagreed with his colleagues and after he had defeated them at Actium, he made himself absolute ruler of Rome.

Secularism a system of philosophy that insists on the careful examination of dogmas and creeds before acceptance and on a person's actions being guided by reason rather than impulse. It was founded 1846 by the English cooperator George Jacob Holyoake (1817–1906).

Sedan, Battle of (1) a battle of the Franco-German War in the Ardennes when the French under Napoleon III surrendered to the Germans, 1 September 1870. (2) German breakthrough at, May 1940.

Seddon, Frederick Henry (1870–1912) English murderer. He was hanged.

Sedgemoor, Battle of a battle of Monmouth's Rebellion, 6 July 1685, between James II and his nephew, the Duke of Monmouth, which was a victory for James. Monmouth was executed 15 July.

Sedgwick, Rev. Adam (1785–1873) English geologist.

Sedgwick, Robert (d.1656) major-general of Massachusetts forces.

Sedley, Sir Charles (*c.*1639–1701) English writer (*Bellamira* 1687).

Seed drill, invented 1731 by the English agricultural writer Jethro Tull (1674–1741).

Seed Testing scientific method originated 1869 by the German plant physiologist Friedrich Nobbe (1830–1922).

Seeley, Sir John Robert (1834–95) English historian and writer who advocated imperial federation. His books include *Ecce Homo* (1865) and *The Expansion of England* (1883).

Segovia, Andrés [Marquis of Salobreña] (1894–1987) Spanish guitarist. An internationally recognized virtuoso, he initiated a revival of interest in the classical guitar.

Seguier, William (1771–1843) English artist and first Keeper of the National Gallery.

Seiber, Mátyás (1905–60) composer (*Ulysses* 1949).

Seismograph earth tremor reader invented by the Chinese Chang Heng 132.

Sejanus, Lucius Aelius (d.31) Roman prefect, minister of Tiberius. He was executed.

Selborne, Roundell Palmer, Earl of (1812–95) Lord Chancellor.

Selby, William (1738–98) English-born organist and composer.

Selden, John (1584–1654) English jurist (*Table Talk* 1689).

Selenium an element with the property of conducting electrity more easily when exposed to light than when in the dark. It was discovered 1817 by the Swedish chemist Baron Berzelius (1779–1848).

Selenous acid first obtained 1827 by the German chemist Eilhard Mitscherlich (1794–1863).

Seleucid dynasty founded by Seleucus I and ruled Syria 312–64 BC with its capital at first at Babylon.

Seleucid era began 1 September 311 BC.

Seleucus I [Nicator] (*c.*356–280 BC) king of Syria (312–280 BC) and founder of the Seleucid dynasty. He was the son of Antiochus, a Macedonian officer of Philip II, and accompanied Alexander the Great on his expedition to Asia and after Alexander's death acquired the wealthy and important satrapy of Babylonia. Through a series campaigns he gradually extended his power over all the eastern provinces that had formed part of the empire of Alexander, from the Euphrates to the banks of Oxus and Indus. His capital was at first at Babylon but he founded Antioch 312 BC, to where he moved his capital. He was murdered during an attempt to invade Macedonia and was succeeded by his son, Antiochus I.

Seleucus II [Callinicus] (d.227 BC) king of Syria (246–226 BC) who succeeded his father, Antiochus II. His mother Laodice had had his father, stepmother Berenice and their infant son put to death, which antagonized his people and brought about an invasion of Syria by Ptolemy VII of Egypt, the brother of Berenice. He was accidentally killed by a fall from his horse while trying to regain Asia Minor from Attalus I of Pergamus and was succeeded by his son, Seleucus III.

Seleucus III [Ceraunus] (d.223 BC) king of Syria (226–223 BC) who succeeded his father, Seleucus II. He continued his father's campaign to regain Asia Minor from Attalus I of Pergamus but was assassinated. He was succeeded by his brother Antiochus III.

Seleucus IV [Philopator] (d.175 BC) king of Syria (187–175 BC) who fought at the battle of Magnesia with his father, Antiochus III, and succeeded him three years later as king of a diminished empire. He was assassinated by one of his ministers and was succeeded by his brother, Antiochus IV.

Seleucus V (d.125 BC) king of Syria (125 BC). The eldest son of Demetrius II and Cleopatra (4), he assumed the throne immediately on learning of the death of his father, but his mother was angry that he had taken such a step without her authority and caused him to be assassinated. He was succeeded by his brother, Antiochus VIII.

Seleucus VI (d.95 BC) king of Syria (96–95 BC) and eldest of the five sons of Antiochus VIII. On the death of his father, he immediately assumed the sovereignty but his claims were resisted by his uncle, Antiochus IX, who marched from Antioch against him. In a decisive battle that ensued in 95 BC, Antiochus was totally defeated and killed and Seleucus was for a short time undisputed ruler. But Antiochus X, the son of Antiochus IX, rebelled against him, defeated him in battle and expelled him from Syria.

Selfridge's Oxford Street department store, London, opened 15 March 1909. Founded by the American merchant Gordon Selfridge (1858–1947), who had retired from business in the USA in 1903 and come to England in 1906.

Self-starter for cars developed 1911 by the inventor Charles Franklin Kettering (1876–1958).

Selim I (1465–1521) sultan of Turkey (1512–21).

Selim II (1524–74) sultan of Turkey (1566–74).

Selim III (1762–1808) sultan of Turkey (1789–1808). He was strangled.

Seljuk *or* **Jalalian era** began 15 March 1079.

Selkirk, Alexander (1676–1721) Scottish sailor who was the prototype for Robinson Crusoe. He took part in buccaneering expeditions in the South Seas and in 1704, having quarrelled with his captain, was put ashore, at his own request, on the island of Juan Fernandez. He lived there alone for four years and four months, and was then taken off by the captain of a privateer. He returned home in 1712 and rose to be a lieutenant in the navy before his death.

Sellers, Peter (1925–80) English comedy actor and entertainer. One of the founders of the Goon Show (*see* Spike Milligan). He made several films in the UK, e.g. *The Ladykillers* (1955) and achieved further popularity as Inspector Clouseau in such films as *The Pink Panther* (1963).

Selous, Frederick Courteney (1851–1917) English explorer. He was killed.

Selwyn College, Cambridge University, founded in memory of Bishop George Augustus Selwyn 1882.

Selwyn, George Augustus (1809–78) first bishop of New Zealand (1842–67).

Semaphore signalling pioneered 1666 by Lord Worcester; developed 1792 by Claude Chappé and 1796 by Lord George Murray; perfected 1803 by Admiral Home Riggs Popham.

Semmelweiss, Ignatz Philipp (1816–65) Hungarian discoverer of antisepsis.

Semmering Pass in the Alps, railway constructed 1848–54.

Sempill, Robert (*c.*1595–*c.*1665) Scottish poet (*Life and Death of Habbie Simpson* 1640).

Senancour, Étienne Pivert de (1770–1846) French writer (*Obermann* 1804).

Seneca (*c.*54 BC– AD 39) Roman orator.

Seneca [Lucius Annaeus Seneca] (*c.*4 BC–65 AD) Roman dramatist and Stoic philosopher. His verse tragedies were very influential on Elizabethan dramatists such as Shakespeare. He was for a time tutor to Nero, by whose orders he had finally to commit suicide.

Senefelder, Alois (1771–1834) German inventor 1798 of lithography.

Senior, Nassau William (1790–1864) English economist.

Senlac, Battle of *or* **Battle of Hastings** between the Normans under Duke William of Normandy and the English under Harold II, 14 October 1066. William was victorious and Harold was killed—beginning of the Norman Conquest of England.

Sennacherib (d.681 BC) king of Assyria (705–681 BC) and son of Sargon II. He besieged Jerusalem, 701 BC, but failed to take the city because of an outbreak of plague. He returned to Nineveh where he was assassinated by his sons.

Sennett, Mack [Michael Sinnott] (1880–1960) Canadian-born American film director and producer. He produced the manic 'Keystone Cop' comedies, which achieved international success. He also produced Charlie Chaplin's first films.

Sensory and motor nerves distinguished 1807 by Sir Charles Bell (1774–1842).

Sentinum, Battle of a battle of the Third Samnite War, when the Romans defeated the Samnites and their allies 295 BC.

Septuagint the oldest Greek version of the Old Testament believed to have been made in Alexandria by 70 people in 270 BC. It was used by Hebrews generally in the time of Christ and quoted from by the authors of the New Testament.

Sequoyah (*c.*1770–1843) American Indian leader of the Cherokee nation.

Serapeum, ruins of, discovered 1850 by the French Egyptologist Auguste Ferdinand François Mariette (1821–81).

Serbia ruled by Turks 1459–1829; occupied by Austrians 1915–18; republic of the former Yugoslavia 1918–91.

Serfs a feudal system of employment corresponding to the slaves of ancient times. Serfs were attached to the land, were not allowed to leave an estate and could be bought and sold with it. It gradually disappeared, remaining longest in the mining industris, which were not completely freed from it until the 18th century in Scotland. In France serfdom was abolished in the Revolution, in Prussia serfs were emancipated in 1807 and in Russia they were liberated from Imperial Russian domination 1861 by order of Alexander II.

Sergius I, Saint pope (687–701).

Sergius II pope (844–847).

Sergius III pope (904–911).

Sergius IV pope (1009–12).

Sertorius, Quintus (d.72 BC) Roman general and administrator in Spain. A follower of Marius, he led a rebellion against Sulla, 76–72 BC, that was suppressed by Pompey. He was assassinated.

Servetus, Michael [Miguel Serveto] (1511–53) Spanish theologian. He was burnt at the stake.

Service, Robert William (1876–1958) English-born writer (*Songs of a Sourdough* 1907).

Servile Wars, Sicily 103–101 BC; Italy 73–71 BC.
Sesostris I (d.1933 BC) king of Egypt (1980–1933 BC).
Sesostris II (d.1887 BC) king of Egypt (1906–1887 BC).
Sesostris III (d.1849 BC) king of Egypt (1887–1849 BC).
Sesshu, Toyo (1421–1507) Japanese painter.
Sessions, Roger (1896–1985) American composer (*Montezuma* 1947).
Seti I (d.1292 BC) king of Egypt (1313–1292 BC).
Sethos I king of Egypt who conducted wars against the Libyans, Syrians and Hittites 1350 BC
Seti II (d.1205 BC) king of Egypt (1209–05 BC).
Settle, Elkanah (1648–1724) English poet and playwright (*The Empress of Morocco* 1671).
Seurat, Georges (1859–91) French painter, a leading neo-Impressionist. He developed the system of pointillism in which the painting is built up from tiny areas of pure colour. His works include *Une Baignade* (1884).
Seven Days' Battles, near Richmond, Virginia, American Civil War, 26 June to 2 July 1862.
Seven Sleepers of Ephesus seven Christians who were allegedly imprisoned in a cave during the Decian persecution *c*.247. They fell asleep and woke 200 years later, in the reign of Theodosius II, whom they spoke with and then died after blessing the people.
Seventeen year locust a cicada whose development from egg to adult needs 17 years.
Seven Weeks' War between Prussia and Austria (and her allies) 1866.
Seven Wise Men of Greece seven philosophers or statesmen of ancient Greece who lived in the 5th century BC and are generally held to be Periander of Corinth, Pittacus of Mitylene, Thales of Miletus, Solon of Athens, Bias of Priene, Chilo of Sparta and Cleobulus of Lindus.
Seven Years' War (1756–63) between Prussia (and England) and Austria for the possession of Silesia, which was part of the territory of Maria Theresa of Austria. The war involved France, Russia and Sweden, and ended in favour of Prussia.
Sévérac, Déodat de (1873–1921) French composer (*Le Parc aux cerfs*).
Severinus pope ((640).
Severn, Joseph (1793–1879) English painter (*Spectre Ship*).
Severn Bridge carrying the M4 motorway opened 1966.
Severn Crossing opened 1996.
Severn tunnel, England, construction begun 1873; completed 1886.
Severus (146–211) Roman emperor (193–211). He died in Britain.
Severus (d.307) Roman emperor (306–307).
Sévigné, Marquise de (1626–96) French writer (*Lettres*).
Seward, Anna ('The Swan of Litchfield') (1747–1809) English poet and letter-writer.
Sewell, Anna (1820–78) English writer (*Black Beauty* 1877).
Sewing machine models patented by Charles Weisenthal 1755 and Thomas Saint 1790; Thimonnier produced a machine 1830; models patented by Newton and Archbold 1841; Singer used Howe's needle for his model 1850.
Sexred (d.616) king of Essex (616) *see* Appendix.
Sextant invented 1731 by the Englishman John Hadley (1682–1744).
Seychelles island group in the Indian Ocean, probably discovered by the Portuguese *c*.1500; annexed by France 1744; ceded to Britain 1814; became an independent republic within the Commonwealth 1976.
Seymour of Sudeley, Thomas Seymour, Baron (*c*.1508–1549) Lord High Admiral. He was executed.
Seymour, Edward, Earl of Hertford and Duke of Somerset (*c*.1506–1552) (The Protector). He was beheaded.
Sforza, Francesco (1401–66) Duke of Milan.
Shackleton, Sir Ernest Henry (1874–1922) Anglo-Irish explorer. He served in Robert Scott's Antarctic expedition, and commanded two further expeditions (1908–1909, 1914–16). His last expedition to Antarctica began in September 1921. He died in the course of it and was buried in South Georgia.
Shadwell, Thomas (*c*.1642–1692) English writer (*Bury Fair* 1689).
Shaftesbury, Anthony Ashley Cooper, 1st Earl of (1621–83) English politician.
Shaftesbury, Anthony Ashley Cooper, 3rd Earl of (1671–1713) English philosopher.
Shaftesbury, Anthony Ashley Cooper, 7th Earl of (1801–85) English philanthropist.
Shah Jehan (d.1666) Mogul emperor of Delhi (1627–58) and builder of the Taj Mahal.
Shakers, Society of religious movement seceded from Quakers 1747 under James and Jane Wardley; first settlement in America founded 1776 by Ann Lee (1736–84).
Shakespeare, William (1564–1616) English dramatist and poet. His status as the greatest of all poets and dramatists has rarely been challenged. His plays are generally divided into three groups. The first group (late 1580s–*c*.1594) consists of histories, e.g. the *Henry VI* trilogy, early comedies such as *The Two Gentlemen of Verona*, and the tragedy of *Romeo and Juliet*. The second group (*c*.1595–*c*.1599) includes

histories such as *King John, Henry IV Parts I and II*, the comedies *A Midsummer's Night's Dream* and *As You Like It*, and the tragedy *Julius Caesar*. The third group (*c*.1600–*c*.1612) includes the great tragedies *Hamlet, Othello, King Lear, Macbeth, Antony and Cleopatra, Coriolanus* and *Timon of Athens*, the so-called "dark comedies," *Troilus and Cressida, All's Well That Ends Well*, and *Measure for Measure*, and tragicomedies such as *The Winter's Tale* and *The Tempest*. Shakespeare's other major works are the narrative poems *Venus and Adonis* (1593) and *The Rape of Lucrece* (1594), and the magnificent *Sonnets*, which feature a romantic triangle between the poet (Shakespeare) a dark lady (identity unknown) and a beautiful young nobleman (possibly the Earl of Southampton).

Shakespeare Memorial Theatre new building opened at Stratford-on-Avon, 23 April 1932.

Shalmaneser I king of Assyria 1330 BC.

Shalmaneser III king of Assyria (858–824 BC) who subdued Babylon and Syria 860 BC.

Shamshi-Adad king of Assyria (824-811 BC), son of Shalmeneser III.

Shang Yin dynasty, China, 1766 to 1122 BC.

Shankar, Ravi *see* RAVI SHANKAR.

Shankly, Bill [William Shankly] (1913–81) Scottish footballer and manager. Regarded as one of the outstanding football managers of the century, he transformed Liverpool into one of the most successful clubs of modern times. A renowned football fanatic, he once notoriously observed that football was more important than life or death.

Sharp, Cecil James (1859–1924) English collector of English folk songs and dances.

Sharp, Granvillle (1735–1813) English anti-slavery pioneer.

Sharp, James (1613-79) Scottish clergyman who signed the National Covenant against Charles I in 1638 and was imprisoned in 1651-52. He was made Archbishop of St Andrews in 1660 after the Restoration and was soon seen as someone who had betrayed the cause of the Covenanters and became a much despised figure. He was murdered by twelve Covenanters on 3 May.

Sharp, William ('Fiona Macleod') (1855–1905) Scottish novelist (*The Immortal Hour*1900).

Sharpeville Massacre shooting by South African police of anti-apartheid marchers protesting against Pass Laws, 70 killed, 190 injured, 21 March 1960.

Shaw, George Bernard (1856–1950) Anglo-Irish dramatist and critic. He began his literary career as a drama, literary and music critic in the 1880s, and after a false start in novel-writing, began writing plays in the 1890s. The plays, e.g. *Man and Superman* (1903), *Major Barbara* (1905) and *Pygmalion* (1913), have been very successful thanks to Shaw's mastery of witty dialogue. He was awarded the Nobel prize for literature in 1925.

Shaw, Martin (1876–1958) English composer (*Mr Pepys* 1926).

Shaw, Richard Norman (1831–1912) Scottish architect.

Shearer, Moira (1926–) Scottish ballerina.

Shee, Sir Martin Archer (1770–1850) Irish painter (*Prospero and Miranda*).

Shee, Sir William(1804–68) first British Roman Catholic judge since the Revolution.

Sheffield University founded 1879 as Firth College by the English manufacturer Mark Firth (1819–80); constituted a university college 1897; achieved university status 1905.

Sheldonian Theatre Oxford theatre built 1669 by the archbishop of Canterbury, Gilbert Sheldon (1598–1677).

Shelley, Mary Wollstonecraft (1797–1851) English novelist, wife of Percy Bysshe Shelley. Her masterpiece is *Frankenstein, or the Modern Prometheus* (1818), a Gothic fantasy that has also been hailed as the first science fiction novel.

Shelley, Percy Bysshe (1792–1822) English poet. His talent for public scandal emerged at Oxford University, where he was expelled for co-writing a tract entitled *The Necessity of Atheism* (1811), in which year he eloped with Harriet Westbrook. Two years later, he published his poem *Queen Mab*, which celebrates a future republican millenium of free love and vegetarianism. In 1814, he eloped with Mary Godwin (*see* Mary Wollstonecraft Shelley) and her step-sister, Jane 'Claire' Clairmont. Harriet committed suicide by drowning in 1816, in which year he married Mary. Shelley and his entourage moved to Italy in 1818, where he drowned in a sailing accident. His poems are among the greatest of English Romantic poetry. The highlights are: *Prometheus Unbound* (1820); *Adonais* (1821), his elegy on the death of Keats; and several of the finest poems in the English language, notably *Ode to the West Wind* and *To a Skylark* (both 1820).

Shenstone, William (1714–63) English poet (*The Schoolmistress* 1742).

Sheppard, Jack (1702–24) English highwayman. He was hanged.

Sheraton, Thomas (1751–1806) English cabinetmaker.

Sheridan, Richard Brinsley (1751–1816) Irish dramatist and politician, noted for his superb comedies of manners, *The Rivals* (1775) and *School for Scandal* (1777), both of which are firm repertory favourites. His other major play is *The Critic* (1779), a burlesque satirizing the conventions of tragedy. He was also highly regarded for his oratory in parliament.

Sherman, General William Tecumseh (1820–91) American general (march to the sea, November–December 1864).

Sherriff, Robert Cedric (1896–1975) English-born dramatist (*Journey's End* 1928).

Sherrington, Sir Charles (1859–1952) British physiologist.

Sherwood, Robert Emmet (1896–1955) American playwright (*The Petrified Forest*).

Sheshonk Libyan king of Egypt who conquered Palestine 950 BC.

Shi'a Islamic religious movement founded *c.*658.

Shiloh, Battle of American Civil War battle, 6–7 April 1862.

Shinwell, Lord Emanuel ('Manny') (1884–1986 British Labour politician).

Ship steam first used for propulsion 1775 in France; the American *Clermont* launched 1807; Henry Bell's *Comet* began to ply on the Clyde 1812; first steam-propelled (*Savannah*), crossed the Atlantic 1819; first steamship to ply the Atlantic the *Royal William* 1833; iron began to replace wood for the hulls 1840; first ocean-going iron ship (*The Great Britain*), built 1843 by the British engineer Isambard Brunel (1806–59); screw propellor ousted the paddle wheel *c.*1860; the *Great Eastern*, the largest of iron ships, made her first trip in 1860; iron began to give way to steel 1873; steam turbine appeared 1896; first turbine-propelled (*Turbinia*), invented 1897 by the British engineer, Sir Charles Parsons (1854–1931); internal combustion engine first used 1904; first gas-turbine propelled (HMS *Grey Goose*), fitted with two Rolls-Royce RM 60 engines 1955; first guided-missile (HMS *Girdle Ness*), commissioned 1956.

Ship canals Sault Ste Marie, USA, opened 1855; Suez 1869; Amsterdam 1876; Welland, Canada 1887; Panama 1914; Corinth 1893; Manchester 1894; Kiel 1895.

Ship Money first levied in England 1007. Also levied without Parliament's consent 1634–36 by King Charles I.

Shipton, Mother English witch and prophet reputed to have been born *c.*1487 as Ursula Southill and to have died 1561.

Shirley, James (1596–1666) English playwright (*The Traitor* 1631).

Shirley, Sir Anthony (1565–*c.*1635) English adventurer.

Shockley, William Bradford (1910–89) American physicist. He shared, with Bardeen and the Chinese-born American physicist **Walter Brattain** (1902–87), the 1956 Nobel prize for physics for his development of the junction transistor.

Sholem Aleichem, *see* ALEICHEM, SHOLEM.

Shore, Jane (d.*c.*1527) mistress of King Edward IV.

Shorthand a method of rapid writing using signs invented 1588 by the Englishman Dr Timothy Bright (1551–1615); introduction 1837 of phonetic system devised by Isaac Pitman (1813–97).

Shorthouse, Joseph Henry (1834–1903) English novelist (*John Inglesant* 1881).

Shostakovich, Dimitri Dimitriyevich (1906–75) Russian composer. Many of his works, e.g. the opera *Lady Macbeth of Mtensk* (1934), were attacked for their disregard of socialist realism. His works include 15 symphonies, 15 string quartets and song cycles.

Shrewsbury, Treaty of recognizing Llywelyn ap Gruffydd's overlordship of Wales, signed 1265.

Shrove Tuesday first day of Lent and the day before Ash Wednesday.

Shute, Nevil [Nevil Shute Norway] (1899–1960) English-born novelist who settled in Australia. His novels include *A Town Like Alice* (1949).

SI *see* SI UNITS.

Siam *see* THAILAND.

Sibelius, Jean (1865–1957) Finnish composer. His works, which include *Finlandia* (1899), reflect his strong Finnish nationalism and often draw on the Finnish traditional epic, *Kalevala.*

Siberch, John, of Siegburg, set up the first printing press in Cambridge 1521.

Sicilian Vespers massacre of French residents in Sicily, 31 March 1282.

Sicily an island hanging from the toe of Italy and the largest island in the Mediterranean, now an autonomous region of Italy. Carthaginian attack repelled by Sicilian Greeks at battle of Himera 480 BC; Hamiclar Barca became Carthaginian commander in Sicily 247 BC; Sicily became the first Roman province 241 BC after Roman victory over Carthage at the naval battle of Aegates Islands; conquered by Arabs in 8th century, by Normans in 11th century; ruled by Aragonese 1301–1713, by Bourbons 1735–1860.

Sickert, Walter Richard (1860–1942) German-born painter (*Victor Lecour* 1922).

Siddons, Mrs Sarah (1755–1831) English actress who was the first great tragic actress of the English stage. She began her career as a child and at the age of nineteen married William Siddons, an actor in the company of her father, Roger Kemble. Her first appearance at Drury Lane was a failure but in 1782, as Isabella in *The Fatal Marriage*, she won success. She retired in 1812.

Sidgwick, Henry (1838–1900) English philosopher and champion of women's rights.

Sidmouth, Henry Addington, Viscount (1757–1844) statesman.

Sidney Sussex College, Cambridge University, founded under the will of the Lady Frances Sidney, Countess Dowager of Sussex, 1596.

Sidney, Algernon (1622–83) English democrat. He was executed.

Sidney, Sir Philip (1554–86) English poet, soldier and courtier. His works include *Arcadia* (1590), the first major English pastoral poem; the sonnet sequence *Astrophel and Stella* (1591), which inspired a host of imitations; and *A Defence of Poetry* (1595), a spirited defence of English as a medium for writing great poetry. He went to the Netherlands in 1585 and was appointed governor of Flushing. He died in action against the Spaniards at Zutphen.

Siebold, Philipp Franz von (1796–1866) German ethnographer and naturalist (particularly with regard to Japan).

Siegen, Ludwig von (*c.*1609–1680) Dutch-born engraver and inventor (1642) of the mezzotint process.

Siemens, Ernst Werner von (1816–92) German electrical engineer.

Siemens, Sir William (1823–83) German-born electrical engineer.

Siena, University of, founded 1247.

Sienkiewicz, Henryk (1846–1916) Polish novelist (*Quo Vadis?* 1896).

Sierra Leone West African country, earliest English settlement 1787; British colony 1808–1960; gained independence within the Commonwealth 1961; declared a republic 1971.

Sièyes, Emmanuel Joseph (1748–1836) French statesman.

Sigeberht (1) (d.*c.*634) king of East Anglia (631–634) *see* Appendix.

Sigeberht (2) (d.759) king of Wessex (756–757) *see* Appendix.

Sigeberht I (d.653) king of Essex (617–653) *see* Appendix.

Sigeberht II king of Essex (653–660)

Sigebert (d.575) king of the Franks. He was assassinated.

Sigeherd (d.*c.*709) king of Essex (695–709) *see* Appendix.

Sigered (d.825) king of Essex (798–825) *see* Appendix.

Sigeric king of Essex (758–798) *see* Appendix.

Sighere (d.*c.*695) king of Essex (665–695) *see* Appendix.

Sigismund I (1467–1548) king of Poland (1506-1548).

Sigismund II (1520–72) king of Poland (1548–72).

Sigismund III (1566–1632) king of Poland (1587–1632).

Sigismund (1368–1437) Holy Roman emperor (1433–37).

Sign language for deaf and dumb people developed 1765 by the French priest Charles Michel, Abbé de l'Epée (1712–89).

Signac, Paul (1863–1935) French painter (*Le Pont des Arts* 1914).

Signorelli, Luca (*c.*1442–1523) Italian painter (*Eternal Destiny of Man*).

Sigurdsson, Jón (1811–79) Icelandic statesman.

Sihanouk, Prince Norodom (1922–) Cambodian statesman, formerly (elected) king of Cambodia (1941–55). He abdicated (in favour of his father) to become prime minister (1955–60) after independence from France in 1955, becoming head of state in 1960. He was deposed by a military coup in 1970 and fled to China, forming an alliance with Pol Pot's Khmer Rouge, who seized Cambodia in 1975. He again became head of state in 1975 and was deposed by Pol Pot the following year. After the Vietnamese invasion of 1979, Sihanouk formed a government in exile, in an uneasy alliance with the Khmer Rouge.

Sikh religion, founded by the Indian religious leader Nanak (1459–1538).

Sikh Wars, India, between the British and the Sikhs, 1845–46, 1848–49.

Sikkim under British control 1861–1947; became Indian protectorate 1950, and state in 1975.

Sikorski, Wladyslaw (1881–1943) Polish general and statesman. Premier of the Polish government in exile during the Second World War and commander in chief of the Free Polish armed forces.

Sikorsky, Igor Ivan (1889–1972) Russian-born American aeronautical engineer. He built the first four-engined aircraft in 1913 and the first successful helicopter in 1939.

Silesia a Bohemian fief 1335–1740; Prussian 1740–1871; German 1871–1945; Polish since 1945.

Silesian Wars, between Prussia and Austria 1740–42, 1744–45 and 1756–62.

Silicones, study developed 1899–1941 by the English chemist Frederick S. Kipping (1863–1949); practical applications discovered 1941 by J. F. Hyde.

Silk, artificial made 1883 by the English chemist Sir Joseph Wilson Swan (1828–1914). Industry founded *c.*1885 by the French scientist Hilaire, Comte de Chardonnet (1839–1924).

Silk traditionally invented 2640 BC; silkworms brought to Constantinople *c.*AD 550; first silk mill in USA established 1839.

Silurian period of Earth history, 350 million years ago.

Silurist, The' (Henry Vaughan) (1622–95) poet.
ilverius, Saint pope (536–537).
ilvester I, Saint pope (314–336).
ilvester II [Gerbert] pope (999–1003).
ilvester III pope (1045).
ilvester IV anti-pope (1105).
ilvestrians monastic order founded by St Silvester (d.1267).
imenon, Georges (1903–89) Belgian novelist, creator of 'Inspector Maigret'.
imeon I tsar of Bulgaria (reigned 893–927).
imeon Stylites, Saint (d.*c*.459) a Syrian monk who, near Antioch, lived on a pillar three feet in diameter at the top as a method of penance. He must have come down at times, for he healed the sick by touch and took a somewhat acrimonious part in politics.
imhath Torah (Rejoicing of the Law) Jewish holiday, 23rd day of Tishri.
imnel, Lambert (*c*.1475–died after 1525) pretender.
imon, Sir John (1816–1904) British public health pioneer.
imon, John, Viscount (1873–1954) British Liberal lawyer and statesman who after a career at the bar was appointed Attorney-General in 1913 and Home Secretary in 1915. He served in the army 1917–18. Elected leader of the Liberal Party in 1922, in 1931 he headed a Liberal National party to support Ramsey MacDonald's National Government in the general election and became Foreign Secretary. During the Second World War he was Lord Chancellor in Churchill's coalition government (1940–45)
imon de Montfort (*c*.1208–1265) English baronial leader. He was killed in battle.
imon Maccabaeus Jewish leader and a bro her of Judas Maccabaeus, who became leader of the Jews 143 BC
implicius pope (468–483).
implon Pass over the Alps, built 1800–1807; tunnel built 1898–1906.
impson, Sir James Young (1811–70) Scottish physician who introduced anaesthetics in childbirth *c*.1847.
impson, Maxwell (1815–1902) British chemist.
impson, Wallis *see* WINDSOR, DUKE OF.
imson, William (1800–1847) Scottish painter (*Solway Moss-Sunset* 1831).
inatra, Frank [Francis Albert Sinatra] (1915–) American singer and film actor. Regarded as one of the finest modern popular singers, with a finely tuned jazz-like sense of phrasing.
inclair, Upton (1878–1968) American novelist (*Boston* 1928).
inding, Christian (1856–1941) Norwegian composer (*Rustle of Spring*).
Sind War between British and Baluchi forces, March 1843.
Singapore founded 1819 by the British administrator Sir Stamford Raffles (1781–1826; held by Japanese 1942–45; independent state within the Commonwealth since 1959; part of the Federation of Malaysia from 1963; became independent republic 1965.
Singer, Isaac Bashevis (1904–91) Polish-born American Yiddish writer. Much of his fiction deals with the now vanished world of Polish Judaism, e.g. *The Magician of Lublin*. He was awarded the 1978 Nobel prize for literature.
Sinigaglia, Leone (1868–1944) Italian composer (*Danze Piemontese*).
Sinn Fein political party founded 1905 by the Irish patriot Arthur Griffith (1872–1922).
Siphon principle discovered 1577 by the Scottish mathematician William Welwood (d. after 1622).
Sirisius, Saint pope (384–399).
Sisinnius pope (708).
Sisley, Alfred (1839–99) French painter of English extraction. Influenced by the Impressionists Renoir and Monet, he painted mainly carefully composed and sensitively coloured landscapes. His works include *Le Canal du Loing*.
Sismondi, Jean Charles Leonard de (1773–1842) Swiss-born economist and historian.
Sitting Bull (*c*.1837–1890) American Indian chief. He was killed 1890).
Sitwell, Dame Edith (1887–1964) English writer (*Bath*1932).
Sitwell, Sir Osbert (1892–1969) English writer (*Miracle on Sinai* 1933).
Sitwell, Sacheverell (1897–1988) English writer (*Southern Baroque Art* 1924).
SI units (Système International d'Unités) accepted standard of scientific units (metre (m), kilogram (kg), second (s), ampere (A), kelvin (K), mole (mol) and candela (cd), first proposed 1960.
Siward the Strong (d.1055) earl of Northumberland).
Six Day War between Israel and Arab coalition, ended 10 June 1967.
Six-shooter, automatic invented 1836 by the American inventor Samuel Colt (1814–62).
Sixtus I, Saint pope (115–125).
Sixtus II, Saint (d.258) pope (257–258). He was martyred.
Sixtus III, Saint pope (432–440).
Sixtus IV [Francesco della Rovere] (1414–84) pope (1471–84).
Sixtus V [Felice Peretti] (1521–90) pope (1585–90).
Skanderbeg [Iskander Bey or George Castriota] (*c*.1403–1468) Albanian leader.
Skeat, Walter William (1835–1912) English philolo-

gist who was the first professor of Anglo-Saxon at Cambridge and did much to popularize the study of the origins of English. He published his *Etymological English Dictionary* in 1882.

Skelton, John (*c.*1460–1529) English poet (*Phyllyp Sparowe* 1542–46).

Skinners Company London livery company founded in the 12th century; first charter granted by King Edward III 1327.

Skryabin *see* SCRIABIN.

Skyscraper a tall steel-framed building. The first was erected in Chicago 1884–85 and designed by the American architect William Le Baron Jenney (1832–1907).

Skywriting a method of advertising in which an aeroplane emits letters in smoke from a special apparatus. It was first done in England in 1922 over Epsom Downs by the British aviator J. C. Savage.

Slater, Oscar (*c.*1872–1948) German-born victim of wrongful imprisonment (1909–28) for murder.

Slavery declared illegal in Britain 1772; Abolition Act passed 1807; abolished in British possessions 1834; in French possessions 1848; in the USA 1863.

Slaves first negro, introduced into an English colony, landed at Virginia 1620.

Slave trade, British, abolished 1805–1807.

Sledda (d.*c.*605) king of Essex (587–605) *see* Appendix.

Sleeping cars on railways invented *c.*1864 by the American financier George Mortimer Pullman (1831–97).

Slimming by the elimination of starch in diet made popular by the English undertaker William Banting (1797–1878).

Sloane, Sir Hans (1660–1753) Irish-born physician.

Sluter, Claus (d.1406) Dutch sculptor (*Well of Moses*).

Smallpox eradicated by World Health Organization 1980.

Smart, Christopher (1722–71) English poet (*Song to David* 1763).

Smeaton, John (1724–92) English civil engineer and designer 1759 of the Eddystone Lighthouse and 1768–90 of the Forth-Clyde Canal.

Smedley, Francis Edward (1818–64) English novelist (*Frank Fairlegh* 1850).

Smetana, Bedrich (1824–84) Bohemian composer (*The Bartered Bride* 1866).

Smiles, Samuel (1812–1904) Scottish writer and biographer. His didactic *Self-Help* (1859) was a best-seller of its time. He also wrote *Lives of the Engineers* and a *History of Ireland.*

Smirke, Sir Robert (1781–1867)English architect (The British Museum).

Smith, Adam (1723–90) Scottish economist and philosopher. His book *Inquiry into the Nature and Causes of the Wealth of Nations* (1776), with its advocacy of free trade was of huge influence in the development of modern capitalist societies.

Smith, Bernard (*c.*1630–1708) German-born organ builder.

Smith, Bessie [Elizabeth Smith] (1894–1937) American blues singer, nicknamed the 'Empress of the Blues'. She became very popular with jazz audiences in the 1920s.

Smith, Sir Francis Pettit (1808–74) English inventor.

Smith, George Joseph (1872–1915) English murderer (The Brides in the Bath). He was hanged.

Smith, Ian [Douglas] (1919–) Zimbabwean politician. He was prime minister of Rhodesia (1964–79), and declared UDI (unilateral declaration of independence) from Britain in 1965 in order to maintain white minority rule. Majority rule came in 1979, with Bishop Abel Muzorewa (1925–) serving as caretaker premier (1979–80). Mugabe's Zanu party won the 1980 election. Smith resigned his leadership of his party in 1987.

Smith, Joseph (1805–44) American founder 1827 of the Mormon Church. He was murdered.

Smith, Dame Maggie (1934–) British film and stage actress (*The Prime of Miss Jean Brodie* 1967).

Smith, Stevie [Florence Margaret Smith] (1902–71) English poet and novelist. Her graceful, melancholic, and occasionally fiercely funny verse has been much admired.

Smith, Sydney (1771–1845) British clergyman and writer who is remembered more for his wit than for the books that he wrote or for his advocacy of social reform and emancipation of the Catholics. When he was canon of St Paul's Cathedral, the question of paving the churchyard with wood came up. It could be quickly done, he said, if the dean and chapter would only put their heads together.

Smith, William 'father of British geology' (1769–1839).

Smithsonian Institution, Washington DC, established 1846 through the endowment of the French-born scientist James Smithson (1765–1829).

Smolensk, Battle of between the French and the Russians, 16–17 August 1812.

Smollett, Tobias [George] (1721–71) Scottish surgeon and novelist. He served in the Royal Navy as a ship's surgeon and took part in an attack upon a Spanish port in the West Indies. In the early 1740s, he set up a surgical practice in London. His picaresque novels, of which the most important are *The Adventures of Roderick Random* (1748), *The Adventures of Peregrine Pickle*, and his masterpiece, *The Expedition of Humphrey Clinker*, are cleverly plotted satirical works rich in characterization, which achieved lasting popularity. His works influenced Dickens.

Smuts, Jan Christiaan (1870–1950) South African statesman and philosopher. He commanded Boer forces during the Boer War, and became prime minister (1919–24, 1939–48).

Smybert, John (1688–1751) Scottish-born artist (*Bishop Berkeley and his Family* 1731).

Smyth, Dame Ethel (1858–1944) English composer (*The Wreckers* 1909).

Snow, Sir C[harles] P[ercy] (1905–80) English scientist and writer (*The Masters* 1951).

Snow, John (1813–58) British anaesthetist.

Snowden, Philip Snowden, 1st Viscount (1864–1937) British Labour statesman who was chairman of the Independent Labour Party 1903–1906 and Chancellor of the Exchequer 1929–31. In July 1931 he put before the House of Commons the serious financial position of the nation, which led to the resignation of the Labour Government and the formation of a National Government in October.

Snowdonia first British national park founded by gift of 300 acres near Snowdon to the National Trust 21 January 1935.

Snyders, Frans (1579–1657) Flemish painter (*Stag-Hunt*).

Soane, Sir John (1753–1837) English architect who designed the original Bank of England. He bequeathed to the nation his house in Lincoln's Inn Fields, London, with all his furniture, pictures books and art treasures. It is now a museum.

Soap opera originated in Chicago *c.*1928.

Soap tax imposed in England 1712; abolished 1853.

Sobers, Gary [Sir Garfield St Auburn] (1936–) West Indian cricketer. Regarded as one of the finest all-rounders of all time.

Sobieski, John [John III] (1624–96) king of Poland (1674–96).

Social Democratic Party (SDP) British political party founded in 1981 by 'gang of four' defectors from the Labour Party: David Owen, Shirley Williams, Roy Jenkins and William Rodgers; dissolved 1988 and merged with the Liberals to form the Social and Liberal Democratic Party.

Social insurance first begun in Germany 1883; begun in Britain 1911; Beveridge Report on Social Security 1942; system reorganized 1946.

Socialist parties founded: Germany 1869; France (several) 1870s and 1880s; Portugal 1875; Denmark 1878; Spain 1879; Belgium 1885; Holland and Switzerland 1888; Sweden 1889; Norway 1890; Italy 1892; Russia 1898; Finland 1899. In England, Labour Representation Committe formed 1900 became Labour Party of Great Britain 1906.

Social War a revolt of the Italians cities against Rome 90 BC. The Roman franchise was granted to some Italians and soon afterwards to all 89 BC

Society for Promoting Christian Knowledge founded 1698 by the English philanthropist Dr Thomas Bray (1656–1730).

Society for Propagating the Gospel in Foreign Parts founded in London 1701.

Society for Psychical Research founded in London 1882.

Society for the Prevention of Cruelty to Animals, Royal founded in London 1824.

Society for the Prevention of Cruelty to Children, National founded in London 1884.

Society for the Prevention of Cruelty to Children in USA founded 1874 by the American lawyer Elbridge Thomas Gerry (1837–1927).

Society Islands island group in Polynesia, discovered 1607 by the Portuguese explorer Pedro Fernandez de Queiros (1560–1614; became French protectorate 1843 and colony 1880.

Society of Antiquaries of Scotland founded 1780.

Society of Antiquaries founded in London 1707, reconstituted 1717, granted royal charter 1751.

Society of Friends (Quakers) founded 1647 by George Fox (1624–90).

Society of Indexers founded in London by G. Norman Knight 1957.

Socotra island in the Indian Ocean, part of South Yemen; ceded to Britain 1878 and formally annexed 1886.

Socrates (470–399 BC) Greek philosopher, the tutor of Plato. The sources of his teachings are many and widely varied, but it is Plato's Socrates, with a gift for answering questions with another question, who has come down to posterity in Plato's 'Socratic' dialogues. The central theme in Socrates' thinking is a quest for truth through rigorous self-examination. He was forced to commit suicide by the Athenians for supposedly corrupting youths through teaching them 'impiety'.

Soddy, Frederick (1877–1956) English scientist.

Sodium discovered 1807 by the English scientist Sir Humphry Davy (1778–1829).

Sodoma, Giovanni (1477–1549) Italian painter (*Christ Scourged*).

Solar compass invented 1836 by the American William Austin Burt (1792–1858).

Solar parallax deduced 1639 by the English astronomer Jeremiah Horrocks (*c.*1617–1641).

Solar year length determined by the Greek astronomer Hipparchus (*fl.* 160–125 BC).

Sol-fa, tonic invented *c.*1845 by the English musician Sarah Ann Glover (1785–1867).

Solferino, Battle of a battle between the French and the Sardinians and Austrians in Italy, 24 June 1859. The Austrians were defeated and forced to cede most of Lombardy, and a unified Italy began to emerge.

Solidarity (*Solidarnosc*) Polish trade union formed 22 September 1980 by Lech Walesa who headed the popular campaign for democratic reform which led to free elections in 1989; Walesa was elected president in December 1990.

Solid fuel injection principle invented 1890 by the English engineer Herbert Ackroyd-Stuart.

Solomon (d.930 BC) king of Israel (970–930) and son of David who ruled over a strong, wealthy and extensive kingdom. He built the Temple at Jerusalem and an opulent royal palace, using forced labour. The political outcome was restlessness among the slave labour and open revolt on his death, with the eventual break-up of the kingdom into king of Israel in the north and Judah in the south.

Solomon Islands independent state and member of the Commonwealth; discovered 1568 by the Spanish navigator Alvaro de Mendana; British protectorate established 1893–99.

Solon (*c.*640–*c.*558 BC) Greek statesman and one of the Seven Wise Men of Greece. An Athenian, he was one of the greatest lawmakers of history, introducing his legislation in Athens 594 BC. As chief magistrate with practically unlimited powers, he divided his countrymen into four classes, according to wealth, laid the foundations of Athenian democracy and broke the oppressive rule of the aristocrats.

Solstice, summer longest day, 21 or 22 June, according to the year; **winter** shortest day, 21 or 22 December, according to the year.

Solti, Sir Georg (1912–) Hungarian-born British conductor. His recording of Wagner's Ring cycle was particularly renowned.

Solvay process ammonia process for making sodium carbonate invented 1863 by the Belgian industrial chamist Ernest Solvay (1838–1922).

Solzhenitsyn, Aleksandr Isayevich (1918–) Russian novelist and historian. He exposed the corruption and cruelty of Russian society in works such as *One Day in the Life of Ivan Denisovich* (based on his experiences in a Soviet labour camp and published in the USSR during a brief thaw in cultural restrictions), and *The First Circle* and *The Gulag Archipelago* (1973–75), which had to be published abroad. He was awarded the Nobel prize for literature in 1970, and was deported from the USSR in 1974. He settled in Vermont in the USA, and returned to Russia in 1994.

Somalia Italian protectorate 1899–1941; British military administration 1941–49; UN trusteeship 1950–60; united with former British Somaliland to form an independent republic 1960.

Somaliland, British *see* BRITISH SOMALILAND.

Somaliland, French *see* DJIBOUTI.

Somaliland, Italian *see* SOMALIA.

Somerled (d.1164) king of Man (1158–64) *see* Appendix.

Somers, Sir George (1554–1610) English discoverer 1609 of the Bermudas.

Somerset, Edward Seymour, Duke of (The Protector) (*c.*1506 beheaded 1552).

Somerset, Robert Carr, Earl of (*c.*1590–1645) Scottish politician.

Somerville College, Oxford University, founded 1879.

Somerville, Mary (1780–1872) British scientist.

Somerville, William (1675–1742) English poet (*The Chase* 1735).

Somme, Battle of the First World War battles, 24–25 September 1914 and July-October 1916.

Sondheim, Stephen [Joshua] (1930–) American songwriter and composer. He studied with Hammerstein and wrote the lyrics for Bernstein's *West Side Story*, before writing the music and lyrics for several musicals, e.g. *A Funny Thing Happened on the Way to the Forum, A Little Night Music* (1973) and *Into the Woods*.

Sontag, Susan (1933–) American writer and critic (*Illness as Metaphor* 1978).

Sontius, River scene of the battle between Theodoric, king of the Ostrogoths, and Odoacer, 15 March 496.

Sophia (1630–1714) electress of Hanover.

Sophia Alekseievna (1657–1704) regent of Russia (1682–89).

Sophia Charlotte (1668–1705) queen of Prussia.

Sophia Dorothea (1666–1726) electress of Hanover.

Sophists philosophical teachers who appeared in Greece in the period immediately preceeding Socrates and contemporary with him in the latter part of the 5th century BC. Their philosophy was one of criticism of those who had gone before. It created nothing creative or formative, and its tendency was chiefly sceptical about previous philosophies but it rendered considerable service to science and literature. Some of them were rhetoricians and grammarians and supplied the earliest models of Greek prose.

Sophocles (*c.*496–406 BC) Greek dramatist. Seven of his *c.*120 plays are extant. He was the most popular of the three great Athenian dramatists (the others being Aeschylus and Euripides). The plays include *Oedipus Rex*, *Oedipus at Colonus*, and *Antigone*. He introduced a third actor and made the actors more important than the chorus in developing the plot of a drama.

Sophonisba (*fl* 3rd century BC) queen of Numidia.

Sopwith, Sir Thomas [Octave Murdoch] (1888–1989) English aeronautical engineer. He designed and built the Sopwith Camel, one of the most successful fighter planes of World War I.

Sorabji, Cornelia (1866–1954) Indian barrister.

Sorbonne a university in Paris founded 1253 by the French priest Robert de Sorbon (1201–74) originally as a theological college. It was closed during the Revolution and made the home of the French Academy by Napoleon and subsequently rebuilt.

Sordello Italian troubadour lived in the 13th century (b.c.1422).

Sorel, Agnes (d.1450) mistress of King Charles VII of France.

Sorel, Georges (1847–1922) French political theorist (*Reflexions sur la Violence* 1908).

Sorolla y Bastida, Joaquin (1863–1923) Spanish painter (*King Alfonso*).

SOS international distress call signal adopted by the International Radiotelegraph Conference 1912.

Sotheby's London auction rooms founded by Samuel Baker 1744.

Soufflot, Jacques Germaine (1709–80) French architect.

Soult, Nicolas Jean de Dieu (1769–1851) statesman and marshal of France.

Sound recording first done by machine 1876 (Edison's phonograph); first gramophone disk made 1887 by Berliner.

Sousa, John Philip (1854–1932) American composer (*El Capitan* 1896).

South, Robert (1634–1716) English court preacher.

South, Sir James (1785–1867) English astronomer.

South Africa, Union of came into being 31 May 1910; achieved independence 1961.

Southampton, Henry Wriothesley, Earl of (1573–1624) patron of William Shakespeare.

Southampton, Thomas Wriothesley, Earl of (1505–50) statesman.

Southampton University founded 1902; achieved university status 1952.

South Carolina discovered 1497 by John Cabot; settled permanently 1670; re-admitted to the Union 1868.

Southcott, Joanna (1750–1814) English self-styled prophet.

South Dakota first reached 1743 by the French family Vérendrye; admitted to the Union 1889.

Southeast Asia Collective Defence Treaty signed at Manila 8 September 1954.

Southerne, Thomas (1660–1746) Irish-born playwright (*Oroonoko* 1696).

Southey, Robert (1774–1843) English poet. Closely associated with Wordsworth and Coleridge, he was poet laureate 1813–43. His works include *Joan of Arc* (1796).

South Pole first reached 14 December 1911 by the Norwegian explorer Roald Amundsen (1872–1928).

South Sea Bubble a financial scheme put forward in 1719 by the South Sea Company (incorporated 1711) to take over the National Debt in return for exclusive rights of trading the coasts of South America. The shares rose tremendously in value and a general enthusiasm for speculation in many wildcat ventures followed. The result was a financial collapse, which burst the Bubble in 1720 and brought ruin to thousands. It was exposed as a fraud in 1721.

Southwell, Robert (*c.*1561–1595) English poet and Jesuit martyr. He was hanged.

Southwood, Julius Salter Elias, Viscount (1873–1946) British newspaper publisher.

Souvestre, Emile (1806–54) French novelist (*Derniers Bretons* 1835–37).

Soweto (Southwest Township) racially segrated urban area southwest of Johannesburg, South Africa.

Soyer, Alexis (1809–58) Reform Club chef.

Space shuttle first re-usable manned spacecraft (US) launched 12 April 1981.

Space-time concept first mooted by the Dutch scientist Hendrik Antoon Lorentz (1853–1928).

Spain conquest by Carthage began 237 BC; Saguntum captured by Hannibal 219 BC; conquest by Scipio 206 BC; Roman provinces formed 133 BC; Muslim invasion 711; last Muslims expelled 1492; ruled by Hapsburgs 1516–1700, by Bourbons 1700–1808, 1814–70, 1874–1931; republics 1873–74, 1931–39; dictatorship of Primo de Rivera 1923–30; Franco regime 1939–75; King Juan Carlos acceded to the thone November 1975; new democratic constitution 1977–78.

Spanish Armada assembled 1587; defeated by the English 29 July 1588.

Spanish Civil War began 16 July 1936; ended 31 March 1939.

Sparta an ancient Greek city in the Peloponnese: Messenia conquered by Sparta 740 BC, 685 BC and 550 BC and Sparta supreme in the Peloponnese; Peloponnesian War 431–404 BC between Athens and allies and Sparta and allies; Spartans set up the Thirty Tyrants; Spartan fleet destroyed by a combined Persian and Athenian fleet at Cnidus 394 BC; Spartans under Agesilaus defeat confederacy against them at Coronea 394 BC; peace of Antalcidas between Sparta and Persia 387 BC; Sparta defeated by Thebes at Leactra 371 BC; Sparta defeated by Thebes at Mantinea 362 BC; Spartans defeated at Megalopolis by Macedonian regent Antipater 331 BC; Agis IV attempts to reform Sparta 245 BC;

Cleomenes III became the last king of Sparta 236 BC.

Spartacus (d.71 BC) a Thracian soldier and freebooter who was taken prisoner and sold to a trainer of gladiators. He organized a break-out from the gladiatorial school at Capua and became leader of a revolt of gladiators and slaves 73–71 BC that spread from the south of Italy to the Alps. He defeated the Romans in battle several times but was ultimately defeated in a battle near the Siluras river, in which he was killed.

Spassky, Boris Vasilyevich (1937–) Russian chess player. He was world champion (1969–72).

Speaker of the House of Commons the officer in the House of Commons who presides over debates of the House and is elected by the House. The Speaker must be a member of parliament but does not speak in debates or vote at divisions as the position is politically neutral. His or her chief duty is to see that debates are orderly and there is not appeal from his or her decisions. The post was instituted in 1377. The first woman Speaker, Betty Boothroyd, was elected 1993.

Specific gravity principle discovered by the Greek scientist Archimedes (287–212 BC).

Spectacles a device used to bend rays of light inwards or outwards to bring them to a focus in the retina of the eye. They were probably invented by the Chinese and were known in Europe in the 14th century.

Spectator, The British periodical, first, 1711–12, edited by the English writer Joseph Addison (1672–1719 and Sir Richard Steele (1672–1729; British periodical, second, founded 1828 by Robert Rintoul (1787–1858).

Spectrograph invented 1919 by the English experimental physicist Francis William Aston (1877–1945).

Spectroheliograph for photographing the sun invented 1910 by the American astronomer George Ellery Hale (1868–1938).

Spectrum the oblong figure or stripe formed by a beam of light emitted by some luminous body, such as the sun, received through a narrow slit, passed through a prism, and thus separated into its constituent rays. The spectrum of sunlight was discovered in 1666 by Sir Isaac Newton (1642–1727).

Spectrum analysis the analysis of a spectrum in which light from incandescent vapours or gases is examined so that the lines that cross the spectrum band and differ in position, etc, for different substances can be determined. It was originated in 1859 by the German scientists Robert Wilhelm Bunsen (1811–99) and Gustav Robert Kirchhoff (1824–87).

Spee, Maximilian, Graf von (1861–1914) German naval commander. He died in a naval battle.

Speed, John (*c.*1552–1629) English map-maker.

Speke, John Hanning (1827–64) English discoverer 1862 of the source of the Nile.

Spellman, Cardinal Francis J. (1889–1967) archbishop of New York (1939–67).

Spence, Sir Basil (1907–76) Indian-born Scottish architect. He is famous for a few highly prestigious buildings, such as Coventry Cathedral (1951–62), and notorious for some disastrous council housing.

Spencer, Lady Diana *see* CHARLES, PRINCE.

Spencer, Herbert (1820–1903) English philosopher who built up a system of philosophy that applied to life, ethics, social development and political and religious institutions the evolutionary theory evolved by Darwin in regard to zoology. His works include *Man versus the State* (1884).

Spencer, Sir Stanley (1891–1959) English painter. An isolated figure in modern art, he is best known for his series of religious paintings (*Resurrection, Cookham* 1922–27), and, in his capacity as a war artist, his *Shipbuilding on the Clyde* series of panels.

Spender, Stephen (1909–) English poet.

Spengler, Oswald (1891–1936) German philosopher (*The Decline of the West* 1918–22).

Spenser, Edmund (*c.*1552–1599) English poet, noted particularly for his long allegorical poem *The Faerie Queene* (1589–96), which describes the adventures of 12 knights (who represent 12 virtues). Many of the adventures begin at the court of Gloriana, the Faerie Queen (an idealized version of Elizabeth I).

Sperry, Elmer Ambrose (1860–1930) American inventor.

Spielberg, Steven (1947–) American film director and producer. His many films include some of the most successful ever made, e.g. *Jaws* (1975), *E.T.*, *Raiders of the Lost Ark* and *Jurassic Park* (1993).

Spin, aeronautic, first voluntary, performed 1915 by English pilot J. C. Brooke; first scientifically investigated 1917 by English physicist F. A. Lindemann.

Spinello Aretino (d.*c.*1410) Italian painter (*Madonna and Saints* 1391).

Spinning frame, Arkwright's invented 1768 by the English inventor Sir Richard Arkwright (1732–92).

Spinoza, Benedict [Baruch Despinoza] (1632–77) Dutch philosopher (*Ethics*).

Spiral nebulae discovery publicly announced 1850 by the astronomer the Earl of Rosse (1800–1867).

Spiritualism, modern, began at Hydeville, USA, in 1847–48.

Spitfires last fly-past over London commemorating the Battle of Britain, Sunday, 20 September 1959.

Spithead British Fleet mutiny at, 16 April 1797.

Spock, Dr [Benjamin McLane] (1903–) American pediatrician. He advocated a 'permissive', non-authoritarian approach to the raising of infants, which was popular in the 1960s. His books include *The Common Sense Book of Baby and Child Care* (1946).

Spode, Josiah (1754–1827) English potter.

Spohr, Ludwig (1784–1859) German composer and violinist who conducted court concerts at Gotha, was attached to the theatre in Vienna, and finally, from 1822, was musical director to the court of Hesse-Cassell. He wrote mainly for the violin but also wrote symphonies and an oratorio, *The Last Judgment.*

Spoonerisms originated by the English don the Rev. William Archibald Spooner (1844–1930).

Spotsylvania Courthouse, Battle of American Civil War battle, 8–21 May 1864.

Spottiswoode, John (1565–1639) archbishop of St Andrews.

Spring *c.*21 March to 21 June in the northern hemisphere.

Spurgeon, Charles Haddon (1834–92) English Baptist preacher who was a gifted and influential speaker whose eloquence, sincerity and humour gave him a great hold over his congregations. He was so popular that eventually the Metropolitan Tabernacle, of which he was pastor, was built with seating for 6,000 people. Fifty volumes of his sermons were printed.

Spurius Cassius first Agrarian Law (Land Reform) at Rome passed by Spurius Cassius 486 BC

Spurs, Battle of the between the English and the French, 16 August 1513.

Sputnik series of Russian earth satellites first launched 4 October 1957.

Spyri, Johanna (1827–1901) Swiss writer (*Heidi*).

Squarcione, Francesco (1394–1474) Italian painter (*Madonna with Child*).

Squire, Sir John (1884–1958) English writer.

Sri Lanka formerly Ceylon; a British colony from1802; gained independence in 1948; became a republic within the Commonwealth 1972 and renamed Democratic Socialist Republic of Sri Lanka.

SSAFA (Soldiers', Sailors' and Airmen's Families Association) founded in London 1885; incorporated by royal charter 1926.

Staël, Mme de (1766–1817) French writer (*Delphine* 1802).

Stafford, Edward, Duke of Buckingham (1478–1521) Lord High Constable. He was beheaded.

Stafford, Henry, Duke of Buckingham (*c.*1454–1483) politician. He was beheaded.

Stahl, Georg Ernst (1660–1734) German propounder (1731) of the phlogiston theory.

Stainer, Sir John (1840–1901) English composer and organist. He was appointed organist of Magdalen College, Oxford, in 1859, and of St Paul's Cathedral in 1872. He composed much church music and some cantatas, of which *The Crucifixion* (1887) is the best known.

Stainless steel steel alloyed with smaller proportions of nickel and chromium to make it resistant to tarnishing and corrosion. It was invented 1916 by the Englishman Harry Brearley at Sheffield.

Stair, John Dalrymple, Earl of (1673–1747) soldier and diplomat.

Stalin, Joseph [Josef Vissarionovich Dzhugashvili] (1879–1953) Soviet dictator. Born in Georgia, he was expelled in 1899 from an orthodox seminary in Tiflis for expounding Marxism. After the Bolshevik Revolution, he manoeuvred his way into absolute power, shrewdly playing off his 'rightist' allies against Trotsky and other 'leftists'. He forcibly collectivized Soviet agriculture in the 1930s and developed the Soviet Union's industrial base, using (and killing) many millions of prisoners as slave labour. His purges of the 1930s destroyed most of the surviving old Bolsheviks, as well as the army leadership. He signed a peace treaty with Hitler in 1939, and seized Poland's eastern territories after Hitler's September invasion. Forceful resistance from the Red Army, notably in the defence of Leningrad, the battle of Stalingrad, and in massive infantry and tank battles, led directly to the defeat of Hitler's regime and the occupation of eastern Europe by Stalin's forces.

Stamp Act passed 1764; repealed 1766.

Stamp booklets first used in Britain 1904.

Stamp duty introduced in England 1694.

Stamped envelopes, first British, designed by the Irish artist William Mulready (1786–1863); issued 1840.

Standard, Battle of the between the English and the Scottish, 22 August 1138.

Standard Oil Company founded 1870 by the American financier John Davison Rockefeller (1839–1937).

Standish, Myles (1584–1656) English colonizer of New Plymouth.

Stanford, Sir Charles Villiers (1852–1924) Irish composer who produced many operas, orchestral works and compositions for piano and violin. He became organist of Trinity College, Dublin, at the age of twenty and professor of Music at Cambridge at the age of thirty-five. His works include *The Canterbury Pilgrims* (1884).

Stanford University university in California founded 1891 through an endowment from the American railway builder Leland Stanford (1824–93).

Stanhope, Lady Hester [Lucy] (1776–1839) English traveller. She lived for many years with her uncle, William Pitt, and on his death in 1806 received a government pension of £1200. In 1810 she left England, visited various places in the East and then settled in Syria, establishing herself in the deserted Convent of Mar Elias in the Lebanon. She adopterd the style and dress of an Arab chief.

Stanhope, Philip Dormer, Earl of Chesterfield (1694–1773) statesman.

Stanislaus I (1677–1766) king of Poland (1705–1709, 1733).

Stanislaus II (1732–98) king of Poland (1764–95).

Stanislavsky, Konstantin Sergeivich (1863–1938) Russian director and actor, who was co-founder of the Moscow Art Theatre in 1897. The influence of his theory of acting (later dubbed 'method') has been immense. His theory is contained in such works as *An Actor Prepares* (1929) and *Building a Character* (1950).

Stanley, John (1713–86) English organist and composer (*Zimri* 1760).

Stanley, Sir Henry Morton [John Rowlands] (1841–1904) Welsh journalist and explorer. In 1859 he went to New Orleans and was employed by a Mr H. M. Stanley, whose name he took. He served in the American Civil War with the Confederates and was captured and released. He went to Abyssinia with the British forces in 1867–68 as war correspondent for the *New York Times*. In 1869 he was commissioned to find David Livingstone in Africa, and met him at Ujiji on Lake Tanganyika 10 November 1871. During the next sixteen years he did much African exploration and in 1887 was sent from the west coast to relieve Emin Pash in equatorial Africa, where he had been isolated after the fall of Khartoum. He was a member of parliament 1895–1900.

Stannary Parliament, Cornwall, last held at Truro 1752.

Stanton, Mrs Elizabeth Cady (1815–1902) American champion of women's rights.

Star, The British newspaper founded 1888; absorbed by the *Evening News* 1960.

Star Chamber an English prerogative court of civil and criminal jurisdiction inaugurated in the 14th century. It had jurisdiction over forgery, perjury, riots, fraud, libel and conspiracy, and could inflict any punishment except death. Its process was summary, and, in the reigns of James I and Charles I, often iniquitous. It was abolished by the Long Parliament 1641.

Stark, James (1794–1859) English painter (*The Valley of the Yare*).

Stark effect in polarization of light discovered 1913 by the German physicist Johannes Stark (1874–1957).

Starr, Ringo [Richard Starkey] (1940–) English rock drummer and singer. He was the Beatles' drummer (1962–70).

Stationers' Company London livery company incorporated 1557; charter confirmed by Queen Elizabeth I 1559; monopoly ended 1842.

Statius (d.96) Latin poet (*Silvae*).

Statue of Liberty in New York harbour designed 1876 by the French sculptor Frédéric Auguste Bartholdi (1834–1904); unveiled 28 October 1886.

Staunton, Howard (1810–74) English chess player.

Stavisky, Alexandre (1886–1934) French swindler.

Stead, William Thomas (1849–1912) English editor and reformer. He was drowned at sea.

Steamboat first, the *Charlotte Dundas* built 1801 by the British engineer William Symington (1763–1831); first practical, invented 1787 by the American inventor John Fitch (1743–98).

Steam engine invented 1698 by the English military engineer Captain Thomas Savery (*c.*1650–1715).

Steam hammer invented 1839 by the Scottish engineer James Nasmyth (1808–90).

Steam plough invented 1850–60 by the English engineer John Fowler (1826–64).

Steam pumping engine invented 1705 by the English mechanic Thomas Newcomen (1663–1729); perfected 1767 by the Scottish engineer James Watt (1736–1819).

Steam turbine driving high-speed electric generator invented 1884 by Sir Charles Parsons (1854–1931).

Stearin fat formed from glycerine and stearic acid discovered by the French scientist Michel Eugène Chevreul (1786–1889).

Steel, Sir David [Martin Scott] (1938–) Scottish Liberal politician. He became leader of the Liberal Party in 1976 and, with David Owen, the SDP (1981–88).

Steel cast by the crucible process invented *c.*1750 by the English clockmaker Benjamin Huntsman (1704–76).

Steele, Sir Richard (1672–1729) Anglo-Irish essayist and dramatist. With Addison, he contributed many notable essays to the *The Tatler* and *The Spectator*. His plays were moral, Christian responses to the excess of Restoration drama and had a strong influence on 18th-century drama.

Steel rails first made *c.*1858 by the British engineer Sir John Brown (1816–96).

Steen, Jan (1626–79) Dutch painter (*Music master*).

Steer, Philip Wilson (1860–1942) English painter (*Chepstow Castle*).

Stein, Gertrude (1872–1946) American writer (*The Autobiography of Alice B. Toklas* 1933).

Stein, Sir Aurel (1862–1943) Hungarian-born archaeologist in Asia.

Steinbeck, John (1902–68) American author (*The Grapes of Wrath* 1939). He was awareded the 1962 Nobel prize for literature.

Steiner, Rudolf (1861–1925) Hungarian-born Austrian

philosopher and educationist. Influenced by theosophy, he formed his own movement of 'anthroposophy' in 1912, dedicated to developing the innate human capacity for spiritual perception, through activities such as art and dance.

Steinitz, William (1836–1900) German-born chess champion.

Steinmetz. Charles Proteus (1865–1923) German-born electrical engineer.

Steinway G., Sons piano manufacturers, firm founded Brunswick *c.*1825; New York 1853; London 1875; Hamburg 1880.

Stellar parallax study developed and advanced by the German astronomer Wilhelm Struve (1793–1864).

Stendhal [Marie Henri Beyle] (1783–1842) French novelist (*Le Rouge et le Noir* 1831).

Steno, Nicolaus (1631–86) Danish scientist.

Stephen (*c.*1097–1154) king of England (1135–54) *see* Appendix.

Stephen, Sir James Fitzjames (1829–94) English jurist and writer.

Stephen, Sir Leslie (1832–1904) English writer and editor of the *Dictionary of National Biography*.

Stephen I, Saint pope (254–257).

Stephen II pope (752).

Stephen III pope (752–757).

Stephen IV pope (768–772).

Stephen V pope (816–817).

Stephen VI pope (885–891).

Stephen VII (d.897) pope (896–897). He was murdered.

Stephen VIII pope (928–931).

Stephen IX pope (939–942).

Stephen X [Frederick] pope (1057–58).

Stephen I, Saint (*c.*977–1038) king of Hungary (997–1038).

Stephen II (1100–1131) king of Hungary (1114–31).

Stephen III (1161–73) king of Hungary.

Stephen IV (d.1166) king of Hungary (1162).

Stephen V (1239–72) king of Hungary (1270–72).

Stephen Harding, Saint (d.1134) founder of the Cistercian Order.

Stephens, Alexander Hamilton (1812–83) American statesman.

Stephens, George (1813–95) English runic archaeologist.

Stephens, James (1882–1950) Irish writer (*The Crock of Gold* 1912).

Stephenson, George (1781–1848) English civil engineer and inventor. He worked as a colliery engineer and then began building steam locomotives to haul coal and introduced a notable improvment in design by sending the exhaust steam up the chimney to increase the draught through the furnace. He was appointed engineer of the Darlington to Stockton-on-Tees, the first public railway in England, and also built the Manchester-Liverpool Railway. He also invented a miner's safely lamp independently of Sir Humphry Davy.

Stephenson, Robert (1803–59) English civil engineer who was the son of George Stephenson. His most notable feats were the construction of the tubular bridge across the Menai Straits (completed in 1854) and a similar bridge, the Victoria Bridge, across the St Lawrence River in Canada (1854–60).

Stephen the Great (1431–1504) prince of Moldavia.

Stepniak, Sergei [Sergei Mikhailovich Kravchinski] (1852–95) Russian revolutionary emigre and writer.

Stereochemistry study initiated 1874 by the Dutch scientist Jacobus Hendricus van't Hoff (1852–1911).

Stereoscope invented *c.*1838 by the English scientist Sir Charles Wheatstone (1802–75).

Stereotype process the making of casts from set-up type for use in a printing press. It was invented 1725 by the Scottish inventor William Ged (1690–1749).

Sterling, John (1806–44) Scottish writer (*The Election* 1841).

Sterling taken off the British gold standard 20 September 1931.

Sterne, Laurence (1713–68) Irish-born English novelist. His novel *The Life and Opinions of Tristram Shandy* (1759–67) is noted for its eccentric style and humour.

Stethoscope invented by the French physician René Théophile Hyacinthe Läennec (1781–1826).

Stetson hats manufactured by the American industrialist John Batterson Stetson (1830–1906).

Steuben, Frederick William, Baron von (1730–94) German-born soldier in American service.

Stevens, Alfred (1818–75) English painter and sculptor (Wellington monument 1856–92).

Stevens, Henry (1819–86) American bibliographer, London.

Stevens, John (1749–1838) American inventor 1813 of the ironclad.

Stevenson, Adlai (1900–1968) American politician.

Stevenson, David (1815–86) Scottish civil engineer.

Stevenson, Robert (1772–1850) Scottish engineer.

Stevenson, Robert Louis [Balfour] (1850–94) Scottish novelist, poet and essayist. He trained as an advocate in Edinburgh, but decided in his twenties to be a writer. By the time his first important fictional work, *Treasure Island* (1883), had been published he had established himself as an author of note with essays, poems and two travel books, *Travels with a Donkey in the Cevennes* (1879) and *The Silverado Squatters* (1883). His masterpiece is *The Strange Case of Dr Jekyll and Mr Hyde* (1886), a disturbing story of dual personality. Other works include *Kidnapped* (1886), *The Master of Ballantrae* (1889), and the unfinished *Weir of Hermiston* (1896). He settled in Samoa, where he died.

Stevenson, Thomas (1818–87) Scottish engineer and meteorologist.

Stewart, Arabella (1575– 1615) the great-great-granddaughter of Henry VII and heir to the English throne after James VI and I. On James's accession a conspiracy was formed for making her queen. Her private marriage to William Seymour (grandson of the Earl of Hertford) alarmed the court, and they were both imprisoned. She died in the Tower.

Stewart, Balfour (1828–87) Scottish meteorologist.

Stewart, Prince Charles Edward [Louis Philip] (1720–88) also known as 'Bonnie Prince Charlie' or the 'Young Pretender', he led the Jacobite revolt against the Hanoverian King George III in 1745, fleeing Scotland when his Highland soldiers were defeated at Culloden in 1746. He died in Rome.

Stewart, Dugald (1753–1828) Scottish philosopher.

Stewart, Jackie [John Young Stewart] (1939–) Scottish racing driver. He was world champion 1969, 1971 and 1973, and he retired in 1973.

Stewart, Robert, Duke of Albany (*c.*1340–1420) regent of Scotland.

Stiegel, Henry William (1729–85) American pioneer glass manufacturer.

Stieler, Adolf (1775–1836) German cartographer.

Stifter, Adalbert (1805–68) Bohemian-born writer (*Studien* 1844–51).

Stigand (d.1072) archbishop of Canterbury.

Stilicho, Flavius (d.408) Roman general. He was assassinated.

Still, Andrew Taylor (1828–1917) American founder (1874) of osteopathy.

Stillingfleet, Edward (1635–99) bishop of Worcester (1689–99).

Stirling, James (1) (1692–1770) Scottish mathematician.

Stirling, James (2) (1926–) Scottish architect. His works include Neuestaatsgalerie in Stuttgart.

Stirling, James Hutchison (1820–1909) Scottish philosopher.

Stirner, Max [Kaspar Schmidt] (1806–56) German anarchist (*The Ego and His Own*).

Stockhausen, Karlheinz (1928–) German composer. Regarded as the leading exponent of twelve-tone music, he also used electronic sounds in his work.

Stockmar, Christian Friedrich, Baron von (1787–1863) adviser to Queen Victoria.

Stockton, Frank R. (1834–1902) American novelist and short-story writer (*The Lady or the Tiger?* 1884).

Stoicism philosophical system founded in the 4th century BC. by Zeno of Citium (340–270 BC), an Athenian. From Greece, stoicism found its way to Rome, where it became a rule of life and had many eminent adherents, including Cato, Cicero and Seneca. Stoicism was essentially an ascetic doctrine, urging the effort to free oneself from bodily passions and so rise nearer to the divine, taking good or ill that might come with 'an equal mind'.

Stoker, Bram (1847–1912) Irish writer (*Dracula* 1897).

Stokes, Margaret McNair (1832–1900) Irish archaeologist.

Stokes, Sir George Gabriel (1819–1903) Irish-born physicist.

Stokowski, Leopold (1882–1977) British-born American conductor. A popularizer of classical music, he is best known for his collaboration with Walt Disney on the film *Fantasia*.

Stolberg, Friedrich Leopold, Graf zu (1750–1819) German poet (*Timoleon* 1784).

Stolypin, Piotr Arkadevich (1863–1911) Russian statesman. He was assassinated.

Stone, Lucy (1818–93) American champion of women's rights and abolitionist.

Stone, Nicholas (1586–1647) English architect.

Stone Age the very early period in the evolution of the human race during which the use of metals was as yet unknown, and stones, more or less shaped articially, were used for tools and weapons. The Stone Age is subdivided into periods, according to the quality of the workmanship revealted by the stones. **Old** between ten thousand and one million years ago; **Middle** between 4,500 and 10,000 years ago; **New** between 4,000 and 4,500 years ago. It was succeeded by the Bronze Age.

Stonehenge a prehistoric monument of the Stone Age or possibly the Bronze Age, standing on Salisbury Plain, near Salisbury. Construction began 1860 BC. It was presented to the nation in 1918.

Stopes, Marie [Charlotte Carmichael] (1880–1958) Scottish scientist and birth-control pioneer. She began her career as a palaeobotanist, but the breakdown of her marriage led her to the study of sex education, in which field she soon became a world authority. She established a birth control clinic in Holloway in London (1920), which gave free contraceptive advice to the poor.

Stoppard, Tom (1937–) Czech-born British dramatist. His plays, e.g. *Rosencrantz and Guildenstern are Dead* (1966), are noted for their sharp, witty wordplay and fast, cleverly plotted action.

Storm, Theodor (1817–88) German writer (*Gedichte* 1852).

Storting Norwegian parliament founded 1814.

Stoss, Veit (1438–1533) German sculptor (*Annunciation*).

Stothard, Thomas (1755–1834) English painter (*The Canterbury Pilgrims*).

Stow, John (1525–1605) English antiquary (*Survey of London* 1598).

Stowe, Mrs Harriet [Elizabeth] Beecher (1811–96) American novelist. Her great anti-slavery novel *Uncle Tom's Cabin, or, Life Among the Lowly* (1852) has been described as a factor leading to the American Civil War.

Stowe Collection of manuscripts now in the British Museum, collected by the English antiquary Thomas Astle (1735–1803).

Strabo (*c.*64 BC–*c.*AD 22) Greek geographer who wrote a 17-volume account of the geography of Europe, Asia and Africa, including information political events, chief cities and important people.

Strachey, John St Loe (1860–1927) English editor of *The Spectator* (1896–1925).

Strachey, Lytton (1880–1932) English writer (*Eminent Victorians* 1918).

Stradella, Alessandro (*c.*1645–1682) Italian composer (*Esther*). He was murdered.

Stradivari, Antonio (*c.*1644–1737) Italian violin-maker from Cremona. He was Nicolo Amati's pupil, remaining with him until 1700 when he set up for himself. He settled the typical pattern of the Cremona violin, and his Stradivarius instruments have never been equalled.

Strafford, Thomas Wentworth, Earl of (1593–1641) British statesman who was lord deputy of Ireland (1632–39) where he ruled in an absolutist manner. He was impeached by the Long Parliament in 1640 and executed.

Strand Magazine, The launched 1891 by Sir George Newnes, it was one of the first to make use of illustrations produced by photographic processes. Arthur Conan Doyle's stories of Sherlock Holmes appeared in the Strand and other writers included Kipling,, J.B. Priestley, Agatha Christie and P.G. Wodehouse.

Strang, William (1859–1921) British artist (*Rudyard Kipling*).

Strange, Sir Robert (1721–92) Scottish engraver.

Straparola, Giovanni Francesco (*c.*1495–*c.*1557) Italian writer (*Piacevoli notti* 1550–54).

Strasbourg European city ceded to France under the Treaty of Ryswyck 1697.

Stratford, John de (d.1348) archbishop of Canterbury (1333–48).

Strathclyde a Celtic kingdom of ancient Scotland, which grew from the 5th century to dominate south-west Scotland and northern England with its capital at Dumbarton. In the 11th century it was incorporated in the Scottish kingdom but lingered on for many years as a principality granted to the heir apparent to the Scottish throne.

Strathcona and Mount Royal, Donald Alexander Smith, Baron (1820–1914) Scottish-born statesman in Canada.

Straus, Oskar (1870–1954) Austrian composer (*The Chocolate Soldier* 1908).

Strauss, Johann (the Elder) (1804–49) Austrian composer who was a prolific and popular composer of dance music. He collected a orchestra with which he toured Europe and wrote 400 waltz tunes.

Strauss, Johann (the Younger) (1825–99) Austrian violinist, conductor and composer. One of a musical family, he wrote light music, especially Viennese waltzes, e.g. the 'Blue Danube' waltz, and 16 operettas, e.g. *Die Fledermaus* (1874).

Strauss, Richard (1864–1949) German composer and conductor. His works include a series of richly orchestrated tone poems, e.g. *Also Sprach Zarathustra*, several operas, e.g. *Elektra* and *Der Rosenkavalier* (1911), and *Four Last Songs*.

Stravinsky, Igor Fyodorovich (1882–1971) Russian composer. He composed ballet scores for Diaghilev, e.g. *Petrushka* (1911) and *The Rite of Spring* (1913), the first performance of the latter provoking a riot but now regarded as a milestone in modernist music. He later composed several austerely neoclassical works, such as the opera-oratorio *Oedipus Rex* (1927), which also displayed the influence of Schoenberg's serial techniques.

Street, George Edmund (1824–81) English architect.

Street lighting in England, first oil 1681; first gas *c.*1812; first electricity *c.*1880.

Streptomycin first isolated 1943 by the Russian-born scientist Selman Abraham Waksman (1888–1973), who was awarded the 1952 Nobel Prize.

Stresemann, Gustav (1878–1929) German statesman.

Stretcher bearers introduced *c.*1792 by the Baron Pierre François Percy (1754–1825).

Stribling, Thomas Sigismund (1881–1965) American novelist (*The Store* 1932).

Strickland, Agnes (1796–1874) English historian (*Lives of the Queens of England* 1840–48).

Strijdom, Johannes Gerhardus (1893–1958) prime minister (1954–58) of the Union of South Africa.

Strike, General in Britain, 3–13 May 1926.

Strindberg, Johan August (1849–1912) Swedish dramatist and novelist. His highly innovative works, e.g. the play *Miss Julie* (1888), have influenced many 20th-century dramatists.

Strip cartoons originated by the German artist Wilhelm Busch (1832–1908).

Stroheim, Erich von (1886–1957) film director and actor.

Strongbow, Richard, [Richard de Clare, 2nd Earl of Pembroke and Strigul] (d.1176) English soldier who in 1170 helped Dermot, king of Leinster, to retrieve his domains that had been subjugated by Rory O'Connor and also took Dublin, Waterford and other places. Strongbow married the daughter of Dermot and on his death ascended the throne of Leinster. There was an immediate rebellion, and a further invasion by Rory, and Strongbow hastened to England where he acknowledged the overlordship of Henry II who crossed to ireland in 1172 with an army and occupied all the strong places. Strongbow subsequently served in France (1173) and received Leinster again from Henry II.

Strontium a silvery white metallic element discovered 1808 by the English chemist Sir Humphry Davy (1778–1829) and named from the parish of Strontian in the Scottish Highlands where it was found.

Struensee, Johann Friedrich (1731–72) German-born statesman in Denmark. He was executed.

Strutt, Joseph (1749–1802) English antiquary.

Struve, Friedrich Georg Wilhelm (1793–1864) German astronomer.

Struve, Peter Berngardovich (1870–1944) Russian writer and politician.

Strychnine discovered 1818 by the French chemists Pierre Joseph Pelletier (1788–1842) and Joseph Bienaimé Caventou (1795–1877).

Strype, John (1643–1737) English historian (*Cranmer* 1694).

Stuart, John McDouall (1815–66) Scottish explorer, first (1860) to reach the centre of Australia.

Stuart, John [Earl of Bute](1713–92) statesman.

'Stuart, La belle' [Frances Teresa Stuart, Duchess of Richmond and Lennox] (1647–1702) mistress of Charles II.

Stubbs, George (1724–1806) English painter and engraver, best known for his paintings of horses, e.g. *Mares and Foals.*

Stubbs, Henry (1632–76) English writer (*The Commonwealth of Oceana* 1660).

Stukeley, William (1687–1765) English antiquary.

Sturdee, Sir, Frederick Charles Doveton (1859–1925) Admiral of the Fleet (1859–1925).

Sture, Sten (*c.*1440–1503) regent of Sweden and founder of the University of Uppsala.

Sturge, Joseph (1793–1859) English reformer and philanthropist.

Sturluson, Snorri (1179–1241) Icelandic historian (*Heimskringla*). He was killed.

Sturt, Charles (1795–1869) English explorer of Australia. While an army captain, in 1828 he discovered the Rivers Macquarie, Castlereagh and Darling, and explored the Murrunbidgee. In 1830 he discovered the Murray, and in 1844 penetrated nearly to the centre of the continent.

Stuyvesant, Peter (*c.*1602–1682) Dutch governor of New Amsterdam (now New York).

Stylites, Simeon, Saint *see* SIMEON STYLITES, SAINT.

Stylites or pillar saints Christian ascetics who exposed themselves on pillar tops as a method of penance or self-torture, introduced by St Simeon Stylites.

Suaebhard (d.692) king of Kent (690–692) *see* Appendix.

Suarez, Francisco de (1548–1617) Spanish theologian.

Submachine gun invented 1921 by the American inventors John Taliaferro Thompson (1860–1940) and John N. Blish.

Submarine first navigable, invented 1620 by the Dutch scientist Cornelis Jacobszoon Drebbel (1572–1633; first British model launched at Barrow 2 October 1901; first atomic-powered, US submarine *Nautilus,* launched 21 January 1954.

Submarine telephone system first long-distance, laid across the Atlantic 1956.

Submarine warfare in First World War declared by Germany, 4 February 1915.

Sucre, Antonio José de (1795–1830) South American liberator and president of Bolivia (1826–28). He was assassinated.

Sudan achieved self-government 1953; independence as a democratic republic proclaimed 1956.

Sudermann, Hermann (1857–1928) German playwright (*Die Ehre* 1888).

Sue, Eugène (1804–57) French novelist (*Le Juif errant* 1844–45).

Suetonius (75–160) Roman historian.

Suez Canal in Egypt, concession granted 1855 to French engineer Ferdinand de Lesseps (1805–94); construction begun April 1859; opened 17 November 1869; British occupation of Canal Zone 1882; convention signed 1888; British evacuated Zone 1955; canal nationalized by Egyptian Government July 1956; British and French invasion of Zone November 1956; forces withdrawn December 1956.

Suffren St Tropez, Pierre André de (1729–88) French admiral.

Sugar, grape, discovered 1799 by the French scientist Joseph Louis Proust (1754–1826).

Sugar in beet discovered 1747 by the German physicist Andreas Sigismund Marggraf (1709–82).

Suger (*c.*1081–1151) French statesman.

Suggia, Mme Guilhermina (1888–1950) Spanish cellist.

Sui dynasty, China, 581–618.

Suicides buried at crossroads transfixed by a stake until 1834.

Sukkoth (Feast of Tabernacles) Jewish holiday, 15th day of Tishri.

Sulawesi *or* **Celebes** an island in eastern Indonesia.

Suleiman sultan of Adrianople (1402–10).

Suleiman I (1494–1566) sultan of Turkey (1520–66).

Suleiman II (1641–91) sultan of Turkey (1687–91).

Sulfanilamide first synthesized 1908 by the German scientist P. Gelmo.

Sulla, Lucius Cornelius (138–78 BC) Roman statesman and soldier who served in the Jugurthine and Cimbrian Wars and for his services in the Social War (90–89 BC) was appointed consul in 88. He was obliged to flee Rome, however, to avoid Marius, who was violently jealous of him. At length he drove the latter to Africa, expelled the armies of Mithridates VI from Europe in the First Mithridatic War and compelled him to make peace. He returned to Rome with a large army 83 BC and after much bloodshed was proclaimed dictator in 82 BC. He resigned in 79 BC.

ullivan, Sir Arthur (1842–1900) English composer who collaborated with Sir W. S. Gilbert in he production of series of comic operas, e.g. *The Mikado* (1885), which are unique in their combination of tuneful music with literary wit. He wrote compositions of other kinds, e.g. anthems, oratorios and songs.

ullivan, Sir Edward (1822–85) Lord Chancellor of Ireland (1883–85).

Sully, Maximilien de Béthune, Duc de (1560–1641) French statesman and first Minister of Henri IV. He won distinction at the battle of Ivri in 1590 and afterwards helped the king to resist the intrigues of the Catholic League, becoming controller of finance in 1597 and holding many other offices. After the murder of Henri IV he retired in 1611 and was made Marshal of France in 1634 by Richelieu.

ully-Prudhomme, René François Armand (1839–1907) French poet (*L'Idéal* 1865).

ulphonamide drugs first produced 1935 (Prontosil) and 1938 (M&B).

umatra Indonesia settled *c.*1510 by the Portuguese; taken over by the Dutch *c.*1596 onwards; included in the independent Republic of Indonesia, established 1949.

umeria an ancient state of southern Babylonia, of which Meslim, king of Kish, became overlord 4000 BC; Lugai-Zaggisi, ruler of Umma and king of Erech, became overlord 2800 BC; Ur dynasty established by Ur-Engur 2400 BC; empire expanded over the whole of Babylonia Elam conquered by Dungi; Ur dynasty overthrown because of Elamite invasion 2300 BC and Isin dynasty established by Ishbi-Ura.

ummer 21 June to 21 September in the northern hemisphere.

Summer solstice *see* SOLSTICE.

Summer Time, British introduced 21 May 1916; made permanent institution by House of Commons vote, 17 July 1925.

Sumner, John Bird (1780–1862) archbishop of Canterbury (1848–62).

Sumter, Fort, Battle of American Civil War battle, 12–14 April 1861.

Sun distance from earth first reliably calculated 1673 by Cassius and Riches; rotation first observed 1610 by Galileo.

Sunday schools founded in Gloucester 1780 by the English publisher and reformer Robert Raikes (1735–1811).

Sunday Times, The British newspaper founded 1822.

Sung dynasty in China 960–1279.

Sun spots discovered by Joannes Fabricius (1587–1615).

Sun Yat-sen *or* **Sun Zhong Shan** (1866–1925) Chinese nationalist leader and statesman. He played a leading role in the overthrow of the Manchu dynasty and became the first president of the Republic of China in 1911–12.

Superconductivity of metals discovered 1911 by the Dutch scientist Heike Kamerlingh Onnes.

Superman comic strip hero first appeared in print 1938.

Suppé, Franz von (1819–95) Austrian-born composer (*Poet and Peasant*).

Supremacy, Acts of separating the Anglican from the Catholic Church, signed by Henry VIII in 1534 and by Queen Elizabeth in 1559.

Surgeons' Company founded in London 1746.

Surgical instruments, steam sterilization of, introduced 1886 by the German scientist Ernst von Bergmann (1836–1907).

Surinam (formerly Netherlands Guiana) first settled by the English 1630; ceded to the Netherlands 1667; became self-governing 1954 and fully independent 1975.

Surrealism art movement manifesto issued 1924 by the French poet André Breton (1896–1966).

Surrey, Henry Howard, Earl of (*c.*1517–1547) English poet and soldier. He was beheaded.

Surtees, Robert Smith (1803–64) English novelist (*Handley Cross* 1843).

Susa an ancient city north of the Persian Gulf, which was capital of Elam and the Persian empire. Alexander the Great reached Susa in his campaigns 325 BC and here organized the mass marriage of himself and his officers with women of the Persian aristocracy.

Suso, Heinrich (1300–1366) German mystic (*Das Büchlein der Wahrheit c.*1329).

Sussex, Thomas Radclyffe, Earl of (*c.*1526–1583) lord lieutenant of Ireland (1560–64).

Sussex the Anglo-Saxon kingdom of the South Saxons which became part of Mercia in the 9th century.

Sutherland, Graham [Vivian] (1903–80) English painter. He was an official war artist (1941–45) and subsequently became a portrait painter of note.

Sutherland, Dame Joan (1926–) Australian soprano. She became one of the world's leading bel canto operatic sopranos.

Suttee *or* **Sati** an old Hindu custom in India which required widows of high-caste Hindus to throw themselves on to the funeral pyres of their husbands. A widow to failed to do so was regarded as an outcast. It was made illegal in 1829.

Sutter, John Augustus (1803–80) American pioneer.

Sutton, Thomas (1532–1611) English founder (1611) of Charterhouse School.

Sutton Hoo, Suffolk, ship-burial treasure discovered 1939.

Suvorov, Aleksandr Vasilievich (1729–1800) Russian field marshal.

Svalbard Archipelago Norwegian sovereignty recognized 1920; officially incorporated in Norway 1925.

Svendsen, Johan (1840–1911) Norwegian composer (*Norwegian Rhapsody*) and violinist.

Sverdrup, Otto (1855–1930) Norwegian explorer in the Arctic.

Sverrir (d.1202) king of Norway (1177–1202).

Svevo, Italo [Ettore Schmitz] (1864–1928) Italian writer.

Swabian League, The Great formed by Frederick III 1488; disintegrated 1534.

Swalfred (d.*c*.712) king of Essex (695–709) *see* Appendix.

Swammerdam, Jan (1637–80) Dutch scientist.

Swan, Sir Joseph Wilson (1828–1914) English pioneer in electric lighting and photography.

'Swan of Lichfield, The' *see* SEWARD, ANNA.

Swanson, Gloria (1899–1983) American film star (*Sunset Boulevard* 1950).

SWAPO [South West Africa People's Organization] founded 1959 to oppose South Africa's rule; won majority in 1989 elections in Nambia.

Swarthmore College university in Pennsylvania founded by the Society of Friends 1864.

Swaziland protected by the South African Republic 1894–99; administered by the governor of the Transvaal 1903–1907; administered by a British High Commissioner from 1907; gained independence 1968.

Sweden Christian since *c*.1000; ruled by Vasas 1521–1810, by Bernadottes since 1810.

Swedenborg, Emanuel (1688–1772) Swedish scientist and theologian who devoted himself to engineering and science until he was forty-five. He then claimed to have received revelations from God, on which he based doctrines that were accepted by a large number of people. His writings include *Heavenly Arcana* (1749–56).

Swedenborgian Church organized 1788 by Robert Hindmarsh (1759–1835).

'Swedish Nightingale' *see* LIND, JENNY.

Sweelinck, Jan (1562–1621) Dutch organist and composer (*Cantationes Sacrae*).

Sweet, Henry (1845–1912) English philologist.

Sweyn Forkbeard (d.1014) king of England (1013–14) *see* Appendix.

Swete, Henry Barclay (1835–1917) British theologian.

Sweynheym, Conrad (*fl* 15th century) pioneer German printer in Italy.

Swift, Jonathan (1667–1745) Anglo-Irish divine, poet and satirist. His first important satirical works, published in 1704, were *The Battle of the Books*, a defence of the merits of classical literature against the claims of the moderns, and *A Tale of a Tub*, an attack on religious extremism. In politics, Swift began as a Whig but soon became a staunch Tory. He became Dean of St Patrick's Cathedral in Dublin in 1713 and published several tracts defending the Irish poor against their overlords, including the avage *A Modest Proposal* (1729). His masterpiece is *Gulliver's Travels* (1726), which culminates in Gulliver's voyage to the Houyhnhnms ('whinims'), intelligent horses whose nobility is contrasted with the brutality of humanity.

Swinburne, Algernon [Charles] (1837–1909) English poet and critic, noted for his sensuous verse which frequently created scandal, not just for their sexuality but for the author's clear dislike of Christianity. His works include *Atalanta in Calydon* (1865).

Swithhelm (d.665) king of Essex (660–665) *see* Appendix.

Swithin, Saint (d.862) bishop of Winchester (852–862) and patron saint of Winchester Cathedral from the 10th to the 16th century.

Swithin's Day, St 15 July. If rain falls on this day it is supposed to rain for six weeks afterwards.

Swithred king of Essex (746–758) *see* Appendix.

Switzerland state formed 1291–1798; unified Helvetic Republic established 1798; present area and neutrality achieved 1815.

Sybota, Battle of a naval battle of the Peloponnsian Wars between Corinth and Athens 433 BC, victory at which was claimed by both sides.

Sydenham, Thomas (1624–89) English physician and medical pioneer.

Sydney, New South Wales, founded 1788.

Sydney Harbour Bridge officially opened 19 March 1932.

Sydney Opera House completed 1973, designed by the Danish architect Joern Utzon (1918–) who won the international competition for its plan 1956.

'Sylva, Carmen' pseudonym of Elizabeth, queen of Romania (1843–1916).

Sylvester, Joshua (1563–1618) English writer and translator (mainly from the French).

Sylvester I, Saint (d.335) pope (313–335).

Sylvester II [Gerbert of Aurillac] (*c*.940–1003) pope (999–1003) who was a great promoter of learning and wrote a number of works, particularly on arithmetic and geometry.

Symbolism artistic and literary movement originated in Paris 1886–89.

Symington, William (1763–1831) British marine engineer.

Symmachus, Saint pope (498–514).

Symonds, John Addington (1840–93) English writer and translator.

Symons, George James (1838–1900) English meteorologist.

Syndicalism revolutionary doctrine formulated by Fernand Pelloutier (1867–1901).

Synge, [Edmund] John Millington (1871–1909) Irish dramatist, noted for his poetic rendering of Irish peasant speech. His masterpiece is *The Playboy of the Western World* (1907), a highly controversial comedy.

Synod of the clergy first held in England at Hertford 673.

Synthetic geometry theory developed by the Swiss mathematician Jakob Steiner (1796–1863).

Synthetic oil production initiated 1850 by the Scottish scientist James 'Paraffin' Young (1811–83).

Syphilis bacillus discovered 1905 by the German scientists Erich Hoffman (1868–1959) and Fritz Schaudinn; curative drug 'Salvarsan' discovered 1908 by the German bacteriologist Paul Ehrlich (1854–1915).

Syracuse an ancient seaport on the east coast of Sicily founded in the 8th century BC. During the Peloponnesian war it was besieged 415 BC by the Athenians but they were defeated in a naval battle there and forced to lift the siege; the Romans under Marcellus captured the city from the Carthaginians 212 BC during the Second Punic War (when Archimedes was killed); destroyed by an earthquake 1693; again nearly destroyed 1757; surrendered to Neapolitan troops 1849.

Syracuse University a university in New York State founded 1849; moved to present site 1870.

Syria a region in the Middle East bounded by the Mediterranean, the Taurus, the Euphrates and the Arabian Desert, which was subdued by Shalmaneser II, king of Assyria, 860 BC; Egyptian power in Syria overthrown by Babylon 605 BC at battle of Carchemish; Seleucid dynasty founded by Seleucus I 312 BC; Syrians defeated by the Romans at battle of Magnesia 190 BC; Syrian garrison expelled from Jerusalem 175 BC; Syria conquered by Pompey and made a Roman province 64 BC; now a country in southwest Asia that borders the Mediterranean Sea in the West; ruled by Turks 1517–1918; under French mandate 1920–41; became independent 1944; joined Egypt in the United Arab Republic 1958–61; government dominated by the Arab Socialist Renaissance (Ba'ath) Party; president Hafez el-Assad has held power since 1970.

Széchenyi, Count Stephen (1791–1860) Hungarian statesman. He committed suicide.

Szymanowski, Karol (1883–1937) Polish composer (*Symphonie Concertante* 1933).

T

Tabari, Abu Ja'far (839–*c.*923) Arab historian.

Tabernacles, Feast of (Sukkoth) Jewish holiday, 15th day of Tishri.

Table turning in Spiritualist seances began in the USA 1848, reached Europe 1852.

Tabora capital of Western Province, Tanzania, founded by Arab slave and ivory traders *c.*1820.

Tabriz capital of Azerbaijan Province, Iran, reputed to have been founded by Zobeidah, wife of Harun-el-Rashid, 791.

Tacitus (d.276) Roman emperor (275–276).

Tacitus, Cornelius (*c.*55–*c.*116) Roman historian whose works, e.g. *Agricola*, *Germania* and *Annals*, throw much light on the history of the early Roman empire. His style is concise, his opinions pithy and his character sketches masterly.

Tacoma Narrows American suspension bridge, collapsed after construction 1940.

Taddeo di Bartolo (*c.*1362–*c.*1422) Sienese painter.

Tadema, Sir, Lawrence Alma- (1836–1912) Dutch-born painter.

Taffeta in its earliest form introduced into England in the 14th century.

Taft, William Howard (1857–1930) 27th US president (1909–13).

Taganrog Sea of Azov port founded 1769 on the site of a fortress erected by Peter the Great 1698.

Taglioni, Maria (1804–84) Italian ballerina.

Tagore, Rabindranath (1861–1941) Indian poet and philosopher whose works include *Gitanjali* (1912). He wrote in both Bengali and English and was awarded the Nobel prize for literature in 1913. He was knighted in 1915 but resigned his title in 1919 to show his disapproval of British methods of dealing with rioters.

Tahirites ruling family in Khorassan, Persia 813–872.

Tahiti the largest of the Society Islands in French Polynesia, discovered 1767 by the English naval captain Samuel Wallis (1728–1804).

Taillefer (*fl* 11th-century) a bard who is said to have struck the first blow at the battle of Hastings 1066.

Taine, Hippolyte (1828–93) French historian.

Tait, Archibald Campbell (1811–82) Scottish clergyman who became headmaster of Rugby (1842–50) on the death of Thomas Arnold, dean of Carlisle (1850–56), bishop of London (1856–68) and archbishop of Canterbury (1868–82), the first Scot to become archbishop.

Taiwan (formerly Formosa) ceded to Japan by China 1895; seized by Chiang Kai-shek 1945 and held after evacuation of Chinese mainland in 1949.

Tajikistan former Soviet Socialist Republic (admitted to the USSR 1929), declared independence from the Soviet Union 6 September 1991.

Taj Mahal a mausoleum at Agra, India, built 1632–43 by Emperor Shah Jehan (d.1666) in honour of his favourite queen, Mumtaz Mahal. It stands on a marble platform on the banks of the Jumna and is itself constructed of white marble, much decorated inside. It is regarded as the finest extant example of Mogul art.

Talana Hill scene near Dundee, north Natal, of the first Battle of the Boer War, 20 October 1899.

Talavera, Battle of a battle of the Peninsular War between, 27–28 July 1809, when the French were defeated by the British under Wellington.

Talbot, William Henry Fox (1800–1877) English pioneer in photography. Invented instantaneous photography 1851.

Taliesin (*fl* 6th century) Welsh bard.

'Talkies' (talking films) a film that reproduces sound as well as views and motions by means of a narrow recorded sound track occupying a narrow strip at the side of the film, first shown in commercial cinemas 1928.

Talking books for the blind first sponsored 1934 by the American lawyer Robert Forsythe Irwin (1892–).

Tallage special tax on English towns first levied in the reign of King Henry I, ceased with the 1332 levy, formally abolished 1340.

Tallahassee capital of Florida, reputed to have been founded by the Spaniards 1638.

Talleyrand-Périgord, Charles Maurice de (1754–1838) French cleric, diplomat and statesman who escaped to America during the Reign of Terror in France and returned to become Napoleon's foreign minister 1797–1807. As foreign minister again, 1814–15, he brought Louis XVIII to the throne while Napoleon was on Elba, but when Napoleon escaped he retired into private life until 1830 when he became the French ambassador in London until 1834.

Tallien, Jean Lambert (1769–1820) French Revolutionary leader.

Tallinn Estonian city, founded by Waldemar II of Denmark 1219.

Tallis, Thomas (*c.*1505–1585) English composer (*Song of Forty Parts*).

Talma, François Joseph (1763–1826) French actor and one of the first to advocate realism in scenery and custume. He became a friend of Napoleon, Chénier and Danton, and helped found the Théâtre de la République.

Talmud the collection of ancient Jewish laws not derived directly from Moses but observed as traditional. Rabbinical thesaurus, recension completed during the 5th century; first complete edition published 1520–23 by the Christian printer Daniel Bomberg (d.1549).

Talorcen (d.657) king of Picts *see* Appendix.

Talorgen (d.787) king of Picts 9785–787).

Tamar Bridge linking Devon and Cornwall completed 1961.

Tamerlane *or* **Timur the Lame** (*c.*1336–1405) Mongol conqueror who was born near Samarkand and raised himself to its throne in 1369. He first organized his kingdom and then started on his raids, conquering nearly all of Persia, India, Syria and Asia Minor. He died while invading China.

Tammany (*fl* mid-17th century) American Indian chief of the Delaware tribe who is said to have had a motto, 'Unite in peace for happiness, and in war for defence'.

Tammany Hall New York political organization founded *c.*1789. Tammany Hall Scandal took place 1870.

Tancred (*c.*1078–1112) Norman crusader who distinguished himself on the First Crusade and was made the hero of *La Gerusalemme liberata* by Tasso.

Tandy, James Napper (1740–1803) United Irishman.

Tanganyika former East African state; German territory 1884–1914; conquered by British forces 1914–18; mandated territory of the League of Nations 1920–46; United Nations trusteeship 1946; gained independence 1961; united with Zanzibar 1964 as the United Republic of Tanzania.

Tanganyika, Lake discovered 1858 by the English explorers Burton (1821–90) and John Hanning Speke (1827–64).

T'Ang dynasty in China 618–906.

Tangier ruled by Portugal 1471–1662, England 1662–84, Morocco 1684–1904; international zone created 1923, terminated 1956; made summer capital of Morroco and free port 1962.

Tank Corps of the British Army, formation authorized 28 July 1917.

Tanks mobile forts propelled by caterpillar tracks for attacking or supporting infantry. They were tested and so named 29 January 1916 and first used by the British Army on the Somme 15 September 1916.

Tannenberg, Battle of between Teutonic Order and Poles 1410; and between the Germans and the Russians 26–31 August 1914.

Tanner, Thomas (1674–1735) English antiquary (*Notitia Monastica* 1695).

Tannhaüser (*fl* 13th century) German knight and minnesinger who became the hero of a German legend and personified the regret of the people for the old paganism and its stern treatment by the Church.

Tantalum a rare white hard and heavy metallic element, able to stand great heat without fusing, discovered 1802 by A. G. Ekeberg.

Tanzania East African republic formed by the union of Tanganyika and Zanzibar 1964.

Taoism religious movement thought to have been founded by the Chinese sage Lâo-tsze, who lived in the late 7th and early 6th centuries BC.

Tarkington, Booth (1869–1946) American writer (*Penrod* 1914).

Tarleton, Sir Banastre (1754–1833) English general in the American War of Independence.

Tarlton, Richard (d.1588) English actor.

Tarquin [Lucius Tarquinius Superbus] (534–510 BC) Roman king.

Tartini, Giuseppe (1692–1770) Italian violinist and composer (*Trillo del Diavolo*).

Tasman, Abel Janszoon (*c.*1603–*c.*1659) Dutch navigator.

Tasmania discovered 1642 by the Dutch navigator Abel Janszoon Tasman (*c.*1603–*c.*1659).

Tassili rock paintings Sahara discovered 1938 by the Camel Corps officer Lieutenant Brenans.

Tasso, Torquato (1544–95) Italian poet whose best-known work is *La Gerusalemme Liberata* ('Jerusalem set free' 1576), which centres on the First Crusade. He also wrote lyrics, dalogues and plays, e.g. *Aminta* (1573).

Tata, Jamsetji Nasarwanji (1839–1904) Indian pioneer industrialist and philanthropist.

Tate, Sir Henry (1819–99) English manufacturer and philanthropist.

Tate, Nathum (1652–1715) Irish-born poet laureate (*Panacea* 1700).

Tate Gallery in London officially opened 21 July 1897; founded by the English manufacturer Sir Henry Tate (1819–99); re-assumed its original name 1932.

Tatham, Charles Heathcote (1772–1842) British architect.

Tati, Jacques [Jacques Tatischeff] (1908–82) French comedy actor and film maker. An ex-rugby player, he became an international comedy star with his Monsieur Hulot creation, an engagingly incompetent character at odds with the modern world. Five Hulot films were made, including *Mr Hulot's Holiday* (1953) and *Mon Oncle* (1958). He also made *Jour de Fête* (1949).

Tatler, The British periodical, 1709–11, edited by the Irish-born writer Sir Richard Steele (1672–1729).

Tattersall's London horse auction and sporting centre founded 1776 by the English horse-auctioneer Richard Tattersall (1724–95).

Tatum, Art[hur] (1910–56) American jazz pianist. He was an acclaimed virtuoso of jazz piano music in the 'swing' mode.

Tatum, Edward Lawrie (1909–75) American biochemist. With the American geneticist George Wells Beadle (1903–89), he demonstrated that biochemical reactions in cells are controlled by particular genes. With Lederberg, he discovered the phenomenon of genetic recombination in bacteria. All three shared the 1958 Nobel prize for physiology or medicine.

Tauber, Richard (1892–1948) Austrian-born operatic singer.

Tauchnitz, Karl Christoph Traugott (1761–1836) German publisher and printer who set up a business of his own in Leipzig in 1796. In 1809 he began his editions of the Classics, and in 1816 he introduced stereotyping into Germany.

Taussig, Frank William (1859–1940) American economist.

Tavener, John Kenneth (1944–) English composer. He studied under Lennox Berkeley, and became noted particularly for his religious compositions, e.g. the cantata *Cain and Abel*.

Taverner, John (*c*.1490–1545) English composer. He taught at Oxford University and is best known for his religious works.

Tavernier, Jean Baptiste (1605–89) French traveller and merchant in the East.

Taxi cabs first official recognition of their existence shown in the draft of proposed cab regulations for London, issued by the Home Secretary 21 January 1907.

Taylor, A[lan] J[ohn] P[ercivale] (1906–90) English historian. Often a controversial figure (he argued that the Second World War was produced by accident as much as by Hitler's design), he was admired by his peers for his research and insight into modern European history, and became the historian best known to the British public through his live lectures to television audiences. His books include *The Origins of the Second World War* (1961).

Taylor, Alfred Swaine (1806–80) English medical jurist (*The Principles and Practice of Medical Jurisprudence* 1865).

Taylor, Elizabeth (1932–) English-born (of American parents) American film actress. Her films as a child include *National Velvet* (1944) and *Little Women* (1949). Regarded as one of the most beautiful film stars of her generation, her films include *Cat on a Hot Tin Roof* (1958) and *Who's Afraid of Virginia Woolf?* (1966). The latter film co-starred her 5th husband, Richard Burton, whom she married twice.

Taylor, Jeremy (1613–67) English theologian and writer who was th son of a Cambridge barber. He was made a Fellow of All Souls College, Oxford, and rector of Uppingham. His works include *Holy Living* (1650) and *Holy Dying* (1651).

Taylor, John ('The Water-Poet') (1580–1653) English writer (*The Pennyles Pilgrimage* 1618).

Taylor, Zachary (1784–1850) 12th US president (1849–50).

Tay Railway Bridge first opened 1878, collapsed under a train, 28 December 1879, killing 75 people; second opened 1887.

Tchaikovsky, Peter Ilyich (1840–93) Russian composer. Notable for his strong melodic sense and rejection of an overtly nationalistic and 'folk' approach to composition, his works include tone poems, a violin concerto, operas, e.g. *Eugene Onegin* (1879), the ballets *Swan Lake* and *The Sleeping Beauty*, and the so-called 'Pathétique Sixth Symphony.

Tea a drink made from the dried leaves and small shoots of a shrub that is native to China and India, traditionally invented 2737 BC by the Chinese emperor Shen Nung; reached Holland 1610; first recorded reference in Britain 1658; Indian tea reached Britain 1839. Black tea is allowed to ferment before the leaves are rolled and dried; green tea is made from unfermented leaves.

Teach, Edward ('Blackbeard') (d.1718) English pirate. He was killed.

Technetium (Masurium) discovered 1925 by I. and W. Noddack. Confirmed by C. Perrier and E. Segré of the University of California, 1937.

Tecumseh (1768–1813) American Indian Chief. He was killed in battle.

Tedder, Arthur William, Baron (1890–1967) marshal of the Royal Air Force.

Te Deum a Latin hymn used in services of thanksgiving to God, (the 'Ambrosian Chant') probably composed in the 5th century.

Teheran Conference Second World War conference between the Allied statesmen Roosevelt, Stalin and Churchill, 28 November to December 1943.

Teilhard de Chardin, Pierre (1881–1955) French Jesuit theologian, philosopher and palaeontologist. He developed a theory of evolution which he claimed was compatible with Roman Catholic teaching.

Teixeira, Pedro (d.1640) Portuguese explorer in South America.

Te Kanawa, Dame Kiri (1944–) New Zealand soprano. She is regarded as one of the world's leading operatic sopranos.

Tel Aviv-Jaffa the largest city of Israel and the main financial centre, founded 1909, capital 1948–50.

Telegraph a system for transmitting messages over long distances using electricity, wires and a code, invented 1832 by the American inventor Samuel Morse (1791–1872).

Telegraph, ocular, invented 1792 by the French engineer Claude Chappe (1763–1805).

Telegraph cable first laid across English Channel 1851; first Atlantic, laid 1857.

Telegraph line, first practical, patented 1837 by the English inventors Sir William Fothergill Cooke (1806–79) and Sir Charles Wheatstone (1802–75); first, set up between Washington and Baltimore 1844 by the American inventor Samuel Morse (1791–1872); monopoly granted to Post Office 1869.

Tel-el-Kebir, Battle of a battle in northeast Egypt on 18 September 1882, which was a victory by troops under Sir Garnet Wolseley over Arabi Pasha.

Telemann, George Philipp (1681–1767) German composer. A highly prolific composer of the Baroque era, his works include over 40 operas and over 40 Passions.

Telepathy communication between people's minds of thoughts and feelings without the need for speech or proximity, first so named 1882 by the English writer Frederick William Henry Myers (1843–1901).

Telephone the instrument that transmits speech at a distance, invented 1860 by Reis; patented 1876 by the Scottish-born inventor Alexander Graham Bell (1847–1922).

Telephone exchange first commercial exchange in US 1878.

Telephone service, first automatic, inaugurated in London 1927.

Telescope a tubular optical instrument that uses a combination of lenses to magnify distant objects, traditionally invented by Roger Bacon in the 13th century; model presented 2 October 1608 to Dutch General Estates by the optician Hans Lippershey (d.1619).

Telesphorus, Saint pope (125–136).

Teletext a broadcast system for displaying information on a TV which is continuously updated, Ceefax® (BBC) and Oracle® (ITV) first introduced 1973.

Television the transmission of visual images and accompanying sound through electrical and sound waves, first demonstrated 1926 by the Scottish inventor John Logie Baird (1888–1946); **colour** first publicly demonstrated in Glasgow 1927; the two-colour system demonstrated 1944 by the Scottish inventor John Logie Baird (1888–1946); **commercial** began in Britain 1955; **satellite** began in the UK 1989.

Television broadcast, first BBC experimental 1929; first BBC experimental programme broadcast 1932; first satellite broadcast 1962 (via Telestar).

Telford, Thomas (1757–1834) Scottish civil engineer who built roads, harbours, canals and bridges. His works include the Menai suspension bridge (1825), the Caledonian Canal and the Gota Canal in Sweden.

Tell, William mythical Swiss patriot of the 14th century who was forced by an Austrian governor to shoot his crossbow at an apple placed on the top of his son's head.

Teller, Edward (1908–) Hungarian-born American nuclear physicist. Known as the 'father of the hydrogen bomb' for his ground-breaking work in that field.

Tellier, Charles (1828–1913) French inventor 1867 of the refrigerator.

Tellurium white metal-element discovered by Reichenstein 1782.

Telstar I and II the first privately owned communications satellites, launched 1962–65.

Tempest, Marie (1864–1942) English actress.

Templars, Order of the Knights a Crusading order founded *c.*1118 for the protection of pilgrims in Palestine and afterwards for the defence of the Holy Sepulchre. The knights wore a white cloak with a red eight-pointed (Maltese) cross on the left shoulder. Philip IV of France massacred the 54 chief knights in 1310 and Pope Clement V abolished the order in 1312.

Temple, Shirley (1928–) American film actress and Republican politician. She became the world's leading child film star (*Curly Top* 1935) and later developed a career in politics.

Temple, Sir William statesman and writer (1628–99).

Temple a building in ancient Jerusalem erected by the Jews for the worship of Jehovah and the central shrine of Jewish worship for a thousand years. It was built three times. The first was begun *c.*961 BC by Solomon, taking seven years to build, and was destroyed by Nebuchadnezzar 586 BC; the second was built on the same site and dedicated 515 BC by returned exiles from the Babylonian Captivity. It was despoiled by Antiochus IV and in 165 BC was cleansed and restored to normal worship, an event that is still celebrated in the festival of Hanukkah, or Feast of Lights. The third Temple was a complete reconstruction of the second building, begun by Herod the Great in 20 BC. It was destroyed by Titus AD 70.

Temple Bar a building that originally stood between Fleet Street and the Strand in London and divided the City from Westminster, built 1672 by Sir Christopher Wren (1632–1723); re-erected at Theobalds Park, Essex, 1878.

Teng Hsiao-p'ing *see* DENG XIAO PING.

Teniers, David (the Elder) (1582–1649) Flemish painter who studied with Rubens. His works include *Temptation of St Anthony*).

Teniers, David (the Younger) (1610–90) Flemish painter who became tutor of Don John of Austria. Like his father, he specialized in the depiction of fairs, rustic sports, etc, as well as religious works.

Tenison, Thomas (1636–1715) archbishop of Canterbury (1694–1715).

Tennant, Smithson (1761–1815) English chemist and discoverer (1804) of iridium.

Tennessee state of the USA, first settled 1757; admitted to the Union 1796.

Tennessee University, USA, founded at Knoxville 1794.

Tennessee Valley Authority, USA, established 1933.

Tenniel, Sir John (1820–1914) self-taught English artist who made his name as illustrator of Lewis Carroll's *Alice's Adventures in Wonderland* (1865). He was the chief cartoonist for *Punch* for more than fifty years (1850–1901).

Tennis, Lawn origins in outdoor real tennis played in France in 18th century. Invented as 'sphairistike' by Major Wingfield in 1874, and Lawn Tennis Association formed 1888.

Tennis, Royal played in France in 11th century; played in England by Henry VII as early as 1497.

Tennis Court Oath of the French Revolution, 20 June 1789.

Tennyson, Alfred, Lord [1st Baron Tennyson] (1809–92) English poet. He first came to public notice with *Poems, Chiefly Lyrical* (1830). Subsequent volumes established him as a highly popular poet, and he was appointed poet laureate in in 1850, the year in which he published his great elegy for his dead friend A. H. Hallam, *In Memoriam* (1850). He became a much respected public figure, with several of his poems, e.g. 'Locksley Hall' (1842), being regarded as oracular statements on the spirit of the age.

Tenzing Norgay *see* HILLARY, EDMUND.

Terbium a metallic element discovered by the Swedish chemist Karl Gustav Mosander (1797–1858).

Ter Borch, Gerard (1617–81) Dutch painter (*Guitar Lesson*).

Terence (*c.*185–*c.*159 BC) Roman playwright ad poet who was originally a Carthaginian slave brought to Rome and freed by his master. He wrote six comedies, e.g. *Phormio*, based on originals by the Greek playwright, Menander.

Teresa, Mother *see* THERESA, MOTHER.

Teresa, Saint [Teresa de Cepeda y Ahumada] (1515–82).

Terpander 'Father of Greek music' lived in the 7th century BC.

Territorial Army inaugurated at Buckingham Palace 1907. Yeomanry and Volunteer Force units transferred to the newly constructed Territorial Force 1958.

Terry, Dame Ellen (1848–1928) English actress who made her first appearance at the age of eight in Charles Kean's productions of The Winter's Tale and King John. She made her London debut in 1863.

Terry, Sir Richard (1865–1938) English composer of church music.

Tertiary Period in Earth history between 1 and 70 million years ago.

Tertullian (*c.*155–*c.*220) Roman theologian who is the earliest father of the Church whose works are extant. His most famous book is the *Apologeticus* (197).

Teschen, The Peace of averting war between Austria and Prussia, signed 13 May 1779.

Test Act a law passed 1673 to curb Catholic influence at the court of Charles II and extended to peers 1678. Every office holder swore an oath to uphold the Protestant faith by taking the oaths of Supremacy and Allegiance. It was repealed 1828–29.

Test-tube baby first (Louise Brown), born in London 1978.

Tet offensive major Vietcong offensive against towns and cities in South Vietnam 30 January 1968 (Vietnamese New Year 'Tet').

Tetrazzini, Luisa (1871–1940) Italian operatic soprano born in Florencre. She toured Europe, the USA and South America and made her London debut in 1907.

Tetzel, Johann (1455–1519) German ecclesiastic.

Teutoburg Forest, Battle of the between the Cherusei and the Romans AD 9.

Teutonic Knights military order of Crusaders founded 1189–91.

Teutons an ancient Germanic people who moved to southern Gaul in the 2nd century BC. They allied themselves with the Cimbri to invade Italy and were annihilated by a Roman army under Marius at Aix 102 BC.

Tewfik Pasha (1852–92) Khedive of Egypt.

Texas state of the USA, proclaimed a republic 1836; admitted to the Union 1845.

Texas Rangers mounted military police formed 1836.

Texas University founded in Austin 1883.

Textile Institute founded in Manchester 1910.

TGV [Trains à Grande Vitesse] French high-speed train first introduced 27 September 1981 between Paris and Lyon.

Thackeray, William Makepeace (1811–63) Indian-born English novelist and essayist, noted particularly for the witty social satire of both his novels and his non-fiction works, e.g. *The Book of Snobs* (1846–47), a funny description of the varieties of snobbery. His masterpiece is *Vanity Fair* (1847–48), a decidedly non-moralistic tale of the opportunistic 'anti-heroine' Becky Sharp, set during the Napoleonic wars. His other works include the novels *Pendennis* (1850) and *Henry Esmond* (1852).

Thailand former name Siam (until 1939 and 1945–49), absolute monarchy until 1932; constitutional monarchy from 1932.

Thales (*c.*624–*c.*548 BC) Greek statesman and philosopher who was born in Miletus and is said to have studied in Egypt. He held that moisture was the elemental principle of everything.

Thalidomide sedative drug used in pregnancy 1957–61, found to cause severe birth defects, 1962, and removed from the market.

Thallium metallic element discovered 1861 by the English scientist Sir William Crookes (1832–1919).

Thames river steamboat service inaugurated 1905.

Thames Tunnel constructed 1825–43 by the French-born engineer Sir Marc Isambard Brunel (1769–1849).

Thanksgiving Day a legal holiday observed on the fourth Thursday of November in the USA, commemorating the 1623 harvest. The first national Thanksgiving Day was 26 November 1789.

Thapsus, Battle of a battle of the civil war between Caesar and Pompey where the republicans were defeated by Caesar in Africa 46 BC. Cato committed suicide rather than survive the republic.

Thatcher, Margaret Hilda (1925–) English Conservative stateswoman. She became MP for Finchley in 1959 and, as secretary of state for education and science (1970–74) ended provision of free school milk. She defeated Heath in the Tory leadership campaign of 1975, becoming the first woman to lead a major British political party. As prime minister (1979–1990), she launched an ideological crusade (dubbed 'Thatcherism') against what she perceived as the entrenchment of socialism in Britain, the principal elements of her attack being free-market policies and the privatization of nationalized industries. Her period of office was marked by rising unemployment and by the Falklands War of 1982, the success of which many believed to be the decisive factor in the Conservative's huge election victory of 1983 over Foot's Labour party. Her policies were widely disliked by her political opponents and by moderate Tories, the latter forming small resistance groups around figures such as Heath and Michael Heseltine (1933–). Increasing dissension within her cabinet, over such issues as the highly controversial Community Charge (or Poll Tax) and the disarray of the Health Service, led to her resignation in 1990 and the election of Major as prime minister.

Thayer's Law of Camouflage defined 1910 by the American painter Abbott Henderson Thayer (1849–1921).

Theatre a building where plays are peformed. Theatres were among the chief public buildings in classical times but disappeared with the decline of the ancient drama. The first modern theatres were in Italy, at Florence and Para, built in the second half of the 16th century. The first permanent English theatre was opened in London 1576.

Theatre, first television, opened at Brighton 1953.

Theatre footlights first used in Britain 1672.

Theatre-in-the-round first used in cinematography by Grimion Samson at the Paris Exhibition 1900.

Theatre lighting, first gas, 1803 (Lyceum, London); first electric, 1846 (Opera, Paris).

Theatres, English, closed by the Puritans 1642; reopened 1660.

Thebes the chief city of Boeotia in ancient Greece: Thebes under Epaminondas defeated by Sparta at Leactra 371 BC in the Wars of Greek City States; Sparta defeated by Thebes at Mantinea 362 BC but Epaminondas killed; Athens and Thebes defeated by Philip of Macedon at Chaeronea 338 BC and Philip became supreme in Greece; Thebes captured by Alexander, who destroyed the city except for the house of Pindar 335 BC.

Thelwall, John (1764–1834) English reformer.

Themistocles (*c.*525–*c.*459 BC) Greek general and statesman in Athens. On the second invasion of Greece by Xerxes, he obtained the command of the Athenian fleet by bribery and tricked Xerxes into the battle of Salamis 480 BC, which the Athenians won. He was afterwards accused of treachery and fled to the Persian court.

Theobald (d.1161) archbishop of Canterbury.

Theocritus (*c.*310– *c.*260 BC) Greek pastoral poet from Syracuse. Some thirty idylls attributed to him still survive.

Theodora (d.548) Byzantine empress.

Theodore anti-pope (687).

Theodore I pope (642–649).

Theodore II pope (897–898).

Theodore I (1557–98) tsar of Russia (1584–98).

Theodore II (1589–1605) tsar of Russia (1605). He was murdered.

Theodore III (1661–82) tsar of Russia (1676–82).

Theodore of Mopsuestia (*c.*350–*c.*428) Syrian theologian.

Theodore of Tarsus (602–690) archbishop of Canterbury (668–690).

Theodoret (393–458) Syrian theologian.

Theodoric (1) (Theodoric the Great) (*c.*454–526) king of the Ostrogoths or Eastern Goths (493–526) who as a youth lived in Constantinople as a hostage. In 493 he induced Odoacer, king of the Visigoths (Western Goths) to share his authority with him, and then by the murder of Odoacer he became sole ruler of the Goths and Italy. He was nominally a Christian and a wise ruler.

Theodoric (2) anti-pope (1100).

Theodosius I (*c.*346–395) Byzantine emperor (379–395).

Theodosius II (401–450) Byzantine emperor (408–450).

Theodosius III Byzantine emperor (716–717).

Theognis (*fl* 6th and 5th centuries BC) Greek poet.

Theophrastus (*c.*371 d.*c.*287 BC) Greek philosopher.

Theosophical Society founded in the USA 1875 by the Russian-born Mme Helena Blavatsky (1831–91); in Britain by the English leader Annie Besant (1847–1933).

Thera (modern Thira) a volcanic island of the Cyclades group of islands in Greece. Its Proto-Mycenean civilization was destroyed by volcanic upheaval 2000–1700 BC.

Theresa of Avila, Saint (1515–82) a Carmelite nun in Spain who was canonized by Pope Gregory XV. She was the author of several devotional works, including an autobiography.

Theresa of Calcutta, Mother [Agnes Gonxha Bojaxhiu] (1910–) Yugoslavian-born Roman Catholic nun and missionary. She founded the Order of the Missionaries of Charity in Calcutta in 1950. Venerated by many people as a living saint, her work in Calcutta with orphans and the dying led to her being awarded the 1979 Nobel Peace Prize.

Thérèse of Lisieux, Saint (Little Flower of Jesus) (1873–97).

Thermidor French Revolutionary calendar month of July-August.

Thermionic emission observed 1883 by the American scientist Thomas Alva Edison (1847–1931).

Thermionic valve a diode invented 1904 by J. A. Fleming; triode developed 1907 by Lee de Forest; tetrode developed 1916 by von Schottky.

Thermionics study developed by the English physicist Sir Owen Willans Richardson (1879–1959).

Thermochemistry study developed by the German scientist Germain Henri Hess (1802–50).

Thermodynamics study founded by the German scientist Rudolf Julius Emanuel Clausius (1822–88).

Thermoelectricity discovered 1821 by the German physicist Thomas Seebeck (1770–1831).

Thermopylae, Battle of between Greeks and Persians 480 BC, when the Persians defeated the Greeks.

Thibaut IV (1201–53) king of Navarre and troubadour.

Thicknesse, Philip (1719–92) English soldier and writer.

Thierry, Augustin (1795–1856) French historian.

Thiers, Louis Adolphe (1797–1877) French statesman who became first president 1871–73 of the third republic following the fall of France in the Franco-Prussian war and had to draw up the treaty of peace, suppress the insurrection at the loss of Alsace and Lorraine, and to pay the indemnity.,

Thimonnier, Barthélemy (1793–1859) French tailor and inventor (1830) of a sewing machine.

Third Republic in France, 1871–1940.

Third-class travel on British Railways abolished 3 June 1956.

Thirkell, Angela (1890–1961) English writer (*Love Among the Ruins* 1948).

Thirty-nine Articles of the Church of England agreed by Convocation 1563; enforced by Parliament 1571; revised 1604.

Thirty Tyrants thirty men to whom the government of Athens was given by the Spartans in 404 BC after the city was taken by the Spartan army under Lysander at the end of the Peloponnesian War; they were overthrown 403 BC.

Thirty Years' War religious wars in Germany 1618–48 that broke out between the Protestant and Catholic parties. The Swedes intervened in 1630 to help the Protestants, who also had the assistance of France in crushing the German emperor. The war left France as the leading military power in Europe.

Thistle, Order of the founded by James III of Scotland *c.*1480; revived in 1687 and 1703.

Thistlewood, Arthur (1770–1820) English conspirator and murderer. He was hanged.

Thomas, Ambroise (1811–96) French composer (*Mignon* 1866).

Thomas, Dylan [Marlais] (1914–53) Welsh poet. His best-known single work is *Under Milk Wood* (1954), a radio drama in poetic prose.

Thomas à Becket *see* BECKET, THOMAS À.

Thomas à Kempis *or* **Thomas of Kempen** (*c.*1397–1471) German theologian who retired to an Augustine monastery in Holland when he was twenty. He is regarded as the author of *The Imitation of Christ*, but this is sometimes attributed to his contemporary, Gerson.

Thomas Aquinas, Saint (*c*.1225–74) Italian theologian and philosopher. His writings, e.g. *Summa Theologiae*, established the need for both reason and faith in Christianity, and have become a cornerstone in the teachings of the Roman Catholic Church.

Thomas Cook's travel agents founded 1841 by the English pioneer Thomas Cook (1808–92).

Thomas of Erceldoune ('Thomas the Rhymer') (*fl* 13th century) Scottish prophet and writer.

Thomas of Kempen *see* THOMAS À KEMPIS.

Thomason, George (d.1666) English bookseller and collector of contemporary pamphlets.

Thompson, David (1770–1857) English-born explorer in Canada.

Thompson, Edith (1893–1922) English murderess. She was hanged.

Thompson, Francis (1859–1907) English poet (*The Hound of Heaven* 1893).

Thompson, John Taliaferro (1860–1940) American inventor 1921 of the submachine ('Tommy') gun.

Thomson, Elihu (1853–1937) English-born engineer.

Thomson, Sir George Paget (1892–1975) English physicist. He shared the 1937 Nobel prize for physics with the American physicist **Clinton Joseph Davisson** (1881–1958) for their (independent) discovery of the diffraction of electrons by crystals.

Thomson, James (1700–1748) Scottish poet whose best-known work is his series of poems, *The Seasons* (1726–30). His others works include the *Castle of Indolence*. He was the author of *Rule Britannia*.

Thomson, Sir Joseph John (1856–1940) English physicist. He was awarded the 1906 Nobel prize for physics for his discovery (1906) of the electron, one of the most significant discoveries in physics. Seven of his assistants went on to win Nobel Prizes.

Thomson, Robert William (1822–73) Scottish engineer and inventor 1845 of pneumatic tyres.

Thomson, Virgil (1896–1989) American composer (*Four Saints in Three Acts* 1934).

Thomson, William *see* KELVIN, WILLIAM THOMSON, BARON.

Thoreau, Henry David (1817–62) American philosopher who in 1845 built a hut near Walden Pond, Concord, and lived there as a hermit for two years. His advocacy of self-sufficiency and passive resistance to tyranny has been very influential, Gandhi being his most notable admirer. His writings include *Walden* (1854).

Thoresby, John (d.1373) statesman and archbishop of York (1351–73).

Thoresby, Ralph (1658–1725) English antiquary.

Thorium radioactive element discovered 1828 by the Swedish chemist Baron Jöns Jakob Berzelius (1779–1848).

Thorndike, Dame Sybil (1882–1976) English actress.

Thornton, Robert (1623–78) English antiquary.

Thornton, William (d.1827) British-born architect of the US Capitol (1793–1827).

Thorvaldsen, Bertel (1770–1844) Danish sculptor.

Thothmes I king of Egypt (1557–1501 BC).

Thothmes II king of Egypt (1501 BC).

Thothmes III king of Egypt (1501–1447 BC).

Thothmes IV king of Egypt (1420–1411 BC).

Thou, Jacques Auguste de (1553–1617) French statesman and historian. Henri IV employed him in several important negotiations and in 1593 made him his principal librarian. He became Chief Justice in 1595 and during the regency of Marie de' Medici he was one of the directors-general of finance. He wrote a voluminous history of his own times, *Historia sui Temporis*, comprising the events from 1545 to 1607, which is remarkable for its impartiality.

Thrace an ancient country situated astride the borders of modern Bulgaria, Greece and Turkey in the Balkans: conquered by Persia 512 BC and 492 BC; conquered by Alexander the Great 335 BC

Thrale, Mrs Hester Lynch (Mrs Piozzi) (1741–1821) friend of Dr Samuel Johnson.

Thrasybulus (d.*c*.390 BC) Greek statesman. He was killed.

Three Choirs Festival annual West Country festival founded 1724.

Three-Mile Island accident nuclear power plant in Pennsylvania that went critical and threatened to explode, 28 March–27 April1979.

Threshing machine, first, invented 1784 by the Scottish millwright Andrew Meikle (1719–1811).

Throckmorton, Sir Nicholas (1515–71) English diplomat.

Thucydides (*c*.460–*c*.398 BC) Greek historian and politician. He was a prominent commander in the Peloponnesian War but was exiled for alleged remission in duty. As an historian he wrote *History of the Peloponnesian War*. He was indefatigable in collecting facts, severe in sifting them and very terse in recording them, and in the power of analysing character and actions he has probably never been surpassed.

Thulium a metal of the rare earths discovered 1879 by Per Teodor Cleve.

Thurber, James [Grover] (1894–1961) American humorist, cartoonist and essayist, much of whose work first appeared in *New Yorker* magazine, including his most famous story, 'The Secret Life of Walter Mitty'. Other works include *The Middle-aged Man on The Flying Trapeze*).

Thurloe, John (1616–68) English statesman.

Thurlow, Edward Thurlow, Baron (1731–1806)

English lawyer and politician who became Lord Chancellor (1778–83, 1783–92)

Thurstan (d.1140) archbishop of York.

Thutmosis I (d.*c*.1500 BC) king of Egypt of the 18th dynasty who completed his conquest of Nubia 1560 BC.

Thutmosis III (d.*c*.1450 BC) king of Egypt of the 18th dynasty who conquered Syria and penetrated into Assyria 1515 BC.

Tiananmen Square central square in Beijing, site of massacre of student pro-democracy protestors by Chinese troops, 3–4 June 1989.

Tiberius (42 BC– AD 37) second Roman emperor (AD 14–37) who succeeded Augustus (*see* OCTAVIAN), whose daughter he had married. He was a good soldier and in many ways a good ruler, but his suspicious nature made him cruel, although not as cruel as the historian Tacitus has painted him.

Tibullus, Albius (*c*.54–18 BC) Roman poet.

Tichborne, Chidiock (*c*.1558–1586) English conspirator. He was executed.

Tichborne Claimant, The Australian butcher, Arthur Orton (1834–98), who claimed the Tichborne inheritance 1871–72. He was tried for perjury 1873–74 and imprisoned 1874–84.

Tickell, Thomas (1686–1740) English poet (*Colin and Lucy*).

Ticker-tape machine invented by the American inventors, Thomas Alva Edison (1847–1931) and Franklin Leonard Pope (1840–95).

Tieck, Ludwig (1773–1853) German novelist (*Magelone* 1796).

Tiepolo, Giovanni Battista (1696–1770) Italian artist, the greatest decorative fresco painter of the Rococo period. His works include *St Catherine of Siena*).

Tiffany, Charles Lewis (1812–1902) American jeweller.

Tiglath-Pileser I (*fl* 12th century BC) king of Assyria 1120 BC.

Tiglath-Pileser III (d.727 BC) king of Assyria (745–727 BC) who subdued Babylon 729 BC and raised Assyria to its greatest power.

Tigranes (140–55 BC) king of Armenia (96–55 BC) and of Syria (83–69 BC). He was offered the kingdom by the Syrian people, who were worn out by the civil wars that followed the death of Antiochus X, and accordingly ruled over Syria until he was defeated by Lucullus in 69 BC.

Tigranocerta, Battle of a battle of the Third Mithridatic War 69 BC, which was a Roman victory under Lucullus.

Tillett, Benjamin (1860–1943) English labour leader.

Tillich, Paul [Johannes] (1886–1965) German-born American theologian and philosopher. His highly influential writings address the problems of matching traditional Christianity with an increasingly secular society.

Tillotson, John (1630–94) archbishop of Canterbury (1691–94).

Tilly, Johann Tserklaes, Count of (1559–1632) Imperial general. He was killed.

Tilsit, Treaty of between Napoleon and Russia and Prussia, July 1807.

Timaeus Greek philosopher lived in the 5th and 4th centuries.

Time and Tide British periodical founded 1920 by Lady Rhondda (1883–1958).

Times, The British newspaper founded in London 1785 by the English merchant John Walter (1739–1812); present name since 1788. It was among the first newspapers to be printed by steam (1814) and the first to use mechanical typesetting.

Timoleon (*c*.410–*c*.337 BC) Greek statesman.

Timon of Athens lived in the 5th century BC.

Tinbergen, Jan (1903–) Dutch economist (brother of Niko Tinbergen). He shared the 1969 Nobel prize for economics with the Norwegian economist **Ragnar Frisch** (1895–1973) for their work in the field of econometrics.

Tinbergen, Niko[laas] (1907–88) Dutch ethologist (brother of Jan Tinbergen). He shared the 1973 Nobel prize for physiology or medicine (with Lorenz and Karl von Frisch) for his ground-breaking studies of animal behaviour.

Tincommius (*fl* 1st century BC) king of the Atrebates tribe *see* Appendix.

Tindal, Mathew (1653–1733) English theologian.

Tintoretto [Jacopo Robusti] (1518–94) Italian painter, the last of the great Venetian artists. He is noted for his dynamic, highly imaginative use of lighting and highlighting. His works include *The Miracle of St Mark*.

Tippecanoe, Battle of a battle between the Americans and the Indians, 7 November 1811.

Tippett, Sir Michael (1905–) English composer. His works include several operas, e.g. *The Midsummer Marriage* (1955), the oratorio *A Child of our Time*, symphonies, song cycles and chamber music.

Tippoo Sahib (1749–99) sultan of Mysore. He was killed in battle.

Tiptoft, John, Earl of Worcester 'the Butcher of England' (*c*.1427 executed 1470).

Tirpitz German warship destroyed by the British Navy in World War II, 12 November 1944.

'Tirso de Molina' [Gabriel Téllez] (1571–1648) Spanish playwright (*El Burlador de Sevilla* 1630).

Tisserand, François Félix (1845–96) French astronomer.

Tissue culture devised 1907 by the American biologist Ross Harrison (1870–1959).

Titanic Atlantic passenger liner that sank on her maiden voyage, 15 April 1912; wreckage located 500 miles south of Newfoundland September 1985, and explored July 1986.

Titanium a white metallic element discovered 1791 under the name Menachinite by the English scientist the Rev. William Gregor (1761–1817). Called Titanium 1795.

Tit-Bits British periodical designed to produce light but instructive reading, founded in Manchester 1881 by George Newnes (1851–1910), transferred to London 1885.

Titian [Tiziano Vecelli] (*c.*1490–1576) Venetian painter, one of the great figures of world art. He studied with Giovanni Bellini and worked with Giorgione, whom he succeeded as the master of Venetian painters for some 60 years. His works include *Sacred-and Profane Love*. He died of the plague at the age of ninety, having painted to the very end.

Tito, Marshal [Josip Broz] (1892–1980) Yugoslav statesman (prime minister 1945–53, president 1953–80). He fought with the Bolsheviks during the Russian civil war and became secretary-general of the Yugoslav Communist Party in 1937. In 1941, after the German invasion of Yugoslavia, he organized a partisan force to fight the occupiers and succeeded in diverting British aid from other guerrilla forces to his own. After the war, he established a Communist government and broke with Stalin. He succeeded in preserving a fragile Yugoslav unity, but 11 years after his death the break-up of the Yugoslav state began with Slovenia, then Croatia, declaring independence from the Serbian-dominated state in 1991.

Titus (40–81) Roman emperor (79–81) who served under his father, Vespasian, before the latter became emperor in 69. He took Jerusalem in 70 and became emperor himself nine years later. He was an enlightened and benevolent ruler. He built large public baths and completed the Colosseum, which had been begun by his father.

Tobacco the prepared leaves of a broad-leaved plant native to North America which are smoked, chewed or taken as snuff. It was brought to England in the 16th century by Sir Walter Raleigh, who cultivated the plant in Ireland as it was prohibited in England until 1886. It was introduced into France in 1560 by the French ambassador to Portugal, Jean Nicot (1530–1600).

Tobacco pipe, Indian, brought by Ralph Lane, first governor of Virginia, to Sir Walter Raleigh 1586.

Tobruk taken in the Second World War by the British, 22 January 1941; recaptured after an eight months siege by Rommel, 21 June 1942.

Tocqueville, Alexis Charles Henri Clérel de (1805–59) French politician and writer whose works include *La Démocratie en Amérique* (1834) and *L'Ancien Régime et la Révolution* (1856).

Togo, Heihachiro (1847–1934) Japanese admiral who came to prominence in the Chinese-Japanese War by sinking the transport Kowshing in 1894. He commanded the Japanese navy during the Russo-Japanese War 1904–1905 and destroyed the Russian fleet at Tsushima in May 1905.

Togodummus (*fl* 1st century AD) high king of British tribes *see* Appendix.

Togoland surrendered by Germany to the British and French 1914; divided into British Togoland and French Togoland by the League of Nations 1922; British Togoland joined Ghana 1957; French Togoland became independent as Togo 1960.

Tojo, Hideki (1885–1948) Japanese soldier. He became minister of war (1940–44) and prime minister (1941–44). He resigned in 1944, and was executed as a war criminal.

Toleration, religious, granted to German rulers by the Peace of Augsburg 1555; in Transylvania by John Sigismund 1568; in France by Edict of Nantes 1598; in England by the Act of Toleration 1639.

Tolkien, J[ohn] R[onald] R[euel] (1892–1973) South African-born British fantasy writer and scholar. Probably the most influential (and best-selling) fantasy writer, the works on which his fame rests are *The Hobbit* and *Lord of the Rings* (1954–55).

Toller, Ernst (1893–1939) German playwright. He committed suicide.

Tolpuddle Martyrs six agricultural labourers who were convicted of taking illegal oaths because they formed a trade union (organized by the Methodist preacher George Loveless 1833) and sentenced to seven years' transportation to Australia. There was public outrage at the severity of the sentence and they were eventually pardoned.

Tolstoy, Count Leo [Nikolayevich] (1828–1910) Russian novelist, dramatist, short-story writer and philosopher. He served as a soldier during the Crimean War and first became prominent as a writer through his descriptions of the siege of Sebastopol. His spiritual self-questioning resulted in some of the world's greatest works of fiction, notably *War and Peace* (1864–68), a panoramic epic of the Napoleonic invasions of Russia, and *Anna Karenina* (1877) a tragic tale of adulterous love which raises profound questions about personal social morality.

Tom Thumb [General Charles Sherwood Stratton] (1838–83) American dwarf.

'Tom Thumb, The' first railway engine built 1830 in the USA, constructed by the American inventor Peter Cooper (1791–1883).

Tomato brought from South America to Europe in 16th century.

Tomkins, Thomas (1743–1816) British calligrapher (*The Beauties of Writing* 1777).

Tommasini, Vincenzo (1878–1950) Italian composer (*Medea* 1906).

Tommy gun invented 1921 by the American inventors John Taliaferro Thompson (1860–1940) and John N. Blish.

Tompion, Thomas (1639–1713) English clockmaker.

Tone, [Tjeobald] Wolfe (1763–98) Irish politician who, inspired by the doctrines if not the practices of the French Revolution, founded the Society of United Irishmen in 1790. In 1795 he had to flee to the USA to avoid a charge of treason, and from there went to France where he became a brigadier in Hoche's projected invasion of Ireland. He wa eventually captured on board a French ship and sentenced to death but he committed suicide in prison.

Tonga island group in the South Pacific discovered by the Dutch 1616, and by Abel Janszoon Tasman 1643; proclaimed a British Protectorate 1900; gained independence 1970.

Tonic sol-fa system invented *c.*1845 by the English musician Sarah Ann Glover (1785–1867).

Tonson, Jacob (*c.*1656–1736) English publisher.

Tonti, Henri de (*c.*1650–1704) Italian-born explorer in North America.

Tontine annuity system introduced *c.*1653 by the Italian banker Lorenzo Tonti (*c.*1633–*c.*1689).

Tooke, John Horne (1736–1812) English politician and writer (*The Diversions of Purley* 1786–98).

Toplady, Augustus Montague (1740–78) English divine and hymn-writer (*Rock of Ages* 1775).

Tories British political group first so named 1679.

Toronto University in Canada founded 1827.

Torpedo a self-propelling submarine offensive weapon that carries an explosive charge, invented by the American engineer Herschel Clifford Parker (b.1867).

Torpedo, Submarine invented 1866 by the English engineer Robert Whitehead (1823–1905).

Torquemada, Tomás de (1420–98) leader (1483) of the Spanish Inquisition.

Torrens, Sir Robert Richard (1814–84) Irish-born statesman in Australia.

Torres Vedras, Lines of lines of fortification built 1810 by Wellington about 24 miles northwest of Lisbon. They consisted of two lines of fortification, the outer being 29 and the inner 24 miles in length.

Torricelli, Evangelista (1608–47) Italian inventor of the barometer.

Torrigiano, Pietro (1472–1522) Italian sculptor (*Henry VII's Tomb*).

Torvill, Jayne (1957–) and **Dean, Christopher** (1958–) English ice-dance skaters. They became world champions (1981–83) and Olympic champions (1984).

Toscanini, Arturo (1867–1957) Italian conductor. Regarded as one of the most authoritarian conductors of all time, he was renowned for his devotion to authenticity and for his remarkable musical memory.

Tosti, Sir Francesco Paolo (1846–1916) singing master to the British royal family and composer.

Tostig (d.1066) earl of the Northumbrians. He was killed.

Tottel, Richard (d.1594) English publisher (*Miscellany* 1557).

Toulon scene of the sabotaging of the French Fleet in the Second World War, 27 November 1942.

Toulouse-Lautrec, Henri [Marie Raymond] de (1864–1901) French painter and lithographer. Influenced by van Gogh and Degas, his subjects were café clientele, prostitutes and cabaret performers in and around Montmartre.

Tourneur, Cyril (*c.*1575–1626) English playwright (*The Atheist's Tragedy c.*1611).

Tourniquet invented in the Thirty Years' War by the German surgeon Fabriz von Hilden (1560–1634).

Tourniquet, screw, invented by the French surgeon Jean Louis Petit (1674–1750).

Tours, Battle of between Charles Martel and the Saracens 732.

Toussaint l'Ouverture, François Dominique (*c.*1743–1803) Haitian statesman. Born a slave on the island of Santo Domingo (now Haiti), he showed such military skill after the insurrection of 1791 that the French appointed him governor-general 1794. He eventually became president of the Haiti republic and governed so well that commerce and agriculture flourished. Napoleon became jealous of him and sent an expedition that took him prisoner, and he died in a French prison.

Tovey, Sir Donald (1875–1940) English musicologist.

Townshend, Charles Townshend, Viscount (1674–1738) British statesman and agricultural pioneer.

Toynbee, Arnold (1852–83) British economist and social reformer who from 1875 took up his residence in Commercial Road, Whitechapel and devoted the rest of his short life to helping the poor by living among them, his health giving way under the strain. After his death, the inspiration of his example led to the founding of Toynbee Hall.

Toynbee, Arnold Joseph (1889–1975) British historian and nephew of Arnold Toynbee. His works include A *Study of History* (1934–54).

Toynbee Hall a residential settlement in London founded 1885 as a memorial to the British social reformer Arnold Toynbee.

Trachoma main cause of blindness, virus first isolated by the Chinese scientist F. F. T'ang 1957.

Tracts for the Times Oxford Group tracts issued in defence of the Church of England as a divine institution 1833 to 1841.

Tracy, Spencer (1900–1967) American film and stage actor. Noted for his straightforward, yet commanding, performances, e.g. *Captains Courageous* (1937), he had a long personal and professional relationship with Katharine Hepburn.

Trade Unions the modern equivalent of the medieval craft guilds that resulted from the industrial developments of the 19th century. Their aim is to improve the status of their members and their conditions of work and pay. They were forbidden by law in 1800 but legalized by stages in 1824, 1859, 1869, 1871 and 1901.

Trades Union Congress (TUC) the major association of the trade unions in Great Britain, formed 1868.

Trafalgar, Battle of between the British fleet under Lord Nelson and Collingwood, and French and Spanish fleets, 21 October 1805. The British victory that resulted, although married by the death of Nelson, relieved England of fear of invasion and her for many years unchallenged mistress of the seas.

Traherne, Thomas (*c.*1637–1674) English poet.

Trajan (*c.*54–117) Roman emperor (98–117). As a soldier he gained such distinction in the Parthian and German wars that he was adopted by the Emperor Nerva as his colleague and successor. As emperor in 101 he led out his legions to battle in person, the first emperor to do so, and converted Dacia, Armenia and Mesopotamia into Roman provinces. He was a just and enlightened ruler.

Tramway a street railway, said to get its name from James Outram, a mining engineer, who in 1776 laid down cast-iron rails for mine trucks to run on. These 'Outram-ways' were first used for passenger traffic in the USA, in New York, 26 November 1832; first introduced into England by G. F. Train 1860; first English electrified tramway, Leeds 1891; last tram in London ran 6 July 1952.

Trans-Siberian railway construction begun 1891, completed 1906.

Transandine railway tunnel between Chile and Argentine opened 1910.

Transatlantic cable first laid 1858.

Transatlantic cable signal, first, received 14 December 1901 at St John's, Newfoundland, by the Italian radio pioneer Guglielmo Marconi (1874–1937).

Transatlantic flight first non-stop solo flight (Long Island to Paris) made 20–21 May 1927 by the American aviator Charles Augustus Lindbergh (1902–74). First woman Transatlantic flier, Amelia Earhart (1898–1937), flew Newfoundland to Wales 18 June 1928.

Transatlantic telephone cables between the United Kingdom, Canada and the USA inaugurated 1956.

Transcendental Club formed in USA 1836.

Transistors first demonstrated by scientists of the Bell Telephone Laboratories 1948.

Transvaal colonized by the Boers after 1836; independence recognized by Britain 1852; annexed by Britain 1877; independence restored 1881; reconquered 1902; joined South Africa 1910.

Transvaal gold-bearing lode discovered 1883.

Transverse-propelled ship first (the *Oriana*) launched 1959.

Transylvania ruled by Austria 1698–1848, 1849–67; by Hungary 1867–1920; by Romania 1920–40, 1947–.

Trappist Order a religious order that toop its name from the narrow valley of La Trappe in Normandy in which it was founded in the 12th century. It was reorganized in 1664 by Armand de Rancé (1626–1700) under rules of great severity, which enforce perpetual silence on its members. Many Trappists were expelled from France in 1880.

Trasimeno, Battle of Lake between Hannibal and the Romans 217 BC.

Trebia, Battle of a battle of the Second Punic War 218 BC, which was a victory for Hannibal.

Trebizond Black Sea port founded 756 BC (as Trapezoz); site of Empire of Comneni 1204–1461; captured by Turks 1461 and renamed Trabzon.

Tree, Sir Herbert Beerbohm (1853–1917) English actor-manager.

Treitschke, Heinrich von (1834–96) German historian.

Trelawny, Edward John (1792–1881) English writer.

Trelawny, Sir Jonathan (1650–1721) bishop of Winchester (1707–21).

Trent, Council of Catholic ecumenical council held 1545 to 1563.

Trevelyan, George Macaulay (1876–1962) English historian. His highly readable works include *History of England* (1926) and *English Social History* (1944) and several biographies.

Trevisa, John of (1326–1412) English writer and translator.

Trevithick, Richard (1771–1833) English mining engineer who was the first person to use a steam locomotive to haul a train, in 1804 at Merthyr Tydfil.

Trianon, Treaty of between Hungary and the Allies, signed 4 June 1920.

Triassic period in Earth history 195 million years ago.

Trieste ruled by Austria 1382–1918, by Italy 1918–45; free territory 1942–54; partitioned by Italy and Yugoslavia 1954.

Trinity College, Cambridge University, founded by King Henry VIII 1546.

Trinity College, Oxford University, founded 1555 by Sir Thomas Pope (d.1559).

Trinity Hall, Cambridge University, founded by William Bateman, bishop of Norwich, 1350.

Trinity House the institution in London that is responsible for the upkeep of the lighthouses around the coasts of England, the buoying of channels and the granting of certificates to polites. It has its origins in the medieval Guild of Mariners, developing into the Corporation of Trinity House of Deptford Strond which was granted its first charter by King Henry VIII 1514.

Triode valve (audion) invented 1906 by the American inventor Lee de Forest (1873–1961).

Triple Alliances in Europe 1668, 1717, 1820, 1827, 1881, 1882.

Tristan da Cunha group of Atlantic islands discovered March 1506 by the Portuguese navigator Tristão da Cunha (*c.*1460–*c.*1540; settled 1810, annexed by Britain 1816.

Triumvirate joint rule by three people, in Rome three magistrates appointed equally to govern the state with absolute power. This system of rule gave a fatal blow to the expiring independence of the Roman people. The First Triumvirate was a private league between Pompey, Crassus and Caesar in 60 BC to carry out their own plans, and led to civil war. The Second Triumvirate 43 BC was a similar league between Octavian, Mark Antony and Lepidus through which the Romans totally lost their liberty. Octavian disagreed with his colleagues, and after he had defeated them, he made himself asolute ruler in Rome.

Trolleybus first used in England 1909.

Trollope, Anthony (1815–82) English novelist whose more than 50 books are dominated by two main novel sequences: the 'Barsetshire' novels, which focus on the provincial lives of the gentry, clergy and middle classes (e.g. *Barchester Towers* 1857) and the 'Palliser' novels of political life. His mother was Frances Trollope.

Trollope, Mrs Frances [né Milton] (1780–1863) prolific English writer, whose works include *Domestic Manners of the Americans* (1832). She was the mother of Anthony Trollope.

Trotsky, Leon [Lev Davidovich Bronstein] (1879–1940) Russian revolutionary leader. An advocate of 'permanent revolution', he believed that socialism could not be built in one country alone, and supported the Mensheviks against Lenin's Bolsheviks. Forced into exile by Stalin in 1929, he was later assassinated by a Russian agent.

Troubadors early poets in Provence and the inventors or adaptors of a type of lyric poetry that was devoted to stories of romantic gallantry and was very intricate in its metre. They flourished from the 11th to the 13th centuries and spread from the south of France to the north of Italy and into Catalonia and Aragon. Many of them were knights, and some of them seem to have been women.

Troy an ancient city in Asia Minor, a few miles south of the Dardenelles. There have been nine cities on the same site at different periods, the seventh being the one besieged by the Greeks in the Trojan War in the mid-13th century BC. The site at Hissarlik was discovered 1801 by the English archaeologist Sir William Gell (1777–1836); excavations carried out 1870–90 by the German archaeologist Heinrich Schliemann (1822–90).

Troy ounce for precious metals and stones legalized in Britain 1853.

Truck Act prohibiting payment in kind passed by Parliament 1831.

Trudeau, Pierre Elliott (1919–) Canadian statesman (prime minister 1968–79, 1980–84).

Trueman, Freddy [Frederick Sewards Trueman] (1931–) English cricketer. He was a notable fast bowler.

Truffaut, François (1932–84) French film director, critic and actor. One of the *Cahiers du Cinema* group of film critics, his first film, the semi-autobiographical *The Four Hundred Blows* (1959), was widely praised. His other films include *Jules et Jim* (1961), *The Wild Child* (1970) and *Day for Night* (1973). He also acted in a number of his own films and those of others, e.g. Spielberg's *Close Encounters of the Third Kind.*

Truman, Harry S (1884–1972) American Democratic statesman. He became 33rd president of the US (1945–52) after Franklin D. Roosevelt's death, and authorized the dropping of the atom bombs on Hiroshima and Nagasaki. He initiated the change in US foreign policy towards the Soviet Union expressed as the 'Truman doctrine', a policy of containment of communism and aid towards groups or nations resisting communism, and approved the Marshall Plan of aid for Britain and Western Europe.

Trumbull, John (1756–1843) American painter.

Trunk call dialling first introduced in Britain at Bristol, 5 September 1959.

Truth British periodical founded 1877 and edited by the English scholar Henry Labouchere (1831–1912); ceased publication 1957.

ryphon, Diodotus (d.137) a usurper of the Syrian throne during the reign of Demetrius II. After the death of Alexander Balas, 146 BC, Tryphon first set up Antiochus, the infant son of Alexander, as a pretender against Demetrius, but in 142 BC he murdered Antiochus and reigned as king himself. He was defeated and put to death by Antiochus VII, the brother of Demetrius.

sushima, Naval battle of between the Japanese and Russian fleets, 27 May 1905.

uberculosis bacillus discovered 1882 by the German bacteriologist Robert Koch (1843–1910).

UC *see* TRADES UNION CONGRESS.

ucuman, Congress of declared the independence of Argentina, 9 July 1816.

uke, Sir Brian 'Master of the Postes' (d.1545).

ukultininib king of Assyria conquered Babylonia 1290 BC.

ulane University in New Orleans founded 1834.

ulip mania a period in the 17th century in Holland when the prices of tulips rose to enormous figures, as much as £460 being paid for a single bulb.

ull, Jethro (1674–1741) English agricultural pioneer and inventor of the seed drill 1731.

ungsten a grey metallic element that is very hard and difficult to melt. It was discovered 1781 by the Swedish chemist Carl Wilhelm Scheele (1742–86); isolated 1783 by the Spanish chemist Fauste d'Elhuyar (1755–1833); ductile tungsten discovered 1906 by the American scientist William David Collidge (b.1873).

uning fork said to have been invented 1711 by the English trumpeter and lutenist John Shore (d.1752).

unney, Gene [James Joseph Tunney] (1897–1978) American ex-world heavyweight champion.

unstall, Cuthbert (1474–1559) Master of the Rolls and bishop of Durham (1530–59).

upper, Martin (1810–89) English author who began to publish his Proverbial Philosophy in 1838. It proved to be immensely popular. He also wrote verse of a second-rate quality.

urbine the first reaction turbine, which makes use of the expansive force of a fluid as it flows between fixed and moving vanes, was built 1839; the steam turbine was invented 1884 by the British engineer Sir Charles Parsons (1854–1931) and used for generating electricity and then applied to ship propulsion.

urbojet, first (the De Havilland Comet), entered airline service 1958.

urboprop airliner, first (the Bristol Britannia), entered scheduled service 1 February 1957.

urboprop engine, first (the Rolls-Royce Dart), 1947.

urenne, Henri de la Tour d'Auvergne, Vicomte de (1611–75) French soldier. He was killed in battle.

Turgenev, Ivan Sergeyevich (1818–83) Russian novelist, short-story writer and dramatist. His novels, e.g. his masterpiece *Fathers and Sons* (1862), explore such major issues of Russian life as serfdom and revolutionary change. The best known of his plays is *A Month in the Country* (1850).

Turgot (d.1115) bishop of St Andrews.

Turgot, Anne Robert Jacques (1727–81) French statesman.

Turina, Joaquin (1882–1949) Spanish composer (*Sinfonia Sevillana*).

Turing, Alan Mathison (1912–54) English mathematician. Regarded as one of the most important computer theoreticians, he developed the concept of an idealized computer called the 'Universal Automaton' (later called the 'Turing Machine'). The computer, he posited, would be able to modify its own program through a sequence on paper tape of 1s and 0s. Turing also took part in the vitally important code-breaking project at Bletchley Park in World War II, which deciphered the German 'Enigma' codes. He committed suicide.

Turks rebelled against Avars 552, defeated Byzantine army 1071, defeated by Mongols 1243; Ottomans crossed Dardanelles 1345, defeated Serbs at Kossovo 1389, defeated by Timur 1402, captured Constantinople 1453. Ottoman Empire collapsed 1922 and republic of Turkey proclaimed 1923.

Turner, Joseph Mallord William (1775–1851) English painter. Precociously talented, he exhibited his first work aged fifteen. After a trip to Italy in 1819 he became interested in gradations of shifting light and atmosphere. The works of the next two decades represent his finest period, Constable describing paintings such as *The Fighting Téméraire* (1839) as 'airy visions painted with tinted steam'. He found an influential champion in Ruskin.

Turner, Thomas (1749–1809) English potter who introduced (1780) the willow pattern.

Turpin, Dick (1705–39) English highwayman. He was hanged.

Tussaud's, Mme London waxworks opened 1835 by the Swiss-born showperson Mme Marie Tussaud (1760–1850).

Tutankhamun king of Egypt (1361–1352 BC) of the 18th dynasty. His tom was discovered 1922 by Lord Carnarvon and Howard Carter after many years of excavation in the Valley of the Kings. It was one of the most sensational finds in the history of archaeology, as for the first time a tomb of an Egyptian king was found in an apparently untouched condition, so revealing fully the magnificence attending a pharaoh's burial. The tomb consists of four chambers and contained many treasures.

Tutu, Desmond (1931–) South African Anglican archbishop and anti-apartheid campaigner. He was awarded the 1984 Nobel Peace Prize.

Twain, Mark [pseud. of Samuel Langhorne Clemens] (1835–1910) American novelist, short-story writer and humorist. His two most famous novels, *The Adventures of Tom Sawyer* (1876) and *The Adventures of Huckleberry Finn* (1884), have become classics of children's literature.

Twelfth Night (Old Christmas Day or The Feast of the Three Kings) celebrated on night of 5 January. It corresponds to the Protestant festival of the Epiphany.

Twelve Tables a code of laws drawn up 450 BC by the Decemvirs in Rome, which were approved by the senate and the Comitia Tributa and written on metallic tables and set u in the place where the people met . They were originally Ten Tables (451 BC) with two added the following year.

Two Thousand Guineas race at Newmarket first run 1809.

Tycho Brahe (1546–1601) Danish astronomer.

Tyler, John (1790–1862) 10th US president (1841–45).

Tyler, Wat (d.1381) English rebel leader. He was killed.

Tynan, Kenneth (1920–80) British theatre critic and writer.

Tyndale, William(*c.*1494–1536) English Protestant martyr and translator of parts of the Bible who came under the influence of Erasmus while at Cambridge. He began the printing of his translation of the New Testament in 1525 and when it was completed began the translation of the Old Testament. The Pentateuch was published in 1530. He was arrested for heresy in 1535, imprisoned and put to death by strangling. His body was then burnt at the stake. *See also* MORE, SIR THOMAS.

Tyndall, John (1820–93) Irish-born scientist.

Typewriter model constructed 1873 by Sholes and Glidden; first modern version (Underwood) constructed 1898 by F. X. Wagner.

Typhoid fever bacillus described by Eberth 1880.

Typhus bacillus described by Ricketts 1910.

Tyrant of Athens *see* PISISTRATUS.

Tyre an ancient seaport and trading city of the Phoenicians on an island off the coast of Palestine. It was besieged unsuccessfuly by the Assyrians 719–713 BC but taken and demolished by Nebuchadnezzar 585 BC. The people removed to an opposite island where they built a new city that was taken by Alexander the Great 332 BC with much difficult after a seven-month siege.

Tyres *see* PNEUMATIC TYRES.

Tyrrell, Anthony (1552–*c.*1610) English spy.

Tytila (d.*c.*593) king of East Anglia (*c.*578–*c.*593) *see* Appendix.

Tzetzes, John (*c.*1110–1180) Byzantine scholar.

U

U-2 incident shooting down of US military spy plane by Soviet missiles over Russia, 1 May 1960; pilot Gary Powers was exchanged for a Soviet agent two years later.

Ubaldini, Petruccio (*c.*1524–*c.*1600) Italian-born writer and illuminator.

Uberweg, Friedrich (1826–71) German philosopher.

Uccello, Paolo (*c.*1396–1475) Italian artist (*Deluge c.*1445).

Udall, Nicholas (1505–56) English playwright (*Ralph Roister Doister c.*1553).

Uen (d.*c.*839) king of Picts (837–839) *see* Appendix.

UFO [Unidentified Flying Object] first 'noticed' by the American Kenneth Arnold, June 1947.

Uganda British Protectorate 1894–96; gained independence 1962; became republic 1967.

Ugolino da Siena (*fl* 14th century) Italian painter.

Uhde, Fritz von (1848–1911) German painter.

Ukraine former Soviet Socialist Republic, declared independence December1991.

Ulfilas (*c.*311–383) translator of the Bible into Gothic.

Ulloa, Francisco de (d.*c.*1540) Spanish navigator of the Californian coast.

Ulpianus (d.*c.*228) Roman jurist. He was killed.

Ulster former kingdom in Northern Ireland divided 1921 into Northern Ireland (Antrim, Armagh, Down, Fermanagh, Londonderry and Tyrone) and the Republic of Ireland (Cavan, Donegal and Monaghan).

Umberto I (1844–1900) king of Italy (1878–1900). He was assassinated.

Umberto II (1904–83) king of Italy (1946).

Unamuno, Miguel de (1864–1937) Spanish writer.

Underground railroad system by which negro slaves were enabled to escape through the northern states of America, 1825 onwards.

Underground railway first opened in London 1863 (Metropolitan Railway); first electric line opened 1890 (City & South London Railway).

Undset, Sigrid (1882–1949) Norwegian novelist (*Kristin Lavransdatter*).

UNESCO (United Nations Educational, Scientific and Cultural Organization) established 4 November 1946.

UNICEF (United Nations Children's Fund) established 1946.

Unidentified Flying Objects *see* UFO.

Uniformity, Acts of 1549, 1552, 1559, 1662.

Union, Act of between England and Scotland 1707; between Britain and Ireland 1800.

Union, Decree of (*Laetentur caeli*) uniting the Latin and Greek churches, issued 6 July 1439.

Union of Soviet Socialist Republics formed 1922 from Russian empire and other Soviet republics in the Baltic created after 1917 revolution; Soviet empire enlarged 1924–45; 1985 new policies of *perestroika* (reorganization) and *glasnost* (openness) introduced by president Mikhail Gorbachev; Baltic and other constituent republics pressed for independence; 19 August 1991 hardliners attempted military coup to restore communist authority; 29 August communist party banned by Russian president Boris Yeltsin; formation of the Commonwealth of Independent States (CIS) 8 December 1991; Gorbachev resigned as Soviet president and USSR ceased to exist 26 December 1991.

Union Pacific Railway the first railway across the central part of the American continent, which was begun at Omaha, on the Missouri river in 1864 and on 10 May 1869 met the Central Pacific Railway, which had been built eastwards through the Sierras from San Francisco.i

United Boys' Brigade of America founded 1887.

United Church of Christ formed in the USA through the union of the General Council of the Congregational Christian Churches with the Evangelical and Reformed Church 1957.

United Kingdom (Great Britain) formed 1801.

United Nations formed 1942; organization set up 1945.

United States of America declared independence 1776; constitution established 1787.

Universal Postal Union founded at Bern, 9 October 1875.

University College of London University opened 1828.

University College of Oxford University once believed to have been founded 872; in existence by 1170.

UNO *see* UNITED NATIONS.

Unuist king of Picts (820–834) *see* Appendix.

Updike, John [Hoyer] (1932–) American novelist and critic. His best-known work is the 'Rabbit' sequence, i.e. *Rabbit Run* (1960), *Rabbit Redux* (1971), *Rabbit is Rich* (1981) and *Rabbit at Rest* (1990), which describes the troubles of a middle American in his progress through the changing fabric of American society.

Ur (Ur of the Chaldees) an ancient centre of early civilization near the mouth of the Euphrates and capital city of the Sumerians: A dynasty was 2400 BC established by Ur-Engur, who was succeeded by his son, Dungi, who extended the empire over the whole of Babylonia and also conquered Elam. It was overthrown 2300 BC. Ur has been the scene of many remarkable archaeological discoveries.

Uranus the seventh planet in distance from the sun, discovered 13 March 1781 by the German-born astronomer William Herschel (1738–1822).

Urban II [Odo] (d.1099) pope (1088–99) who instigated the First Crusade 1095.

Urban VI [Bartolomeo Prignano] (*c.*1318–1389) pope (1378–89) whose policies led to the French cardinals electing an antipope, creating the Great Schism in the Church in the West.

Urban VIII [Maffeo Barberini] (1568–1644) pope (1623–44) who extended the power of the Church by taking part in military warfare by support Richelieu against the Hapsburgs in the Thirty Years' War and who condemned Galileo for his support of the Copernican astronomical theory.

Ur-Engur king of Ur (2400–2382 BC) who established a dynasty.

Urfey, Thomas d' (*c.*1653–1723) English playwright (*The Comical History of Don Quixote* 1694–96).

Urien (*fl* 5th century) British prince *see* Appendix.

Ur-Nina king of Lagash in Sumeria (3000 BC) who founded a dynasty and built temples and canals .

Urquhart, Sir Thomas (*c.*1611–1660) Scottish writer and translator.

Urquiza, Justo José de (1800–1870) president of Argentina (1854–60). He was assassinated.

Ursinus, Zacharias (1536–83) German theologian who, with Caspar Olevianus (1536–87), published (1563) the Heidelburg Catechism.

Ursuline Order of nuns founded 1535.

Urukagina king of Lagash (2800 BC) who was a great reformer. Lagash was defeated and destroyed by Lugai-Zaggisi, ruler of Umma and king of Erech, who became overlord of all Sumeria.

Uruguay independence established 1828.

Ussher, James (1581–1656) archbishop of Armagh and writer.

USSR *see* UNION OF SOVIET SOCIALIST REPUBLICS.

Ustinov, Sir Peter [Alexander] (1921–) British actor, director, dramatist and raconteur (of Russian-French parentage). His plays include *The Love of Four Oranges* (1951) and *Romanoff and Juliet* (1956). Other works include an autobiography, *Dear Me* (1977). He is best known as an engaging raconteur.

Utah state of the USA, settled 1847; organized as a Territory 1850; admitted to the Union 1896.

Utah University in Salt Lake City founded 1850; reopened under present name 1867.

Utamaro, Kitagawa (1753–1806) Japanese artist.

U Thant (1909–74) Burmese diplomat (secretary general of the UN 1962–71).

Utilitarianism the ethical theory that makes the greatest happiness of the greatest number the supreme end to aim at and regards the sense of right and wrong as being derived from humankind's experience of what does or does not benefit the race. The great exponents of utilitarianism in England were Jeremy Bentham (1748–1832) and John Stuart Mill (1806–73).

Utrecht, Peace of a peace signed 1713 between England France that ended the war of the Spanish Succession, which had been fought to prevent the union of the French and Spanish crowns and included he battles of Blenheim, Ramillies and Malplaquet. By the Treaty, Philip, grandson of Louis XIV, was acknowledged king of Spain, and Louis undertook to give no further support to the exiled Stuarts.

Utrillo, Maurice (1883–1955) French painter.

Uttman, Barbara (1514–75) German woman who introduced (1561) pillow lace-making into Germany.

Uurad (d.842) king of Picts (839–842) *see* Appendix.

V

Vaccination a method of inoculating against smallpox pioneered by Lady Mary Wortley Montagu (1689–1762); revived 1796 by Edward Jenner (1749–1823).

Vacuum flask a glass vessel with hollow sides from which air has been almost completely exhausted, invented by the Scottish scientist Sir James Dewar (1842–1923). The absence of air prevents loss of heat through the ja·ket by conduction while the silvering of the interior of the jacket delays loss by radiation.

Vadimonian Lake, Battle of the a battle in which the Romans defeated the Gauls and Etruscans, and Rome became ruler of northern Italy 283 BC.

Vaihinger, Hans (1852–1933) German philosopher.

Valdivia, Pedro de (d.1554) Spanish conquistador in Chile. He was killed.

Valency, double isomerism study developed 1893 by the Swiss chemist Alfred Werner (1866–1919).

Valens. Flavius (328–378) Byzantine emperor (364–378) who was at war with the Goths during the whole of his reign apart from one period of peace (370–377). He was killed in battle against the Goths.

Valentine pope (827).

Valentine, Saint (d.*c*.270) a saint of the Roman calendar, said to have been martyred. The custom of choosing valentines on his day (14 February) has been only accidentally associated with him.

Valentine's Day, St 14 February; originally young people of both sexes met on St Valentine's Eve to draw by lot one of a number of names of the opposite sex. The men were bound to the service of their valentine for a year.

Valentinian I (321–375) Roman emperor (364–375).

Valentinian II (371–392) Roman emperor (375–392).

Valentinian III (419–455) Roman emperor (425–455). He was assassinated.

Valentino, Rudolph [Rodolfo Guglielmi di Valentina d'Anton-guolla] (1895–1926) Italian-born American film actor. He became the leading screen personification of the romantic hero in many silent films, e.g. *The Son of the Sheik*. He died of peritonitis.

Valera, Eamon de (1882–1975) Irish statesman who was a commander of the rebel forces in the Irish rebellion of 1916. He was sentenced to death, reprieved and released in 1917. He was imprisoned again in 1918 but escaped to the USA in 1919, where he raised money to promote an Irish Republican government. He was president of Sinn Fein 1917–25 and a bitter opponent of the Irish Treaty of 1922. He became leader of the opposition and champion of a policy of complete separation from England. His party came to power in 1932 and he was prime minister 1927–48, 1951–54 and 1957–59 and president 1959–73.

Valerian, Publius Licinius Roman emperor (253–260) who was taken prisoner by the Persians in 260 and whose fate after this is unknown.

Valéry, Paul (1871–1945) French writer.

Valle-Inclán, Ramón del (1870–1936) Spanish novelist.

Vallet, Edouard (1876–1929) Swiss painter (*Sunday in the Valais* 1919).

Vallotton, Félix (1865–1925) Swiss painter (*The Rape of Europa* 1908).

Valois dynasty ruled France 1328–1589.

Valparaiso Chile founded 1536.

Vanadium a toxic silvery white metallic element discovered by Sefström 1830.

Van Allen, James Alfred (1914–) American physicist. He discovered, through detectors on the US satellite *Explorer I*, the Van Allen radiation belts outside the Earth's atmosphere.

Vanbrugh, Sir John (1664–1726) English dramatist and architect, noted for his witty comedies, e.g. *The Relapse: or, Virtue in Danger*, with its instantly recognizable characters of Lord Foppington, Miss Hoyden and Sir Tunbelly Clumsey (1696), and *The Provok'd Wife* (1697). As an architect, he became Comptroller of the Royal Works in 1702 and built many country mansions, including Castle Howard and Blenheim Palace, the building of the latter bringing him into unpleasant relations with the Duchess of Marlborough and being a source of worry, expense and litigation for years.

Van Buren, Martin (1782–1862) American lawyer and statesman who became 8th US president (1837–41). The difficulties that his administration had to face were chiefly connected with the deposit of State funds in private banks, and his method of dealing with these brought about his defeat at the next election in 1840.

Vancouver, George (1758–98) British navigator who

accompanied Captain Cook on his second and third voyages (1772–74, 1776–79) and gave his name to the large island off the coast of British Columbia, which he surveyed 1791–92.

Vandals a German confederation, probably allied to the Goths, who occupied the country south of the Baltic, between the Oder and Vistula rivers. They invaded Silesia, Pannonia, Moravia and Dacia. In 406 they crossed the Rhine 406 and invaded Gaul and from there entered Spain 409. They seized Seville and Carthagena, and crossed to Africa 429 where they founded a kingdom and revived the maritime glories of Carthage. Genseric also conquered Sicily, Sardinia and Corsica, and sacked Rome in 455. The kingdom of the Vandals was overthrown in 534 when they were defeated by Belisarius, the general of Emperor Justinian.

Vanderbilt, Cornelius (1794–1877) American financier who amassed a fortune in shipping and railroads. He founded Vanderbilt University.

Vanderbilt University in Tennessee founded 1872.

Van Der Meer, Jan (1628–91) Dutch painter.

Van der Post, Sir Laurens [Jan] (1906–) South African novelist, travel writer and mystic. His works are strongly influenced by Jung and display a strong sympathy for the 'primitive' peoples of the world. His novels include *The Seed and the Sower* (1963), based on his experiences a a prisoner of war of the Japanese in World War II and filmed as *Merry Christmas, Mr Lawrence*. His travel books include two African classics, *Venture to the Interior* and *The Lost World of the Kalahari*.

Van Doren, Carl (1885–1950) American writer.

Van Dyck, Sir Anthony (1599–1641) Flemish-born painter who became court painter to Charles V and was knighted. He painted many portraits and some mythological and historical pieces and was also a fine etcher.

Vane, Sir Henry (1613–62) English Puritan statesman and writer who was governor of Massachusetts 1636–37 and as a member of Parliament one of the leaders of the Long Parliament. After the Restoration he was executed.

Van Eyck, Jan (*c.*1385–1441) Dutch painter. A master in the medium of oil painting, his paintings are both realistic and charged with a serene, spiritual atmosphere.

Van Gogh, Vincent *see* GOGH, VINCENT VAN.

Vanhomrigh, Esther (1690–1723) Dean Swift's 'Vanessa'.

Van Loon, Hendrick(1882–1944) American writer (*Story of Mankind* 1921).

Vanuatu (formerly New Hebrides) island group in the South Pacific, discovered by the Portuguese navigator Pedro Fernandez de Queiras (*c.*1560–1614).

Varèse, Edgard (1883–1965) French-born American composer and conductor. His compositions are noted for their combination of the extreme registers of instruments with taped and electronic sounds.

Vargas Llosa, Mario (1936–) Peruvian novelist and politician whose novels include *The Time of the Hero* (1963), a satire on Peruvian society, the historical novel *The War of the End of the World* (1984) and *The Storyteller* (1990), a powerful fable on power and the rights of the Peruvian Indians. He ran for the presidency unsuccessfully in 1990.

Varro, Marcus Terentius (116–27 BC) Roman writer.

Vasari, Giorgio (1511–74) Italian painter, writer and architect, noted particularly for his *Lives of the Most Eminent Painters, Sculptors and Architects*, an invaluable source book for the lives of Renaissance artists.

Vasco da Gama (*c.*1460–*c.*1525) Portuguese explorer and navigator.

Vascular surgery initiated by the French surgeon Alexis Carrel (1873–1945).

Vatican the palace of the popes at Rome, which received its name from the hill on which it stands. It has been the papal residence since 1377. The present building was begun *c.*1450.

Vatican Council Catholic general council held 1869–70.

Vaughan, Henry (1622–95) ('The Silurist') Welsh poet.

Vaughan, William (1577–1641) colonizer of Newfoundland.

Vaughan Williams, Ralph (1872–1958) English composer. Like Holst, he was heavily influenced by traditional English music, particularly English folk song. His works include the choral *Sea Symphony*, *Fantasia on a Theme by Thomas Tallis*, operas (e.g. *Hugh the Drover* 1911–14), ballet music and song cycles.

Vauxhall Gardens in London open from *c.*1661 to 1859.

Vedas the oldest sacred writings of Hinduism, which are in Sanskrit and are thought to belong to the period 1500–1000 BC.

VE Day Victory in Europe, 8 May 1945.

Veblen, Thorstein (1857–1929) American sociologist.

Veidt, Conrad (1894–1943) German-born British film actor who specialized in demoniacal roles in the 1920s and later, in Hollywood, as Nazi commanders, e.g. in *Casablanca* (1943).

Veii an ancient Etruscan city northwest of Rome, which was captured and destroyed by the Romans 400 BC.

Velàzquez *or* **Velàsquez, Diego Roderiguez de Silva y** (1599–1660) Spanish painter. His earliest paintings were *bodegones*, a type of genre painting peculiar to Spain, consisting largely of domestic scenes, e.g. *An Old Woman Cooking Eggs* (1618). On Rubens' advice he travelled to Italy in 1628, where he was influenced by Titian and Tintoretto, developing a lighter palette and finer brushwork. His works include the portrait of *Pope Innocent X* (1650), *Surrender of Breda* (1634–35) and *The Rokeby Venus*.

Venezuela independence proclaimed 1811, secured 1830.

Venice independent republic under rule of doges 697–1797; ruled by Austria 1797–1805, 1815–48, 1849–66.

Venizelos, Eleutherios (1864–1936) Greek statesman who led an successful insurrection against Turkish rule of Crete. The dominant figure in Greek politics from 1910 to 1920 he founded the Balkan League in 1912 and in 1914 attempted to take Greece into the First World War but was vetoed by King Constantine. When Constantine was dethroned by Britain and replaced by Alexander, Venizelos reorganized the government and declared war against Germany 1917.

Vercellae, Battle of a battle in which the Cimbri, who were moving towards Rome, were defeated by the Romans under Marius 101 BC.

Vercingetorix (d.*c*.45 BC) leader of the Gauls in the Gallic Wars who was defeated and captured by Caesar at Alesia 52 BC. He was executed.

Verdi, Giuseppe (1813–1901) Italian composer. His post-1850 operas, which include *Rigoletto* (1851), *Il Trovatore* (1853), *La Traviata* (1853), *La Forza del Destino* (1862), *Aida* (1871), *Otello* (1887) and *Falstaff* (1893), were hugely popular and remain constant favourites within the repertory of most opera companies. He became a deputy in the first Italian parliament of 1860.

Verdun, Battle of a battle of the First World War between the Germans and the French, February-April 1916

Vere, Edward de, Earl of Oxford (1550–1604) poet.

Vereeniging, Treaty of between English and Boers, signed 1902.

Verhaeren, Emile (1855–1916) Belgian poet.

Verlaine, Paul (1844–96) French poet, regarded with his friend and lover Rimbaud as an early Symbolist. Collections of his verse include *Romances Without Words*.

Vermeer, Jan *or* **Johannes** (1632–75) Dutch painter. He is best remembered for his small-scale intimate interior scenes, carefully composed and lit, usually by daylight through a window.

Vermont state of the USA, first settled 1724; admitted to the Union 1791.

Verne, Jules (1828–1905) French novelist, whose innovative fantasy novels, e.g. *Voyage to the Centre of the Earth* (1864) and *20,000 Leagues Under the Sea* (1969), are regarded as the earliest great science fiction novels.

Veronese [Paolo Cagliari] (1528–88) Italian painter who was a contemporary of Titian and Tintoetto in Venice. He is noted as a colourist and for his rich, fetrtile imagination. Among his masterpieces is *The Marriage at Cana*.

Versailles, Treaty of between the Allied and Associated Powers on the one side and Germany on the other was signed 28 June 1919 and came infor force on 10 January 1920. The USA refused to ratify it. It provided for the cession of Alsace-Lorraine to France and of Posen and part of east Prussia to Poland, the surrender of all German colonies, the occupation of the Rhine zone for fifteen years, limitation of German armaments and military forces, and reparations to the Allies for damage done by Germany. It also embodied the Covenant of the League of Nations.

Vertue, George (1684–1756) English engraver.

Verwoerd, Hendrik Frensch (1901–66) South African politician and prime minister (1958–66). He fostered apartheid, banned the African National Congress (1960) and took South Africa out of the Commonwealth in 1961.

Vespasian [Titus Flavius Vespasianus] (11–79) sixth Roman emperor (69–79). In 43 ad he came to Britain and conquered the Isle of Wight. A fine soldier, after his succession he restored and maintained peace in the Roman world. The second year of his reign was marked by the fall of Jerusalem. The Colosseum in Rome was begun by him.

Vespucci, Amerigo (1451–1512) Italian Florentine explorer who sailed with Christopher Columbus on his third voyage and organized expeditions which he commanded. He was the first European explorer to enter the Antarctic regions and to see the constellation called the Southern Cross. The continent of America was named after him.

Vestris, Mme [Lucia Elizabeth Mathews] (1797–1856) actress.

Veto the right of refusing assent to legislation, abolished in the Polish Diet 1791; last used by a British sovereign, Queen Anne, in 1707; established in UN Security Council 1945.

Vianney, Jean Marie (The Curé d'Ars) (1787–1859) French priest.

Viceroy title of British colonial ruler of India 1858–1947.

Vichy place of French government 1940–47.

Vicky [Victor Weisz] (1913–66) German-born British

cartoonist. He was one of the leading left-wing political cartoonists and caricaturists of his day.

Vico, Giambattista (1668–1744) Italian writer.

Victor Emmanuel II (1820–78) king of Italy (1870–78) who was the first king of a united Italy, formed out of previously more or less independent states. he was the son of Victor Emmanuel I, king of Sardinia.

Victoria (1819–1901) queen of Great Britain and Ireland (1837–1901) and empress of India (1876–1902). *See* Appendix.

Victoria and Albert Museum in London opened 18 May 1852.

Victoria Cross premier British decoration for valour, founded by Queen Victoria 1856.

Victorian Order, Royal founded by Queen Victoria 1896.

Vidal, [Eugene Luther] Gore (1925–) American novelist, dramatist and critic. His American historical fiction provides an unofficial and waspishly entertaining alternative history of the US and its leaders, e.g. *Burr* (1973) and *1876* (1976). His work includes several important essay collections, e.g. *The Second American Revolution* (1982) and *Armageddon* (1987).

Video recorders first domestic system (Sony Betamax) introduced 1975.

Vidocq, François Eugène (1775–1857) French criminal and detective.

Vienna besieged by Turks 1529 and 1683.

Vienna, Congress of 1814–15 to determine the settlement of Europe after the abdication of Napoleon in April and the conclusion of the first Peace of Paris in May.

Vietnam socialist republic in Southeast Asia; conquered by France 1858–84, and incorporated as part of French Indochina (with Laos, Cambodia and Annam); occupied by Japanese 1940–45; French authority restored 1945, but Vietminh resistance led to defeat of French 1954; country partitioned at Geneva conference 1954 between North Vietnam and South (Republic of) Vietnam; war between North and South escalated 1956–65; US troops supported the South 1965–73; Paris Peace Accords 1973 ended US involvement, but further fighting led to the defeat of the South in March 1975; united socialist republic established 1976.

Vietnam War *see* VIETNAM.

Vieuxtemps, Henri (1820–81) Belgian violinist and composer.

Vigfússon, Gudbrandur (1828–89) Icelandic philologist who was called to England in 1864 to completge the *Icelandic-English Dictionary* (1869–74) and in 1884 was appointed reader in Scandinavian at Oxford.

Vigny, Alfred de (1797–1863) French poet, novelist and dramatist who was associated with the Romantic movement in French literature but stood apart from its main stream.

Vikings Scandinavian sea rovers who lived in *viks*, or creeks, and who in the 8th to 10th centuries ravaged the coasts of Britain and France. They were also known as Danes, Norsemen and Northmen. They were fought and conquered in England by Alfred the Great but under Canute they established themselves firmly in England, and, under Rollo, in Normandy. Vikings from Greenland are thought to have discovered America *c.*997.

Villa, Pancho (*c.*1878–1923) Mexican rebel leader.

Villa-Lobos, Heitor (1887–1959) Brazilian composer and conductor. His popular works, e.g. *Vidapura* (1918), combined elements of traditional Brazilian music with the European classical tradition.

Villiers, Barbara, Countess of Castlemaine Duchess of Cleveland (1641–1709).

Villiers, George, Duke of Buckingham (1628–87) courtier and statesman.

Villiers, George, Duke of Buckingham (1592–1628) English courtier. He was assassinated.

Villon, François(1431–63?) French lyric poet. The little that is known of his life indicates a violent, unstable personality. He graduated from the University of Paris, became involved with a criminal gang and killed a priest, being eventually pardoned. He was banished from Paris in 1463, and nothing is known of him after this date. His best-known work is the 'Ballad of Ladies of Long Ago', with its haunting refrain, *'Mais où sont les neiges d'antan?'* ('But where are the snows of yesteryear?').

Vinegar Bible so-called for its 'Parable of the Vinegar' (i.e. Vineyard), published 1717.

Vintners Company London livery company, origins uncertain; first recorded reference 1321; Letters Patent granted 1363; first charter 1437.

Violin playing first made the subject of formal tuition 1730 by the Italian violinist Francesco Geminiani (1687–1762).

Virchow, Rudolf German founder of the science of modern pathology (1821–1902).

Virgil [Publius Vergilius Maro] (70–19 BC) Roman poet and one of the most influential poets of all time. He published his *Georgics*, poems that deal with agriculture and country life, in 30 BC and spent the rest of his life writing his masterpiece, the epic poem the *Aeneid,* which charts the progrss of the Trojan hero Aeneas from the fall of Troy to the founding of the Roman state.

Virginia state of the USA, first settled 1607, entered the Union 1788.

Viroids isolated 1971.

Viruses existence of discovered 1897 by Martinus Beijerinck, Dutch botanist.

Viscellinus, Spurius Cassius (d.485 BC) Roman statesman and lawmaker who drew up and passed the first Agrarian Law for land reform in Rome 486 BC. He was charged with trying to gain regal power, tried and executed.

Visconti [di Modrone], Count Luchino (1906–76) Italian film director. He began his career as a stage designer, then worked as an assistant to Renoir. His films include *The Damned* (1969) and *Death in Venice* (1971), both starring Bogarde.

Vishnevskaya, Galina *see* ROSTROPOVICH, MSTISLAV.

Vitalis, Ordericus (1075–*c.*1143) English historian.

Vitellius, Aulus (15–69) Roman emperor (69) who was remarkable for his gluttony. He was appointed commander of the legions in Lower Germany by Galba, and on the death of the latter he was problaimed emperor by his troops. Six months later Vespasian was called to the throne and Vitellius was deposed and executed.

Vitruvius [Marcus Vitruvius Pollio] (*fl* 1st century BC) Roman architect who worked in the time of Julius Caesar and Augustus and wrote his work, *De Architectura, c.*13 BC.

Vivaldi, Antonio (*c.*1676–1741) Italian composer (*La Stravaganza*).

Vivisection law regulating passed 1876.

Vodka manufacture of prohibited in Russia 1914–25.

Volta, Alessandro (1745–1827) Italian physicist who was an early experimented in electricity and invented the earliest form of electric battery, the voltaic pile. The unit of electric potential, the volt, is named after him.

Voltaire [pseud. of François Marie Arouet] (1694–1778) French philosopher, poet, historian, essayist, dramatist and essayist. He was banished from France for his anti-clerical opinions and lived for some years at the court of Frederick the Great. Regarded as one of the most important of the French philosophers of the Enlightenment, his most influential single work is the *Philosophical Letters* (1734), a collection of witty, acerbic attacks on the tyranny of the *ancien régime.* His writings, with those of Rousseau (with whom he disputed bitterly), are often described as the main intellectual roots of the French Revolution. His other works include the remarkable novel *Candide* (1759), which takes a markedly pessimistic view of human endeavour.

Volunteers of America founded by Generals Ballington Booth and Maud Ballington Booth 1896.

Von Braun, Wernher (1912–77) German-born American rocket engineer, he designed the V–1 and V–2 rocket bombs for Germany and later the Saturn moon rockets in the US.

Vonnegut, Kurt, Jr (1922–) American author (*Slaughter-house Five* 1969).

Von Neumann, John (1903–57) German mathematician.

Von Stroheim, Erich (1886–1957) film director and actor.

Vortigern (*fl* 5th century) British tribal king of Kent (*c.*450) *see* Appendix.

Vostok I first manned space flight (USSR), 12 April 1961, crewed by Yuri Gagarin; Vostok 6 carried the first woman into space, Valentina V. Tereshkova, 16–19 June 1963.

Vulcanization of rubber patented 1843 by the English merchant Thomas Hancock (1786–1865).

Vulgate the Latin translation from Hebrew (the Old Testament) and Greek (the New Testament) of the Bible, which was made 382–405 by St Jerome. After revisions at various periods, the Vulgate was adopted by the Roman Catholic Church in 1598 under Pope Clement VIII.

Waals, Johannes Diderik van der (1837–1923) Dutch scientist and Nobel prize winner.

Wade, George (1673–1748) English soldier and engineer who assisted in suprressing the Jacobite rising of 1715 and was later commissioned to build 800 miles of roads in Scotland to enable troops to move about more readily in case of another rising. One of his roads ran along the line of the present Caledonian Canal and another through the Pass of Glencoe. These were the first real roads in Scotland.

Wadham College, Oxford University, founded 1612 by bequest of Nicholas Wadham (d.1609).

Wafd Egyptian political party, formed 1919.

Wagner, Cosima (1837–1930) wife of Richard Wagner.

Wagner, [Wilhelm] Richard (1813–83) German composer. He achieved great success with his third opera, *Rienzi* (1842). The operas that followed, *The Flying Dutchman* (1843) and *Tannhäuser* (1845), were not so popular and, in trouble with the authorities for his radical sympathies, he fled to Paris. He established his own theatre in Bayreuth in 1876, where he staged his *Ring of the Niebelung* cycle. His strongly Romantic works revolutionized opera, with their use of leitmotif and dramatic power (*Lohengrin*, 1848).

Wagram, Battle of a battle between Napoleon and the Austrians 5–6 July 1809 in which Napoleon inflicted a severe defeat of the Austrians within sight of the towers of Vienna.

Wain, John (1925–) English novelist (*Hurry on Down* 1953).

Wainewright, Thomas Griffiths (1794–1852) the English poisoner and artist.

Waitangi, Treaty of signed with the Maoris in New Zealand, 6 February 1840.

Waksman, Dr Selman Abraham (1888–1978) Russian-born discoverer 1943 of streptomycin. Awarded Nobel prize 1952.

Walburga, Saint (*c*.710–*c*.777) English Abbess of Heidenheim. She joined St Boniface on his mission to Germany.

Wacheren Expedition an expedition in 1809 involving an army of 40,000 British soldiers under Lord Chatham, eldest son of the Earl of Chatham, sent to destroy the French fleet in the Scheldt estuary and capture Antwerp. Chatham took Flushing, failed to take Antwerp and landed many of his troops on the island of Walcheren, where thousands of them died from malaria and from which the remainder had to be evacuated.

Walcott, Derek [Anton] (1930–) St Lucian-born West Indian poet and dramatist who has lived most of his life in Trinidad. His poetry includes *Omeros*, a reworking in a Caribbean setting of themes from Homer's *Odyssey* and *Iliad* and Dante's *Divine Comedy*. His plays draw on Creole traditions and imagery. He was awarded the Nobel prize for literature in 1992.

Waldenses a Christian heretic sect founded *c*.1176 by Peter Waldo of Lyons, a rich merchant. They established themselves in the Cottian Alps and on account of their denunciation of the Church were persecuted in France, Germany and Italy. They joined the Reformation movement in the 16th century.

Waldheim, Kurt (1918–) Austrian diplomat. After service as a Nazi intelligence officer in the Second World War he entered the Austrian diplomatic service and became secretary-general of the United Nations (1972–82) and president of Austria (1986–). Revelations about his role in the Nazi genocide machine in Yugoslavia during the war surfaced in the late 1980s.

Waldteufel, Emil (1837–1915) French composer of dance music (*Estudiantina*).

Wales finally subdued by England 1284 (rebelled 1400–1410); united with England 1536–47; first archbishop of (the bishop of St Asaph), enthroned 1 June 1920.

Walesa, Lech (1943–) Polish trade union leader and statesman. He became the leader of the free trade union, Solidarity, in 1980, which forced substantial concessions from the Polish government. After the imposition of martial law in 1981, Solidarity was banned and he was imprisoned (1981–82). After his release, he was awarded the 1983 Nobel Peace Prize. A skilled negotiator, Walesa succeeded in getting Solidarity re-legalized, and, in 1989, in the first free elections in eastern Europe since the 1940s, a Solidarity government was formed with Walesa as president.

Walker, George (1618–90) Irish clergyman and governor of Londonderry, he was killed in action at the battle of the Boyne.

Walkinshaw, Clementina (*c.*1726–1802) mistress of the Young Pretender Charles Edward Stewart.

Wall, Max [Maxwell George Lorimer] (1908–90) British comedian famous for his eccentric dance routine but who also appeared in revue, radio, television and film, and proved himself to be an able straight actor.

Wallace, Alfred Russel (1823–1913) Welsh naturalist. Independently of Darwin, he devised a theory of evolution by natural selection, which Darwin acknowledged. He differed from Darwin in holading that selection could not account for the higher faculties of human beings.

Wallace, Edgar (1875–1932) English crime novelist. He was a war correspondent in the Boer War and editor of a Johannesburg newspaper before turning to writing. He was a prolific writer, and his books, e.g. *Four Just Men*, became immensely popular.

Wallace, Lew[is] (1827–1905) American soldier, politician and writer who served on the Federal side in the American Civil War, was governor of Utah (1878–81) and minister to Turkey (1881–85). His religious novel, *Ben Hur* (1880), was an immediate best-seller and has been filmed twice.

Wallace, Sir William(*c.*1274–1305) Scottish leader who led Scotland's fight for independence. He and his troops won a victory against the English at Stirling Bridge in 1297, and started to advance towards English border counties and attack them. But Edward I's retaliation at Falkirk in 1298 brought their defeat. Wallace attempted to enlist French support in 1299. In 1305 he was captured near Glasgow and hanged, drawn and quartered.

Wallace Collection, The a collection of pictures, miniatures, armour, French furniture, bronzes and porcelain in London, bequeathed by the widow of Sir Richard Wallace (1818–90) on condition that it should be suitably housed. Hertford House in Manchester Square, the Wallaces' home, was bought and reconstructed for the collection and opened in 1900.

Wallenstein, Albrecht von (1583–1634) Bohemian soldier. He was assassinated by Irish and Scottish officers in his company.

Waller, Edmund (1606–87) English poet and politician who became a member of parliament in 1621. A cousin of John Hampden and a relative by marriage of Oliver Cromwell, he was a member of the Long Parliament, which met in 1640. In 1643 he was one of the commissioners appointed to negotiate with Charles I and became involved in Waller's Plot to secure London for the king. He was arrested and in 1644 banned from parliament and banished from the country. He lived in France but returned to England after his banishment was revoked in 1651. He became a member of parliament in 1661 after the Restoration. A collection of his poems was published in 1645, and his best-known works are 'Go, Lovely Rose' and 'On a Girdle'. He also wrote poems in praise of both Cromwell and Charles II.

Waller, Fats [Thomas Wright Waller] (1904–43) American jazz pianist and composer, he was an exponent of the 'stride' school of jazz piano and noted for his humorous lyrics.

Waller, Sir William soldier and politician (*c.*1597–1668).

Wall Game held at Eton College on St Andrew's Day, 30. November.

Wallis, John English mathematician (1616–1703).

Wallis, Samuel (1728–1804) English naval captain and discoverer (1767) of Tahiti.

Wallis, Sir Barnes [Neville] (1887–1979) English aeronautical engineer. He designed the 'bouncing bombs' used in the famous 'Dambuster' bombing raids of 1943.

Wall Street Journal American financial broadsheet established 1889.

Walpole, Horace [4th Earl of Orford] (1717–97) English author and politician, son of Sir Robert Walpole. A member of parliament from 1741 until 1768, he was noted for his vast correspondence and for his fascination with the 'Gothic', which expressed itself in his conversion of his house, Strawberry Hill, into a pseudo-medieval castle. He wrote the Gothic novel *The Castle of Otranto* (1764), which spawned a host of imitations.

Walpole, Hugh (1884–1941) New Zealand-born novelist who wrote prolifically and whose works, e.g. *Rogue Herries* (1930), were very popular.

Walpole, Sir Robert [1st Earl of Orford] (1676–1745) English statesman. As Chancellor and First Lord of the Treasury he was, effectively, Britain's first prime minister from 1721–42, George I having little interest in the government of Britain. His son was Horace Walpole.

Walpurga, Saint *see* WALBURGA, SAINT.

Walsh, John (d.1736) English publisher of music.

Walsingham, Sir Francis British statesman (*c.*1530–1590).

Walsingham, Thomas (d.*c.*1422) English historian (*Chronica Majora*).

Walter, Bruno [Bruno Walter Schlesinger] (1876–1962) German-born American conductor. Noted for his concerts and recordings of the great German Romantic composers, he is particularly associated with the works of his friend Mahler.

Walter, John English merchant and founder 1785 of *The Times* (1739–1812).

Walther von der Vogelweide (d.*c.*1230) German minnesinger and poet (*The Palestine Song*).

Walton, Sir Earnest *see* COCKCROFT, SIR JOHN DOUGLAS.

Walton, Izaak (1593–1683) English author, best known for *The Compleat Angler*, a treatise on the art of angling.

Walton, Sir William [Turner] (1902–83) English composer. His works include a setting of Edith Sitwell's poem *Façade* for voice and instruments. His other works include the oratorio *Belshazaar's Feast* (1930–31) and several film scores, e.g. for Olivier's *Henry V* (1944).

Wan Li period in China 1573–1619.

Warbeck, Perkin French-born pretender to the English crown (1474–99). He was recognized as the dowager Duchess of Burgundy as her nephew, Richard of York, who had been murdered in the Tower. He made several attempts to gain the throne by invading England but was finally captured and executed.

Warburg Institute of the University of London founded by Professor Aby Warburg (1866–1929).

Warburton, William (1698–1779) bishop of Gloucester (1759–79).

Ward, Mrs Humphry [Mary Augusta Arnold] (1851–1920) Tasmanian-born English novelist who was the granddaughter of Thomas Arnold. Her first novel was *Robert Elsmere* (1888) and subsequent works included The Case of Richard Meynell (1911).

Warham, William (*c.*1450–1532) archbishop of Canterbury (1504–32).

Warhol, Andy [Andrew Warhola] (*c.*1926–87) American pop artist and film-maker. He became the prime exponent of Pop Art in the early 1960s with his deliberately mundane works such as his reproductions of Campbell's soup cans and his repetitive portraits of contemporary icons, such as Presley, Mao and Marilyn Monroe. His films include the three-hour *Sleep*.

Warlock, Peter [Philip Heseltine] (1894–1930) English composer (*The Curlew*).

Warner, Sylvia Townsend (1893–1978) English writer (*Lolly Willowes* 1926).

Warren, Robert Penn (1905–89) American author (*All the King's Men* 1946).

Warren Commission 1963 tribunal investigating the assassination (November 1961) of US President John F. Kennedy, headed by Chief Justice Earl Warren (1891–1974).

Wars of the Roses *see Roses, Wars of the*.

Warwick. Richard Neville, Earl of ('Warwick the Kingmaker') (1428–71) English nobleman. gained his name by the enormous influence that he had on the fortunes of the rival parties during the Wars of the Roses. It was he who gave the orders 'spare the people but slay their leaders', which had a tremendous effect on the social politics of Henry VII's reign. Originally a Yorkist, he later became a Lancastrian and was killed at the battle at Barnet.

Washington, Booker T[aliaferro] (*c.*1859–1915) American educationist and social reformer who was born a slave and worked to improve educational and social opportunities for black Americans.

Washington, George (1732–99) American general and 1st president of the United States (1789–97). He led forces against the French in 1754, when he had to withdraw in the face of superior numbers, making a masterly retreat. After reorganizing the local militia, he retired into private life, from which he emerged as representative of Virginia at the first (1744) and second (1775) Continental Congresses. He became commander of the American armed forces during the War of Independence in 1775 and led them to victory. After the Philadelphia Convention of 1787, he was elected president of the new country for two terms (1789–97) but refused to be nominated for a third.

Washington a state of the USA, created a Territory 1853; admitted to the Union 1889.

Washington, Treaty of between the USA and Great Britain, signed 1871.

Washington Conference a conference held 1921–22 that resulted in various treaties to limit armaments, the most important of which was the Naval Agreement between Britain, the USA, France, Italy and Japan. The conference was the first practical step towards disarmament taken after the First World War.

Washington DC capital of USA, founded 1791.

Wassermann, August von (1866–1925) German scientist and inventor 1906 of the Wassermann Test, the reaction test for syphillus.

Wassermann, Jakob (1873–1933) German novelist (*Die Juden Von Zindorf* 1897, *Christian Wahnschaffe* 1919).

Water first analysed 1783 by the French chemist Antoine Laurent Lavoisier (1743–94).

Water closets invented 1596 by the English poet Sir John Harington (1561–1612).

Watergate Washington headquarters of the US Democratic Party burgled by operatives of the Nixon White House 17 June 1972; their discovery and subsequent White House cover-up led to Nixon's resignation in August 1974.

Waterloo, Battle of a battle fought on 18 June 1815 near Brussels in Belgium, in which Napoleon suffered defeat at the hands of Wellington and Blücher. It was one of the decisive battles of history as it finally shattered the power of Napoleon.

Waterloo Bridge London, old bridge built by the Scottish engineer John Rennie (1761–1821). New bridge opened to vehicles 1942; formally opened 1945.

Watermarks in paper, first known example made *c.*1282.

'Water Poet, The' [John Taylor] (1580–1653) English writer (*The Pennyles Pilgrimage* 1618.

Waterproof clothing invented 1823 by the Scottish chemist Charles Macintosh (1766–1843).

Watling Street the Roman road from Dover through Canterbury and London to Chester, with branches to York and Carlisle. It was the line of division between the Danes and the Saxons in the Treaty of Wedmore between Alfred the Great and Guthrum in 878. Traces of it still remain.

Watson, George Lennox (1851–1904) British yacht designer.

Watson, James Dewey (1928–) American biologist. He and Francis Crick discovered the 'double helix' structure of DNA, for which they shared (with Maurice Wilkins) the 1962 Nobel prize for physiology or medicine.

Watson, Richard (1737–1816) bishop of Llandaff and scientist.

Watson-Watt, Sir Robert Alexander (1892–1973) Scottish physicist. He played a major role in the development of radar.

Watt, James (1736–1819) Scottish engineer and inventor. His improvements to the steam engine led directly to the rapid expansion of the Industrial Revolution.

Watt, Robert (1774–1819) Scottish physician and bibliographer.

Watteau, Jean-Antoine (1684–1721) French painter, an outstanding exponent of Rococo art, who worked as a decorative painter in Paris before winning fame and entering the Academy in 1717. His best-known works are *fêtes galants*, figures in pastoral settings, a genre in which he excelled, and his work is noted for a delicacy of colour and sensitivity of composition not achieved by his imitators.

Watts, Charlie *see* JAGGER, MICK.

Watts, George Frederick (1817–1904) English painter and sculptor who began exhibiting at the Royal Academy at the age of twenty. He excelled in portraits and pictures with a symbolic meaning, and he left some of his best paintings to the nation. His works include *Paolo and Francesca* (1848).

Watts, Isaac (1674–1748) English clergyman and hymn-writer who became famous for his sermons as well as his hymns, which include *Jesus Shall Reign* and *O God, our Help in Ages Past*.

Waugh, Evelyn [Arthur St John] (1903–66) English novelist known for his brilliant satires, e.g. *Vile Bodies* (1930) on the brittle postwar world of upper-class England, *Scoop* (1938) on war reporting, and *The Loved One* (1948) on Californian burial practices. His work also had a deeper tone, resulting from his conversion to Catholicism in 1930. His best-known novel, *Brideshead Revisited* (1945), although still a satire displays a growing spiritual concern. His masterpiece is his *Sword of Honour* trilogy, based on his own experiences with the Communist partisans in Yugoslavia in World War II.

Wavell, Archibald Percival Wavell, Earl (1883–1953) viceroy of India (1943–47). He was killed.

Wave mechanics defined 1923 by the French scientist Prince Louis de Broglie (1892–1987).

Wayne, John [Marion Michael Morrison] (1907–79) American film actor. A screen actor of outstanding presence, he is best known as the star of many classic westerns (*She Wore a Yellow Ribbon* 1949).

Waynflete, William of (*c.*1395–1486) bishop of Winchester and founder 1458 of Magdalen College, Oxford.

Weather map first drawn 1820 by the German astronomer and physicist Heinrich Wilhelm Brandes (1777–1834).

Weather prediction study founded by the French scientist Jean Baptiste Pierre Antoine de Monet, Chevalier de Lamarck (1744–1829).

Webb, Matthew (Captain Webb) (1848–83) English sailor who became a profession swimmer and was the first person to swim the English Channel (from Dover to Calais), in August 1875, taking $21^{3}/_{4}$ hours, a record that stood for 36 years. He lost his life attempting to swim the Niagara rapids.

Webb, Beatrice [Potter] (1858–1943) and **Webb, Sidney James** [Baron Passfield] (1859–1947) English social reformers and economists. Married in 1892, the Webbs were, with George Bernard Shaw and H. G. Wells, the leading propagandists of Fabian socialism. They co-founded the London School of Economics (1895), founded the *New Statesman* (1913) and produced many of pamphlets and articles.

Weber, Carl Maria Ernst von (1786–1826) German composer, conductor and pianist. He is considered to be the creator of German romantic opera, using French opera as a framework and introducing German themes. He had a colossal influence on subsequent composers up to, and including, Wagner. His works include the operas *Der Freischütz, Euryanthe* and *Oberon*, two symphonies, concertos, piano sonatas and many songs.

Weber, Max (1864–1920) German sociologist. Regarded as one of the founders of sociology, he devised the concept of 'ideal types' of real situations for comparative purposes (*The Protestant Ethic and the Spirit of Capitalism* 1904–05).

Webern, Anton von (1883–1945) Austrian composer and one of the leading (*Passacaglia* 1908) exponents of the serial form of composition.

Webster, John (*c*.1578–*c*.1632) English dramatist, noted for two very powerful tragedies, *The White Devil* and *The Duchess of Malfi*. His bleak and chilling dialogue has rarely been matched.

Webster, Noah (1758–1843) American lexicographer who has left an enduring name as the compiler of the first scientifically planned English dictionary. The original edition took him 21 years to compile (1807–28).

Wedekind, Frank (1864–1918) German writer.

Wedgwood, Josiah (1730–95) English potter.

Wedmore, Treaty of 878 a treaty that ended the long struggle between Alfred the Great and Guthrum, the leader of the Danes. By the terms of the treaty the Danes were assigned all the country east of Watling Street, called the Danelagh, and had to acknowledge Alfred's Suzerainty. During the peace that followed Alfred built up a strong navy and army.

Week the seven days from midnight on Saturday to midnight the following Saturday; adopted in the Roman empire from Jewish custom *c*.500.

Wei dynasty China 368 to 557.

Weight reduction by the elimination of starch in diet popularized by the English undertaker, William Banting (1797–1878).

Weil, Simone (1909–43) French philosopher. From an intellectual Jewish family, she chose to live as a farm and industrial labourer during the 1930s, and worked for the Republican forces during the Spanish Civil War. She later developed a strong interest in Roman Catholic mysticism. She worked for the French Resistance in London, where she starved herself to death in sympathy with the inmates of the Nazi camps.

Weill, Kurt (1900–1950) German composer, noted especially for his collaborations with Brecht, e.g. *The Threepenny Opera* (1928). He fled from Germany in 1935, settling in the US.

Weimar Republic Germany 1918–33).

Weinberg, Steven (1933–) American physicist. He devised a theory of the unity of the forces operating on elementary particles that was independently arrived at by the Pakistani physicist Abdus Salam (1926–) and later developed by the American physicist Sheldon Glashow (1932–). All three shared the 1979 Nobel prize for physics.

Weingartner, Felix (1863–1942) conductor.

Weishaupt, Adam (1748–1830) German philosopher and founder 1776 of the Illuminati.

Weizmann, Chaim [Azriel] (1874–1952) Russian-born chemist and Israeli statesman and Zionist leader. A distinguished scientist, he participated in the negotiations for a Jewish homeland and became first president of Israel (1949-52).

Welles, [George] Orson (1915–85) American stage and film director and actor. He achieved notoriety with his radio production of H. G. Wells's *War of the Worlds* in 1938, which sparked off mass panic in the US. He co-wrote, produced and directed one of the greatest films of all time, *Citizen Kane*, based on the life of Hearst. His other films include *The Magnificent Ambersons*, *Macbeth* and *Othello*. His other acting roles include, most notably, Harry Lime in Reed's masterpiece, *The Third Man*.

Wellington, Arthur,1st Duke of [Arthur Wellesley] (1769–1852) Anglo-Irish soldier and statesman, nicknamed the 'Iron Duke'. In 1794–95 he served in Flanders and in 1796 went to Bengal just as war was declared against Tippoo Sahib. He distinguished himself as a commander in India, and was appointed commander of the British forces during the Peninsular War of 1808–14, opening the campaign at the Douro and with victory at Talavera. In 1810 the battle of Busaco was followed by the defence of the lines of Torres Vedras, and in 1811 he won the battle of Salamana. In 1814 he routed Soult's best troops at Toulouse, and soon afterwards Napoleon abdicated. In 1815 he led the Allied forces to victory against Napoleon at Waterloo. Respected for defeating Napoleon, he became Tory prime minister (1828–30) and opposed reform, but later served under Sir Robert Peel (1834–41, 1846).

Wells, H[erbert] G[eorge] (1866–1946) English novelist and short-story writer who began his working life as a draper's apprentice before studying science at London University. His science fiction works include several classics, e.g. *The Time Machine* (1895), *The War of the Worlds* (1898) and *The Shape of Things to Come* (1933). He was a propagandist with the Webbs and others for Fabian socialism, and his novels on contemporary themes generally address their subject matter from a 'progressive' viewpoint, e.g. *Ann Veronica*, and sometimes with a comic or satirical element, e.g. *Love and Mr Lewisham, Kipps* and *The History of Mr Polly*.

Wells, Fargo & Co. American express company founded 1852).

Welsbach mantle (1858–1929) invented by the Austrian chemist Baron von Welsbach.

Welsh literature recorded before 600.

Welwyn Garden City built 1920

Wembley Exhibition (British Empire Exhibition) Wembley, opened 23 April, closed 1 November 1924.

Wenlock Abbey a ruined Cluniac convent in Shropshire, originally founded as a nunnery at the end of the 7th century by St Milbarga, a granddaughter of Penda of Mercia. It was refounded after the Norman Conquest.

Wentworth, William Charles (1793–1872) Australian pioneer.

Werfel, Franz (1890–1945) Austrian writer.

Werner, Alfred (1866–1919) Swiss chemist who developed (1893) the study of double valency.

Wesker, Arnold (1932–) English playwright whose Jewish background features strongly in his work (*Roots* 1959).

Wesley, Charles (1707–88) English evangelist and hymnwriter, he formed a small group of devout Anglicans who subsequently became known as 'Methodists', which name was used to describe the expanding movement, and which remained within the Church of England in Wesley's lifetime. His hymns include *Jesu, Lover of My Soul.*

Wesley, John (1703–91) English evangelist. The 15th son of the poet and clergyman, Samuel Wesley, and brother of Charles Wesley, he joined his brother's Methodist group.

Wesley, Samuel (1662–1735) English poet and clergyman and father of John and Charles Wesley.

Wessex the Anglo-Saxon kingdom in southwest England of the West Saxons. Under Egbert, power was established over the whole south of England, East Anglia, Mercia and Northumbria. Until after the Norman Conquest, Winchester, the capital of Wessex, was the capital of England.

West, Benjamin (1738–1820) American painter (*The Death of General Wolfe* 1771).

West, Mae (1892–1980) American vaudeville artist, dramatist and film actress. Several of her plays were banned for obscenity, notably *Sex*, for which she was also briefly imprisoned. She became a major star, renowned for her sardonic wit and powerful sexuality, with such films as *She Done Him Wrong* (1933) and *I'm No Angel* (1933).

West, Rebecca [Cicely Fairfield] (1892–1983) English writer (*The Meaning of Treason* 1949).

West Bank former Jordanian territory west of the river Jordan occupied by Israel 1967.

Western Australia founded 1829; reached overland 1875 on third attempt (1875–76) by the Australian explorer Ernest Giles (1835–97).

West Indies the islands of the Caribbean Sea, which were discovered by Columbus in 1492 and named 'Indies' because he thought he had reached India. Slaves were introduced in 1525 to take the place of the native Caribs who had been decimated by the cruelty of Spanish planters. Other European nations, especially the English, French and Dutch, began to intrude into the area in the 17th century, English superiority being decided by a naval battle off Dominica in 1728 when Admiral Rodney almost annihilated the French fleet.

Westminster, Statute of regulating British Commonwealth relations passed 1931.

Westminster Abbey [Collegiate Church of St Peter] a church in London built on the site of a Benedictine monastery in the Norman style by Edward the Confessor (1050–65), part of which remains in the pyx house and the south side of the cloisters, but the main building as it now stands was begun by Henry III and practically completed by Edward I. Additions were made down to the time of Henry VII, who built the chapel called after him, and Sir Christopher Wren designed the upper parts and two western towers. Almost all English monarchs since William I have been crowned in the Abbey.

Westminster Assembly religious body that sat 1643–49.

Westminster Cathedral, England, opened 1903; consecrated 1910.

Westminster Gazette, The British newspaper founded 1892; absorbed into *The Daily News* 1928.

Westphalia, kingdom of existed 1807–14.

Westphalia, Peace of ending the Thirty Years War, signed 1648.

West Virginia a state of the USA, separated from Virginia 1861, admitted to the Union 1863.

Wetterhorn 12,162 ft. peak near Grindelwald, first climbed by the Swiss guides Bannholzer and Jaun 1844.

Weyden, Rogier van der (*c.*1400–1464) Flemish painter (*The Last Judgment*).

Weyman, Stanley John (1855–1928) English barrister who became an author of historical novels. He published *The House of the Wolf* in 1890 and followed it up with *A Gentleman of France*, which won him a wide public for the many novels that subsequently appeared.

Weyprecht, Karl (1838–81) German discoverer 1873 of Franz Josef Land in the Arctic.

Whaling Commission, International set up 1946 to regulate the whaling industry and stop overfishing.

Wharton, Henry (1664–95) English scholar.

Wheatstone, Sir Charles (1802–75) English scientist who, in 1836 in conjunction with others, produced the first practical electric telegraph. He also invented the Wheatstone bridge, a device for measuring the electrical resistance of a circuit and in 1867 appeared his mechanical transmitter of telegraphic messaged, which was operated by a paper tape previously machine-punched with groups of holes corresponding respectively to letters, figures or signs and capable of sending words at the rate of hundreds a minute.

Whigs British political group first so named 1679. A group who were agitating for the exclusion of James, Duke of York because of his Catholicism, they stood for the principles of limited monarchy and the importance of parliament. They split in 1791. Many became leading members of the new Liberal Party in the middle of the next century. The word is of Scottish origin and was first applied to the Covenanters of the southwest of Scotland.

Whistler, James Abbott McNeill (1834–1903) American painter. He settled in London in 1859, where he was influenced by the Pre-Raphaelites and by Japanese art. He became famous as a portraitist, with works such as *Arrangement in Grey and Black*, a portrait of his mother. He became involved in a court case with Ruskin, who had sneered at Whistler's work in a review of an 1877 exhibition (Whistler was awarded a penny damages).

Whiston, Joseph (d.1780) London bookseller.

Whitaker's Almanack founded 1868 by the English publisher Joseph Whitaker (1820–95). It has been issued annually since, in practically its original form.

Whitby, Synod of held 664.

White, Gilbert (1720–93) English clergyman and naturalist who became a Fellow of Oriel College, Oxford, in 1744. He declined promotion and in his latter years was curate in his native village, Selborne. His *Natural History and Antiquities of Selborne* (1789) is an English classic.

White, William Hale ['Mark Rutherford'] (1831–1913) English writer (*Catherine Furze* 1893).

White Lotus Day commemorating the death of the founder of the Theosophical Society, Mme Blavatsky (1831–91).

White Russia Soviet republic declared 1919.

White Ship, The sank with Prince William 1120.

Whitefield, George (1714–40) English clergyman. He met the Wesleys at Oxford and joined the Methodists but left *c.*1740 to found the Calvinist Methodists. He was a popular preacher in both England and the USA.

Whitehead, Alfred North (1861–1947) British philosopher.

Whitehead, Robert (1823–1905) English inventor and torpedo manufacturer.

Whiteman, Paul (1891–1967) American jazz conductor.

Whitlam, Edward Gough (1916–) Australian statesman (prime minister 1972–75).

Whitley Councils concerning British labour conditions largely founded 1917 by John Henry Whitley (1866–1935), Speaker of the House of Commons.

Whitman, Walt[er] (1819–92) American poet. His collection, *Leaves of Grass*, was first published in 1855 and the book is regarded as the most important single volume of poems in American literature. His experiences in the American Civil War, during which he nursed wounded Federal soldiers, are reflected in *Drum Taps* (1865).

Whitsunday (Pentecost) seventh Sunday after Easter.

Whittier, John Greenleaf (1807–92) American poet, called the 'laureat of ab olition' because much of his poetry championed the freeing of the slaves. Other works include *The Two Angels* and *At Last*.

Whittingham, Charles (1767–1840) English printer.

Whittington, Dick [Sir Richard Whittington] (*c.*1358–1423) the son of a Gloucestershire knight who by the age of twenty-two had established himself in London as a prosperous merchant. Before he was forty he had been elected Lord Mayor of London twice. He restored St Bartholomew's Hospital as his own expense and lent large sums of money to the three kings in whose reigs he lived, being knighted for his services by Henry V.

Whittle, Sir Frank (1907–) English aeronautical engineer. He designed the first operational jet engine for aircraft and the first successful flight was made in a Gloster in 1941.

Whitworth, Sir Joseph (1803–87) English mechanical engineer and inventor who in 1841 proposed a standardized pitch and diameter for metal screw threads that were adopted as standard in the UK.

Whymper, Edward (1840–1911) English climber (1865) of the Matterhorn.

Whyte-Melville, George John (1821–78) Scottish soldier and writer who served in the Coldstream Guards (1839–49) and joined the Turkish contingent during the Crimean War. He began his literary career in 1850, writing novels, many of which feature hunting, on which he was an authority. His books, which became very popular, include *Digby Grand* (1853), his first novel, and *Holmby House* (1859), an historical novel set at the time of the English Civil War. He died in a hunting accident.

Wickham, Sir Henry (1846–1928) pioneer rubber planter.

Widor, Charles Marie Jean Albert (1844–1937) French organist and composer who taught at the Paris Conservatoire. His works include operas, ten organ 'symphonies' (his famous toccata comes from the fifth), piano concertos and chamber music.

Wien, Wilhelm (1864–1938) German physicist and exponent of the theory of radiation.

Wieniawski, Henri (1835–80) Polish violinist and composer (*Légende*).

Wiglaf king of Mercia (827–840) *see* Appendix.

Wihtred king of Kent (690–725) *see* Appendix.

Wilberforce, Samuel (1805–73) English clergyman and son of William Wilberforce. He was an eloquent preacher and had a reputation as a wit and became bishop of Oxford (1845–69) and Winchester (1869–73).

Wilberforce, William (1759–1833) English philanthropist and politician. His long campaign to end the slave trade in Britain led to its abolition in 1807. He then devoted his efforts to the abolition of the trade altogether.

Wild, Jonathan (*c.*1682–1725) English receiver and informer who was hanged.

Wilde, Oscar [Fingal O'Flahertie Wills] (1854–1900) Irish dramatist, poet, essayist and wit. He first came to notice in the late 1870s, and lived up to the 'Bunthorne' image of an aesthete presented in Gilbert and Sullivan's comic opera *Patience*. After the publication of *Poems* (1881), he made a highly successful tour of America, published his children's stories *The Happy Prince and Other Tales* in 1888, with his only novel *The Picture of Dorian Gray* following in 1890. The first of his great plays, *Lady Windermere's Fan*, appeared in 1892). The succeeding plays, *A Woman of No Importance* (1893), *An Ideal Husband* (1895) and *The Importance of Being Earnest* (1895), established him as the most important dramatist of the age, with their superbly witty dialogue and biting satire. He was jailed for homosexuality (1895–97), and during his imprisonment wrote *De Profundis*. After his release, Wilde fled to France, where he wrote *The Ballad of Reading Gaol* (1898) and died in poverty.

Wilder, Billy [Samuel Wilder] (1906–) Austrian-born American film director and screenwriter. He emigrated to the US in the 1930s, winning Oscars for *The Lost Weekend*, *Sunset Boulevard* and *The Apartment*. Other films include *Double Indemnity*, *The Seven Year Itch* and *Some Like it Hot*.

Wilder, Thornton (1897–1975). American author and playwright (*The Bridge of San Luis Rey* 1927, *Our Town* 1938)

Wilfrid, Saint (634–710) English divine.

Wilhelm, Karl Friedrich (1815–73) German composer (*Die Wacht am Rhein* 1854).

Wilhelmina (1880–1962) queen of the Netherlands (1890–1948), her reign lasting longer than any other European monarch. In 1901 she married Henry, Duke of Mecklenbverg Schwerin, who took the title of Prince Consort. She abdicated in favour of her daughter, Juliana, in 1948.

Wilhelmshaven first German military port, opened officially 17 June 1869.

Wilkes, John (1727–97) English politician.

Wilkins, Sir Hubert (1888–1958) Australian explorer.

Wilkins, Maurice Hugh Frederick (1916–) New Zealand physicist and biologist. His research into DNA structure resulted in Crick and Watson's discovery of the 'double helix' structure of DNA, for which Wilkins, Crick and Watson shared the 1962 Nobel prize for physics.

Willett, William (1856–1915) English builder who for years advocated advancing the clock by one hour in summer, earning him the title of 'Father of Daylight-Saving'. Twice he managed to get a bill introduced in the House of Commons but on both occasions it was thrown out. He did not live quite long enough to see his idea made law by an Act of Parliament that came into operation on 22 May 1916.

William (William the Lion) (1143–1214) king of Scots (1165–1214) *see* Appendix.

William I ('William the Conqueror') (*c.*1027–1087) conqueror of England (1066–87) *see* Appendix.

William II (William Rufus) (*c.*1056–1100), king of England (1087–1100) *see* Appendix.

William III (William of Orange) (1650–1702) king of England, Scotland and Ireland (1689–1702) *see* Appendix.

William IV (1765–1837) king of the United Kingdom of Great Britain and Ireland (1830–37) *see* Appendix.

William I (1797–1888) king of Prussia (1861–88) and emperor of Germany (1871–88). He succeeded his brother and was proclaimed emperor 1871.

William II (1859–1942) emperor of Germany (1888–1918). He abdicated.

William II (William of Orange) (1626-50) stadholder and captain-general of the Netherlands. He married Mary, daughter of Charles I. His posthumous son became William III of Great Britain and Ireland.

William and Mary, College of Williamsburg, Virginia, founded 1693 by the English colonist William Randolf (1650–1711).

William II Land in Antarctica discovered 1903 by the German explorer Erich von Drygalski (1865–1949).

William of Malmesbury (*c.*1095–1143) English historian.

William of Ockham (d.*c.*1349) English philosopher.

William of Wykeham (1324–1404) bishop of Winchester and founder 1379 of New College, Oxford, and 1382 of Winchester College.

William the Lyon (1143–1214) king of Scotland (1165–1214) *see* Appendix.

William the Silent (1533–84) Prince of Orange who freed the Netherlands from the yoke of Spain. He was assassinated.

Williams, Sir George (1821–1905) founder 1844 of the YMCA, London.

Williams, Ralph Vaughan *see* VAUGHAN WILLIAMS, RALPH.

Williams, Tennessee (1911–83) [Thomas Lanier Williams] American playwright whose dominating themes often involve the frustration over the constrictions of some outside element or force on the protagonists' lives, usually involving sex, and set in the surroundings of the Deep South. He first achieved fame with *The Glass Menagerie* (1945). He was awarded the Pulitzer prize for*A Streetcar Named Desire* in 1948, and again in 1955 for *Cat on a Hot Tin Roof.* In addition he wrote poetry, short stories, a novel and the scripts for several films.

Williams, Walter (1843–1960) last surviving veteran (Confederate) of the American Civil War.

Williamson, Malcolm (1931–) Australian-born British composer. Master of the Queen's Music since 1975, his works include several operas and music for film and television.

Willow pattern a very popular pattern for dinner services and china introduced into England from China 1780 by the English potter Thomas Turner (1749–1809). It illustrates an old legend about a girl whose father was a mandarin. Outside her room was a willow tree (the catkins of which represent it in the design), and not far from it a fruit tree. The girl fell in love wither her father's secretary, a poor man, and he sent her a letter floating in a nutshell (typified by the boat) asking her to run away with him. The three people seen crossing the bridge are, first, the girl, carrying a bundle of flax; second, the man, with her box; and last, the pursuing father with a whip. The lovers escaped, were turned into the doves seen at the top of the design, and lived happily ever after.

Wilmot, John *see* Rochester, 2nd Earl of.

Wilson, Sir Angus (1913–91) English writer (*Hemlock and After* 1952).

Wilson, 'Beau' [Edward] (d.1694) London man about town. He was killed.

Wilson, Sir [James] Harold [Baron Wilson of Rievaulx] (1916–95) English Labour statesman. He served in the Second World War as a civil servant and became an MP in 1945. He held various ministerial posts before succeeding Gaitskell as Labour leader in 1963). He was prime minister (1964–70, 1974–76). Originally on the soft left of his party, he became a defender of US policy on Vietnam and imposed a statutory incomes policy to deal with the a balance of payments crisis in the mid–1960s. He unexpectedly resigned in 1976, with Callaghan succeeding him as prime minister.

Wilson, John (1595–1673) English lutenist and composer.

Wilson, John ['Christopher North'] (1785–1854) Scottish writer (*Recreations* 1842).

Wilson, [Thomas] Woodrow (1856–1924) American Democratic statesman. He was 28th president of the USA (1913–21). Re-elected in 1916 on a policy of neutrality, he declared war on Germany following the sinking of US vessels. His 'fourteen points' speech of January 1918 set out US conditions for ending the war, including the disbandment of the German, Austro-Hungarian and Ottoman empires, and imposed the armistice with Germany on Britain and France.

Wilson Cloud Chamber invented 1911 by the Scottish scientist Charles Thomson Rees Wilson (1869–1959), Nobel prize 1927.

Wilson's Fourteen Points announced by President Wilson 8 January, accepted by Germany 27 October 1918.

Wilton carpet introduced into Britain from the USA *c.*1878.

Winchester Cathedral, England, constructed *c.*1079 to 1093.

Windmill first mentioned in Persia in 7th century; first mentioned in England in 1191.

Windsor adopted by the British royal family as the family title 17 July 1917 instead of Saxe-Coburg.

Windsor, Duke of [formerly Edward VIII] (1894–1972) English monarch (1936). Highly popular with the British public for his apparent concern at the lot of the unemployed, he abdicated to marry the American divorcée, Wallis Simpson (1896–1986), after Baldwin had made plain his opposition to the notion of Mrs Simpson becoming queen. He married her in 1937, after which they lived in exile, the Duke becoming governor of the Bahamas during the Second World War.

Windsor Castle English royal residence, the building of which was begun by William I as a round tower on the site of a much more ancient fortress. This was replaced by the present round Tower in Edward III's reign. Henry I made it a palace, and Henry III enlarged and strengthened it. Many additions have been made to it by his successors. It was badly damaged by fire in 1992.

Wingate, Orde Charles (1903–44) British soldier. He was killed in an air crash.

Winslow, Edward (1595–1655) English governor of Plymouth Colony.

Winstanley, Gerrard (*fl* 1648–52) English communist.

Winterhalter, Franz Xaver (1806–73) German-born painter (*The Prince Consort*).

Winthrop, John (1588–1649) English governor of Massachusetts.

Winthrop, John (1606–76) English governor of Connecticut.

Wireless telegraphy *see* RADIOTELEGRAPHY

Wisconsin state of the USA, first settled 1670; created a Territory 1836; admitted to the Union 1848.

Wiseman, Cardinal Nicholas (1802–65) first archbishop of Westminster.

Witchcraft, last trial for (of Jane Wenham d.1730) in England 1712; last in Scotland 1722; statutes against witchcraft repealed 1736.

Witan *or* **witenagemot** ('the meeting of wise men') the great national council in Saxon times. It was composed of the chief clery and nobility, who were in no real sense representative. It elected the king out of the members of the royal family and helped him to govern both at home and in his foreign relations. Each kingdom under the Heptarchy had its own witan, but on the unionof the whole of England under Egbert in 827 the separate witans were merged in a single central witan.

Wittelsbach dynasty ruled Bavaria 1180–1918.

Wittgenstein, Ludwig [Josef Johann] (1889–1951) Austrian-born British philosopher. He studied under Bertrand Russell (1912–13) who observed that he was soon learning as much from his pupil as he had taught him. On the outbreak of the First World War, he returned to Austria to serve as an artillery officer and was captured. While a POW, he wrote and sent to Russell his *Tractatus Logico-Philosophicus*, a series of aphoristic propositions on the boundaries of language and philosophy in relation to the world. During the 1920s, influenced by Tolstoy's asceticism, he gave his considerable inherited wealth away and worked as a schoolteacher. His posthumous *Philosophical Investigations* retracts the confident assertions of the *Tractatus*, focusing instead on the concept of language as a series of games in which 'The meaning of the word is its use in language.'

Wodehouse, Sir P[elham] G[renville] (1881–1975) English-born novelist and short-story writer. His most famous literary creations are Bertie Wooster and his butler Jeeves, e.g. *Right Ho, Jeeves* (1934). He also wrote many lyrics for musicals in collaboration with composers such as Jerome kern and Irving Berlin. Internted by the Nazis during the Second World War, he foolishly made some innocuous broadcasts from Germany, which led to his being branded a traitor. Both Evelyn Waugh and George Orwell wrote spirited defences of him, effectly disproving the treason charges.

Woffington, Peg (*c.*1714–1760) Irish-born actress.

Wolcot, John ['Peter Pindar'] (1738–1819) English writer (*The Lousiad* 1785).

Wolf, Hugo (1860–1903) Austrian composer (*Der Corregidor* 1896).

Wolfe, James (1727–59) English general. He had his first experience of warfare in the Low Countries, where he took part in the battles of Dettingen and Fontenoy. After service in America against the French, he was put in command of an expedition against Quebec, the French stronghold, in 1759. He scaled the Heights of Abraham with his troops and was morally wounded in the battle, which he won the next day. His opponent, Montcalm, also died in the battle.

Wolf-Ferrari, Ermanno (1876–1948) Italian-born composer (*I Gioielli della Madonna* 1911).

'Wolf of Badenoch, The' [Alexander Stewart, Earl of Buchan and Lord of Badenoch] (*c.*1343–*c.*1405). Son of King Robert II and overlord of Badenoch. His continued attacks on Moray earned him his nickname.

Wollstonecraft, Mary (1759–97) Anglo-Irish writer and social reformer (*Vindication of the Rights of Women* 1792) advocating sexual equality and equal rights to education for women. In 1797 she married William Godwin and gave birth to a daughter, Mary (Mary Wollstonecraft Shelley), but died soon afterwards.

Wolsey, Cardinal Thomas (*c.*1475–1530) English cleric and statesman. He was made a privy councillor (1511) by Henry VIII, who then appointed him archbishop of York (1514–30) and lord chancellor (1515–29). Instructed by the king in 1527 to negotiate with the pope the annulment of the king's marriage, his failure after two years of pressurizing Rome led to his dismissal as lord chancellor (being succeeded by Sir Thomas More). He died on the journey from York to London to face charges of treason.

Women's Legion voluntary British wartime organization of drivers founded by the Marchioness of Londonderry (1879–1959).

Women's suffrage New Zealand 1893, Australia 1902, Finland 1907, Norway 1913, Britain 1918 (when women of thirty and over were enfranchised) and 1928 (when women gained equality with men), USA 1920, France 1944, Italy 1945.

Wood, Anthony à (1632–95) English antiquary.

Wood, Mrs Henry [Ellen Price] (1814–87) English novelist who is best known for her melodrama, *East Lynne* (1861) which had great success. She also founded the *Argosy*, a monthly magazine, in 1867.

Wood, Sir Henry [Joseph] (1869–1940) English conductor. He founded the London Promenade Concerts (the 'Proms') in 1895, which he conducted until his death.

Woods and Forests, His Majesty's *see* Civil List.

Woolf, [Adeline] Virginia (1882–1941) English novelist and critic. Her novels, including *To the Lighthouse*, *Mrs Dalloway* and *Orlando*, are written in a fluid, poetic style using stream of consciousness narration and are recognized as being among the greatest and most innovative of the 20th century. She was also a very fine literary critic and essayist. She committed suicide by drowning herself.

Woolsack a large square bag of wool covered with red cloth on which the Lord Chancellor sits in the House of Lords. It was first used in the time of Edward III to remind the peers of the great importance of the trade to England and the consequent necessity of keeping friendly with Flanders.

Worcester, Battle of between Parliamentary and Royalist forces 3 September 1651.

Worcester Cathedral built 1084–89; burnt 1202; restored 1218.

Worcester porcelain manufactured since 1781).

Worde, Wynkyn de (d.*c*.1534) Alsace-born pioneer printer in England.

Wordsworth, Dorothy English writer (1771–1855) sister and companion of William Wordsworth. Her own work, such as her *Journals* of their tours around Britain, shows a grasp of poetic imagery and acute observation that is said to have been of great influence to both her brother and his friend Coleridge. She had a nervous breakdown in 1829 from which she never fully recovered.

Wordsworth, William (1770–1850) English poet. The main figure of the English Romantic movement, his work successfully blended the personal with the natural and social worlds into a coherent whole. He and Coleridge wrote *Lyrical Ballads* (1798) together, which began with Coleridge's *Ancient Mariner* and ended with *Tintern Abbey*, heralding a new era of poetry, the Romantic Revival, with nature as prime inspiration for the poet. He became poet laureate in 1843.

Work, Henry Clay (1832–84) American composer (*Marching Through Georgia*).

Worker-priest movement French, instituted 1943, banned by the Vatican 1959.

World Association of Girl Guides and Girl Scouts formed in London 1928.

World Bank [International Bank for Reconstruction and Development] to encourage investment in the Third World, established 1945.

World Council of Churches constituted 23 August 1948.

World Cup, soccer 1930 Montevideo, Uruguay (winner Uruguay); 1934 Rome, Italy (winner Italy); 1938 Paris, France (winner Italy); 1950 Rio de Janeiro, Brazil (winner Uruguay); 1954 Berne, Switzerland (winner W. Germany); 1958 Stockholm, Sweden (winner Brazil); 1962 Santiago, Chile (winner Brazil); 1966 London, England (winner England); 1970 Mexico City, Mexico (winner Brazil); 1974 Munich, W. Germany (winner W. Germany); 1978 Buenos Aires, Argentina (winner Argentina); 1982 Madrid, Spain (winner Italy); 1986 Mexico City, Mexico (winner Argentina); 1990 Rome, Italy (winner W. Germany); 1994 USA (winner Brazil).

World Health Organization constitution drawn up 1946; confirmed as a specialized agency of the United Nations 1948.

World War I 28 July 1914 to 11 November 1918.

World War II 1 September 1939 to 15 August 1945.

Worms, Diet of an assembly of the princes of the Holy Roman empire and Emperor Charles V called in 1521 at Worms in southwest Germany to condemn Martin Luther.

Worth, Charles Frederick (1825–95) English-born couturier who founded *haute couture*. He trained as a tailor in London before going to Paris in 1846. In 1858 he set up in business with a Swedish partner and, thanks to the patronage of the Empress Eugénie, soon established a reputation as.the leading designer in Europe. After the Franco-Prussian War of 1870–71, his partner retired, leaving him to carry on the business with his sons.

Wotton, Sir Henry (1568–1639) English diplomat and writer.

Wren, Sir Christopher (1632–1723) English architect who was educated at Oxford and became a Fellow of All Souls in 1653. He became professor of astronomy at Gresham College in 1657 and in 1660 Savilian professor of astronomy at Oxford. One of the founders of the Royal Society he was commissioned to rebuild St Paul's Cathedral after the Great Fire of London in 1666. It was begun in 1675, and his son laid the last stone in 1705. He also designed the modern part of Hampton Court Palace, the hospitals of Chelsea and Greenwich and many churches in the City of London.

Wright, Frank Lloyd (1869–1959) American architect who regarded as one of the greatest modern architects. He sought to develop an architecture with traditionally American 'organic' values of harmony between a building and its environment. His buildings include the Guggenheim Museum of Art in New York (1959).

Wright, Joseph (Joseph Wright of Derby) (1734–97) English painter whose works incude genre painting, portraits and landscapes, the outstanding features of which are his extraordinary lighting effects.

Wright, Orville (1871–1948) and **Wright, Wilbur** (1867–1912) American aviators and brothers. Cycle manufacturers, they designed and built the first heavier-than-air flying machine. They flew their first plane 17 December 1903.

Wuffa (d.*c*.578) king of East Anglia (571–*c*.578) *see* Appendix.

Wulfhere (d.675) king of Mercia (657–675) *see* Appendix.

Wulfstan (d.1023) archbishop of York.

Wulfstan, Saint (*c*.1012–1095) bishop of Worcester.

Wyatt, Sir Thomas (the Elder) (1503–42) English lyric poet.

Wyatt, Sir Thomas (the Younger) (*c*.1521–1554) English rebel, son of the poet Sir Thomas Wyatt. He was executed.

Wycherley, William (*c*.1641–1715) English dramatist noted for the witty dialogue of his popular Restoration comedies (*The Country Wife* 1675).

Wyclif *or* **Wycliffe, John** (*c*.1320–1384) English religious reformer. His version of the Bible was the first complete translation into English from Latin and (the early version) was completed *c*.1382–84; the later version completed *c*.1388. This was because he believed it was the right of everyone to be able to read the Bible. He attacked the abuses carried out by the Church and its very constitution. His supporters came to be known as Lollards.

Wykeham, William of (1324–1404) bishop of Winchester and founder (1379) of New College, Oxford, and 1382 of Winchester College .

Wyman, Bill *see* JAGGER, MICK.

Wynkyn de Worde (d.*c*.1534) Alsace-born pioneer printer in England.

Wyoming state of the USA, first settled 1834; Territory 1868; admitted to the Union 1890.

XYZ

Xavier, Saint Francis *see* FRANCIS XAVIER, SAINT.

Xenon a gaseous element present in extremely small quantities in the atmosphere, discovered 1898 by Ramsay and Travers.

Xenophon (*c.*430–355 BC) Greek historian and essayist who was one of the early disciples of Socrates. In 401 BC he joined (not in a military capacity) the Greek mercenaries under Cyrus the Younger in his rebellion against Artaxerxes II, and after the Cyrus's death at Cunaxa, the chief Greek officers having been assassinated, he led the famous retreat of the 10,000 through mountainous regions for five months until they reached Trebizon. This expedition forms the subject of his best-known work, the *Anabasis*. He also wrote the *Hellenica*, an account of the later stages of the war between Athens and Sparta, and *Memorabilia*, a defence of Socrates.

Xerography basic principles discovered in 1938 by the American inventor Chester Floyd Carlson (1906–68).

Xerxes I (c519–465 BC) king of Persia (485–465 BC) who succeeded his father, Darius I. In his invasion of Greece, he crossed the Hellespont on a bridge of boats a mile long, and when the bridge was destroyed by a storm, he ordered 200 lashes to be given to the sea as a punishment. His huge army took a week to cross the bridge and marched on unopposed as far as Thermopylae, where Leonidas and a small force kept it in check long enough to enable the Athenians to emark in their fleet safely and make all preparations for the battle of Salamis. His 1200 warships could not manoeuvre in the narrow straits, and the Athenians inflicted an overwhelming defeat that saved Europe from Persian conquest. The remnant of the army was annihilated in the following year at Plataea, and Xerxes himself was murdered.

Xiamen *see* AMOY.

X-rays discovered 1895 by the German scientist Wilhelm von Rontgen (1845–1923).

XYZ Mission to arrange Franco-American treaty 1798.

Yale, Elihu (1648–1721) American administrator who was brought to Enland when he was four years old and afterwards rose in the service of the East India Company to be governor of Madras. He bequeathed a large amount of money to Yale College.

Yale locks invented by the American inventor Linus Yale (1821–68).

Yale University in Connecticut founded as the Collegiate School of Connecticut in 1701; first called Yale College 1716; moved to New Haven 1717; chartered 1745; Yale University since 1887. It was named after Elihu Yale.

Yalta, Conference of Second World War leaders' conference, February 1945.

Yamagata, Prince Aritono (1838–1922) Japanese soldier and statesman who organized the Japanese army on modern lines during the last two decades of the 19th century and so contributed greatly to the defeat of Russia by Japan i the war of 1904–1905, during which he commanded the First Army Corps. In 1889 and 1898 he was prime minister of Japan and in 1907 was honoured with the title of prince.

Yamamoto, Gombei (1852–1933) Japanese prime minister (1913–14, 1923).

Yankee a word meaning an American the commonly accepted derivation of which is that it represents 'English' as pronounced by American Indians when they first came into contact with the early English settlers. It was afterwards used by Americans of the inhabitants of the New England states, and later, during the Civil War, was applied to the northerners by the southerners. Outside the USA it stands for Americans generally.

Yankee Doodle a popular American song and tune that is supposed to have been of Dutch origin and introduced into America by British soldiers in the middle of the 18th century. During the American War of Independence it was adopted by the colonists as one of their favourite songs. The words are believed to have been written by an English army surgeon.

Yard an imperial standard length established in Britain 1844 and defined 1963 as exactly 0.9144 metre.

Yarrow, Sir Albert Fernandez (1842–1932) English engineer and inventor and founder in 1866 of the Yarrow & Co. shipbuilding firm in London. In 1906 the business was moved to the Clyde, where it built many warships, merchant ships and river vessels. Yarrow made a large fortune but was a generous benefactor, gifting money to the National Physical Laboratory and the Royal Society to fund scientific research.

Yeardley, Sir George (*c.*1580–1627) governor of Virginia.

Year of confusion first of the Julian Calendar and including 80 extra days, 46 BC.

Yeats, W[illiam] B[utler] (1865–1939) Anglo-Irish poet and dramatist. His early works reflect his concern with Irish myth and legend. His play, *Cathleen ni Houlihan* (1902) demonstrated his support of Irish patriotism, and he later feared it had sent men to their deaths against the British. Following Irish independence, he became a member of the Irish senate. He was awarded the Nobel prize for literature in 1923. His brother, Jack Yeats [John Butler Yeats] (1870–1957) was an illustrator, particularly of comic strips and children's books, before turning to painting and writing.

Yellow Book, The English quarterly literary journal in which appeared many outstanding contributions by late 19th-century writers and artists, published 1894 to 1897.

Yellow fever an infectious tropical fever caused by virus transmitted by certain mosquitoes, the cause beig discovered 1900 by the American bacteriologist Walter Reed (1851–1902).

Yellowstone National Park a national park in Wyoming, USA, the first area in the USA to be designated a national park, 1872. It is famous for its geysers and its scenery.

Yeltsin, Boris Nikolayevich (1931–) Russian politician. A member of the Communist party since 1960, he was brought into the Soviet Politburo by Gorbachev in 1985, in which year he was appointed head of the Moscow party organization. His subsequent assault on the ingrained inefficiency and corruption of that body resulted in his demotion from the post and from the Politburo. In the free elections of 1989, he was elected to the Congress of People's Deputies, and won an overwhelming majority of votes in the Russian presidential election of 1990. He was re-elected president 1996.

Yeomen of the Guard a royal bodybuard for the English monarch, founded 1485 by Henry VII, the members of which wear Tudor uniform. Its duties are now purely ceremonial. The 'Beefeaters' of the Tower of London are not Yeomen of the Guard, but they are allowed to wear the uniform without its shoulder belt.

Yevtushenko, Yevgeny Aleksandrovich (1933–) Russian poet (*Babi Yar* 1961).

Yiddish language earliest known document dated 1396.

YMCA [Young Men's Christian Association] an organization for the physical, social and spiritual development of boys and young men, which was founded in London 1844 by Sir George Williams (1821–1905).

Yokohama Japanese port first opened to foreign trade through the intervention of Commodore Perry, 1859.

Yom Kippur War *see* ARAB-ISRAELI WARS.

Yonge, Charlotte Mary (1823–1901) English writer who wrote many novels, the best known of which is *The Heir of Redclyffe* (1853), and also several works on historical subjects.

York Minster the cathedral at York, the present structure of which was erected mainly 1291–1345, with important additions in the middle of the 15th century. It was damaged by fire in 1823, 1840, 1984.

Yorktown, Virginia, Siege of in which Cornwallis surrendered to Washington 1781.

Yosemite National Park a national park in central California, USA, designated 1890. It contains the Yosemite Valley, which is six miles long and from half a mile to one and a half miles wide, with granite crags rising on each side from 3000 to 6000 feet, and the Yosemite Falls, a waterfall with a direct plunge of 1500 feet, a broken cascade of 626 feet and another direct plunge of 400 feet.

Youmans, Vincent (1898–1946) American composer (*No, No Nanette* 1924).

Young, Arthur (1741–1820) English agricultural administrator and writer.

Young, Brigham (1801–77) American Mormon leader who was a painter and glazier by trade. He joined the Mormons in 1832 and was ordained one of the twelve 'apostles' to preach its doctrines in the eastern USA. After the lynching of Joseph Smith, the founder of Mormonism, by a mob in 1844, Young was elected president. He led the migration of the Mormons from their city of Nauvoo in Illinois to Salt Lake, Utah, where he founded Salt Lake City in 1847. In 1849 he was appointed governor of Utah Territory, but his advocacy of polygamy brought him into collision with the government, who sent large armed forces against the 'saints'. After the American Civil War he was arrested for polygamy. At his death he left a large fortune to his many wives.

Young, Edward (1683–1765) English poet and dramatist, whose best-known work is *Night Thoughts* (1742), which was written following the death of his wife.

Young, James 'Paraffin' (1811–83) Scottish chemist and founder 1856 of the paraffin industry.

Young, Thomas (1773–1829) English scientist and Egyptologist who contributed to the establishment of the wave theory of light and helped to decipher the Rosetta Stone.

Young Italy nationalist group founded 1831 by Giuseppe Mazzini (1805–72).

Young Men's Christian Association *see* YMCA.

Young Women's Christian Association *see* YWCA.

Youth Hostels Association founded 1930.

Ypres a city in Belgium which was one of the chief centres of British resistance during the First World War. It lay on the direct route to Calais and other Channel ports and was fiercely bombarded and reduced to ruins early in the war. Three battles were fought near the city. It was rebuilt after the war and has a memorial to the soldiers who died.

Ypres, Battle of battles of the First World War: (1) 19 October–22 November 1914, in which a German offensive to break through the British lines was defeated. (2) 22 April–25 May 1915, when again a German offensive was defeated. It was during this battle that gas was first used in an attack by the Germans. (3) 31 July–10 November, a series of battles in which the British were the attackers. They succeded in enlarging the Ypres salient, which projected into the country held by the Germans, and was commanded by higher ground.

Ysaÿe, Eugène (1858–1931) Belgian violinist and conductor.

Ytterbium chemical element discovered 1878 by the French scientist Jean Charles Gallisard de Marignac (1817–94).

Yttrium chemical element discovered by the scientist Johan Gadolin 1794.

Yüan dynasty in China 1280–1368.

Yugoslavia a kingdom formed out of the former kingdoms of Serbia and Montenegro, and parts of Austria and Hungary, which was proclaimed 1 December 1918; constitution established 1921; monarchist dictatorship 1929–41; Communist regime 1945–80; in 1991 the constituent republics of Slovenia, Croatia and Bosnia Hezogovnia declared independence and fierce fighting errupted between Serbs, Croatians and Muslims.

Yukon a Territory in northwest Canada in which the river of the same name rises. Its capital is Dawson, near which are the Klondyke goldfields, the discovery of which in 1897 led to a goldrush.

Yule, Sir Henry (1820–89) Scottish administrator in India.

Yuletide the Christmas festival.

Yung Chêng period in China 1723–35.

Yung Lo period in China 1403–24.

YWCA [Young Women's Christian Association] the counterpart of the YMCA, an organization for the physical, social and spiritual development of young women, which was founded in London 1877 by Lady Kinnaird (1816–88).

Zachary, Saint pope (741–752).

Zagreb University in Croatia founded 1669.

Zaharoff, Sir Basil (1849–1936) Turkish-born cosmopolitan financier and armaments manufacturer of Greek descent and British nationality.

Zaïre a country in west central Africa: established 1885 as the Belgian colony of Congo Free State; Belgian Congo 1908; independent 1960.

Zama, Battle of the final battle of the Second Punic War 202 BC, when Hannibal was completely defeated near Carthage by Publius Cornelius Scipio, who had invaded Africa, obliging Hannibal to evacuate Italy in order to hurry home for the defence of Carthage.

Zambia a country in central Africa: administered by the British South Africa Company by 1900; unified as Northern Rhodesia 1911; made a British protectorate 1924; part of Federation of Rhodesia and Nyasaland 1953–63; gained independence within the Commonwealth 1964.

Zamenhof, Lazarus Ludovic (1859–1917) Polish inventor (1887) of Esperanto.

Zandonai, Riccardo (1883–1944) Italian composer (*Francesca da Rimini* 1914).

Zangwill, Israel (1864–1926) English Jewish novelist. He was educated and taught at the Jews' Free School in London before turning to writing. One of his most popular novels was *Children of the Ghetto* (1892).

Zanzibar an island lying off the east coast of Africa, in the Indian Ocean: first visited by the English 1591; united with Pemba under one sovereign, Seyyid Said bin Sultan 1822; placed under British protection by the sultan and formally declared a British protectorate 1890; constitutional government established 1891; slavery abolished by the sultan 1897; new constitution granted 1956; became independent within the Commonwealth 1963, and a republic 1964; joined Tanganyika to form United Republic of Tanzania 1964.

Zapata, Emiliano (*c.*1879–1919) Mexican revolutionary leader. He was murdered.

Zapf, Hermann (1910–) German type designer.

Zarubin, Georgi (1900–1958) Soviet Deputy Foreign Minister.

Zedekiah (618–*c.*587 BC) the last king of Judah (597–587 BC). When Jerusalem was taken by Nebuchadnezzar 597 BC he took the king, Jehoiachin, to Babylon and made Zedekiah a vassal king. Zedekiah rebelled, however, and Nebuchadnezzar's army once again besieged Jerusalem, finally taking the city in 587 BC. Zedekiah fled but was captured at Jericho and taken to Babylon. It was the end of the royal house of David in Jerusalem and the kingdom of Judah.

Zeebrugge a Belgian seaport on the seaward end of a ship canal running to Bruges. It was an German important submarine base in the First World War and scene of the Zeebrugge Raid. In 1987, the car ferry *Herald of Free Enterprise* capsized off Zeebruge with the loss of 188 lives.

Zeebrugge Raid a raid of the First World War, 22 April 1918, when the British Navy launched a night attack against the mole protecting the harbour and under cover of it scuttled a ship in the entrance to the canal with the object of closing it to submarines, which was only partially successful.

Zeeman, Pieter (1865–1943) Dutch scientist (discovered the Zeeman effect 1896). He was awarded the 1902 Nobel prize.

Zeffirelli, Franco (1923–) Italian stage and film director and designer. His films include *Romeo and Juliet* and the TV film *Jesus of Nazareth*.

Zeiss, Carl (1816–88) German optical instrument manufacturer and founder of the firm of that name.

Zela, Battle of (1) a battle of the Third Mithridatic War between Rome and Mithradates VI, king of Pontus, 67 BC. It was a Pontic victory but Mithridates was wounded. (2) a battle of the Wars of the First Triumvirate 47 BC, when Caesar defeated Pharnaces, king of Pontus.

Zemstvos Russian provincial assemblies formed 13 January 1864.

Zen Buddhism founded *c.*520 when Bodhi-Dharma (480–528) went to China.

Zeno (d.491) Roman emperor (474–491) at Constantinople who succeeded his son, Leo II, grandson of Leo I, who died as a child. Theodoric gave him permission to dethrone Odoacer, which led to the establishment of the Ostrogothic kingdom in Italy.

Zenobia (d.*c.*285) queen of Palmyra (266–273). She was the wife of Odenathus, whom Gallienus appointed as governor of the East. When her husband was murdered in 266, she conquered Egypt and called herself Queen of the East. Her ambition roused Aurelian against her, and after a stubborn resistance she was defeated by him in 273 and taken to Rome where she spent the rest of her life.

Zeno of Citium (340–270 BC) Greek philosopher and founder of the Stoic school, who was born in Cyprus and settled and taught in Athens, where he set up his school in the *Stoa Poikile* ('painted porch'). His writings are all lost, but in his ehtical system, the nature of moral obligation was recognized as unconditional, virtue as the onlyd good, and vice, not pain, as the only evil. Developed by his successors, Stoicism became the creed of the noblest of the Romans until Christianity was generally accepted. He is said to have committed suicide.

Zeno of Elea (*c.*490–*c.*430 BC) Greek philosopher who taught at Athens. Pericles is said to have been one of his pupils. He was a favourite disciple of Parmenides and is introduced as discussing philosophy with his master in Plato's dialogue of that name.

Zeppelins invented 1900 by the German Count Ferdinand von Zeppelin (1838–1917). Zeppelin L21 destroyed at Cuffley, 3 September 1916; L33 in Essex, 24 September 1916.

Zero, absolute approximately achieved 1921 at Leyden University's physical laboratory.

Zetkin, Klara (1857–1933) German communist leader.

Zeuss, Johann Kaspar (1806–56) German pioneer (1853) in the study of Celtic philology.

Zeuxis (*fl* late 5th century BC) Greek painter who lived in Ephesus. He belonged to the Asiatic school, of which the distinguishing points were accurate imitation and the representation of physical beauty. None of his works survive.

Zhivkov, Todor (1911–) Bulgarian Communist statesman. Prime minister (1962–71) and president (1971–89). Under his rule, Bulgaria became the most servile of the satellites of the Soviet Union.

Zhou En Lai *see* CHOU EN-LAI.

Zhukov, Georgi Konstantinovich (1896–1974) Soviet field marshal.

Zhukovskii, Vassily Andreievich (1783–1852) Russian poet.

Ziegfeld, Florenz (1869–1932) American producer of the Ziegfeld Follies (from 1917).

Zimbabwe formerly Southern Rhodesia (until 1964) and Rhodesia (1964–79), British colony founded by British South Africa Company 1890; joined with former Northern Rhodesia and former Nyasaland to form Federation of Rhodesia and Nyasaland 1953–63; Ian Smith prime minister 1964–79 (declared unilateral independence from Britain 1965); proclaimed a republic 1970; gained independence 1980.

Zimbabwe Ruins the stone ruins of a settlement in the Mashonaland region of Zimbabwe, discovered 1868 by Adam Renders, the chief of a series of ruins along the Sabi river, which may have been a depot for troops employed to protect gold miners, of whose work there are traces. They were explored in 1891 by Theodore Bent, who considered that they belonged to a very early Arabian settlement.

Zimbalist, Efrem (1889–1985) Russian-born violinist.

Zimisces, John (*c.*925–976) Byzantine emperor (969–976).

Zincography illustration process invented in Paris 1850.

Zingarelli, Nicola Antonio (1752–1837) Italian composer (*Giulietta e Romeo* 1769).

Zinoviev Letter forged instructions for Communist uprising in Great Britain, published October 1924. Supposedly written by Grigori Zinoviev, Russian revolutionary leader (1883–1936) who was shot.

Zinzendorf, Nikolaus Ludwig (1700–1760) German leader of the Moravian Community.

Zionist Congress, first world, held at Basle 1897.

Zionist Movement founded 1897 by Theodor Herzl (1860–1904).

Zirconia a mineral discovered 1789 by the German chemist Martin Heinrich Klaproth (1743–1817).

Zirconium a chemical element isolated 1824 by the Swedish chemist Baron Berzelius (1779–1848).

Zizka, John (*c.*1370–1424) Hussite leader.

Zoë (d.1050) Byzantine empress (1028–50).

Zoega, Georg (1755–1809) Danish-born archaeologist.

Zoffany, John (1725–1810) English-born painter.

Zog [Ahmed Beg Zogu] (1895–1961) king of Albania (1928–39).

Zola, Emile (1840–1902) French novelist. Regarded as the most prominent exponent of Naturalism in the novel, and a highly able propagandist for socialism and for social justice. His novels include *Thérèse Raquin* (1866). He championed the cause of Alfred Dreyfus, publishing the pamphlet, *J'accuse* (1898), a step that compelled him to flee to England for a time but resulted in Dreyfus's final acquittal and release at a retrial. Zola was accidentally suffocated by gas while asleep.

Zollverein German Customs Union formed 1834.

Zomba city in southern Malawi founded *c.*1880; capital of Malawi since 1971.

Zoological Society founded in London 1826 by Sir Stamford Raffles (1781–1826).

Zorn, Anders (1860–1920) Swedish artist.

Zoroaster (Zarathustra) (*c.*628–*c.*551 BC) Persian religious leader and founder of Zoroastrianism. The fundamental idea of his doctrine was the existence from the first of a spirit of good, Ormuzd (or Ahura Mazda), and a spirit of evil, Ahriman (or Angro Mainyush), represented by darkness. These two are in perpetual conflict over the soul of man, but Ormuzd will ultimately triumph.

Zorrilla, José (1817–93) Spanish poet (*Don Juan Tenorio* 1844).

Zosimus (*fl* mid 5th century) Greek historian active.

Zosimus, Saint pope (417–418).

Zsigmondy, Richard (1865–1929) Austrian pioneer in the development of colloid chemistry.

Zucchi, Antonio Pietro (1726–95) Italian painter.

Zuckerman, Sir Solly (1904–84) South African-born anatomist.

Zuckmayer, Carl (1896–1977) German playwright (*Der Hauptmann von Köpenick* 1931).

Zuider Zee a former inlet of the North Sea in the north coast of the Netherlands: reclamation of inundated land planned 1891 by the Dutch engineer and statesman Dr Cornelius Lely (1854–1929); inaugurated 1 May 1919; last gap closed 28 May 1932; repaired 1945.

Zukor, Adolph (1873–1976) Hungarian-born film industry pioneer.

Zuloaga, Ignacio (1870–1945) Spanish painter.

Zululand a former kingdom of the Zulus in northeastern Natal, South African. It was taken by the British 1879 after the First Zulu War and the defeat of Cetewayo, but the subsequent reorganization did not work successfully, and in 1882 Ceteway was restored. Annexed to Natal 30 December 1897.

Zulu War, First 1879.

Zulu War, Second 1906.

Zumalacárregui, Tomás (1788–1835) Spanish general.

Zurbaran, Francisco de (1598–1662) Spanish painter (*Apotheosis of St Thomas Aquinas*).

Zutphen, Battle of an attack by the British on a Spanish convoy in the Netherlands, September 1586, in which the poet Sir Philip Sidney was killed.

Zweig, Arnold (1887–1968) German novelist (*Sergeant Grischa* 1927).

Zweig, Stefan (1881–1942) Austrian writer. He committed suicide.

Zwingli, Huldreich *or* **Ulrich** (1484–1531) Swiss religious reformer who was originally a priest. In 1518 he became preacher at Zurich Cathedral and eventually made it Protestant. After Luther and Calvin, he became the most influential of the Protestant reformers. He was killed in a engagement near Zurich when cantons that had remained Roman Catholic waged war on him.

Zymose yeast-cell fermenting agent discovered 1903 by the German scientist Eduard Buchner (1860–1917).

Chronology of World History

Chronology of World History

4000
- Meslim, king of Kish, becomes overlord of Sumeria (southern Babylonia).

3000
- Early Minoan Age of Cretan civilization begins.
- Ur-Nina founds a dynasty at Lagash in Sumeria; builds temples and canals.
- Fourth Egyptian Dynasty founded by Snefru; later kings of the dynasty, Cheops, Chephren and Mycerinus, build the Great Pyramids at Gizeh.

2900
- Eannatum becomes king of Lagash: conquers Umma, Kish Opis, Erech, Ur; repels the Elamites.

2850
- Fuhi becomes first emperor of China.

2800

Urukagina becomes king of Lagash: a great reformer; Lagash defeated and destroyed by Lugai-Zaggisi, ruler of Umma and king of Erech, who becomes overlord of all Sumeria.

2650

Sargon founds Akkadian Empire in Mesopotamia.

2600

Naram-Sin, son of Sargon.

2500-2000

Legendary period of the second city on the site of Troy; destroyed by fire.

580

In Egypt the pharoahs begin to build pyramids

400

Dynasty of Ur in Sumeria established by Ur-Engur, he reigns for eighteen years; Dungi, his son, who reigns for fifty-eight years, extends his empire over the whole of Babylonia and also conquers Elam.

300

Asshur, the oldest Assyrian city, founded not later than this date.

Dynasty of Isin in Sumeria, established by Ishbi-Ura; overthrow of Ur due to Elamite invasion.

2290
- Sixth Dynasty in Egypt ends the ancient empire: Pepy I conquers Palestine; Pepy II reigns ninety-four years, longest reign in the world's history.

2144
- Gudea ruler of Lagash for twenty years.

2100
- First Dynasty of Babylon established, by Sumu-Abu, after fall of Isin; the Sumerians finally give way to the Semites.

2000
- Twelfth Egyptian Dynasty begins, with Thebes as capital.

2000-1850
- Middle Minoan Age in Crete.

2000-1800
- Twelfth Egyptian Dynasty: Amenemhet I, Usertesen I, Amenemhet II, Usertesen II, Usertesen III (conquered Nubia), Amenemhet III, Amenemhet IV and Queen Sebknofru all great builders.

2000-1700
- Proto-Mycenean civilization of the island of Thera; destroyed by volcanic upheaval.

2000
- Hammurabi, the greatest king of the first Babylon dynasty: noted for agricultural improvements and law reform.

1860
- Construction of Stonehenge begins in Britain.

1840
- Ismi-Dagan, oldest known ruler of Assyria.

1800-1100
- Late Minoan Age in Crete.

1800-1200
- Babylon ruled by Kassite invaders.

1800
- Hyksos rule in Egypt begins.

1700-1000
- Mycenaen civilization in Greece.

1700
- Assyria becomes independent of Babylonia around this time.

1600
- Amasis I finally drives the Hyksos from Egypt and founds the New Empire; conquers Palestine and Phoenicia.

1600-1100
- The Sixth city on the site of Troy (Homeric Troy).

1560
- Thutmosis I of Egypt completes conquest of Nubia.

***c*.1523-*c*.1027**
- Shang dynasty, CHina.

1515
- Thutmosis III of Egypt: conquers Syria and penetrates to Assyria.

1450
- Amenophis III of Egypt: noted temple-builder.

1415
- Amenophis IV of Egypt: replaces the old religion by sun worship.

1410
- Conflict between Assyria and Babylonia begins.

1355
- Rameses I begins Nineteenth Dynasty in Egypt.

1350
- Sethos I of Egypt: wars against Libyans, Syrians and Hittites.

1330
- Shalmaneser I, king of Assyria.

1300-1000
- Hellenic conquests in Greece.

1290
- Tukultininib, king of Assyria: conquers Babylon-ia.
- Raneses II succeeds his father Seti

1285
- Rameses II, the most celebrated king of Egypt; wages long war with the Hittites, retains Palestine, Battle of Kadesh; greatest builder among the Egyptian kings.

1273
- Meneptah, king of Egypt: wars against Libyans and Asiatic pirates.

1200
- Rameses III of Twentieth Egyptian Dynasty, king till 1166.

1120
- Tiglathpileser I, king of Assyria.

1100
- Herihor, high priest of Ammon: seizes the throne of Egypt; deposed by a Tanite Dynasty.

***c*.1027-256**
- Chou dynasty, China.

1000
- David becomes king of Israel.
- Iron Age begins.
- *Rigveda* (India).

970
- Solomon becomes king of Israel.

950
- Sheshonk, Libyan king of Egypt: conquers Palestine.

930
- Hebrew kingdom is divided on death of Solomon: Jeroboam I becomes king of Israel in the north; Rehoboam becomes king of Judah in the south.

884
- Asurnasirpal III becomes king of Assyria.

869
- Ahab becomes king of Israel.

860
- Shalmaneser II, king of Assyria: subdues Babylon and Syria.

858
- Shalmaneser III, son of Ashirnaspiral II, king of Assyria (until 824)

854
- Battle of Karkar: Benhadad of Damascus and Ahab of Israel defeated by Shalmaneser III.

850
- Carthage founded as a Phoenician colony (traditional).

842
- Jehu becomes king of Israel.

838
- Shalmaneser III makes futher attempt to conquer Assyria.

824
- Death of Shalmaneser III, his son Shamshi-Adad succeeds.

811
- Death of Shamshi-Adad. Babylon is defeated and power is restored to Assyria. His son Adad-Nirari III too young to rule and power is with Sammuramat, his mother.

806
- Adad-Nirari III, king of Assyria; invades Damascus

797
- Jehoash, king of Israel, successfully repels Syrian attacks.

782
- Jeroboam II, king of Israel: defeats Syria and increases prestige of Israel.

776
- The first Olympiad in Greece.

753
- Legendary date of the Foundation of Rome by Romulus (21 April).

***c*.750-700**
- Homer's Illiad and Odyssey date from about this period.

745
- Tiglath-Pileser III raises Assyria to greatest power.

740
- Conquest of Messenia by Sparta (first Messenian War).

738
- Menahem, king of Israel.

734
- Ahaz, king of Judah.

729
- Tiglath-Pileser III subdues Babylon.

721
- Sargon, king of Assyria, takes Samaria and transports a large number of the Israelites to Mesopotamia and Media; the northern kingdom of Israel never revives.
- Merodachbaladan ends Assyrian power in Babylon and reigns as king for twelve years.

720
- Hezekiah becomes king of Judah: noted religious reformer and skilful leader.

716
- Gyges, king of Lydia.

705
- Sennacherib, king of Assyria.

701
- Sennacherib fails in his attack on Jerusalem.

700
- Deioces founds the Medean monarchy; Midas, king of Phrygia; Gyges, king of Lydia.

685
- Second Messenian War; Messenians again defeated by Sparta.

683
- End of monarchy in Athens.

680
- Esarhaddon, king of Assyria.

670
- Esarhaddon defeats Taharka, Ethiopian king of Egypt, and captures Memphis.

668
- Asurbanipal, king of Assyria: Babylon again subdued; Elam overthrown.

660
- Psammetichus, aided by Gyges of Lydia, makes Egypt independent again.

647
- Phraortes, king of Media.

637
- Josiah, king of Judah: noted religious and political reformer.

628
- Birth of Zoroaster around this time.

625
- Nabopolassar, king of Babylon.

624
- Cyaxares, king of Media.

621
- Legislation of Draco at Athens.

617
- Neco, king of Egypt.

612
- Nineveh captured and destroyed by Nabopolassar of Babylon and Cyaxares of Media; end of the Assyrian Empire.

610
- Battle between Cyaxares of Media and Alyarres of Lydia stopped by an eclipse of the sun

608
- Battle of Megiddo between Josiah, king of Judah

and Neco, king of Egypt: Josiah is defeated and killed.

605
- Battle of Carchemish; Egyptian power in Syria overthrown by Babylon.
- Nebuchadnezzar, king of Babylon.

597
- Jerusalem taken by Nebuchadnezzar; Jehoiachin, the king, Ezekiel, the prophet, and others taken to Babylon; Zedekiah made king of Judah.

596
- Apries (Hophra), king of Egypt.

594
- Legislation of Solon at Athens.

586
- Zedekiah's revolt against Babylonian rule; Jerusalem taken and destroyed by Nebuchadnezzar.

585
- Tyre taken by Nebuchadnezzar.

584
- Astyages, king of Media.

570
- Athens conquers island of Salamis.

569
- Amasis II, king of Egypt after a rebellion against Apries.

563
- Buddha born in India.

562
- Death of Nebuchadnezzar.

561
- Evil-Merodach, king of Babylon.

560
- Croesus, king of Lydia: subdues Greek cities in Asia Minor.
- Pisistratus becomes Tyrant of Athens (expelled 555 BC).

555
- Nabonidus, king of Babylon.

551
- Confucius born in China.

550
- Sparta becomes supreme in the Peloponnesus.
- Cyrus conquers Media and founds the Persian Empire.
- Second Tyranny of Pisistratus at Athens (expelled 549 BC).

546
- Cyrus conquers Lydia.
- Asiatic Greek cities conquered by Persia.

540
- Pisistratus again Tyrant of Athens until his death (527 BC).

538
- Cyrus conquers Babylon.

529
- Cambyses, king of Persia.

527
- Hippias and Hipparchus in power at Athens.

525
- Persian conquest of Egypt.

521
- Darius I, king of Persia.

520
- Persian conquest of Babylon.

515
- Dedication of the New Temple at Jerusalem after the return from the Babylonian Captivity.

512
- Persian conquest of Thrace.

510
- Pisistratid Tyranny at Athens ends; Hippias, son of Pisistratus expelled; Athens joins Peloponnesian League.

508
- Treaty between Rome and Carthage.

507
- Reforms of Cleisthenes at Athens.

500
- End of monarchy at Rome: Republic founded.

499
- Asiatic Greeks revolt from Persia.

497
- Athenians assist in the burning of Sardis.

493
- First Secession of Plebeians at Rome; Tribunes of the Plebs first appointed.

492
- Persians conquer Thrace and Macedonia.

490
- Battle of Marathon: Persians defeated by Greeks under Miltiades; Aeschylus flourishes at this time.

486
- First Agrarian Law (Land Reform) at Rome passed by Spurius Cassius Viscellinus.
- Xerxes, becomes king of Persia on the death of his father Darius I.

483
Deaths
Gautama Siddharta Buddha, Indian founder of Buddhism.

480
- Battle of Thermopylae: Persians defeat Greeks (Leonidas).
- Battle of Salamis: Athenians under Themistocles defeat Persians in naval battle.
- Battle of Himera: Carthaginian attack on Sicily repelled by Sicilian Greeks.

479
- Battle of Plataea: Persians defeated by Greeks under Pausanias.
- Battle of Mycale: Greek naval victory over the Persians.

477
- Confederacy of Delos founded by Athens for defence against Persia.

471
- Lex Publilia passed at Rome; Tribunes to be chosen by the Comitia Tributa (popular assembly).

465
- Battle of the Eurymedon: Persians defeated by Greeks under Cimon.
- Artaxerxes I, king of Persia.

463
- Democratic reform at Athens; powers of the Areopagus limited by Ephialtes.

462
- Influence of Pericles begins at Athens; Sophocles and Euripides flourish around this time.

458
- Long Walls to Piraeus built by Athens.
- Ezra returns with many Jews from Babylon to Jerusalem.

456
- Athens conquers Aegina.

Deaths
Aeschylus, Greek dramatist.

454
- Athenian expedition to Egypt fails after initial successes.

453
- Treasury of Confederacy of Delos removed to Athens; Athenian Empire at its height.

450
- Decemvirs drew up laws of the Twelve Tables at Rome.

448
- Second Secession of the Plebeians at Rome; great increase in powers of Comitia Tributa.

447
- Battle of Coronea, Athens loses Boeotia.
- Building of Parthenon begins.

445
- Lex Canuleia at Rome legalized marriage between Patricians and Plebieans.
- Nehemiah begins rebuilding walls of Jerusalem.

*c.*443
Deaths
Pindar, Greek musician and poet.

433
Deaths
Herodotus, Greek historian.

433-404
- Peloponnesian War begins. Athens and allies against Sparta and allies; Thucydides its historian: naval battle of Sybota, both sides claim victory.

429
- Naval battle of Corinth: Athenian victory. Naval battle of Naupactus: Athenian victory

429-427
- Spartans beseige Plataea: the city surrenders.

428-427
- Battle of Mytlilene: Athenians victorious as city surrenders.

426
- Battle of Olpae: Athenian victory.

425
- Athenians are beseiged at Pylos by Spartans based at Sphacteria, but manage to mount a counter-seige at Sphacteria in which the Spartans surrender.

424
- Battle of Delium: Athenian defeat.

423
- Darius II, king of Persia.

422
- Battle of Amphipolis: Athenian defeat.

421
- Peace of Nicias between Athens and Sparta ends the first part of the Peloponnesian War.

418
- Peloponnesian War resumes. Battle of Mantinea: Athenians defeated by Spartans.

413
- Athenian defeat in a naval battle at Syracuse.

411
- Naval battle of Cynossema: Athenian victory.

410
- Naval battle of Cyzicus: Athenian victory.

407
- Naval battle of Notium: Athenian defeat.

406
- Naval battle of Mytilene: Athenian defeat.

Deaths

Euripides, Greek dramatist.

405
- Battle of Aegospotami: naval victory of Sparta under Lysander over Athens.

Deaths

Sophocles, Greek tragedian.

404
- Peloponnesian War ends. Spartans enter Athens and set up the Thirty Tyrants.
- Artaxerxes II, king of Persia.

403
- Thirty Tyrants overthrown at Athens.

401
- Battle of Cunaxa: a force of Greeks help Cyrus in his rebellion against Artaxerxes II, among them Xenophon.

400
- Etruscan city of Veii captured by Romans.

399
- Socrates executed.

398
- First Punic War of Dionysius of Syracuse.

394
- Corinthian War. Battle of Coronea: Spartans under Agesilaus defeat confederacy against them. Battle of Cnidus: Spartan fleet destroyed by a combined Persian and Athenian fleet.

390
- Rome burned down by Gauls under Brennus.

387
- Peace of Antalcidas between Sparta and Persia.

Deaths

Aristophanes, Greek dramatist.

371
- Battle of Leactra: Sparta defeated by Thebes under Epaminondas.

366
- Licinian Laws passed at Rome; first Plebeian consul.

362
- Battle of Mantinea: Sparta defeated by Thebes (Epaminondas killed).

359
- Artaxerxes III, king of Persia.
- Philip II becomes king of Macedonia.

347

Deaths

Plato, Greek philosopher.

343-340
- First Saminite War waged by Rome.

340-338
- Rome conquers Latium.

339
- Publilian Laws at Rome; decrees of Comitia Tributa to bind whole people; one Censor to be a Plebeian.

338
- Battle of Chaeronea: Athens and Thebes defeated by Philip of Macedon, who becomes supreme in Greece.
- Arses, king of Persia.

336
- Philip II assassinated and succeeded by his son Alexander the Great.

336
- Alexander the Great becomes king of Macedon.
- Praetorship at Rome thrown open to Plebeians.
- Alexander elected supreme general of the Greeks.

335
- Alexander's campaign in Thrace and Illyria.
- Alexander captures Thebes (in Boeotia) and destroys it except the house of Pindar.
- Memnon of Rhodes opposes Alexander's lieutenant Parmenion in Asia Minor.
- Darius III, king of Persia.
- Aristotle begins teaching at Athens.

334
- Alexander crosses the Hellespont into Asia.

- Battle of the Granicus: Alexander defeats the Persians.
- Alexander captures Sardis and conquers Lydia.
- Capture of Ephesus.
- Siege and capture of Miletus.
- Siege and capture of Halicarnassus.

333
- Alexander at Phrygia; cuts the Phrygian knot.
- Battle of Issus: Alexander defeats Darius.

332
- Siege and capture of Tyre.
- Capture o Gaza.
- Alexander enters Egypt.

331
- Alexander founds Alexandria.
- Alexander visits the temple of Zeus Ammon.
- Battle of Arbela (Gaugamela): Darius again defeated.
- Babylon submits to Alexander.
- Battle of Megalopolis: Spartans under Agis defeated by Macedonian regent Antipater.

330
- Alexander at Persepolis.
- Alexander at Ecbatana.
- Death of Darius III: end of the Persian Empire.

330-327
- Alexander conquers Hyrcania, Gedrosia, Bactria, Sogdiana.

327
- Alexander enters India.
- Second Samnite War between Rome and the Samnites begins.

326
- Alexander crosses the Indus near Attock.
- Battle of the Hydaspes: the Punjab conquered.

325

Alexander at Susa where he organises mass marriage of himself and his officers with women of the Persian aristocracy

323
- Alexander dies at Babylon aged 32.

323
- Ptolemy I founds the dynasty of the Ptolemies in Egypt; makes Alexandria the intellectual centre of the Hellenic world; Euclid flourishes in his reign.

322
- Lamian War; Antipater of Macedonia defeats insurgent Greeks at Battle of Crannon.

Deaths

Aristotle, Greek philosopher.

321
- The Samnites capture a Roman army at the Caudine Forks.

312
- The Seleucid Dynasty in Asia founded by Seleucus I (Nicator); capital at first Babylon.

304
- Second Samnite War ends.

301
- Battle of Ipsus determines distribution of Alexander's Empire among his generals.

300
- Antioch founded by Seleucus Nicator as capital of his Syrian kingdom.

300
- Lex Ogulnia at Rome provides for Plebeian Pontiffs and Augurs.

300
- Zeno, founder of Stoicism and Epicurus, founder of Epicureanism, flourish at this time.

298
- Third Samnite War begins.

295
- Battle of Sentinum: Romans defeat Samnites and allies.

295
- Pyrrhus becomes king of Epirus.

294
- Demetrius I becomes king of Macedonia.

290
- Third and Last Samnite War ends: Rome ruler of central Italy.

287
- Third Secession of the Plebs at Rome.

286
- Lex Hortensia at Rome makes the popular assembly (Comitia Tributa) the supreme legislative power.

285
- Ptolemy II becomes king of Egypt.

283
- Battle of the Vadimonian Lake: Romans defeat Gauls and Etruscans; Rome ruler of northern Italy.

280
- Pyrrhus invades Italy; Romans defeated in Battle of Heraclea.

- Achaen League revived in Greece.
- Gauls invade Greece.

279
- Battle of Asculum: Pyrrhus again defeats Romans.

275
- Battle of Beneventum: Romans defeat Pyrrhus and drive him from Italy.

266
- Rome ruler of all Italy.

264
- First Punic War (Rome v. Carthage) begins.

262
- Battle of Agrigentum: Roman victory.

260
- Battle of Mylae: Roman naval victory.

256
- Romans invade Africa.

255
- Romans under Regulus heavily defeated by Carthaginians in Africa.

251
- Battle of Panormus: Romans defeat Carthaginians.

246
- Ptolemy III becomes king of Egypt.
- Hamilcar Barca assumes Carthaginian command in Sicily.

245
- Aratus becomes leader of the Achaean League.
- Agis IV attempts to reform Sparta.

241
- Battle of Aegates Islands: Roman naval victory over Carthage; First Punic War ends with cession of Sicily to Rome.
- Sicily becomes the first Roman province.

240
- Livius Andronicus, the first Roman poet stages the first comedy in latin literature.

239
- Rome seizes Sardinia and makes it a province.

237
- Carthage begins conquest of Spain.

236
- Cleomenes III, the last king of Sparta.

222
- Conquest of Cisalpine Gaul by Rome completed.
- Ptolemy IV, king of Egypt; beginning of Egypt's decline.
- Cleomenes III defeated by Achean League at Battle of Sellasia.

221-206

Ch'in dynasty, China rules after destroying the Chou dynasty in 256 and several other rival states afterwards.

220
- Philip V, king of Macedon.

219
- Hannibal, the great Carthaginian leader, captures Saguntum in Spain.

218
- Second Punic War begins; Hannibal crosses the Alps into Italy.
- Battle of the Trebia: Hannibal victorious.

217
- Battle of Lake Trasimene: Hannibal victorious.

216
- Battle of Cannae: Hannibal victorious.

214
- First Macedonian War; Romans victorious over Philip V; war ends in 205.
- Great Wall of China constructed.

212
- Romans under Marcellus capture Syracuse.

Deaths

Archimedes, Greek mathematician.

208
- Philopoemen becomes leader of the Achaean League.

207
- Hasdrubal, brother of Hannibal, crosses the Alps into Italy; defeated and killed in Battle of Metaurus.

206
- Conquest of Spain by Scipio.

206-AD 9
- Former Han dynasty rules China.

204
- Ptolemy V, king of Egypt; period of anarchy.
- Scipio carries the war into Africa.

202
- Battle of Zama: Hannibal completely defeated near Carthage by the elder Scipio; end of Second Punic War.

200
- Roman poets Ennius and Plautus flourish at this time.
- Second Macedonian War begins.

198
- Battle of Avus: Roman victory.

197
- Battle of Cynoscephaloe: Roman victory ended Second Macedonian War.

196
- Romans proclaim freedom of Greece.

190
- Battle of Magnesia: Romans defeat Antiochus the Great of Syria.

181
- Ptolemy VI, king of Egypt.

175
- Antiochus IV becomes king of Syria.

171
- Third Macedonian War begins. Battle of Larissa: Macedonian victory
- Battle of Pelusium: Antiochus Epiphanes takes Memphis.

170
- Roman poet Terence flourishes at this time.

168
- Battle of Pydna; Perseus of Macedonia crushed; end of Third Macedonian War.

166

Deaths

Mattathias, the Jewish priest who led revolt of Jews against Hellenizing policy of Antiochus Epiphanes; succeeded by his son, Judas Maccabaeus.

161
- Judas Maccabaeus killed at Elasa; succeeded by his brother Jonathan.

149
- Fourth Macedonian War.
- Third Punic War begins.

147
- Roman victory under Mummius at Corinth; Macedonia becomes a Roman province.

146
- Greece becomes a Roman province.
- Carthage destroyed; Roman province of Africa formed.
- Ptolemy VII, king of Egypt.

143
- Simon, a brother of Judas Maccabaeus, becomes leader of the Jews.

142
- Syrian garrison expelled from Jerusalem.

140
- Roman conquest of Lusitania (Portugal).

135
- John Hyrcanus, leader of the Jews.

133
- Roman provinces in Spain formed.
- Attalus III, king of Pergamom, bequeathes his dominions to Rome; province of Asia formed.

133
- Tiberius Gracchus becomes tribune of the Plebs at Rome; attempted to solve the land problem.

123
- Gaius Gracchus, brother of Tiberius, becomes tribune of the Plebs; further land reform.

121
- Gaius Gracchus killed in a riot.

120
- Roman province in Southern Gaul (hence Provence).

117
- Cleopatra III rules Egypt jointly with her son Ptolemy VIII.

111
- War between Rome and Jugurtha, king of Numidia in Africa; Roman generals, Metellus and Marius.

107
- Ptolemy IX, king of Egypt.

106
- Jugurtha defeated and captured by Marius.

102
- Barbarian Teuto .s moving to invade Italy defeated by Marius at Aix.

101
- Barbarian Cimbri moving towards Rome defeated by Marius at Vercellae.

90
- Social War: revolt of the Italians Cities against Rome.

89
- Roman franchise granted to some Italians; soon afterwards to all.
- Death of Ptolemy IX.

88
- First Mithridatic War begins. Rome v. Mithridates VI (the Great), king of Pontus, in Asia Minor; Sulla the Roman general. Battle of Cyzicus: Roman victory.
- Civil War in Rome: Marius v. Sulla; immediate occasion was rivalry for the command in Asia.

87
- Massacres in Rome by Marius and Cinna.

86
- Battles of Chareonea and Milletopolis: Roman victories

Deaths

Gaius Marius, Roman soldier.

85
- First Mithridatic war. Battle of Orchomanes in Boeotia: Roman victory.

84
- End of first Mithridatic War.

Deaths

Lucius Cornelius Cinna, Roman patrician and politician and supporter of Marius is killed in a mutiny.

83-82
- Second Mithridatic War.

83
- Sulla returns to Rome; many citizens executed.

82
- Sulla made dictator of Rome; makes the constitution more aristocratic.
- Battle of Halys: Pontic victory over Murena.

79
- Sulla resigns (d.78).

76-71
- Pompey suppresses the rebellion of Sertorius, a follower of Marius, in Spain.

75
- Cicero, the orator, comes into prominence at Rome.

74
- Third Mithridatic War begins; Roman leaders Lucullus and Pompey. Naval battle of Chalcedon: Pontic victory

73-71
- Revolt of gladiators and slaves under Spartacus.

72
- Battle of Cabria: Roman victory.

69
- Battle of Tigranocerta: Roman victory.

67
- Battle of Zela: Pontic victory, but Mithridates is wounded.

66
- Battle of Nicopolis: Roman victory under Pompey.

64
- Pompey conquers Syria and makes it a Roman province. Third Mithridatic War ends.

63
- Pompey takes Jerusalem.
- The conspiracy of Catiline exposed and foiled by Cicero.

60
- First Triumvirate: Caesar, Pompey and Crassus.

58
- Caesar begins the conquest of Gaul; the Helvetii defeated at Bibracte; Ariovistus, the German leader, defeated.

55
- Julius Caesar's first invasion of Britain.

54
- Caesar's second invasion of Britain.

53
- Battle of Carrhae: Crassus defeated and killed by Parthians.

52
- Battle of Alesia: Vercingetorix, leader of the Gauls, defeated and captured by Cæsar.

50
- Conquest of Gaul complete.

49
- Cæsar crosses the Rubicon and invades Italy.

48
- Battle of Pharsalia: Cæsar defeats Pompey (Pompey murdered soon afterwards in Egypt).

48-47
- Caesar in Egypt; under the influence of Cleopatra, Queen of Egypt.

47
- Battle of Zela: Caesar defeats Pharnaces, king of Pontus.

46
- Battle of Thapsus: the republicans defeated by Caesar in Africa; Cato commits suicide rather than survive the republic.
- Calendar reformed by Caesar.

45
- Battle of Munda: Pompey's sons defeated in Spain by Caesar.

44

- Caesar made Perpetual Dictator.
- Assassination of Caesar.

43

- The Second Triumvirate constituted: Octavius, Antony and Lepidus; Cicero executed.

42

- Battle of Philippi: Brutus and Cassius, the leaders of the revolt against Caesar, are defeated and they commit suicide.

40

- Virgil and Horace, the Roman poets, flourish about this time.

31

- Battle of Actium: Antony and Cleopatra defeated in naval battle by Octavius.

30

Suicide of Antony and Cleopatra; Egypt becomes a Roman province.

29

- Temple of Janus closed, denoting a world at peace - the first time for 200 years; Livy, the great historian flourishes at this time.

27

- The Senate gives Octavius the title of Princeps of the Roman State; beginning of the Principate, an Empire under the forms of the old republic.
- Senate gives Octavius the title of Augustus.
- Beginning of Roman Empire with Augustus in the form of the Principate.

23

- Readjustment of the authority of Augustus.

20

- Restoration of Temple at Jerusalem begun by Herod the Great.

4

- Death of Herod the Great; Herod Antipas becomes tetrarch of Galilee and Perea; Herod Archelaus becomes ethnarch of Judaea, Samaria and Idumea.

***c*.4**

- Probable date of the birth of Jesus Christ in Judea.

AD

9

- Roman army under Varus defeated in Germany by Arminius: Teutonic Civilization saved from absorption by Rome.

9-23

- Hsin dynasty rules China.

14

- Death of Emperor Augustus, Tiberius becomes emperor of Rome.

17

Deaths

Livy, Roman historian.

18

Deaths

Ovid, Roman poet.

25-220

- Later Han dynasty rules China.

26

- Pontius Pilate becomes Roman procurator of Judaea.

29

- Jesus is renowned as a preacher and for his miracles.

Deaths

Livia, wife of Emperor Augustus. Her son Tiberius refuses to allow her to be deified.

30

- Probable date of crucifixion of Jesus Christ.

31

- Sejanus, minister of Tiberius, executed.

37

- Death of Tiberius: Caligula becomes emperor of Rome.

40

- Caligula declares himself a god; he is assassinated by two Praetorian tribunes.

41

- Claudius becomes emperor.
- Herod Agrippa I recognized as king of Judaea and Samaria.

43

- Roman invasion of Britain begins under Aulus Plautius.
- Death of Cymbeline (or Cunobelinus), king of the Catuvellauni and ally of the Romans. Succeeded by his son Caractacus who resisted the Romans.
- Battle of the Medway: Romans defeat the Britons under Caractacus, king of the Catuvellauni.
- First recorded mention of Icknield Way, natural road of Celtic origin from Berkshire Down to the Fens.

44

- Death of Herod Agrippa I; Judea governed afterwards by Roman procurators.

47
- Construction begun by the Romans of Fosse Way from Lincoln to Exeter as a frontier line against raiding forces.

50
- St Paul begins missionary work in Europe.
- Battle of Shropshire: Romans defeat Britons under Caractacus; Caractacus flees.

51
- Romans captured Caractacus.

54
- Nero becomes emperor; last of the Caesar family
- The philosopher Senecca flourishes at this time.
- Caractacus died in captivity in Rome around this time.

61
- St Paul arrives in Rome.
- Anglesey conquered by the Romans.
- Revolt of the Iceni against the Romans, led by Boadicea (or Boudicca); defeated by Suetonius Paulinus.

62
- Boadicea commits suicide by poisoning herself.

63

Deaths

St Paul at Rome.

64
- Great fire in Rome.

65
- First persecution of Christians at Rome.
- Death of Senecca, Roman philosopher.

68
- Galba usurps the Empire.
- Nero, Roman emperor, commits suicide to save himself from execution by the Paetorian Guards who rise against him to make Galba emperor.

69
- Otho murders and displaces Galba.
- Vitellius proclaimed emperor at Cologne; defeats Otho and accepted as emperor.

70
- Vespasian becomes emperor by the defeat of Vitellius; first of the Flavian emperors.
- Jerusalem destroyed by Titus; Jewish revolt suppressed.

***c*.70**
- The Iron Age fort of Maiden Castle, Dorset, destroyed.

78
- Agricola begins his conquest in Britain.

79
- Titus, son of Vespasian, becomes emperor.
- Herculaneum and Pompeii destroyed by eruption of Vesuvius.
- Tacitus, Roman historian, flourishes at this time.

80
- Colosseum completed at Rome.

81
- Domitian, son of Vespasian, becomes emperor.
- Death of Titus, Roman emperor: he is succeeded by his brother Domitian.

84
- Battle of Mons Graupius or Battle of the Grampians: Caledonians defeated by Romans under Agricola; Agricola completes conquest of Britain.

86-90
- Dacians under Decebalus successful against Roman armies; bought off by Domitian.

90
- Domitian expels Epictetus, the Stoic, and other philosophers from Rome.

93

Deaths

Gnaeus Julius Agricola, Roman statesman and soldier.

95
- Persecution of Christians.

96
- Domitian murdered: Nerva becomes Roman emperor. Nerva chooses Trajan as his successor.

98
- Trajan (a native of Spain) becomes emperor.

100

The Mexican pyramids of the sun and moon are built at Teotihuacan.

106
- Conquest of Dacia completed by Trajan.

107
- Persecution of Christians.

114
- Trajan at war with Parthians; the Roman Empire reaches its greatest extent.

117
- Hadrian becomes emperor of Rome; visits all the

provinces of the empire; abandons Trajan's conquests beyond the Euphrates.

122
Roman Governor, Aulus Platorius Nepos builds Hadrian's Wall across northern England from the Solway to the Tyne to keep out the Scots.

125
Persecution of Christians.

126
Hadrian's Wall completed.

131
Revolt of Jews under Barcochba.

136
Jewish revolt suppressed; dispersion of the race.

138
Antoninus Pius becomes emperor of Rome.

140
Construction of a Roman theatre at Verulamium (St Albans).
Building of the Antonine Wall from the Forth to the Clyde begins.

142
Completion of the Antonine Wall.

148
A Parthian monk, An Shigao, initiates the first translation of Buddhist texts into Chinese.

155
Polycarp, Bishop of Smyrna, suffers martyrdom.

161
Marcus Aurelius becomes Roman emperor.

163
Justin Martyr, one of the earliest Fathers of the Christian Church, suffers martyrdom at Rome.

165
The plague in Italy.

166
The Parthians defeated in Roman invasion.
Construction of the first church in Britain, at Glastonbury.

169
War with the German tribes Quadi and Marcomanni.

173
Greek writer and historian, Pausanias finishes writing his *Itinerary*.

174
Aurelius defeats the Quadi ('The Thundering Legion').

177
- Persecution of Christians; Irenaeus, a Father of the Church at Lyons about this time.

180
- Death of Marcus Aurelius: Commodus, son of Marcus Aurelius, becomes Roman emperor.
- Defeat of the Romans in Caledonia: they retreat behind Hadrian's Wall.
- The Goths migrate from the Baltic to the shores of the Black Sea and the Crimea.

192
- Commodus strangled; Pertinax becomes emperor.

193
- Murder of Pertinax by the Praetorian Guards.
- The Empire sold to Didius Julianus by the Praetorian Guards; general revolt in the provinces.
- Julianus executed; Severus Septimius becomes emperor of Rome (until 211).

194
- Battle of Issus: Pescennius Niger, Severus's rival, defeated and killed.

197
- Battle of Lyons: Clodius Albinus, a rival of Severus Septimius, defeated after ruling in Britain over three years.

200
- Tertullian, Latin Father of the Church and Clement of Alexandria, a Greek Father, flourish around this time.

202
- Persecution of Christians.

204
- Origen, a Greek Father of the Church, begins teaching at Alexandria.

210
- Severus strengthened Hadrian's Wall across Britain.

211
- Death of Severus at York; his sons Caracalla and Geta become joint emperors.

212
- Geta, joint emperor of Rome murdered.
- Roman citizenship conferred upon all free men.

217
- Caracalla murdered; Macrinus becomes emperor.

218
- Heliogabalus becomes emperor; tries to establish worship of Syrian sun-god.

220-265
- Wei dynasty, China.

221-263
- Shu dynasty, China

222
- Alexander Severus becomes emperor after murder of Heliogabalus.

222-280
- Wu dynasty, China.

229
- Sassanid Empire begins in Persia with Ardashir I, who overthrew the Parthians; he re-establishes the Zoroastrian religion.

231
- Alexander Severus at war with Persia.

235
- Alexander Severus murdered; Maximian becomes emperor.

238
- The elder and the younger Gordian proclaimed joint emperors in Africa, acknowledged by the Senate; defeated and killed after thirty-six days' reign; Balbinus and Maximus proclaimed joint emperors by the Senate and associated with the third Gordian; Maximin murdered by his own troops; Maximus and Balbinus murdered, leaving the third Gordian sole emperor.

243
- Battle of Resaena: Gordian defeats the Persians under Sapor I.

244
- Gordian murdered by his mutinous soldiers; Philip (an Arabian) becomes Roman emperor.

249
- Decius becomes Roman emperor, after defeating and killing Philip.

250
- Invasion of Moesia by the Goths
- Cyprian, Bishop of Carthage, Latin Father of the Church.
- Persecution of the Christians.

251
- Battle of Forum Trebonii: Decius defeated and killed in Moesia by Gothic invaders; Gallus becomes emperor and buys off the Goths.

253
- Aemilianus routs the Goths and is proclaimed emperor; Gallus murdered; Aemilianus defeated and overthrown by Valerian.

254

Origen, the Christian theologian and philosopher dies as a result of torture he suffered by Decian persecution in 250ad.

260
- Valerian defeated and taken prisoner at Edessa by Sapor, king of Persia; his son Gallienus becomes sole emperor. The Goths ravage the east of the Empire. General disorder and revolt (the so-called Thirty Tyrants). Postumus establishes a so-called Gallic Empire.

265-36
- Western Chin dynasty, China.

266
- Odenathus, after raising Palmyra to a position of power and repelling the Persians, is murdered; his widow Zenobia rules on behalf of her son and makes extensive conquests.
- The Goths pillage Thrace, Macedonia and Greece.

268
- Claudius becomes emperor.

269
- Battle of Naïssus: Claudius defeats the Goths and saves the Empire from destruction.

270
- Aurelian becomes emperor; Dacia granted to the Goths.
- St Anthony, the first Christian Monk, becomes an ascetic in Egypt.

Deaths

Plotinus, Egyptian-born Roman philosopher, who revived and extended the works of Plato.

271
- Battle of Châlons: Tetricus defeated and the 'Gallic Empire' ended.

272
- Aurelian destroys the power of Palmyra and takes Zenobia prisoner.

275
- Aurelian assassinated; Tacitus elected emperor by the Senate.

276
- Probus becomes emperor.

277
- Probus expels the Almanni from Gaul.

79

Probus expels the Burgundians and the Vandals from Rhaetia.

82

Probus assassinated; Carus becomes emperor.

83

Carus succeeded by his two sons, Carinus and Numerian, as joint emperors.

84

Diocletian becomes emperor.

86

Maximian chosen by Diocletian as his colleague.
Carausius appointed to protect British shore against Frankish and Saxon pirates; proclaims himself emperor in Britain in 287 and recognized.

93

Constantius Chlorus and Galerius created Caesars, with a share in governing the Empire: Rome ceases to be real capital, being replaced by the four towns Nicomedia, Sirmium, Milan and Trier, one for each Augustus and Caesar. These four divisions afterwards become the Prefectures of the East, Illyricum, Italy and Gaul.
Carausius murdered in Britain by Allectus sets himself up as emperor in Britain.
Rebuilding of Hadrian's Wall and York.

96

Allectus defeated and killed by Constantius Chlorus.

03

Persecution of Christians.
Church established at St Albans.

04

St Alban the first Christian martyr in Britain.

04-439

Sixteen Kingdoms dynasty, China

05

Abdication of Diocletian and Maximian.

06

Constantine the Great proclaimed emperor of Rome, on the death of his father Constantius at York. Severus made joint emperor by Galerius; Maxentius, son of Maximian, declared emperor at Rome.

07

Severus executed by Maximian; Licinius made joint emperor Galerius; Maximian also proclaimed emperor; six emperors at one time.

10

Maximian executed by Constantine.

311

- Death of Galerius, Roman emperor.

312

- Constantine invades Italy; Maxentius's army defeated in Battle of Turin and in Battle of Verona.

312

- Battle of the Milvian Bridge (at Rome): Constantine captures Rome; death of Maxentius.

313

- Licinius defeats Maximin; death of Maximin soon afterwards.
- Edict of Milan grants freedom to Christians.

314

Deaths

Tiridates, king of Armenia, who had become a Christian.

315

- Battle of Cibalis: Constantine defeats Licinius.
- Battle of Mardia: Licinius is again defeated; a Treaty of Peace concluded.
- Constantine declares Christianity the official religion of the Roman Empire.

317-420

- Eastern Chin dynasty, China.

320

- St Pachomius founds the first Christian monastery in Egypt.
- Goths conquer Dacia and raid Thrace.

322

- Constantine defeats the Goths in Dacia.

323

- Battle of Adrianople: Liciunius defeated by Constantine.
- Battle of Chrysopolis: Licinius defeated by Constantine and dies soon afterwards.

324

- Constantine sole Roman emperor; he adopts Christianity.

325

- Council of Nicaea, the first General Council of the Christian Church; held in the presence of Constantine; the doctrines of Arius condemned, chiefly through the influence of Athansius.

328

- Constantine founds a new capital at Byzantium under the name of Constantinople or New Rome.

330

- Constantinople dedicated.

331
Constantine orders that all pagan temple-treasures throughout the empire are confiscated

332
- Constantius, son of Constantine, defeats the Goths in Moesia.

337
- Death of Constantine; his sons, Constantius, Constantine II and Constans, divide the Empire.

337
- The Empire at war with Persia under Sapor II.

340
- Constantine II killed in attacking the territories of Constans.

341
- Ulfilas begins the conversion of his fellow Goths to Arian Christianity; his translation of the Bible in Gothic is the oldest teutonic literary work.

348
- Battle of Singara: Romans defeated by Persians.

350
- Constans murdered in a revolt by Magnetius, who assumes the purple.
- Third Siege of Nisbis: Sapor II unsuccessful.
- Hermanric becomes king of the Goths and establishes a Gothic Empire in Central Europe.

351
- Battle of Mursa: Magnentius defeated by Constantius.

353
- Battle of Mount Seleucus: defeat of Magnentius, who then commits suicide; Constantius sole emperor.

356
- Julian (the Apostate) begins campaign in Gaul against the Alamanni, Franks and others.
- Constantius II orders that all pagan temples in the empire must be closed.

357
- Battle of Strassburg: Julian defeats the Alamanni.

359
- Amida captured by Sapor II.

359
- Julian subdues the Franks.

360
- Singara and Bezabde captured by Sapor II.

361
- Julian becomes emperor; tries to restore Paganism as the state religion.

363
- Julian campaign against Persia leads to his death; Jovian emperor.
- Jovian makes a humiliating peace with Persia.

364
- Valentinian I becomes emperor.
- Valentinian divides the Empire into eastern and western, making Valens eastern emperor.

365
- Revolt of Procopius against Valens.

366
- Procopius defeated and executed.
- Alamanni invade Gaul; defeated by Jovinus.
- War against the Visigoths under Athanaric begins.

367
- Hadrian's Wall overrun by Pictish invasion.

368
- Valentinian defeats the Alamanni in the Black Forest and fortifies the Rhine.

369
- Theodosius drives back the Picts and Scots from southern Britain.
- Repair of Hadrian's Wall.

370
- Basil the Great, a pioneer of monasticism, becomes Bishop of Caesarea.

372
- St Martin, a pioneer of monasticism, becomes Bishop of Tours.
- Huns under Balamir begin westward movement from the Caspian steppes; they defeat and absorb the Alans.

373
- Theodosius suppresses a revolt in Africa.

374
- Huns attack the Ostrogoths of Hermanric's kingdom and conquer them. Hermanric commits suicide.
- War against the Quadi and Sarmatians.
- St Ambrose becomes Bishop of Milan.

375
- Huns attack Athanaric and the Visigoths.
- Gratian and Valentinian II, sons of Valentinian I, become western emperors.

376
- Visigoths under Fritigern permittted by Valens to settle in Thrace; they successfully revolt because of oppression.

378
- The Alamanni defeated by Gratian near Colmar.

- Battle of Adrianople: Romans defeated by Goths and Valens killed.
- Massacre of Gothics in Asia by the Romans.
- Gregory Nazianzen accepts the mission of Constantinople.

379
- Theodosius the Great becomes eastern emperor.

380
- Theodosius baptised in the Orthodox faith; suppresses Arianism in Constantinople and begins persecution of heretics.

381
- Second General Council of the Church, at Constantinople.

382
- Theodosius makes terms with the Goths and enlists them in his service.

383
- Revolt of Magnus Maximus in Britain; he invades Gaul and murders Gratian; treaty between Theodosius and Magnus Maximus, leaving the latter in possession of Gaul, Spain and Britain.
- Hadrian's Wall again overrun by Picts.

385
- Priscillian, a Spanish bishop, is executed at Träves for heresy by Maximus.
- St Jerome works on the Latin translation of the Bible (the Vulgate).

386
- Conversion of St Augustine.
- Ostrogoths defeated on the Danube.

386-581
- Northern Wei dynasty, China

387
- Sedition of Antioch severely punished by Theodosius.
- Maximus invades Italy; Valentinian flees to Theodosius.

388
- Maximus defeated and executed by Theodosius.

390
- Sedition of Thessalonica punished by massacre; Theodosius compelled by St Ambrose to do humble penance at Milan.
- Paganism prohibited under heavy penalties.

392
- Death of Valentinian II, strangled by Arbogast, a Frankish general in the imperial service; Eugenius usurps western Empire at the instance of Arbogast.

394
- Theodosius defeats Eugenius and becomes sole emperor; Eugenius is killed and Arbogast commits suicide.
- Olympic Games finally abolished.
- Consecration of St Ninian as a bishop.

395
- Death of Theodosius the Great, Roman emperor : final division of the Empire into East and West: Honorius becomes western emperor and Arcadius eastern emperor.

396
- Alaric, the Visigothic leader, invades Greece.

397
- Alaric defeated in Greece by Stilicho, master-general of the western armies, of Vandal race.
- St Ninian builds a monastery at Whithorn and begins to Christianize the Picts of Galloway in Scotland.

398
- Alaric made master-general of eastern Illyricum and also proclaimed king of the Visigoths.
- St Chrysostom becomes Archbishop of Constantinople.

399
- Revolt of Ostrogoths in Asia Minor under Tribigild: joined by Gainas, a Goth, who is military minister of the eastern Empire.
- Buddism spreads through China.

400
- Alaric invades Italy; Honorius flees from Rome.
- Claudian, the last of the Roman poets, celebrates Stilicho's victories.

401
- Gainas defeated by Fravitta, a loyal Goth; beheaded later by the Hunnish king.

402
- Battle of Pollentia: Stilicho defeats Alaric.

403
- Battle of Verona: Stilicho again victorious over Alaric.

404
- Honorious makes Ravenna his capital.
- Gladiatorial contests abolished.

405
- Italy invaded by a Germanic host under the Pagan Radagaisus: Florence is besieged: the invaders are

defeated and their leader is killed by Stilicho.
- St Patrick begins the conversion of the Irish.

407
- Revolt of British army: Constantine declared emperor.

408
- Constantine acknowledged in Gaul and Spain.
- Theodosius II eastern emperor; government conducted first by Anthemius, then by Pulcheria, sister of the emperor.
- Stilicho disgraced and assassinated.
- Alaric besieges Rome; bought off.

409
- Second Siege of Rome by Alaric; Ostia captured: Attalus made emperor by Alaric, with himself as master-general of the west.
- Spain invaded by Suevi, Vandals, Alans, etc.

410
- Alaric degrades Attalus; Rome besieged and sacked; Italy ravaged; death of Alaric.
- Honorius calls upon Britain to defend itself; Britain sets up a provisional government, as does Armorica (Brittany).

411
- Constantius regains Gaul for Honorius.

413
- Heraclian invades Italy from Africa; defeated and executed.

414
- Atawulf, successor of Alaric, after conquering in Gaul, marches to Spain in order to recover it for the Empire; he is assassinated next year at Barcelona.
- St Jerome finishes translating the Bible from Hebrew to Latin, which he began in 377.

418
- Visigoths under Wallia reconquer Spain for the Empire.

419
- Visigoths granted lands in Aquitania under the Empire: Visigothic kingdom of Toulouse established.
- Theodoric I becomes king of the Visigoths.

420
- The Indian classic, *The Ring of Sakuntula* by Kalidása is published.

420-479
- Liu Sung dynasty, China.

422
- Eastern Empire successful against Persia.

423
- Death of Honorius; usurpation of the western Empire by John.

425
- Emperor John beheaded at Aquileia: Valentinian III becomes emperor, with his morther Placidia as guardian.

427
- Chlodio first known king of the Franks, on the lower Rhine.
- Aëtius, a general of Valentinian III, deceives Boniface, another general of the Empire, into revolting in Africa.

428
- Boniface invites the Vandals to invade Africa.

429
- The Vandals under Gaiseric invade Africa from Spain.

430
- Boniface, repenting, opposes the Vandals unsuccessfully.

431
- Third General Council of the Church, at Ephesus.

432
Deaths
St Ninian, bishop, missionary and earliest known Christian leader in Scotland.

437
- Burgundian kingdom on the Upper Rhine overthrown by Aâtius: the Burgundians granted lands in Savoy.

439
- Carthage taken by the Vandals.

440
- Leo I (the Great) Pope (d.461).

445
- Huns under Attila attack the eastern Empire.

446
- 'The Groans of the Britons': unsuccessful appeal of the Britons to Aetius for help against the invading Saxons.
- Treaty between Attila and Theodosius.

448
- Meroveus becomes king of the Franks—hence Merovingian dynasty.

449
- Beginning of invasions by Jutes, Angles and Saxons.

- Hengist and Horsa invades and settles in Kent.

450
- Marcian becomes eastern emperor as husband of Pulcheria.

451
- Attila and the Huns, with Ostrogothic subjects, invade Gaul.
- Battle of Châlons or the Catalaunian Fields or Maurica: Aëtius in alliance with the Visigoths under Theodoric I and the Franks under Meroveus repel Attila and save western Europe from the Huns; Theodoric is killed.
- Fourth General Council of the Church, at Chalcedon.

452
- Attila invades Italy and destroys Aquileia; the city of Venice originated with fugitives.

453
- Death of Attila and end of his Empire; the Ostrogoths free again.
- Theodoric II, king of the Visigoths.

454
- Aëtius murdered by Valentinian III.

455
- Battle of Aylesford or Aegelsthrep: Jutes are victorious over Britons under Vortigern, but the Jutish leader Horsa is killed.
- Valentinian III assassinated at the instance of Maximus: Maxiums becomes emperor.
- Gaiseric and the Vandals march against Rome; Maxiums assassinated when attempting flight; Rome sacked by the Vandals.
- Avitus made emperor by the Visigoths.

c.463

Deaths

St Patrick, bishop, missionary, and patron saint of Ireland.

456
- Avitus deposed by Rikimer, a Goth in the service of the Empire who had defeated the Vandals by sea and land; he is recognized as Patrician of Rome.
- Sardinia occupied by the Vandals.
- Visigoths conquer most of Spain: Toledo becomes their capital.

457
- Rikimer makes Majorian western emperor; Leo I becomes eastern emperor.
- Childeric becomes king of the Franks.

460
- Majorian's great fleet for invasion of Africa destroyed by Gaiseric in the Bay of Carthagena, through treachery.

461
- Rikimer compels Majorian to abdicate and makes Libius Severus a purely nominal emperor; Marcellinus revolts in Dalmatia and Aegidius in Gaul.

465
- Death of Severus; no western emperor for two years.

466
- Euric becomes king of the Visigoths.

467
- Anthemius becomes western emperor.

468
- Leo's expedition against the Vandals fails.
- Sardinia recovered from the Vandals.

469
- The Vandals occupy Corsica.

472
- Olybrius made western emperor by Rikimer, who sacks Rome and massacres Athemius; deaths of Rikimer and Olybrius.
- Glycerius emperor for a brief period; Julius Nepos made emperor by Leo I.

474
- Leo II eastern emperor; succeeded by Zeno.

475
- The Patrician Orestes leads the barbarian confederates against Nepos in Ravenna; Nepos flees to Dalmatia.
- Romulus Augustulus, son of Orestes, proclaimed western emperor.
- Odoacer, a Goth, leads a revolt of the barbarian allies, who proclaim him king of Italy: besieges Orestes in Pavia and executes him.

476
- Romulus Augustulus forced to resign the Empire.
- Zeno, at the instance of the Senate, made Odoacer Patrician of Italy.
- Odoacer obtains Sicily from the Vandals for tribute.

477
- South Saxons under Aelle settle in England.

478
- Ostrogoths under Theodoric the Great invade Greece.

479-502
- Southern Ch'i dynasty, China.

480
- Julius Nepos assassinated in Dalmatia; no successor appointed. End of the western Empire.

481
- Dalmatia annexed by Odoacer.
- Clovis becomes king of the Franks and begins the Merovingian dynasty (descendants of Meroveus); Tournai his capital.

484
- Sardinia recaptured by the Vandals.

485
- Death of Euric, king of the Visigoths; the Visigothic kingdom at its greatest extent.

486
- Battle of Soissons: Syagrius, son of Aegidius, Roman ruler of a kingdom with Paris as its centre, defeated by Clovis and his kingdom is annexed.

488
- Theodoric the Great commissioned by the emperor Zeno to recover Italy for the Empire.

489
- Battle of Aquileia: Theodoric defeats Odoacer.

489
- Battle of Verona: Theodoric defeats Odoacer.

490
- Odoacer again defeated by Theodoric.

491
- Clovis subdues the Thuringi.
- Anastasius I becomes emperor at Constantinople.

492
- Isaurian War begins and occupies Anastasius till 496.

493
- Theodoric captures Ravenna and puts Odoacer to death; beginning of Ostrogothic kingdom of Italy.

495
- West Saxons settled in England under Cerdic and Cynric.

496
- Clovis subdues the Alamanni.

496
- Clovis converts from Paganism to Catholicism.

500
- Clovis defeats Gundobald, king of the Burgundians, near Dijon.
- Scots under Fergus Mor crosses from Ireland to found kingdom of Dalriada in Scotland.

501
- Death of Fergus Mor, a king of the Scots, ruler of the kingdom of Dalriada.

502
- War between the Empire and Persia (ended 506).

502-557
- Liang dynasty, China.

504
- Theodoric's general Pitzia defeats the Gepids and makes them subject allies.

507
- Battle of Vouillé (near Poitiers): Clovis defeats the Visigoths and kills their king, Alaric II.

508
- Clovis made a Roman consul by the Emperor Anastasius.
- Peace between Theodoric and the Empire after a short war arising out of the Gepid war of 504.

510
- Clovis annexes Aquitania from Visigoths.
- Theodoric checks Clovis, wins Provence for the Ostrogoths and saves a small part of Gaul for the Visigoths.
- Theodoric rules the Visigothic kingdom as protector of his grandson Amalaric: Gothic power at its height.

511
- Death of Clovis; the Frankish kingdom divided among his four sons, Thierry, Childebert, Chlodomir and Clotaire, with capitals at Metz, Paris, Orleans and Soissons.

516
- Battle of Mount Badon: Britons defeat the Saxons. Saxon advance in Britain checked for many years by Britons (possibly under King Arthur).

518
- Justin I becomes emperor.

520
- The Christian Era introduced about this time in Italy by Dionysius Exiguus.

522
- War between the Empire and Persia.

*c.*523-524
- Boethius writes *Consolatio Philosophiae* (The Consolation of Philosophy) during his imprisonment for treason.

524
- Boethius the philosopher executed by Theodoric on a charge of treason.

525
- Symmachus, father-in-law of Boethius, executed by Theodoric the Great.

526
- Remorse and death of Theodoric the Great, king of the Ostrogoths.
- Destructive earthquake at Antioch: great loss of life.
- East and Middle Saxons settled in England about this time.

527
- Accession of Justinian I to the Empire.

529
- Justinian suppresses the Athenian Schools of Philosophy.
- Justinian's Code of Civil Law is prepared under the direction of Tribonian.

530
- Gelimer becomes king of the Vandals.

531
- Chosroes I becomes king of Persia.
- The Franks subdue the Thuringians in central Germany; also the Bavarians.

532
- The Nika at Constantinople: a destructive revolt due to the rivalry of the Blue and Green circus factions. Belisarius' troops massacre 30, 000 of the rebels
- Peace concluded between Justinian and Persia.
- Franks invade Burgundy.

533
- War between the Empire and the Vandals: Carthage captured by Belisarius and Gelimer taken prisoner.
- Justinian's *Institutes* published; also the *Pandects* or *Digest*.

534
- Conquest of Burgundy by the Franks: end of the Burgundian kingdom.
- Africa recovered for the Empire; the Vandal kingdom at an end.
- Malta becomes a province of the Byzantine Empire.

535
- Moors defeated in Africa by Solomon, colleague of Belisarius.
- Amalasuntha, Queen of the Ostrogoths; strangled by Theodatus; a pretext for Justinian's invasion.
- Belisarius subdues Sicily.

536
- Belisarius invades Italy and takes Naples; Witigis becomes king of the Sostrogoths; Belisarius enters Rome.

537
- Justinian builds and dedicates the Cathedral of St Sophia in Constantinople.
- The Ostrogoths, under Witiges, besiege Belisarius in Rome. The siege fails.
- Belisarius deposes the Pope Sylverius; the see sold to Vigilius.

538
- Siege of Rome raised.
- Burgundians destroy Milan; Franks invade Italy.
- Buddhism arrives at the court of the Japanese emperor.

539
- Belisarius takes Ravenna.
- Bulgarian invasion of Macedonia and Greece; Slavs invade Illyricum and Thrace.

540
- Recall of Belisarius.
- Chosroes I invades Syria.
- The Goths revolt in Italy.

541
- Justinian ends the Roman consulship.
- Chosroes I captures Antioch and expels many of its people; Belisarius sent to defend Asia against him.
- The Goths victorious in Italy under Totila. Byzantine rule in Italy brought to an end.

542
- Plague in Europe.
- Belisarius drives Chosroes across the Euphrates.
- Battle of Septa: Visigothic invasion of Africa defeated.

543
- Rebellion of the Moors begins (ends 558).

  Deaths

  St Benedict, organizer of western monasticism at Monte Casino (in Italy).
- Franks invade Spain and besiege Saragossa; heavily defeated by the Visigoths.

544
- Belisarius again in Italy.

545
- The Turks ascendant in Tartary.

546
- Totila captures Rome.

547
- Belisarius recovers Rome.
- English kingdom of Bernicia founded by Ida.

548
- Final recall of Belisarius from Italy.

549
- The Goths again take Rome; Sicily, Sardinia and Corsica captured; Greece invaded.
- Siege of Petra begins (ended 551).
- Beginning of Colchian or Lazic War (ended 556).

550-577
- Northern Ch'i dynasty, China.

551
- Germanus leads an army to Italy against the Goths; he dies.
- End of the Roman Senate.
- Introduction of silk cultivation into Europe.

552
- Narses made commander against the Goths.
- Battle of Tadino: Totila defeated and killed.

553
- Narses recovers Rome.
- Battle of Mons Lactarius: the Goths under Teias defeated and Teias killed.
- Fifth General Council of the Church, at Constantinople.
- Invasion of Italy by Franks and Alamanni under Lothaire and Buccelin.

554
- Battle of Casilinum: The Alamannic invaders defeated by Narses.
- Part of southern Spain recovered for the Empire by this date.
- End of the Ostrogothic kingdom; Italy becomes the Exarchate of Ravenna under the Empire.

557-581
- Norhtern Chou dyansty, China.

557-589
- Ch'en dynasty, China.

558
- Avar embassy to Justinian: the Avars employed against the Bulgarians and Slavs.
- Clotaire I sole king of the Franks.
- Another outbreak of plague in Constantinople.

559
- Bulgarians under Zabergan invade Macedonia and Thrace and threaten Constantinople; defeated by Belisarius.

560
- Kingdom of Deira founded in Britain by Aella.

561
- The Frankish monarchy divided among the four sons of Clotaire I, namely, Charibert I, Guntram, Sigebert I and Chilperic I (capitals, Paris, Orleans, Reims and Soissons).

562
- Peace concluded between Justinian and Persia.

Deaths
Procopius, Byzantine historian.

563
- St Columba lands in Iona to Christianize the Picts of Scotland.

565
- Justin II becomes emperor: the Empire becoming Greek instead of Latin.

Deaths
Justinian, Byzantine emperor.
Belisarius, Byzantine general.

566
- Avar embassy to Justin II.
- Lombards and Avars destroy the Gepid kingdom.

568
- The Lombards under Alboin begin to conquer in Italy and establish a kingdom.
- Leovigild becomes king of the Visigoths.

570
- The Persians conquer Yemen in Arabia.
- Beginning of the Avar Empire under Baian in the Danube lands vacated by the Lombards.
- Birth of Mohammed.

571
- The Lombards take Pavia and make it their capital; Italy now partly imperial and partly Lombard.

572
- Renewal of war between Persia and the Empire.

573
- Alboin murdered at the instance of his wife Rosamond; Clepho becomes king of the Lombards.

573
- Battle of Arderydd: Christian party gains the victory in the kingdom of the Strathclyde Britons.

574
- Clepho murdered; the Lombards ruled for ten years by a number of independent dukes.

575
- Synod of Drumceatt in Ireland: Columba got Aidan recognized as independent king of Dalriada.

577
- Battle of Deorham: the West Saxons under Ceawlin defeats Britons; Saxon advance resumes.

578
- Tiberius II becomes emperor.

579
- Hormuz succeeds Chosroes I as king of Persia.

581
- Slavs invade Greece and Thrace: defeated by Priscus.

581-618
- Sui dynasty, China.

582
- Maurice becomes emperor.

584
- Battle of Fethanleag: Britons defeated by West Saxons.
- Autharis becomes king of the Lombards, but the duchies of Spoleto and Beneventum in the centre and south remain practically independent; three invasions of Franks and Alamanni repelled.

585
- The Visigoths conquer and absorb the Suevic kingdom in northwest Spain.
- St Columban leaves Ireland to Christianize Burgundy, etc.

586
- Reccared becomes king of the Visigoths: under him the Visigoths abandon Arianism and become Catholic Christians.

588
- The kingdom of Northumbria formed by the union of Bernicia and Deira with Ethelric as its first king.

590
- Gregory the Great becomes Pope (till 604): greatly increases the powers of the Bishop of Rome by taking advantage of the confusion and disunion of Italy.
- Revolt of Bahram in Persia; Hormuz deposed: Chosroes II becomes king of Persia, but has to flee to the Romans for help; Roman general Narses (not the conquereor of Italy) defeats Bahram and recovers his kingdom for Chosroes II.

592
- Agilulf becomes king of the Lombards.

595
- The Emperor Maurice has to fight against the Avars (till 602).

597

Deaths

St Columba, Irish monk, missionary and apostle in Scotland.

598
- Augustine, sent by Gregory the Great, converts Ethelbert and the kingdom of Kent to Catholic Christianity; becomes first archbishop of Canterbury.

601

Deaths

St David, bishop of Menevia patron saint of Wales.

602
- Phocas becomes emperor: Maurice executed.

603
- Battle of Degsastan: Northumbrians under Tethelfrith defeat Scots under Aidan.

Deaths

St Kentigern or St Mungo, who evangelized the Strathclyde Britons.

604

Deaths

St Augustine, first archbishop of Canterbury.

609
- Mohammed preaches at Mecca.

610
- Heraclius overthrows Phocas and becomes emperor; the Empire hard pressed by Persians, Avar and Slavs.

611
- Persians capture Antioch.

613
- Clotaire II becomes sole king of the Franks.
- Persians take Damascus and overruns Syria.
- Battle of Chester: Northumbrian Ethelfrith defeats Welsh.

614
- St Gall, from Ireland, settles in east Switzerland.

616
- Persians take Alexandria and subdue Egypt.
- Asia Minor conquered by the Persians.

617
- Edwin becomes king of Northumbria (until 633).
- Persians capture Chalcedon, opposite Constantinople.

***c*.617**
- Edinburgh founded by Edwin, king of Northumbria.

618-907
- T'ang dynasty, China

621
- Swinthila becomes king of the Visigoths; recovers Southern Spain from the Empire.

622
- Heraclius begins his great campaigns against the Persians under Chosroes II.

- The Hejira, or flight of Mohammed from Mecca to Medina.

626
- Penda becomes king of Mercia.
- Constantinople unsuccessfully attacked by the Persians in league with the Avars.

627
- Edwin, king of Northumbria, embraces Christianity under the influence of Paulinus, who becomes first archbishop of York.
- Battle of Nineveh: Heraclius's final victory over the Persians.

628
- Battle of Cirencester: Penda of Mercia defeats the West Saxons.
- Chosroes II deposed and murdered; peace between Persia and the Empire.
- Mohammed's message to all rulers calling upon them to embrace Islam.

629
- Submission of Mecca to Mohammed; first battle between Moslems and the Empire, near the Dead Sea.

630
- Dagobert I becomes sole king of the Franks.

632
- Mohammed succeeded by Abu-Bekr, the first Caliph; beginning of the Caliphate.
- Arabia conquered by the Moslems by this date.

Deaths
Mohammed, founder of Islam.

633
- Battle of Heathfield: Edwin overthrown and slain by Penda, heathen king of Mercia, in alliance with Welsh under Cadwalla.

634
- Battle of Heavenfield or Hexham: Oswald defeats Britons and slays Cadwalla and becomes king of Northumbria.
- Battle of Ajnadain (near Jerusalem): Moslems under Khaled defeat the army of Heraclius.
- Omar becomes Caliph.

635
- The Moslems capture Damascus.
- St Aidan goes to Holy Island (Lindisfarne) from Iona to re-Christianize Northumbria.

636
- Donald Breac, king of Dalriada, invades Ireland and is beaten at the Battle of Magh Rath.
- Battle of Yermuk: Moslem victory over Imperial troops seals fate of Syria.
- Rotharis becomes king of the Lombards; a great legislator.

637
- Battle of Cadesia: Moslems defeat the Persians and conquer western Persian provinces.
- Moslems capture Ctesiphon in Persia.
- Moslems capture Jerusalem: the Temple becomes a mosque.

638
- Moslems capture Aleppo and Antioch.

639
- Death of Dagobert I, last notable Merovingian king of the Franks; Mayors of the Palace become the real rulers in Austrasia (eastern division of kingdom), Neustria (western division) and Burgundy; nominal kings called *rois fainéants* ('do-nothing kings').

640
- Moslems begin conquest of Egypt under Amru.

641
- Heraclius succeeded in the Empire by his sons, Constantine III and Heracleonas.
- Battle of Nehavend: Moslems defeat Persians and overthrow the Sassanid Dynasty; last Sassanid king, Yezdegerd III, dies a fugitive in 651.

642
- Constans II emperor.
- Moslems occupy Alexandria.
- Battle of Maserfeld (Oswestry): Oswald of Northumbria defeated and killed in battle by Penda of Mercia.
- Battle of Strathcarron: the Dalriada Scots are defeated by the Strathclyde Britons. Donald Breac, king of Dalriada, is killed.

644
- Othman becomes Caliph.

647
- Moslems begin conquest of Africa.

649
- Moslems conquer Cyprus.

653
- Aribert becomes first Catholic king of the Lombards.

654
- Moslems conquer Rhodes.

655
- Great naval victory of Moslems over Greeks off Lycian coast.

- Battle of the Winwaed: Penda, king of Mercia defeated and slain by the Northumbrian forces under Oswy.

656
- Othman murdered; Ali becomes Caliph.

659
- Wulfhere becomes king of Mercia and restores Mercian power.

660
- Sect of Paulicians, followers of St Paul, founded in Armenia by Constantine.

661
- Ali murdered; Moawiya first of the Ommiade Caliphs, with seat at Damascus.

662
- Emperor Constans II goes to Italy and tries to recover part of it.

664
- Synod of Whitby: Oswy, ruler of the Northumbrians, decides to favour Roman against Celtic Christianity.

668
- Constantine IV becomes emperor, after Constans II is assassinated in Italy.

Deaths

Samo, a Frank who had founded a Slav kingdom in the Danube valley, after a long reign.

669
- Theodore of Tarsus reached England as archbishop of Canterbury; introduced Greek learning and organized the English Church.

670
- English poet Caedmon flourishes at this time.
- Aquitaine about this time breaks away from Frankish rule.

671
- Egfrith becomes king of Northumbria.

672
- Wamba the last great king of the Visigoths.

673
- First Arab siege of Constantinople begins.
- First synod of clergy held in England at Hertford.

675
- Slavs and Bulgars overrun Macedonia.

677
- Arabs abandon the siege of Constantinople and agree to pay tribute; Greek fire used by defenders.

679
- Bulgarians under Isperich occupy Moesia and settle there.

680
- Sixth General Council of the Church, at Constantinople; continues into 681.

c.680

Deaths

Caedmon, the father of English poetry.

683
- Battle of Glenmarreston: Scots under king of Dalriada defeats invading Angles.

685
- Battle of Nechtansmere (20 May): Egfrith of Northumbria defeated and slain by the Picts under Brude; Northumbria never recovers its power.
- Justinian II becomes emperor.

687
- Battle of Tertry: Pepin of Heristal, the Austrasian Mayor of the Palace, defeats the Neustrian Mayor of the Palace and becomes virtual ruler over the whole Frankish kingdom.

Deaths

St Cuthbert, bishop of Lindisfarne and apostle of the Lothians.

688
- Ine becomes first great king of Wessex: a lawmaker.

689
- Pepin defeats the Frisians.

690
- St Willibrord, an Anglo-Saxon, becomes Bishop of Frisia, which he converts to Christianity.

693
- Battle of Sebastopolis: Greeks defeated by the Moslems.

695
- Leontius usurps the Empire.

697
- First doge of Venice elected.

698
- Moslems capture Carthage.
- Tiberius III usurps the Empire.

c.700-730
- Probable time of the writing of *Beowulf.*

705
- Justinian II recovers the Empire and perpetrates great cruelties.

709
- Pepin defeats the Alamanni.

Deaths

St Wilfrid, bishop of York and Ripon.

710
- Moslem conquest of Africa complete.
- Moslems begin conquest of Transoxiana; they reach India.
- Roderick becomes king of the Visigoths.
- First Moslem invasion of Spain.

711
- Second Moslem invasion of Spain under Tarik; Visigothic kingdom overthrown in Battle of Xeres or Guadalete or Lake Janda; Toledo, the capital, captured; oppressed Jews welcome invaders.
- Justinian II executed; Philippicus becomes emperor.

712
- Liutprand becomes king of the Lombards; aims at unifying Italy under the Lombard monarchy.

713
- Batttle of Segoyuela: Moslems again victorious over Visigoths; King Roderick killed.
- Anastasius II usurps the Empire.
- Aelfwald becomes king of East Anglia.

714
- Death of Pepin of Heristal, ruler of the Franks: his son Charles Martel is chosen as duke of the Austrasian Franks.

716
- Theodosius III usurps the Empire.

717
- Leo III (the Isaurian) becomes emperor.
- Second Arab siege of Constantinople begins by land and sea under Moslemah, brother of the Caliph Soliman; Moslems routed in 718 with the help of the Bulgarians and by means of Greek fire.
- Battle of Vincy: Charles Martel, son of Pepin of Heristal, defeats the Neustrians and becomes virtual ruler of the Franks.
- Church of Iona confirmed to Roman Catholicism.

718
- Charles Martel ravages the country of the Saxons (in north Germany).

720
- Moslems cross the Pyrenees and capture Narbonne.

721
- Moslem attack on Toulouse repelled by Eudes (Eudo), Duke of Aquitaine.

722
- St Boniface, an Anglo-Saxon, goes as Papal missionary to Germany under the protection of Charles Martel.

724
- Charles Martel ravages Frisia.

725
- Moslems take Carcassonne and Nimes.
- Charles Martel fights the Bavarians.

726
- Leo III begins his campaign against the worship of images, promulgating the Iconoclastic controversy; he is opposed by Pope Gregory II.

731
- Pope Gregory III summons a council at Rome which condemns the Iconoclasts; this breach between the Pope and the Empire makes the Roman Republic virtually independent of the Empire but under Papal influence.
- Moslems under Abderrahman advance to conquer France.
- Completion of the Venerable Bede's *Ecclesiastical History.*

732
- Battle of Tours or Poitiers: Charles Martel defeats and drives back the Moslems.

733
- Ethelbald of Mercia becomes overlord of Wessex, etc.

737
- Angus MacFergus, king of the Picts, subdues the Scots of Dalriada.

739
- Pope Gregory III appeals to Charles Martel for help against the Lombards, who, under Liutprand, are besieging Rome.

740
- Ethelbald of Mercia becomes overlord of East Anglia.
- Constantine V becomes emperor.

741
- Death of Charles Martel: Frankish kingdom divided between his sons Pepin the Short and Carloman.

747
- Carloman becomes a monk, leaving Pepin sole master of the Franks.

750
- Ommmiade dynasty of Caliphs overthrown and replaced by the Ambassides.
- Cynewulf, Anglo-Saxon poet.

51

Pepin III (the Short), with the consent of Pope Zacharias, is crowned king of the Franks at Soissons, superseding the nominal Merovingian Childeric III: beginning of the Carolingian Dynasty.

Ravenna captured by the Lombards under King Aistulf: end of the Exarchate.

52

Battle of Burford: Cuthred of Wessex defeats Ethelbald of Mercia.

54

Pope Stephen II concludes an alliance with Pepin, whom he anoints as king of the Franks and Patrician of the Romans.

Pepin invades Italy and repels the Lombards under Aistulf; he grants the lands of the Exarchate to the Pope; beginning of the temporal power of the papacy.

Iconoclastic Synod, Constantinople.

55

Abderrahman founds the Emirate (afterwards Caliphate) of Cordova in Spain as a secession from the Abbasside Caliphate.

56

Pepin again in Italy to subdue the Lombards.

Strathclyde subdued by Angus the Pictish king and Eadbert of Northumbria.

57

Offa becomes king of Mercia and makes himself overlord of England.

58

Pepin III fights heathen Saxons between the Rhine and the Elbe.

59

Pepin III takes Narbonne from the Moslems.

60

Pepin III begins conquest of Aquitaine; completed in 768.

66

The Abbassides remove the Caliphate to Baghdad.

68

Aed Find becomes king of Scots.

Death of Pepin III; Frankish kingdom divided between his sons Charlemagne (Charles the Great) and Carloman.

70

Dissolution of the monasteries by the eastern emperor.

71

Death of Carloman; Charlemagne sole king of the Franks.

772

- Charlemagne begins his wars against the Saxons.

773

- Desiderius, king of the Lombards, attacks the Pope, Adrian I, who appeals to Charlemagne.

774

- Charlemagne captures Pavia and overthrows the Lombard kingdom; he is crowned king of the Lombards; renews Pepin's donation of territory to the Pope.

775

- Leo IV becomes emperor.

776

- Charlemagne again in Italy to repress the Lombards.

777

- Battle of Bensington: Offa of Mercia defeats Cynewulf of Wessex.

778

- Aed Find, king of Scots, dies.
- Charlemagne invades Spain and takes Pampeluna; origin of the Spanish March (established 795). His rearguard cut to pieces by Basques at Roncesvalles: Roland killed.

780

- Constantine VI becomes emperor, with his mother Irene as regent. The latter opposes the Iconoclasts.

781

- Eastern Empire abandons claims to the pontifical state in Italy.

782

- Alcuin, a British scholar, goes to Aachen (Aix-la-Chapelle) to organize the palace school of Charlemagne.
- The eastern Empire pays tribute to the great Caliph Haroun-al-Raschid.

784

- Construction of Offa's Dyke as a Welsh border defence by Offa.

786

- Cynewulf, king of Wessex, murdered by Cyneheard, brother of Sigebert ofWessex.

787

- Seventh General Council of the Church, at Nicaea.
- Peter's Pence, the annual offering to the pope, first sent.

788

- Charlemagne finally conquers Bavaria, Duke Tassilo is deposed.

789
- Constantin I becomes king of the Picts.

790
- Constantine VI proclaimed sole emperor.

793
- First Danish raid on Britain, at Lindisfarne.

795
- First attack of the Norsemen or Northmen on Ireland.

796
- Offa, king of Mercia. He is succeeded by his son Egfrith, who dies the same year.
- Charlemagne conquers the Avars.

797
- Irene blinds Constantine VI and rules alone.

798
- The Norsemen ravaged the Isle of Man.

800
- Charlemagne crowned Holy Roman emperor by Pope Leo III in St Peter's at Rome on Christmas Day.

801
- Charlemagne receives an embassy from Haroun-al-Raschid.

802
- Nicephorus I dethrones Irene and becomes eastern emperor.
- Egbert becomes king of the West Saxons (until 839).
- First Norse raid on Iona.

804
- Charlemagne completes the conquest of the Saxons and compels them to accept Christianity.

Deaths

Alcuin, English scholar.

806
- The Norsemen raid Iona, this time murdering 68 monks.

807
- The Norsemen attack west coast of Ireland.

810
- The Frisian coast is ravaged by Vikings.

811
- Nicephorus I killed in a war against the Bulgarians under Krum; Michael I becomes eastern emperor, after Stauracius reigned a few months.

Deaths

Abu Nuwas, Arab poet.

812
- Michael I acknowledges Charlemagne as western emperor.

813
- Michael I defeated by Bulgarians and dethroned; Leo V becomes eastern emperor.
- Death of Charlemagne: Louis I of France becomes king of the Franks and western emperor.

817
- Partition of Aachen: Louis I divides his kingdom among his sons.

818
- Bernard, king of Italy, nephew of Louis I, revolts; he is defeated and executed.

820
- Eastern emperor Leo V murdered; Michael II becomes eastern emperor.
- Norse raids on Ireland: beginning of worst period.

824
- Iona raided by the Norsemen for the third time.

825
- Battle of Gafulford: Egbert of Wessex conquers the West Welsh (in Cornwall).
- Battle of Ellandune: Egbert of Wessex defeats Beornwulf of Mercia.
- Kent conquered about same time and East Saxons submit.

826
- Crete taken by the Moslems.

827
- Moslem conquest of Sicily begins.

829
- Egbert of Wessex conquers Mercia.
- Theophilus becomes eastern emperor.

833
- The Field of Lies: Louis I compelled by his sons to abdicate.

834
- Vikings sack Dorstadt and Utrecht.
- Danish raids in Britain recommenced: Sheppey attacked.

835
- Louis I restored to his kingdom.

836
- Vikings sack Antwerp; attack Dorsetshire.

837
- Battle of Hengestesdun: Egbert of Wessex defeats a combination of Danes and West Welsh.

838
- Norsemen under Thorgils captures Dublin, after desolating much of Ireland.

39

Ethelwulf becomes king of Wessex and England.

40

Moslems made conquests in Southern Italy.

Death of Louis I; Lothair I, the eldest son, becomes western emperor.

41

Death of Alpin, king of Scots: his son Kenneth I (Mac-Alpin) becomes king

Vikings under Oscar sack Rouen.

Battle of Fontenoy: Louis the German and Charles the Bald, sons of Louis I, defeat their brother Lothair I.

42

Louis the German and Charles the Bald exchange the Oaths of Strassburg in Romance and German, the earliest document of the French and German languages.

Moslems capture Bari in South Italy and make it their base.

Michael III becomes eastern emperor under the guardianship of his mother Theodora, who finally restores image-worship.

43

Treaty of Verdun: the Frankish Empire partitioned between Louis the German (eastern or German part), Charles the Bald (western or French part; Charles II of France) and Emperor Lothair I (Italy and a part between France and Germany): the beginning of France and Germany as distinct states.

Kenneth I MacAlpin, king of the Scots, also becomes king of the Picts: beginning of Scottish kingdom.

44

Vikings raid Spanish coast, but are driven off.

45

Battle of Ballon: Charles the Bald defeated by Bretons.

Malachy I, king of Meath, defeats and slays Thorgils, Norse king of northern Ireland.

Vikings destroy Hamburg; Paris partly destroyed by Vikings under Ragnar.

46

Danes defeated in Somerset.

Moslems sack Rome.

48

Norsemen defeated in Ireland.

Vikings take Bordeaux.

Battle of Ostia: Moslems defeated in naval battle at mouth of Tiber, largely owing to Pope Leo IV.

850

- John Scotus (Erigena), an Irish scholar and theologian, flourishes about this time at the court of Charles the Bald.

851

- Battle of Juvardeil: Bretons defeat Charles the Bald.
- Danish attack on England under Roric; Canterbury burnt; London plundered.
- Battle of Aclea or Ockley: Ethelwulf of Wessex completely defeats the Danish invaders.

853

- Danes land in Thanet.

855

- Death of Emperor Lothair I; his son Louis II becomes emperor and king of Italy; another son, Lothair, becomes king of Lotharingia or Lorraine (the central kingdom of his father); and a third son, Charles, becomes king of Provence.
- Edmund becomes king of East Anglia (until 870).
- Danes wintered in Sheppey.

858

- Death of Ethelwulf. His son Ethelbald becomes king of Wessex and England.
- Death of Kenneth I MacAlpin, king of the Scots. His brother Donald I becomes king of Scots.
- Nicholas I becomes pope; final breach between eastern and western Churches.

860

- Death of Ethelbald. Ethelbert becomes king of Wessex and England.
- Danes under Weland capture Winchester, capital of Wessex; then defeated.

862

- Aed Finnliath becomes high king of Ireland.
- Death of Donald I, king of Scots. His nephew becomes king as Constantine I.
- Swedish invasion of Russia under Rurik; a state founded with Novgorod as capital, afterwards Kiev, the origin of Russia; Swedes becomes absorbed by the Slavs.

Deaths

St Swithin, bishop of Winchester.

863

- Death of Charles, king of Provence; his kingdom falls mostly to Emperor Louis II, king of Italy.

864

- Boris, king of Bulgarians, baptised as a Christian.

865

- Death of Ethelbert. Ethelred I becomes king of Wessex and England.

- Russian attack on Constantinople.
- Danes wintered in Thanet.

866
- Robert the Strong, count of Anjou, is killed in battle against the Vikings.
- Emperor Louis II routs the Moslems.
- 'Great Army' of Danes under Ingwar and Hubba in East Anglia.

867
- Danes capture York: Northumbrian kingdom overthrown.
- Scotland ravaged by Danes from Ireland under Olaf the White, king of Dublin.
- Michael III murdered; Basil I becomes eastern emperor, founding Macedonian dynasty.

868
- Battle of Killineery: Aed Finnliath defeated the Norsemen in Ireland.
- Moslems capture Malta.

869

Deaths

Lothair, king of Lorraine.

870
- Danes from Northumbria invade East Anglia; death of St Edmund, king of East Anglia, in Battle of Hoxne or Thetford.
- Olaf the White from Ireland invade Strathclyde and take Dumbarton. Artgal, king of Strathclyde, flees.
- Treaty of Mersen: Lorraine divided between Charles the Bald and Louis the German; France and Germany conterminous.
- Eighth General Council of the Church, at Constantinople.

Deaths

Al-Kindi, Arabian philosopher.
Gottschalk, German theologian and poet.

871
- Danes invade Wessex; capture Reading; defeated in Battles of Englefield and Ashdown by West Saxons under Ethelred supported by Alfred; Danes are successful in Battles of Basing and Merton against West Saxons; Battle of Marden indecisive.
- Death of Ethelred I, king of Wessex, after being wounded at the Battle of Merton. His brother becomes king of Wessex as King Alfred (Alfred the Great).
- Battle of Wilton: Alfred defeated by the Danes, who wintered in London.
- Olaf the White, from Ireland, invades Strathclyde and takes Dumbarton.
- Emperor Louis II captures Bari, the Moslem headquarters in south Italy, with naval help from the eastern Emperor Basil I.

872
- Curfew introduced at Oxford by Alfred to reduce fire risks.
- Battle of Halfsfjord: Harold Haarfager becomes sole king of Norway.

874
- Iceland colonized by Norwegians.
- Danes put an end to the Mercian kingdom.

875
- Norse earldom of Orkney established by Harold Haarfager.
- Danish attacks on Wessex renewed.
- Battle of Dollar: Danish defeat of Constantine I, king of Scots.
- Thorstein the Red, son of Olaf the White, conquers a large part of Scotland; killed.
- Cearbhall, Lord of Ossory, becomes king of Dublin.
- Death of Emperor Louis II; Charles the Bald becomes western emperor.

876
- Death of Louis the German: Charles the Fat becomes German king.
- Battle of Andernach: Charles the Bald defeated.

877
- Battle of Dollar: Constantin II of Scotland defeated by Vikings.
- Battle of Forgan: Constantin II defeated and killed by Vikings.
- Danes divide up Mercia.
- Death of Charles the Bald: his son, Louis II (the Stammerer), becomes king of France.

878
- Moslems take Syracuse, almost completing conquest of Sicily.
- Danes under Guthrum attack Wessex; Battle of Chippenham (January): Guthrum inflicted heavy defeat on King Alfred's Wessex army. Alfred is forced to flee.
- Battle of Ethandun or Edington: Guthrum defeated by Alfred.
- Treaty of Wedmore brought peace between Alfred and the Danes for fifteen years; Guthrum baptised as a Christian; England divided between the two peoples.

879
- Battle of Forgan: Constantine I, king of Scots, defeated and slain by Norsemen. Constantine succeeded by his brother Aed.

- Murder of Aed, king of Scots, possibly by his cousin who becomes joint king with Eocha as Giric I.
- Death of Louis II; Louis III and Carloman, his sons, become joint kings of France.
- Boso becomes independent king of Burgundy or kingdom of Arles.

881
- Charles the Fat crowned emperor at Rome.
- Vikings sack Aachen.
- Battle of Saucourt: Louis III and Carloman defeat the Vikings.

882
- Death of Louis III; Carloman sole king of France.
- Treaty of Elsloo: Charles the Fat reaches agreement with the Vikings.

884
- Death of Carloman, king of France: Charles the Fat chosen king of France; reunion of most of Charlemagne's Empire.

885
- Vikings under Rollo besiege Paris.

886
- Alfred recovers London from the Danes.
- Paris saved from the Vikings by Odo, Count of Paris.
- Leo VI becomes eastern emperor.

887
- Charles the Fat deposed; final break-up of Frankish Empire.

887
- On deposition of Charles the Fat, Arnulf becomes king of Germany and Odo, Count of Paris, king of West Franks.
- Louis the Blind succeeds Boso as king of Cisjuran Burgundy (Arles); Rudolph I founds kingdom of Transjuran Burgundy farther north.

888
- Berengar of Friuli becomes king of Italy.
- Third siege of Paris by Vikings; bought off by Odo.
- Odo defeats Vikings in Champagne.
- Moslems or Moors settle on Provençal coast and penetrate inland.

889
- Battle of Dundurn: Giric I killed in battle by Donald II, the first to be called king of Scotland rather than of Dalriada or Picts.

891
- Battle of Louvain: Arnulf, king of Germany, defeats the Vikings.
- Guido of Spoleto becomes emperor and king of Italy after defeating Berengar.

893
- Danish invasion of England under Hastein; Danes defeated at the Battles of Farnham and Bemfleet.
- Civil War between Odo and the Carolingian Charles the Simple; the latter admitted to a share in the kingdom.
- Simeon founds a great Bulgarian Empire, which falls to pieces after his death.

895
- Alfred the Great captures the Danish fleet.
- Arnulf overthrows Guido and becomes king of Italy.
- Magyars under Arpád invade Hungary, where they settle permanently.

896
- Arnulf crowned emperor at Rome.

898
- Charles the Simple becomes king of France on the death of Odo.

899
- Death of Alfred the Great. His elder son becomes king of England as Edward the Elder.
- Arnulf succeeded as German king by Louis the Child.

900
- Death of Donald II, king of Scots, in battle against the Norse. His cousin becomes king as Constantine II.

901
- Louis the Blind (of Provence) crowned emperor as Louis III.

902
- Battle of the Holme: Edward the Elder defeats the Danes of Northumbria.

903
- Magyars reach the Elbe.

904
- Constantine II of Scotland expels the Danes.
- Sergius III becomes Pope; degradation of the papacy under the influence of Theodora, wife of Theophylact, consul of Rome and her daughter Marozia.
- Moslems raid Salonica.

905
- Louis the Blind is blinded by Berengar.
- The *Kokin Wakashu* is completed; an anthology of pure Japanese poetry.

906
- Magyars complete conquest of Hungary.

906-960
- The rule of the Five Dynasties, China.

907
- Magyars invade Bavaria.
- Russian fleet under Oleg attacks Constantinople.

907-979
- The rule of the Ten Kingdoms, China

908
- Magyars ravage Thuringia.

909
- Magyars ravage Suabia.
- Fatimite Caliphate founded in North Africa by Obaidallah.

910
- Danish Invasion of Britain. Battle of Tettenhall (5 August): Edward the Elder severely defeats the Danes.
- Battle of Augsburg: Louis the Child defeated by the Magyars.
- Foundation of Cluny Abbey in eastern France; becomes the centre of a monastic reformation.

911
- Conrad I of Franconia succeeds Louis the Child as German king.
- Charles the Simple acquires Lotharingia or Lorraine.
- Moslems destroy the Greek fleet.
- Treaty of St Clair-sur-Epte; the Vikings, under Rollo, allowed by Charles the Sinple to settle in the land that becomes Normandy.
- Danish Invasion of Britain. Battle of Wednesfield: Danes defeated by West Saxons under Edward the Elder.

912
- Constantine VII becomes eastern emperor; his uncle Alexander being regent and joint emperor.

913
- Kingdom of Leon founded.
- Magyars penetrate to Rhine.

914
- Bulgarians capture Adrianople.

915
- Berengar crowned emperor.

916
- Edward the Elder and his sister Ethelfled, the Lady of the Mercians, recover Eastern Mercia from the Danes.
- Battle of Tempsford: Danes heavily defeated by Edward the Elder.
- Battle of Maldon: Edward the Elder victorious over the Danes; East Anglia recovered.

917
- Edward the Elder's victories over the Danes continue; death of Ethelfled.
- Battle of Garigliano: Moslems defeated by Romans under Theophylact and Alberic, husband of Marozia.
- Pope John X forms a league against the Moors in South Italy.
- Battle of Garigliano: Moslems defeated by Romans under Theophylact and Alberic, husband of Marozia.
- Pope John X forms a league against the Moors in South Italy.

918
- Henry I (the Fowler) becomes the German king; beginning of Saxon line.

919
- Romanus I becomes co-emperor in the East with Constantine VII.
- Edward the Elder receives the homage of all the northern kings.

922
- Robert I, Duke of France, brother of Odo, crowned king of France, Charles the Simple having been displaced.

923
- Battle of Soissons: Robert I, king of France, killed, though victorious over Charles the Simple's supporters; Hugh the Great becomes Duke of France and Rudolph I of Burgundy becomes king of France; Charles the Simple made prisoner.

923
- Moslem fleet destroyed at Lemnos.

Deaths

Rhases, Arab physician.

924
- Nine years' truce between Henry I and the Magyars; Magyars ravage Italy.
- Berengar, emperor and king of Italy, assassinated.
- Death of Edward the Elder. His illegitimate son Elfward becomes king of Wessex and Mercia but died within a few months. He is succeeded by his half-brother Ethelstan (or Aethelstan).

926
- Hugh of Provence becomes king of Italy.

927
- William Longsword succeeds Rollo as Duke of Normandy.
- Odo becomes Abbot of Cluny and starts the Cluniac reformation.

Deaths
Simeon I, tsar of Bulgaria.

928
- Henry I takes Brandenburg from the Slavs.

929
- Emirate of Cordova becomes a Caliphate; there now exist three Caliphates.
  Deaths
  Al-Battani, Arab astronomer.
  Charles the Simple.

932
- Alberic, son of Marozia, expels Hugh of Provence from Rome and becomes head of the commune.

933
- Battle of Merseburg: Henry I defeats the Magyars.
- The two Burgundian kingdoms (Cisjuran and Transjuran) united.

934
- Haakon I becomes king of Norway.

936
- Otto I (the Great) becomes German king.
- Louis IV (d'Outremer) becomes king of France.

937
- Magyars invade Burgundy and Aquitaine.
- Battle of Brunanburh: Ethelstan defeated a combination of Scots, Danes and Northumbrians.

938
- Alan of the Twisted Beard expels Normans from Brittany.
  Deaths
  Marozia, thrice-married Roman noblewoman dies in prison.

939
- Otto I conquers Lorraine.
- Death of Ethelstan. His half-brother becomes king of the English as Edmund I (until 946).

940
- Edmund makes peace with Olaf, leader of the Vikings who have taken York.
- Harold Bluetooth becomes king of Denmark.

941
- Russian raid defeated by Byzantine fleet.

942
- Richard the Fearless becomes Duke of Normandy.

943
- Malcolm I becomes king of Scots on the abdication of his cousin, Constantine II.

944
- Battle of Wels: Magyars defeated by Bavarians.
- Romanus I deposed.

***c*.945**
- Dunstan becomes abbot of Glastonbury.

946
- Murder of Edmund I by Leofa, an exiled thief. His brother Edred becomes king of the English (until 955) as Edmund's sons are too young.
  Deaths
  Tsuraguki, Japanese poet.

947
- Magyars again invade Italy and Aquitaine.
- Erik Bloodaxe, deposed as king of Norway, comes to England and seizes Northumbria from Edred.

947-1125
- The Liao dynasty rules the extreme north of China.

948
- Edred suppresses a Northumbrian rebellion led by Erik Bloodaxe.

950
- Berengar of Ivrea becomes king of Italy.
  Deaths
  Alfarabi, Arab philosopher.

951
- Otto I invades Italy and makes Berengar do homage.

951-979
- Northern Han dynasty, China.

952
Deaths
Constantine II ,king of Scots (abdicated 943), in a monastery in St Andrews.

954
- Edred invades Northumbria and kills Erik Bloodaxe in an ambush. Northumbria given to Oswulf as an earldom.
- Malcolm I of Scotland dies in battle; succeeded by Indulf, who made Dunedin (or Edinburgh) Scottish.
- Lothair becomes king of France.
  Deaths
  Alberic, son of Marozia, the head of the Roman commune.

955
- Battle of Augsburg (Lechfeld): Otto I defeats Magyars and the Slavs. East Mark (afterwards Austria) refounded.
- Death of Edred. His nephew Edwy (or Eadwig) becomes king of the English.

956
- Death of Hugh the Great; succeeded as Duke of France by his son, Hugh Capet.
- Dunstan exiled by Edwy. He goes to Flanders and Ghent.

957
- Renunciation by the Mercians and Northumbrians of Edwy (or Eadwig) in favour of Edgar, his brother. Edwy rules south of the Thames.

958
- Romanus II eastern emperor.

959
- Death of Edwy. Edgar becomes king of the English.
- Dunstan recalled.
- Dunstan becomes archbishop of Canterbury.

960-1126
- Sung dynasty, China.

961
- Otto I again in Italy; crowned king of Italy at Pavia.
- Nicephorus takes Crete from the Moslems.
- Haakon I of Norway killed in battle.

962
- Death of Indulf. Dubh, son of Malcolm I, becomes king of Scots.
- Otto crowned western emperor at Rome: revival of Holy Roman Empire after a period of decline.
- Byzantine victories under Nicephorus over Moslems in Asia Minor.
- Mieczyslaw I becomes ruler of Poland; accepts Christianity in 966.

963
- Basil II eastern emperor, with Nicephorus II (Phocas) and Constantine VIII as co-emperors.

964
- Nicephorus Phocas begins conquest of Cilicia from the Moslems.

966
- Murder of Dubh, king of Scots. Cuilean becomes king.

968
- Nicephorus Phocas conquers Northern Syria.

969
- Nicephorus Phocas murdered by his nephew John Zimisces, who becomes co-emperor.

971
- Death of Cuilean, king of Scots, in battle against the Britons of Strathclyde. Kenneth II becomes king of Scotland.
- John Zimisces drives back the Russians from Thrace and other Balkan lands.

972

Deaths

Sviatoslav, the Russian ruler.

973
- Edgar created 'emperor of Britain' at a ceremony in Bath.
- Otto II becomes emperor in the West.

975
- Death of Edgar, king of England. His eldest son becomes king as Edward the Martyr.

976
- Death of John Zimisces; Basil II comes into power.
- Samuel becomes king of Bulgaria; he made extensive conquests and built up a Bulgarian Empire.
- Otto II deposes Henry the Quarrelsome, Duke of Bavaria.

978
- Lothair of France invades Lorraine.
- Murder of Edward the Martyr. His half-brother, Ethelred II the Unready, becomes king of England at the age of ten.

980
- Battle of Tara: Malachy II, king of Meath, defeat the Danes in Ireland.
- Battle of Luncarty: Scots under Kenneth II defeat Danes.
- Vikings attack Southampton, Thanet, and Chester.
- Otto II goes to Italy; aims at conquering southern Italy.
- Vladimir I (St Vladimir) becomes Russian ruler.

982
- Greenland discovered by the Norwegians.
- Otto II heavily defeated in Italy by combined Byzantine and Moslem forces.

983
- Otto III becomes German king.

985
- Duke Henry of Bavaria restored.

986
- Death of Harold Bluetooth of Denmark; Sweyn Forkbeard becomes Danish king.
- Louis V becomes king of France.

987
- Death of Louis V; Hugh Capet, son of Hugh the Great, becomes king of France, with Paris as capital: founder of the long Capetian dynasty.

988

- Russian Duke Vladimir becomes a Christian.

Deaths

St Dunstan, prelate and archbishop of Canterbury.

990

- Pax Ecclesiae, restricting private warfare, introduced in southern France.

991

- Olaf Tryggveson of Norway raids the British Islands (till 994).
- Battle of Maldon between the Danes and Anglo-Saxons; Danes are victorious and bought off by Ethelred II the Unready with first payment of Danegeld tax (abolished 1163).

992

- Boleslaus I becomes ruler of Poland.

993

- Danes sack Bamburgh.

994

- Sweyn Forkbeard and Olaf Tryggveson attack London but are driven off. Ethelred again buys them off.

995

- Murder of Kenneth II, king of Scotland. Constantine III (possibly his murderer) becomes king.
- Olaf Tryggveson becomes Olaf I, king of Norway; imposes Christianity on his people.

996

- Richard the Fearless succeeded by Richard the Good as Duke of Normandy.
- Robert II (the Pious) becomes king of France.
- Otto III crowned emperor at Rome.

997

- Stephen I becomes ruler of Hungary.
- Vikings again attack Wessex.
- Murder of Constantine III, king of Scotland, by Kenneth III, who becomes king and shares the throne with his son, Giric II.

998

- Battle of Veszprem: Stephen I of Hungary victorious over rebels; takes title of king, which the Pope confirms in 1001.
- Crescentius, patrician of Rome, executed: Otto III master of Rome.

999

- Gerbert of Aurillac becomes pope as Silvester II.

1000

- Battle of Svold: Norwegians defeated in naval battle by combined Swedes and Vikings; Norway divided between the conquerors.
- Leif Ericsson discovers Vinland, part of Canada.
- Revival of legal studies at Bologna: celebrated university founded later.
- Battle of Glenmama: Malachy II and Brian Boru, Irish rivals, combined and defeated the Danes.

1001

- Danes again bought off from Wessex.

1002

- Ethelred II marries Emma, daughter of Richard, Duke of Normandy.
- Massacre of Danes in England on St Brice's Day (13 November).
- Brian Boru, king of Munster, becomes high king of Ireland.
- Henry II, son of Henry the Quarrelsome, becomes German king.
- Ardoin of Ivrea crowned king of Italy.
- The Moslems take Sardinia.

1003

- Boleslaus I of Poland conquers Bohemia.
- Sweyn Forkbeard again invades England.

1004

- Ardoin overthrown in Italy: Henry II becomes king of the Lombards.

1005

- Battle of Monzievaird: Kenneth III and Giric II killed by Kenneth's cousin, Malcolm, who becomes king of Scots as Malcolm II.

1006

- Boleslaus I of Poland gave up Bohemia.

1007

- Danes again bought off from England by Ethelred II.
- Ship money first levied in England.

1009

- Another Danish invasion of England.
- Danes under Sweyn besieged Nairn and defeats Malcolm II at Battle of Kinloss.

1010

- Danes under Sewyn are defeated by Malcolm at Battle of Mortlack and forced to withdraw.

1012

- Ethelred II again buys off Danes.

1013

- Sweyn Forkbeard again invades England; Ethelred II flees to Normandy; Danish conquest.

1014

- Death of Sweyn Forkbeard; his son Canute succeeds

him. Ethelred returns to England and begins struggle with Canute for the throne.
- Battle of Clontarf between the Irish and the Danes (23 April): Danes heavily defeated by Brian Boru, high king of Ireland, but Brian himself is killed. He is succeeded as high king by Mael Sechnaill II.
- Sutherland and Caithness come under the control of Malcolm II.
- Olaf II (St Olaf) becomes king of Norway.
- Crushing defeat of Bulgaria by Basil II, followed by death of Samuel, king of Bulgaria; his Empire collapses.
- Henry II crowned emperor at Rome.

1015
- Death of Vladimir I of Russia.
- Duchy of Burgundy annexed to the French monarchy by Robert II.

1016
- Death of Ethelred II the Unready, king of England. His son Edmund II Ironside chosen as king by Saxons and fights against Canute at Battles of Pen Selwood and Assandun, or Ashingdon. He is defeated at Assandun; partition of kingdom arranged, but death of Edmund, after only 7 months as king, leaves Canute sole king (until 1035).
- Malcolm II acquires Strathclyde. Malcolm II's grandson, Duncan (I) installed as king of Strathclyde.

1017
- Marriage of Canute and Emma of Normandy, widow of Ethelred II.

1018
- Basil II, the Bulgar-slayer, completes the conquest of Bulgaria.
- Battle of Carham: Malcolm II, king of Scots, annexes Lothian.

1022
- Catharist heretics burned at Orleans.

1023
- Death of Mael Sechnaill II, high king of Ireland. Civil war over the succession leads to the end of royal rule in Ireland.

1024
- Death of Henry II, Holy Roman emperor.
- Conrad II elected German king: first of Franconian emperors.

1025
- Constantin VIII sole eastern emperor.
- Death of Boleslaus I, king of Poland.

1027
- Conrad II crowned emperor at Rome.
- Truce of God, restricting private war, first proclaimed in southern France.

1028
- Romanus III eastern emperor.
- Fall of Caliphate of Cordova.
- Ferdinand I (the Great) becomes king of Castile.

1030
- Normans begin conquest of Southern Italy or Apulia.
- Battle of Stiklestad: Norway overthrown and annexed by Denmark.
- Seljuk Turks begin aggression in Asia Minor.

1031
- Henri I becomes king of France.

1032
- Lusatia recovered from Poland by Emperor Conrad II.
- Duchy of Burgundy bestowed on King Henry's brother Robert: line lasts till 1361.

1033
- Kingdom of Burgundy annexed to emperor by Conrad II.

1034
- Michael IV becomes eastern emperor.
- Death of Malcolm II, king of Scots. His grandson becomes king as Duncan I.

1035
- William the Conqueror becomes Duke of Normandy.
- Death of Canute. His illegitimate son, Harold I 'Harefoot' Knutsson, becomes regent while Canute's legitimate son, Hardicanute, defends Denmark against the Norwegians.

1037
- Norway recovers its independence from Denmark.
- Bretislav I Prince of Bohemia (conquers Moravia, Silesia, much of Poland).
- Harold I 'Harefoot' Knutsson becomes king of the English (until 1040).

Deaths

Avicenna, Arab physician and philosopher.

1038
- Ferdinand I of Castile acquires Leon.

Deaths

Alhazen, Arab physicist.

1039
- Henry III German king.
- Unsuccessful siege of Durham by Duncan I, king of Scots.

1040
- Death of Harold I 'Harefoot' Knutsson: Hardicanute becomes king of the English (until 1042).
- Duncan I killed by Macbeth, nephew of Malcolm II, who proclaims himself king of the Scots (until 1057).
- Lady Godiva, wife of the Earl of Mercia, rides naked through the streets of Coventry.

1041
- Bohemia made subject to the Empire.
- Michael V becomes eastern emperor.
- The Danish soldier Siward the Strong is made Earl of Northumbria.

1042
- Emperor Michael V deposed: Constantine IX becomes eastern emperor.
- Death of Hardicanute. His half-brother, Edward the Confessor, son of Ethelred II, becomes king of the English.

1043
- Unsuccessful Russian expedition against Constantinople.

1044
- Henry II defeats Hungarians.
- Seljuks capture Edessa.

1045
- Marriage of Edward the Confessor and Edith, daughter of Godwin, Earl of Wessex.

1046
- Anarchy in Rome: three rivals for Papacy: Henry III called in and chooses Clement II, who crowns him emperor.
- The Norman Robert Guiscard arrives in Italy.

1047
- Battle of Val-des-Dunes: William of Normandy, aided by King Henri I, defeats rebel nobles.

1049
- Harold Hardrada becomes king of Norway.

1050
- Emund succeeds Anund as king of Sweden.

1051
- Emperor Henry III subdues Hungary.
- Fall of Earl Godwin in England because of his anti-Norman views. Edward promises English succession to William, Duke of Normandy.

1052
- Earl Godwin's triumphant return.
- Edward the Confessor founds Westminster Abbey.

1053
- Battle of Civitella: Robert Guiscard, the Norman, defeats Papal forces; makes agreement with Pope Leo IX.

Deaths

Godwin, earl of the West Saxons: his son Harold becomes Earl of Wessex.

1054
- Scotland invaded by Siward.
- Battle of Dunsinane: defeat of Macbeth by Siward, Earl of Northumberland fighting for Malcolm, son of Duncan.
- Battle of Mortemer: William of Normandy defeats the French royal forces.
- Breach between eastern and western churches complete.
- Theodora becomes eastern Empress.

Deaths

Yaroslav the Great, Grand Duke of Russia.

1055
- Seljuk Turks under Togrul Beg occupy Baghdad and restore authority of the Caliph.

Deaths

Siward: Tostig becomes earl of the Northumbrians.

1056
- Henry IV becomes German king.
- Michael VI becomes eastern emperor: last of the Macedonian dynasty.

1057
- Isaac I (Comnenus) eastern emperor after dethroning Michael VI: first of the Comneni.
- Macbeth killed by Malcolm, son of Duncan, at the Battle of Lumphanan (15 August). Macbeth's stepson, Lulach, becomes king of Scotland.

1058
- Battle of Varaville: William of Normandy defeats the French royal forces.
- Boleslaus II becomes king of Poland.
- Lulach ambushed and killed by Malcolm, who becomes king of Scotland as Malcolm III Canmore.

1059
- Constantine (X) Ducas eastern emperor.
- Method of papal election settled.
- Robert Guiscard obtains title of Duke of Apulia and Calabria from Pope Nicholas II, subject to Holy See.

1060
- Norman invasion of Sicily begins under Count Roger: Messina taken.
- Death of Henri I, king of France: Philip I becomes king of France under the guardianship of the count of

Flanders, Baldwin V (rules alone from 1067).
• Steinkel succeeds Emund as king of Sweden.

1063
• William of Normandy conquers Maine.

1064
• Seljuks conquer Armenia.
• Ferdinand I takes Coimbra from Portugal.

1065
• Alfonso VI succeeds Ferdinand I as king of Castile and Leon.
• Revolt against Tostig. Morcar becomes Earl of the Northumbrians.
• Consecration of Westminster Abbey (Collegiate Church of St Peter).

1066
• Death of Edward the Confessor (6 January). His brother-in-law, Harold, Earl of Wessex, claimed the throne as Harold II.
• Battle of Stamford Bridge (25 September): Harold, king of the English, defeats Norwegian invasion: Harold Hardraade, king of Norway, and Tostig, former earl of the Northumbrians, killed.
• Norman Conquest. Battle of Hastings on Senlac Hill between the Normans and the English (14 October):William the Conqueror (William I) victorious and Harold slain: Norman Conquest of England begins.
• With the conquest the Channel Islands (formerly part of Normandy) becomes attached to England.
• Haakon the Red becomes king of Sweden: Olaf Kyrre becomes king of Norway.

1067
• Michael VII and Romanus IV eastern emperors.
• Anglo-Saxon revolt against the Normans crushed.
• Work begins on the building of the Tower of London.

1069
• North of England subdued by William I.
• Malcolm III Canmore of Scotland marries Margaret of the English royal family.
• Malcolm III invades England.

1070
• Duchy of Bavaria given to Count Welf.
• Revolt by Hereward the Wake against William I the Conqueror (quashed 1071).
• Malcolm III again invades England.
• Construction of Canterbury Cathedral begins (completed 1495).

1071
• Battle of Manzikert: Seljuks under Alp Arslan defeat forces of Romanus IV, who is captured: Asia Minor lost to eastern Empire.
• Normans capture Bari, last Greek possession in Italy.
• Normans take Palermo.
• Norman conquest of England complete.

1072
• William the Conqueror invades Scotland. Treaty of Abernethy: Malcolm III of Scotland does homage to William the Conqueror. Malcolm's son, Duncan, is taken to England as a hostage.

1073
• Saxon revolt against the Empire.
• Hildebrand becomes Pope as Gregory VII.

1074
• Peace of Gerstungen between Henry IV and the Saxons.

1075
• Seljuks capture Jerusalem.
• Henry IV reduces the Saxons.
• Gregory VII issues his decrees on clerical celibacy and investiture of prelates.

1076
• Emperor Henry IV summons a synod of German bishops at Worms, which declares Gregory VII deposed; Gregory VII declares Henry IV deposed and excommunicated.
• Sancho Ramirez of Aragon becomes king of Navarre.
• *Monologion* written by St Anselm, giving the philosophical reasoning behind religious belief.

1077
• Humiliation of Emperor Henry IV by Gregory VII at Canossa in Tuscany; Rudolph of Suabia elected German king; civil war results.
• Ladislas I (St Ladislas) becomes king of Hungary.

1078
• Nicephorus III eastern emperor, after displacing Michael VII.
• St Anselm finishes *Proslogion*, which gives the ontological argumant for the proof of the existence of God

1079
• Malcolm III invades England but is defeated.
• New Forest made a royal hunting ground by William the Conqueror.

1080
• Rudolph of Suabia defeated and killed. Seljuks capture Nicaea.

1081
• Alexius I (Comenus) eastern emperor; beginning of

continuous dynasty of Comneni.
- Battle of Durazzo: Normans under Robert Guiscard defeat Emperor Alexius I.

1083
- Henry IV enters Rome.
- Battle of Larissa: Emperor Alexius I defeats Normans.

1084
- Alfonso VI recovers Toledo from the Moors.
- Carthusians founded at Chartreuse, near Grenoble, by St Bruno.
- Henry IV crowned emperor in Rome by anti-pope Clement III; Gregory VII saved by Robert Guiscard; Rome sacked.

1085
- Emperor Alexius I recovers Durazzo from Normans.
- Death of Gregory VII.

1086
- Battle of Zalaca: Alfonso VI defeated by Almoravides under Yusuf.
- Preparation of Domesday Book completed (began 1085).

1087
- Death of William the Conqueror in France as the result of a fall from his horse (9 September). His second son William Rufus becomes king of England.

1088
- Bohemia under Vratislav is made a kingdom by the emperor.
- Supporters of Robert, elder son of William I, rebels in Normandy.

1089
- Completion of building of Worcester Cathedral (began 1084).

1090
- Count Roger of Sicily takes Malta from the Moors.
- William Rufus invades Normandy and defeats the rebels. The duchy of Normandy given to Robert in lieu of the English crown.

1091
- Norman conquest of Sicily completed.
- Emperor Alexius I defeats the Petchenegs.
- Malcolm III Canmore invades England but is forced to submit to William Rufus (William II).

1092
- William Rufus annexes southern Cumbria to England.
- Seljuk Empire broken up into parts on death of Malik Shah.
- Consecration of Lincoln Cathedral (construction began 1086).

1093
- Malcolm III Canmore again invades England. Battle of Alnwick (13 November): Scots defeated by the English; Malcolm and his eldest son are killed. Malcolm's brother Donald III Bane becomes king of Scotland.
- Magnus Barefoot becomes king of Norway.
- Anselm becomes archbishop of Canterbury.
- Construction completed of Winchester Cathedral (began *c.*1079).

1094
- Duncan, son of Malcom III, becomes king of Scotland as Duncan II after overthrowing Donald III Bane; Duncan is killed, and Donald regains the throne.
- Rodrigo Diaz, called El Cid, takes Valencia from the Moors.
- Construction of Norwich Cathedral begins (completed *c.*1150).

1095
- Pope Urban II advocates a crusade, to recover the holy places, at Council of Clermont.
- Coloman, great reforming king of Hungary.
- Count Henry of Burgundy marries Theresa of Leon, receiving County of Portugal as dowry; beginning of Portuguese state.
- Foundation of Durham Cathedral.

1096
- First Crusade sets out: led by Godfrey of Bouillon, his brother Baldwin, Raymond of Toulouse, Bohemond of Otranto and a Tancred; preceded by popular forces under Peter the Hermit and Walter the Penniless.

1097
- Edgar, son of Malcom III, defeats Donald III Bane and imprisoned and blinded him. Edgar becomes king of Scotland.
- Frankish County of Edessa founded in Syria.
- Crusaders capture Nicaea and win Battle of Doryloeum.
- Anselm, quarrelling with William Rufus over Church property, leaves the kingdom.

1098
- England invades Wales to subdue a rebellion.
- Magnus Barefoot, king of Norway, invades Orkneys and Sudreys.
- Crusaders take Antioch: Principality of Antioch formed under Bohemond.
- Cistercians founded by St Robert at Citeaux, near Dijon.

1099
- Crusaders take Jerusalem.

- Crusaders win Battle of Ascalon.

1100
- Baldwin I succeeds his brother Godfrey of Bouillon as ruler of Jerusalem and takes title of king.
- William Rufus shot by an arrow and killed while hunting in the New Forest (2 August). His youngest brother becomes king of England as Henry I.
- Charter of Liberties proclaimed.
- Marriage of Henry I and Edith (Matilda), sister of King Edgar of Scotland.

Deaths

Donald Bane, deposed and imprisoned Scots king.

1101
- Treaty of Alton: Robert of Normandy recognizes his younger brother Henry I as king of England.

1102
- Magnus Barefoot, king of Norway, devastates Sudreys and conquers Isle of Man: the Scottish king Edgar recognizes his claim to the Western Islands.
- Boleslaus III becomes king of Poland.

1103
- Death of Magnus Barefoot.

1104
- Revolt of Henry (afterwards Henry V), son of Henry IV, Holy Roman emperor.
- Alfonso I (the Battler) becomes king of Aragon.
- Crusaders capture Acre.
- Building of Gloucester Cathedral completed (begun 1072).

1106
- Henry I invades Normandy and in the Battle of Tinchebrai defeats his brother, Robert of Normandy, and gains the duchy.
- Henry V becomes German king.
- Lothair of Supplinburg appointed Duke of Saxony.

1107
- Death of Edgar, king of Scots. His brother becomes king as Alexander I.
- Battle of Durazzo: Emperor Alexius defeats the Normans under Bohemond.
- Council of Troyes.

1108
- Louis VI (the Fat) becomes king of France.

1109
- Crusaders capture Tripoli (in Syria).

Deaths

St Anselm of Canterbury, philosopher.

1110
- Crusaders capture Beirut.
- Introduction in England of Pipe Rolls, annual rolls for recording exchequer payments, by Roger, bishop of Salisbury.

1111
- Henry V crowned emperor at Rome.

1112
- Theresa rules alone over Portugal on death of Count Henry.

1114
- Saxon rebellion against Empire.
- Marriage of Matilda (Maud), daughter of Henry I, and Henry V, Holy Roman emperor.

1115
- Peter Abelard begins teaching at Paris.
- St Bernard becomes Abbot of Clairvaux.
- Consecration of St Albans Abbey (construction began 1077).

Deaths

Countess Matilda of Tuscany: her estates left to the papacy.

1116
- Henry V in Italy.

1118
- John II eastern emperor.
- Alfonso I of Aragon captures Saragossa.

Deaths

Florence of Worcester, historian.

1119
- Order of Templars founded.
- Battle of Brenneville (Brémule): Louis VI defeated by the English under Henry I.

1120
- Knights of St John (or the Hospitallers) acquire a military character.
- Battle of Cutanda: Almoravides defeated by Alfonso I of Aragon.
- Sinking of *The White Ship* (25 November): Prince William, Henry I's son, drowned. Empress Matilda (Maud), his daughter, and wife of Emperor Henry V is named as heir.

1122
- Concordat of Worms settles the controversy between Empire and Papacy about investiture of bishops.

1123
- Emperor John II defeats the Serbians and exterminates the Petchenegs.
- First Lateran Council of the Church.
- Foundation of St Bartholomew's Hospital in London by Rahere.

Deaths

Omar Khayyam, Persian poet and scientist.

1124

Death of Alexander I, king of Scots. His brother becomes king as David I (until 1153).

Emperor John II defeats the Hungarians.

Boleslaus III of Poland converts the Pomeranians.

Christians, with help of Venice, captures Tyre.

1125

Empress Matilda (Maud) widowed by the death of Henry V, the Holy Roman emperor: end of Franconian line of emperors.

1125

Lothair of Supplinburg elected German king as Lothair II.

1126

Emperor John II successful against Seljuks.

Henry the Proud becomes Duke of Bavaria.

Pierre de Bruys burned for heresy.

1126-1234

Chin dynasty, China.

1127

Conrad of Hohenstaufen proclaimed German king in rivalry with Lothair II: flees to Italy.

Roger II, Count of Sicily, also becomes Duke of Apulia.

Deaths

Guilhem, Count of Poitiers, first of the Troubadour poets.

1127-1279

Southern Sung dynasty, China.

1128

Marriage of Empress Matilda (Maud) and Geoffrey Plantagenet, Count of Anjou.

Conrad crowned king of Italy.

Theresa deposed in Portugal: Alfonso I becomes count.

Holyrood Abbey, Edinburgh, founded by David I.

1130

Roger II assumes style of king of Sicily as Roger I.

1132

Fountains Abbey founded by the Cistercians.

1133

Birth of a son (later Henry II) to Geoffrey Plantagenet and Matilda.

Lothair II crowned emperor at Rome. Beginning of alliance between kingdom of Jerusalem and Emir of Damascus.

- First Bartholomew Fair held at West Smithfield London on St Bartholomew's Day (24 August) (last held 1855).

1134

- Conrad yields to Lothair II.
- Battle of Braga: death of Alfonso I of Aragon and Navarre: Navarre and Aragon again separated.
- Sverker becomes king of Sweden: amalgamates Swedes and Goths.

1135

- Death of Henry I from fever while in France (1 December). His nephew Stephen persuaded the archbishop of Canterbury that he is the legitimate heir instead of Henry's daughter, Matilda, and becomes king of England.
- Alfonso VII becomes king of Castile and Leon.

1136

- Stephen subdues baronial revolts.
- Melrose Abbey founded by David I.

1137

- Emperor John II defeats Armenians.
- Louis VII becomes king of France.
- Queen of Aragon marries Raymond, Count of Barcelona; Aragon greatly extended.
- Henry the Proud of Bavaria obtains Duchy of Saxony.

1138

- David I of Scotland invades England on behalf of Matilda: Battle of the Standard, Northallerton (22 August): defeat of the Scots.
- Conrad III elected German king, never actually crowned emperor: first of the Hohenstaufen line.
- Normans capture Naples.

1139

- Matilda (Maud) lands in England at Arundel and secured a base in the West Country, aided by Earl Robert of Gloucester.
- Battle of Ourique: Alfonso I of Portugal defeats the Moors and takes title of king.
- Henry the Lion becomes Duke of Saxony.
- Pope Innocent II compelled to recognize Norman kingdom of Sicily and South Italy.
- Second Lateran Council of the Church.
- Geoffrey of Monmouth's *History of the Britons* in existence: the basis of the Arthurian romances.
- Boleslaus III; his Polish realm is divided into four principalities.

1140

- Beginning of Guelf versus Ghibelline contest in Germany about this time; later mostly in Italy.

- Vienna becomes capital of Austria.

1141
- Battle of Lincoln (February): Matilda captures Stephen; Matilda proclaimed queen. Matilda falls out with the Bishop of Winchester after having briefly regained his support and besieged him. Stephen's queen, Matilda of Boulogne, besieges and defeats Matilda. Stephen is exchanged for Earl Robert of Gloucester and crowned king (December).

1142
- Matilda besieged at Oxford but escaped.
- Treaty of Frankfort between Conrad and his opponents: Henry the Lion confirmed in Duchy of Saxony and Bavaria given to Henry Jasomirgott, Margrave of Austria.

c.1143

Deaths

Peter Abelard, French theologian and philosopher.

1143
- Manuel I becomes eastern emperor.
- Alfonso I of Portugal recognized by Peace of Zamora as independent of Spain.
- Democratic revolution at Rome against nobles and the pope's temporal power.

Deaths

William of Malmesbury, English historian.

1144
- Turks recapture Edessa (end of the Christian principality).

1145
- Battle of Farringdon: Stephen defeats Matilda.
- Arnold of Brescia at Rome to direct the revolution.

1146
- Second Crusade inspired by St Bernard.
- Matilda leaves for Normandy, which Geoffrey Plantagenet had conquered in her absence.

1147
- Henry the Lion, Duke of Saxony, conquers lands beyond the Elbe.
- Emperor Conrad III and Louis VII of France set out on Second Crusade. France governed by Abbé Suger.
- Alfonso I of Portugal captures Lisbon.
- King Roger of Sicily invades Greece.
- Arnold of Brescia supreme in Rome.
- Geoffrey of Monmouth writes *Historia Regum Britaniae*, a fictitious history of Britain. Introduces the figure of King Arthur to European literature.

1148
- Matilda leaves England and returns to Normandy.
- Failure of Second Crusade against Damascus.
- Construction completed of He ford Cathedral (began 1079 on Anglo-Saxon crypt).

1149
- Normans expelled from island of Corfu.

1150
- Albert the Bear becomes Margrave of Brandenburg, the precursor of Prussia.
- Eric IX becomes king of Sweden.
- Carmelites (White Friars) founded about this time at Mount Carmel by Berthold.
- University of Salerno founded, based upon a much older medical school.
- Approximate date of *Nibelungenlied.*

1151
- Henry of Anjou becomes Duke of Normandy.
- Henry the Lion becomes Duke of Bavaria.

1152
- Louis VII divorced Eleanor of Aquitaine; she marries Henry of Anjou (later Henry II) and brings Aquitaine to him.
- Frederick I (Barbarossa) German king.

1153
- Death of David I, king of Scotland. His grandson, the son of the Earl of Northumberland, becomes king as Malcolm IV.
- Henry Plantagenet of Anjou, son of Matilda (Maud), invades England. Treaty of Winchester or Wallingford: succession of Henry to the English throne assured.

1154
- Death of Stephen (24 October). Henry of Anjou becomes king of England as Henry II (19 December).
- Frederick Barbarossa invades Italy.
- Nureddin, Turkish ruler of Mosul, captures Damascus.
- William I (the Bad) becomes king of Sicily and Naples.
- Nicholas Breakspear becomes pope as Adrian IV, first and only English pope (4 December).

Deaths

Geoffrey of Monmouth, English churchman and historian.

1155
- Thomas à Becket appointed chancellor of England.
- Arnold of Brescia hanged and burned at the command of Pope Adrian IV, to whom he had been handed over by the emperor.
- Frederick Barbarossa crowned emperor in Rome by the Pope.

- Pope Adrian IV's papal bull, Laudabiliter, gave Henry II the right to invade Ireland.
- Wace's *Roman de Brut* completed.

1156
- Bavaria confirmed to Henry the Lion; Austria created as a duchy.
- Franche-Comté (County of Burgundy) gained for the Empire by marriage.

1157
- Castile and Leon separated at death of Alfonso VII.
- Waldemar I becomes king of Denmark.
- Birth of a third son (later Richard I) to Henry II and Eleanor of Aquitaine (8 September).
- Henry II takes back from Scotland the territories of Northumberland, Cumberland and Westmoreland.

1158
- Bohemia finally made a kingdom under Vladislav II.
- Alfonso VIII becomes king of Castile.
- Second invasion of Italy by Frederick Barbarossa.
- Somerled expelled the Norse from the Isle of Man and becomes Lord of the Isles.
- Carlisle and Norwich granted charters by Henry II.

1159
- Peter Lombard, noted theologian, Bishop of Paris.
- Milan besieged by Frederick Barbarossa.
- Death of Pope Adrian IV (Nicholas Breakspear), the only Englishman to be elected pope (1 September).

1160
- Chrétien de Troyes, French poet of Arthurian romances, flourishes at this time.
- Frederick Barbarossa excommunicated by Pope Alexander III.

1161
- Edward the Confessor canonized as St Edward by Pope Alexander III.

1162
- Frederick Barbarossa destroys Milan.
- Alfonso II becomes king of Aragon.
- Thomas à Becket appointed archbishop of Canterbury.

1163
- Frederick Barbarossa invades Italy for the third time.
- Danegeld tax abolished (first levied in 991).

1164
- Somerled of the Isles invades southern Scotland: died at Renfrew.
- Royal proclamation of the Constitutions of Clarendon issued.

1165
- Death of Malcolm IV. His brother becomes king of Scotland as William the Lion.

1166
- Fourth Invasion of Italy by Frederick Barbarossa.
- William II (the Good) becomes king of Sicily and Naples.
- Assize of Clarendon. Establishment of trial by jury.

1167
- Birth of the sixth and youngest son (later King John) of Henry II and Eleanor of Aquitaine (24 December).
- Lombard League formed against Frederick Barbarossa.
- Frederick Barbarossa enters Rome; forced to withdraw because of the plague.
- Oxford University founded.

1169
- Wendish pirates overthrown in Rügen.

1170
- Waldensians founded in southern France by Peter Waldo.
- Invasion of Ireland by Strongbow, Raymond Le Gros and others. Waterford and Dublin conquered.
- University College, Oxford, in existence by this date.
- Thomas of Brittany writes his version, the earliest surviving version, of the legend of Tristan around this time.

Deaths
- Thomas à Becket, archbishop of Canterbury, murdered by four knights acting on the orders of Henry II (29 December).

1171
- Henry II lands in Ireland and received submission of many chiefs.
- Saladin becomes ruler of Egypt, superseding Fatimite dynasty and founding the Ayyubite.

1173
- The Princes' Rebellion. Revolt against Henry II by his sons, Henry, Richard and Geoffrey. Their supporters are defeated by the king's forces at Battle of Fornham St Geneviève.
- Frederick Barbarossa invades Italy for fifth time.
- Bela III made king of Hungary by Emperor Manuel.
- Canonization of Thomas à Becket.

1174
- William the Lion of Scotland mount an expedition to retrieve Northumbria from England and besiege Alnwick Castle. Defeated and captured by English; imprisoned at Falaise Castle in Normandy; released under Treaty of Falaise on doing homage for his kingdom.

- Saladin takes Damascus: Moslem power in Asia again consolidated.
- Destruction of Canterbury Cathedral by fire (5 September).

1175
- Limerick taken by Raymond Le Gros.

1176
- Battle of Legnano: Lombard League completely defeats Frederick Barbarossa.

1177
- Treaty of Venice: a truce between Frederick Barbarossa, the Pope and the Lombard League.

1179
- Third Lateran Council of the Church.
- Aberdeen granted charter by William the Lion.

1180
- Marie de France, French poetess, flourishes at this time.
- War between Emperor Frederick and Henry the Lion, Duchy of Bavaria given to Otto of Wittelsbach.
- Alexius II eastern emperor.
- Philip II (Augustus) becomes king of France.

Deaths
John of Salisbury, English scholar and cleric.

1182
- Banishment of Jews decreed in France.
- Canute VI becomes king of Denmark.
- Massacre of Latins in Constantinople.

1183
- Peace of Constance: definite agreement between emperor, Pope and Lombard League.
- Emperor Alexius murdered; Andronicus I becomes eastern emperor.
- Turkish ruler Saladin takes Aleppo.

1185
- Emperor Andronicus I overthrown: Isaac II (Angelus) eastern emperor.
- Sancho I follows Alfonso I as king of Portugal.
- William II of Sicily takes Salonica, but fails to keep it.

1186
- Guy of Lusignan becomes king of Jerusalem.
- Saladin completes consolidation of Turkish power.
- Bulgarians recover independence of the Empire.

1187
- Battles of Tiberias and Hattin: Saladin victorious over Christians. Jerusalem taken by Saladin.

1189
- Henry II invades France: defeated in battle by his son Richard and Philip II of France. Henry died thereafter at Tours (6 July). His third son becomes king of England as Richard I, Coeur de Lion.
- Tancred becomes king of Sicily and Naples.
- Third Crusade begins: joined by Emperor Frederick, Philip Augustus and Richard I. Siege of Acre begins.
- Legal memory dated from accession of Richard I (1 September).
- Independence of Scotland bought back from England by William the Lion for 10,000 marks.
- Fire rules drawn up by the City of London.
- Office of Lord Mayor of London said to have been founded.

1190
- Henry VI German king.
- Order of Teutonic Knights founded.
- Trouvères flourishes at this time at the court of Marie of Champagne.

Deaths
Chrétien de Troyes, French court poet.

1191
- Henry VI crowned emperor at Rome.
- Henry VI invades southern Italy: fails against Naples.
- Crusaders take Acre.
- Richard I took Cyprus and sold it to the Templars; resold to Guy of Lusignan, king of Jerusalem.
- Crusaders under Richard reinforced force besieging Acre (June). Battle of Arsouf (September): Saracen attack under Saladin withstood by Crusaders under Richard I. Richard sailed for England (October). King Philip returns to France.

1192
- Pope Celestine III declared the Scottish Church to be independent under Rome.
- Agreement between Richard I and Saladin. Richard captured by Duke Leopold of Austria on his way home and handed over to Henry VI, Holy Roman emperor, who demands a heavy ransom.

1193
- Death of Saladin, sultan of Egypt and Syria.
- Philip Augustus attacks Normandy.

1194
- Henry VI conquers kingdom of Sicily and Naples (claimed in right of his wife) and annexes it to Empire.
- Richard I ransomed and released.
- Anglo-French Wars. Battle of Freteval: English under Richard I defeats French under Philip II in Normandy.

- Portsmouth granted a charter by Richard I.

1195
- Emperor Isaac II deposed: Alexius III eastern emperor.
- Cyprus becomes a kingdom under Guy of Lusignan's brother Amaury.

1196
- Christians lose Jaffa.
- Peter II becomes king of Aragon.

1197
- Anglo-French Wars. Battle of Gisors: Richard I defeats French under Philip II near Paris.

1198
- Death of Roderic O'Connor, king of Connaught and last high king of Ireland.
- Philip Suabia and Otto IV of Brunswick rival emperors.
- Frederick, son of Henry VI, crowned king of Sicily.
- Ottacar I becomes king of Bohemia.
- Innocent III becomes Pope.
- Completion of St David's Cathedral, Wales.

Deaths

Averroes, Arabian scholar.

1199
- Death in France of Richard I from wounds received in battle (6 April). His brother John becomes king of England.

1200
- King John divorces his first wife, Isabel of Gloucester, and marries Isabel of Angoulême.
- Mariner's Compass known in Europe soon after this date.
- Saxo Grammaticus, Danish historian, flourishes at this time.
- Walter Map, English author, flourishes at this time.
- Cambridge University founded.

***c*.1200**
- The legendary English hero Robin Hood may have lived at this time.

Deaths

Chu-Hsi, Chinese philosopher.

Procopius, Byzantine historian.

1201
- Philip of Suabia under Papal ban.
- Fourth Crusade starts from Venice.
- Knights of the Sword founded to convert the Letts.
- Denmark conquers Holstein and Hamburg.

Deaths

Archbishop Absalon, Danish statesman.

Reynaud de Coucy, French poet.

1202
- Llewelyn ap Iorwerth united kingdom of Gwynedd.
- Crusaders take Zara on behalf of Venice, at instance of the Doge Henry Dandolo. Waldemar II succeeds Canute VI as king of Denmark: captures Lübeck, Schwerin.
- France conquers Anjou, Maine, Normandy, etc, from England.
- Worcester Cathedral burned (restored 1218).
- Donnybrook Fair in Ireland licensed by King John.

Deaths

Eleanor of Aquitaine, widow of Henry II and mother of Richard I and John.

1203
- Emperor Isaac II restored by Crusaders along with Alexius IV.
- Wolfram von Eschenbach, German poet, flourishes at this time.

1204
- France conquers Anjou, Maine, Normandy from England.
- Alexius V is made eastern emperor, then replaced by Baldwin I of Flanders, the first Latin emperor: beginning of Latin Empire of Constantinople.
- Crete given to Venice.

Deaths

Moses Maimonides, Jewish religious philosopher.

1205
- Emperor Baldwin defeated and captured by Bulgarians at Adrianople and executed.
- Andrew II becomes king of Hungary.
- Walter De Grey becomes chancellor of England (until 1214).

1206
- Walther von der Vogelweide, German poet, flourishes at this time: the greatest of the Minnesingers.
- Stephen Langton nominated as archbishop of Canterbury (until 1228) rather than John's preferred candidate.

1207
- Birth of a son (later Henry III) to King John (1 October).

1208
- Philip of Suabia murdered: Otto IV sole western emperor.
- Albigensian crusade begins: first crusade against heresy.
- Innocent III placed England under interdict (until 1213).
- Great Yarmouth granted charter (18 March) by King John.

- Liverpool created a borough (28 August).

1209
- Otto IV in Italy: crowned emperor at Rome.
- King John excommunicated.
- Construction of first London Bridge completed (begun 1176).
- Peace of Norham between England and Scotland.

1210
- Genghis Khan, Mongol leader, invades China.
- University of Paris founded about this time.
- Franciscan Order (Grey Friars) founded by St Francis of Assisi.
- Otto IV is excommunicated by the Pope, but successfully completes conquest of Sicily.
- Gottfried von Strassburg, German poet, writes *Tristan und Islode*, a version of the Tristan legend based on the poem by Thomas of Brittany (*c*.1170).

1211
- Alfonso II becomes king of Portugal.

1212
- Battle of Navas de Tolosa: Almohades is defeated heavily by a combination of all the Christian kings of Spain and Portugal under Castile.
- Children's Crusade—thousands of children travel from Germany and France to recapture Jerusalem from the Turks; as a consequence of this endeavour, many are shipped to North Africa and sold into slavery.
- Frederick II crowned German king.

1213
- James the Conqueror becomes king of Aragon.
- Battle of Muret: defeat of the Albigenses: Peter II of Aragon killed.
- Parliament called for the first time by King John as an advisory body.
- Cardinal Pandulf arrived in England as commissioner from Pope Innocent III. King John surrenders and does homage for his kingdom. Papal inderdict lifted.

  Deaths

  Villehardouin, French historian of the Fourth Crusade.

1214
- Battle of Bouvines: Philip of France defeats John of England, Otto IV and others.
- Death of William the Lion, king of Scots. His son becomes king as Alexander II (until 1249).
- Battle of Bouvines: Philip of France defeats John of England, Emperor Otto IV, etc.

  Deaths

  Alfonso VIII of Castile.

1215
- Magna Carta signed and sealed reluctantly by King John (15 June). Outbreak of civil war, the Barons' War, when the Pope declares that John need not heed the terms of the Magna Carta.
- Dominican Order (Black Friars) founded at Toulouse by St Dominic.
- Fourth Lateran Council of the Church abolishes trial by ordeal.
- First Lord Mayor's Show held in London.

1216
- Barons' War. Louis, heir of the French king,is called in by English barons against John because of his failure to honour the terms of the Magna Carta. Louis lands in England (May).
- Death of John (19 October): his young son becomes king of England as Henry III. William Marshall, Earl of Pembroke, becomes regent.

1217
- Ferdinand III (the Saint) becomes king of Castile.
- Crusade led by Andrew of Hungary.
- Haakon IV becomes king of Norway.
- Barons' War. Fair of Lincoln (20 May): Prince Louis of France defeated.

1217-1223
- Ghengis Khan's general in the Far East conquers all of Northern China except Honan.

1218
- Death of Otto IV; Frederick I becomes western emperor.
- Waldemar II of Denmark captures Reval.
- Ivan Asen II, Bulgarian king: conquers Albania, Epirus, Macedonia and Thrace; capital, Tirnovo.
- Restoration of Worcester Cathedral.
- Ghengis Khan invades and conquers Khwarazm.

1219
- Damietta taken by John de Brienne, king of Jerusalem.

1220
- Frederick II crowned emperor at Rome.
- Approximate date of the *Owl and Nightingale* and of the *Queste del St Graal*.

  Deaths

  Hartmann von der Aue, German poet.

  Saxo Grammaticus, Danish historian.

***c*.1221**
- English glass industry established.

1221
- Ghengis invades and conquers Caucasia.
- Dominicans settle at Oxford.

- Crusaders abandon Damietta.

1222
- Ghengis invades and conquers Persia
- Introduction of a poll tax in England.
- Golden Bull, the Great Charter of Hungary.

1223
- Louis VIII becomes king of France.
- Sancho II becomes king of Portugal.

Deaths
Giraldus Cambrensis, Welsh writer.

1224
- Ghengis invades and conquers Russia.
- Mongols advance into Russia; Russians defeated in Battle of Kalka.
- Franciscans settle at Oxford and Cambridge.
- Death of Cathal O'Connor, king of Connaught, last provincial monarch in Ireland.

1225
- English take Gascony.
- Frederick II assumes the title of king of Jerusalem in right of his wife.

1226
- Lombard League renewed against Frederick II.
- Louis IX (St Louis) becomes king of France.
- Waldemar II of Denmark compelled to surrender most of the Danish conquests.
- Reputed foundation of St Edmund Hall, Oxford University.

Deaths
St Francis of Assisi, Italian monk, founder of the Franciscan order.

1227
- Battle of Bornhõved: Frederick II defeats Denmark.
- Ottoman Turks settle in Angora under Ertoghrul.
- Frederick II sets out on a crusade, then excommunicated.

Deaths
Genghis Khan, Mongol conqueror.

1228
- Frederick II sets out on Fifth Crusade.
- French king gives the County of Venaissin, near Avignon, to the Papacy.
- First recorded life assurance bond.

1229
- Frederick II procures cession of Jerusalem to the Christians; crowned king of Jerusalem.
- James of Aragon conquers the Balearic Islands.
- Papal victory over Frederick II's troops in Italy.
- Treaty of Meaux: submission of the County of Toulouse and the Albignesians.
- First recorded mention of the Royal Mint.

1230
- Franciscans in Paris.
- Teutonic Knights begins to settle in Prussia.
- Wenceslas I becomes king of Bohemia.
- Final Union of Castile and Leon.
- Ottocar I, king of Bohemia

1231
- Privilege of Worms: German princes recognized by emperor as virtually independent.
- Cambridge University organized and granted Royal Charter.

1232
- Dismissal by Henry III of Hubert de Burgh, his most able adviser.
- Pope Gregory IX establishes the monastic inquisition.

1234
- Marshal Rebellion, led by Richard Marshal, Earl of Pembroke, against Henry III's employment of foreigners in government is defeated (began 1233).
- The Yuan dynasty succeeds the Chin in North China and goes on to rule till 1368.

1235
- War against Lombard League.
- Bela IV becomes king of Hungary.
- The cathedral of Notre Dame in Paris is finished (started 1163).

1236
- Marriage of Henry III and Eleanor of Provence.
- Cordova conquered by the Christians.

***c*.1237**
- French poet Guillaume de Lorris composes *Roman de la Rose* around this time.

1237
- Battle of Cortenuova: Lombard League defeated by Frederick II.
- Ryazan sacked by Mongols under Batu Khan.

1238
- James of Aragon conquers Valencia.
- The Mongols settle in Russia (The Golden Horde), with capital at Sarai; Kiev taken.
- Consecration of Peterborough Cathedral (building began 1117).

1239
- Frederick II excommunicated.
- Birth of a son (later Edward I) to Henry III and Eleanor of Provence.

1240
- Mendovg becomes ruler of Lithuania.
- Death of Llewelyn ap Iorwerth, king of Gwynedd. His son Dafydd ap Llywelyn becomes king.

1241
- Invasion of Hungary and Poland by Batu Khan: Silesian princes defeated in Battle of Liegnitz; Pesth captured.

1242
- Mongols defeated at Olmütz and Neustadt.
- Anglo-French Wars. Battles of Taillebourg (21 July) and Saintes: Louis IX defeats Henry III of England.

1244
- End of Albigensian Persecution.
- Christians finally lose Jerusalem.

1245
- First Church Council of Lyons.
- Frederick II excommunicated and declared deposed by Innocent IV.

Deaths

Alexander of Hales, philosopher and theologian.

1246
- Death of Dafydd ap Llywelyn, king of Gwynedd. The principality is divided among his nephews.
- Provence joined to France.
- Henry Raspe, Landgrave of Thuringia, elected German king at the instigation of the Pope.

1247
- Frederick II besieges Parma (defeated 1248).
- Death of Henry Raspe; William II, Count of Holland, elected German king by Papal party.
- Foundation of Bedlam (Bethlehem Hospital), London, by Simon Fitzmary.

1248
- Rhodes taken by Genoa.
- Earl Birger virtual ruler of Sweden; Stockholm founded.
- Alfonso III succeeds Sancho II of Portugal.
- St Louis started Sixth Crusade.
- Christians conquer Seville.
- Charter granted to Oxford University by Henry III.

1249
- Death of Alexander II, king of Scots. His eight-year-old son becomes king as Alexander III.
- St Louis of France takes Damietta; then defeated and captured at Mansourah; released on giving up Damietta.
- Margaret, wife of Malcolm III Canmore, canonized.

1250
- Conrad IV becomes German king.
- Sorbonne founded in Paris.
- Beginning of Mameluke rule in Egypt.
- Manfred, natural son of Frederick II, regent of Naples and Sicily.
- *The Harrowing of Hell*: oldest known dramatic work in English, a dramatic poem drawn from the (apocryphal) gospel of Nicodemus.

1251
- Emperor Conrad IV in Italy.
- Conrad and Manfred take Capua and Naples.
- Marriage of Alexander III, king of Scots, and Margaret, eldest daughter of Henry III of England.

1252
- Alphonso X becomes king of Castile.
- Innocent IV approves torture for the discovery of heresy.

1253
- Struggle between Venice and Genoa begins.
- Ottacar II becomes king of Bohemia.

Deaths

Robert Grosseteste becomes bishop of Lincoln.

1254
- Death of Conrad IV: his son Conradin proclaimed king of Sicily.
- St Louis returns to France.

1255
- League of Rhenish towns formed, supported by William of Holland.
- Bavaria divided into Upper and Lower.

1256
- St Bonaventura becomes general of the Franciscans.
- Death of William of Holland: double election to Empire of Richard of Cornwall and Alphonso X of Castile: the period 1256-73 known as the Interregnum in the history of the Empire.
- First form of Hanseatic League.

1258
- Mad Parliament meets in Oxford. Provisions of Oxford forced by barons on Henry III to limit his power.
- Manfred crowned king of Sicily.
- Mongols capture Baghdad and destroy the Abbasside Caliphate.
- Consecration of Salisbury Cathedral (building began 1220).

1259
- Death of Ezzelino de Romano, tyrant who supported Frederick II in Italy.
- Second Tatar raid on Poland.

- Ratification of the Treaty of Paris (Treaty of Abbeville) (December): peace between Louis IX and Henry III, English claims to several French territories relinquished.

Deaths

Matthew Paris, English monk and historian.

1260

- Battle of Montaperti: Florentine Guelfs defeated by Ghibellines of Sienna; Ghibellines supreme in Florence.
- Mongols take Damascus.
- Battle of Kressenbrunn: Ottocar II of Bohemia defeats Bela, king of Hungary and obtains Carinthia, Istria.

1261

- Tatar invasion of Hungary repelled by Bela IV.
- Latin Empire of Constantinople overthrown: Michael VIII becomes eastern emperor: beginning of Palaeologian dynasty.
- Charles of Anjou accepts the crown of Sicily from the Pope.
- Henry III renounces the Provisions of Oxford.

1262

- First Visconti lord of Milan.

1263

- Norse Invasion of Scotland. Battle of Largs (2 October): Scots victory; death of Haakon IV (December); succeeded by Magnus VI.
- Portugal reaches present limits and attains complete independence.

***c.*1263**

- Foundation of Balliol College, Oxford, by John de Balliol.

1264

- Barons' War. Battle of Lewes (14 May): Henry III defeated by Simon de Montfort; Mise of Amiens: Louis IX arbitrated between Henry III and the English barons, deciding in favour of former.
- Battle of Trapani: Venetian victory over Genovese fleet.
- First recorded reference to the administrative and judicial post of justice of the peace.

1265

- Burgesses first called to English parliament by Simon de Montfort.
- Barons' War. First English Battle of Evesham (4 August): Simon de Montfort defeated and slain by royal army under Prince Edward. End of Barons' War. Restoration of Henry III.
- Signature of the Treaty of Shrewsbury, giving recognition of Llewelyn II's overlordship of Wales.
- Christians conquer Murcia; only Granada left to Moors in Spain.

1266

- Treaty of Perth: Hebrides and Isle of Man ceded by Norway to Scotland.
- Battle of Benevento: defeat and death of Manfred; Charles of Anjou becomes master of Sicily and Naples.
- Ghibellines expelled from Florence.

1268

- Christians lose Antioch.
- Battle of Tagliacozzo: Conradin defeated by Charles of Anjou and afterwards executed; end of Hohenstaufen line.

1270

- St Louis on Eighth Crusade: dies at Tunis; Philip III (the Bold) becomes king of France.
- Stephen V becomes king of Hungary.

1271

- Prince Edward of England goes to Acre (returns in 1272).
- Marco Polo, Venetian traveller, sets out on his journey through Asia to China (1271-95).

1272

- Ladislas IV becomes king of Hungary.
- Death of Henry III (16 November). His elder son, Prince Edward, returns from the crusades and becomes king of England as Edward I (nicknamed Longshanks).

1273

- Rudolph of Hapsburg elected German king.

1274

- 'Little' Battle of Châlons: a tournament between French and English knights that develops into a battle. Edward I nearly killed.
- Kublai Khan fails to conquer Japan.
- Foundation completed (started 1274) of Merton College, Oxford, by Walter de Merton, bishop of Rochester.
- Dominicans settle at Cambridge.
- Second Church Council of Lyons effects a temporary union of the eastern and western Churches.

Deaths

St Thomas Aquinas, scholastic theologian.

1275

- First Statute of Westminster.
- Magnus Ladulas becomes king of Sweden.
- Marco polo in the service of Kublai Khan as an envoy (till 1292).

Deaths
Margaret, queen of Alexander III, king of Scots.

1276
- Peter III becomes king of Aragon.

1277
- Edward I invades Wales.

1278
- Statute of Gloucester decreeing necessity of trial before the granting of tne royal pardon.
- Battle of Marchfield, (Dürnkrut): Ottocar II of Bohemia killed; Czech Empire dismembered; Wenceslas II becomes king of Bohemia.
- Jean de Meun continues *The Roman de la Rose* about this date.

Deaths
Nicola Pisano, Italian sculptor.

1279
- Statute of Mortmain.
- Diniz becomes king of Portugal.

John Peckham becomes archbishop of Canterbury (until 1292).

1279-1368
- Yuan dyansty, founded by Kublai Khan, rules all of China.

1280
- Trouvère poetry comes to an end.
- Eric II becomes king of Norway.

Deaths
Albertus Magnus, German scholastic philosopher.

1282
- Andronicus II eastern emperor.
- Sicilian Vespers: massacre of French in Sicily; Sicily separated from kingdom of Naples and obtained by king of Aragon.
- Hapsburgs established in the Duchy of Austria.
- Hertford College, Oxford, founded (as Hertford Hall).

1283
- Prussia subjugated by Teutonic Knights.
- Annexation of Wales to England by Edward I. Edward secured the border with England.

Deaths
Saadi, Persian poet.

1284
- Battle of Meloria: Genoa crushes Pisa.
- Sancho IV becomes king of Castile.
- Queen of Navarre marries the eldest son of Philip III of France: Navarre then joined to France till 1328.
- Birth of a third son (later Edward II) to Edward I and Eleanor of Castile (25 April).
- Foundation of Peterhouse, Cambridge, by Hugh de Balsham, bishop of Ely.

1285
- Statute of Winchester and Second Statute of Westminster.
- Philip IV (the Fair) becomes king of France.
- Charles II becomes king of Naples; Alfonso III becomes king of Aragon.
- First justices of the peace installed in England.

1286
- Death of Alexander III, king of Scotland. Margaret, Maid of Norway, his only grandchild and daughter of Erik, king of Norway, becomes queen of Scotland.

1288
- Pope declares a crusade against Ladislas IV of Hungary.
- Osman I succeeds Ertoghrul as leader of Ottoman Turks.

1289
- Christians lose Tripoli.

1290
- Third statute of Westminster (*Quia Emptores*).
- Treaty of Brigham between Scotland and Edward I, arranged the marriage of Margaret, Maid of Norway, and Edward of Caernarvon, son and heir of Edward I, and the joint rule of the two separate nations.
- Death by drowning of Margaret, Maid of Norway, while on her way from Norway to Scotland. The Treaty of Brigham is negated, and there is dispute over the succession.
- Isle of Man comes under English government.
- Ladislas IV of Hungary murdered.
- Jews expelled from England.

Deaths
Eleanor of Castile, wife of Edward I.

1291
- Fall of Acre: end of Christian power in Syria and Palestine.
- Everlasting League of Uri, Schwyz and Unterwalden: beginning of the Swiss Republic.
- James II becomes king of Aragon.

Deaths
Emperor Rudolph of Hapsburg.
Eleanor of Provence, widow of Henry III.

1292
- Adolf of Nassau elected German king.
- John Balliol chosen as king of Scotland (until 1296) by Edward I.

1294

- Boniface VIII becomes Pope.
- Death of Guiraut Riquier, last of the Troubadours.
- Guienne seized by France.
- Venetian fleet defeated by Genoa.
- The king of Aragon abandons Sicily, but Sicily under Frederick III refuses to be joined to Naples.

Deaths

Roger Bacon, philosopher and pioneer of science.
Kublai Khan, founder of Mongol dynasty in China.

1295

- Model English Parliament summoned by Edward I.
- Edward I invades France.
- Beginning of Franco-Scottish Alliance.
- Anglesey conquered by the English.

1296

- Edward I invades Scotland. Wars of Scottish Independence. Battle of Dunbar (27 April): Edward I defeats John Balliol; Berwick sacked. John Balliol renounces the kingdom of Scotland. Edward I proclaimed king of Scotland. The Stone of Scone (Coronation Stone) is taken to Westminster Abbey by Edward I.
- Bull of Clericis Laicos issued by Boniface VIII: extravagant Papal claims.
- Ferdinand IV becomes king of Castile.

1297

- Wars of Scottish Independence. Battle of Stirling Bridge or Battle of Cambuskenneth (11 September): victory of Sir William Wallace over English army as it crossed the River Forth.

1298

- Adolf of Nassau defeated and killed at Gelheim by Albert I, Duke of Austria, who had been elected German king.
- Wars of Scottish Independence. Battle of Falkirk between the English and Scots (22 July): Edward I defeats Wallace, who is forced to flee.

1299

- Battle of Curzola: Venice defeated by Genoa.
- Treaty between Venice and the Turks.
- Haakon V becomes king of Norway.

1300

- Wenceslas II of Bohemia becomes king of Poland, later also of Hungary.
- Boniface VIII proclaims a Jubilee.

1301

- Edward of Caernarvon (later Edward II), son of Edward I, is created first Prince of Wales (7 February).
- Albert of Austria ravages the Palatinate and Mainz.
- Charles of Valois overthrows the Bianchi (White) Guelfs in Florence and drives Dante into exile.

1302

- End of the War of the Sicilian Vespers; Frederick III recognized as king of Sicily by the Peace of Caltabellotta.
- French States-General meet for the first time.
- Battle of Courtrai: Flemish victory over France.

Deaths

Cimabue, Italian painter.

1303

- Edward I again conquers Scotland.
- Robert Mannyng's *Handlynge Synne,* an early English poem, is published.
- Avoirdupois system of measurement supersedes the merchants' pound in England.

Deaths

Boniface VIII, pope.

1305

- Betrayal and execution in London of Sir William Wallace (23 August).
- Wenceslas III becomes king of Bohemia.

1306

- Robert the Bruce crowned king of Scotland.
- Wars of Scottish Independence. Battle of Methven (19 June): Scots under Bruce defeated by the English.
- Jews expelled from France.
- Wenceslas III of Bohemia murdered: end of dynasty.
- Vladislas I becomes Duke of Great Poland: reunites Great and Little Poland.

1307

- Death of Edward I near Carlisle (7 July). His son becomes king of England as Edward II (until 1327).
- Wars of Scottish Independence. Battle of Loudon Hill (10 May): Scots under Bruce defeat English.
- Philip IV of France seizes the property of the Knights Templars.

1308

- Edward II forced by barons to exile his favourite, Piers Gaveston, but Gaveston returns.
- Murder of Albert of Austria: Henry VII (of Luxemburg) elected German king. Henry VII conquers Bohemia (1308-10).
- Marriage of Edward II and Isabella of France.

Deaths

Duns Scotus, scholastic philosopher and theologian.

1309

- Robert becomes king of Naples.

1310

- Clement V begins residence in Avignon: beginning of Babylonish Captivity of Popes (till 1377).

1310

- Henry VII goes to Italy.
- Arpad dynasty in Hungary succeeded by dynasty of Anjou in person of Charles I.
- Knights of St John or Hospitallers seize Rhodes.
- John of Luxemburg, son of Henry VII, elected king of Bohemia.
- Lords Ordainers group of English noblemen comes into power (until 1316).

1311

- Church Council of Vienna.
- Edward again forced to exile Gaveston.

Deaths

Arnold of Villanova, Italian physician and alchemist.

1312

- Henry VII crowned emperor at Rome.
- Abolition of Templars finally decreed by Pope Clement V, under pressure from Philip IV of France.
- France obtains the Lyonnais.
- Gaveston returns to England and is executed near Warwick Castle.

1313

- Alfonso XI becomes king of Castile.

1314

- Battle of Bannockburn (24 June): English defeated and Scottish independence vindicated by Robert the Bruce.
- Birth of a son (later Edward III) to Edward II and Isabella (13 November).
- Louis X becomes king of France.
- Louis IV of Bavaria and Frederick Duke of Austria rival claimants of the Empire.
- Exeter College, Oxford, founded by Walter de Stapeldon, bishop of Exeter.
- Dante Alighieri writes the Divine Comedy (till 1321).

1315

- Battle of Morgarten: a great Swiss victory over Leopold, Duke of Austria.
- Gedymin ruler of Lithuania: annexes Kiev, Chernigov, etc.

1316

- Philip V (the Tall) becomes king of France.
- Edward Bruce becomes high king of Ireland at the invitation of the earl of Tyrone as a counter to Edward II (May).
- Conquest of Ireland. Battle of Athenry (August): English defeat the O'Connor clan.

1317

- Anglo-Scottish Wars. Battle of Inverkeithing: English defeated by Scots.

1318

- Truce between Swiss and Hapsburgs.
- Battle of Dundalk (5 October) between Scots and English in Ireland; Edward Bruce defeated and slain.
- Siege of Berwick by Edward II begins.

1319

- Wars of Scottish Independence. Battle of Chapter of Mitton (20 September): Scots defeat English in Yorkshire; siege of Berwick raised by Edward II.
- First Union of Sweden and Norway: Magnus VII common king.
- Completion of St Andrews Cathedral (begun 1159).

1320

- End of War between France and Flanders.
- Vladislas I revives royal dynasty in Poland.
- The Declaration of Arbroath seeking recognition of the independence of Scotland drawn up by nobles and sent to the Pope, who recognized Robert the Bruce.

1321

- Edward II forced by the barons to exile his favourites, Hugh le Despenser and his son, also Hugh.
- Death of Dante Alighieri, Italian poet.

1322

- Battle of Boroughbridge: Edward II defeats his kinsman Thomas of Lancaster.
- The Despensers recalled to England by Edward II. The elder Despenser made Earl of Winchester by Edward.
- Wars of Scottish Independence. Battle of Byland: Robert the Bruce defeats Edward II.
- Battle of Mühldorf: Frederick of Austria defeated and taken prisoner by Louis of Bavaria.
- Charles IV (the Fair) becomes king of France.

1323

- Truce established between England and Scotland for thirteen years.
- James I of Aragon conquers Sardinia from the Pisans.
- Emperor Louis IV, deposed and excommunicated by John XXII, appeals to a Council.

1324

- Death of Marco Polo, Venetian traveller.

1325

- Frederick of Austria relinquishes claim to Empire.
- Alphonso IV becomes king of Portugal.

1326
- Isabella, estranged queen of Edward II, and her lover, Roger Mortimer, arrive in England with an army to overthrow the Despensers.
- The Despensers are captured and executed.
- Brussa taken by the Ottoman Turks and becomes their capital.
- Orkhan succeeds Osman as leader of the Ottoman Turks.
- First Scottish Parliament (at Cambuskenneth).
- Foundation of Oriel College, Oxford, by Edward II.
- Clare College, Cambridge, founded as Union Hall.
- Scots College founded in Paris.
- Gunpowder known by this date.

1327
- Orkhan takes Nicomedia.
- Alfonso IV becomes king of Aragon.
- Edward II deposed by Isabella and Mortimer (January) and murdered at Berkeley Castle (21 September). His son becomes king as Edward III. For the remainder of his minority *de facto* power is in the hands of Isabella and Mortimer.

Deaths

Eckhart, German mystic.

1328
- Treaty of Northampton: England recognizes the complete independence of Scotland (May).
- Marriage of David, son of Robert the Bruce by his second wife, and Joan, sister of Edward III of England (July).
- Andronicus III becomes eastern emperor, after persuading his grandfather Andronicus II to abdicate.
- Philip VI becomes king of France: beginning of Valois dynasty: Navarre separated.
- Battle of Cassel: Flemish insurgents under Jacob van Artevelde defeated by Philip VI.
- Louis IV is crowned emperor at Rome and deposes Pope John XXII.

1329
- Battle of Pelekanon: Andronicus III defeated by Ottoman Turks.
- Death of Robert the Bruce from leprosy (7 June). His son becomes king of Scotland as David II.

1330
- Sir James Douglas killed in battle in Spain while carrying the embalmned heart of Robert the Bruce on crusade.
- Roger de Mortimer, Earl of March, lover of Queen Isabella, the queen mother, hanged. Isabella is pensioned off.
- Ottoman Turks take Nicaea: Janissaries organized.
- Battle of Kustendil: Bulgaria conquered by Serbia.
- Walachia begins to gain independence from Hungary.

1331
- King John of Bohemia in Italy.

1332
- Edward Balliol invades Scotland: Battle of Dupplin Moor (12 August): Scottish regent, Earl of Mar, slain. David II flees to France. Edward Baliol crowned king of Scotland at Scone. He accepts Edward III as overlord and flees to Carlisle because of opposition of Scottish lords.
- Parliament is divided into the two Houses of Lords and Commons for the first time.
- Lucerne joins the Swiss League.
- Battle of Plowce: Vladislas I defeats the Teutonic Knights.

1333
- Casimir III (the Great) king of Poland: acquires Galicia.
- Edward Balliol again invades Scotland.
- Wars of Scottish Independence: Battle of Halidon Hill (19 July): Scots defeated by Edward III.
- John de Stratford becomes archbishop of Canterbury (until 1348).

1335
- Edward III invades Scotland.
- Zurich joins the Swiss League.
- Internal free trade established in England.

1336
- Peter IV becomes king of Aragon.
- City of Aberdeen burnt by Edward III.
- Clare College, Cambridge, refoun ed.

1337
- Peter II becomes king of Sicily.
- Jacob van Artevelde forms a league of Flemish cities with Ghent as leader; they join England in the war against France.
- Hundred Years' War between France and England begins (ended 1453).

Deaths

Giotto, Italian painter.

1339
- Edward Balliol driven from Scotland.
- Wars of Scottish Independence. Siege of Dunbar by the English withstood by the Countess of March.
- Battle of Laupen: Nobels overthrown in Berne.

1340
- Emperor Louis IV reunites Bavaria under him.
- Battle of Rio Salado: Spanish and Portuguese repel an African invasion.

- Waldemar IV becomes king of Denmark.
- Hundred Years' War. Battle of Sluys (24 June): English naval victory over France.
- Edward III claims throne of France.

c.1340
- The illuminated Luttrell Psalter produced.

1341
- David II returns to Scotland to claim his throne.
- John V eastern emperor.
- Foundation of The Queen's College, Oxford, by Robert de Eglesfield.
- Petrarch crowned poet on the Capitol, Rome.

1342
- Louis the Great becomes king of Hungary.
- Duke of Athens appointed head of Florentine state: expelled the following year.

1343
- Joanna I, wife of Andrew of Hungary, becomes queen of Naples.
- Charles I (the Bad) becomes king of Navarre.
- Haakon VI becomes king of Norway.

1344
- Suabian League of cities formed.

1345
- Order of the Garter founded about this date.
- Andrew of Hungary assassinated.
- Jacob van Arteveide assassinated.
- Emperor Louis takes possession of Holland, etc.
- Completion of the building of York Minster (began 1291; important additions made c.1450).

1346
- Anglo-Scottish Wars 'Bishops' War'. Battle of Newburn (28 August): English Northern Levies defeated by Scots under Leslie; Battle of Neville's Cross between the Northern Levies and the Scottish armies (17 October): Scots defeated and David II captured and held in Tower of London.
- Hundred Years' War. Siege of English garrison at Aiguillon; abandoned by Duke of Normandy (August); Battle of Crécy (26 August): English victory over French: King John of Bohemia killed. Siege of Calais begins (August).
- Battle of Zara: Venetians defeat Hungarians.
- Charles becomes king of Bohemia.

1347
- Hundred Years' War. Battle of Crotoye: French fleet attempting to reach Calais defeated by English; Calais surrenders to the English (4 August).
- John VI (Cantacuzenus) becomes co-emperor in the East.
- Foundation of Pembroke College, Cambridge (as House or Hall of Valence-Mary), by Mary de St Paul, the widow of the Earl of Pembroke.
- Cola di Rienzi becomes Tribune in Rome.
- Corsica transferred from Pisa to Genoa.

1348
- Hundred Years' War. Truce between England and France (until 1350).
- Charles IV (of Bohemia) German king.
- Battle of Epila: Peter IV of Aragon establishes his power over the nobles.
- Great Plague in Italy.
- The Black Death plague appears in England.
- Gonville and Caius College, Cambridge, founded as Gonville Hall by Edmund Gonville (present name assumed 1557).
- Giovanni Boccaccio begins the writing of *The Decameron.*

c.1348
- The Order of the Garter founded by Edward III: motto 'Honi soit qui mal y pense'.

1349
- Bavaria again divided.
- Persecution of Jews in Germany.
- Fall of Rienzi.

Deaths

William of Occam, nominalist philospher and supporter of Louis IV against the Pope.

1350
- Edward III invades France.
- John becomes king of France.
- Peter the Cruel becomes king of Castile.
- The Black Death in Scotland.
- Black Rod first appointed in the House of Lords.
- Foundation of Trinity Hall, Cambridge, by William Bateman, bishop of Norwich.
- Dafydd ap Gwilym, greatest of Welsh poets, flourishes.

1351
- Zurich joins the Swiss League.
- Statute of Labourers attempts to regulate wages and prices at 1340 levels.

1352
- Glarus and Zug join the Swiss League.
- Corpus Christi College, Cambridge, founded by the Guilds of Corpus Christi and of the Blessed Virgin Mary.

Deaths

Laurence Minot, English poet.

1353
- Berne joins the Swiss League.
- Battle of the Bosphorus: Venice defeated by Genoa.
- Statute of Praemunire places restraints on Papal authority in England.

1354
- New League of the Rhine.
- Rienzi killed in a riot.

1355
- Charles IV crowned emperor in Rome.
- Conspiracy of Marino Faliero in Venice foiled.
- Death of Stephen Dushan, king of the Serbians: break-up of Serbian Empire.

1356
- Burnt Candlemas: Edward III burns every town and village in Lothian.
- The Golden Bull settles the mode of electing the Holy Roman emperor.
- War between Venice and Hungary.
- Hundred Years' War. Battle of Poitiers between the French and the English (19 September): English victory over France won by the Black Prince; King John of France a prisoner.

1357
- Treaty of Berwick (October): David II released by Edward III in return for a ransom.
- Pedro I becomes king of Portugal.

1358
- Turks under Suleiman take Gallipoli.
- Peace between Hapsburgs and the Swiss League.
- Treaty of Zara: peace between Venice and Hungary: Venice makes large cessions.
- Revolution in Paris: Étienne Marcel, provost of Paris merchants, leads a reform movement.
- Battle of Sapienza: Venice defeated by Genoa.
- Jacquerie or Peasants' Revolt in France.
- Boccaccio completes *The Decameron* (begun in 1348).

1359
- Amurath (Murad) I becomes Turkish Sultan.
- Turks cross the Hellespont.

1360
- Hundred Years' War. Treaty of Brétigny: truce between England and France. Edward III gains Calais, Guienne, Gascony and Poitou in return for giving up his claim to the French throne.
- Moldavia independent of Hungary by this date.

1361
- Battle of Adrianople: Turks defeat the emperor and capture the town.
- Waldemar IV of Denmark recovers Scania and conquers Gotland.
- Duchy of Burgundy expires with Philip de Rouvre.
- Marriage of Edward, the Black Prince and Joan of Kent (Fair Maid of Kent).

1362
- English becomes language of Parliament and the law courts in England.
- Quarter sessions established by statute.
- Turks conquer Philippopolis.
- Appearance of *Piers Plowman*, great English alliterative poem, attributed to William Langland.

1363
- Timour (Tamerlane), the Tatar leader, begins conquests in Central Asia.
- The king of France creates his son, Philip the Bold, duke of Burgundy.

Deaths

Ranulf Higden, English chronicler.

1364
- Hundred Years' War. Hostilities resume after death of John of France. Battle of Cocherel (May): Navarrese and English force defeated by French; Siege of Auray: English besiegers attacked by French (27 September) but withstand the attack.
- Crete revolts against Venice.
- Charles V becomes king of France.

1365
- Peter I of Cyprus takes Alexandria, Tripoli, etc, but does not retain his conquests.
- Albert of Mecklenburg supersedes Magnus as king of Sweden.

1366
- Statute of Kilkenny: English attempt to impose English law in Ireland.
- Peter the Cruel expelled from Castile by his brother Henry of Trastamara.
- Amadeus VI of Savoy takes Gallipoli from the Turks and Varna from the Bulgarians.
- Simon Langham becomes archbishop of Canterbury (until 1368).

1367
- A son (later Richard II) born to the Black Prince (6 January).
- A son (later Henry IV) born to John of Gaunt (3 April).
- Hundred Years' War. Battle of Navarrete (3 April): Henry of Trastamara defeated and Peter the Cruel restored to Castilian throne with the aid of the Black Prince.
- Ferdinand makes Lisbon capital of Portugal.

- Adrianople becomes Turkish capital.
- Construction of Exeter Cathedral completed (began 1261).

1368

- Battle of Montiel: death of Peter the Cruel; succeeded by Henry of Trastamara.

Deaths

Orcagna, Italian painter, sculptor and architect.

1368-1644

Ming dynasty, the last indigenous Chinese dynasty, founded by Zhu Yuangzhang.

1369

- Venetians repel Hungarian invasion.
- Charles V declares war against England.
- Flanders passes by marriage to the Duchy of Burgundy.
- Geoffrey Chaucer writes *The book of the Duchess.*

1370

- Limoges sacked.
- Louis of Hungary elected king of Poland.

1371

- Death of David II. His nephew becomes the first Stewart king of Scotland as Robert II.
- Turks defeat Louis of Hungary.

1372

- Hundred Years' War. English fleet attempting to relieve La Rochelle defeated by Spanish fleet (22 June); siege and capture of Chizai by French (July).

1373

- Charles IV gains Brandenburg and Lower Lusatia by treaty.
- Bertrand du Guesclin reduces Brittany.

1374

Deaths

Petrarch, Italian poet and pioneer of humanism.

1375

- Waldemar IV of Denmark succeeded by Margaret.

Deaths

Giovanni Boccaccio, Italian writer.

1376

- The Good Parliament.
- *The Bruce* composed by Scottish poet John Barbour.

Deaths

Edward, the Black Prince.

1377

- Death of Edward III (21 June). His grandson becomes king of England as Richard II (22 June). John of Gaunt, his uncle, becomes regent.
- Poll tax imposed in England.
- John Wyclif summoned before bishop of London for writing *De Domino Divino*.
- Institution of the post of Speaker of the House of Commons.
- Pope Gregory XI returns to Rome.

1378

- Great Schism in the Papacy begins: Urban VI and Clement VII both elected and strongly supported.
- Wencelsas IV becomes king of Bohemia.
- War of Chioggia between Venice and Genoa begins.

1379

- Poll tax again imposed in England.
- Battle of Pola: Venice defeated by Genoa. Chioggia taken.
- John I becomes king of Castile.
- Foundation of New College, Oxford, by William of Wykeham.

1380

- Poll tax imposed in England by Richard II.
- Gerhard Groot founds Brethren of the Common Life at Deventer.
- Venice wins Chioggia back and captures Genoese fleet.
- Charles VI becomes king of France.
- Battle of Kulikovo: Russian victory over Golden Horde under Dimitri Donskoi of Moscow.
- John Wyclif begins to attack doctrine of transubstantiation.

1381

- Charles of Durazzo conquers Naples: Queen Joanna murdered in 1382.
- League of German Free Cities.
- End of the war between Venice and Genoa.
- Treaty of Turin between Venice and Hungary: Venice cedes Dalmatia.
- First English Navigation Act.
- Peasants' Revolt in England under Wat Tyler in protest at the poll tax of 1380; Tyler killed by the mayor of London (15 June).

Deaths

John Ball, English priest and peasants' leader, by execution.

1382

- Death of Louis the Great of Hungary; period of disorder follows.
- Battle of Roosebeke: Philip van Artevelde and the Flemish insurgents defeated by the French: Philip killed.
- Moscow taken by Mongols.
- Maillotin Revolt in Paris, etc.

Earthquake Council in London condemns Wyclif.
Lollards, church reformers and followers of John Wyclif, active after now and in the early 15th century.

.1382-84

Completion of Wyclif's early version of the Bible, the first translation of the Bible into English.

1384

- Union of Heidelberg: peace between Count of Würtemberg and the Suabian League.
- Chaucer writes *House of Fame*.

Deaths

John Wyclif, English religious reformer.

1385

- Gian Galeazzo Visconti sole ruler of Milan.
- Battle of Aljubarrota: Portuguese victory over Castilians.
- John I becomes king of Portugal.
- Chaucer writes *Troilus and Criseyde*

1386

- Battle of Sempach: Swiss victory over Austria: Leopold of Austria killed.
- Charles VI of France declares war against England.
- Death of Charles III of Naples: anarchy follows.
- Vladislas II becomes both king of Poland and Grand Duke of Lithuania: beginning of Jagellon dynasty.
- Charles VI of France declared war against England.
- Alliance between England and Portugal confirmed by Treaty of Windsor.

1387

- Barons against Richard II. Battle of Radcot Bridge: forces of the Lords Appellant under the Earl of Derby (later Henry IV) defeat the troops of Richard II. The Lords Appellant take control of government.
- Birth of a son (later Henry V) to the Earl of Derby (later Henry IV).
- Hundred Years' War. Battle of Margate (24 March): defeat of an invading French and Castilian fleet by the Earls of Arundel and Nottingham.
- John I becomes king of Aragon.
- Charles III (the Noble) becomes king of Navarre.
- Sigismund becomes king of Hungary.
- Geoffrey Chaucer begins *The Canterbury Tales* (completed 1400).

1388

- Wars of Scottish Independence. Battle of Otterburn (Battle of Chevy Chase) between Scots and English (15 August): Scottish victory over English under Hotspur.
- The Merciless Parliament condemns friends of Richard II to death (February-May).
- Battle of Naefels: victory of Swiss canton Glarus over Austrians.
- Count of Würtemberg defeats the Suabian League.
- Rhenish Towns defeated at Worms by Elector Palatine Rupert.

*c.*1388

- Posthumous completion of Wyclif's later version of the Bible.

1389

- Richard II takes over government of England.
- Battle of Kossovo: Serbians overthrown by Turks; Amurath I killed; Bajazet I succeeds him and obtains from the Caliph the title of Sultan.

1390

- Henry III becomes king of Castile.
- Death of Robert II of Scotland. Robert III becomes king. His brother, the duke of Albany, becomes regent because of the king's physical disability.
- John Gower begins *Confessio Amantis* (finished 1393).

1391

- Manuel II eastern emperor.
- Massacre of Jews in Spain.

1392

Deaths

Earl of Oxford, court favourite.

1393

- Great Statute of Praemunire in England.
- Turks capture Philadelphia, in Asia Minor; also Tirnovo, in Bulgaria.

1394

- Hapsburgs recognize the independence of the Swiss League.

1395

- Gian Galeazzo Visconti obtains from emperor title of Duke of Milan.
- Martin I becomes king of Aragon.
- Timour conquers the Kipchaks on the Volga.
- Turks, after taking Salonica and Larissa, besiege Constantinople.

1396

- Richard II attempts to conquer the west of Ireland.
- Fight at the North Inch in Perth between the Clans Chattan and Kay.
- Turkish conquest of Bulgaria completed.
- Battle of Nicopolis: Crusading army of Hungarians, etc, under King Sigismund, defeated by Turks.
- Thomas Arundel becomes archbishop of Canterbury (until 1414).

1397

- Richard II takes revenge on the Lords Appellant by executing or expelling.
- Dick Whittington becomes Lord Mayor of London.
- Union of Kalmar between Norway, Sweden and Denmark: Eric VII (XIII of Sweden) recognized as king.

1398

- Duke of Albany forced to resign as regent in Scotland. Regency conferred on David, Duke of Rothesay, eldest son of Robert III.
- Timour conquers Northern India.
- Rome submits to complete authority of the pope, who is supported by Ladislas, king of Naples.
- Richard le Scrope becomes archbishop of York (until 1405).

1399

- Death of John of Gaunt, Duke of Lancaster (3 February). Richard II withholds his inheritance. Richard forced to abdicate (29 September) by Henry IV, son of John of Gaunt, who is chosen king of England by Parliament (30 September). Richard is imprisoned at Pontefract Castle.

1400

- Death of Richard II in prison.
- Revolt of Owen Glendower in Wales (until 1410).
- Wenceslas of Bavaria is deposed: Rupert, Elector Palatine, elected German king.

Deaths

Geoffrey Chaucer, English poet (25 October).

1401

- Owen Glyndwr begins a campaign for independence for Wales.
- Rupert fails in Italy.
- Compact of Vilna: partial separation of Poland and Lithuania.

Deaths

William Sawtrey burned in England for heresy under a new statute, *De Heretico Comburendo*, against heretics, particularly Lollards.

1402

- Death of the Duke of Rothesay in Falkland Palace. Duke of Albany recovers the regency.
- Anglo-Scottish Wars. Battle of Homildon Hill (September): Scots defeated by English under Sir Henry Percy ('Hotspur').
- Battle of Angora: Timour defeats Bajazet I and makes him prisoner; Turkish pressure on the Empire relieved.

1403

- Owen Glyndwr joins the Percys in revolt against Henry IV. Battle of Shrewsbury (21 July): Royalists under Henry IV defeat Sir Henry Percy ('Hotspur'); he is killed.

1404

- John the Fearless becomes D[illegible] of Burgundy.
- The Parliament of Dunces meet at Coventry.
- Owen Glyndywr sets up a Welsh parliament.

1405

- Death of Timour; his empire falls apart.
- Insurrection against Henry IV led by the Earl of Nottingham and Richard le Scrope, archbishop of York. It is suppressed and Scrope executed.
- French troops land in Wales to help Owen Glyndwr.

1406

- James, young son of Robert III, king of Scotland, sent to France to escape the intrigues of his uncle, the Duke of Albany. His ship is captured by the English off Flamborough Head and he is taken as a prisoner to London. Death of Robert III. James proclaimed king as James I but not allowed to return to Scotland.
- John II becomes king of Castile.

1407

- Duke of Orleans murdered by a Burgundian.
- Rome occupied by Ladislas of Naples.

Deaths

John Gower, English poet.

1408

- Earl of Northumberland killed in battle.

1409

- Sicily joined to Aragon by marriage.
- Council at Pisa: both Popes deposed; Alexander V elected.

1410

- Battle of Tannenberg: Teutonic Knights overthrown by Poland and Lithuania.
- Ferdinand becomes the Catholic king of Aragon.

Deaths

Jean Froissart, French historian.

1411

- Scottish Civil Wars. Battle of Harlaw (24 July): Highlanders under Donald, Lord of the Isles, defeated by a Lowland force under Earl of Mar.
- Sigismund of Hungary elected German king.
- Battle of Rocca Secca: Louis of Anjou defeats Ladislas of Naples.
- Construction of the Guildhall in London begins.

1412

- Treaty between Hapsburgs and Swiss League renewed.

- Jan Hus of Bohemia excommunicated.
- Battle of St Cloud: Burgundian party in France defeat Armagnacs (followers of Orleans); Treaty of Auxerre concluded.
- St Andrews University founded.

1413
- Ladislas of Naples sacks Rome.
- Mohammed I becomes Turkish sultan.
- Death of Henry IV (20 March). His son becomes king of England as Henry V.

1414
- Council of Constance meet.
- Treaty of Arras between Burgundians and Armagnacs.
- St Andrews University founded in Scotland.

1415
- Council of Constance condemns Jan Hus, who is burned; Bohemian nobles protest.
- Count Frederick of Hohenzollern obtains Brandenburg and title of Elector.
- Portugal takes Ceuta.
- Hundred Years' War. Henry V invades France. Battle of Agincourt (25 October): Henry V defeats French but withdrew to Calais.

1416
- Hundred Years' War. Battle of the Seine Mouth (15 August): English fleet withstands attack by French blockading fleet to get supplies to besieged Harfleur.
- Alfonso V (the Magnanimous) becomes king of Aragon: also king of Sicily and Naples.

Deaths

Owen Glyndwr, Welsh rebel leader.

Jerome of Prague, a follower of Huss, burned.

1417
- Henry V takes Caen.
- End of Papal Schism: Martin V sole Pope.

Deaths

Execution by burning of Sir John Oldcastle, leader of the Lollards, for heresy.

1418
- Hundred Years' War. Siege of Rouen laid by Henry V.
- End of Council of Constance, without touching the reform question.
- Burgundians capture Paris.
- Date of earliest known woodcut.

1419
- Hundred Years' War. Henry V captures Rouen (19 January).
- Duke of Burgundy murdered at Montereau; Philip the Good succeeds. Burgundians join the English.
- War between Empire and Bohemia begins.
- Sigismund becomes king of Bohemia, but is not accepted by the people.

1420
- Death of Andrew of Wyntoun, author of a metrical chronicle of Scotland.
- Battle of Vysehrad: Bohemians defeat Sigismund.
- Treaty of Troyes: Henry V of England recognized as heir to crown of France.

1421
- Battle of Baugé: Scottish victory over English.
- Birth of a son (later Henry VI) to Henry V (6 December).
- Amurath II Turkish Sultan.
- Sigismund declared deposed in Bohemia.

1422
- Battle of Deutschbrod: Bohemian victory over Sigismund.
- The infant Henry VI becomes king of England on death of Henry V from dysentry (31 August) and of France on death of Charles VI; Charles VII in France called 'King of Bourges'.
- John of Lancaster and Humphrey, Duke of Gloucester, head a council of regency and govern (until 1437).

1423
- Hundred Years' War. Battle of Cravant (31 July): Armagnac force under the Earl of Buchan defeated by English and Burgundians under the Earl of Salisbury.
- Treaty of London: freedom of James I of Scotland agreed in return for a ransom and hostages.
- Sigismund crowned emperor at Rome.
- Francesco Foscari becomes doge of Venice.
- *The Kingis Quair* is written by James I of Scotland.

1424
- James I of Scotland set free under the terms of the Treaty of London.
- Hundred Years' War. Battle of Verneuil (17 August): English under Duke of Bedford defeat the French.
- Treaty between Venice and Florence against Milan.

1425
- John VII eastern emperor.

1426
- Dom Henrique of Portugal (Prince Henry the Navigator) charts the west coast of Africa and engages in slave trade.
- Battle of Aussig: Bohemian victory over the Empire.

Deaths
Hubert van Eyck, Flemish painter.

1427
- Bohemians under Procopius completely defeat the Empire: Germany invades.

1428
- Turks take Salonica.
- Hundred Years' War. Siege of Orléans begun by English under Duke of Bedford (12 October).

1429
- Hundred Years' War. Battle of the Herrings or Battle of Rouvray (12 February): French attack on English defeated; Battle of Patay (18 June): French under Joan of Arc and Duc d'Alençon defeat the English; Joan of Arc enters Orléans (April) and raises siege (7 May); Charles VII crowned at Rheims.

Deaths
Masaccio, Italian painter.

1431
- François Villon, French poet, born.
- Battle of Taus: Bohemian victory over Empire.
- Council of Basle begins.
- Joan of Arc burned at Rouen (30 May, canonized 1920).

1432
- Carmagnola executed by Venetians for treason in the war against Milan.

1433
- Sigismund crowned emperor at Rome.

1434
- Battle of Lipan: conflict between different Hussite parties in Bohemia; Procopius killed.
- Cosimo de' Medici in power in Florence

Deaths
Vladislav II of Poland.

1435
- Treaty of Arras between Burgundy and Charles VII.
- Alfonso the Magnanimous reunites the Two Sicilies.

1436
- Charles VII regains Paris.
- Council of Basle practically concedes the demands of the Bohemians.
- Sigismund recognized as king of Bohemia.
- Charles VIII elected king of Sweden.

1437
- Henry VI assumes control of government.
- James I of Scotland assassinated at Perth by disgruntled nobles and descendants of Robert II (20 February). His six-year-old son becomes king as James II.
- Council of Basle transferred by Pope to Ferrara.
- All Souls' College, Oxford, founded by Henry Chichele.

1438
- Albert V of Austria becomes king of Hungary and Bohemia; elected also German king as Albert II.
- Pragmatic Sanction of Bourges: Charles VII of France establishes independence of French Church.
- Amurath II invades Hungary; opposed by John Huniades.
- Alfonso V becomes king of Portugal.

1439
- Pragmatic Sanction of Mainz.
- Eric VII of Denmark is deposed, Christopher III of Bavaria elected king.
- Formal union of Greek and Latin Churches arranged by Council of Basle sitting in Florence.

1440
- Bruges crushed by Duke Philip.
- Frederick III German king.
- Praguerie revolt in France: nobles against king.
- Ladislas V (Postumus) becomes king of Bohemia and Hungary; Vladislas III of Poland a rival in Hungary.
- Frederick II Elector of Brandenburg.
- Invention of Printing with movable types by Johan Gutenberg of Mainz.
- The Azores discovered.

1441
- King's College, Cambridge, founded by Henry VI.
- Thomas à Kempis writes *De Imitatione Christi* about this date.

Deaths
Jan van Eyck, Flemish painter.

1442
- Birth of a son (later Edward IV) to Richard, Duke of York.

1443
- Turks defeated by Albanians under Scanderbeg.
- Battle of Nissa: Turks defeated by John Huniades.

1444
- Peace of Szegedin: Amurath II surrenders control of Serbia, Walachia and Bosnia to Hungary.
- Battle of Varna: Turkish victory over Hungary; King Vladislas III killed.

1446
- Death of Brunelleschi, Italian pioneer of Renaissance architecture.

1447
- Amurath II defeated by Scanderbeg.

- Casimir IV becomes king of Poland and grand duke of Lithuania.

1448

- Constantine XI eastern emperor.
- French regain Anjou and Maine.
- End of the Union of Kalmar: Christian I becomes king of Denmark.
- Concordat of Vienna between the Emperor Frederick III and the Pope: obedience of German people to Rome pledged.
- Battle of Kossovo: John Huniades defeated by the Turks.
- Christ's College, Cambridge, founded by Henry VI (as God's-House).
- Foundation of Queens' College, Cambridge, by Queen Margaret of Anjou.

1449

- End of the Council of Basle.

1450

- Cade's Rebellion. Rebels led by Jack Cade defeat royal troops at Sevenoaks (18 June), enter London (4 July) but are defeated at London Bridge (5 July). Cade flees and is killed at Heathfield by Sheriff of Kent (12 July).
- Hundred Years' War. Battle of Formigny (25 April): English defeated by French: Normandy recovered.
- Francesco Sforza becomes Duke of Milan.
- Papal Jubilee.

1451

- French recover Guienne.
- Mohammed II Turkish Sultan.
- Foundation of Glasgow University.

1452

- Birth of a son (later Richard III) to Richard, Duke of York (2 October).
- James II of Scotland murders the Earl of Douglas at Stirling Castle. Scottish Civil War follows.
- Frederick III crowned emperor by Pope Nicholas V in Rome: the last coronation of an emperor at Rome.

1453

- Turks capture Constantinople: end of the Easter or Byzantine Empire.
- Austria created an Archduchy.
- Ladislas V of Hungary becomes king of Bohemia also.
- Hundred Years' War. Battle of Castillon (17 July) English defeated by French in last battle of the War; Bordeaux becomes French (19 October).
- Wars of the Roses. Battle of Stamford Bridge (August), the first battle of the War.

1454

- Peace of Lodi between Venice and Milan.
- First known document printed from movable types: at Mainz.
- Prussia incorporated in Poland.
- Henry IV becomes king of Castile.
- Richard, Duke of York, made Protector because of Henry VI's mental illness.

1455

- Duke of York dismissed as Protector and rebelled against Henry VI. Wars of the Roses: First Battle of St Albans (22 May): Yorkist victory under York.
- Scottish Civil War. Battle of Arkenholm (12 May): House of Douglas overthrown in Scotland when James II defeats the rebel Douglas brothers; Archibald Douglas is killed in battle, Hugh Douglas captured and James, Earl of Douglas, forced to flee to England.
- Appearance of Halley's Comet (named after Edmund Halley).

  Deaths

  Fra Angelico, Italian religious painter.
  Lorenzo Ghiberti, Italian sculptor.

1456

- Turkish attack on Belgrade repelled by John Huniades.

1457

- End of Foscari's dogeship: Venice begins to decline.
- Death of Ladislas V of Hungary and Bohemia.
- Birth of a son (later Henry VII) born to Edmund, Earl of Richmond (28 January).
- First recorded mention of golf in Scotland.

1458

- Matthias Corvinus, son of John Huniades, elected king of Hungary; George Podiebrad elected king of Bohemia.
- Death of Alfonso the Magnanimous: Two Sicilies again separated.
- John II becomes king of Aragon. Ferdinand I becomes king of Naples.
- Magdalen College, Oxford, founded by William of Wayneflete, bishop of Winchester.

1459

- Turks conquer Serbia.

1460

- Anglo-Scottish Wars. James II laid siege successfully to the English-held Roxburgh Castle. James killed by an exploding cannon (3 August). His young son becomes king of Scotland as James III.
- Wars of the Roses. Battle of Northampton (10 July): Lancastrians under Henry VI defeated by Yorkists

under Earl of Warwick; Battle of Wakefield (30 December): Lancastrian victory over Yorkists under Richard, Duke of York. Death of the Duke of York.
- Turks conquer the Morea.
- Denmark obtains Schleswig and Holstein.
- William Dunbar, Scottish poet, born.

1461
- Wars of the Roses. Battle of Mortimer's Cross (2 February): Yorkist victory; Second Battle of St Albans (17 February): Lancastrian victory; Henry VI deposed (5 March) and flees to Scotland; Battle of Ferrybridge (28 March): Lancastrian victory over Yorkists; Battle of Towton (29 March): Yorkist victory made Edward IV, son of the Duke of York, king of England.
- Empire of Trebizond destroyed by Turks.
- Death of Charles VII, king of France: Louis XI succeeds.
- Ivan III (the Great) ruler of Moscow.
- Pragmatic Sanction of Bourges revoked.

1462
- Battle of Puck: Polish victory; Prussia conquered.

1463
- War begins between Venice and the Turks.
- Turks acknowledge Scanderbeg as ruler of Albania.

1464
- Henry VI returns to England.
- Wars of the Roses. Battle of Hedgeley Moor (25 April): Lancastrians defeated by Yorkists; Battle of Hexham (15 May): Yorkist victory over Lancastrians.
- Turks conquer Bosnia.
- Death of Cosimo de' Medici of Florence: succeeded by his son Piero.

Deaths
Roger van der Weyden, Flemish painter.

1465
- League of Public Welfare formed by French nobles against Louis XI.
- Henry VI imprisoned (until 1470).
- Refoundation of Queens' College, Cambridge, by Elizabeth Widville, consort of Edward IV.

1466
- Treaty of Thorn between Poland and the Teutonic Knights; Poland dominant and master of Prussia.

Deaths
Donatello, Italian sculptor.

1467
- Turks conquer Herzegovina.
- Charles the Bold becomes duke of Burgundy.

1468
- Orkney annexed by default to Scotland.
- War declared against Bohemia by Hungary.

1469
- Wars of the Roses. Battle of Edgeworth (26 July): Edward IV's troops defeated; Edward IV captured (August) and escapes (September).
- Shetland annexed to Scotland.
- Matthias Corvinus, king of Hungary, crowned king of Bohemia by Papal legate.
- Lorenzo de' Medici begins rule in Florence along with his brother Giuliano.
- Marriage of Ferdinand of Aragon and Isabella of Castile.

Deaths
Fra Fillippo Lippi, Italian painter.

1470
- Truce between Hungary and Bohemia.
- Turks take Negropont.
- Three northern kingdoms reunited under Christian I of Denmark.
- Henry VI restored as king of England (until 1471).
- Wars of the Roses. Battle of Empingham ('Battle of Loosecoat Field') (12 March): Edward IV defeats rebels under Sir Robert Wells.

1471
- Wars of the Roses. Battle of Barnet (14 April): Yorkist victory. Warwick the Kingmaker killed; Edward IV reclaims throne; Battle of Tewkesbury (4 May): Yorkist victory.
- Henry VI imprisoned in Tower of London and murdered there (21 May). His son is taken to Brittany for safekeeping.
- Orkney and Shetland formally annexed to the Scottish Crown as part of the dowry of Margaret, daughter of Christian I of Denmark and wife of James III.
- Death of George Podiebrad of Bohemia; Prince Vladislav of Poland elected king.
- Sixtus IV becomes Pope; notorious for nepotism and abuses.
- Ivan the Great conquers Novgorod.

Deaths
Thomas à Kempis, author of the *Imitation of Christ*.

1472
- Philip de Comines joins Louis XI.

1473
- Venice obtains Cyprus.

Charles the Bold consolidates Burgundian power in Netherlands.
- Foundation of St Catherine's College, Cambridge, by Robert Woodlark, Provost of King's College.

1474

- Scutari successfully defended against Turks.
- Ferdinand the Catholic king of Castile.
- Everlasting Compact: Swiss independence recognized.

1475

- Battle of Racova: Stephen the Great of Moldavia defeats the Turks.
- Edward IV invades France to help Charles the Bold: Treaty of Pecquigny arranged with Louis XI.
- First book printed in English language (*Recuyell of the Histories of Troye*) by William Caxton at Bruges.

*c.*1480

- Foundation of the Order of the Thistle by James III of Scotland.

1476

- William Caxton sets up his printing press at Westminster.
- Battle of Granson: Swiss defeat Charles the Bold.
- Battle of Morat: Swiss defeat Charles the Bold.
- Battle of Toro: Portugal defeated by Ferdinand of Castile.

1477

- Battle of Nancy: Charles the Bold defeated and killed; end of the Duchy.
- Mary, daughter of Charles the Bold, marries Maximilian, afterwards emperor.

1478

- Plot of the Pazzi in Florence: Giuliano de' Medici killed; Lorenzo's position strengthened.
- Treaty of Olmütz between Hungary and Bohemia: Moravia, Silesia and Lusatia ceded to former.

1479

- Treaty of Brünn between Poland and Hungary.
- Treaty of Constantinople between Venice and Turkey.
- Ferdinand the Catholic becomes Ferdinand II of Aragon: Aragon and Castile united.
- Battle of Guinegate: French defeated by Maximilian.

1480

- Turks occupy Otranto for a short time; fail against Rhodes.
- Caxton prints *The Chronicles of England.*
- Parachute invented by Leonardo da Vinci.

1481

- Spanish Inquisition established by Ferdinand the Catholic, with Torquemada as its chief.
- John II becomes king of Portugal.
- Hand becomes king of Denmark.
- Bajazet II becomes Turkish Sultan.

1481-1483

- Botticelli, Ghirlanaio, Perugino, Pinturrichio, Signorelli and others paint frescoes in the Sistine Chapel, Rome

1482

- Scotland loses Berwick to England.
- Treaty of Arras between France and the Netherlands: Louis IX receives Duchy of Burgundy, Franche-Comté, Picardy, etc.

1483

- Charles VIII becomes king of France.
- Death of Edward IV, king of England (9 April). His 12-year-old son Edward becomes king as Edward V but reigns for only 77 days. He and his brother Richard are declared illegitimate by their uncle, the Duke of Gloucester, who had been appointed Protector of the kingdom by Edward IV and who takes the throne as Richard III (26 June). Edward V and Richard, the Princes in the Tower, disappear, probably murdered in the Tower at their uncle's instigation.
- Rebellion by Duke of Buckingham against Richard III crushed.

1484

- Council of the North established to govern the north of England.
- Introduction of bail for defendants in legal courts.
- English first used for parliamentary statutes.

1485

- Matthias Corvinus takes Vienna.
- The Mad War in France.
- Partition of Leipzig: henceforward two Saxon lines.
- Battle of Bosworth (22 August): Richard III defeated and killed. Henry VII becomes king of England, first of the Tudor dynasty.
- Formation of the Yeomen of the Guard.
- Cardinal John Morton becomes archbishop of Canterbury (until 1500).
- The *Morte d' Arthur* by Sir Thomas Malory printed by Caxton.

1486

- Bartholomew Diaz doubles Cape of Good Hope.
- Frederick the Wise becomes elector of Saxony.
- John becomes Elector of Brandenburg.
- Marriage of Henry VII and Elizabeth, daughter of Edward IV, uniting the Houses of York and Lancaster.

1487

- Revolt of Lambert Simnel against Henry VII by pretending to be Edward Plantagenet, son of the Duke of Clarence; Battle of Stoke (16 June): royal troops un-

der Henry VII defeats rebels under Earl of Lincoln.
- Matthias Corvinus master of Austria, Styria and Carinthia.

1488
- Barons' Rebellion. Battle of Sauchieburn (18 June): death of James III of Scotland at the hands of rebel nobles, led by his son, James, and accession of James as James IV.
- Venice obtains Cyprus.

Deaths
Verrocchio, Italian sculptor.

1490
- Death of Matthias Corvinus, king of Hungary; Vladislav II of Bohemia elected: Hungarians expelled from Austrian duchies by Emperor Maximilian.
- Maximilian obtains Tirol.

1491
- Maximilian invades Hungary: Treaty of Pressburg.
- France obtains Brittany by marriage.
- Birth of a second son (later Henry VIII) to Henry VII.

1492
- Christopher Columbus discovers the West Indies.
- Henry VII invades France: Treaty of Étaples.
- Ferdinand the Catholic conquers Granada: end of Moorish power in Spain.
- Expulsion of Jews from Spain.
- Alexander VI becomes Pope: scandalous reign.
- Death of Casimir IV of Poland.

Deaths
Lorenzo de' Medici.

1493
- Maximilian I becomes German king.
- Pope Alexander VI divides newly explored lands between Spain and Portugal.
- Treaty of Senlis: France gives Maximilian Artois and the County of Burgundy.
- End of the Lordship of the Isles. James IV assumes the title.

1494
- Sir Edward Poynings becomes Lord Deputy of Ireland.
- Lollards of Kyle in Scotland, pioneers of Reformation.
- Turks driven out of Styria.
- The Medici expelled from Florence.
- Charles VIII of France invades Italy.
- Treaty of Tordesillas between Spain and Portugal.
- Aldus Manutius printing at Venice.

Deaths
Hans Memling, Flemish painter.
Pico de Mirandola, Italian painter.

1495
- Introduction in Ireland of Poynings' Law to regulate Irish government by Sir Edward Poynings: Parliament of Ireland made entirely dependent on that of England.
- Manuel becomes king of Portugal.
- Charles VIII conquers Naples.
- Battle of Fornovo: French advance in Italy checked.
- Holy League against France between Ferdinand, the Pope, the emperor, etc.
- King's College, Aberdeen, founded by Bishop William Elphinstone as St Mary's College (renamed in honour of James IV).
- Play of *Everyman* not later than this date.
- Canterbury Cathedral completed.

1496
- First of several fruitless invasions of England and Ireland by Perkin Warbeck, who claimed to be Richard, Duke of York, the younger of the two Princes in the Tower, and claimant to Henry VII's throne.
- Magnus Intercursus: a commercial treaty between England and Netherlands.
- Philip, son of Emperor Maximilian I and Mary of Burgundy, marries Juana, daughter of Ferdinand and Isabella of Spain.
- Magnus Intercursus: a commercial treaty between England and Netherlands.
- Jesus College, Cambridge, founded by John Alcock, bishop of Ely.

1497
- Turks devastate Poland.
- Capture of Perkin Warbeck after an attempt on Cornwall (October). He is confined in the Tower of London.
- Killing of Sir James Ormonde ('Black James'), Lord Treasurer of Ireland.
- The Scottish Parliament passes education legislation.
- Leonardo da Vinci finishes *The Last Supper.*
- John Cabot discovers Labrador, Newfoundland and South Carolina.
- Royal tennis played in England by Henry VII.

1498
- Vasco da Gama reaches India by sea.
- Louis XII becomes king of France.
- Erasmus at Oxford.
- Building of Holyrood Palace, Edinburgh, begins.

Deaths
Girolamo Savonarola, Italian reformer executed in Florence.

1499
- Vicente Pinzon and Amerigo Vespucci reach America.

- Battle of Sapienza: Venetian fleet totally defeated by Turks.
- Louis XII conquers Milan; Ludovico il Moro overthrown.
- War between Ivan the Great and Alexander of Lithuania.
- Peace of Basle: Swiss League virtually recognized as independent of the Empire.
- Execution by hanging of Perkin Warbeck (23 November).

1500
- Battle of Vedrosha: Lithuanians routed by Russians.
- Poedro Cabral discovers Brazil.

1501
- France and Spain arrange joint conquest and partition of kingdom of Naples; then fall out over the spoils.
- Alexander becomes king of Poland: final union with Lithuania.

1502
- Massacre of the Orsini at Rome by Pope Alexander VI and his son Caesar Borgia.

1503
- Battle of Garigliano: French defeated by Spanish in Italy.
- Julius II becomes Pope; Caesar Borgia overthrown.
- Marriage of James IV of Scotland and Margaret Tudor, daughter of Henry VII of England.
- William Dunbar composes his most famous poem *The Thrissil and the Rois* in honour of the marriage of James IV and Margaret Tudor.
- Leonardo da Vinci paints *Mona Lisa*.

1504
- Treaty of Blois between Louis XII and Maximilian I.
- William Warham becomes archbishop of Canterbury.
- Michelangelo finishes the statue of *David* (started 1501).

1505
- Almeida becomes Portuguese Viceroy in India.
- Basil III becomes Tsar of Moscow.
- Christ's College, Cambridge, refounded and enlarged by Lady Margaret Beaufort.

1506
- Sigismund I becomes king of Poland.
- Philip, husband of Juana, is recognized as king of Castile: dies same year.

Deaths

Chrisopher Columbus.

Andrea Mantegna, Italian painter.

1507
- Machiavelli in power at Florence.
- Margaret, daughter of Maximilian, becomes governor-general of Netherlands.
- Louis XII takes Genoa.
- First printing press in Scotland set up in Edinburgh by Andrew Myllar.

1508
- Maximilian assumes at Trent the title of Roman emperor elect, without waiting for coronation at Rome.
- League of Cambrai formed against Venice, comprising France, Empire and the Pope Julius II.
- *Romance of Amadis de Gaul* published around this time.
- Michelangelo and Raphael working at Rome for Julius II: culmination of Renaissance Art.

Deaths

Robert Henryson, Scottish poet.

1509
- Death of Henry VII (21 April): his second son succeeds him as Henry VIII, king of England.
- Marriage of Henry VIII and Catherine of Aragon, widow of Henry's brother, Prince Arthur (11 June).
- Spaniards under Cardinal Ximenes defeat Barbary pirates and take Oran.
- Battle of Agnadello: Venetians defeated by French.
- Florence finally subdues Pisa.
- Emperor Maximilian fails to take Padua.
- Great earthquake in Constantinople.
- Publication of *Praise of Folly* by Erasmus.
- Gentlemen-at-Arms established as the sovereign's personal bodyguard by Henry VIII.

1510
- Venice reconciled to the Pope.
- Albuquerque captures Goa in India for Portugal.
- Erasmus begins lecturing on Greek at Cambridge University.

Deaths

Sandro Botticelli, Italian painter.

1511
- Albuquerque takes Malacca.
- Holy League of Pope, Venice, and Spain: joined by Henry VIII.
- Foundation of St John's College, Cambridge, by Lady Margaret, Countess of Richmond and Derby.

1512
- Selim I becomes Sultan of Turkey.
- Imperial Diet at Cologne: last reforming Diet.
- Battle of Ravenna: Gaston de Foix victorious against Holy League but killed: artillery first decides a battle.

- Holy League restores the Medici in Florence.
- League between the Pope and the emperor.
- Admiralty founded.

1513

- Anglo-French Wars. Battle of Guinegate or Battle of the Spurs (16 August): English under Henry VIII defeats French.
- Anglo-Scottish Wars. Battle of Flodden (9 September): English victory over Scots: James IV killed; his young son becomes James V, king of Scotland.
- Franco-Venetian League renewed.
- Maximilian allies with Henry VIII against France.
- Battle of Novara: Swiss defeat the French.
- Christian II becomes king of Denmark.
- Leo X (of Medici family) becomes Pope.
- Vasco Núñez de Balboa discovers the Pacific Ocean.
- Machiavelli *The Prince.*

1514

- Greek New Testament of Erasmus.
- First Charter granted to Trinity House by Henry VIII.

Deaths

Donato Bramante, Italian architect.

1515

- Cardinal Thomas Wolsey becomes Lord Chancellor of England.
- Francis I becomes king of France.
- Charles, grandson of Maximilian, becomes Governor of the Netherlands.
- Navarre incorporated with Castile.
- Congress of Vienna: marriage treaties between Maximilian and Vladislav of Hungary.
- Battle of Marignano: French defeat Swiss and recover Milan.

1516

- Church Concordat between Francis I and Leo X.
- Death of Ferdinand the Catholic: Charles I (afterwards Emperor Charles V) becomes king of Castile, Aragon and other regions.
- Louis II becomes king of Hungary.
- Barbarossa, the pirate leader, captures Algiers.
- Treaty of Noyon: between France, Spain and the Holy Roman Empire.
- Everlasting League between the Swiss and French.
- Birth of a daughter (later Mary I) to Henry VIII and Catherine of Aragon (18 February).
- Corpus Christi College, Oxford, founded by Richard Foxe.
- Publication of *Utopia* by Sir Thomas More.

Deaths

Hieronymus Bosch, Dutch painter.

1517

- Treaty of Rouen between Scotland and France.
- Turks occupy Cairo and overthrow the Mamelukes: Turkish sultan henceforth caliph.
- Martin Luther publishes his Ninety-five Theses at Wittenberg (a protest against the indulgences of the Roman Catholic church): beginning of Reformation.
- The Royal College of Physicians founded by Thomas Linacre.

1518

- Melanchthon becomes Professor of Greek at Wittenberg.
- Zwingli becomes People's Priest at Great Minster of Zurich.

1519

- Death of Emperor Maximilian: Charles V elected king of the Romans.
- Ferdinand Magellan starts on voyage round the world.

Deaths

Leonardo da Vinci, Italian engineer and artist.

1520

- Field of the Cloth of Gold: conference between Henry VIII and Francis I of France (6 June).
- Suleiman the Magnificent becomes Sultan of Turkey.
- Christian II of Denmark, having overthrown Sten Sture, is crowned king of Sweden.
- Luther excommunicated.
- The Meaux Preachers pioneer the Reformation in France.
- Stockholm Bath of Blood.
- Hernando Cortés conquers Mexico.

***c.*1520**

Deaths

William Dunbar, Scottish poet

1521

- Treaty of Bruges between Emperor Charles V and Henry VIII.
- Henry VIII created Defender of the Faith by Pope Leo X for answering Luther.
- Battle of Villalar: Spanish revolt crushed by Charles V.
- Ferdinand, brother of Charles V, given the government of the Austrian Hapsburg dominions.
- Milan occupied by the troops of Charles V and the Pope.
- Turks capture Belgrade.
- Luther at Diet of Worms: placed under the ban of the Empire.

1522

- Treaty of Windsor: between Charles V and Henry VIII.

- Adrian VI becomes Pope: last non-Italian Pope.
- Battle of the Bicocca (near Milan): French defeated by Imperialists and compelled to evacuate Lombardy: Francesco Sforza set up in Milan.
- Turks conquer Rhodes.
- The Knights' War: Franz von Sickingen, a German Lutheran knight, fails to capture Trier.

1523

- Charles Brandon, Duke of Suffolk, invades France.
- Revolt against Christian II causes his flight from Denmark: Frederick I becomes king.
- Franz von Sickingen defeated and killed.
- Gustavus Vasa becomes king of Sweden (Gustavus I): Union of Kalmar ended.
- Albert of Brandenburg, last Grand Master of Teutonic Order, becomes Lutheran.
- Clement VII (of the Medici family) becomes Pope.
- First recorded insurance policy.

1524

- Catholic Swiss League formed.
- Beginning of Peasants' Revolt in Germany.
- French invasion of Lombardy (Bayard killed).
- Invasion of France by Duke of Bourbon; fails to take Marseilles; pursued to Italy.
- Order of Theatines founded.
- Protestantism banned in Scotland.
- Death of Hans Holbein the Elder, German painter.

1525

- Clement VII's agreement with Francis I.
- Battle of Pavia: Francis I defeated by Charles V and made prisoner; hand firearms triumphant.
- Mass abolished at Zürich.
- Massacre of Weinsberg by revolting German peasants: rebels crushed in several fights.
- Albert of Brandenburg makes his dominions the hereditary Dukedom of Prussia.
- Peace between England and France.
- Christ Church, Oxford, founded.
- William Tyndale's translation of the New Testament completed in Germany.
- Lefèvre's French New Testament condemned to be burned.

1526

- Treaty of Madrid between Charles V and Francis I: Francis set free.
- Lutheran Alliance completed, with Landgrave Philip of Hesse as its moving spirit.
- League of Cognac against emperor by Francis I, Pope, Florence, Venice and others.
- Milan surrenders to the Imperialists.
- Beginning of Danish breach with Rome.
- Battle of Mohács: Hungary overthrown by the Turks: King Louis II drowned.
- Battle of Panipat: Moslem conquest of India by Babar begun: Mogul Empire founded.
- John Zapolya and Ferdinand of Austria both elected king of Hungary: Zapolya defeated by Ferdinand at Tokay.
- Ferdinand elected king of Bohemia.
- Order of Capuchins founded.
- Building of Fountains Abbey completed.

1527

- Sack of Rome by Imperialist troops under Duke of Bourbon.
- Second expulsion of Medici from Florence.
- Västeras Recess: beginning of official Swedish Reformation.
- French under Lautrec invade Italy.
- Alliance between Henry VIII and Francis I.
- Publication of *History of Scotland* by Hector Boece.

Deaths

Niccolò Machiavelli, Italian writer, political philosopher and diplomat.

1528

- England and France declare war against the Empire.
- Naples besieged by French and Genoese.
- Genoese under Andrea Doria desert French, capture Genoa and establish a republic.
- Patrick Hamilton burned for heresy in Scotland.

Deaths

Albrecht Dürer, German painter and engraver.

1529

- Henry VIII's divorce trail begins: transferred to Rome by the Pope.
- Fall of Cardinal Wolsey when he is accused of treason: Sir Thomas More becomes Lord Chancellor (until 1533).
- Diet of Speir: Protest against its decisions by Lutheran Princes and cities: hence name of Protestant.
- Berquin burned for heresy in France.
- Zurich declares war on Lucerne and Catholic allies: Peace of Kappel arranged.
- Treaty of Barcelona: between Pope and emperor.
- Conference of Marburg between Luther and Zwingli: failure.
- Unsuccessful siege of Vienna by Turks.
- Peace of Cambrai ('Ladies' Peace'): between Francis I, the emperor, and England.

1530

- Compact between Charles V and Clement VII: Charles crowned emperor by Pope at Bologna; the last to be crowned emperor.
- Florence surrenders to the Medici after a long siege.
- Schmalkaldic League of Protestant German Princes formed.

- The Grisons League obtains the Valtelline.
- Diet of Augsburg: Phillipp Melanchthon prepares the anti-Zwinglian Confession of Augsburg.
- Tetrapolitana Confession (Zwinglian) prepared by cities of South Germany under influence of Martin Bucer.

Deaths

Cardinal Wolsey on his way to the Tower of London (29 November).

1531

- Battle of Kappel: Catholic Swiss cantons victorious over Protestant: Ulrich Zwingli killed.
- Second Peace of Kappel between the two religious parties in Switzerland.
- Murder of James Inglis, abbot of Culross.
- Appearance of Halley's Comet (named after Edmund Halley).

1532

- 'Submission of the Clergy' to Henry VIII in England.
- The Court of Session, central court of civil justice, established by James V in Scotland.
- Agreement of Nuremberg: Protestants guarantee peace till next Diet of General Council.
- End of Florentine Republic: Alessandro de' Medici made Duke.
- Francisco Pizarro conquers Peru.
- Resignation of Sir Thomas More as Chancellor.
- Ariosto writes *Orlando Furioso*.
- *Pantagruel* is written by François Rabelais

1533

- Secret marriage of Henry VIII and Anne Boleyn (25 January); Anne Boleyn publicly named queen of Henry VIII; Cranmer declared Catherine of Aragon's marriage null; Anne Boleyn crowned; Henry VIII excommunicated by Pope.
- Birth of a daughter (later Elizabeth I) to Henry VIII and Anne Boleyn.
- Thomas Cromwell becomes chief minister.
- Death of Frederick I of Denmark: disputed succession.
- Treaty of Peace between Turkey and Austria.
- Ivan IV (the Terrible) becomes tsar.
- Marriage of Henri, Duke of Orléans (to be Henri II) to 14-year-old Catherine de' Medici.
- Thomas Cranmer becomes archbishop of Canterbury.
- Completion of St James's Palace (begun 1532) by Henry VIII.

1534

- Anabaptist revolution in Münster under John of Leyden (soon suppressed).
- Geneva adopts the Reformation.
- First Voyage of Jacques Cartier to Canada.
- Revolution in Lübeck under Wullenwever.
- Battle of Lauffen: Philip of Hesse, leader of the Schmalkaldic League, defeats Ferdinand's forces in Württemberg.
- Barbarossa II captures Tunis.
- Grevefeide or Count's War in Denmark.
- Act of Supremacy in England (17 November) separating Anglican Church from the Catholic Church, signed by Henry VIII, who becomes Supreme Head of the English Church.
- Paul III becomes Pope.
- The Paris Placards against the mass: severe persecution.
- Luther's German Bible completed.
- Peter's Pence, the annual offering to the pope, abolished.
- Rabelais writes *Gargantua*.

1535

- Barbarossa II defeated and Tunis taken by Emperor Charles along with Andrea Doria, Venice, Knights of Malta and others.
- Execution by beheading of Bishop Fisher and Sir Thomas More (6 July) because they will not accept the Act of Supremacy.
- Henry VIII declared deposed by Pope Paul III in the first Bull of Deposition.
- Thomas Cromwell becomes Vicar-General for Henry VIII.
- Publication of the English Bible of Miles Coverdale (first complete one).

1536

- The Act of Union unites England and Wales.
- Treaty between Francis I of France and Suleiman sultan of Turkey.
- Savoy conquered by French.
- Imperialists invade Province, but repelled.
- Christian III enters Copenhagen as king.
- Anne Boleyn beheaded for adultery (19 May); Henry VIII married Jane Seymour (30 May); Jane Seymour proclaimed queen.
- First act for dissolution of the monasteries ordered by Henry VIII in England.
- Pilgrimage of Grace, Yorkshire insurrection under Robert Aske and John Pickering.
- William Tyndale burned for heresy in the Netherlands (6 October).
- Lincolnshire Insurrection against religious and fiscal oppression (suppressed 1536-37).
- Calvin's *Institutes*.
- Concord of Wittenberg between Luther and Zwinglians.
- Calvin at Geneva.

Deaths

Catherine of Aragon (7 January).
Desiderius Erasmus of Rotterdam, humanist scholar.

1537

- Christian III takes possession of Norway.
- A Papal Commission reports on reform.
- Suleiman of Turkey devastates Corfu in his war with Venice.
- End of Lübeck attempt at city-Empire: Wullenwever executed.
- Birth of a son (later Edward VI) to Henry VIII and Jane Seymour: Jane Seymour díes several days later.
- Robert Aske and John Pickering, leaders of the Pilgrimage of Grace, executed.

1538

- Defensive League against the Turks between the emperor, Pope, Ferdinand and Venice.
- Calvin expelled from Geneva.
- Catholic League of Nürnberg.
- Truce for ten years between Francis I, Charles V and the Pope.
- Suleiman annexes part of Moldavia.
- Turkish fleet sails against India; Yemen captured.
- Naval flight in the Ambracian Gulf: Barbarossa defeats forces of emperor, Pope, Venice and Genoa.
- Marriage of James IV of Scotland and Mary of Lorraine, daughter of the Duke of Guise.

1539

- Society of Jesus (Jesuits) founded by Ignatius Loyola.
- Act of the Six Articles against heresy in England.

1540

- Anne of Cleves married (January) and divorced (July) by Henry VIII.
- Thomas Cromwell beheaded.
- Marriage of Henry VIII to Catherine Howard, his fifth wife.
- Charles V punishes Ghent severely for rebellion.
- Peace between Venice and the Turks.
- Severe Edict of Fontainebleau against heresy.
- Jacques Cartier discovers the St Lawrence River.
- First recorded horse racing event in Britain (9 February) at Chester.

c.1540

- Apricots first planted in England around this time.

1541

- Henry VIII given the title 'King of Ireland' by the Irish Parliament.
- Suleiman virtually annexes Hungary.
- Failure of Spanish attack on Algiers
- Religious Conference at Ratisborn: failure.
- Calvin finally settles in Geneva.
- Hernando De Soto discovers the Mississippi.

Deaths

Execution of Margaret Pole, Countess of Salisbury, mother of Reginald Pole, at the order of Henry VIII.

Theophrastus Paracelsus, Swiss physician and alchemist.

1542

- Anglo-Scottish Wars. Battle of Solway Moss (14 December): English defeat Scots.
- Death of James V: his infant daughter Mary Stewart becomes queen of Scotland as Mary Queen of Scots: Earl of Arran Regent.
- Catherine Howard, fifth wife of Henry VIII, beheaded for adultery (13 February).
- Roberval attempts to found a French colony in Canada.
- French attack Artois and Flanders.
- Brunswick lands overrun by the Schmalkaldic League's forces.
- Imperialist forces under Joachim of Brandenburg fail to take Pesth from the Turks.
- Council of Trent opened.
- Inquisition set up in Rome.
- Magdelene College, Cambridge, founded.

Deaths

Sir Thomas Wyatt, English poet.

1543

- Betrothal of the infant Mary of Scotland to Edward, son and heir of Henry VIII, the Greenwich Treaty; repudiated by Scots Parliament.
- Catherine Parr becomes sixth wife of Henry VIII (12 July).
- Charles V victorious in his war against Duke William of Cleves.
- Suleiman takes Gran, Stuhlweissenburg and others.
- Barbarossa and the French fleet capture Nice city, but not the citadel.
- Vesalius, the anatomist, publishes his chief work.

Deaths

Nicolas Copernicus, Polish astronomer.

Hans Holbein the Younger, German painter.

1544

- Bologne taken by English.
- The 'Rough Wooing': English troops under the Earl of Hertford invade Scotland; Edinburgh burned.
- Peace of Crépy: between emperor, England, and France. Title of Defender of the Faith for Henry VIII continued by Parliament.
- Battle of Ceresole: French defeat Spanish forces in Lombardy.
- Edict calling upon all subjects in the hereditary Hapsburg lands to accept Confession of Louvain.

1545

- The 'Rough Wooing'. Battle of Ancrum Moor (17 February): Scottish victory over English.
- Massacre of the Waldenses.

- Brunswick territories appropriated by Schmalkaldic League.
- Council of Trent again opened.
- The *Mary Rose* sinks in the Solent (19 July, raised 1982).

1546

- Ban of the Empire against Philip of Hesse and the Elector John Frederick of Saxony.
- Execution of the Fourteen of Meaux in France.
- Ernestine Saxony invaded and occupied by Maurice of Albertine Saxony and Ferdinand: Elector John Frederick recovers his territory and invades that of Maurice.
- Religious conference at Ratisbon: futile.
- Diet of Ratisbon: Protestants repudiate Council of Trent and demand a National Council.
- George Wishart burned as a heretic in Scotland.
- Cardinal Beaton murdered to avenge Wishart and St Andrews Castle captured.
- Anne Askew tortured and burned for heresy in London.
- Foundation of Trinity College, Cambridge, by Henry VIII.

Deaths

Martin Luther, German religious reformer.

1547

- Death of Henry VIII (28 January): Edward VI becomes king of England (until 1553): Earl of Hertford (created Duke of Somerset) becomes Protector of the realm.
- The 'Rough Wooing'. Battle of Pinkie (10 September): English under Somerset victorious over Scots under Huntly; English took Edinburgh. Capitulation of St Andrews: John Knox a French galley slave.
- Failure of revolt against Andrea Doria of Genoa.
- Practically all South German cities subdued by Emperor Charles by this date; Duke Henry regains Brunswick; Catholicism re-established in Cologne.
- Council of Trent removed to Bologna by the Pope.
- Henri II becomes king of France.
- Battle of Mühlberg: Charles V defeats Elector John Frederick and takes him prisoner; the electoral dignity transferred to Maurice of Albertine Saxony.
- Philip of Hesse surrenders to Charles V.
- Chambre Ardente created in France.
- Brittany united to the French kingdom.
- Earl of Surrey executed for treason.
- Marriage of Lord Seymour and Catherine Parr, widow of Henry VIII.
- Execution of Jaime de Enzines at Rome: first Italian death for heresy.
- English replaces Latin in English Church services.
- Somerset repeals the English laws against heresy.
- Inquisition established in Portugal.

1548

- Suleiman victorious against Persia.
- Sigismund II (Augustus) becomes king of Poland.
- The Bohemian Brethren, expelled from Bohemia, settle in Poland.
- Interim religious compromise drawn up by a committee chosen by Charles V and proclaimed as an Edict.
- Mary Queen of Scots sent to France.

Deaths

Catherine Parr in childbirth (7 September).

1549

- France declares war against England.
- Somerset as social reformer: Enclosures Commission appointed.
- Ket's Rebellion in eastern England over land enclosures, led by Robert Kett, suppressed by royal troops at Battle of Duffindale; Kett hanged.
- Arundel's Rebellion. Battle of Farrington Bridge (27 July): rebels defeated by royal troops; Battle of St Mary's Clyst (4 August): rebel attack on royal army defeated; Arundel abandoned siege of Exeter; Battle of Sampford Courtney (17 August): rebels under Arundel finally defeated.
- France declares war against England.
- Imprisonment of Somerset: Warwick (later Duke of Northumberland) in power as Protector.
- Parliament declared enclosures legal.
- First Act of Uniformity in England makes the Catholic mass illegal.
- The Anabaptist religious movement (founded 1522) reached England.
- First Book of Common Prayer sanctioned by Parliament and published (9 June): the wedding ring finger changed from right hand to left.

Deaths

Lord Seymour, brother of Somerset, executed for treason for seeking to marry Elizabeth.

1550

- Julius III becomes Pope.
- Dragut the corsair defeated by Charles and headquarters in Tunisia taken.
- Severe placard against heresy in the Netherlands.
- Persecution of Catholics and heretics in England.
- Anglo-French Wars. Battle of Jersey: French fleet besieging St Helier defeated by English.
- Peace between France and England: Boulogne given back to France.

1551

- Council of Trent resumes at Trent.
- Turks capture Tripoli from Knights of St John.
- Turco-Hungarian war renewed after a truce.

- Magdeburg capitulates to the Elector Maurice.

Deaths

Martin Bucer, German religious reformer.

1552

- Treaty of Chambord between Henry II and the Protestant German princes.
- French invade and occupy Lorraine.
- Council of Trent suspended.
- Charles V's flight from Maurice of Saxony across the Brenner Pass.
- Treaty of Passau: Protestant position secured.
- Kazan annexed by Ivan IV.
- Second Act of Uniformity in England.
- Second Book of Common Prayer published.

Deaths

- Edward Seymour, 1st Duke of Somerset executed due to the plotting of the Earl of Warwick (afterwards the Duke of Northumberland).

1553

- Death of Edward VI from tuberculosis (6 July): Lady Jane Grey, great-niece of Henry VIII and daughter-in-law of the Earl of Northumberland, proclaimed queen by Northumberland but recognized only by King's Lynn and Berwick; Mary Tudor also proclaimed; Northumberland executed and Mary proclaimed as Mary I.
- Battle of Sievershausen: Elector Maurice defeats Albert Margrave of Brandenburg, but is killed.
- Battle of Steterburg: Albert of Brandenburg defeated by Duke Henry of Brunswick.
- Michael Servetus, an anti-Trinitarian, burned for heresy in Geneva by Calvin.
- Sir Hugh Willoughby and Richard Chancellor set out in search of northeast passage: Willoughby is lost: but Chancellor found the White Sea and Archangel Passage.

Deaths

François Rabelais, French writer.

1554

- Wyatt's Rebellion. Announcement of Mary I's intention to marry Philip of Spain provoked a rebellion in Kent led by Sir Thomas Wyatt. Insurgents defeated at Wrotham Heath (January); Wyatt executed.
- Execution by beheading of Lady Jane Grey and her husband, Lord Guildford Dudley (12 February) by Mary Tudor.
- Mary Tudor marries Philip, heir of Charles V.
- Mary of Lorraine (or Guise), becomes regent of Scotland.
- Battle of Schwarzach: Albert of Brandenburg defeated by Duke Henry of Brunswick and driven as a fugutive to France.
- Astrakhan annexed by Ivan IV.
- Cardinal Reginald Pole arrives in England: Parliament decides in favour of returning to the old religion.

1555

- Marcellas II becomes Pope; dies a few months later; Paul IV succeeds; Counter-Reformation in the Papal chair.
- Charles V abdicates sovereignty of Netherlands at Brussels: Philip II succeeds.
- Vaudois become Calvinists.
- Union of Bohemian Brethren and Calvinists in Poland.
- Religious Peace of Augsburg: Cujus regio, ejus religio.
- John Rogers burned for heresy in England; many others follow.
- Bishop Hugh Latimer and Bishop Nicholas Ridley of London burned at the stake in England for heresy (16 October).
- Foundation of St John's College, Oxford.
- Foundation of Trinity College, Oxford, by Sir Thomas Pope.
- Muscovy Company founded by Richard Chancellor to trade with Russia.

1556

- Charles V abdicates sovereignty in Spain and Italy: Ferdinand I becomes emperor.
- Peace of Vaucelles between Philip and France.
- Battle of Panipat (second): Mogul conquest of India made secure.
- Akbar becomes Mogul emperor in India.
- Thomas Cranmer, archbishop of Canterbury, burned at the stake for heresy (21 March). Cardinal Pole becomes archbishop of Canterbury.
- Richard Chancellor, instigator of the Muscovy Company, dies in a shipwreck.

Deaths

Nicholas Udall, English playwright, author of the comedy *Ralph Roister Doister*.

1557

- War declared between England and France to support Spain.
- Battle of St Quentin: French defeated by Spanish under Duke of Savoy and Egmont.
- Colloquy of Worms: no result.
- Livonia conquered by Ivan IV.
- First bond of the Lords of the Congregation, organization of Scottish Protestantism.

Deaths

Anne of Cleves, fourth wife of Henry VIII.

1558

- English expelled from Calais, last of the French possessions (7 January).

- Mary Queen of Scots marries the French dauphin, Francis.
- Death of Mary I (Mary Tudor) (17 November). Her half-sister becomes queen of England as Elizabeth I.
- Battle of Gravelines: Egmont again defeated by the French.

Deaths

Reginald Pole (17 November), cardinal and papal legate, succeeds Cranmer as Archbishop of Canterbury (1556).

1559

- Third Act of Uniformity and Act of Supremacy in England, signed by Elizabeth, settled the question of religion. Elizabeth becomes head of the English Church.
- Mary Queen of Scots becomes queen of France on the accession of her husband.
- Death of Christian III of Denmark: Frederick II succeeds.
- Auto-da-fé at Valladolid: first one against heresy.
- Francis II becomes king of France with the death of his father Henri II.
- Philip leaves the Netherlands: Margaret of Parma Regent.
- Colloquy of Westminster.
- Treaty of Cateau-Cambresis: a European settlement between the Empire, France, and England.
- First Papal Index of Prohibited Books: great opposition.
- Pius IV Pope.
- John Knox returns to Scotland where he introduces Presbyterianism.
- Matthew Parker becomes archbishop of Canterbury (until 1575).
- Elizabethan *Book of Common Prayer* published (revised 1662).
- Completion by John Foxe of *Foxe's Book of Martyrs* (begun 1554).

1560

- Treaty of Berwick (27 February): the Scottish protestant Lords of the Congregation are promised English aid against the French.
- Elizabeth sends Lord Grey with an army to help the Scottish Lords of the Congregation.
- Death of Mary of Guise, the Scottish regent.
- Mary Queen of Scots widowed by the death of Francis II of France.
- The Treaty of Edinburgh, enacting peace between England and Scotland, signed: French forces to quit Scotland.
- Sussex becomes Lord Lieutenant of Ireland (until 1564).
- Tumult of Amboise.
- Death of Gustavus Vasa, king of Sweden: succeeded by Erik XIV.
- Charles IX becomes king of France.
- Scottish Parliament abolishes Roman Catholicism in Scotland.
- Establishment of the Reformed Church of Scotland.
- First Book of Discipline in Scottish Church.

Deaths

Amy Robsart, wife of Robert Dudley, later Earl of Leicester, in a fall.

1561

- Abortive Protestant Conference at Naumberg: Lutherans and Calvinists irreconcilable.
- Vaudois rebellion suppressed by Savoy.
- Reval becomes Swedish.
- The Colloquy of Poissy: a form of French National Church Council.
- Teutonic Order submits to Poland.
- Mary Queen of Scots lands in Scotland.

1562

- Edict of January: first legal recognition of Protestantism in France.
- Council of Trent resumes at Trent.
- Massacre of Vassy: First War of Religion in France begins.
- Huguenots take Orleans.
- French royalists occupy Rouen.
- Battle of Dreux: indecisive royalist victory in France.
- English force lands to help the Huguenots in France: Le Havre occupied.
- Treaty of Prague between emperor Ferdinand and Suleiman the Magnificent.
- Emmanuel Philibert of Savoy obtains Turin and makes it his capital.
- Treaty of Hampton Court between Elizabeth and the Prince de Condé (signed 21 September).
- Battle of Corrichie: rebel troops under Earl of Huntly defeated by Mary's troops under Moray, half-brother of Mary; Huntly killed.

1563

- Edict of Amboise ends First War of Religion.
- Le Havre evacuated by the English.
- Swedes defeat Danes off Bornholm.
- Northern Seven Years' War declared by Denmark.
- Charles IX declared of age in France.
- End of Council of Trent: The Counter-Reformation complete.
- Agreement by Convocation of the Church of England of the Thirty-nine Articles.
- Plague in London.

Deaths

Francis, Duke of Guise, leader of the Catholic party fighting the Huguenots, is murdered in a suburb of Orléans.

1564

- Papal Decree confirming decrees of Council of Trent.
- Treaty of Troyes between France and England.
- Treaty of Lausanne adjusts boundaries between Berne and Savoy.
- Cardinal Granville recalled from the Netherlands.
- Philip orders decrees of Trent to be enforced in the Netherlands.
- Maximilian II becomes emperor.
- Anti-Trinitarians in Poland.
- Calvinism established in Palatinate by the Elector Frederick III.
- Puritan opposition of anglicanism.
- Tridentine Index of Prohibited Books.

Deaths

John Calvin, French theologian.
Michelangelo, Italian artist.

1565

- Mary Queen of Scots marries Lord Henry Darnley (29 July); Moray flees to England.
- Failure of Turkish attack on Malta.
- Bayonne Conference between France and Spain.
- Trent Decrees and Placards against heresy begin to be enforced in Netherlands.
- Revival of Catholicism in Poland.
- First punishments of Puritans in England.

1566

- Birth of a son (later James VI of Scotland and James I of England) born to Mary Queen of Scots and Lord Darnley (19 June).
- The Culemberg Banquet in Brussels:Vivent les Gueux first heard.
- Iconoclastic outbreaks in the Netherlands.
- Conference at Dendermonde between William the Silent, Lewis of Nassau, Egmont, Horn; Egmont and Horn not prepared to resist Philip.
- Death of Suleiman the Magnificent in Hungary: Selim II succeeds as Sultan.
- 'The Compromise' signed by many Netherland nobles, pledging them to oppose the Inquisition.
- 'The Request' presented to a Netherlands Assembly by Lewis of Nassau and Brederode, embodying the principles of the 'Compromise'.
- First organized Lord Mayor's Show in London.

Deaths

- David Rizzio, Italian musician and secretary of Mary Queen of Scots, murdered in a conspiracy involving Lord Darnley and a group of nobles.

Nostradamus, French astrologer.

1567

- Murder of Lord Darnley (10 February) near Edinburgh. Mary Queen of Scots marries James Hepburn, Bothwell.
- Mary Queen of Scots taken prisoner by Scottish nobles at the bloodless Battle of Carberry Hill, imprisoned in Lochleven Castle, and compelled to abdicate.
- Scottish Parliament declared Mary guilty of murder and to have forfeited the crown: the infant James VI proclaimed king of Scotland. Moray becomes regent.
- Shane O'Neill defeated and killed in Ireland.
- Rout of John de Marnix at Austruweel.
- Valenciennes taken by Royal forces.
- William of Orange goes into exile.
- Murder of the Sture by Erik XIV of Sweden.
- Arrest of Egmont and Horn after Alva had arrived in Netherlands as Captain-General; Council of Troubles created: Alva becomes Regent and Governor-General.
- Enterprise of Meaux.
- John Casimir, second son of Elector Palatine Frederick, leads a force into France to help the Huguenots.
- Battle of Saint Denis between Huguenots and Catholics: indecisive.

1568

- Mary Queen of Scots escaped from Lochleven: defeated by Moray at the Battle of Langside (13 May); flees to England. Imprisoned by Elizabeth I.
- William of Orange proclaimed an outlaw.
- La Rochelle opens its gates to the Huguenots.
- Condé raises the seige of Orleans.
- Peace between the emperor and the Turks.
- Peace of Longjumeau ends the Second War of Religion in France.
- Battle of Heiligerlee: Lewis of Nassau defeated Spanish.
- Execution of Egmont and Horn.
- Revolt of Moriscos in Granada: suppressed with great slaughter.
- Douay College founded by Father Allen.

1569

- Erik XIV deposed by Swedish Diet: John III becomes king.
- States-General summoned at Brussels: Alva fails to get all his taxes.
- Battle of Jarnac: Huguenots routed: Condé captured and shot dead.
- Union of Lublin: Poland and Lithuania incorporated.
- Cosimo de' Medici created grand duke of Tuscany by the pope.
- Battle of Moncontour: Huguenot defeat.
- Spanish treasure ships seized at Falmouth and Southampton.

- Beggars of the Sea first appear.
- Gerard Mercator makes a revolutionary new map of the world, which is the foundation of modern cartography.

Deaths

Pieter Breughel the Elder, Flemish painter.

1570

- Assassination of Regent Moray; Lennox becomes regent of Scotland.
- Elizabeth I declared deposed by Pope Pius V in the second Bull of Deposition.
- Peace of Saint-Germain ends Third War of Religion: La Rochelle becomes Huguenot headquarters.
- Concensus of Sadomir: Union of Bohemian Brethren, Lutherans and Calvinists in Poland.
- Northern Seven Years' War ended by Peace of Stettin.
- Incorporation of Oxford University by Elizabeth I.

1571

- Beggars of the Sea forbidden to use English ports.
- Thirty-nine Articles enacted in England by parliament.
- Regent Lennox murdered in Scotland: Earl of Mar becomes regent.
- Triple Alliance of Spain, Venice and Pope against Turks.
- Turks land in Cyprus.
- Battle of Lepanto: Don John of Austria wins naval victory over Turks.
- Khan of Crimea invades Russia and burns Moscow.
- Ridolfi conspiracy discovered by William Cecil.
- Beginning of penal legislation against Catholics in England.
- Foundation of Jesus College, Oxford, by Hugh Price.
- Opening of the Royal Exchange, founded by Sir Thomas Gresham.

Deaths

Benvenuto Cellini, florentine artist

1572

- Defensive alliance between France and England.
- Execution of the rebel Earl of Northumberland by beheading.
- Death of Regent Mar in Scotland: Morton succeeds.
- Death of Sigismund II of Poland.
- Beggars of the Sea capture Brell; also Flushing, etc.
- Lewis of Nassau invades the Netherlands from France; takes Valenciennes and Mons.
- Edict of Rochelle ends Fourth War of Religion.
- William the Silent invades the Netherlands from the East: takes Roermond: Brussels shut against him.
- States of Holland at Dort recognize William the Silent as Stadtholder.
- Henri of Bourbon becomes king of Navarre.
- St Bartholomew's Day Massacre in Paris: Admiral Coligny murdered, fourth War of Religion follows.
- Alva recovers Mons.
- Sack of Malines, Zutphen and Naarden by Spanish troops.
- Siege of Haarlem begun by Don Frederick of Toledo.

Deaths

John Knox (24 November), Scottish religious reformer.

1573

- Compact of Warsaw secures absolute religious liberty in Poland.
- Venice cedes Cyprus to Turks.
- Surrender of Haarlem.
- Siege of Alkmaar: dykes cut: siege raised.
- Battle of Enckhuysen: Spanish fleet defeated by Dutch.
- Duke of Anjou elected king of Poland.
- William the Silent declares himself a Calvinist.
- Alva recalled from the Netherlands: Don Luis Requesens succeeds.
- Pacification of Perth. Edinburgh Castle surrendered by Kirkcaldy of Grange and Maitland of Lethington.

1574

- Huguenot rising begins Fifth War of Religion.
- Battle of Bergen: Dutch naval victory.
- Spaniards surrender Middelburg.
- Battle of Mookerheide: Lewis of Nassau killed.
- Plot of Vincennes.
- Flight of Anjou from Poland.
- Relief of Leyden after long seige.
- The Gerusalemme Liberata of Tasso.
- Henri III becomes king of France.
- Murad III becomes sultan of Turkey.

1575

- Anjou declared deposed in Poland: Maximilian II elected by Senate, Stephen Bathory by Diet; latter elected king of Poland.
- Escape of Monsieur to join Huguenots.
- Battle of Dormans: Huguenot defeat.
- John Casimir again in France.

1576

- Henri of Navarre (future Henri IV) escapes to the Huguenots and abjures Catholicism.
- Death of Requesens: Don John of Austria becomes Governor of Netherlands.
- Union of Holland and Zeeland completed.
- Edict of Beaulieu ends Fifth War of Religion (Peace of Monsieur).
- Rudolph II becomes emperor.
- The League formed by French Catholics.
- Pacification of Ghent.

- Revolt of Spanish troops in Netherlands: Sack of Antwerp and 'Spanish Fury'.
- Opening of the first permanent English theatre, in London.

Deaths

Titian, Venetian painter.

1577

- French king repudiates Edict of Beaulieu: Sixth War of Religion begins.
- Union of Brussels.
- 'Perpetual Edict': agreement between Netherlands and Don John of Austria.
- Don John seizes Namur.
- Peace of Bergerac: Edict of Poitiers: end of Sixth War of Religion.
- William the Silent enters Brussels.
- Drake's voyage round the world in the *Golden Hind* begins (13 December, completed 1580).
- Publication of Holinshed's *Chronicles*.
- Discovery of the siphon principle by William Welwood.

1578

- Morton resigns the regency of Scotland, but afterwards takes possession of the king.
- Battle of Gemblours: Alexander of Parma's victory.
- Battle of Alcazat-Kebir: King Sebastian of Portugal killed in Morocco; Henry succeeds.
- Battle of Verden: Poles and Swedes defeat Russians.
- State entry of Archduke Matthias into Brussels as Governor, with William the Silent as Lieutenant-General.
- Duke of Anjou accepts title of 'Defender of the Liberties of the Netherlands'.
- Alexander of Parma becomes governor of Netherlands.
- Fausto Sozzini (Socinus) in Transylvania and Poland.

1579

- League of Arras for protection of Catholic religion in Hainault, Douay and Artois.
- Union of Utrecht: Dutch republic formed.
- Publication of Spenser's *The Shepherd's Calendar* and Lyly's *Euphues*, the Anatomy of Wit.

1580

- Philip of Spain obtains Portuguese crown on death of King Henry.
- Seventh War of Religion begins; ends in same year by Peace of Fleix.
- Charles Emmanuel succeeds Emmanuel Philibert as Duke of Savoy.
- Robert Parsons and Edmund Campion, Jesuit missionaries, arrive in England.
- First collection of the *Essays* of Montaigne.
- Colonization of Ireland. Battle of Glen Malone: Irish clans defeated English settlers.
- Francis Drake completes first English circumnavigation of the world (26 September).

Deaths

John Heywood, English dramatist.

***c*.1580**

- Congregational Movement founded by Robert Browne.

1581

- Philip puts a price on the head of William the Silent.
- William the Silent provisionally accepts the title of Count of Holland.
- Philip II abjured by Brabant, Flanders, Utrecht, Gelderland, Holland and Zeeland.
- The Apology of William the Silent.
- Poles and Swedes take Narva.
- Battle of Terceira: naval victory of Santa Cruz over Don Antonio.
- Francis Drake knighted by Elizabeth I on his ship, the *Golden Hind* (4 April).
- Second Book of Discipline in Scotland.
- *Defense of Poesy* and *Arcadia* by Sir Philip Sidney are published.
- Publication of *Galatea* by Cervantes.
- The English trading venture, the Levant Company, founded.

Deaths

Edmund Campion, Jesuit missionary to England, hanged (beatified 1886).

James Morton Scottish regent for James VI (1572-80) put to death for his alleged part in the murder of Darnley.

1582

- Raid of Ruthven (22 August): James VI of Scotland a prisoner of the English in Ruthven Castle (until June 1583).
- Peace between Poland and Russia: former gained Livonia, etc.
- Anjou inaugurated at Antwerp as Duke of Brabant.
- Pope Gregory XIII introduces new style in dating by Bull.
- Anjou accepted as Lord of Friesland, Duke of Gelderland and Count of Flanders.
- Marriage of William Shakespeare and Anne Hathaway (27 November).
- Edinburgh University founded.

Deaths

George Buchanan, Scottish scholar and historian, and tutor of James VI.

1583

- 'French Fury' at Antwerp: Anjou sacks Antwerp.
- Truce of Pliusa between Russia and Sweden.
- William the Silent accepts the hereditary Countship of Holland and Zeeland.
- Newfoundland annexed by Britain: Sir Humphrey Gilbert's voyage to found a colony there. During the voyage home his ship sank off the Azores and all perished (9 September).
- Whitgift becomes archbishop of Canterbury to suppress Puritanism.
- Cambridge University Press founded by Thomas Thomas.

Deaths

Earl of Desmond, Gerald Fitzgerald, rebelled against Elizabeth and was executed as a traitor.

Edward Arden, English High Sheriff, hanged.

1584

- William the Silent assassinated at Delft by Gérard.
- Death of Ivan IV: succeeded by Theodore I, with Boris Godunoff as real ruler of Russia.
- Association formed to protect Elizabeth.
- Sir John Perrot becomes Lord Deputy of Ireland (until 1588).
- Episcopacy established in Scottish Church by James VI.

Deaths

- Lord William Ruthven, one of the conspirators in the Raid of Ruthven, executed by beheading.

1585

- Treaty of Joinville against Henri of Navarre between Spain and the Catholic League.
- Sixtus V becomes pope.
- Treaty of Nemours between Henri III and the Catholic League: latter victorious: Eighth War of Religion (War of the Three Henrys) follows.
- Papal Bull against Henri of Navarre and Condé.
- Drake commissioned for reprisals in West Indies. Caragena in Colombia captured by him.
- North Carolina first settled (permanently 1663).
- Earl of Leicester lands in Holland with a force to support the Dutch (December).
- Babington Plot to murder Elizabeth I devised by Anthony Babington.
- English Act against Jesuits, seminary priests, etc.
- Suppression of provincial printing offices by order of the Star Chamber (23 June).
- Foundation of Oxford University Press.

1586

- Babington Plot exposed by Walsingham (August): Babington executed.
- Trial of Mary Queen of Scots for treason (14–15 October).
- Alliance between Elizabeth and James VI for defence of Protestantism.
- Leicester made Governor-General of United Provinces.
- Death of Sir Philip Sidney from wounds sustained in an attack on Spanish convoy at Zutphen in the Netherlands (September).

Deaths

Sir Philip Sidney, English writer and soldier.

1587

- Execution of Mary Queen of Scots by beheading at Fotheringhay Castle (8 February).
- Anglo-Spanish War. Drake's expediton to Cadiz where he destroyed over 100 Spanish vessels to delay sailing of Spanish Armada (19 April).
- Leicester leaves Holland (August).
- Alexander of Parma captures Sluys.
- Sigismund, son of John III of Sweden, elected king of Poland.
- Battle of Coutras: victory of Henri of Navarre.
- Sir Walter Raleigh's second expedition to the New World lands in North Carolina (11 August); first child born in the New World of English parents, Virginia Dare (18 August).
- Davis Strait, Greenland, discovered by John Davis.
- Introduction of potatoes into England.

1588

- Duke of Guise enters Paris: Henri III flees.
- Guise murdered in Henri III's antechamber; his brother, the Cardinal, executed; other Leaguers arrested.
- Christian IV becomes king of Denmark.
- Anglo-Spanish War. Spanish Armada set sail from Lisbon (20 May); defeated on 29 July; Armada forced to return to Spain by sailing north round Scotland.
- 'Martin Marprelate' Puritan tracts begin (ended 1589): attacks on bishops.
- The Gambia sold to English merchants by the Portuguese.
- Invention of shorthand by Dr Timothy Bright.

Deaths

Earl of Leicester, Robert Dudley, English statesman of poisoning.

1589

- Duke of Aumale declared lieutenant-general of France; occupies Paris.
- Truce between Henri III and Henri of Navarre.
- Henri III assassinated: Henri of Navarre becomes king as Henri IV; beginning of Bourbon Dynasty.
- Battle of Arques: Henri IV victorious.

- Galileo experiments with falling objects at leaning tower of Pisa.
- Failure of Drake's expedition against Portugal.

1590
- Dutch capture Breda.
- Battle of Ivry: Henri IV triumphant.
- Savoyard forces invade Provence: Duke of Savoy enters Aix.
- Catholic reform completed (commenced *c*.1522).
- Publication of Spenser's *Faerie Queene* (Ist three books).

1591
- Torgau Alliance of Protestant princes to aid Henry IV.
- Henri IV excommunicated by the Pope.
- Dutch under Maurice and William Lewis of Nassau take Zutphen; then Deventer and Nimeguen.
- Murder of Tsarevitch Dimitri in Russia.
- Francis Vieta of Paris founds modern algebra.
- Anglo-Spanish War. Battle of the Azores (August): Spanish fleet defeats English fleet.
- Shakespeare writes *Henry IV* and probably *Richard III* and *Comedy of Errors* around this time.

1592
- Clement VIII becomes pope.
- Death of Alexander of Parma: Archduke Ernest succeeds in Netherlands.
- Sigismund, king of Poland,also becomes king of Sweden : Charles Regent of Sweden.
- Presbyterianism fully established in Scotland.
- Thomas Kyd writes *Spanish Tragedy.*
- Shakespeare may have written *The Taming of the Shrew* around this time.

Deaths

Michel de Montaigne, French author.

1593
- Upsala Council: Swedish Reformation.
- Maurice of Nassau takes Geertruidenburg.
- Henri IV's conversion to Catholicism: 'Paris vaut une messe'.
- Anti-Puritan Statute in England: many flee to Holland.
- English Acts against Popish recusants.
- Marischal College, Aberdeen, founded by George Keith, 5th Earl Marischal.
- Probable date of the writing of Shakespeare's *Two Gentlemen of Verona* and the poem *Venus and Adonis*.
- British statute mile established by law.

Deaths

Christopher Marlowe, English playwright, in a tavern brawl (30 May).

1594
- French invade Savoy.
- Henry IV enters Paris.
- Huntly's Rebellion. Battle of Glenlivet (4 October): rebels defeat royal troops of James VI.
- First performance of Shakespeare's *Comedy of Errors* and *Titus Andronicus:*
- Earliest known performance of Marlowe's *Dr Faustus*.

Deaths

Tintoretto, Italian painter.

1595
- Henri IV declares war on Spain.
- Death of Archduke Ernest, Governor of Netherlands.
- Peace of Teusin between Sweden and Russia.
- Battle of Groenloo: Maurice of Nassau's victory.
- Henri IV absolved by the Pope.
- Peasant insurrection in Upper Austria.
- Probable date of the writing of Shakespeare's *Romeo and Juliet* and *Richard II. Loves Labour's Lost* written and performed around this time.

Deaths

Torquato Tasso, Italian poet.

1596
- Archduke Albert made Governor of Netherlands.
- Archduke Albert captures Calais.
- Henri IV takes La Fère.
- Mohammed III defeats Archduke Maximilian in a three days' battle.
- Triple Alliance between England, France, and United Provinces.
- English expedition to Cadiz: Cadiz captured.
- Sir Robert Cecil becomes Secretary of State.
- The Lambeth Articles concerning predestination and election drawn up by John Whitgift, archbishop of Canterbury.
- Publication of second three books of Spenser's *Faerie Queene*.
- Shakespeare writes *A Midsummer Night's Dream.*
- Foundation of Sidney Sussex College, Cambridge, by the terms of the will of Lady Frances Sidney, Countess Dowager of Sussex.
- Invention of the water closet by Sir John Harington.
- Galileo invents the thermometer.

Deaths

Sir Francis Drake (28 January).

1597
- Battle of Turnhout: Maurice of Nassau's victory.
- Spaniards take Amiens (soon recovered).
- Polish suzerainty over Moldavia recognized by Sultan.
- Sully becomes Finance Minister of France.
- Serfdom introduced in Russia.

- Publication of *The Ecclesiastical Polity* of Richard Hooker.
- Shakespeare writes *King John, The Merchant of Venice*, and *The Merry Wives of Windsor.*

1598
- Edict of Nantes: Protestant liberties secured in France.
- Netherlands erected by Philip II into a sovereign state under Archduke Albert; Albert marries Philip's daughter Isabel.
- Peace of Vervins between France and Spain.
- Philip III becomes king of Spain.
- Battle of Stangebro: Charles of Sweden defeats Sigismund.
- Death of Theodore I: Boris Godunoff becomes tsar.
- Shakespeare's Henry IV is published.

1599
- Sigismund deposed in Sweden: Charles IX becomes king.
- Sweden conquers Finland.
- Earl of Essex becomes Lord Deputy of Ireland: disgraced on his return.
- Shakespeare writes *Julius Caesar*, *Henry V*, *As You Like It* and *Much Ado About Nothing*. Probable that first version of *Hamlet* was written at this time

Deaths
Edmund Spenser, English poet.

1600
- Estonia seeks the protection of Charles IX.
- Battle of Nieuport: Maurice of Nassau's desperate victory.
- Charles IX invades Livonia.
- Birth of a son (later Charles I) to James VI of Scotland and Anne of Denmark (19 November).
- Gowrie Conspiracy in Scotland.
- East India Company founded in England (dissolved 1858).
- Dr William Gilbert publishes *De Magnete,* his pioneer work describing the magnetism of the Earth.

Deaths
Giordano Bruno, Italian philosopher, burned for heresy.

1601
- Great English Poor Law Act passed.
- O'Neill's Rebellion. Kinsale taken by Spanish troops supporting rebels (September). Royal troops besiege Kinsale and defeat Spaniards and Irish rebels at Battle of Kinsale (24 December).
- Valladolid becomes capital of Spain (till 1606).
- Treaty of Lyons between France and Savoy: Savoy keeps Saluzzo, but cedes other territory.
- Siege of Ostend begun by Spinola (surrendered 1604).
- Poland reconquers Livonia.
- Dutch East India Company founded.
- Shakespeare writes *Twelfth Night* and *Troilus and Cressida.*
- First use of fruit juice as a preventative of scurvy by James Lancaster.

Deaths
Rebellion and execution for treason of Robert Devereux, 2nd Earl of Essex.
Tycho Brahe, Danish astronomer.
Thomas Nashe, English poet and dramatist.

1602
- Execution of Marshal Biron.
- Treaty between France and the Grisons regarding the Valtelline.
- Arminius becomes a professor at Leyden: rivalry with Gomarus.
- Savoy fails to take Geneva.
- First performance of Shakespeare's *Hamlet.* Publication of *the Merry Wives of Windsor.*
- Opening of the Bodleian Library founded (1598) by Sir Thomas Bodley.
- Galileo discovers the laws of gravitation and oscillation.

1603
- Death of Elizabeth I (24 March). James VI of Scotland becomes king of England as James I of England: Union of the Crowns.
- The False Dimitri appears in Poland to claim tsardom.
- Earl of Tyrone submits: Ireland conquered.
- Translation of Montaigne's *Essays* into English by John Florio.
- Shakespeare may have written *All's Well that Ends Well* at this time.

1604
- Peace between England, Spain and the Netherlands.
- Scottish Civil Wars. Battle of Glen Fruin: Highlanders defeated royal force under Duke of Argyll.
- Maurice of Nassau takes Sluys.
- The False Dimitri invades Russia.
- Revision of the Thirty-nine Articles.
- Hampton Court Conference of clergy failed to reach agreement between Puritans and High Churchmen.
- Shakespeare writes *Othello* and *Measure for Measure.*

1605
- Paul V becomes pope.
- The False Dimitri accepted as tsar on death of Boris.
- Battle of Kirkholm: Poles defeat Charles IX of Sweden.
- The Gunpowder Plot to blow up the Houses of Parliament discovered (5 November).
- Cervantes' *Don Quixote* (1st part) published.
- Shakespeare writes *King Lear.*

1606

- Treaty of Venice between the Austrian Archdukes: Archduke Matthias becomes head of House of Austria.
- Venice under Papal Interdict.
- The False Dimitri killed: Vasili Shuiski becomes tsar.
- Peace of Zsitva-Torok between Empire and Turks: Imperial tribute to Turks abolished.
- Grand Remonstrances of Sandomir against Sigismund of Poland: its supporters suppressed.
- Adoption of the Union Jack as the flag of England (12 April).
- Execution by hanging of Guy Fawkes, one of the instigators of the Gunpowder Plot (31 January).
- The London Company chartered to colonize in Virginia.
- Shakespeare writes *Anthony and Cleopatra* and *Macbeth*.

Deaths

John Lyly, English novelist and dramatist.

1607

- Proposals to unite Scotland and England rejected by English parliament.
- Swedish power begins to be restored in Estonia.
- Battle of Gibraltar: Heemskerk annihilates Spanish fleet.
- Earls of Tyrone and Tyrconnel leave Ireland forever with their families.
- London Company colonizes Virginia. Establishment of the first permanent English settlement at Jamestown (13 May).
- Shakepeare writes *Timon of Athens*.
- Appearance of Halley's Comet (named after Edmund Halley).

1608

- Alliance of Pressburg: Hungarian and Austrian Estates united against Emperor Rudolph.
- Evangelistic Union formed by German Protestant Princes, headed by Christian of Anhalt.
- Emperor Rudolph cedes Hungarian crown and territorial dominion in Austria and Moravia to Archduke Matthias.
- Quebec founded by French under Champlain.
- Shakespeare writes *Coriolanus*.

1609

- Alliance between Charles IX and tsar against Poland.
- Death of Duke John William of Jülich and Cleves.
- Twelve Years' Truce between Spain and Holland: Spain concedes freedom of Indian trade.
- Rudolph's Letter of Majesty in Bohemia.
- Edict against the Moriscos in Spain.
- Barbary Corsairs defeated at Tunis by Spain and France.
- Catholic Union (or League) formed at Munich under Maximilian of Bavaria.
- English Baptist Church formed at Amsterdam (and 1611 in London).
- Publication of Shakespeare's *Sonnets*.
- Johannes Kepler begins publishing his astronomical laws.
- Galileo invents the telescope about this time.
- Bermuda settled by British (formally taken over 1684).

1610

- James VI and I dissolves his first Parliament: constitutional struggle begins.
- Plantation of Ulster with English and Scottish colonists begins.
- Assassination of Henri IV of France: succeeded by Louis XIII.
- Battle of Klutsjino: Russians defeated by Poles and tsar overthrown: Wladislav, son of Sigismund of Poland, crowned tsar.
- Maurice of Nassau took Jülich.
- Frederick V becomes Elector Palatine.
- Publication of the Douai Bible, first English Catholic translation of the Bible, complete (began 1609).
- Shakespeare writes *Cymbeline*.
- Dutch bring tea to Europe (from China) for first time.
- Hudson's Bay discovered by Henry Hudson.

Deaths

Michelangelo Caravaggio, Italian painter.

1611

- War of Kalmar between Denmark and Sweden begins.
- Matthias crowned king of Bohemia and Emperor Rudolph resigns Bohemian crown.
- Gustavus Adolphus becomes king of Sweden: Oxenstierna his chief statesman.
- The Authorized Version of the Bible published.
- Shakespeare writes *Winter's Tale* and *The Tempest*.
- James VI and I creates the title of baronet.

1612

- Death of Emperor Rudolph II: Matthias elected emperor.
- Evangelical Union of Princes concludes treaty with England.
- Turks recover Moldavia.
- James VI and I establishes episcopacy in Scotland.
- English factory founded at Surat in India.
- Wadham College, Oxford, founded by bequest of Nicholas Wadham.

1613

- Peace of Knäred ends the War of Kalmar.
- Michael Romanoff becomes tsar: beginning of the Romanoff dynasty in Russia

- Frederick V, Elector Palatine, marries Elizabeth, daughter of James I and VI.
- Marriage in Virginia of Pocahontas, daughter of an American Indian chief, and John Rolfe.
- Shakespeare writes *Henry VIII.*

Deaths

El Greco, Cretan-born painter

1614

- Addled Parliament in England sat (5 April), dissolved by James I (7 June); it passes no bills.
- Last meeting of French states-general until 1789.
- Alliance between Sweden and United Provinces.
- Jülich and Cleves divided between the two claimants by treaty of Xanten.
- Napier of Merchiston introduced logarithms.

1615

- Treaty between Empire and Turks.
- The Spanish Marriages: double alliance of French and Spanish royal families.
- Sir Thomas Roe becomes resident English ambassador at court of Great Mogul in India.
- Death in prison of Arabella Stewart, heir to the English throne.
- Charles Emmanuel of Savoy defeated in Lombardy by Spanish viceroy.
- Dutch destroy Spanish fleet in East Indies and gain command of Moluccas.
- First newspaper (in Germany) appears.
- Second part of Don Quixote by Cervantes is published.
- Circulation of blood discovered by William Harvey.

1616

- Fall of Somerset, favourite of James VI and I: Buckingham in power.
- Cardinal Richelieu becomes foreign and war minister.
- John Rolfe and Pocahontas come to England.
- Edict of Inquisition against Galileo.
- Ben Jonson becomes first poet laureate.
- Baffin Bay discovered by William Baffin (*c.*1584–1622).
- Dutch bring coffee to Europe (from Mocha) for the first time.

Deaths

William Shakespeare, English dramatist (23 April).
Miguel de Cervantes Saavedra, Spanish writer.

1617

- Peace of Stolbova between Sweden and Russia: Russia renounces Esthonia and Livonia; Sweden surrenders Novgorod.
- Richelieu out of office: Luynes in power.
- Ferdinand of Styria crowned king of Bohemia.
- Peace of Madrid between Austria and Bohemia.
- Treaty of Pavia between Savoy and Spain relating to Lombardy.
- War between Sweden and Poland.
- Henry Briggs introduces decimal notation.

Deaths

John Napier, Scottish mathematician (4 April).

1618

- Ferdinand of Styria proclaimed king of Hungary.
- Bohemian Protestants set up a provisional government.
- Failure of Osuna's conspiracy against Venice.
- Fall of Cardinal Klesl.
- Duke of Prussia added to Electorate of Brandenburg.
- Synod of Dort: the Arminian Remonstrants crushed in the United Provinces.
- The Five Articles of Perth accepted by a pseudo General Assembly.
- Epsom salts discovered.

Deaths

Sir Walter Raleigh executed for treason by beheading (29 October).

1619

- Death of the Emperor Matthias: Ferdinand II elected.
- Execution of Oldenbarnveldt, the Dutch statesman.
- George William becomes Elector of Brandenburg.
- Emperor Ferdinand declared deposed from Bohemian throne and Elector Palatine Frederick V elected king of Bohemia.
- Bethlen Gabor of Transylvania, in alliance with Bohemians, occupies most of Upper Hungary.
- Agreement between Emperor Ferdinand and Maximilian of Bavaria.
- Batavia founded as capital of Dutch East Indies.
- Slavery introduced in Virginia.

Deaths

Nicholas Hilliard, English painter.

1620

- Frederick V ordered to quit the emperor's dominions.
- Massacre of Protestants in the Valtelline.
- Tilly, the general of the Catholic League, enters Upper Austria.
- Spinola invades the Palatinate.
- Battle of the White Hill: Tilly defeated Christian of Anhalt and Thurn: Prague taken.
- Battle of Cécora: Poles heavily defeated by Turks when attempting to recover Moldavia.
- Huguenots formulate their demands at La Rochelle: war followed.
- The Pilgrim Fathers set sail in the *Mayflower* for New England (6 September, arrived 21 December/16 December OS).
- Massachusetts first settled.

- The *Novum Organum* of Francis Bacon.
- Manufacture of coke patented by Dud Dudley.
- Epsom races first run around this time.

1621

- English Parliament attacks monopolies; dissolved after Protestation of its Rights.
- Five Articles of Perth passed by Scottish Parliament.
- Fall of Francis Bacon.
- Philip IV becomes king of Spain, with Olivarez as chief minister.
- Treaty of Madrid between Spain and France: the Valtelline restored to Grisons.
- Evangelical Union of Princes dissolved.
- Riga taken by the Swedes.
- End of Twelve Years' Truce between Spain and United Provinces.
- Dutch West India Company founded.

1622

- Articles of Milan: Grisons renounce the Valtelline.
- Battle of Wimpfen: Tilly victorious.
- Battle of Höchst: Tilly defeats Christian of Halberstadt.
- Battle of Fleurus: victory of Mansfield and Christain of Halberstadt.
- Treaty of Lindau: Austrian supremacy in the Valtelline strengthened.
- Treaty of Montpellier between Louis XIII and Huguenots.
- First English newspaper appears.

1623

- Abolition of the right of sanctuary for criminals in England.
- Ratisbon Conference: Maximilian got Frederick's electoral dignity.
- Treaty of Paris: France, Venice and Savoy unite to restore Valtellines.
- Prince Charles and Buckingham in Madrid.
- Expulsion of Protestant clergy from Bohemia.
- Battle of Stadtlohn: Tilly defeats Christian of Halberstadt.
- Dutch conquer Formosa.
- First collected edition of Shakespeare's plays is published.

  Deaths

  William Byrd, English composer.
  William Jaggard, publisher of Shakespeare's works.
  Anne Hathaway, widow of William Shakespeare.

1624

- Dutch take Bahia in Brazil from Portugal (soon recovered).
- Richelieu becomes chief minister of France.
- Massacre of Amboina.
- Protestants deprived of all rights in Bohemia.
- French occupy the Valtelline.
- Monopoly Act in England: patents protected.
- Foundation of Pembroke College, Oxford (as Broadgates Hall).

1625

- Death of James VI and I (27 March). His son becomes king of England, Scotland and Ireland as Charles I.
- Parliament gives Charles I tonnage and poundage for one year only.
- Treaty of Southampton: between England and the United Provinces.
- Failure of English expedition to Cadiz.
- Triple Alliance between England, Denmark and Holland.
- Barbados formally occupied by the English.
- Huguenots seize Blavet and the royal ships.
- Frederick Henry becomes Prince of Orange.
- Wallenstein becomes Imperialist commander-in-chief: enters Lower Saxony.
- Spinola takes Breda.
- Montmorency seizes islands of Ré and Oléron.
- Swedes overrun Livonia.
- French colony of Cayenne founded; French also colonize St Kitts.
- Post of Master of the King's Musick originated. Nicholas Lanier first Master.
- The size of bricks standardized in England around this time.

1626

- English Treaty with Huguenots.
- Impeachment of Buckingham.
- Forced loan in England; Sir John Eliot and others imprisoned.
- Battle of Wallhof: victory of Gustavus Adolphus over the Poles.
- Battle of Dessau Bridge: Wallenstein defeats Mansfield.
- Treaty of Monzon between France and Spain regarding the Valtelline.
- Swedish invasion of Prussia.
- Tilly takes Göttingen.
- Battle of Lutter: Tilly defeats Christian IV of Denmark.
- Peace of Pressburg between Wallenstein and Bethlen Gabor.
- English settlement of Barbados.

  Deaths

  Francis Bacon, Lord Verulam, English philosopher and statesman (9 April).

1627

- Anglo-French Wars. St Martin, capital of Ile de Ré in

the Bay of Biscay unsuccessfully besiged by the Duke of Buckingham (17 July–29 October); retreating English troops suffer bad losses.
- Treaty of Alliance between France and Spain.
- Duke of Buckingham's expedition to La Rochelle in aid of Huguenots.
- Wallenstein occupies Schleswig and Jutland.
- Disputed succession in Mantua.

1628
- Petition of Right, protecting the 'rights and liberties of the subject', passed by Parliament and received Royal Assent of Charles I.
- Treaty between Sweden and Denmark.
- Unsuccessful siege of Stralsund by Imperialist troops under Arnim.
- Hein, Dutch naval leader, captures Spanish treasure fleet.
- Capitulation of La Rochelle: final failure of the Huguenot cause.
- Harvey published *De Motu Cordis*, revealing his discovery of the circulation of the blood.
- Massachusetts Bay Company granted territory.

Deaths
- Buckingham, favourite of James VI and I, murdered by John Felton (23 August): Felton hanged.

1629
- Peace between England and France.
- Charles I dissolves his third parliament and begins eleven years of arbitrary government.
- French invasion of Italy in support of Duke of Nevers' claim to Mantua.
- Edict of Restitution in Germany.
- Peace of Lübeck between Wallenstein and Denmark.
- Frederick Henry of Orange reduces Bois-le-Duc.
- Truce between Sweden and Poland for six years: Sweden gains Livonia and other territories.
- Spinola at war in Lombardy.

Deaths

Cardinal Pierre de Berulle, French theologian.

Bethlen Gabor of Transylvania

1630
- Treaty of Madrid between England and Spain.
- Settlement of Surinam (Netherlands Guiana) by the English.
- Dutch take Pernambuco.
- French invasion of Savoy: Death of Charles Emmanuel.
- Gustavus Adolphus lands in Germany: conquers Pomerania.
- Mantua and Casale captured by Spain.
- Dismissal of Wallenstein.
- Birth of a son (later Charles II) to King Charles I and Henrietta Maria of France (29 May).

1631
- Treaty of Bärwalde between France and Sweden.
- Protestant Convention at Leipzig.
- Gustavus Adolphus takes Frankfort-on-the-Oder.
- Spain's ignominious peace with France.
- Fall of Magdeburg to Imperialists.
- Battle of the Slaak: Dutch destroy Spanish fleet.
- Alliance between Gustavus Adolphus and John George of Saxony.
- Battle of Breitenfield: Tilly defeated by Gustavus Adolphus.
- Gustavus Adolphus conquers Franconia and takes Mainz.
- Saxons invade Lusatia and occupy Prague.
- Treaties of Cherasco: settlement of Mantuan succession.
- New Hampshire founded by John Mason.

Deaths
- John Donne, English poet.

1632
- Mannheim taken by Bernard of Weimar (in Swedish service).
- Gustavus takes Nürnberg.
- Battle of the Lech: Gustavus defeats Tilly, who is mortally wounded.
- Gustavus takes Augsburg and Munich.
- Wallenstein resumes command and recaptures Prague.
- Frederick Henry of Orange reduces Maestricht.
- Battle of Lützen: Gustavus victorious but killed: Pappenheim mortally wounded.
- Christina, daughter of Gustavus, becomes queen of Sweden.
- Rembrandt paints *The Anatomy Lesson of Doctor Tulp.*

Deaths

Sir John Eliot, English parliamentarian, in prison.

1633
- Alliance of Heilbronn: Palatinate restored to heir of Frederick V.
- French occupy Lorraine.
- Bernard of Weimar takes Ratisbon.
- Wallenstein invades Brandenburg and then Bavaria.
- Southern Netherlands reverts to Spain on death of Isobel.
- Birth of a second son (later James II) to Charles I and Henrietta Maria.
- Sir Thomas Wentworth, 1st Earl of Strafford, becomes Lord Deputy of Ireland.
- William Laud becomes archbishop of Canterbury (until 1645).
- Publication of *Poems* by John Donne.

Deaths

George Herbert, English poet.

Philaret, Russian monk-statesman.

1634

- Wallenstein deposed (murdered soon after).
- King Ferdinand of Hungary recaptures Ratisbon.
- Battle of Nördlingen: Imperialist victory: Heilbronn Alliance broken up.
- Treaty of Paris between France and Sweden: Oxenstierna, Swedish Chancellor, against it.
- French Academy founded.
- William Prynne, English Puritan pamphleteer, condemned for his *Histriomastix*.
- Ship money begins to be demanded by Charles I without the consent of parliament.
- Maryland settled.
- First performance of the Oberammergau Passion Play

1635

- Alliance between France and the United Provinces.
- Treaty of Compiègne between France and Sweden.
- War declared by France against Spain.
- Treaty of Prague between the becomes emperor and Saxony: widely accepted: Sweden and France isolated.
- Battle of Livigno: Duke of Rohan's victory over the Austrian and Spanish forces in the Valtelline.
- Battle of Mazzo: Rohan's victory in the Valtelline.
- Compact at Stuhmsdorf between Sweden and Poland.
- Saxony declares war on Sweden.
- Compact between France and Bernard of Weimar.
- Imperialists take Mainz.
- Battle of Goldberg: Banér and Torstensson, Swedish generals, keep the Saxons out of Mecklenburg.
- Pierre Corneille, French playwright writes *Medea.*
- Connecticut first settled.
- Invention of the flintlock around this time.

Deaths

Lope de Vega, Spanish dramatist.

1636

- Brandenburg declares war on Sweden.
- Treaty of Wismar between France and Sweden.
- Battle of Wittstock: Banér's victory over Saxons and Imperialists.
- Pierre Corneille writes *Le Cid.*
- John Hampden refuses to pay ship money.
- Hackney carriages in use by now in London.
- First settlement of Rhode Island.

1637

- Death of Ferdinand II; Ferdinand III elected, becomes emperor.
- Rising of Grisons against France.
- Frederick Henry of Orange recaptures Breda.
- Dutch conquests from Portuguese in West Africa.
- Publication of Descartes' *Discours de la Méthode.*
- Laud's *Liturgy* published in Scotland: popular indignation.
- John Hampden condemned by the judges.

Deaths

Ben Jonson, English poet and playwright (6 August).

1638

- War declared by France against Austria.
- Battles of Rheinfelden (two): victories of Bernard of Weimar.
- Battle of Wittenweier: Bernard's victory.
- Bernard of Weimar takes Breisach.
- Establishment of Presbyterianism in Scotland again. The National Covenant signed in Scotland. The Glasgow Assembly meet.
- British Honduras (now Belize) settled by the English.
- Descartes invents analytical geometry.

1639

- 'Perpetual Peace' of Milan between Austria and the Grisons.
- Van Tromp destroys Spanish, attacking Armada in the Downs.
- First Bishops' War: ended by Peace of Berwick between England and Scotland.
- Act of Toleration in England established religious toleration.
- First printing press established in America.

1640

- Catalonia revolt against Spain.
- Braganza proclaimed king of Portugal as John IV.
- Frederick William, the 'Great Elector', becomes ruler of Brandenburg.
- Van Diemen conquers Malacca.
- The Short Parliament in England (April-May).
- Second Bishops' War begins: ended by Treaty of Ripon: a parliament is called.
- Long Parliament meets (November): purged 1648, expelled 1653, recalled 1659, dissolved 1660.
- Impeachment of Archbishop Laud.

Deaths

John Ford, English dramatist.

Peter Paul Reubens, Flemish painter.

1641

- Spanish royal forces repelled from Barcelona.
- Truce of Stockholm between Brandenburg and Sweden.
- Execution of Strafford.
- Charles I sets out for Scotland.
- Irish Rebellion. Drogheda besieged (December) by rebels under Owen Roe O'Neill.
- Abolition by the Long Parliament of the Star Cham-

ber, English court of prerogative inaugurated in the 14th century.

- Grand Remonstrance indictment of Charles I voted and published by English Parliament (November).

Deaths

Flemish-born court painter Sir Anthony van Dyck (9 December).

1642

- English Civil War. Outbreak when Charles I raises his standard at Nottingham (22 August); Battle of Edgehill between Charles I and the Parliamentary forces (23 October): victory claimed by both sides. Portsmouth surrenders to parliament.
- Irish Rebellion: O'Neill ends siege of English garrison at Drogheda (March).
- Conspiracy of Cinq-Mars against Richlieu discovered: Cinq-Mars executed: Richelieu dies shortly afterwards.
- Battle of Breitenfield: Torstensson defeats the Imperialists.
- Attempt to seize the Five Members of the Commons.
- General Assembly of Confederated Catholics in Kilkenny.
- The English religious movement Fifth Monarchy Men active (until 1661).
- Richard Lovelace writes*To Althea, from Prison*.
- Rembrandt paints *The Night Watch*.
- English theatres closed by the Puritans (until 1660).
- Abel Tasman's voyage: discovery of Van Dieman's Land (now Tasmania) (24 November; rediscovery of New Zealand (13 December).

Deaths

Cardinal Richelieu, French prelate and statesman.

1643

- English Civil War. Battle of Stratton.(16 May): Royalist victory over Parliamentary troops; Battle of Chalgrove Field, Oxfordshire (18 June): between the Royalists and the Parliamentarians; John Hampden killed; Battle of Adwalton Moor or Atherton Moor (30 June): Parliamentary forces under the Fairfaxes defeated; Battle of Lansdowne (5 July): Royalist victory over Parliamentarians under Waller; Battle of Roundway Down (13 July): Sir William Waller's Parliamentary army destroyed; Royalists under Prince Rupert storm Bristol; Battle of Newbury (20 September): drawn: Falkland killed. Battle of Winceby: victory of Sir Thomas Fairfax and Oliver Cromwell.
- Westminster Assembly begins its sessions.
- Battle of Ross: Irish rebels defeated by Ormonde.
- Solemn League and Covenant: agreement between English parliament and the Scots.
- Fall of Olivarez.
- Louis XIV becomes king of France.
- Battle of Rocroi: D'Enghien's victory.
- French take Thionville.
- Severe defeat of Spanish fleet by French off Carthagena.
- Torstensson, Swedish general, invades Denmark.
- English Parliament abolishes Episcopacy.
- First English medal struck by Charles I.
- Rediscovery of Tonga by Tasman.

Deaths

John Pym, parliamentary leader.

1644

- English Civil War. Battle of Alresford (29 March): Parliamentarians under Sir William Waller defeat the Royalists with heavy losses; Battle of Selby (11 April): Royalists defeated by Parliamentarians under Sir Thomas Fairfax; Battle of Copredy Bridge (29 June): defeat of Waller; Battle of Marston Moor (2 July): Parliamentary victory over Royalists due to Cromwell, aided by Scots; Battle of Tippermuir (1 September): Scottish Royalists under Montrose victorious over Covenanters; Capitulation of Parliamentary army under Essex at Battle of Lostwithiel (2 September); Battle of Aberdeen (13 September): Covenanters defeated by Royalist troops under Montrose; Second Battle of Newbury (27 October): Parliamentary success.
- Scots enter England under Alexander Leslie, Earl of Leven.
- Parliament captures York.
- Battle of Kolberg Heath; defeat of Christian IV of Denmark in naval battle.
- French take Gravelines.
- Battle of Freiburg: D'Enghien and Turenne defeat Imperialist general Mercy.
- Turenne takes Mainz.

1645

- Uxbridge negotiations between Charles I and Parliament.
- New Model Army organized under Sir Thomas Fairfax.
- English Civil War. Battle of Inverlochy (2 February): Montrose's victory over Covenanters and Campbells; Battle of Auldearn (9 May): Montrose's victory over Covenanters; Battle of Naseby between Parliamentarians and Royalists (14 June): victory of Fairfax and Cromwell over Charles I and Rupert; Battle of Alford (2 July): Montrose's Royalist victory over the Covenanters; Battle of Langport (10 July): Parliamentarian victory under Fairfax; Battle of Kilsyth (15 August): Montrose's victory over Covenanters; Battle of Philiphaugh (13 September): Montrose defeated by Covenanters under David

- Leslie; Battle of Rowton Heath (24 September): Parliamentary defeat of Royalist cavalry.
- Self-denying Ordinance.
- Royalists sack Leicester.
- Fairfax takes Bristol.
- Battle of Jankau: Torstensson's victory.
- Battle of Herbsthausen: Mercy defeats Turenne.
- Battle of Allerheim: D'Enghein and Turenne defeat Mercy (last killed).
- Peace of Brömsebro between Sweden and Denmark and United Provinces.
- Swedish general Wrangel takes Bornholm.
- French conquests in Catalonia.

Deaths

Henry Morse, Jesuit missionary is executed.

William Laud, Archbishop of Canterbury is executed by beheading (10 January).

1646

- D'Enghiem (Condé) takes Dunkirk.
- Fairfax takes Exeter and Oxford.
- Charles I surrenders to the Scottish army.

1647

- William II succeeds Frederick Henry of Orange in United Provinces.
- Masaniello heads revolt in Naples against Spain.
- Charles I handed over to English Parliament.
- Cornet Joyce carries off Charles I.
- 'Heads of the Proposals' prepared by Ireton.
- Army marches on London.
- 'The Agreement of the People' prepared by the English republican and democratic group, the Levellers.
- Charles I escapes to Carisbrooke Castle.
- 'The Engagement' between Charles I and the Scots.
- Irish Rebellion. Battle of Dunganhill (8 August): Irish rebels defeated by English.
- Foundation of the Quakers (Society of Friends) by George Fox.

1648

- Commons passes 'Vote of No Addresses'.
- Scots begin the second Civil War (April).
- English Civil War. Battle of Preston (17–19 August): Cromwell defeats the Scots under Hamilton.
- Fairfax takes Colchester.
- Failure of Newport negotiations between Parliament and Charles I.
- Charles I declines terms offered by the army.
- Pride's Purge of the Long Parliament (6 December): Presbyterian royalist members expelled from the House by General Thomas Pride; remnant named Rump Parliament.
- Naples revolt suppressed by Don Juan of Austria.
- Frederick III becomes king of Denmark.
- Battle of Zusmarshausen: Wrangel and Turenne defeat the Imperialists.
- Assembly of the Hall of St Louis to discuss French situation.
- Battle of Lens: Condé defeats the Spaniards.
- Rising in Paris.
- Peace of Westphalia ends Thirty Years' War.
- Declaration of Saint-Germain: demands of the Fronde granted.
- The Diggers group of English communists active between now and 1652: among them Gerrard Winstanley.
- Publication of *Hesperides* by Robert Herrick.

1649

- Execution of Charles I (30 January). Commonwealth republican regime in England (until 1653).
- English Parliament abolishes the House of Lords and the monarchy.
- The Levellers are crushed by Cromwell.
- Charles II proclaimed king of Scotland.
- Irish Campaign. Battle of Rathmines (2 August): Roundhead troops in Dublin defeat Royalists under the Marquis of Ormonde; Cromwell besieges and sacks Drogheda (12 September) and captures Wexford.
- First War of the Fronde in France (quickly ended by Treaty of Rueil).
- Sorbonne condemns Jansenism.

1650

- English Civil War. Battle of Carbisdale (27 April): Orkney Royalists and Swedish mercenaries under Montrose defeated by Parliamentarians; Montrose captured by David Leslie and executed by hanging (21 May).
- Agreement of Breda between Charles II and the Scots.
- Cromwell leaves Ireland, leaving Ireton in command.
- Scottish Campaign. Battle of Dunbar (3 September): English under Cromwell defeat the Scots under Leslie.
- Birth of a son (later William III) posthumously to William II of Orange (4 November).
- Arrest of Condé and other princes in France.
- Coffee brought to England around this time.

1651

- Parliament of Paris votes the release of Condé and the princes and demands dismissal of Mazarin; princes released; Mazarin flees.
- Condé in revolt.
- William III succeeds William II in United Provinces.
- English Civil War. Charles II crowned at Scone

(January). Battle of Worcester (3 September): Scottish Royalists under Charles II defeated by Parliamentarians under Cromwell; Charles flees to France.
- Navigation Act passed by English Parliament.
- Publication of *The Leviathan* by Thomas Hobbes.
- Foundation of the religious sect of Muggletonians by the tailors Lodowicke Muggleton and John Reeve.

1652
- George Monck subdues Scotland.
- Act for Settling of Ireland.
- Anglo-Dutch Wars. Battle of Dover (29 November): Van Tromp defeats Blake off Dungeness.
- English Admiral Robert Blake defeats De Ruyter in naval battle off coast of Kent.
- Battle of Saint-Antoinne: Turenne against Condé.
- Provisional Fronde government in Paris: soon overthrown.
- Capitulation of Barcelona.
- Dutch settlement at Cape of Good Hope.
- France surrenders Dunkirk and Gravelines.
- Nukon, an ecclesiastical reformer, becomes patriarch of Moscow.
- Bengal becomes an English settlement about now.

Deaths

Inigo Jones, English architect.

1653
- Anglo-Dutch Wars. Battle of Portland (18–20 February): Dutch under Van Tromp defeated by Blake; Battle of Leghorn (31 March): naval victory of Dutch fleet over English; Battle of Texel (2–3 June): British fleet defeat Dutch. Van Tromp is killed.
- Rupert's Royalist fleet destroyed.
- Monck and Blake defeat Dutch off the Gabbard.
- Rump Parliament (residue of Long Parliament) dissolved by Cromwell (20 April).
- Barebone's Parliament meets, 4 July to 12 December (named after Praise-God Barebone, one of its members.
- Cromwell accepts the Instrument of Government and becomes Protector (16 December).
- Mazarin returns to Paris.
- Johan De Witt becomes Grand Pensionary of Holland: the Orange family excluded.
- Publication of *The Compleat Angler* by Izaak Walton.

1654
- Abdication of Christina of Sweden: Charles X becomes king.
- Dutch lose Brazil.
- Peace between England and Holland.
- General Monck made governor of Scotland (until 1660) by Cromwell.

1655
- Sweden declares war on Poland.
- Charles X takes Warsaw and Cracow.
- Treaty of Westminster between France and England.
- Anglo-Spanish War begins with capture of Jamaica from Spain by the British under Penn and Venables (May).

1656
- Anglo-Spanish War. Blake captures the Plate fleet. Blake destroys Spanish fleet at Tenerife.
- Treaty of Paris between England and France.
- Foundation of the Grenadier Guards (30 May).
- Treaty of Königsberg between Charles X and Frederick William of Brandenburg; Treaty of Marienburg later and that of Labiau still later in same year.
- Warsaw recovered by Poles.
- Battle of Valenciennes: Turenne defeated by Condé and Don John.
- Battle of Warsaw: Poles defeated by Swedes and Brandenburgers: Warsaw recaptured.
- Mohammed Kiuprili becomes vizier of Turkey.
- First recorded mention of tea in Britain.

1657
- Act of Union between Scotland and England: annulled at Restoration.
- Cromwell accepts the Humble Petition and Advice, and assumes the title of lord protector after refusing that of king.
- Treaty of Paris between England and France.
- Death of Emperor Ferdinand III: Leopold I elected next year.
- Blake destroys Spanish fleet at Tenerife.
- Alliance between Austria and Poland.
- Denmark declares war against Sweden.
- Charles X invades Holstein.
- Treaty of Wehlau: Brandenburg joins Austria and Poland.

1658
- Death of Cromwell from pneumonia (3 September): Richard Cromwell becomes lord protector (until 1659).
- Swedes conquer most of Denmark.
- Peace of Roeskilde between Sweden and Denmark.
- Battle of the Dunes: Turenne defeats Condé and Don John and captures Dunkirk and Gravelines.
- League of the Rhine formed, including France.
- Second Danish War of Charles X.
- Copenhagen relieved by the Dutch.
- Mohammed Kiuprili conquers Transylvania.
- Aurangzeb becomes Mogul becomes emperor in India.

1659

- Battle of Elvas: Portuguese defeat the Spaniards.
- Peace of the Pyrenees between France and Spain.
- Concert of the Hague: Holland, France and England against Sweden.
- Dutch take Nyborg and capture a Swedish force.
- Rump Parliament (Long Parliament) reassembled.
- Abdication of Richard Cromwell.
- Coldstream Guards raised.
- Cheques first used, the date on the first known to have been drawn being 6 February.

1660

- Monck arrives in London and demands a dissolution of Parliament; Long Parliament dissolved, and a new Parliament, the Cavalier Parliament, meets (until 1678).
- Fourth Act of Uniformity.
- General Letter Office established by Act of Parliament.
- Clarendon becomes chief minister (until 1667).
- Death of Charles X of Sweden.
- Peace of Oliva ends Swedo-Danish wars.
- Restoration of Charles II (29 May—Oak Apple Day). Reopening of theatres in Britain.
- Organization of the Royal Society of London (granted Royal Charter 1662).
- Composition of light discovered by Newton.
- The formula of laudanum developed by Thomas Sydenham.

Deaths

Diego de Silva Velásquez, Spanish artist.

1661

- Treaty between England and Portugal: England obtains Tangier and Bombay as a marriage dowry.
- Death of Mazarin: Louis XIV assumes role of own minister.
- Peace between Holland and Portugal.
- Peace of Kardis between Sweden and Russia.
- Savoy Conference failed to make agreement between Puritans and other Churchmen.
- Board of Trade founded in London (now Department of Trade and Industry and incorporating since 1992 the Department of Energy).
- Episcopacy established in Scotland by decree.
- Corporation Act: first of a series of Acts against Puritans.
- Island of St Helena appropriated by the British East India Company.
- Hand-struck postage stamps first used.
- Opening of Vauxhall Gardens in London around this time (closed 1859).

1662

- Patronage restored by Scottish parliament.
- Royal Society incorporated (22 April).
- Treaty between England and Holland.
- Act for the Settlement of Ireland.
- Dunkirk sold to France by Charles II.
- Alliance between France and Holland.
- Birth of a daughter (later Mary II) to James, Duke of York (later James II) and Anne Hyde.
- Act of Uniformity in England: leads to ejection of many clergy: beginning of English Nonconformity.
- Press Act in England.

Deaths

Blaise Pascal, French philosopher and scientist.

1663

- Turks begin war against Austria.
- Battle of Amegial: Spaniards under Don John defeat Portuguese and their English allies.
- First Drury Lane Theatre in London opened.

1664

- English expedition seizes New Netherland and changes New Amsterdam to New York, after James, Duke of York (8 September); Richard Nicolls becomes first governor of New York (until 1667).
- Battle of St Gothard: Turks under Ahmed Kiuprili defeated by Imperialists under Montecuculi.
- Jean Baptiste Colbert becomes chief minister under Louis XIV.
- Treaty of Vasvar between Turks and the Empire.
- First Conventicle Act in England.
- Molière writes *Tartuffe*.
- Formation of the Royal Marine Corps (as the Duke of York and Albany's Maritime Regiment of Foot).
- French East India Company founded.

Deaths

Francisco Zurbaran, Spanish painter.

1665

- Battle of Lowestoft (3 June) between English and Dutch fleets: English victory over Dutch.
- Buccaneers' Raids. Porto Bello sacked by Henry Morgan.
- Battle of Montes Claros: Portuguese defeat Spaniards.
- Charles II becomes king of Spain.
- Five Mile Act restricts nonconformist ministers from going within five miles of their places of ministry and also prevents them from teaching (repealed 1812).
- Birth of a second daughter (later Queen Anne) to the Duke of York (later James II) and Anne Hyde (6 February).
- Great Plague in London.

Deaths

Nicolas Poussin, French painter.

1666

- Louis XIV declares war against England.
- Anglo-Dutch Wars. Battle of the Downs (1–3 June): battle between English and Dutch fleets; Battle of the Goodwins (1–4 July): Monck and Rupert defeated by De Ruyter in Four Days' Naval Battle; Battle of North Foreland (4 August): Dutch fleet defeated by English under Monck and Rupert.
- Covenanters' Rising. Battle of Rullion Green (November): Scottish Covenanters defeated by royal troops.
- Quadruple Alliance: Holland, Brandenburg, Denmark and Brunswick-Lüneburg.
- Great Fire in London (2-6 September): Fleet Prison burns down.
- Fire insurance pioneered by Nicholas Barbon, son of Praise-God Barebone.
- Molière writes *Le Misanthrope*.
- Semaphore signalling pioneered by Lord Worcester.
- Discovery of the spectrum of sunlight by Newton.

Deaths
Frans Hals, Dutch painter

1667

- Act of English parliament against Irish cattle trade.
- Anglo-Dutch Wars. Battle of St Kitts (10 May): British victory over French and Dutch fleets; Battle of Sheerness (7 June): Dutch fleet in the Thames.
- Peace of Breda between England and the United Netherlands.
- Surinam (Netherlands Guiana) ceded by England to the Netherlands.
- Fall of Clarendon in England.
- Dutch conquer Surinam and Tobago.
- War of Devolution in regard to Spanish Netherlands.
- Lille taken by French.
- Publication of *Paradise Lost* by John Milton.
- Boyle's Law discovered by Robert Boyle.
- Fire plugs first put into water mains.

1668

- Cabal ministry formed (ended 1673) by Charles II: the name comes from the names of members: Clifford, Ashley (Shaftesbury), Buckingham, Arlington, Lauderdale.
- Triple Alliance: England, Holland and Sweden.
- Spain recognizes independence of Portugal.
- France conquers Franche-Comté.
- Peace of Aix-la-Chapelle between France and Spain.
- Abdication of John Casimir of Poland.
- Dryden becomes the first poet laureate (13 April, resigned 1689).

1669

- Michael Korybut Wisniowiecki becomes king of Poland.
- Turks conquer Crete.
- Secret Treaty between Louis XIV and the Elector of Brandenburg.
- Ormonde recalled from Ireland: restored in 1667.
- The Sheldonian Theatre built at Oxford by Gilbert Sheldon, archbishop of Canterbury.

Deaths
Rembrandt, Dutch painter.

1670

- Secret Treaty of Dover between Charles II and Louis XIV to re-establish Catholicism in England: also a sham public treaty.
- Second Conventicle Act in Britain.
- Christian V becomes king of Denmark.
- Treaty between Holland and Brandenburg.
- Hudson's Bay Company chartered by Charles II.
- South Carolina and Wisconsin settled permanently.

1671

- Leaders of a Hungarian Conspiracy executed.
- Buccaneers' Raids. Henry Morgan attacks Panama City (18 January) and plunders it; withdraws with plunder and prisoners (24 February).
- Attempt to steal the crown jewels from the Tower of London by Colonel Thomas Blood (9 May).
- Death of Anne Hyde, wife of James, Duke of York (later James II).

1672

- Stop of the Exchequer in England.
- First Declaration of Indulgence issued.
- England declares war against Holland.
- Treaty between Sweden and England.
- Anglo-Dutch Wars. Battle of Southwold Bay (7 June): De Ruyter defeats an Anglo-French fleet under the Duke of York.
- Treaty between Sweden and France; also one between Sweden and England.
- War between France and Holland.
- Alliance between the emperor and Brandenburg.
- Johan De Witt resigns post of Grand Pensionary of Holland.
- Murder of Johan and Cornelius De Witt.
- Alliance between emperor and Holland.
- Footlights first used in British theatres.
- Leather hose invented for fire-fighting.

1673

- Test Act passed, barring Roman Catholics from holding public office: Cabal ministry dissolved: Danby in power.
- Charles II cancels Declaration of Indulgence.
- Anglo-Dutch Wars. Battles of Schooneveld: De Ruyter against Rupert: both drawn. Battle of Kykduin: De Ruyter defeats Anglo-French fleet.
- Death of King Michael of Poland.

- Battle of Khoczim: John Sobieski defeats Turks.
- William of Orange takes Bonn: French have to evacuate Netherlands.
- Marriage of James, Duke of York (later James II) and Mary of Modena.

Deaths

Molière, French playwright.

1674

- John Sobieski elected king of Poland.
- Franche-Comté conquered by France.
- Battle of Sinsheim: Turennne defeats the Imperialists and devastates the Palatinate.
- Battle of Seneff: indecisive conflict between William of Orange and Condé.
- Battle of Enzheim: Turenne's victory.
- Sweden at war with Brandenburg.
- Pondicherry founded by French in India.
- Sivaji crowns himself an independent Mahratta sovereign in India: wars with Aurangzeb.
- Peace between England and Holland.
- Second Drury Lane Theatre in London opened.

Deaths

John Milton, English poet (8 November).

1675

- Shaftesbury organizes an opposition in Parliament: beginning of Whig Party.
- Letters of Intercommuning in Scotland against Covenanters.
- Battle of Calmar: Turenne defeats the Great Elector and conquers Alsace.
- Battle of Fehrbellin: Great Elector's decisive victory over Sweden.
- Turenne killed.
- Battle of Lemberg: Sobieski defeats the Turks.
- War of Scania begins between Sweden and Denmark.
- Dr John Fell appointed bishop of Oxford.
- Building of the Royal Observatory at Greenwich, founded by Charles II, betgan (10 August, moved to Sussex in the 1950s).

1676

- Battle of Öland: Swedish naval disaster.
- Danes conquer Scania.
- Treaty of Zurawna between Turkey and Poland.
- Kara Mustafa succeeds Ahmed Kiuprili as Vizier of Turkey.
- Theodore II Tsar of Russia.
- French found Chandernagore in India.
- Bacon's Rebellion, American revolt in Virginia led by Nathaniel Bacon.
- Binomial Theorem invented before now by Newton.

1677

- Battle of Landskrona: Charles XI victorious over Danes.
- Turkey at war with Russia.
- Stettin capitulates to the Great Elector.
- Marriage of William of Orange and Mary, daughter of James, Duke of York (later James II) (4 November).

Deaths

Benedict Spinoza, Dutch philosopher.

1678

- End of Cavalier Parliament.
- Treaty between England and Holland.
- Unsolved murder of the MP Sir Edmund Berry Godfrey. Invention by Titus Oates of the 'Popish Plot' to murder Charles II: cause of agitation 1678-81.
- Extension of the Test Act to peers.
- Beginning of the Exclusion Struggle against the succession of James, Duke of York (ended 1681).
- Peace between France and Holland.
- Swedes expelled from Germany.
- Publication of Pilgrim's Progress by John Bunyan (1st part).

1679

- Exclusion Bill introduced by English parliament.
- Covenanters' Rising. Battle of Drumclog (11 June): Covenanters defeat John Graham of Claverhouse; Battle of Bothwell Bridge (22 June): Covenanters defeated by the English under the Duke of Monmouth.
- Habeas Corpus Act becomes law in England (27 May): principle previously stated in Magna Carta and confirmed by Petition of Right.
- Meal Tub Plot: a fictitious plot to prevent the accession of James, conceived by Thomas Dangerfield: Dangerfield found guilty of perjury.
- Treaty of St Germain between Brandenburg and Sweden.
- Treaty of Fontainebleau between Denmark and Sweden.
- Peace of Nimeguen: treaties between France, Spain, Holland and Empire.
- The Great Elector makes an alliance with France.
- Fall of Danby.
- Archbishop Sharp murdered by Scottish Covenanters.
- Black Letter first used for English newspaper titles.
- The Tories first so named.
- The Whigs so named around this time.

1680

- Petitioners (political group connected with the

Whigs) and Abhorrers for and against Exclusion Bill: beginning of English party system.
- House of Lords rejects Exclusion Bill.
- Covenanters' Rising. Sanquhar Declaration: Charles II disowned by strong Covenanters. Battle of Aird's Moss: Richard Cameron killed.
- Buccaneers' Raids. John Coxon defeated and captured Spanish vessels at Panama.

1681
- French occupy Strassburg.
- Donald Cargill executed in Scotland.
- Oil lighting first used in streets in London.

Deaths

Pedro Calderon de la Barca, Spanish dramatist.

1682
- Revolt of Hungary.
- Death of Theodore II: Tsarevna Sophia becomes Regent for Ivan and Peter.
- Thomas Dongan, Earl of Limerick, made governor of New York.
- Ashmolean Museum, Oxford, opened (founded *c.*1677 by Elias Ashmole.
- Advocates' Library, Edinburgh (now National Library of Scotland) founded.
- Appearance of Halley's Comet
- Foundation of Pennsylvania by the English Quaker William Penn.

1683
- Siege of Vienna by Turks under Kara Mustafa: relieved by John Sobieski.
- Battle of Parkány (Oct 7): Turks defeat Poles.
- Battle of Parkány (Oct 9): Turks defeated by Austrians and Poles: Gran captured.
- Kara Mustafa executed.
- Birth of a son in Germany (later George II) to George (later Elector of Hanover and George I) (10 November).
- City of London charter forfeited.
- Rye House Plot by Whigs to assassinate Charles II discovered.
- Execution of Algernon Sidney and Lord Russell for alleged involvement in the Rye House Plot.
- Opening of the Ashmolean Museum, Oxford, the first museum in Britain (6 June).

Deaths

Izaak Walton, English writer (15 December).

1684
- Holy League against Turks between Austria, Poland and Venice.
- French take Luxemburg.
- Truce of Ratisbon between Louis XIV and Emperor Leopold.
- Publication of the second part, and whole work, of *Pilgrim's Progress* by John Bunyan.
- The Law of Gravity established by Isaac Newton.

1685
- Death of Charles II from apoplexy (6 February). His brother becomes king as James VII of Scotland and II of England.
- Duke of Monmouth, illegitimate son of Charles II and Lucy Walter, proclaims himself king and leads Monmouth's Rebellion (11 June to 6 July); Battle of Sedgmoor (6 July) between James II and the Duke of Monmouth: defeat of Monmouth; Execution of Monmouth by beheading (15 July). Jeffreys and the Bloody Assizes: 320 rebels executed, including the Earl of Argyll, and 800 transported.
- Alliance between Great Elector and Holland.
- Venetians under Francesco Morosini begin conquest of Morea.
- Battle of Gran: Charles of Lorraine defeats the Turks.
- Buda captured from the Turks.
- Revocation of Edict of Nantes in France: great emigration of the Huguenots.

1686
- James II disregards the Test Act and appoints Catholics to public office.
- Second Treaty between Frederick William and the emperor.
- Augsburg Alliance to maintain Treaties of Westphalia and Nimeguen.
- Tyrconnel commander-in-chief in Ireland.

1687
- Venetians capture Corinth
- Battle of Mohacs: Imperial victory by Charles of Lorraine and Lewis of Baden over Turks.
- Venetians take Athens.
- Mohammed IV supplanted by Suleiman II.
- Tyrconnel becomes viceroy of Ireland.
- Second Declaration of Indulgence.
- Buccaneers' Raids. Naval encounter between buccaneering ships and Spanish ships (27 April–3 May).
- Invention of the repeating watch by Daniel Quare.
- Revival of the Order of the Thistle.
- Death of Nell Gwyn, mistress of Charles II (13 November).

1688
- Birth of a son (later James Stewart, the 'Old Pretender') to James II and Mary of Modena, his second wife (10 June).
- Invitation to William of Orange and Mary to ascend the throne.
- William of Orange lands in England (November);

flight of James II to France: the 'Glorious Revolution'.
• Outbreak of the War of the Grand Alliance (ended 1697) between France and the Allies (Austria, the Netherlands, England, Spain and certain German states): in England called King William's War.
• Frederick III becomes elector of Brandenburg.
• Belgrade taken by the elector of Bavaria.
• Seven Bishops put on trial for sedition for opposing James II's policy of religious toleration under the terms of the Declaration of Indulgence are acquitted.
• First allusion to Lloyd's of London (as Edward Lloyd's Coffee House) (February).

Deaths

John Bunyan, English author (31 August).

Execution of James Renwick, last Covenanting martyr.

1689

• House of Commons declares the English throne vacant: William and Mary are declared joint sovereigns (13 February) and crowned (11 April).
• Scottish Parliament declares that James has forfeited the Scottish crown: William and Mary are chosen.
• Declaration of Rights in England (February). Bill of Rights, based on Declaration of Rights, passed by parliament in England (October). Royal powers limited.
• War of the English Succession. Ex-King James II lands in Ireland. Siege of Londonderry by James II begins (19 April), ultimately relieved (30 July); Battle of Newtown Butler (31 July): James's army defeated: Sligo fell, but recovered by Sarsfield.
• Jacobite Rebellion. Battle of Killiecrankie (27 July): Jacobites defeat royal force but with many casualties on both sides, Claverhouse killed in hour of victory; Battle of Dunkeld (21 August): rebel attack defeated.
• First Battle of Bantry Bay: French attempted the invasion of Ireland.
• The Palatinate devastated by forces of Louis XIV.
• Louis XIV declares war against Spain.
• Sophia's rule overthrown in Russia.
• Abolition of poll tax in Britain.
• Members of the British clergy who refuse to take the oath of allegiance are called Nonjurors (until 1805).
• Toleration Act grants freedom of worship to Protestant dissenters.
• First perforfmance of the opera *Dido and Aeneas* by Henry Purcell.

Deaths

1st Baron George Jeffreys, English judge. in the Tower of London (18 April).

Christine, former Queen of Sweden

1690

• War of the English Succession. Battle of Beachy Head (30 June–10 July): French naval victory by Tourville over England and Holland; Battle of the Boyne in Ireland (1 July) between William III and James II: James defeated and flees to France: commander in chief of British forces in Ireland, Schomberg, killed.
• Jacobite Rebellion. Battle of Cromdale: rebels finally overcome.
• First Siege of Limerick (soon raised).
• Scottish Parliament abolishes the Lords of the Articles and lay patronage and re-establishes Presbyterianism finally: Scottish parliament becomes a real power in Scotland.
• Battle of Fleurus: French victory by Luxembourg over Dutch and allies.
• Belgrade recaptured by the Turks.
• Publication of *Essay Concerning Human Understanding* by John Locke.

1691

• War of the Engli
h Succession. Battle of Aughrim (12 July): Willia
III's
t oops defeated Irish and French troops supporting
ames II. Galway surrenders to William's forces.
econd Siege of Limerick: capitulated (October); T-
reaty of Limerick (October): freedom of worship for C
tholics.• Athlone taken by Ginckell (or Ginkel). • B
ttle of Aughrim: Ginckell defeats
S Ruth (who is killed). •
F ench take Mons. • Battle of Szalankemen: Turks de
eated by
L wis of Baden. • John Tillotson becomes archbish
p of Canterbur
(until 1694).

Deaths

George Fox, founder of the Society of Friends (13 January).

1692

• Massacre of Glencoe (13 February): Government troops massacred families of the Clan MacDonald whose leader, MacIan, had been late taking an oath of loyalty to William III.
• War of the Revolution/English Succession. Battle of La Hogue (19–20 May): Russell's naval victory over French; Battle of Steenkerke or Steinkirk (3 August): unsuccessful attack by the English under William III on the French under Luxembourg.
• Louis XIV takes Namur.
• Nathum Tate becomes poet laureate.

1693

• War of the English Succession. Battle of Lagos (17 June): French naval attack on Dutch and English

fleet under Sir George Rooke; Battle of Neerwinden (29 July): English under William III defeated by French under Luxembourg.
- Battle of Marsaglia: Duke of Savoy defeated by Catinat.
- Dutch take Pondicherry.
- The Cabinet form of government formally instituted by William III and its principles developed by Sir Robert Walpole.
- The 'Alfred Jewel' found at Athelney (now in the Ashmolean Museum, Oxford).
- National Debt created in England by Charles Montagu.

1694
- National Debt comes into effect in England.
- Bank of England founded by William Paterson.
- Triennal Act in England.
- Death of Queen Mary from smallpox (28 December); William III becomes sole sovereign.
- Thomas Tenison becomes archbishop of Canterbury.
- Introduction of stamp duty in England.
- Opening of the Royal Hospital, Chelsea (designed by Christopher Wren).

1695
- Fénelon becomes Bishop of Cambrai.
- Mustapha II Sultan.
- William III takes Namur.
- Freedom of Press established in England.
- Darien Scheme proposed by William Paterson.
- Anti-Catholic legislation in Ireland.
- Bank of Scotland founded by the Scottish Parliament (1 November).

Deaths
Henry Purcell, English composer (21 November).

1696
- Russia takes Azoff.
- Death of Ivan V: Peter the Great rules alone.
- Duke of Savoy joins France.
- Recoinage Act.
- Assassination Plot against William III detected.
- First settlement at Princeton, New Jersey.

1697
- Charles XII king of Sweden.
- Elector of Saxony elected king of Poland as Augustus II.
- Battle of Zenta: Turks defeated by Prince Eugene.
- Irish Parliament refuses full ratification of the Articles of Limerick.
- Treaty of of Ryswick (September) ends the War of the Grand Alliance between France and the Allies.
- Official opening of St Paul's Cathedral (2 December).
- First public concert hall in London opened (Hickford's Room, Haymarket).

Deaths
John Aubrey, English author.

1698
- Revolt of the Strieltzy in Russia suppressed.
- First Treaty of Partition (of Spanish dominions) between Louis XIV and William III.
- New East India Company founded in England.
- Darien Scheme expedition to found a Scottish colony set out for Panama.
- Publication of Collier's *Short View of the Immorality and Profaneness of the English Stage.*
- Foundation of the Society for Promoting Christian Knowledge (SPCK) by Dr Thomas Bray.
- Invention of the steam engine by Captain Thomas Savery.

1699
- Treaty of Carlowitz between Austria, Venice, Poland and Turkey:
- Austria gains Hungary, Poland Podolia, Venice Dalmatia and Morea.
- Death of Joseph Ferdinand of Bavaria: Spanish Succession reopened.
- Frederick IV becomes king of Denmark.
- Convention between Denmark and Russia.
- Alliance of Denmark and Poland against Sweden.
- Russia signs treaty with Poland for partition of Sweden.
- Second Partition Treaty.
- English legislation against Irish woollen industry.
- Treaty of Carlowitz between Turks and Allies is signed.

Deaths
Jean Racine, French dramatist.

1700
- War of the Spanish Succession. Battle of Saragossa (20 August): Spanish attack on Allied troops withstood.
- Thirty Years' Truce between Russia and Turkey.
- Great Northern war begins: Russia and Poland against Sweden.
- Peace of Traventhal between Denmark and Sweden.
- Last Will of Charles II of Spain makes Duke Philip of Anjou his heir.
- Death of Charles II of Spain: Louis XIV accepts the dead king's will: War of Spanish Succession begins.
- Battle of Narva: Charles XII defeats Russians.
- Act of Resumption in Ireland.
- First performance of *The Way of the World* by Congreve.
- The first Eddystone Lighthouse completed (begun 1698, swept away 1703).

Deaths
Dryden, English poet and playwright (1 May).

1701

- War of the Spanish Succession. Battle of Chiari (1 September): troops under Prince Eugène defeat French and Spanish forces under Villeroi.
- Brandenburg erected into the kingdom of Prussia: Frederick III first king as Frederick I.
- Prince Eugene invades Italy.
- Battle of Dünamunde: Charles XII defeats Russians and Saxons: Courland occupied.
- Grand Alliance concluded between England, Holland and the Holy Roman emperor.
- Death ofJames VII in France (17 September). Louis XIV recognizes his son as James III of England.
- Act of Settlement in England, securing Hanoverian succession to the throne and barring Catholics from the throne.

Deaths

Captain William Kidd, Scottish merchant and Privateer, hanged for piracy (23 May).

1702

- War of the Spanish Succession. Battle of Vigo Bay (12 October): British and Dutch fleet under Rooke destroy Franco-Spanish fleet; Marlborough takes Liege; failure of English attack on Cadiz.
- Death of William III after falling from a horse (8 March). His sister-in-law succeeds as Queen Anne.
- Battle of Errestièr: Swedes defeated by Russians.
- Eugene raids Cremona and captures Villeroi.
- Charles XII at Warsaw.
- The Allies take Kaiserswerth.
- Battle of Hummelshof: Swedes defeated by Russians.
- Battle of Klissow: Charles XII defeats Poles and Saxons: Cracow captured.
- Battle of Friedlingen: Lewis of Baden defeated by Villers.
- Camisard Rebellion (Huguenot) in central France.
- First English daily newspaper founded (11 March)—*The Daily Courant* (ran until 1735).

1703

- War of the Spanish Succession. Marlborough takes Bonn; Battle of Höchstädt: Villars defeats Germans; Savoy joins Grand Alliance; Battle of Speyerbach: Allies defeated by Tallard.
- Battle of Scharding: Austrians defeated by Bavarians.
- Battle of Pultusk: Charles XII defeats Saxons.
- St Petersburg founded by Peter the Great.
- Act of Security in Scotland (Royal Assent next year).
- Revival of the Order of the Thistle.
- Methuen Treaty between England and Portugal: another Methuen Treaty (commercial) later in same year, negotiated by John Methuen (27 December).
- Buckingham Palace built by the Duke of Buckingham (rebuilt 1825-37).
- Establishment of the ecclesiastical fund, Queen Anne's Bounty.

Deaths

Samuel Pepys, English diarist (26 May).

1704

- War of the Spanish Succession. Battle of Donauwörth (2 July): Marlborough's victory; Gibraltar captured by British under Rooke (24 July); Battle of Malaga (24 August): drawn naval battle between Anglo-Dutch under Rooke and French under Toulouse; Battle of Blenheim between the English and the French (13 August): Marlborough and Eugène defeat Tallard and the Elector of Bavaria. Marlborough occupies Trier.
- Alien Act in England.
- Stanislaus Leszczynski made king of Poland by Charles XII.
- Russians take Dorpat and Narva.
- Rooke captures Gibralter.
- Battle of Malaga: drawn naval battle between Rooke and Toulouse.
- Warsaw recaptured from Charles XII.
- Invention of the negus hot drink of sweet wine and water by Colonel Negus.

1705

- War of the Spanish Succession. Battle of Alicante (29 June): British naval and marine forces seized Alicante; Battle of Cassano (16 August): victory of Prince Eugène over the French; Barcelona besieged (14 September) and captured by British under the Earl of Peterborough (9 October).
- Marriage of Prince George (later George II) and Caroline of Anspach.
- Harley and Bolingbroke become ministers in England.
- Death of Leopold I: Joseph I elected emperor.
- Battle of Gemaurhof: Swedes defeat Russian attempt on Coutland.
- Building of Blenheim Palace begins (completed 1722).
- Invention of the steam pumping engine by Thomas Newcomen.

Deaths

Titus Oates, English conspirator (13 July).

1706

- War of the Spanish Succession. Allies take Madrid (soon evacuated). Battle of Ramillies (23 May): British under Marlborough crush French under Villeroi.

Marlborough takes Ostend.
- Battle of Fraustadt: Swedish victory.
- Battle of Turin: Eugene defeats the investing army: French evacuate Piedmont.
- Peace of Altranstädt between Saxony and Sweden: Stanislaus recognized as King.
- Execution of Patkul.
- Battle of Kalisch: Swedes defeated by Russians and Saxons.

Deaths

Pierre Bayle, French philosopher.

1707
- Treaty of Union between Scotland and England: Union of the Parliaments (1 May).
- War of the Spanish Succession. Battle of Almanza (25 April): British defeated in Spain by Marshal Berwick. Battle of Stolhoffen (22 May): French victory; Battle of Toulon (17 July): naval attack by Dutch and British fleets unsuccessful. Eugene abandons attempt on Toulon.
- Convention of Milan: France abandons North Italy.
- Perpetual Alliance between Prussia and Sweden.
- Death of Aurangzeb: Mogul Empire in decline.
- Last use of the veto by a British sovereign.
- Foundation of the Society of Antiquaries (reconstituted 1717, granted Royal Charter 1751).
- First performance of *The Beaux' Stratagem* by George Farquhar.

1708
- Harley and Bolingbroke out of office: ministry entirely Whig.
- War of the Spanish Succession. Battle of Oudenarde (or Audenarde) between the English and the French (ll July): Marlborough defeats Vendôme; Siege of Lille by Allied troops under Prince Eugène begins (12 August); Battle of Wynandael (28 September): British convoy supplying Lille defeat French attack; Lille surrenders (25 October); Leake and Stanhope take Minorca from Spain (returned 1802) and Sardinia.
- Battle of Holowczyn: Charles XII defeats Russians.
- Battle of Lyesna: Swedes under Levenhaupt defeated by Russians.
- Cossack leader Mazepa joined Charles XII.
- Union of the two British East India Companies.
- Legal protection of ambassadors in England introduced.

1709
- War of the Spanish Succession. Siege of Tournai by the British under the Duke of Marlborough begins (8 July); surrenders (2 September); Battle of Malplaquet between the Allies and the French (11 September): hard-won victory by Marlborough and Prince Eugène. Allies take Mons.
- Battle of Pultawa: Charles XII defeated by Peter the Great and flees to Turkey.
- Alliance between Denmark and Augustus of Poland and Saxony.
- New League against Sweden is formed between Augustus and Peter the Great.
- First Barrier Treaty between Britain and Holland.
- Danish invasion of Scania.
- First Copyright Act passed.
- First publication of *The Tatler* (12 April, until 1711), edited by Steele.
- The process of pig iron production improved by Abraham Darby.
- The second Eddystone Lighthouse completed (begun 1708, burned down 1755).

1710
- War of the Spanish Succession. Siege of Douai (25 April–26 June): town taken from French by Prince Eugène; Battle of Almenara (10 July): Spanish defeated by Allied troops under General Stanhope; Madrid again occupied by Allies; Battle of Brihuega (9 December): British under the Earl of Stanhope defeated by the French.
- Harley and Bolingbroke again in office.
- Battle of Helsingborg: Danes are defeated and driven out of Sweden.
- Russians take Viborg, Riga, Pernau and Reval.
- Battle of Saragossa: Spaniards defeated by Starhemberg.
- Impeachment by English parliament of Dr Henry Sacheverell for a sermon against religious toleration.

1711
- War between Russia and Turkey.
- Death of Emperor Joseph: Charles VI elected emperor.
- Peace of the Pruth between Russia and Turkey.
- Marlborough dismissed.
- First publication of *The Spectator*, edited by Addison and Steele (1 March).
- Completion of the building of St Paul's Cathedral (begun 1675) by Sir Christopher Wren.
- Incorporation of the South Sea Company.
- Ascot Race Meeting first held (11 August).
- Invention of the tuning fork by John Shore.

1712
- Peers created in British Parliament to pass peace clauses.
- War of the Spanish Succession. Battle of Denain (24 July): Allied forces under the Earl of Albemarle de-

feated by Villars.
- Battle of Gadesbusch: Swedish victory over Danes.
- Imposition of soap tax (abolition 1853).
- Last trial for witchcraft in England (of Jane Wenham).
- Lay patronage restored in Scottish Church against Scottish opinion.

1713
- Charles XII's defence against Turks at Bender.
- Death of Frederick I of Prussia: Frederick William I succeeds.
- Pragmatic Sanction of Charles VI to settle Austrian Succession.
- Swedish forces capitulate at Oldenburg.
- Peace of Adrianople between Russia and Turkey.
- Papal Bull Unigenitus condemns Jansenism.
- Second Barrier Treaty between Britain and Holland.
- Signature of the Treaty of Utrecht (11 April) ends War of the Spanish Succession: Acadia, Newfoundland, Nova Scotia, St Kitts-Nevis ceded by France to Britain; Gibraltar and Minorca ceded by Spain to Britain. Victor Amadeus of Savoy becomes king of Sicily.

1714
- Death of Anne (1 August): end of the Stewart succession. George I, elector of Hanover, son of Sophia, granddaughter of James VI and I, becomes king of Great Britain: beginning of the Hanoverian dynasty.
- Quarrel between Harley (Earl of Oxford) and St John (Lord Bolingbroke): former dismissed.
- Peace of Rastadt between Austria and France: accepted by Empire in Peace of Baden.
- Peter the Great conquers Finland.
- Whig Ministry: Townshend, Stanhope, Walpole, etc.
- Publication of *The Rape of the Lock* by Alexander Pope.

1715
- Jacobite Rebellion in Scotland and northern England, an attempt to restore the throne to James Edward Stewart, 'the Old Pretender', son of James II; Battle of Preston (13 November): Jacobites defeated and their army surrenders; Battle of Sheriffmuir (13 November): indecisive battle between Jacobites and Royalists; James Edward lands at Peterhead (22 December).
- Commercial treaty between Britain and Spain.
- Riot Act passed.
- Death od Louis XIV: Louis XV becomes King of France.
- Denmark cedes Bremen and Verden to Hanover.
- Third Dutch Barrier Treaty.
- Doggett's Coat and Badge Prize, rowing competition on the Thames, founded by Thomas Doggett.

1716
- Triple Alliance: France, Britain and Holland.
- Septenniel Act of Britain: general elections to be held every seven years.
- Treaty of Westminster between Britain and the emperor.
- Commercial treaty between Britain and Holland.
- Prussia captures all Swedish Pomerania.
- Battle of Peterwardein: Turks defeated by Prince Eugene.
- Turks conquer Morea.
- John Law establishes Banque générale in France.

Deaths

Gottfried Wilhelm Leibnitz, German philosopher.

1717
- Whig Split: Stanhope becomes chief minister.
- Triple Alliance: France, Britain, and Holland.
- Spanish conquest of Sardinia.
- Battle of Belgrade: Turks defeated by Prince Eugene.
- Bangorian controversy.
- The Mother Grand Lodge of Freemasonry inaugurated in London (24 June).
- Louisiana Company founded by John Law. Inauguration of the Mississippi Scheme as the 'Western Company' by John Law.

1718
- Britain declares war against Spain.
- Charles VI joins Triple Alliance, making it a Quadruple Alliance.
- War of the Quadruple Alliance. Battle of Cape Passero or Messina (31 July): British fleet under Admiral Sir George Byng defeats Spanish fleet.
- Peace of Passarowitz between the Empire and the Turks.
- Death of Charles XII of Spain.
- Victor Amadeus of Savoy becomes king of Sardinia instead of king of Sicily.

Deaths
- William Penn, English Quaker reformer (30 July).
- Edward Teach ('Blackbeard'), pirate, killed off the coast of North Carolina (22 November).

c.1718
- Inoculation for smallpox introduced into England by Lady Mary Wortley Montagu.

1719
- Act passed empowering the English Parliament to pass laws for Ireland.
- France declares war against Spain.
- Treaty of Vienna between George I, Austria and Saxony.

- Treaty of Stockholm between Hanover and Sweden.
- Fall of the Spanish minister Alberoni.
- Publication of *Robinson Crusoe* by Daniel Defoe, based on the life of Alexander Selkirk.

Deaths

Joseph Addison, English essayist (17 June).
John Flamsteed, first Astronomer Royal (31 December).

1720

- Atterbury's plot to restore the Stewarts.
- Birth in Rome of a son, Charles Edward Stewart (later the 'Young Pretender' or 'Prince Charlie'), to James Edward Stewart, the 'Old Pretender' (31 December).
- Richard Philips becomes governor of Nova Scotia (until 1749).
- Quadruple Alliance joined by Spain, Denmark, and Poland.
- Failure of Law's Banque générale in France.
- Treaties between Sweden and Prussia and between Sweden and Denmark.
- Collapse of the South Sea Company: South Sea Bubble (exposed as fraud 1721).
- Outbreak of Plague in Marseilles and southern France.

1721

- Treaty of Madrid between Spain and France.
- Peace of Nystad between Peter the Great and Sweden: Sweden ceases to be a first-rate power.
- Walpole becomes prime minister (3 April, until 12 February 1742): office of prime minister introduced (legally recognized 1905).

1722

- Peter the Great takes Baku.
- Bank of Scotland founded by John Holland, who becomes first governor.
- Last trial for witchcraft in Scotland.
- Fire engines first acquired by a London insurance company.
- Guy's Hospital in London founded by Thomas Guy.
- The compensated pendulum invented by George Graham.

1723

- Ostend East India Company chartered by Charles VI.
- Abolition of the right of sanctuary in England for civil offenders.

Deaths

Sir Christopher Wren, English architect (25 February); he is buried in St Paul's Cathedral.

1724

- Abdication of Philip V of Spain: Luis's short reign: re-accession of Philip V.
- First settlement of Vermont.
- Foundation of the Three Choirs Festival.
- Publication of Jonathan Swift's *Drapier's Letters*.

1725

- First Treaty of Vienna between Austria and Spain.
- Catherine I succeeds Peter the Great in Russia.
- Order of the Bath founded by George I.
- Alliance of Herrenhausen (or Hanover) between Britain, France, and Prussia.
- The Black Watch, Highland regiment, formed (becomes Royal Highland Black Watch 1739).
- Invention of the stereotype process by William Ged.

1726

- Treaty of Wusterhausen between Austria and Prussia.
- Alliance of Herrenhausen joined by Sweden and Denmark.
- Completion of St Martin-in-the-Fields in London (begun 1722) by James Gibbs.
- Publication of *Gulliver's Travels* by Jonathan Swift.
- First circulating library opened in Edinburgh.
- Invention of the chronometer by John Harrison.

1727

- Death of George I in Osnabrück of a stroke (10 June). His only son becomes king of Britain as George II (11 June).
- Spain declares war against Britain.
- Peter II becomes tsar of Russia.
- First Indemnity Act for Nonconformists in England.
- Publication of James Thomson's *Summer.*
- First boxing title fight held in London (6 June).

Deaths

Sir Isaac Newton, English scientist (20 March).

1728

- Convention of the Pardo ends war between Spain and Britain.
- First performance of *The Beggar's Opera* by John Gay.

1729

- The Ostend Company abolished.
- Treaty of Seville between Britain, France and Spain.
- Foundation of Robert Gordon's College, Aberdeen (becomes Robert Gordon Institute of Technology, then the Robert Gordon University 1992).
- Last burning to death of a woman as a punishment (legally abolished 1790).
- Beginning of Methodist revival in Britain.
- Aberration of light discovered by James Bradley.

Deaths

Death of Congreve, English dramatist.

1730

- Anne becomes tsarina of Russia.
- Victor Amadeus, king of Sardinia, abdicates: succeeded by Charles Emmanuel.
- Christian VI becomes king of Denmark.
- Colly Cibber appointed poet laureate.

1731

- Spain denounces the Treaty of Seville.
- Second Treaty of Vienna: emperor ratifies Treaty of Seville: Spain afterwards accedes.
- Britain and Holland guarantee the Pragmatic Sanction.
- Invention of the seed drill by Jethro Tull.
- Invention of the sextant by John Hadley.

Deaths

Daniel Defoe, English writer (26 April).

1732

- Foundation of Georgia in North America as a colony by James Oglethorpe.
- Invention of pinchbeck, an alloy of copper and zinc, by Christopher Pinchbeck.

1733

- Walpole, British prime minister, compelled to withdraw his Excise Bill.
- Death of Augustus II of Poland: Stanislaus Leszczynski elected king, also Augustus III: War of Polish Succession follows.
- Battle of Bitonto: Spanish victory in Italy over Austrian forces.
- Treaty of Turin between France and Sardinia.
- Treaty of the Escurial: First Family Compact between France and Spain.
- Invention of the flying shuttle by John Kay.
- Jethro Tull *writes The Horse-Hoeing Husbandry* encouraging improved agricultural techniques.

1734

- Sir Robert Walpole is the first prime minister to live in 10 Downing Street (22 September).
- *Lloyd's List and Shipping Gazette* founded.

Deaths:

Lady Abigail Masham, favourite of Queen Anne
Rob Roy (Robert MacGregor), Scottish outlaw.

1735

- Abdication of Stanislaus Leszczynski: Augustus III elected King of Poland.
- War begins between Russia and Turkey.

1736

- Porteous Riots in Edinburgh (8 September) when soldiers are ordered by Captain John Porteous to fire into a crowd that have been watching the execution of a smuggler. Porteous is later hanged by a mob.
- Military rank of field marshal introduced.
- Repeal of statues against witchcraft.

1737

- Third Treaty of Vienna ends War of the Polish Succession: Don Carlos established as King of Naples.

1738

- Parties of Hats and Caps first appear in Sweden.
- Birth of a son (later George III) to Frederick Louis, Prince of Wales (4 June).
- Foundation of the first Methodist association (May) by John and Charles Wesley.

1739

- Peace of Belgrade: Austria sacrifices to Turks all the achievements of Peace of Passarowitz.
- Treaty of Constantinople ends Russo-Turkish war.
- Portobello in West Indies captured by Vernon.
- The War of Jenkin's Ear breaks out between Britain and Spain, caused by British breaking Spanish monopoly of South American trade.

Deaths

Dick Turpin, highwayman (7 April), execution by hanging.

1740

- War of Jenkin's Ear. Unsuccessful British raid on Cartagena; circumnavigation of the world by Anson seeking Spanish ships; War of the Austrian Succession absorbs War of Jenkin's Ear (ends 1748); Porto Bello in Panama captured from Spain by a British fleet (21 November).
- Frederick II (Frederick the Great) becomes king of Prussia.
- Ivan VI becomes tsar of Russia.
- Death of Charles VI: War of Austrian Succession begins, to prevent accession of his daughter, Maria Theresa.
- Invasion of Silesia by Frederick the Great.
- Grenadier Guards organized permanently.
- Publication completed (began 1739) of *A Treatise of Human Nature* by David Hume.
- Publication of Samuel Richardson's *Pamela.*
- *Rule, Britannia* composed by Thomas Arne to words by James Thomson.

1741

- Battle of Mollwitz: Frederick the Great's victory over Austrians.
- Treaty of Breslau between France and Frederick the Great.
- Sweden declares war against Russia.
- Battle of Vilmanstrand: defeat of Swedes.
- Convention of Klein-Schnellendorf: Maria Theresa abandons Lower Silesia to Frederick.

- Frederick's allies capture Prague and Frederick invades Moravia.
- Elizabeth becomes Tsarina of Russia.
- Royal Military Academy established at Woolwich (13 April).
- Platinum discovered in England by William Brownrigg.

Deaths

Jethro Tull, English agriculturist (21 February).

1742

- Charles VII elected emperor.
- Battle of Chotusitz: Austrians defeated by Frederick the Great.
- Resignation of Robert Walpole: John Carteret, Earl Granville, in power.
- First performance of Handel's *Messiah* in Dublin (13 April).
- Opening of Ranelagh pleasure gardens in London (closed 1803).

Deaths

Edmund Halley, English astronomer.

1743

- War of the Austrian Succession. Battle of Dettingen (16 June): British and Allies under George II defeat French. Last time a British sovereign leads troops in battle.
- Treaty of Worms between Austria, Britain, and Sardinia.
- Battle of Campo Santo: Spanish defeated.
- Peace of Berlin between Austria, Prussia and Saxony.
- Peace of Abo between Sweden and Russia.
- Treaty of Fontainebleau: Second Family Compact between France and Spain.
- Sheffield plate invented.

1744

- War of the Austrian Succession. Battle of Toulon (21 February): British fleet under Admiral Mathews defeated by French-Spanish fleet; Britain captures Louisburg from America.
- War declared between Britain and France.
- Union of Frankfort between Prussia, Hesse-Cassel and Elector Palatine.
- Invasion of Bohemia by Frederick the Great.
- Pelham ministry in Britain.
- Foundation of Sotheby's auction rooms.
- First General Conference of the Methodists.

Deaths

- Alexander Pope, English poet (30 May).

1745

- Jacobite Rebellion. Prince Charles Edward Stewart lands in Scotland and raises his father's standard at Glenfinnan (19 August); Battle of Prestonpans or Gladsmuir between the Jacobites and government forces (21 September): Prince Charles Edward victorious over English royal forces under Sir John Cope; Siege of Carlisle begun (9 November) by Jacobites under Prince Charles Edward; city surrendered (14 November).
- War of the Austrian Succession. Battle of Fontenoy between the French and British (11 May): defeat of British by Marshal Saxe; Outbreak of King George's War between Britain and France in North America (ended 1754); British took Cape Breton.
- Death of Charles VII: Francis I, husband of Maria Theresa, elected emperor.
- Treaty of Füssen between Austria and Bavaria.
- Alliance between Austria and Russia.
- Battle of Hohenfriedberg: Frederick the Great victorious.
- Battles of Sohr and Hennersdorf: Frederick the Great victorious.
- Battle of Kesselsdorf: Prussian victory over Austrians and Saxons.
- Battle of Basignano: French and Spanish victory in Italy: Milan captured.
- Treaty of Dresden between Prussia and Austria.
- First medal given to all ranks: King George II's medal (also in 1746).
- First performance of the national anthem, *God Save the King*, at the Drury Lane Theatre (28 September).
- First recorded women's cricket match held in Surrey (25 July).
- Jacobite glass manufactured (until 1765).

Deaths

Jonathan Swift, English author.

Sir Robert Walpole, Earl of Orford, English statesman (18 March).

1746

- Jacobite Rebellion. Battle of Falkirk between the Young Pretender and General Hawley (17 January): Prince Charles victorious; Battle of Culloden or Drummossie Moor (16 April): Jacobites under Prince Charles finally crushed by the Duke of Cumberland (last battle fought in Britain); Prince Charles escapes to France, aided by Flora MacDonald and others (20 September).
- Britain takes Cape Breton.
- War of the Austrian Succession. France captures Madras (25 September).
- Franco-Sardinian Alliance.
- Milan retaken from the French and Spaniards with aid of Charles Emmanuel of Sardinia: all Piedmont and Lombardy recovered.
- Brussels taken by Marshal Saxe.

Frederick V becomes king of Denmark

Franco-Danish Alliance.

Battle of Piacenza: Austrian victory.

Treaty of St Petersburg between Russia and Austria.

Ferdinand VI becomes king of Spain.

Battle of Roucoux: Marshal Saxe defeats the Allies: Netherlands secured.

Foundation of the Surgeons' Company.

Manufacture of Bow porcelain begins (ended 1776).

747

War of the Austrian Succession. Battle of Cape Finisterre (3 May): British fleet under Admiral Anson defeat French; Battle of Lauffeldt (2 July): Austrians and British under the Duke of Cumberland defeated by French under Marshal Saxe; Battle of Cape Finisterre (2 October): British fleet under Admiral Hawke defeat French.

William IV becomes stadtholder of United Provinces.

Treaty between Prussia and Sweden.

Secession of the Society of Shakers from the Quakers.

748

French take Bergen-op-Zoom.

War of the Austrian Succession. Siege of French-held Pondicherry in India begun by British fleet and land forces (30 August); siege abandoned (October); Battle of Havana (12 October): indecisive naval battle between British and Spanish squadrons.

Treaty of Aix-la-Chapelle: War of Austrian Succession ended.

Henry Fielding appointed first British stipendiary magistrate.

749

Dupliex makes the Carnatic French.

Carnatic War. Battle of Devicotta: capture of the fortress.

Halifax, Nova Scotia, founded: named in honour of George Montagu Dunk, 2nd Earl of Halifax.

Treaty of Aquisgran between Britain and Spain: commercial.

Publication of Henry Fielding's *Tom Jones*.

The Ohio Company, English colonizing organization, chartered.

750

Joseph becomes king of Portugal.

Bill for the Prohibition of Colonial Manufactures before parliament.

Chiltern Hundreds first granted as grounds for resignation to MPs.

Publication of *Elegy* by Thomas Gray.

Beginning of manufacture of Bristol porcelain (ended 1880) and Derby porcelain.

Deaths

Johann Sebastian Bach, German composer.

c.1750

- Invention of steel cast by the crucible process by Benjamin Huntsman.

1751

- Carnatic War. Seizure (August) and defence of Arcot by Clive; Battle of Arnee: French force defeated by British and Maratha troops under Clive and treasure seized.
- Manufacture of Doctor Wall (Worcester) porcelain begins (ended 1783).
- The *Encyclopédie* begins to appear in France.

1752

- Treaty of Aranjuez between Spain and Austria regarding Italy.
- Carnatic War. Battle of Chingleput: capture of French garrison by Clive.
- Seven Years' War. Battle of Bahur (August): defeat of French and Indian troops in India by British and Muslim troops.
- Britain adopts the Gregorian, or New Style calendar (14 September), superseding the Julian or Old Style calendar, the eleven days being 'lost', 3–11 September.
- Last Stannary Parliament in Cornwall held at Truro.

1753

- Carnatic War. Battle of Golden Rock (7 August): British defeat French; Battle of Sugar-Loaf Rock (20 September): successful British attack on French army besieging Trichinopoly; Battle of Seringham: British defeat French and Maratha forces.
- British Museum founded (opened 16 January 1759).

1754

- Carnatic War. Batte of Tondeman's Woods (14 February): supply convoy to Trichinopoly captured by Hyder Ali.
- Prelude to Seven Years' War. Battle of Youghioghenny (27 May): American force under Washington attacks and defeats French.
- Newcastle ministry in Britain.
- Clandestine marriages abolished in England.
- Foundation of the Royal Society of Arts.
- Foundation of the Royal and Ancient Golf Club of St Andrews.
- Modern form of the heliometer invented by John Dollond.
- Development of the theory of quantitive analysis by Joseph Black.

Deaths

Henry Fielding, English novelist and dramatist (8 October).

1755

- Convention of St Petersburg between Britain and Russia.
- Prelude to Seven Years' War. Battle of Monongahela River (9 July): General Braddock's forces destroyed by French and Indians in America; Siege and capture of French fort at Beauséjour by British and Massachusetts volunteers (4–16 June); Battle of Lake George (8 September): French attack defeated by New England militia.
- Great Lisbon earthquake.
- Publication of *Dictionary of the English Language* by Dr Johnson.
- Period of canal construction begins (until 1827).

1756

- Convention of Westminster between Britain and Prussia (16 January).
- Britain declares war against France (15 May): Seven Years' War begins (ends 1763). Calcutta besieged (16 June) by Surajah Dowlah and small British garrison seized (20 June); 146 survivors detained in the 'Black Hole' (20-21 June): 23 survive; Minorca taken from the British by the French because of failure of British fleet under Byng; Siege and surrender of British at Oswego in North America to the French (11–14 August).
- Treaty of Versailles between France and Austria.
- Battle of Lobositz: Frederick the Great against the Austrians: indecisive.
- Russia adheres to Treaty of Versailles.
- Devonshire and Pitt (afterwards Earl of Chatham) form a ministry (4 December).
- Publication of *A Philosophic Inquiry into the Origin of our Ideas of the Sublime and Beautiful* by Edmund Burke.
- Construction of the Bridgewater Canal from Worsley to Manchester begins (completed 1761).
- Mortar developed by John Smeaton.

c.1756

- Printing on porcelain developed in Liverpool and Worcester.

1757

- New Treaty of Versailles between France and Austria.
- Convention of Klosterzeven: Hanoverian army to be disbanded.
- Devonshire-Pitt cabinet falls (5 April). Ministry of Newcastle and Pitt (29 June). Coalition government.
- First settlement of Tennessee, USA.
- Seven Years' War. Clive captures Calcutta (2 January); Admiral Byng executed by firing squad at Portsmouth (14 March); Siege and capture of Chandernagore by Clive (14–24 March); Battle of Prague: Frederick the Great defeats the Austrians (6 May); Battle of Kolin: Frederick the Great defeated by Austrians under Daun (18 June); Battle of Plassey between Lord Clive and Indian rebel forces (23 June): Clive's victory over Surajah Dowlah; Battle of Hastenbeck (26 July): Hanoverians under Duke of Cumberland beaten by French; Battle of Gross-Jägerndorf: Prussians defeated by Russians (30 July); Siege and capture of British Fort William Henry (4–9 August): by French, Canadians and North American Indians; capitulation of British at Kloster Zeven (8 September); Battle of Rossbach: Frederick the Great defeats the French (5 November); Battle of Breslau: Prussians defeated by Austrians (22 November); Battle of Leuthen: Prussian victory over the Austrians (5 December).

1758

- Seven Years' War. Battle of Ile d'Aix (4 March): French squadron defeated by British under Sir Edward Hawke; French expedition to North America delayed; Battle of Fort St David (29 April): naval battle in India between French and British fleets; outcome indecisive; Second Battle of Fort St David in India (14 May): successful siege of British fortress by French forces; British captured Louisburg (8 June) with troops and fleet; Battle of Ticonderoga (8 July): British attack on French under Montcalm failed; Battle of Carrical (2 August): engagement of British and French fleets off the coast of India; outcome indecisive; Battle of Zorndorf: drawn between Frederick the Great and the Russians (25 August); Battle of Fort Frontenac (27 August): British gained control of Lake Ontario from French; Battle of Grant's Hill (14 September): British forces defeated by French; Battle of Rajahmundry (9 December): British defeat French; Battle of Hochkirch: Frederick the Great defeated by Austrians (14 October); Battle of Madras (16 December): Madras regained from the French; Clive becomes governor of Bengal.
- Appearance of Halley's Comet.

1759

- Charles III King of Spain.
- Seven Years' War. Siege and capture of the French at Masulipatam north of Madras by the British (March); Siege of Quebec by British under General Wolfe begins (27 June); Siege and capture of French fort at Niagara by British (24 July); Battle of Montmorenci in North America (31 July): British attack on French position defeated; Battle of Minden (1 August): French defeated by Ferdinand of Brunswick, Hanover saved; Battle of Trincomalee (10 August): inconclusive naval engagement between British and French fleets off India; Battle of Kunersdorf:

Frederick the Great defeated by Russians (12 August); Battle of Quebec (Battle of the Heights of Abraham) (13 September): Britain defeat French; Wolfe and Montcalm both killed; Quebec surrendered (17 September); Battle of Quiberon Bay (20 November): British fleet under Hawke annihilated French fleet.
- Battle of Kay: Prussians defeated by Russians.
- Anglo-Dutch Conflict in India. Battle of Hooghly (24 November): Dutch ships and troops defeated by British in India.
- Jesuits expelled from Portugal and Brazil.
- Kew Gardens, London, established by Princess Augusta, Dowager Princess of Wales.
- Opening of the British Museum to the public (15 January).
- Completion of the third Eddystone Lighthouse (designed by John Smeaton).
- Invention of a ribbing machine for the manufacture of stockings by Jedediah Strutt.

Deaths

George Friederic Handel, German composer (14 April).

1760
- Seven Years' War. Battle of Wandiwash (22 January): British under Sir Eyre Coote defeat French in India; Siege of Pondicherry begins; Battle of Ste Foy (27 April): British defeated by French; Battle of Quebec: French laid siege to Quebec; siege abandoned after arrival of British squadron that cut the French lines of supply (16 May); Capitulation of Montreal: Britain master of Canada; Battle of Warburg (31 July): French defeated by British and Prussians; Battle of Torgau: Frederick the Great defeats the Austrians (3 November).
- Death of George II (25 October): his grandson becomes king of Britain as George III.
- Russians occupy Berlin.
- Battle of Landshut: Prussian force annihilated: fall of Glatz.
- Battle of Leignitz: Frederick defeats the Austrians.
- First British school for the deaf and dumb set up in Edinburgh by Thomas Braidwood.

Deaths

Laurence, Earl Ferrers executed by hanging (5 May): last nobleman to be executed in Britain; first use of hangman's drop.

1761
- Seven Years' War. Pondicherry surrenders to British (15 January).
- Battle of Panipat: Mahrattas defeated by Afghans in India: the Mogul Empire now only a shadow.
- Spaniards invade Portugal.
- Treaty of San Ildefonso: Third Family Compact between France and Spain.
- Marriage of George III and Princess Charlotte Sophia of Mecklenburg-Strelitz.
- Fall of Pitt. Bute becomes prime minister.
- Opening of the Bridgewater Canal (17 July).

1762
- Britain declares war against Spain (4 January).
- Seven Years' War. Siege and capture of Havana by British (5 June); Manila, Martinique, etc, also captured by Britain. Battle of Wilhelmsthal: British and Hanoverian victory over France. Battle of Lutternberg: British and Hanoverians defeat the French.
- Birth of a son (later Prince Regent and George IV) to George III (12 August).
- Peter III becomes tsar of Russia; Catherine II tsarina soon afterwards.
- Prussia concludes peace with Russia and Sweden: alliance between Russia and Prussia.
- Battle of Freiberg: Prussians defeat the Austrians.
- First demonstration of the compressibility of water by John Canton.
- Cigars introduced into Britain from Cuba.

***c.*1762**
- Cheques issued by English banker Lawrence Childe.
- Publication of *Du Contrat Social* by Jean Jacques Rousseau.

1763
- Bute resigns office in Britain: Grenville ministry formed (7 April).
- Seven Years' War ended by Peace of Hubertusburg between Prussia, Austria and Saxony (15 February), and Treaty of Paris between France, Spain and Britain (10 February): Britain gains Canada, Nova Scotia, Cape Breton, St Vincent, Dominica, Tobago, Grenada, etc, regained Minorca; Pondicherry restored to French; Illinois ceded by France to Britain; Ontario, Canada, becomes British territory.
- Conquest of Bengal. Battle of Morshedabad (24 July): British defeat the deposed Nawab of Bengal and occupied the city; British capture Bengali fort at Oondwa Nullah (September).
- Whiteboy outbreaks in Ireland.
- Beginning of Pontiac's Rebellion (ended 1764) led by Pontiac, American Indian chief.
- Almack's club (established as Brooks's 1778) founded by William Almack (d.1781).

1764
- John Wilkes expelled from House of Commons (19 January) for attacks on the British monarchy.
- Battle of Buxar: Britain gains Oude and other territories in India.

- Stanislaus Poniatowski elected King of Poland.
- Jesuits expelled from France.
- Latent existence of heat established by Joseph Black.
- Lloyd's Register of shipping first prepared.

c.1764

- Invention of the spinning jenny by James Hargreaves.

1765

- Joseph II becomes emperor.
- Birth of a third son (later William IV) to George III and Queen Charlotte (21 August).
- Stamp Act passed by British Parliament (23 March, repealed 1766).
- Rockingham Ministry formed (16 July, until 1766).
- First volume published of *Blackstone's Commentaries,* legal guide by Sir William Blackstone (completed 1769).
- Opening of Sadler's Wells Theatre, London (reconstruction 1879; closure 1916; reopening 1931).

1766

- Death of James Francis Edward Stewart the 'Old Pretender' in Rome (1 January).
- Repeal of Stamp Act (11 March), but Declaratory Act passed declaring Britain's right to tax the colonies.
- Chatham and Grafton formed Ministry, Chatham prime minister (12 July, until 1767).
- Isle of Man becomes a Crown Colony.
- Falkland Islands occupied by British.
- France annexes Lorraine.
- North Dakota first settled.
- Christie's auctioneers founded and first sale held (5 December).
- Publication of Oliver Goldsmith's *Vicar of Wakefield.*
- Construction of the Grand Trunk Canal begun by James Brindley.

1767

- Tax on tea and other duties imposed by British Parliament on America (May).
- First Mysore War. Battle of Trincomalee (3 September): British withstood attack by Hyder Ali; Battle of Trincomalee (26 September): British defeat Hyder Ali; Siege of Ambur by Hyder Ali begins (10 November); relieved (6 December).
- Treaty of alliance between Prussia and Russia.
- Spain expels the Jesuits.
- British Nautical Almanac first published.
- Newcomen's steam pumping engine perfected by James Watt.
- Discovery of Pitcairn Island in the Pacific Ocean by Philip Carteret.
- Discovery of Tahiti by Captain Wallis.

1768

- Corsica bought by France from Genoa.
- Renewal of alliance between Russia and Prussia.
- Confederation of Bar formed in Poland.
- Russia invades Poland.
- Turks declare war against Russia.
- Chatham retires: Grafton head of ministry.
- First Mysore War. Attack at Ooscata by Hyder Ali repulsed (23 August).
- Establishment of the Royal Academy (10 December): its first president is Joshua Reynolds.
- The water spinning frame invented by English inventor Arkwright.
- Beginning of Captain Cook's first voyage (ends 1771).

Deaths

Laurence Sterne, English novelist (18 March).

1769

- Russians defeat Turks and occupy Moldavia and Bucharest.
- First of *Letters of Junius* published.
- First practical boring machine invented by John Smeaton.
- Cook's expedition reached New Zealand (7 October).

1770

- Lord North becomes British prime minister (until 1782) after resignation of Grafton (28 January).
- Spaniards attack British in Falkland Islands. Falkland Islands ceded to Britain by Spain (January).
- The 'Boston Massacre' (5 March): five rioters killed in Boston, Massachusetts by British troops.
- Battle of Tchesmé: Turkish fleet destroyed by Russia.
- Foundation of the Radcliffe Observatory, Oxford University, by the executors of John Radcliffe.
- Astley's Circus founded by Philip Astley.
- Portland Vase, Roman funerary urn (now in the British Museum), bought by Sir William Hamilton.
- Manufacture of Chelsea-Derby porcelain begins (ended 1784).
- Botany Bay, New South Wales, discovered (28 April) by Captain Cook. Captain Cook declares New South Wales as British (23 August).
- Cook Strait, New Zealand, discovered by Captain Cook.
- First crossing of Barren Grounds, Canada, begun by Samuel Hearne (completed 1772).
- Discovery of Lake Tana in Ethiopia as the source of the Blue Nile by James Bruce (14 November).
- Publication of Edmund Burke's *Thoughts on the Present Discontents.*

Deaths

Thomas Chatterton, English poet, commits suicide.

1771

- Parliament of Paris exiled.
- Gustavus III King of Sweden.
- Russia occupies the Crimea.

Deaths

Tobias Smollet, Scottish novelist.

1772

- Royal Marriage Act in Britain.
- Slavery declared illegal in Britain.
- First Partition of Poland between Russia, Austria and Prussia.
- Gustavus III re-establishes absolutism in Sweden.
- Struensee, Danish reforming statesman, executed: Guldberg in power.
- Manufacture of Caughley porcelain begins (ends 1799).
- Discovery of nitrogen by Daniel Rutherford.
- Laughing gas (nitrous oxide) discovered by Joseph Priestley (first used as an anaesthetic 1844).
- Beginning of Captain Cook's second voyage (ends 1775).

1773

- First Mysore War. Siege and capture of fortress of Tanjore by British troops (20 August–16 September).
- Boston Tea Party, American revolutionary protest against unfair British taxation (16 December).
- Warren Hastings becomes first governor-general of Bengal.
- Alliance between France and Sweden.
- Pugachoff's insurrection in Russia.
- Jesuit Order suppressed by Pope Clement XIV.
- Indian Regulating Act passed concerning East India Company.

1774

- Louis XVI becomes king of France.
- Turgot becomes finance minister of France.
- Battle of Shumla: Russians rout Turks.
- Treaty of Kutchuk-Kainardji between Russia and Turkey.
- Hansard record of parliamentary debates begun by Luke Hansard.
- Retaliatory legislation to Boston Tea Party by British Parliament (28 March). The first Continental Congress meet in Philadelphia to protest at the repressive British legislation.
- Quebec Act passed concerning the territory and government of the Province of Quebec.
- Battle of Point Pleasant between American Indians and the Virginia militia (10 October).
- Oxygen and ammonia gas discovered by Joseph Priestley.
- Chlorine disovered by Karl Wilhelm Scheele.
- Discovery of New Caledonia in the South Pacific by Captain Cook (annexed by France 1853).
- Discovery of Norfolk Island in the South Pacific by Captain Cook.

Deaths

Baron Robert Clive of Plassey, English soldier and colonial administrator commits suicide (22 November).

1775

- War of American Independence begins (ends 1783). Battle of Lexington (19 April): American victory; Washington becomes commander-in-chief of American troops (15 June); Battle of Bunker Hill (17 June): Americans defeated.
- First Maratha War. Battle of Aras (18 May): British defeat the Marathas.
- Spaniards attack Algiers.
- Commercial steam engines produced by Watt and Boulton.

1776

- Parliament passes a Prohibitory Act against American commerce.
- War of American Independence. Americans forced out of Canada (March); Declaration of Independence by American colonies (4 July).
- Spaniards attack Sacramento.
- Publication of the first volume of Edward Gibbon's *Decline and Fall of the Roman Empire.*
- Publication of Adam Smith's *Wealth of Nations.*
- St Leger horse race first run at Doncaster.
- Foundation of Tattersall's horse auction and sporting centre by Richard Tattersall.
- The properties of hydrogen discovered by Henry Cavendish.
- Beginning of Captain Cook's third voyage (11 July, ends 1779).

Deaths

David Hume, Scottish philosopher.

1777

- War of American Independence. Battle of Princeton (3 January): British under Cornwallis defeated by Americans under Washington; British siege and capture of fortress of Ticonderoga (22 June–5 July); Battle of Brandywine (11 September); British defeat Americans and seize Wilmington; Battle of Germantown (3 October): British defeat Americans; Battle of Stillwater or Battle of Saratoga (7–17 October): British under General Burgoyne defeated by Americans; Burgoyne surrenders.
- Maria I becomes queen of Portugal along with Pedro III.
- Necker becomes finance minister of France.

- Suspension of the Habeas Corpus Act (February).
- First performance of *The School for Scandal* by Richard Sheridan (8 May).
- Christmas Island discovered by Captain Cook.

1778

- War of American Independence. Battle of Carenage Bay: French fleet defeated by the British; the British seized St Lucia; Battle of Monmouth in New Jersey (28 June): British defeated by Washington; Battle of Onessant (27 July): inconclusive naval battle between British and French squadrons; Battle of Pondicherry (10 August) British naval defeat of French; Pondicherry captured by the British (September).
- Treaty of the Pardo between Spain and Portugal.
- Bavarian War of Succession begins.
- Treaty of Paris between France and America (6 February). Treaty between Holland and America.
- Roman Catholic Relief Act passed.
- Discovery of the Sandwich Islands (later Hawaii) by Captain Cook (18 January).

Deaths:

Thomas Arne, English composer (5 March).

William Pitt the Elder, Earl of Chatham, English statesman (11 May).

Giambattista Piranesi, Italian etcher and architect.

Voltaire, French writer.

1779

- First Maratha War. Battle of Wargaom (12 January): British withstand Maratha attack.
- War of American Independence. Spain declares war against Britain (16 June); Siege of Gibraltar begins (relieved 1783); Battle of Grenada (6 July): unsuccessful British naval attempt to regain Grenada from French; Battle of Penobscot Bay (14 July): British squadron defeat American squadron.
- Treaty of Teschen between Austria and Russia ends War of Bavarian Succession.
- Irish Volunteers first formed.
- Construction completed (began 1773) of the first iron bridge at Coalbrookdale, Ironbridge, Shropshire.
- Spinning mule (Crompton's mule) invented by Samuel Crompton.
- The Oaks horse race first run at Epsom.

Deaths

Captain James Cook, English navigator and explorer, murdered in the Sandwich Islands (14 February).

David Garrick, English actor (20 January)

Thomas Chippendale, English cabinet-maker.

1780

- First Maratha War. British take fortresses at Ahmadabad (15 February) and Gwalior (3 August); British massacred by Tippu Sahib at Perembacum (10 September); British besieged and captured Bassein (13–14 November); British defeat Marathas at Deeg.
- Armed Neutrality formed against Britain by Russia and Prussia (10 March).
- War of American Independence: Charleston taken by British (May); Battle of Camden (16 August): the British under General Cornwallis defeat the Americans.
- First Mysore War. Siege of British at Tellicherry begins (June); attack by Tippu Sahib defeat by British at Ponani (19 November); Siege of British fort at Wandiwash begins (December).
- Britain declares war against Holland (20 November).
- Joseph II sole emperor of Austria on death of Maria Theresa.
- Alliance of Austria and Russia against Turkey.
- Hyder Ali conquers Carnatic.
- Gordon Riots (2-9 June), instigated by a petition against the Roman Catholic Relief Act led by Lord George Gordon.
- Foundation of Bampton Lectures at Oxford University, by John Bampton: annual series.
- Rebuilt Fleet Prison destroyed.
- Foundation of Sunday schools by Robert Raikes.
- Foundation of the Society of Antiquaries of Scotland.
- Hectograph duplicating process invented by James Watt.
- Introduction of the willow pattern on pottery by Thomas Turner.
- The Derby horse race first run at Epsom (4 May).

Deaths

Bernardo Canaletto, Italian painter.

1781

- First Mysore War. Siege of Wandiwash lifted by Hyder Ali after arrival of British reinforcements (22 January); Battle of Porto Novo (1 July): British under Sir Eyre Coote advancing on Cuddalore defeat Hyder Ali; Battle of Pollicore (27 August): British defeat Mysore troops under Hyder Ali; Battle of Sholingur (27 September): British defeat Hyder Ali; Siege and capture of Mysore garrison (21 October–3 November).
- War of American Independence. Battle of Guildford Courthouse (15 March): British victory over Americans; Battle of Cape Henry (16 March): French fleet defeated by British fleet; Battle of Porto Praia Bay, Cape Verde (16 April): French attack on British squadron defeated; Battle of Dogger Bank (15 August): British fleet defeated by Dutch; Battle of

Chesapeake Bay (5 September): British defeated by French; Battle of Lynn Haven Bay (5 September): failure of British naval attack on French fleet; Battle of Eutaw Springs (8 September): futile victory of British over Americans; Siege of Yorktown (September): Cornwallis surrendered to Washington (19 October).
- Patent of Tolerance issued by Joseph II.
- Serfdom abolished by Joseph II.
- French attack on Jersey defeated by Pierson.
- Rodney's victories in West Indies.
- French admiral De Grasse captures Tobago.
- Discovery of the planet Uranus by William Herschel (13 March).
- Manufacture of Worcester porcelain begins.

1782

- First Mysore War. British reinforcements relieved Tellicherry (18 January); Battle of Arnee (7 June) between British under Sir Eyre Coote and Mysore troops under Hyder Ali: outcome indecisive; death of Hyder Ali (7 December); succeeded by Tippu Sahib.
- First Maratha War ended by Treaty of Salbai (17 May).
- Resignation of Lord North (19 March); second Rockingham ministry formed. Death of Rockingham (1 July); succeeded by Shelburne. Coalition government.
- Ireland. Declaration of Rights by Grattan: Irish legislative independence; Repeal of Poynings' Law.
- War of American Independence. Minorca taken from British by Spain (5 February); Battle of Dominica (12 April): British fleet defeat French, Rodney's victory De Grasse in West Indies saves Jamaica; Battle of Trincomalee (12 April): inconclusive naval battle between British and French fleets off India; Battle of Pondicherry (20 June): inconclusive naval battle between French and British; Battle of Trincomalee (3 September): second inconclusive battle between British and French fleets.
- Spain suppresses rebellion in Peru.
- Evacuation of Barrier fortresses by Dutch.
- French capture Minorca and various West Indian islands.
- Relief of Gibraltar by Howe.
- Sinking of *The Royal George* at Portsmouth.
- Fleet Prison rebuilt.
- James Watt patents his steam engine.

1783

- Resignation of Shelburne (24 April); coalition ministry of Portland, Fox and North; Fox's India Bill rejected by the House of Lords; William Pitt in power (19 December, until 1801): at twenty-four Britain's youngest prime minister.
- First Mysore War. Siege of British garrison at Mangalore begun by Tippu Sahib.
- War of American Independence. Battles of Cuddalore in India: First (13 June) British defeat French and take Cuddalore; Second (20 June): British fleet unable to secure sea access to Cuddalore; Treaty of Versailles between Britain, France, Spain and America, ends the War of American Independence (3 September): Britain recognizes independence of American colonies; St Vincent and other West Indian possessions ceded to Britain by France, who recover possession in the east. Spain kept Minorca; Bahamas becomes British colony (until 1964).
- First Chamber of Commerce in Britain founded in Glasgow.
- Catherine II annexes the Crimea.
- Foundation of the Order of St Patrick by George III.
- Completion of the rebuilding of Newgate Prison in London (begun 1770).

Deaths

Lancelot 'Capability' Brown, landscape gardener (6 February).

1784

- Dissolution of parliament (4 March); after elections Pitt in power with large majority. India Act of William Pitt established control of the East India Company by the government (August).
- First Mysore War. British garrison at Mangalore surrendered to Tippu Sahib.
- Peace of Versailles between England and Holland (20 May).
- Bernstorff in power in Denmark.
- Treaty of Constantinople between Russia and Turkey: Crimea finally passes to Russia.
- First balloon ascent in Britain.
- Invention of the puddling furnace by Henry Cort.
- Invention of the threshing machine by Andrew Meikle.
- Mail coaches first run, between London and Bristol (2 August).
- Imposition of a tax on bricks (lifted 1850).
- The Honourable Company of Edinburgh Golfers, the first golf club, founded.

Deaths

Dr Samuel Johnson, English writer and lexicographer (13 December).

1785

- Resignation of Warren Hastings and return to England (June).
- Home Office founded by now.
- Marriage of the Prince of Wales (later George IV) and Mrs Maria Fitzherbert (15 December); marriage invalid but they remain together until 1811.
- Sweden declares war against Russia.

- Battle of Hogland: Russian naval victory over Sweden.
- The Fürstenbund (League of Princes) formed by Frederick the Great.
- Danish attack on Sweden.
- Treaty of Fontainebleau abrogates Barrier Treaty of 1715.
- The Diamond Necklace Affair in France.
- Penang, peninsular Malaysia, ceded to the East India Company by the Sultan of Kedah.
- Foundation of *The Times* by John Walter under the name of *The Daily Universal Register* (adopts present name 1788).
- First balloon crossing of the English Channel by Blanchard and Jeffries (7 January).
- First lifeboat designed by Lionel Lukin, English coach-builder.
- The power loom invented by Edmund Cartwright.

1786

- Death of Frederick the Great: succeeded by Frederick William II.
- Commercial Treaty between Britain and France (26 September).
- Botany Bay becomes British penal settlement for transportation.
- Robert Burns publishes first volume of poems (9 December).
- The existence of the Indo-European language postulated by Sir William Jones.
- Manufacture of Chamberlain porcelain (ends 1840).

Deaths

George Hepplewhite, English cabinet-maker.

1787

- Disturbances in Austrian Netherlands.
- Invasion of Holland by Prussia.
- Assembly of Notables meet in France.
- Austria and Russia declare war against Turkey.
- Impeachment of Warren Hastings by Edmund Burke.
- First English settlement in Sierra Leone.
- MCC (Marylebone Cricket Club) founded (first match held 1788).

1788

- War between Sweden and Russia.
- Convention of Uddevalla: Danes evacuate Sweden.
- Charles IV King of Spain.
- Russians take Ochakoff from the Turks.
- First motion in House of Commons for abolition of slave trade.
- King George III suffers a serious bout of insanity (probably caused by the disease porphyria).
- Trial for impeachment of Warren Hastings for corruption (February).
- Triple Alliance between Britain, Holland and Prussia.
- First convicts transported to Australia arrive at Sydney (26 January).
- Publication of *The Times* begins (1 January), replacing *The Daily Universal Register*.
- Publication completed of *The Decline and Fall of the Roman Empire* (begun 1766) by Edward Gibbon.
- Completion of first steam flour mill, at Blackfriars, London, by John Rennie (burned down 1791).
- Linnean Society, London, founded by James Smith.

Deaths

Charles Edward Stewart, 'Bonnie Prince Charlie', 'the Young Pretender', in Rome (31 January).

Thomas Gainsborough (2 August).

1789

- Bread Riots in France.
- Gustavus III makes Swedish monarchy virtually absolute.
- States-general meet in Versailles (4 May).
- Third Estate declares itself a National Assembly (17 June).
- Joseph II cancels the liberties of Brabant.
- Oath of the Tennis Court.
- Union of the Three Estates.
- Committee of the Constitution appointed.
- Fall of Necker.
- Fall of the Bastille (14 July).
- Battle of Focsani: Turks defeated by Austrians and Russians.
- King recalls Necker.
- Great reforming session of National Assembly on August 4: feudal tenures abolished, etc.
- Declaration of the Rights of Man.
- Battle of Rimnik: Turks defeated by Austrians and Russians.
- Émeute in Paris: mob marches to Versailles: King and National Assembly go to Paris (October).
- Austrians take Belgrade.
- Church lands nationalized by National Assembly (November).
- Assignats first issued (December).
- George Washington elected first President of the US.
- Selim III becomes Sultan of Turkey.
- Second Mysore War. Battle of Travancore (28 December): British troops withstood attack by Tippu Sahib.
- Mutiny of the crew of the *Bounty* led by Fletcher Christian against Captain Bligh (28 April).
- British attacked by Spaniards at Nootka Sound, British Columbia (June).
- Publication of *The Natural History and Antiquities of Selbourne* by Gilbert White.
- Publication of William Blake's *Songs of Innocence*.

1790

- Belgian Republic constituted (January): suppressed in November.
- Alliance between Prussia and Turkey.
- French National Assembly deprives monastic vows of force and suppresses religious orders.
- Leopold II becomes emperor.
- Convention of Reichenbach: ends war between Austria and Turkey and Russia: war between Prussia and Austria averted.
- Suppression by France of a revolt in San Domingo.
- Treaty of Werelå between Russia and Sweden.
- Civil constitution of the clergy enacted in France.
- Resignation of Necker in France.
- National Assembly issue a decree imposing an oath on the clergy.
- Second Mysore War. Battle of Calicut (10 December): British victory over Mysore troops led by Hussein Ali.
- Berlin Convention of England, Holland and Prussia regarding Belgium (9 January).
- Nootka Sound Convention between Britain and Spain (28 October).
- Mutineers from the *Bounty* settle on Pitcairn Island.
- Publication of *Reflections on the Revolution in France* by Edmund Burke.
- Forth and Clyde Canal completed (begun 1768) by John Smeaton.
- Manufacture of Coalport porcelain begins.

Deaths

John Howard from jail fever in Russia; the economist Adam Smith (17 July).

1791

- Split in the Whigs.
- Constitutional Act for Canada (6 May); Ontario organized as Upper Canada.
- Ireland. Wolfe Tone founds the Society of United Irishmen.
- Second Mysore War. Battle of Arikera or Carigat (13 May): Tippu Sahib defeated by British troops under General Lord Cornwallis.
- National Assembly decrees abolition of slavery in West Indies.
- New Polish constitution granted by Stanislaus Poniatowski: throne made hereditary.
- Flight of Louis XVI to Varennes.
- Massacre of the Champ de Mars.
- Treaty of Sistova between Austria and Turkey.
- Conference of Pillnitz between emperor and Prussian King to arrange for support of Louis XVI.
- Fresh slave revolt in San Domingo.
- New French Constitution enacted (September).
- Union of Avignon and the Venaissin to France decreed.
- Louis XVI takes the oath to the new Constitution.
- End of National Assembly (30 September): Legislative Assembly begins next day.
- Treaty of Drottningholm between Sweden and Russia.
- Decree against the émigrés: vetoed by Louis XVI.
- Decree against non-juring priests: vetoed by Louis XVI.
- Establishment of the Ordnance Survey of Great Britain.
- Joseph Priestley's house in Birmingham burned down by mob.
- First publication of *The Observer* newspaper, the oldest Sunday newspaper (4 December).
- Thomas Paine's *Rights of Man* and Sir James Mackintosh's *Vindiciae Gallicae*: replies to Burke's *Reflections*.
- Discovery of titanium (under the name menachinite) by Rev. William Gregor: named titanium 1795.

Deaths

Selina Hastings, Countess of Huntingdon, founder of the 'Countess of Huntingdon's Connexion', a Calvinist-Methodist sect (now part of the United Reformed Church)

John Wesley, English evangelist and founder of Methodism (2 March).

Mirabeau, French political writer.

Wolfgang Amadeus Mozart, Austrian composer.

1792

- Treaty of Jassy: ends war between Russia and Turkey: Russia obtained Crimea.
- Alliance between Austria and Prussia.
- Francis II becomes emperor.
- Assassination of Gustavus III of Sweden: Gustavus IV succeeds.
- A Jacobin ministry in power in France.
- 'Society of the Friends of the People' founded in Britain.
- France declares war against Austria (20 April).
- Russia invades Poland and Lithuania.
- Insurrection in the Tuileries at Paris: the Tuileries later taken by the mob.
- Longwy taken from the French by the Allies: then Verdun.
- September Massacres in Paris.
- Battle of Valmy: Dumouriez defeats Prussians.
- National Convention replaces Legislative Assembly (21 September).
- Monarchy abolished in France.
- French take Nice, Spires and Mainz.
- Battle of Jemappes: Dumouriez defeat Austrians: Brussels occupied by French.

- National Convention offers its protection to all nations struggling for freedom.
- Opening of Scheldt to commerce.
- Trial of Louis XVI begun.
- Second Mysore War. Siege of Seringapatam begun (5 February) by British and Indian troops led by Lord Cornwallis; Tippu Sahib surrendered (16 February); end of war (March).
- Outbreak of the bubonic plague in Egypt kills 800,000.
- Introduction of money orders in Britain (1 October).
- Completion of publication (began 1791) of *The Rights of Man* by Thomas Paine.
- Rouget de Lisle *La Marseillaise*.
- Publication of Mary Wollstonecraft's *Rights of Women*.
- Coal-gas lighting invented by William Murdock.

Deaths

Robert Adam, Scottish architect (3 March).
Lord North, English statesman (5 August).
Sir Joshua Reynolds, English painter (23 February).

1793

- Committee of General Defence in France.
- Execution of Louis XVI (21 January).
- Second Partition of Poland.
- Royalist insurrection in the Vendée.
- French take Aix-la-Chapelle.
- Revolutionary Tribunal created in Paris.
- Battle of Neerwinden: French defeated by Austrians: Brussels evacuated by French (18 March).
- French evacuate the Netherlands.
- Dumouriez deserts to the Austrians.
- First Committee of Public Safety.
- The Girondists proscribed.
- Vendéans fail to take Nantes.
- Battle of Chatillon: Republican forces defeated in west of France by rebels.
- Second or Great Committee of Public Safety: more extreme. The Reign of Terror.
- Assassination of Marat by Charlotte Corday.
- Prussians take Mainz.
- Allies take Valenciennes.
- Toulon surrenders to Admiral Hood.
- French relieve Dunkirk.
- End of the Lyons revolt.
- Battle of Wattignies: French under Jourdan victorious over Austrians (15–16 October).
- Battle of Cholet: defeat of Vendéans (17 October).
- Execution of Marie Antoinette (16 October).
- Battle of Château Gontier: western French rebels victorious under La Rochejaquelin.
- Lyons massacres.
- The Girondists executed.
- Notre Dame consecrated to the worship of Reason.
- Diet of Grodno agrees to partition of Poland and revokes the new Polish constitution.
- New Republican Calendar comes into force in France.
- Battle of Kaiserslautern: Hoche fails against the Austrians in a three days' battle.
- Law of 14 Frimaire makes Committee of Public Safety supreme in France.
- Battle of Le Mans: Vendéans crushed.
- French recover Toulon: Napoleon Bonaparte distinguishes himself.
- Battle of Savenay: Kléber finally defeats the Vendéans.
- First Coalition of Allies against France. France declared war against Britain and Holland (1 February).
- French Revolutionary Wars. Toulon surrendered to Admiral Hood (28 August). French besieged and recover Toulon (18 December): Napoleon Bonaparte distinguished himself; British take Tobago from the French.
- £5 notes first issued by the Bank of England (15 April).
- First free settlers arrived in New South Wales.
- William Godwin's *Political Justice*.
- Manufacture of Davenant porcelain begins (ended 1882).

Deaths

Lord George Gordon, anti-Catholic agitator, in prison (1 November).

1794

- Hoche master of the Palatinate.
- Execution of the Hébertists.
- Manifesto of Kosciusko in Poland against Prussia and Russia.
- Battle of Raslawice: Kosciusko defeats Russians.
- Execution of Dantonists.
- Russians evacuate Warsaw.
- Jourdan takes Charleroi.
- Battle of Rawka: Poles defeated by Prussians.
- Feast of the Supreme Being in Paris organized by Robespierre.
- Law of 22 Prairial strengthens Revolutionary Tribunal.
- Prussians take Cracow.
- Battle of Fleurus: hard-won victory by Jourdan over Austrians under Coburg.
- The Ninth Thermidor: fall of Robespierre.
- Execution of Robespierre, Saint-Just and others.
- French capture Fuenterrabia.
- Britain captures Corsica.
- Battle of Maciejowice: Kosciusko routed and taken prisoner by Russians: Russians recapture Warsaw.
- Jacobin Club closed in Paris.

- French conquer all the North Catalonian fortresses.
- British capture Martinique, St Lucia and other territories.
- Suspension of Habeas Corpus Act for eight years.
- William Pitt's coalition with the Portland Whigs.
- French Revolutionary Wars. Treaty of the Hague between Britain, Holland and Prussia (19 April); Battle of the Glorious First of June or Battle of Ushant (1 June): British fleet under Howe defeat the French fleet; island of St Lucia taken from French by British fleet (4 April); Battle of Tourcoing (17 May): British under Duke of York defeated by the French; Battle of Guadeloupe (3 July): island of Guadeloupe gained from the French by a British force; recaptured by French (10 December); Prussia withdrew from Treaty of the Hague.
- The Gordon Highlanders raised.
- Publication of *The Mysteries of Udolpho* by Mrs Radcliffe.
- Third Drury Lane Theatre in London opened.

Deaths

Edward Gibbon, English writer (16 January).
Antoine Laurent Lavoisier, French chemist.

1795

- Marriage of the Prince of Wales (later George IV) and Princess Caroline of Brunswick.
- Warren Hastings acquitted (23 April).
- Ireland. Orange Society (Orangemen), Irish Protestant association, founded in Ireland.
- French Revolutionary Wars. Triple Alliance of Britain, Austria and Russia; French troops conquered Holland and established the Batavian Republic; British take Ceylon and Malacca from Dutch (February); French recaptured St Lucia (June); Cape Town taken by British from Dutch (September).
- Treaty between emperor and Catherine the Great of Russia for partition of Turkey, Venice, Poland and Bavaria.
- Peace of La Jaunaie with Royalist rebels in western France.
- Insurrection of 12 Germinal in Paris: 'Bread and the Constitution of 1793'.
- Treaty of Basle between France and Prussia: Holland and Spain accede later.
- Insurrection of 1 Prairial in Paris.
- Revolutionary Tribunal abolished in France.
- 'White Terror' in southern France.
- Death of the French dauphin in prison.
- Bilbao taken by French.
- Constitution of the Year III proclaimed (23 September).
- Belgium incorporated in France.
- Insurrection of Vendémiaire in Paris suppressed.
- The Directory installed in France (3 November).
- Battle of Loano: French victory over Austrian and Sardinian forces.
- Abdication of Stanislaus Poniatowski in Poland.
- French troops conquer Holland and establish the Batavian Republic.
- The consumption of lime juice made compulsory in the Royal Navy as a preventative of scurvy.
- Navigation of the River Niger by Mungo Park.

Deaths

James Boswell, Scottish author (19 May).

1796

- Birth of a daughter, Princess Charlotte, to the Prince of Wales and Princess Caroline. The Prince of Wales deserts Caroline, and she settles abroad.
- French Revolutionary Wars. Saldanha Bay taken from the Dutch by the British (17 August); British evacuate Corsica; British reconquer St Lucia from French and take Demerara from the Dutch; Spain declares war on Britain (5 October); French under Hoche attempt the invasion of Ireland at Bantry Bay but fail (December).
- Napoleon Bonaparte appointed to command the Army of Italy.
- Armistice of Cherasco: neutrality of Sardinia.
- Conspiracy of Babeuf frustrated in Paris.
- Battle of Lodi: Bonaparte defeats Austrians.
- French occupy Milan, but abandon siege of Mantua.
- Battle of Solferino: Bonaparte defeats Austrians under Wurmser.
- Treaty of San Ildefonso between France and Spain.
- Archduke Charles defeats Jourdan in Bavaria and drives him across the Rhine.
- Cispadane Republic founded by Bonaparte: includes Modena, Bologna and Ferrara.
- Battle of Arcola: Bonaparte's desperate victory over Austrians under Alvintzy.
- Paul I becomes tsar of Russia.
- Battle of Lonato: Austrians defeated by French under Augereau.
- John Quincy Adams elected President of US.
- Revival of vaccination against smallpox by Edward Jenner (14 May).
- Semaphore signalling developed by Lord George Murray.
- The carbon composition of diamonds demonstrated by Smithson Tennant.
- The hydraulic press invented by Joseph Bramah.

Deaths

Robert Burns, Scottish poet (21 July).

1797

- Mutiny in British fleet at Spithead (16 April): demands granted.Mutiny in British fleet at the Nore against poor pay and conditions, led by Richard Parker (23 May–30 June): special legislation against it. Parker hanged.

- French Revolutionary Wars. Battle of Cape St Vincent (14 February): Spanish fleet defeated by Jervis; Britain takes Trinidad from France (17 February); Battle of Camperdown (11 October): Dutch fleet under De Winter on its way to link up with the French to land in Ireland defeated by British fleet under Admiral Duncan.
- Third and Final Partition of Poland.
- Bonaparte takes Mantua.
- Pope submits to Bonaparte.
- Rising against French in Verona.
- Battle of Neuwied: Austrians defeated by Hoche (18 April).
- Preliminaries of peace at Loeben between Austria and Bonaparte.
- French enter Venice.
- Genoa becomes Ligurian Republic under French influence.
- Cisalpine Republic established by Bonaparte in Lombardy.
- Cispadane Republic unites to Cisalpine Republic.
- Treaty between France and Portugal.
- Coup d'état of 18 Fructidor in France.
- Peace of Campo Formio: Venice given to Austria: Ionian Islands to France: Austria surrenders Netherlands and recognizes Cisalpine Republic.
- Valtelline annexed to Cisalpine Republic.
- Frederick William III King of Prussia.
- Paul I made Protector of the Knights of Malta.
- Congress of Rastatt.
- Cash payments suspended in Britain.
- £1 banknotes issued for the first time by the Bank of England (26 February).
- The mass of the Earth first calculated by Henry Cavendish.

Deaths

Edmund Burke, Irish statesman and philosopher (9 July).

John Wilkes, English politician (26 December).

1798

- Irish Rebellion. Battle of Ballymore (3 June): Irish rebels attack and defeat English force; Battle of New Ross (5 June): rebel attack defeated; Battle of Arklow (9 June): rebel attack repulsed; Battle of Vinegar Hill (21 June): British under General Lake attack Irish rebels and defeat them; death by suicide of Wolfe Tone.
- French Revolutionary Wars. Bonaparte's Egyptian expedition set sail; Malta taken by French (12 June); Battle of the Pyramids (21 July): French victory in Egypt; Bonaparte enters Cairo; Battle of the Nile or Battle of Aboukir Bay (1 August): British under Nelson destroy French fleet under Brueys; Siege of Valletta in Malta by British and Maltese begins (September); French invasion of Ireland fails (27 October); Minorca captured by British (November); Alliance between Russia and Britain (24 December).
- French occupation of Bern: Swiss Confederacy replaced by Helvetic Republic.
- Fall of Godoy in Spain.
- Sieyès elected a French Director.
- Bonaparte's Egyptian expedition sets sail: Malta taken.
- Bonaparte takes Alexandria.
- French occupy citadel of Turin.
- Battle of the Pyramids: French victory in Egypt: Bonaparte enters Cairo.
- France at war with Turkey: Russian fleet in Mediterranean to help Turks.
- Conscription introduced in France.
- Roman Republic declared, with aid of France: temporal power of Pope overthrown.
- Rebellion in Cairo.
- Paul I made Grand Master of the Knights of Malta.
- Ferdinand IV of Naples enters Rome: retaken by French.
- Abdication of Charles Emmanuel IV of Savoy.
- Flight of Ferdinand of Naples.
- Alliance between Russia and Turkey: soon joined by Britain.
- Publication of Malthus's *Essay on the Principle of Population.*
- *Lyrical Ballads* of Wordsworth and Coleridge.
- Bass Strait between Australia and Tasmania discovered by George Bass.
- Bleaching powder discovered by Smithson Tennant.
- First planned human experiment to test an hypothesis based on observation undertaken by Edward Jenner.

Deaths

George Vancouver, English explorer and navigator (10 May).

1799

- French occupation of Naples: Parthenopean Republic created.
- Bonaparte's Syrian campaign begins: Jaffa taken.
- Austria declares war against France.
- French Revolutionary Wars. Siege of Acre by French fails (17 March); Battle of Stockach: Jourdan defeated by Archduke Charles (25 March).
- French Revolutionary Wars/Napoleonic Wars. Battle of Bergen: British and Russians defeated in Holland;

Battle of Novi between the Allies and the French (15 August); Battle of Alkmaar (2 October): British and Russian troops under the Duke of York defeat the French; Convention of Alkmaar: Britain to evacuate Holland; British take Surinam from Dutch.

- Third Mysore War. Attacks by Tippu Sahib on British forces at Sidassir (6 March) and Malavilly (20 March) repulsed; British stormed Seringapatam (3 May): Tippu Sahib, sultan of Mysore, killed.
- Congress of Rastatt ends without result.
- Milan taken by Russians and Austrians under Suvóroff.
- Allies enter Turin.
- Battle of Modena: French under Macdonald defeat Austrians.
- Naples capitulates to Bourbons.
- Suvóroff defeats Macdonald and overthrows the Italian republics.
- Battle of Aboukir: French victory in Egypt over Turks (25 July).
- Allies take Mantua.
- Battle of Novi: French routed: Joubert killed (15 August).
- British force lands in Holland under Duke of York.
- Battle of Bergen-op-Zoom: British and Russians defeated in Holland (19 September).
- Battle of Zürich: Russians defeated by Masséna: Suvóroff driven out of Switzerland (4–7 June).
- Bonaparte deserts Egyptian army, leaving Kléber in command and lands in France.
- 18 Brumaire: Directory overthrown by Bonaparte.
- Consulate established in France: Bonaparte, Cambacérès and Lebrun consuls.
- British take Surinam from Dutch.
- Repressive legislation in Britain against combinations and corresponding societies.
- Income tax introduced in Britain by Pitt (9 January).
- Repressive legislation in Britain against political associations and combinations (12 July).
- Foundation of Sandhurst Royal Military College by the Duke of York.
- Foundation of the Royal Institution of Great Britain.

Deaths

Joseph Black, Scottish chemist.

George Washington, first President of the US.

1800

- Union of Britain and Ireland under the Act of Union as the United Kingdom (Great Britain) (2 July): abolition of Irish Parliament.
- The province of Wellesley, peninsular Malaysia, added to Penang.
- French Revolutionary Wars/Napoleonic Wars. British capture Malta from the French (12 June); Siege of Valletta ended (5 September).
- Russia, Prussia, Denmark and Sweden form Northern Confederacy against Britain (16 December).
- Treaty of El Arish between Kléber and the Turks: French to evacuate Egypt.
- Pius VII becomes pope.
- Battle of Heliopolis: Kléber defeats the Turks (20 March).
- Godoy restored in Spain at instance of Napoleon.
- Napoleon crosses the Great St Bernard Pass into Italy: occupies Milan.
- Masséna capitulates in Genoa.
- Assassination of Kléber in Egypt.
- Battle of Marengo: Austrian victory turned into French victory by Desaix, who is killed (14 June).
- Battle of Höchstädt: Moreau defeats Austrians under Kray (19 June).
- Battle of Hohenlinden: Moreau defeats Austrians under Archduke John (3 December).
- Second Armed Neutrality: Russia, Sweden, Denmark and Prussia.
- Thomas Jefferson elected US President.
- Mutiny of the *Danae*.
- Foundation of the Royal College of Surgeons.
- Beginning of Robert Owen's social reforms at New Lanark.
- First shipment of the Elgin Marbles brought from the Parthenon in Athens to London by Lord Elgin (completed 1803).
- Electric light first produced by Sir Humphry Davy.
- Use of high-pressure steam pioneered by Richard Trevithick.

Deaths

William Cowper, English poet.

1801

- The Act of Union becomes effective (1 January).
- William Pitt the Younger resigns: Addington becomes prime minister.
- Madras state in India brought under British rule by now.
- Napoleonic Wars. Battle of Aboukir (8 March): British troops under Abercromby land at Aboukir in Egypt and defeat French troops; Battle of Alexandria (21 March): Abercromby defeats French, but is killed: Cairo surrenders to British: French evacuates Egypt. Battle of Copenhagen between the British and Danish fleets (2 April): Nelson destroyed Danish fleet, using his blind eye not to see the signal to break off the fight; Battle of Algeçiras Bay (8 July): naval battle between the French and British.
- Dissolution of the Northern Confederacy. Treaty of St Petersburg between Russia and Britain.
- Toussaint L'Ouverture master of San Domingo.

- Peace of Lunéville between France and Austria: France gains Belgium, Luxemburg, Piedmont and other territories.
- Kingdom of Etruria founded by Napoleon in Tuscany.
- Treaty of Florence between France and Naples.
- Constitution of Malmaison imposed on Switzerland by France.
- Treaty of Badajos between Spain and Portugal: Napoleon angry.
- Paul I murdered: Alexander I Tsar.
- British embargo on Russian, Danish and Swedish vessels in British ports.
- Danish embargo on British ships in Danish ports.
- Treaty of St Petersburg between Russia and Britain.
- Denmark accepts Russo-British Treaty.
- Chateaubriand's Génie de Christianisme: a Catholic revival.
- Publication of the first census made in Britain (29 June).
- The element columbium (niobium) isolated by Charles Hatchett.

1802

- Cisalpine Republic called Italian Republic.
- Peace of Amiens.
- Sweden accepts Anglo-Russian treaty.
- Concordat between Napoleon and the Pope.
- Legion of Honour created.
- Constitution of the Year X: Napoleon First Consul for Life (4 August).
- France annexes Piedmont.
- Treaty between France and Russia.
- French Marshall Ney sent to crush Switzerland.
- Ceylon becomes a British colony.
- Treaty of Bassein between Britain and the Peshwa: leads to Second Maratha War.
- Treaty of Amiens between Great Britain, France, Spain and the Netherlands (25 March): an unstable settlement; Minorca returned to Spain.
- First British Factory Act.
- *Edinburgh Review* founded (October): organ of Whigs.
- *Charlotte Dundas*, the first practicable steamboat, built by William Symington.

1803

- Cobbett begins unofficial publication of Parliamentary reports (publication taken over by Hansard report 1811).
- Second Maratha War. Battle of Aligarh (29 August): capture of the fortress and arsenal by British troops; Battle of Delhi (11 September): British victory; Battle of Assaye (23 September): British and Indian troops won a bloody victory; Siege of Agra begins (4 October): British troops besiege the fortress; the garrison surrenders (18 October); Battle of Laswari (1 November): Sind's army defeated by British under General Lake; Battle of Argaon (28 November): Wellesley (later Duke of Wellington) defeats the Marathas.
- Orissa, India, conquered by the British.
- Balearic Islands ceded to Spain by the British.
- Britain declares war against France.
- Act of Mediation replaces Helvetic Republic by a Swiss Confederation.
- United States purchases Louisiana from Napoleon, who had taken it from Spain.
- First publication of *Debrett's Peerage* by John Debrett.
- Dalton's Law of partial pressures defined by John Dalton.
- Discovery of the metallic element osmium by Smithson Tennant and of the metallic elements palladium and rhodium by William Wollaston.
- Early locomotive constructed by Richard Trevithick. Opening of the first public railway (Wandsworth to Croydon).
- Semaphore signalling perfected by Admiral Popham.

Deaths

Edward Despard is executed for Despard's Plot against the British government

Robert Emmet, Irish rebel, hanged (20 September).

1804

- Pitt the Younger again prime minister (until 1806).
- Second Maratha War. Battle of Delhi (7–16 October): Maratha siege of British garrison is unsuccessful; Battle of Farrukhabad (14 November): defeat of Marathas; Battle of Deeg (11–23 December): British siege successful.
- Napoleonic Wars. Battle of Surinam (5 May): British captured Dutch garrison. Napoleon makes Spain declare war against Britain (12 December).
- Napoleon's legal legislation.
- Duc d'Enghien shot.
- Empire established in France: Napoleon becomes emperor.
- Execution of Cadoudal and others for conspiracy in Paris.
- Revolt of Servia against Turkey: Kara George elected leader.
- Foundation of the Royal Society of Painters in Watercolours.
- Construction of the Caledonian Canal across Scotland by Thomas Telford begins (completed 1822).
- Discovery of iridium by Smithson Tennant.
- Opening of the Rochdale canal, constructed by John Rennie.

- Establishment of the first savings bank at Rotherham.

Deaths

Immanuel Kant, German philosopher.

Joseph Priestley, English scientist (6 February).

1805

- Napoleonic Wars. Battle of Cape Finisterre (22 July): Franco-Spanish fleet under Villeneuve defeated by British fleet under Admiral Sir Robert Calder; Battle of Trafalgar between the British and the Franco-Spanish fleet (21 October): Nelson destroys Franco-Spanish fleet but is killed in the action; Battle of Austerlitz: Napoleon defeats Austro-Russian army (2 December).
- Napoleon crowns himself King of Italy at Milan.
- Ligurian Republic annexed to France.
- Russo-Austrian Treaty.
- Parma and Piacenza annexed to France.
- Capitulation of Austrian general Mack in Ulm.
- Napoleon enters Vienna.
- Treaty of Vienna between France and Prussia: Prussia to get Hanover.
- Peace of Pressburg between France and Austria: Bavaria and Württemberg become kingdoms: Austria loses Venice and Tyrol.
- Armour plate first proposed for ships of war by Sir William Congreve.
- Trooping of the Colour first held in London (4 June).
- Endowment to Oxford University of the Newdigate Prize for English verse by Sir Roger Newdigate.
- Sir Walter Scott's *Lay of the Last Minstrel.*
- Completion of the Grand Junction Canal (begun 1793).
- The percussion detonator for firearms invented by the Scottish minister Alexander Forsyth.

Deaths

Friedrich von Schiller, German writer.

1806

- Death of William Pitt the Younger (23 January): Ministry of 'All the Talent' formed (resigned 1807) under Grenville and including Fox.
- Napoleonic Wars. New Treaty between France and Prussia. Prussia compelled to exclude British ships from Prussian ports: Britain declared war against Prussia; British occupy Buenos Aires, but forced by townspeople to surrender; Battle of Maida (6 July): British defeat French in southern Italy. Battle of Jena: Napoleon defeats Prussia (14 October); Battle of Auerstädt: Davout defeats Prussia (14 October).
- Berlin Decrees against Britain (21 November): beginning of the imposition of the Continental System closing continental ports against British imports.
- Venetia annexed to kingdom of Italy.
- Joseph Bonaparte declared King of the Two Sicilies.
- Prussia annexes Hanover.
- Louis Bonaparte becomes King of Holland.
- Confederation of the Rhine formed by Napoleon: the confederated states secede from the empire.
- Francis II resigns the empire and becomes Francis I, emperor of Austria: End of Holy Roman Empire.
- Murat occupies Warsaw.
- Treaty of Posen: Saxony joins Confederation of the Rhine and becomes a kingdom.
- Russia supresses Bucharest.
- Carbon paper patented by Ralph Wedgwood (7 October).

Deaths

George Stubbs, English painter.

Charles James Fox, English politician (13 September).

1807

- Tory ministry of Portland and Perceval.
- Bill passed by British Parliament abolishing the slave trade.
- Napoleonic Wars. British Order in Council in reply to Berlin Decrees. British capture Montevideo (3 February) and then retroceded it;Battle of Eylau: Napoleon against the Russians: indecisive (8 February). Russia and Prussia join the Continental System (July); British capture island of Heligoland from Denmark (31 August); British bombardment and capture of Copenhagen (5 September): Danish fleet surrenders; Milan Decree issued by Napoleon extending ban on British goods (7 December); the Caribbean islands of St Thomas and St Croix taken from the Danish by a British military and naval force (21 and 25 December).
- Britain accedes to Convention of Bartenstein to help Prussia and Sweden.
- Battle of Friedland: Napoleon defeats the Russians (14 June).
- Treaty of Tilsit between France and Russia.
- Convention of Fontainebleau between Napoleon and Spain for partition of Portugal.
- French troops cross into Spain.
- Kingdom of Westphalia founded by Napoleon for Jerome.
- Serfdom abolished in Prussia.
- Russian breach with Britain.
- Flight of Portuguese royal family to Brazil.
- Selim III of Turkey dethroned: Mustafa IV becomes sultan.
- Downing College, Cambridge, built.
- Discovery of potassium and sodium by Humphrey Davy.

- Distinction between sensory and motor nerves made by Charles Bell.
- First recorded journey of the Mumbles Railway, Swansea, the oldest British passenger railway (closed 1 January 1960).
- Shore-to-ship lifeline, fired by mortar, invented by George Manby.
- Ascot Gold Cup horse race initiated.

1808

- Sierra Leone becomes a British colony (until 1960).
- Peninsular War between the Allies and Napoleon (ended 1814); British force lands in Portugal under Wellington. Palafox's defence of Saragossa: French repelled (June). Capitulation of French at Baylen (19 July). Battle of Rolica (17 August): British and Portuguese under Wellington defeat French; Battle of Vimiero (21 August): Wellington defeats Junot; Battle of Espinosa (10 November): French victory over Spanish troops under General Blake. Second siege of Saragossa (December, surrenders following year).
- French seize Pampeluna and Barcelona.
- Joachim Murat becomes king of Naples.
- Joseph Bonaparte made king of Spain.
- Russia invades Finland.
- Charles IV of Spain abdicates: Ferdinand VII becomes king.
- National insurrection in Spain.
- Etrurian kingdom annexed to France.
- Mahmud II Sultan of Turkey after murder of Mustafa IV.
- Joseph evacuates Madrid.
- Convention of Cintra: French evacuate Portugal.
- Convention of Erfurt: Napoleon and Russia.
- Napoleon takes Madrid.
- Frederick VI becomes king of Denmark.
- Papal States partly annexed to kingdom of Italy.
- James Madison elected US President.
- Goethe completes first part of *Faust*.
- Discovery of the elements barium, boron, calcium, magnesium and strontium by Sir Humphrey Davy.

1809

- Perceval becomes prime minister (until 1812).
- Signature of friendship treaty between British and Sikhs (25 April).
- Peace of the Dardanelles between Britain and Turkey.
- Napoleonic Wars. USA brought in legislation against trade with Britain (January); Martinique taken from the French by the British (24 February); Battle of Abensberg: Napoleon defeats Austrians (20 April). Battle of Eckmühl: Napoleon defeats Archduke Charles (22 April). Battle of Aspern: Napoleon defeated by Archduke Charles: Lannes killed (21–22 May). Battle of Wagram: Napoleon defeats Austrians (6 July). Walcheren Expedition (28 July–23 December): British besieges Flushing, which surrenders (16 August), but expedition to take Antwerp fails; Austria joins Continental System (14 October).
- Peninsular War. Battle of Corunna (16 January): French attack to prevent embarkation of British army defeated by General Moore; Moore is killed; French under Marshal Soult take Oporto (28 March); Battle of Medellin: French under Victor defeat Spanish (28 March). Battle of Douro (12 May): Wellington drives Soult out of Oporto; Battle of Talavera between the French and the English (27-28 July): French under Victor defeated by Wellington.
- Deposition of Gustavus IV of Sweden: Charles XIII succeeds.
- Austrians occupy Warsaw for a time.
- Napoleon in Vienna.
- Napoleon annexes Rome and Papal States to French Empire: Pius VII a prisoner.
- Andreas Hofer and the Tyrolese take Innsbruck.
- Revolts in Quito and other places in Spanish South America.
- Treaty of Fredrikshamn: Sweden cedes Finland to Russia.
- Peace of Schönbrunn between France and Austria.
- Battle of Alba de Tormes: Spaniards defeated.
- French take Gerona after long siege.
- Treaty of Jonköping ends war between Sweden and Denmark.
- French naturalist Lamarck originates theory of evolution.
- Opening of Dartmoor Prison (24 May), originally for French prisoners of war.
- Christian Tract Society founded by Robert Aspland.
- The *Quarterly Review* founded by John Murray: organ of the Tories.
- Study of aerodynamics founded by Sir George Cayley.
- The Two Thousand Guineas horse race first run at Newmarket.

Deaths

Thomas Paine, Anglo-American author, in New York (8 June).

1810

- Napoleonic Wars. Sweden joins Continental System (January); Battle of Ile de France (3 December): Mauritius taken from the French by the British.
- Peninsular War. Battle of Busaco (27 September): Wellington defeats Massena; Coimbra with its garrison taken by British; Wellington retires behind the lines of Torres Vedras; Fontainebleau Decrees by

Napoleon against British goods (October).
- Treaty between Sweden and France: Sweden adopts Continental System.
- Napoleon divorces Josephine.
- Soult takes Seville.
- Andreas Hofer shot.
- Caracas Junta appointed in South America.
- Revolution in Buenos Aires.
- Holland annexed to France.
- Ney takes Ciudad Rodrigo.
- Masséna invades Portugal.
- France annexes northwestern Germany.
- Foundation of the Independent Order of Oddfellows temperance society in Manchester.
- The Luddites, machine wreckers, active (until 1818).
- Chiswick Press founded in London by Charles Whittingham.
- First British landing on Rockall Island, off the Outer Hebrides.

*c.*1810

- Orange Free State, South Africa, first settled.

1811

- George III incapacitated by insanity: the Prince of Wales, later George IV, becomes Prince Regent.
- Peninsular War. Battle of Sabugal (3 April): British under Wellington defeat French; Battle of Fuentes D'Oñoro (8 May): Massena fails against Wellington; Wellington takes Almeida; Battle of Albuera (16 May): Allied armies under Sir William Beresford defeat French under Marshal Soult; Siege of Tarragona completed by the French (28 June); attacks by French under Suchet on British-held fortress of Sagunto fail (23 September, 18 October); besieged by French and surrenders (26 October); Russia and Britain agree secretly to break the Continental System (December).
- French take Tortosa.
- France annexes duchy of Oldenburg: leads to breach with Russia.
- Soult takes Badajoz.
- Masséna retreats from Portugal.
- Caracas Congress proclaims independence of Spain.
- Massacre of the Mamelukes: Mehemet Ali supreme in Egypt.
- Chilian revolution.
- Sir George Prevost becomes governor-general of Canada (until 1816).
- Appearance of the Primitive Methodist sect.
- Bell Rock Lighthouse completed (begun 1807).
- First ichthyosaurus to be brought to scientific notice by Mary Anning.
- First county cricket match played by women (3 October).

1812

- War of 1812 between Britain and the United States. US declares war on Britain (18 June); Battle of Queenston Heights (13 October): severe defeat of the Americans.
- Peninsular War. Wellington besieges and captures Ciudad Rodrigo (8–15 March); Battle of Badajoz: attack begins (17 March 1812) on fortress by Wellington's army and Portuguese troops; fortress and town captured (7 April), enabling Wellington's advance into Spain; Battle of Salamanca (22 July): British under Wellington defeats French under Marmont; Wellington enters Madrid (12 August).
- Napoleonic Wars. Napoleon occupies Swedish Pomerania. Napoleon invades Russia (24 June). Battle of the Borodino: Napoleon against the Russians under Kutusoff: drawn (7 September). Napoleon enters Moscow (14 September): city in flames. Napoleon evacuates Moscow (18 October). Napoleon in Paris (19 December) ahead of the remnant of his army.
- Caracas destroyed by earthquake.
- Treaty of Bucharest between Russia and Turkey.
- Revolutionists capitulate under Miranda in Caracas.
- Crossing of the Berezina (26 November).
- Assassination of Spencer Perceval by Francis Bellingham in the House of Commons (11 May): Lord Liverpool becomes prime minister (until 1827).
- Five Mile Act repealed.
- Manitoba organized as the Red River Settlement.
- Fourth Drury Lane Theatre in London opened.
- Publication of *Childe Harold's Pilgrimage* by Lord Byron.
- First gas company, the Gas Light and Coke Company, granted charter.
- Goodwood Cup first run.

*c.*1812

- Gas lighting first used as street lighting.

1813

- Peninsular War. Battle of Castella (13 April): Allied troops under Sir John Murray defeat French under Marshal Suchet; Battle of Vittoria (21 June): Allied troops under Wellington defeat French under Marshal Jourdan and King Joseph Bonaparte; Siege and capture of San Sebastian by the British (10–31 July); French-held citadel surrendered (9 September); Battle of Colde Maya (25 July): French defeat of British; Battles of the Pyrenees: (25 July–2 August): Wellington defeats Soult; Battle of Dennewitz (6 September): French under Ney defeated by Prussians; Battle of Nivelle (10 November): Wellington defeats French; Battle of the Nive (13 December): British and Portuguese under Wellington defeats French under Marshal Soult; Wellington invades France (22 December).

- Napoleonic Wars. Battle of Leipzig (Battle of the Nations) (16-19 October): Napoleon defeated by the Allies; Leipzig taken.
- Battle of Gross-Görschen: Napoleon defeats Russians and Prussians. Battle of Bautzen: Napoleon defeats the Russians and Prussians (20–21 May). Armistice of Pläswitz concluded at instance of Napoleon. Battle of Gross-Beeren: French defeated by Prussians (23 August). Battle of Katzbach: Blücher defeats Napoleon (26 August). Battle of Dresden: Napoleon defeats the Allies (26–27 August). Battle of Kulm: Allies defeat French (29–30 August). Battle of Leipzig (Battle of the Nations) (16–19 October): Napoleon defeated by the Allies: Leipzig taken. Wellington takes Pampeluna. Treaty of Valençay: Napoleon gives crown of Spain to Ferdinand. Formation of the Quadruple Alliance of the Allies (Austria, Britain, Prussia and Russia) against Napoleon. Austria declares war against Napoleon (12 August).
- Treaty of Reichenbach.
- French take Vilna.
- Russians invade Germany.
- Alliance between Russia and Prussia.
- Treaty of Stockholm between Sweden and Britain.
- Bolivar enters Caracas as liberator.
- Turks reconquer Serbia: Kara George flees.
- War of 1812. Battle between the British frigate *Shannon* and the American *Chesapeake* (29 May); Battle of Lake Erie (10 September): American fleet defeat a British fleet; Battle of Chrysler's Farm (11 November): British defeat of American force; British forced out of Detroit.
- Publication of *Pride and Prejudice* by Jane Austen.
- Invention of 'Puffing Billy', pioneer locomotive by William Hedley.

1814

- Peninsular War. Battle of Orthez (27 February): British under Wellington defeat French under Soult.
- Napoleonic Wars. Battle of La Rothière (1 February): Blücher defeats Napoleon; Battle of Craonne (7 March): French defeat of Allied armies; Treaty of Chaumont between Russia, Austria, Prussia, and Britain (9 March); Battle of Laon (10 March): Allies defeat Napoleon; Battle of Arcis-sur-Aube (20 March): French defeated by Allied armies; Allies occupy Paris (March 31); Battle of Toulouse (10 April): Wellington defeats Soult; abdication of Napoleon (11 April); Treaty of Paris (Treaty of Fontainebleau), ending the Napoleonic Wars, accepted by Napoleon: banished to Elba (April 13); renewal of the Quadruple Alliance of the Allies (Austria, Britain, Prussia and Russia) against Napoleon (20 November).
- War of 1812. Battle of Chippewa (5 July): American defeat of British force; Battle of Lundy's Lane (25 July): American attempt to take British position failed; The White House and the Capitol in Washington burned by British troops (24 August); Battle of Lake Champlain (11 September): British fleet defeated by Americans; British launch first of several unsuccessful attacks on New Orleans, unaware of peace agreement (December); Treaty of Ghent (signed 24 December) ends the war.
- Malta annexed to Britain under the terms of the Treaty of Paris; Cape Province, South Africa, bought by Britain; Rodrigues ceded to Britain by Portugal; St Lucia and Seychelles ceded to Britain by France.
- Treaty of Kiel: Denmark surrenders Norway to Sweden.
- Treaty of Chaumont between Russia, Austria, Prussia and Britain.
- Louis XVIII enters Paris (3 May).
- Ferdinand of Spain issues proclamation against the Constitution: Liberal deputies arrested.
- First Peace of Paris (30 May).
- Fall of Montevideo.
- Bolivar heavily defeated: abandons Caracas.
- Society of Jesus reconstituted by Pope Pius VII.
- Congress of Vienna opens.
- Peruvian invasion overthrows Chilian republic.
- Hetairia Philike founded at Odessa: Greek national movement begins.
- Opening of the Congress of Vienna (1 October, lasted until 9 June 1915).
- Gurkha War. Siege of Kalunga (October): Gurkha fort taken by British troops.
- Publication of Sir Walter Scott's *Waverley*.
- Early locomotive constructed by George Stephenson.
- Present ground of the Marylebone Cricket Club opened. First matched played there 22 June.

Deaths

Marquis de Sade, French writer.

1815

- Gurkha War. Battle of Jitgurh (14 January): Gurkhas defeat British troops; Battle of Almorah (25 April): British victory over Gurkhas.
- War of 1812. Last attack on New Orleans by British, unaware of peace agreement (8 January): defeated by Americans under Andrew Jackson.
- Napoleon lands in France (March 5): the Hundred Days begins; Louis XVIII flees from Paris (19 March) and Napoleon enters next day; Battle of Tolentino (2 May): Murat overthrown in Italy; Battle

of Quatre-Bras (16 June) between the British and the French: Wellington defeats Ney (June 16); Battle of Ligny (16 June): Blücher defeated after hard fight; Battle of Waterloo (18 June): Napoleon defeated by Wellington and Blücher; abdication of Napoleon (June 22); Allies enter Paris (7 July): Louis XVIII restored next day; Napoleon surrenders to the British (July 15) and exiled to St Helena; Treaty of Paris (November): Concert of Europe established between Britain, Russia, Prussia and Austria.
- Revolt in the Vendée.
- Battle of St Gilles: Vendéans defeated and La Rochejaquelin killed.
- Richelieu Prime Minister of France.
- William I of Holland becomes King of the Netherlands.
- Second Serbian revolt against Turkey: under Milosh Obrenovitch.
- Spanish force lands at Cumaná in South America under Morillo.
- Brazil declared a separate kingdom.
- Final Act of Congress of Vienna (9 June).
- Holy Alliance between Russia, Austria and Prussia.
- Alexander I grants a Polish constitution.
- Morillo invades New Granada: Bolivar flees.
- First of the Corn Laws passed in Britain and in 1828 and 1842 (repealed 1844 and 1869).
- Introduction into Britain of the quadrille dance.
- Invention of the safety lamp for miners by Sir Humphry Davy.

Deaths

Emma Hamilton, mistress of Lord Nelson (15 January).

1816

- Gurkha War. Battle of Mukwanpur (27 February): attack by Gurkha forces repelled by British with heavy losses.
- Annexation of Tristan da Cunha (settled 1810) by Britain (14 August).
- Bombardment of Algiers by British ships to halt slavery.
- Death of mad Queen Maria I of Portugal: John VI proclaimed king of Portugal, Brazil and the Algarves.
- Independence of the Argentine provinces proclaimed.
- James Monroe elected US President.
- Luddite anti-machinery riots.
- Radical meeting at Spa Fields broken up.
- First portable fire extinguisher invented by George Manby, a barrack-master.
- Macadamized roads invented by John Macadam.
- The kaleidoscope invented by David Brewster.

Deaths

Richard Brinsley Sheridan, Irish playwright and politician (7 July).

c.1816

- Whigs use name of Liberal Party (adopted officially in 1830s).

1817

- Third Maratha War. Battle of Kirkee (5 November): Marathas under Baji Rao defeated by Colonel Burr; Battle of Sitabaldi (24 November): attack by the rajah of Nagpur withstood by British-led troops; Battle of Mahidpur (21 December): British defeat of the Marathas.
- Battle of Chacabuco (12 February): San Martin defeats the Royalists in South America.
- Simon Bolivar captures Angostura.
- Serbian autonomy recognized by Turkey.
- Ali Pasha of Janina at the height of his power.
- Seditious Meetings Act in Britain passed by Castlereagh, suspending Habeas Corpus Act.
- Acquittal of the publisher William Hone: important development in the freedom of the press.
- Publication of Ricardo's *Principles of Political Economy*.
- *Blackwood's Magazine* founded in Edinburgh.
- Kalium (potassium) discovered by Sir Humphrey Davy.

Deaths

Jane Austen, English novelist (18 July).

Captain Bligh, English mariner (7 December).

Princess Charlotte, daughter of George IV and wife of Leopold of Saxe-Coburg.

1818

- Third Maratha War. Battle of Korygaom (1 January): Maratha attack on British defeated; Battle of Ashtee (18 February): rout of Maratha army; Siege of Asirghar begun by British (18 March), garrison surrendered (7 April); Siege of Chanda (9–11 May): British troops take Maratha fortress; Battle of Sholapur (10 May): Peshwa's army finally defeated. End of last Maratha War in India; Maratha power completely destroyed.
- Battle of Maipú: Chilian independence.
- Charles XIV (Bernadotte) becomes king of Sweden and Norway.
- Prussia becomes a free trade area.
- Bavaria obtains a constitution: also Baden.
- Decazes chief minister in France.
- Congress of Aix-la-Chapelle: France admitted to the Concert of Europe.
- Institution of Civil Engineers founded (granted Royal Charter 1828).

- Completion by Mary Wollstonecraft Shelley of the novel *Frankenstein* (begun 1816).
- Publication of *Family Shakespeare* by Bowdler.
- Soporific properties of ether discovered by Faraday (first used as an anaesthetic 1846).

1819
- Treaty of Frankfort completes work of Congress of Aix-la-Chapelle.
- Carlsbad Decrees: reaction in Germany.
- Bolivar occupies Bogotá.
- Birth of a daughter (later Queen Victoria) to the Duke of Kent and Princess Mary Louisa Victoria of Saxe-Coburg-Gotha (24 May).
- The Six Acts in Britain restricting right of meeting, etc.
- Foundation of Singapore by Stamford Raffles.
- Burlington Arcade, London, opened (20 March).
- Peterloo Massacre at reform meeting near Manchester (16 August): eleven killed by soldiers dispersing the meeting.
- Radical meeting at Bonnymuir dispersed.
- First crossing of the Atlantic by a steam-powered ship, the *Savannah* (24 May–20 June).
- First rubber factory built in London by Thomas Hancock, who patented the vulcanization of rubber.
- Cash payments resumed in Britain.

Deaths

James Watt, Scottish engineer and inventor (19 August).

1820
- Death of George III (29 January). The Prince Regent becomes king of Britain as George IV.
- Failure of George IV's Divorce Bill. He is unable to divorce Caroline.
- Spanish Revolution breaks out.
- Murder of the Duke of Berry in France.
- Fall of Decazes in France: Richelieu again chief minister.
- Ferdinand of Spain decides to adopt the Constitution of 1812.
- Revolt in Naples.
- Democratic insurrection in Lisbon.
- The Missouri Compromise on the slavery issue in the US.
- Cato Street Conspiracy to assassinate the members of the British Cabinet discovered (23 February): the leader, Arthur Thistlewood, and four others executed.
- First British settlers in South Africa (10 April).
- Congress of Troppau: Britain and France dissented from the reactionary protocol.
- Foundation of the Royal Astronomical Society (chartered 1831).

1821
- Coronation of George IV (19 July): Queen Caroline is barred from attending.
- Congress of Laibach.
- Prince Ypsilanti invades Moldavia to rouse the Greeks against Turkey.
- Battle of Rieti (March): Neapolitan constitutionalists defeated by Austrians.
- Revolt in Piedmont.
- Greek revolt in the Morea.
- Patriarch Gregorius and two bishops hanged by Turks.
- John VI returns from Brazil to Lisbon.
- Greeks under Ypsilanti defeated in Wallachia.
- San Martín enters Lima and proclaims independence of Peru.
- Battle of Carabobo (24 June): Bolivar defeats the royalist forces and occupies Caracas.
- Richelieu resigns in France: Royalist reaction under Villèle.
- Iturbide declares for an independent Mexican Empire.
- Mehemet Ali begins conquest of Soudan.
- Foundation of the *Manchester Guardian* (named changed to *The Guardian* 1959).
- Discovery of plesiosaurus remains by Mary Anning.

Deaths

John Keats, English poet, from tuberculosis in Rome (23 February).
- Queen Caroline, deserted wife of George IV.
- Napoleon Bonaparte, emperor of France (5 May).

1822
- Suicide of Lord Castlereagh: Canning succeeds him.
- Congress of Verona: Britain dissents from coercion of Spain.
- Massacre in Scio by the Turks.
- Lima occupied by the royalists.
- Battle of Pichincha: Sucre frees Quito.
- Iturbide proclaimed emperor of Mexico.
- US recognizes national independence of Colombia, Chile, Buenos Aires and Mexico.
- Dom Pedro proclaimed emperor of Brazil.
- Brazil declared as an independent empire.
- Ali Pasha surrenders to the Turks and is murdered.
- Hetton railway line, Co. Durham, first mineral railway in Britain and first railway on a prepared surface (built by George Stephenson) opened.

Deaths

Antonio Canova, Italian sculptor.

Percy Bysshe Shelley, English poet, by drowning in Italy (8 July).

1823
- France, Russia, Austria and Prussia demand the abo-

lition of 1812 Constitution in Spain.
- Louis XVIII declares war against Spanish rebels.
- Britain recognizes the Greeks as belligerents.
- The French invade Spain and enter Madrid.
- Bolivar enters Lima.
- Leo XII becomes Pope.
- President Monroe's message: beginning of Monroe Doctrine.
- Iturbide abdicates in Mexico owing to military revolt of Santa Ana.
- Birkbeck College, London University, founded (as the London Mechanics' Institution) by Dr George Birkbeck.
- Foundation of the Royal Society of British Artists.
- Foundation of *The Lancet* medical journal by Thomas Wakley.
- Invention of the waterproof coat by Charles Macintosh.
- The dynamo invented by William Sturgeon.
- Establishment of the Baltic Exchange in London.
- Rugby football begins to be played at Rugby School (legalized 1846).

Deaths
Edward Jenner, English physician (26 January).

1824
- Laws against combinations repealed in Britain (and in 1825). Trade unions become legal.
- First Ashanti War. First Battle of Accra: Ashanti victory over British troops.
- First Burma War. British forces take Burmese positions at Kemendine (10 June), Kamarut (8 July) and Kokein (12 December).
- Portuguese settlement of Malacca comes under British rule.
- Mehemet Ali takes part against the Greeks.
- Dom Miguel assumes government of Portugal, but compelled by the Powers to withdraw.
- Conference of St Petersburg on Eastern Question between Russia and Austria.
- Battle of Junin: Bolivar victorious.
- Charles X King of France.
- Battle of Ayacucho: Sucre decisively defeats Royalists.
- John Quincy Adams elected US President.
- Athenaeum Club founded in London.
- Foundation of the Royal Society for the Prevention of Cruelty to Animals.
- Foundation of the Royal Naval Lifeboat Institution by Sir William Hillary (4 March).
- Foundation of the National Gallery in London.
- *Westminster Review* started: organ of Radicals.
- Imperial standard measure of the gallon legalized.
- Portland cement patented by Joseph Aspdin (21 October).

Deaths
Lord Byron, George Gordon, 6th Baron Byron of Rochdale, British poet, from fever in Greece, fighting for Greek independence from Turkey (19 April).

1825
- Financial crisis in Britain.
- First Ashanti War. Second Battle of Accra: British victory over Ashanti.
- First Burma War. Battle of Donabew (7–25 March): British seizes Burmese stockades; Battle of Watigaon (15 November): British attack on Burmese fails; Battle of Pagahar: British defeat Burmese.
- Britain recognizes independence of Buenos Aires, Colombia and Mexico.
- Ibrahim, son of Mehemet Ali, lands in Morea to help Turkey.
- Consecration of Charles X at Reims.
- Nicholas I becomes tsar.
- December rising in Russia suppressed.
- Actinometer invented by Sir John Herschel.
- Electromagnet invented by William Sturgeon.
- Opening of the Stockton and Darlington Railway, the first public steam railway (27 September).
- Navigation Laws partly repealed.

1826
- First Ashanti War. Ashanti invasion of Gold Coast. Battle of Dodowah: Ashanti defeated by British.
- Straits Settlements of Malaya formed from Penang, Wellesley, Malacca and Singapore.
- Protocol of St Petersburg regarding Greece: between Britain and Russia; end of defence of Missolonghi.
- Death of John VI of Portugal.
- Russian ultimatum to Turkey demanding evacuation of principalities of Moldavia and Wallachia.
- Revolt of the Janissaries in Constantinople crushed.
- Chief Decembrists hanged in Russia.
- Massacre of the Janissaries in Constantinople.
- Jesuits return to France.
- Treaty of Akkerman: Turkey agrees to Russian demands.
- *Burke's Peerage* founded by Sir John Burke.
- Completion of Menai suspension bridge (begun 1818) by Thomas Telford.
- Foundation of the Zoological Society in London by Sir Stamford Raffles.
- Invention of the reaper by Patrick Bell.

1827
- Canning becomes prime minister: Whig coalition. Death of Canning (8 August): Goderich becomes prime minister.
- Foundation of Ottawa, Canada, (as Bytown) by John By.
- Greek War of Independence. Battle of Navarino be-

tween the Allied and Egyptian fleets (20 October): Treaty of London regarding Greece: between Britain, Russia, and France (6 July). Turkish fleet destroyed by Allied fleet under Codrington.

- Martignac chief minister in France.
- Turkey denounces Treaty of Akkerman.
- Press Censorship established in France.
- Publication of *Shepherd 's Calendar* by John Clare.
- *The Evening Standard* newspaper founded (asbsorbed the *St James's Gazette* 1905).
- Bright's disease identified by Dr Richard Bright.
- Charles Babbage begins work on his 'analytical engine', the prototype for modern computers (completed 1847).
- First suggestion of feasibility of contact lenses by Sir John Herschel (first made in Germany in 1887).
- Wooden friction matches invented by John Walker.

Deaths

Ludwig van Beethoven, German composer.

William Blake, English poet and artist (12 August).

1828

- Repeal of Test and Corporation Acts.
- Wellington becomes prime minister (26 January, until 1830).
- Protocol of London: Britain, France and Russia.
- O'Connell elected for Clare.
- Andrew Jackson elected US President.
- Capodistrias elected Greek President.
- Dom Miguel lands at Lisbon as regent.
- Russia invades Turkey.
- Dom Miguel takes title of king of Portugal: reign of terror.
- Ibrahim evacuates the Morea.
- Foundation of London University (chartered 1836). Opening of University College, London University.
- Opening of Regent's Park, London (27 April).
- Thomas Arnold becomes headmaster of Rugby.
- *Athenaeum* periodical begins publication (absorbed into *The Nation* 1921).
- Foundation of *The Spectator* (second) by Robert Rintoul.
- Brownian Motion in physics discovered by Robert Brown.
- Invention of the Nicol prism for the polarization of light by William Nicol.
- Marble Arch built.
- Darling River in Australia discovered by Charles Sturt.

1829

- Catholic Emancipation Act passed in Britain (April); Catholics allowed access to Parliament.
- Final repeal of the Test Act.
- Functions of the Bow Street Runners superseded by the setting up of the Metropolitan Police Force by Peel as Home Secretary (19 June).
- Pius VIII becomes pope.
- Polignac becomes chief minister in France.
- Treaty of Adrianople between Russia and Turkey: Greece recognized as independent: Serbian autonomy secured: Danubian principalities practically independent states.
- Fourth marriage of Ferdinand of Spain (to Maria Christina of Naples): beginning of Carlist movement.
- William Lloyd Garrison begins the abolitionist movement in US.
- The practice of suttee made illegal in India.
- Foundation of King's College, London University.
- The Catholic Apostolic Church (or Irvingites) sect founded by Edward Irving.
- Concertina invented.
- Completion of St Katharine's Dock, Port of London, by Thomas Telford.
- First scheduled omnibus service in London (4 July, from Marylebone Road to the Bank).
- The manufacture of steel pen nibs perfected by Josiah Mason and Joseph Gillot.
- The Rainhill locomotive trials (6 October): victory of George and Robert Stephenson's 'Rocket', the first successful high-speed locomotive.
- Oxford and Cambridge Boat Race first held (10 June).

Deaths

Sir Humphrey Davy, English chemist, at Geneva (29 May).

1830

- Death of George IV (26 June). His brother becomes king of Britain as William IV.
- Wellington succeeded by Earl Grey as prime minister (until 1834).
- Conference of London recognizes Belgian independence.
- The July Revolution in Paris: Louis Philippe becomes king.
- Belgian revolt against Holland: Belgian provinces proclaim their independence.
- Algiers captured by France.
- Insurrection in Poland.
- Milosh hereditary prince of Serbia.
- Victor Hugo *Hernani*.
- Foundation of the Plymouth Brethern religious sect by the Rev. John Darby.
- Royal Geographical Society founded by Sir John Barrow.
- The principles of induction discovered by Michael Faraday.

c.1830

- First prefabricated house built as a toll house on the West Bromwich to Birmingham road (dismantled 1926).

Deaths

William Huskisson, former President of the Board of Trade, by being run over by a train at the opening of the Manchester-Liverpool railway (15 September).
William Hazlitt, English author.

1831

- Second Reading of first Reform Bill carried in House of Commons by majority of 1 (March 21); hostile amendment carried (April); Parliament dissolved (April 22); majority for Reform elected.
- House of Lords rejects first Reform Bill in its second form (8 October).
- Truck Act passed, prohibiting payment in kind.
- Polish Diet declares the Romanoffs excluded from the sovereignty.
- Gregory XVI becomes pope.
- Revolution in the Papal States.
- Battle of Grochov (25 February): Russians defeat Poles.
- Casimir Périer ministry in France.
- Austrian troops help pope to suppress rising in Bologna.
- Abdication of Pedro I in Brazil: Pedro II succeeds.
- Leopold of Saxe-Coburg elected as Leopold I, king of the Belgians.
- French squadron in the Tagus: Portuguese fleet surrenders.
- Dutch invasion of Belgium.
- Assassination of Capodistrias.
- Polish revolution crushed: the kingdom ended.
- Mehemet Ali invades Syria: siege of Acre.
- Charles Albert becomes king of Sardinia.
- Young Italy founded by Giuseppe Mazzini.
- British Guiana in northeast South America becomes a British colony.
- British Association for the Advancement of Science founded.
- Opening of second London Bridge, designed by John Rennie (1 August, begun 1824).
- Hackney carriages regularized by the Carriage Act.
- The laws of electromagnetic induction defined by Faraday.
- HMS *Beagle* begins five-year scientific circumnavigation of the world with Charles Darwin aboard (27 December).
- Enderby Land, Antarctica, discovered by John Biscoe.
- King William Island, Arctic, discovered by James Clark Ross.
- North magnetic pole located by James Clark Ross.

Deaths

Georg Wilhelm Friedrich Hegel, German philosopher.

1832

- British Cabinet recommended creation of peers to pass Reform Bill: King William IV refuses: Wellington fails to form a ministry: king then agrees: Lords pass the Bill. First Reform Bill becomes law (4 June) and greatly increases electoral franchise.
- Dod's *Parliamentary Companion* founded by Charles Dod.
- General election: Whig triumph.
- Kingdom of Greece erected by Convention of London: Otho of Bavaria becomes king.
- Ibrahim takes Acre.
- Ibrahim takes Damascus.
- Pedro's expedition lands in Portugal.
- Ibrahim conquers all Syria.
- The Pope condemns the teaching of Lamennals.
- Soult ministry in France, including the doctrinaires (Guizot, Thiers, etc).
- Antwerp capitulates to French.
- Battle of Koniah: Egyptians and Syrians under Ibrahim defeat Turks.
- Crete placed under Egypt.
- Establishment of shore stations in Otago, New Zealand.
- Book jackets first used in England (in general used by 1890).
- Durham University founded.
- Electroplating invented by George Elkington.

Deaths

Jeremy Bentham, English philosopher
Johann Wolfgang von Goethe, German writer.
Sir Walter Scott, Scottish novelist and poet (21 September).

1833

- Factory Act forbade employment of children below the age of nine.
- Act for Emancipation of British colonial slaves.
- Election of the first Quaker MP.
- Falkland Islands claimed by Britain as a Crown Colony.
- Russian squadron in the Bosphorus.
- Convention of Kutaya: Mehemet Ali recognized by Turkey as Pasha of Syria, etc.
- Battle of Cape St Vincent: Napier destroys the Miguelist fleet.
- Treaty of Unkiar Skelessi: alliance between Russia and Turkey.
- Terceira defeats Miguelists near Lisbon.

- Siege of Oporto raised by Miguelists.
- Dom Pedro enters Lisbon.
- Death of Ferdinand of Spain: succeeded by his daughter Isabella II.
- Convention of Münchengrätz between Russia, Austria and Prussia in aid of Turkey (secret).
- Treaty of Berlin between Austria, Prussia and Russia.
- Launch of the Oxford Movement by John Keble (14 July).
- Thomas Carlyle *Sartor Resartus*.
- *Sartor Resartus* by Thomas Carlyle.
- Electrolysis investigated by Michael Faraday.

Deaths

Edmund Kean, English actor.

Thomas Telford, Scottish civil engineer (2 September).

William Wilberforce, English philanthropist (29 July).

1834

- Abolition of slavery in British possessions.
- Lord Grey resigns: Lord Melbourne becomes prime minister.
- Poor Law Act in England reforms Poor Law system. Introduction of workhouses.
- William IV dismisses Melbourne and summons Peel.
- Treaty between Britain, Spain, Portugal and France: Austria, Russia and Prussia become Carlist.
- Battle of Asseiceira: Miguelists finally defeated by Pedroists in Portugal: Maria II established as queen.
- The island of St Helena becomes a British Crown Colony.
- Tolpuddle Martyrs transported for trade union activity.
- End of the practice of burying suicides at crossroads, transfixed by a stake.
- Palace of Westminster destroyed by fire except Westminster Hall and St Stephen's Chapel (16 October).
- The Veto Act passed by the Scottish General Assembly.
- The hansom cab patented by Joseph Hansom (23 December).

Deaths:

Samuel Taylor Coleridge, English poet (25 July).

Charles Lamb, English essayist (27 December).

1835

- Municipal Reform Act.
- Peel resigns: Melbourne recalled (in office until 1841).
- Ferdinand I becomes emperor of Austria.
- Carlists fail to capture Bilbao.
- Sir George Airy made Astronomer Royal.
- Foundation of Madame Tussaud's Waxworks in London by Mme Marie Tussaud.
- Appearance of Halley's Comet (named after Edmund Halley).
- Cuneiform writing first deciphered by Sir Henry Rawlinson.
- Electric telegraph invented.
- First surviving photograph taken by William Fox Talbot.
- Bear-baiting and bull-baiting prohibited by Act of parliament.

Deaths

James Hogg, Scottish poet.

John Nash, English architect.

1836

- Thiers ministry in France: then Guizot ministry.
- Bilbao again relieved by Espartero from Carlist attack.
- Martin Van Buren elected US President.
- Beginning of Chartist movement (ended *c.*1858).
- Adelaide, South Australia founded (named after Queen Adelaide).
- Beginning of the Great Trek of Boers in South Africa, away from British territory in Cape Colony to the Orange Free State. Transvaal first colonized by Boers.
- Tolpuddle Martyrs pardoned.
- Non-religious marriages made legal.
- Orange Lodges dissolved.
- Acetylene discovered by Edmund Davy.
- Appointment of the first Registrar-General, Thomas Lister.
- Invention of the screw propeller by Francis Pettit Smith.

1837

- Death of William IV (20 June). His niece Victoria becomes queen of Britain.
- French-Canadian Rebellion in Canada under Papineau and Mackenzie; rebels victorious at Battle of St Denis, but defeated at the Battles of St Charles and St Eustache.
- Molé ministry in France.
- Indian Post Office established (24 July).
- The registration of births, marriages and deaths made compulsory in England and Wales (1 July).
- Publication completed of *The Posthumous Papers of the Pickwick Club* by Charles Dickens (begun 1836): his first novel.
- Opening of Euston Railway Station, first in London (20 July).
- Discovery of the polarization of heat by James Forbes.
- Invention of the railway ticket dating machine by Thomas Edmondson.
- Publication of *Stenographic Sound Hand* by Isaac

Pitman, demonstrating Pitman's shorthand (15 November).

- The first practical telegraph line patented by William Cooke and Charles Wheatstone.
- The invention of penny postage by Rowland Hill (who put it into effect in 1840).
- Grand National horse race first run at Liverpool.

Deaths

John Constable, English painter (31 March).

Giacomo Leopardi, Italian poet.

Alexander Sergeievich Pushkin, Russian poet.

1838

- Act of Parliament brings the Public Records under the superintendence of the Master of the Rolls.
- Anti-Corn Law League founded by Richard Cobden and John Bright.
- People's Charter published.
- Afrikaner-Zulu War. Massacre of Boers by Zulu chief Dingaan. Battle of Dingaan's Day (16 December): Boer revenge on Zulus.
- Lord Durham becomes governor-general of Canada.
- Grace Darling rescues survivors of the *Forfarshire* (7 September).
- Foundation of the Peculiar People religious movement in London.
- Opening of the National Gallery in London (9 April).
- Invention of the bicycle by Kirkpatrick Macmillan.

- **c.1838**

- Invention of the stereoscope by Charles Wheatstone.

1839

- Peel becomes prime minister: resigns on Bedchamber question when Victoria rejects the proposal that some of her Whig Ladies of the Bedchamber be replaced by Conservatives: Melbourne resumes office.
- Petition by Chartist movement rejected by Parliament (also in 1842 and 1848).
- Rebecca Riots in Wales destroys tollhouses and tollgates.
- Durham's Report on Canada submitted to British Parliament.
- First Afghan War begins (ends 1842). Khelat captured by British (13 November).
- Treaty of London: final adjustment of Belgian frontiers and recognition by Holland.
- War renewed between Sultan of Turkey and Mehemet Ali: Sultan's army invades Syria.
- Soult ministry in France.
- Battle of Nezib: Ibrahim's decisive victory over the Turks.
- Abdul Mejid becomes sultan of Turkey.
- Prince Milosh abdicates in Serbia.
- French conquest of Algeria completed.
- Christian VIII King of Denmark.
- Aden annexed to British India.
- Indian tea reaches Britain for the first time.
- First publication of *Bradshaw's Railway Guide* (Great Britain) by George Bradshaw (25 October, discontinued 1961).
- Invention of the steam hammer by James Nasmyth.
- The Grove cell electric battery invented by William Grove.
- Cunard steamship company founded (4 May).
- Cesarewitch Stakes, Newmarket, first run.
- Grand National first run at Aintree (26 February).
- First Henley Regatta at Henley-on-Thames held (14 June).

1840

- Treaty of Waitangi between Captain Hobson and Maori chiefs in New Zealand (6 February); New Zealand proclaimed a British colony (21 May).
- Union Act for Canada: responsible government granted: an epoch in colonial history.
- Beirut bombarded by Sir Charles Napier.
- Convention of London: Four Powers to Act against Mehemet Ali in Egypt: France stands aloof; British and Turkish troops attack and destroyed Acre; Egyptians defeated.
- Outbreak of the Opium War between Britain and China on opium question (ended 1842).
- O'Connell revives the Repeal Association.
- Marriage of Queen Victoria and Prince Albert of Saxe-Coburg (10 February).
- William Henry Harrison elected US President.
- Thiers ministry in France.
- End of the Carlist war in Spain.
- Frederick William IV becomes king of Prussia.
- Convention of London: four Powers to Act against Mehemet Ali.
- Reactionary constitution imposed in Hanover.
- Christina abdicates the regency in Spain.
- Resignation of Thiers.
- Crete restored to Turkey.
- Acre taken by allied fleet.
- War between Britain and China on opium question.
- Abdication of William I in Holland: William II succeeds.
- End of convict transportation to New South Wales.
- Penny postage introduced in Britain by its inventor, Rowland Hill (10 January); Adhesive postage stamps first used (6 May); stamped envelopes issued.
- Livingstone begins his work in Africa.
- London Library founded (opened 1841).
- Introduction of the term 'scientist' by William Whewell, Master of Trinity College, Cambridge.
- Lake Eyre, South Australia, discovered by Edward Eyre.

1841

- Melbourne, defeated after a dissolution, resigns: Peel becomes prime minister (until 1845).
- Richard Moody made first governor of the Falkland Islands (until 1849).
- Birth of a son, Albert Edward (later Edward VII), to Queen Victoria and Prince Albert (9 November); created Prince of Wales (8 December).
- Hong Kong ceded to Britain by China.
- John Tyler becomes president of US on death of Harrison.
- Mehemet Ali submits to Sultan: becomes hereditary Pasha of Egypt.
- Espartero becomes Spanish Regent.
- Foundation of Thomas Cook's, travel agents, by Thomas Cook.
- First publication of *Punch* (17 July) by Ebenezer Landells and Mark Lemon.
- Completion of construction (began 1811) of Plymouth breakwater, designed by John Rennie.
- Foundation of the Pharmaceutical Society of Great Britain (incorporation by Royal Charter 1843).
- Joule's Law of electrical energy pronounced by James Joule.
- Standardization of screw threads by Joseph Whitworth.
- The term 'hypnotism' first introduced by James Braid.
- Mount Erebus, volcanic mountain in Antarctica, discovered by Sir James Clark Ross.

1842

- Assam conquered by the British.
- First Afghan War. British army evacuating Kabul attacked at Khoord Kabul Pass (8 January) and at Jugdulluk (12 January); Siege of British at Jellalabad begins (11 March); British defeated at Khojah Pass (28 March); Battle of Maidan (14 September): Afghans defeated.
- Treaty of Nanking (29 August): end of the Opium War. Hong Kong leased to Britain by China (20 January); New Territories, Kowloon and Stonecutters Island added 1898.
- Death of Duke of Orleans: Regency Act in France.
- Alexander Karageorgevich becomes prince of Serbia.
- Claim of Right by Scottish Church.
- Foundation of Mudie's Library (existed until 1937) by Charles Mudie.
- The *Illustrated London News* begins publication (14 May).
- *The Nation* begins publication in Dublin.
- Blueprint process for copying plans, etc, first used by Sir John Herschel.
- King Edward VII Land, Antarctica, sighted by James Clark Ross.

Deaths

Thomas Arnold, English educator.

Stendhal, French novelist.

1843

- Sind Conquest. Battle of Miani (17 February): hard-fought British defeat of Beluchi forces. Battle of Dubba (24 March): British defeat Beluchi forces. Battle of Hyderabad (24 August): Beluchis defeated; Napier's conquest of Sind complete.
- First Afghan War. Relief of British at Jellalabad (18 April).
- Gwalior Campaign. Battle of Maharajpur (29 December): British victory.
- Natal declared British.
- The Gambia made an independent British Crown Colony.
- Entente cordiale between France and Britain.
- Rebecca Riots in Wales.
- First International Peace Congress held in London.
- Counter-revolution in Spain: flight of Espartero: Narvaez in power.
- The MacNaghten Rules formulated as the legal definition of insanity after the trial for murder of Daniel MacNaghten.
- Foundation of the Evangelical Union by James Morison.
- Free Church founded in Scotland by the Disruption: Dr Thomas Chalmers the leader.
- Khaki first worn by the Queen's Own Corps of Scouts and Guides (becomes general in second Afghan War).
- William Wordsworth becomes poet laureate (6 April) after the death of Robert Southey (21 March).
- First Christmas cards produced in Britain.
- *The Economist* magazine founded by James Wilson.
- First publication of the *News of the World* (1 October).
- Building of the first ocean-going iron ship (the *Great Britain*) by Isambard Kingdom Brunel; launched by Prince Albert 19 July.
- Opening of the Thames Tunnel (begun 1825), the world's first underwater tunnel, built by Sir Marc Isambard Brunel, still in use by London Underground.
- Foundation of the Royal College of Surgeons in London (21 June).
- Foundation of the world's first agricultural experimental station at Rothamsted by John Lawes.
- Hydroelectricity discovered by Michael Faraday.
- Patent granted to Thomas Hancock for the vulcanization of rubber (21 November).

- The Royal Hunt Cup horse race first ran at Ascot.

1844

- Railway Act. Bank Charter Act.
- Annexation of Natal to Cape Colony.
- James Knox Polk elected US President.
- Oscar I becomes king of Sweden and Norway.
- France annexes Tahiti.
- Otto compelled to grant a constitution in Greece.
- Fleet Prison pulled down.
- Foundation of the YMCA (Young Men's Christian Association) by George Williams.
- First co-operative store opened by the Rochdale Society (21 December): origin of Co-operative Societies.
- Establishment of the Imperial standard weight of the pound and standard measure of the yard.

Deaths

John Dalton, English scientist (27 July).

1845

- Peel forced to resign. Lord John Russell fails to form a ministry.
- First Sikh War. Battle of Mudki (18 December): failure of Sikh attack on British troops; Battle of Ferozeshah (21 December): bloody draw between the British and Sikhs.
- Catholic Sonderbund formed in Switzerland.
- Failure of the potato crop (until 1849): great distress in Ireland, etc.
- Portland Vase deliberately destroyed in the British Museum (7 February).
- Experiments on the polarization of light made by Michael Faraday.
- Invention of the Moon alphabet for the blind by Dr William Moon.
- The pneumatic tyre is patented by Robert Thomson (10 December).
- Position of the planet Neptune predicted by John Couch Adams.
- The *Great Britain* sets out from Liverpool on her maiden voyage, to New York (26 July).

Deaths

Elizabeth Fry, English Quaker prison reformer (12 October).

.1845

- Hydraulic crane invented by William Armstrong.
- Tonic sol-fa system invented by Sarah Glover.

846

- Repeal of the Corn Laws.
- Defeat and resignation of Peel: Russell forms a ministry (until 1852).
- First Sikh War. Battle of Aliwal (28 January): British victory over the Sikhs; Battle of Sobraon (10 February): British defeat Sikhs. End of war.
- Kashmir recognizes British supremacy.
- Entente cordiale between Britain and France broken off on question of Spanish marriages.
- Pius IX becomes pope.
- Austria absorbs Cracow.
- War between US and Mexico because of annexation of Texas by former.
- Foundation of Manchester University (as Owens College) by John Owens.
- Foundation of Secularism by George Holyoake.
- Marriage of Robert Browning and Elizabeth Barrett.
- Publication of *Book of Nonsense* by Edward Lear.
- *The Daily News* founded (merged with *News Chronicle* 1930).

1847

- Ten Hours Act in Britain.
- Lord Elgin becomes governor-general of Canada (until 1854): makes responsible government a reality.
- Austrian occupation of Ferrara.
- Federal Diet in Switzerland declares dissolution of Sonderbund.
- Swiss Federal general Dufour takes Fribourg and Lucerne and crushes the Sonderbund.
- Mexico occupied by US troops.
- French defeat and capture Abd-el-Kader in Algeria.
- Foundation of the Oratory, Birmingham.
- Excavation completed (began 1845) of Nineveh, the Assyrian capital, by Sir Austen Layard.
- Publication of *Jane Eyre* by Charlotte Brontë, *Wuthering Heights* by Emily Brontë and *Agnes Grey* by Anne Brontë.
- Publication of *Vanity Fair* by Thackeray.
- Chloroform first used as an anaesthetic.
- James 'Paraffin' Young begins experimenting with the distillation of oil distilled from coal and shale (completed 1850).

Deaths

Daniel O'Connell, Irish politician (15 May)

Sir John Franklin, British explorer, while attempting to discover the Northwest Passage (11 June).

1848

- Transportation of leaders of Young Ireland.
- Battle of Boomplaatz (29 August): Boers defeated by Sir Harry Smith, governor of the Cape of Good Hope. Orange Free State proclaimed British Territory.
- Dalhousie made governor-general of India (until 1856).
- First officially organized settlement in Otago, New Zealand.

- Second Sikh War. outbreak in India (ends 1849) between the British and the Sikhs: Punjab annexed. Battle of Kineyri (18 June): Sikhs defeated and flee to Multan; Battle of Suddasain (1 July): Sikh attack on British-led forces defeated; Siege of Multan begins (July).
- Austrians crush disturbances in Milan.
- Rising in Palermo: Sicily soon freed, except fortress of Messina.
- Constitutional edict in Naples.
- Frederick VII King of Denmark.
- Demand for a German National Parliament formulated in Baden Chamber.
- Constitution granted in Tuscany.
- February Revolution in Paris: Republic proclaimed: Lamartine a leader.
- Guizot dismissed.
- Louis Philippe abdicates.
- Neuchâtel proclaimed a Republic.
- Constitution granted in Piedmont.
- Insurrection in Vienna: resignation and flight of Metternich: End of Absolutist Reaction.
- Constitution granted in Rome: Republic proclaimed, with Mazzini at its head.
- Hungary gains the People's Charter: virtual autonomy.
- Successful insurrection in Berlin.
- Successful revolution in Milan.
- Venice proclaimed a Republic.
- Charles Albert invades Lombardy (25 March).
- Tuscany declares war against Austria.
- Tuscan forces invade Lombardy.
- Pope disclaims the Italian cause.
- Prussia occupies Schleswig and invades Jutland.
- Neapolitan constitution dropped.
- Flight of Emperor Ferdinand.
- German National Assembly at Frankfort.
- Battle of Goito: Piedmontese victory over Austrians.
- Radetzky overruns Venetia.
- National Workshops in Paris: soon abolished.
- Cavaignac suppresses a Paris insurrection.
- Archduke John elected Reichsverweser by Frankfort Assembly.
- Reichstag meets at Vienna.
- Battle of Custozza: Charles Albert defeated by Radetzky.
- Union of Venetia and Piedmont declared: soon overthrown.
- Radetzky reoccupies Milan.
- Salasco armistice.
- Truce of Malmoe between Denmark and Prussia.
- New Swiss Federal constitution.
- Hungary invaded by Jellachich, Ban of Croatia.
- Austria declares war against Hungary.
- Vienna again in revolution.
- Battle of Schwechat: defeat and retreat of Hungarian army.
- Vienna falls to Windischgrätz.
- New Dutch constitution.
- Flight of Pius IX to Gaeta.
- Ferdinand forced to abdicate: Francis Joseph becomes Austrian emperor.
- Prince Louis Napoleon Bonaparte elected President of France for four years.
- Treaty of Guadalupe Hidalgo cedes New Mexico, California and Texas from Mexico to the US.
- Gold discovered in California.
- Zachary Taylor elected US President.
- Chartist demonstration in London a fiasco.
- Publication of *The Communist Manifesto* by Karl Marx.
- John Bird Sumner becomes archbishop of Canterbury (until 1862).
- Continental *Bradshaw* established.

Deaths

George Stephenson (12 August).
Lord Melbourne (24 November).
Emily Brontë (19 December).

1849

- Second Sikh War. Multan stormed (2 January) and surrendered (22 January); Battle of Chilianwala (14 January): British and Indian troops under Lord Gough defeat the Sikhs; Battle of Gujerat (22 February): British and Indian troops under Gough crush the Sikhs; Battle of Ramnuggur (22 November): British attempt to dislodge Sikh army unsuccessful.
- Battle of Kápolna: Hungarians defeated in bloody battle.
- William III King of Holland.
- Battle of Novara: Radetzky defeats Charles Albert.
- Charles Albert abdicates in favour of Victor Emmanuel II.
- Frankfort Assembly choses King of Prussia as German emperor: King of Prussia declines.
- Schleswig-Holstein War re-opened.
- Twenty-eight German States accept Frankfort Constitution of the empire.
- Hungary declares itself a republic, at instance of Kossuth.
- Prussia rejects the Frankfort Constitution.
- French under Oudinot land in Italy to suppress Roman Republic: Garibaldi repels them at first, but Rome falls.
- Russia helps Austria to suppress Hungarian revolution.
- Revolt in Bavarian Palatinate.

Prussians suppress revolt in Dresden.
Revolt in Baden: Provisional Government formed.
Sicilian revolution crushed by Naples.
Haynau's brutality at Brescia.
Austrians enter Florence.
Garibaldi repulses the Neapolitans.
Hungarians under Görgei take Budapest.
Windischgrätz suppresses the Prague insurrection.
Austrians take Budapest.
Prussians suppress Baden revolution.
Battle of Segesvár: Hungarians under Bem routed.
Death of Mehemit Ali: Abbas I succeeds in Egypt.
Battle of Szöreg:Haynau defeats Hungarians.
Battle of Temesvar: Hungarians defeated.
Abdication and flight of Kossuth.
Surrender of Görgei and a Hungarian army at Világos.
Venice surrenders to Austrians.
Flight of pope to Gaeta.
Complete repeal of Navigation Laws in Britain (and 1854).
Cockfighting made illegal.
Foundation of the Royal London Homeopathic Hospital by Dr Frederick Quin.

Deaths

Queen Adelaide, widow of William IV (2 December).
Anne Brontë, English novelist (28 May).
Edgar Allan Poe, US author.

850

Millard Fillmore becomes US President on death of Taylor.
Erfurt Parliament called by Prussia.
Saxony and Hanover withdraw from the Three Kings' League.
Pius IX returns to Rome.
Dispute between Greece and Britain over Don Pacifico.
Peace of Berlin ends Schleswig-Holstein War.
Cavour Prime Minister in Piedmont.
Olmütz 'Punctuation': Austria and Prussia adjust Hesse-Cassel question.
First British Public Library Act passed (superseded by the Act of 1919), permitting the establishment of public libraries in England.
Christian Socialism founded by John Ludlau.
Foundation of the Meteorological Office in London by James Glaisher.
Opening of the first reformatory in Britain at Redhill.
The Koh-i-Noor diamond presented to the British regalia by the East India Company.
Publication of Tennyson's *In Memoriam*.
Collodion process invented by Frederick Archer.

- Discovery of the spiral nebulae announced by the Earl of Rosse.
- Initiation of synthetic oil production by James Young.
- Process of mercerising invented by John Mercer.
- The hydraulic pressure accumulator invented by William Armstrong.

Deaths

Sir Robert Peel, British statesman, following a riding accident (2 July).
William Wordsworth (23 April), poet laureate. Lord Tennyson appointed poet laureate (19 November).

c.1850

- First kindergarten in England opened.

1851

- Palmerston dismissed from Foreign Office for unauthorized recognition of the French coup d'état.
- Catholic hierarchy restored in Britain and Holland.
- Secret Alliance between Austria and Prussia.
- First Australian goldfield opened.
- Louis Napoleon's coup d'état in France: victorious on a plebiscite.
- Austrian constitution abolished.
- The Great Exhibition in London (1 May-15 October) held in the Crystal Palace (designed by Joseph Paxton), Hyde Park, London.
- Publication of cheap editions of music pioneered by Henry Litolff.
- Publication of *Lavengro* by George Borrow.
- Development of the mathematical theory of determinants by William Spottiswoode.
- Discovery of the organic base pyridine by Thomas Anderson.
- First telegraph cable laid across the English Channel.
- Invention of instantaneous photography by William Fox Talbot.
- Marble Arch (built 1828) re-erected at Cumberland Gate, Hyde Park.
- The first envelope-making machine invented by Warren de la Rue.
- Gold found in the Blue Hills, New South Wales, Australia, leading to a gold rush (February).

Deaths

Mary Shelley, English writer (1 February)
Joseph Mallord William Turner, English painter.

1852

- Coalition government. Fall of Derby ministry. Russell defeated: Derby becomes prime minister.
- Annexation of Lower Burma by Britain.
- Signature of the Sand River Convention (17 January): Britain recognizes independence of Transvaal.
- Hereditary empire restored in France: Lòuis Napoleon becomes Napoleon III (November 22).

- Enrico Tazzoli hanged in Italy: 'Mantuan Trials'.
- Franklin Pierce elected US President.
- Great Ormond Street Hospital for children opened for patients (14 February).
- Last duel fought in England at Priest Hill, Surrey.
- Compilation of *Roget's Thesaurus* by Peter Mark Roget.
- Harriet Beecher Stowe *Uncle Tom's Cabin*.
- Opening of the Victoria and Albert Museum in London.
- Invention of quaternions vector analysis by William Hamilton.
- Alpaca fabrics first manufactured in England by Sir Titus Salt.

Deaths

Arthur Wellesy, Duke of Wellington, English soldier and politician (14 September).

1853

- Aberdeen coalition ministry with Earl of Aberdeen as prime minister.
- Orange River Sovereignty abandoned by Britain.
- Abolition of soap tax (imposition 1712).
- American naval commander Perry in Japan.
- Montenegrins defeat Turkish expedition against them.
- Pedro V King of Portugal.
- Chetham's Library, Manchester, founded by Humphrey Chetham.
- Newspaper advertisement duty abolished.
- The troy ounce measure for precious metals legalized in Britain.
- David Livingstone discovers the Victoria Falls.

1854

- Ecclesiastical Titles Bill in Britain: abortive.
- Orange Free State established as independent.
- British and French troops occupy the Piraeus.
- Crimean War. British and French troops land in the Crimea; the Allies (Britain, Turkey and France) and Russia (ended 1856); Battle of the Alma (20 September): Russians defeated; Siege of Sebastopol begins (28 September); Battle of Balaklava (25 October) between the Russians and the British the outcome of which is indecisive: Charge of the Light Brigade; Battle of Inkerman between the Russians and British (5 November): Russians defeated.
- Missouri Compromise repealed in US.
- German Zollverein practically complete.
- Said Pasha ruler in Egypt.
- Revolt in Madrid: Espartero becomes premier.
- Cigarettes introduced into Britain.
- Crystal Palace moved to Penge.
- Institute of Chartered Accountants of Scotland chartered.
- Voyage of discovery of the Northwest Passage completed (began 1850) by Robert McClure.

1855

- Aberdeen defeated and resigns: Palmerston becomes prime minister.
- Suppression of Donnybrook Fair in Ireland.
- Crimean War. Sardinia joins Britain and France in Crimean War; death of Lord Raglan (28 June); Battle of the Great Redan (8 September): unsuccessful British attack on southern defences of Sebastopol; Siege of Sebastopol ends with seizure (9 September).
- Alexander II becomes tsar of Russia.
- Letters of Marque, granted to allow private persons to fit out armed ships in wartime, abolished by the Declaration of Paris.
- Building of Balmoral Castle completed.
- Jews' College, London, founded by Nathan Adler, Chief Rabbi.
- Last Bartholomew Fair held at West Smithfield London on St Bartholomew's Day (began 1133).
- The registration of births, marriages and deaths made compulsory in Scotland.
- Newspaper stamp tax abolished.
- *The Daily Telegraph* newspaper refounded by Joseph Moses Levy (29 June).
- Addison's disease discovered by Thomas Addison.
- Cellulose nitrate, first synthetic plastic material, invented by Alexander Parkes. Celluloid patented by Alexander Parkes.
- Study of astrophysics founded by Sir William Huggins.
- Creation of the first registered trademark, the Red Badge of Bass & Co.'s Pale Ale.

Deaths

Charlotte Brontë, English novelist (31 March).

1856

- James Buchanan elected US President.
- Crimean War: ended by signature of the Treaty of Paris (30 March).
- Annexation of Oude to British India.
- British Guiana issued the most valuable postage stamp (only one copy known) in February.
- Natal made a British colony.
- Norfolk Island in the South Pacific settled (becomes an external territory of Australia 1913).
- Foundation by Queen Victoria of the Victoria Cross, the premier decoration for valour (29 January), made from the iron of Russian cannon used by the Russians at Sebastopol.
- Elizabeth Garrett Anderson qualifies as first British woman doctor.
- Publication of *Tom Brown's Schooldays,* by Thomas Hughes.
- Anilines dyes discovered by William Henry Perkin.

- Bessemer converter invented by Henry Bessemer.
- Origination of the paraffin industry by James 'Paraffin' Young.

Deaths

Heinrich Heine, German poet.

1857

- Prince Albert created Prince Consort.
- Bank Charter Act suspended.
- Lord Canning becomes governor-general of India. Indian Mutiny. Outbreak at Meerut when troops who object to biting off the ends of cartridges greased with animal fat are court-martialled (10 May); Massacre of Cawnpore (6 June): members of the English garrison and their families murdered by rioters; Jhansi captured by mutineers (June); Residency at Lucknow defended by the Duke of Cornwall's Light Infantry (1 July); Mutineers defeated by British force advancing on Cawnpore at Aong and Pandu Naddi (15 July); Defeat of rebels at Maharajpur (16 July) and Onao (28 July); Battle of Agra (2 August): British garrison forced back into the fort; Battle of Nujufghur (24 August) rebels defeated by British force; Battle of Agra (October): British force put rebels to flight. Sir Henry Havelock's relief of Lucknow begins (19 September). Delhi besieged by British (from 8 June); palace taken (20 September). Battle of Secunderbagh (16 November): rebel stronghold stormed by British and Indian troops. Campbell relieved garrison at Lucknow (19 November). Mutineers defeated at Goraria (23–24 November) and Pandu Naddi (26 November). Battle of Cawnpore (6 December): British under Sir Colin Campbell rout the mutineers.
- Arrow incident in China leads to war: Palmerston defeated in Parliament: appeals to the country and obtains a majority.
- Prussia relinquishes control over Neuchâtel.
- Britannia Royal Naval College founded at Portland (transferred to Dartmouth 1863).
- International Code of Signals devised by the British government (amended 1901).
- Merger as the United Methodists of a group of Methodist sects (added to in 1907).
- Foundation of the National Portrait Gallery (opened 1859).
- Publication of *Barchester Towers* by Anthony Trollope.
- The Halle Orchestra in Manchester established by Sir Charles Halle.
- First telegraph cable laid across the Atlantic.

Deaths

Honoré de Balzac, French novelist.

1858

- Orsini's attempt on life of Napoleon III.
- Palmerston defeated on Orsini question: Derby Premier.
- The Jewish Disabilities Removal Act passed, allowing Jewish members of the House of Commons (to the House of Lords 1885).
- British Columbia constituted a British Crown Colony (2 August).
- Indian Mutiny. Mutineer-held palace of Musa Bagh at Lucknow captured by British (19 March); Relief of the city of Lucknow finally achieved (21 March); Mutineers besiged at Kotah (22 March) and captured (30 March) by Lord Roberts; Jhansi recaptured by British (2 April); Battle of Azimghur (15 April): British and Sikh troops defeated rebels; British besieged and captured Kalpi (19–23 May); Battle of Baduli-ki-Serai (8 June): mutineers defeated by British force; Battle of Gwalior (17–19 June): Sir Hugh Rose defeated mutineers.
- Government of India transferred to the Crown: title of viceroy implemented; Lord Canning becomes first viceroy; East India Company dissolved.
- US treaty with Japan.
- The Fenians (Irish Republican Brotherhood), an Irish-American revolutionary movement founded in the USA.
- Treaty of Aigun: Russia obtains from China a large part of Amur basin.
- Cavour and Napoleon III meet at Plombières.
- Big Ben hour bell cast (10 April).
- First regular public concert by the Halle Orchestra (30 January).
- Opening of Covent Garden Theatre (now the Royal Opera House) in London (15 May).
- Bishop Rock Lighthouse completed.
- First Atlantic cable completed (5 August).
- First meeting of the General Medical Council held (23 November).
- Geologists' Association founded (17 December).
- Launch of the *Great Eastern*, designed by Isambard Kingdom Brunel (31 January).
- London divided into postal districts.
- The Darwin's theory of evolution by natural selection first read to the Linnean Society of London (1 July).
- Discovery of Lake Victoria by John Speke (3 August).
- Discovery of Lake Tanganyika by Burton and Speke.

Deaths

Robert Stephenson, English engineer (12 October)
Robert Owen, Welsh industrialist and social reformer (17 November).

c.1858

- Steel rails first made by the industrialist John Brown.

1859

- Lord Palmerston again prime minister (until 1865).
- Formation of Queensland, Australia, into a separate colony.
- Milosh restored as Prince of Serbia.
- War between Austria and Piedmont: Austria invades Piedmont.
- Italian Wars of Independence: Battle of Montebello (20 May): Austrians defeated by Piedmontese.
- Battle of Palestro (30 May): Austrians defeated by Piedmontese.
- Battle of Magenta (4 June): French defeat Austrians and free Milan.
- Battle of Melegnano: French defeat Austrians.
- Battle of Solferino (24 June): Austrians defeated by French and Piedmontese.
- Peace of Villafranca between France and Austria; Italy gains Lombardy.
- The duchies declare for union with Piedmont.
- Union of Moldavia and Wallachia under Prince Cuza: joint state becomes known as Romania.
- Spain at war with Morocco.
- Treaty of Zürich completes the Villafranca peace.
- Charles XV becomes king of Sweden and Norway.
- John Brown's attack on Harper's Ferry.
- London Irish Volunteer Rifles formed (25 November).
- Volunteer movement arose in Britain: the Royal Naval Reserve (Volunteers) Act leads to the formation of the Royal Naval Reserve.
- Big Ben into service (31 May).
- Closure of Vauxhall Gardens in London (opened *c.*1661).
- Corps of Commissionaires founded by Sir Edward Walter for employment of ex-soldiers (13 February).
- Dr Elizabeth Blackwell becomes first US registered woman doctor.
- The district nursing movement introduced in Britain by William Rathbone.
- First Cruft's dog show held in Newcastle.
- *Chambers's Encyclopaedia* founded by William Chambers (completed 1868).
- First publication of Darwin's *Origin of Species*, *On Liberty* by John Stuart Mill, Meredith's *Ordeal of Richard Feverel* and *The Rubáiyát of Omar Khayyám* by Edward Fitzgerald.
- The kinetic theory of gases postulated by James Clerk Maxwell.
- Lake Nyasa (now Lake Malawi) discovered by David Livingstone.

Deaths

Isambard Kingdom Brunel, English civil engineer (15 September).

Thomas de Quincey, English author.

Alexis de Tocqueville, French author.

1860

- Lords reject repeal of paper duties: Gladstone overcomes their opposition.
- Maori Wars begin in New Zealand (ended 1870).
- Commercial Treaty between Britain and France negotiated by Richard Cobden.
- Treaty of Tientsin ends war in China: more ports opened.
- Abraham Lincoln elected US President.
- Secession of Southern States: Civil War in US begins.
- Tuscany and Emilia declare for union with Piedmont.
- Treaty of Turin between France and Piedmont: France given Nice and Savoy.
- Revolution in Sicily: Garibaldi lands.
- Battle of Calatafimi: Garibaldi's victory.
- Garibaldi enters Palermo.
- Battle of Milazzo: Garibaldi victorious.
- Garibaldi invades Italy: enters Naples, from which Francis II had fled.
- Piedmontese army in kingdom of Naples.
- Naples and Sicily vote for annexation to Piedmont.
- Meeting of Garibaldi and Victor Emmanuel II: former salutes latter as King of Italy.
- Marches and Umbria vote for annexation to Piedmont.
- The Liberal Decrees in France.
- Michael becomes Prince of Serbia.
- Launch of HMS *Warrior*, the first British iron-clad warship (29 December).
- Aberdeen University formed by the amalgamation of King's College and Marischal College.
- Foundation by Florence Nightingale of the first British training school for nurses at St Thomas's Hospital, London.
- Ruskin completes *Modern Painters*.
- First transportation by sea of petroleum from the USA to Europe arrives in London.
- Foundation of the Institution of Naval Architects.
- Introduction of trams into England, at Birkenhead (30 August).
- Linoleum invented by Frederick Walton.
- An incandescent electric lamp invented by Swan.
- Centre of Australia first reached by John McDouall Stuart.
- Last bare-knuckle prize fight held in England (17 April).

1861

- Death of Prince Albert, the Prince Consort, from typhoid (14 December).
- Bahrain becomes British protectorate.
- France, Britain and Spain intervene in Mexico.
- American Civil War. Confederate States constituted in southern US: Jefferson Davis President. Fort Sumter capitulates to the Confederates: first shot in American Civil War. Battle of Bull Run: Northern army defeated by Confederates.
- William I becomes King of Prussia.
- Fall of Gaeta.
- First manifesto of serf emancipation in Russia.
- Kingdom of Italy proclaimed (17 May).
- Lebanon constitution.
- Abdul Aziz becomes Sultan of Turkey.
- Luiz I King of Portugal.
- Debate at Oxford University on Darwin's theory of natural selection between Thomas Huxley ('Darwin's Bulldog' (for), and Bishop Wilberforce (against).
- Introduction of the Post Office Savings Bank (16 September).
- Completion of publication (began 1849) of Lord Macaulay's *History of England*.
- Publication of *The Golden Treasury* anthology by Palgrave.
- Discovery of the metallic element thallium by William Crookes.
- Invention by Joseph Reade of Reade's kettledrum, a condenser for the microscope.
- The study of colloidal chemistry initiated by Thomas Graham.
- Gold found in the Otago, New Zealand.
- First British Golf Open championship held at Prestwick (26 September).

Deaths

Elizabeth Barrett Browning, English poet, in Florence (30 June).
Count Camillo Cavour, Italian statesman.

1862

- American Civil War. Battle of Shiloh: Confederates defeated by Halleck. Second Battle of Bull Run: Confederates under Lee defeat Northern army. Battle of Antietam: Confederates under Lee and Northern army under McClellan: drawn.
- French troops enter Mexico: Maximilian of Austria proclaimed emperor.
- Seven Days' Battles: Federal victories.
- Garibaldi at Palermo.
- *The Alabama* sets out from Britain.
- Garibaldi invades southern Italy.
- Battle of Aspromonte: Garibaldi defeated and taken prisoner.
- Montenegrin war ended by Convention of Scutari.
- Bismarck becomes Prussian minister.
- Lincoln's first Emancipation Proclamation.
- King Otho deposed in Greece.
- Battle of Fredericksburg: Northern army under Burnside completely defeated.
- British Honduras (now Belize) declared a British colony.
- Cotton famine in Lancashire.
- Land registry established (reformed 1875; now operating under Land Registration Acts 1925-88).
- First Lambeth Bridge in London opened.
- Speke and Grant discover sources of the River Nile.

Deaths

Henry David Thoreau, US author.

1863

- Marriage of the Prince of Wales (later Edward VII) and Princess Alexandra of Denmark (10 March).
- Fenian Secret Society founded in Ireland to set up Irish republic.
- First Ashanti War begins (ended 1864).
- American Civil War. Battle of Murfreesborough: Confederates defeated by Rosecrans. Battle of Chancellorsville: Lee defeats Northern army under Hooker: Stonewall Jackson killed. Battle of Gettysburg: Lee defeated by Northern army under Meade. Vicksburg captured for the North by Ulysses S. Grant. Battle of Chickamauga: Northern army defeated in fierce battle. Battle of Chattanooga: Confederates defeated by Grant.
- Uprising in Poland against Russia.
- Ismail Pasha succeeds in Egypt.
- New constitution proclaimed for Schleswig and Holstein: indignation in Germany.
- Prince William of Schleswig-Holstein elected king of Greece as George I.
- Christian IX becomes king of Denmark.
- Saxon and Hanoverian troops invade Holstein.
- Broadmoor criminal lunatic asylum opened (27 May).
- Carbolic first used as a disinfectant by Lister.
- Opening (10 January) of the first underground railway, the Metropolitan Railway in London between Paddington and Farringdon Street.
- English Football Association formed (26 October).
- The world's first heavyweight boxing championship held (8 December).

Deaths

Ferdinand Delacroix, French painter.
William Thackeray, English novelist (24 December).

1864

- American Civil War. Battles of the Wilderness and Spotsylvania: indecisive struggles between Lee and Grant. Battle of Cold Harbour: Grant defeated by Lee. Battle of Franklin: Confederates under Hood crushingly defeated. Battle of Nashville: Hood defeated by Northern army under Thomas.
- Sherman captures Savannah.
- Britain cedes the Ionian Islands to Greece.
- War declared against Denmark by Prussia and Austria.
- Russia completes subjugation of the Caucasus.
- Geneva Convention regarding sick and wounded in war.
- End of Taiping Rebellion in China.
- Danish government hands over Schleswig and Holstein to Prussia and Austria.
- Atlanta captured by Sherman.
- Pius IX issued the Bull Quanta Cura and the Syllabus: Papal war against modern enlightenment and progress.
- Café Royal founded in London (bombed 1940).
- International Working Men's Association founded in London.
- Building of Albert Memorial, Hyde Park, begins (completed 1876).
- Opening of the Clifton Suspension Bridge, Bristol (8 December).
- Cotton's knitting frame invented by William Cotton.
- First publication of *British Pharmacopoeia.*
- The existence of electromagnetic waves established by James Clerk Maxwell.
- Lake Albert Nyanza discovered by Sir Samuel Baker.

Deaths

John Clare, English poet.

1865

- Birth of a second son (later George V) to the Prince of Wales (later Edward VII) and Princess Alexandra (3 June).
- Death of Lord Palmerston (18 October). Russell becomes prime minister.
- American Civil War. Richmond evacuated by the Confederates. Lee surrenders at Appomattox: end of American Civil War.
- Assassination of Lincoln: Andrew Johnson becomes US President.
- Thirteenth Amendment of US Constitution abolishes slavery.
- Convention of Gastein between Prussia and Austria.
- Leopold II King of the Belgians.
- Russia acquires Tashkent.
- Red Flag Act introduces the first road speed limit (5 July).
- Foundation of the Salvation Army by William Booth (2 July).
- Publication of *Alice's Adventures in Wonderland* by Lewis Carroll, illustrated by Tenniel.
- Building begins on Blackfriars Bridge, London (completed 1869).
- Completion of the metropolitan drainage system in London (began 1855), carried out by Joseph Bazalgette.
- The Matterhorn first climbed by Edward Whymper (13 July).

1866

- Russell retires following defeat on his franchise bill (June). Gladstone introduces a Reform Bill: the Adullamites helpes the Conservatives to defeat it: Derby ministry follows Russell's resignation.
- Habeas Corpus Act suspended in Ireland.
- Isle of Man gains home rule.
- Jamaica established as a British colony. The Gambia incorporated in the West African settlements.
- Howard League for Penal Reform founded in memory of John Howard.
- Treaty between Prussia and Italy.
- Austria declares war against Prussia.
- Italy declares war against Austria.
- Battle of Custozza: Italians defeated by Austrians.
- Battle of Lissa: naval defeat of Italians by Austrians.
- Hanoverians capitulate to Prussia.
- Battle of Königgrätz (Sadowa): Austrians under Benedek defeated by Prussians.
- Preliminaries of Nikolsburg between Austria and Prussia.
- Treaty of Prague between Prussia and Austria ends Seven Weeks' War.
- Treaty of Vienna between Austria and Italy: Italy obtains Venetia.
- Prince Charles becomes ruler of Romania.
- French withdraw from Rome.
- First Atlantic telegraph cable successfully laid by the SS *Great Eastern* (completed 7 September).
- Foundation of the Royal Aeronautical Society (as the Aeronautical Society of Great Britain; name changed 1919).
- Invention of the submarine torpedo by Robert Whitehead.
- Last major epidemic of cholera in England.
- London Salvage Corps founded.
- 'Black Friday' in London: financial crisis.

1867

- Resignations of ministers because of Disraeli's Reform Bill.
- Second Reform Act passed as moulded by the Liberal majority. Electoral franchise doubled to over two million.

- Abyssinian Expedition begun by British troops from India (ended 1868).
- British North America Act (1 July) creates Dominion of Canada: beginning of federation in the Empire. Nova Scotia and Ontario become Provinces.
- Fenian (Irish Republican Brotherhood) attacks in London, Manchester, etc.
- Turkey agrees to withdraw her garrisons from Serbia.
- French withdraw from Mexico.
- Luxembourg made neutral.
- Title of Khedive granted by Sultan to the Viceroy of Egypt.
- Maximilian shot in Mexico.
- North German Confederation formed.
- Russia sells Alaska to US.
- Battle of Mentana: French help to defeat Garibaldi.
- Barnardo's Homes founded by Dr Thomas Barnardo.
- First Lambeth Conference of Anglican bishops convened.
- Karl Marx's *Das Kapital,* is published.
- Louisa May Alcott's *Little Women,* is published.
- First operation under antiseptic conditions performed by Lister in Glasgow (18 June).
- Building of Albert Hall, Kensington, in memory of Prince Albert begins (completed 1871).
- First demonstruation of dynamite by Alfred Nobel in Surrey (14 July).
- Initiation of the Queensberry Rules for boxing with gloves, by Lord Queensberry.

Deaths

Charles Pierre Baudelaire, French poet.
J.A.D. Ingres, French painter.

1868

- Disraeli becomes prime minister on Derby's retirement: defeated on question of disestablishing Irish Church.
- General election in Britain: Liberal triumph: Gladstone's first ministry (9 December, until 1874).
- Formation of the Trades Union Congress (TUC). First Congress held 2–6 June.
- President Andrew Johnson impeached in US: Ulysses S. Grant elected President.
- Shogunate abolished in Japan: Mikado resumes the government.
- Prince Michael of Serbia assassinated: Milan becomes prince.
- Treaty between Russia and Bokhara giving Samarkand to former.
- Isabella II dethroned in Spain.
- Hungarian autonomy established.
- Foundation of St Catherine's Society, Oxford University.
- Last public execution held in London (26 May).
- Foundation of the Press Association in London (29 June).
- First publication of *Whitaker's Almanack* by Joseph Whitaker (10 December).
- Publication of *The Moonstone* by Wilkie Collins.
- Development of the theory of radio waves (discovered by Hertz) by James Clerk Maxwell.
- Helium discovered spectroscopically by Joseph Lockyer.
- Invention of photochromolithography by William Griggs.
- Opening of the Metropolitan District Railway in London between Mansion House and South Kensington.

1869

- Government passes the Disestablishment Act to disestablish and disendow the Church of Ireland.
- Annexation of the Nicobar Islands in the Bay of Bengal by Britain.
- Red River Rebellion in Canada under Louis Riel begins: suppressed by Wolseley in 1870.
- Archibald Tait becomes archbishop of Canterbury (until 1882).
- Buchan's days weather predictions defined by Alexander Buchan.
- First publication of *Nature* periodical edited by Joseph Lockyer.
- Foundation of the Metaphysical Society by Sir James Knowles.
- Introduction of the term 'agnostic' by Thomas Huxley.
- Opening of Girton College, Cambridge, as the College for Women (16 October). Acquired present name and site in 1872.
- Opening of the Suez Canal (17 November).
- Telegraph monopoly given to the Post Office.
- The Labour Representation League (one of the forerunners of the Labour Party) organized.

Deaths

Hector Berlioz, French composer.

1870

- Bankruptcy Act: abolished imprisonment for debt.
- Education Act for England and Wales: primary education compulsory.
- Ending of the Maori Wars in New Zealand (began 1860).
- Home Rule for Ireland League founded by Isaac Butt.
- Irish Land Act.
- Red River Rebellion in Canada under Louis Riel: suppressed by Wolseley.

- Manitoba, formerly the Red River Colony, admitted to the Dominion of Canada (12 May).
- Ollivier ministry in France.
- Bismarck modifies the Ems telegram.
- Franco-Prussian War. France declares war (14 July): beginning of Franco-Prussian War. Battle of Wörth: Macmahon defeated by Crown Prince Frederick. Battle of Spicheren: French defeated. Battle of Colombey: German failure: battle drawn. Battle of Vionville: drawn. Battle of Gravelotte: Bazaine defeated. Battle of Sedan: Capitulation of French army under Macmahon: the emperor a prisoner.
- French troops finally abandon Rome: Rome occupied by Italian troops and becomes capital of the kingdom.
- Republic proclaimed in France.
- Revolution in Paris: Provisional government of National Defence.
- Bulgarian Exarchate established.
- Leopold of Hohenzollern accepts offer of Spanish crown: candidature soon withdrawn: France insists on promise not to renew it.
- Capitulation of Bazaine in Metz.
- Russia denounces Black Sea clauses of Treaty of Paris.
- Germans driven out of Orleans, but re-occupy it later.
- Prim assassinated in Madrid.
- Amadeo I King of Spain.
- Formation of the Old Catholics religious movement (until 1871).
- Disestablishment and disendowment of the Church of Ireland.
- Keble College, Oxford, erected in memory of John Keble.
- Institute of Accountants (later Institute of Chartered Accountants) in England and Wales founded.
- Introduction of the postcard and the halfpenny postage stamp (1 October).
- Foundation of the Red Cross Society in Britain (4 August).
- America's Cup first competed for by yachts. American *Magic* defeat British *Cambria* (8 August).

Deaths

Charles Dickens, English novelist (9 June).

1871

- German Empire created at Versailles.
- Bombardment of Paris: capitulation.
- Battle of Le Mans: Germans defeat Chanzy.
- Armistice between France and Germany.
- Bourbaki's army disarmed in Switzerland.
- National Assembly at Bordeaux: ratifies peace and deposes Napoleon III.
- Paris Commune set up: notable buildings destroyed.
- Treaty of Frankfort between France and Germany.
- Treaty of Washington: Alabama claims submitted to arbitration.
- Paris Commune suppressed with great cruelty.
- Thiers becomes president of the French Republic.
- Legal recognition of trade unions in Britain (29 June).
- British Columbia becomes a Province of the Dominion of Canada.
- Conference of London modifies Treaty of Paris of 1856.
- Infantry rank of ensign and cavalry rank of cornet abolished.
- Foundation of the Institution of Electrical Engineers (as The Society of Telegraph Engineers).
- The Tichborne Claimant: beginning of Arthur Orton's claim of the Tichborne inheritance.
- Institution of the practice of photographing prisoners (2 November).
- Abolition of religious tests at Oxford University.
- Publication completed of *Encyclopaedia Britannica* (began 1768) and *Middlemarch* by George Eliot (began 1870).
- Bank Holiday Act (25 May); first bank holiday held on Whit Monday (29 May).
- Opening of the Royal Albert Hall by Queen Victoria (29 March).
- Meeting of Stanley and Livingstone at Ujiji (10 November).
- Foundation of the Rugby Union (26 January).

Deaths

Sir John Herschel, English astronomer (11 May).

1872

- Ballot Act passed: made voting by secret ballot compulsory.
- Self-government in Cape Colony.
- Education Act for Scotland.
- League of the Three Emperors.
- Oscar II King of Sweden and Norway.
- Geneva award in Alabama case.
- Rebellion against Spain in the Philippines.
- College erected in Aberystwyth.
- The ship *Mary Celeste* found derelict in the Atlantic (5 December).
- C. P. Scott becomes editor of the *Manchester Guardian* (until 1929).
- Unveiling of the Albert Memorial in London (1 July).

Deaths

Grillparzer, Austrian dramatist.

Samuel F.B. Morse, US inventor.

1873

- Second Ashanti War begins (ends 1874).
- Foundation of Oxford University Observatory.
- Abdication of Amadeo in Spain: Republic proclaimed.
- Russia takes Khiva.
- The Kulturkampf in Germany.
- Macmahon president in France.
- German troops evacuate France after indemnity had been paid.
- Formation of the Scottish Football Association (13 March).

Deaths

Livingstone, Scottish explorer and missionary, in Africa (1 May).

Sir Edwin Landseer, English painter (1 October).

*c.*1873

- Badminton first played in England.

1874

- Second Ashanti War. Battle of Amoaful (31 January): Ashantis defeated by British forces under Sir Garnet Wolseley; Kumasi captured from Ashanti and Gold Coast established as a British colony.
- Disraeli becomes prime minister after a general election (until 1880).
- Patronage Act repealed in Scotland.
- Fiji becomes a British colony (until 1970).
- New Federal Constitution for Switzerland.
- Treaty between Germany and Russia.
- Alfonso XII King of Spain.
- Leeds University founded (granted university status 1904).
- Tichborne Claimant: end of Orton's trial for perjury (he is imprisoned until 1884).
- Invention of the safety bicycle by H. J. Lawson.

1875

- Insurrection in Herzegovina.
- Britain annexes the Fiji Islands.
- Russia obtains Sakhalin.
- Treaty between Japan and Korea.
- Foundation of the Universal Postal Union in Bern (9 October).
- Birmingham University founded as Mason College by Sir Josiah Mason.
- Mrs Emma Anne Paterson becomes the first woman to be admitted to the Trade Union Congress.
- First intelligible telephone communication made by Bell (5 June).
- First observation of the photoelectric property of selenium by Willoughby Smith.
- English Channel first swum by Captain Matthew Webb (25 August).
- Western Australia first reached overland by Ernest Giles at his third attempt.

1876

- Queen Victoria proclaimed Empress of India under the terms of Disraeli's Royal Titles Act.
- Disraeli buys Khedive's shares in Suez Canal for Britain. International control begins in Egypt.
- Rutherford Hayes elected US President.
- Russia annexes Khokand.
- Bulgarian massacres.
- Serbia declares war against Turkey.
- Murad V becomes Sultan on deposition of Abdul Aziz: soon replaced by Abdul Hamid II.
- Bristol University founded as University College (granted Royal Charter 24 May 1909).
- Regulation of vivisection established by law.
- The British medical profession opened up to women through the efforts of Sophia Jex-Blake.
- Telephone patented by Bell.
- The Plimsoll Line, devised by Samuel Plimsoll, comes into force to establish the limit to which a ship may be loaded.
- Manchester November Handicap horse race first run 1876.

Deaths

George Sand, French author.

1877

- Britain annexes Transvaal.
- The Indian Empire proclaimed.
- Russo-Turkish War begins.
- Romania declared independent.
- Siege and capture of Plevna.
- Satsuma rebellion in Japan.
- Porfirio Diaz becomes President of Mexico.
- Great Indian famine.
- Library Association of the United Kingdom established.
- New Forest scheduled as a National Park.
- Formation of the Ambulance Association (later St John's Ambulance Brigade) by the Red Cross (24 June).
- Cleopatra's Needle taken from Egypt to London by Sir Erasmus Wilson.
- Foundation of *Truth* magazine.
- Publication of *Black Beauty* by Anna Sewell.
- Stanley explores the Congo.
- First day of first Wimbledon lawn tennis championships (9 July).

Deaths

Gustave Courbet, French painter.

1878

- Second Afghan War begins (ends in 1880); British

- defeated Aghans guarding the Peiwar Kotal Pass (2 December).
- Cyprus placed under British administration by Turkey (12 July).
- Humbert I King of Italy.
- Russians take Adrianople: Montenegrins take Antivari, Dulcigno, etc.
- Leo XIII becomes Pope.
- Austria occupies Bosnia and Herzegovina.
- Treaty of San Stefano between Russia and Turkey.
- Treaty of Berlin replaces Treaty of San Stefano: Serbia and Romania independent; Bulgaria autonomous; Macedonia restored to Turkey.
- Dog licences required in Britain by Act of Parliament.
- Cleopatra's Needle erected on the Embankment in London (12 September).

c.1878

- Introduction of the Axminster and Wilton carpet into Britain from USA.

1879

- First Zulu War. Battle of Isandhlwana (22 January): overwhelming defeat of British troops and Natal volunteers by Zulus; Battle of Rorke's Drift (22–23 January): Zulu attack defeated; Battle of Inhlobane Mountain (28 March): British attack on Zulus defeated; Battle of Kambula (29 March): Zulu attack on British defeated; Battle of Ulundi (4 July): British defeated Zulus; Cetewayo captured (28 August).
- Second Afghan War. Battle of Ahmed Khel: attack on British force repulsed; Battle of Charasiab (6 October): British attack on and defeat of Afghan force.
- Abolition of outlawry in Britain.
- Irish Land League founded by Michael Davitt.
- Prince Alexander first prince of Bulgaria.
- Alliance of Austria and Germany.
- Grévy president in France.
- Dual control in Egypt: Britain and France.
- Collapse of the Tay railway bridge carrying the Edinburgh to Dundee train (28 December); ninety people killed.
- Foundation of Sheffield University (as Firth College) by Mark Firth.
- Foundation of Somerville College, Oxford, in memory of Mary Somerville, St Anne's College, Oxford, and Lady Margaret Hall, Oxford.
- John Henry Newman created a cardinal (converted to Catholicism 1845).
- First publication of the *Liverpool Echo* (27 October).
- Henry George's *Progress and Poverty*.
- Reconstruction of Sadler's Wells Theatre.
- Incandescent electric lamp patented by Edison.
- Invention of an apparatus for determining the flashpoint of petroleum by Frederick Abel.

1880

- Gladstone prime minister (until 1885) after a general election.
- Captain Boycott, Lord Erne's English land agent in Co. Mayo 'boycotted' (from 24 September).
- Revolt of Boers in the Transvaal.
- Second Afghan War. Battle of Maiwand (27 July): British defeated; Battle of Kandahar (1 September): British victory under Lord Roberts ends war.
- Britain recognizes Abdurrahman as Amir of Afghanistan.
- James Garfield elected US President.
- Turkey cedes part of Thessaly to Greece.
- Montenegro obtains Dulcigno.
- Greenwich Mean Time made legal time for Britain.
- Institute of Chartered Accountants chartered.
- Publication begins of the *St James's Gazette* newspaper (absorbed by the *Evening Standard* 1905).
- First telephone directory in Britain issued (15 January).
- The volcanic mountain Chimborazo in Ecuador first climbed by Edward Whymper.
- Amateur Athletic Association founded.

Deaths

George Eliot, English novelist (22 December).
Jacques Offenbach, French composer.

1881

- First Boer War. Battle of Lang's Neck (28 January): British attack on Boers defeated; Battle of Ingogo (8 February): British attack on Boers defeated; Battle of Majuba Hill (27 February): British defeated by Boers; Transvaal independence recognized.
- North Borneo made a British protectorate.
- Revolt in Egypt against the British and French over the Suez Canal; Alexandria bombarded by British fleet and Egyptian forts destroyed (11–12 July).
- Irish Land Act.
- Revolt of the Mahdi in the Sudan.
- Murder of Tsar Alexander II: Alexander III succeeds.
- France occupies Tunis.
- Murder of President Garfield: Chester Arthur becomes president of US.
- Gambetta chief minister in France.
- Romania declares itself a kingdom.
- French protectorate on Upper Niger.
- Introduction of postal orders in Britain (1 January).
- Nottingham University opened as University College (achieved university status 1948).
- Foundation of *TitBits* periodical by George Newnes.
- *The Evening News* newspaper founded (absorbs *The Star* 1960).
- Electric light first used domestically in Britain.
- First electric power station in England opened at Goldalming.

Deaths

Thomas Carlyle, Scottish historian and writer (5 February).

Benjamin Disraeli, Earl of Beaconsfield, English statesman (19 April). That day named Primrose Day because of Disraeli's fondness for the flower.

Fyodor Mikhailovich Dostoyevsky, Russian novelist.

1882

- Triple Alliance formed: Austria, Germany and Italy.
- St Kitts-Nevis and Anguilla made a British colony (until 1967).
- Ireland. Phoenix Park murders in Dublin: the murder of the newly appointed chief secretary for Ireland, Lord Frederick Cavendish, and of the permanent undersecretary, Thomas Henry Burke, by Irish patriots (6 May). 'Kilmainham Treaty' between Gladstone and Parnell (May).
- Egyptian Revolt. Battle of Kassassin (28 August): British defeated Egyptian attack; British fleet bombards Alexandria; Britain occupied the Suez Canal Zone (until 1955); Battle of Tel-el-Kebir: Wolseley defeated Arabi Pasha.
- Serbia declares itself a kingdom.
- War between Serbia and Bulgaria.
- Arabi Pasha Egyptian minister: national revolt against misgovernment.
- Hague Convention established a three-mile limit for territorial waters.
- Foundation of Selwyn College, Cambridge, in memory of the first bishop of New Zealand, George Selwyn.
- Foundation of the London Polytechnic by Quintin Hogg.
- Foundation of the Royal University of Ireland in Dublin (superseding the Queen's University in Ireland).
- Foundation of the Society for Psychical Research.
- Term 'telepathy' coined by Frederick Myers.
- Foundation of the Church Army by Rev. Wilson Carlile.
- Foundation of the *Dictionary of National Biography* by George Smith (first published 1885-1901).
- The fourth Eddystone Lighthouse completed.
- Gold found at Barberton, South Africa.
- Institution of 'the Ashes' in cricket.

Deaths

Charles Darwin, English naturalist (19 April).

Anthony Trollope, English novelist (6 December).

Ralph Waldo Emerson, US poet.

Henry Wordsworth Longfellow, US poet.

1883

- Foundation of the Primrose League, British Conservative organization by Lord Randolph Churchill.
- Married Women's Property Act becomes law.
- Sir Edward Sullivan becomes Lord Chancellor of Ireland (until 1885).
- Sudan Campaign. Egyptian force under General Hicks massacred by Mahdists at Kashgal (3 November); British withdraws from Sudan.
- French protectorate in Annam.
- Treaty of Ancon (20 October).
- Foundation of the Fabian Society.
- Germany begins national insurance.
- Inland parcel post begins in Britain (1 August).
- The Boys' Brigade founded in Glasgow by William Smith (4 October).
- Publication of *Treasure Island* by Robert Louis Stevenson.
- Artificial silk made by Sir Joseph Wilson Swan.
- Discovery of gold-bearing lode in Transvaal.
- The Eclipse Stakes horse race first run at Sandown Park.

Deaths

Gustave Doré, French artist.

Edouard Manet, French painter.

Karl Marx, German social and political theorist, in London (14 March).

Ivan Turgenev, Russian novelist.

Richard Wagner, German composer.

1884

- Third Reform Act (followed by redistribution next year).
- British Somaliland made a British protectorate (until 1960).
- Convention of London between Britain and the Transvaal: Boer independence strengthened.
- Establishment of British protectorate over Papua, southern area of Papua New Guinea.
- Berlin Conference of the Powers regarding Africa.
- Sir Evelyn Baring (Lord Cromer) becomes consul-general in Egypt.
- Sudan Campaign. Mahdist siege of General Gordon's garrison in Khartoum begins; British defeated Mahdists at Battle of Tamai (13 March) and Battle of Trinkitat or El Teb (29 March).
- Three Emperors' League revived.
- Russia annexes Merv.
- Germany and Britain appropriate parts of New Guinea.
- French in Tonkin.
- Berlin Conference of the Powers regarding Africa.
- Stephen Grover Cleveland elected US president.
- Greenwich Mean Time made prime meridian of the world.
- Foundation of the National Society for the Preven-

tion of Cruelty to Children (NSPCC) by Rev. Benjamin Waugh.
- The term 'Industrial Revolution' for the period of 1760 to 1840 coined by Arnold Toynbee.
- Completion of Revised Version of the Bible.
- Artificial leather first manufactured in Britain.
- Invention of a steam turbine to drive a high-speed electric generator by Charles Parsons.
- Three-wheeled motorcycle built by Edward Butler.
- Gold found at Witwatersrand, South Africa.

1885
- Salisbury becomes prime minister (until 1886).
- Bechuanaland becomes a British protectorate.
- Indian National Congress founded.
- Lord Roberts becomes commander-in-chief India (until 1893).
- Riel's Second Rebellion in Canada under Louis Riel: rebels withstood attack at Battle of Fish Creek (24 April); Battle of Batoche (9–12 May): rebels defeated; Riel executed.
- Sudan Campaign. Battle of Abu Klea (17 January): British troops withstood attack by a Mahdist force; Battle of Gubat or Abu Kru (19 January): British troops withstand Mahdist attack to reach the Nile; fall of Khartoum (26 January): General Gordon, governor of the Sudan (from 1877) killed; Battle of Kirbekan (10 February): British attack and defeat Mahdist-held heights of Kirbekan; Battle of Hashin (20 March): British defeat of Mahdist army; Battle of Tofrek (22 March): Mahdist attack on British and Indian troops failed.
- Congo Free State constituted by the Powers.
- Russians and Afghans in conflict at Penjdeh.
- Treaty of Tientsin between France and China.
- Regency of Maria Christina in Spain.
- Italians occupy Massowah.
- Bulgaria absorbs eastern Roumelia.
- Serbia declares war against Bulgaria and suffers defeat.
- Daimler invents his petrol engine.
- Foundation of Toynbee Hall in London in memory of Arnold Toynbee.
- First performance of *The Mikado* by Gilbert and Sullivan.
- Publication of *King Solomon's Mines* by H. Rider Haggard.
- Manganese steel discovered by Robert Hadfield.
- Rover 'safety' bicycle appeared.
- Legalization of professional football (20 July).

1886
- Canadian Pacific Railway completed.
- Gladstone becomes prime minister. He introduces his first Home Rule for Ireland Bill: defeated in Commons.
- Salisbury again prime minister (until 1892).
- Royal Niger Company formed.
- The Plan of Campaign in Ireland.
- Britain annexes Upper Burma.
- Alfonso XIII born to be king of Spain.
- Treaty of Bucharest settles Serbo-Bulgarian War.
- Abdication of Prince Alexander in Bulgaria: Stambuloff the leading statesman.
- Refoundation at Oxford University of Mansfield College (formerly Spring Hill College, Birmingham).
- The game of bridge is played in England.
- Cruft's dog show first held in London (10 March).
- Publication of *Little Lord Fauntleroy* by Frances Hodgson Burnett.
- Construction completed (began 1873) of the Severn tunnel.
- Official opening of the Mersey railway tunnel by the Prince of Wales (20 January).
- The *Gluckauf*, prototype of an oil tanker, built on Tyneside.
- Gold rush in the Transvaal, South Africa.
- The present Hockey Association formed.

1887
- The Labour Electoral Association (one of the forerunners of the Labour Party) formed by the TUC.
- First Colonial Conference of the prime ministers of dominions.
- The Maldives in the Indian Ocean came under British protection.
- Prince Ferdinand elected ruler of Bulgaria.
- Treaty between France and China.
- Marie François Carnot president in France.
- Jubilee of Queen Victoria.
- Opening of the second Tay Bridge, the longest railway bridge in Britain (20 June).

1888
- Foundation of the Scottish Labour Party by Keir Hardie.
- British protectorate declared over parts of Borneo, Brunei.
- The Gambia again made an independent British Crown Colony.
- Signature of convention on Suez Canal.
- Christmas Island annexed by Britain.
- Parnell Commission to investigate Parnell's authorship of a letter in *The Times* playing down the Phoenix Park murders. Vindication of Parnell.
- William Henry Harrison elected US President.
- Frederick III German emperor: soon succeeded by William II.
- Treaty between Russia and Korea.

- A series of unsolved murders committed on women in London by 'Jack the Ripper'.
- County Councils created in Britain.
- Gregg's shorthand invented by John Gregg.
- Foundation of *The Star* newspaper (absorbed by *The Evening News* 1960).
- First detection of radio signals.
- The pneumatic tyre perfected by John Boyd Dunlop.
- Formation of the English Football League (22 March). Matches first played 8 September.
- Formation of the Lawn Tennis Association.

1889

- Ministry of Agriculture, Fisheries and Food (formerly Board of Agriculture) formed.
- British South Africa Company formed.
- Charles Stewart Parnell involved in the O'Shea divorce case.
- Abdication of Milan in Serbia: Alexander becomes King.
- Flight of General Boulanger: end of Boulangism in France.
- Franco-Russian entente.
- Pedro II deposed in Brazil: Brazil becomes a Republic.
- Carlos I King of Portugal.
- Treaty between Italy and Abyssinia.
- Foundation of the Museums Association in London.
- Foundation of the Women's Franchise League by Mrs Emmeline Pankhurst.
- Influenza pandemic (until 1890).
- Publication completed (began 1879) of Grove's *Dictionary of Music and Musicians*.
- Publication of *Three Men in a Boat* by Jerome K ;Jerome.
- Lake Edward in Uganda discovered by Sir Henry Stanley.

Deaths

Robert Browning, English poet (12 December).
Wilkie Collins, English novelist (23 September)

1890

- Formal declaration of Zanzibar as a British protectorate following the sultan placing it under British protection.
- Britain cedes Heligoland to Germany.
- Sherman Anti-Trust Act in US.
- Wilhelmina Queen of Holland.
- Fall of Bismarck.
- French protectorate over Madagascar.
- First Japanese Parliament.
- Publication of *The Golden Bough* by Sir James Frazer.
- *The Daily Graphic* newspaper founded (absorbed by *Daily Sketch* 1925).
- First comic paper, *Comic Cuts*, published (17 May).
- Forth Rail Bridge completed (begun 1883) by William Arrol, to designs by John Fowler and Benjamin Baker. Officially opened by the Prince of Wales (4 March).
- Invention of the solid fuel injection principle by Herbert Ackroyd-Stuart.
- Opening of the first electric underground public railway line (City and South London Railway) (18 December) between King William St and Stockwell.

Deaths

Cardinal Newman, English poet and churchman (11 August).

1891

- Agreement between Britain and Portugal regarding East Africa.Nyasaland (now Malawi) constituted as the British Central Africa Protectorate. Establishment of constitutional government in Zanzibar. Foundation of the British colony of Southern Rhodesia by the British South Africa Company.
- Baccarat case tried in June: Prince of Wales gave evidence concerning gambling at Tranby Croft.
- The Baptist Union of Great Britain and Ireland formed.
- Trans-Siberian Railway begun.
- Great famine in Russia.
- Completion of New Scotland Yard by Norman Shaw.
- Foundation of the Romanes Lectures at Oxford University by George Romanes.
- First charity street collection made in Manchester for lifeboats (8 October).
- The Kelmscott Press founded by William Morris (wound up1898).
- Cordite, invented by Abel and Dewar, adopted by the Government.
- Electrification of trams in England begins in Leeds.
- Synthetic rubber first produced by William Tilden.
- Telephone service between London and Paris opened.
- Foundation of the National Sporting Club.

Deaths

Thomas Cook, pioneering English travel agent (18 July)
Georges Seurat, French painter.
Charles Stewart Parnell, Irish politician (6 October).

1892

- Gladstone prime minister (until 1894) after a general election.
- Keir Hardie elected Member of Parliament (until 1895).
- Gilbert and Ellice Islands in the Western Pacific proclaimed a British protectorate (annexed by Britain 1915 and remained a colony until 1975; achieved full independence as Kiribati 1979).
- Grenfell Mission founded in Labrador by Wilfred Grenfell.

- Cleveland again elected US President.
- Indian Councils Act.
- Abbas II becomes khedive of Egypt.
- Panama scandals in France.
- France annexes the Ivory Coast.
- Bibliographical Society founded in London.
- Foundation of Reading University (as the University Extension College).
- Foundation of *The Westminster Gazette* newspaper (absorbed by *The Daily News* 1928).
- Linotype first made in England.
- 'Gentleman Jim' Corbett becomes the first world heavyweight boxing champion under Queensberry Rules (7 September).

Deaths

Alfred, Lord Tennyson, English poet (6 October).

1893

- The Independent Labour Party founded by Keir Hardie.
- Durand Line defining the frontier between India and Afghanistan determined.
- Establishment of the Solomon Islands as a British protectorate (until 1899).
- Gladstone's second Home Rule for Ireland Bill rejected by the Lords.
- Marriage of the Duke of York (later George V) and Princess Mary of Teck (6 July).
- Matabele War in Rhodesia.
- Natal granted responsible government.
- The Gaelic League founded in Dublin.
- Bering Sea arbitration between Britain and the United States.
- New Zealand adopts woman suffrage.
- Foundation of St Hilda's College, Oxford.
- First performance of *The Second Mrs Tanqueray* by Sir Arthur Wing Pinero.
- World's first elevated railway opened at Liverpool (4 February).

1894

- Gladstone resigns: Rosebery becomes prime minister. Harcourt's budget introduced death duties (2 August).
- Birth of a son (later Edward VIII) to Prince George (later George V) and Princess Mary.
- Nicholas II becomes tsar.
- Murder of President Carnot in France: Casimir-Périer elected successor.
- Trial and condemnation of Dreyfus in France.
- Armenian massacres.
- War between Japan and China: latter easily defeated.
- Return of King Milan in Serbia.
- Use permitted of postcards with adhesive stamps.
- British protectorate over Uganda (until 1896).
- Motor vehicles become common.
- First publication of *The Yellow Book* quarterly (until 1897).
- Publication of *The Prisoner of Zenda* by Anthony Hope.
- Official opening by Queen Victoria of the Manchester Ship Canal (21 May, construction began 1887).
- Opening of Tower Bridge in London (30 June).
- The inert gas argon discovered by Lord Lister and Sir William Ramsay.
- Opening of the first Penny Bazaar (Marks and Spencer's) in Manchester (28 September).

Deaths

Oliver Wendell Holmes, US author.
Christina Rossetti, English poet.
Robert Louis Stevenson, Scottish writer, in Samoa (3 December).

1895

- Salisbury again prime minister (until 1902): Conservative victory at general election.
- Chitral Campaign in India. British force defeated Indians at Malakand Pass (3 April).
- Federation of Malaya formed.
- Jameson Raid, Transvaal, led by Dr Leander Starr Jameson (29 December to 2 January 1896): Cecil Rhodes forced to resign as prime minister of South Africa. British ultimatum to the Transvaal.
- Third Ashanti War begins (ends 1900).
- Birth of a second son (later Duke of York and George VI) to Prince George (later George V) and Princess Mary.
- Franco-Russian alliance.
- François Félix Faure president in France.
- Murder of Stambuloff in Bulgaria.
- Armenian massacres.
- X-rays discovered by Röntgen.
- Booksellers Association of Great Britain and Ireland founded as the Associated Booksellers (assumes present name 1948).
- Foundation of the National Trust for places of historic interest or natural beauty.
- First performance of *The Importance of Being Earnest* by Oscar Wilde.
- Foundation of the London Promenade Concerts by Sir Henry Wood (6 October).
- Helium obtained by William Ramsay.
- Wireless telegraphy brought about by Marconi.
- Secession of Rugby League from Rugby Union (as Northern Union; name changed 1922).

Deaths

Friedrich Engels, German political philosopher, in London (5 August).

1896

- Sudan Campaign. Battle of Ferkeh (7 June): Egyp-

tian and British troops under Kitchener defeated Mahdists.
- Franco-British treaty regarding Siam.
- William McKinley elected US president.
- France annexes Madagascar.
- Insurrection in Crete: international intervention.
- Battle of Adowa: Italians heavily defeated in Abyssinia.
- Outbreak of plague in India.
- Foundation by Queen Victoria of the Royal Victorian Order.
- Alfred Austin becomes poet laureate.
- Publication of A *Shropshire Lad* by A. E. Housman.
- *The Daily Mail* newspaper founded by Lord Northcliffe (4 May).
- Alpha and beta rays discovered by Lord Rutherford.
- Marconi patents wireless telegraphy (2 June).
- Gold found in Rabbit Creek in the Klondike, Canada (17 August); beginning of gold rush.

Deaths

Edmund de Goncourt, French author.

1897

- Northwest Frontier Campaign. Revolt of tribes on Indian northwest frontier; Battle of Dargai (20 October): Heights of Dargai stormed by British. Indian frontier rebellion ended.
- Sudan Campaign. Battle of Abu Hamed (7 August): Mahdist troops defeated by Egyptian troops under British officers.
- Queen Victoria's Diamond Jubilee.
- Zululand annexed to Natal (30 December).
- Massacre in Crete: international occupation.
- War between Greece and Turkey: Turkey victorious.
- Autonomy proclaimed for Crete.
- Germany seizes Kiaochow in China.
- Philippine revolt against Spain.
- Constitution of Sheffield University as a university college.
- Foundation of the Royal Automobile Club as the Automobile Club of Great Britain (10 August).
- Official opening of the Tate Gallery (21 July).
- Publication of *Dracula* by Bram Stoker.
- Electron discovered by Joseph John Thomson.
- Invention of the first turbine-propelled ship by Charles Parsons.
- The national standard metre established in Britain.

1898

- Irish Local Government Act.
- Lord Minto made governor-general of Canada (until 1904).
- Sudan Campaign. Battle of Atbara (8 April): British and Egyptian army under Sir Herbert Kitchener defeats Mahdists; Fashoda Incident when French occupies British fort (10 July); Battle of Omdurman (2 September): Kitchener's army defeats Dervishes; Sudan reconquered.
- Britain obtains 99-year lease of Hong Kong from China (9 June). Britain obtains Wei-hai-wei and new territories of Hong Kong on lease from China.
- US declares war against Spain.
- US annexes Hawaii.
- The French under Marchand at Fashoda.
- Dargai stormed: Indian frontier rebellion ended.
- Treaty of Paris between Spain and US: Spain loses all her American possessions and also the Philippines.
- Russia obtains Port Arthur from China.
- Prince George of Greece High Commissioner in Crete.
- Oscar Wilde *The Ballad of Reading Gaol.*
- Henry James *The Turn of the Screw.*
- H. G. Wells *The War of the Worlds.*
- Idea of garden cities introduced into England by Sir Ebenezer Howard.
- Official opening of the Tate Gallery (21 July), founded by Sir Henry Tate.
- Radium isolated by Marie and Pierre Curie; together they work on magnetism and radioactivity.
- Definition by Oliver Lodge of the basic principles of selective radio tuning.
- Discovery of the element xenon and the inert gas krypton by William Ramsay and Morris Travers; the gaseous element neon discovered by Ramsay.

Deaths

Aubrey Beardsley, English illustrator.
Lewis Carroll, English author (14 January)
William Gladstone, British statesman (19 May).

1899

- United Irish League formed.
- Lord Curzon becomes viceroy of India (until 1905).
- The Gulf state of Kuwait becomes a British protectorate.
- Second Boer War (11 October, ended 31 May 1902). *October*: beginning of sieges of the British by the Boers at Mafeking (12) and Kimberley (15); British garrison at Mafeking commanded by Baden-Powell; Battle of Talana Hill or Battle of Dundee, north Natal (20), Boers defeated; Battle of Elandslaagte (21): Boers defeated; British troops prevent Boer attack on forces retreating from Talana Hill (24); Battle of Farquhar's Farm at Ladysmith (29): British defeated by Boers.
November: Siege of British at Ladysmith begins (2); Battle of Graspan or Enslin (25): successful British attack on Boer position; Battle of Modder River (28): Boers defeated by Lord Methuen.

December: Battle of Stormberg (10): British defeated by Boers; Battle of Magersfontein: Boers defeated Methuen (11); Battle of Colenso (15): British attack on Boers failed.

- Battle of the Tugela: Boers defeat Buller.
- Loubet President in France.
- First Peace Conference at The Hague.
- End of Dreyfus affair in France.
- Germany and the US annexe and share Samoa Islands.
- Venezuela boundary question settled.
- The Khalifa defeated and killed in the Sudan.
- Wladyslaw Reymont *The Promised Land*.
- Edward Elgar *Enigma Variations*.
- Foundation of the National Physical Laboratory.
- John Rylands Library founded in Manchester by the widow of John Rylands.
- Revival of morris dancing led by Cecil Sharp who saw a demonstration of it at Headington, Oxford (26 December).
- Gold discovered in Klondyke.

Deaths

Robert Bunsen, German chemist.

Alfred Sisley, French painter.

1900

- Second Boer War. *January*: Boers attack Ladysmith (6); Field Marshal Lord Roberts takes command of British forces (10); Battle of Spion Kop (19–24): Boers defeat General Buller in his second attempt to relieve the siege of Ladysmith.

  February: Battle of Vaalkranz (5–7): Buller's third attempt to break Boer lines failed; Kimberley relieved (15); Battle of Paardeberg (18–27): Boers under Cronje defeated by British under Kitchener and surrender to Lord Roberts; Relief of Ladysmith (28).

  March: Battle of Driefontein (10): British under Roberts defeat Boers; Boers defeated by British at Karee (29); British troops ambushed by Boers at Sanna's Post (31). *April*: British defeated at Battle of Reddersberg (3); British besieged by Boers at Wepener (9); relieved (25).

  May: Relief of Mafeking (17); Annexation of Orange Free State (26); Boer victory at Battle of Lindley (27); unsuccessful British attack on Boers at Senekal (29).

  June: Battle of Diamond Hill (11–12): British attack under Roberts on Boers successful.

  August: Battle of Elands River (4–15): Boer attack on Australians relieved by Kitchener; Battle of Dalmanutha (21–28): British defeat Boers and entered Machadodorp.

  October: Annexation of Transvaal (25).
- The Labour Party founded (as the Labour Representation Committee) in London (27-28 February): present name adopted 1906. Ramsay MacDonald named as its secretary.
- Unionist victory at general election ('Khaki Election', 28 September-16 October).
- Tonga in the South Pacific becomes a British protectorate.
- Victor Emmanuel III King of Italy after assassination of Humbert I.
- World Exhibition opens in Paris.
- William McKinley re-elected as US President.
- Russia annexes Manchuria.
- Royal Niger Company's territories taken over by the Crown. British protectorate over Lagos and Nigeria.
- Boxer Rising: Chinese attack on foreign legations in Peking (13 June and July). Peking taken by international force.
- Charter granted to Birmingham University.
- United Free Church of Scotland founded by union of Free and United Presbyterian Churches.
- Excavations started at Knossos on Crete by Sir John Evans, leading to his discovery of the Minoan Civilization.
- First performance of *The Dream of Gerontius* by Sir Edward Elgar.
- Opening of the Wallace Collection in London.
- Publication of *The Daily Express* begins.
- Central London electric railway opened (27 June).
- Development of the thermionic valve by John Fleming.
- Davis Cup for tennis first competed for (8 August): won by the US.

Deaths

Gottlieb Daimler, German motor car designer.

Sir Charles Grove, British musicologist.

Casey Jones, US railway engineer.

Friedrich Nietzsche, German philosopher.

John Ruskin, British art critic (20 January)

Sir Arthur Sullivan, British composer (22 November)

Oscar Wilde, Irish writer, in Paris (30 November).

1901

- Death of Queen Victoria (22 January): Prince of Wales becomes king as Edward VII. His son George becomes Prince of Wales (later George V).
- Second Boer War. *June*: denunciation of use of concentration camps as prison camps for Afrikaner women and children by Campbell-Bannerman (14).

  October: Boers invade Cape Colony.
- Commonwealth of Australia founded (1 January).
- Britain annexes Ashanti, former West African kingdom, and incorporated it within the colony of the Gold Coast (25 September).

- Northwest Frontier Province of North Pakistan made part of British India (until 1947).
- Taff Vale decision of Lords affecting legal position of trade unions.
- William McKinley assassinated: Theodore Roosevelt becomes US President.
- Philippine revolt suppressed by the US.
- Student rioters in St Petersburg dispersed by Cossacks.
- Peking Treaty ends Boxer Rebellion in China.
- Trans-Siberian Railway opened.
- First Nobel Prizes awarded in fields of literature, chemistry, physics, peace and medicine.
- British Standards Institution founded as the Engineering Standards Committee (incorporated by Royal Charter 1929).
- Launch of the first Royal Navy submarine (2 October).
- Radio signals first sent across the Atlantic by Marconi (from Cornwall to Newfoundland, 12 December).
- Boxing legalized in England.

Deaths

Henri de Toulouse-Lautrec, French painter.

1902

- Resignation of Salisbury: Balfour becomes prime minister (until 1905).
- Empire Day (later Commonwealth Day) first celebrated on Queen Victoria's birthday (24 May).
- Second Boer War. Signature of the Treaty of Vereeniging between Britain and the Boers ends the war (31 May).
- Anglo-Japanese Alliance.
- Treaty between China and Russia over Manchuria.
- Treaty of Vereeniging ends Boer War.
- Aswan dam completed in Egypt.
- Foundation of the Order of Merit by Edward VII (23 June).
- Foundation of Southampton University (gains university status 1952).
- British Academy granted charter (8 August).
- Cancer Research Institute founded.
- Education Act for England and Wales: keen opposition by Nonconformists.
- King Edward VII Land, Antarctica, identified by Robert Scott.
- Coronation Cup horse race first run at Epsom.

Deaths

Friedrich Krupp, German steel magnate.

Cecil Rhodes, South African statesman (26 March). Rhodes Scholarships at Oxford University provided for by his will.

Émile Zola, French writer.

1903

- Chamberlain resigns as Secretary for the Colonies in order to advocate Protection.
- Irish Land Purchase Act.
- Pius X becomes pope.
- King Alexander I and Queen Draga of Serbia murdered: Peter I becomes king.
- Anti-Semitic pogroms in Russia.
- US recognizes Panama as independent republic and leases the Canal Zone.
- Turkish troops massacre Bulgarians in Macedonia.
- Orville and Wilbur Wright fly heavier-than-air aircraft at Kitty Hawk.
- Demolition of Newgate Prison completed (begun 1902).
- First session of Manchester University formally opened (6 October).
- Foundation of the militant Women's Social and Political Union by Mrs Emmeline Pankhurst and Christabel Pankhurst to agitate for votes for women.
- Letchworth, first garden city in England, founded.
- The evidence of fingerprints first used in securing a criminal conviction (13 September).
- Opening of Westminster Cathedral (consecrated 1910).
- Randall Davidson becomes archbishop of Canterbury (until 1928).
- First performance of *Man and Superman* by Bernard Shaw.
- Publication of *The Riddle of the Sands* by Erskine Childers.
- Publication of *The Daily Mirror* begins (2 November).
- British car registration introduced.
- Sugar Convention abolished sugar bounties.
- Commander Robert Falcon Scott and Lieutenant Ernest Shackleton travel farther towards the South Pole than any previous expedition.
- Internal secretion of hormones discovered by William Bayliss and Ernest Starling.

Deaths

Dr Richard Gatling, US rapid-fire gun inventor.

Paul Gaugin, French painter.

Camille Pissarro, French artist.

Herbert Spencer, English philosopher.

James McNeill Whistler, American-born painter (17 July).

1904

- Anglo-French Entente signed, aimed at solving all outstanding grievances.
- Somali Expedition. Battle of Jidballi (10 January): British attack and defeat Somali forces.
- British military expedition to Tibet captures Lhasa (3

August). Anglo-Tibetan Treaty signed giving Britain exclusive trading rights (7 September).
- Dogger Bank incident between Britain and Russia: settled peaceably.
- Triple Entente between England, France and Russia established (until 1917).
- Russo-Japanese War begins.
- US occupation of Cuba ends.
- Theodore Roosevelt wins US presidential election.
- Rebellious tribesmen massacre German settlers in South West Africa.
- Booklets of stamps first issued in Britain (16 March).
- Licensing Act for England and Wales.
- Abbey Theatre, Dublin, founded (burned down 1952, rebuilt 1966).
- First concert of the London Symphony Orchestra.
- First performance of *Peter Pan* by James Barrie.
- Diode valve invented by Sir John Fleming.
- Electrification of the Metropolitan Railway in London between Baker Street and Harrow.
- Northern Underground Line in London opened (as the Great Northern and City Railway).

Deaths

Frederic Bartholdi, French sculptor.
Anton Chekhov, Russian writer.
Antonin Dvoràk, Czech composer.
Theodor Herzl, Hungarian-born Zionist.
Paul Kruger, Boer leader.
Henri Fantin-Latour, French painter.
Friedrich Siemens, German industrialist.
Sir Henry Morton Stanley, British explorer.

1905

- Russo-Japanese War: Japanese capture Port Arthur (5 January); Russians routed by Japanese at Battle of Mukden (10 March); Battle of Tsushima: Russian navy destroyed (28 May); Japanese capture Sakhalin (31 July); Treaty of Portsmouth ends conflict (5 September).
- Russian Grand Duke Sergei killed in bomb attack.
- Earthquake in India claims 10,000 victims.
- Norway separated from Sweden: Haakon VII becomes king of Norway.
- Riots in St Petersburg crushed by Tsarist police (22 January); first workers' soviet formed; sailors mutiny on battleship 'Potemkin' (27 June); revolt by students and workers in Moscow crushed by Tsarist troops (30 December).
- Legal recognition of office of prime minister.
- Liberal leader, Campbell-Bannerman, becomes prime minister.
- Sinn Fein formed by Arthur Griffith (28 November).
- Districts of Alberta and Saskatchewan become Provinces of Canada.
- Lord Minto made viceroy of India (until 1910).
- Dartmouth College (Britannia Royal Naval College) opened.
- Automobile Association founded (26 June).
- Sheffield University gains university status.
- Aldwych Theatre opened.
- Publication of *Kipps* by H. G. Wells.
- Dreadnought warships introduced by Lord Fisher.
- Inauguration of a river steamboat service on the Thames.

Deaths

Dr Thomas John Barnardo, Irish-born doctor and philanthropist (19 September).
Sir Henry Irving, British actor.
Jules Verne, French writer.

1906

- General election in Britain: overwhelming Liberal victory. First Labour Members of Parliament.
- First Duma (elects parliament with limited powers) convened in Russia.
- San Francisco destroyed by earthquake and fire.
- Algeciras Conference on Franco-German crisis over Morocco: dispute settled in favour of France.
- Mount Vesuvius erupts leaving hundreds dead.
- Armand Fallières president in France.
- Frederick VIII becomes king of Denmark.
- Simplon Tunnel opened for railway traffic.
- Self-government granted to Transvaal in South Africa.
- Beginning of construction of Rosyth naval base in Scotland.
- Trades Disputes Act reverses Taff Vale decision.
- Women's suffrage movement in Britain gathers strength.
- *John Bull* magazine founded by Horatio Bottomley (12 May).
- Opening of the Bakerloo Line of the London Underground (10 March) and the Piccadilly Line (15 December).
- Official opening of the Vauxhall Bridge in London (26 May).
- Discovery of vitamins by Frederick G. Hopkins.

Deaths

Pierre Curie, French physicist.
Henrik Ibsen, Norwegian playwright.
Albert Sorel, French historian.

1907

- Earthquake devastates Kingston in Jamaica.
- Lawyer Mahatma Gandhi leads civil disobedience movement ('Satyagraha') in South Africa.
- Second Hague Peace Conference.
- Belgian parliament votes to annexe the Congo and

end absolute rule over the central African territory by King Leopold.
- Gustavus V succeeds Oscar II as king of Sweden.
- Cunard ship *Mauretania*, the world's largest liner, leaves Liverpool on her maiden voyage.
- Cullinan diamond (found in 1905) presented to Edward VII on behalf of the people of Transvaal (9 November).
- Mahatma Ghandi leads civil disobedience movement in South Africa.
- New Zealand declared a Dominion within the British Empire (26 September).
- Self-government granted to Orange River Colony as the Orange Free State.
- Second Hague Peace Conference.
- Territorial and Reserve Forces Act. Inauguration of the Territorial Army at Buckingham Palace (26 October).
- Boy Scout movement, devised by Lord Baden-Powell, begins with first camp in Dorset (August).
- Small Holdings and Allotments Act for England and Wales.
- Foundation of *The Nation* periodical (absorbed into the *New Statesman* 1931).
- First official recognition of taxi cabs.
- The Cunard ship *Mauretania*, the world's largest liner, sailed on her maiden voyage.
- First TT motorycycle race held on the Isle of Man (28 May).
- Brooklands motor racecourse opened (6 July, closed 1939).

Deaths

Edvard Grieg, Norwegian composer.
William Howard Russell, British journalist.
Dmitri Mendeleev, Russian chemist.
William Thomson, Lord Kelvin, British physicist (17 December).

1908

- Carlos I of Portugal and Crown Prince Luiz assassinated: Manuel II becomes king.
- Young Turks revolutionary movement forces Sultan Abdul Hamid II to restore the Turkish constitution.
- Bulgaria declares independence from Ottoman Empire.
- Austria annexes Bosnia-Herzegovina.
- Over 200,00 people killed in earthquake in southern Italy and Messina in Sicily, the most violent tremor ever recorded in Europe.
- William Howard Taft elected US President.
- Ford Motor Company produces first 'Model T' motor car.
- In Paris, Henri Farman makes the first aeroplane flight with a passenger.
- King Edward VII visits Russia: the first monarch to do so.
- Resignation of Campbell-Bannerman because of ill health; Asquith becomes prime minister (8 April, until 7 December 1916). Death of Campbell-Bannerman (22 April).
- Mass demonstration of suffragettes in Hyde Park, London.
- Beginning of the London Naval Conference on war at sea (ends 1909).
- Launch of the first British diesel submarine (16 May).
- First woman mayor in England: Elizabeth Garrett Anderson elected mayor of Aldeburgh (9 November).
- Foundation of the National Farmers' Union (10 December).
- Old Age Pensions introduced in Britain.
- British Red Cross Society receives Royal Charter.
- Boy Scouts founded by Lord Baden-Powell.
- Opening of the Public Trustee Office in London.
- Opening of the Rotherhithe to Stepney tunnel under the Thames (12 June).
- Franco-British Exhibition in London.
- Opening of the fourth official modern Olympic Games in London (13 July).
- The first unofficial Olympic Winter Games held in London.
- Publication of *The Wind in the Willows* by Kenneth Grahame.
- Geiger counter invented by Hans Geiger and Lord Rutherford.

Deaths

Henri Becquerel, French physicist.
Joel Chandler Harris, US author.
Nikolai Rimsy-Korsakov, Russian composer.
Rev. Benjamin Waugh, founder of the National Society for the Prevention of Cruelty to Children.

1909

- Radical budget ('People's Budget') introduced by Lloyd George as Chancellor of the Exchequer (April): rejected by the Lords (November). Introduction of a Bill to curb the power of the House of Lords. Trade Boards Act to deal with sweated labour. Osborne Judgment preventing use of trade union funds for political action.
- The Old Age Pensions Act comes into force (1 January).
- Signature of Declaration of London, concerning maritime law.
- Union of South Africa formed.
- Japanese statesman Prince Hirobumi Ito assassinated.

- Deposition of Abdul Hamid II: Mohammed V Sultan.
- North Pole reached by US explorer Commander Robert E. Peary.
- Young Turks celebrate as Turkish parliament forces Sultan Abdul Hamid to abdicate infavour of reformist Mehemet V.
- Port of London Authority established.
- First Rally and Conference of the Boy Scout movement (4 September).
- King's Police Medal instituted by Royal Warrant.
- Queen's College, Belfast, becomes Queen's University, Belfast.
- Foundation of the National University of Ireland in Dublin (31 October), previously the Royal University of Ireland.
- *The Daily Sketch* founded by Edward Hulton.
- First crossing of the English Channel by aeroplane (27 July) by Blériot: rapid development of aviation.
- Trolleybus first used.
- Anglo-Persian Oil Company (now British Petroleum) formed.
- Foundation of US department store Selfridge's in Oxford Street, London, by Gordon Selfridge (15 March).
- South magnetic pole reached by the Shackleton Expedition (16 January).
- Lonsdale Boxing Belt founded by Lord Lonsdale.

Deaths

Geronimo, Apache chief.
George Meredith, British writer (18 May).
John Synge, Irish playwright.

1910

- General election (January): Liberal victory: the Liberals cling on to power as the crisis over the People's Budget and the power of the House of Lords escalate. Lloyd George's budget passed.
- The creation of the Union of South Africa (31 May); creation of the Orange Free State and Transvaal as Provinces of South Africa; merger of Natal in the Union of South Africa.
- Death of Edward VII from bronchitis (6 May): his son becomes king of Britain as George V.
- Japan annexes Korea.
- Montenegro declares itself a kingdom.
- King Manuel overthrown in Portugal: republic proclaimed.
- Constitutional Conference between Government and Opposition regarding Lords' veto: failed.
- Airmail post first organized in Britain.
- Girl Guides Association founded by Sir Robert Baden-Powell.
- Labour Exchanges established in Britain.
- Appearance of Halley's Comet (named after Edmund Halley): first time it is photographed.
- Isotopes first identified by Joseph John Thomson.
- Foundation of Textile Institute in Manchester.
- Captain Robert Falcon Scott sets out on expedition to the South Pole (15 June).

Deaths

Henri Dunant, Swiss founder of the Red Cross.
William Holman Hunt, British painter.
Julia Ward Howe, US women's campaigner.
Robert Koch, German bacteriologist.
Samuel Langhorne Clemens (Mark Twain), US writer.
Florence Nightingale, British nursing pioneer (13 August).
Henri Rousseau, French painter.
Count Leo Tolstoy, Russian writer.
Dr Crippen, hanged for the murder of his wife in London (23 November).

1911

- Andrew Bonar Law chosen to succeed Balfour as leader of the Conservative Party.
- Coronation of George V (23 June).
- Parliament Act passed after King George V agrees to creation of peers on advice of prime minister: absolute veto of Lords ends. National Insurance Act passed (14 December). Payment of Members of Parliament introduced in Britain.
- Ramsay MacDonald elected chairman of the Labour Party to succeed Keir Hardie.
- Zambia unified as Northern Rhodesia.
- Great labour unrest, culminating in a national railway strike.
- Sidney Street Siege: armed troops and police besiege an Anarchist hideout in a house in Sidney Street, London.
- French move to suppress revolt in Morocco.
- Mexican dictator Porfirio Diaz deposed by rebels.
- Assassination of Peter Stolypin, the Russian Premier.
- Italy declares war against Turkey over Italian claim on Tripoli: Tripoli annexed by Italy.
- Chinese revolution: Manchu dynasty overthrown (October); Dr Sun Yat Sen elected president of the new Chinese Republic (December).
- Franco-German Teaty recognizes French demand for protectorate in Morocco.
- Copyright Act establishes protection of an author's work for fifty years after death.
- English Folk Dance Society founded by Cecil Sharp (succeeded 1932 by English Folk Dance and Song Society).
- Development of the self-starter mechanism for cars by Charles Kettering.

- First escalator in England installed at Earls Court Station.
- Invention of the Wilson Cloud Chamber by Charles Wilson.
- Amundsen reaches the South Pole (14 December) ahead of Scott.

Deaths

Sir William Gilbert, British librettist (29 May).
Gustav Mahler, Austrian composer.

1912

- Ireland. Mass rallies in Ulster to protest at proposals for Home Rule for Ireland (January); Third Home Rule for Ireland Bill passed by the Commons (May); 'Solemn Covenant' to oppose Home Rule signed at a mass rally of Ulster loyalists led by Sir Edward Carson (September).
- Welsh Disestablishment Bill introduced: passed through Commons but rejected by Lords.
- Democrat Woodrow Wilson elected US president.
- End of Ching dynasty in China.
- Yoshihito becomes emperor of Japan.
- Right of France to establish a protectorate over Morocco ceded in Fez Treaty.
- Peace of Ouchy between Italy and Turkey signed in Switzerland: Italy acquires Tripoli.
- War between Turkey and the Balkan States: Bulgarian and Serbian forces inflicts a series of defeats on Turkey.
- Establishment of the Royal Flying Corps (14 May).
- Establishment of Queen Alexandra's Day (26 June).
- Frederick Seddon hanged for murder.
- Militant suffragettes riot in the West End of London.
- National strike of coal-miners in Britain: settled by passage of Coal Mines (Minimum Wage) Act which establishes the principle of a minimum wage.
- The *Titanic* sinks in the Atlantic on her maiden voyage (15 April): a loss of 1,513 lives.
- Beginning of National Insurance in Britain (15 July).
- *The Daily Herald* newspaper first published (16 April).
- First Royal Command performance held in London (1 July).
- Announcement of the 'discovery' of Piltdown man (18 December, proved a hoax 1953/55).
- Development of the theory of isotopes by Frederick Soddy.
- First crossing of the English Channel of an aeroplane piloted by a woman, the American Harriet Quimby.
- Identification of the proton unit of positive charge, the hydrogen nucleus of the atom, by Rutherford.
- Discovery in Antarctica of King George V Land by Douglas Mawson and of Queen Mary Land by Captain Davis.
- Robert Scott reaches the South Pole (18 January) but discovers that Amundsen had reached it on 14 December 1911. Scott and his companions die on the return journey.

Deaths

General Booth, founder of the Salvation Army (20 August); he is succeeded as General by his son, William Bramwell Booth.
Lord Lister, British pioneer of antisepsis (10 February).
August Strindberg, Swedish playwright.
Samuel Coleridge-Taylor, British composer.
Jules Massenet, French composer.
Wilbur Wright, US pioneer aviator.

1913

- Young Turks depose government of the Grand Vizier, Kiamil Pasha in Turkey.
- Raymond Poincaré elected president of French Republic.
- King George I of Greece murdered: Constantine I succeeds.
- Treaty of Bucharest settles Balkan wars: increases of territory to Serbia, Greece, Montenegro, Bulgaria and Romania; Turkey loses Macedonia, part of Thrace, Albania and most of the islands; Albanian kingdom founded.
- Panama Canal completed.
- Last renewal of Triple Alliance.
- Second Irish Volunteers formed.
- Introduction of sickness, unemployment and maternity benefit (15 January).
- Bodies of explorers Captain Robert Falcon Scott and companions discovered in the Antarctic.
- Emily Duncan appointed first British woman stipendiary magistrate (16 May).
- Trades Union Act empowered trade unions to raise political fund, safe-guarding rights of minorities.
- Opening of the first Chelsea Flower Show in London (20 May).
- Foundation of the *New Statesman* periodical.

Deaths

Alfred Austin, British poet laureate. Robert Bridges succeeds him as poet laureate.
Rudolf Diesel, German engineer.

- Emily Davison, suffragette, after she throws herself in front of the king's horse during the Derby (4 June).

1914

- World War I (28 July–11 November 1918). *June*: Murder of Archduke Francis Ferdinand, heir to Austrian throne, in Sarajevo, capital of Bosnia (28). *July*: Austria declares war against Serbia (28). *August*: Germany declares war against Russia (l);

Germany declares war against France (3); German invasion of Belgium (4); Britain declares war against Germany in support of France and Belgium (4); British Expeditionary Force lands in France under Sir John French and suffers heavy casualties at the Battle of Mons (20-31); Japan declares war on Germany (23); Battle of Heligoland between British and German fleets (27–28); Russians routed at Battle of Tannenberg on eastern front (31).

September: Germans capture Rheims (5); Battle of the Marne (5-9); trench warfare begins on Aisne salient (13); three British cruisers sunk by a U-boat (22).

October: First Battle of Ypres (12-11 November).

November: Battle of Coronel: British squadron defeated by Germans (1); Britain declares war against Turkey and annexes Cyprus (5); Death of Lord Roberts in France (14).

December: Royal Navy destroys German squadron in the Battle of the Falkland Islands (8); British protectorate over Egypt (17) and Kuwait proclaimed (17). Lord Kitchener becomes British Secretary for War. Germany surrenders Togoland to Britain and French; German areas of Papua New Guinea come under Australian control.

- Buckingham Palace conference on the future of Ireland called by George V.
- Irish Home Rule Act creates a separate parliament in Ireland with some MPs in Westminster. Home Rule Bill and Welsh Disestablishment Bill passed, but operation suspended till end of World War I.
- Mutiny of the Curragh, Ireland (March).
- The Simla Conference of British, Chinese and Tibetan representatives delineated the northeast frontier of India, named after the British representative, Sir Henry McMahon.
- Foundation of Rotary International in Britain.
- Cub Scout movement begins (2 February).
- Formation of the Royal Naval Air Service (23 June).
- First flag day held in England (3 October).

Deaths

Henri Alain-Fournier, French writer.

August Macke, German painter.

Sir John Tenniel, British artist.

1915

- World War I. *January*: institution of the Military Cross (l); Turkish army surrenders to Russians in Central Asia (5); German Zeppelin raid on Norfolk towns (19); British sink German battleship *Blucher* in North Sea (24).

February: German submarine blockade of Britain begins (2); Imperial troops repulse Turkish attack on Suez Canal (2); French begin offensive in Champagne on Western Front (12).

March: Britain declares blockade of German ports (l); Battle of Neuve Chapelle (10-13); naval attack on Dardanelles aborted (22).

April: Second Battle of Ypres (22-25 May); Germans use gas for the first time on the Western Front (22); British, ANZAC and French troops land at Gallipoli (25).

May: sinking of the Cunard liner *Lusitania* (7); Battle of Aubers Ridge (9-25); Italy declares war on Austria (22); British coalition government formed under Asquith (26); first air raid on London (31).

June: British pilot Reginald Warneford awarded Victoria Cross for destroying a Zeppelin (8); Austrians re-take Lemburg, capital of Galicia, from the Russians (23).

July: Germans advance farther into Poland (3); General Botha accepted surrender of all German forces in South West Africa (9).

August: Allied forces meet stubborn resistance at Gallipoli (13); Italy declares war against Turkey (20); Brest-Litovsk falls to the Germans (30).

September: Allies breech German lines at Champagne and at Loos in Flanders (26); Turks defeated at Kut-el-Amara in Mesopotamia (28).

October: Russia begins campaign against Bulgaria (8); British nurse Edith Cavell executed by Germans as a spy (12).

November: Italians suffer heavy losses at Isonzo River (10); Serbia occupied by German-Austrian and Bulgarian forces (28).

December: Sir Douglas Haig replaces Sir John French as British commander on the Western Front (15); French and British troops occupy Salonika (13); Allied troops begin evacuation of Gallipoli (20).

- Foundation of St Dunstan's Home for blinded soldiers and sailors by Sir Arthur Pearson.
- Requirement for photographs in passports introduced (1 February).
- Women's Institute organization founded in Britain (11 September).

Deaths

Rupert Brooke, British poet, from blood poisoning (23 April).

Paul Ehrlich, German doctor and discoverer of diptheria antitoxin.

W. G. Grace, English cricketer, who had scored a hundred centuries between 1864 and 1895 (23 October).

(James) Keir Hardie, British politician and founder of the Labour Party (26 September)

Alexander Skryabin, Russian composer.

1916

- World War I. *January*: conscription introduced in Britain (6); withdrawal of troops from Gallipoli completed (8); Montenegro captured by Austrians (20); tanks first tested and named (29).
  February: Allies complete occupation of Germany colony of Cameroons (18); Battle of Verdun between Germans and French begins (21).
  April: British forces surrender to Turks after fall of Kut-el-Amara (29).
  May: Battle of Jutland between the British and German fleets, only major sea battle of the war, in which both sides claim victory (31); official adoption of daylight saving (pioneered by William Willett) as British Summer Time to conserve coal stocks (21).
  June: Lord Kitchener drowned when cruiser *Hampshire* is struck by a mine off Orkney (6); Arab revolt against Turkish rule (21); Russians led by General Brusilov capture Galicia from the Austrians (23).
  July: Battle of the Somme (1 July–18 November); Russians rout Turkish army at Erzinjan (27).
  August: Italians capture Gorizia (10); Field Marshall Paul von Hindenburg appointed Chief of German General Staff (27); Romania declares war against Austria and Germany (27).
  September: tanks first used by the British Army on the Western Front (15); Allies launch new offensive in the Balkans (18); destruction of Zeppelin L21 at Cuffley (3) and Zeppelin L33 in Essex (24).
  October: Allies occupied Athens (16); Captain T. E. Lawrence arrives in Jeddah to offer British support for Arab revolt against Turkey (16); Second Battle of Verdun begins (24).
  November: Battle of the Somme (ends 18 November); Austro-Hungarian Emperor Franz Josef dies (21).
  December: General Joffre replaces General Robert Nivelle as head of French forces on the Somme (3); Asquith resigns and Lloyd George forms war cabinet as new prime minister (7); end of the Battle of Verdun (16).
- Ireland. Easter Rising in Ireland, led by Padraic Pearse (23–29 April). Arrest of Roger Casement (24 April), executed for treason (3 August). Padraic Pearse court-martialled and shot.
- US troops defeat Mexican rebels led by Pancho Villa (31 March).
- Woodrow Wilson re-elected US president (November).
- The Persian Gulf State of Qatar becomes a British protectorate (until 1971).
- ANZAC Day first celebrated in London (25 April).
- Foundation of the National Savings Movement (19 February).
- Closure of Sadler's Wells Theatre, London.
- Discovery of Proxima Centauri, the star nearest Earth, by Robert Innes.
- Invention of stainless steel by Harry Brearley.
  Deaths
  Sir Joseph Beecham, British pharmaceuticals manufacturer.
  George Butterworth, British composer.
  Henry James, American-born British writer (28 February).
  Jack London, US author.
  Henrik Sienkiewicz, Polish writer.
- 'Mad Monk' Gregory Rasputin murdered by Russian nobles (30 December).

1917

- World War I. *February*: unrestricted submarine warfare begins (1).
  March: British troops occupy Baghdad (11); British defeat Turks near Gaza (27); Women's Army Auxiliary Corps founded (28).
  April: United States declares war on Germany (6); Battle of Arras (9–14); Vimy Ridge captured by Canadian troops (10); German government helps Bolshevik leader Vladimir Lenin return to Russia (16).
  June: Messines Ridge taken by British (7); German aircraft carries out first bombing raid on London (14); first American troops land in France (26); General Edmund Allenby assumes Palestine command (29).
  July: authorization given for the formation of the British Army's Tank Corps (28); third Battle of Ypres begins (31). Mustard gas first used by the Germans (July).
  August: French break German lines at Verdun on 11-mile front (20).
  September: Germans expel Russians from Riga (17).
  October: French victory on the Aisne (23); Italians routed by Austrians at Battle of Caporetto (24).
  November: Passchendaele captured by British (6); Bolshevik Revolution: Kerensky overthrown (7); Balfour Declaration recognizing Palestine as national home for the Jews (8); Hindenburg lines smashed on 10-mile front (20)
  December: Jerusalem taken by the British (9); Russo-German armistice (15); Russo-German armistice (15); Bolsheviks open peace talks with Germans at Brest-Litovsk (22).
- Russia: *March*: Tsar Nicholas II abdicates and provisional government established (16).
  July: provisional government crushes Bolshevik uprising (16); Alexander Kerensky appointed Russian prime minster (22).

September: Kerensky proclaims Russia a republic (15); the ex-Tsar and his family are moved to Siberia (30).

November: Bolshevik Revolution: Kerensky overthrown (7).

- Order of the British Empire founded by George V. First DBE (Dame of the British Empire) created: Marchioness of Londonderry, founder and director of the Women's Legion.
- Balfour Declaration, in favour of the creation of a Jewish national home in Palestine, made by the British government (2 November).
- Constitution of Newfoundland as a Dominion (created a Province 1949).
- Adoption of the name Windsor instead of Saxe-Coburg-Gotha by the British royal family (17 July).
- Foundation of the Whitley Councils regarding British labour conditions mainly by John Whitley, Speaker of the House of Commons.
- First investigation of the aeronautic spin by Frederick Lindemann.

Deaths

Colonel William F. Cody ('Buffalo Bill').

Edgar Degas, French painter.

Scott Joplin, US ragtime pianist and composer.

Auguste Rodin, French scultptor.

1918

- World War I. *January*: President Wilson outlines to Congress American war aims in his Fourteen Points (8/9); Lenin creates Red Army (28).

  February: Demoralized Russian army attacked by Germans in Estonia as Brest-Litovsk peace talks stall (20).

  March: Treaty of Brest-Litovsk (3); German offensive against British on the Somme opened (21); Battle of Arras (21–4 April).

  April: establishment of the Royal Air Force from the Royal Flying Corps and Royal Naval Air Service (1); second German offensive against British (9–25); Ferdinand Foch appointed commander of Allied armies (14); British naval raid on Belgian ports of Zeebrugge and Ostend (23/22); the League of Nations founded (28).

  May: Battle of the Aisne begins (27): Germans attack British and French.

  June: German advance on the Aisne halted (6).

  July: Last German offensive against the French (15).

  August: Allied offensive near Amiens results in German collapse (8).

  September: Turkish army destroyed at Megiddo (19); Battle of Passchendaele in Belgium (28); Bulgarians sign armistice (29); Allied breakthrough along the whole Western Front (30); Congress of Aix-la-Chapelle opens (30).

  October: T. E. Lawrence leads Arabs into Damascus (1); conquest of Palestine from the Turks completed; Germany accepts President Wilson's Fourteen Points (23); Italian advance (24); surrender of Turkey (30).

  November: Austria accepts peace terms (4); Socialist republic declared in Bavaria (7); Kaiser abdicates and escapes to Holland (9); armistice signed by Germany (11); German fleet surrenders at sea (14); Congress of Aix-la-Chapelle closed (21).

  December: Rhineland occupied by Allied troops (6–9).
- Russia: Conflict between Bolshevik Red Army and anti-Bolshevik White forces begins (June). Ex-Tsar and his family shot by Bolsheviks in cellar in Ekaterinburg (16 July).
- Ireland. Irish Parliament formed in Dublin. Sir John French made lord lieutenant of Ireland (until 1921).
- The Labour Party adopts its constitution.
- Women over thirty allowed to vote for the first time, conditional on educational and property qualifications, at the general election ('coupon election') (14 December): Liberal win; Lloyd George becomes prime minister of a Liberal government.
- Election of the first woman to the House of Commons when Countess Markievicz is elected as Sinn Fein member for a Dublin constituency: she refuses to take the oath of alliegiance to the king and therefore cannot take her seat.
- Influenza pandemic (until 1919).
- Leicester University founded (as the Leicester, Leicestershire and Rutland College); renamed University College, Leicester in 1927; gains university status 1957.
- National Savings stamps first issued for sale (8 July).
- Publication of *Eminent Victorians* by Lytton Strachey.

Deaths

Guillaume Apollinaire, French poet.

Claude Debussy, French composer.

Gustav Klimt, Austrian painter.

Wilfred Owen, British poet, in World War I.

Egon Schiele, Austrian painter.

1919

- World War I aftermath. Peace Conference in Paris (18 January); interned German fleet of battleships scuttled at Scapa Flow, Orkney (21 June); Germany signs Treaty of Versailles (28 June); the signatories of the Treaty of Versailles subscribe to the League of Nations (28 June); signature of the Treaty of Neuilly between the Allies and Bulgaria (27 November). Treaty of St. Germain: dissolution of the Austro-Hungarian Empire.
- Lloyd-George announces plan for the partition of Ireland.

- Dail Eireann, Irish Free State Chamber of Deputies, formed in Dublin (January); Irish Republican Army formed: Irish Volunteers merged with IRA.
- Nancy Astor becomes first woman MP to take her seat in the House of Commons (1 December).
- Amritsar massacre of protesting Indians, 380 dead and over 1200 wounded by British troops under General Dyer (13 April).
- British mandate in Iraq (until 1921).
- Former West African German colony of Cameroon divided into British Cameroons and French Cameroun (united as a republic 1961).
- Outbreak of Third Afghan War (3 May): signature of the Treaty of Rawalpindi (8 August) ends the war.
- Communist 'Sparticist' uprising surpressed in Berlin, leaders Rosa Luxemburg and Karl Liebknecht arrested and then killed.
- Third International founded in Moscow.
- Red Army close to victory over White forces in the civil war in Russia.
- Benito Mussolini founds Fascist party in Italy, Fasci de Combattimento.
- Jan Christian Smuts becomes prime minister of South Africa after death of Louis Botha.
- President Wilson suffers a stroke.
- John Alcock and Arthur Brown fly non-stop across the Atlantic.
- Formation of the Rover Scouts movement.
- The term 'dole' applied to unemployment payments by *The Daily Mail.*
- Disestablishment of the Church of Wales.
- First publication of the periodical *John O'London's Weekly* (until 1954; revived 1959).
- A daily air service between London and Paris inaugurated (25 August).
- Atom split by Lord Rutherford; he is also the first to observe nuclear disintegration of nitrogen atoms.
- Invention of the spectrograph by Francis Aston.
- John Alcock and Arthur Brown flew non-stop across the Atlantic, arrived in County Galway 15 June.
- First airship crossing of the Atlantic: R34 lands in New York State 6 July.

Deaths

Sir John Alcock, English aeronautical pioneer following a plane accident (18 December).

Andrew Carnegie, Scottish-born American philanthropist (11 August).

Auguste Renoir, French artist.

1920

- Conscription ends in Britain (30 April).
- Ireland. Government of Ireland Act: unacceptable to the south; administration of Northern Ireland by separate parliament and executive government established in the Act. 'Black and Tans' auxiliary police used for the first time against Irish republicans (2 January, ceased 1921). 'Bloody Sunday': IRA kill fourteen British soldiers in Ireland. Death in prison of the Irish patriot Terence MacSwiney following a hunger strike (1 November).
- Kenya annexed to the British Crown as a colony (8 July).
- League of Nations comes into effect (1 January): Germany, Austria, Russia and Turkey excluded; American Senate voted against US membership. Signature of the Treaty of Trianon between Hungary and the Allies (4 June); Treaty of Sèvres concludes peace with Turkey and dissolve the Ottoman Empire (10 August).
- 18th Ammendment to US constitution banning sale of alcohol goes into force: beginning of Prohibition.
- Warren G. Harding elected US President.
- Peace Treaty ratified in Paris.
- French troops occupy the Ruhr.
- Treaty of Sévres concludes peace with Turkey and dissolves Ottoman Empire.
- Rebel leader Pancho Villa surrenders to Mexican government.
- Russian civil war ends with triumph of the Bolshevik Red Army.
- King Constantine of Greece returns to Athens.
- Opening of the Royal Air Force College (5 February).
- Admission of women to degrees at Oxford University.
- Building of Welwyn Garden City.
- First World Jamboree of Boy Scouts held in London.
- Foundation of the Communist Party of Great Britain.
- Foundation of the Royal Institute of International Affairs.
- Horatio Bottomley imprisoned for fraud (until 1927).
- Roscoe 'Fatty' Arbuckle, actor, charged with rape and murder of actress Virginia Rappe in Hollywood.
- Enthronement of the first archbishop of Wales (1 June)
- First publication of *Time and Tide*, founded and edited by Lady Rhondda.
- First significant example of a documentary film appeared: *Nanook of the North* by Robert Flaherty.
- Montagu Norman becomes governor of the Bank of England.
- Cenotaph, memorial to the death of both World Wars in Whitehall, London, unveiled (11 November).

Deaths

Amedeo Modigliani, Italian artist.

1921

- Ireland. Anglo-Irish Treaty setting up the Irish Free State, signed (6 December); Irish Free State estab-

lished; division of the former kingdom of Ulster into Northern Ireland (Antrim, Armagh, Down, Fermanagh, Londonderry and Tyrone) and the republic of Ireland (Cavan, Donegal and Monaghan).
- Limitation of Armaments Conference begins in Washington (12 November, ended 6 February 1922).
- Opening of the first Indian parliament (3 January); Lord Reading becomes viceroy of India (until 1926).
- Anglo-Afghan Treaty concluded in Kabul by the Dobbs Mission (22 November).
- British troops sent to quell rioting in Egypt.
- Japanese Premier Takashi Hara assassinated.
- Crown Prince Hirohito named regent of Japan.
- Eduard Benes prime minister of Czechoslovakia.
- Spanish Prime Minister Eduardo Dato assassinated.
- Anti-Bolshevik mutiny of Russian sailors at Kronstadt naval base.
- Lenin's New Economic Policy introduces limited free enterprise in Soviet Union.
- Reparations Commission fixes Germany's liability at 200 billion gold marks (£10 billion).
- British Legion (made Royal British Legion in 1971) founded by Earl Haig (14 May): it organized Poppy Day, first held 11 November.
- First English birth control clinic opened in London.
- First English woman barrister qualified (25 May).
- Foundation of PEN International, world association of writers, in London.
- Foundation of the British Broadcasting Company.
- Insulin isolated by Frederick Banting and Charles Best.
- King George V Dock, London, opened.

Deaths

Enrico Caruso, Italian opera singer.

John Boyd Dunlop, British inventor of the pneumatic tyre (23 October).

Georges Feydeau, French playwright.

Engelbert Humperdinck, German composer.

1922

- Ireland. Execution of Erskine Childers, Irish patriot; Michael Collins killed by Republicans (22 August).
- Lloyd George resigns. Andrew Bonar Law becomes prime minister of a Conservative government after a general election (17 November).
- League of Nations divided Togoland into British Togoland and French Togoland.
- Abolition of the British protectorate over Egypt (6 February); recognition of independence (15 March).
- Palestine proclaimed a British mandate (until 1948).
- Cardinal Achille Ratti, archbishop of Milan elected Pope Pius XI.
- Four Power Pacific Treaty ratified by US Senate.
- Treaty of Rapallo between Germany and USSR restoring full diplomatic relations.
- Walter Rathenau, German foreign minister, assassinated.
- King Constantine of Greece abdicates: succeeded by George II.
- Friedrich Ebert re-elected German president.
- Mussolini's 'March on Rome': Fascist government formed.
- Tomb of Tutankhamun discovered.
- James Joyce *Ulysses*.
- First skywriting in England carried out over Epsom Downs.
- Establishment of 2LO broadcasting station in London (11 May). Regular broadcasts begin 14 November. Daily news broadcasts begin 23 December.
- Introduction of the radio licence (1 November).
- Completion of *The Forsyte Saga* (began 1906) by John Galsworthy.
- Publication of *Just William* by Richmal Crompton.
- Publication of*The Waste Land* by T. S. Eliot.
- Discovery of the tomb of the ancient Egyptian pharoah Tutankhamun by Howard Carter (26 November).

Deaths

Alexander Graham Bell, Scottish-born American inventor of the telephone.

Alfred Harmsworth, Lord Northcliffe, British newspaper proprietor (14 August).

Marcel Proust, French author.

Sir Ernest Shackleton, British Antarctic explorer, in South Georgia (5 January)

1923

- Japanese earthquake: 300,000 dead in Tokyo and Yokohama.
- Miguel Primo de Rivera dictator in Spain after army coup.
- French troops occupy the Rhineland to secure reparations.
- King George II deposed by Greek army.
- Calvin Coolidge President of US after death of Harding.
- Teapot Dome oil scandal in US.
- Turkish republic proclaimed with Mustapha Kemal as first president.
- Hitler's attempt to overthrow the Weimar Republic in Munich (the 'Beer Hall Putsch') fails.
- Catastrophic inflation in Germany: mark drops to 4 trillion to the US dollar.
- Bonar Law resigns because of illness; Stanley Baldwin succeeds as prime minister (22 May).
- General election (6 December): Conservatives won but as a minority government. Labour had the second highest number of seats.

- Establishment of the first British local Record Office at Bedford.
- Marriage of Lady Elizabeth Bowes-Lyon and the Duke of York, later George VI (26 April).
- Big Ben chimes broadcast for the first time (31 December).
- First publication of *Radio Times* (28 September).
- Sir Arthur Bliss made Master of the King's Musick.
- First English FA Cup final played at Wembley (28 April).

Deaths
Sarah Bernhardt, French actress.
Gustav Eiffel, French engineer.
Jaroslav Hasek, Czech writer.
Katherine Mansfield, New Zealand-born writer.
Wilhelm Röntgen, pioneer of X-rays.

1924

- Baldwin's Conservative government resigns. King George V asks Ramsay MacDonald to form the first Labour government (23 January); the new government recognizes the USSR (1 February).
- Publication of the Zinoviev Letter purporting to be from Grigori Zinoviev, Russian leader of the Communist International, with plans for a Communist uprising in Britain (25 November).
- General election (29 October): overwhelming Conservative victory; Baldwin becomes prime minister for the second time (until 1929).
- Vladimir Ilyich Lenin, founder of the USSR, dies.
- Greece proclaimed a republic: King George II deposed by Greek parliament.
- Mussolini's Fascists gain convincing victory in Italian general election.
- J. Edgar Hoover appointed director of the Federal Bureau of Investigation.
- Assam (incorporated into Bengal by 1914) becomes separate province.
- Zambia made a British protectorate.
- Dawes Plan for restructuring the payment of German reparations to the Allies agreed at the London Conference. French and Belgians agree to the evacuation of the Ruhr.
- ASLIB (the Association of Special Libraries and Information Bureaux) founded.
- British Empire Exhibition (Wembley Exhibition) held at Wembley, London (23 April-1 November).
- Consecration of Liverpool Cathedral (19 July): building began 1904.
- First appearance of a crossword in a British newspaper, *The Sunday Express*.
- First transmission of radio photographs from Britain to the US.
- Plans for a tunnel under the English Channel abandoned by the British government.
- Cheltenham Gold Cup horse race first run.

Deaths
Frances Hodgson Burnett, British author.
Joseph Conrad, Polish-born British author (3 August).
Gabriel Fauré, French composer.
Anatole France, French author.
Franz Kafka, German author.
E. E. (Edith) Nesbit, British children's author.
Giacomo Puccini, Italian composer.

1925

- Dominions Office founded (assumes name of Commonwealth Relations Office in 1947).
- Cyprus becomes a British Crown Colony.
- Signature in London of the Treaty of Locarno, guaranteeing peace and frontiers in Europe (16 October).
- Field Marshall Paul von Hindenburg elected president of Germany.
- Rheza Khan king of Persia.
- Tennessee school teacher John T. Scopes is found guilty of teaching evolution in a state school and fined $100.
- Adolph Hitler *Mein Kampf*.
- F. Scott Fitzgerald *Great Gatsby*.
- British Summer Time made a permanent institution by House of Commons vote (17 July).

Deaths
Queen Alexandra, widow of King Edward VII (20 November).
William Jennings Bryan, US Democratic politician.
H. Rider Haggard, British author of *King Solomon's Mines* (14 May).
John Singer Sargent, US artist.

1926

- Abdul Aziz ibn Saud proclaimed king of the Hejaz and names the province Saudi Arabia.
- Hitler Youth founded in Germany.
- Ali Reza Khan crowned shah of Persia with title King Pahlavi.
- Jósef Pilsudski stages coup and siezes power in Poland
- Germany admitted to the League of Nations.
- Hirohito succeeds his father, Yoshihito, as emperor of Japan.
- Birth of a daughter (later Elizabeth II) to the Duke and Duchess of York (later King George VI and Queen Elizabeth) (21 April).
- Miners on strike (1 May–27 November); TUC call General Strike in support, which disrupts industry for nine days (3-13 May).
- Canada associated as a member of the British Commonwealth of Nations.
- The Earl of Halifax is made viceroy and governor-general of India.

- British troops end occupation of the Rhineland.
- Imperial Defence College for senior army, navy and air force officers founded.
- Incorporation by Royal Charter of SSAFA—the Soldiers', Sailors' and Airmen's Families Association (founded 1885).
- Legitimacy by marriage of parents made legal in England.
- Reading University receives university status.
- Publication of *A Drunk Man Looks at a Thistle* by Hugh MacDiarmid; of his memoir *The Seven Pillars of Wisdom* by T. E. Lawrence ('Lawrence of Arabia'); and of *Winnie the Pooh* by A. A. Milne.
- Invention of television and first demonstration made by John Logie Baird (27 January).
- First Grand Prix motor race held in Britain at Brooklands (7 August).
- English Channel first swum by a woman, Gertrude Ederle (6 August).

Deaths

Eugene Debs, US socialist leader.
Harry Houdini (Ernst Weiss), Hungarian-born US escapologist.
Claude Monet, French artist.
Annie Oakley, US sharpshooter.
Rainer Maria Rilke, Austrian poet.
Rudolph Valentino, Italian-born US film star.

1927

- Canberra inaugurated as the new capital of the Australian Commonwealth.
- Tomas Masaryk re-elected president of Czechoslovakia.
- In Chinese civil war, Nationalist forces under Chiang Kai-Shek conquer Shanghai.
- Leon Trotsky and Grigori Zinoviev expelled from the Soviet Communist Party by Stalin.
- Italian-born anarchists Sacco and Vanzetti executed in US for armed robbery depite worldwide protests of their innocence.
- Captain Charles Lindbergh makes first solo non-stop flight across the Atlantic.
- Al Jolson stars in first talking film, *The Jazz Singer*.
- Allied military control of Germany ended.
- Menin Gate, Belgium unveiled: memorial to the British who fell in the Ypres salient, World War I.
- British Broadcasting Corporation (formerly British Broadcasting Company) constituted under Royal Charter (1 January).
- First automatic traffic lights set up (5 November).
- Charles Wilson shares the Nobel Prize for physics.
- First non-stop solo transatlantic flight made by Lindbergh.
- First public demonstration of colour television in Glasgow.
- Inauguration of the first automatic telephone service in London. Transatlantic telephone service begins (7 January).
- Champion Hurdle race at Cheltenham first run.
- Greyhound racing begins in Britain at White City (20 June).
- Oxford and Cambridge Boat Race first broadcast (2 April).
- Sir Malcolm Campbell becomes holder of world speed records on land and water.

Deaths

Isadora Duncan, US dancer.
Death of Jerome K Jerome, British writer.

1928

- Earthquake destroys Corinth in Greece.
- Chinese Nationalist forces led by Chiang Kai-shek take Peking (July); Chiang Kai-shek becomes President of Republic of China (October).
- Herbert Hoover elected US president.
- First Five Year Plan begins in USSR.
- Hirohito crowned emperor of Japan.
- Amelia Earhart is the first woman to fly the Atlantic.
- Professor Alexander Fleming of St Mary's Hospital, London discovers Penicillin.
- Under terms of the Women's Suffrage Bill (7 May), women allowed to vote on the same basis as men (over twenty-one).
- Kellog-Briand pact renouncing war signed in Paris by 65 states (27 August).
- Formation of the World Association of Girl Guides and Girl Scouts.
- Release of Oscar Slater after a campaign involving Conan Doyle and others against his wrongful imprisonment (for murder in 1909).
- 'Talkies' (moving pictures with sound) first shown in cinemas.
- Institution of the Malvern Festival.
- Publication of censored *Lady Chatterley's Lover* by D. H. Lawrence.
- First transatlantic flight made by a woman, Amelia Earhart (Newfoundland to Wales, 18 June).
- Penicillin, the first antibiotic, discovered by Alexander Fleming of St Mary's Hospital, London.
- Piccadilly Circus underground station opened in London.
- First transmission of colour television made by John Logie Baird (3 July).

Deaths

Herbert Asquith, British statesman (15 February)
Earl Haig, British soldier (20 January)
Thomas Hardy, English novelist and poet (11 January)
Leos Janacek, Czech composer.
Emmeline Pankhurst, English Suffragette leader (14 June).

Sir George Trevelyan, British statesman and historian.

1929

- King Alexander I declares himself dictator of Yugoslavia.
- St Valentine's Day Massacre in Chicago.
- Mussolini signs Lateran Treaty with Pope Pius XI establishing independent Vatican City.
- Trotsky expelled from the USSR.
- Aristide Briand premier of France.
- Wall Street Crash causes slump in US economy: Great Depression begins.
- Airship *Graf Zeppelin* flies around the world in 21 days.
- Ernest Hemingway *A Farewell to Arms.*
- General election (30 May): Labour minority government; Ramsay MacDonald becomes prime minister (until 1935) and forms second Labour Government.
- Abolition of Poor Law system.
- Foundation of St Peter's Hall, Oxford.
- Margaret Bondfield becomes first woman privy councillor.
- Courtauld Institute of Art established in London.
- Ealing Studios established as Associated Talking Pictures.
- Term 'documentary film' introduced.
- *The Daily Herald* newspaper placed under the joint control of Odhams and the TUC.
- *The Listener* weekly first published (16 January): publication ceased 1991.
- Beginning of regional broadcasting with the opening of Brookmans Park transmitting station (21 October).
- First experimental television broadcast by the BBC.
- First trials held (14 October) of R101, the British dirigible designed by Barnes Wallis (16 December).
- Frederick Hopkins shares the Nobel Prize for physiology and medicine.
- The existence of a fifth dimension affirmed by Sir Owen Richardson.
- Foundation of the Pony Club movement (1 November).

Deaths

Carl Benz, German engineer.
Sergei Diaghilev, Russian impresario.
Wyatt Earp, US marshal.
Lillie Langtry, British actress (12 February).
Lord Rosebery, British statesman (21 May).
Gustav Stresemann, German statesman.

1930

- Gandhi begins his civil disobedience campaign against British rule in India (12 March).
- Publication of the Simon Report on India (24 June); Round Table Conference held in London on subject of India (12 November–19 January); Lord Willingdon becomes viceroy of India.
- The independence of Iraq recognized by Britain (30 June).
- Ratification of the London Naval Treaty between Britain, USA, France, Italy and Japan on naval disarmament.
- Stalin's collectivization of agriculture in USSR accelerated at enormous human cost.
- Ras Tafari becomes Emperor Haile Salassie of Ethiopia.
- Last French troops withdraw from the Rhineland.
- Nazis come second in German general election.
- Mandate policy in goverment White Paper on Palestine suggests halting Jewish immigration.
- R.101 disaster: world's biggest airship explodes in France on maiden flight to India, killing 48 people.
- Uruguay wins first World Cup football competition.
- Planet Pluto discovered by C.W. Tombaugh.
- Nylon discovered in US by Wallace Carrothers of the Du Pont company.
- Foundation of the Youth Hostels Association.
- Unemployment in the UK reaches two million.
- Formation of the *News Chronicle* by the amalgamation of *The Daily News* and *The Daily Chronicle.*
- John Masefield appointed poet laureate.
- Amy Johnson becomes the first woman to fly solo from England to Australia (6–24 May).

Deaths

Arthur Balfour, British statesman (19 March)
Lon Chaney, US actor.
Sir Arthur Conan Doyle, British author (7 July).
D. H. Lawrence, British author (2 March).

1931

- King Alfonso abdicates and Spain is declared a republic.
- US gangster Alphonse Capone jailed for income tax evasion.
- Empire State Building completed in New York.
- New Party founded by Sir Oswald Mosley along Facist lines (28 February).
- Britain abandons the gold standard (21 September) and devalues the pound.
- Financial crisis leads to coalition government under Ramsay MacDonald (25 August); Ramsay MacDonald replaced as leader of the Labour Party (28 August).
- General election (27 October): a second coalition national government formed under Ramsay MacDonald.
- Statute of Westminster passed to regulate British

Commonwealth relations (January); becomes law (11 December)

- End of the civil disobedience campaign in India (March); Gandhi attends the second India Conference in London (1 December).
- Mutiny over pay cuts at Invergordon naval base (15 September).
- First publication of the Highway Code (14 April).
- Foundation of the National Trust for Scotland for places of historic interest or natural beauty.
- Reopening of Sadler's Wells Theatre, London (6 January).
- The *New Statesman* absorbs *The Nation*.
- King George V Dock, Glasgow, opened.

Deaths

Bix Beiderbecke, US jazz musician.
Arnold Bennett, British writer (27 March).
Thomas Alva Edison, US inventor.
Anna Pavlova, Russian ballerina.

1932

- British Union of Fascists founded by Sir Oswald Mosley, replacing the New Party (December).
- Irish election (16 February); Eamon de Valera elected president of Ireland (9 March).
- The Independent Labour Party under James Maxton seceded from the Labour Party.
- Arrest of Gandhi in India (4 January)
- Lausanne Pact between the Allies and Germany signed (July).
- Japanese capture Shanghai.
- Manchukuo, Japanese puppet regime, established in Manchuria.
- Kidnappers abduct Charles Lindbergh's baby son.
- Second Five Year Plan begins in USSR.
- Paul von Hindenburg narrowly defeats Hitler in German presidential contest; Nazis win majority of seats in Reichstag (July); Hitler fails in attempt to become Chancellor (August); Nazi setback.
- Assassination of French President Paul Donner; replaced by Albert Lebrun.
- Olivier Salazar elected premier of Portugal.
- Franklin D. Roosevelt elected US president in landslide victory.
- Foundation of the Methodist Church of Great Britain and Ireland, uniting the Wesleyan Methodist, Primitive Methodist and United Methodist Churches (20 September).
- Sydney Harbour Bridge opened in Australia.
- Opening of a new building for the Shakespeare Memorial Theatre in Stratford-on-Avon (23 April).
- Publication of *Brave New World* by Aldous Huxley.
- First experimental television programme broadcast by the BBC; Annual Christmas Day broadcast by the monarch instituted by George V; speech written by Rudyard Kipling.
- First solo transatlantic flight by a woman when Amelia Earhart flies from Newfoundland to Londonderry (21 May).
- Atomic nucleus split by Sir John Cockcroft and Dr Walton, releasing atom's energy.
- Neutrons, nuclear particles, discovered by James Chadwick.
- Piccadilly Circus lit by electricity for the first time.

Deaths

George Eastman, US industrialist.
Kenneth Grahame, British author (6 July).
John Philip Sousa, US musician.
Edgar Wallace, British crime writer, in Hollywood (10 February).

1933

- Adolf Hitler appointed chancellor of Germany (January); Reichstag building in Berlin destroyed by fire (February); commercial boycott of Jews begins and violence against Jews and their property escalates (April); Germany becomes one-party state as Hitler bans all political opposition (June); use of concentration camps for Jews and opponents of the regime confirmed (August); Germany withdraws from the League of Nations (October) and walks out of the Geneva Disarmament conference (November).
- Communist uprising in Spain
- Japan withdraws from the League of Nations.
- Economic legislation in US to combat the Great Depression.
- End of Prohibition in US.
- Formation of the Popular Front, cooperation by leftwing parties against Fascism (until 1939).
- Irish elections (24 January); oath of allegiance removed from the constitution (May).
- *Codex Sinaiticus* purchased from the Soviet government.
- Discovery of the Tassili rock paintings by Lieutenant Brenans, an officer in the Camel Corps.
- Foundation of the British Film Institute in London.
- Discovery of polythene by ICI chemists.
- Charter granted to the National Playing Fields Association.

Deaths

John Galsworthy, British author (31 January).
Adolf Loos, Austrian architect.

1934

- Leopold III becomes king of the Belgians after death of Albert I.
- Hitler eliminates rivals in the SA (Storm Troopers' Association) in the 'Night of the Long Knives'.
- Austrian chancellor Englebert Dollfuss is assasinated by Nazis.

- Death of President Hindenburg: Hitler announces the end of the republic and beginning of the Third Reich with himself as Führer and Reich Chancellor.
- King Alexander of Yugoslavia and Louis Barthou, French foreign minister, assassinated in Marseilles.
- Assassination of Sergei Kirov and purge of the Communist Party in USSR.
- Formation of the Scottish Nationalist Party.
- Civil disobedience campaign in India suspended by Gandhi (7 April).
- Initiation of the Peace Pledge by the Rev. Dick Sheppard.
- Opening of the Police Training College at Hendon (10 May).
- The Iron Age fort of Maiden Castle, Dorset, excavated.
- Glyndebourne Festival Opera founded by John Christie.
- Publication of *I, Claudius* by Robert Graves and *Right Ho, Jeeves* by P. G. Wodehouse.
- Official opening of the Mersey tunnel between Liverpool and Birkenhead (18 July, begun 16 December 1925).
- Launch of the Atlantic passenger liner *Queen Mary* (26 September).
- First women's cricket test match held in Australia (28 December).

Deaths

Marie Curie, Polish-born French physicist.
Frederick Delius, British composer (10 June).
Sir Edward Elgar, British composer (23 February).
Roger Fry, British painter and art critic.
Gustav Holst, British composer (25 May).

1935

- Saar plebiscite for return to Germany.
- Bruno Hauptmann sentenced to death for kidnapping and murder of US aviator Charles Lindbergh's baby son.
- Germany repudiates Versailles Treaty and accelerates rearmament programme.
- Jews banned from public office in Germany.
- Mussolini invades Abyssinia: League of Nations imposes ineffectual economic sanctions against Italy.
- US Senator Huey Long assassinated.
- Long March of Communists from Nationalist-held areas in southern China ends: Mao Tse-tung establishes Soviet state in northern China.
- Retirement of Ramsay MacDonald; Baldwin succeeds him as prime minister and forms a new National Government (7 June).
- John Buchan becomes governor-general of Canada (until 1940).
- Germany repudiates the Treaty of Versailles and accelerates rearmament programme.
- Introduction of 30-mile speed limit in built-up areas (12 March) and of driving tests (1 June).
- Alcoholics Anonymous (AA) founded.
- Approval of (29 January) and implementation of (1 April) the Green Belt Scheme for London.
- The first National Park in Britain started with a gift of 300 acres near Snowdon.
- British Council established (chartered 1940).
- First practical demonstration of radar by a team led by Robert Watson-Watt (26 February).

Deaths

Death of Colonel T. E. Lawrence, 'Lawrence of Arabia', British soldier and author, in a motor-cycle accident (19 May).

1936

- German remilitarization of the Rhineland.
- Italy annexes Abyssinia.
- Spanish army led by General Franco revolts against the Republican government: Spanish Civil War begins.
- Mussolini and Hitler announce the Rome-Berlin Axis.
- Stalin initiates the great purges that are to last for two years and cost up to 10 million lives
- F. D. Roosevelt re-elected US President by landslide.
- Death of King George V from bronchitis (20 January): Edward VIII becomes king (January) and abdicates (10 December) to marry American divorcee Wallis Simpson. His brother, the Duke of York, becomes king as George VI (12 December).
- Irish Republican Army proclaimed illegal (19 June).
- Constitution of Orissa and Sind as separate Provinces of India (1 April).
- Italy annexes Abyssinia: Haile Selassie lives in exile in England (until 1941) during the Italian occupation of Ethiopia.
- End of the British protectorate of Egypt (ratified 22 December); the Anglo-Egyptian Treaty established an alliance allowing use of the Suez Canal for twenty years.
- Opening of the first British open prison in, New Hall in Yorkshire (27 May).
- Jarrow 'hunger' march of unemployed people leaves Jarrow (5 October) and reaches London (11 November).
- Crystal Palace destroyed by fire (30 November).
- Publication of *General Theory of Employment, Interest and Money* by John Maynard Keynes.
- First television broadcast by the BBC (21 August); high-definition broadcast begins (2 November).

Deaths

G. K. Chesteron, British author (14 June).

Alexander Glazunov, Russian composer.

Rudyard Kipling, British poet and author (18 January).

Ivan Pavlov, Russian physiologist.

1937

- Guernica bombed by German air force in Spanish Civil War.
- German airship *Hindenburg* explodes on landing in New Jersey.
- Japanese begin attempted conquest of China; Shanghai bombed (August); forces of Chiang Kai-shek unite with Mao's Communists to combat Japanese threat (September).
- Stalin stages show trials of ex-colleagues in Moscow and purges army generals.
- Marriage of the Duke of Windsor (formerly Edward VIII) and Mrs Wallis Simpson in France (3 June).
- Neville Chamberlain becomes prime minster (until 1940) after the resignation of Stanley Baldwin (28 May).
- Aden made Crown Colony.
- Constitution of Punjab as an autonomous province.
- Publication of a plan for the partition of Palestine (7 July).
- Irish Free State renamed Eire (December).
- Divorce for grounds other than adultery made legal in England.
- Foundation of Nuffield College, Oxford, by Lord Nuffield.
- Inter-Regional Spelling Competition becomes the first British quiz programme broadcast (25 November).
- *Lilliput* periodical founded by Stefan Lorant.
- First test-bed run of a jet engine developed by Frank Whittle.
- The 999 telephone emergency service begins (1 July).
- Wimbledon lawn tennis championship first televised (21 June).

Deaths

Sir James Barrie, British author (19 June).

George Gershwin, US composer.

Jean Harlow, US actress.

Ramsay MacDonald, British statesman (9 November).

Guglielmo Marconi, Italian engineer.

Maurice Ravel, French composer.

John D. Rockefeller, US oil tycoon.

Lord Ernest Rutherford, British scientist (19 October).

Bessie Smith, US blues singer.

1938

- Austria annexed by Germany.
- Japanese bomb Canton.
- Germans march into Czechoslovakia.
- Kristallnacht: Jewish homes and businesses are attacked and looted throughout Germany (November); all Jewish property is confiscated (December).
- John Logie Baird demonstrates the colour television
- Signature of an agreement between Britain and Eire (25 April); last British troops depart (11 July).
- Munich Pact made (29 September) between Neville Chamberlain, the French premier Daladier, Hitler and Mussolini appeased over Czechoslovakia: the fate of Sudetenland determined.
- Singapore naval base opened (14 February); mobilization of the British fleet (27 September).
- Wavell becomes commander in chief in the Middle East (until 1941).
- Foundation of the Women's Voluntary Service (WVS) by the Marchioness of Reading (16 May); created Royal Women's Voluntary Service in 1966.
- FA Cup final first televized (30 April).
- Empire Exhibition held in Glasgow (May).
- Coal industry taken over by the state.
- Holidays with pay enforced by law.
- The Iona Community founded by the Rev. George Macleod.
- First publication of *Picture Post* periodical (ceased publication 1958).
- Publication of *Brighton Rock* by Graham Greene.
- Sir John Rothenstein becomes director of the Tate Gallery (until 1961).
- Launch of the Atlantic passenger liner *Queen Elizabeth* (27 September).
- Low-voltage fluorescent lighting available.

Deaths

Gabriele d'Annunzio, Italian soldier and poet.

Karel Capek, Czech writer.

Constantin Stanislavsky, Russian stage director.

1939

- Madrid falls to Nationalist forces led by General Franco (March): end of the Spanish Civil War.
- Bohemia and Moravia annexed by Hitler.
- Britain signs treaty of mutual assistance with Poland.
- Conscription introduced in Britain.
- Mussolini invades Albania.
- Italy and Germany sign alliance.
- Germany and USSR sign Non-Agression Pact.
- Britain signs treaty of mutual assistance with Poland (24 March); denounced by Hitler (28 April).

Emergency Powers Bill (24 August) passed by parliament; conscription of men introduced (August, until 1960); evacuation of children begins; gas masks issued to civilians in Britain; Ministry of Information set up (abolished 1946).

- World War II begins (ends 15 August 1945). *Septem-*

ber: Hitler invades Poland (1); Britain and France declare war on Germany (3); British liner *Athenia* is sunk off the Irish coast by a German submarine (4); first enemy air raid on Britain (6); British Expeditionary Force lands in France (11); Warsaw capitulates and Nazi-Soviet pact signed in Moscow for partitioning of Poland (29).
October: the *Royal Oak* torpedoed in Scapa Flow by German ships with the loss of 810 lives (14).
November: Finland attacked by Russia.
December: Battle of the River Plate (13-17 December): *Graf Spee*, German warship, scuttled in Montevideo harbour after being trapped by British cruisers (17).

- Beginning of 'Phoney War' (ended March 1940).
- John Steinbeck *The Grapes of Wrath*.
- James Joyce *Finnegan's Wake*.
- Henry Miller *Tropic of Cancer*.
- George VI becomes first British monarch to visit North America.
- Discovery of ship burial treasure at Sutton Hoo.
- BBC Home Service begins broadcasting (1 September).
- Introduction of identity cards in Britain (30 September).

Deaths
Douglas Fairbanks, US actor.
Sigmund Freud, Austrian psychoanalyst, in London (23 September).
William Butler Yeats, Irish poet and playwright, in France (28 January).

1940

- World War II. *January*: introduction of food rationing (8, ended 1953); Finnish Winter War.
February: Battle of the Altmark (16).
March: Finns defeated by Red Army.
April: Hitler invades Denmark and Norway (9): British troops join fighting in Norway.
May: Holland, Belgium and Luxembourg suffer German blitzkrieg; resignation of Neville Chamberlain as prime minister (10); Churchill becomes prime minister (11 May, until 1945) of a coalition National Government; British troops encircled on the French coast around Dunkirk (31); Home Guard founded as LDV (Local Defence Volunteers) (14), new name adopted July.
June: evacuation of British army from Dunkirk completed (4); Italy declares war on Britain and France (10); Paris captured by the Germans (14); France accepts terms for an armistice (22).
July: Channel Islands occupied by Germany (1); Battle of Britain begins (10).
August: British Somaliland attacked by Italy (7); Britain begins night bombing of Germany.
September: Blitz on London begins; Battle of Britain ends in victory for the Allies (15); the George Cross and the George Medal instituted (23); Japanese invade Indochina.
October: Bucharest occupied by Axis troops.
November: Greek troops repel Italian attacks; Coventry bombed in worst air raid of the war, 1,000 killed; Coventry Cathedral (built in the 15th century) destroyed (rebuilt 1954-62).
December: Sidi Barani captured by British troops in North Africa; General Archibald Wavell begins destruction of Italian forces in the Western Desert; Germans dropped incendiary bombs on London.
- Strips of metal first added to Bank of England £1 notes (29 March) and ten-shilling notes (2 April) to make forgery more difficult.

Deaths
John Buchan, British author and governor-general of Canada (11 February).
Neville Chamberlain, British statesman (9 November).
Francis Scott Fitzgerald, US novelist.
Harold Harmsworth, Lord Rothermere, British newspaper baron.
Paul Klee, German artist.
Sir Joseph John Thomson, British physicist (30 August).
Leon Trotsky, revolutionary socialist.

1941

- World War II. *January*: Tobruk taken by Commonweath troops (22).
February: Benghazi captured (7); Mogadishu in Somaliland captured by Imperial troops (26); General Erwin Rommel's Afrika Korps land in Tripoli.
March: Lease-Lend (US aid to Britain programme, proposed 1940) signed by President Roosevelt (11) (made reciprocal 1942); British raid on Lofoten Islands off Norway (4); Italian fleet virtually destroyed by British in Battle of Cape Matapan, off Crete (28); Rommel begins campaign in North Africa (30).
April: Benghazi captured by Rommel (3); Addis Ababa captured by Imperial troops (4); Germans occupy Yugoslavia (17); Athens captured by Germans (27); British and Commonwealth troops land in Crete; Ethiopia (conquered by Italy 1935-37) invaded by British forces.
May: Rudolf Hess parachutes into Scotland (10); heavy German bombing raid on London; destruction of the House of Commons (11); Germans invade Crete, and British forces withdraw (20); German battleship *Bismarck* sinks HMS *Hood* (24); *Bismarck* sunk (27).
June: clothes rationing begins (2); Germany attacks Russia (20).

July: US troops take over Iceland (7): Smolensk falls to German advance in Russia (16); Syrian capital Damascus surrenders to Allied forces (21); Japanese troops move into Thailand and Cambodia, and occupy Saigon (27).

August: Atlantic Charter signed by Churchill and Roosevelt (11); British and Russian troops attack Iran (25); Syria occupied by British and French (25); the Dnepropetrovsk dam blown up by the Russians to halt German advance (27).

September: intense fighting around Leningrad (12); Kiev falls to the Germans (19); in London General de Gaulle announces the formation of a French provisional government in exile (25).

October: Germans attack Moscow (6); Soviet government leaves Moscow (20); Germans take Kharkov in the Ukraine (25).

November: *Ark Royal* sunk by Italian torpedo (13); Eighth Army begins first offensive in Libya (18); Russians re-take Rostov (30).

December: conscription of women in Britain (4, until 1947); German attack on Moscow stalls (4); Japanese attack Pearl Harbour (7); Britain and USA declare war on Japan (8); Britain declares war on Finland, Romania and Hungary (8); Japanese forces land in Malaya (8); Philippines invaded by Japanese (10); sinking of *Repulse* and *Prince of Wales* (10); . Benghazi recaptured by British (24); Hong Kong surrenders to Japanese (25).

- First flight of the first British jet-propelled aircraft (15 May).
- Bailey bridge invented by Donald Bailey.
- First Outward Bound sea school opened at Aberdovey (autumn).

Deaths

Lord Robert Baden-Powell, British founder of the Scouting movement (8 January).

Henri Bergson, French philosopher.

Amy Johnson, British airwoman, when she crashed into the Thames in the cargo plane she is piloting for the Air Transport Auxiliary (5 January)

James Joyce, Irish author (13 January).

Rabindranath Tagore, Indian author.

Virginia Woolf, British author, by suicide (drowning) (28 March).

1942

- World War II. *January*: Manila captured by Japanese (2); Japanese forces land in New Guinea and Solomon Islands (23); German and Italian troops take Benghazi.

February: Introduction of soap rationing (9); Singapore falls to the Japanese (15); Battle of Java Seas (28).

March: Java surrenders to the Japanese (9); German U-boat base at St Nazaire attacked by British commandoes (27); RAF begins intensive bombing campaign against Germany (28).

April: George Cross awarded to the people of Malta (16); US B-52s bomb Tokyo (18).

May: Battle of the Coral Sea (4–8); Britain signs alliance with Russia (26); Rommel launches offensive in Libya (27); 1,000 RAF bombers raid Cologne (31).

June: US routs Japanese navy in Battle of Midway Island (3–7); Czech village of Lidice destroyed by Germans in reprisal for assassination of Reinhard Heydrich (10); recapture of Tobruk by Rommel (20/21) following an eight-month siege.

July: Sebastopol falls to the Germans (1); RAF makes first daylight raid on the Ruhr (16).

August: General Bernard Montgomery assumes command of the Eighth Army (6); Germans advance on Stalingrad (6); US forces attack Solomon Islands (7); Allied raid on Dieppe (19); Battle of Alam el Halfa (30): Rommel's attempt to break the Alamein Line to Cairo defeated by Eighth Army.

September: Germans clear the Warsaw Jewish ghetto (2); Germans halted at Stalingrad (8); Madagascar falls to British forces (18); Eighth Army seizes key German positions near El Alamein (30).

October: Battle of El Alamein (23-4 November): Allies victorious, Rommel in full retreat (30).

November: Allies invade North Africa at Algiers, Casablanca and Oran (8); Benghazi recaptured by British (20); Germans defeated near Stalingrad (26); French fleet scuttled in Toulon harbour (27).

December: Physicists led by Enrico Fermi at Chicago University achieve first controlled nuclear chain reaction (2); Admiral Darlan, Vichy leader in North Africa, assassinated (24).

- Formation of the United Nations (organization established 1945).
- Beveridge Plan published (20 November): scheme for national insurance devised by Lord Beveridge.
- Foundation of Oxfam (Oxford Committee for Famine Relief).
- First broadcast of Desert Island Discs (29 January).
- First discoveries made of the Mildenhall Treasure of Roman silver tableware near Mildenhall, Suffolk (continue into 1943).

Deaths

John Barrymore, US actor.

Carole Lombard, US actress.

Stefan Zweig, Austrian author.

1943

- World War II. *January*: Tripoli taken by the Eighth

Army (23); Casablanca Conference of Allied powers (14-20): between Franklin Roosevelt and Churchill at which 'unconditional surrender' formula is agreed; US bombers make their first attack on Germany (27); Germans surrender at Stalingrad (31). *February*: Japanese cleared from Guadalcanal in the Solomon Islands (9); Kharkow retaken by the Russians (16).
March: Battle of the Bismarck Sea (1–3/2-4); Rommel almost surrounded by US and British forces in North Africa (26).
April: Mass grave of Polish officers discovered by Germans in Katyn forest near Smolensk.
May: remaining German and Italian forces surrender to Allies in North Africa (12); RAF Dambuster raid on the Ruhr dams (17); Wavell appointed viceroy of India (18, until 1947).
June: French Committee for National Liberation formed in Algiers.
July: Allied invasion of Sicily (10); Germans routed in Battle of Kursk (13); Mussolini overthrown (25).
August: Sicily falls to the Allies (17); Quebec Conference (11-24); Mountbatten appointed Supreme Allied Commander in South-East Asia (25).
September: Allies invade Italian mainland (3); Italy surrenders (8); US forces land at Salerno, near Naples (10); Germans occupy Rome (10); Smolensk taken by the Russians (25).
October: Naples falls to Allies (1); Russians cross the Dneiper and capture Zaporozhie and Dnepropetrovsk (29).
November: Kiev taken by the Russians (6); Teheran Conference between Roosevelt, Stalin and Churchill (28).
December: General Dwight D. Eisenhower chosen as supreme commander of Allied invasion of Europe (24); sinking of the German battleship *Scharnhorst* off North Cape by the British Navy (26).

- Nuffield Foundation formed by Lord Nuffield (13 February).
- Sir John Barbirolli becomes conductor of the Halle Orchestra.

Deaths

Leslie Howard, British actor and director, in a plane crash (1 June).

Sergei Rachmaninov, Russian composer.

Thomas 'Fats' Waller, US jazz pianist.

Beatrice Potter, British children's author (22 December).

Beatrice Webb, British socialist and writer (30 April)

1944

- World War II. *January*: Allied landings at Anzio (22-25); Russians raise German siege of Leningrad (19).
February: US forces land on the Marshall Islands (1); Russians destroy ten German divisions on the Ukrainian front (17); beginning of strategic bombing of Germany.
March: Monte Cassino destroyed by Allied bombing (15); Allied force lands in Burma (19); General Orde Wingate killed in an air crash.
April: General de Gaulle appointed head of the Free French Forces (9); Russians drive Germans from the Crimea (16).
May: Sevastopol captured by the Russians (9); Monte Cassino falls to the Allies (18); 47 Allied airmen shot after mass escape from Stalag Luft III prison camp in Silesia.
June: Allied forces enter Rome (4); Normandy Offensive (codename Operation Overlord) begins on D-Day: Allied troops land in Normandy (6); first V–1 rocket falls on England (18).
July: Minsk captured by Russians (3); Caen falls to the Allies (9); Bomb Plot fails to kill Hitler (20); Guam captured by Americans (21).
August: Warsaw uprising (1); Allied troops enter Florence (11); Allies land in southern France (15); Paris liberated (23); Romania declares war on Germany (25).
September: Antwerp and Brussels taken by Allies (4); Boulogne taken by Allies (7); Bulgaria declares war on Germany (7); V–2 rockets begin to fall on England (8); Allies enter German soil (11); Allied landings near Arnhem (17); Battle of Arnhem (19-28); US forces attack Japanese near Manila (21); British troops land in Greece (24).
October: Warsaw rising crushed by Germans (3); British troops land on mainland Greece (5); Rommel commits suicide (14); Athens occupied by Allies (14); Aachen taken by Allies (20); Red Army liberates Belgrade (20); Battle of Leyte Gulf, Japanese sea power destroyed (25); Naval Battle of the Philippines (23-25).
November: Home Guard disbanded (1); British troops capture Salonika (1); sinking of the German warship *Tirpitz* by RAF bombs (12).
December: Civil war begins in Athens (6); German counter-offensive in the Ardennes ('Battle of the Bulge') (16–22); Budapest surrounded by Red Army (26).
- Education Act for England and Wales.
- PAYE (Pay As You Earn) introduced in Britain by Sir Cornelius Gregg (6 April).
- Pluto underwater oil pipeline from the Isle of Wight to France first in action (12 August).
- Cancellation of the thirteenth official modern Olympic Games scheduled to be held in London.

Deaths
Sir Edwin Lutyens, British architect.
Glen Miller, US band leader.
Piet Mondrian, Dutch artist.
Edvard Munch, Norwegian artist.
Heath Robinson, British humorist (13 September).
Sir Henry Wood, British conductor (19 August).

1945

- World War II. *January*: US troops land Luzon in Philippines (11); Warsaw captured by Russians (17); Hungary declares war on Germany (21); Red Army liberates Auschwitz (27); Ledo road from Burma to China reopened (28).
  February: Allied conference at Yalta (4); bombing of Dresden (14); US forces land on Iwo Jima (19).
  March: Cologne captured by Allies (6); Marshall Tito takes power in Yugoslavia (6); Allies cross the Rhine (25).
  April: US invades Okinawa (1); Red Army enters Vienna (11); death of President Roosevelt (12); American troops and Red Army link up in Germany (27); Mussolini and his mistress show by Italian partisans (28); Allies penetrate Berlin (30); Hitler and his mistress commit suicide (30).
  May: Germans surrender in Italy (2); Berlin captured by Red Army (2); Rangoon falls to the British (3); war against Germany ended officially, Victory in Europe (VE Day) (8); naval air attacks on Japan (28).
  June: arrest of William Joyce ('Lord Haw-Haw') for treason for broadcasting propaganda from Germany; San Francisco Conference of the United Nations (25-26 June), charter signed (26).
  July: Polish government in Warsaw recognized by Allies (5); Labour wins landslide in general election: Clement Atlee becomes prime minister (until 1951); Potsdam conference and Agreement (17 July-2 August).
  August: atom bomb first used in warfare on Hiroshima (6) and Nagasaki (9); Russia declares war against Japan and advances into Manchuria (8); unconditional surrender of Japan (14); VJ Day (15). Hong Kong re-occupied by British (30).
  September: Second World War ends officially (2).
  November: de Gaulle elected President of France (13); Nuremburg Trials begin (20 November).
- The United Nations comes into existence formally 24 October.
- Introduction of Family Allowance (15 June, later Child Benefit).
- Publication of *Brideshead Revisited* by Evelyn Waugh.

Deaths
Bela Bartok, Hungarian composer.
David Lloyd George, British Liberal statesman (26 March).
General George S. Patton, US commander.
Anton von Webern, Austrian composer.

1946

- General Assembly of the United Nations meets in New York for the first time.
- Leon Blum forms Socialist government in France.
- Juan Péron elected president of Argentina.
- Abdication of Victor Emmanuel III as king of Italy; his son Umberto II reigns briefly then leaves the country after referendum in favour of a republic under premier, de Gasperi.
- King David Hotel, British military HQ in Jerusalem, bombed by Jewish terrorists (22 July).
- Civil war between Nationalists and Communists resumes in China.
- Biro pen, invented by Hungarian journalist Ladislao Biro, goes on sale.
- Bank of England nationalized (1 March).
- Execution by hanging of William Joyce ('Lord Haw-Haw') for treason by broadcasting Nazi propaganda from Germany (3 January).
- The term 'Iron Curtain' used in a speech by Sir Winston Churchill (5 March) at Fulton, Missouri, to describe the barrier descending across Europe.
- War Crimes Tribunal, World War II, at Nuremberg ended; executions carried out 16 October.
- Ceylon gains independence.
- Malacca incorporated in the Malayan Union.
- British protectorate of Jordan ended and it becomes an independent kingdom.
- Creation of the Royal Military Academy at Sandhurst by the combination of Sandhurst and Woolwich (2 April).
- Execution by hanging of Neville Heath for murder.
- Introduction of television licences in Britain (1 June).
- Formation of the Young Conservatives (6 July).
- Introduction of bread rationing (22 July).
- New Bodleian Library opened in Oxford.
- Thirty-three football fans crushed by collapsed barriers at Burnden Park in Bolton (9 March).
- Premiere of *A Matter of Life and Death* by Michael Powell and Emeric Pressburger.
- The Arts Council of Great Britain (formerly the Council for the Encouragement of Music and the Arts, founded 1940) incorporated.
- ENIAC (Electronic Numerical Integrator and Calculator), first electronic computer, publicly demonstrated (February).

Deaths
John Logie Baird, British scientist and pioneer of television (14 June)
John Maynard Keynes, British economist (21 April).
H. G. Wells, British author (13 August).

1947

- Cominform, a new international Communist organization, established in Belgrade.
- UN determines the partition of Palestine.
- Coal industry nationalized (1 January).
- GATT (General Agreement on Tariffs and Trade) signed by 23 nations.
- The Marshall Plan for post-war recovery in Europe inaugurated by George Marshall, US Secretary of State (22 September).
- Marriage of Princess Elizabeth and Prince Philip, Duke of Edinburgh, formerly Philip Mountbatten (20 November).
- Lord Mountbatten appointed last viceroy of India to oversee the transfer of power to the independent governments of India and Pakistan (20 February).

  India gained independence within the British Commonwealth and separated into the separate dominions of Pakistan and India (15 August); Bengal and Punjab divided between India and Pakistan.
- Burmese premiere U Aung San and six ministers are assassinated (July 19).
- Groundnut scheme in Tanganyika begins.
- Foundation of St Benet's Hall, Oxford.
- Raising of the school-leaving age to 15 (1 April).
- The Edinburgh International Festival of Music and Drama launched (24 August).
- First performance of Tennessee Williams' *A Streetcar Named Desire.*
- First British nuclear reactor built at Harwell.
- First turboprop engine in use (in the Rolls-Royce Dart).
- North Channel between Northern Ireland and Scotland first swum by Tom Blower of Nottingham.

Deaths
Stanley Baldwin, Earl Baldwin of Bewdley, British Conservative statesman (14 December).
Pierre Bonnard, French artist.
Henry Ford, US car manufacturer.
Max Planck, German physicist.
Sidney Webb, British Socialist and author (13 October)

1948

- Mahatma Gandhi assassinated.
- Communists seize power in Czechoslovakia.
- Marshall Plan for $17 billion in economic aid to Europe passed by US Senate.
- State of Israel established with Chaim Weizmann as president.
- Russian blockade of Berlin: Western airlift of supplies begins.
- North Korea becomes a republic: Koreans now divided between Communist North, led by Kim Il Sung, and Republic of Korea in the south, led by Syngman Rhee.
- Harry S Truman elected US President.
- Birth of Charles, Prince of Wales (14 November).
- British Union of Fascists revived as British Union Movement by Sir Oswald Mosley.
- Plural voting discontinued by Act of Parliament.
- The Independent Labour Party ceases to have parliamentary representation.
- The Malayan Union becomes the Federation of Malaya.
- Burma becomes independent and leaves the British Commonwealth (4 January).
- Ceylon becomes a dominion within the British Commonwealth (4 February)
- British mandate in Palestine ended; Palestine partitioned between Jordan and the new state of Israel (14 May).
- Establishment of the Organization for European Economic Cooperation (OEEC) (16 April): superseded by the Organization for Economic Cooperation and Development (OECD) 1960.
- Russian blockade of Berlin (18 June): Western airlift of supplies begin.
- British Railways inaugurated (1 January), amalgamating existing regional railway companies under national ownership.
- Opening of the first supermarket in Britain, in London (12 January).
- Bread rationing ended (29 July).
- Electricity industry nationalized (1 April).
- The National Health Service comes into effect (5 July).
- Alcoholics Anonymous founded in Britain (15 July).
- The Institute of Contemporary Arts founded in London.
- Opening of the world's first port radar system at Gladstone Dock, Liverpool (30 July).
- Production of the Morris Minor car, designed by Alex Issigonis, begins (12 October).
- Opening of the fourteenth official modern Olympic Games in London (29 July).
- First British Grand Prix run at Silverstone (28 September).

Deaths
Sir Malcolm Campbell, British racing driver (31 December).
Sergei Eisenstein, Soviet film director.
Mohammed Ali Jinnah, Pakistani statesman.
Franz Lehar, Austrian composer.

1949

- People's Republic of China founded with Mao Tse-tung as leader (October); Chinese Nationalist government establishes headquarters on Formosa (December).
- Berlin blockade lifted (12 May); German Federal Republic created with Bonn as capital (23 May); Konrad Adenauer elected first Chancellor of the FDR (August); Soviet sector becomes German Democratic Republic (October).
- Pandit Nehru elected Prime Minister of India.
- Republic of Eire proclaimed in Dublin.
- Eire leaves the British Commonwealth (18 April).
- Recognition of George VI as head of the Commonwealth (27 April).
- North Atlantic Treaty signed in Washington DC (4 April, amended in London by protocol 17 October 1951), setting up the North Atlantic Treaty Organization (NATO), mutual defence pact between 12/13 European nations and the USA.
- Council of Europe comes into effect (5 May).
- Berlin blockade lifted (6 October).
- Test flight of the Canberra jet bomber (13 May).
- Foundation of University College of North Staffordshire at Keele.
- End of clothes rationing (15 March).
- Nationalization of the gas industry (1 May).
- First appearance of The Goon Show comedy series on BBC radio (ran until 1960).
- Weather forecast first televised (29 July).
- Publication of Simone de Beauvoir's *The Second Sex*.
- First performance of Arthur Miller's *Death of a Salesman*.
- Publication of *Nineteen Eighty Four* by George Orwell.
- First flight of the Comet, the first jet-propelled airliner (27 July) and the Brabazon, the largest British aircraft (4 September).
- The Nature Conservancy is set up.
- Plans announced for twelve National Parks in England and Wales.

Deaths

Tommy Handley, British comedian (9 January).
Margaret Mitchell, US author.
Richard Strauss, German composer.

1950

- Labour win general election, the first to be televised (24 February).
- The Stone of Scone (Coronation Stone) stolen from Westminster Abbey by Scottish Nationalists (25 December, retrieved 1951).
- India becomes a republic within the British Commonwealth (26 January).
- Britain recognizes Communist China.
- Sino-Soviet Alliance signed.
- Senator Joseph McCarthy begins Communist witchhunt in US.
- US starts building hydrogen bomb.
- North Korea invades South Korea (25 June): US military forces dominate UN forces, led by General MacArthur, sent to repel Communist advance (June–July); Britain sends troops (August); UN landings at Inchon (September); UN forces capture Communist capital Pyongyang (October); massive Chinese offensive in North Korea (November); Chinese take Pyongyang (December).
- Vietnam partitioned between Communist North and regime in the south under Emperor Bao Dai.
- China invades Tibet.
- Klaus Fuchs found guilty of betraying secrets of atomic bomb constructions to Russia (February).
- Submarine HMS *Truculent* sunk in the Thames following a collision (12 January).
- End of petrol rationing (26 May) and soap rationing (9 September).
- Introduction of Legal Aid in Britain (2 October).
- Foundation of St Anthony's College, Oxford.
- The docking of horses' tails prohibited by law.
- *The Archers* radio serial first broadcast by the BBC.
- Nobel Prize for literature awarded to Bertrand Russell.
- Publication of *The Lion, the Witch and the Wardrobe* by C. S. Lewis.
- Link between cigarettes and lung cancer established.
- The first gas turbine-powered car built by the Rover Company.
- First Outward Bound mountain school opened in Eskdale.
- The Peak District designated the first National Park in England (28 December).
- Execution by hanging of Timothy Evans for the murder of his infant daughter while living in the house of John Christie; the charge of murdering his wife is not heard.

Deaths

Edgar Rice Burroughs, US author.
Al Jolson, US entertainer.
Sir Harry Lauder, Scottish comedian (26 February).
Heinrich Mann, German author.
Vaslav Nijinsky, Russian ballet dancer.
George Orwell (Eric Blair), British author (21 January).
Cesare Pavese, Italian author.

George Bernard Shaw, Irish author and playwright (2 November).
Kurt Weill, German composer.

1951

- Korean War: Seoul captured by Communist forces (4 January); General MacArthur sacked by Truman after threatening invasion of China (April); cease-fire talks begin (July); truce-line established along the 38th parallel (November).
- Vietminh guerillas suffer heavy losses in offensive against the French in Tonkin.
- Treaty of Paris creates European Coal and Steel Community (18 April).
- Winston Churchill prime minister after Conservative victory in general election (25 October).
- 22nd Amendment to the US Constitution limits presidents to two terms, a maximum of eight years in office.
- Julius and Ethel Rosenberg sentenced to death for passing wartime atomic secrets to Russia.
- Libya gains independence.
- Stone of Scone found at Forfar (13 April).
- British diplomats and spies, Guy Burgess and Donald Maclean, escape to the Soviet Union (26 May).
- British troops seized Suez Canal Zone (19 October).
- Festival of Britain held (3 May-30 September).
- Nationalization of railways (1 January).
- First Miss World contest in London (19 April).
- First party political broadcast on television, for the Liberal Party (15 October).
- Introduction of zebra pedestrian crossings (31 October).
- First performance of the opera *Billy Budd* by Benjamin Britten.

Deaths

Ernest Bevin, British Labour statesman (14 April).
André Gide, French author.
William Randolph Hearst, American newspaper magnate.
Sinclair Lewis, US author.
Ivor Novello, British actor and composer (6 March).
Arnold Schoenberg, Austrian-born US composer.
Ludwig Wittgenstein, Austrian philosopher.

1952

- Japan regains sovereign status.
- US launches air strikes against North Korea as peace talks stall.
- State of Emergency declared in Kenya after series of Mau Mau terrorist killings.
- General Neguib leads coup and seizes power in Egypt; King Farouk abdicates in favour of his infant son.
- Riots in South Africa against apartheid laws.
- US tests first hydrogen bomb on Eniwetok atoll in the Pacific.
- Dwight D. Eisenhower elected US President.
- Death of King George VI (6 February): succession of his daughter as Elizabeth II.
- Sovereignty of Ethiopia handed over by Britain.
- Vincent Massey appointed as first Canadian governor-general of Canada (until 1959).
- European Defence Community established (27 May).
- Abolition of identity cards (21 February).
- Lynmouth devastated by floods (16 August).
- Minoan Script B form of Mycenaean Greek first deciphered by Michael Ventris.
- *Waiting for Godot* by Samuel Beckett published.
- Publication of Anne Frank's *Diary*.
- Publication of Ernest Hemingway's *The Old Man and the Sea.*
- First performance of *The Mousetrap* by Agatha Christie (25 November).
- Last tram runs in London (6 July).
- Britain tests its first atomic bomb (3 October).
- Myxomatosis introduced to destroy rabbits in Britain.

Deaths

Paul Eluard, French poet.
Eva ('Evita') Peron, Argentine political activist.
George Santayana, Spanish philosopher.

1953

- Marshall Tito elected President of Yugoslavia.
- General Naguib declares republic in Egypt.
- Stalin dies: Nikita Krushchev emerges as Soviet leader after power struggle.
- Atom spies Julius and Ethel Rosenberg executed in US.
- Korean War ends: armistice signed at Panmunjom
- Russia tests hydrogen bomb.
- Mau Mau leader Jomo Kenyatta jailed in Kenya.
- French Legionnaires capture Dien Bien Phu.
- Agreement signed for laying of the first transatlantic telephone cable.
- Death of Queen Mary, widow of George V (24 March).
- Coronation of Queen Elizabeth II in Britain (2 June).
- Nyasaland (now Malawi) federated with Southern and Northern Rhodesia to form the Federation of Rhodesia and Nyasaland (1 August, until 1963).
- Korean Truce formally ending the Korean War between the United Nations and North Korea signed (27 July).
- End of sweet (4 February) and sugar rationing (26 September).

- Amnesty granted to World War II deserters (23 February).
- Execution of John Christie for murdering four women (15 July); Christie admitted to murdering six other women, including the wife of Timothy Evans.
- Opening of the first television theatre, in Brighton.
- First broadcast of the Panorama programme by BBC television (12 November).
- Sir Arthur Bliss made Master of the Queen's Musick.
- Agreement signed for laying of the first transatlantic telephone cable.
- The double helix structure of DNA (deoxyribonucleic acid) first identified by James D. Watson and Francis Crick.
- Launch of the royal yacht *Britannia*.
- Summit of Mount Everest reached (29 May) by Sir Edmund Hillary and Tenzing Norgay.

Deaths

Hilaire Belloc, British author (16 July).
Kathleen Ferrier, English contralto (8 October)
Eugene O'Neill, US playwright.
Sergei Prokofiev, Soviet composer.
Django Reinhardt, jazz guitarist.
Dylan Thomas, Welsh poet (9 November).
Hank Williams, US country singer.

1954

- Colonel Gamel Abdul Nasser seizes power in Egypt.
- St Lawrence Seaway approved by Eisenhower.
- French defeated by Vietminh forces at Dien Bien Phu (May); Geneva Agreement divides Vietnam into North and South along 17th Parallel.
- US Supreme Court rules against racial segregation in state schools.
- South East Asia Treaty Organization (SEATO) established.
- Senator McCarthy's anti-Communist Senate hearings televised in US: McCarthy eventually censured and condemned by Congress (December).
- Anti-polio vaccine developed by Dr Jonas E. Salk begins intensive trials.
- Anti-British rioting in Cyprus by supporters of EOKA (National Organization of Cypriot Combatants), demanding union with Greece.
- Britain agreed to withdraw troops from the Suez Canal Zone (19 October). Colonel Gamel Abdul Nasser seized power in Egypt (November).
- End of food rationing in Britain (3 July).
- Eurovision—first large-scale television link-up between European countries (6 June).
- First broadcast and publication of *Under Milk Wood* by Dylan Thomas.
- Publication of *Lord of the Flies* by William Golding and *Lucky Jim* by Kingsley Amis.
- Bill Haley and the Comets *We're Gonna Rock Around the Clock*.
- First four-minute mile run (6 May) by the medical student Roger Bannister.

Deaths

Lionel Barrymore, British actor.
Enrico Fermi, Italian physicist.
Wilhelm Furtwangler, German conductor.
Auguste Lumière, French cinema pioneer.
French artist Henri Mattisse.
Alan Turing, British inventor of the Turing Machine, who made important theoretical contributions to computer science, by suicide.

1955

- Civil war between rival factions in Saigon, South Vietnam.
- Italy, West Germany and France establish European Union.
- East-West Geneva Conference.
- Warsaw Pact signed by USSR and Eastern Bloc nations.
- Germany becomes member of NATO.
- Eighty spectators die in crash disaster at Le Mans.
- Civil Rights campaign emerges in US South; Blacks begin bus boycott in Alabama.
- First publication of Vladimir Nabokov's *Lolita*.
- Sir Anthony Eden becomes prime minister (6 April, until 1957) after resignation of Churchill; general election (26 May) won by the Conservatives.
- Clement Attlee resigns as Labour Party leader (7 December) and is replaced by Hugh Gaitskell.
- Formal annexation by the Royal Navy of Rockall Island.
- State of emergency declared in Cyprus after violent demonstrations against British rule.
- Nationalization by Egypt of the Suez Canal. British evacuation of Suez Canal Zone.
- Execution of Ruth Ellis by hanging for the murder of her lover (13 July): the last woman to be hanged in Britain.
- Commercial television begins in Britain (22 September).
- Beginning of the exposure as a fraud of Piltdown man, discovered 1912 (21 November).
- First experimental fast-breeder nuclear reactor started at Dounreay.
- First gas turbine-powered ship (HMS *Grey Goose*).
- Hetton, the oldest mineral railway line, Co. Durham (built by George Stephenson) closed.
- Completion of the aircraft carrier HMS *Ark Royal* (25 February).
- The hovercraft patented by its inventor, Christopher Cockerell (12 December).

Deaths
James Dean, US actor.
Albert Einstein, German-born US physicist.
Sir Alexander Fleming, British scientist (11 March).
Arthur Honegger, Swiss composer.
Fernand Leger, French artist.
Thomas Mann, German novelist.
Charlie Parker, US jazz musician.
Maurice Utrillo, French painter.

1956

- Nikita Khruschev denounces Stalin at 20th Communist Party Congress.
- Race riots in Alabama.
- Pakistan becomes Islamic republic.
- Uprising in Hungary against Soviet control crushed by Soviet tanks.
- Fidel Castro lands in Cuba to lead rebellion against President Batista.
- US film star Grace Kelly marries Prince Rainier III of Monaco.
- Jo Grimond becomes leader of the Liberal Party (until 1967).
- Barbados and Jamaica become part of the British Caribbean Federation.
- British deport Archbishop Makarios, leader of the Greek-Cypriot community, to the Seychelles (9 March).
- Grant of a new constitution in Zanzibar.
- Sudan becomes independent republic (1 January).
- Suez Crisis: Britain evacuates Suez Canal Zone (18 June); Colonel Nasser, president of Egypt, seizes the Suez Canal and nationalizes it (26 July); Israel attacks Egypt (29 October); Anglo-French forces bomb Egyptian military targets (30 October); Allied forces retake Canal Zone (6 November); UN-imposed cease-fire (8 November); Canal blocked (16 November); British forces withdrawn after financial pressure from the US (23 November).
- Abolition of third-class travel on British Railways (3 June).
- ERNIE (Electronic Random Number Indicating Equipment) used to select winning numbers in Premiums Bonds, first issued for sale by the Department of National Savings (1 November).
- Annual Kate Greenaway Medal award for illustration of children's books instituted in memory of Kate Greenaway.
- First experimental transmission of colour television made from Alexandra Palace.
- First performance of *Look Back in Anger* by John Osborne (May).
- Commissioning of the first guided-missile ship (HMS *Girdle Ness*).
- Official opening of Calder Hall atomic power station (17 October).
- First Atlantic telephone cable opened for traffic.

Deaths
Sir Max Beerbohm, British author and cartoonist (20 May).
Bertold Brecht, German playwright.
Walter de la Mare, British poet (22 June).
Alfred Kinsey, US sociologist.
Sir Alexander Korda, Hungarian-born British film director (23 January).
A. A. Milne, British children's author (31 January).
Jackson Pollock, US artist.

1957

- Treaty of Rome, signed by France, Germany, Italy and the Benelux nations, inaugurates the European Community.
- Suez Canal reopened.
- Tunisia becomes republic after Bey is deposed by Premier Bourguiba.
- President Eisenhower sends National Guard into Little Rock, Arkansas to enforce school desegregation.
- Harold Macmillan becomes prime minister (until 1963) after resignation of Sir Anthony Eden (9 January).
- The Gold Coast gained independence within the British Commonwealth as Ghana (6 March); British Togoland joined Ghana.
  Establishment of the West Indies Federation (1 August).
  Malaya becomes independent as a sovereign member state of the British Commonwealth (31 August, joined Malaysia 1963).
- Euratom (European Atomic Energy Authority) established by Treaty of Rome (25 March).
- European Economic Community established by Treaty of Rome (25 March), made up of France, Germany, Italy and the Benelux nations.
- First British hydrogen bomb dropped over Christmas Island (15 May).
- First Premium Bond draw by ERNIE (1 June).
- Publication of Jack Kerouac's *On the Road.*
- Publication of *Room at the Top* by John Braine.
- *Truth* magazine ceased publication.
- Sputnik I (4 October) and Sputnik II (3 November) put into orbit round the earth by Russia.
- Jodrell Bank radio telescope went into operation (11 October).
- The entry into scheduled airline service of the first turboprop airliner (the *Bristol Britannia*).
- The sedative drug Thalidomide first prescribed for pregnant women.

Deaths
Humphrey Bogart, US actor.
Constantin Brancusi, Romanian sculptor.
Christian Dior, French fashion designer.
Jimmy Dorsey, US band leader.
Oliver Hardy, US comedian.
Diego Rivera, Mexican painter.
Dorothy L. Sayers, British detective story writer (18 December).
Jean Sibelius, Finnish composer.
Erich von Stroheim, Austrian actor and film director.
Arturo Toscanini, Italian conductor.

1958

- Egypt and Syria proclaim union as United Arab Republic.
- Alaska becomes 49th US State.
- Dr Vivian Fuchs completes first overland crossing of Antarctica.
- French Nationalist settlers rebel in Algeria.
- King Faisal of Iraq assassinated.
- Cardinal Giuseppe Roncalli becomes Pope John XXIII.
- Fifth Republic established in France with General Charles de Gaulle as first president.
- US nuclear submarine 'Nautilus' sails under the ice-cap at the North Pole.
- Prince Charles created Prince of Wales by Queen Elizabeth II (26 July).
- Women peers appointed to the House of Lords first take their seats (21 October).
- EOKA terrorists step up campaign against British in Cyprus. Anti-British riots.
- European Nuclear Energy Agency founded within OEEC (1 February).
- The Yeomanry and Volunteer Force of the Territorial Army transferred to the Territorial Force.
- Campaign for Nuclear Disarmament (CND) founded by Bertrand Russell and Canon Collins (17 February); organized its first march from London to Aldermaston (7 April).
- Opening of the Planetarium in London (21 March).
- Presentation of the first Duke of Edinburgh Awards (4 June).
- The last presentation of debutantes to the Queen (July).
- Introduction of parking meters in Westminster, London (July).
- The Litter Act comes into force (7 August).
- Race riots in the Notting Hill Gate area of London and in Nottingham (September).
- First performance of *The Birthday Party* by Harold Pinter.
- Publication of *Picture Post* ceased.
- Award of the Nobel Prize for chemistry to Frederick Sanger.
- Development and manufacture of the hovercraft, invented by Christopher Cockerell, undertaken.
- Entry into airline service of the first turbojet (the De Havilland Comet).
- First heart pacemaker inserted.
- First oil tanker of 100,000 deadweight tonnage built.
- Opening of Gatwick Airport (9 June).
- Opening by Harold Macmillan of the first motorway in Britain, the Preston bypass (5 December).
- Thalidomide drug implicated in birth defects (December).
- First drive-in bank in Britain opened in Liverpool (January).
- Empire Games are held in Cardiff (July).
- Seven members of Manchester United football team killed in a plane crash at Munich airport (6 February).

Deaths
Sir William Burrell, Scottish shipping magnate and art collector.
Ronald Colman, British actor (19 May).
Robert Donat, British actor (9 June).
Dame Christabel Pankhurst, British suffragette (13 February)
Tyrone Power, US actor.
Marie Stopes, British pioneer of family planning (2 October)
Ralph Vaughan Williams, British composer (16 August)

1959

- Fidel Castro overthrows Batista regime and takes power in Cuba.
- Indira Gandhi becomes president of Congress Party in India.
- Hawaii becomes 50th US State.
- China supresses uprising in Lhasa: Dalai Lama flees.
- Conservatives re-elected under Harold Macmillan win general election.
- European Free Trade Association inaugurated as rival trading bloc to European Community.
- Archbishop Makarios elected as the first president of the new Republic of Cyprus.
- Conservatives under Harold Macmillan win general election (8 October).
- Agreement by Greece, Turkey and Britain on Cyprus (February)
- Singapore becomes an independent state within the British Commonwealth (3 June).
- European Free Trade Association (EFTA) inaugurated as a rival trading bloc to European Economic Community (3 May).

- Last fly-past of Hurricane bombers and Spitfire fighters over London to commemorate the Battle of Britain (20 September).
- Introduction of the postcode in Britain (3 October).
- Main section of the MI motorway from London to Birmingham officially opened (2 November).
- Empire Day becomes Commonwealth Day (24 May).
- Hugh Carleton Greene becomes director-general of the BBC (until 1969).
- The Mermaid Theatre becomes the first English theatre to be opened in the City of London since the Restoration (28 May).
- Opening of Chapelcross nuclear power station in Dumfriesshire (2 May).
- First Dover-Calais crossing by hovercraft (25 July).
- Introduction of telephone trunk call dialling in Britain (5 September).
- Launch of the *Oriana*, the first transverse-propelled ship.
- Maiden voyage made of the British *Auris*, the world's first gas turbine-powered oil tanker.
- The first heliport in Britain opened in London (23 April).
- British Motor Corporation launches the Mini (August).
- Loch Lomond first swum by Commander Gerald Forsberg, a distance of 22 miles.

Deaths

Raymond Chandler, US author.
Lou Costello, US comedian.
John Foster Dulles, US statesman.
Sir Jacob Epstein, British sculptor (21 August).
George Grosz, German-born US artist.
Errol Flynn, US actor.
Billie Holliday, US singer.
Buddy Holly, US singer.
Cecil B. de Mille, US film director.
Sir Stanley Spencer, British artist.
Frank Lloyd Wright, US architect.

960

American U-2 spy plane shot down over Soviet territory.

Adolf Eichmann captured by Israeli secret service Mossad in Argentina.

Belgian Congo granted independence as Congo Republic under president Patrice Lumumba (1 June); Congolese army mutiny (6 June); Katanga province declares itself independent from Congo and civil war begins (July); Congolese army takes power under Colonel Mobutu (September); Congolese army in conflict with UN troops (November); ex-premier Lumumba arrested (December).

- US nuclear submarine *Triton* completes first underwater circumnavigation of the globe.
- Charles van Doren and 12 other contestants arrested for perjury in testifying that they are not given the answers in advance to questions on top US TV quiz '21'.
- John Fitzgerald Kennedy elected US President.
- First publication of Harper Lee's *To Kill a Mockingbird.*
- 'Wind of Change' speech by Harold Macmillan to the South African Parliament in Cape Town (3 February).

Sharpeville Massacre in South Africa (21 March): 56 Africans killed by police.

- Somalia united with the British Somaliland to become the Somali Republic (1 July).
- The Gold Coast and British Togoland (united in 1957) becomes the independent republic of Ghana within the British Commonwealth (1 July).
- British rule ends and Cyprus becomes an independent republic (16 August): Archbishop Makarios elected as the first president of the new republic.
- Nigeria becomes an independent country within the British Commonwealth (1 October).
- Launch of the *Dreadnought*, Britain's first nuclear-powered submarine (21 October).
- Marriage of Princess Margaret and Antony Armstrong-Jones (later Lord Snowdon) (6 May).
- Churchill College, Cambridge, opened.
- Mumbles Railway, Swansea, the oldest British passenger railway closed (1 January).
- Introduction of MOT (Ministry of Transport) tests on motor vehicles (12 September).
- Introduction of traffic wardens in London (15 September).
- Foundation of the Royal Shakespeare Company.
- *News Chronicle* incorporated in *The Daily Mail.*
- Publication of the complete *Lady Chatterley's* Lover by D. H. Lawrence (2 November): '*Lady Chatterley*' trial in London: Penguin Books found not guilty of publishing obscene material.
- *Coronation Street* first shown on television (9 December).
- First proposal of SI units (Système International) as internationally accepted standard of scientific units: metre, kilogram, second, ampere, kelvin, mole and candela.
- Nobel Prize for physiology or medicine awarded to Sir Peter Medawar and Sir Frank Burnet for work on immunological tolerance.
- English Football League matches first televised (10 September).

Deaths

Aneurin Bevan, Welsh Labour statesman (6 July).

Albert Camus, French author.

Clark Gable, US actor.

Sylvia Pankhurst, British suffragette.

Boris Pasternak, Soviet author.

Mack Sennett, US film director.

Nevil Shute, English-born Australian writer (12 January).

1961

- In referendum French and Algerian voters support De Gaulle's policy of home rule for Algeria.
- US severs diplomatic relations with Cuba.
- President Kennedy establishes US Peace Corps.
- Soviet cosmonaut Major Yuri Alexeyevitch Gagarin becomes first man in space.
- US-armed Cuban exiles stage unsuccessful invasion of Cuba at Bay of Pigs.
- Berlin Wall constructed.
- UN Secretary-General Dag Hammarskjöld killed in plane crash.
- Adolf Eichmann sentenced to death for war crimes at trial in Jerusalem.
- Britain begins negotiations to join the European Community.
- British police arrest members of the Portland spy ring (January).
- Jamaica leaves the West Indies Federation (19 September).
- Northern Cameroons joins the Federation of Nigeria (1 June). Sierra Leone (27 April) and Tanganyika (9 December) becomes independent within the British Commonwealth. Union of South Africa withdraws from the Commonwealth (15 March) and becomes a republic (31 May). Kuwait becomes completely independent.
- The Organization for Economic Cooperation and Development (OECD) established in Paris (30 September), succeeding the Organization for European Economic Cooperation (OEEC).
- Amnesty International founded.
- The farthing ceases to be legal tender in Britain (1 January).
- The Pill, oral contraceptive, goes on sale in Britain.
- Introduction of mini cabs in London (6 March).
- Black-and-white £5 notes issued by the Bank of England cease to be legal tender (13 March).
- Opening of betting shops (1 May).
- Enthronement of Dr Ramsey as hundredth archbishop of Canterbury (27 June).
- First publication of Joseph Heller's *Catch 22*.
- First performance of the review *Beyond the Fringe* at the Edinburgh Festival with Alan Bennett, Peter Cook, Jonathan Miller and Dudley Moore.
- Completion of the Tamar Bridge linking Cornwall and Devon.

Deaths

Sir Thomas Beecham, British conductor (8 March).

Gary Cooper, US actor.

(Samuel) Dashiell Hammett, US author.

George Formby, British comedian.

Ernest Hemmingway, US author.

Augustus John, British painter (31 October).

Carl Jung, Swiss psychoanalyst.

James Thurber, US author.

1962

- US steps up miltary aid to South Vietnam.
- Adolf Eichmann hanged for Nazi war crimes.
- France recognizes independence of Algeria.
- Riots in Deep South as University of Mississippi enrols black student James Meredith.
- Uganda and Tanganyika gain independence.
- Cuban Missile crisis.
- Trans-Canada Highway opened.
- Western Samoa becomes independent within the Commonwealth (1 January). Dissolution of the West Indies Federation (31 May): Jamaica (5 August) and Trinidad and Tobago (31 August) become independent within the Commonwealth. Uganda becomes independent within the Commonwealth (9 October); Tanganyika becomes a republic within the Commonwealth (9 December).
- Consecration of Coventry Cathedral (15 May, begun 1951), designed by Basil Spence.
- Establishment of the National Theatre in London with Sir Laurence Olivier as director (9 August).
- Nobel Prize for medicine and physiology awarded to Francis Crick and James D. Watson for their double-helix model of the structure of DNA.
- Telstar communications satellite launched (10 July): first live transatlantic television broadcast.
- Thalidomide withdrawn from the market after discovery that it causes severe birth defects.
- World's first passenger hovercraft enters service.

Deaths

Niels Bohr, Danish nuclear physicist.

William Faulkner, US author.

Herman Hesse, German-born Swiss author.

Charles Laughton, British actor (15 December).

Marilyn Monroe, US actress.

Richard Tawney, British socialist historian.

George Trevelyan, British historian (21 July).

Victoria Sackville-West, British writer.

1963

- President de Gaulle of France vetoes British entry into the European Community.

- Civil Rights demonstrations in Birmingham, Alabama: Martin Luther King arrested.
- Cardinal Giovanni Battista Monitine elected Pope John XXIII.
- 200,000 join civil rights 'Freedom March' on Washington DC.
- Buddhist riots in Saigon.
- Russia puts first woman in space, Lieutenant Valentina Tereshkova.
- Sir Alec Douglas Home succeeds Harold Macmillan as prime minister.
- Test Ban Treaty signed by Britain, US and Russia.
- President John F. Kennedy assassinated by Lee Harvey Oswald in Dallas, Texas: succeeded by Vice President Lyndon Baines Johnson.
- Lee Harvey Oswald shot by nightclub owner Jack Ruby at Dallas police headquarters.
- Military coup overthrows regime of President Ngo Dinh Diem in South Vietnam.
- Defection of Kim Philby to the Soviet Union (January).
- Unexpected death of Hugh Gaitskell, leader of the Labour Party (18 January): succeeded by Harold Wilson (14 February).
- The Profumo Affair: resignation (5 June) of John Profumo, Secretary of State for War, after lying to Parliament about an affair with a call girl, Christine Keeler, who is also involved with a Russian diplomat.
- The Profumo Affair and ill health forces Macmillan to retire (10 October); succeeded by Sir Alec Douglas-Home, formerly Lord Home (30 November).
- Aden joins the South Arabian Federation (21 March). Formation of the Federation of Malaysia (16 September): made up of Malaya, Singapore, Sabah and Sarawak. Nigeria becomes a republic (1 October) within the British Commonwealth. British protectorate of Zanzibar ends and it becomes independent (9 December). Kenya gains independence within the British Commonwealth (12 December).
- Violent clashes between Turkish and Greek Cypriots in Cyprus: UN peace forces intervene (22 December).
- President de Gaulle of France vetoes British entry into the European Economic Community (29 January).
- Test Ban Treaty signed by Britain, US and Russia (5 August).
- Britain agrees to buy Polaris missiles from the US.
- Beeching Report recommends extensive cuts in British railway branch lines (27 March).
- Great Train Robbery (8 August): £2.5 million stolen from the Glasgow to London mail train (12 of the gang are tried and convicted in 1964).
- *Doctor Who*, children's TV series, begins.
- Publication of *The Spy Who Came in from the Cold* by John Le Carré.
- The Beatles pop group founded (disbanded 1970).
- Opening of the Dartford Tunnel under the Thames (18 November).

Deaths

Georges Braque, French Cubist painter.
Jean Cocteau, French artist and writer.
Robert Frost, US poet.
Paul Hindemith, German composer.
Aldous Huxley, British writer (22 November).
Max Miller, British comedian.
Lord Nuffield, British motor car manufacturer and philanthropist (22 August).
Edith Piaf, French singer.
Francis Poulenc, French composer.
Dinah Washington, US blues singer.
William Carlos Williams, US poet.

1964

- Constantine II becomes king of Greece on death of King Paul I.
- Violent clashes between Turkish and Greek Cypriots in Cyprus: UN peace forces intervene.
- Gulf of Tonkin Incident: US destroyers allegedly attacked by North Vietnamese torpedo boats; President Johnson orders air strikes against the North.
- Warren Commission finds Lee Harvey Oswald acted alone in assassination of President Kennedy.
- Jawaharl Nehru, Indian Prime Minister since independence, dies after heart attack.
- Black Nationalist leader Nelson Mandela sentenced to life imprisonment in South Africa.
- President Johnson signs Civil Rights Act.
- Soviet leader Nikita Khrushchev deposed; replaced by Leonid Brezhnev as Communist party leader and Alexei Kosygin as prime minister.
- Martin Luther King awarded Nobel Peace Prize.
- Lyndon Johnson wins landslide victory in US presidential election.
- Harold Wilson becomes prime minister (until 1970) after a general election (15 October).
- Zanzibar becomes a republic (12 January) and joined Tanganyika to form the United Republic of Tanzania (27 April). Southern Rhodesia renamed Rhodesia (until 1979); Ian Smith becomes prime minister (8 April). Nyasaland (now Malawi) becomes independent within the Commonwealth (6 July). Malta becomes independent (21 September). Northern Rhodesia becomes the independent republic of Zambia within the British Commonwealth (24 October). Kenya becomes a republic within the Common-

wealth (12 December) with Jomo Kenyatta as president.

- Last hangings in Britain (13 August): Peter Allen and John Walby.
- First broadcast of Radio Caroline radio station (28 March) and of the BBC2 television channel (21 April). Opening of Radio Manx, first British commercial radio station (23 November).
- Official opening of the Forth Road Bridge (4 September, begun 21 November 1958).
- Blue Streak, first British rocket launched into space at Woomera, Australia (5 June).
- World land speed record set by Donald Campbell in Australia (17 July).

Deaths

Lord Beaverbrook, Canadian-born British newspaper tycoon (9 June).

Brendan Behan, Irish playwright.

Ian Fleming, British novelist and creator of James Bond (12 August).

Alan Ladd, US actor.

Peter Lorre, US actor.

Harpo Marx, US comedian.

General Douglas MacArthur, US soldier.

Sean O'Casey, Irish playwright.

Flannery O'Connor, US novelist.

Cole Porter, US composer.

1965

- Militant Black leader Malcolm X assassinated in New York.
- President Johnson sends marines into Vietnam.
- Race riots in Watts, Los Angeles.
- India and Pakistan at war over disputed territory of Kashmir.
- Singapore separates from Malyasia.
- General de Gaulle wins French presidential election.
- Resignation of Sir Alec Douglas-Home as leader of the Conservative Party: Edward Heath becomes its first elected leader.
- The Gambia gains independence as a kingdom within the British Commonwealth (18 February). The Maldives in the Indian Ocean becomes independent (26 July). Singapore separated from Malaysia (9 August). Rhodesia declared unilateral declaration of independence (UDI) (11 November); Ian Smith's regime declared illegal. Britain imposes oil embargo.
- Free-trade pact between Britain and Eire (14 December).
- Opening of the Pennine Way from Derbyshire to Roxburghshire (23 April).
- Abolition of the death penalty for murder in Britain (9 November).
- Formation of the Greater London Council (1 April).
- Television advertising of cigarettes banned (31 July).
- Opening of the Post Office Tower, tallest building in Britain (7 October).
- Introduction of a speed limit of 70 miles per hour on motorways (22 December).
- Confederation of British Industries (CBI) founded.
- Starting stalls first used in horse races, at Newmarket (8 July).

Deaths

Sir Winston Leonard Churchill, British Conservative statesman (24 January).

Nat King Cole, US singer.

T. S. Eliot, American-born British poet (4 January).

Stan Laurel, British-born US comedian (23 February).

Le Corbusier (Charles Edouard Jeanneret), Swiss-born French architect.

Albert Schweitzer, German-born French doctor and missionary.

1966

- Indira Gandhi becomes prime minister of India.
- Mao Tse-tung proclaims 'Cultural Revolution' in China.
- Prime Minister Dr Hendrik Verwoerd assassinated in South Africa and is succeeded by B. J. Vorster.
- President de Gaulle announces that France is to withdraw her troops from NATO.
- General election (31 March): Labour win. The first Welsh Nationalist member of parliament, Gwynfor Evans, takes his seat (21 July) after a by-election.
- Opening of Parliament first televised (21 April).
- Bechuanaland becomes fully independent as Botswana (30 September). British protectorate ended and Basutoland (now Lesotho) becomes independent (4 October). British Guiana becomes the independent republic of Guyana within the Commonwealth. Barbados becomes independent within the Commonwealth (30 November).
- Aberfan disaster in Wales (27 October): 144 people killed, including 116 children, by a collapsing slag heap.
- Moors murderers Myra Hindley and Ian Brady sentenced to life imprisonment (6 May).
- Special Christmas stamps issued for the first time (1 December).
- First publication of Truman Capote's *In Cold Blood.*
- First performance of *Rosencrantz and Guildenstern are Dead* by Tom Stoppard.
- Official opening of the Severn Bridge (8 September).
- Introduction of breathalyser tests.
- Launch of Britain's first Polaris submarine, *Resolution* (16 September).

- Discovery of gas fields in the North Sea (May).
- The first non-stop solo voyage around the world begun by Francis Chichester (27 August).
- The first Britons to row across the Atlantic, Captain John Ridgway and Sergeant Chay Blyth, (arrive 3 September).
- Football World Cup held in England: won by the England team (30 July).

Deaths

André Breton, French poet and author.
Lenny Bruce, US comedian.
Montgomery Clift, US actor.
Walt Disney, US animator.
Alberto Giacometti, Italian sculptor.
Buster Keaton, US actor and director.
Evelyn Waugh, British novelist (10 April).

1967

- Six Day War between Israel and Arab nations: Israel takes territory from Egypt, Jordan and Syria.
- 50,000 demonstrators against the Vietnam War gather at the Lincoln Memorial in Washington DC.
- Ernesto ('Che') Guevara shot dead in the Bolivian jungle.
- Eastern region of Nigeria breaks away as independent state of Biafra.
- US airforce intensifies bombing of North Vietnam.
- Christian N. Barnard performs first heart transplant in Groote Schuur Hospital, Cape Town.
- Fire kills three US astronauts in Apollo spacecraft on launch pad.
- Expo 67 opens in Montreal.
- Abortion Bill passed by parliament (25 October).
- Jeremy Thorpe elected leader of the Liberal Party after the retirement of Jo Grimond (18 January).
- Colony status of Antigua ended. Uganda becomes a republic (8 September). Last British troops leave Aden (30 November); Aden becomes part of People's Republic of Southern Yemen. St Lucia gained self-government.
- The first Scottish Nationalist member of parliament, Winifred Ewing, takes her seat (2 November) after a by-election.
- Britain reapplies to join the European Economic Community.
- Renationalization of the steel industry (28 July).
- Introduction of majority jury verdicts in English courts; first instance in Brighton (5 October).
- First British ombudsman, Sir Edmund Compton, takes office (1 April).
- Opening of the Roman Catholic Cathedral in Liverpool (14 May).
- Colour television first broadcast by BBC2 (1 July).
- Radio 1 first broadcast by the BBC (30 September).
- Opening of the first local radio station, Radio Leicester (8 November).
- North Sea gas first pumped ashore in Co. Durham (4 March).
- The oil tanker *Torrey Canyon* goes aground off Land's End causing major pollution of the coastline (30 March).
- Launch of the first British satellite, Ariel III (5 May).
- Cunard liner *Queen Elizabeth II* launched by Queen Elizabeth II (20 September).
- The first non-stop solo voyage around the world completed by Francis Chichester (28 May): he is knighted by Elizabeth II.

Deaths

Konrad Adenauer, German statesman.
Clement Attlee, British Labour statesman (8 October)
Donald Campbell, British car and speedboat racer, killed in jet-powered boat *Bluebird* crash on Lake Coniston while attempting to break the world waterspeed record (4 January).
John Coltrane, US jazz musician.
Brian Epstein, manager of the Beatles, by committing suicide.
Sir Victor Gollancz, British publisher and founder of the Left Book Club (8 February).
J. Vivien Leigh, British actress (8 July).
René Magritte, Belgian artist.
John Masefield, British poet laureate (12 May); succeeded by Cecil Day Lewis.
J. Robert Oppenheimer, US nuclear physicist.
Joe Orton, British playwright, murdered by his lover, Kenneth Halliwell, who commits suicide.
Dorothy Parker, US author and critic.
Claude Rains, US actor.
Arthur Ransome, British author.
Carl Sandburg, US poet.
Siegfried Sassoon, British poet (1 September).
Spencer Tracy, US actor.

1968

- Tet (New Year) Offensive in Vietnam: Vietcong launch widespread attacks against southern cities.
- Alexander Dubcek named First Secretary of Czechoslovak Communist Party; begins reform of socialist system.
- US President Johnson announces he will not seek reelection.
- Martin Luther King assassinated in Memphis hotel.
- Robert Kennedy assassinated in Los Angeles hotel.
- Student riots and street-fighting in Paris.
- Soviet tanks move into Prague to surpress 'Prague Spring' reform programme.
- Violent anti-Vietnam war demonstrations disrupt

Democratic Party Convention in Chicago.
- Richard M. Nixon elected US President.
- Enoch Powell makes his 'rivers of blood' speech on immigration (6 May).
- Race Relations Act comes into force (26 November).
- Mauritius becomes an independent nation within the British Commonwealth (12 March). Swaziland becomes independent as a kingdom within the British Commonwealth (6 September).
- Collapse after a gas explosion of the high-rise building Ronan Point, killing three people.
- Introduction of two levels of postal service, first and second class (16 September).
- Issue of 5p and 10p decimal coins (23 April).
- Opening of the University of Ulster at Coleraine, Northern Ireland (1 October).
- Violent anti-Vietnam war demonstrations in London (17 March).
- Publication of *2001, A Space Odyssey* by Arthur C. Clarke.
- Opening of the new Euston Station (14 October).
- The first heart transplant operation in Britain is carried out (3 May).
- MCC tour of South Africa cancelled by the South African prime minister, John Vorster, because of the presence in the English team of the player Basil D'Oliviera.
- European Cup first won by an English team, Manchester United (29 May).

Deaths

Enid Blyton, British children's author (28 November).
Jim Clark, British racing driver, in a crash during the German Grand Prix (7 April).
Tony Hancock, British comedian, in Australia by suicide (24 June).
Mervyn Peake, British author and artist.
Upton Sinclair, US author.

1969

- Jan Palach, Czech student, burns himself to death in protest against Soviet occupation of Prague.
- Golda Meir becomes president of Israel.
- General de Gaulle resigns as French president: George Pompidou elected to replace him.
- Yassar Arafat appointed leader of the Palestine Liberation Organization.
- Neil Armstrong, commander of US spacecraft Apollo 11, becomes the first man on the moon.
- Chappaquiddick Incident: Senator Edward Kennedy fails to report car accident in which his passenger, Mary Jo Kopechne, is killed.
- Sharon Tate, pregnant wife of film director Roman Polanski, is brutally murdered in Beverly Hills mansion by Charles Manson gang.
- Colonel Muammar Gaddafi seizes power in Libya.
- 'Vietnam Moratorium': largest ever anti-Vietnam war demonstrations in the US.
- Nigeria bans Red Cross aid for starving Biafrans.
- Investiture of Prince Charles as Prince of Wales at Caernarvon Castle (1 July).
- Northern Ireland Crisis. Eruption of violence between Protestant and Catholic communities in Northern Ireland: British troops are sent to suppress conflict (August); a 'peace wall' is constructed between the two communities in Belfast (28 September); the formation of the Ulster Defence Regiment is agreed by Parliament (18 December).
- Formation of St Vincent and the Grenadines into a British Associated State (until 1979).
- Voting age lowered from 21 to 18 (17 April).
- Television broadcasting in colour begins (14 November).
- Introduction of the 50p decimal coin (14 October).
- First publication of Kurt Vonnegut's *Slaughterhouse Five.*
- First publication of Philip Roth's *Portnoy's Complaint.*
- British-built supersonic *Concorde* makes maiden flight (9 January).
- Oil discovered in the British and Norwegian sectors of the North Sea.

Deaths

Richmal Crompton, British children's author, creator of William.
Otto Dix, German artist
Judy Garland, US actress and singer.
Walter Gropius, German architect.
Brian Jones, British rock musician, member of the Rolling Stones.
Jack Kerouac, US author.
John Wyndham, British author.

1970

- Biafran Civil War ends with Biafran capitulation to Nigerian Federal forces.
- Gambia gains independence.
- President Nixon sends US troops into Cambodia.
- Four students killed by National Guard during anti-Vietnam war demonstration at Kent State University, Ohio.
- Salvador Allende elected President of Chile.
- Palestinian commandos hijack and blow up three airliners at Dawson's Field, Jordan.
- Anwar Sadat succeeds Gamel Abdul Nasser as President of Egypt.
- Typhoon and tidal wave kill 150,000 in East Pakistan.

- First publication of Germaine Greer's *The Female Eunuch.*
- Northern Ireland Crisis. Riots in the Catholic Bogside district of Londonderry; troops seal it off (29 March); first use of rubber bullets by the army in Belfast (2 August); Democratic Unionist Rev. Ian Paisley becomes a Stormont (April) and Westminster member of parliament (June); foundation of the liberal Alliance Party (April); the Social Democratic and Labour Party (SDLP) launched by Gerry Fitt and John Hume as a moderate nationalist party (21 August).
- Conservatives win general election (19 June) and Edward Heath becomes prime minister (until 1974).
- Britain makes third application to join European Economic Community.
- Guyana becomes a republic (23 February).
- Rhodesia proclaimed a republic (2 March).
- Tonga (4 June) and Fiji (10 October) gained independence within the British Commonwealth.
- High Court award of damages to children with birth defects caused by the drug Thalidomide (23 March).
- Decimal postage stamps first issued for sale in Britain (17 June).
- The ten-shilling banknote goes out of circulation (20 November).
- Publication of *The Female Eunuch* by Germaine Greer.
- Split of The Beatles pop group (April).
- Return of the *Great Britain* to Bristol from the Falklands (23 June).

Deaths

Sir John Barbirolli, British conductor (29 July).
General Charles de Gaulle, French statesman.
E(dward) M(organ) Forster, British novelist (7 June).
John Dos Passos, US author.
Eva Hesse, German-born US sculptor.
Jimi Hendrix, US guitarist.
Ian MacLeod, British Conservative politician (20 July)
Yukio Mishima, Japanese author.
Erich Maria Remarque, German author.
Mark Rothko, US artist.
Bertrand Arthur William Russell, British philosopher (2 February)

1971

- Fighting in Vietnam spreads to Laos and Cambodia.
- General Idi Amin seizes power from President Milton Obote in Uganda.
- Lieutenant William L. Calley Jr found guilty of massacre in My Lai village, Vietnam in 1968.
- 'Pentagon Papers' exposing secret history of US involvement in Vietnam begin to appear in the *New York Times.*
- Civil war in Pakistan after East Pakistan declares itself independent as the new state of Bangladesh.
- Jean-Claude Duvalier succeeds his father, Francois 'Papa Doc' Duvalier, as president of Haiti.
- China is admitted to the United Nations.
- Attica prison revolt: 10 warders and 32 prisoners die in five days of mayhem.
- India defeats Pakistan in two-week war.
- Earthquake in Los Angeles kills 51 people.
- Introduction of decimal currency in Britain (15 February).
- Northern Ireland Crisis. James Chichester-Clark resigned as prime minister of Northern Ireland and is succeeded by Brian Faulkner (21 March); Britain sends more troops and introduces internment (imprisonment without trial) to combat IRA terrorism (August).
- Agreement signed to prepare Rhodesia's legal independence from Britain and settle issue of transition to African majority rule.
- Declaration of Sierra Leone as a republic.
- East Bengal fights war of independence and becomes Bangladesh.
- Bahrain (British protectorate from 1861) and the Persian Gulf State of Qatar becomes independent.
- Open University inaugurated.
- Sixty-six football fans crushed by collapsed barrier at Ibrox Park stadium in Glasgow (2 January).

Deaths

Louis Armstrong, US jazz trumpeter.
Gabrielle 'Coco' Chanel, French fashion designer.
Harold Lloyd, US film actor and comedian.
Ogden Nash, US poet.
Igor Stravinsky, Russian composer.

1972

- Bangladesh (East Pakistan) established as independent state.
- President Nixon visits Russia and China.
- Five burglars arrested in Democratic National Headquarters in the Watergate Building in Washington DC: beginning of Watergate Affair.
- George Wallace, governor of Alabama, paralysed after assassination attempt.
- Lon Nol takes power in Cambodia.
- Ireland, Britain and Denmark become full members of the European Community.
- Japanese terrorists massacre 25 people at Lod International airport, Tel Aviv.
- Last US combat troops withdraw from South Vietnam: US bombing of North Vietnam and Viet Cong supply routes in the south intensifies.
- 'Black September' Arab terrorists kill two Israeli atheletes at Munich Olympics.

- Idi Amin expels 50,000 Ugandan Asians with British passports.
- Earthquake in Managua, Nicaragua kills 10,000.
- Philippine President Marcos declares martial law to combat so-called 'Communist rebellion'.
- Northern Ireland Crisis. Bloody Sunday, Londonderry, Northern Ireland (30 January): British paratroopers fire on civil rights demonstrators, killing thirteen. Parliament of Northern Ireland suspended and replaced by direct rule from London.
- Ceylon becomes a republic within the British Commonwealth and renamed Democratic Socialist Republic of Sri Lanka (22 May).
- Idi Amin expelled 50,000 Ugandan Asians with British passports.
- Nobel Peace prize awarded to Amnesty International.

Deaths

Maurice Chevalier, French actor and singer.
J. Edgar Hoover, FBI director since 1924.
Dr Louis Leakey, British anthropologist.
Cecil Day Lewis, British novelist and poet laureate (22 May). Sir John Betjeman appointed poet laureate (10 October).
Ezra Pound, US poet.
The Duke of Windsor (formerly Edward VIII) in Paris (28 May).

1973

- Cease-fire in Vietnam agreed at Paris peace conference.
- Yom Kippur War: Egyptian forces launch surprise attack on Israeli positions along Suez Canal.
- Top Nixon aids, including H.R. Haldemann and John D. Ehrlichman, resign as Watergate scandal penetrates the Oval Office (April); Senate Watergate hearings begin (May).
- President Salvador Allende killed during military coup in Chile.
- Greek army seizes power in Athens overthrowing President George Papadopoulos.
- Arab oil countries increase prices and cut production in protest at US support of Israel in Yom Kippur War.
- Publication of Alexandr Solzhenitsyn's *Gulag Archipelago*.
- Britain and Ireland joined the European Economic Community (the Common Market) (1 January).
- Miners' strike brings government announcement of three-day week to conserve fuel stocks (13 December).
- Bahamas becomes independent country within the British Commonwealth (10 July). British Honduras ren amed Belize.
- First woman allowed on to the floor of the London Stock Exchange (26 March).
- VAT (Value-Added Tax) introduced in Britain (1 April).
- British Library established.
- Introduction of teletext for displaying information on a TV screen.
- First commercial radio station (London Broadcasting) begins transmission (8 October).
- Red Rum wins the Grand National (31 March).

Deaths

W(ystan) H(ugh) Auden, British poet (28 September).
Elizabeth Bowen, Irish writer.
Sir Noel Coward, British playwright (26 March).
John Ford, US film director.
Bruce Lee, Kung Fu film star.
Pablo Picasso, Spanish artist.
Edward G. Robinson, US actor.
John Ronald Reuel Tolkien, British author (2 September)

1974

- Bloodless coup in Portugal: dictatorship ended by military intervention and democratic reforms inaugurated.
- Syria and Israel agree to cease-fire on the Golan Heights.
- Turkish invasion of Cyprus.
- President Nixon resigns as White House tape recordings implicate him in Watergate cover-up and Senate moves to impeach him; Gerald Ford sworn in as new president.
- Greek military junta collapses and ex-Premier Constantine Karamanlis returns from exile to head new government.
- President Haile Salassie overthrown by coup in Ethiopia.
- Edward Heath resigns, and Harold Wilson leads minority government after snap election (March); Labour wins second election with tiny majority (October); Wilson prime minister until 1976.
- IRA bombs kill 21 and injure 120 in two Birmingham pubs.
- Grenada becomes fully independent within the Commonwealth (7 February).
- Disappearance of Lord Lucan after the murder of his children's nanny and the attempted murder of his wife (7 November).
- Covent Garden fruit market moves to Nine Elms (8 November).
- First large-scale prototype fast-breeder nuclear reactor at Dounreay.

Deaths

Duke Ellington, US jazz musician.
Samuel Goldwyn, US film producer.

Vittorio de Sica, Italian film director.

Eric Linklater, British novelist.

Walter Lippman, US journalist.

1975

- Angola achieves independence from Portugal (January); civil war breaks out (November).
- Saigon surrenders to North Vietnamese troops.
- Communist Khmer Rouge seize control of Cambodia: Pol Pot regime inaugurates 'Year Zero'.
- Beirut erupts in civil war between Christians and Moslems.
- Spain reverts to monarchy after the death of General Franco: Prince Juan Carlos crowned as King Juan Carlos I.
- Suez Canal reopens for first time since 1967 Arab-Israeli War.
- Terrorists led by Carlos the Jackal raid Vienna headquarters of the Organization of Petroleum Exporting Countries (OPEC).
- Internment (detention without trial) ends in Northern Ireland.
- Margaret Thatcher elected first woman leader of the Conservative Party.
- Referendum held on Britain's entry to the European Community (5 June); result in favour of staying in the Community.
- First live broadcast of House of Commons debate.
- Introduction of the first domestic video recorders (Sony Betamax).
- The Equal Pay Act and the Sex Discrimination Act comes into effect (27 December).
- Dr Donald Coggan becomes archbishop of Canterbury (25 January).
- Rev. David Sheppard becomes bishop of Liverpool.
- North Sea oil first pumped ashore in Britain (11 June).

Deaths

Sir Arthur Bliss, British composer and Master of the Queen's Musick (27 March).

Sir Neville Cardus, British music critic and cricket writer.

Sam Giancana, Chicago Mafia boss.

Susan Hayward, US actress.

Graham Hill, British racing driver, in a plane crash (29 November).

Sir Julian Huxley, British scientist and philosopher.

Aristotle Onassis, Greek shipping magnate.

Dimitri Shostakovich, Russian composer.

Thornton Wilder, US writer.

Sir P(elham) G(renville) Wodehouse, British-born US author and creator of Jeeves (14 February).

1976

- President Isabel Peron overthrown by Argentine military in bloodless coup.
- US celebrates its bicentennial.
- Dr Mario Soares elected prime minister of Portugal.
- North and South Vietnam reunified as Socialist Republic of Vietnam with Hanoi as capital: Saigon renamed Ho Chi Minh City.
- Death of Chairman Mao Tse-tung.
- Jimmy Carter elected US President.
- Israeli commandos rescue 103 hostages held at Entebbe airport, Uganda, by pro-Palestinian hijackers.
- Widespread anti-apartheid riots in black townships of South Africa.
- Harold Wilson resigns: succeeded as prime minister by James Callaghan (until 1979).
- Jeremy Thorpe resigns as leader of the Liberal Party; David Steel elected to replace him.
- Ian Smith accepts British proposal for majority rule in Rhodesia, ending eleven years of illegal independence.
- Seychelles becomes an independent republic within the Commonwealth (28 June).
- Opening of the National Exhibition Centre at Birmingham by Elizabeth II (2 February).
- Publication of *The Selfish Gene* by Richard Dawkins.
- First scheduled supersonic passenger service inaugurated: two Concorde airliners take off simultaneously from London and Paris (21 January).

Deaths

Dame Agatha Christie, British crime writer (12 January).

Benjamin Britten, British composer (4 December).

Max Ernst, German-born French artist.

John Paul Getty, US oil tycoon.

Howard Hughes, US tycoon.

Chou En-lai, Chinese Premier.

Fritz Lang, German film director.

Laurence Stephen Lowry, British painter (23 February)

Man Ray, US artist and photographer.

André Malraux, French writer and politician.

Field Marshal Bernard Law Montgomery, Viscount Montgomery of El Alamein, British commander (24 March)

Paul Robeson, US singer and Black activist.

1977

- Moraji R. Desai becomes prime minister of India after resignation of Indira Gandhi.
- Menahem Begin becomes prime minister of Israel after resignation of Yitzhak Rabin.

- Convicted murderer Gary Gilmore executed by firing squad in Utah State prison: first convict to be executed in the US in ten years.
- Egyptian President Anwar Sadat visits Israel, the first visit by an Arab leader since the Jewish state was founded in 1948.
- Two Jumbo jets collide at Tenerife airport: 574 passengers killed in world's worst aviation disaster.
- Prime minister of Pakistan, Zulfikar Ali Bhutto, overthrown by General Zia ul-Huq.
- South African black leader Steve Biko beaten to death in prison cell at Port Elizabeth.
- US Space Shuttle makes maiden flight on top of a Boeing 747.
- Liberal and Labour parties form Lib-Lab Pact.
- Award of the Nobel Prize for chemistry to Frederick Sanger.
- Red Rum wins the Grand National for the third time, a record (2 April).

Deaths

Maria Callas, Greek soprano.
Sir Charles Chaplin, British actor and director (25 December).
Joan Crawford, US actress.
Bing Crosby, US singer and actor.
Peter Finch, Australian-born actor (14 January).
Julius 'Groucho' Marx, US actor and comedian.
Vladimir Nabokov, Russian-born US author.
Anais Nin, US author.
Elvis Presley, US rock singer, of a drug overdose at the age of forty-two.
Terence Rattigan, British playwright (30 November)

1978

- Former Italian prime minister Aldo Moro is kidnapped and murdered by Red Brigade terrorists.
- Military junta seizes power in Afghanistan.
- US establishes full diplomatic relations with People's Republic of China.
- Pieter Willem Botha Prime Minister of South Africa after resignation of John Vorster.
- Military coup in Bolivia.
- Prime Minister of Israel Menaham Begin and Egyptian President Anwar Sadat agree on framework for Middle East peace treaty at Camp David summit, organized by President Carter.
- Shah of Iran imposes martial law to surpress anti-government demonstrations.
- Cardinal Luciani elected Pope John Paul I; he dies after 33 days in office and is succeeded by Polish Cardinal Karol Wojtyla as Pope John Paul II.
- Members of the People's Temple, a US religious cult led by Rev. Jim Jones, commit mass suicide in Guyana.
- Beginning of 'Winter of Discontent', a time of pay freezes and strikes under the Callaghan Labour government.
- Ecu international currency unit adopted by the European Community.
- The *in vitro* fertilization technique first used successfully: first 'test-tube baby', Louise Browne, born (25 July).

Deaths

Charles Boyer, French actor.
Jacques Brel, Belgian singer.
Jomo Kenyatta, Kenyan statesman.
Margaret Mead, US anthropologist.

1979

- Shah of Iran is driven into exile by supporters of Moslem leader Ayatollah Khomeini who returns to Tehran after 14 years in exile.
- Vietnam invades Cambodia and crushes Khmer Rouge regime: evidence emerges of mass killings under leader Pol Pot.
- Regime of Idi Amin collapses in Uganda.
- Egypt and Israel sign peace treaty sponsored by President Carter.
- Leonid Brezhnev and President Carter sign SALT-2 arms limitation treaty.
- Accident at Three Mile Island nuclear plant in Pennsylvania.
- Sandinista rebels overthrow dictator General Anastasio Samosa in Nicaragua.
- Supporters of Ayatollah Khomenei attack US embassy in Tehran and seize Marines and staff as hostages.
- Soviet troops invade Afghanistan.
- General election: Labour defeated by Conservatives. Margaret Thatcher becomes first British woman prime minister (4 May, until 1990).
- Nationalist hopes for devolution killed by referendum results: a majority vote against a Welsh Assembly, and only 33 per cent for a Scottish Assembly, short of the 40 per cent required.
- Lancaster House agreement arranges cease-fire in the guerrilla war in Rhodesia and elections to effect transfer to Black majority rule in a new state to be called Zimbabwe.
- St Lucia and St Vincent gain full independence within the Commonwealth.
- Robert Runcie becomes archbishop of Canterbury (until 1990).
- Earl Mountbatten of Burma murdered by an IRA bomb (27 August).
- Sir Anthony Blunt, Surveyor of the Queen's Pictures, revealed as Soviet spy, the 'fourth man' in the Burgess, Maclean and Philby affair; stripped of his knighthood.

Deaths

Dame Gracie Fields, British actress and singer (27 September).
Herbert Marcuse, German-born US philosopher.
Mary Pickford, US actress.
Jean Renoir, French film director.
Nelson Rockefeller, US politician.
Jean Seberg, US actress.
John Wayne, US actor.

1980

- US military bid to rescue hostages held by Iranians in Tehran embassy aborted due to mechanical failures.
- Archbishop Romero shot in San Salvador, El Salvador.
- Sanjay Gandhi, the 33-year-old youngest son of Indira Gandhi, killed in plane crash.
- Polish strikers led by Lech Walesa win concessions from Communist government on trade union rights; Solidarity, central workers' organization, formed with Lech Walesa as leader.
- Iraq attacks Iranian oil installations at Abadan: Iraq-Iran War begins.
- Ronald Reagan elected US President.
- Michael Foot succeeds James Callaghan as Labour Party leader.
- Rhodesia gained independence as Zimbabwe. Robert Mugabe elected prime minister of Zimbabwe.
- SAS storm Iranian embassy in London to release hostages held by terrorists.
- British Telecom (BT) created when the telephone service split from the Post Office (privatized as a public limited company 1984).
- Jeremy Thorpe, former leader of the Liberal Party, acquitted in conspiracy trial.
- John Lennon assassinated in New York by Mark David Chapman (8 December).
- Modernized *Book of Common Prayer* published.
- Publication of *Rites of Passage* by William Golding.

Deaths

Joy Adamson, Austrian-born naturalist, murdered by Kenyan tribesmen.
Sir Cecil Beaton, British photographer and designer.
Jimmy Durante, US comedian.
Sir Alfred Hitchcock, British film director (29 April).
Oscar Kokoschka, Austrian artist.
Steve McQueen, US actor.
Henry Miller, US writer.
Sir Oswald Mosley in France, British fascist politician (3 December)
Jean-Paul Sartre, French philosopher.
Peter Sellers, British actor and comedian (24 July).
Mae West, US actress.

1981

- Iran releases US embassy hostages after 444 days in captivity.
- General Jarulzelski appointed prime minister in Poland as strikes and demonstrations led by Solidarity intensify (February); martial law declared (December).
- Presiden Reagan wounded in assassination attempt outside Hilton Hotel, Washington.
- Pope John Paul II survives assassination attempt by Turkish gunman in St Peter's Square, Rome.
- French elect François Mitterrand as new president.
- Egyptian President Anwar Sadat assassinated at military parade in Cairo.
- Hunger strike by IRA prisoners at the Maze Prison in Northern Ireland; ten die.
- The Social Democratic Party (SDP) founded by the 'gang of four', four defectors from the Labour Party: David Owen, Shirley Williams, Roy Jenkins and William Rodgers.
- Belize becomes independent 21 September. Independence of Bechuanaland as Botswana. Independent state of Antigua and Barbuda set up.
- Peter Sutcliffe convicted of 'Yorkshire Ripper' murders.
- Prince Charles marries Lady Diana Spencer in St Paul's Cathedral: 700 million watch on television worldwide (29 July).
- Rioting in Brixton, Liverpool and Manchester in response to allegedly heavy policing.
- Official opening of the Humber Estuary Bridge (17 July).

Deaths

Samuel Barber, US composer.
Karl Bohm, Austrian conductor.
Bill Haley, US rock singer.
William Holden, US actor.
Bob Marley, Jamaican reggae star.
Jessie Matthews, British actress and singer.
Bill Shankly, Scottish footballer and manager (29 September).
Albert Speer, German architect.
Natalie Wood, US actress.

1982

- Barbican Centre arts complex opens in London.
- Israel invades Lebanon in reprisal for Palestinian guerilla activities (June); Israeli forces drive the PLO out of Beirut (August); Lebanese Christian militia massacre hundreds in Palestinian refugee camps of Sabra and Chatila in West Beirut.
- Leonid Brezhnev dies; Yuri Andropov becomes Soviet leader.
- Princess Grace of Monaco (Grace Kelly) killed in car crash.

- Birth of a son, Prince William, to the Prince and Princess of Wales (21 June).
- Argentina invades the Falkland Islands in the South Atlantic (British Crown Colony since 1833) (2 April); Margaret Thatcher sends Task Force (5 April); Argentine cruiser *General Belgrano* sunk by torpedoes (2 May); HMS *Sheffield* hit by Exocet missile (4 May); first land battles between Argentinian and British troops (21 May); Argentine attack on two British supply ships off Bluff Cove (7 June); Argentinians surrender (14 June).
- Raising of the *Mary Rose* from the Solent (11 October, sank 1545).
- Unemployment in Britain reaches over three million.
- Women's Peace Camp established at Greenham Common in Berkshire to protest against planned siting of US Cruise missiles at nearby US military base.
- First visit to Britain of a reigning pope: arrival of John Paul II (28 May).
- Britain's fourth television channel, Channel Four, goes on air.
- Thames flood barrier raised for the first time.

Deaths
Ingrid Bergman, Swedish actress.
Rainer Werner Fassbinder, German film director.
Henry Fonda, US actor.
Glenn Gould, Canadian pianist.
Theolonis Monk, US jazz pianist.
Carl Orff, German composer.
Romy Schneider, Austrian actress.
Jacques Tati, French film director and actor.

1983

- 'Star War' defence system proposed by President Reagan.
- 'Hitler Diaries' exposed as fake after extracts are published in the German news magazine *Stern* and the *The Sunday Times*.
- Benigno Aquino, leading opponent of President Marcos, assassinated at Manila airport.
- Soviet Union shoots down Korean Airlines' Boeing 747 flight 007, with the loss of 269 lives over Sakhalin Island off Siberia: Soviets claim the aircraft was on a spying mission.
- Shia Muslim suicide bombers kill 241 Marines and 58 French paratroopers in Beirut by driving trucks filled with explosives into their compounds.
- Civilian rule restored in Argentina with the inauguration of Raul Alfonsin as president.
- Margaret Thatcher re-elected in landslide general election.
- Neil Kinnock elected leader of the Labour Party.
- Brunei achieves independence.
- US troops invade Grenada to remove Cuban presence from the island.
- The wearing of front seat-belts in cars made compulsory (31 January).
- 'Hitler Diaries' exposed as fake after extracts published in the German news magazine *Stern* and *The Sunday Times*.
- The Nobel Prize for literature awarded to William Golding, author of *The Lord of the Flies*.

Deaths
Luis Buñuel, Spanish film director.
George Cukor, US film director,
Arthur Koestler, Hungarian-born British writer, and his wife by suicide.
Joán Miró, Spanish artist.
David Niven, British actor.
Sir Ralph Richardson, British actor.
Gloria Swanson, US actress.
Sir William Walton, British composer (8 March).
Dame Rebecca West, British author.

1984

- Konstantin Chernenko succeeds Yuri Andropov as Soviet Communist Party leader.
- Pierre Trudeau resigns as Canadian prime minister.
- Discovery of the Aids virus announced in Washington.
- Prime Minister of India, Indira Gandhi, assassinated by Sikh bodyguards; she is suceeded by her son Rajiv.
- Gas leak from a chemical processing plant in Bhopal, India kills over 2,000 people.
- European Union established by treaty (February).
- Bomb attack by the IRA on a Brighton hotel used by Conservative politicans during the Party Conference (12 October): five killed.
- Diplomatic ties with Libya severed after the shooting of WPC Yvonne Fletcher outside the Libyan embassy in London.
- BBC TV report on the famine in Ethiopia prompts massive aid effort.
- Miners' national strike against pit closures begins.
- York Minster badly damaged by fire (9 July).
- HIV (human immuno-deficiency virus) discovered as cause of Aids.
- Death of the poet laureate Sir John Betjeman (19 May). Ted Hughes becomes poet laureate.

Deaths
William 'Count ' Basie, US jazz band leader.
Richard Burton, British actor.
Truman Capote, US author.
Diana Dors, British actress.
Marvin Gaye, US singer.
Lillian Hellman, US author and playwright.
Joseph Losey, US film director.
James Mason, British actor.

Eric Morecambe, British comedian.
Sam Peckinpah, US film director.
J. B. Priestley, British author and playwright.
Sir Arthur Travis ('Bomber') Harris, British commander of the RAF during World War I.
Francois Truffaut, French film director.
Johnny Weismuller, US actor and athlete.

1985

- Mikhail Gorbachev appointed new leader of the Soviet Union: begins to initiate wide-ranging liberal reforms (Glasnost) and economic restructuring (Perestroika).
- President Reagan and Soviet leader Mikhail Gorbachev establish rapport at Geneva summit.
- House of Lords proceedings televised for the first time.
- Miners vote to end year-long national strike.
- Wreckage of the *Titanic* located 550 miles south of Newfoundland (September): explored July 1986.
- Live Aid Concert raises £40 million in aid for famine victims in Ethiopia.
- Summit of Everest reached by Chris Bonington.
- British football teams banned indefinitely from European competition after 38 people die as Liverpool fans rioted at Heysel Stadium, Brussels.

Deaths
Laura Ashley, British fashion designer.
Yul Brynner, US actor.
James Cameron, British journalist and author.
Marc Chagall, Russian-born French painter.
Robert Graves, British poet.
Rock Hudson, US actor.
Philip Larkin, British poet.
Sir Michael Redgrave, British actor.
Orson Welles, US actor and director.

1986

- US space shuttle Challenger explodes on take-off killing crew of seven.
- Swedish Prime Minister Olof Palme assassinated in Stockholm.
- Ferdinand Marcos overthrown and replaced by Mrs Corazon Aquino as president of the Philippines.
- US launches air strikes against terrorist targets in Libya.
- Russian nuclear reactor at Chernobyl is seriously damaged by fire and contaminates a wide area.
- President Reagan denies any knowledge of 'Irangate' scandal whereby profits from US weapons sales to Iran are used covertly to fund the Contra rebels fighting the left-wing Sandinista government in Nicaragua.
- Cabinet ministers Michael Heseltine and Leon Brittain resign over the Westland Affair.
- Jeffrey Archer resigns as chairman of the Conservative Party after allegations of payments to a prostitute.
- Single European Act signed (February).
- Appearance of Halley's Comet (named after Edmund Halley).
- Construction of the Channel Tunnel begins.

Deaths
Simone de Beauvoir, French author.
Jorge Luis Borges, Argentine author.
James Cagney, US actor.
Benny Goodman, US jazz clarinettist.
Cary Grant, British-born US actor.
Henry Moore, British sculptor.
Otto Preminger, US film director.

1987

- Former SS officer Klaus Barbie, the 'Butcher of Lyons', is sentenced in a court in Lyons to life imprisonment for war crimes.
- Rudolph Hess found dead in Spandau prison after apparently hanging himself.
- President Reagan and Mikhail Gorbachev sign treaty to arrange for the dismantling of Soviet and US medium-and shorter-range missiles.
- Princess Anne created Princess Royal.
- General election (14 June): Margaret Thatcher reelected for third term as prime minister.
- Government announces plans to introduce the Community Charge, a poll tax to replace the rates system for funding local services.
- David Owen resigns as leader of the SDP in opposition to talks about merging with the Liberals.
- IRA bomb kills eleven people at Remembrance Day service in Enniskillen, Northern Ireland (8 November).
- Terry Waite, special envoy of the archbishop of Canterbury, is kidnapped in Beirut by members of the militant Islamic group Hezbollah.
- The car ferry *Herald of Free Enterprise* capsizes off Zeebrugge with the loss of 188 lives.
- The Order of the Garter opened to women.
- 'Black Monday' in the City of London: over £100 billion wiped off the value of shares on the stock market.

Deaths
Fred Astaire, US dancer and actor.
Rita Hayworth, US actress.
John Huston, US film director.
Danny Kaye, US actor and comedian.
Lee Marvin, US actor.
Jacqueline du Pre, British cellist, from multiple sclerosis.
Andy Warhol, US artist.

1988

- Intifada uprising by West Bank and Gaza Arabs against Israeli occupation begins.
- Iran and Iraq agree a cease-fire to end eight years of conflict.
- Floods in Bangladesh kill 300 and leave over 20 million people homeless.
- Canadian sprinter Ben Johnson is found guilty of using drugs and is stripped of his gold medal for the 100 metres at the Seoul Olympics.
- George Bush elected US President.
- President Gorbachev announces dramatic reduction in Red Army strength in speech to the United Nations.
- Earthquake in Armenia kills over 100,000 people.
- Copyright Act.
- Merger of the Liberal Party and the Social Democratic Party to form the Social and Liberal Democratic Party (SDLP).
- Lockerbie Disaster: a terrorist bomb destroys Pan Am flight 103, which crashes on to a Scottish village killing 244 passengers, 15 crew and 11 on the ground (21 December).
- Piper Alpha disaster: 167 workers killed by explosion on an oil rig in the North Sea.
- The National Theatre becomes the Royal National Theatre.
- Publication of A *Brief History of Time* by Stephen Hawking.

Deaths

Sir Frederick Ashton, British ballet choreographer.
Enzio Ferrari, Italian racing car magnate.
Richard Feynman, US physicist.
Trevor Howard, British actor.
Roy Orbison, US singer.
Kenneth Williams, British comedy actor.

1989

- Emperor Hirohito dies and is succeeded by his son Crown Prince Akihito.
- Soviet troops leave Afghanistan after ten-year occupation.
- Supertanker *Exxon Valdez* spills cargo of oil in Price William Sound, Alaska, the worst oil spillage in US history.
- People's Liberation Army crush student pro-democracy demonstration in Tiananmen Square in Peking.
- Poland elects Tadeusz Mazowiecki first non-Communist Prime Minister.
- Vietnamese troops leave Cambodia after eleven years of occupation.
- Hungary announces changes to its constitution to allow free elections.
- The Berlin Wall is dismantled as political reform in East Germany allows free movement of East German citizens to the west.
- Communist leadership in Czechoslovakia resigns; playwright Vaclav Havel is elected as president to prepare for free elections.
- Romanian dictator Nicolai Ceausescu and his wife Elena are executed by firing squad as Communist rule collapses.
- National Assembly in Bulgaria approves liberal political reforms in response to mass demonstrations.
- US troops invade Panama to oust dictator Manuel Noriega.
- Nigel Lawson, Chancellor of the Exchequer, resigns from the government over differences on economic policy.
- Poll tax implemented as Community Charge in Scotland.
- Privatization of water authorities in England.
- Guildford Four (Gerard Conlon, Carole Richardson, Patrick Armstrong and Paul Hill) convicted of IRA pub bombings in 1974, based on confessions fabricated by the police, are released.
- Hillsborough Stadium disaster in Sheffield (15 April): 95 football fans crushed to death at Liverpool vs Nottingham Forest match.
- House of Commons proceedings first televised. Satellite television begins in Britain.
- *Fatwa* (order to kill) instituted by Ayatollah Khomeni against the author Salman Rushdie for supposedly blasphemous content of his novel *Satanic Verses*: Rushdie goes into hiding.

Deaths

A. J. Ayer, British philosopher.
Lucille Ball, US comedienne.
Samuel Beckett, Irish writer.
Irving Berlin, US songwriter.
Salvador Dali, Spanish artist.
Bette Davis, US actress.
R. D. Laing, British psychiatrist.
Herbert von Karajan, Austrian condutor.
Daphne du Maurier, British novelist.
Lord Olivier, British actor.
Georges Simenon, Belgian novelist.

1990

- Ban on African National Congress (ANC) lifted in South Africa; Black nationalist leader Nelson Mandela freed from prison in Cape Town after 27 years; Mandela and ANC enter talks with President F. W. de Klerk about political future of the country.
- Sandinista government in Nicaragua defeated in democratic elections by National Opposition Union

led by Senora Violeta Chamorro.
- Boris Yeltsin elected president of the Republic of Russia.
- Iraq invades Kuwait (August): UN imposes economic sanctions to persuade Saddam Hussein to withdraw his forces: UN resolution imposes ultimatum on Iraq to withdraw from Kuwait by 15 January 1991 (November).
- West and East Germany are reunited (October); Helmut Kohl elected Chancellor of reunited Germany (December).
- Britain joins the ERM (Exchange Rate Mechanism) for the stabilization of currency in the European Monetary System (October).
- Britain rejects timetable for a single European currency by the year 2000 at EC summit in Rome.
- Margaret Thatcher withdraws from Conservative Party leadership contest and is replaced by John Major.
- David Owen disbands Social Democratic Party because of lack of support.
- Poll tax implemented as Community Charge in England. Anti-poll tax march in London turns into a riot.
- Brian Keenan, one of several Western hostages held by militant Islamic groups in Beirut, freed after 1,597 days in captivity.
- GATT (General Agreement on Tariffs and Trade) signed by 96 nations.
- Operation Desert Shield: military operation by US and UN Allies in Kuwait to deter further Iraqi attacks on Kuwait after the Iraqi invasion of Kuwait (2 August)
- George Carey made archbishop of Canterbury.
- Channel Tunnel excavation teams from English and French sides meet in the middle.

Deaths

Leonard Bernstein, US composer and conductor.
Aaron Copland, US composer.
Sammy Davis Jr, US entertainer.
Greta Garbo, Swedish-born actress.
Ava Gardner, US actress.
Rex Harrison, British actor.
Barbara Stanwyck, US actress.
A. J. P. Taylor, British historian.
Paul Tortellier, French cellist.
Irving Wallace, US writer.

1991

- Gulf War begins with operation 'Desert Storm', a massive air assault with bombs and missiles on Iraq by British, US and Saudi forces (17 January); land war begins (24 February) and Iraq capitulates after 100-hour conflict.
- Soviet troops crack down on Baltic states as demands for independence intensify.
- Last of the apartheid laws in South Africa are abolished.
- Saddam Hussein suppresses Kurd revolt in northern Iraq.
- Prime Minister of India Rajiv Gandhi assassinated.
- Boris Yeltsin elected president of Russia.
- Violence escalates in Yugoslavia as the Serbian-dominated federal army attempts to suppress demands for independence by Slovenia and Croatia (June); Dubrovnik besieged by army (October).
- The Soviet Union comes to an end: President Gorbachev is temporarily ousted by hardline Communists opposed to his reform program and then reinstated after Boris Yeltsin leads popular resistance to coup leaders (August); Russia, Byelorussia, Ukraine and eight other former Soviet republics form the Commonwealth of Independent States (8 December); Gorbachev resigns (25 December).
- The British government replaces the Community Charge with a new Council Tax, based on property values.
- British hostages in Beirut released by Islamic fundamentalist group Hezbollah: John McCarthy (August) and Terry Waite (November) and Jackie Mann.
- Czech-born British publisher Robert Maxwell drowned at sea: his publishing empire collapses with massive debts.

Deaths

Dame Peggy Ashcroft, British actress.
Miles Davis, US jazz musician.
Dame Margot Fonteyn, British dancer.
Graham Greene, British novelist.
Sir David Lean, British film director.
Freddie Mercury, British rock star.

1992

- European Commission recognizes independence of breakaway republics Croatia and Slovenia, legitimizing the disintegration of the former Yugoslavia (January); Bosnia-Herzegovina votes for independence (March); fighting between the Serb-dominated Yugoslav army and the secessionist republics intensifies; revelation of emaciated Moslem prisoners in Serbian camps in Bosnia confirms Serbian policy of 'ethnic cleansing' from Serb-dominated areas (August).
- Race riots in Los Angeles, after police beat black motorist Rodney King.
- Judge Giovanni Falcone, Italy's chief anti-Mafia investigator, murdered by the Mafia in Palermo.
- US Marines land in Somalia to curb Somali warlords

and allow humanitarian aid for famine victims to be distributed.

- Bill Clinton is elected US President.
- Abolition of the Community Charge.
- Britain forced to withdraw from the ERM (September).
- Education Act for England and Wales.
- General election won by the Conservatives (8 April). Neil Kinnock resigns as Labour Party leader; John Smith elected to succeed him.
- Prince Charles and Diana the Princess of Wales announce their separation.
- Windsor Castle badly damaged by fire.
- Privatization of the coal industry.

Deaths

Isaac Asimov, US science-fiction writer.
Francis Bacon, British artist
Richard Brooks, US film director.
Marlene Dietrich, German-born US actress.
Denholm Elliot, British actor.
Alex Haley, US author.
Benny Hill, British comedian.
Frankie Howerd, British comedian.
Robert Morley, British actor.
Anthony Perkins, US actor.
Sanjit Ray, Indian film director.

1993

- Czechoslovakia is split into Slovakia and the Czech Republic.
- President Bush and President Yeltsin sign START-2 treaty cutting nuclear arsenals by two thirds.
- Two Los Angeles police officers found guilty of beating black motorist Rodney King.
- FBI siege of Branch Davidian cult headquarters at Waco, Texas ends in mass suicide as building is deliberately set on fire.
- Lord Owen and Cyrus Vance peace plan for division of Bosnia abandoned.
- Violence in South African black townships escalates as 1994 date for democratic elections is announced: President de Klerk and ANC leader Nelson Mandela ratify new democratic constitution (November).
- Flooding in US mid-West causes $5 billion damage.
- Sarajevo placed under UN rule.
- PLO-Israeli peace deal agreed after secret negotiations: Palestinians given control in Gaza and Jericho: Yasser Arafat signs mutual recognition agreement with Israel.
- Jordan and Israel sign peace accord for dealing with disputes.
- State of Emergency declared in Moscow: President Boris Yeltsin uses military force to oust opponents from the Russian parliament building.
- European Union inaugurated as Maastricht Treaty comes into force.
- Inauguration of the Single European Market.
- John Major replaces Norman Lamont with Kenneth Clarke as Chancellor of the Exchequer in a Cabinet reshuffle.
- Ratification of the Treaty of Maastricht, providing a timbetable for European political, economic and monetary union (July).
- Government admits to clandestine meetings with the IRA (November); Downing Street Declaration on Northern Ireland by John Major and Albert Reynolds, Irish taoiseach, opens the way to all-party talks (December).
- Betty Boothroyd becomes first woman Speaker of the House of Commons.
- Buckingham Palace opened to the public. Queen Elizabeth II agrees to pay tax on private income.
- The oil tanker *Braer* runs aground off Shetland.

Deaths

John Birks (Dizzy) Gillespie, US jazz musician.
Anthony Burgess, British author, composer and critic.
Sir William Golding, British author.
William Randolph Hearst, US newspaper magnate.
Audrey Hepburn, US actress.
Rudolf Nureyev, Russian-born ballet dancer.
Albert Sabin, US virologist.

1994

- Serb forces withdraw from around Sarajevo as NATO threatens air strikes against their artillery positions.
- Italian media tycoon Silvio Berlusconi becomes prime minster of Italy (March); resigns (December).
- Massacres of Tutsis by Hutus in Rwanda leaves estimated 500,000 dead and 1.5 million homeless.
- Nelson Mandela leads African National Congress to victory in South; African elections (April); Mandela inaugurated as first black president (May).
- Israel and PLO sign pact ending Israeli occupation of Gaza Strip and Jericho.
- President Kim Il Sung dies and is succeeded by his son Kim Jong Il as North Korean leader.
- Jordan and Israel sign peace treaty.
- US forces invade Haiti to oust military government.
- Roll-on roll-off car ferry *Estonia* sinks in Baltic with loss of 900 lives.
- Russia invades breakaway Caucasian state of Chechenia.
- IRA announces cease-fire in Northern Ireland, opening way for political settlement (August); Loyalists announce cease-fire (October); peace talks begin between government and Sinn Fein (December).

- John Smith, leader of Labour Party dies; Tony Blair is elected to succeed him.
- Queen Elizabeth II visits Russia.
- National Lottery begins (November). Sunday shopping introduced in England.
- Completion of a new opera house for Glyndebourne Festival Opera.
- Channel Tunnel opened.

Deaths

Sir Harold Acton, British author and historian.
Lindsay Anderson, British film director.
Cab Calloway, US band leader.
John Candy, Canadian actor.
Elias Canetti, Bulgarian-born British author.
Joseph Cotton, US actor.
Peter Cushing, British actor.
Robert Doisneau, French photographer.
Derek Jarmann, British filmmaker.
Burt Lancaster, US actor.
Harry Nilsson, US singer-songwriter.
Richard M. Nixon, US statesman.
Henri Mancini, US composer.
Jacqueline Kennedy Onassis.
John Osborne, British actor and playwright.
Sir Karl Popper, British philosopher.
Dennis Potter, British television dramatist.
Madeleine Renaud, French actress.
Fernando Rey, Spanish actor.
Cesar Romero, US actor.
Telly Savalas, Greek-born US actor.
Mai Zetterling, Swedish actress.

1995

- Frederick West, alleged serial killer, hangs himself in prison (1 January) while awaiting trial, leaving his widow, Rosemary West, to stand trial (3 October–22 November). She is found guilty of the murder of ten young women and girls and jailed for life.
- The Princess of Wales is interviewed by Martin Bashir on BBC's Panorama programme (20 November).
- Queen Elizabeth II visits South Africa
- President Clinton visits Northern Ireland (November), the first US president to do so.
- Gerry Adams, leader of Sinn Fein, visits US, culminating in a meeting with President Clinton in the White House (March).
- Barings, the merchant bank, collapses after rogue trader, Nick Leeson, loses an estimated £17 billion on the Japanese futures market; Leeson is later found guilty of fraud and sentenced to six and a half years imprisonment (December).
- Oklahoma: the Alfred P. Murrah building (offices of the Federal government) is bombed with the loss of 158 lives; two members of a white supremacist movement are arrested and later indicted for the bombing.
- Actor and former football star O. J. Simpson stands trial in Los Angeles for the murder of his estranged wife and her friend (in 1994); the trial highlights racial tensions in US society; Simpson is found not guilty after a nine month hearing (Oct).
- Nato forces bomb Serb held positions in Sarajevo in response to Bosnian Serb attack on Sarajevo market two days earlier; bombing later suspended to enable resumption of peace talks; Bosnian peace talks held at Dayton, Ohio (November).
- Israeli Prime Minister Yitzakh Rabin is assassinated by right wing extremist Yigal Amir; he is succeeded by Shimon Peres.
- A nerve gas is released in the Tokyo subway during the morning rush hour killing ten people and injuring over 5000 (March); a second attack occurs in April in Yokahama; the leader of a religious cult is arrested and admits to the attacks (May).
- Celebrations to mark the fiftieth anniversary of VE day take place throughout UK.
- Japanese city of Kobe is hit by an earthquake with the loss of over 5000 lives.

Deaths

Kingsley Amis, British novelist
Robert Bolt, British playwright
Dean Martin, US actor
Gerald Durrell, British author and conservationist
Michael Hordern, British actor
Louis Malle, French film director
Elizabeth Montgomery, US actress
Sir Stephen Spender, British poet and novelist

Appendix

British Kings and Queens

British Kings and Queens

Introduction

Roman Britain

The British islands first became known to the Romans through Julius Caesar's two expeditions in 55 BC and 54 BC. The main island was generally known by them as *Britannia*, but it was not until the time of Claudius, nearly a hundred years later, that the Romans made a serious attempt to convert Britain into a Roman province. There is evidence to suggest that there were tribal rulers in Britain as early as 4500 years ago, but the contemporary records of the Romans give the first clear proof that there were Iron Age tribal kings and queens. The tribes were migrants from mainland Europe who spoke Celtic tongues akin to Gaelic, Irish and Welsh and used coins similar to those used in Greece and Rome. Among these tribes were the Atrebates (based around Sussex), Brigantes (who founded York as their capital), Catuvellauni (based around Hertfordshire), Regni (based in Sussex) and the Iceni (based around Norfolk and Suffolk). After the Roman conquests some of the leaders of these tribes were made 'client' rulers under Rome and retained their power; others such as Boudicca of the Iceni tribe rebelled and were crushed.

The heart of Roman rule was in the southeast of England, but Roman armies also came into contact with the tribes of the north. The battle at 'Mons Graupius', thought to have been in Aberdeenshire, gave the Romans a temporary foothold, but the rugged terrain, as much as the resistance of the tribes, meant they had to retire behind the wall built in AD 120 by Hadrian, between the Solway and the Tyne. Thus the southern part of the island alone remained Roman and became specially known as Britannia while the northern portion was distinctively called Caledonia.

Eight Roman emperors were proclaimed in Britannia, and it became an important part of the Empire, but by 400 attacks from northern Europe, Scotland and Ireland had almost exhausted the resources of the province. Hadrian's Wall was abandoned and troops withdrawn from important outposts until, around 415, the formal rule of the Romans ended.

Early English Kings

After the Romans withdrew, Romano-British rulers had to defend their territories against attack from fierce northern tribesmen. They also had to contend with invasions by Germanic tribes eager to drive them out and settle new lands. From what are now called the Netherlands, Germany, Denmark and France came the Angles, Saxons and Jutes to set up hundreds of petty states. The rulers of these states claimed the war god Woden as their ancestor and, with the consent of a council of advisers known as the *witan* or *witenagemot*, bequeathed their crowns to their sons.

In time the larger of these states swallowed the smaller until, around 700, there were about forty established statelets. Eventually a group of the seven most prominent states emerged, generally referred to as the *Heptarchy*, which dominated most of the southern part of Britain. This consisted of the kingdoms of Kent, the South Saxons (in Surrey and Sussex), the East Angles (East Anglia), the East Saxons (Essex and Middlesex), the West Saxons or Wessex (Devon, Dorset, Somerset and part of Cornwall), Northumbria (Northumberland, York and Durham and also southeast Scotland) and the kingdom of Mercia (which included Gloucester, Leicester and Chester). To the north were the Picts and Scots, to the west were the Celts of Wales. The Britons fleeing the European invaders had settled in Strathclyde (the southwest of Scotland) and Cornwall. The battle for supremacy between these seven kingdoms persisted until at length Wessex overran Mercia, Sussex and all the lands south of the Humber, and the whole came to be known as England, or Angleland.

These were uncertain times, however, and the Angle kings were frequently defeated by the ambitions of Danish invaders. Their advance was checked for a time by Alfred the Great (who also ensured that those he defeated were converted to Christianity), and many were diverted to northern France where their settlements became Normandy. Alfred was the first to bring about some form of national unity among the Anglo-Saxons, but his descendants could not claim to rule all England, and fought against the Danes, with varying degrees of success, to maintain power. By 1016 England had again been made to submit to foreign rule as the Danish king, Canute, made England part of a greater northern European empire. When this empire finally collapsed, England was left disunited, a state of affairs that was finally exploited by a Norman, Duke William of Normandy, who began his conquest by defeating the English forces at Hastings in 1066.

Picts and Scots

The inhabitants of the northern lands, known to the Romans as Caledonians and to the Britons as the people of Albion, could be distinguished as Goidels (or Gaels) and Picts. The Gaels were of a similar stock to the British, and, since the 18th century, British and Gaels have alike been termed 'Celtic'. This usage originated in the discovery of an affinity between the language of Brittany and those of the Welsh and of the Scottish Highlanders. It is, however, important to make a distinction between the Brythonic Celts of Wales, Cumbria and Strathclyde, and the Goidelic Celts or Gaels of the Northern Highlands. By the 6th century these northern tribes were more commonly known as Picts, which means literally 'painted people'.

As well as the Picts, a body of Celts from Ireland, known as Scots, had, by the middle of the 6th century, settled in what is the present-day county of Argyll and founded the kingdom of Dalriada. This kingdom consisted of Argyll, part of Northern Ireland and the islands of the Inner Hebrides.

The amalgamation of the Scots, Picts, Britons and Angles into one kingdom was a slow and lengthy process. The foundation for the ultimate union of the Scots and the Picts was laid by St Columba, who travelled to the already christianized kingdom of Dalriada in 563. The actual occasion of the union of Scots and Picts, however, was to come via a combination of factors. Dynastic intermarriage, religious unity and Scandanavian aggression all played their part, but it was the strong leadership of

Kenneth mac-Alpin, king of Scots, which finally brought the kingdoms together. Under his guidance the Scots became the dominant force in the land, and the idea of the Picts as an independent people largely died out.

The amalgamation of the Lothians and of Strathclyde with Alba (the kingdom of Picts and Scots) was delayed for two centuries. Strathclyde was finally merged through dynastic inheritance, but it took the collapse of Nothumbrian power and the consolidation of England under the successors of Alfred the Great to unite the Scots and Angles. Successive monarchs of Alba tried to add Lothian to their dominions, but it was not until 1018 that it was finally annexed and the whole of the historical kingdom of Scotland was ruled by one king, who maintained the title of 'king of Scots'.

Early Welsh Kings

Previous to the Roman occupation, Wales appears to have been chiefly inhabited by three British tribes, called the Silures, Dimaetae, and Ordovices. During the latter period of the Roman occupation the subjected part of the island was divided into four provinces, of which one, including the country from the Dee to the Severn, was called *Britannia Secunda*. It was after the invasion of the Saxons that the country aquired a distinctive national character as the refuge of the vanquished Britons who were gradually driven to the west. From this period until the final conquest of the country by Edward I, there is little but a succession of petty wars between the rival chiefs or kings into which both countries were divided during a great part of the Saxon period, or the more systematic efforts of the larger monarchy to absorb the smaller. By war and marriage three main territories were established: Gwynedd in North Wales; Powys in the central region; and Deheubarth in South Wales. Of the three, Gwynedd spread its influence the farthest, and sometimes dominated all Wales. By 1200, however, Welsh kings had been reduced to lords and princes owing homage to the king of England. The last of the Welsh princes, Llewllyn, who revolted against Edward I, was defeated by the earl of Mortimer in 1284. Since that time the principality has been incorporated with England, and Wales has given the title of Prince of Wales to the heir apparent of the British Crown.

Early Irish Kings

As in Western Europe generally, the earliest inhabitants of Ireland are believed to have been of Iberian race and therefore akin to the modern Basques. They were followed by the Celts, different tribes who probably arrived at different times. Among these the Scots were the latest, and subsequently got the upper hand, so that their name became generally applied to all the inhabitants. The land was divided into five principal kingdoms—Ulster, Munster, Leinster, Connaught and Meath—which were each divided in turn into lesser divisions or chiefdoms. Each king or chieftain desired to become the *Ard-Ri* (high king) of the whole island, but for centuries no one achieved any real degree of supremacy.

Following the introduction of Christianity and Christian literature by St Patrick, Ireland became an important seat of learning. Its internal condition, however, was far from satisfactory. Divided among a number of hostile kings or chiefs, it had been long torn by internal wars and for nearly two centuries ravaged by the Danes, numbers of whom settled in the country, when, in the beginning of the 11th century, Brian Boru united the greater part of the island under his sceptre and subdued the northern invaders. After the death of Brian, the island relapsed into its former state of division and anarchy. In this state of matters, Henry II of England obtained a Papal Bull giving him the right to subdue it. In 1172 Henry entered Ireland himself, and partly through the favour of the clergy, the great princes did homage to him and acknowledged his supremacy. Many Norman barons and their followers now settled in the country, but the English power was far from being established over it. For long, only a part was recognized as English territory (generally known as 'the Pale'), and this was governed by various nobles subject to a viceroy. The greater part of the island remained unconquered, and English supremacy was threatened frequently by rebellions of Irish chiefs and barons. It was not until the reign of Henry VIII that the title of 'king', instead of 'lord', of Ireland was properly established. The chieftains of Ulster remained fiercely independent, however, and continued to seek allies on the continent to rid Ireland of the English. During the reign of Elizabeth I they were eventually forced to flee, and this 'Flight of the earls' became a turning point in the history of England's involvement in Ireland for it was then that the 'Plantation'—the settlement of English and Scottish Protestants in Ulster—began.

Ireland remained under English, and then British, kings and queens until the time of Edward VIII's abdication in 1936. Independence was finally achieved in that year when the Irish Free State abolished the monarchy and formally became a republic. British monarchs continue to reign over Northern Ireland, comprising most of what had been the ancient kingdom of Ulster.

A

Aed (d.879) king of Scots (879). The son of Kenneth mac-Alpin, he succeeded his brother Constantine I as king but reigned for less than a year. He was reputedly murdered by his first cousin, Giric, the son of Donald I, a rival for the throne.

Aed Find (d.*c*.778) king of Scots (768–778). He invaded the Pictish heartland early in his reign but the results of his efforts are not known.

Aed Finnliath (d.*c*.879) high king of Ireland (862–868). In 861 he joined with a Norse force against the ruling high king, Mael Sechnailli. On his death a year later, Aed became high king and turned against his former allies. Over the next five years of his reign he was greatly troubled by inroads made by the Vikings but won an important battle against them at Killineery in 868.

Aelfwald (d.749) king of East Anglia (713–749). An under-king of Mercia under the powerful Ethelbald from 740.

Aelle (1) (d.*c*.514) king of Sussex. According to the *Anglo-Saxon Chronicle* he established the South Saxon kingdom after landing around 477 and defeating a force of Britons at a place called Cymenesora. With his third son Cissa he beseiged an old Roman fort at Pevensey held by Britons in 491 and massacred the occupants. He came to be regarded as *Bretwalda*, or overlord, among the Anglo-Saxon kings of southern England although at this time the success of the invaders was not certain and the title was little more than honorary.

Aelle (2) (d.588) king of Deira (*c*.560–588). A son of Ida, he was the first king of this small kingdom (roughly Humberside) to establish independence from Bernicia (roughly Northumberland). On his death, the kingdom was taken by his brother, Ethelric (who ruled Bernicia after his father), and his two sons fled the kingdom. Ethelric became the first king of Northumbria.

Aelle (3) (d.867) king of Northumbria (866–867). He was chosen to be king following the removal of the unpopular Osbert. Soon afterwards, a large Norse army that had invaded in 865 took advantage of the royal infighting to seize York, the chief city of Northumbria. After resolving their dispute, Osbert and Aelle mounted a joint attack in 867. They were at first successful, but at length lost their army in a climactic battle. Osbert was killed in the fighting but Aelle was sacrificed to the Norse war god Odin in a gruesome ritual. The leader of the Norsemen, Ivar the Boneless, justified the killing by falsely claiming that Aelle had slain his father by throwing him into a pit of vipers.

Aesc (d.512) king of Kent (488–512). Son of Hengest and nephew of Horsa, the first Jutish kings of Kent, in 488 his father died and Aesc succeeded to the kingdom. He was regarded as a powerful commander and many of his battles against the Welsh and the men of Kent are recorded in the *Anglo-Saxon Chronicle*. Although his father and uncle are regarded as the first kings, Aesc, also given as 'Oisc', provided the dynastic name of 'Oiscingas'.

Aescwine (1) king of Essex (*c*.527–*c*.587). He is thought to have been the founder of the small kingdom of East Saxons, which, with London as its capital, was later absorbed by Wessex.

Aescwine (2) king of Wessex (674–676). He was the son of Cenfus and a descendant of King Coel.

Aiden (Mac Gabrain) (d.606) king of Scots (*c*.575–606). Ordained at Dunadd by his cousin Colum Cille (St Columba) in what was probably the first Christian coronation in Britain, Aiden was a descendant of Fergus Mor and did much to consolidate the kingdom of Dalriada. Influenced by St Columba, he sought an alliance with the king of the O'Neill dynasty in Ulster to protect the monastic community founded by St Columba on the small island of Iona. This was acheived at Druim Cett soon after Aiden's coronation. Sometime between 580 and 585 he captured Orkney and the Isle of Man respectively, thus extending his kingdom. During his reign he fought many battles against the Picts, Britons and Angles but was finally defeated in 603 by Ethelfrith at Degsastan, near Liddesdale. As Aiden lost most of his army and a son in the battle, the Northumbrian ruler was free to advance farther north and west. At his death, Aiden was over seventy years old and was succeeded by his son Eochaid.

Alchred *or* **Elhred** king of Northumbria (765–774). Claiming to belong to the Bernician royal house, he deposed Ethelwold Moll in 765. He is known to have been a supporter of missions to Europe and was in contact with the Frankish king Charlemagne. Deposed in favour of Ethelred, he sought shelter among the Picts.

Aldfrith (d.705) king of Northumbria (685–705). The son of Oswy's mistress, Aldfrith combined statesman-like qualities with a reputation as a man of letters. In his pursuit of learning it is said he exchanged an estate in return for a book that had been brought by a monk from Rome. He was succeeded by his eight-year-old son, Osred.

Aldwulf (1) king of East Anglia (663–713). He was the son of Ethelhere and a Northumbrian princess, Hereswith of Deira.

Aldwulf (2) king of Sussex. He reigned briefly *c.*765 and is known to have made a land grant to the Church.

Alexander I (the Fierce) (*c.*1078–1124) king of Scots (1107–24). Fifth son of Malcolm III (Canmore), the first king of all Scotland, and Margaret of England, he was born at Dumbarton and succeeded his elder brother Edgar as king. He ruled only that part of the kingdom to the north of the Forth and Clyde as the south (Cumbria, Strathclyde and southern Lothian) had been bequeathed to David, his younger brother, for him to govern as earl. As a devout patron of the church, Alexander did much to strengthen the religious independence of his kingdom. He revived the see at Dunkeld, established an Augustinian priory at Scone and an abbey on the island of Inchcolm. During his reign many new castles were built, including a new royal castle at Stirling.

He maintained good relations with Henry I and encouraged Norman settlement in lowland Scotland, where feudalism was introduced as a system for holding land and castles built in the Norman style. He took an active part in Henry's campaign against the rebellious Welsh kings in 1114 and married Sybilla, Henry's illegitimate daughter. The marriage produced no legitimate offspring, although descendents of his natural son, Malcolm Mac-Heth, later made unsuccessful claims to parts of Caithness. He was succeeded by his younger brother David I on his death at Stirling. He was interred at Dunfermline's Abbey Church.

Significant events of Alexander I's reign

- 1112 Berwick-upon-Tweed becomes the first royal burgh in Scotland.
- 1114 With Alexander's help Henry I receives oaths of obedience from Welsh kings.

Alexander II (1198–1249) king of Scots (1214–49). The son of William I, 'the Lion', and Ermengarde de Beaumont, he was born at Haddington and succeeded his father at the age of sixteen. His accession was immediately disputed, and an army was gathered by Donald mac-William, a rival to the throne. They soon landed from Ireland but were defeated by the earl of Mar who ordered the execution of the leaders.

During Alexander's reign there was no serious conflict with England and he was married to King John's eldest daughter, Princess Joan, in 1221, but the relationship was far from stable. As the young Scottish king had red hair, John boasted of how he would 'hunt the red fox cub from his lair', but John was being forced by his barons to sign the Magna Carta and Alexander stood firmly with them. Following a successful campaign in the north of England, the barons paid homage to Alexander, but following King John's death the barons broke the agreements made with Alexander, and he raised an army against them. He was unsuccessful and, constrained to come to terms with England, had to do homage to the new king, Henry III. He was an able politician however, and gave up his claims to Northumberland, Westmore-land and Cumberland in order to agree the peace. This led to the Treaty of York of 1237, which fixed the borders between the two countries roughly where they are today and Alexander received estates in northern England worth £200 a year. It was an uneasy peace, however, and it was seven years until the relationship improved with the betrothal of Henry's three-year-old daughter, Margaret, to Alexander's son and heir.

He was an intelligent and energetic monarch. As well as being a good soldier, he governed wisely and introduced measures to modernize the administration of his kingdom. As a devoted patron of the church he was responsible for the founding of several important monasteries and abbeys. Despite these progressive achievements, he was still very much a king of his times. This was demonstrated by his punishment of those present at the brutal murder of Bishop Adam of Caithness, when he ordered that the hands and feet of eighty men be cut off.

Princess Joan died childless in 1238. Alexander's second wife, Marie de Coucy, daughter of Baron de Coucy of Picardy, provided his successor, Alexander III.

Alexander died after falling ill with a fever at Kerrera, an island opposite Oban, whilst on route to join his naval fleet for an expedition in which he hoped to wrest the Hebrides from King Haakon IV of Norway. He is buried at Melrose Abbey.

Significant events of Alexander II's reign

- 1215 Alexander receives homage of the northern English barons.
- 1216 King John dies of dysentery. Henry III ascends his father's throne.
- 1221 Alexander marries Henry's sister, Joan.
- 1237 Treaty of York fixes Scottish border with England.

Alexander III (1241–85) king of Scots (1249–85). The

only son of Alexander II and Marie de Coucy, he succeeded his father when still only eight years of age. He married Princess Margaret, eldest daughter of Henry III of England, to whom he had been betrothed, two years later. Rival court factions jostled for position during his minority, and rebel lords, led by the Comyns of Monteith and Buchan, attempted to take control of the government when Alexander was sixteen by holding the king hostage. This angered Henry III of England who offered to keep an army in northern England until the difficulty was resolved. Negotiations at Jedburgh finally settled the matter and the Comyns were reconciled to their rivals in government and to the English king. Later the same year a council of ten people was chosen to care for Alexander until he reached his majority in 1262 and the dispute between Henry, the Comyns and the Scottish government was formally ended.

It was not long after assuming full powers that Alexander began to assert his position as king. Like his father, he was eager to bring the Hebrides under his sway, and this he was able to accomplish in a few years after defeating an invasion force led by the Norse king, Haakon, at Largs. He bought the Isle of Man and the Hebrides from Norway's Magnus VI for £2666, and in 1266 signed the Treaty of Perth, which established his control over all the Western Isles. This brought to an end nearly four centuries of Norse domination of the Hebrides. For the first time the mainland and islands of Scotland had been brought together under one sovereign, although Orkney and Shetland still belonged to Norway.

Alexander was strenuous in asserting the independence both of his kingdom and of the Scottish Church, but his relationship with England remained peaceful. At his wedding, when he was only ten years old, he is said to have nearly been tricked into doing homage to Henry but had the presence of mind to evade Henry's approaches. The king of England never gave up, however, and continued to appeal to Alexander. Following Henry's death, Alexander attended Edward I's coronation only after receiving written confirmation that the independence of the kingdom of Scotland would not be compromised. For the rest of his reign he managed to keep on good terms with his neighbour, despite refusing to do homage except for those lands he held in the north of England.

Alexander's main difficulty was in securing a successor. His wife's death in 1275 was followed by that of his two sons, David and Alexander, both childless. In order to secure the succession, he married Yolande of Dreaux, but less than six months later, while riding in the dark along the cliffs between Edinburgh and Kinghorn in Fife to meet his wife, his horse stumbled and threw him. The body of the last Celtic king was found at the foot of the cliffs the next morning. The marriage of his daughter Margaret to Eric II of Norway had brought a daughter, however, and this infant, Margaret, the Maid of Norway, had been recognized as heir to the throne by parliament two years before. She was proclaimed queen of Scotland, despite the unpopularity of female succession, but died on the sea crossing from Norway and never put foot on Scottish soil.

Significant events of Alexander III's reign

- 1263 Alexander defeats Norse invaders at Battle of Largs.
- 1266 Alexander gains control of the Hebrides under the Treaty of Perth.
- 1274 Alexander attends coronation of Edward I of England.
- 1285 Margaret, the Maid of Norway, is recognized as heir presumptive.

Alfred the Great (849–899) king of Wessex (871–899). Alfred was born at Wantage in Berkshire, his father being Ethelwulf, son of Egbert, king of the West Saxons. He succeeded his brother Ethelred in 871, at a time when the Danes, or Norsemen, had extended their conquests widely over the country; they had completely overrun the kingdom of the West Saxons (or Wessex) by 878. Alfred, the king of Wessex, was obliged to flee in disguise. At length he gathered a small force and having fortified himself on the Isle of Athelney, formed by the confluence of the Rivers Parret and Tone amid the marshes of Somerset, he was able to make frequent raids on the enemy. It was during his time here that he, according to legend, disguised himself as a harper and entered into the camp of King Guthrum. Having ascertained that the Danes felt themselves secure, he returned to his troops and led them against the enemy. He gained such a decided victory that fourteen days afterwards the Danes begged for peace. This battle took place in May 878 near Edington in Wiltshire. Later he took London and repulsed a Danish seaborne invasion. Alfred allowed the Danes who were already in the country to remain, on condition that they gave hostages, took a solemn oath to quit Essex, and embraced Christianity. Under these terms, known as the Peace of Wedmore, their king, Guthrum, was baptized, together with thirty of his followers. In return they received that portion of the east of England now occupied by the counties of Norfolk, Suffolk, and Cambridge, as a place of residence. By this time all outside of Danish-ruled England also recognized Alfred as king of all England.

The few years of tranquillity (886–893) which followed were employed by Alfred in rebuilding the towns that had suffered most during the war, particularly London. He consolidated his power by raising around thirty forts, including Oxford and Hastings. He also set about training his people in arms and in agriculture; in improving the navy; in systematizing the laws and internal administration; and in literary labours and the advancement of learning. He re-established the monasteries (as a youth he had twice visited the pope in Rome and had been devoutly Christian since) and schools sacked by the Danes and caused many manuscripts to be translated from Latin. He himself translated several works into Anglo-Saxon, such as the Psalms, *Aesop's Fables*, Boethius on the *Consolation of Philosophy*, the *History of Orosius* and Bede's *Ecclesiastical History*. He also drew up several original works in Anglo-Saxon and initiated the translation of Latin records to form the *Anglo-Saxon Chronicle*.

These labours were interrupted, about 894, by a invasion of Norsemen, who, after a struggle of three years in which they tried to settle lands in the south of England, were finally driven out. Alfred died in 899 and is buried at Winchester. He had married, in 868, Alswith, the daughter of a Mercian nobleman, and left three daughters and two sons, Edward, who succeeded him, and Ethelward, who died in 922. Their descendants ruled England until 1066.

Alpin (d.*c*.840) king of Scots (*c*.837–*c*.840). This semi-legendary king ruled Dalriada for only a short period before being killed by an unknown assailant. He was the 34th king of Dalriada and is thought to have been the son of Eochaid 'the Venomous', perhaps by a Pictish mother, and the father of Kenneth mac-Alpin and Donald I.

Alric king of Kent (747–762). He succeeded his brother Eadbert I as joint ruler with his other brother, Ethelbert II.

Anarawd king of Gwynedd (878–916). The son of Rhodi Mawr, he shared with his five brothers the rule of lands won by his father. In 885 he made an alliance with the Norse king of Dublin against the other kings of Wales who were themselves allied with Alfred of Wessex. This made him the most powerful ruler in Wales and the alliance held for eight years before he finally made peace with Alfred.

Androco (*fl.*1st century AD) high king of the British tribes. Son of Caswallon, he ruled the Catuvellauni tribe based around Hertfordshire and followed his father as the high king of the various tribes he had united against the Romans.

Anna (d.654) king of East Anglia (*c*.633–654). A devout Christian son of Ine, he produced four daughters known for their piety. He was killed in battle fighting Penda of Mercia.

Anne (1665–1714) queen of England and later Great Britain and Ireland (1702–14). The second daughter of James II, then duke of York, and Anne Hyde, daughter of the earl of Clarendon. With her father's permisson she was educated according to the principles of the English Church. In 1683 she married Prince George, son of King Ferdinand III of Denmark and brother of King Christian V of Denmark. On the arrival of the Prince of Orange in 1688, Anne wished to remain with her father, but she was prevailed upon by Lord Churchill (afterwards duke of Marlborough) and his wife to join the triumphant party. After the death of William III she ascended the English throne and was crowned at Westminster Abbey.

Her character was essentially weak, and she remained distant from the new political parties, called the Whigs and the Tories, although she presided over meetings of the Cabinet. Most of the principal events of her reign are connected with the War of the Spanish Succession. The18th century had opened with a series of events in Europe that made war inevitable as it was essential for England to have an Austrian, instead of a French prince, ascend the Spanish throne. The commander of the English army, the Duke of Marlborough was a brilliant soldier, arguably the best ever produced by England, and he soon routed a combined French and Bavarian army at Blenheim. The queen rewarded him with the estate on which was built Blenheim Palace. Two years later Marlborough drove the French from the Netherlands following victory at Ramillies, and King Louis sued for peace. Instead of negotiating a treaty with the French, however, England negotiated an Act of Union with Scotland. In May 1707 the two parliaments of Scotland and England, not without some difficulty, were finally united. The united kingdoms came to be called Great Britain, which had as its symbolic flag the Union Jack.

Meanwhile the war with the French was vigorously prosecuted. British forces defeated the French at Oudenarde and continued to seize valuable French colonies elsewhere. At home, however, there were disputes within the government as the Tories, who had never been in favour of the government funding wars that served the financial interests of the Whigs, took control of the Commons. Anne then fell out with her old friend, the Duchess of Marlborough, and came under the influence of the Tories. Marlborough was soon recalled from Europe and the Treaty of Utrecht negotiated with the French. Austria was to have the Spanish Netherlands, the crowns of Spain and France were to be united, and Britain was to retain the valuable colonies of Gibraltar, Nova Scotia, Newfoundland and Minorca.

England was still divided, however, as Anne wanted to secure the succession to her brother James against the wishes of the Cabinet. The Act of Settlement eventually assigned the crown to James I's Protestant descendants of the House of Hanover if Anne were to die childless. Grieved at the disappointment of her wishes, she fell into a state of weakness and lethargy, and died. She was the last of the Stuart monarchs.

The reign of Anne was distinguished not only by the brilliant successes of the British army, but also on account of the number of excellent writers who flourished at this time, among whom were Pope, Swift, and Addison. Anne bore her husband many children, all of whom died in infancy, except one son, the Duke of Gloucester, who died at the age of twelve.

Significant events of Anne's reign

- 1702 War of the Spanish Succession begins.
  The first daily newspaper, *The Daily Courant*, is printed in London.
- 1704 Battle of Blenheim.
- 1704 Gibraltar is taken from Spain by Sir George Rook.
- 1705 Barcelona is taken by the earl of Peterborough.
- 1706 Battle of Ramillies.
- 1707 Act of Union creates Great Britain.
- 1708 Battle of Oudenarde.
  Prince George of Denmark dies.
- 1708 Minorca falls to English troops.
- 1709 Battle of Malplaquet.
- 1710 Tory administration takes power.
- 1711 Marborough is relieved of his post.
- 1713 War of the Spanish Succession is ended by the Treaty of Utrecht.
  For the last time in England a death sentence for witchcraft is carried out.
- 1714 Sophia of Hanover dies, her son George becomes heir to England's throne.

Artgal (d.871) king of Strathclyde. His kingdom was subject to raids from Norse invaders and in 870 they sacked Dumbarton, an important stronghold on the Dublin to York trade route. He escaped capture but was later put to death on the orders of Constantine I.

Arthur (*fl.*5th or 6th century AD) a possibly mythical Celtic warrior king of post-Roman Britain who may have organized resistance against the Saxon invaders. He is cited in legend with having won a battle over the Saxons at 'Mount Baden' and is supposed to have been buried at Glastonbury. The legends of King Arthur appear in Welsh literature of the 10th century and also feature in Geoffrey Monmouth's *History of the Kings of Britain* in the 12th century. Later writers contributed to the tales, most famously Sir Thomas Mallory, whose work, *Le Morte d'Arthur*, was adapted from the French Arthurian romances.

Athelstan *see* **Ethelstan.**

B

Balliol *or* **Baliol, Edward** (1287–1364) king of Scots (1332–41). The son of John Balliol, he was held prisoner in Normandy and England after his father's abdication. When Robert the Bruce of Scotland died, leaving his young son David as heir, Balliol became Edward III's candidate for the throne, although he was also acknowledged by many Scots as the heir. Soon after the coronation of David II he landed a considerable army at Kinghorn in Fife and with the support of dispossessed English and Scottish nobles and many mercenary soldiers, he defeated the earl of Mar's army at Dupplin Moor. David II fled to France where he was to remain until he was seventeen. Balliol was eventually crowned at Scone in 1332 and, as he accepted Edward III as overlord of his kingdom, put Scotland in the control of England. This proved unacceptable to a great many Scots lords, and he had to flee to Carlisle where he survived as a powerless king during the minority of David II. His enthonement had nonetheless entailed the surrender of much of lowland Scotland to England and the country was thrown into civil war with rival factions of nobles contesting estates. An army led by Scots lords attempting to end the Siege of Berwick was subsequently defeated by an English army at Halidon Hill in 1333. Edward's army advanced again in 1334 and, after taking Roxburgh, forced the Scots lords to accept Balliol as their king. He had no real power but remained a puppet of the English king until David II returned from France. Balliol was eventually dismissed with a pension by Edward III in 1356 and died on his family estate (Bailleul) in Picardy, France, in 1364.

Significant events of Edward Balliol's reign

- 1332 Battle of Dupplin Moor. Balliol is crowned at Scone.
- 1333 Edward III invades and defeats Scots at Halidon Hill.
- 1334 Balliol accepted as king by Scots lords.
- 1337 The Hundred Years' War begins.
- 1341 Edinburgh Castle regained from the English.
- 1342 David II regains the throne of Scotland.

Balliol *or* **Baliol, John** (1249–1313) king of Scots (1292–96. The son of Devorguilla Balliol, John married the daughter of the earl of Surrey and owned vast estates in both England and Scotland. His claim to the throne in 1291 was contested by a dozen rivals (known as the Competitors), including Robert Bruce of Annadale, the grandfather of Robert I. The Guardians of Scotland, fearing a civil war, asked Edward I of England to intervene. Edward took advantage of the situation and demanded allegiance and custody of several important castles before deciding on Balliol. Edward continued to make demands of the Scots, and his interventions soon became intolerable. After demanding Scots troops for a war with France, the Community of the Realm persuaded Balliol to renounce his allegiance. The Auld Alliance with France was renewed in 1295, and Edward invaded Scotland in retaliation. Following his defeat at Dunbar, John sued for peace and surrendered at Stracathro in July 1296. He was forced to relinquish the crown, and the English forces that overran Scotland took away or burned many records and removed the Stone of Destiny (the Coronation Stone of Scone) to Westminster Abbey. Imprisoned in the Tower of London, Balliol was later given Bailleul, his ancestral home in France, where he died in 1313. His son, Edward Balliol, later renewed the claim to Scotland's throne with the support of England.

Significant events of John Balliol's reign

- 1295 Franco-Scottish treaty begins the Auld Alliance
- 1296 Balliol is deposed.
- 1296 Edward I invades Scotland.

Bealdred king of Kent (807–825). He ruled as an under-king of Mercia under the control of Cuthred's brother, Coenwulf. He was driven out in 825 by Egbert of Wessex, who soon afterwards became overlord of the East Angles as well as Kent, Surrey, Sussex and Essex.

Beli (d.722) king of Strathclyde. He successfully defended his kingdom from attacks by Oengus, king of the Picts. His son and successor, Tewdwr, later won an important battle against the Picts at Mugdock, near Glasgow, in 750.

Beonna king of East Anglia (*c.*760). He is known to have issued a coinage during his reign.

Beonred king of Mercia (757). The successor to the throne of Ethelbald of Mercia, he was challenged by Offa, a cousin of the former king. Disorder followed, and the confederacy of kingdoms that had been built by Ethelbald was weakened as the two rivals fought.

It was only a matter of months before Offa deposed him.

Beorhtwulf (d.853) king of Mercia (840–853). He succeeded Wiglaf as king and endured a period of sustained Viking attacks. He was finally routed in 852 when over 350 ships stormed London and Canterbury, and he died a year later. He was succeeded by his son Burgred.

Beornwulf (d.827) king of Mercia (823–827). He deposed Ceolwulf in 823 and soon afterwards led an army into Wessex. After some initial success he was defeated by Egbert and later killed near Swindon. He was succeeded by Ludeca, previously an ealdorman.

Beortric (d.802) king of Wessex (757–802). He married Eadburga of Mercia, a daughter of Offa, and was succeeded by Egbert.

Berhtun (d.686) king of Sussex (686). Ruling for less than a year, he was killed during an invasion of Kent.

Boudicca *or* **Boadicea** (d.62) queen of the Iceni tribe. Wife of Prasutagus, a client of Rome, whose lands in Norfolk and Suffolk were taken by the Romans after his death. Homes and estates were burned and plundered, Boudicca was flogged and her daughters raped. In retaliation she gathered a large army and led a violent rebellion that took London, St Albans and Colchester while the Roman governor Paulinus was in Wales. When Paulinus returned he violently suppressed the rebellion, and the defeated Boadicea killed herself with poison.

Bred (d.842) king of Picts (842). He ascended the throne on the death of his father, Uurad, but his reign did not last the year as he was deposed by his brother, Kineth.

Brian Boru (*c*.941–1014) king of Munster (976–1014), high king of Ireland (1002–14). He took the title of high king after defeating his great rival, Mael Sechnaill II, the last of the O'Neill kings, at Athlone. After extending his kingdom to take in much of southern Ireland, he put an end to Norse ambitions in Ireland by his victory at the Battle of Clontarf (1014) near Dublin. The losses suffered in this conflict were great, and in the confusion Brian Boru was killed in his tent by defeated and fleeing Danes. Mael Sechnaill quickly reclaimed the title of high king, but after his death in 1024 no king was able to secure the position for any notable period of time for over 150 years. This effectively ended royal rule in Ireland.

As well as being a soldier Brian Boru was a patron of education and religion. He established monasteries and encouraged the preservation of the old Irish sagas as well as the writing of poetry and prose. Three O'Brien descendents remained kings of Munster until the next century (1119). Their main kingdom disappeared in 1194, but the O'Briens remained kings of north Munster until 1543. The kingdom then became an earldom under Henry VII. It remained an earldom until 1741 when the eighth earl died childless.

Bridei I (d.586) king of Picts (556–586). His royal court at Inverness was visited by St Columba, but he did not convert to Christianity.

Bridei II (d.641) king of Picts (635–641). A brother of Garnard.

Bridei III (d.692) king of Picts (671–692). The son of Drest I's sister, he was the first of the Pictish kings to be recognized overlord of all Pictland after defeating King Egfrith of Northumbria in the battle of Nectansmere in 685. Egfrith had installed his cousin Drest as ruler of the Picts in order to consolidate his power in the north.

Bridei IV (d.706) king of Picts (696–706). The son of Drest's sister.

Bridei V (d.763) king of Picts (761–763). The brother of Oengus.

Bruce, Edward (1276–1318) high king of Ireland (1315–18). He was one of the five sons of Robert, Earl of Carrick, and Marjorie, Countess of Carrick, and the younger brother of Robert I of Scotland (his three other brothers were executed following Robert's defeats at Methven and Dalry). A fearless commander, he aided his brother during his guerilla-style campaign of raids on English-held castles. By mid-1308, Edward had overrun Galloway, while his brother had control of much of the north. He failed in his attempt to take Stirling in 1313 and made a truce with Philip de Mowbray which made Bannockburn inevitable.

Invited to Ireland, where he had grown up, in 1315 by the king of Tyrone he led an army in a difficult campaign for a year before being crowned high king of Ireland. His tactic of destroying everthing in his path as he progressed through Ireland made him a widely unpopular figure. He failed to take Dublin despite assistance from his brother and was killed in battle at Dundalk along with many of his supporters. He married Isabel of Atholl and had two sons.

Brude (d.845) king of Picts (843–845). The son of Uurad's sister, he ascended the throne after killing his uncle, Kineth. He was converted to Christianity by St Columba.

Burgred king of Mercia (853–874). The son of Beorhtwulf, he married Ethelswith, daughter of Ethelwulf of Wessex, and with the assistance of the latter frequently raided north Wales. He made two treaties with the Viking Great Army (868 and 872) only to be driven from it from Repton to exile in Rome, where he died. He was buried in the Church of St Mary in the English quarter.

C

Cadwalla (*c*.658–689) king of Wessex (685–688). A member of the Wessex royal family who was forced into exile early in life, he returned in 684 and after establishing himself in Wessex attacked and subjugated the kingdom of Sussex. He also annexed the Isle of Wight and made advances as far as Kent. He was converted to Christianity and after he abdicated made a pilgrimage to Rome where he was baptised in the presence of the pope.

Cadwallon (d.633) king of Gwynedd (*c*.625–633). An ally of King Penda of Mercia, he helped defeat Edwin of Northumbria in a battle at Hatfield Chase, near Doncaster, in 633. He was killed at Hexham by Edwin's nephew, Oswald, who had returned from exile among the Scots.

Canute (*c*.994–1035) king of England (1016–35), Denmark and Norway. He was the son of Sweyn Forkbeard. Following the death of Ethelred, the kingdom of England fell into confusion, and Canute renewed Danish attacks. He began by devastating the eastern coast and extended his ravages in the south, where, however, he failed to establish himself until after the battle of Ashingdon and the assassination of the Saxon choice for king, Edmund. He was accepted as king of the whole of England in 1016. At Harold's death in 1018 he gained Denmark, and in 1031 he conquered Norway, thus becoming ruler of a great Danish empire. Malcolm III of Scotland admitted Canute's superiority and Sweden also was vassal to him.

Canute, who began his reign with barbarity and crime, afterwards became a humane and wise monarch. He restored the English customs at a general assembly and ensured to the Danes and English equal rights and equal protection of person and property, and even preferred English subjects for the most important posts. His power was confirmed by his marriage to Emma of Normandy, Ethelred's widow. He died at Shaftesbury, leaving Norway to his eldest son, Sweyn, England to Harold I, and Denmark to the third, Hardicanute.

Significant events of Canute's reign

- 1016 Edmund Ironside is chosen as king by the Saxons.
  Edmund Ironside killed after the Battle of Ashingdon.
  Canute becomes king of all England.
- 1017 Marriage of Canute and Emma of Normandy.
  Canute creates four earldoms—Wessex, Mercia, Northumbria and East Anglia.
- 1027 Canute makes a pilgrimage to Rome.

Caradoc *or* **Caratalus** (d.*c*.54) king of the Catuvellauni tribe. A son of Cunobelinus, he resisted the Romans (by whom he was known as **Caratacus**) from AD 43 to 47 but was eventually captured and taken to Rome in chains. His brother Togodummus was probably killed at the Battle of the Medway in AD 43.

Cartimandua (*fl.*1st century) queen of the Brigantes tribe, a leader of one of the largest British tribes, which had York as its centre.

Caswallon (d.*c*.60) high king of the British tribes. Leader of the Catuvellauni tribe, which settled in what is now Hertfordshire, he fought rival tribes to become high king and united them against the first Roman invasions.

Cathal O'Connor (d.1224) king of Connaught (1202–24). The last provincial monarch in Ireland, he resisted the advances of Henry III until his death.

Ceawlin (d.*c*.593) king of Wessex (577–591). The son of Cynric, he succeeded his father to the leadership of the West Saxons and began advancing north of the Thames. In 577 he defeated Ethelbert of Kent at Wibbandum, killing two of his sons, and was recognized as *Bretwalda*, overlord of all the Anglo-Saxon kings. His turbulent reign came to an end following a power struggle in Wessex, and he died in exile.

Cenfus king of Wessex (674). A grandson of Ceolwulf.

Cenred king of Mercia (716–718). He succeeded the murdered King Osred.

Centwine king of Wessex (676–685). A brother of Cenwahl.

Cenwahl king of Wessex (643–672). The son of Cyneglis, he married a sister of Penda but had to flee from the Mercian king after abandoning her. He extended his territory after Penda's death and won an important victory in 658 at Peonnan, near Exeter. Advancing farther into Devon he is said to have 'put the Britons to flight as far as the sea'. He then lost Oxfordshire to Mercia, which also seized the Isle of Wight and lands in Hampshire, and accepted baptism while in exile at the court of King Anna of East Anglia. He ended his turbulent reign by going on pilgrimage in Rome; his successor Ine followed him thirty-seven years later. In Wessex he built the Old Minster, Winchester (648), and was buried there.

Ceol king of Wessex (591–597). He came to the throne after the abdication of Ceawlin.

Ceolred king of Mercia (709–716). The son of Ethelred, he succeeded Coenred and earned a reputation as a spoiler of monasteries. He also fought Ine of Wessex at Woodborough in Wiltshire in 715.

Ceolwulf (1) king of Wessex (597–611). He succeeded his brother, Ceol, and in 607 defeated the South Saxons who had gained lands in the kingdom following the abdication of Ceawlin.

Ceolwulf (2) (d.760) king of Northumbria (729–737). A brother of Cenred, he was temporarily deposed in 731 when a rival faction seized him and had him tonsured as a monk. Bede's *Ecclesiastical History of the English People* was dedicated to him.

Ceolwulf I king of Mercia (821–823). He succeeded his brother, Coenwulf, but reigned for only two years before being deposed by Beornwulf.

Ceolwulf II king of Mercia (874–*c*.880). The last Mercian king, he was chosen by the Danish overlords to rule the subordinate western half of the kingdom. He was deposed.

Ceorl king of Mercia (*c*.606–626). Related to Pybba, his daughter married the dominant king of Northumbria, Edwin.

Cerdic king of Wessex (519–534). Recorded as the first king of the West Saxons, he landed near Southampton in 494 and fought the Britons for control of the area. He is known to have killed a British king in 508 and had a further victory at Charford on the Avon in 519. By 530 he also had control of the Isle of Wight. His son, Cynric, succeeded him.

Charles I (1600–1649) king of Great Britain and Ireland (1625–49). The son of James I (James VI of Scotland) and Anne, daughter of King Ferdinand II of Denmark, Charles was born at Dunfermline Palace (the last sovereign to be born in Scotland), and was never expected to become king as he was second in line to the throne after his brother, Henry, Prince of Wales. He became heir apparent after his brother died and was created Prince of Wales at the age of twelve. In early 1625, he succeeded to the throne and was crowned at Westminster Abbey. In the same year he was married by proxy to Henrietta Maria, daughter of Henry IV of France.

Charles proved himself to have inherited his father's inflexible convictions about the role of the monarchy in relation to parliament. As he had Catholic sympathies, he favoured the new High Church party of William Laud, soon to be made archbisop of Canterbury, against the dominant parliamentarians of the time. The first parliament that he summoned, being more disposed to state grievances than grant supplies, was dissolved after financially crippling Charles. The next year (1626) a new parliament was summoned but proved no more tractable than before, and it too was soon dissolved. In 1628 a series of military and naval disasters compelled the king to call a new parliament, which showed itself as much opposed to arbitrary measures as its predecessor, and, after voting the supplies prepared the Petition of Rights. This was essentially a reminder to Charles of what parliament took to be the traditional liberties of the people and asserted that any loan or tax forced by the king was illegal without the permission of parliament. Charles was constrained to pass the Petition into law. But the assassination of the duke of Buckingham, Charles's supporter, and the determined spirit with which parliament resisted the king's claim to levy tonnage and poundage on his own authority led to a rupture, and Charles again dissolved parliament, resolving to try and reign without one. In this endeavour he was supported by the earl of Strafford and William Laud, archbishop of Canterbury, as his chief counsellors. With their help Charles continued to rule for eleven years without summoning a parliament, using the arbitrary courts of High Commission and Star Chamber as a kind of cover for pure absolutism, and raising money by unconstitutional or doubtful means. He made various attempts to get estates into his possession on the pretext of invalid titles, and in May 1635, the city of London estates were sequestered. In 1637 John Hampden began the career of resistance to the king's arbitrary measures by refusing to pay ship money, the right to levy which, without authority of parliament, he was determined to bring before a court of law. His cause was argued for twelve days in the Court of Exchequer; and although he lost it by the decision of eight of the judges out of twelve, the discussion of the question produced a very powerful impression on the public mind.

During this period Archbishop Laud began to enforce his High Church discipline, and Puritans, forced into exile, founded colonies in America. It was in Scotland, however, that Charles's insensitivity and arrogance came to the fore. He was crowned in Edinburgh with full Anglican ceremonial in 1633, and this lost him the goodwill of a number of his Scottish subjects. In 1636 the new Book of Canons was issued by the king's authority, and this attempt by Charles to introduce an Anglican liturgy into Scotland produced great opposition. The Presbyterian nobility in Scotland attempted to obstruct this imposition in parliament but soon found that the influence of the bishops was too great. The following year saw the introduction of the Book of Common

Prayer, and it became apparent that Charles was acting without consultation. After repeated petitions to the king, frustration led to the drawing up and subscription of the National Covenant in 1638. Thousands gathered in Edinburgh to sign this declaration of faith and obedience to the reformed religion of Scotland. Soon the Covenanters were buying arms and preparing to defend their beliefs on the battlefield, and Charles was forced to seek a settlement. Suspension of the Code and Prayer Book and the calling of a General Assembly in Glasgow did not calm the Covenanters, however, and they proceeded to abolish episcopacy and defy Charles by refusing to disarm. Charles attempted to reassert himself by force of arms, but lack of money and troops frustrated his efforts. He was also forestalled by the effective deployment of men and arms by the Covenant army, and hostilities did not begin immediately. Charles sought instead, through an agreement reached at Berwick, to begin consultations with a view to negotiating a peaceful settlement.

The Covenanters would not disband, however, and were adamant over the abolition of the bishops. In 1640 a parliament was summoned and Charles tried again to get military support. Again he was disappointed, and an army of Covenanters moved south, taking Newcastle and occupying the northern English counties, remaining there until Charles paid an indemnity to secure their return north. Again parliament was summoned, and the stormy sessions that followed resulted in Charles agreeing to the Act of Attainder, under which Charles's chief minister, the earl of Strafford, was executed. In early 1642 Charles decided to resist and attempted to arrest the parliamentary leaders. He failed, the City of London gave refuge to the parliamentarians, and Charles left his capital to raise the royal standard in Nottingham in August. The king had on his side the great bulk of the gentry, while nearly all the Puritans and the inhabitants of the great trading towns sided with parliament.

Early successes by the king resulted in parliament making a Solemn League and Covenant with the Scots, in return for whose help they promised to impose Presbyterianism on England. The first action, the battle of Edgehill, gave the king a slight advantage, but nothing very decisive happened until the Battle of Marston Moor, in 1644. The parliamentary army by this stage was composed of Scots, Roundheads, and Sir Thomas Fairfax's and Oliver Cromwell's New Model Army. The latter army fought with great vigour, representing as it did the fervour of the extreme Puritan sects, and went on to route the royalists at the Battle of Naseby. This completed the ruin of the king's cause, and Charles at length gave himself up to the Scottish army at Newark. The parliamentarians who favoured moderation in the face of mounting religious extremism had been displaced by Cromwell, however, and when the Scots decided to surrender Charles they had little influence on his fate. When the moderate Covenanters realized that their hopes for a Presbyterian settlement in England would be better served by a having a legitimate sovereign than by the turbulent Cromwell, they rallied in support of Charles. This 'Engagement' was a failure, however, and the defeat of the royalist army at Preston (1648) sealed the king's fate. Cromwell was soon able to coerce parliament and the more hesitating of the Presbyterians into bringing Charles to trial for high treason against the people.

Although Charles repeatedly refused to recognize the court, he had the sentence of death pronounced against him. All interposition being in vain, he was beheaded before the Banqueting House in Whitehall, meeting his fate with an admirable obstinacy that seemed dignified and courageous. The execution of the king produced a feeling of revulsion throughout the country, and Cromwell had to maintain his minority rule by force.

Charles had nine children, notably Charles II and James VII. He was buried in St George's Chapel, Windsor Castle.

Significant events of Charles I's reign

- 1626 Parliament dismissed by Charles.
- 1627 England declares war on France.
- 1628 Assassination of Buckingham.
- 1628 Charles reluctantly agreed the Petition of Rights.
- 1629 Charles dismisses parliament again, this time for eleven years.
- 1632 Van Dyck becomes court painter.
- 1637 New Book of Common Prayer is published.
- 1638 National Covenant pledged in Scotland.
- 1640 The Short Parliament (three weeks) is called.
  The Long Parliament (until 1660) is called.
- 1641 Abolition of the Star Chamber.
- 1642 Civil War begins.
- 1644 Solemn League and Covenant signed.
  Battle of Marston Moor.
- 1645 Battle of Naseby.
- 1646 Scots surrender Charles to English parliament.
- 1648 Royalist Scots invade England.
- 1649 England is declared a republic.
  Parliament tries and executes Charles.

Charles II (1630–1685) king of Great Britain and Ireland (1660–85). The eldest surviving son of Charles I and Henrietta Maria of France, and the brother of James, Duke of York, later James VII. He was sent into exile in France after the battle of Edgehill (1645) and was there tutored by Thomas Hobbes, among others. After his father's execution he immediately assumed the royal title. At the time, however, Cromwell was all-powerful in England, and he accepted an invitation from the Scots, who had proclaimed him their king. He sailed from Holland and was crowned at Scone (1651), making him the last king to be crowned in Scotland. It would still be ten years before the restoration of the monarchy in England, but in Scotland at least the Stuart succession remained unbroken, although Charles never revisited Scotland after 1660.

An early attempt to take back the throne was frustrated by divisions among the royalist parties, and Charles reluctantly had to sign the Covenant to appease the strongest faction. Eventually he took to the field with the English royalists, who, having gathered an army, encountered Cromwell at Worcester and were totally defeated. With great difficulty Charles escaped to France. Richard Cromwell succeeded his father in 1658 but almost immediately abdicated in the face of growing discontent with the Puritan austerities of the time. The popular Restoration, effected without a struggle by General Monk, set Charles on the throne after the Declaration of Breda, his entry into the capital being made amidst universal acclamations.

He was a witty and stylish man, and seemed at first to characterize the anti-Puritan mood of the country, becoming known by many as the 'Merry Monarch'. Within two years he married the Infanta of Portugal, Catherine of Braganza, and for a time his measures, mainly counselled by the Chancellor, Lord Clarendon, were prudent and conciliatory. In this favourable climate Charles re-established much of the royal prerogative. The privileges of the Anglican Church were restored and a pro-Catholic policy began to appear, excluding Nonconformists from holding municipal office and forcing Puritans to accept the doctrines of the Church of England. But the extravagance and licentious habits of the king soon involved the nation as well as himself in difficulties. Dunkirk was sold to the French to relieve his pecuniary embarrassment, and war, caused by commercial rivalry, broke out with Holland. A Dutch fleet entered the Thames, and burned and destroyed ships as far up as Chatham. The great plague in 1665 and the Great Fire of London, which burned 13,000 houses to the ground the following year, added to the disasters of the period. Amid such calamities there were mutterings of idolatry having taken root in a licentious court.

A triple alliance between England, Holland and Sweden, for the purpose of checking the ambition of Louis XIV, followed, but the extravagance of the king made him willing to become a mere pensioner of Louis XIV, with whom he arranged a private treaty in 1670. This was the Treaty of Dover, by which he declared himself a Catholic and agreed to restore Catholicism in return for secret subsidies from Louis XIV of France. After this Charles issued a declaration attempting to free both Protestant dissenters and Roman Catholics from some of their disabilities. Parliament countered this with the Test Act, which was designed to keep Roman Catholics out of public office. In 1674 parliament also reversed Charles's foreign policy by breaking off relations with France and making peace with the Dutch.

Alarm over the 'Popish Plot' of 1678, in which an Anglican parson, Titus Oates, disclosed a Catholic plot to murder Charles and restore Catholicism to England, led to further difficulties between Charles and parliament. The plot was soon revealed to be a fabrication, but the resulting furore led parliament to attempt to exclude Charles's Catholic brother James from the throne. The question of the succession was settled only after the passing of the Habeas Corpus Act in 1679, which established important measures for protecting individual rights. A new parliament that assembled in 1680 had to be dissolved following further difficulties with the king, and yet another, which met the following year at Oxford. Finally, Charles, like his father, determined to govern without a parliament, and after the discovery of an assassination conspiracy (the Rye House Plot of 1683) and the execution of Lord Russell and Algernon Sidney, Charles became as absolute as any sovereign in Europe, although political stability was maintained until his death. England, however, was deeply divided and uncertain of the future and thus unable to take a full part in European affairs. Advances were nonetheless made during his reign in the fields of science and architecture, areas in which Charles took great interest, encouraging and supporting the work of men like Isaac Newton, Robert Boyle and Christopher Wren.

Charles II died from the consequences of an apoplectic fit and converted to Catholicism on his deathbed, having received the sacrament according to the rites of the Roman Catholic Church. He had no legitimate children but was well known for his love of women. His many mistresses included the famous Nell Gwynn and several others were raised to the highest ranks of nobility. Six of the thirteen illegitimate sons he had by them were made dukes—

Monmouth (by Lucy Walters), St Albans (by Nell Gwynn), Richmond (by Louise de Querouaille), and Cleveland, Grafton and Northumberland (by Barbara Villiers).

Significant events of Charles II's reign

- 1660 Restoration of Charles to the throne. Samuel Pepys diary is begun.
- 1661 Parliament meets at Westminster.
- 1662 Act of Uniformity compels Puritans to accept Church of England doctrines. The Royal Society receives its charter.
- 1665 Two-year-long war begins with Holland. London struck by plague.
- 1666 Great Fire of London.
- 1670 Secret Treaty of Dover with France.
- 1672 War resumes with Holland.
- 1673 Test Act introduced to keep Catholics from office.
- 1675 Creation of the Royal Observatory. Building of St Paul's Cathedral is begun.
- 1678 Popish Plot results in the persecution of Catholics.
- 1679 Habeus Corpus Act introduced. Whig and Tory first used as names for political parties.
- 1681 Exclusion Bill attempts to exclude James from the succession.
- 1683 Rye House Plot to murder the king is uncovered.

Cinioch (d.631) king of the Picts. Son of Gartnart's sister, the dates of his reign are not known.

Ciniod king of Picts (763–775). Son of Oengus's sister.

Cissa king of Sussex (*c*.514). He participated in the Siege of Pevensey in 491 and succeeded his father, Aelle. He gave his name to Chichester (Cissa's-ceaster), the royal capital. Nothing more is known of him as the *Anglo-Saxon Chronicle* does not mention the South Saxons again until 661.

Coel (Old Coel the Splendid) (*fl.*5th century) British tribal king. The 'Old King Cole' of nursery-rhyme fame, he was overlord of several British tribes and ruled much of lowland Scotland. His descendants ruled the kingdom of Strathclyde.

Coenred king of Mercia (704–709). He was the eldest son of Wulfhere. On his father's death the throne was taken by Ethelred as he was then too young to rule. In 697 there were rebellions south of the Humber, and he was declared king there in 702. Two years later Ethelred died, and Coenred succeeded him as king of Mercia. He was unsuited to the royal life, however, and abdicated in 709 in favour of Ethelred's son, Ceolred. Soon afterwards, he left England to become a monk in Rome and dedicated the rest of his life to spiritual works.

Coenwulf king of Mercia (796–821). He was a descendant of Penda's youngest brother. Worcestershire is first mentioned in a land grant he made to Bishop Deneberht sometime between 814 and 820.

Cogidummus (*fl.*1st century) king of the Regni tribe. A client king of the Romans, he called himself the legate of the emperor in Britain and built himself a palace at Fishbourne, near Chichester.

Commius (*fl.*50) king of the Atrebates tribe. Leader of a tribe that settled in what are now Hampshire and Sussex after fleeing Gaul.

Conall king of Picts (787–789). The son of Alpin II's sister, he succeeded Talorgen but was deposed within two years by Constantine.

Constantine (d.820) king of Picts (789–820). The first Constantine to rule in Scotland, he was the son of Alpin II's sister. He asserted his authority over the Scots of Dalriada sometime after 811, a task that was made easier by the frequent Viking attacks of the period.

Constantine I (d.878) king of Scots (862–877). Thought to have been the son of Kenneth Mac-Alpin, he succeeded Kenneth's brother, Donald, to the throne and bore the title of Constantine I although he was not the first king of that name in Scotland. During his reign his kingdom was frequently attacked by Viking forces sailing from Ireland. Following a landing in Fife in 879, his forces were routed at Dollar, and in a further engagement at Forgan he lost his life. He was succeeded by his brother, Aed, who soon afterwards was murdered by a rival to the throne. Constantine's sister had married Run, the British king of Strathclyde, and their son, Eocha, became king after Aed.

Constantine II (d.952) king of Scots (900–942). After defeating the Danes, who had killed his predecessor, Donald II, he held an ecclesiastical court at Scone for the settlement of the rule and discipline of the Celtic Church. In diplomatic affairs he was the first Scottish king to acknowledge an English king as overlord (Edward the Elder, son of Alfred the Great, in 924) but this may only have been for expediency, as an ally against Norse aggression. An invasion by Ethelstan, son of Edward, led to a counter-invasion by the Scots, which resulted in the Battle of Brunanburgh, near the Humber, in 937. The Northumbrians were the victors despite Constantine having received the assistance of a Norse force from Dublin. He abdicated in 942, leaving the throne to his cousin, Malcolm I, and spent the final years of his life as abbot at St Andrews.

Constantine III (d.997) king of Scots (995–997). The grandson of Constantine II and son of Cuilean, his reign was short and turbulent. It is thought he may have been murdered by Kenneth III after having had Kenneth II murdered two years previously.

Cormac mac-Art (d.*c*.360) high king of Ireland. A semi-legendary warrior king who reigned from Tara, where he is said to have quarrelled with the local Druids after converting to Christianity. He choked to death on a fishbone, and folklore has it that a Druid curse was to blame.

Creoda (d.593) king of Mercia (*c*.585–593). The first named king of the Mercians, he is thought to have been the son of Icel, the first continental Angle king to settle in Britain.

Cuilean (d.971) king of Scots (966–971). He was killed in battle fighting the Britons of Strathclyde.

Cunedda (*fl*.4th century) Welsh tribal king. He was settled by the Romans in north Wales where he defended the country against attacks from Ireland. Kings of Gwynedd claim descent from him.

Cunobelinus (*fl*.1st century) high king of the British tribes, Shakespeare's Cymbeline. He was recognized by Augustus as the leader of the Catuvellauni tribe and high king of many others. He became an ally of the Romans and ruled from Camulodonum (Colchester). His sons later resisted the Romans.

Cuthred (d.756) king of Wessex (740–756). He defeated Ethelbald of Mercia at Burford in Oxfordshire in 752.

Cyneglis (d.641) king of Wessex (611–643). He failed in a plot to murder Edwin of Northumbria in 626, and in 628 he was defeated in a territorial dispute with Penda of Mercia. Towards the end of his reign he was converted to Christianity.

Cynewulf (d.786) king of Wessex (757–786). A client of Offa of Mercia, he was murdered while visiting his mistress by Cyneheard, a brother of Sigeberht of Wessex, who believed that he was plotting to exile him. Cyneheard was killed by Cynewulf's bodyguards.

Cynric king of Wessex (534–560). He extended his kingdom by fighting the Britons at Salisbury in 552 and at Banbury, near Swindon in 556. He was succeeded by his son, Ceawlin.

D

Dafydd ap Llywelyn (d.1246) king of Gwynedd (1240–46). The second son and successor of Llywelyn ap Iorwerth, he attempted to take back lands lost to the English but was forced to do homage to Henry III and to give up all the territories won by his father since 1215. He titled himself 'Prince of Wales' in 1244 and died after uniting other Welsh rulers in a second attempt to restore the kingdom. The Baron's War in England enabled him to marry Simon de Montfort's daughter, but he died without an heir, and his principality was divided among the sons of his elder brother.

Dafydd ap Opwain (d.1194) king of Gwynedd (1170–94). He married Henry II's illegitimate half-sister, Emma.

David I (the Saint) (*c*.1081–1153) king of Scots (1124–53). Sixth son of Malcolm III Canmore's second marriage to Margaret, sister of Edgar the Aetheling, his early years were spent at the English court of Henry I, and in 1100 his sister married the king. Their daughter became Queen Matilda. On the death of his elder brother Edgar, David inherited that part of Scotland below the Forth-Clyde line. However, another brother, Alexander I, succeeded Edgar, and he disputed David's right to this territory until David strengthened his position with the support of Henry. After Alexander's death in 1124 he quickly established himself throughout his kingdom by initiating a simple form of centralized government. He was the first to introduce feudal institutions to his native land and was the first Scottish king to strike his own coinage. He also vigorously promoted education and agriculture and regularly gave informal audience to the poor in all the languages of the realm. During David's reign around a dozen royal burghs were created, including Perth and Aberdeen.

Amidst baronial revolts in England, David twice took an army south to support his niece Matilda against Stephen, her rival claimant for the English crown. During one of his incursions he was defeated at the Battle of the Standard near Northallerton in Yorkshire (1138).

David also acquired a considerable reputation for sanctity. While prince of Cumbria he had begun the re-establishment or restoration of the Glasgow bishopric, and after he became king founded the bishoprics of Aberdeen, Ross, Caithness, Brechin and Dunblane. Among the religious houses that date from his reign are Holyrood, Melrose, Jedburgh, Kelso, Dryburgh and Newbattle. His services to the Church procured for him the popular title of saint, but the endowments so taxed the royal domains and possessions that James VI famously characterized him as 'ane sair sanct for the crown'.

In old age he spent his time gardening and establishing apple orchards. He died at Carlisle, and was succeeded by his eldest grandson, who, as Malcolm IV, inherited a peaceful and flourishing kingdom.

David II (1324–71) king of Scots (1329–71 with interruptions). He was born at Dunfermline, the son of Robert I (the Bruce) by his second wife, Elizabeth de Burgh. At the age of four he was married to Joan, sister of Edward III of England, then only three years older. He succeeded to the throne on the death of his father and was acknowledged as king by the greater part of the nation.

During his minority he was troubled by those his father had disinherited, who supported the claim of Edward Balliol, the son of John Balliol, to the throne. Balliol was backed by Edward III of England, and at first was successful at the Battle of Dupplin Moor (1332), being crowned at Scone soon afterwards. David fled to France following a later defeat at Halidon Hill (1333) but eventually returned to Scotland at the age of seventeen and succeeded in driving Balliol from Scotland. Still, however, the war was carried on with England with increasing rancour, until at length David was wounded and taken prisoner at the Battle of Neville's Cross, near Durham (1346). After being detained in captivity for eleven years, he was ransomed for 100,000 merks, to be paid in annual instalments, but in place of making the payments he made the offer of leaving his kingdom to an English heir. Following opposition from his nobles, this plan was disallowed by the Scottish parliament, which disliked the idea of a formal union of the crowns.

David married Margaret Drummond in 1363 following the death of Joan, but died at Edinburgh Castle seven years later without having produced an heir.

Significant events of David II's reign

- 1332 David deposed by Edward Balliol.
- 1333 Edward III invades Scotland.
- 1341 David II returns to claim the throne.

- 1346 Battle of Neville's Cross. David captured and held in the Tower of London.
- 1348 Scotland afflicted by the Black Death.
- 1357 The Treaty of Berwick. David returns to Scotland.
- 1363 David II offers the Scottish throne to Edward III.

Donald I (d.862) king of Scots (858–862). The son of Alpin and brother of Kenneth I, he reputedly applied the laws of Dalriada to Pictland. Donald died at Scone, leaving the throne to Kenneth I's son, Constantine I.

Donald II (d.900) king of Scots (889–900). The son of Constantine I, he was the first king of both the Scots and Picts to be referred to as *ri alban* or 'king of Alba'. His kingdom was repeatedly ravaged by the Norse, and he was killed in battle near Dunnottar. He was succeeded by Constantine II.

Donald III Bane (1031–1100) king of Scots (1093–1100). Donald, whose sobriquet 'Bane' means 'fair', retreated to the Hebrides on the death of his father, Duncan I, at the hands of his rival, Macbeth. Donald's brother, later Malcolm III, took refuge in England. Macbeth was himself overthrown (1054) and killed by Malcolm, who then became king of Scots. During his exile in the Hebrides Donald Bane had been exposed to Celtic culture and, under Malcolm's rule, had nursed a hatred of the increasing English influence he saw in the Scottish court. On Malcolm's death, Donald seized the throne, at the age of sixty-two, and attempted to reverse the anglicization of the court. His position was soon threatened, however, by Malcolm's son, Duncan II, who had been trained as a Norman knight during his period of detention as a hostage in England. An invasion led by Duncan, with the backing of an English and French army, dethroned Donald in 1094, but Donald regained the throne when Edmund, another of Malcolm's sons, killed Duncan. Malcolm's other surviving son, Edgar, then had Donald blinded and imprisoned in 1097. He died three years later and became the last Scottish king to be buried on Iona.

Donald Breac (d.642) king of Scots (*c*.635–642). The tenth king of Dalriada, he invaded Ireland in 636 and was soundly beaten at the battle of Magh Rath (Moira). This was said to have activated the curse of St Columba on Scots kings who fought their own kinsmen. After returning to Scotland he was killed in a battle with the Strathclyde Britons at Strathcarron. These defeats led to a sharp decline in the influence of Dalriada in Scotland.

Drest I king of Picts (663–671). The brother of Gartnait, he was ousted by a faction of the Picts who resented the influence and expansionist policies of his uncle, Egfrith, the Northumbrian king. He was succeeded by Bridei III who crushed Egfrith's army at Nechtansmere in 685.

Drest II (d.729) king of Picts (724–729). The son of Nechton's sister, he was one of four who claimed the title of king in 724 following the decision of Nechtan to abdicate. He was killed by his cousin Oengus in 729.

Drest III (d.780) king of Picts (780). The son of Alpin II's sister.

Drest IV (d.837) king of Picts (834–837). He was the son of Uen.

Drust (d.848) king of Picts (845–848). One of the sons of Uurad.

Dubh (d.966) king of Scots (962–966). The son of Malcolm I, he was killed in battle.

Duncan I (1010–40) king of Scots (1034–40). The son of Crinan, abbot of Dunkeld, and Bethoc, daughter of Malcolm II, Duncan succeeded his grandfather and founded the Dunkeld dynasty. When he became king of Scots he was already the king of Strathclyde and therefore inherited a kingdom larger than any held by his predecessors. A rash and hot-headed king, he was not particularly successful in battle, and in 1039 fruitlessly besieged Durham. He was also twice defeated in battle by his cousin Thorfinn, earl of Orkney, before being killed by a rival for the throne, Macbeth, *mormaer*, or steward, of Moray at Forres, near Elgin, in 1040. He married a cousin of the earl of Northumberland and had two sons who both became kings—Malcolm III Canmore and Donald Bane. After their father's murder the two brothers fled the kingdom.

Duncan II (1060–1094) king of Scots (1094). The eldest son of Malcolm III from his first marriage, his father had given him as a hostage to William II in 1072, and he grew up in Normandy before being set free and knighted in 1087. Soon afterwards, he married Octreda of Northumberland. On the death of his father, he was seen as the true heir, and with support from the English king, William II, under whose banner he was then serving, he led an Anglo-Norman army north. He defeated his uncle, Donald III Bane, to become king, but his reign was short and difficult as there was much resentment of his English supporters. Within a matter of months he was slain in battle by his half-brother, Edmund, at Mondynes near Dunnottar, and Donald Bane regained power. Donald was soon afterwards deposed by another of Malcolm's sons, Edgar.

Dyfnwal I (d.934) king of Strathclyde (*c*.920–934). He recognized the Wessex king, Edward the Elder, as overlord in 925.

Dyfnwal II (d.975) king of Strathclyde (934–*c*.973). He killed the king of Scots, Culiean, in battle in 971 and died whilst on a pilgrimage to Rome.

EF

Eadbert (d.768) king of Northumbria (737–758). He came to the throne after the abdication of his cousin Ceolwulf. His brother, Egbert, had been made archbishop of York, and they governed Church and state in union. In 740 he led a campaign against the Picts, and in his absence Ethelbert, king of Mercia, ravaged parts of his kingdom. He soon recovered his lands and went on to add parts of Strathclyde to his kingdom. In 756 he was defeated by the Strathclyde Britons, and two years later he resigned his crown in favour of his son, Oswulf. Soon afterwards, he entered the monastery of St Peter's at York and remained there until his death.

Eadbert I (d.748) king of Kent (725–748). Joint ruler of the kingdom with his brother, Ethelbert II.

Eadbert II Praen (d.*c*.810) king of Kent (796– 798). Despite having become a monk, Eadbert strongly contested the Mercian domination of Kent, and on the death of Offa he became king. He was supported by his nobles and condemned by the Church, which favoured Mercia. In 798 Coenwulf invaded Kent, captured the king, and caused him to have his hands cut off and his eyes burned out. Coenwulf then imposed Cuthred as an under-king, and the independent existence of Kent was brought to an end.

Eadric (d.688) king of Kent (*c*.685–687). Joint ruler with the East Saxon, Suabhard, under the over-lordship of the South Saxons.

Eadwig *see* **Edwy**.

Eanfrith (d.634) king of Bernicia (633–634). The son of Ethelfrith, he married a Pictish princess, and their son, Talorcen, became king of the Picts. He was killed by the Welsh king, Cadwallon.

Eanred (d.850) king of Northumbria (809–841). A son of Eardwulf, he did homage to Egbert of Wessex in 827.

Eardwulf (1) (d.762) king of Kent (747–762). The son of Eardbert, he was a joint ruler of the kingdom with Ethelbert II.

Eardwulf (2) king of Northumbria (796–809). He deposed Osbald and was succeeded by his son, Enred.

Edbald (d.640) king of Kent (616–640). On succeeding his father, Ethelbert, he promptly renounced Christianity, which had been introduced to the kingdom by St Augustine in his father's reign. He married his stepmother before taking a daughter of the Frankish king, Theudebert II of Austrasia, as his queen.

Edgar (1) (944–975) king of Mercia and Northumbria (957–975) and of England (959–975). The second son of Edmund I, he replaced Edwy as ruler of Northumbria and Mercia after nobles who were discontented with his brother transferred their allegiance. Edwy still held the lands south of the Thames, but these came into Edgar's kingdom following Edwy's early death. In 973 he was created 'emperor of Britain' at a ceremony in Bath conducted by the Archbishop of Canterbury. The same year he was supposedly rowed on the River Dee by six or eight kings as an act of subservience. These kings included Malcolm of Strathclyde, Kenneth II of Scots, Maccus of the Isle of Man, and up to five Welsh kings. It is probable that this was a conference to discuss borders in which the Scots recognized English control over Bernicia in Northumberland in return for Edgar's acknowledgement of their rule of the Lothians.

In contrast to his brother, he was known for his piety and reinstated Dunstan as archbishop of Canterbury as well as making him his chief adviser. Acting under Edgar's patronage, Dunstan led a revival of Benedictine monasticism and reformed the church. In order to secure the loyalty of his clerics forty, abbeys were founded in Edgar's reign and laws introduced that punished non-payers of taxes due to the Church. He also reformed the administration of the country, codified the laws of the land and clarified the boundaries between shires. He also struck a new coinage and licensed towns to mint the new silver pennies. He married twice to daughters of his ealdormen and kept a mistress. His legitimate sons were Edward (the Marytr), Edmund (the Aetheling) and Ethelred II (the Unready).

Edgar (2) (1074–1107) king of Scots (1097–1107). The fourth son of Malcolm III's second marriage, on his father's death he went to the English court where he was sheltered by William II. He returned to Scotland in 1096, and with the help of English troops he defeated his uncle, Donald Bane, at Roscobie in Fife in early 1097. He became king in October of the same year and afterwards was practically a dependant of William II and Henry I of England. Shortly after he took the throne, his kingdom was threatened by the king of Norway, Magnus Barelegs, who brought a considerable fleet into western waters and forced Edgar to cede 'all the isles around which a ship could sail', including Kintyre. Pursuing a pro-English policy, he settled the first English knight in Lothian and married his sister Matilda to Henry I in 1100. He died unmarried, and the kingdom passed to his brother, Alexander I. The 'king with the Saxon name' was buried in Dunfermline.

Edmund (St Edmund) (*c*.840–870) king of East Anglia (*c*.855–870). East Anglia's last Anglo-Saxon king, he was defeated and martyred by Danish invaders at Haegelisdum (Hellesdon in Norwich or Hoxne in Suffolk) in 870. Seeking to avert war he had tried to negotiate with the Danes but his stipulation that they convert to Christianity before making peace offended them. As a consequence, on his capture he was subjected to the 'blood eagle' rite and beheaded. He became protector of sailors and for a time was England's patron saint.

Edmund I (921–946) king of England (939–946). The eldest son of Edward the Elder and Edgifu, he succeeded his half-brother Ethelstan as king. Having commanded well at Brunanburgh, he reclaimed those parts of the kingdom lost after his brother's death to the Norse king, Olaf II. He also subdued Strathclyde, which he bestowed on Malcolm I, king of Scots, on the condition of him doing homage for it. This secured the Anglo-Scottish border. He was slain by Leofa, an exiled thief, while keeping the feast of St Augustine of Canterbury (26 May) at Pucklechurch and was buried at Glastonbury. He married twice and had two sons who became kings—Edgar and Edwy.

Edmund II Ironside (983–1016) king of England (1016). The eldest surviving son of Ethelred II and Elfled, this warrior prince was nicknamed 'Ironside' for his bravery against the Danes. He attempted to oppose Canute's invasion of Wessex in late 1015 but could not hold Northumbria when Canute moved against it early the following year. On his father's death, Edmund was chosen king by a council of Anglo-Saxon kings and ealdormen (the Witan) in London and proclaimed in early 1016. Canute, however, had already been elected king by a majority of Witan members gathered at Southampton. Edmund marched into Wessex and won three of the four battles there, relieving a besieged London, but support from the Mercian king Edric did not arrive, and his cause was lost. He was finally defeated at Assandun in Essex (1016) and forced to surrender the midland and northern counties to Canute after a meeting at Olney where the two rivals agreed to partition England. He died at London of natural causes (although later sources claim he was murdered) after a reign of only seven months and was buried at Glastonbury. His infant sons fled Canute's invasion and settled in Hungary.

Edred (923–955) king of England (946–955). The youngest son of Edward the Elder and Edgifu, he succeeded to the throne following the murder of his brother, Edmund I, in 946 as Edmund's two sons were too young to reign. Because of ill-health the government of the kingdom appears to have been carried out by his mother and his chief minister, Abbot Dunstan. Despite his poor health, Edred was able to quell a rebellion of the Northumbrian Danes under Erik Bloodaxe (948), but it was not until 954 that he was able to secure Northumbria again as part of his kingdom. This he achieved through a bloody invasion, which resulted in the death of the usurper king. Edred committed Northumbria to Oswulf as an earldom. He died while still in his early twenties and was buried at Winchester.

Edward I (Hammer of the Scots) (1239–1307) king of England (1272–1307) and Wales (1283–1307). He was the eldest surviving son of Henry III and Eleanor of Provence. The contests between his father and the barons called him early into active life. By 1265 Simon de Montfort had become leader of the opposition to Henry and had formed a parliament that represented not only the knights of the shires but the burgesses of the towns that supported him as well. Prince Edward restored the royal authority within months by defeating and killing de Montfort at the Battle of Evesham. He then proceeded to Palestine, where he showed great valour, although no conquest of any importance was achieved. He returned on his father's death after further campaigns in Italy and France with a reputation as an excellent soldier and was crowned amid much public rejoicing at Westminster Abbey in 1274. The new king was immediately popular among the people as he identified himself with the growing tide of nationalism that was sweeping the country. The other side to this popular nationalism was displayed later in his persecution and banishment of the Jews, which was the culmination of many years of anti-semitism in England. The spirit of nationalism also led to England looking to its borders. The mountainous land to the west had never been completely subdued, and following an uprising against English influence Edward began a war with Llewellyn, Prince of Wales, which ended in the annexation of that principality to the English crown in 1283. He secured the new principality by building nine castles along the border and created his eldest son, Edward, Prince of Wales in 1301.

From the earliest days of his reign Edward showed great vigour as well as a degree of severity in his administration, especially in his policy of limiting the encroachment of the barons and the Church. This was achieved by restricting baronial privileges and prohibiting gifts of land to the Church. His harsh treatment of those in power whom he found to be corrupt also gave him the support of the common people, and his reforms of the administration were brought about only with their backing. Under his guidance the great common law courts consisting of the King's Bench, Exchequer and Common pleas, took shape. He also called the Model Parliament, which, with nobles, churchmen and commoners, foreshadowed representative government.

Edward's great ambition, however, was to gain possession of Scotland, but the death of Margaret, the Maid of Norway, who was to have been married to Edward's son, for a time frustrated the king's designs. The contested succession soon gave him the opportunity to intervene, however, and he was invited by the Scots to choose between the thirteen competitors for the throne. His choice, John Balliol, was induced to do homage for his crown to Edward at Newcastle but was forced by the indignation of the Scottish people to throw off Edward's overlordship. An alliance between the French and the Scots followed, and Edward, then at war with the French king over possession of Gascony, marched his army north. He entered Scotland in 1296, devastated it with fire and sword, which earned him the sobriquet 'Hammer of the Scots', and removed the symbolic Stone of Destiny from Scone.

Edward assumed the administation of the country, but the following summer a new rising took place under William Wallace, the son of a knight. His successes, notably at Stirling Bridge, recalled Edward to Scotland with an army of 100,000 men. He defeated Wallace's army at Falkirk, and the supporters of Scottish independence went into hiding, but their leader was at length betrayed and executed in London as a traitor. The unjust and barbaric execution of Wallace made him a national hero in his homeland, and resistance to England became paramount among the people. All Edward's efforts to reduce the country to obedience were unavailing, and with the crowning of Robert Bruce, Earl of Carrick, as Robert I of Scotland, the banner of independence was again unfurled. In 1306 an enraged Edward assembled another army and marched against Bruce but only reached Burgh-on-Sands, a village near Carlisle, where he died.

He was married twice—to Eleanor of Castile, by whom he had sixteen children, and Margaret of France, by whom he had three. Twelve memorials to his first wife stand between Nottingham and London to mark the journey taken by her funeral cortege. He was buried at Westminster Abbey.

Significant events of Edward I's reign

- 1277 Edward mounts an invasion of Wales.
- 1282 Llywelyn, last independent Prince of Wales, is killed at Builth.
- 1284 Statute of Rhuddlan brings Wales under English rule.
- 1285 The first Justices of the Peace installed.
- 1290 England banishes the Jews.
  Margaret, Maid of Norway, dies before reaching Scotland.
- 1292 John Balliol is chosen by Edward to become Scotland's king.
- 1295 The Model Parliament is assembled. Edward mounts an invasion of France.
- 1296 The Scots are vanquished by Edward's invading army and Balliol is deposed.
- 1297 William Wallace gains victory over Edward at Stirling Bridge.
- 1298 Wallace defeated at Battle of Falkirk.
- 1301 Edward makes his son, Edward, the Prince of Wales.
- 1305 Wallace is executed in London.
- 1306 Robert Bruce becomes king of Scots.

Edward II (1284–1327) king of England and Wales (1307–27). The only surviving son of Edward I and Eleanor of Castile, he was born at Caernarvon Castle and became the first English prince of Wales. He succeeded his father in 1307 and was crowned at Westminster Abbey the same year. He was of a mild disposition but indolent and fond of pleasure. With little contact with his father and surrounded by sisters, he became very reliant on his friends and fiercely loyal to them, regardless of court or public opinion. As king, this weakness for his personal favourites, Piers Gaveston and, later, the two Hugh Despensers, father and son, infuriated the powerful nobles. By the Ordinances of 1311 the barons forced Edward to banish Gaveston and executed him as a public enemy when he disobeyed and returned for the second time.

Two years after this Edward assembled an immense army to check the progress of Robert I (Robert the Bruce) in Scotland, who had been threatening an invasion of England. With superior tactical awareness, Bruce routed the assembled feudal forces of Edward at Bannockburn, near Stirling Castle. Barely escaping the field with his life, it soon became apparent to Edward that his father's plans for a united kingdom stood little chance of success.

Over the next few years his problems extended from France, where his duchy of Aquataine was overrun by French soldiers, to Ireland, where Bruce had devastated the countryside and threatened the prosperity of the English of the Pale. By 1320 the king also had new favourites, the two Hugh

Edward III

Despensers. Their influence over the king provoked a rebellion by the barons, led by the powerful earl of Lancaster, which was defeated at Boroughbridge in Yorkshire. Finally, in 1326, the exiled baron Roger Mortimer invaded England with his mistress, Edward's estranged wife, Isabella, to seize power. Their army was completely successful, and Edward was deposed. The Despensers, father and son, were captured and executed. Edward was imprisoned in Kenilworth, and then Berkeley Castle in Gloucestershire, and eventually murdered on the orders of Isabella and Mortimer. His death was particularly gruesome as the order for his execution stipulated that no external marks should be left that would betray violence. The only way to do this was by disembowelment with a red hot iron inserted into the rectum, a conventional form of death for homosexuals at the time.

He had four children by Isabella, and his son, Edward, became king after him. He was buried at Gloucester Cathedral.

Significant events of Edward II's reign

- 1308 Piers Gaveston is exiled for the first time.
- 1312 Gaveston is put to death.
- 1314 Edward is defeated by Robert the Bruce at Bannockburn.
- 1320 Hugh Despenser and his son receive the favour of the king.
- 1322 Barons' revolt is defeated at Boroughbridge.
- 1327 Isabella and Mortimer depose the king. The Despensers are executed.

Edward III (1312–77) king of England and Wales (1327–77). The eldest son of Edward II and Isabella of France, he was born at Windsor Castle and succeeded to the throne at the age of fourteen. During his minority, a council was elected to govern, but his mother's lover, Roger Mortimer, held the principal power in the state. The pride and oppression of Mortimer led to a general confederacy against him, and to his seizure and execution in 1330. Isabella received a yearly pension and quietly retired from public life.

After many years of domestic squabbles, Edward was finally in a position to improve England's international standing. First he turned his attention to Scotland. His claimant for the Scottish throne, Edward Balliol, the son of John Balliol, defeated David II's army and seized the throne, forcing the Scots king into exile. A Scots army then took Balliol by surprise at Annan in Dumfriesshire and expelled him over the border. Edward, having levied a well-appointed army, invaded Scotland and defeated David II's regent, Donald, at Halidon Hill. This victory produced the restoration of Edward Balliol, who was, however, again expelled.

The ambition of the English king was diverted from Scotland by the prospect of succeeding to the throne of France. To this end Edward initiated the Hundred Years' War in 1337, which was to last intermittently until 1453. Collecting an army and accompanied by his son, the Black Prince, he crossed over to France. There he devastated the northern and eastern territories and declared himself king of France. Memorable victories followed in the Battle of Sluys, in the Battle of Crécy and at the Siege of Calais. In the meantime David II, having recovered the throne of Scotland in 1346, invaded England with a large army. The campaign was a disaster, however, and he was defeated and taken prisoner at Neville's Cross, near Durham, by a much inferior force.

In 1348 a truce was concluded with France, but on the death of King Philip, in 1350, Edward again invaded France, plundering and devastating. Recalled home by a Scottish inroad, he retaliated by carrying fire and sword from Berwick to Edinburgh. In the meantime the Black Prince had penetrated from Guienne to the heart of France, fought the famous Battle of Poitiers, and taken King John II prisoner. A truce was then made, the Treaty of Brétigny, which gave Edward possession of Calais, Guienne, Gascony and Poitou in return for giving up his claim to the throne. When King John died, however, and Charles V became king of France, the two countries resumed hostilities. Edward again crossed over to France and laid waste the provinces of Picardy and Champagne, but at length consented to a peace. This confirmed him in the possession of several provinces and districts of France, which were entrusted to the Prince of Wales (the Black Prince), but gradually all the English possessions in France, with the exception of Bordeaux, Bayonne, and Calais, were lost.

The Black Prince died in 1376 and Edward, suffering in his later years from senile dementia, died the following year. He had thirteen children by Philippa of Hainault.

Significant events of Edward III's reign

- 1330 Mortimer is put to death.
- 1332 Parliament is divided into the two Houses of Lords and Commons for the first time.
- 1333 David II defeated at Halidon Hill.
- 1337 The Hundred Years' War begins.
- 1340 French navy is defeated at Battle of Sluys.
- 1346 David II is captured at Neville's Cross.
- 1346 The French are routed at the Battle of Crécy.
- 1347 Calais is taken by England.
- 1349 The Black Death reaches England.

- 1356 The French are defeated at Poitiers.
- 1357 David II is released from captivity.
- 1362 English replaces French as the official language of government and the courts.
- 1366 Statute of Kilkenny imposes English law in Ireland.
- 1376 The Black Prince dies.

Edward IV (1442–83) king of England and Wales (1461–83). The son of Richard Plantagenet, Duke of York, and grandson of Edmund, Earl of Cambridge and Duke of York, fourth son of Edward III, he became the first Yorkist king after ousting Henry VI in the dynastic civil wars later called the Wars of the Roses. The rival line of Lancaster descended from John of Gaunt, the third son of Edward III. The York line had intermarried with the female descendants of Lionel, the second son, which gave it the preferable right to the crown. Before reaching his twenties, Edward led an army against the Lancastrian supporters of Henry VI and defeated them at the Battle of Mortimer's Cross. This avenged the death of his father, 'the Protector', Richard, Duke of York, a claimant to the throne. He was then proclaimed king by his cousin Warwick 'the Kingmaker' and drove Henry north. Edward owed Warwick his crown, however, and hostility soon began to develop between them. Edward had allowed Warwick to govern the kingdom, but Edward's marriage to Elizabeth Woodville, the widow of a commoner and daughter of Sir Richard Neville, caused a rift as Warwick felt his position to be threatened. Warwick rebelled against his king, defeated him at Edgecote and left England after a brief period of reconciliation. On his return he allied with the wife of Henry VI, Margaret, to restore the deposed king. Their army caused Edward to flee the realm, but he returned the following year to defeat and kill Warwick at the Battle of Barnet. Margaret was also soon defeated at the Battle of Tewkesbury, and her son, Edward, was captured and killed. Henry VI was held in the Tower of London where he was later murdered on Edward's orders.

Once he was restored, Edward secured his throne from any further Lancastrian attack by quashing rebellions in the north and began to prove himself as an able ruler in his own right. He set about improving the royal finances, which had suffered greatly under Henry VI (he was the first monarch to be solvent at his death for over three hundred years), and establishing good trading relationships abroad. He endeavoured to keep his country out of foreign entanglements and after a short campaign in France withdrew with payments. Recognizing the value of wool and cloth, he worked hard to improve trade with German cities, and England enjoyed a period of much greater prosperity in the second half of his reign than it had in the first. Law enforcement was similarly improved, and he won the respect of his commoners by establishing the Court of Requests, which heard complaints against greedy landlords.

The dynastic disputes were not completely forgotten, however, and as the Lancastrians were no longer a threat, York turned against York. Edward's two younger brothers, the dukes of Gloucester and Clarence, both had their eyes set on the throne, and Clarence, who had at one time allied himself with the Lancastrians, was accused of treason. He was sent to the Tower, where he was later found murdered. After Edward's death, Gloucester claimed the throne and had himself crowned as Richard III.

Edward had ten children by Elizabeth Wood-ville and was succeeded by Edward V, who, along with his brother Richard, was declared to be illegitimate and deprived of the throne.

Significant events of Edward IV's reign

- 1461 Edward defeats the Lancastrians at Mortimer's Cross.
- 1464 Edward is married to Elizabeth Wood-ville.
- 1469 Warwick deposes Edward.
- 1470 Henry VI regains the crown.
- 1471 Edward restored.
- 1476 William Caxton brings the printing trade to England.
- 1471 Duke of Clarence murdered in the Tower.

Edward V (1470–1483) king of England and Wales. (1483). The eldest son of Edward IV and Elizabeth Woodville, he became Prince of Wales in 1471 and was in his thirteenth year when he succeeded his father. Within weeks of becoming king, he fell victim to an uncle's ambitions. Richard of Gloucester had been appointed by his dying brother, Edward IV, as Protector of the kingdom during his heir's minority. He had resented the king's marriage to Elizabeth Woodville, however, and sought to become king himself. The young prince had been brought up with his brother, Richard, under the power of the Woodville family at Ludlow Castle on the Welsh border. Suspecting that the Woodvilles would remove him from his office as Protector, Gloucester ordered that the senior members be arrested; Edward's grandfather, Earl Rivers, and an uncle were killed and his mother forced to seek shelter in Westminster Abbey. Gloucester then placed Edward and his younger brother in the Tower of London, which at that time was a royal residence as well as a prison.

Before the coronation could take place Gloucester declared that the two princes were illegitimate. He had been informed by the bishop of Bath and Wells that when Edward IV had married their mother he had been betrothed to Lady Eleanor Butler. A betrothal constituted the same commitment as marriage, and consequently Edward IV's marriage was declared void and his sons illegitimate. Parliament had little choice but to agree, and soon after Edward should have been crowned, Gloucester was proclaimed king and took the title Richard III.

Edward and Richard vanished, and although no evidence has ever been found, they were undoubtedly murdered in the Tower. Two skeletons were found in 1674 and given a full forensic examination in 1933, but their identity has never been properly established. They were most probably killed by Richard's close associate, Henry Stafford, Duke of Buckingham, or by Henry Tudor, 2nd earl of Richmond.

Edward VI (1537–53) king of England and Ireland (1547–53). The only son of Henry VIII by Jane Seymour, he was born at Hampton Court Palace and on his father's death was only nine years of age. He was too young to shape government and during his minority this was done by two Protectors—firstly Edward Seymour, Duke of Somerset, and then John Dudley, Duke of Northumberland. He grew up with a rooted zeal for the doctrines of the Reformation and made the Catholic mass illegal by the Act of Uniformity in 1549. He also ordered that icons and statues of saints be removed and destroyed and that church walls be whitewashed to cover up paintings. Objections to his reforms led to widespread disquiet and in Devon and Cornwall to a revolt that was put down with severity. His reign also produced the first *Book of Common Prayer*, written by Thomas Cranmer, Archbishop of Canterbury, and the later named Thirty-Nine Articles of Religion.

His reign was, on the whole, tumultuous and unsettled. In an attempt to secure Scotland, an English army invaded and defeated the Scots at the Battle of Pinkie. Despite this victory, the 'Rough Wooing', as the attempt to marry Mary, Queen of Scots, was later called, failed. In 1551 the Protector Somerset, who had hitherto governed the kingdom with energy and ability, was deposed by the intrigues of Dudley, Duke of Northumberland, who became all-powerful. Somerset was executed two years later. At the end of 1552 Edward contracted tuberculosis, of which he would die the following year. Dudley induced the dying Edward to set aside the succession of his sisters, Mary and Elizabeth, and settle the crown upon Lady Jane Grey, to whom he had married his son, Lord Guildford Dudley. The king died, aged fifteen, at Greenwich Palace in 1553, and Lady Jane was proclaimed queen, although her reign was to be very brief.

Significant events of Edward VI's reign

- 1547 Duke of Somerset is appointed Protector of England.
  Scots defeated at the Battle of Pinkie.
- 1549 First Act of Uniformity passed.
- 1550 John Dudley deposes Duke of Somerset and becomes Protector.
- 1553 Lady Jane Grey named as successor to the throne.

Edward VII (1841–1910) king of the United Kingdom of Great Britain and Ireland and British dominions overseas; emperor of India (1901–10). The eldest son of Queen Victoria and Prince Albert of Saxe-Coburg-Gotha, he was born at Buckingham Palace and created Prince of Wales in 1841. He was educated under private tutors and at Edinburgh, Oxford and Cambridge. He visited Canada and the United States in 1860 and underwent military training at the Curragh camp in 1861. Promoted to the rank of general in 1862, he visited Palestine and the East, and the next year took his seat in the House of Lords. In 1863 he was married in St George's Chapel, Windsor Castle, to Princess Alexandra, eldest daughter of Christian IX of Denmark, and from this time onwards he discharged many public ceremonial functions. Many of these duties he undertook in the place of Victoria, who felt she could not trust him with domestic political affairs. This strained relationship meant that he was not given access to any state papers, cabinet reports or diplomatic correspondence. Excluded from his mother's circle of advisers, he became more frequently seen at society events, and, although he appeared to remain happily married, it was known that he had had many affairs with actresses and society beauties (he had thirteen known mistresses). As well as a socialite, he was a keen sportsman and enjoyed gambling, shooting and yachting. He also took a keen interest in horse-racing (he owned one Grand National and three Derby winners), motor cars (all his cars displayed the royal coat of arms on the sides), and the theatre, which benefited greatly from his patronage. He also had a strong attachment to France, which, while he was Prince of Wales, annoyed his mother, who preferred Prussia. By the end of Victoria's reign the diplomatic relationship with France was strained by territorial disputes. Soon after becoming king, however, Edward met the French president, Emile Loubert, in an effort to improve relations. This friendly meeting laid the foundation of the *Entente Cordiale* of the following year, which settled many of the old disputes.

Edward succeeded to the throne on the death of Victoria in 1901 and was crowned the following year at the age of fifty-nine. A well-loved king, he did much to popularize the monarchy in his nine-year reign. His love of foreign travel and public ceremonial established a more ambassadorial style of monarchy, which came to replace the traditional political role of the head of state. His death from bronchitis in 1910 was felt keenly by all strata of society.

Significant events of Edward VII's reign

- 1901 Australia is granted dominion status.
- 1902 Order of Merit is created by Edward.
- 1903 The first flight is made by Wilbur and Orville Wright.
  The Women's Social and Political Union is formed by Emmeline Pankhurst.
- 1904 *Entente Cordial* is reached between Britain and France.
- 1907 *Entente Cordial* reached between Russia and Britain.
- 1908 The 4th Olympic Games are held in London.
  Triple Entente is reached between Britain, France and Russia.
- 1909 Old age pensions introduced.
  Parliament Bill introduced to curb the power of the House of Lords.

Edward VIII (1894–1972) king of Great Britain and Ireland and British Dominions overseas; emperor of India (1936). The son of George, Duke of York (later George V) and Princess Mary of Teck, he was educated in England and France and joined the army on the outbreak of the First World War. When it was over he made several extended tours of Europe. He was popular with the public because of his great charm and concern for the plight of the unemployed during the recession. Ceremonial duties bored him, however, and he was notoriously bad at keeping appointments. His private life met with the disapproval of his father, whom hw succeeded in January 1936. Before his coronation he made it clear he intended to marry Mrs Wallis Simpson, an American who in 1935 was embarking on her second divorce. The marriage was opposed by the archbishop of Canterbury and the prime minister, Stanley Baldwin, who held a similar opinion of Edward's private life to Edward's father. Rather than force a constitutional crisis, Edward decided to abdicate after reigning for 325 days. He was never crowned. Edward and Mrs Simpson were created Duke and Duchess of Windsor when they married at Chateau Conde, near Tours, in 1937 and, apart from the years of the Second World War, when he served as governor of the Bahamas, they lived in France. He remained on good terms with his royal relatives, but Mrs Simpson was never accepted. The duke died in 1972; the duchess in 1986. They had no children.

Edward the Confessor (St Edward) (*c*.1003–1066) king of England (1042–66). The eldest son of Ethelred II and Emma of Normandy, he was born at Islip, in Oxfordshire, and lived in exile in Normandy from 1013 to 1042 while the Danes ruled England. On the death of his maternal brother, Hardicanute the Dane, he was called to the throne and thus renewed the Saxon line.

He restored the Norman influence in England as, not unnaturally, he had returned more French than English, and brought with him his Norman clergy and supporters. He moved the royal residence from the walled city of London to the palace of Westminster, and this, more than anything else, ensured the return of a Dane to the throne after his death. London had been the wealthiest city in the land and became the centre for discontent with his rule among the powerful anti-Norman party. The real power devolved to his father-in-law, Godwin, Earl of Wessex, and Edward was forced to remove him from government and place his own Norman supporters in high office. After a dispute in Dover, Godwin left for France in 1051 and returned a year later to take London by force. After a period of confrontation Godwin was reconciled with the king, but died shortly afterwards, leaving his son, Harold, to became Earl of Wessex. Harold returned from exile in Ireland and had little difficulty in assuming his father's position of influence. During Godwin's time in exile, however, Edward had appealed for Norman help to reassert his authority and had promised the throne of England to William, Duke of Normandy (*see* William (I) the Conqueror) in return. There was little support for such a succession in England, and on Edward's death in 1066 Harold took the throne, claiming that his succession had been accepted by the dying king some time beforehand. This was contested by William, who asserted that Edward had confirmed his earlier promise some two years before his death. The succession dispute led directly to the Norman conquest of England.

Edward was a weak and superstitious but well-intentioned king, who, despite his Norman upbringing, acquired the respect of his subjects by his monkish sanctity and care in the administration of justice. His legacy was the abbey at Westminster, and he was canonized by Pope Alexander III in 1161.

Edward the Elder (870–924) king of Wessex (899–924). The son of Alfred the Great, he inherited Wessex from his father and defeated a Danish-backed claimant for the throne. His reign was distinguished by a series of successes over the Danes as he took control of the Danish-held Five Boroughs (Nottingham, Derby, Lincoln, Leicester and Stamford).

He fortified many inland towns (including Manchester in 919) and acquired dominion over Mercia, which had been allied to his father's kingdom. With Mercian support he extended his authority to run from the English Channel to the Humber. In the north he subdued the Strathclyde king, Dyfnwal, and several Welsh tribes, who later sought his protection from the Norse. Among his many sons and daughters by three wives were Elfward, Ethelstan, Edmund I and Edred, who all became kings. He was buried at Winchester New Minster.

Edward the Martyr (St Edward) (*c*.963–978) king of England (975–978). The only son of Edgar and his first wife, Ethelfled, he succeeded his father at the age of twelve. His succession was disputed by supporters of Edgar's second son by his second wife, Ethelred, and he began his reign amid a power struggle. The opportunity was taken by some members of the royal court to regain the power lost when Edgar increased the land-holding and authority of the Church. Attacks on monasteries and Church property by secular landowners became more frequent, especially in the north of the country, where it was compounded by opposition to southern rule. Edward was guided by the powerful Archbishop Dunstan but seemed powerless to stop the seizures of monastic estates and other church lands.

He was assassinated after only three years on the throne by a servant of his stepmother at her home, Corfe Castle in Dorset. Travelling alone to the castle, he was seized from behind while waiting at the gates and stabbed. It is generally held that his stepmother ordered the assassination in order to make Ethelred king. Pity caused by his innocence and misfortune induced people to regard him as a martyr, and miracles supposed to occur at his tomb later led him to be venerated as a saint

Edwin (d.633) king of Northumbria (617–633). The heir to the kingdom of Bernicia, he formed an alliance with King Redwald of East Anglia on his return from exile and defeated his rival, King Ethelfrith, in battle on the River Idle. He became *Bretwalda*, overlord of all Anglo-Saxon kings. He married Ethelburga, daughter of Ethelfrith, in 625 and embraced Christianity, being baptised at York in 627. He was finally defeated in 633 at Hatfield Chase by an alliance of Welsh and Mercians, under Penda. The city of Edinburgh derives its name from being Edwin's northern outpost.

Edwy *or* **Eadwig** (940–959) king of England (955–959). The eldest son of Edmund I and Elfgifu, he succeeded his uncle Edred to the throne in at the age of fifteen. He promptly earned himself a reputation as a corrupt and incompetent ruler by leaving the coronation feast with two women. It is said that he was dragged from his bedchamber by Dunstan, Abbot of Glastonbury, and forced to return to the table. Edwy later exiled him for his pains. His unpopularity led the Northumbrians and Mercians to renounce their allegiance to Edwy in favour of his brother, Edgar, in 557. From then on he ruled only over the area south of the Thames.

Egbert III (775–839) king of Wessex (802–839). His early years were spent in exile at the court of Charlemagne. As king of Wessex he defeated Beornwulf of Mercia and was recognized by Northumbria in 829 as *Bretwalda*, or overall ruler, of all Anglo-Saxon kings in England, except in Kent. He made Wessex the leading kingdom in the land and laid the basis for future unification. Under King Wiglaf, however, Mercia re-established independence in 830, and thereafter Egbert was effective ruler of Wessex only and its dependent kingdoms of Surrey, Sussex, Kent and Essex.

Egbert I (d.873) king of Bernicia (867–873). He was installed as ruler of this kingdom in Northumbria by the Vikings.

Egbert II (d.878) king of Bernicia (876–878). He was the last of the Viking-installed rulers.

Egbert I king of Kent (664–673). He extended his kingdom to include Surrey.

Egbert II king of Kent (765–780). He failed to win independence from the Mercian overlords at the Battle of Otford in 766.

Egfrith (1) (d.685) king of Northumbria (670–685). The son of Oswy and Eanfled of Deira, on succeeding to the throne he consolidated his kingdom by driving the Mercians back across the Humber. In the north his expansionist policies were strongly resisted by the Picts, and in 685 his army was destroyed at Nechtansmere, near Forfar in Angus. He was killed in the battle.

Egfrith (2) (d.796) king of Mercia (787–796). Son of the powerful Offa, he survived his father only by 141 days, having ruled jointly with him since 787.

Egric (d.637) king of East Anglia (634–637). A kinsman who took the throne when Sigebert entered a monastry. He was killed fighting Penda during a Mercian invasion.

Elfward (d.924) king of Wessex (924). An illegitimate son of Edward the Elder, his reign lasted only a few months. His half-brother Ethelstan succeeded him.

Elfwold (d.788) king of Northumbria (779–788). The grandson of King Edbert, he deposed Ethelred to take the throne. He was murdered by a supporter of the rival dynasty and buried in Hexham church.

Elhred *see* **Alchred**.

Elizabeth I (1533–1603) queen of England and Ireland

(1558–1603). The only child of Henry VIII and Anne Boleyn, she was born at Greenwich Palace and almost immediately declared heiress to the crown. After her mother had been beheaded (1536), both she and her half-sister, Mary, were declared illegitimate, and she was finally placed after her half-brother, Edward, and Mary in the order of succession. On the accession of Edward VI, Elizabeth was committed to the care of the queen-dowager, Catherine Parr. After the death of Catherine and the execution of her consort, Thomas Seymour, Elizabeth was closely watched at Hatfield, where she received a classical education under William Grindal and Roger Ascham.

At the death of Edward, Elizabeth vigorously supported the title of Mary against the pretensions of Lady Jane Grey, but throughout her sister's whole reign she was an object of suspicion and surveillance. In self-defence, she made every demonstration of zealous adherence to the Roman Catholic faith, but her inclinations were well known. When Mary died, Elizabeth was immediately recognized as queen by parliament. The accuracy of her judgment showed itself in her choice of advisers—Matthew Parker, a moderate divine (archbishop of Canterbury 1559), aiding her in ecclesiastical policy, while William Cecil assisted her in foreign affairs. The first great object of her reign was the settlement of religion, to effect which a parliament was called on 25 January and dissolved on 8 May, its object having been accomplished. The nation was prepared for a return to the reformed faith, and parliament was at the bidding of the court. The ecclesiastical system devised in her father's reign was re-established, the royal supremacy asserted, and the revised Prayer Book enforced by the Act of Uniformity. While, however, the formal establishment of the reformed religion was easily completed, the security and defence of the settlement was the main object of the policy and the chief source of all the struggles and contentions of her reign. Freed from the tyranny of Mary's reign, the Puritans began to claim predominance for their own dogmas, while the supporters of the established church were unwilling to grant them even liberty of worship. The Puritans, therefore, like the Catholics, became irreconcilable enemies of the existing order, and increasingly stringent measures were adopted against them. But the struggle against the Catholics was the more severe, chiefly because they were supported by foreign powers, so that while their religion was wholly prohibited, even exile was forbidden them, in order to prevent their intrigues abroad. Many Catholics, particularly priests, suffered death during her reign; but simple nonconformity, from whatever cause, was pursued with the severest penalties, and many more clergymen were driven out of the Church, by differences about the position of altars, the wearing of caps, and such like matters, than were forced to resign by the change from Rome to Reformation.

Elizabeth's first parliament approached her on a subject that, next to religion, was the chief trouble of her reign, the succession to the crown. They requested her to marry, but she declared her intention to live and die a virgin, and she consistently declined in the course of her life such suitors as the Duc d'Alençon, Prince Erik of Sweden, the Archduke Charles of Austria, and Philip of Spain. While, however, she felt that she could best maintain her power by remaining unmarried, she knew how to temporize with suitors for political ends and showed the greatest jealousy of all pretenders to the English succession.

With the unfortunate Mary, Queen of Scots were connected many of the political events of Elizabeth's reign. On her accession the country was at war with France. Peace was easily concluded (1559), but the assumption by Francis and Mary of the royal arms and titles of England led to an immediate interference on the part of Elizabeth in the affairs of Scotland. She entered into a league with the Lords of the Congregation, the leaders of the reformed party, and throughout her reign this party was frequently of use to her in furthering her policy. She also gave early support to the Huguenot party in France and to the Protestants in the Netherlands, so that throughout Europe she was looked on as the head of the Protestant party. This policy roused the implacable resentment of Philip of Spain, who strove in turn to excite the Catholics against her both in her own country and in Scotland. The detention of Mary in England (1568–87), where she fled to the protection of Elizabeth, led to a series of conspiracies, beginning with that under the earls of Northumberland and Westmore-land and ending with the Babington plot, which finally forced the reluctant Elizabeth to order her execution. Mary's death (1587), although it has stained Elizabeth's name, tended to confirm her power among her contemporaries. The state of France, following the accession of Henri IV, who was helped by Elizabeth, removed any danger from the indignation that the execution had caused in that country; and the awe in which King James VI of Scotland stood of Elizabeth and his fear of interfering with his own right of succession to England made him powerless.

Philip of Spain was not so easily appeased, Mary's execution giving an edge to his other grievances. Elizabeth's fleets had galled him in the West Indies and her arms and subsidies had helped to deprive him of the Netherlands. Soon his Armada was prepared, ready to sail for England. Accordingly he called the queen of England a murderess and refused to be satisfied even with the sacrifice she seemed prepared to make of her Dutch allies. The Armada sailed in 1588, but the great naval force was broken up by English fireships and sent in retreat up the east coast and round the rocky shoreline of northern Scotland. It is not known how many of the ships returned to Spain, but at least one-third of the crews, 11,000 men, were lost at sea. The war with Spain dragged on until the close of Elizabeth's long reign.

During her reign the splendour of her government at home and abroad was sustained by such men as Cecil, Bacon, Walshingham and Throg-morton, but she had personal favourites of less merit who were often more brilliantly rewarded. Chief of these were Dudley, whom she created earl of Leicester and whom she was disposed to marry, and Essex, whose violent passions brought about his ruin when he rebelled against the government. He was beheaded in 1601, but Elizabeth never forgave herself his death. She died two years later of blood poisoning from a tonsillar abscess, having named James VI of Scotland as her successor.

Significant events of Elizabeth I's reign

- 1558 Cecil appointed chief secretary of state.
- 1559 Matthew Parker appointed archbishop of Canterbury.
  Elizabeth becomes head of the English Church via the Act of Supremacy.
- 1560 Treaty of Berwick promises Scottish Protestants English aid against French.
  William Cecil appointed Chief Secretary of State.
- 1563 15,000 die in the Plague of London.
- 1568 Mary, Queen of Scots, is imprisoned by Elizabeth.
- 1580 Francis Drake returns to England having circumnavigated the world.
- 1586 Mary, Queen of Scots stands trial for treason
- 1587 Mary, Queen of Scots is executed.
- 1588 The Spanish Armada is destroyed.
- 1601 Earl of Essex is executed.

Elizabeth II (1926–) queen of the United Kingdom of Great Britain and Northern Ireland and other realms and territories; head of the Commonwealth and head of state for sixteen of its members (1952–). Elizabeth was born in London, the elder daughter of George VI (then Duke of York) and Lady Elizabeth Bowes-Lyon. She was privately educated and at the outbreak of the Second World War, under the threat of bombing, the princess and her sister Margaret were moved from London to Windsor Castle (Buckingham Palace was bombed on 12 September 1940). As a girl she had no expectations of becoming queen, but the abdication of Edward VIII meant her father reluctantly became George VI. In 1944, at the age of eighteen, she trained with the Auxiliary Transport Service, becoming a capable driver. She married in 1947 Philip Mountbatten (son of Prince Andrew of Greece and made Duke of Edinburgh on his marriage) and had four children; Charles, born 14 November 1948 (made Prince of Wales in 1969), Anne, born 15 August 1950 (made Princess Royal in 1987), Andrew, born 19 February 1960 (later to become Duke of York), and Edward, born 10 March 1964. Elizabeth acceded to the throne on the death of her father on 6 February 1952 (whilst on tour in Africa) aged twenty-five and was crowned at Westminster Abbey on 2 June 1953.

The queen's full title in the United Kingdom is: 'Elizabeth the Second, by the Grace of God, of the United Kingdom of Great Britain and Northern Ireland and of Her other Realms and Territories Queen, Head of the Commonwealth, Defender of the Faith'. Her right to this title derives from the common-law rules of heredity and from legislation such as the Act of Settlement made in 1700, which states that only Protestant descendants of Electress Sophia of Hanover, granddaughter of James I, may succeed to the throne. The succession can be changed only if all the members of the Commonwealth that recognize the queen as sovereign consent to the change. Only if this happens can someone other than the eldest son of the sovereign succeed to the throne.

As head of state of one of the last remaining constitutional monarchies, Elizabeth's duties include the opening of parliament and, as commander of the British armed forces, the inspection of the Trooping of the Colour. She also has the authority to pardon criminals, appoint government ministers and judges, and, as head of the Church of England, it is she who appoints bishops. All these decisions are made, however, only with the advice of her government. In her long reign she has seen several prime ministers come and go, and all cabinet papers pass before her, as does all important diplomatic correspondence. She also sees the prime minister once a week and gives advice on government affairs that is rarely ignored.

A hard-working ambassador for the United Kingdom, the queen has made state visits worldwide, a feature of these being her informal 'walkabouts', which enable her to have direct contact with the public. During her reign she has done much to bring the monarchy closer to the people, but as a result she and her family have been subjected to almost constant invasions of privacy by the world's media. The strain of being the most photographed family in the world has taken its toll on the relationships and marriages of the younger Windsors.

Significant events of the reign

- 1955 Churchill resigns as prime minister and Anthony Eden takes his place.
  Nationalization of the Suez Canal.
- 1957 Macmillan becomes Prime Minister.
- 1960 Nigeria and Cyprus gain independence.
- 1963 Macmillan government collapses.
- 1964 Harold Wilson becomes prime minister.
  Launch of the Cunard liner *Queen Elizabeth II*.
- 1969 Charles invested as Prince of Wales.
  British troops deployed in Ulster to control sectarian disturbances.
- 1970 Edward Heath becomes prime minister
- 1973 Britain joins the European Economic Community.
- 1974 Harold Wilson returns as prime minister.
- 1976 Harold Wilson resigns as prime minister and James Callaghan takes his place.
- 1979 Margaret Thatcher becomes first British woman prime minister.
- 1980 Rhodesia gains independence as Zimbabwe.
- 1981 Prince Charles marries Lady Diana Spencer.
- 1982 Britain goes to war with Argentina over control of the Falkland Islands.
- 1990 Rioters in London protest against the Community Charge (Poll Tax).
  Margaret Thatcher resigns as prime minister and John Major takes her place.
- 1991 Gulf War threatens Middle East relations.
- 1992 Windsor Castle damaged by fire.
  Charles and Diana announce separation
- 1993 The queen agrees to pay tax on private income.
- 1994 The queen visits Russia.
- 1995 The queen visits South Africa.
- 1996 Charles and Diana divorce.

Enfrith (d.633) king of Bernicia (633). The eldest son of Ethelfrith, he married a Pictish princess but was killed after reigning for less than a year by the Welsh king, Cadwallon, at a battle near Doncaster.

Enred (d.*c*.841) king of Northumbria (809–*c*.841). A son of Eardwulf, he succeeded his father in 809 and in 829 made a formal submission to Egbert of Wessex. He maintained his kingdom without recorded incident for more than thirty years.

Eocha (d.889) king of Scots (878–889). The son of Run, king of Strathclyde, and grandson of Kenneth mac-Alpin, he ruled jointly with his cousin, Giric I, the son of Donald I, before being deposed.

Eochaid I (the Yellow-Haired) (d.*c*.629) king of Scots. The son and successor of Aiden.

Eochaid II (the Crook-Nose) (d.*c*.679) king of Scots.

Eochaid III (d.*c*.733) king of Scots. He was the last to rule in Irish Dalriada.

Eochaid IV (the Venomous) (d.*c*.737) king of Scots (733–737). He married a Pictish princess and his son, Alpin, was the father of Kenneth mac-Alpin who became the first king of the Dalriadan Scots and the Picts.

Eormenric (d.*c*.560) king of Kent (*c*.540–560). He was a son of Aesc.

Eorpwold (d.627) king of East Anglia (*c*.617–627). A son of Redwald, he was converted to Christianity by Edwin of Northumbria and murdered by a rival to the throne.

Eppilus (*fl*.1st century AD) king of the Atrebates tribe. One of the three sons of Commius who divided his kingdom and used the Roman title *Rex* meaning 'king'.

Erconbert (d.664) king of Kent (*c*.660–664). He married Sexburga, one of the four daughters of King Anna of East Anglia.

Eric (d.918) king of East Anglia (900–902). He succeeded his father, Guthrum, and was killed fighting Edward the Elder's army. He was the last Dane to rule the kingdom of East Anglia.

Erik Bloodaxe (d.954) king of York (947–954). After being deposed as king of Norway in 934 he fled to England and seized Northumbria from Edred in 947. He was killed along with his brother and a son in an ambush at Stainmore by Edred's army.

Ethelbald (1) (d.757) king of Mercia (716–757). By 731 Ethelbald had established himself as *Bret-walda*, or overlord, of all the kingdoms south of the Humber and styled himself *Rex Britanniae*, 'king of Britain'. He was nonetheless troubled by frequent Welsh raids and had the fortifications of Wat's Dyke built as a bulwark against aggression. He was murdered by his bodyguard in 757 and is buried at Repton, Derbyshire.

Ethelbald (2) (834–860) king of Wessex (858–860). He ascended the throne on the death of his father, Ethelwulf, but reigned for only two years. He married his stepmother, Judith. He is buried at Sherborne Abbey, Dorset.

Ethelbert I, Saint (d.616) king of Kent (560–616). Ruler of all England south of the Humber, he married Bertha, daughter of the Frankish king Charibert, *c*.589. He became the first baptised Anglo-Saxon king after receiving St Augustine's mission from

Rome in 597, which landed at Ebbsfleet, near Ramsgate. He made Canterbury the centre of Christianity in southern England and is buried there in the monastery of St Peter and St Paul. He was succeeded by Edbald, who temporarily renounced Christianity and married his stepmother.

Ethelbert II (d.762) king of Kent (725–762). The son of Wihtred and Cynegyth, he reigned jointly until 748 with his brother, Eadbert, and then with his half-brothers, Alric and Eardwulf.

Ethelbert (d.792) king of East Anglia (792). He was executed by his father-in-law, King Offa of Mercia, and is the patron saint of Hereford Cathedral.

Ethelbert (836–865) king of Wessex (857–865). The third son of Ethelwulf, he succeeded his elder brother Ethelstan in the eastern side of the kingdom in 857, and in 860, on the death of his brother, Ethelbald, became sole king. He was troubled by the inroads of the Danes, who sacked Kent and crushed Winchester during his reign. He is buried at Sherborne Abbey in Dorset.

Ethelfrith (d.617) king of Northumbria (604–617). The third of Ida's six sons, he reigned in Bernicia from 592 and seized Deira in 604. In his efforts to expand his realm he defeated King Aiden of the Dalradian Scots at Degastan, near Liddesdale, in 603. He also took Chester from the Welsh in 613. He married three times and had seven sons and three daughters.

Ethelheard (d.740) king of Wessex (726–*c*.740). He succeeded Ine as king in 726 although his connection to him is unknown. A land charter he made to Bishop Fortherne in 739 first mentions Devon.

Ethelhere (d.654) king of East Anglia (654). A younger brother of Anna, he reigned for only a few months before being killed in the Battle of Winwaed fighting the South Saxons with Penda of Mercia.

Ethelred king of Mercia (675–704). A brother of Wulfhere, he abdicated to become a monk.

Ethelred I (d.796) king of Northumbria (774–796). The son of Ethelwold (Moll), he deposed Alchred, who had deposed his father, in 774. He earned a reputation as a tyrant after having several of his nobles executed for treachery and was briefly deposed by Elfwold, the grandson of King Edbert. He returned to the throne in 790 after imprisoning Osred, nephew of Elfwold. Osred later escaped and Ethelred was murdered at Corbridge at Hadrian's Wall. Osbald, one of those who conspired against him, took the throne.

Ethelred II king of Northumbria (841–850). He was the son of Eanred.

Ethelred I (St Elthelred) (840–871) king of Wessex (865–871). The son of Ethelwulf, he succeeded his brother, Ethelbert, at a time when the Danes were threatening the conquest of the whole kingdom. He died in consequence of a wound received in action against the Danes at the Battle of Merton in 871 and was succeeded by his brother, Alfred. Ethelred's devout Christianity was recognized in his popular title of St Ethelred.

Ethelred (II) the Unready (*c*.968–1016) king of England (978–1016). The son of Edgar and Emma of Norway, he succeeded his brother, Edward the Martyr, and, because of his lack of vigour and capacity, earned the name of 'the Unready'. In his reign he began the practice of buying off the Danes by presents of money. After repeated payments of tribute (known as Danegeld), he effected, in 1002, a massacre of the Danes, but this led to Sweyn gathering a large force together and ravaging the country. The Danes were again bribed to depart, but following a new invasion, Sweyn obliged the nobles to swear allegiance to him as king of England. Ethelred fled to Normandy but returned after the death of Sweyn in 1004, when he was invited to resume the government. He died in London in the midst of a struggle with Canute, his Danish rival for the throne. He married twice, and among his children were Edmund II and Edward the Confessor. His second marriage, to the daughter of the second duke of Normandy, formed an Anglo-Norman connection that provided a basis for the Norman invasion of 1066.

Ethelric king of Bernicia (568–572). A son of the Saxon king Ida, Ethelric ruled Bernicia, which, with Deira, ruled by his brother Aelle, later formed the kingdom of Northumbria. Bernicia supplied most of the kings in the merged kingdom.

Ethelstan (895–939) king of Wessex and Mercia (924–939). The eldest son of Edward the Elder and Egwina, he was crowned at Kingston-on Thames and became the first Saxon king with effective control of all England (with the exception of Cumbria). He was an able ruler, and with the combined forces of Mercia and Wessex was victorious during his wars against the Danes of Northumbria, and the Scots and Irish by whom they were assisted, at Brunanburh, an unidentified site in Cumbria, in 937. In this battle a son of the king of Scots and five Irish kings were killed, shattering the Viking-Scots coalition. He also summoned a number of Welsh princes to Hereford and imposed a tribute on them, as well as fixing the border between his kingdom and that of the princes at Wye. He became, therefore, in name at least, the overlord of Celtic kingdoms in Cornwall, Scotland and Wales.

Ethelstan sought to ease the plight of his poorer subjects through some of the many laws he introduced, which punished theft and corruption. He established a corps of clerks that is thought to have foreshadowed the civil service, as well introducing a national coinage. He also strengthened relations with continental rulers through the marriages of four of his sisters to dukes in France and to the Holy Roman Emperor Otto I the Great. He is buried in Malmesbury Abbey in Wiltshire.

Ethelwalh king of Sussex (before 685). He received the Isle of Wight from Wulferhere of Mercia in 661 and in turn gave Wilfred the bishopric of Selsey.

Ethelweard king of Mercia (*c*.837–850).

Ethelwold (1) king of Mercia (654–663). He was the youngest brother of Anna.

Ethelwold (2) (Moll) king of Northumbria (759–765). He defeated his rival for the throne, Oswin, in 761 but was deposed by Elhred (who claimed to be a descendant of Ida, the founder of the Bernician dynasty) four years later.

Ethelwulf (800–858) king of Wessex (839–858). He succeeded his father, Egbert, and was chiefly occupied in repelling Danish incursions. He is best remembered for his donation to the clergy, which is often quoted as the origin of the system of tithes. Alfred the Great was the youngest of his five children.

Fergus Mor (d.501) king of Scots. He was the ruler of the kingdom of Dalriada in Argyll, which also included the Inner Hebrides and part of northern Ireland. He led a group of his people, the 'Scots', from Antrim in northern Ireland to settle in western Scotland around 500 and is credited with introducing the Gaelic language to Scotland, as well as the term 'Scot' from which the country was later to take its name. All kings of Dalriada for the following 343 years claimed descent from either Fergus or Loarn, his brother or half-brother.

G

Garnard (d.635) king of Picts (631–635). He was the son of Cinoich's sister.

Gartnait (d.663) king of Picts (657–663). He was the son of Talorcen's sister.

Gartnart (d.597) king of Picts (*c.*586–597). He was the son of Bridei I's sister,

George I (1660–1727) king of Great Britain and Ireland (1714–27), elector of Hanover (1698–1727). The son of the first elector of Hanover, Ernest Augustus, by Sophia, daughter of Frederick, Elector Palatine, and granddaughter of James I, he inherited the throne through his mother following the Act of Succession of 1701, which conferred the succession on her heirs.

In 1682 he was married to Sophia Dorothea of Zell, whom, in 1694, on account of suspected adultery with Count Königsmark, he caused to be imprisoned and kept in confinement for the rest of her life. In 1698 he succeeded his father as elector of Hanover (electors were princes of the Holy Roman Empire who elected the emperor). He commanded the imperial army in 1707 during the War of the Spanish Succession and ascended the throne of Great Britain on the death of Queen Anne in 1714. He arrived in Britain at the age of fifty-four, and, as he spoke only German, had a very limited knowledge of the kingdom. It was a difficult succession as there were many who wanted the Stuart dynasty to continue, and within a year he was faced with a Scottish-led Jacobite rebellion. The attempt to place the 'Old Pretender', James II's son, James Edward Stuart, on the throne was a failure, however, as a series of tactical errors led to the Jacobite army being defeated at the Battle of Sherrifmuir.

More than most monarchs, George needed good advisers and men he could trust in government. Sadly, the leading men of the day were mostly corrupt and sought to take advantage of a political system that was almost entirely devoid of integrity. The poor character of the nation at large was exposed by the disaster involving the South Sea Company. Thousands invested in this trading company, but in 1720 the South Sea Bubble, as it came to be known, burst. Most of the investors lost their money, and the government was engulfed in scandal. A radical change was required in the financial administration of the country, and it was only with the appointment of Sir Robert Walpole as First Lord of the Treasury that confidence was restored. For twenty-one years Walpole oversaw the restructuring of government and became, in effect, the first prime minister. The king came to depend on him and his Whig ministry, although, because he could not speak English, he could not preside over meetings of the cabinet.

The private character of George I was bad, but he showed much good sense and prudence in government, especially of his German dominions, and was an able military leader. Other than his patronage of Handel, he had little time for the arts and was widely disliked for his treatment of his wife and for his many mistresses. He died of a stroke while visiting his German possessions. By Sophia Dorothea he had a son, George, afterwards George II of England, and a daughter, Sophia, the mother of Frederick the Great.

Significant events of George I's reign

- 1715 Jacobites are defeated at Sherrifmuir.
- 1716 Septennial Act allows for general elections to be held every seven years.
- 1720 Collapse of the South Sea Company.
- 1721 Sir Robert Walpole becomes first prime minister.
- 1726 The first British circulating library opens in Edinburgh.
  Jonathan Swift's *Gulliver's Travels* is published.
- 1727 Sir Isaac Newton dies.

George II (1683–1760) king of Great Britain and Ireland (1727–60). The only son of George I and Sophia Dorothea of Celle. In 1708, then only electoral prince of Hanover, he distinguished himself at the Battle of Oudenarde, in the War of the Spanish Succession, under Marlborough. He succeeded his father to the English throne and inherited to the full his father's predilection for Hanover. For the first twelve years, however, he was well served by his prime minister, Robert Walpole, who kept England out of foreign entanglements, and their relationship can be said to have laid the foundations of constitutional monarchy.

After 1739 Britain was involved in almost continous warfare—first with Spain, then with France during the War of the Austrian Succession, and then again with France during the Seven Years'

War. The events in Europe led to the resignation of Walpole in 1742, for he was no war minister, and his place was taken for the next twenty years by Henry Pelham and his brother, the duke of Newcastle. With the British army engaged in Flanders, the Scottish Jacobites took the opportunity to attempt again the restoration of a Stuart to the thone. This time it was the 'Young Pretender', Charles Edward Stuart, the son of James Edward Stuart. He landed from France in the Highlands of Scotland and raised an army among the clan chiefs loyal to the Stuarts. The Jacobite army was at first successful, taking Edinburgh with little difficulty and routing an English army at Prestonpans, before advancing south. Support hoped for in the north of England never materialized, however, and following a long and tiring retreat, the Jacobites were crushed by the British army, now returned from Flanders, under the command of William, Duke of Cumberland, son of George II, at the Battle of Culloden. In the aftermath, 'Bonnie Prince Charlie' escaped to France, leaving his Highland supporters to face deportation or execution. Many clan chiefs lost their estates and possessions, and the Highlands of Scotland, which had for so long remained distant from royal authority, were at last brought under control.

There was further success for George in the victories of the Seven Years' War. The year 1759 saw France lose important territories in North America, and its stronghold, Quebec, was taken by General Wolfe. In India Clive defeated the French at Plassey and Madras, giving the East India Company control of the vast province of Bengal. By 1763 France had ceded all Canada to Britain and retained only two small trading posts in India. The last years of George's reign saw Britain well on its way to becoming a truly world power.

The reign was also notable for the number of great men in art, letters, war and diplomacy who then adorned Britain. George II had a keen interest in music and continued his father's patronage of Handel, but he was a king of very moderate abilities and ignorant of science or literature. He nevertheless won respect for his military abilities—at the Battle of Dettingen during the War of the Austrian Succession (1743) he became the last British king to lead his troops into battle. In matters of state he was guided by his wife, Caroline of Ansbach, who was far more cultured and intelligent than her husband. By Caroline he had three sons and four daughters, notably Frederick, Prince of Wales, Anne, William, Duke of Cumberland, Mary and Louisa.

Significant events of George II's reign

- 1732 A royal charter founds Georgia.
- 1738 The Methodist movement is founded by John and Charles Wesley.
- 1740 War of Austrian Sucession begins.
- 1742 Handel's *Messiah* first performed.
- 1743 George leads troops at Dettingen.
- 1745 Jacobites gain victory at Prestonpans.
- 1746 The Battle of Culloden crushes the Jacobite rising.
- 1753 The British Museum is founded.
- 1757 Robert Clive secures Bengal for Britain. William Pitt becomes Prime Minister.
- 1759 Quebec is taken by James Wolfe.

George III (1738–1820) king of Great Britain and Ireland (1760–1820). From 1801 he became king of the United Kingdom of Great Britain and Ireland, elector of Hanover (*de facto* until 1803). The eldest son of Frederick Louis, Prince of Wales, by the Princess Augusta of Saxe-Coburg-Gotha, he succeeded his grandfather, George II, in 1760. In the following year he married the Princess Charlotte Sophia of Mecklenburg-Strelitz. The sixty years of his reign are filled with great events, amongst which are the acceleration of the Industrial Revolution; the Wilkes controversy; the American Revolution, the result of which the king felt acutely; the French Revolution and the Napoleonic Wars that followed, comprising the long struggle that ended at Waterloo; and the Irish Rebellion of 1798.

He was the first Hanovarian monarch to be raised in England, and he took a great interest in government, although he was also thought by many to interfere too much. He had a succession of prime ministers, most of whom met with the king's disapproval. In 1770 he appointed Lord North, and they established a good working relationship that lasted until 1783. After the losses Britain suffered in the American War of Independence, however, North was held responsible, and George also had to shoulder some of the blame. William Pitt the Younger replaced North and guided Britain through the troubled times following the French Revolution. The victories of Waterloo and Trafalgar in the Napoleonic Wars restored some British pride, but the death of Nelson, Britain's greatest naval commander, was keenly felt, as were the social consequences of twenty-two years of continous war with France.

In Ireland a rebellion in 1798 was followed by Pitt's attempt to solve the Irish problem by passing an Act of Union, similar to that of Scotland one hundred years earlier, whereby Ireland returned members to the British parliament. But these members were Protestant, as Catholics, although they had the vote, could not sit in parliament. George denied Pitt's attempts to give them this right, and, after the bribing of the Irish Protestants, the assembly in Ireland dissolved itself and the country became governed by a Protestant parliament of the newly formed United Kingdom at Westminster.

By this time, however, George had lost the ability to rule because of a disease that had the appearance of a slowly worsening mental illness. It is now thought that he had a rare and incurable ailment called porphyria, in which the victim suffers delusions and displays symptoms of delirium. In the last nine years of his life the attacks became more frequent, and he died deaf, blind and in a state of permanent derangement.

George III was a man of conscientious principles and of a plain, sound understanding, although his narrow patriotism and his obstinate prejudices were often hurtful to British interests. His tastes and amusements were plain and practical, and he enjoyed touring the country. His special interest in agriculture earned him the nickname 'Farmer George'. With Queen Charlotte he had fifteen children, nine being sons. His son George had been made Prince Regent in 1811 and succeeded to the throne on his father's death as George IV.

Significant events of George III's reign

- 1769 James Cook begins his first voyage around the world.
- 1773 'Boston Tea Party' sparks protest against unfair British taxation in America.
- 1774 The first Continental Congress meets in Philadelphia to protest at repressive British legislation.
- 1775 American War of Independence begins. The first commercial steam engines are produced by Watt and Boulton.
- 1783 Britain acknowledges the independence of the American Colonies. William Pitt the Younger becomes prime minister.
- 1789 The French Revolution.
- 1791 First publication of Thomas Paine's *Rights of Man*.
- 1793 Britain and France go to war.
- 1800 Act of Union with Ireland.
- 1803 Napoloenic Wars commence.
- 1805 Nelson dies in the Battle of Trafalgar.
- 1810 Prince George becomes Regent.
- 1815 Battle of Waterloo ends the Napoleonic Wars. The Corn Laws are passed.
- 1819 The Peterloo Massacre—reform campaigners in Manchester are killed.

George IV (1762–1830) king of the United Kingdom of Great Britain and Ireland (1820–30). The eldest son of George III and Charlotte Sophia, in 1811 George became regent and, on the death of his father nine years later, king. He distinguished himself while regent as a great patron of the arts—the first George about which that could be said—and his intelligent patronage fostered painting, literature and Regency architecture. His extravagant tastes in food and wine were well known, but in the early part of his life these weaknesses did not harm his popularity.

His secret marriage to Maria FitzHerbert, a Catholic, caused problems, however, as the 1701 Act of Settlement prohibited the succession of a Catholic to the throne. Forced by parliament to choose an official wife, he married his cousin, Caroline of Brunswick, and had his huge debts paid off in return. The couple soon parted amid accusations of adultery on both sides. George lost his good standing with the people, however, when he openly accused his wife of infidelity at a public trial and forbade her from attending his coronation.

The most significant event of his reign was the Catholic Relief Act of 1829, which finally allowed Catholics access to parliament. There were also important advances made in criminal law and labour relations. George had little interest in politics however, and spent the majority of his time as king indulging himself with drink, food and his many mistresses. His dissipated life and his extravagance alienated him from the affection of the nation, and the image of the monarchy as a moral influence was greatly tarnished. He died in a state of obesity from internal bleeding and liver damage. As his only daughter, Princess Charlotte, wife of Leopold of Saxe-Coburg (afterwards king of the Belgians) died childless in 1817, he was succeeded by his brother, William IV.

Significant events of George IV's reign

- 1820 Cato Street Conspiracy to assassinate the cabinet is discovered. Queen Caroline is tried and George sues for divorce on grounds of adultery.
- 1824 The National Gallery is founded in London.
- 1825 The world's first railway service, the Stockton and Darlington Railway, opens. Legalization of Trade Unions.
- 1828 Duke of Wellington becomes prime minister.
- 1829 Establishment of the Metropolitan Police Force by Robert Peel takes place. The Catholic Relief Act passed.

George V (1865–1936) king of Great Britain and Ireland and of the overseas British dominions, emperor of India (1910–36). Second son of Edward VII and Queen Alexandra of Denmark, he was born at Marlborough House and, after being educated by a private tutor, he and his elder brother, Prince Albert Victor, became naval cadets and as midshipmen visited many parts of the world. George attained the rank of commander in 1891, but his brother's death in 1892, which placed him in direct succession to the crown, led to his practical withdrawal from a naval career. Created Duke of York in 1892, the following year he married Princess Victoria Mary, daughter of the duke of Teck. On the death of Queen Victoria and accession of Edward VII, he became Duke of Cornwall, and later in the year was created Prince of Wales.

He ascended the throne in the middle of a constitutional crisis caused by the House of Commons attempting to limit the powers of the House of Lords, and within four years he was also leading the nation in the First World War. Although he was related to Kaiser Wilhelm II, he had no objections to his government's decision to engage Germany in war. He quickly gained the admiration of the public by visiting the troops on the Western Front and openly disapproving of Wilhelm's military gesturing. In 1917 he changed the British royal family's name from the German Saxe-Coburg-Gotha to the English Windsor.

As well as carrying out his royal duties with great conscientiousness, he made important contributions to the handling of political problems of the day. Shortly before the outbreak of the war, he summoned a conference of party leaders at Buckingham Palace for the purpose of solving the Irish question. This was an important step towards the postwar creation of the Irish Free State. Later, during the 1931 financial crisis, he intervened to persuade the leading political parties to form a national coalition government.

On Christmas Day 1932 George broadcast a message to the nation (which had been written by Rudyard Kipling) and established a tradition that has been maintained every year since. His hobbies were shooting and stamp-collecting—his collection is well known to philatelists. In later life he suffered ill-health and almost died from septicaemia, or blood poisoning, in 1928. He never fully regained his former vigour and died of bronchitis eight years later. He was succeeded by Edward VIII, who abdicated before being crowned, in favour of his brother, George VI.

Significant events of George V's reign

- 1911 Parliament Act ensures the sovereignty of the House of Commons.
  National Insurance Act passed.
- 1912 Sinking of the SS *Titanic*.
- 1914 First World War breaks out.
- 1916 Easter Rising in support of Irish independence takes place in Dublin.
  David Lloyd George becomes prime minister.
- 1917 The Russian Revolution.
- 1918 Women over thirty gain the vote.
  Irish Parliament formed in Dublin.
- 1919 The first woman MP to take her seat, Lady Astor, is elected to parliament.
- 1921 Ireland partitioned.
- 1924 First Labour government takes power under Ramsay MacDonald.
- 1926 General Strike called by the trade unions.
- 1928 Women over twenty-one get the vote.

George VI (1895–1952) king of the United Kingdom of Great Britain and Northern Ireland and British dominions overseas, the last emperor of India (1936–52); head of the Commonwealth (1949–52). Second son of George V and Queen Mary, Prince Albert, as he was then known, served in the navy and air force until 1919 and attended Trinity College, Cambridge, until 1920. He was called to the throne in 1936 on the abdication of his brother, Edward VIII.

Unprepared for the role of king, George nevertheless carried out his duties with great conscientiousness and became a popular figurehead for the nation during the Second World War. He struggled with a speech impediment in his early years but worked hard to overcome it in order to perform his duties with the sense of authority that he knew was expected of him. He lived in London for the duration of the war despite frequent bombing raids and visited the troops in North Africa and France.

In 1939 he became the first British monarch to visit North America and restored much of the reputation lost by the monarchy following his brother's abdication. The postwar years saw a Labour government transforming Britain into a welfare state, and George became head of the Commonwealth of Nations, following the fragmentation of the empire.

He opened the 1951 Festival of Britain but died the following year after an operation for lung cancer. He had two daughters by Lady Elizabeth Bowes Lyon (now the Queen Mother), and was succeeded by the elder, Queen Elizabeth II.

Significant events of George VI's reign

- 1939 Second World War breaks out.
- 1940 Dunkirk evacuation takes place.
  Winston Churchill becomes prime minister.
  Battle of Britain prevents German invasion.
- 1941 Pearl Harbour bombing brings the USA into the war.
- 1944 D-Day—Allied forces land in Normandy and force German retreat.
- 1945 Germany is defeated and war ends in Europe.

Japan surrenders and Second World War ends.
United Nations founded.
Labour Government elected.

- 1947 India and Pakistan gain independence.
- 1948 Establishment of the National Health Service.
- 1951 Festival of Britain opens.

Giric I (d.889) king of Scots (878–889). The cousin of Aed, whom he is thought to have murdered to take the throne, he ruled jointly with Eocha, who was king of the Britons of Strathclyde and Kenneth I's grandson. He was defeated and killed in battle at Dundurn by Donald II.

Giric II (d.1005) king of Scots (997–1005). He was the son of Kenneth III, with whom he shared the throne. Both were killed by Malcolm II in battle at Monzievaird in order to secure his succession to the throne.

Godfred (Crovan) (d.1095) king of the Isle of Man (1079–95). The island kingdom had been held by Orkney rulers since *c.*990 when Godfred landed in 1079. He founded a dynasty of Norse kings that ruled the island until 1265. The legacy of Godfred's kingdom is reflected in the island's present self-governing status.

Grey, Lady Jane (1537–1554) queen of England and Ireland (for nine days in 1553). The daughter of Henry Grey, Marquis of Dorset, and Lady Francis Brandon, the daughter of Henry VIII's younger sister, Mary, Lady Jane Grey was the unfortunate victim of a scheme designed by Dudley, Duke of Northumberland, her father-in-law, to give his family the succession. He persuaded the dying king, Edward VI, to settle the succession on Northumberland's daughter-in-law and her male heirs in order to stop the throne being taken by either Mary, Queen of Scots, or Mary Tudor, both of whom were Catholics. When the king died in 1553 the country would have nothing to do with Northumberland, and Edward's sister, Mary Tudor, was proclaimed by the Lord Mayor of London. Lady Jane Grey was never crowned and had been recognized only by King's Lynn and Berwick before being imprisoned in the Tower. She was later beheaded for treason along with her husband.

Gruffydd ap Cynan (b.1055) king of Gwynedd (1081–1137). Although born in Ireland, he invaded his ancestral kingdom three times from 1075. He secured it briefly in 1081 before he was captured and imprisoned in Chester. He escaped, reconquered Gwynedd, and resisted two attempts by William II to capture him again. He finally rendered homage to Henry I.

Gruffydd ap Llywelyn (d.1062) king of Gwynedd (1039–63). He briefly ruled all Wales when he annexed Deheubarth in 1055. After several years spent raiding the English border, he was captured by a Wessex army at Rhuddlan in 1062 and beheaded. His descendants ruled the kingdom of Powys until 1269.

Guthrum (d.890) king of East Anglia (880–890). A Danish army commander who first attacked Wessex in 878, he was defeated by Alfred at Ethandune and made the Treaty of Wedmore. The treaty required Guthrum and his men to embrace Christianity and accept baptism. With Alfred acting as sponsor, they honoured their oaths and were baptised at the River Aller in Somerset. Guthrum then became king of East Anglia and settled at Cirencester.

H

Halfran (Ragnarson) (d.895) king of York (875–883). In 875 he founded the kingdom of York, which had thirteen Norse rulers in eighty years.

Hardicanute [Hardaknut Knutsson] (1018–42) king of England (1040–42) and Denmark. The only son of Canute and Emma of Normandy and the rightful successor to Canute, he was consolidating his dominion over Denmark when his half-brother, Harold, usurped his English throne in 1035. He came to the throne on Harold's death in 1040. Hardicanute's short and unpopular reign is noteworthy for its violence—he had Worcester burned for killing royal tax collectors, he murdered the earl of Northumbria, and abused the body of his dead brother, Harold I, by having it flung into a bog. He collapsed at a drunken wedding banquet and died shortly afterwards. He was succeeded by Edward the Confessor.

Harold I (Harefoot) (1016–40) king of England (1035–40). The second son of Canute and Elgifu, he succeeded his father to the throne of England. Despite being his illegitimate son, he proclaimed himself king and had a rival claimant, Aetheling, son of Ethelred, blinded and killed. His countrymen, the Danes, maintained him upon the throne while his half-brother was in Denmark. He exiled Emma, mother of Hardicanute, and defended his kingdom against vigorous attacks from the Welsh and Scots.

Harold II (1020–66) king of England (1066). The second son of Godwin, Earl of Kent, and Gytha, sister of Canute's Danish brother-in-law, he was made powerful by inheriting his father's lands in Wessex and Kent and was a rival to Edward the Confessor for the whole kingdom of England. He successfully defeated Welsh incursions and took control of Hereford before he was shipwrecked in 1064. He was then held by Duke William of Normandy (later William the Conqueror) and gained his release only by promising to help secure the English crown for William. Harold himself had been named as successor by the dying Edward, however, and in early 1066 he stepped into the vacant throne. Claims of a bequest of Edward in favour of Duke William of Normandy led the latter to call upon him to resign the crown. Harold refused, and William prepared for invasion. William also incited Harold's hostile brother, Tostig, to land on the northern coast of England in conjunction with the king of Norway. The united fleet of these chiefs sailed up the Humber and landed a large body of men, but at Stamford Bridge, in Yorkshire, they were totally routed by Harold, whose brother Tostig fell in the battle. Immediately after the battle, Harold heard of the landing of William of Normandy at Pevensey in Sussex, and went there with all the troops he could muster. It was a forced march of over 250 miles completed in nine days, but in the engagement that followed at Senlac, near Hastings, they were narrowly defeated. Harold died on the field, supposedly killed by an arrow, with two of his brothers. With his death there also ended England's six hundred years of rule by Anglo-Saxon kings.

Hengest king of Kent (455–488). The first of the Jutish kings of Kent, he ruled jointly with his brother Horsa. After being invited by the British king, Vortigern, to help force back the northern Picts, Hengest, along with his brother, turned on the Britons and founded what is referred to in the *Anglo-Saxon Chronicles* as the first Saxon kingdom. His son, Aesc, succeeded him.

Henry I (1068–1135) king of England (1100–35). Often surnamed 'Beauclerk' (fine scholar), he was the youngest son of William the Conqueror and Matilda of Flanders. Henry was hunting with the king William II, when the king was accidentally killed. He immediately rode to London and claimed the throne before he could be challenged by his elder brother, Robert Curthose of Normandy, then absent on a crusade. He soon re-established by charter the laws of Edward the Confessor and did away with the legal abuses William II had let go unchecked. He then introduced measures to stop the seizure of Church lands and married Matilda, a Saxon daughter of Malcolm III of Scotland, thus conciliating in turn his people, the Church and the Scots. Robert landed an army but was pacified with a pension and the promise of succession in event of his brother's death. Soon afterwards, however, Henry invaded Normandy, captured Robert and imprisoned him in Cardiff Castle. The last years of his reign were very troubled. In 1120 his only son, William, was drowned returning from Normandy, where, three years later, a revolt occurred in favour of Robert's son. The Welsh also were a source of disturbance, but he was a capable commander and was never seriously threatened.

In the later years of his reign he was able to

strengthen the Norman system of government and administration of justice. He also won from the Church the agreement that the bishops should acknowledge the king as overlord of their extensive secular holdings. Henry appointed as his heir his daughter, Matilda, whom he had married first to Emperor Henry V and then to Geoffrey Plantagenet of Anjou. This laid the basis for a much enlarged kingdom, but Stephen took the throne from the rightful heir, Matilda, when Henry died of fever in France.

Significant events of Henry I's reign

- 1100 Charter of Liberties proclaimed.
  Henry marries Matilda of Scotland.
- 1101 Robert of Normandy recognizes Henry I as king in the Treaty of Alton.
- 1104 Crusaders capture Acre.
- 1106 War breaks out with Normandy.
- 1120 Henry's heir, William, is drowned.
- 1129 Matilda marries Geoffrey Plantagenet, Count of Anjou.

Henry II (1133–89) king of England (1154–89). The first of the Plantagenet line, Henry was born in Normandy, the son of Geoffrey, Count of Anjou, and Matilda, daughter of Henry I. Invested with the duchy of Normandy by the consent of his mother in 1150, he succeeded to Anjou, and in 1151, by marriage with Eleanor of Aquitaine, the divorced wife of King Louis VII of France, gained Guienne and Poitou. In 1152 he invaded England to make his claim to the throne, but a compromise was effected by which Stephen was to retain the crown and Henry to succeed at his death.

He began his reign by destroying the castles, or 'dens of thieves' as he called them, built by rebellious barons in Stephen's time. A man of immense energy, he soon stamped his character on his vast kingdom that stretched from Scotland to the Pyrenees. He intended to reform the powers of the Church and began by installing Thomas à Becket as archbishop of Canterbury. The Constitutions of Clarendon, which placed limitations on the jurisdiction of the Church over crimes commited by the clergy, were contested by Becket, however, and he fled the kingdom after quarrelling with the king. They were later reconciled but quarrelled again, and Becket was murdered in Canterbury Cathedral by four knights who took Henry's request 'Will someone not rid me of this turbulent priest?' a little too literally. Although sufficiently submissive after Becket's death in the way of penance, Henry gave up only the article in the Constitutions of Clarendon that forbade appeals to the court of Rome in ecclesiastical cases.

Henry began the settlement of Ireland in 1166 after responding to a request by the king of Leinster to resolve a dynastic dispute. His support was commanded by Richard de Clare, Earl of Pembroke, commonly known as Strongbow, who successfully established England's claim to rule Ireland and forced the subservience of all Ireland's regional kings to Henry, who created himself First Lord of Ireland. An earlier papal bull, *Laudabiliter*, made by Pope Adrian IV in 1155, had given the approval of the Roman Church for an invasion to bring the Irish Church under its control.

Henry's last years were embittered by his sons, to whom he had assigned various territories. The eldest, Henry, who had been not only declared heir to England, Normandy, Anjou, Maine and Touraine but actually crowned in his father's lifetime, was induced by the French monarch to demand of his father the immediate resignation either of the kingdom of England or of the dukedom of Normandy. Queen Eleanor excited her other sons, Richard and Geoffrey, to make similar claims; William I of Scotland gave them support. A general invasion of Henry's dominions was begun in 1173 by an attack on the frontiers of Normandy and an invasion of England by the Scots, attended by considerable disturbance in England. Henry took prompt action. William of Scotland was captured and forced to acknowledge the English king as overlord. Henry's sons, however, once more became turbulent, and although the deaths of Henry and Geoffrey reduced the number of centres of disturbance, the king was forced to accept humiliating terms from Richard and Philip of France.

Henry II ranks among the greatest English kings both in soldiership and statecraft. He partitioned England into four judiciary districts and appointed itinerant justices to make regular excursions through them. He revived trial by jury and established it as a right, but by the time of his death he was a defeated king, worn out by family revolts.

Significant events of Henry II's reign

- 1155 Thomas à Becket appointed chancellor of England.
  Pope Adrian IV's papal bull gives Henry the right to invade Ireland.
- 1162 Becket appointed archbishop of Canterbury.
- 1164 The Constitutions of Clarendon issued.
- 1166 Trial by jury is established at the Assize of Clarendon.
- 1168 Oxford University founded.
- 1170 Becket is murdered.
- 1171 Henry is acknowledged as Lord of Ireland.
- 1173 Becket is canonized.

Henry III (1207–1272) king of England (1216–72). The eldest son of John by Isabel of Angoulême, he was born at Winchester and succeeded his father at the age of nine. At the time of his accession, the dauphin of France, Louis, at the head of an army supported by a faction of English nobles had assumed the reins of government, but he was compelled to quit the country by the earl of Pembroke, who was guardian of the young king until 1219. The Treaty of Lambeth followed, which established peace between France, the English barons and supporters of Henry. But as Henry approached manhood he displayed a character wholly unfit for his station. He discarded his most able minister, Hubert de Burgh, and falsely accused him of treason. After 1230, when he received homage in Poitou and Gascony, he began to bestow his chief favours upon foreigners and installed many of them in government.

His marriage in 1236 to Eleanor of Provence increased the dislike of him felt by his subjects, and although he received frequent grants of money from parliament on condition of confirming the Great Charter, his conduct after each ratification was as arbitrary as before. At length the nobles rose in rebellion under Simon de Montfort, Earl of Leicester and husband of the king's sister, and in 1258, at a parliament held at Oxford, known in history as the Mad Parliament, the king was obliged to sign the body of resolutions known as the Provisions of Oxford. A feud arose, however, between Montfort and Gloucester, and Henry recovered some of his power. War again broke out, and Louis was called in as arbitrator, but his award was favourable to the king, and Leicester refused to submit to it. A battle was fought near Lewes, in which Henry was taken prisoner. A convention, called the Mise of Lewes, provided for the future settlement of the kingdom, and in 1265 the first genuine House of Commons was summoned. Leicester, however, was defeated and killed in the battle of Evesham, and Henry retained the throne.

He was a selfish and petulant king, with few of the personal qualities required to command respect or obedience. In some respects, however, he redeemed himself as patron of the arts. He established the first three colleges of Oxford and initiated improvements to Westminster Abbey and the construction of Salisbury Cathedral. His son, Edward I, succeeded him.

Significant events of Henry III's reign

- 1227 Henry takes control of the government; Hubert de Burgh remains as adviser.
- 1232 Hubert de Burgh is dismissed; Peter des Riveaux becomes Treasurer of England.
- 1234 A revolt led by Richard Marshall is defeated.
- 1258 The Provisions of Oxford are prompted by a rebellion led by Simon de Montfort.
- 1261 Henry renounces the Provisions.
- 1264 The Barons' War begins.
- 1265 'Mad Parliament' called.
  Montfort killed at the Battle of Evesham.

Henry IV (1367–1413) king of England and Wales (1399–1413). Henry was the eldest son of John of Gaunt, Duke of Lancaster, fourth son of Edward III, by Blanche of Lancaster, daughter of Henry, Duke of Lancaster, great-grandson of Henry III. In the reign of Richard II he was made Earl of Derby and Duke of Hereford, but having in 1398 preferred a charge of treason against Thomas Mowbray, Duke of Norfolk, he was banished with his adversary. In the 1390s Henry took part in crusades in Lithuania and Prussia. On the death of John of Gaunt in 1399, Richard withheld Henry's inheritance, and Henry, landing in England, deposed the king and had him imprisoned at Pontefract Castle. The recognition of Henry IV as king by parliament was followed by Richard's death in prison the following year by self-inflicted starvation.

Henry was king by conquest and election by parliament, however, and not by heredity. For this reason he had to accept a degree of subservience to his peers and to conciliate the Church accepted the *De Heretico Comburendo*, a statute that persecuted heretics, notably the followers of John Wycliffe, known as the Lollards. His position was precarious, and there were several plots to depose him, which led to the executions of several noblemen. An insurrection in Wales, however, under Owen Glyndwr proved more formidable. Glyndwr was a descendant of the last independent Prince of Wales and sought full independence for his principality. He launched a guerilla campaign against the English in 1401 and made a treaty with France who sent an army to help him. For the next ten years all attempts to subdue him failed.

Henry was also troubled by the Scots and the Percy family of Northumberland. In 1402 the Scots were decisively defeated by the Percies at Homildon Hill and their leader, the earl of Douglas, was captured. An order from Henry not to permit the ransom of Douglas and other Scottish prisoners was regarded as an indignity by the Percies, who let Douglas free, made an alliance with him, and joined Glyndwr. The king met the insurgents at Shrewsbury, and the battle ended in defeat for the Percies. The earl of Northumberland was pardoned, but a few of the insurgents were executed. A new insurrection, headed by the earl of Nottingham and Richard Scrope, archbishop of York, broke out in 1405 but was suppressed. The same year, James, the son and heir of King Robert III of Scotland, was captured at sea on his way to France and imprisoned in England. The rest of Henry's reign was comparatively untroubled, and he eventually died after contracting a leprosy-like illness. He was succeeded by his son, Henry V.

Significant events of Henry IV's reign

- 1400 Richard II dies in prison.
  Geoffrey Chaucer dies.
- 1401 Statute of *De Heretico Comburendo* leads to many being burned at the stake.
- 1403 The Percy family rebellion is defeated at Shrewsbury.
- 1404 Glyndwr sets up Welsh parliament.
- 1405 French troops land in Wales.
- 1411 Construction of the Guildhall in London begins.

Henry V (1387–1422) king of England and Wales (1413–22). The only surviving son of Henry IV and Mary de Bohun, he showed a wisdom in kingship in marked contrast to a somewhat reckless youth. As Prince of Wales he had fought against Welsh rebels and prided himself on his abilities as a soldier. On becoming king he acted quickly to thwart an attempt by a group of nobles to place his cousin, Edmund Mortimer, Earl of March, on the throne (the Cambridge Plot). He also carried on the persecution of the Lollards and sent many to their deaths. Like his father, his claim to the throne was doubtful, and he busied himself with foreign affairs in order to divert attention from domestic difficulties.

The struggle in France between the factions of the dukes of Orleans and Burgundy afforded Henry a tempting opportunity for reviving the claims of his predecessors to the French crown. He accordingly landed near Harfleur in 1415, and although its capture cost him more than half his army, he decided to return to England by way of Calais. A large French army endeavoured to intercept him at the plain of Agincourt but was completely routed. It is thought that as many as 6,000 Frenchmen died while fewer than 400 English lost their lives. A year later the French were defeated at sea by the Duke of Bedford.

In 1417 the liberal grants of the Commons enabled Henry once more to invade Normandy with 25,000 men. The assassination of the duke of Burgundy, which induced his son and successor to join Henry, greatly added to his power, and the alliance was soon followed by the famous Treaty of Troyes, by which Henry engaged to marry the Catherine of Valois and to leave her father, Charles VI, in possession of the French crown on condition that it should go to Henry and his heirs at his death. He returned in triumph to England, but on the defeat of his brother, Duke of Clarence, in Normandy by the Earl of Buchan, he again set out for France, drove back the army of the dauphin, and entered Paris. All his great projects seemed about to be realized when he died of fever at Vincennes, at the age of thirty-five, having reigned for ten years.

An adventurous, headstrong leader, Henry pursued his policies with great zeal and proved himself to be a shrewd military tactician as well as an able politician. His campaign in France had the effect of uniting his nobles in a common cause, thus diverting attention from domestic plots to dethrone him. His ten-month-old son, Henry VI, succeeded him as king of both England and France.

Significant events of Henry V's reign

- 1415 The Cambridge Plot is thwarted.
  Battle of Agincourt.
- 1416 Welsh leader Glyndwr dies.
- 1420 The Treaty of Troyes makes Henry heir to the French throne

Henry VI (1421–71) king of England and Wales (1422–61, 1470–71). The only son of Henry V and Catherine of Valois, he succeeded to the throne on the death of his father when he was less than one year old. In his minority, the government of the kingdom was placed in the hands of his uncle, Humphrey, Duke of Gloucester, who was made protector of the realm of England. A few weeks after Henry's succession, Charles VI of France died, and, in accordance with the Treaty of Troyes, Henry was proclaimed king of France. Another uncle, John, Duke of Bedford, was appointed regent of France. The war that followed at first proved favourable to the English, but by the heroism of Joan of Arc, who claimed to have been inspired by a vision telling her to drive the English from France, the confidence of the French people was restored. Joan of Arc was captured and burnt at the stake in Rouen, but Henry eventually lost all his possessions in France with the exception of Calais.

When Henry assumed personal rule at the age of fifteen, the government of England was being conducted by rival ministers of the houses of York and Lancaster. The fact that Henry suffered from bouts of mental illness gave these houses greater power, and their rivalry increased. In 1453, his wife, Margaret of Anjou, bore him a son, but within the year his mind had failed him to such a degree that he had to submit to the rule of a protector, Richard, Duke of York. Fighting soon broke out between the houses of York and Lancaster, the rival factions in government, and the appointment of York was annulled the following year, the king having recovered his faculties. York retired to the north, and being joined by his adherents, marched on London. He encountered and defeated the king's Lancastrian army at St Albans, the first battle of the thirty years' War of the Roses. The king again becoming deranged, York was once more made protector. Four years of peace followed, but the struggle was soon renewed. A Yorkist army led by Richard Neville, Earl of Warwick, defeated the Lancastrian forces at Bloreheath, but they recovered to win over the Yorkists at Ludford. The Lancastrians then declared York a traitor at a session of Parliament held in Coventry. Neville's army in return defeated the Lancastrians at Northampton and captured Henry. Following this victory, York was restored as protector and Henry's wife fled to Scotland. She returned with an army that defeated the Yorkists at Wakefield and killed their leader, Richard of York, who was replaced by his son, Edward, as Duke of York. His army then defeated the Lancastrians at Mortimer's Cross, and Warwick engaged Margaret's forces at the second Battle of St Albans. Warwick was unsuccessful at first but finally defeated Margaret's army at the Battle of Towton and declared Edward, Duke of York, as king.

Further revolts by the Lanacastrians were suppressed, and Henry was captured and imprisoned in the Tower of London following Warwick's victory at the Battle of Hexham. Edward owed his crown to Warwick, however, and it was inevitable that the next stage of the struggle would be between the kingmaker and the king. After gaining the upper hand at Edgecote, Warwick was at length banished by the king, only to return, allied with Margaret, to attempt a restoration of Henry. This they achieved in 1470, but it was to be a brief affair. Edward soon returned and defeated Warwick at the Battle of Barnet and Margaret at the Battle of Tewkesbury. Warwick and Henry and Margaret's son, Edward, were both killed in the fighting, and shortly afterwards Henry was murdered in the Tower. The Wars of the Roses did not end until 1485, when the Lancastrian heir and claimant to the throne, Henry Tudor (Henry VII), defeated Richard III, the brother of Edward IV.

Henry VI had been a pious and well-intentioned but hopelessly incompetent ruler. Throughout his life he had been deeply religious and had a passion for education and building. His principal claim to remembrance is that he founded Eton College and King's College, Cambridge.

Significant events of Henry VI's reign

- 1422 Henry becomes king of France on the death of Charles VI.
- 1429 Joan of Arc begins the rout of the English.
- 1431 Joan of Arc is burned at the stake.
- 1437 Henry VI assumes control of government.
- 1453 The English are expelled from France, ending of the Hundred Years' War.
- 1454 Richard, Duke of York, becomes protector.
- 1455 Wars of the Roses begin when Richard is dismissed as protector and rebels against Henry.
- 1461 Richard's son Edward deposes Henry.
- 1470 Henry briefly regains the crown.

Henry VII (1457–1509) king of England (1485–1509). The first of the Tudor kings, Henry was the son of Edmund, Earl of Richmond, son of Owen Tudor and Catherine of France, widow of Henry V. His mother, Margaret, was the only child of John, Duke of Somerset, grandson of John of Gaunt. After the Battle of Tewkesbury he was taken by his uncle, the Earl of Pembroke, to Brittany, and on the usurpation of Richard III was naturally turned to as the representative of the house of Lancaster. In 1485 he assembled a small body of troops in Brittany and, having landed at Milford Haven, defeated Richard III at Bosworth. Henry was proclaimed king on the field of battle, his right being subsequently recognized by parliament. In 1486 he married Elizabeth, daughter of Edward IV and heiress of the house of York, and thus united the claims of the rival houses of York and Lancaster.

His reign was troubled by repeated insurrections, of which the chief were those headed by Lord Lovell (1486) and the impostures of Lambert Simnel (1487) and Perkin Warbeck (1496–99). In order to strengthen England's prestige, he made important marriage alliances. He brought about a match between the Infanta Catherine, daughter of Ferdinand of Aragon and Isabella of Castile, and his eldest son, Arthur. On the death of Arthur, in order to retain the princess's dowry, he obtained papal dispensation to allow his son Henry (later Henry VIII) to marry the widow, an event that, in its sequel, led to a separation from Rome. He married his eldest daughter to James IV, king of Scots, from which marriage there ultimately resulted the union of the two crowns.

The problem of the English barons was still present, however, and he set about breaking their power by reviving the Court of Star Chamber. This prevented the barons from raising private armies and allowed them to be tried if they broke the law. He also did much to strengthen England's commercial activities and took an interest in the development of trading in North America. His fiscal policies were criticized as being largely for the benefit of the royal exchequer, and in his later years this avarice became increasingly marked. Two exchequer judges, Empson and Dudley, were employed in all sorts of extortion and chicanery in order to augment the royal purse. His reign, however, was in the main beneficial. Its freedom from wars permitted the development of the internal resources of the country. His policy of depressing the feudal nobility, which proportionably elevated the middle ranks, was highly profitable. For a time, however, the power lost by the aristocracy gave an undue preponderance to that of the crown.

A cultured man, Henry also brought European scholars to England, patronized the printer William Caxton, and initiated what came to be called the 'revival of learning'. In his later years he suffered from arthritis and gout, and died aged fifty-two.

Significant events of Henry VII's reign

- 1485 Henry defeats Richard III at Bosworth and is declared king of England.
  The Yeoman of the Guard is formed.
- 1486 Houses of York and Lancaster are joined with the marriage of Henry to Elizabeth of York.
- 1487 A rebellion on behalf of the pretender Lambert Simnel is thwarted.
- 1492 Henry defeats another attempt to dethrone him led by Perkin Warbeck.
  America discovered by Columbus.
- 1497 John Cabot discovers Newfoundland.
- 1502 Henry's daughter is married to James IV of Scotland.

Henry VIII (1491–1547) king of England (1509–47) and Ireland (1542–47). The second son of Henry VII and Elizabeth of York, he succeeded his father as king at the age of eighteen. Although well educated and opinionated, the young king at first had no enthusiasm for politics or personal rule. He chose instead to leave the business of government to his very capable chancellor, Cardinal Thomas Wolsey, who administered with great skill and increased England's trade and standing abroad.

Henry strained the finances of his kingdom, however, through a series of costly wars. The success of the English at the Battle of the Spurs (1513) was followed by no adequate result, the taking of Tournai being the only fruit of this expensive expedition. In the meantime, success attended the English army at home, with James IV of Scotland being completely defeated and slain at the Battle of Flodden in 1513. Henry, however, granted peace to the queen of Scotland, his sister, and established an influence that rendered his kingdom long secure on that side. Soon afterwards he made peace with France, retaining Tournai and receiving a large sum of money.

After the election of Charles V to the German Empire, both Charles and the French king, Francis I, sought alliance with England. A friendly meeting took place between Henry and Francis at the Field of the Cloth of Gold (1520), but the interest of Charles preponderated, and Henry soon afterwards again declared war against France.

In 1529 Henry determined to divorce his wife, Catherine of Aragon, who was older than he, had borne him no surviving male heir, only a daughter (later Mary I) and had, moreover, been in the first place the wife of his elder brother. The last of these points was the alleged ground for seeking divorce, although Henry was probably influenced largely by his attachment to Anne Boleyn, one of the queen's maids of honour. Wolsey, for his own ends, had at first been active in promoting the divorce but drew back and procrastinated when it became apparent that Anne Boleyn would be Catherine's successor. This delay cost Wolsey his power and the papacy its authority in England. Wolsey was accused of treason but died before he could be brought to trial. He was succeeded by Sir Thomas More, who, however, could not bring himself to support Henry's divorce and resigned.

Henry eagerly took the advice of Thomas Cranmer, afterwards archbishop of Canterbury, to refer the case to the universities, from which he soon got the decision that he desired. In 1533 his marriage with Catherine was declared null and an anticipatory private marriage with Anne Boleyn declared lawful, and as these decisions were not recognized by the pope, two Acts of parliament were obtained, one in 1534 setting aside the authority of the chief pontiff in England, the other in 1335 declaring Henry the supreme head of the Church. But although Henry discarded the authority of the Roman Church, he adhered to its theological tenets, and while, on the one hand, he executed Bishop Fisher and Sir Thomas More for refusing the oath of supremacy, he brought many of the reformers to the stake. Finding that the monks and friars in England were the most direct advocates of papal authority, and a constant source of disaffection, he suppressed the monasteries by Act of parliament, and thereby inflicted an incurable wound on the Catholic religion in England. The fall of Anne Boleyn, who had borne a daughter (later Elizabeth I) in 1533 and a stillborn son early in 1536, was, however, unfavourable for a time to the reformers.

Henry then married Jane Seymour, and the birth of a son in 1537 fulfilled his wish for a male heir. The death of the queen was followed in 1540 by Henry's marriage with Anne of Cleves, the negotiations of which were conducted by Thomas Cromwell. The king's dislike of his wife, which resulted in another divorce, became extended to the minister who had proposed the union, and Cromwell's disgrace and death soon followed. A marriage with Catherine Howard in 1541 proved no happier, and in 1542 she was executed on a charge of infidelity. In 1543 he married his sixth wife, Catherine Parr, a lady secretly inclined to the Reformation, who survived the king.

In the meantime Scotland and France had renewed their alliance, and England became again involved in war. James V ravaged the borders but was defeated at Solway Moss in 1542, and in 1544 Boulogne was captured, Henry having again allied himself with Charles V. Charles, however, soon withdrew, and Henry maintained the war alone until 1546. War and his sense of isolation now so much aggravated his natural violence that his oldest friends fell victim to his tyranny. The Duke of Norfolk was committed to the Tower, and his son, the earl of Surrey, was executed.

During his reign it is estimated that Henry had at least seventy thousand people executed for various offences. As well as the brutality shown to his subjects, he also frequently proved himself to be disloyal to his wives and advisers. His driving ambition, however, was to secure a male heir for the throne, and he cared little about his public image so long as this goal was acheived. His only son by Jane Seymour, Edward VI, succeeded him.

Significant events of Henry VIII's reign

- 1509 Henry marries Catherine of Aragon.
- 1513 James IV of Scotland is killed at the Battle of Flodden.
- 1515 Thomas Wolsey is made chancellor of England.
- 1517 Martin Luther protests against the indulgences of the Roman Catholic church at Wittenberg.
- 1520 Francis I of France meets Henry at the Field of the Cloth of Gold.
- 1529 Cardinal Wolsey is accused of treason.
  Sir Thomas More becomes chancellor of England.
- 1532 Sir Thomas More resigns.
- 1533 Archbishop Thomas Cranmer annuls Henry and Catherine's marriage.
  Henry marries Anne Boleyn.
  The pope excommunicates Henry.
- 1534 Act of Supremacy makes Henry the head of the Church in England.
- 1535 Sir Thomas More does not accept the Act of Supremacy and is put to death.
- 1536 Anne Boleyn is executed; Henry marries Jane Seymour.
  The Act of Union unites England and Wales.
  Dissolution of the monasteries begins.
- 1537 Jane Seymour gives birth to a son and dies several days later.
- 1540 Henry marries Anne of Cleves and divorces her six months later.
  Henry marries Catherine Howard.
- 1542 Catherine Howard is charged with treason and put to death.
- 1543 Henry marries Catherine Parr.

Hlothere (d.685) king of Kent (673–685). The younger brother of Egbert I, he was sole ruler and then, from 676, joint ruler with Suaebhard of Essex. Early in his reign he faced an invasion from Mercia and died in battle during a later South Saxon conquest.

Horsa (d.455) king of Kent (455). With his brother Hengest he became joint ruler after being invited by Vortigern to help fight off raids from the north. The first Jutish kings soon established themselves despite Horsa's early death in battle at Aegelsthrep (Aylesford, near Maidstone)

Hywel ab Idwal (the Bad) king of Gwynedd (979–985). A descendant of Rhodi Mwar, he deposed his father, Iago ap Idwal.

Hywel Dda (the Good) (d.950) king of Gwynedd (904–950). A grandson of Rhodi Mwar, he briefly united north and south Wales under his governorship. By marriage to princess Elen, daughter of the king of Dyfed, he secured that kingdom (*c*.904) and soon extended his realm into the area of south Wales known as Deheubarth. He also absorbed Powys but had to acknowledge Edward the Elder and later Ethelsatan as overlords in light of threatened invasions by the Danes. The law code that he is credited with initiating (the Laws of Hywel) still survives in a 13th-century manuscript, and he was the only Welsh ruler to issue a coinage. He went on a pilgrimage to Rome in 928.

I J

Iago I ab Idwal (d.*c*.980) king of Gwynedd (950–979). He was deposed by his son, Hywel ab Idwal.

Iago II ab Idwal (d.*c*.1040) king of Gwynedd (1023–39). He was the grandson of the first Iago and father of Gruffydd ap Cyan.

Ida (d.*c*.568) king of Bernicia (547–568). According to the *Anglo-Saxon Chronicle*, he captured the Bernician stronghold of Banburgh and, with his son Aelle as king of Deira, effectively ruled most of Northumbria. This name for this kingdom comes from *Northanhymbre*, the Old English for 'people north of the River Humber'.

Idwal Foel (Idwal the Bald) king of Gwynedd (916–942). The son of Anarawd, he was killed rebelling against Edmund II of England. Hywel Dda succeeded him.

Indulf king of Scots (954–962). He succeeded his uncle, Malcolm I, to the throne and abdicated eight years later in favour of Duff, Malcolm's son. He died at St Andrews and was buried at Iona

Ine (d.*c*.728) king of Wessex (688–726). One of the most powerful Wessex rulers, he defeated the South Saxons in battle in 722 and 725 and the Cornish Britons in 710. He set up a port at Southampton and founded the monastery at Glastonbury (his sister, Cuthburh, founded a monastery at Wimborne in Dorset). His greatest achievement, however, was the important law code he compiled between 690 and 693, which reveals a growing sophistication in the consideration of the concepts of kingship and royal authority. He abdicated and retired to Rome.

James I of England. *See* **James VI** of Scots.

James I (1394–1437) king of Scots (1406–37). The son of Robert III by Annabella Drummond. Following the death of James's brother, Robert wished him to be taken to France in order to escape the intrigues of his uncle, the first duke of Albany. The ship in which he was being conveyed was captured by an English squadron off Flamborough Head, and the prince was taken prisoner to London, where he received an education from Henry IV. To relieve the tedium of captivity, he applied himself literary pursuits and distinguished himself as a poet. Robert III died in 1406, but James was not allowed to return to his kingdom until a ransom had been paid and hostages handed over to act as security. After the Treaty of London he was freed and crowned at Scone. Before his departure, he married Joan Beaufort, daughter of the earl of Somerset. On his return to Scotland he had the second duke of Albany and his son Murdoch executed as traitors, and proceeded to carry on vigorous reforms, and, above all, to improve his revenue and curb the ambition and lawlessness of the nobles. The nobility, headed by the earl of Atholl, exasperated by the decline of their power, formed a plot against his life, and assassinated him at Perth in 1437, where he was buried. His collection of poems, *The King's Quair* ('king's book'), entitles him to high rank among the followers of Chaucer. He was succeeded by his son James II.

Significant events of James I's reign

- 1406 James is captured by the English en route to France and is held in the Tower.
- 1423 Treaty of London agreed.
- 1424 James is freed on a ransom.

James II (1430–60) king of Scots (1437–60). The surviving twin son of James I and Queen Joan, he was only seven years old when his father was assassinated. He was the first king to be crowned at Kelso Abbey rather than Scone. During his minority the kingdom was distracted by struggles for power between his guardians, Sir Alexander Livingston and Sir William Crichton, and the great house of Douglas. Crichton had the Earl Douglas murdered at what would come to be known as the 'Black Dinner' at Edinburgh Castle with the young king in attendance. After assuming his full powers as king, James still found his position menaced by the Douglas family, and he invited the 8th Earl Douglas to Stirling Castle to persuade him to abandon a league of nobles that had been formed in opposition to the crown. The interview ended in the king stabbing his guest and his bodyguard killing him. The civil war that followed was won by James, and three years later parliament announced the forfeiture of the Douglas territories.

Having finally brought the nobles under control, James, who, because of a birthmark was nicknamed 'Fiery Face', consolidated his kingdom to the point where even the Lords of the Isles were involved in his attempt to take back Roxburgh from the English. He was killed by the bursting of a cannon at this siege. By his wife, Mary of Gueldres, he had four sons and was succeeded by the eldest, James III.

Significant events of James II's reign

- 1450 Glasgow University is founded.
- 1455 James II defeats the 'Black' Douglas family.

James II (1633–1701) king of Great Britain and Ireland (1685–88). The second son of Charles I and Henrietta Maria of France, he was immediately created Duke of York. During the Civil War he escaped from England and served with distinction in the French army under Turenne and in the Spanish army under Condé. At the Restoration in 1660 he obtained the command of the fleet as Lord High Admiral. He had previously married Anne, daughter of Chancellor Hyde, afterwards Lord Clarendon. In 1671 she died, leaving two daughters, Mary and Anne, both of whom were subsequently sovereigns of England and Scotland. Having openly avowed the Roman Catholic faith, after passing of the Test Act, which prevented Roman Catholics from holding public employment, he was obliged to resign his command. He was afterwards sent to Scotland as Lord High Commissioner, where he persecuted the Covenanters.

He succeeded his brother as king in 1685, and at once set himself to attain absolute power. His conversion to Catholicism had made him unpopular, however, and a rebellion was initiated by the duke of Monmouth (his nephew). This was easily put down (the Battle of Sedgmoor in 1685 was the last to be fought on English soil) and encouraged the king in his arbitrary measures. After a series of trials, known as the Bloody Assizes, 320 rebels were executed and 800 transported as slaves.

He then accepted a pension from Louis XIV to help effect his purposes, especially that of restoring the Roman Catholic religion. The Declaration of Indulgence followed, which led to the imprisonment of seven bishops who opposed the suspension of penal laws against Roman Catholics. The bishops were later found not guilty of the charge laid at them, that of sedition, and were freed. Things came to a head in the Revolution of 1688, which immediately followed the birth of a male heir by the king's second wife, Mary of Modena (the child was the future 'Old Pretender', recognized by Jacobites as James III of England and James VIII of Scotland). Fearing a Catholic tyranny, the king's opponents invited his son-in-law, William of Orange, to claim the throne. He landed in November 1688. James found himself completely deserted and fled to France, where he was received with great kindness and hospitality by Louis XIV. Parliament declared James to have abdicated soon afterwards, and William accepted the throne. James attempted the recovery of Ireland, but the Battle of the Boyne, fought in 1690, compelled him to return to France. All succeeding projects for his restoration proved equally abortive, and he spent the last years of his life in ascetic study. He died of a stroke at St Germain in 1701.

Significant events of James II's reign

- 1685 Monmouth fails to depose the king. Bloody Assizes follow.
- 1686 James disregards the Test Act and Catholics are appointed to public office.
- 1688 William III lands in England and James flees to France.
  James is deemed by Parliament to have abdicated.

James III (1451–88) king of Scots (1460–88). The son of James II and Mary of Gueldres, he succeeded his father at the age of nine, the kingdom during his minority being governed in turn by Bishop Kennedy and the Boyd family. James throughout his reign was much under the influence of favourites, and he quarrelled with his brothers. One, the earl of Mar, was reputedly murdered, and another, the duke of Albany, was forced to flee to France. Albany obtained English aid and later invaded Scotland with hopes of being crowned as Alexander IV. When James marched to meet him, the nobles seized and hanged some of his favourites, including Cochrane, an architect, who was specially unpopular. Albany was proclaimed 'Lieutenant General of the Realm' but was soon afterwards expelled.

James continued to be on bad terms with his nobles, and was eventually defeated by a rebellion led by his son, later James IV, in 1469. After a military defeat at Sauchiburn, near Stirling, the king was murdered, allegedly by a soldier disguised as a priest. By his marriage with Margaret, daughter of Christian I of Denmark and Norway, he brought Orkney and Shetland into the kingdom of Scotland. They had three sons.

Significant events of James III's reign

- 1470 Work begins on the Great Hall at Stirling Castle.
- 1472 Scotland gains Orkney and Shetland from Norway as a royal wedding dowry.
- 1482 Scotland loses Berwick to the English.
- 1488 James IV leads the rebel noblemen at the Battle of Sauchieburn.

James IV (1473–1513) king of Scots (1488–1513). The son of James III, he was in his sixteenth year when he succeeded to the throne and was, either voluntarily or by compulsion, on the side of the nobles who rebelled against his father. He was not judged to require a regent, and, feeling great remorse for the manner in which he became king, carried out his duties admirably. During his reign the ancient enmity between the king and the nobility seems to have ceased. His frankness and bravery won him the people's love, and he ruled with vigour, administered justice with impartiality, and passed important laws. Henry VII, then king of England, tried to obtain a union with Scotland by political measures, and in 1503 James married his daughter, Margaret. This was later to become the basis for Stuart rule in England. A period of peace and prosperity followed. French influence, however, and the discourtesy of Henry VIII in retaining the jewels of his sister and in encouraging the border chieftains hostile to Scotland, led to angry negotiations that ended in war.

Siding with France in 1513, James invaded England with a large force and, despite papal excommunication and his advisers' pleas for caution, engaged in battle. Together with many of his nobles he died at the Battle of Flodden, having fought at the heart of the battle. He was the last British king to die in battle, and it was later said of him that he was 'more courageous than a king should be'.

He is credited with sponsoring Renaissance values in Scotland and did much to broaden education in his kingdom. But by leaving an heir to the throne, James V, who was barely more than a year old, he had put Scotland's independence in jeopardy.

Significant events of James IV's reign

- 1493 James subdues the last Lord of the Isles and assumes the title himself.
- 1495 Aberdeen University founded.
- 1496 The Scottish Parliament passes education legislation.
- 1503 James marries the daughter of Henry VII, Margaret Tudor.
- 1507 Scotland's first printing press is set up in Edinburgh by Andrew Myllar.
- 1513 James invades England.

James V (1512–1542) king of Scots (1513–42). James succeeded his father, James IV, who had died at the Battle of Flodden when he was only eighteen months old. His cousin, the duke of Albany, a Frenchman by birth and education, was the regent during his childhood. Because of Albany's incompetence and the intrigues of the queen mother, Margaret of England, the period of his long minority was one of lawlessness and gross misgovernment. James assumed the reins of government in his seventeenth year. James V was culturally literate (he renovated several palaces, including Linlithgow) but was morally wanting, having at least six illegitimate children and reputedly keeping low company. In order to increase his wealth, he married Madeleine, daughter of Francis I of France, in 1537, but she died just seven months later. After her death James married Mary of Lorraine, daughter of the duke of Guise, and obtained a large dowry.

James was able to exploit the fears of the pope that Scotland would follow England in making the king head of the church. In return for his commitment to Rome, James received the right to appoint bishops and benefited from payments from the Church. Henry VIII, having broken with Rome and eager to gain his nephew over to his views, proposed an interview at York, but James never came, and it is known that Henry hoped to kidnap him. A rupture took place between the two kingdoms, and war was declared. James was badly supported by his nobles, and after some initial success in holding off an English invasion, his army was crushed at Solway Moss. The defeat destroyed him, and he died a broken king only seven days after the birth of his daughter, Mary, who became queen of Scots.

Significant events of James V's reign

- 1532 The Court of Session, central court of civil justice, is established.
- 1537 James marries Madeleine de Valois, but she dies shortly afterwards.
- 1538 James marries Mary of Guise.
- 1542 Mary of Guise gives birth to Mary, later Mary, Queen of Scots.
- 1542 The Scots invade England and are routed at the Battle of Solway Moss.

James VI of Scots and I of England (1566–1625) king of Scotland (1567–1625) and of England and Ireland (1603–25). The only son of Mary, Queen of Scots, and Henry Stuart, Lord Darnley. When James succeeded Elizabeth I as king of England, he had already been on the throne in Scotland for thirty-six years. He was first crowned at Stirling, aged thirteen months, and at his coronation endured a lengthy sermon from John Knox. His childhood was passed under the direction of the earl of Mar and the tuition of the great scholar George Buchanan. He had much trouble with his nobles, a party of whom made him captive at Ruthven Castle in 1582, but a counter party soon set him free. These disputes were connected with the ecclesiastical controversies of the period, James, from his youth onwards, being determined to destroy the power of the Presbyterian clergy. When his mother's life was in danger, he did not exert himself to any great extent on her behalf and when her execution took place he did not venture upon war. In 1589 he married Princess Anne of Denmark. James took an active interest in the North Berwick witch trials of 1591, in which several witches were accused of provoking a storm in the Firth of Forth as the king was returning from Denmark with his bride. It was probably the earl of Bothwell, an enemy of the king, who was behind these events. Bothwell was imprisoned but later escaped. He had little time for the nobility of Scotland, preferring instead to be a king of the commoners. He was also a firm believer in the Divine Right of Kings, the doctrine that states that kings are appointed by God and are therefore unanswerable to other men.

In 1603 James succeeded to the crown of England on the death of Elizabeth, and proceeded to London taking with him his favourites from the Scottish court, which somewhat alienated the English courtiers. One of the early events of his reign was the Gunpowder Plot, in which a group of fanatical Catholics hoped to blow up the king and all his ministers. He soon allowed his lofty notions of divine right to become known, got into trouble with parliament, and afterwards endeavoured to rule as an absolute monarch, levying taxes and demanding loans in an arbitrary manner. In matters of religion he succeeded in establishing Episcopacy in Scotland and forced English Puritans to conform to the Anglican Church. He also began the plantation of Scottish and English settlers in Ireland (1611) and curbed the powers of Catholic nobles who objected to their country being treated like a colony.

James was man of peace, however, and sought at all costs to keep his people out of war. This led to a decline of the navy and a loss of influence overseas as the government did little to support the new colonies. In 1621 the Thirty Years' War of Religion, which involved almost all Europe, began, and one of the Protestant leaders was the German prince who had married James's daughter Elizabeth (this alliance also ultimately brought the present royal family to the throne). He wished to marry his son, Charles, Prince of Wales (later Charles I), to a Spanish princess, but this was blocked by parliament, and war was declared against Spain.

James, although possessed of some good abilities, had many defects as a ruler, prominent among them being subservience to unworthy favourites. He was also vain, pedantic and gross in his tastes and habits. He was well educated and enjoyed being called 'the British Solomon'. Henri IV of France is thought to have coined his more enduring nickname, 'the wisest fool in Christendom'. In his reign the authorized translation of the Bible was executed. He died at Hertfordshire of kidney failure, leaving seven children.

Significant events of James's reign

- 1591 The North Berwick witch trials.
- 1603 James VI of Scotland ascends the English throne to become James I of England.
- 1605 The Gunpowder Plot is thwarted. Shakespeare writes *King Lear*.
- 1607 The English Parliament rejects proposals to unite Scotland and England. The colony of Virginia is founded.
- 1611 Publication of the Authorized Version of the Bible.
- 1614 James dissolves the 'Addled Parliament', which failed to pass any legislation.
- 1616 Shakespeare dies.
- 1618 Accused of treason, Sir Walter Raleigh is put to death.
- 1620 The Pilgrim Fathers reach Cape Cod in the *Mayflower* and found New Plymouth.

John (1167–1216) king of England (1199–1216). The youngest son of Henry II by Eleanor of Aquitaine. Being left without any particular provision, he got the name of 'Sans Terre' or 'Lackland', but his brother, Richard I, on his accession conferred large possessions on him. He obtained the crown on the death of Richard in 1199, although the French provinces of Anjou, Touraine and Maine declared for his nephew, Arthur of Brittany, who was linearly the rightful heir, then with the king of France. A war ensued in which John recovered the rebelling provinces and received homage from Arthur. In 1201 some disturbances again broke out in France, and the young Arthur, who had joined the malcontents, was captured and confined in the castle of Falaise and afterwards in that of Rouen, where he died. John was universally suspected of his nephew's death, and the states of Brittany summoned him before Philip of France to answer the charge of murder. In the war that followed John lost Normandy, Anjou, Maine and Touraine.

In 1205 his great quarrel with Pope Innocent III began regarding the election of the archbishop of Canterbury, for which post the pope had nominated Stephen Langton, but John refused to recognize him. The result was that Innocent III laid the whole kingdom under an interdict, and in 1211 issued a bull deposing John. Philip of France was commissioned to execute the decree and was already preparing an expedition when John made abject submission to the pope, even agreeing to hold his kingdom as a vassal of him (1213). John's arbitrary proceedings led to the rising of his nobles, and he was compelled to sign the Magna Carta, or Great Charter, in 1215. This charter set out to curtail abuses of royal power in matters of taxation, religion, justice and foreign policy. But John did not mean to keep the agreement, and, obtaining a bull from the pope annulling the charter, he raised an army of mercenaries and waged war. The barons, in despair, offered the crown of England to Prince Louis of France, who accordingly landed at Sandwich in 1216, and, after capturing the Tower of London, was received as lawful sovereign. The issue was still doubtful when John was taken ill and died of dysentery at Newark later that year.

Significant events of John's reign

- 1202 Wars with the French king, Philip II, begin.
- 1206 Pope Innocent III nominates Stephen Langton as archbishop of Canterbury.
- 1208 The pope's interdict prohibits almost all church services in England.
- 1209 John is excommunicated.
- 1212 Pope proclaims that John is not the rightful king of England.
- 1213 John gives way to the pope's demands.
- 1214 French defeat the English at Bouvines. English barons meet at Bury St Edmunds.
- 1215 John reluctantly signs the Magna Carta. Civil war breaks out when the pope declares that John need not heed the terms of the Magna Carta.
- 1216 The French join the fray at the invitation of the barons.

KL

Kenneth (I) mac-Alpin (d.858) king of Scots (841–858) and Picts (*c*.844–858). The son of Alpin, king of Dalriadan Scots, he united the kingdoms of Scots and Picts by exploiting a period of Pictish weakness due in part to devastating Scandinavian attacks on Pictland, although he also had a claim to the Pictish kingship by maternal descent. An ambitious and warlike ruler, Kenneth had completely conquered the Picts by 846. In order to eliminate any opposition to his rule it is thought that he asked the heads of important Pict families to dine with him around this time and had them killed when they fell into a concealed pit he had had dug behind the benches on which they were invited to sit.

He moved the centre of his kingdom as part of the general Dalriadic migration into the lands of the Picts, possibly installing the new centre at Forteviot, the old Pictish centre. In 849 he moved the relics of St Columba to Dunkeld and either founded or enlarged a religious centre there. Kenneth's reign was not a peaceful one, and he made frequent raids on Lothian and on the Saxons and was raided by Britons, Danes and Vikings.

Kenneth also established Scone as a royal and holy centre and made it the place for the inauguration of kings of Alba, as the kingdom was then known. Although it cannot be said with any certainty, it has been suggested that it was he who brought the symbolic Stone of Destiny to Scone. On his death through illness he was succeeded by his brother, Donald I.

Kenneth II (d.995) king of Scots (971–995). The son of Duff, he succeeded Cuilean in 971. During his reign he was able to secure Lothian as part of his kingdom by recognizing Edgar, king of England, as his overlord. He was murdered in 995 under mysterious circumstances following a dispute regarding the succession. He was succeeded by Constantine III, but his son later took the throne as Malcolm II.

Kenneth III (d.1005) king of Scots (997–1005). He ruled jointly with his son, Giric II, and both were killed in battle at Monzieviard by Malcolm II, who then ascended the throne.

Kineth (d.843) king of the Picts (842–843). The son of Uurad, he is thought to have killed his brother Bred to take the throne. He in turn was usurped and murdered by Brude, his nephew.

Lywelyn ap Gruffydd (Llwelyn the Last) (d.1282) prince of Wales (*c*.1260–1282). The eldest son of Gruffydd, he styled himself 'Prince of Wales' and received recognition from Henry III of England in 1267. His kingdom embraced Gwynedd, Powys and Deheubarth but after refusing to do homage to Edward I in 1276, he lost all his lands except the western part of Gwynedd. His brother provoked another war in 1282, and Llywelyn died in a skirmish at Builth. He is buried at the monastery of Cyn Hir. He was succeeded by his son Daffydd ap Llywelyn.

Llywelyn ap Iorwerth (Llwelyn the Great) (d.1240) king of Gwynedd (1202–40). He reunited the formerly divided kingdom of Gwynedd in 1202 and came to dominate all other Welsh princes. He successfully evaded the attempts of King John to subdue him and exploited a civil war in England to take control of Powys. He was recognized as Wales's strongest ruler in 1218 and gave himself the title of Lord of Snowdon.

Ludeca king of Mercia (827). An ealdorman who succeeded Beornwulf, he reigned briefly before being killed in battle along with five of his earls.

Lulach (1032–58) king of Scots (1057–58). He was installed as king on the death of Macbeth, his stepfather. Within seven months he was ambushed and killed by Malcolm III at Strathbogie. His death was the result of an ongoing dispute as to which branch of the royal line should legitimately hold the throne of Scotland. Lulach's descendents, including his son Malsnechtai, would continue to challenge the mac-Malcolm dynasty's legitimacy without success for a century.

MN

Macbeth (1005–57) king of Scots (1040–57). A nephew of Malcolm II, he was one of three kings who came to dominate 11th-century Scotland. He was heriditary *mormaer* (ruler) of Moray and slew his cousin, King Duncan, at Bathgowan, near Elgin, in 1040, and proclaimed himself king. In 1050 he is said to have gone on a pilgrimage to Rome. At the death of their father, the sons of Duncan had taken refuge—Malcolm (later Malcolm III) with his uncle Siward, Earl of Northumbria, and Donald Bane in the Hebrides. With Siward's aid, Malcolm invaded Scotland in 1054. A battle was fought at Dunsinane, but it was not until 1057 that Macbeth was finally defeated and slain at Lumphanan in Aberdeenshire. He was married to Gruach, granddaughter of Kenneth III, and his stepson, Lulach, reigned briefly after his death before being killed by Malcolm who then claimed the throne.

The legends that gradually gathered round the name of Macbeth were collected by John of Fordun and Hector Boece, and reproduced by Holinshed in his *Chronicle*, where they were found by Shakespeare.

Mael Sechnaill I (d.862) high king of Ireland. His reign was threatened in 861 when his rival, Aed Finnliath, joined with the Norse kings. He survived their attacks but died the following year and Aed became high king.

Mael Sechnaill II (d.1023) high king of Ireland (1002–23, interrupted). He abdicated in favour of Brian Boru in 1014 following his defeat at the Battle of Clontarf. Brian Boru was killed in his tent shortly after the battle, however, and Mael Sechnaill was able to regain the title. Following Mael Sechnaill's death a civil war broke out over the succession and his sons were unable to secure the high kingship. This indirectly ended royal rule in Ireland, as for over 150 years no one could unite the various kingdoms.

Malcolm I (d.954) king of Scots (943–954). The son of Donald II, he succeeded to the throne on the abdication of his cousin Constantine II. His kingdom was constantly under threat from hostile Norwegian forces both to the north (in Caithness and the Northern Isles under Erik Bloodaxe) and to the south. He was granted Cumbria by Edmund in return for recognition of Edmund's sovereignty. He attempted to stamp his authority on the northern lands but without success and was killed in battle by the men of Moray. He was succeeded by his nephew, Indulf.

Malcolm II (*c*.954–1034) king of Scots (1005–34). The son of Kenneth II, he ascended the throne after killing his cousin, Kenneth III, who contested the inheritance in battle at Monzievaird. On Earl Sigurd of Orkney's death in 1014, at the hands of Brian Boru at Clontarf in Ireland, his son, Thorfinn, became a vassal of Scotland and his lands in Sutherland and Caithness came under Malcolm's control. In the early years of his reign Malcolm set about attempting to annexe Bernicia and mounted raids on Northumbria. A victory over the Angles with the assistance of Owen, king of Strathclyde, at Carham on the Tweed in 1018 secured Lothian as part of Scotland. With Lothian and Strathclyde (probably made a subkingdom during Owen's reign) now under his control, Malcolm had extended his kingdom to include the old lands of Alba and the English-speaking lands to the south. When Owen died childless in 1016 Malcolm's grandson, Duncan, succeeded him as king of Strathclyde. Malcolm II had no sons, and on his death Duncan I became king of all Scotland.

Significant events of Malcolm II's reign

- 1005 Kenneth III killed at Monzievaird.
- 1014 Sutherland and Caithness secured as part of Scotland.
- 1016 Duncan installed as king of Strathclyde.
- 1018 Battle of Carham secures the Lothians as part of Scotland.

Malcolm III Canmore (1031–93) king of Scots (1058–93). The 'Canmore' of his title means 'big head' or 'chief'. During the reign of Macbeth, young Malcolm was under the protection of his uncle, Siward, and spent his early years in exile in Northumberland. He then visited the court of Edward the Confessor, and with the English king's aid Malcolm took the Scottish crown with the defeat of Macbeth at Dunsinane Hill in 1054 and the subsequent killing of both Macbeth (at Lumphanan in 1057) and Macbeth's stepson Lulach, who had assumed the crown on his stepfather's death. Malcolm married twice. His first wife, Ingibiorg, widow of Earl Thorfinn II of Orkney, died in 1069, leaving a son who would later become Duncan II. Malcolm then married Margaret, sister of the Anglo-Saxon prince, Edgar the Aetheling, who had fled the Norman invasion with her brother. Margaret had six sons by Malcolm, three of whom would become kings—Edgar, Alexander I and David I. Under Margaret's influence, the Scottish court accepted English language and customs as the norm. The queen, an educated woman and devout Christian, encouraged religious reform, and her piety would lead to her canonization in 1249.

The king and queen welcomed, and indeed encouraged, the influx of refugees from William the Conqueror's regime, which was a dangerous policy as the Norman king could see the potential menace of the pretender, Edgar the Aetheling, to the English throne residing in a hostile nation whose monarch was married to his sister. Malcolm had already made incursions into Northumbria and Cumbria (in 1069 and in 1070) when, in 1072, William invaded Scotland. William forced the Scots king to accept the Treaty of Abernethy whereby Malcolm was obliged to acknowledge the English king as overlord. Malcolm's son Duncan was taken to England as a hostage. However, in spite of the treaty, Malcolm once again marched into England, only to be soundly defeated (1079). In 1091 Malcolm was again forced to submit to an English king, William I's successor, William II. Malcolm met his death in an ambush in 1093 on yet another expedition into England and was not long survived by his wife, Margaret, who, already ill, died four days after hearing of her husband's death. Malcolm, buried with his wife at Dunfermline, was succeeded by his brother, Donald III. His reign began more than two centuries' almost unbroken rule by the house of Dunkeld.

Malcolm IV (the Maiden) (1141–65) king of Scots (1153–65). The grandson of David I and eldest of the three sons of Henry, the earl of Northumberland, he ascended the throne on David I's death aged only twelve. He had been proclaimed as heir before David's death and had toured the country to ensure that his succession was acceptable. At first the kingdom he inherited was peaceful, but there was resentment of David's Normanizing policies, and this carried over into Malcolm's reign. In 1157 Henry II took back the territories of northern England (Northumberland, Cumberland and Westmorland) that had been granted to David I. Malcolm nevertheless went to France the following year to fight for Henry (for which he received a knighthood), and this was taken by many as a sign of unacceptable subordination. In the west the Lord of the Isles, Somerled, founder of the Mac-donald clan, tried to extend the boundaries of his territory and sailed up the Clyde, but Malcolm was able to defeat him. To the north the rebellious men of Moray and Galloway were also contained.

Malcolm, nicknamed 'the Maiden' because he did not marry, was probably the last Gaelic-speaking monarch. Weakened by the exigences of kingship, he died in his early twenties at Jedburgh Abbey and was succeeded by his younger brother, William I (the Lion).

Margaret (Maid of Norway) (1283–90) queen of Scotland (1285–90). The daughter of Erik II of Norway and Margaret, daughter of Alexander III, Margaret was declared heiress to the Scottish throne in 1284 whilst still an infant, all her grandfather's other children having died. When Alexander died accidentally two years later, Margaret, aged only three, being the sole surviving descendant of the mac-Malcolm line, became queen. The Treaty of Brigham (1290) arranged the marriage of Margaret and Edward of Caenarvon, son and heir of Edward I of England, and guaranteed Scotland's separate existence from England, although the two nations were to be jointly ruled. Margaret set sail from Norway in September 1290 but died a short time after reaching Orkney, never setting foot on the Scottish mainland. The Treaty of Brigham was naturally negated by Margaret's death and, with no legitimate successor to the past three generations of Scottish kings, bitter disputes over the succession ensued. During the interregnum the claim to the throne was contested by many 'competitors', the main rivals being John Balliol and Robert Bruce, Earl of Annandale. After conferences at Norham and Berwick in 1291, Edward I, the English king, found in favour of John Balliol, who was crowned king of Scots at Scone in 1292.

Mary I (1516–58) queen of England and Ireland (1553–58). The only surviving daughter of Henry VIII by Catherine of Aragon, Mary was declared illegitimate when she was born but was restored to her rights when the succession was finally settled in 1544. The first undisputed female sovereign of England, she ascended the throne in early 1553, after an abortive attempt to set her aside in favour of Lady Jane Grey. One of her first measures was the reinstatement of the Roman Catholic prelates who had been superseded in the reign of her half-brother, Edward VI. Her marriage to Philip II of Spain, united as it was with a complete restoration of Catholic worship, produced much discontent. Insurrections broke out under Cave in Devon, and Wyatt in Kent, which, although suppressed, formed sufficient excuse for the imprisonment of her sister Elizabeth in the Tower, and the execution of Lady Jane Grey and her husband, Lord Guildford Dudley. England was declared to be reconciled to the pope, and *De Heretico Comurendo*, the Act against heretics was revived. Nearly 300 people perished at the stake, including the bishops Cranmer, Latimer and Ridley. The daily burnings repulsed the people, however, and the martyrs who perished in the fires of Smithfield in London, where most of the burnings were held, secured the triumph of Protestantism in England.

The people were also angry that England, once a powerful independent power, appeared to have become little more than a province of Spain. Philip II dragged England into a war with France which ended in the humiliating loss of Calais in 1558 after it had been held by England for over 200 years; and Spain, with its detested Inquisition, replaced France as the enemy of the English people. This disgrace told acutely upon Mary's disordered health, and she died shortly afterwards. Feasting and dancing in the streets followed the death of the hated 'Bloody Mary' and the announcement of the succession of her Protestant half-sister, Elizabeth.

Significant events of Mary's reign

- 1554 The announcement of Mary's intention to marry Philip II of Spain provokes an unsuccessful rebellion.
  Lady Jane Grey and her husband are put to death.
  Mary marries Philip II of Spain.
  Mary repeals Edward VI's religious laws and the persecution of Protestants begins.
- 1556 Thomas Cranmer, archbishop of Canterbury, is burned as a heretic.
- 1557 England enters into war with France.
- 1558 England loses Calais.

Mary II (1662–94) queen of England, Scotland and Ireland (1689–94). The elder daughter of James, Duke of York (afterwards James II) by his wife Anne Hyde, daughter of Lord Clarendon, she married in 1677 her cousin William, Prince of Orange. She was a popular princess in Holland and when the Revolution dethroned her father, she was declared joint possessor of the throne with William, on whom all the administration of the government devolved. This unique arrangement lasted until her death, after which William ruled by himself.

During the absence of William in Ireland in 1690, and during his various visits to the Continent, Mary managed at home with extreme prudence and, unlike her husband, was well liked by the people. She died childless and is buried in Westminster Abbey.

Significant events of Mary II's reign

- 1689 Toleration Act grants freedom of worship to Protestant dissenters.
  A Scottish revolt is crushed.
  Bill of Rights limits regal power.
  In Ireland Catholic forces loyal to James II besiege Londonderry.
- 1690 James is defeated at the Battle of the Boyne.
- 1691 Treaty of Limerick allows freedom of worship for Catholics.
- 1692 The Massacre of Glencoe.
- 1694 The Bank of England is established.

Mary, Queen of Scots (1542–87) queen of Scotland (1542–67). The ill-fated Mary Stuart was born at Linlithgow Palace, the daughter of James V by Mary of Lorraine, a princess of the family of Guise. Her father dying when she was only seven days old, Mary was crowned at Stirling and the regency was, after some dispute, vested in the Earl of Arran (from 1554 in her mother, Mary of Guise). In 1543 the infant was betrothed to the six-year-old Edward, son and heir of Henry VIII, but that agreement was soon repudiated by the Scots. In retaliation Henry invaded Scotland (1544 and 1545) in what became known as the 'Rough Wooing', and following the defeat of the Scots at Pinkie, his armies occupied large parts of southeastern Scotland. Mary was sent to the island priory of Inchmahome for safety, and the Scots asked the French for help. It was duly given on the condition that Mary be sent to France, and in 1558 she was married to the dauphin, afterwards Francis II.

Mary had made a secret agreement before the marriage, however, that, should she die without issue, her kingdom should fall to the French crown. Her husband died seventeen months after his succession to the crown, in December 1560, and in the minority of his brother, Charles IX, power rested with Catherine de' Medici, the dowager queen and Mary's mother-in-law. She was not on very good terms with Mary, and three years after the accession of Elizabeth to the English throne, the widowed queen returned to Scotland.

Mary was heir presumptive to the English crown, and Roman Catholics who did not accept the legality of Henry VIII's marriage to Elizabeth's mother, Anne Boleyn, thought that Mary had a better claim to the throne. But when she returned to Scotland, she found that the influence of the Presbyterians was paramount in her kingdom. Although inclined to have Roman Catholicism again set up in Scotland, after a vain attempt to influence the leader of the Scottish Reformation, John Knox, she resigned herself to circumstances, quietly allowed her half-brother, the Protestant Earl of Moray, to assume the position of first minister, surrounded herself with a number of other Protestant advisers, and dismissed the greater part of her French courtiers. She even gave these ministers her active support in various measures that had the effect of strengthening the Presbyterian party, but she still continued to have

Mass performed in her own private chapel at Holyrood Palace, in Edinburgh. At first her subjects were quiet, she herself was popular, and her court was one of the most brilliant in Europe.

The calamities of Mary began with her marriage to her cousin, Lord Darnley. He was a Roman Catholic and immediately after the marriage the Earl of Moray and other of the Protestant lords combined against the new order of things. They were compelled to take refuge in England, and the popularity of Mary began to decline. In addition to this, Darnley proved a weak and worthless profligate, and almost entirely alienated the queen by his complicity in the brutal murder of her secretary, David Rizzio, although a reconciliation seemed to be effected between them about the time of the birth of their son, afterwards James VI of Scotland and I of England in 1556.

About the close of the same year, however, Darnley withdrew from the court, and in the meantime the earl of Bothwell had risen high in the queen's favour. When the young prince James was baptised at Stirling Castle in December 1566, Bothwell did the honours of the occasion, and Darnley, James's father, was not even present. Once more, however, an apparent reconciliation took place between the king and queen. Darnley had fallen ill and was in Glasgow under the care of his father. Mary visited him and took measures for his removal to Edinburgh, where he was lodged in a house called Kirk o' Field, close to the city wall. He was there tended by the queen herself but during her absence at Holyrood the house in which Darnley lay was blown up by gunpowder.

The circumstances surrounding the crime were very imperfectly investigated, but popular suspicion unequivocally pointed to Bothwell as the ringleader, and the queen herself was suspected, suspicion becoming still stronger when she was carried off by Bothwell, with little show of resistance, to his castle of Dunbar, and secretly married to him. A number of the nobles now banded together against Bothwell, who succeeded in collecting a force, but at Carberry Hill, where the armies met, his army melted away. The queen was forced to surrender herself to her insurgent nobles, Bothwell making his escape to Dunbar, then to the Orkney Islands, and finally to Denmark.

The confederate nobles first conveyed the queen to Edinburgh and then to Loch Leven Castle, where she was placed in the custody of Lady Douglas, mother of the earl of Moray. A few days later, a casket containing eight letters and some poetry, all said to be in the handwriting of the queen, fell into the hands of the confederates. The letters, which have come down to us only in the form of a translation, show, if they are genuine, that the writer was herself a party to the murder of Darnley. They were held to afford unmistakable evidence of the queen's guilt, and she was forced to sign a document renouncing the crown of Scotland in favour of her infant son and appointing the earl of Moray regent during her son's minority. After remaining nearly a year in captivity, Mary succeeded in escaping from Loch Leven, and, assisted by the few friends who remained loyal to her, made an effort for the recovery of her power.

Defeated by the regent's forces at the Battle of Langside, she fled to England four days later and wrote to Elizabeth entreating protection and a personal interview. This the latter refused to grant until Mary should have cleared herself from the charges laid against her by her subjects. At the end of 1568, commissioners of Elizabeth at York and Westminster heard representatives of Mary and her opponents, with a view as to whether or not she should be restored. No decision was formally made, and for one reason or another Elizabeth never did grant Mary an interview, preferring instead to keep her in more or less close captivity in England, where her life was passed in a succession of intrigues for achieving her escape.

For more than eighteen years Mary continued to be the prisoner of Elizabeth, and in that time the place of her imprisonment was frequently changed, her final prison being Fotheringay Castle in Northamptonshire. During this time there were a series of allegations that she was involved in pro-Catholic plots to depose Elizabeth. She was at last accused of being implicated in the Babington Plot against Elizabeth's life and, having been tried by a court of Elizabeth's appointing, was in late 1586 condemned to be executed. There was a long delay before Elizabeth signed the warrant, but her hand had at last been forced, and this was done in February the following year. Mary received the news with great serenity and was beheaded a week later at Fotheringay.

Authorities are more agreed as to the attractions, talents and accomplishments of Mary Stuart than as to her character. Contemporary writers who saw her unite in testifying to her beauty and the charm of her manners and address. She was witty in conversation, and ready in dispute. In her trial for alleged complicity in the Babington Plot she held her ground against the ablest statesman and lawyers of England. She was buried at Peterborough Cathedral until transferred in 1612 by her son to Henry VII's Chapel at Westminster.

Significant events of Mary's reign

• 1548 Mary is sent to France.

- 1554 Mary of Guise becomes Regent.
- 1558 Mary marries the Dauphin Francis
- 1559 The Scottish Reformation begins with John Knox's return from exile.
  Mary becomes queen of France on the accession of her husband (now Francis II of France).
- 1560 Francis II dies.
- 1561 Mary returns to Scotland.
- 1565 Mary marries Lord Darnley, her cousin.
- 1566 David Rizzio, Mary's secretary, is murdered.
- 1567 Lord Darnley is murdered.
  Mary is married to JamesHepburn, Earl of Bothwell.
  A rebellion by Scottish lords forces Mary's abdication.

Matilda (Empress Maud) (1102–67) queen of England (1141, uncrowned). The daughter of Henry I of England and Matilda, the daughter of Malcolm III of Scotland, she was married to Henry V, the Holy Roman Emperor, at the age of twelve and ruled Germany as empress until the death of her husband in 1125. She married Geoffrey Plantagenet of Anjou in 1128 and gave birth to three children, including Henry Plantagenet who would later become Henry II of England.

She was named as heir to the English throne when Henry I's only son, William, met his death on the *White Ship*, which was smashed onto rocks when returning to England from Normandy in 1120. Henry I had much persuading to do to make his barons accept his daughter as heir, twice calling his nobles together to obtain their oath to stand by Matilda. However, the existence of another potential claimant to the throne was to produce complications for the succession. Stephen, whose mother, Adela of Flanders, was the daughter of William the Conqueror and whose father was Stephen of Blois, the leader of the Norman barons with substantial estates in England, believed that he was the rightful male heir, his elder brother having set aside any claim he may have had. On the death of Henry I, Stephen, who had sworn loyalty to Matilda along with the rest of the nobility of England, hurried from Blois to claim the throne and, with the aid of his brother Henry, Bishop of Winchester, was installed as king. However, the early support that Stephen enjoyed soon evaporated when it became clear that he was not as effective at government as Henry I had been. Many barons who wished to increase their power and influence began to use Stephen's weakness as king to do so, and some remembered their sworn allegiance to Matilda. Stephen also began to lose the support of the Church. In 1138 David I of Scotland invaded northern England on Matilda's behalf but was defeated at Northallerton at the Battle of the Standard. Civil war broke out in England soon afterwards. In 1139, while her husband invaded Normandy, Matilda invaded England and was welcomed by a grouping of barons who had switched their support from Stephen, including Robert of Gloucester, an illegitimate son of Henry I, who was to prove a useful ally. Matilda set up a base in the West Country and at Bristol, Robert of Gloucester's stronghold, and from there further fermented the general rebellion against Stephen's rule. By 1141 the bishop of Winchester had joined her cause, and in that same year Matilda defeated the king's forces at the Battle of Lincoln and imprisoned Stephen in Bristol Castle. Henry of Winchester proclaimed at a council that divine intervention had indicated God's will that Matilda be queen of England and Normandy. The queen then travelled to London to claim her crown. However, her behaviour when she arrived there did nothing to endear her to the people. She displayed the fiercely arrogant side of her nature to the Londoners and the nobility, ally or otherwise alike, and imposed a heavy tax on the city. She fell out with Henry of Winchester, which led him to abandon her cause and retreat to his palace. Matilda, having come so close to gaining the crown, was chased out, the Londoners demanding Stephen's release. Matilda laid siege to the bishop of Winchester at Wolvesey Palace, hoping to regain his support by force, but was herself besieged by Stephen's queen, Matilda of Boulogne. Matilda escaped but Robert of Gloucester was captured. This was a major blow to Matilda's ambitions as Robert was her military leader. Stephen was released in exchange for Robert, but with Stephen restored as king, Matilda's best chance of claiming the throne had passed. The fighting continued but was now more sporadic in nature and gradually diminished in ferocity over the next few years. Matilda was almost captured at her stronghold at Oxford in December 1142 but managed to escape by stealing away into the winter's night, travelling over six miles on foot in her nightgown to Wallingford, where she obtained a horse. Stephen defeated her forces at the Battle of Farringdon in 1145, but she still fought on, even although her support was growing ever smaller.

The following year Matilda finally gave up the fight and left England for Normandy, which her husband had conquered in her absence. Matilda had failed in her attempt on the English throne but her son, Henry Plantagenet, would be more successful. After invading England in 1153, Henry and Stephen came to an agreement under which Henry would succeed to the throne on the king's death. Stephen died the following year, and Henry II was duly crowned.

Nechton (d.*c*.724) king of Picts (706–724). The brother of Bridei IV, he embraced Christianity and abdicated, leaving four rivals to contest the succession.

Niall of the Nine Hostages (d.405) high king of Ireland (379–405). A semi-legendary figure, he gained his name by holding nine members of different ruling dynasties hostage at the same time to secure his position as high king. He was succeeded by a son, Loeguire, who controlled much of northern and central Ireland in the year of St Patrick's mission (432). Two of Niall's other sons founded the kingdom of Aileach in 400 which had 52 known sovereigns until 1170.

Nunna king of Sussex (*c*.710–*c*.725). He was an underking of Ine of Wessex and participated in his campaign of 710 to bring Kent under his control. He eventually freed his kingdom from subordination and offered refuge to exiles from Wessex. He made land grants to the Bishop of Selsey between 714 and 720, and one of his charters is the first to mention Sussex formally.

O

Octa (d.*c*.540) king of Kent (*c*.512–*c*.540). The grandson of Hengest, he succeeded his father, Aesc.

Oengus (d.761) king of Picts (728–761). He claimed the throne during the civil war that erupted after Nechtan abdicated in 724. He killed his cousin, Drest, one of the four claimants, in 729, and took control of the kingdom of the Dalriadan Scots in 736. He attempted to overrun Strathclyde in 750, but was defeated at Mugdock, near Glasgow. His troubled reign lasted for over thirty years.

Offa (1) (d.*c*.720) king of Essex (709). The son of Sigeherd, he ruled for less than a year before making a pilgrimage to Rome with Cenred of Mercia and Swafred. He became a monk and died there after founding a hostel for English pilgrims just outside Rome.

Offa (2) (d.791) king of Mercia (757–796). A descendant of Penda's younger brother, he defeated his rival claimants to the throne of Mercia in the civil war that followed the death of Ethelbald. After an initial period of unrest that saw the Welsh gain territory, he established Mercian superiority in all England south of the Humber. Rebellions in Kent led to a ten year period (775–785) in which the independence of that kingdom was re-established. He eventually succeeded in conquering Kent, however, and thereafter it was no more than a province of Mercia. By conquest and marriage he reduced Wessex and East Anglia to almost the same status. He issued the first major royal coinage and built a 120–mile long defensive wall to protect Mercia from Welsh attacks, which became known as Offa's Dyke. He was also the first king of Mercia to be recognized as a significant power in Europe, and in 789 Charlemagne asked for one of his daughters as a wife for his son. Offa died at the height of his powers and was succeeded by his son. Concerned that the succession would be disputed, he had his son, Egfrith, consecrated as king before his death. Unfortunately his last wish to secure the dynasty was not fulfilled as Egfrith outlived his father by only a few months.

Olaf the White king of Dublin (853–*c*.854). He styled himself 'king of the Northmen of all Ireland and Britain' after uniting all the Viking leaders in 853.

Olaf the Red (b.*c*.920) king of Dublin (*c*.945–980). Following Ethelstan's death in 939, Olaf invaded Northumbria and compelled his successor, Edmund, to cede him an area of land in the northeast Midlands known as the Five Boroughs. He also gained land in Bernicia, and Edmund had to appeal to the Scots to assist him in keeping Olaf's advances in check. He disputed control of York with his cousin, Erik Bloodaxe, who was finally driven out by Edred in 952. He was the longest reigning king of Dublin.

Olaf Guthfrithson (d.941) king of Dublin. He was an ally of the Scots under Constantine II at the Battle of Brunanburgh in 937. He died in an obscure battle whilst raiding lowland Scotland.

Osbald (d.796) king of Northumbria (796). He was one of the conspirators who killed Ethelred in 796 but reigned for only a few weeks before being ousted by Eardwulf.

Osbert (d.867) king of Northumbria (850–865). He was expelled in favour of his brother, Aelle. Both were killed in a joint attack on York, which had been seized by the Norse while they were fighting over the throne.

Osmund king of Sussex (*c*.765–770). He was an under-king of the powerful Offa of Mercia, who annexed the kingdom in 772.

Osred I (d.716) king of Northumbria (705–716). The young successor of Aldfrith in 705, he earned a reputation as a tyrant and was murdered.

Osred II king of Northumbria (788–790). A nephew of Elfwold, he was imprisoned by Ethelred I and later escaped to the Isle of Man.

Osric (d.729) king of Northumbria (718–729). He was succeeded by his nephew, Ceolwulf.

Oswald (St Oswald) (605–642) king of Northumbria (634–642). The brother of Enfrith, he lived in the Hebrides during Edwin's reign. On his return he established himself as *Bretwalda*, or overlord, of all the Anglo-Saxon kings with his victory over Cadwallon of Gwynedd. He then tried to check the advance of Mercia under King Penda and died fighting him on the Welsh Marches. He was a popular figure and gained the nickname 'Bright Blade' for his abilities in battle. He was also a devout Christian and gave Bishop Aiden the island of Lindisfarne. He was the first Anglo-Saxon king to be canonized; 5 August is his feast day.

Oswin (d.651) king of Deira (642–651). The son of Oswald, he contested the succession with his uncle, Oswy, and took Deira (southern Northumberland) as his kingdom. He was assassinated by his brother at Gilling in 651, and the two kingdoms of Deira and Bernicia were united.

Oswini (d.690) king of Kent (688–690). He ruled jointly with Suaebhard.

Oswulf (d.759) king of Northumbria (759). The son and successor of Edbert, he was killed by his own bodyguard within a year of coming to power.

Oswy (602–670) king of Northumbria (651–670). The brother of Oswald, his time as ruler saw the peak of Northumbrian power. After thirteen years ruling Bernicia in Mercia's shadow, he united his kingdom with Deira by assassinating the ruler, his nephew Oswin, at Gilling. He went on to defeat and kill the powerful Penda of Mercia and many of his under-kings in 655 on the flooded River Winwaed (near Leeds) to become *Bretwalda*, or overlord, of all the Anglo-Saxon kings. He also contributed to the development of religion in England by presiding over the Synod at Whitby in 664 that resolved many of the disputes between the Celtic and Roman Churches. His daughter Alchfled married Peada of Mercia but only after he was persuaded to convert to Christianity.

Owain Gwynedd (1100–1170) king of Gwynedd (1137 –70). He united the kings in the south to resist Henry II's advances into Wales in 1165. His son married Henry's illegitimate half-sister. He is buried in Bangor Cathedral.

Owen (the Bald) (d.*c*.1018) king of Strathclyde. Probably the last king of Strathclyde, he was an ally of Malcolm II of Scotland, whom he helped defeat Earl Uhtred of Northumbria at the Battle of Carham on the River Tweed (1018). It is thought that by this time Strathclyde was a subkingdom of Scotland and Owen only a vassal king.

P

Peada (d.656) king of Middle Anglia (653–656). The youngest son of Penda, he was made an under-king of Middle Anglia, a kingdom created by his father in 653. He married Alchfled, the daughter of Oswy of Bernicia, who slew his father Penda in 655. Oswy gave Peada his daughter on the condition that he be converted to Christianity. In Bede's *Historia Ecclesiastica* it is claimed that Peada was murdered through the treachery of his wife.

Penda (577–655) king of Mercia (626–655). The son of Pybba, this pagan king established Mercian supremacy by defeating the West Saxons at Cirencester in 628 and the then all-powerful Edwin of Northumbria in 633 at Heathfield in Yorkshire with the help of Cadwallon of Gwynedd. It was under Penda that the Mercians evolved from being a tribe to being a powerful people and a formidable enemy. Penda's policy as king was to maintain the independence of his kingdom from Northumbrian domination. This led him to make two very destructive attacks on Northumbria as Oswy of Bernicia attempted to reunite the kingdom. Penda was finally defeated and killed during his last invasion at a battle on the flooded river at Winwaed by the much smaller army of Oswy. He features heavily in Bede's *Ecclesiastical History* where he is portrayed as an anti-hero pagan warrior king.

Prasutagus (d.60) king of the Iceni. He ruled the tribal kingdom as a client of the Romans but when he died his lands were seized, his daughters raped and his wife, Boadicea, flogged. Boadicea led a rebellion that was eventually quashed.

Pybba (d.*c*.606) king of Mercia (*c*.593–*c*.606). He is thought to have been the son of Creoda, the first king of the Mercians. His family of three sons and two daughters founded the Mercian dynasty.

R

Redwald king of East Anglia (*c.*593–*c.*617) and was considered to be *Bretwalda*, or overlord, of all the Anglo-Saxon kings in England. He helped Edwin win the Northumbrian throne in 617 by defeating and killing Ethelfrith at a battle on the River Idle on the Deiran frontier. He converted to Christianity but lapsed back to paganism, supposedly influenced by his wife. The pagan ship burial site at Sutton Hoo near Ipswich is thought to commemorate his death.

Rhodi Mawr (the Great) king of Gwynedd (844–878). He resisted several attacks by the Vikings and came to dominate Powys and Deheubarth in south Wales. He was eventually forced into exile in Ireland by the Vikings and killed in battle by a Mercian army on his return.

Richard I (Couer de Lion or the Lionheart) (1157–99) king of England (1189–99). The third son of Henry II by Eleanor of Aquitaine, he was born at Beaumont Palace, Oxford. In his youth, as duke of Aquitaine, Richard rebelled against his father, finally fighting alongside Philip II of France. On Henry's death at Chinon, Richard sailed to England where he was crowned at Westminster Abbey. Very much a warrior king, Richard spent only six months of his reign in England, and the principal events of his reign are connected with the Third Crusade against Muslim rule in the Holy Land in which he took part, uniting his forces with those of Philip of France. In the course of this crusade he conquered Cyprus, retook Acre and Jaffa and married the Princess Berengaria of Navarre whilst in Cyprus. He failed to take Jerusalem from Saladin but secured access for Christians to the holy places.

Richard left Palestine in 1192 and sailed for the Adriatic but was wrecked near Aguileia. On his way home through Germany he was seized (in spite of his disguise as a woodsman) by the duke of Austria, whom he had offended in Palestine, and was given up as prisoner to Emperor Henry VI. During his seventeen-month captivity his brother, John, headed an insurrection in England, which was suppressed by Richard when he returned in 1194 after the ransom securing his release had been paid. (One legend tells of Richard being found by his favourite minstrel, Blondel, who sang under the walls of each castle he passed on his way back from the crusades to England.)

Richard spent the rest of his life in Normandy fighting Philip II of France. He died of a shoulder wound received whilst besieging the castle of Châlus. Legend has it that he pardoned the archer who had fired the arrow that killed him. Richard, although utterly neglectful of his duties as a king, was a popular figure who owed his fame chiefly to his abilities as a military leader and to his personal bravery.

Significant events of Richard I's reign

- 1189 The Third Crusade is launched.
- 1191 Richard conquers Cyprus but fails to capture Jerusalem.
- 1192 Richard captures Jaffa and makes peace with Saladin.
  Richard is captured by Duke Leopold of Austria.
- 1194 A ransom is paid and Richard travels to England.
  Richard leaves England once more to fight Philip II of France.
- 1199 Richard lays siege to Chalus Castle.

Richard II (1367–1400) king of England and Wales (1377–99). The second and only surviving son of Edward the Black Prince and Joan of Kent and the grandson of Edward III, he was born at Bordeaux, succeeded his grandfather at the age of ten, and was crowned at Westminster Abbey. In the years of his minority the government was in the hands of his uncles, firstly John of Gaunt and later Thomas of Gloucester.

These were troubled times. The continuing cost of the Hundred Years' War (1337–1453), the aftermath of the Black Death and John of Gaunt's misrule culminated in the Peasants' Revolt of 1381. The insurrection, led by Wat Tyler at the head of upwards of 10,000 men, was a reaction to the imposition of a poll tax that weighed heavily on the poor whose wages were being held down by legislation (the Statute of Labourers, 1351, held wages and prices at 1340's levels). First introduced in 1377 and again in 1379, a higher tax was imposed in 1380, with officials being sent into the country to collect arrears. Violence against the tax collectors became common. On 13 June 1381 Tyler and his men reached London, leaving in their wake a trail of destruction, and made their demands of the king, which included the abolishment of serfdom and a pardon for all who had taken part in the rebellion. The young Richard agreed to these demands but, after the danger had passed, his government reneged on the agreement and almost two hundred peasants were killed in the reprisals that followed. Once the unpopular poll tax was abolished, however, Richard found the revolts of his nobles more difficult to contain. The Lords Appellant, under the duke of Gloucester, rebelled against the unpopular government of John of Gaunt and seized control in 1387. Many of Richard's advisers and personal friends were killed or banished. The Lords Appellant ruled until 1389, when the king, having reached his majority, took over the reins of power. Richard's revenge was exacted in 1397 with the killing or banishment of the Lords Appellant, including the exile of Henry of Bolingbroke, son of John of Gaunt. John of Gaunt, Duke of Lancaster, died in 1399, and his estates were confiscated by the king. These acts of despotism infuriated many of the nobles, and in that same year, while Richard was in Ireland attempting to subdue the western part of the country, Henry of Bolingbroke (now Duke of Lancaster on his father's death) landed in England and claimed the throne. Parliament accused Richard of having violated his coronation oaths, and he was deposed in favour of Bolingbroke. Thus the Commons became little more than a pawn in the hands of rival court factions.

The deposed king was imprisoned at Pontefract Castle, where he died the following year, either being murdered or starving himself to death. Richard was married twice, firstly in 1382 to Anne of Bohemia, daughter of Emperor Charles IV, who died in 1394, and then in 1396 to Isabella of France, daughter of King Charles VI (a marriage opposed by the duke of Gloucester), but neither marriage produced children. Something of a tyrant, Richard was nonetheless a feeble ruler who was unable to stamp his royal authority on the kingdom. A lover of the arts, Richard took a particular interest in literature and was a patron of Geoffrey Chaucer. He has also been credited with inventing the handkerchief. He was buried at Kings Langley, Hertfordshire, and reburied in Westminster Abbey in 1413.

Significant events of Richard II's reign

- 1381 The Peasants' Revolt.
- 1389 The Lords Appellant seize power.
  Richard assumes control of government.
- 1394 Richard attempts to conquer the west of Ireland.
- 1397 Reprisals are taken against the Lords Appellant and Bolingbroke is expelled.
  Chaucer writes *The Canterbury Tales*.
- 1398 Richard assumes absolute rule.
- 1399 Duke of Lancaster deposes Richard with the approval of Parliament.

Richard III (1452–85) king of England and Wales (1483–85). The last of the Yorkist kings, he was the youngest son of Richard Plantagenet, Duke of York, and Lady Cecily Neville. On the accession of his brother, Edward IV, he was created Duke of Gloucester, and during the early part of Edward's reign served him with courage and fidelity, taking part in the battles of 1471 against the Lancastrian supporters of Henry VI, the rival to Edward's throne. Marriage to Anne Neville, joint heiress of the earl of Warwick, brought him wealth, although disputes over the inherited estates also caused friction between himself and his younger brother, the duke of Clarence, who married Anne's sister.

From 1480 to 1482 Richard was lieutenant-general in the north, where he won acclaim for his successes over the Scots at Edinburgh and Berwick. On the death of Edward he was appointed Protector of the kingdom, and his nephew, the young Edward V, was declared king. Richard swore loyalty to the king but soon began to pursue his own ambitious schemes. The young king had grown up under the guidance of the powerful Woodville family with whom Richard had not been on good terms since his objection to the marriage of Edward IV to Elizabeth. Before the coronation could take place, therefore, he moved against the leading members of the family. Earl Rivers, the dowager queen's brother, and Sir Robert Grey, a son by her first husband, were arrested and beheaded at Pomfret. Lord Hastings, who was faithful to his young sovereign, was executed without trial in the Tower of London. With the support of the bishop of Bath and Wells Richard then declared that the young King Edward and his brother were illegitimate, as their father had been betrothed to another before he married their mother, and that Richard, as a result, had a legal title to the crown. The duke of Buckingham supported Richard, and parliament had little choice but to offer him the crown. The deposed king and his brother were, according to general belief, smothered in the Tower by order of their uncle. The duke of Buckingham later revolted against Richard, but this came to nothing as the rebellion was crushed and Buckingham beheaded.

Richard governed with vigour and ability and set about making financial and legal reforms, but he was not generally popular and faced increasing opposition to his slight claim to kingship. In 1485 Henry Tudor, Earl of Richmond, head of the house of Lancaster and rival claimant to the throne, landed with a small army at Milford Haven in west Wales and soon gathered support from the disaffected nobility. Richard met him with an army of 8,000 men at Bosworth Field in Leicestershire. Richmond's force was initially smaller, but Lord Stanley and Sir William Stanley joined with the Lancastrians and enabled him to win a decisive victory. Richard wore his crown on the field and is said to have come within a sword's length of Henry before being cut down. His body was subjected to indignities and afterwards buried in Leicester. Henry was crowned on the field. The Wars of the Roses were at last over, and the two warring houses united by the marriage of Henry VII to Edward IV's daughter, Elizabeth. The reconciliation was symbolized by the red and white rose of the House of Tudor.

Richard possessed courage as well as capacity, but his conduct showed cruelty, treachery and ambition. His personal defects were no doubt magnified by the character assassinations of historians loyal to the house of Tudor, but he remains one of the most maligned of English kings. Contrary to Shakespeare's portrayal, there is no evidence that he was a hunchback. He is buried at the Abbey of the Grey Friars in Leicester.

Significant events of Richard III's reign

- 1483 Edward V and his brother are murdered in the Tower.
  Buckingham's rebellion is crushed.
  The College of Arms, which regulates the issue of coats of arms, is established.
- 1484 William Caxton prints *Morte D'Arthur.*
  The Council of the North is established to govern the north of England.
- 1484 Bail for defendants in legal courts is introduced.
  English is used for the first time for parliamentary statutes.
- 1485 Richard III killed at the Battle of Bosworth Field.

Robert (I) the Bruce (1274–1329) king of Scots (1306–29). Considered to be the greatest of the Scottish kings, Robert de Bruce VIII was born in Essex and, as the second earl of Carrick, swore loyalty to Edward I. In 1297 he fought with the English against William Wallace before joining the Scots in their fight for independence. He briefly returned to his allegiance with Edward until 1298, when he again joined the national party and became in 1299 one of the four regents of the kingdom.

In the three final campaigns, however, he resumed loyalty to Edward, and resided for some time at his court, but, learning that the king meditated putting him to death on information given by John Comyn (a rival for the Scottish throne), he fled to Scotland, stabbed Comyn in a quarrel at Dumfries, assembled his vassals at Lochmaben Castle and claimed the crown, which he received at Scone. Twice defeated by the English, he dismissed his troops, retired to Rathlin Island, and was supposed to be dead, when, in the spring of 1307, he landed on the Carrick coast, defeated the earl of Pembroke at Loudon Hill in Ayrshire, and in two years had wrested nearly the whole country from the English. He then in successive years advanced into England, laying waste the country, and, in 1314, defeated at Bannockburn the English forces advancing under Edward II to the relief of the garrison at Stirling. (The Monymusk Reliquary, used by Kenneth mac-Alpin to carry St Columba's relics from Iona to Dunkeld, legend has it, was carried into battle at Bannockburn.) He then went to Ireland to the aid of his brother Edward Bruce, and on his return in 1318, in retaliation for inroads made in his absence, took Berwick and harried Northumberland and Yorkshire.

In the face of continuing English aggression, thirty-one lords and earls met at Arbroath Abbey and wrote to Pope John XXII seeking recognition of Scotland as a sovereign state independent of England (the Declaration of Arbroath, or sometimes called the Declaration of Independence). Hostilities continued until the defeat of Edward near Byland Abbey in 1323, and though in that year a truce was concluded for thirteen years, it was speedily broken. Not until 1328 was the treaty concluded by which the independence of Scotland was fully recognized (Treaty of Northampton).

Bruce did not long survive the completion of his work, dying the following year at Cardross Castle. His heart was buried at Melrose Abbey and his other remains at Dunfermline. He was twice married—first to Isabella, a daughter of the earl of Mar, by whom he had a daughter, Marjorie, mother of Robert II; and then to Elizabeth, a daughter of Aymer de Burgh, Earl of Ulster, by whom he had a son, David II, who succeeded him.

Significant events of Robert I's reign

- 1306 Bruce forced to flee Edward I's army.
- 1307 Edward I dies on his way to Scotland.
- 1314 Battle of Bannockburn.
- 1315 Robert's brother, Edward Bruce, is crowned as high king of Ireland.
- 1320 The Declaration of Arbroath is drawn up and dispatched to the Pope.
- 1323 Bruce enters into a truce with the English.
- 1327 Edward III becomes king of England.
- 1328 The Treaty of Northampton acknowledges the independence of Scotland.

Robert II (1316–90) king of Scots (13–90). The son of Marjorie, daughter of Robert Bruce, and of Walter, Steward of Scotland, Robert II was the first of the Steward (later changed to Stuart) kings. During

David II's period of imprisonment in England, 'Auld Blearie', as he was known on account of his blood-shot eyes, had acted as regent, having been recognized by parliament in 1318 as heir to the throne. On David II's death, he was crowned at Scone. He was married twice, firstly to Elizabeth Mure (1348), who bore him nine children before marriage, and secondly, on Elizabeth's death, to Euphemia Ross, who bore him four children. An Act of Parliament in 1375 settled the crown on his sons by his first wife, Elizabeth, illegitimate by ecclesiastical law. A feeble king, Robert effectively handed over power to his eldest son, John, Earl of Carrick (later Robert III). His reign was comparatively a peaceful one, one of the chief events being the defeat of the English at the Battle of Otterburn in 1388.

Robert III (1337–1406) king of Scots (1390–1406). The eldest son of Robert II and Elizabeth Mure, he was originally called John, but he changed his name on his coronation in 1390. Having been crippled by being kicked by a horse, he was unable to engage in military pursuits, and he trusted the management of government affairs almost entirely to his brother, whom he created Duke of Albany. In 1398 Albany was compelled to resign his office by a party who wished to confer it on the king's eldest son, David, Duke of Rothesay. War was renewed with England in 1402, and an extended raid reached as far as Newcastle, but the Battle of Homildon Hill resulted in a crushing defeat for the Scots. In that year the duke of Rothesay died in Falkland Castle, where he had been imprisoned, commonly believed to have been starved to death at the instigation of Albany. Dread of Albany, who had recovered the regency, induced the king to send his second son, James, to France in 1406, but the ship that carried him was captured by the English, and Henry IV detained him as a prisoner for the next eighteen years. Shortly after hearing of his son's capture, Robert III died heartbroken. He was succeeded by his son, James I.

Rory *or* **Roderic O'Connel** (d.1198) king of Connaught and last high king of Ireland (*c*.1116–86). He sought Anglo-Norman assistance in his fight to take control of Leinster in 1169. An invasion by Richard de Clare, Earl of Pembroke, followed in which Wexford, Waterford and Dublin were captured for England. In 1171 Henry II landed near Waterford to assert his crown rights and receive homage from the native kings. O'Connel recognized Henry as his overlord in 1175.

Run (d.*c*.878) king of Strathclyde. He married a daughter of Kenneth mac-Alpin, the Scots king, and their son, Eocha, followed Constantine and Aed to the throne, thus strengthening ties between the Scots and Britons of Strathclyde.

S

Saebert (d.616) king of Essex (605–616). An early convert to Christianity, he established a bishopric in London in 605. He was succeeded by his sons, Sexred and Saeward.

Saelred (d.746) king of Essex (709–746). He was descended from Sigeberht II. Little is known of him other than that he died a violent death.

Saeward (d.616) king of Essex (616). The son of Saebert, he reigned briefly with his brother, Sexred. After reverting to paganism, the brothers expelled Bishop Mellitus from London and were both killed by the West Saxons as a result.

Sebbi king of Essex (665–695). A joint ruler with his nephew Sighere, he abdicated to take monastic vows in London and is buried at Old St Paul's.

Sexred (d.616) king of Essex (616). The son of Saebert, he reigned jointly with his brother, Saeward. Both were killed by the West Saxons after expelling Bishop Mellitus from London.

Sigeberht (1) (d.*c.*634) king of East Anglia (631–634). Half-brother of Eorpwald, he founded the bishopric of Dunwich for St Felix. He also built the monastery at Burgh Castle on the site of a Roman fort.

Sigeberht (2) (d.759) king of Wessex (756–757). He was deposed by the council of kings and ealdormen (the Witan) and exiled by Cynewulf, who was elected in his place. He was murdered in revenge for the killing of one of Cynewulf's supporters.

Sigeberht I (the Little) (d.653) king of Essex (617–653. He was succeeded by his son, Sigeberht II.

Sigeberht II (the Good) king of Essex (653–660). After his baptism he restored Christianity to the kingdom after a generation of paganism.

Sigeherd (d.*c.*709) king of Essex (695–709). He succeeded his father, Sebbi, and became joint ruler with his brother, Swalfred.

Sigered (d.825) king of Essex (798–825). He was the last king of Essex before the kingdom became absorbed by Wessex.

Sigeric king of Essex (758–798). He ruled as an underking of Mercia before abdicating.

Sighere (d.*c.*695) king of Essex (665–695). Son of Swithelm, he shared the throne with his uncle, Sebbi. He married a Mercian princess.

Sledda (d.*c.*605) king of Essex (587–605). He married a sister of Ethelbert I of Kent.

Somerled (d.1164) king of (the Isle of) Man (1158–64. He was the seventh king of Man and became the first Lord of the Isles after expelling the Norsemen in 1140. His nine male descendants claimed the Hebrides until 1493, and he is considered to be the founder of the powerful MacDonald clan.

Stephen (1096–1154) king of England (1135–54). The son of Stephen, Count of Blois, and Adela, daughter of William the Conqueror, he went to the court of Henry I (his uncle) in 1114 and received the countship of Mortain in Normandy. Despite having sworn loyalty to the Empress Maud (Matilda) when she was named as heir, he was persuaded to claim the throne on Henry's death. After convincing the archbishop of Canterbury that he was the legitimate heir and that he had Henry's approval, he was duly crowned king of England in 1135. However, there was some rancour from Maud's supporters, and several years of unrest ensued. Many barons had sworn loyalty to the empress and some had become disillusioned with Stephen because his leadership was neither as effective nor as strong as Henry I's had been. An invasion of the north of England was undertaken by King David of Scotland on Maud's behalf (1138), but the Scots were crushed near North-allerton at the Battle of the Standard. (Scotland, however, retained Cumberland.) The rebelliousness of his barons was more difficult to deal with; Robert, Earl of Gloucester, an illegitimate son of Henry I, had attended Stephen's court in early 1136 but now turned against him, and several nobles, such as the earl of Chester, were only too willing to exploit the weakness of the king and the divisions in the country to enhance their own power and standing.

Stephen had not shown himself able to deal decisively with insurrection thus far, and this would not change with the coming of his rival for the throne. In September 1139 Matilda arrived in England, landing at Arundel, and was welcomed by a group of barons, including the earl of Gloucester, and with their aid she secured a base in the west country and rallied all those disillusioned with Stephen's reign. Stephen was defeated at the Battle of Lincoln (1141) and imprisoned. The empress proceeded to London, but, when the Londoners called for Stephen's release and rose against her, she was forced to flee to Winchester. There she was besieged by an army raised by Stephen's queen, Matilda of Boulogne. Empress

Matilda escaped, but Robert of Gloucester, who had become central to the campaign, was captured. Stephen regained his liberty, being exchanged in return for Robert, and he returned to the throne.

The following years saw sporadic outbreaks of warfare between the rival factions, with Stephen almost capturing Matilda in her stronghold at Oxford (1142), but the fighting gradually decreased in intensity until 1148 when she returned to Normandy. She had, however, laid the foundations for a successful claim by her son and his descendants. The dispute over the kingship of England continued, and Henry, eldest son of Matilda and later to become Henry II of England, made his third and most successful invasion of England in 1153, backed by a sizeable army. Stephen fought against him but, with the intervention of the Church, which wished to see peace and stability restored, a compromise was reached. It was arranged that Stephen should remain king until his death and thereafter Henry would ascend the throne. Stephen died the following year (1154), never having been able to stamp his authority on the realm or bring his wayward barons to heel. Henry II was duly crowned king of England, the first of the Plantagenet kings.

Significant events of Stephen's reign

- 1135 Stephen becomes king of England.
- 1136 Stephen subdues baronial revolts.
- 1138 Earl of Gloucester defects to Matilda's camp.
  David I of Scotland invades northern England in support of Matilda.
  David loses the Battle of the Standard.
- 1139 Matilda lands in England.
- 1141 Stephen is captured at the Battle of Lincoln and is imprisoned.
  Matilda claims the throne.
  Robert of Gloucester is captured and exchanged for the king.
- 1142 Matilda is besieged at Oxford but escapes.
- 1147 Robert of Gloucester dies.
  Henry Plantagenet unsuccessfully claims the throne.
- 1148 Matilda leaves for Normandy.
- 1149 Henry attempts to take the throne for the second time.
- 1151 Henry becomes Count of Anjou on the death of his father.
- 1153 Treaty of Westminster agrees that Henry will become king on Stephen's death.

Suaebhard (d.692) king of Kent (690–692). Joint ruler with Wihtred.

Swalfred (d.*c*.712) king of Essex (695–709). He succeeded his father, Sebbi, and ruled jointly with his brother, Sigeherd. With his nephew, Offa, he visited Rome in 709.

Sweyn Forkbeard (d.1014) king of England (1013–14), Norway and Demark. The son of Harold Bluetooth of Denmark and Queen Gunild, he built his North Sea empire through conquest and marriage. In 978 he seized his father's kingdom of Denmark and began making raids on England, often demanding protection payments. In 1000 he attacked Norway and became ruler. Two years later King Ethelred of England, fearing that Sweyn's empire would overrun his kingdom, ordered that the Danes settled in England be massacred. This order was impracticable in many areas where the Danes had strongholds, but where the policy was carried out the consequences were terrible. Among the Danes massacred at Oxford was Sweyn's sister, Gunnhild, and Sweyn's resolve to rule England was hardened. The Massacre of St Brice's Day turned support away from Ethelred, and the king executed many who expressed pro-Danish sympathies. Sweyn enjoyed several early successes at Oxford and Winchester but was unable to seize London despite frequent attempts in 994. By late 1013, however, he had devastated fifteen counties and driven Ethelred from England. He was accepted soon afterwards as king of England but died early the following year after a fall from his horse. He had two sons–Harold IV of Denmark and Canute, later king of England.

Swithhelm (d.665) king of Essex (660–665). He was baptised by St Cedd although his kingdom lapsed back to paganism following the arrival of a plague in 664. He was succeeded by his son, Sebbi, and his brother, Sighere, who ruled jointly.

Swithred king of Essex (746–758). He made Colchester the capital of his kingdom.

TU

Talorcen (d.657) king of Picts. He was the son of Eanfrith of Bernicia.

Talorgen (d.787) king of Picts (785–787).

Tincommius (*fl.*1st century BC) king of the Atrebates tribe. He was one of Commius's three sons who divided their father's kingdom and used the title of *Rex*, meaning 'king'. He was recognized by Augustus.

Togodummus (*fl.*1st century AD) high king of British tribes. Son of CUNOBELINUS and brother of CARADOC, he resisted the Romans and was probably killed at the Battle of the Medway.

Tytila (d.*c.*593) king of East Anglia (*c.*578–*c.*593. He was the successor of Wuffa.

Uen (d.c839) king of Picts (837–839). Frequent attacks by the Norse, which claimed Uen, indirectly led to the unification of Pictland and Dalriada. Uen's brothers were also killed, as were most of the members of the major families of the Pictish kingdom, leaving a power vacuum that Kenneth mac-Alpin was later able to exploit to become king of both Picts and Scots.

Unuist king of Picts (820–834). He was the brother of Drest IV.

Urien king of Rheged, a kingdom around the Solway Firth. A British king descended from Coel, he ruled in the late 5th century. One of the last rulers, he fought the Bernicians who were moving north and west from the Humber. The poem *Gododdin* describes one such Bernician attack at Catterick. There is evidence that Urien allied with Strathclyde. He was assassinated by a rival chief.

Uurad (d.842) king of Picts (839–842). Four of his sons claimed the throne after him.

V

Victoria (1819–1901) queen of the United Kingdom of Great Britain and Ireland (1837–1901), empress of India (1876–1901). The only child of Edward, Duke of Kent, fourth son of George III, by his wife, Mary Louisa Victoria, daughter of Francis, Duke of Saxe-Coburg, and widow of Ernest, Prince of Leiningen, was born at Kensington Palace, London. Her prospects of the succession to the crown were somewhat remote—her father might reasonably hope for a male heir; his three elder brothers were alive, and one of them, the duke of Clarence, afterwards William IV, had recently married. The deaths of the princess's father in 1820 and of her cousins, two daughters of the duke of Clarence, in 1819–20, placed her next in the succession to her two elderly uncles, the dukes of York and Clarence. The duke of York died in 1827, and on the accession of William IV in 1830 Victoria became heiress presumptive to the throne.

She had been brought up very quietly, but from 1830 she began to make public appearances, to the annoyance of William, who was on very bad terms with the duchess of Kent. Her coming of age, on her eighteenth birthday, was the occasion of some public rejoicing, and when she succeeded her uncle later that year, she created a favourable impression by the tact and composure she displayed in difficult circumstances. Her accession involved the separation of the crowns of Great Britain and Hanover, the latter passing to the nearest male heir, her uncle, the duke of Cumberland.

In the first years of her reign, Victoria was under the guidance of her Whig prime minister, Lord Melbourne, who devoted himself to the task of training a young girl for her high responsibilities and encouraging her to involve herself in official business. Lord Melbourne and Victoria developed an affectionate relationship, so much so that there were fears that the young queen may become to closely associated with the Whig party. The general election that, by the then existing law followed her accession, gave the Whigs a reduced but adequate majority, but in the summer of 1839 Melbourne's position in the Commons became so weak that he resigned, and the young queen encountered her first political difficulties in a controversy with Sir Robert Peel, who, in taking office, proposed to replace some of the Whig Ladies of the Bedchamber with Conservatives. On her refusal, Peel declined to take office, and Melbourne returned to power for two more years. The queen, who had been taken by surprise and given insufficient time for consideration, afterwards admitted that she had been 'foolish', and no similar difficulty arose again.

The influence of Melbourne diminished after the queen's marriage in 1840 to her cousin, Prince Albert of Saxe-Coburg, whose wide interests and wise counsel had an important effect upon the development of the queen's character, although he never acquired popularity in his adopted country. Their first child, Victoria, the queen's favourite, with whom she would correspond on an almost daily basis for more than forty years following 'Vicky's' marriage to Crown Prince Frederick of Prussia in 1858, was born later the same year, and the Prince of Wales (later Edward VII) the following year. Seven other children followed between 1843 and 1857. Victoria reigned during a period of tremendous change both at home and abroad. Conditions for the poor in the industrial north of the country were growing worse because of economic depression, and calls for political change were voiced by the Chartists whose demands included universal male suffrage and secret ballots, and opposition to the Corn Laws of 1815, which kept the price of bread high by banning cheap imports of corn, rumbled on. The Corn Laws were finally repealed in 1846, but the Chartist demonstration of 1848, the year of revolutions all over Europe, achieved little. The industrialization of Britain moved on apace, and the Great Exhibition of 1851, conceived by Prince Albert, showcased over 100,000 industrial products by more than 13,000 exhibitors, over half of which were British, at the purpose-built Crystal Palace in London.

Britain's empire grew considerably during Victoria's reign. At the height of its expansion the Union Jack flew over one quarter of the world's land surface, taking in Australia, New Zealand, Canada, many colonies in Africa and the far east and the Indian subcontinent. In India, which had been under the administration of the East India Company with limited supervision from the British government since 1600, a native uprising was to have a profound effect on the development of Britain as an imperial power. The East India Company's army in Bengal was an undisciplined unit—grievances over pay, disputes between officers of different castes and rumours that the government wished to convert India to Christianity by force were among the causes of general unrest. In the spring of 1857 a court martial at Meerut of Indian troops who had refused to touch munitions that they believed had been greased with the fat of pigs and cows resulted in their being stripped of their uniforms and led to a mutiny later that year. Three regiments of Indian soldiers freed the prisoners after murdering their guards and marched on Delhi, and, once there, killed every European in sight. The mutiny spread like wildfire. The worst excesses were perpetrated at Cawnpore where over 900 British and loyal Indians, men, women and children, were slaughtered. At length the revolt was overcome and Delhi retaken. The government of India was passed to the British crown, which promised equality and freedom of worship for all. The government that replaced the East India Company was detached from those it ruled with an efficiency and impartiality that would become the model for the rest of the empire's colonies.

Victoria came to be regarded as the figurehead for all of Britain's possessions overseas. She played a considerable part in foreign policy, and on several occasions her personal intervention improved foreign relations, especially with France. No sovereign of this country had left the island since George II (except for the brief visit of George IV to Hanover), but Victoria made royal visits a part of the peace-loving diplomacy of her governments, and she paid special attention both to Louis Philippe and Napoleon III, who owed to her his reception into the royal circles of Europe. Her relations with her ministers during this period were generally cordial, although she had grave disagreements with Palmerston, whose foreign policy she distrusted and whose blunt and bullishly worded dispatches to British ambassadors overseas, sent without her consultation, she resented. Victoria considered the possibilities of dismissing Palmerston but settled instead on the assurance that any such dispatches should first be approved by her. Her desire for the maintenance of peace and her frequent correspondence with the Russian tsar, which was of great help to her government, nevertheless led, just before the outbreak of the Crimean War (1854–56) to many misrepresentations of her attitude, which was supposed to be too friendly to Russia. The queen also displayed a great fondness for Scotland and made two visits there, in 1842 and again in 1844, and oversaw the rebuilding of Balmoral Castle in Speyside, which was her favourite home.

The death of her husband (who in 1857 had been created Prince Consort) from typhoid fever in 1861 changed the whole tenor of the queen's life. Victoria was to wear the black of mourning for the rest of her days, and during the many years of her widowhood she lived in almost complete seclusion. She had been the first sovereign to live in Buckingham Palace, but after 1861 she was rarely in London and preferred Balmoral and Osborne (her home in the Isle of Wight) to Windsor, and her disinclination to appear in public was the subject of numerous complaints.

Her devotion to her other duties was, however, undiminished. She continued to exercise some influence on foreign policy, and advocated neutrality in the Danish War of 1864. She was on terms of intimate friendship with one of the prime ministers of this period of her reign, Disraeli, and his Royal Titles Act of 1876, which conferred on her the title of Empress of India, gave her special pleasure. She did not like Gladstone, and did not conceal her reluctance to ask him to form a government in 1880, and her distrust of his policy was increased by the course of events in Egypt and the Sudan. In the last years of her reign she welcomed the Unionist administrations of 1886 and 1890.

Victoria suffered many family griefs, for two of her children and several of her grandchildren predeceased her. She felt deeply the loss of her son-in-law, Emperor Frederick, in 1888. She had watched with anxiety the aggressive policy of Germany and Bismarck, and had warned her daughter that Britain 'cannot and will not stand' the attempt of the German Empire 'to dictate to Europe', and she trusted that her son-in-law's succession would produce a change in German policy. By the end of the century, however, Germany had begun arming rapidly, and ultimately this was to end in war. Her sorrow was increased by the Emperor William's treatment of his mother, but she remained on cordial terms with her grandson to the end of her life.

Her own domestic griefs rendered her sympathetic to the sorrows of her people, and as she grew older she more than recovered her early popularity and was regarded with affection by the whole empire. This affection was illustrated by the enthusiasm for her person that was shown on the occasions of her jubilees in 1887 and 1897. Her last years were clouded by the outbreak of the Boer War in South Africa (1899–1902) and by the disasters of the opening campaign, but she lived long enough to welcome Lord Roberts on his return in January 1901 after the relief of Mafeking and the annexing of the Transvaal and the Orange Free State. She died less than three weeks later and is buried at Frogmore, near Windsor Castle.

Victoria had reigned for almost sixty-four years,

and few of her subjects could remember when she had not been their monarch. A great sense of loss was felt by the nation at her death. Victoria was a woman of robust physique, remarkable powers of memory, great force of character, deep sympathy, and sincere religious feeling. She was very tenacious of her own opinions but understood thoroughly the position of a constitutional sovereign, and her strong common sense kept her prejudices in check.

Significant events of Victoria's reign

- 1838 Chartists campaign for political reforms.
- 1839 Anti-Corn Law League formed.
- 1840 Penny Post introduced.
  Victoria marries Albert of Saxe-Coburg-Gotha.
- 1841 Robert Peel becomes prime minister.
- 1842 China cedes Hong Kong to Britain by the Treaty of Nanking.
- 1845 Great Famine takes hold in Ireland.
- 1846 Corn Laws are repealed.
- 1848 The year of revolutions in Europe.
  Communist Manifesto written by Karl Marx and Friedrich Engels.
- 1851 Great Exhibition held in Hyde Park, London.
- 1852 Duke of Wellington dies.
- 1853 David Livingstone discovers Victoria Falls.
- 1854 The Crimean War commences.
- 1857 The Indian Mutiny.
- 1858 Government of India is taken over by the British crown.
- 1859 *Origin of the Species* written by Charles Darwin.
- 1861 American Civil War begins.
  Prince Albert dies.
- 1863 Foundation of the Salvation Army.
- 1865 American Civil War ends.
- 1867 Second Reform Act doubles the electoral franchise to over two million.
- 1868 Gladstone becomes prime minister.
- 1869 The Irish Church ceases to exist with the passing of the Disestablishment Act.
- 1870 Education Act makes primary education compulsory.
- 1871 Trade Unions are legalized.
- 1872 The secret ballot is introduced for elections.
- 1876 Victoria is created empress of India.
- 1884 Electoral franchise further extended by third Reform Act.
- 1886 Irish Home Rule Bill defeated in parliament.
- 1887 Victoria's Golden Jubilee year.
  Independent Labour Party is founded.
- 1893 Second Irish Home Rule Bill defeated by the House of Lords.
- 1897 Victoria's Diamond Jubilee year.
- 1899 Boer War begins.

Vortigern (*fl.*5th century) British tribal king of Kent (*c.*450). According to the *Anglo-Saxon Chronicle*, Kent was the first of the Anglo-Saxon kingdoms, founded around 450 by Jutes from Denmark and the Rhineland. 'Vortigern', the title used for an overlord, also came to be used as the name of the tribal leader who is thought to have asked mercenaries from Jutland to help him fight off attacks from northern Picts. Led by the brothers Hengest and Horsa, the Jutes landed at Ebbsfleet, near Ramsgate, and, after driving back the Picts, turned on Vortigern and settled the area themselves.

W

Wiglaf king of Mercia (827–840). He was expelled by the powerful Egbert of Wessex in 827 but regained the throne within a year. He is buried at Repton Monastery in Derbyshire.

Wihtred king of Kent (690–725). He ruled jointly with Suaebhard until 692 and married three times. A strong ruler, he successfully resisted repeated Mercian attempts to control his kingdom.

William I (William the Conqueror) (1027–87) king of England (1066–87). He was born in Normandy, the illegitimate son of Robert, Duke of Normandy, by Arlotta, the daughter of a tanner of Falaise. His father having no legitimate son, William became the heir at his death, Robert of Normandy having made a pilgrimage to Jerusalem from which he did not return. William ruled Normandy with great vigour and displayed tremendous military ability. The opportunity of gaining a wider dominion presented itself on the death of his second cousin, Edward the Confessor, king of England, whose crown he claimed by virtue of Edward's promise, made in 1051, that William would succeed him. Harold had himself sworn loyalty to William after falling into the hands of his rival in 1064. However, on his deathbed Edward named Harold as his successor, and Harold duly accepted the crown. To enforce his claim to the throne, William invaded England with a fleet of many hundreds of ships. The decisive victory at Hastings in 1066, in which Harold was killed, ensured his success.

After being crowned on Christmas Day, William began establishing the administration of law and justice on a firm basis throughout England. He conferred numerous grants of land on his own followers and introduced the feudal constitution of Normandy in regard to tenure and services. At least 78 castles were built in this period. He also expelled numbers of the English Church dignitaries and replaced them with Normans. In the early years of his reign, however, William had to deal with rebellion against his rule from the Anglo-Saxons, many of whom had been dispossessed of their estates in favour of their Norman conquerors. Uprisings in the southwest (1067) and the north (1069–70) of the country were ruthlessly crushed, and the defeat of the rebellion of Hereward the Wake (1070–72) effectively ended Saxon resistance. William also invaded Scotland and forced the Scots king, Malcolm III, to recognize him as overlord at Abernethy, taking his son as a hostage. Towards the end of his reign he instituted in 1085 a general survey of the landed property of the kingdom, the record of which still exists under the title of *Doomsday Book*.

In 1087 William went to war with France, where his son had encouraged a rebellion of Norman nobles. He entered French territory and destroyed much of the countryside, but when he burnt Mantes, his horse trod on a hot cinder and stumbled, and he was thrown forward in his saddle and received an internal injury that caused his death at the abbey of St Gervais, near Rouen. He left Normandy and Maine to his eldest son, Robert, and England to his second son, William II.

Significant events of William I's reign

- 1067 A revolt in the southwest is subdued.
  Work begins on the building of the Tower of London.
- 1069 William subdues the north of England.
- 1070 Hereward the Wake's Saxon rebellion erupts in eastern England.
- 1072 William invades Scotland.
- 1079 Work begins on Winchester Cathedral.
  William is victorious against his son, Robert, at Gerberoi, Normandy.
  The New Forest is made a royal hunting ground.
- 1086 The *Domesday Book* is completed.

William (I) the Lion (1143–1214) king of Scots (1165–1214). The brother of Malcolm IV and the grandson of David I, he became king at the age of twenty-two. His first act as king was to attempt to reclaim Northumbria, which had been taken from Scotland by Henry II in 1154. He mounted an expedition to this end in 1174, timing his move to exploit the strife that the English king was suffering after the murder of Thomas à Becket. However, whilst besieging Alnwick Castle the Scots were taken by surprise by an English force led by Geoffrey of Lincoln and Randulph of Glanville. William was captured and was taken to Henry II at Northampton, with his feet shackled beneath the belly of a horse. Henry, who had that very day finished his public penance for Becket's murder, must have been soothed by the capture of the Scots king. William was imprisoned at

Falaise Castle in Normandy, where the following December, he was obliged to accept the terms of the Treaty of Falaise under which he was to acknowledge the sovereignty of England over Scotland, including himself, his kingdom and the Scottish Church.

Scotland had become a vassal kingdom. The chief Scottish castles were placed under English control, and William's younger brother David, along with more than twenty of the Scottish nobility, were taken hostage to England. William was released a few months later but found on his return that in his absence unrest had broken out. The Celtic chiefs took advantage of William's imprisonment and the resentment felt by them towards the friendships of Scottish kings with their Norman neighbours turned into rebellion. The first uprisings took place in Galloway, where several nobles who had been loyal to William and had marched with him into England now wished for Galloway to be independent from the rest of William's kingdom. The nobles seized the royal castles, expelled the king's men and asked Henry to take Galloway from William and become its overlord. Only too willing to do this, Henry sent envoys to Galloway, but by the time they arrived the nobles had had a falling out. Order was not restored to Galloway for over ten tears.

The Celts of the north also rose during William's imprisonment. The men of Ross attacked Norman settlers who had been granted lands. William, after his release, travelled north to subdue his unruly subjects in 1179 and established two castles in Ross to keep order. Two years later the king was obliged to go north again, this time to subdue a rival for the throne, Donald MacWilliam, who claimed to be the great-grandson of Malcolm III and Ingibjorg. MacWilliam, who had become a powerful chief in the north, was killed at Badenoch, but the rebellion took almost seven years to subdue and temporarily took Ross out of the king's control. With the death of Henry II in 1189, relations with England took a turn for the better. On the accession of Richard I, William was able to buy back Scotland's sovereignty for 10,000 marks, raised by taxation, as the new English king was in dire need of money to fund the Third Crusade. Also, the two remaining castles under English control, Berwick and Roxburgh, were returned to Scotland. With the proclamaiion of Pope Celestine III in 1192 that the Kirk should be independent under the jurisdiction of Rome, the independence of the Scottish Church from Canterbury was restored. The final clause of the Treaty of Falaise was done away with on the agreement of Richard I that William should do homage to the English king only for William's English lands. The independence of Scotland had been regained, but William still had designs on Northumbria, which remained in English hands. He made his claim to Richard on the English king's return from the Crusade, but to no avail. William tried to buy Northumbria, Westmorland and Cumberland from Richard and made the offer of his daughter Margaret as a bride for Richard's nephew, but these attempts were all in vain.

When Richard died and was succeeded by John, William renewed his claims to the new king, but John replied by beginning to build a fortress at the mouth of the River Tweed and shortly afterwards invaded Scotland. William waited for him at Roxburgh Castle, but negotiation took the place of battle, and it was agreed that, in return for 15,000 marks and two of William's heiresses, John would not build a castle on the Tweed. William's lifelong ambition to gain Northumbria was never achieved.

Even although William was unable to realize dominion over Northumbria, his reign can be seen as successful. He regained the independence of Scotland and of the Scottish Church, and, through his encouragement of the growth of towns and the creation of many royal burghs, was able to improve the lives of his subjects. William is also credited with being responsible for the incorporation of the lion rampant into the royal coat of arms. William married Ermengarde de Beaumont in 1186, who bore him three daughters and one son, who was to succeed him as Alexander II. He died at Stirling at the age of seventy-two and is buried at Arbroath Abbey, which he had founded in 1178.

Significant events of William I's reign

- 1174 William invades England but is captured and imprisoned in Normandy.
  Under the Treaty of Falaise Scotland loses its independence from England.
  Revolts break out in Galloway and Ross.
- 1178 Arbroath Abbey is founded.
- 1179 William subdues the rebels in Ross.
- 1186 Order is restored to Galloway.
- 1189 Henry II dies and is succeeded by Richard I.
  William buys Scotland's sovereignty back from England for 10,000 marks.
- 1192 Pope Celestine III declares the Scottish Church to be independent under Rome.
- 1199 Richard I of England is succeeded by John.

William II (William Rufus) (1056–1100) king of England (1087–1100). The third son of William the Conqueror and Matilda of Flanders, he was born in Normandy and gained the nickname 'Rufus' on account of his florid complexion. He was nominated by his father to the English succession in preference to his elder brother Robert. The Norman barons supported Robert, however, and in 1088 attempted to depose William. The rebellion in Normandy was defeated by William, who secured the aid of Lanfranc, Archbishop of Canterbury, and the English nobles, and Robert was given the duchy of Normandy in place of the English crown. This was not the last revolt against his rule that William would have to deal with, as, in 1090, a further rising by his brother necessitated an invasion of Normandy to subdue him. Robert's departure to join the First Crusade in 1096 ensured no further trouble from that quarter.

The Scots, however, proved to be difficult neighbours. An invasion of northern England by Malcolm III of Scotland in 1091 was defeated, and the Scots king was compelled to accept William as overlord. Nonetheless, a further invasion was undertaken by Malcolm two years later. Again the Scots were defeated, and Malcolm III was ambushed and killed, together with his eldest son, Edward, at the Battle of Alnwick. Malcolm's son from his marriage to Ingibjorg, Duncan, who had lived in England since being taken hostage by William the Conqueror in 1072, was dispatched north with William II's support at the head of an English army to wrest the throne from Malcolm's successor, Donald III, in 1094. William's intention was for Duncan to rule Scotland as his vassal, but Duncan spent only a few months on the throne before being killed. In 1097 William sent a second army north, this time with Edgar, a son of Malcolm III and Margaret, who had sworn loyalty to the English king, at its head. This expedition met with greater success, and Edgar was installed as king.

Further warfare was conducted, this time against the Welsh, whose risings against the Norman barons in the border lands resulted in an invasion of Wales being undertaken in 1098. William also encountered trouble in ecclesiastical matters, with which he dealt in a somewhat unscrupulous manner. A characteristic incident was his contention with Anselm, Archbishop of Canterbury, in 1097 regarding Church property and the sovereignty of the pope. Church property was regarded by William as the property of the king, and as such he would not allow the election of abbots to vacant abbeys. Anselm asked for leave to receive the pope's decision on the matter, but this too was contentious, as William had not officially recognized the sovereignty of any pope. At length William did recognize Pope Urban II, but the quarrels between them escalated and resulted in Anselm's exile in France and the loss of all his lands.

William met his death while chasing deer in the New Forest—killed by an arrow shot, accidentally or otherwise, from the bow of a French gentleman named Walter Tyrrel. The crown then passed to William's brother, Henry I.

Significant events of William II's reign

- 1088 Supporters of Robert, William II's brother, rebel in Normandy.
- 1090 William invades Normandy..
- 1093 Malcolm III invades England.
- 1095 Durham Cathedral is founded.
  A revolt by William's northern barons is put down.
- 1096 Robert, William's brother, joins the First Crusade.
- 1097 Archbishop Anselm is exiled.
- 1098 William enters Wales to subdue a rebellion.
- 1099 Jerusalem is captured by the Crusaders.

William III (William of Orange) (1650–1702) king of England, Scotland and Ireland (1689–1702, respectively as William III, II and I). The son of William II of Nassau, Prince of Orange, and Henrietta Mary Stewart, daughter of Charles I of England. During his early life in Holland all power was in the hands of the grand pensionary John De Witt, but when France and England in 1672 declared war against the Netherlands, there was a popular revolt in which Cornelius and John De Witt were murdered, while William was declared captain-general, grand-admiral, and stadt-holder of the United Provinces. In the campaign that followed he opened the sluices in the dykes and flooded the country around Amsterdam, forcing the French to retreat, while peace was soon made with England. In subsequent campaigns he lost the battles of Seneffe (1674) and St Omer (1677) but was still able to keep the enemy in check.

In 1677 he married Mary, daughter of the duke of York, later James II of England, and the Peace of Nijmegen followed in 1678. For some years subsequent to this the policy of William was directed towards curbing the power of Louis XIV, and to this end he brought about the League of Augsburg in 1686. As his wife was heir presumptive to the English throne, he had kept close watch on the policy of his father-in-law, James II, and in 1688 he issued a declaration recapitulating the unconstitutional acts of the English king, and promising to secure a free parliament to the people. He was invited over to England by seven of the leading statesmen, who feared that James II's newly born son would be brought up as a Catholic. He arrived suddenly at Torbay with a fleet of 500 ships and 14,000 troops, and the greater part of the nobility declared in his favour. James fled with his family to France, and William made his entry into London. The throne was now declared vacant, and, upon William and Mary's acceptance of the Declaration of Rights, which defined the limits of regal power and fixed the succession, barring Catholics from the throne, William and Mary were proclaimed joint monarchs of England and Scotland.

The 'Glorious Revolution' was virtually complete in England, but the situation in Scotland was to take a little longer to resolve. A few months after James II's flight, John Graham of Claverhouse, Viscount Dundee, raised the royalist standard and defeated an English army at Killiecrankie. Dundee was killed in the battle, and without his leadership the rebellion's momentum was lost. A further battle took place in August of the same year at Dunkeld, but the outcome was indecisive, although both claimed victory. The rising in Scotland rumbled on for a further ten months until the remaining rebels were overcome at Cromdale in early 1690. However, an incident two years later was to prove a boon for Jacobite propagandists. John Dalrymple, Master of Stair and William III's principal minister in Scotland, was placed in charge of effecting the royal decree that each Highland chief must abandon his loyalty to the deposed king and swear an oath of loyalty to his new king. The deadline for taking this oath was set for 1 January 1692 in Inverary, Argyll, and most of the clan chiefs did as they were asked. MacIan of the Clan MacDonald was late in giving his oath, however, having first travelled mistakenly north to Inverlochy instead of south to Inverary. The oath was eventually given, but a troop of soldiers, acting on Dalrymple's orders, nevertheless set about the slaughter of the two hundred families of the Clan MacDonald who lived at Glencoe. The government inquiry that followed in 1695 was indecisive, but the Scottish parliament decided, at length, that Dalrymple was responsible, and he was subsequently dismissed.

By now, however, attention in Scotland had shifted to consideration of the ill-fated Darien Scheme. Scotland, excluded from any part of the wealth generated in England from its trade with its far-flung colonies, decided to establish a colony of its own. An Act passed in 1693 for the purpose of encouraging foreign trade, together with the setting up of the Company of Scotland, with powers granted by parliament to found new colonies, laid the foundations of the scheme. The site for the proposed colony lay in Spanish territory in Central America, and Spain did not approve of the founding of a 'New Caledonia' on its property. In addition, the area became a swamp in the summer infested with fever. The two expeditions to Darien were catastrophic. Fever claimed the lives of many of the colonists, and the English possessions in the West Indies refused supplies to the stricken colony, which was then closed down by Spanish troops. It was a financial disaster that was widely felt and certainly did nothing to improve Anglo-Scottish relations.

In Ireland the accession of William III was no less troubled than it had been in Scotland. In 1689 the Catholics rose up against William's rule in support of James II, and some 30,000 or more Protestants fled to take refuge in Londonderry. James II landed with a small number of French troops sent by Louis XIV and laid siege to the city. Relief came more than a hundred days later from an English fleet. James and his mostly Irish army moved south, having failed to take Londonderry, to the River Boyne, near Drogheda. In the battle with William III's forces that ensued, James II's army was crushed. James escaped to France and was not to return. William, having defeated the rebellions against his reign, attempted to allow Catholics in Ireland freedom of worship in the Treaty of Limerick (1691), but in this he was thwarted, for the Protestant-dominated Irish parliament subsequently passed harsh laws that effectively made the Catholics second-class citizens.

In the war with France William was less successful than he had been against his enemies at home, but although he was defeated at the Battles of Steenkerke (1692) and Neerwinden (1693), Louis XIV was finally compelled to acknowledge him as king of England at the Peace of Ryswick in 1697. Friction between William and Louis XIV continued, however, the final straw coming on the death of James II in 1701. Louis XIV acknowledged James's son as James III of England—this showed a blatant disregard for the treaty of 1697. In addition to this, Louis banned the import of English goods to France and advised Philip V of Spain to do likewise.

England, Holland, and the Austrian Empire had already combined against Louis XIV in the Grand Alliance of 1701, and the War of the Spanish Succession, to prevent the union of the Spanish and French crowns, was just on the point of beginning when William died from the after-effects of a fall from his horse. A hardworking and able monarch, William III was nevertheless unpopular, probably because of his reserved nature, his poor understanding of the English language and his undisguised preference for his beloved Holland. He was succeeded by his sister-in-law, Anne.

Significant events of William III's reign

- 1689 The Bill of Rights is passed.
  Jacobites defeat government forces at Killiecrankie.
- 1689 James II lays siege to Londonderry.

- 1690 Jacobites are defeated at Cromdale. James II is defeated at the Battle of the Boyne.
- 1691 Treaty of Limerick allows freedom of worship for Irish Catholics. War with France breaks out.
- 1692 The Massacre of Glencoe.
- 1694 Queen Mary dies. William reigns alone.
- 1697 The French war is ended by the Peace of Ryswick.
- 1698 Darien Scheme is launched.
- 1701 Act of Settlement establishes Protestant Hanoverian succession. The exiled James II dies. War of the Spanish Succession begins.

William IV (1765–1837) king of the United Kingdom of Great Britain and Ireland (1830–37). The third son of George III and Charlotte of Mecklenburg-Strelitz, he served in the navy, rising successively to all the grades of naval command, until in 1801 he was made admiral of the fleet. In 1789 he had received the title of duke of Clarence and, after retiring from the navy in 1790, settled down with the actress Dorothea Jordan. He lived a happily domestic life with his mistress, who bore him ten children, although financial needs necessitated her frequent return to the stage. In 1811, however, with the worsening condition of George III and uncertainty over the succession, William left Mrs Jordan and searched for a wife, at length marrying Adelaide of Saxe-Meiningen in 1818.

At the age of sixty-four, he succeeded his brother, George IV, as king, amid much concern over his fitness for the crown—he was given to strong language, was well known for his forthright opinions, and his lack of tact had earned him the nickname 'Silly Billy'. However, his blunt speech and lack of pretence soon won him the affection of the public. He was king during a period of some considerable political upheaval, a few of the great events that render his reign memorable being the passage of the Reform Act, the abolition of slavery in the colonies, and the reform of the Poor Laws. He was the last sovereign to try to chose his prime minister regardless of parliamentary support; replacing Melbourne with Peel in 1834. He died at Windsor Castle after a reign of only seven years. His two daughters by Adelaide of Saxe-Meiningen had died in infancy, and, leaving no other legitimate heir, he was succeeded by his niece Victoria.

Significant events of William IV's reign

- 1830 The first passenger steam railways open.
- 1831 Old London Bridge is demolished.
- 1832 First Reform Act greatly increases the electoral franchise.
- 1833 Factory Act forbids the employment of children below the age of nine. Slavery in British colonies is abolished.
- 1834 The Tolpuddle Martyrs are transported. Workhouses are introduced under the Poor Law.
- 1837 Charles Dickens writes *Oliver Twist.*

Wuffa (d.*c*.578) king of East Anglia (571–*c*.578). He is considered to be the first king of the East Angles. The term 'Wuffings' was applied to all following kings up to the time when the kingdom was merged with Mercia around 800. He was succeeded by his son, Tytila.

Wulfhere (d.675) king of Mercia (657–675). A younger brother of Peada, he led the Mercian campaign to overthrow Northumbrian hegemony and invaded Wessex in 674. He gave the Isle of Wight to King Ethelwalh of Sussex.